# Over 1001 Amazing Places to Go in North America

pil

Publications International, Ltd.

**Melissa Arnold** has been in the travel industry for nearly 30 years, working in hotel/motel management, convention and visitors bureau management, and as a freelance travel editor and writer. Melissa's writing focuses on the city of Baltimore, nostalgia travel, and the scenic roads of America.

**David Lewis** is a Denver-based freelance writer. Formerly, he was columnist and business reporter for the *Rocky Mountain News*, editor of *ColoradoBiz* magazine, business editor of *InternetWeek*, and the voice of classical radio on KVOD-FM in Denver. He also served in the mid-1990s as journalism dean of the American University in Kyrgyzstan in Bishkek, Kyrgyzstan.

**Clark Norton** is a freelance travel writer and a longtime San Francisco resident who now lives in New York. He is the author of *Where Should We Take the Kids?: California* and *Around San Francisco with Kids* and has contributed to several other California travel guides. He currently publishes the Web site SmarterCruising.com.

**Eric Peterson** is a Denver-based freelance writer who has contributed to numerous Frommer's guides covering the American West. Peterson's work has also appeared in *ColoradoBiz*, *Delta Sky*, and the *New York Daily News*.

**Laura Sutherland (with Family Travel Forum*)** is a widely acknowledged authority on family travel and has published several books on the topic. She also writes for a number of publications and Internet sites. Laura lives in Santa Cruz, California, with her husband and two children.
* *Family Travel Forum is a global community of families who share expert reviews, vacation tips, and travel tales through a network of Web sites.*

**Christina Tree** has written roughly a thousand stories about New England for *The Boston Globe* Sunday Travel section. She has also authored six books about the region, updating them through more than a dozen editions. Chris is also a contributing editor to the annual *Yankee Magazine Travel Guide to New England*.

**Jim Yenckel** served as editor and writer for *The Washington Post* for 33 years, the last 16 as its travel writer. He writes a weekly travel column for a chain of newspapers and is a regular contributor to several national magazines, including *Budget Travel*, *Washingtonian*, and *Preservation*.

Map illustrations by Dave and Sam Merrill. Reference maps courtesy of the National Scenic Byways Organization (byways.org). Portions of manuscript courtesy of Exxon Mobil Travel Group and the National Scenic Byways Organization. America's Byways™ is a trademark of the Federal Highway Administration.


Photo Credits
Front cover: **Brand X Pictures** (bottom left); **iStockphoto** (center & top right); **PhotoDisc** (left center & top center); **Shutterstock** (top left). Back cover: **Priscilla Alexander Eastman**
**Accent Alaska:** 293, 296; **age fotostock:** 320, 537, 586; **AIA Houston:** 615; **Alamy Images:** Rough Guides, 605 (top); **Amana Colonies Convention and Visitors Bureau:** 152; **AP Images:** 10, 22, 28, 39, 41, 65, 85, 87, 120, 122, 141, 142, 150, 151, 177, 183, 213; **Art Car Fest:** Harrod Blank, 614 (bottom); **ASA Photographic:** George Lucozzi, 18; **Barker Character, Comic and Cartoon Museum:** 592 (bottom); **Baton Rouge Area Convention and Visitors Bureau:** 124 (bottom left & bottom right); **Ben & Jerry's:** 590 (top); **Bent's Old Fort National Historic Site:** 387; **Bill Johnson Photography:** 118; **Pat & Chuck Blackley:** 529, 544; **Boston Children's Museum:** 591; **Brand X Pictures:** 188, 206, 212; **Branson, Lakes Area Chamber of Commerce:** 155; **© 2006 Busch Entertainment Corporation. Reproduced by permission of Busch Gardens Europe. All rights reserved.:** 599 (top); **Cache Valley Tour Council:** 371; **Cape Fear Coast Convention and Visitors Bureau:** 602 (bottom); **Carnegie Science Center:** 596 (top); **Castle Country Travel Region:** Michael Collier, 364; **Cedar Point, Sandusky, OH:** 607 (top); **© 2006 The Children's Museum of Indianapolis:** Garry Chilluffo, 608 (bottom); **City of Chicago:** 138; **City of Reno:** 616; **City of Sturgis:** 163; **Grant Collier:** 389; **Colorado Tourism Office:** 205 (top); **©Corbis:** 288, 289, 298, 304, 307, 311, 313, 315, 317, 337, 344, 357, 381, 434, 439, 443, 446, 464, 466, 468, 475, 482, 485, 488, 493, 497, 503, 506, 507, 511, 512, 514, 519, 524, 533; **Corpus Christi Convention and Visitors Bureau:** 173 (top & bottom); **Crystal Images Photography and Publishing:** Kathleen M. K. Menke, 175, 255; **DE Tourism Office:** K. Clancy, 535; **Daybreak Imagery:** Richard Day, 454; **Dean Hill Photography:** 538; **DigitalVision:** 217 (right), 220, 223; **Jim Dirden:** 180; **John Domont:** 463; **Dreamstime:** 70; **Don Eastman:** 20, 21, 31 (right), 51, 54, 111 (left), 157, 205 (bottom), 225, 231, 244, 253, 260, 263, 266, 277 (bottom); **Priscilla Alexander Eastman:** 132, 143, 159, 194, 195, 276, 278, 280, 282; **John Elk III:** 341, 362, 382, 402, 411, 559, 568; **Judith A. Erickson:** 67 (left), 147; **Clint Farlinger:** 576; **Fernbank Museum of Natural History:** 603; **Bob Firth:** 424, 425, 427, 428, 432; **Flying Fish Photography:** Dolly Sods, 81; **Folio, Inc.:** Linda Bartlett, 107; Walter Bibikow, 247; Walter P. Calahan, 66, 165 (top); Anthony Coletti, 17; Richard Cummins, 136, 176 (right), 190, 248, 249; Claudia Dhimitri, 271; Steve Dunwell, 24; David Falconer, 88, 252, 267; Paul M. Franklin, 72, 580; David R. Frazier, 185; Mark E. Gibson, 281 (top); Alan Goldstein, 47; Jeff Greenberg, 49; Jim Mattson Photography, 131; D. Johnson, 558; James Lemass, 19 (right), 34 (bottom), 108; Virginia Llewellyn, 75; Matthew Borkoski Photography, 62 (bottom); Al Messerschmidt, 37; Novastock, 286; Richard T. Nowitz, 57, 76, 78, 284; Vivian Ronay, 71 (right); John Skowronski, 67 (right), 71 (left), 73; Catherine Ursillo, 32, 33; **Fort Ticonderoga:** 510; **Franklin Institute:** 595 (bottom); **Getty Images:** 121, 135, 277 (top), 595 (top), 601, 610 (top); Panoramic Images, 134; **Christina Gnadinger:** 600 (top); **Grand Canyon, National Park Service:** 189; **Grand Mesa Scenic Byways:** 384; **Hawaii Visitors and Convention Bureau:** Ron Dahlquist, 269; **Hilton Head Island Visitors and Convention Bureau:** 96; **Bert Hoferichter:** 70; **George W. Hormal:** 565; **Hot Topic Images:** Wendy White, 222; **Ian Adams Photography:** 470, 473; **Idaho Travel Council:** 346; **Illinois Al**
**Visitors and Convention Bureau:** 448; **Illinois Lincoln Highway:** 452; **The Image Finders:** Jim Bar
130; R. Berndt, 399; Mark E. Gibson, 192, 285, 354, 356, 498; Max Hunn, 272; Max & Bea Hunn, 2
Sally McCrae Kuyper, 400; Werner Lobert, 368; Michael Philip Manheim, 283; Patti McConville, 1
Ralph L. Staples, 515, 557; **The Image Works:** 491; **Independent Crop Circle Researchers' Associati**
Jeffrey Wilson, 129; **Index Open:** 8, 11, 29, 46, 58, 61, 216, 221, 275; **Index Stock Imagery, Inc.:** 4
484, 523; Walter Bibikow, 182 (top); Vic Bider, 114 (top); Joe Carini, 268; Gary Conner, 98; Jan
Denk, 191; Mark Gibson, 600 (bottom); Robin Hill, 99; Jack Hoehn, Jr.: 145; Henryk T. Kaiser, 50; On
Photo Communications Inc., 95 (left); Paul Rocheleau, 174; Chris Rogers, 172; Stephen Saks, 97, 1
158 (top); Jim Schwabel, 109, 123; Harvey Schwartz, 246 (bottom); Charles Shoffner, 125; Ran
Taylor, 114 (bottom); Jim Wark, 214; Zephyr Pictures, 80; **International Peace Garden:** 167; **Inter**
**tional Spy Museum:** 597; **International UFO Museum and Research Center:** Rodden's Inc., 182 (b
tom); **iStockphoto:** 16, 27, 40, 42, 63, 92, 95 (right), 101, 104, 137 (right), 148, 160, 161, 196, 200, 2
203, 219 (bottom), 224, 226, 236, 237, 240, 241, 242 (top), 246 (top), 264, 265, 279, 281 (botto
596 (bottom), 609, 612 (bottom), 620, 621, 626, 627 (top); **Jack Olson Photography:** 378, 437; **Jan**
**P. Rowan Photography:** 137 (left), 164, 187, 234, 458, 555, 590 (bottom), 599 (bottom), 608 (top);
**R. West Photography:** 62 (top); **Jim Pickerell Photography:** 13; **Jupiterimages:** David Whitten, 270; **I**
**Jusidman:** 627 (bottom); **Kaleidoscope:** 612 (top); **Kentucky Department of Tourism:** 540; **James Ki**
**kis:** 12, 14, 34 (top), 36, 43, 52, 77, 592 (top); **Kristin Shrake Photography:** 19 (left); **geddisphoto.co**
Larry Geddis, 250; **Laurence Parent Photography:** 339, 374, 396, 471, 477, 504, 505, 566, 570, 5
582; **Legoland California:** 622 (top); **Bruce Leighty:** 45, 153, 166, 193; **James Lemass:** 44; **David Li**
**man:** 169; **Virge Lorents:** 517, 520; **Maine Department of Transportation:** 490, 494; **Makoshika Di**
**saur Museum:** Steve Bury, 229; **Mammoth Site of Hot Springs, SD Inc.:** 613; **MCW Photography, LL**
Michael Wootten, 530, 532; **Al Michaud:** 235, 238; **Microsoft Streets & Trips 2006:** 282; **Annma**
**Mikelski:** 178; **Ken Miller:** 359; **Milwaukee Art Museum:** 146; **Minnesota Department of Transpor**
**tion:** 435; **Minnesota Highway 38 Leadership Board:** 416, 418; **Missouri Department Natio**
**Resources:** 479; **Monterey Bay Aquarium Foundation:** 242 (bottom left); Randy Wilder, (bottom righ
**Sheila Morris:** 86 (left); **Mount Rainier, National Park Service:** Michael Larson, 258, 259; **Pat Mur**
**Collection:** 617; **Museum of Glass:** Russell Johnson, 261; **Museum of the Rockies:** 228 (bottom); Jo
Little (top); **National Park Service:** 82, 94, 112, 113, 116, 117, 158; (bottom), 204, 208, 209, 230, 2
233, 257, 589 (bottom); **National Park Service:** Peter Jones, 186; **National Trust Historical Preservati**
363; **National Underground Railroad Freedom Center:** Farshid Assassi/Assassi Productions, 607 (b
tom); **Naturescapes Gallery:** Dale Malmedal, 201; **G. Alan Nelson:** 413; **New Mexico Tourism:** 4
408; **New York Ausable Chasm:** Tim Bresett, 509; **Nik Wheeler Photography:** 327; **Noah's Ark Wat**
**park:** 610 (bottom); **North Dakota Parks & Recreation Department:** Will Kincaid, 415; **Oakhurst Lin**
551; **Oglebay Resort:** 548; **Oklahoma City National Memorial Foundation:** 181 (bottom left & bott
right); Ann E. Clark (top); **Olympic Parks of Utah:** 618; **Maurcie Parnell:** 456; **Paul Brinker Photog**
**phy:** 449; **PhotoDisc:** 7, 30, 31 (left), 64, 68, 69, 74, 106 (top), 168, 176 (left), 215, 217 (left), 251, 2
622 (bottom), 624 (bottom); **Photri, Inc.:** 295, 578; C.W. Biedel, M.D., 404; **Don Poggensee:** 445; **R**
**sell Poole:** 462; **Positive Image Photography:** Marshall Hill, 165 (right center); **Providence Warwi**
**Convention and Visitors Bureau:** 25; **PunxsutawneyPhil.com:** Alan Freed, 53; **Putnam Cottage:** 5
**Christine Randall:** 500; **Raymond J. Malace Photography:** 111 (right), 133; **Robert D. Rheaume:**
**Richmond Wayne City:** 460; **Roanoke Island Festival Park:** 93; **Randall K. Roberts:** 406; **Roving Pho**
Dave Hodge, 239; **Greg Ryan/Sally Beyer:** 419, 423, 430, 441; **Salt Lake Convention and Visit**
**Bureau:** 218 (right); Eric Schramm (left), 219 (top); **Savannah Convention and Visitors Bureau:** 6
(top); **Scenicutah.com:** Ray Boren, 373, 366, 376; **Schlitterbahn Waterparks:** 614 (top); **Shambh**
**Mountain Center:** 207; **Shutterstock:** 35, 38, 79, 102, 124 (top), 139, 149, 154, 162, 170, 197, 211, 2
245, 256, 262, 274, 593, 598, 606, 616 (bottom), 623, 625; **Skip Willits Fine Art Photography:** 9,
55, 59, 60; **David H. Smith:** 395; **South Padre Island Convention and Visitors Bureau:** 173 (cente
**State of Alabama:** 574, 575; **Scott Stemmermann:** 611; **Stock 'N Trade Photography:** Rick Pohlke, 1
**Stock Solution:** 90, 106 (bottom); **Chuck Summers:** 542; **SuperStock:** 83, 127, 128, 292, 300, 318, 3
335, 379, 391, 409, 412, 421, 487, 495, 501, 525, 526, 556, 584; age fotostock, 86 (right), 126, 1
(center), 619 (top); Ping Amranand, 91; Carmel Studios, 350; Angelo Cavalli, 604; George Goodwin,
Dale Jorgensen, 619 (bottom); Sal Maimone, 198; Wilburn D. Murphy, 171; Prisma, 110; Larry Pros
199; Lynn Radeka, 156; Michael Rutherford, 89; Steve Vidler, 140 (bottom), 184; **Norman Swaffo**
481; **Tahoe Rim Trail Association:** 352; **Taliesin Preservation, Inc. © 2006:** Pedro E. Guerrero, 1
**Thompson Photography:** 210, 303, 326; **Touched By Nature:** Matt Palmer, 15; **Travel Montana:** Don
Sexton, 227; **Larry Ulrich:** 348; **Unicorn Stock Photos:** Jeff Greenberg, 343; Paul Thompson, 489; A
Trulove, 392; **USDA Forest Service:** 119, 605 (bottom); **Vulcan Park Foundation:** M. Lewis Kenne
115; **Janet Warlick:** 561, 563; **waterfallswest.com:** Leon Turnbull, 324; **Raymond Wesley:** 594; **W**
**Virginia State Parks and Forests:** 552; **West Virginia Tourism:** 547, 554; **Courtesy of Western Penns**
**vania Conservancy:** 56; **Deborah A. Weymouth:** 589 (top); **World Ice Art Championship:** Artist, Juni
Nakamura/Nicole Bair, 624 (top); **World of Coca-Cola:** 105; **Tom Zikas:** 353





Louis Weber, CEO
Publications International, Ltd.
7373 North Cicero Avenue
Lincolnwood, Illinois 60712





ISBN-13: 978-1-4127-1610-9
ISBN-10: 1-4127-1610-1

Manufactured in China.

8 7 6 5 4 3 2 1

Library of Congress Control Number: 2008920416

# Contents

*r the reader's convenience, we have arranged this table of contents in alphabetical order by state or country, llowed by the places and scenic drives featured there.*

# Create Your Ultimate Road Trip

North America is a diverse landscape dotted with stunning sites, remarkable attractions, and festive events. The great explorers only scratched the surface of the wonders the continent showcases. Indeed, the snow-capped peak of Denali in Alaska, the mystifying thermal vents in Wyoming's Yellowstone, and the sultry swamps of Florida's Everglades are amazing natural features. Beyond these natural beauties are the relics of ancient civilizations and modern-day masterpieces of engineering, architecture, and art. It's no accident that the continent's natural allure has been enhanced by the best of humankind's creations.

The landscape of the world has been changing since its beginnings, with some of its most astounding features created over millions of years. Our greatest accomplishments seem minor compared with the longevity of their natural counterparts. And whether natural or carefully constructed, these wonders will not last forever—which is as good a reason as any to visit as many of these places as you can—and that's where this book can help.

The first section of *Over 1001 Amazing Places to Go in North America* illuminates hundreds of the most amazing attractions in North America. Each profile comes alive with vibrant descriptions and eye-popping photography. You'll start in New England and work your way south and west across America, and then you'll learn about some of the greatest places to experience in Mexico and Canada. As these locations leap off the page, you just might be inspired to leave behind the comforts of home and see some of these amazing places with your own eyes.

## The Roads Best Traveled

If you do decide to explore the United States, why travel by air? You can't taste the varied flavors of this great nation on a flyover, so pack your imagination and your vehicle for a journey of discovery leading to the heart and soul of America. From the West Coast to the Northeast, the Mountain region to the South and Midwest, the second section of *Over 1001 Amazing Places to Go in North America* presents a diverse and distinctive collection of roadways that will transport you across a vast landscape of mountains, hills, prairies, farmlands, woodlands, valleys, canyons, deserts, and communities large and small that lie between.

Although all the roadways in this second section are scenic, most are special in another way: They have earned recognition from the U.S. Secretary of Transportation as either National Scenic Byways or All-American Roads. These prestigious designations require meeting high standards for combining scenic beauty with recreational, natural, historical, cultural, or archaeological significance. Currently, 126 roadways in 44 states have been named either National Scenic Byways or All-American Roads; these roadways are collectively known as America's Byways, and most are included in this book. National Scenic Byways and All-American Roads have somewhat different criteria to meet, but all represent classic journeys.

### *National Scenic Byways*

To earn the distinction of being designated a National Scenic Byway, a road must possess at least one of six intrinsic qualities—although most feature four or more and many display all six. An "intrinsic quality" is a scenic, recreational, natural, historical, cultural, or archaeological feature that is considered representative, unique, irreplaceable, or distinctly characteristic of an area.

- **Scenic qualities.** Along the byways you'll discover the depth and breadth of scenery in America, combining both natural and manufactured panoramas. But breathtaking vistas are just one aspect. A "scenic quality" may include everything from an electrifying neon landscape to scenes of friends, families, and strangers sharing their stories. It may feature a tableau where ancient or modern history comes alive, or which showcases native arts and culture. And, of course, it often does entail drop-dead-gorgeous picture-postcard views.
- **Recreational qualities.** Many of the byways feature rich recreational opportunities as close as the nearest lake, river, forest, canyon, or mountainside. To qualify as a "recreational quality," an activity must be associated with, and dependent upon, the natural and cultural elements of the corridor's landscape. Such activities might include hiking or biking through an adjoining national

orest, skiing a mountain trail, or fishing or afting a free-flowing river along the route.

**Natural qualities.** A "natural quality" refers o a feature in the visual environment that redates the arrival of human populations nd remains in a relatively undisturbed state. Natural qualities may include geological formations, fossils, land forms, bodies of water, egetation, and wildlife found along the byway.

**Historical qualities.** Many byways are historcal treasure troves, windows to discovery of America's heritage. To win recognition for its historic qualities, a byway's sites must encompass legacies of the past that are distinctly assoiated with physical elements of the landscape, whether natural or artificial. They must also be of such historical significance that they educate he viewer and stir an appreciation of the past.

**Cultural qualities.** A "cultural quality" is evidence and expression of the traditions or cusoms of a group of people. Crafts, music, dance, ituals, festivals, speech, food, special events, and architecture are all potential cultural qualiies awaiting discovery along America's Byways.

**Archaeological qualities.** "Archaeologial qualities" often dip into prehistory. They are physical evidence of historic or prehisoric life that's both visible and capable of being inventoried and interpreted. Along he byways, this evidence may take the form of anything from a dinosaur dig to a cave displaying Native American rock art.

### *All-American Roads*

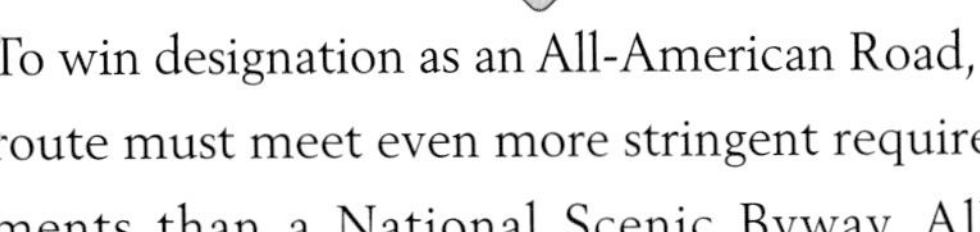

To win designation as an All-American Road, a route must meet even more stringent requirements than a National Scenic Byway. All-American Roads possess multiple intrinsic qualities that are both nationally significant and contain one-of-a-kind features that do not exist elsewhere. The road or highway must also be considered a destination unto itself—providing an experience so exceptional that travelers often consider taking a drive along the roadway a primary reason for their trip.

Whichever trails you choose to follow, you'll discover not only the byways themselves but also their accompanying stories and treasured places. Every byway has outstanding—and often unique—qualities that make it a special path to follow. And each byway's profile includes highlights of area attractions that you won't want to miss. Indeed, the byways are gateways to adventures where no two experiences are the same.

## Youth Is Served

If you have little ones in tow as you travel across North America, you'll love the special third section of this book, "Amazing Places to Take Your Kids." You'll learn about fun amusement and water parks, museums that cater to youngsters, zoos packed with favorite animals, events and festivals tailored to the young, historical sites and monuments that children are learning about in school, and national parks that will stimulate children's interest.

These attractions are grouped by region, so you can plan a trip you and the kids will love. Some of these places are also highlighted in the first section of *Over 1001 Amazing Places to Go in North America*, so you know the whole family will enjoy them.

## Look Before You Leave

Before you hit the road, you'll want to do some quick research to ensure the places you want to go are open. For example, some attractions close for renovation and maintenance, national parks are subject to forest fires and weather-related problems, roads close due to natural disasters, and many facilities close during the winter.

Most states and provinces have Web sites for their tourism boards, where you can find links to popular attractions and other information. You can also find valuable information at the United States National Park Service Web site (www.nps.gov), and many attractions have their own Web sites. If you aren't familiar with using the Internet, your local librarian can help get you started.

No matter which direction you head from any point in North America, you're sure to end up somewhere spectacular. With so many options, you better get packed!

# Acadia National Park

Some say the name "Acadia" came from New England's native Abenaki tribe. Others credit explorer Giovanni da Verrazano, who supposedly called Maine and its environs "Arcadia" after a region in ancient Greece known as a rustic place of perfect peace and quiet—a description that ideally suits Acadia National Park.

Situated off the coast of Maine, Acadia National Park covers nearly half of Mount Desert Island. Originally named Isles des Monts Deserts by explorer Samuel de Champlain in 1604, the island also boasts the towns of Bar Harbor, Southwest Harbor, Mount Desert, and Tremont.

From the coastline, you can see the island's barren mountaintops, sheared off by ancient glaciers. Cadillac Mountain, a granite-topped peak rising 1,532 feet, is the highest mountain along the North Atlantic seaboard. Glaciers created other unique features of Acadia. Look at a topographic map of Mount Desert Island, and you will see that it looks as if it had been gouged by giant bear claws—deep ravines, Long Pond, Echo Lake, Jordan Pond, Eagle Lake, and the seven-mile-long Somes Sound (said to be the only true fjord on the East Coast) all run in parallel lines north to south.

For centuries, the Abenakis fished the sylvan shores of Mount Desert Island; and in the 1800s, farming, fishing, and lumbering provided the local economy. But this way of life changed when artists joined the community in the mid-1850s. Great Hudson River School painters such as Thomas Cole and Frederic Church started showing their landscapes of Mount Desert Island to patrons and friends. Eventually this led to more "rusticators," city dwellers who flocked to the island for a breath of fresh air. At first Bohemians came, followed by the rich and famous. The Astor, Carnegie, Ford, Morgan, Pulitzer, and Vanderbilt families all owned estates on the island and vacationed there during summer. Perhaps the most prominent was John D. Rockefeller, whose estate's 45-mile spiderweb of carriage roads have helped make Acadia a hiking and mountain-biking mecca. Rockefeller gave 11,000 acres to Acadia, including some of its most spectacular coastline.

*Acadia National Park provides splendid views of Maine's rugged coast.*

By 1880, Bar Harbor had 30 hotels, and one ambitious entrepreneur had even built a hotel and a cog railway on Cadillac Mountain. Alarmed by the spiraling development, a group of wealthy islanders began acquiring land to put together what became Acadia National Park in 1919. Today, the park contains more than 40,000 acres and is Maine's only national park.

When visiting this sometimes-crowded island paradise, enjoy carriage rides, sailing, camping, canoeing, fishing, ice-fishing, rowing, cliff-climbing, kayaking, hiking, biking, and more on dozens of trails, beaches, coves, and mountain cliffs. Acadia (and all of Maine's coast) is tormented by wicked weather throughout the winter and early spring, but tourists swarm Acadia and the little nearby towns in the blissful summertime.

Panoramas are plentiful throughout the park. One is Thunder Hole, a coastal rock pounded by huge waves. There's Acadia Mountain Trail, with views of Somes Sound, Echo Lake, and the Cranberry Isles. The pristine Sand Beach lies between rugged coastal rocks and mountains made of tiny crushed shells. Eagle Lake, which spans 425 acres, is the largest on the island. Sieur de Monts Spring symbolizes the preservation of Acadia and features the Wild Gardens of Acadia and the Abbe Museum.

It's hard to go wrong in paradise.

(Opposite page) *Built in 1858, Bass Harbor Head Light marks the entrance to Bass Harbor on the southwest side of Mount Desert Island.*

# Boothbay Harbor

Boothbay Harbor lies along Maine's mid-coast. It's often called the Boating Capital of New England and hosts a summer festival called "Windjammer Days." The harbor is a great place for watching whales and puffins, canoeing, kayaking, hiking, biking, mackerel fishing, and camping. You can cruise to Monhegan Island or see sites such as the Maine Resources Aquarium, the Maine Maritime Museum, or Burnt Island Light, a lighthouse built in 1821.

Boothbay Harbor was incorporated in 1764. Thereafter, the settlement became known for its saw and grist mills and for its shipbuilding industry—more than 500 boats and ships up to 180 feet long were built there. Over time, fishing became more important to the community, which helps explain why today the harbor's symbol is a two-masted fishing schooner, or "pinky."

*Boothbay Harbor celebrates the age of sail each June with Windjammer Days.*

If you can handle some time away from modern luxuries, this rugged area remains one of Maine's most beautiful destinations. A hour's drive from Brunswick, Boothbay Harb is a village of about 2,300 with pleasant sho and boutiques. Its picturesque harbor is exac how many people picture Maine: Fishers ha in lobster traps, and masts gently rock in t distance. The aroma of steamed mussels mix with the salty ocean air. You can rent cove-si cottages; dine in fine restaurants; and brow quaint waterfront souvenir, antique, and cr shops. It also pays to explore the neighbo hoods inland from the harbor.

# Penobscot Bay

Penobscot Bay is Maine's real Down East. While the words "Down East" now refer to the coast of Maine and its culture, the term came from ships sailing downwind from Boston to Maine.

If you're looking forward to exploring the real outdoors, you've found your place. Choose among recreational sports such as fishing for trout, smallmouth bass, or landlocked salmon; hunting bear, moose, deer, grouse, or snowshoe hare; or sailing a three-masted schooner on the bounding main.

The region has Down East civilization, too. Should you seek a vacation spot that has been visited by the rich and famous, from actors to presidential candidates, there are the Penobscot Bay towns of Islesboro, North Haven, and Vinalhaven. If you're eager for a taste of authentic Down East cuisine, the bay area has dinners of lobster and lobster cakes, steamed mussels, corn on the cob, and New England clam chowder, and breakfasts of pancakes and waffles, Maine maple syrup, and Maine blueberry jam.

Penobscot Bay lies just southwest of Acadia National Park and borders Isle au Haut, which in 1943 became the last contribution to Acadia. Towns around the bay include Camden, Bar Harbor, and historic Castine, which was settled by the French in 1613. These nearby towns provide convenient lodging, fine dining, charming shops, and local galleries. There's also Fort Point State Historic Site, which has Fort Point Light (a lighthouse built in 1857), miles of hiking trails, and a gorgeous panorama of the bay and the islands surrounding it.

*The rocky shoreline of Penobscot Bay harbors quaint Maine towns with an authentic Down East feel.*

# White Mountain National Forest

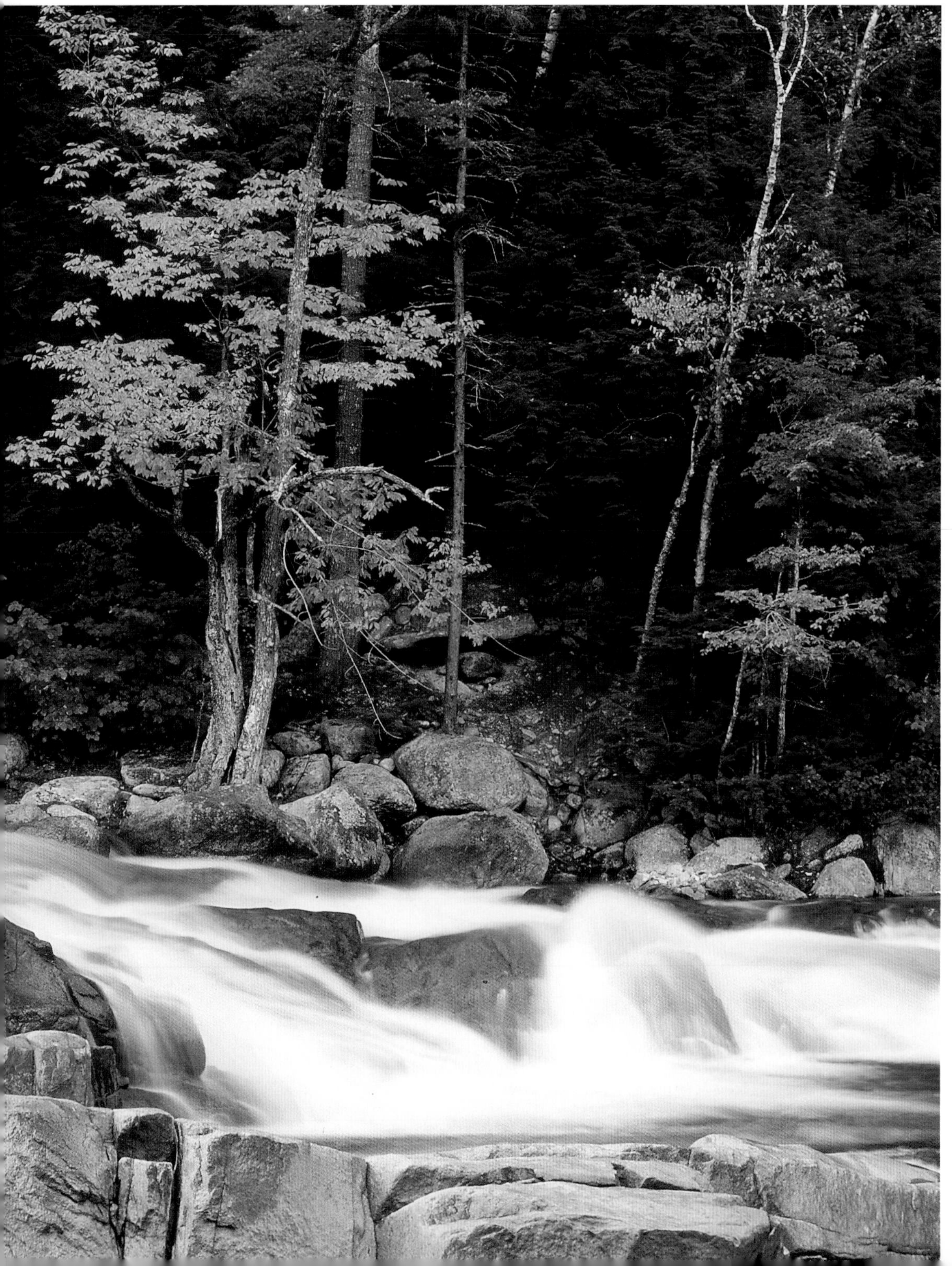

New Hampshire's White Mountain National Forest is the heart of the White Mountains. Mount Washington rises fiercely above the dense woodlands. At 6,288 feet it's the highest mountain in the northeastern United States. On a clear day, you can see into New Hampshire, Maine, Vermont, Massachusetts, and Canada from its peak. The strongest wind of all time was recorded there in 1934—231 miles per hour.

Mount Washington is part of the White Mountains' Presidential Range. The range also included the legendary Old Man of the Mountain—the rock formation remains New Hampshire's state symbol despite the collapse of its famous profile in 2003.

The vast majority of White Mountain National Forest's 800,000 acres are in New Hampshire, with the eastern edge creeping into Maine. The forest is indisputably nature's domain. It may be an easy drive from urban America, but it seems to be a million miles away. Fir, pine, beech, birch, and maple forests are crisscrossed by hiking trails that range from the half-mile Covered Bridge Nature Trail to the Appalachian Trail, which stretches from Maine to Georgia. The forest offers 23 campgrounds. Despite its size, White Mountain National Forest can get crowded, and some advise avoiding it on summer weekends.

*Originating in the White Mountains, the Saco River provides prime stretches for canoeing, kayaking, and tubing.*

# ake Winnipesaukee

*ibrant autumn foliage brightens the shoreline of Lake Winnipesaukee.*

ake Winnipesaukee is New Hampshire's rgest lake. It is 26 miles long and 15 miles cross at its widest point. The driving distance round the lake is 97 miles, though the jagged oreline measures 179 miles around. Dozens f islands scattered like beads throughout the ke's waters add to its scenic splendor.

Like so many of the spectacular natural rmations in North America, Lake Winipesaukee is a glacial phenomenon. It has so become a vacation phenomenon, attracting summer visitors for more than a century. Many come from Boston, which is just a two-hour drive away.

Vacationers are always welcome in the communities that surround Lake Winnipesaukee. The largest is Laconia, where Weirs Beach draws a crowd. Another favorite destination is Wolfeboro, which calls itself the oldest summer resort in America. Sir John Wentworth, colonial governor of New Hampshire, built his summer mansion there in 1769. Many years of local hospitality have yielded a friendly resort with plenty of shopping and culture.

Lake Winnipesaukee is ringed by the Ossipee and Sandwich mountain ranges, allowing other diversions, such as hiking, snowshoeing, fishing, and scuba diving. Among the lake's other attractions are the Canterbury Shaker Village and Kimball's Castle, an 1895 mansion with a panoramic view of "the broads," where Lake Winnipesaukee is 180 feet deep.

# Green Mountains

The Green Mountains of Vermont are full of surprises. The historic mountain range is a great place for caving, hiking, skiing, and gawking—because that's what most visitors do: Whether staring at the snowcapped mountain peaks or Vermont's kaleidoscopic autumn foliage, they gawk, because they must.

The 250-mile-long Green Mountains become the Berkshires to the south, in Massachusetts; to the west is Lake Champlain; and to the east are the White Mountains of New Hampshire. The 385,000-acre Green Mountain National Forest is the public's entry to the mountains. The national forest was formed in 1932 after floods and fires exacerbated by excessive logging threatened the region.

Nowadays, people say the Green Mountains boast six seasons—winter, spring, summer, fall, mud (early spring), and Black Fly (late M[ay] to late July). Avoid those last two! Autum[n] is the Greens' peak season: The fiery-hu[ed] foliage is unforgettable.

## Quick Fact

### *A Fighting Spirit*

Thanks to Ethan Allen and the Green Mountain Boys, the mountain range's name rings in history. Allen was the guerrilla leader who first fought against the Province of New York and later resisted the British, helping lead Vermont to its brief, 14-year independence starting in 1777. Told by his doctor, "General, I feel the angels are waiting for you," Allen is said to have replied, "Waiting, are they? Well . . . let them wait." If that isn't Vermont spirit, what is?

*Historic family farms are sprinkled within the dense forest that sheaths the Green Mountains.*

# Vermont Institute of Natural Science

'here are hundreds of authentic Vermont acation towns where you can get away from : all and enjoy what the state has to offer. But f you are in search of the spirit of the Green Aountain State, you might want to visit Voodstock, Vermont. And if you want to learn bout the heart and soul of little Woodstock, ake a trip a few miles outside of town, past he Quechee Gorge, to the Vermont Institute of Natural Science (VINS).

The VINS Nature Center is the leading New England care center for raptors—owls, falcons, hawks, eagles, and vultures, about 25 species in all—that can no longer survive in the wild. The center receives injured birds from all over the United States and houses them in specially adapted high-ceilinged cages. The Nature Center is artistically designed so that visitors can view the birds and forget that they are in a building at all.

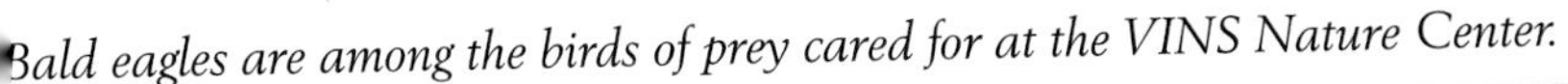

*Bald eagles are among the birds of prey cared for at the VINS Nature Center.*

*Visitors to the center can see raptors, such as this great gray owl.*

Guests also enjoy bird-watching along the center's nature trails.

Meanwhile, back in Woodstock, don't overlook the Billings Farm & Museum, a working dairy farm since the 1870s. Next door is the Marsh-Billings-Rockefeller National Historical Park. Vermont's first national park offers guided tours of the Marsh-Billings-Rockefeller Mansion and its grounds and gardens.

# Lake Champlain

*Sailing is one way to enjoy the pristine waters of Lake Champlain.*

Samuel de Champlain explored so much of New England that it was only fair to name the spectacular Lake Champlain after him. He discovered the lake in 1609 while in the Champlain Valley, which lies between Vermont's Green Mountains and the Adirondack Mountains of New York. Lake Champlain has since served the needs of merchants and mariners, scalawags and soldiers, smugglers and spies, and patriots and traitors. The lake has seen its share of naval conflict, too: Warfare on the lake climaxed in 1814, when troops led by U.S. Commodore Thomas McDonough defeated the British Navy in a fierce fight. During the 19th century, canal boats and steamboats carried coal, timber, iron ore, and grain across the lake. Today, industry has given way to recreation.

Lake Champlain has become a year-round playground featuring boating, hiking, skiing, snowshoeing, snowmobiling, ice climbing, and rock climbing. Bicycling around Lake Champlain is a special favorite, and cyclists take advantage of the Lake Champlain Bikeways' 35 loops and 10- to 60-mile tours.

Bounded by Vermont, New York, and Quebec, the lake's Alburg Peninsula juts southward from Quebec, making it one of the few places in the United States that can only be reached through Canada. A more familiar north crossing extends through Ticonderoga, New York. Just east of the town is Fort Ticonderoga, a sterling 18th-century fort with a museum and guided tours.

# Harvard Square

Iarvard Square is a great place to go if you vant to feel young, hip, and smart. Teeming with Harvard professors, students, and vannabes, "the Square" (as it's universally nown in the Cambridge-Boston area) can ive visitors the sense that they are attending Iarvard without the inconvenience of having o take exams.

The center of Harvard Square is a former ubway kiosk converted into a Harvard-worthy newsstand. The kiosk is surrounded by steps leading down to what is called "the Pit," a pocket-size park dominated by skateboarders. Restaurants, shops, and what may be the highest density of bookstores in the United States fill the remainder of the square.

Harvard Square wasn't always just a hangout. In 1630 it was the village of Newtowne, the first planned settlement in Anglo North America. Newtowne's street plan remains in use today, as do buildings dating from the early 1700s.

The Square is becoming more homogenized as national chains integrate with local shops. But be sure to stroll over to the Grolier Poetry Book Shop and pick up a volume of Robert Lowell or one of 15,000 poetry titles. Or grab a cup of coffee at a local café and enjoy the ambience of the Square.

*An old subway kiosk, now converted to a noteworthy newsstand, stands at the center of Harvard Square.*

# Freedom Trail

Follow the red brick line along the 2.5-mile Freedom Trail and you'll be able to take in 300 years of American history.

The idea for the Freedom Trail came in 1958 from William Schofield, an editorial writer for the *Boston Herald-Traveler*. He hatched the idea of creating a marked line that would transform Boston's mazelike streets into something that tourists could follow. His campaign succeeded and inspired other "trails," including the Constitutional Walking Tour of Philadelphia and Boston's Black Heritage Trail.

There are 16 stops of historic significance along the Freedom Trail. You can start your tour at any of the stops, but the tour officially begins at Boston Common. The 50-acre common was a British troop encampment during the American Revolution. Today's Bostonians think of the common as the centerpiece of the city's Emerald Necklace chain of parks.

From there, the trail moves to the Massa chusetts State House; Park Street Church; an the Granary Burying Ground, where John Han cock, Samuel Adams, and Paul Revere ar buried. It continues on to sites including th Old South Meeting House, where Sam Adam signaled the start of the Boston Tea Party; th Paul Revere House; and Bunker Hill Monu ment, where the ragged colonials held off th British Army.

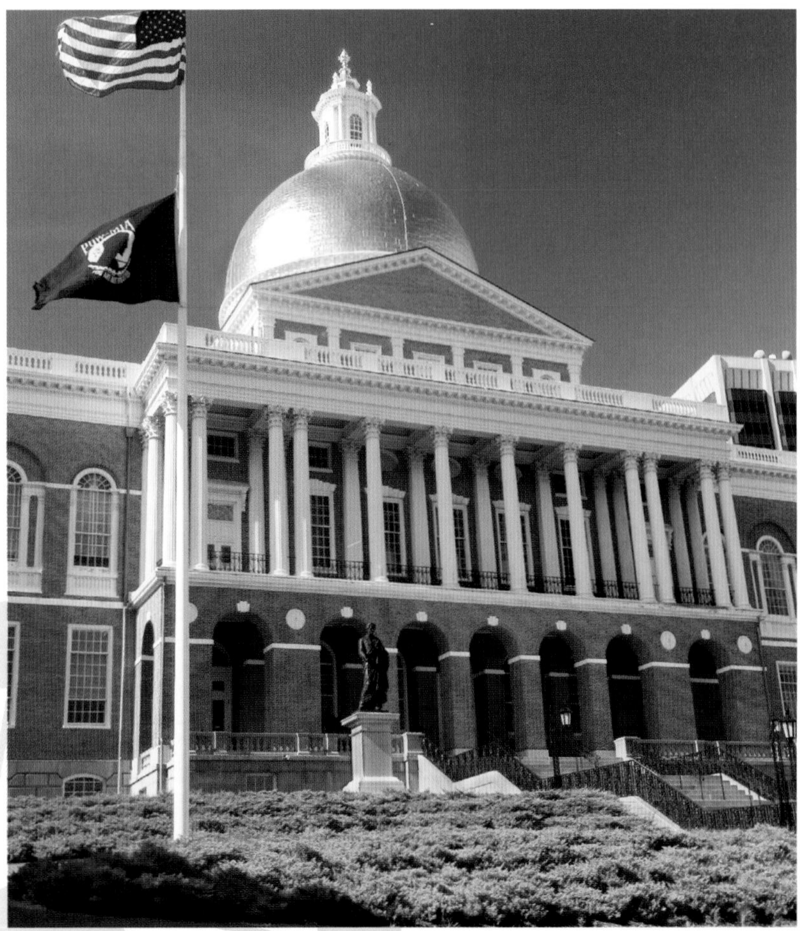

*The Massachusetts State House is the oldest building on Beacon Hill.*

*The Freedom Trail ends at the USS* Constitution, *which became known as "Old Ironsides" during the War of 1812.*

# Fenway Park

Fenway Park reigns as a temple of the Great American Game, despite the decades of misfortunes of its principal occupant, the Boston Red Sox baseball club.

Built in 1912, Fenway is Major League Baseball's oldest park. The stadium's highest capacity is just 36,108 people, and while the team suffered an 86-year dry spell beginning in 1918, Red Sox fans continued to crowd Fenway. Fans were finally rewarded in 2004 (and again in 2007) when Boston won the World Series.

Fenway Park is among the old ballparks that give their fans the feeling that they are surrounded by the legends—if not the ghosts—of ballplayers past. The right-field foul pole became known as "Pesky's Pole" after weak-hitting shortstop Johnny Pesky hit one of his few home runs just beyond it in the 1940s. Then there's a seat in the right-field bleachers painted red to mark the spot where Ted Williams hit the longest measurable home run (502 feet) at the park in 1946.

One caution: Fenway is also the rare major-league park that sells seats with obstructed views. Still, the atmosphere is magical and not-to-be missed when in Boston.

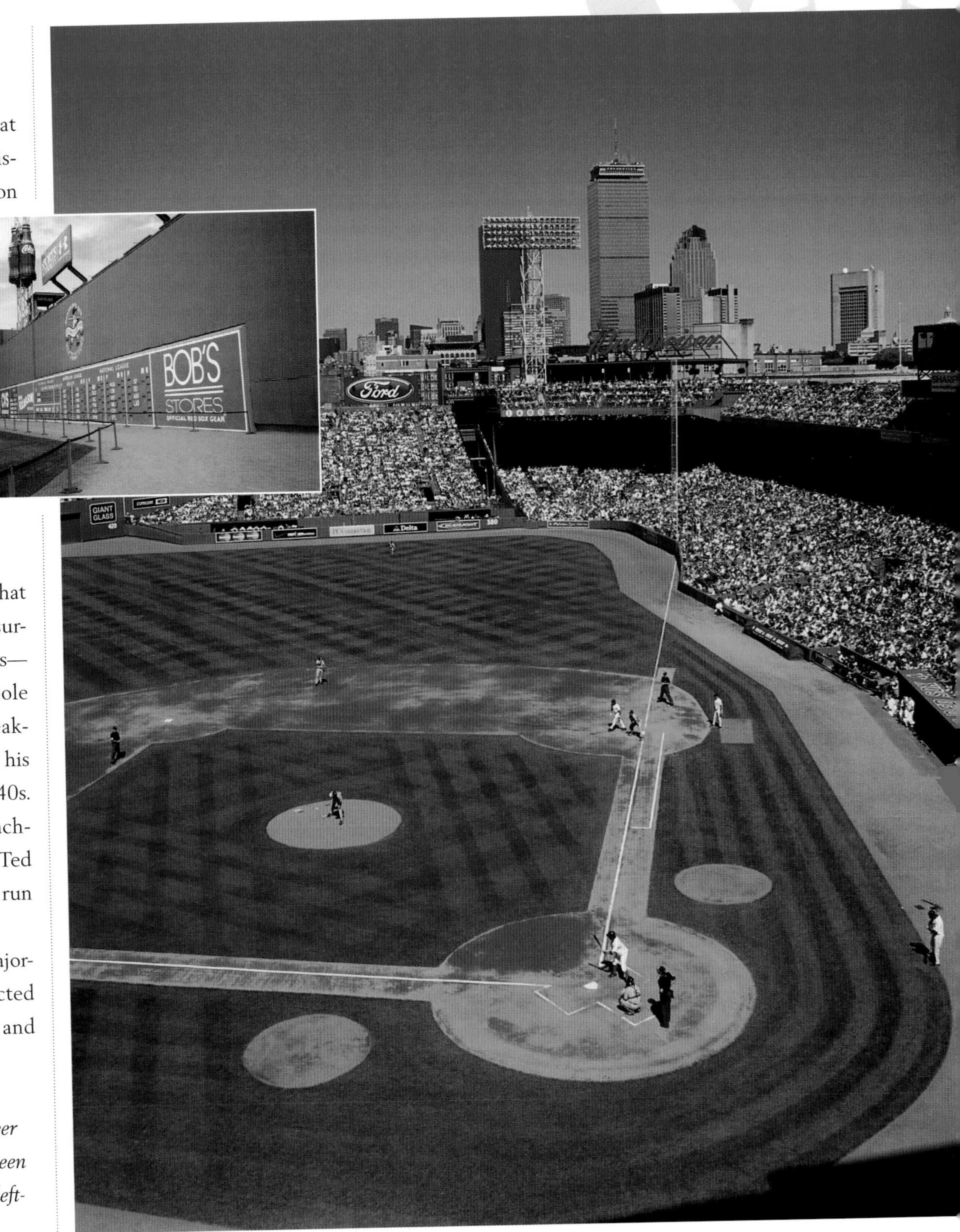


*Fans pack the stands in Fenway Park to cheer on their beloved Boston Red Sox. Painted green in 1947, The Green Monster* (inset) *is the left-field wall at Fenway. It stands 37 feet high.*

# Plymouth Rock

People flock to Plymouth, Massachusetts, to watch whales, relax on the beach, kayak, and see the famous ten-ton granite boulder, Plymouth Rock.

Plymouth Rock is hallowed in American history as the place where the Pilgrims set foot in America. They went on to form the first permanent European settlement in New England. While traveling across the Atlantic, they wrote the Mayflower Compact, the New World's first governing agreement, and signed it in Provincetown Harbor.

However, the claim that the Pilgrims landed at Plymouth Rock may be just that, since the first mention of the site came nearly a century after the *Mayflower* landed. No matter—this is the accepted spot where leaders John Carve William Bradford, and some 100 other Pi grims landed and started Plymouth Colon About half of the colonists died the first yea

"Thus, out of small beginnings . . . as on small candle may light a thousand, so th light here kindled hath shone unto many, Bradford wrote.

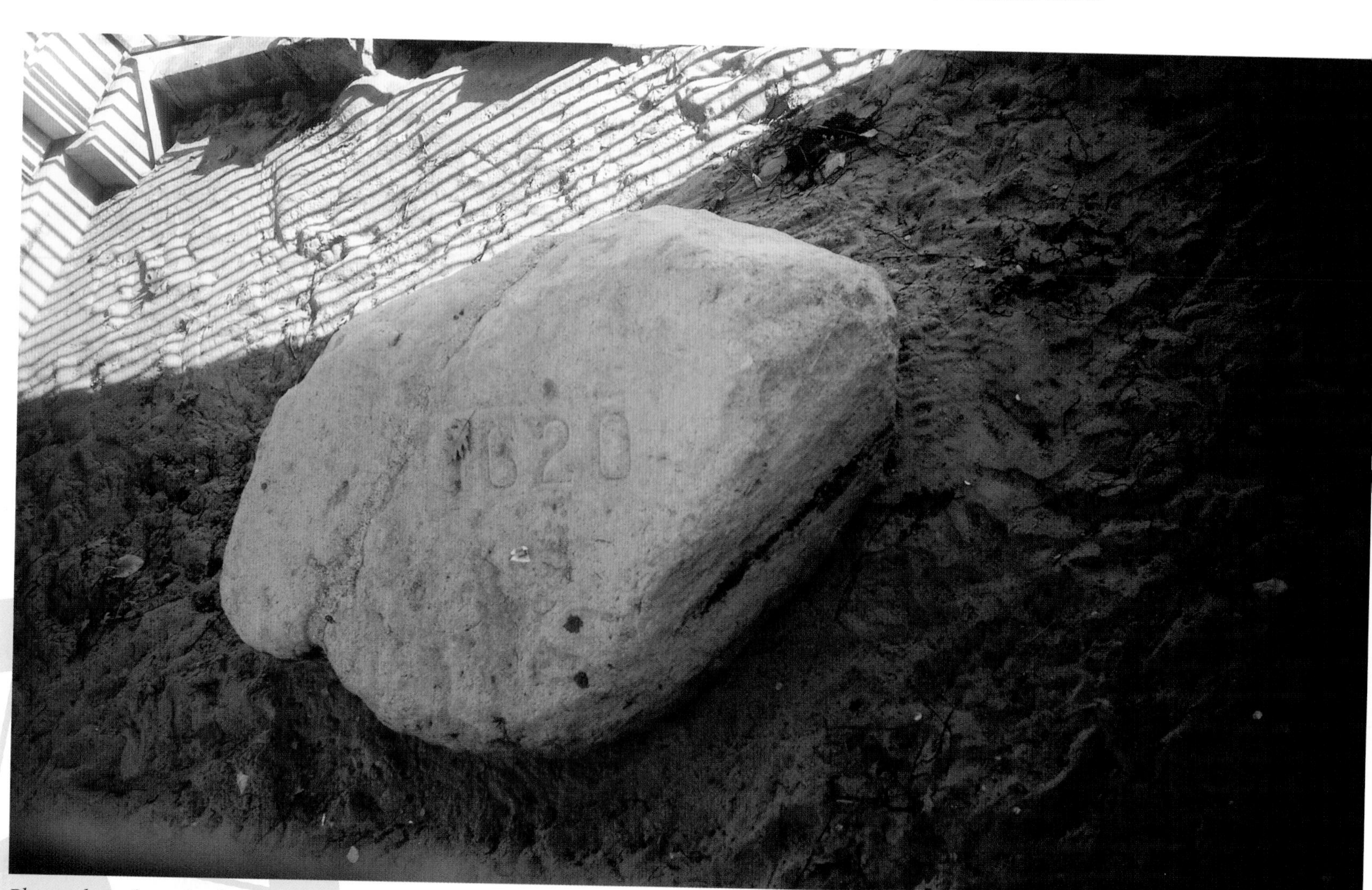


*Plymouth Rock marks the site where the Pilgrims were thought to have landed in 1620.*

# Walden Pond

Henry David Thoreau moved to Walden Pond to get a little peace and quiet and to write. He wrote an account of his time in the cabin he built by the pond and called it *Walden; or, Life in the Woods.* His little book, often credited with creating the conservation movement, changed the world.

"I lived alone, in the woods, a mile from any neighbor, in a house which I had built myself, on the shore of Walden Pond, in Concord, Massachusetts, and earned my living by the labor of my hands only," wrote Thoreau. He lived by the pond for two years, two months, and two days, and then moved back in with Ralph Waldo Emerson and Emerson's family.

In Thoreau's day, the land around the pond was one of the few woods left in the area, which was surrounded by farmland. Today, Walden Pond is part of Massachusetts's Walden Pond State Reservation, which includes the 61-acre pond plus another 2,680 acres known as "Walden Woods."

The park preserves Thoreau's temporary homesite; the original chimney was discovered in 1945, and a replica of the house was built there. Travelers can also linger at the statue of Thoreau, the reservation's The Shop at Walden, or Tsongas Gallery. But check in advance: Only 1,000 people are allowed in at a time.

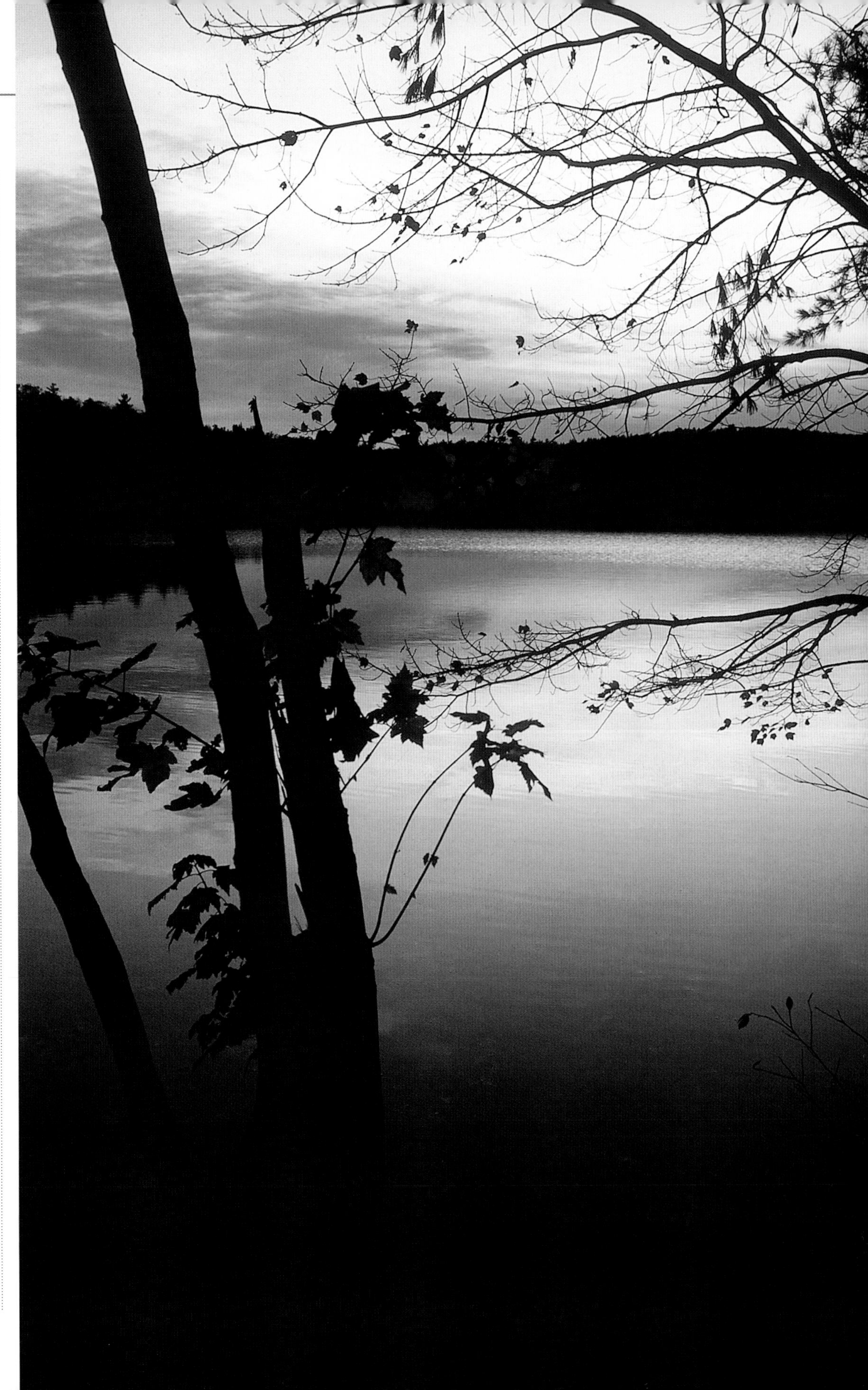

*Walden Pond, seen here at sunset, inspired author Henry David Thoreau's most famous work,* Walden.

# Boston Marathon

The first Boston Marathon was run in 1897. For a sense of perspective, consider that its closest rival, the New York City Marathon, was started in 1970.

The pioneering Boston Athletic Association (BAA) was the primary inspiration for the event. Chartered in 1887, the association provided more than half the U.S. Olympic team for the first modern Olympics in 1896. The next year, it was ready to stage its own BAA Games, the culminating event of which was a

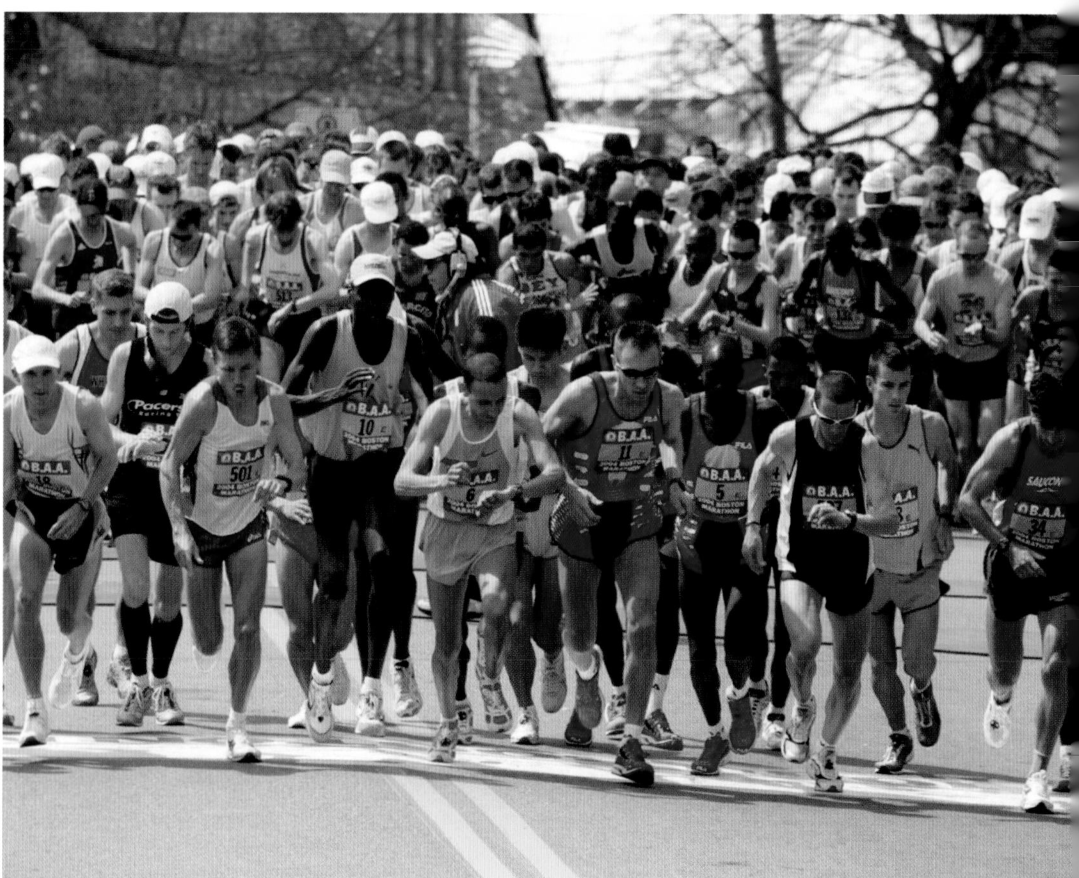


*Runners take off from Hopkinton for the Men's Open.*

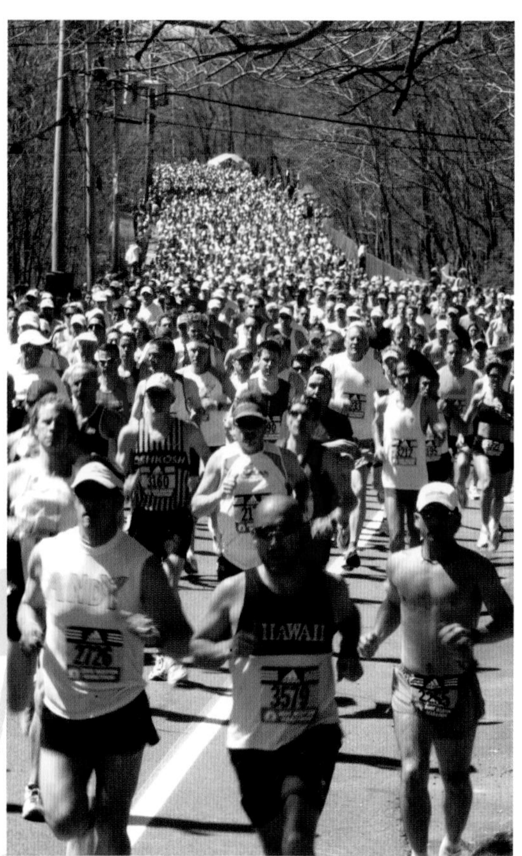


*The Boston Marathon is held each year on Patriots' Day.*

24.5-mile marathon. The first winner was John J. McDermott, who finished in 2:55:10. The fastest finish in a modern Boston Marathon of 26 miles, 385 yards was Robert K. Cheruiyot, in 2006, with a time of 2:07:14. But the most beloved would have to be Johnny A. Kelley, a winner in 1935 and 1945 who finished a record 58 of the 61 Boston Marathons he ran. Kelley died at age 97 in 2004. The most famous loser was amateur Rosie Ruiz, who in 1980 appeared to be the women's winner. But when the videotape was later examined, it revealed that Ruiz had cheated, slipping into the pack about a half-mile from the finish line.

As a matter of tradition, the Boston Marathon is held annually on Patriots' Day, the third Monday in April. So join the roughly half-million spectators who line the marathon route from Hopkinton to Boston each spring to cheer on the runners—especially the rookies. Supply them with water, snacks, and have a ball!

# Boston Harborfest

ndependence Day in Boston is celebrated at mammoth bash called Boston Harborfest, a ix-day patriotic extravaganza that crescendos o a dynamic fireworks display on July 4.

Harborfest has been a favorite of Bostoians and visitors for a quarter-century. Celbrants dress the Cradle of the American evolution with bright trappings of pageantry s Boston revels in its colonial past. There are more than 200 events at the waterfront and downtown areas, including walking tours, lectures, reenactments, and alfresco concerts, plus perennial favorites such as the Chowderfest, Children's Day, tours of the Boston Harbor Islands, and the arrival of the USS *Constitution*, also known as "Old Ironsides," complete with working cannons. About half the events are free.

(Above) *A marching band dressed as British Army Redcoats makes its way down the street during Boston Harborfest.*

At the Harborfest, make your way through crowds of loyalists, royals, and patriots to a favored spot such as the Massachusetts Avenue Bridge to hear the Boston Pops play the 1812 Overture (with traditional cannon fire and church bells). Then watch the fireworks blowout on the Esplanade, the long stretch of parkland along the Charles River.

(Left) *Rebel reenactors ready their reproductions of colonial weapons in a Boston parade.*

# Newport Mansions

Newport is a small city on Aquidneck Island, Rhode Island, in Narragansett Bay. It surely must be the home-viewing capital of the world. Each year, 3.5 million visitors come to the city of 30,000.

Many of the millions of tourists who cross Newport Bridge are drawn by the world's most spectacular collection of mansions, most from the 19th-century Gilded Age of the Astors, Belmonts, and Vanderbilts. Among the most famous, Newport boasts Beechwood, the home of Caroline Schermerhorn Astor, inventor of the American social register. Astor renovated the home in 1881 for $2 million, an inconceivable amount at the time. Today, costumed actors conduct tours there. Stunning, too, is The Breakers, Cornelius Vanderbilt II's summer home, with 70 rooms finished in alabaster and rare marble. The Breakers is also open for tours.

Other reasons to visit Newport include the world-famous JVC Newport Jazz Festival each August and the Newport Folk Festival, not to mention lesser-known fests such as the Newport Waterfront Festivals. These include the Great Chowder Cook-Off and the Spring Boat Show. Then there are the exhibits and tournaments at Newport's International Tennis Hall of Fame.

*Overlooking the Atlantic Ocean, The Breakers is among the most elaborate of Newport's exquisite mansions. It was named for the waves that crash into the rocks below the estate.*

# Benefit Street

If you're touring Providence, Rhode Island, and its antique treasures, the best place to start is Benefit Street, also known as the "Mile of History." The best time to visit Benefit Street is during the Providence Preservation Society's annual June Festival of Historic Houses.

Benefit Street was established in 1756 and became home to Providence's well-to-do merchants. During the next two centuries, however, it crumbled into a tenement slum until the Preservation Society took action to turn the neighborhood into a model for historic restoration worldwide.

Today, almost all of the buildings along the Mile of History have been restored, giving the street the architectural flavor of colonial times. While many of the building interiors are off-limits to the public, visitors can take in the historical ambience of this collection of homes and businesses. One exception is the John Brown House Museum, just around the corner from Benefit Street, which is open for tours.

(Below) *A three-story 18th-century redbrick home with white trim is representative of the restored structures on the "Mile of History."*

(Above) *A historic aura permeates Providence's Benefit Street.*

Not to be confused with John Brown the abolitionist, Providence's John Brown was a politician who completed the mansion in 1788. John Quincy Adams proclaimed the house "the most magnificent and elegant private mansion that I have ever seen on this continent."

Benefit Street was also the haunt of authors Edgar Allen Poe and H. P. Lovecraft. Less unsettling denizens have included the patriots at the Old State House on Benefit Street, where Rhode Island declared its independence from the British Crown two months before the nation's founders did so.

# Block Island

On one side of Block Island is the Atlantic Ocean; on the other, Block Island Sound. The island lies 12 miles off the coast of Rhode Island and about 18 miles from the tip of Long Island, New York. Visitors can sail or fly a private airplane to get there, but most take the ferry. The high-speed ferry has whittled the trip to just half an hour, but why hurry? This retreat offers a kind of time travel, where you can relax and think back to when you had time to skip rocks into the ocean and dig your toes into the sand.

Block Island is a tear-shape isle only three miles wide and seven miles long with about 7,000 acres of rolling hills, sandy cliffs, verdant valleys, timeless beaches, and 365 pocket-size ponds. The signature Victorian homes still set the scene on the inhabited parts of the island. The island's fierce winters guarantee the per manent population will never rise much abov 1,000 residents; in summertime, howeve 10,000 or more occupy the island.

Visit the Block Island North Light, built i 1867 on Sandy Point, and Block Island South east Light, built in 1873 (Southeast Light i the tallest lighthouse in New England). Bot have museums.

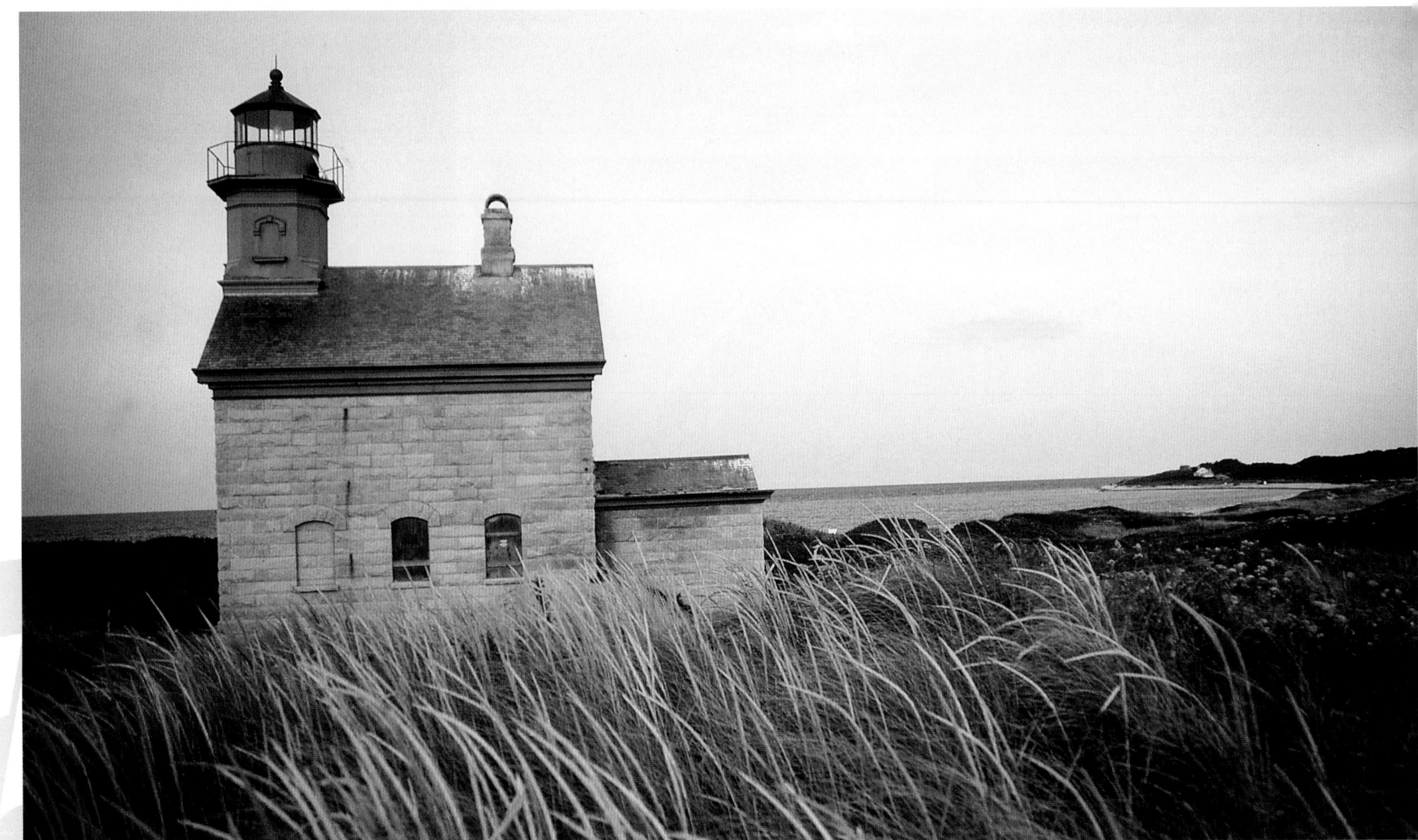

*Block Island North Light operated from 1867 to 1970. In 1989, the lighthouse was restored and now aids ships in navigating near Sandy Point.*

# Stonington Borough Lighthouse

The town of Stonington is the oldest borough in Connecticut (Stonington Borough), settled in 1753 and chartered in 1801. Both the lighthouse and the town represent the history and architecture of an archetypal Connecticut town.

The Stonington Borough Lighthouse Museum is in the restored 30-foot granite tower, which looks as much like a fort as a lighthouse. The beacon was first built on Stonington Point in 1823 to guide the many vessels approaching Stonington Harbor from Long Island Sound. While the original lighthouse eroded and was dismantled, materials from it were saved and used to build the current lighthouse, which was completed in 1840. The lantern was visible up to 12 miles at sea thanks to its 10 oil lamps and parabolic reflectors.

The lighthouse museum is a gateway to Connecticut's past. Six rooms of exhibits testify to the rich and varied history of this coastal region, notable for its Stonington stoneware, which is characteristically splashed with cobalt blue and was made between 1780 and 1834 from clay imported from New York and New Jersey.

The museum also features furniture and portraits that give visitors a peek at the lives of the early blacksmiths, potters, farmers, fishers, merchants, and shipbuilders who lived in Connecticut. One notable portrait is of David Chesebrough, called "King David" in Newport, Rhode Island, for his dominance of the merchant trade. It was painted by John Smibert in Newport in 1732, and hangs over the main room's fireplace mantel. Mystic, Connecticut, with its Mystic Seaport, is about ten minutes away.

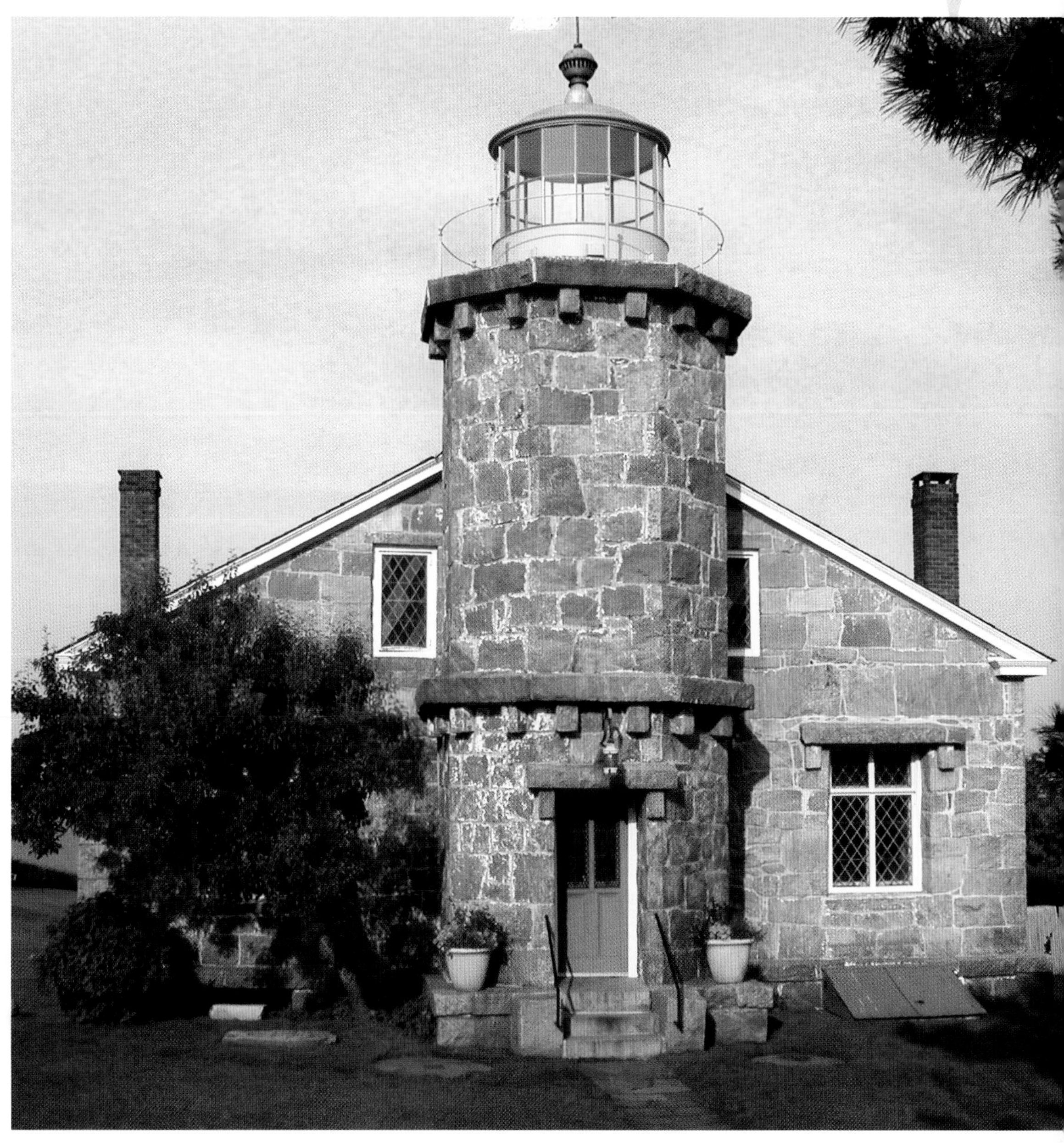

*In 1927, the Stonington Borough Lighthouse was converted to a museum honoring the maritime history of this quaint coastal village.*

# Mystic Seaport

The best way to enter Mystic Seaport, logically enough, is from the sea—best of all in a sailboat. Sure, you can come by car or bus, but it's not quite the same. Sailors who approach Mystic Seaport during the day, slightly dazed by the sun and salt spray, secure their boats and step ashore into a replica of an early-19th-century seafaring town, right down to the costumed actors role-playing strollers, printers, bartenders, teachers, bankers, sailors, sailmakers, chandlers, ship carvers, coopers, mast hoop-makers, and clerks at the Geo. H. Stone General Store. Best of all, visitors who sail into Mystic Seaport may enjoy a walk through the 17-acre town at night, when most tourists and impersonators have gone home. During the day, Mystic Seaport seems as if it's a vision of another century. Under the moonlight, you're sure it is.

Mystic Seaport is in Mystic, Connecticut, which is about a three-hour drive from New York City and two hours from Boston. The seaport is where the Mystic River empties into the Long Island Sound. It is one of a string of Connecticut sea-related enterprises ranging from the nearby New London Naval Submarine Base to the more accessible Mystic Aquarium & Institute for Exploration.

The town of Mystic became a shipbuilding center in the 17th century. Historians say ship-

*The* Charles W. Morgan *is a whaling ship built in 1841 and used until 1921. Mystic Seaport acquired the ship in 1941.*

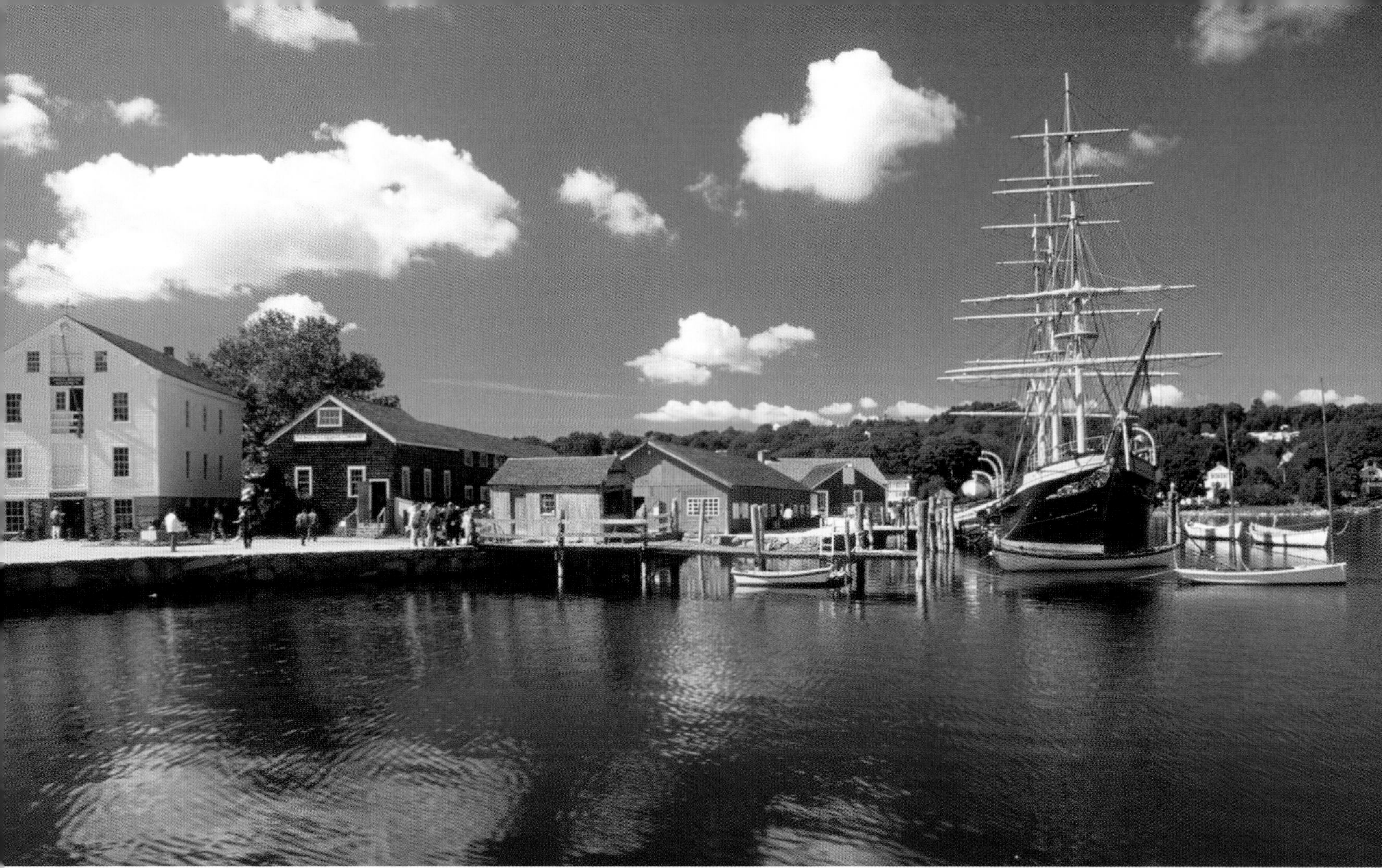

uilders along the Mystic River constructed more than 600 sailing vessels between the ate 1700s and the end of World War I. But by hen the great wooden sailing ships had been utstripped by steam-powered vessels. Mystic's maritime enterprises, like those in most f New England, began to vanish.

Then three visionary Mystic citizens—a octor, a lawyer, and an industrialist—devised plan to turn Mystic Seaport into a living ducational institution designed to preserve eagoing culture. Following this model, Mystic Seaport expanded in the 1940s. Historic uildings—including the Buckingham-Hall House, a coastal farmhouse, the Nautical nstruments Shop, the Mystic Press Printing Office, and the Boardman School one-room schoolhouse—were moved from their original locations in New England and put together to form Mystic Seaport, a model New England seagoing village. Mystic Seaport became one of the first living museums.

The project's leaders swiftly assembled one of today's largest collections of maritime history: There are more than two million maritime artifacts, an impressive selection of maritime photography with more than one million images and 1.5 million feet of film, and an unparalleled collection of almost 500 wooden sailboats. These collections are available at Mystic Seaport's Collections Research Center storage and preservation facility.

*The* Joseph Conrad *is both an exhibit and a training ship for the Mystic Mariner Program at Mystic Seaport.*

The Henry B. duPont Preservation Shipyard, launched in the 1970s, gives Mystic the look and feel of a real seaport. In 1998, the shipyard workers re-created the historic schooner *Amistad*, from keel to topmast. Mystic Seaport also is home port to four ships that are National Historic Landmarks, most notably the *Charles W. Morgan*, a three-masted whaling bark built in 1841 in New Bedford, Massachusetts. "She has outlived all others of her kind," the seaport notes, and she alone is more than worth the price of admission.

# Statue of Liberty

Standing high over New York Harbor since 1886, the majestic Statue of Liberty has been the focal point of countless photographs—and probably as many tears. She stands for freedom, hope, and possibility. But when you visit, don't let the vivid symbolism prevent you from admiring this matchless work of art.

Study the magnificence of the sculpture, alive with dignity, grace, and movement. It seems she is striding forward, torch in one hand, tablet in the other, with her copper gown flowing around her. The crown is regal, the torch a beacon. Her face is that of everyone.

Consider the scale: Physically, Lady Liberty weighs about 225 tons and stands more than 151 feet high. The sculpture is further elevated by the 65-foot-high foundation and the 89-foot-high granite pedestal. (For years she was the tallest structure in New York City.) The statue is classified as a "neoclassical realistic sculpture," but artistry may not be what comes to mind when you examine her 42-foot arm, her 35-foot waist, and her size 879 sandals. She is not only a work of art—she is a feat of engineering.

The statue is a massive iron pylon with a skeletal structure (engineered by Gustav Eiffel of Eiffel Tower fame) clad with copper skin sculpted by Frederic Auguste Bartholdi. Liberty was first erected in France, then dismantled and shipped to Bedloe's Island in New York Harbor. The transfer required 214 crates, and it took American workers four months to reassemble her.

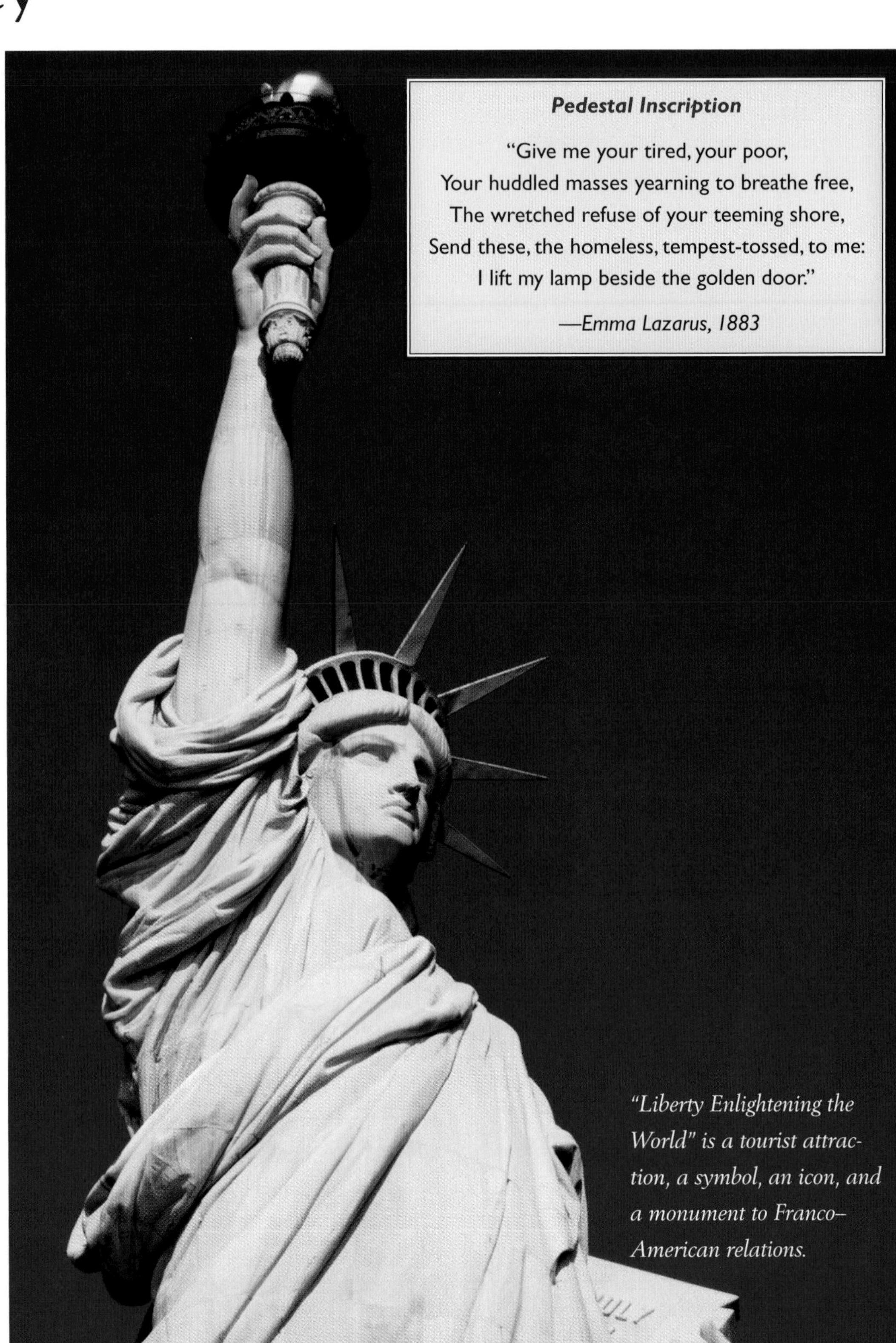

***Pedestal Inscription***

"Give me your tired, your poor,
Your huddled masses yearning to breathe free,
The wretched refuse of your teeming shore,
Send these, the homeless, tempest-tossed, to me:
I lift my lamp beside the golden door."

*—Emma Lazarus, 1883*

*"Liberty Enlightening the World" is a tourist attraction, a symbol, an icon, and a monument to Franco–American relations.*

tially visitors could climb 354 steps and
k out the 25 windows in Lady Liberty's
en-point crown.

You may not know that "Liberty Enlight-
ing the World" (the statue's real name) was
ginally meant to be a lighthouse. But the
ht the Statue of Liberty was to be dedicated
1886, the fog rolled in, the rain poured, and
much anticipated harbor light was at best
n. For years, one electrical system after
other was installed in the torch with limited
ccess. Eventually the goal was given up, and
sculpture was declared a national monu-
nt and turned over to the Department of
Interior.

## Quick Fact

***Statue of Liberty Specifications***

| | |
|---|---|
| Height from base to torch | 151′1″ |
| Ground to tip of torch | 305′1″ |
| Heel to top of head | 111′1″ |
| Length of hand | 16′5″ |
| Index finger | 8′0″ |
| Head from chin to cranium | 17′3″ |
| Head thickness from ear to ear | 10′0″ |
| Distance across each eye | 2′6″ |
| Length of nose | 4′6″ |
| Length of right arm | 42′0″ |
| Thickness of right arm | 12′0″ |
| Thickness of waist | 35′0″ |
| Width of mouth | 3′0″ |
| Length of tablet | 23′7″ |
| Width of tablet | 13′7″ |
| Thickness of tablet | 2′0″ |
| Ground to top of pedestal | 154′0″ |

On July 30, 1916, during World War I, a cache of dynamite was blown up at a nearby New Jersey wharf. It caused damage to the Bedloe site, popping bolts out of Liberty's right arm. The statue was closed for repairs, but the arm (which, of course, included the torch) never reopened to the public. Gutzon Borglum, better known for creating Mount Rushmore, redesigned the torch that year. He added 600 pieces of yellow cathedral glass to enhance the enigmatic light. Today, through the power of many incandescent and mercury vapor lamps, the torch lights up the harbor, shining many times brighter than the moon.

Many sightseeing opportunities have been curbed since the tragedy of September 11, 2001. But you can still get to the island by ferry, walk the grounds, and visit the multilevel pedestal. It holds museums, memorabilia, tributes to the artisans and engineers who created her, pictures, original pieces replaced in a renovation (including the original flame), murals, and much more. Nevertheless, the star of this show is the armature. It sparks awareness of the brilliance of both the sculptor and the engineer who brought Lady Liberty to life.

*From 1892 to 1954, more than 12 million immigrants entered the United States through Ellis Island, which stands in the shadow of the Statue of Liberty.*

# The Solomon R. Guggenheim Museum

"I need a fighter, a lover of space, an agitator, a tester, and a wise man . . . I want a temple of spirit, a monument!" said Hilla Rebay to Frank Lloyd Wright. Rebay was the art advisor to Solomon R. Guggenheim, and the collaboration of these three led to the creation of the fabulous Guggenheim Museum, now known for both its collections and its adventurous architecture.

Guggenheim chose New York City as the site for his new art museum. Wright had reservations about designing the museum for the already overcrowded, overpopulated city, but he reluctantly agreed to the project. The museum opened in 1959.

The Guggenheim Museum remains an iconoclast. Viewed from Fifth Avenue, its exterior is an inverted cone with wide bands rising upward like a child's giant top. Inside, the museum contains an atrium and a spiral ramp where visitors view artwork from a perspective that can be dizzying. Despite its impressiv permanent collection of works by Kandinsk Klee, Calder, Picasso, Rousseau, and man more, visitors sometimes find it a relief t return to the atrium.

Wright's design will forever remain cor troversial, which might be one reason th museum has been so readily adopted by Ne Yorkers—despite Wright's feelings that the city lacked merit.

*Built to showcase avant-garde paintings and sculptures, the Guggenheim Museum is itself a masterpiece.*

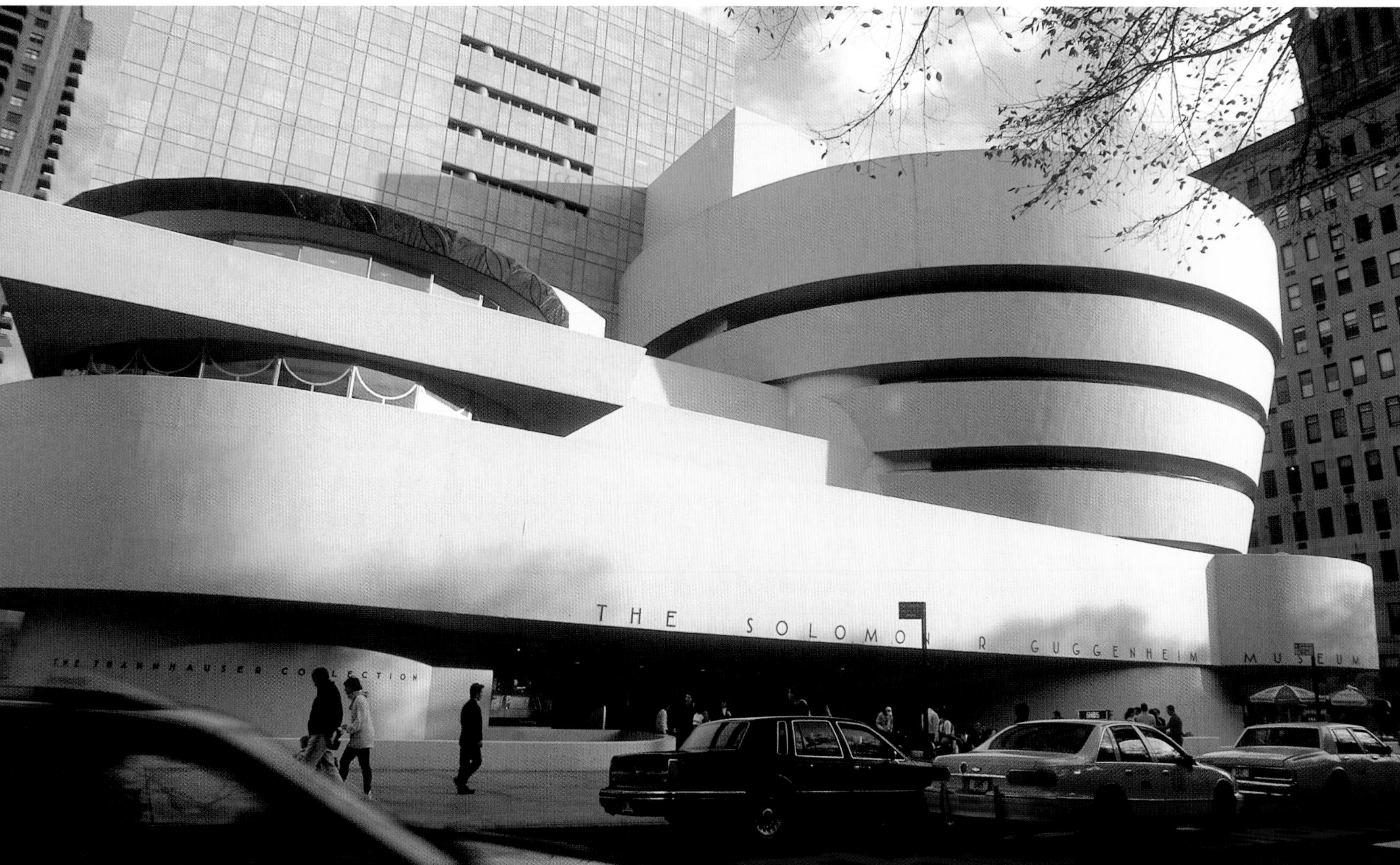

# [T]he Metropolitan Museum of Art

*The American Wing Courtyard at the Met is an interior sculpture garden.*

[A]ny list of the world's most important art [m]useums includes the Metropolitan Museum [o]f Art, better known as "the Met," which [b]oasts one of the world's greatest collections [of]—just about everything.

The museum's two-million-square-foot [b]uilding is a treasure of painting, sculp[tu]re, and decorative art collections, includ[in]g exhibits of American art divided into 24 [b]reathtaking period rooms. The Met also fea[tu]res unsurpassed collections of Dutch Mas[te]rs, Impressionists, and Post-Impressionists from Monet to Mirot, Modigliani, and Matisse. Its massive antiquities collections include ancient Near Eastern art; Greek and Roman art; Asian art; and the art of Africa, Oceania, and the Americas.

More than five million people visit the Met each year. What makes it so appealing? The Fifth Avenue facade and impressive permanent collections give the Met an aura of excellence. But the museum also is in a permanent state of flux, attracting visitors with special temporary exhibits of works culled from influential artists or periods.

Plus, it's a great place to take the family. Children and adults alike enjoy the musical instruments exhibitions, the Costume Institute, and the wonderful Arms and Armor collection, which includes armor for men, women, horses, and children. There's also the mysterious and mind-boggling assemblage of 36,000 Egyptian art objects.

# Central Park

Central Park is the jogging, bicycling, picnicking, and recreational center of life in Manhattan. The park was designed in 1857 by landscape architect Frederick Law Olmsted and his partner Calvert Vaux to be an island of tranquility in the middle of the roiling city.

Today, Central Park hosts activities from alfresco dining while listening to the Metropolitan Opera to strolling through formal gardens or exploring the zoo. There are also spots to fish, play tennis, ice skate, swim, and rollerblade. The park offers horseback riding

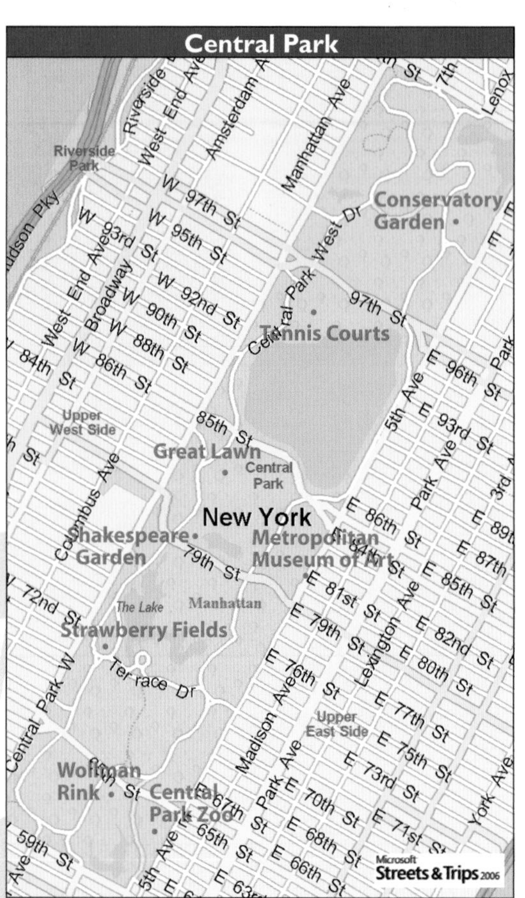

*The elegant cast-iron Pine Bank Bridge is located near the southwest entrance of Central Park.*

and famous horse-drawn carriages. In the summer, the Public Theater presents a Shakespeare in Central Park series, there are rock concerts in the park, and children can ride the carousel. There are many superb restaurants nearby. On the park's east side you'll find the Obelisk (formerly called Cleopatra's Needle) and the Metropolitan Museum of Art; on the west side are the American Museum of Natural History and Strawberry Fields, the section of the park named after the song "Strawberry Fields Forever" in memory of John Lennon. The west entrance to Strawberry Fields contains a memorial to Lennon—a black-and-white mosaic featuring the word "Imagine."

America's first landscaped public park is big enough for all this and much more; it covers 843 acres and is 2.5 miles long and a half-mile wide. Central Park has a 6.1-mile loop for ca that has parallel paths for riders, joggers, ar cyclists during the week, while the park closed to motorists on weekends. The pa earned a reputation for crime decades ago, b those days are long gone. So get out and enjo

*Tourists leave flowers and memorabilia on the "Imagine" mosaic in memory of John Lennon.*

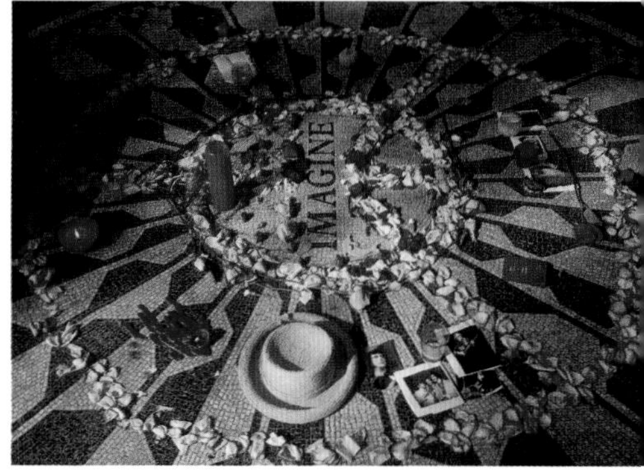

# Ṭimes Square

ʼew York City's Times Square is a blaring, ːectrifying, exhilarating, intoxicating, spotlit :rossroads of the world." Don't believe it? imes Square welcomes 26 million visitors nnually to its stores, hotels, restaurants, the- :ers, and attractions.

Times Square has attracted tourists for a :entury. Its first electric billboard went up 1917, and ever since the square has been ·nonymous with glitz. Today there are more high-technology signs, but the famous electronic newswire still lights up the base of One Times Square, and the ball still drops at the top of the building each New Year's Eve, a tradition since 1907. Times Square remains the heart of midtown Manhattan, in part because the area is a gateway to the city's main theater district, known as Broadway, which extends from 41st Street uptown to the Studio 54 Theatre on 54th Street.

Once upon a time, Times Square had a reputation as the worm at the core of the Big Apple, but the sleaziness was cleaned up in the 1990s and replaced with shops, restaurants, and other tourist-friendly attractions. Many large financial and media firms now have their headquarters in the neighborhood. While as crowded and crazy as ever, Times Square today is an amazing place where visitors can feel comfortable bringing the whole family.

*ʼazzling neon signs and advertisements have made Times Square a New York City icon.*

# Rockefeller Center

Midtown Manhattan's Rockefeller Center is a complex of 19 commercial buildings a few blocks south of Central Park. The center is a shopping mall, an Art Deco icon, a winter wonderland, the backdrop for a television network's morning program, and the only place on earth where you can nurse a cocktail and watch ice-skaters leap and twirl beneath a big, golden statue of Prometheus.

The center of the complex is 30 Rockefeller Plaza, a 70-story building that towers above the skating rink and the adjacent central plaza. Visitors can enjoy glamorous dancing accompanied by a big band in the Rainbow Room or dine next door at the Rainbow Grill, which provides a glistening view past the Empire State Building through its room-spanning vertical windows.

Rockefeller Center is also home to NB studios, which includes the legendary Stud 8H. Arturo Toscanini, the NBC Sympho Orchestra, and *Saturday Night Live* have be filmed there. Or take a tour or see a movie stage show at Radio City Music Hall, the lar est indoor theater in the United States, whe the sky-high-kicking Rockettes have be knocking out audiences since 1932.

*The Plaza at Rockefeller Center is decorated by a golden statue of Prometheus atop a water fountain.*

# United Nations

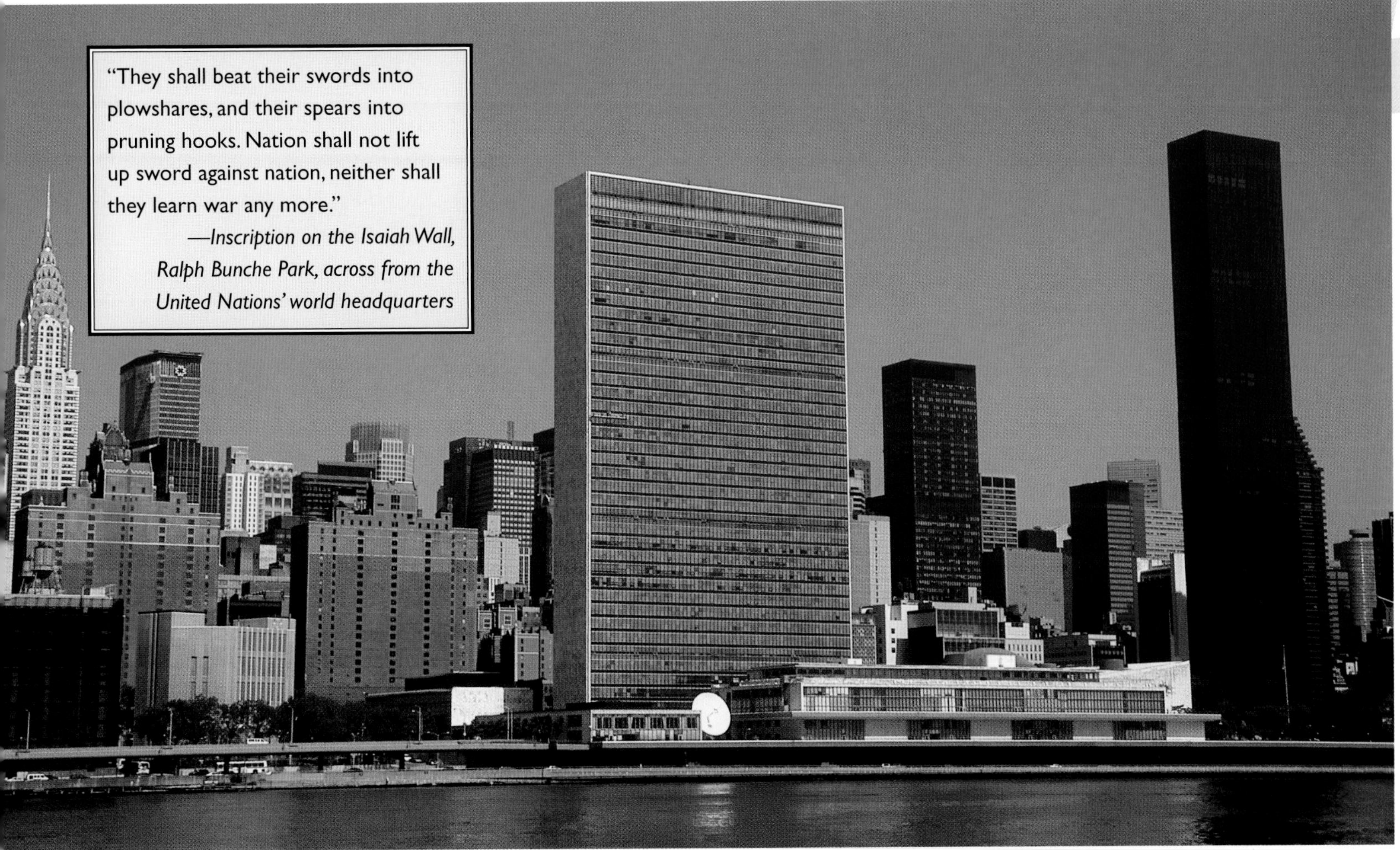

> "They shall beat their swords into plowshares, and their spears into pruning hooks. Nation shall not lift up sword against nation, neither shall they learn war any more."
>
> —*Inscription on the Isaiah Wall, Ralph Bunche Park, across from the United Nations' world headquarters*

The United Nations (UN) was created during a time when the world's nations aspired to work together to bring about peace. The UN's world headquarters is *in*, but not *of*, New York City: It is an 18-acre international zone belonging to its member nations. Visitors may become startled during a tour of the United Nations when they realize they are in what is tantamount to a separate nation-state with its own fire department and post office.

*Offices for the United Nations are located in the Secretariat Building of the United Nations Headquarters.*

UN headquarters is often thought of as the striking glass building on the East River—the high-rise visible in movies and on the news. The complex actually combines four major buildings. Three were completed in 1952: the 39-floor Secretariat building, the General Assembly building, and the Conference building. In 1961, the Dag Hammarskjöld Library was added.

The General Assembly Hall, where representatives of the UN's 192 member nations meet, is the headquarters' largest room, seating more than 1,800. A subdued space, it features the UN emblem (a surprising rarity inside the complex) and abstract murals designed by French artist Fernand Leger.

# Brooklyn Bridge

"That's the first mistake we've made since that guy sold us the Brooklyn Bridge," Stan Laurel says in the film *Way Out West*.

"Buying that bridge was no mistake," rebuts Oliver Hardy. "That's going to be worth a lot of money to us someday."

The Brooklyn Bridge opened on May 24, 1883, linking what would become the boroughs of Brooklyn and Manhattan in New York City. It was an accomplishment of mythic proportions requiring new technologies and new engineering. In its day, the Brooklyn Bridge was the longest suspension bridge in the world with the length of the main span measuring 1,595 feet. Its towers were once the tallest structures in the city.

The design was imaginative: Artists said th Gothic-influenced Brooklyn Bridge demon strated that aesthetics and technology coul coexist. It so inspired the poet Hart Cran that he chose his apartments for their view c the bridge. His masterpiece is the book-lengt poem "The Bridge."

> "O Sleepless as the river under thee,
> Vaulting the sea, the prairies' dreaming sod,
> Unto us lowliest sometime sweep, descend
> And of the curveship lend a myth to God."
>
> —*Hart Crane, excerpt from the poem "The Bridge," 1933*

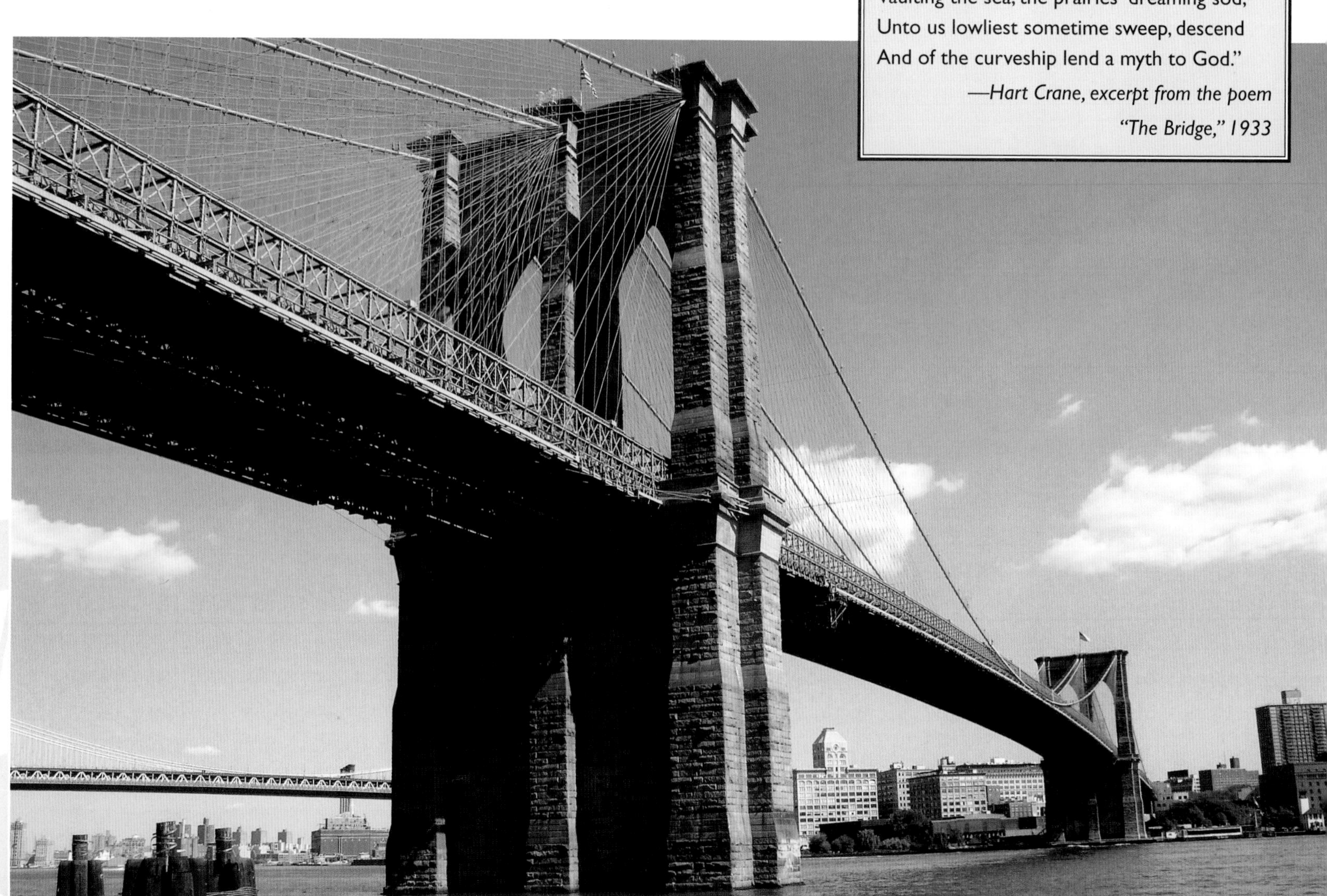

*The Brooklyn Bridge, designed by architect John Augustus Roebling, towers over New York City's East River.*

# Macy's Parade

Macy's Thanksgiving Day Parade requires the support of 10,000 Macy's employees and volunteers. It draws the attention of 2.5 million spectators along the parade line and close to 50 million television viewers. The Macy's parade—with its marching bands, skyscraping balloon characters (some favorites are Spider-Man and Clifford the Big Red Dog), and aircraft carrier-size floats—has the advantage of being able to roll with the times and with the weather. Technology, too, keeps the parade exciting. A recent addition has been the Macy's parade's first square balloon, which was actually a sphere holding together an external square shape with 610 tie lines.

Macy's employees excitedly helped organize the first parade in 1924. There were marching bands and 25 animals borrowed from the Central Park Zoo. A huge crowd lined the parade route, and the event made history. The first balloon appeared at the parade in 1927—a grinning Felix the Cat.

If you're in the area the afternoon before, watch as workers inflate the balloons around 3 P.M. To see the three-hour parade live the next morning, arrive at Central Park West, Columbus Circle, Broadway, or 34th Street between Broadway and Seventh Avenue at about 6:00 A.M. Bring a large mug of hot cocoa, and get ready to feel like a kid again.

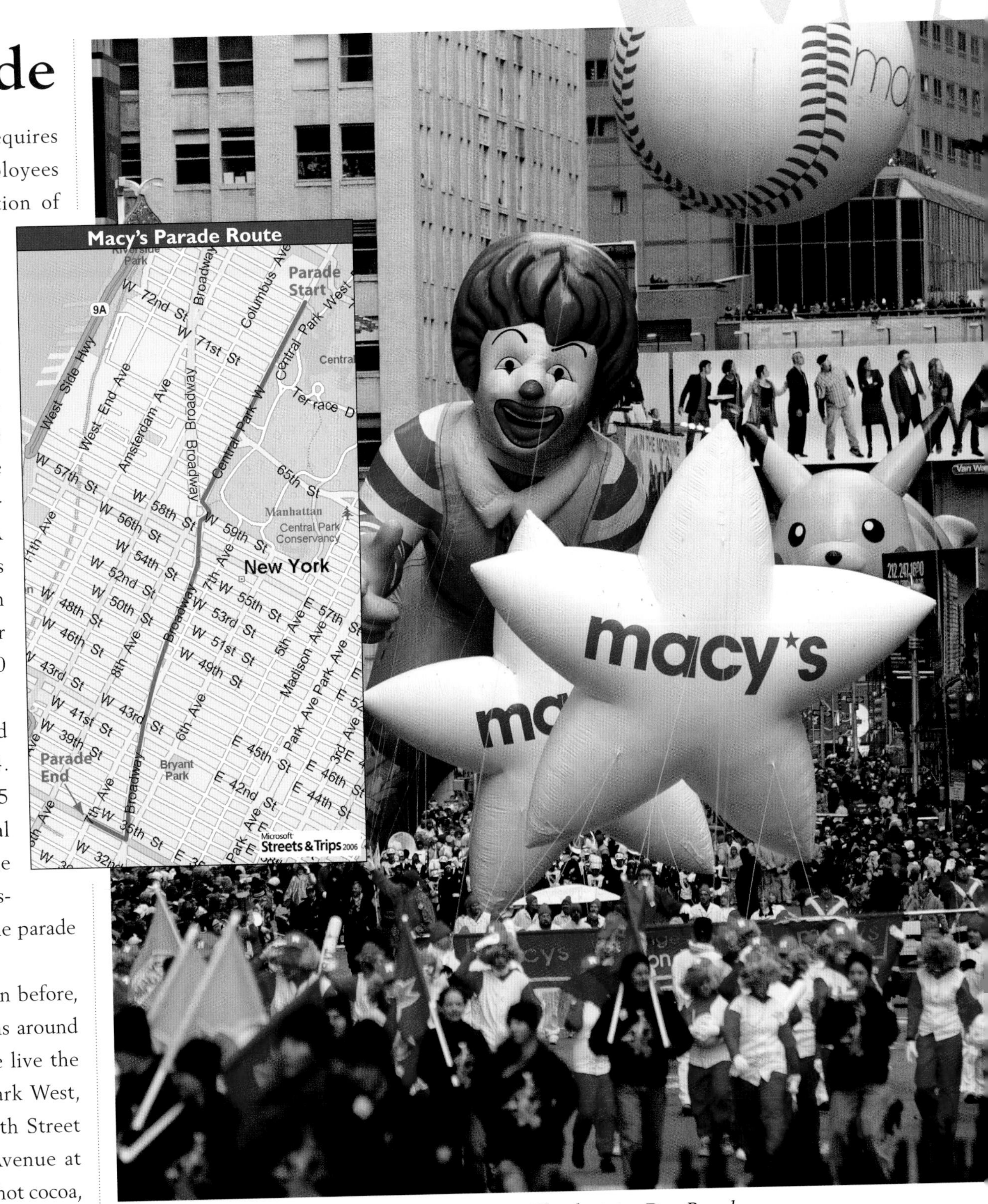


*Crowds gather along Broadway to see the Macy's Thanksgiving Day Parade.*

# Empire State Building

)n a clear day, you can see 80 miles from the bservation deck of the Empire State Building, ll the way to Massachusetts, Connecticut, Jew Jersey, or Pennsylvania, and, of course, ou can see much of New York, the Empire tate. Each year almost four million tourists valk through the building's chrome-and-narble lobby and stand in line, sometimes for nany hours, to ride an express elevator to the op. And it's worth the wait.

Climb the Himalayas, and you will see nore territory. But when it comes to urban iews of the world, the Empire State Building preeminent. This is not only because of the uilding's height but because of the dazzling iews of the New York City skyline. The building overlooks Manhattan and landmarks such s Rockefeller Center, the United Nations, Central Park, the Statue of Liberty, and, seemngly close enough to touch, another Art Deco con, the Chrysler Building.

The Empire State Building takes up about ne-third of the block between 34th Street nd 33rd Street and Fifth Avenue and Herald quare. The building measures 1,453 feet, .5625 inches (443.2 meters) from its base to ne top of its lightning rod. With the World rade Center towers now gone, it is the tallst building in New York and among the ten allest buildings in the world. Nowadays, peole are permitted to visit the spacious 86th floor outdoor observatory, a terrace with a high iron fence. Tourists can also travel to the building's 102nd floor and look out through its 24 tiny windows.

Opposite page) *The Empire State Building ominates the New York City skyline.*

*For more than 40 years the Empire State Building was the tallest building in the world.*

Stories persist that the Empire State Building was built during the Depression to create jobs. Actually, it was the result of a competition between Walter Chrysler, founder of the Chrysler Corporation, and John Jakob Raskob, founder of General Motors Acceptance Corporation. Both wanted to build the tallest building. The Raskob team won the contest with the Empire State Building, but the real winners were New York City and the world.

The building's design, while not as spectacular as the chrome-crowned Chrysler Building, has been recognized since its 1931 opening as an architectural success. Viewed from a distance—say, from across the Hudson River in New Jersey—the Empire State Building looks like a shapely bell tower. (Chief architect William Lamb is said to have based his design on the shape of a pencil.) Its exterior was constructed of limestone and granite and trimmed with aluminum and chrome-nickel steel from the sixth floor setback on up, with long, decorative chrome-nickel steel rails along the corners. The 1950 addition of a television tower only added to the building's impressive, graceful immensity, which helps explain the number of tourists who can be seen daily standing on the Fifth Avenue sidewalk, gaping upward at the skyscraper.

Perhaps the most amazing aspect of the building's history was its rapid design and construction. Thanks to Lamb's ingenious plan, the Empire State Building was built in just over 13 months, setting a record for a building that size. Tragic experience has demonstrated that the design stands up to stress: In 1945 an Army Air Force B-25 bomber struck the building between the 78th and 79th floors, and 14 people died. Witnesses said the building shuddered and then stood still again. The fire was extinguished in 40 minutes.

# Ground Zero

The site of the former World Trade Center towers, now called Ground Zero, has become one of the United States' most revered memorials. Unlike many other memorials, Ground Zero is not naturally aesthetic, and it has no statues, no music, no fountains, no architectural monuments, and no grand memorial. Perhaps Ground Zero is like Gettysburg before it became a national park, or the site where the USS *Arizona* sunk in Pearl Harbor before a memorial was built there.

Yet each week thousands of people come from all over the world to visit this 16-acre site. Some are confused or disappointed when they arrive because Ground Zero is now a construction site where the World Trade Center Transportation Hub is being built (due to be completed in 2009).

On the tour of Ground Zero, guides explain what is currently at the site, where the buildings used to stand, and what the site might look like in the future. For further context, visitors may want to see some of the other remnant of the attacks on September 11, 2001. One i the Ground Zero Memorial in Union Square Another is Fritz Koenig's 45,000-pound stee and-bronze sculpture "Sphere," which ha anchored the fountain at the foot of the tower and is now on exhibit in Battery Park.

*A "Tribute in Light" memorial was held from March 11 to April 13, 2002, to honor victims of the World Trade Center attacks.*

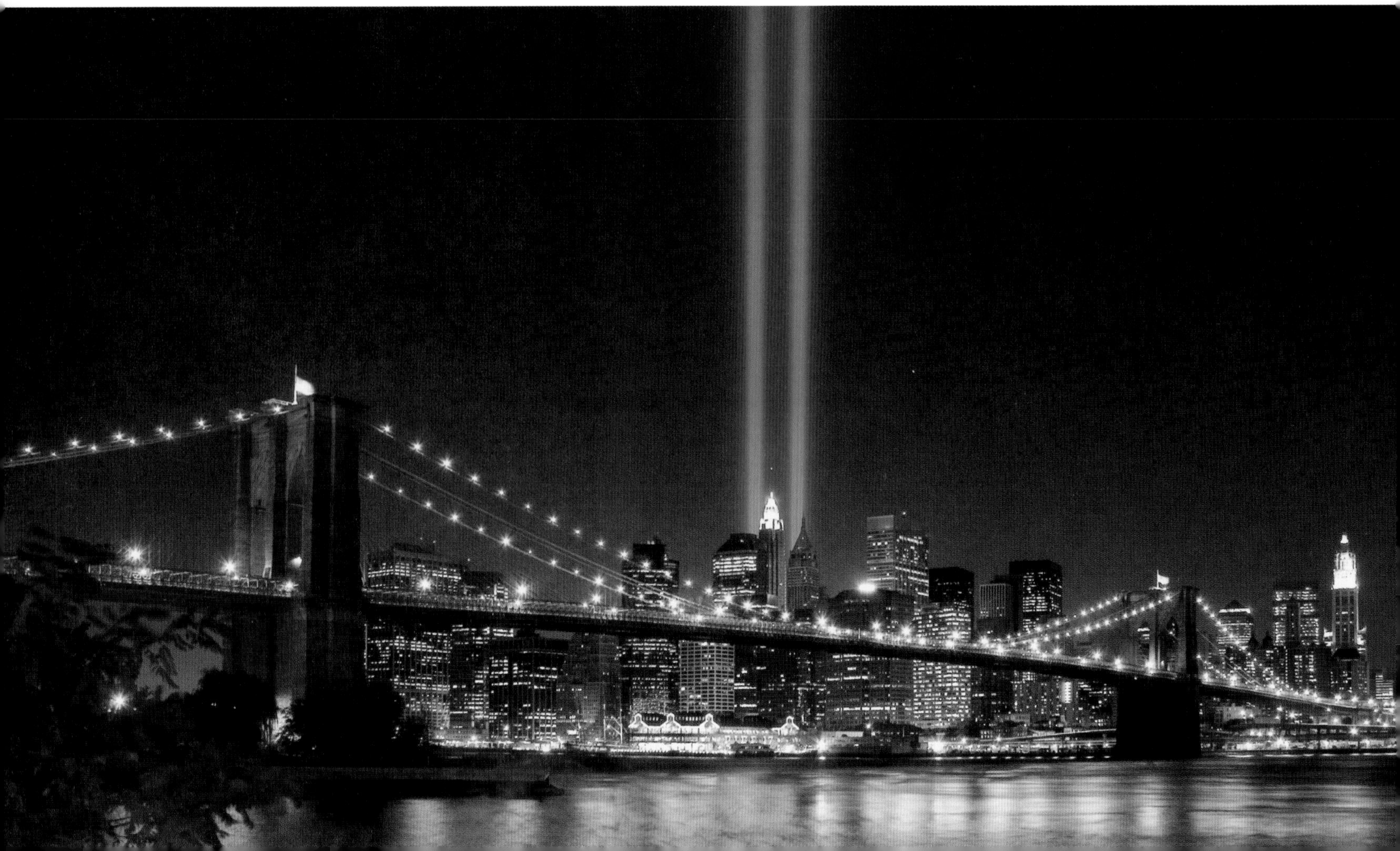

# Chrysler Building

onically, the best place to see the Chrysler uilding is probably from the observation deck f its long-ago archenemy, the Empire State uilding. Sadly, the Chrysler Building closed s observation decks long ago, and so gone are s fabled views of midtown Manhattan and ose-ups of the building's stainless-steel own. The Art Deco spikes, triangular winows, and gargoyles of eagles and wings were ken from the Chrysler hood ornament's esign, and the building's top was modeled ter the Chrysler hubcaps.

Ever since its opening in 1930, the Chrysler uilding has struck observers as the perfect chitectural expression of the Roaring Twenties, hich witnessed a fierce competition to build e tallest skyscraper. The contest was so intense at the Chrysler Building, hailed as the world's llest building by far in 1930, had to yield first ace to the Empire State Building in 1931.

Admire the Chrysler Building from a disnce, then see its lobby. Then (if you can resist opping to shop on Madison Avenue) walk to e restored Grand Central Terminal, the New ork Public Library, or Bryant Park on 42nd reet. From there on Fifth Avenue, which was iginally designed so that its buildings, all e same height, would form a synthetic canon, look downtown: You'll feel like you're on p of the world.

*he Chrysler Building is a masterpiece of Art eco architecture symbolizing the spirit of the oaring Twenties.*

# St. Patrick's Cathedral

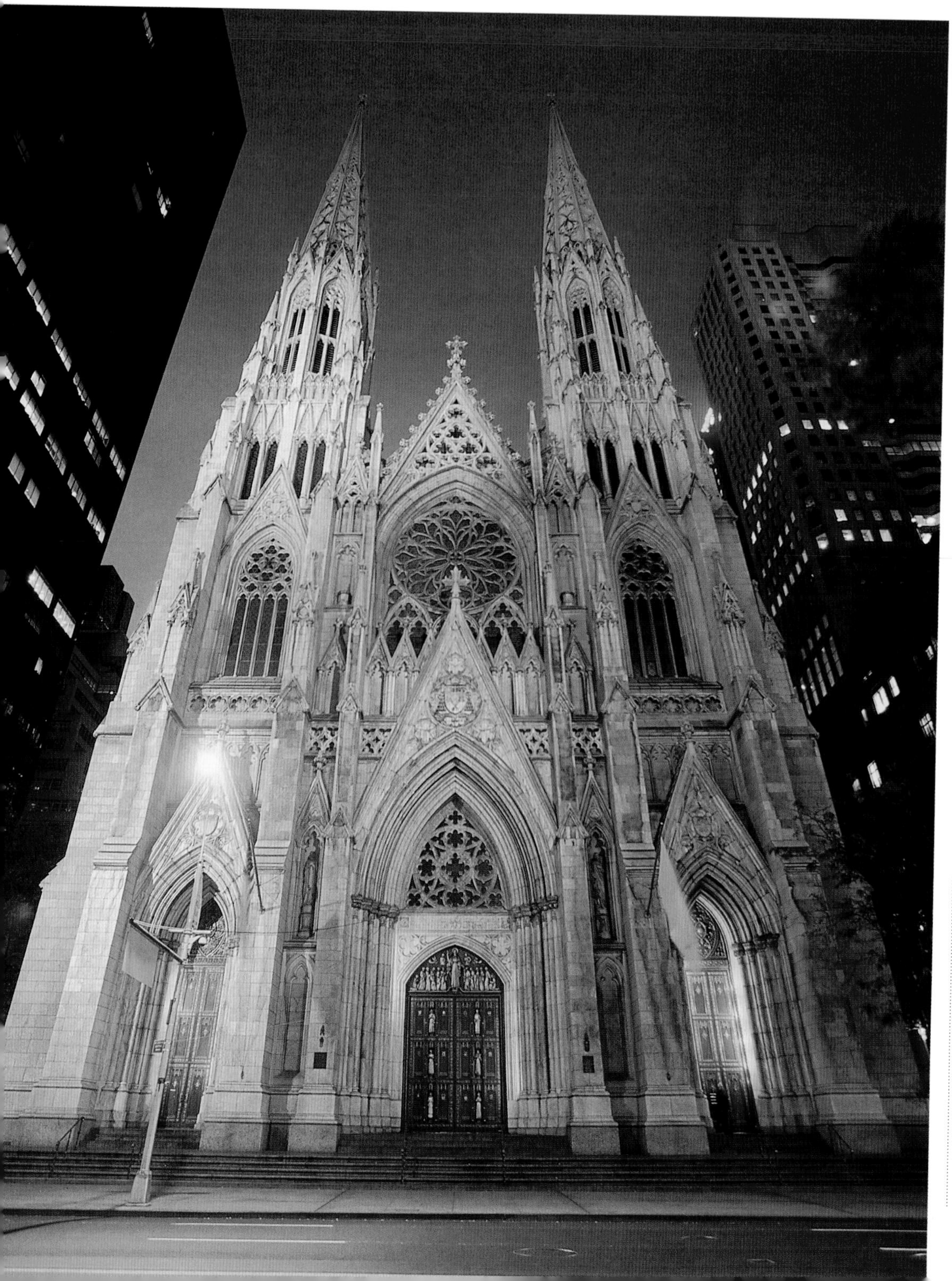

St. Patrick's Cathedral lies in New York Cit across from Rockefeller Center. Technically the cathedral was completed in 1879 afte 20 years of construction. But the cathedral i the seat of the Archbishop of New York, so an archbishop's house and the rectory were added between 1882 and 1884. In the 1880s the cathedral's dramatic spires were completed. Later the great rose window and immense bronze doors on the Fifth Avenue side were added.

On the outside, the cathedral is 400 feet long and 274 feet wide, with spires that rise 330 feet above the street. On the inside, it seats 2,200 and has been the site for the wakes of such greats as Polish Prime Minister Ignace Jan Paderewski, New York Governor Alfred E. Smith, and Senator Robert F. Kennedy.

The cathedral admits both the exalted and the humble; about three million visitors come to admire the catheral each year. Both gawkers and worshipers come to see the St. Michael and St. Louis altar, designed by Tiffany & Company, and the St. Elizabeth altar, designed by Paolo Medici of Rome. There's also the crypt where the former Archbishops of New York are buried under the high altar with their honorary headwear hanging above. St. Patrick's welcomes visitors from 7:00 A.M. to 8:45 P.M. daily, as long as they respect the serenity others seek there.

*St. Patrick's is the largest Gothic-revival-style cathedral in the United States.*

# National Baseball Hall of Fame

Visitors to Cooperstown, New York, enjoy the Farmers' Museum, the Fenimore Art Museum, and in summer, the Glimmerglass Opera. The village was named for author James Fenimore Cooper's father, William Cooper, who founded Cooperstown in 1786. He was the first to explore the lake region that was later immortalized as the setting in his son's *Leatherstocking Tales.*

But only one Cooperstown attraction often draws more daily visitors than the population of the village: the National Baseball Hall of Fame on Main Street, known to baseball fans worldwide simply as "Cooperstown."

In 1905, an official commission erroneously ruled that Abner Doubleday invented baseball in the village of Cooperstown in 1839. Almost 100 years later, a village philanthropist conceived of a hall of fame to celebrate Doubleday's centennial, and the idea took off like a Nolan Ryan fastball.

The hall showcases the plaques of the revered first five inductees: Ty Cobb, Babe Ruth, Honus Wagner, Christy Mathewson, and Walter Johnson. Today, the Hall of Fame's exhibits and archives celebrate the national pastime in countless ways, living up to the hall's motto: "Preserving History, Honoring Excellence, Connecting Generations."

*Outside the Baseball Hall of Fame are bronze statues of Johnny Podres pitching to his Brooklyn teammate Roy Campanella* (right) *during a World Series game.*

# Atlantic City Boardwalk

Just off the mainland of southeastern New Jersey lies Absecon Island, whose marshes and sandy beaches lay undisturbed until 1854. Then the Camden and Atlantic Railroad Line was built there, and Atlantic City was born. Unfortunately, the hordes of vacationers from New York and Philadelphia dragged volumes of sand through too many marbled lobbies. In 1870, Alexander Boardman, a railroad conductor, proposed constructing a wooden walkway to sift out the sand, and the Atlantic City Boardwalk was born. That first boardwalk measured one mile long. By 1883, almost 100 enterprises had sprung up beside it.

Atlantic City built and rebuilt the Boardwalk until the fifth and final version in 1896. It is more than 4 miles long and 60 feet wide and features steel pilings and 40 foot steel beams. The Boardwalk helped make Atlantic City an attractive host for innovative events, such as the first Miss America Pageant in 1921. Later came the legalization of casino gambling in the late 1970s. Today, like Las Vegas, th Boardwalk is open 24 hours a day.

Has the Boardwalk changed all that muc from, say, 1885, when the gasoline engine w invented? It is more modern, but visitors st enjoy a range of distractions, from saltwat taffy and chocolate fudge stands to the Ste Pier's rides and games.

*The Trump Taj Mahal is one of many famous resort-casinos on the Atlantic City Boardwalk.*

# Cape May

Cape May is a peninsula at the southernmost tip of New Jersey and the nation's oldest seaside resort. It was settled by whalers in the 17th century and is now a magnet for visitors from New Jersey, New York, and eastern Pennsylvania. Because a fire swept the little town in 1878, it was rebuilt in the Victorian style of the day, setting the architectural tone for what remains a charming, old-fashioned resort.

Cape May is the gateway to the 30 miles of sandy Atlantic Ocean beaches along the Jersey Cape that connect the resort towns of Ocean City, Sea Isle City, Avalon, Stone Harbor, and the Wildwoods. You'll find plenty of enticing attractions here. Take a nature walk at the Wetlands Institute in Stone Harbor or Leamin's Run Gardens (25 gardens on 30 acres). Visit Historic Cold Spring Village, an Early American living-history museum on 22 acres, or the Cape May County History Museum in the 1755 John Holmes House. The white Cape May Lighthouse towers 157 feet high and serves as a peaceful sentry over the picturesque peninsula.

The cape offers plenty of amusements that have kept fun-lovers coming back for almost 150 years, such as the boardwalk piers in Ocean City and the Wildwoods. You can also charter fishing boats, rent speedboats, kayak, or parasail. And with 30 miles of pure, white sand, it's possible to find some quiet, too.

*Charming Victorian bed-and-breakfast inns are popular with visitors to Cape May.*

# New Jersey Pine Barrens

People who don't know the New Jersey Pinelands National Reserve, better known as the Pine Barrens, probably don't realize how big the forest really is. The 1.1-million-acre national reserve is about the size of Glacier National Park. More than 700,000 people live in Pinelands' communities, yet much of it remains wild.

The barrens comprise impenetrable bogs and marshes with forests of low pine and oak and sporadic stands of cedar and hardwood swamps. And there are the 12,000 acres of mature dwarf pine and oak commonly called the "pygmy forest." Under the barrens, the Cohansey Aquifer contains more than 17 trillion gallons of water—its acidity seeps into the barrens' bogs and swamps and stains the water a tea color. Aboveground, ribbons of water flow to the Atlantic.

Tourists love hiking, biking, boating, and cranberry picking as well as visiting the historic villages of Batsto and Double Trouble. The Pine Barrens has its share of history and legends, such as the Jersey Devil, said to have the head of a horse, large wings, and claws. For the courageous, the New Jersey Pine Barrens offers Jersey Devil tours.

*Pitch pines and blackjack oaks loom over the marshy landscape of the Pine Barrens.*

# Pittsburgh's Three Rivers

*he Duquesne Incline brings tourists atop Mount Washington for a dazzling view of Pittsburgh.*

eople call Pittsburgh the Steel City: The ame dates back to the early 19th century hen the steel industry ruled the city. Back ien, white-collar workers brought an extra irt or blouse to work because a black ring ould form inside their collars by lunchtime. the early 20th century, streetlamps burned l day so residents could see through the noke. Today, the air is clear, and the smoke and ills are mostly gone.

When in Pittsburgh, one of the best ways to see the city is by taking the Duquesne Incline, which, since 1877, has provided public transportation to the top of Mount Washington, a steep hill on the city's south side. Take the incline at night and go to the observation deck overlooking downtown Pittsburgh's Golden Triangle. Fifteen major bridges span the waters of the Allegheny and Monongahela rivers as they flow together to become the Ohio River. The Renaissance City sparkles like a river of stars. You'll not only be rewarded by the view, but by having landed in the middle of Pittsburgh's Restaurant Row.

Opposite Mount Washington, going north across the rivers, is the Andy Warhol Museum, the Carnegie Science Center, PNC Park, and Heinz Field. While you're on the north side of the rivers, check out the National Aviary. It's a warm refuge on a chilly Pittsburgh day.

# Independence National Historic Park and Independence Hall

The United States of America is a relatively young nation, but its history is as illustrious as that of any country, and it should be explored. If you really want to see America, start where the country started: Independence Hall. The area between Fifth and Sixth streets, between Market and Chestnut, in Philadelphia's Center City, is home to the body and spirit of U.S. history.

Independence Hall, which is now part of a 45-acre park (along with 20 or so other buildings), is where America's independence was born. Once called the Pennsylvania State House, this simple building saw the foundations of the Declaration of Independence laid and brought to fruition. It was here that the U.S. Constitution was debated, argued, honed, and signed. (The political debates, the spirit of which continues in today's U.S. legislature, became so heated—and loud—that the windows were always closed, even on hot, humid days in the middle of July.)

Standing in front of Independence Hall, it is difficult to comprehend that this one building, with its subtle charms and small park, is the place where a remarkable gathering of brilliant mind changed the world. It is here that freedo was made possibl Democracy, the keyston of the United States, wa established here. It wa defined here. And it wa celebrated here.

> ***Liberty Bell Inscription***
>
> "Proclaim liberty throughout all the land unto all the inhabitants there of—Lev. XXV, v.x. By order of the Assembly of the Province of Pensylvania [*sic*] for the State House in Philada."

The comely two-stor redbrick building no has a steeple with a cloc in it. But long ago, tha steeple housed a 2,080-pound bell. The bel of course, is the Liberty Bell. It chimed ofte (supposedly annoying the neighbors), bu most notably, it was rung on July 8, 1776, t announce the first public reading of the Declaration of Independence.

The bell was once moved to a church i Allentown, Pennsylvania, where it was hidde under the floorboards to avoid confiscation b British troops. From the beginning, the be was adopted as the symbol for many cause (religious freedom and abolition, to nam two), so it was displayed around the countr After the Civil War, people hoped that seeing it would help to heal the wounds betwee North and South, and so it traveled to fair and exhibitions across the United States.

Now the bell is perhaps best known for it cracks . . . and its silence. No longer hangin

*The Liberty Bell is now displayed in a glass chamber at the Liberty Bell Center, with Independence Hall in the background.*

in the steeple of Independence Hall, it has its own home on the park grounds. The striking history of the bell is available through a video presentation (in several languages) and is sure to get your patriotic heart pumping.

All tours kick off at the Independence National Historic Park Visitor Center (near Market and Arch). The tickets are free, but tours are timed to help manage the crowds. The visitor center will prepare you for an exciting tour (don't expect a square mile of musty musings and memorabilia). The people at the park have gone to great lengths to make history interesting for everyone. There are some artifacts, but there are also high-tech interactive and multimedia exhibits. Some souvenir shops may be of interest. You can even lunch at an outdoor café on the grounds and take in the view that most interests you.

The Independence National Historic Park covers three large city blocks. There are paths (quaint alleys) you can follow to the many historical buildings and fascinating sites, such as Ben Franklin's final resting place in the Christ Church graveyard. The park is tourist-friendly, providing benches, walls, and other seating so you can catch your breath and rest your busy feet. It's hallowed ground you're walking on, so take your time, and try to see as much as you can. It's a visit you'll always remember.

*Construction on the Pennsylvania State House, now called Independence Hall, began in 1732 and was completed 21 years later.*

# Philadelphia's Old City

Philadelphia is made up of many colorful neighborhoods, and Old City is among the most interesting. Laid out by William Penn in 1682, Old City today would surely astonish the great Quaker. It was a lowly waterfront district until artists began buying lofts, restoring dilapidated industrial buildings, and introducing the first theater companies. Soon, architectural firms, art galleries, design firms, restaurants, shops, and bars opened in the neighborhood, all a short stroll from downtown Philly.

The heart of Philadelphia is its Old City neighborhood, where the city began. And the heart of Old City is Elfreth's Alley, the oldest residential street in America. People have lived there since 1702. Three hundred years ago, traders and local merchants lived in the Georgian- and Federal-style buildings on the narrow street, which at just 15 feet wide was sized for horse-drawn carts and pedestrians. Blacksmith Jeremiah Elfreth owned most of the property along the alley and rented his houses to shipbuilders, sea captains, and landlubbers such as pewter smiths.

Today, Old City remains a vibrant neighborhood. Just a short stroll from historic Elfreth's Alley are Christ Church, the Betsy Ross House, and Independence Hall. There's also the Elfreth's Alley Museum, which offers guided tours of the homes built between 1710 and 1825.

*Elfreth's Alley in Philadelphia is the oldest residential street in America.*

# Groundhog Day

Groundhog Day is an American phenomenon. A number of cities boast rodents capable of predicting the advent of spring, but there is only one Punxsutawney Phil.

Punxsutawney Phil is a 20-pound specimen of *Marmota monax* who, on February 2 each year, predicts when spring will arrive. He has also put his western Pennsylvania town on the map while becoming a movie star, especially through roles in films like *Groundhog Day*. Further proof of Phil's status can be found in the form of limited edition Punxsutawney Phil Beanie Babies.

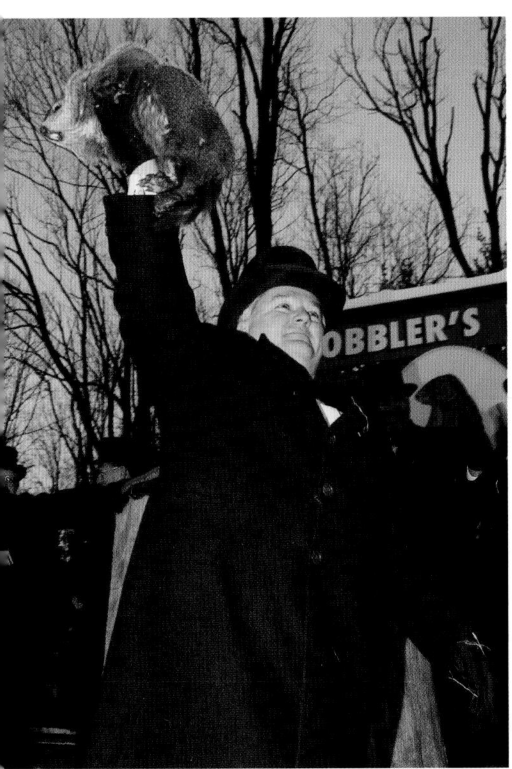


*Phil is consulted each year on Gobbler's Knob before a waiting world.*

(Above) *If Phil sees his shadow on February 2, it's an omen of six more weeks of winter weather.*

Phil today wears his mantle of stardom lightly, thriving on a special diet of dog food and ice cream in his climate-controlled home at the Punxsutawney Library, where he is cared for by his handler, local funeral director Bill Deeley.

Also remarkable is Phil's longevity. The groundhog event was first recorded in 1841. Official Groundhog Day celebrations began in 1886, and the creature was named "Punxsutawney Phil, Seer of Seers, Sage of Sages, Prognosticator of Prognosticators, and Weather Prophet Extraordinary."

*Handler Bill Deeley cares for Phil year-round.*

# Gettysburg

Gettysburg, Pennsylvania, never asked to be a crossroads of history, but it became one nonetheless. The borough is the seat of Adams County, and it was originally purchased in 1736 by the William Penn family from the Iroquois. The Mason–Dixon Line runs just south of Gettysburg. The settlement was named after its founder, General James Getty s. The community prospered, building roads and bridges. Later these structures were used by troops of the North and South during the Battle of Gettysburg. This fateful, pivotal clash during the first three days of July 1863 led to the eventual defeat of the Confederacy.

Gettysburg National Military Park is in the heart and soul of Pennsylvania Dutch country. It will forever be remembered as the place where General George Gordon Meade's Union forces turned back the Confederate Army of General Robert E. Lee, and as the location where President Abraham Lincoln gave his famous address four months later. Gettysburg offers visitors a surprising array of historic battlegrounds, monuments, and activities such as hiking and biking. Gettysburg includes the national park, the adjacent borough, and the next-door Eisenhower National Historic Site. Located about an hour-and-a-half from downtown Washington, D.C., Gettysburg allows visitors to explore a versatile vacationland or

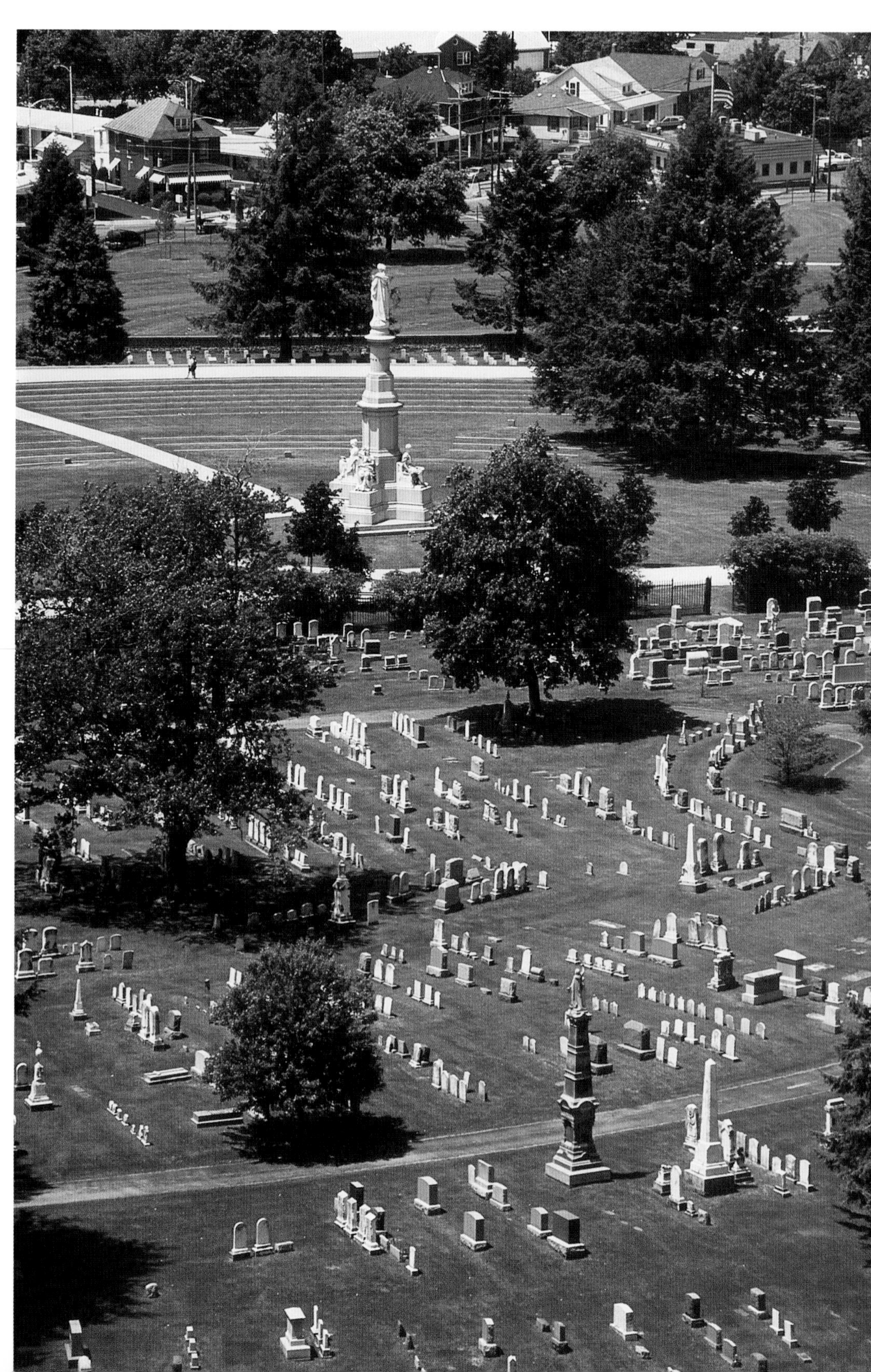

*Gettysburg National Cemetery is shown here from the Gettysburg National Military Park Tower.*

ake a solemn pilgrimage to the hallowed site where 50,000 soldiers were killed, wounded, aptured, or missing in action during the Civil War.

There's also a charming little tourist town next door with attractions such as Gettysburg's American Civil War Museum, the Soldier's National Museum, the Jennie Wade House Museum, the Lincoln Train Museum, and the Gettysburg Battle Theater.

After a visit to the town, continue to the Gettysburg National Military Park Visitor Center, which features the Electric Map program (a 30-minute orientation program, for a fee), and the renowned Gettysburg Museum of the Civil War (free). Then comes the Gettysburg Cyclorama, a 360-degree painting of Pickett's Charge. The cyclorama was unveiled in 1884 by French artist Paul Philippoteaux, who interviewed survivors of the battle to perfect the details of Cemetery Ridge on the battlefield and the "High Water Mark," the point at which the Confederacy penetrated farthest north. (The Parks Service has embarked on a project to rehabilitate the battlefield; the cyclorama is being restored and will be withdrawn from public view until April 2008.) On the other side of the visitor center is the Gettysburg National Cemetery, site of Lincoln's speech and where many Union soldiers are buried.

But the foundation of Gettysburg is really the 6,000-acre battlefield and its more than 1,400 markers and monuments. It is well worth the trip to see the rolling hills and fields where the tide of the Civil War changed. Here Lincoln dedicated the United States "to the great task remaining before us... that this nation, under God, shall have a new birth of freedom—and that government of the people, by the people, for the people, shall not perish from the earth."

*Cannons are positioned on Cemetery Hill as they were during the Civil War.*

## Quick Fact

***The Battle of Gettysburg***

Fighting at Gettysburg lasted just three days, but it was the largest and bloodiest battle of the American Civil War.

On July 1, 1863, Confederate General Robert E. Lee pushed north with his troops to fight on Union ground and to allow the state of Virginia to rebuild after being devastated during previous battles. Lee scored an early victory at the end of the first day, but it was not decisive. Under the command of General George G. Meade, the Union troops were able to hold off Confederate forces by controlling Little Round Top, East Cemetery Hill, and Culp's Hill during the second day. On July 3, Confederate troops tried desperately to regain ground, most famously through Pickett's Charge: a mass infantry assault of nearly 15,000 soldiers marching across an open field, braving artillery fire, in an attempt to take Cemetery Ridge. Nearly 10,000 of these men were killed in the first hour. The Union succeeded in holding off the Confederacy, and Lee retreated the next day.

**Union commander**
General George G. Meade

**Union troops**
approximately 95,000

**Union casualties**
23,040

**Confederate commander**
General Robert E. Lee

**Confederate troops**
approximately 75,000

**Confederate casualties**
22,000–25,000

# Fallingwater

Frank Lloyd Wright is probably the most famous American architect, and his most renowned building is a house in Mill Run, Pennsylvania, called Fallingwater. Wright designed the house in 1935 for Mr. and Mrs. Edgar J. Kaufmann of Pittsburgh. It was completed in 1939.

The location for the building was inspired by Edgar Kaufmann's love for the waterfall on Bear Run, the stream that runs through these serene woods. Wright also recognized the beauty of the location, and immediately visualized a house with cantilevered balconies on the rock bank over the waterfall.

The Kaufmann family used Fallingwater as a vacation and weekend home from 1939 until the 1950s. In 1963, the son, Edgar Kaufmann, Jr., a curator at New York's Museum of Modern Art, entrusted the family home to the Western Pennsylvania Conservancy.

Fallingwater became the gem of Wright's organic architecture school. A 1991 survey of the American Institute of Architects members judged it the all-time-best work of American architecture.

Today Fallingwater is open to the public and contains the original Wright-designed furnishings and the Kaufmanns' superb modern and Japanese art collections. And, of course, there are the exterior views of the place, which suggest that art and nature are not so very far apart.

*The unique balconies of Fallingwater seem to float over the falls.*

# National Aquarium, Baltimore

'he National Aquarium, on the end of Balti- ıore's Pier 3, anchors Baltimore's Inner Har- or. The aquarium is considered the nation's reatest and is certainly entertaining and ıought provoking. It is huge, with more than 0,500 fish and other creatures on display.

You'll rave about the aquarium's exhibi- ions—not to be missed are its 1,200-seat Iarine Mammal Pavilion dolphin show on ier 4 and the Wings in the Water display, which features small sharks, turtles, and dozens of gliding, pinwheeling stingrays that look as if they're dancing on air.

The aquarium has five levels, with more happening on each than at a three-ring circus. The Atlantic Coral Reef exhibit is a 335,000-gallon tank that surrounds you with hundreds of tropical fish swimming around the world's most accurate fabricated coral reef. Step into the South American Rain Forest exhibit, a re-creation of an Amazon River tributary that runs the length of a 57-foot-long acrylic wall with giant river turtles, tropical fish, and dwarf caimans. Or get an up-close look at large sharks in the Open Ocean exhibit, a 225,000 gallon ring-shape tank. Interactive computer stations explain the exhibits.

*Anemones and coral populate the Atlantic Coral Reef exhibit.*

# Baltimore Inner Harbor

Baltimore calls itself "The Greatest City in America," and while some might dispute that, a visit shows why Charm City has every right to burst with pride.

Baltimore's pride and joy is its fantastic Inner Harbor. Not long ago, the city's harbor could have substituted for urban decay's exhibit A. Then, beginning in the early 1960s, a succession of city administrations focused on rehabilitating the old waterfront. They succeeded beyond anyone's wildest dreams, luring many A-list attractions. These range from the Baltimore Orioles' new-yet-classic Camden Yards ballpark to the National Aquarium, the Maryland Science Center, Port Discovery for kids, the Baltimore Maritime Museum, the Baltimore Civil War Museum, the Civil War–era USS *Constellation* (the Navy's last all-sail warship), and much more.

Clearly, the Inner Harbor is designed to satisfy every taste, from the sophisticated to the acquisitive. Shopping centers such as the

*The observation level of Baltimore's World Trad Center gives a 360-degree view of the harbor.*

groundbreaking Harborplace, which occupi 275,000 square feet in two pavilions, mak sure of the latter.

Baltimore Inner Harbor is also home to th Tall Ships, and the best way to see them is th Tall Ship Tour. Another must-see is the To of the World Observation Level on the 27t floor of Baltimore's World Trade Center.

# Assateague Island

ff the coasts of Maryland and Virginia an island of endless white sand sparing in the sunshine. Assateague Island is 7 miles long, and its wild horses have galped along the beach since the 1600s.

The surf is gentle, and stripers, bluefish, eakfish, and kingfish are plentiful. Assateague land is a barrier island, so it has an ocean de, a bay side, and an interior. The center of e island is a bird-watcher's paradise of ponds d marshes, home to wintering snow geese, een-winged teal, northern pintail, American igeon, bufflehead, red-breasted merganser, ld eagles, ospreys, red-tailed hawks, kestrels, d merlins.

(Above) *The horses on Assateague are descendants of domestic horses that reverted back to the wild. They are only about 12 to 13 hands tall—the size of ponies.*

Three stunning public parks share the land's 39,727 acres (48,000 acres counting water boundaries): Maryland's Assateague State Park, Assateague Island National Seashore, and, mainly on the Virginia side, Chincoteague National Wildlife Refuge, which has 14,000 acres of pristine forest, marsh, dunes, and beaches. The refuge also includes three more barrier islands: Assawoman, Metompkin, and Cedar.

The wild horses on the island, made famous by the children's classic novel *Misty of Chincoteague*, are joined not only by deer but by Sikas, Asian elks that have thrived on the island since the 1920s.

*Saltwater marshes provide a habitat for marine wildlife and waterfowl.*

# Chesapeake Bay

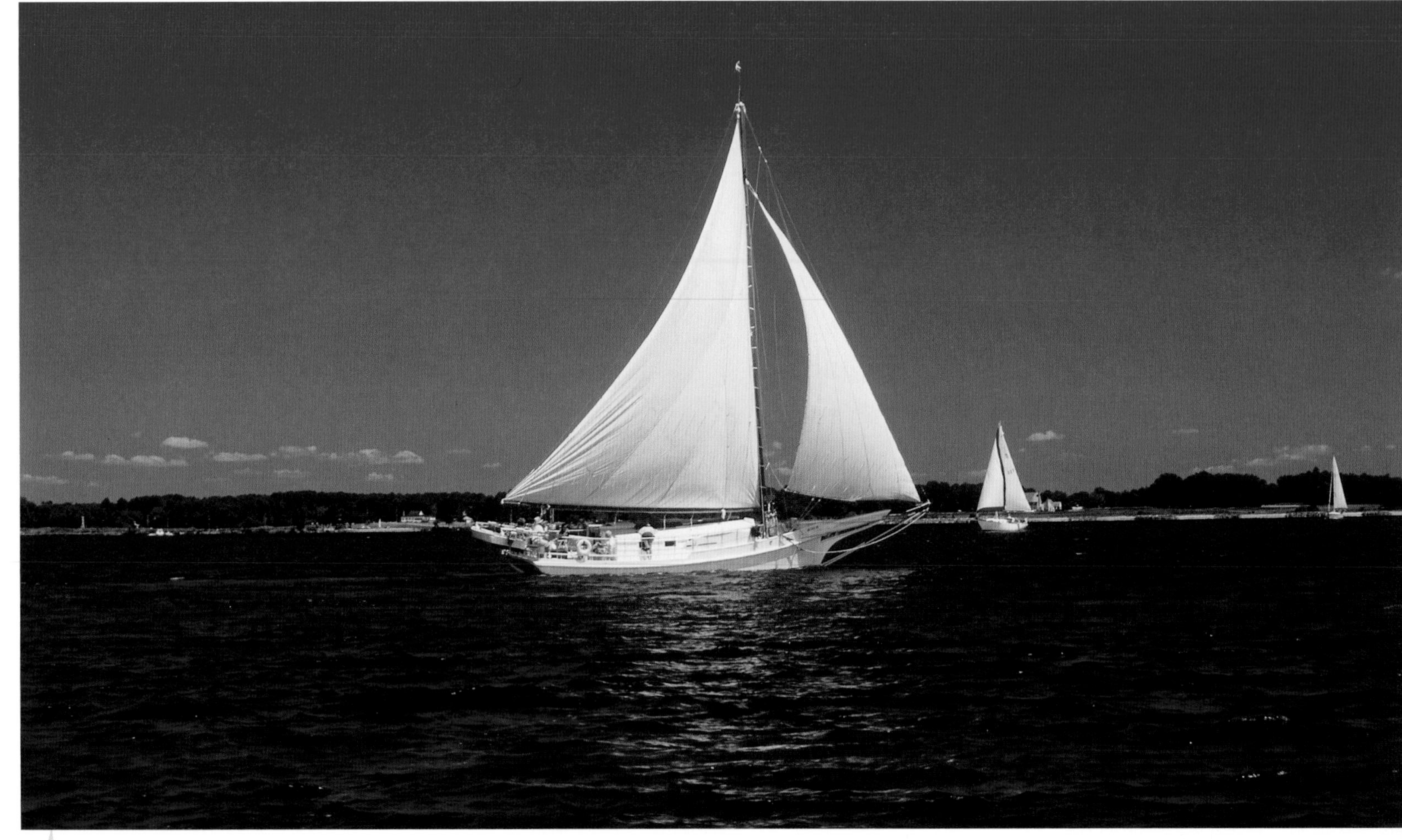

*Skipjacks were introduced to the Chesapeake in the late 19th century to dredge for oysters. Today, some of these versatile old vessels provide tours of the bay.*

Chesapeake Bay, the largest estuary in North America, is shared by Maryland, Virginia, and Delaware. The bay stretches almost 200 miles from the Susquehanna River to the Atlantic Ocean and ranges from 4 miles wide to 30 miles wide. The mighty Chesapeake is spanned by the 23-mile Chesapeake Bay Bridge–Tunnel and the shorter and busier Chesapeake Bridge.

The beautiful bay was once the valley of the Susquehanna River, which helps explain why the bay is surprisingly shallow—most of it is less than six feet deep. Nonetheless, the Chesapeake Bay was the site of the American Revolution's critical naval Battle of the Chesapeake in 1781. It was also the site of the standstill battle between the ironclads CSS *Virginia* and USS *Monitor.*

Giant Chesapeake Bay, called "Great Shel fish Bay" by the Algonquin Indians, has ben fited from recent conservation and restoratic efforts. The devastating pollution of the bay waters has remained a threat since the 197 but no longer greatly detracts from its natur beauty. The bay today is a feast of art exhib tions, waterfront festivals, regattas and race sportfishing contests, and boat shows.

# J.S. Capitol

ocated on the east end of the National Mall, e U.S. Capitol is an icon of 19th-century oclassical architecture that houses the coun-y's legislative branches and stands as a sym-l of the United States. The building's rnerstone was laid on September 18, 1793, d it's been burnt, rebuilt, expanded, and stored since then.

The original building was designed by illiam Thornton, a Scottish-trained physician d neophyte architect whose blueprint was selected by President George Washington. When Congress moved from Philadelphia to Washington, D.C., in 1800, only the north wing of the building was complete. Then in 1814, the building was torched by British troops, but a serendipitous downpour spared its complete destruction. The chambers of the Senate and House, as well as those for the Supreme Court, were ready for use by 1819.

By 1850, an expansion was necessary to accommodate the growing legislature: The wings were lengthened, and the rickety wood-and-copper dome was replaced by the the current stately cast-iron dome.

Today the Capitol has a floor area of about 16.5 acres. It houses the legislative chambers as well as a museum of American art and history.

*The U.S. Capitol's cast-iron dome was designed by architect Thomas U. Walter and constructed from 1855 to 1866. The Statue of Freedom was placed atop the dome in 1863.*

# The National Mall

The National Mall in Washington, D.C., is one of the world's great public places. Its 146 acres of renowned monuments, impressive institutions, and grand government offices draw visitors from around the globe.

By strict definition, "the Mall" means the greensward and adjacent buildings from the Washington Monument to the U.S. Capitol. When you visit there's no need to stick to this definition; instead, enjoy how the Mall connects the White House to the north; the Potomac River, National World War II Memorial, and Lincoln Memorial to the west; the Jefferson Memorial, Franklin D. Roosevelt Memorial, and Tidal Basin (with its glorious cherry trees in spring) to the south; and the U.S. Capitol to the east.

Any one of the dozens of the Mall's world-class museums or memorials is worth its own exploration. It might require a day, a week, or a month to do them justice. The Mall includes the National Archives, the U.S. Botanic Garden, the Ulysses S. Grant Memorial, the U.S. Holocaust Museum, the National Gallery of Art, the Korean War Veterans Memorial, the Vietnam Veterans Memorial, Constitution Gardens, West Potomac Park, and the Reflecting Pool. The National Mall is the center of the center, the magnificent green-and-marble heart of the U.S. capital.

The Mall also encompasses the riches of the Smithsonian Institution, which gives visitors a tour of national treasures, from Ray Charles's

(Below) *The greensward of the Mall extends from the base of the Washington Monument to the steps of the U.S. Capitol and is lined by world-class museums.*

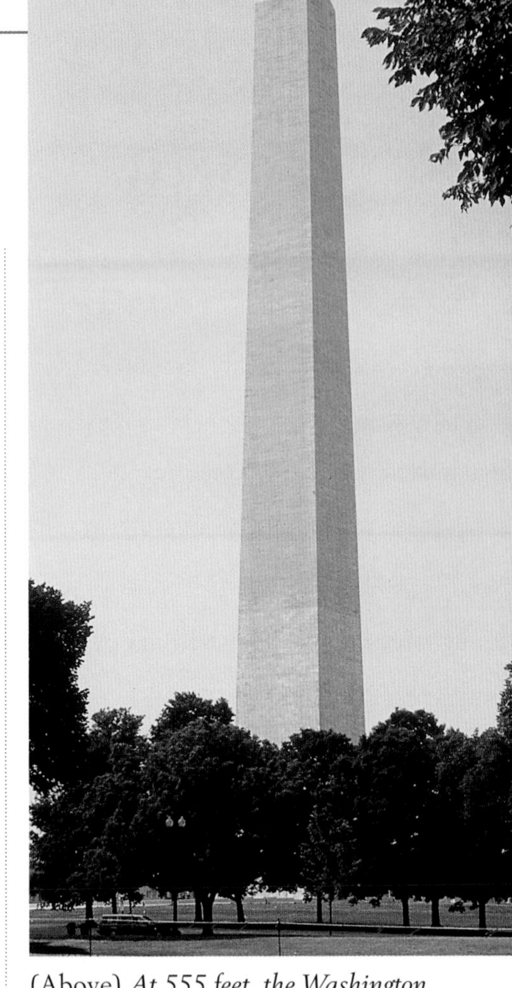

(Above) *At 555 feet, the Washington Monument is the city's tallest structure.*

*ompleted in 2004, the National World War II Memorial honors the 16 million who served in the U.S. armed forces during World War II and the ore than 400,000 who died.*

nglasses to the Hope Diamond. The Smith- nian has 15 museums on the National Mall; s so big that the original "Castle," built in 1855, now merely its office and visitor information nter. Among the Smithsonian museums on e Mall are the National Museum of American istory, the Hirshhorn Museum and Sculpture arden, the National Air and Space Museum, d the National Museum of the American dian. (Admision is free for all Smithsonian useums in Washington, D.C., but tickets need be purchased for IMAX shows.)

Surrounded by the greatness of the ational Mall, it's hard to remember that it as designed in 1791 by architect Pierre L'Enfant as a "Grand Avenue" of gardens and spacious homes interspersed with, not dominated by, monuments, museums, and government buildings. But Washington, D.C., neglected L'Enfant's plan. In 1901, a committee directed by influential architect Daniel Burnham redesigned the Mall with a focus on restoring it to the uninterrupted greensward envisioned by L'Enfant. Since then, the Mall has grown more urban, federal, and monumental, but the landscaped parks, wide avenues, and open spaces of L'Enfant's vision remain.

The National Mall remains at heart a park that means many things to many people. It can be a springtime stroll under the blossoming cherry trees, a getaway in the middle of a political pressure cooker, or a visit to some of the United States' most hallowed documents and precious works of art. Visitors can take it all in bit by bit, spending hours examining a Vermeer painting at the National Gallery of Art, the Rodin sculpture collection at the Hirshhorn, or Dorothy's ruby slippers at the National Museum of American History. Or they can take in the vista of the two miles between the Washington Monument and the Capitol as one great path under the trees that line the Mall and imagine the nation's capital the way L'Enfant did in the District of Columbia's founding.

# The White House

The White House is most amazing for its open-door policy: It is the only residence of a head of state in the world that's open to the public, free of charge. And while visitors can't tour all 132 rooms, they can see some of the more famous ones, including the East, Blue, Green, and Red rooms. (Public tours of the White House are available for groups of ten or more; however, requests must be submitted through your member of Congress six months in advance.)

In 1790, President George Washington laid out his vision for Washington, D.C., to be situated on a plot of land "not exceeding ten miles square . . . on the river Potomac." Washington then worked with city planner Pierre L'Enfant to select the spot for the presidential residence—1600 Pennsylvania Avenue. James Hoban's understated, classical blueprint for the building was selected from a field of nine, and ground was broken in 1792.

Eight years later, John and Abigail Adams became the first residents of the White House—although it wasn't called that until President Theodore Roosevelt gave it that name in 1901. The Adamses made minor changes to the place, as has every president since. In 1949 while Truman was in office, the White House underwent its only major renc vation. The original halls, third floor, and roc were retained, but the rest of the interior w stripped and rebuilt on a new concrete four dation. Since then, several presidents have dec orated the interior differently, but th architecture has remained intact.

Tours typically convene in President's Par South, the 52-acre park better known as th Ellipse. The Ellipse is home to several monu ments and memorials as well as events such the famed Easter Egg Roll in the spring an the lighting of the National Christmas Tre in December.

*The White House, at 1600 Pennsylvania Avenue, has been the president's residence since 1800.*

# U.S. Holocaust Memorial Museum

'he horrors of the Holocaust will never be for-otten. The unspeakable tragedy that took lace in Europe in the 1930s and 1940s must e spoken about so that people never forget.

That is the mission of the U.S. Holocaust Memorial Museum in Washington, D.C. The nuseum is devoted to documenting, studying, nd interpreting the history of the Holocaust. t is also a memorial to the Holocaust's six nillion victims. Beyond educating the public bout the tyranny of Nazi Germany against Europe's Jews, gypsies, and members of other ninority groups, the museum serves to remind visitors that their responsibilities as citizens of a democracy are never to be taken lightly.

*guide discusses the historic photos in the J.S. Holocaust Memorial Museum.*

(Above) *The Tower of Faces contains more than 1,300 photos of Jewish life in the Lithuanian town of Ejszyszki taken between 1890 and 1941.*

Adjacent to the National Mall, the Holocaust Memorial Museum was chartered by Congress in 1980. Its exhibitions focus on artifacts, art, and other evidence of the Holocaust and the death and destruction it wrought. Every spring, a solemn and reflective ceremony is held on the grounds on Holocaust Remembrance Day.

# Supreme Court of the United States

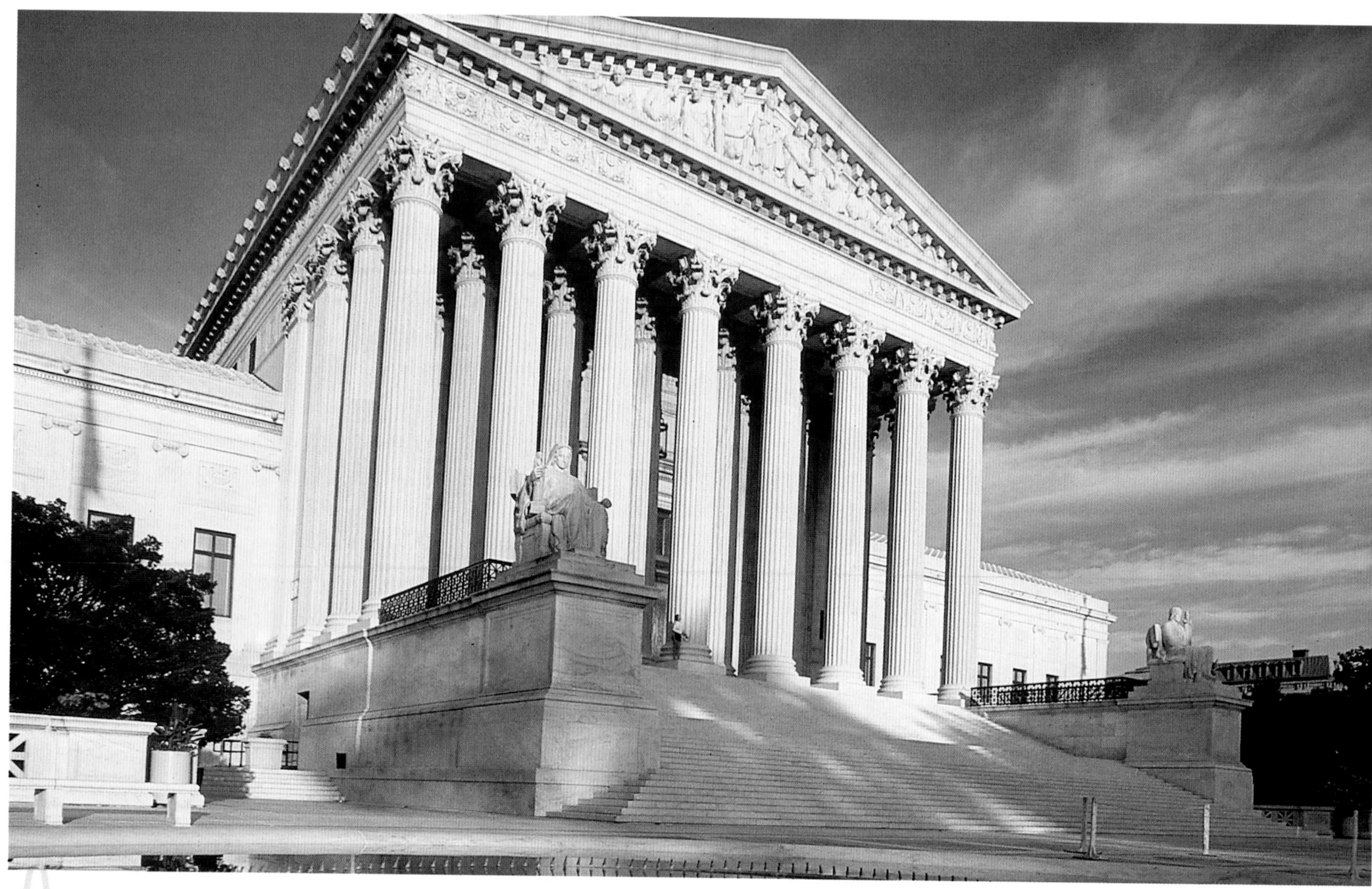

*The classical Corinthian architectural style of the Supreme Court was chosen to accent its dignity.*

The Supreme Court of the United States is the highest court in the nation. Appointed by the president and confirmed by the Senate, the Supreme Court consists of a chief justice and eight associate justices. The justices serve for life, or at least until retirement, and no justice has ever been impeached.

The Supreme Court was established in 1789 by the U.S. Constitution, but it has only occupied the building across from the U.S. Capitol since 1935. Designed by celebrated architect Cass Gilbert, the building is sheathed in marble that was quarried in the United States. On the front, eight rows of imposing pillars stand under the chiseled motto, "Equal Justice Under Law." Inside the courtroom, however, Gilbert decided domestic marble was not good enough for the highest court in the land and would settle for nothing less than the finest marble from Italy's lauded quarries. In this setting, the nine justices make decisions that have shaped and will continue to shape the country.

# Thomas Jefferson Memorial and Franklin Delano Roosevelt Memorial

Located in East Potomac Park on the eastern shore of the Tidal Basin, the Thomas Jefferson Memorial, with its graceful dome, is a striking site. Known as a writer, philosopher, diplomat, and Renaissance man, the third president of the United States left behind a legacy of political ideas and actions that have passed the test of time with flying colors. A statue of Jefferson stands at the center of the rotunda under the dome, and the surrounding walls are inscribed with words from his most lasting and eloquent writings, including personal letters and the Declaration of Independence.

On the west side of the Tidal Basin, the Franklin Delano Roosevelt Memorial pays respect to the nation's 32nd president. Dedicated by President Bill Clinton in 1997, the memorial consists of four outdoor "rooms," each depicting one of FDR's four terms in office. This memorial is not only about the man, but also the tumultuous times through which he guided the nation.

(Above) *The Thomas Jefferson Memorial was dedicated in 1943 on the 200th anniversary of Jefferson's birth.*

(Below) *Sculptures at the Franklin Delano Roosevelt Memorial, such as this one of Roosevelt seated in a wheelchair, were based on photographs of the 32nd president.*

# Lincoln Memorial

At the center of the Lincoln Memorial is a sculpture of Abraham Lincoln, seated with resolve but as if reserving judgment. One hand is clenched, one open. His gaze seems to change with the light but remains focused across the Reflecting Pool to the Washington Monument and the National Mall beyond. He seems to look toward the future and not flinch from it.

The Lincoln Memorial leads visitors to contemplate what Lincoln accomplished and what he stood for. No poet (including Walt Whitman) and no biographer (including Carl Sandburg) has expressed this as well as Lincoln himself in his addresses at his second inauguration and at Gettysburg. Both speeches are carved into the walls of the memorial.

Similar to the Washington Monument, building the Lincoln Memorial was a prolonged process. Congress formed the Lincoln Monument Association in 1867. The original design was for a 12-foot statue of Lincoln surrounded by 6 large equestrian and 31 pedestrian statues. But a lack of funding derailed the initial project, and construction on the current memorial didn't begin until Lincoln's birthday in 1914.

The memorial was made from Indiana limestone and yule marble from Colorado. It was completed in 1922. It is unlike any other structure on the National Mall. The choice of a neoclassical Greek rather than Roman desig stirred dismay.

The memorial is majestic in scale an impressive in its ability to share Lincoln vision. The base covers roughly the sam area as a football field. The statue measur 19 feet wide by 19 feet tall—its size was sharp increased when sculptor Daniel Chest French realized it would be overwhelmed b the memorial's size. The building has 36 Dor columns, one for each state during Lincoln presidency. The memorial has attracted crow since its creation and has hosted historic gath erings including Marian Anderson's 193 Easter Sunday concert, an early turning poi

*Millions of people come to visit the Lincoln Memorial each year. Here they crowd the steps and many look up in awe.*

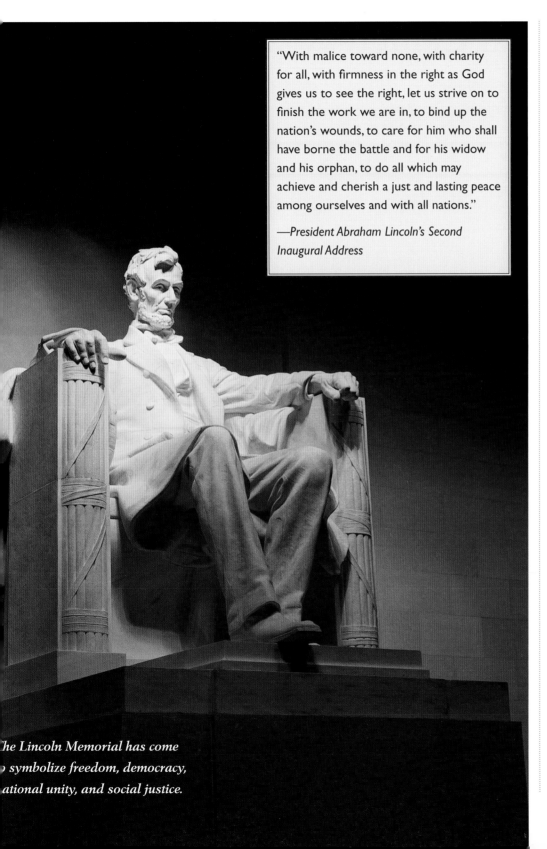

"With malice toward none, with charity for all, with firmness in the right as God gives us to see the right, let us strive on to finish the work we are in, to bind up the nation's wounds, to care for him who shall have borne the battle and for his widow and his orphan, to do all which may achieve and cherish a just and lasting peace among ourselves and with all nations."

*—President Abraham Lincoln's Second Inaugural Address*

***he Lincoln Memorial has come symbolize freedom, democracy, ational unity, and social justice.***

*The inscription honors the 16th U.S. president.*

in the Civil Rights Movement, and Martin Luther King, Jr.'s, "I Have a Dream" speech culminating the historic march on Washington for civil rights in 1963.

The words carved into the marble of the Lincoln Memorial long ago came true: "In this temple, as in the hearts of the people for whom he saved the Union, the memory of Abraham Lincoln is enshrined forever."

# Arlington National Cemetery

Nearly four million visitors come to Arlington National Cemetery each year. Most come to pay respect to their loved ones, to honor the leaders interred here, or to thank the more than 300,000 people buried here, many of whom were soldiers killed in the line of duty.

The original 200 acres were designated as a military cemetery on June 15, 1864. Soldiers and veterans from every war the United States has fought, from the Revolutionary War to the war in Iraq, are buried here (those who died prior to the Civil War were reinterred in Arlington after 1900).

(Below) *Tomb Guard sentinels, which are volunteers from the elite 3rd U.S. Infantry, guard the Tomb of the Unknowns 24 hours a day, 365 days a year.*

(Above) *Rows of headstones mark the graves of the soldiers and veterans buried in Arlington National Cemetery.*

Three unknown soldiers—from World War I, World War II, and the Korean War—are buried at the never-officially-named Tomb of the Unknowns. (The Vietnam veteran who had been buried here was identified in 1998 and his body was returned to his family in St. Louis.) President John F. Kennedy is buried in Arlington. His grave is marked by the Eternal Flame, designed so that a constant spark of electricity ignites the gas, keeping the flame alive through rain and wind.

# Washington National Cathedral

Pierre L'Enfant, Washington, D.C.'s first city planner, conceived of a national church in 1791. In his writings, L'Enfant described his vision of a cathedral "intended for national purposes, such as public prayer, thanksgiving, funeral orations, etc., and assigned to the special use of no particular Sect or denomination, but equally open to all." However, it took some time for L'Enfant's vision to come to pass. The foundation was laid in 1907, but the building was not actually finished for 83 years. Its western towers were completed in 1990.

The National Cathedral has been a focal point for spiritual life in the nation's capital since it opened in 1912. Every president has attended services here while in office. Many people have gathered at the church to mourn the passing of leaders or mark momentous events in world history.

The National Cathedral is a grand structure with intricate architectural details. With towers 676 feet above sea level and a facade adorned with more than 250 angels and more than 100 gargoyles, the church deserves its lofty title.

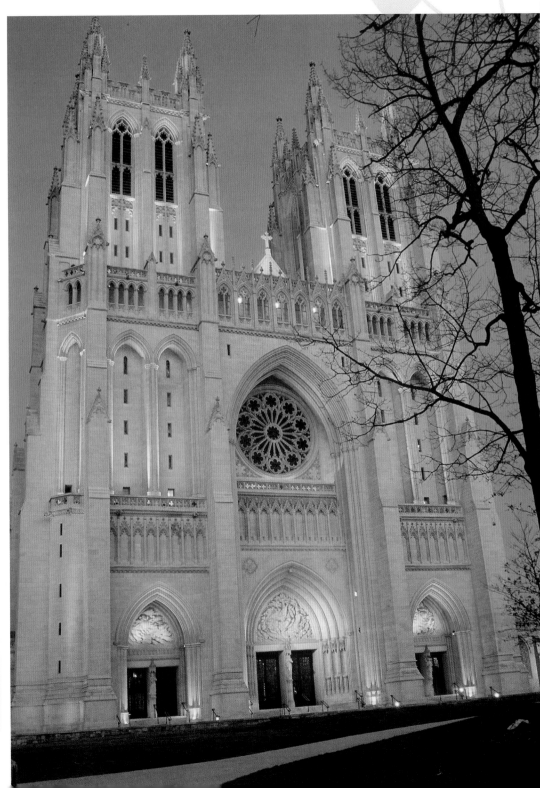

*The National Cathedral is the sixth-largest cathedral in the world. Its High Altar* (below) *is made from stones quarried near Jerusalem.*

# National Cherry Blossom Festival

*Cherry trees bloom each spring along the Tidal Basin in Washington, D.C.*

In 1912, Tokyo Mayor Yukio Ozaki gave Washington, D.C., a gift of 3,000 cherry trees to beautify its streets. Since 1935, the city has commemorated the trees' blooming in late March or early April with one of its biggest festivals. Participants from the United States and Japan kick off the festival with a parade on Constitution Avenue. The festivities continue for two more weeks, with such events as a ten-mile run, concerts, and Sakura Matsuri, a Japanese street festival.

The cycle of giving has continued. In 1965, First Lady Lady Bird Johnson accepted a gift of 3,800 more trees. Then in 1981, Japanese horticulturists came to Washington, D.C., to collect cuttings, which were then planted where a flood had wiped out numerous cherry trees in Japan. In 1999, more cherry trees were planted around the Tidal Basin; their common ancestor was a 1,500-year-old tree from the Gifu province in Japan.

# Fourth of July Fireworks

Independence Day in the nation's capital is an all-day affair. The morning of July 4 begins with a bustling parade on Constitution Avenue with patriotic floats, military units, marching bands, and important political figures.

While there are all sorts of activities—from art shows to puppet theater—the big event is the evening festivities: one of the country's biggest fireworks displays. This work of incendiary art has an ideal setting above the Reflecting Pool on the National Mall, with the majestic backdrop of some of the country's most beloved monuments and memorials. The multihued fireworks extravaganza is a feast for the ears as well as the eyes: The evening also includes a concert by the National Symphony Orchestra. More than 450,000 people "ooh" and "aah" over the fireworks in person, and millions more take in the spectacle on television. After all, what better place is there to celebrate the birth of the United States than in its capital city?

*Each year, on July 4, a dazzling display of fireworks lights up the sky above Washington, D.C.*

# Monticello

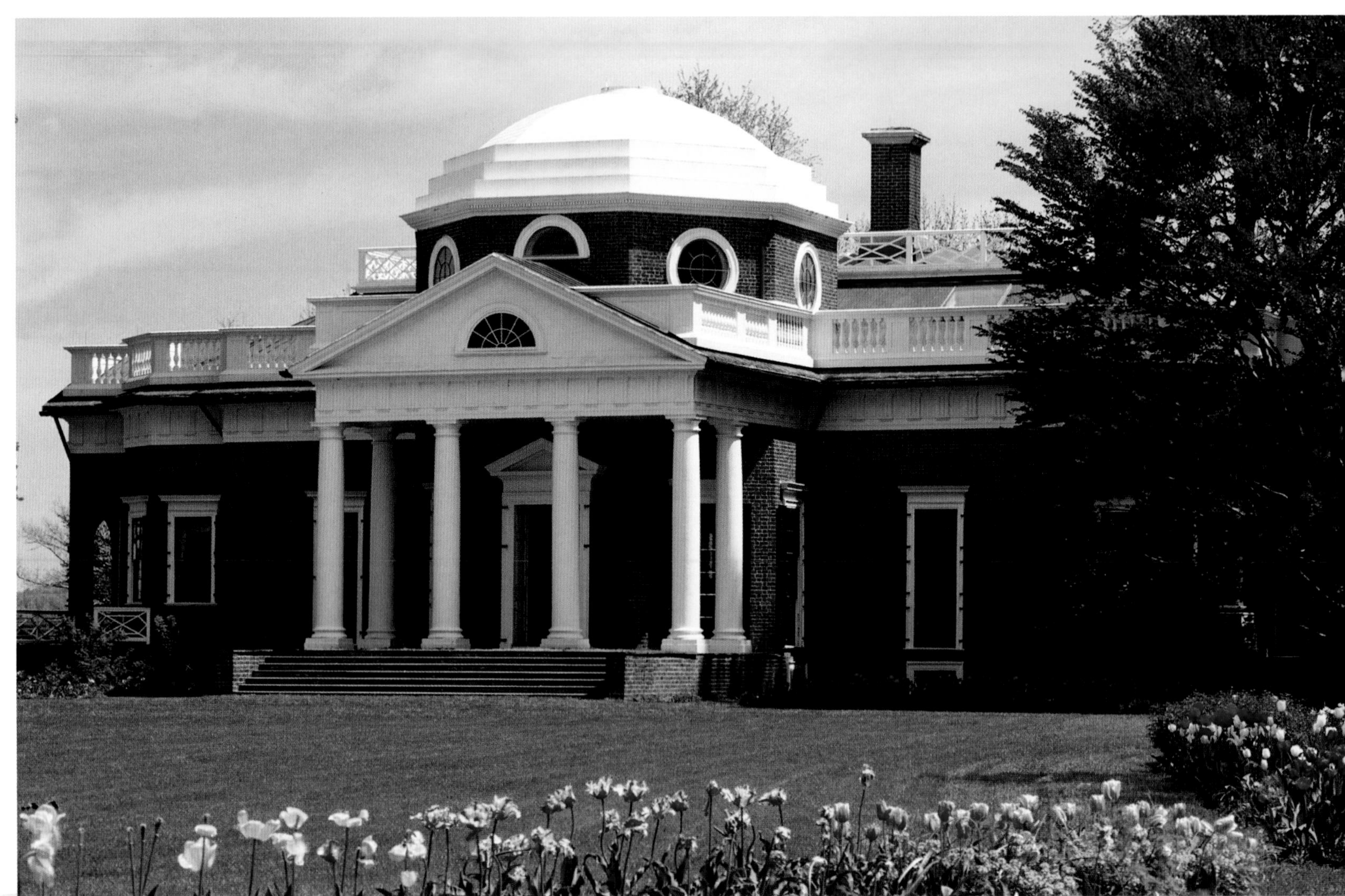

Monticello, the Virginia home of American founder Thomas Jefferson, is a Roman neoclassical masterpiece. Jefferson moved onto the property in 1770, but the mansion was not completed until 1809, after Jefferson's second term as president.

The domed building features east- and west-facing porticos that bookend an entrance hall and parlor. Jefferson, ever the tinkerer and innovator, made all sorts of improvements to Monticello to maximize space and light. The 43-room mansion has 13 skylights, including one over Jefferson's bed.

On the tour of Monticello, you'll have a chance to see Jefferson's mansion up close. The house was the centerpiece of Jefferson's plantation, which totaled 5,000 acres at its peak. About 130 slaves worked the land, tended livestock, cooked, and cleaned there during Jefferson's life.

*The west front of Jefferson's Monticello may seem familiar—it was exclusively featured on the back of the U.S. nickel from 1938 to 2003.*

# Mount Vernon Estate and Gardens

Mount Vernon was home to George Washington, the first president of the United States. The land in eastern Virginia was given to George Washington's great-grandfather in 1674, and it remained in the family for seven generations.

Washington spent five years at Mount Vernon as a child and later lived there as an adult with his wife, Martha. The plantation grew to 8,000 acres while Washington served as commander in chief during the Revolutionary War. While Washington was best known as a military and political leader, he also left a strong architectural legacy: He designed and built many of the structures at Mount Vernon, including the famed mansion with its distinctive two-story portico.

The estate is now 500 acres, 50 of which are open to the public. In Washington's day, Mount Vernon was essentially a self-sustaining community, and a considerable amount of this heritage is still showcased today.

*Washington and his family lived in the "Mansion House Farm" section of Mount Vernon.*

# Colonial Williamsburg

Williamsburg, Jamestown, and Yorktown make up Virginia's Historic Triangle. Known as Colonial Williamsburg, the area is the world's largest, and possibly greatest, living-history museum. Nowhere else is more care taken to create, re-create, and maintain a semblance of pre-Revolutionary life in the United States than here. Actors wear period clothing and interact with each other and the visiting public to simulate life in Williamsburg during the 17th century.

## Quick Fact

***Jamestown and Yorktown***

These locations were the backdrop for two definitive moments in U.S. history. Jamestown was the first permanent English settlement in the New World. And the decisive battle in the Revolutionary War was fought at Yorktown.

Jamestown was founded in 1607—13 years before the Pilgrims landed at Plymouth Rock. While in Jamestown, visit the living-history area. There are replicas of three ships that sailed across the Atlantic to Virginia, re-creations of the colonists' fort and a Powhatan village, and a "riverfront discovery" area describing the commerce of Jamestown in the early 1600s.

The Yorktown Victory Center commemorates the Siege of Yorktown in 1781. The British surrendered at this battle, ending the six-year Revolutionary War.

Jamestown was the first capital of Virginia, but it lay in a low marsh area that compromised defenses against both hostile native people and malaria-carrying mosquitoes. The Army moved some soldiers to nearby Middle Plantation, five miles away on a high point between the James and York rivers. In 1693, King William III and

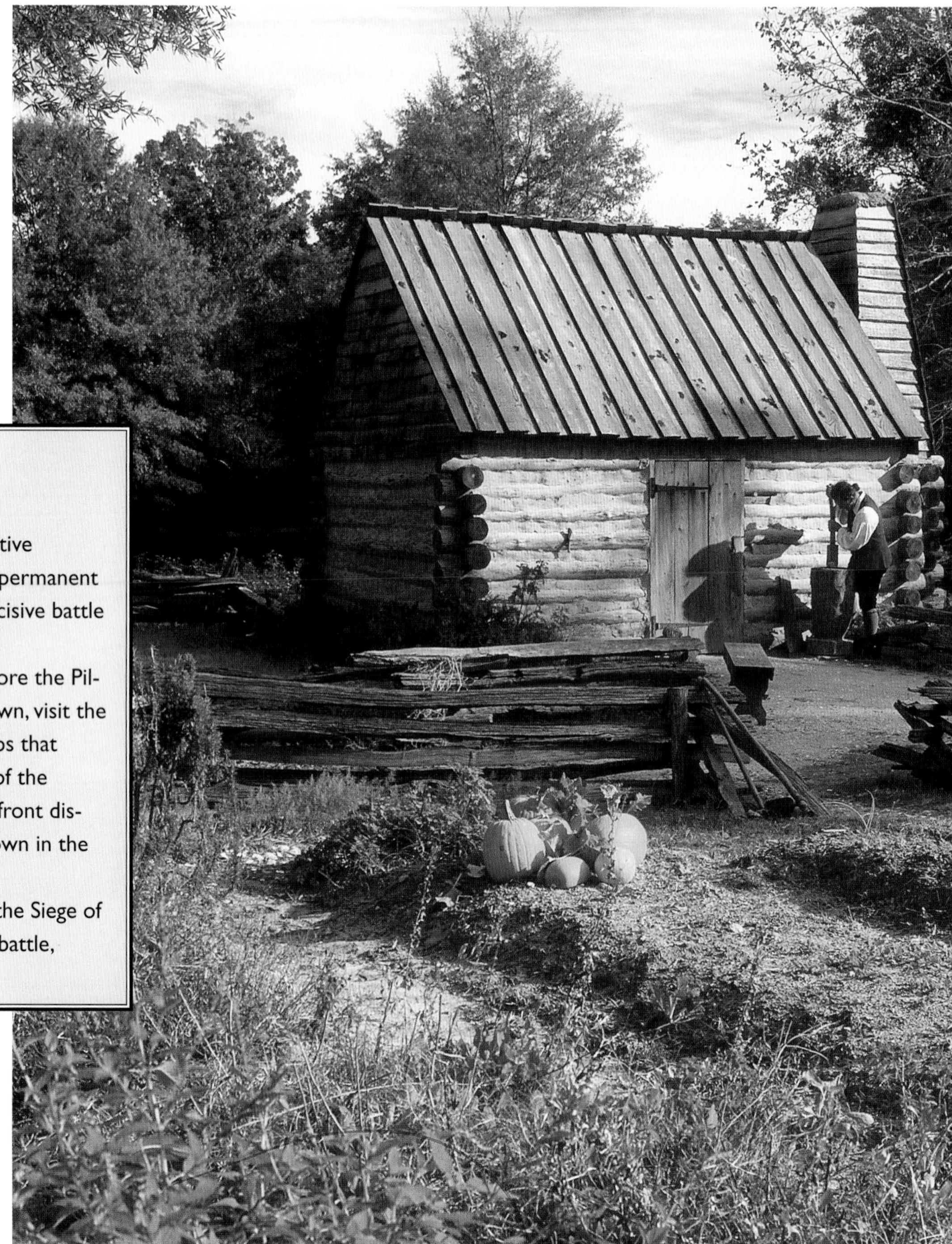

*The Yorktown Victory Center gives visitors a look at life on a 1780s Virginia farm.*

*oday the Colonial Williamsburg Fifes and Drums are boys and girls ages 10 to 18 who carry on the tradition of military music.*

ueen Mary II granted a charter to the College William and Mary, the colonies' second uni-rsity (Harvard was the first). In 1699, the set-ement was renamed Williamsburg after the ng and was declared the new colonial capital. onstruction soon began on a new statehouse id governor's house. And so Williamsburg mained for nearly a century, until 1780, when overnor Thomas Jefferson moved the capital Richmond.

Fast-forward to the 20th century. Williams-ırg's neglected center, the old capital, was st decaying until a local pastor persuaded hn D. Rockefeller, Jr., to take an interest. ockefeller quietly bought property and privately financed a plan for the city's restoration. When the time came, he unveiled the idea to universal applause.

The result is today's 301-acre colonial village, where 88 original buildings were restored or repaired and nearly 500 buildings and outbuildings were reconstructed. Colonial Williamsburg is a living museum, meaning while tourists visit museums, they are also invited to immerse themselves in another century and its homes, handicrafts, clothing, stores, taverns, gardens, and jails, as well as its people.

A great way to arrive at Colonial Williamsburg is to drive the nearby Colonial Parkway, which connects Yorktown to Jamestown via Williamsburg. The parkway's 23 miles of picturesque scenery through the Colonial National Historic Park have been protected from roadside development. Even traffic signs are minimized.

For an authentic 17th-century thrill, visitors can stay in period accommodations in Colonial Williamsburg. The Colonial Houses program offers accommodations inside the old city at 28 guesthouses, which are authentically furnished and range in size from one room in a tavern to a 16-room home. The adjacent Williamsburg Lodge, built by John D. Rockefeller, Jr., and listed on the National Register of Historic Places, is equally as exciting.

# Virginia Beach

Virginia Beach is a modern magnet for outdoors buffs—namely surfers, anglers, golfers, and boaters. The city is a favorite getaway with attractions ranging from amusement parks and miniature golf courses to historic sites and vibrant art. The beach is a wide, sandy strip on the central Atlantic coast, fronted by a three-mile boardwalk and oceanfront resorts with all the trimmings.

The big event here is the Neptune Festival, which has been held annually in late September since 1974. It's now one of the biggest festivals on the entire East Coast, drawing hordes to surfing contests, concerts, "Boardwalk Weekend," and the ever-popular North American Sandsculpting Championship.

Thanks to its location at the mouth of Chesapeake Bay, Virginia Beach also has made history. Just north on Route 60 is Fort Story, home to the Cape Henry Lighthouses. The original lighthouse, built in 1792, was the first lighthouse structure authorized, completed, and lighted by the federal government. While the old lighthouse still stands, a new lighthouse was added in 1878.

The first Europeans—a party that included Captain John Smith—landed at Cape Henry on April 26, 1607. In 1621, they settled what is now Virginia Beach. The Cape Henry Memorial Cross at Fort Story commemorates where these colonists made landfall.

*The new Cape Henry Lighthouse stands an impressive 164 feet tall.*

# Mabry Mill

The wonderfully preserved Mabry Mill is one of the most popular attractions on the Blue Ridge Parkway.

'he historic fixture of Mabry Mill lies alongide Virginia's sublime stretch of the Blue :idge Parkway. It's located on Rocky Knob, a eautiful mountain known for its crystalline uartz formations and apple orchards.

The mill's namesake, Ed Mabry, began contruction on the complex in 1905. The mill vas an active gristmill and sawmill in the early part of the 20th century. The complex also included a blacksmith's shop, a whiskey still, and a wheelwright's shop.

In modern days, Mabry Mill has emerged as a living-history center with regular demonstrations of old-fashioned smithing, spinning, and weaving techniques. A short hike on the Mountain Industry Trail reveals what life was like in rural Virginia a century ago. Hikers may also glimpse turtles, ducks, and other wildlife. Better yet, on Sunday afternoons there are festive events with traditional music and dancing.

# Shenandoah Valley

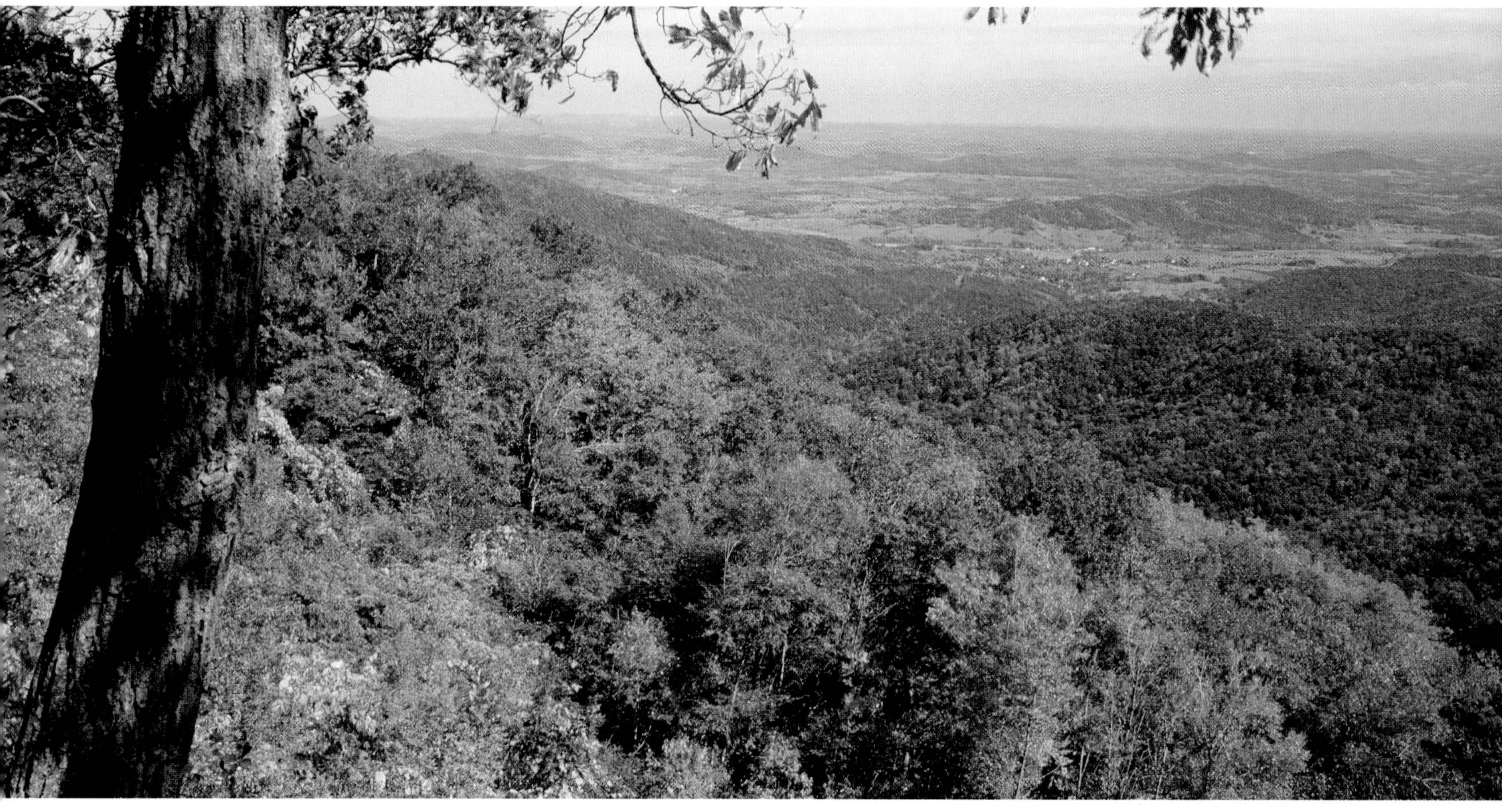

*The lush Shenandoah Valley stretches from Harpers Ferry, West Virginia, to Roanoke and Salem, Virginia.*

For years, the Blue Ridge Mountains seemed an insurmountable obstacle to the westward expansion of the United States. Many pioneers stopped cold in their tracks, but a spectacular sight greeted those who made it to the top of the ridge—the lovely Shenandoah Valley. This green paradise of endless forests and meadows cut by winding rivers and streams was so inviting that the valley seemed to hold all the promise of the West.

Shenandoah is in large part protected as a national park. It's also a place where people have lived for many generations. When the park was established in 1935, much of the area consisted of eroded hillsides, worn farmland, and thin second- or third-growth forests. Today, the forests are mounting a comeback, sheathing the scars of grazing, farming, and logging. Native wildlife is returning, as well; black bears, raccoons, and opossums (America's only marsupial), roam here, just as the did in pioneer days.

Skyline Drive runs along the crest of th Blue Ridge, providing 75 overlooks and mag nificent vistas of forests, mountains, and th valley. For a real treat, visit the valley in th spring or fall to see the fabulous blossomin flowers or autumn leaf displays. More tha 500 miles of trails wind through the valle including part of the Appalachian Trail. Ther are also numerous waterfalls—a dozen in th park drop more than 40 feet.

# Monongahela National Forest

he Monongahela National Forest in West Vir- nia is one of the largest tracts of protected astern woodlands. This naturally makes it a ecca for outdoorspeople of all stripes—fish- s, hikers, mountain bikers, and paddlers. When visiting, make good use of the forest's extensive network of backcountry trails. The landscape is dotted with highland bogs and dense thickets of blueberries. The forest is made up of five different federally designated wilderness areas at elevations ranging from 900 feet above sea level to 4,861 feet atop Spruce Knob, the loftiest peak in the entire state.

*he Monongahela National Forest covers 19,000 rugged acres.*

The size and scope of Monongahela is impressive by any standard, and so is the breadth of life in the forest. Black bears, foxes, beavers, woodchucks, opossums, and mink are among the mammals found there. There are also dozens of types of fish in the streams, more than 200 feathered species in the skies and the treetops, and 75 types of trees rooted there.

# Harpers Ferry National Historic Park

Harpers Ferry, at the confluence of the Shenandoah and Potomac rivers in Virginia, West Virginia, and Maryland, has played a fascinating role in U.S. history.

The town emerged in the 1830s at the railroad hub where northern and southern lines connected. Harpers Ferry is best known for abolitionist John Brown's raid on an arsenal there in 1859. He believed that with the weapons stored there, the slaves could fight for their own freedom. Its location also made it a key target in the Civil War: In 1861, shortly after Virginia seceded from the Union, Northerners set fire to its strategic structures to keep them out of Confederate hands.

When the Civil War ended, Harpers Ferry became a focal point during Reconstruction. The town made many early attempts at integrating former slaves into society. This was marked most notably by the 1867 establishment of Storer College, one of the first integrated schools in the United States.

*The small but historically important town of Harpers Ferry, West Virginia, has a population of just more than 300.*

Now designated Harpers Ferry Nation[al] Historical Park, this spot is a popular way st[a]tion for hikers traveling the Appalachia[n] Trail. The town offers numerous historical re-creations and other living-history events. Visitors also come to fish, go rafting, or explore the surrounding forest.

# Mammoth Cave

Iammoth Cave is hidden below the forested ills of southern Kentucky. This is the world's ırgest network of caverns. There are more than 50 miles of underground passages on five dif- erent levels—and that's just what's been ıapped thus far.

The full extent of Mammoth Cave is still unknown. New caves and passageways are being discovered to this day. The underground frontiers of this spectacular labyrinth extend deeper and deeper into a netherworld that almost defies belief.

The underground wonderland of spectacular Mammoth Cave is made up of limestone, which dissolves when water seeps through the ground. As the water works its way downward, the limestone erodes, forming the honeycomb of underground passageways, amphitheaters, and rooms that make up Mammoth Cave, as well as its dazzling array of stalagmites, stalactites, and columns.

Native Americans first explored the great cave about 4,000 years ago. European settlers stumbled upon it in the 1790s, and guides have been turning interested tourists into amateur spelunkers ever since.

*'he stalagmites and stalactites of Mammoth ˜ave are the product of water seeping down- ɪard for many millennia.*

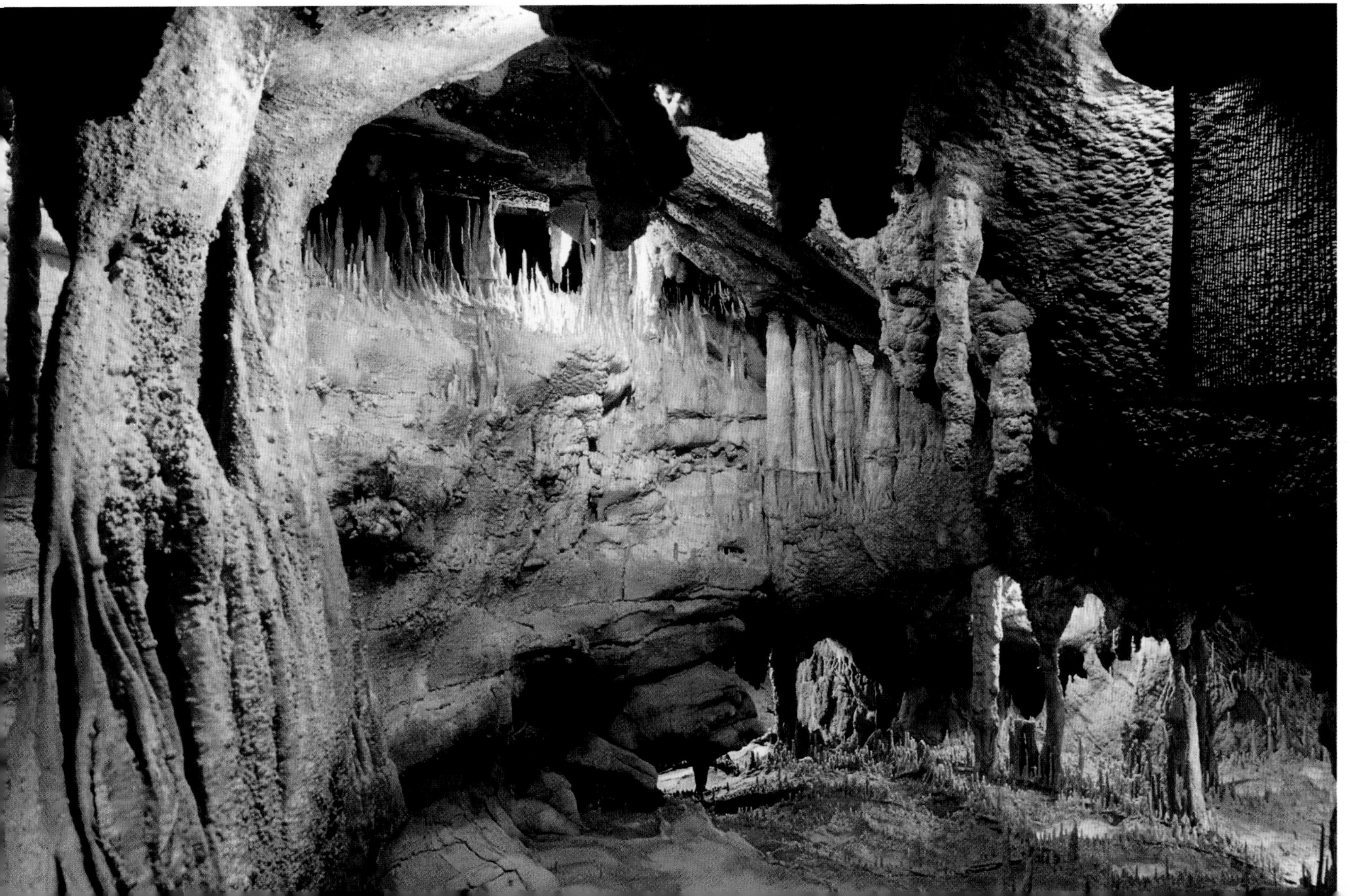

# Kentucky Derby

It's called "the most exciting two minutes in sports" and features 20 world-class athletes culled from a field of more than 30,000. Perfectly chiseled, they line up. A bell sounds. And they're off!

The athletes in question are three-year-old thoroughbred horses. The winner covers the 1.25-mile track at Churchill Downs in Louisville, Kentucky, in just about two minutes at a gallop averaging almost 40 miles per hour.

The first "jewel" of the three races collectively known as the Triple Crown (along with the Preakness Stakes and the Belmont Stakes), the Kentucky Derby is no ordinary sporting event. It's a raucous party, a longstanding tradition, and a vibrant pageant. The race caps the three-week Kentucky Derby Festival, which includes steamboat and balloon races, spectacular fireworks, marathons, and the lively Pegasus Parade.

Run every May since 1875, the Derby is steeped in tradition. In many ways, these time-honored traditions and their year-to-year evolutions are just as amazing as the actual race.

The most visible tradition at the "Run for the Roses" might be the derby hat. Spectators have worn formal attire to the race since its 19th-century founding, and the icing on the cake has always been the women's headgear, wide-brimmed and adorned with flowers or other ornaments. It's said that you don't choose your hat to match your outfit on Derby Day, but your outfit to match your hat! While more modest styles prevailed in the 1870s, today's derby hats are emblems of excess: the bigger, more colorful, and gaudier, the better Even men get in on the act nowadays with wilder hats every year.

More than 150,000 people attend the Derby each year. "Millionaire's Row," frequented by Very Important People of every stripe, is one place from which spectators can view the action. Another spot is the infield; this area is much rowdier and muddier and can hold up to 80,000 people. A flash of silk and a cloud of dust are about all you can expect to see from here, though.

A prevailing tradition at the Derby is th mint julep. This Southern cocktail—consistin of mint, crushed ice, sugar, and bourbon—ha long been the refreshment of choice for th spectators at Churchill Downs.

Mint juleps are perfect for wash ing down a bowl of savory burgoo, th Derby's traditional Kentuckian stev Served from vast iron kettles that som times measure ten-feet across, burgo is a time-tested stew that has no estab lished recipe but usually includes lamb okra, lima beans, and plenty of spices. It said that a spoon should stand straigh up in a bowl of good burgoo.

The traditional silks worn by th jockeys have their origins in early 18th century England, where riders' color would denote the duke, earl, or king fo whom they raced. Now the silks are symbol of the horse's owner.

It's also traditional for a long shot t pay off at Churchill Downs. Only tw favorites have won in the last 26 years. I 2005, a 50-to-1 long shot won the race.

Legends of races past seem to gallop along side the contenders. Secretariat is often men tioned as the greatest athlete in Kentuck Derby history. In 1973, the legendary thor oughbred ran the race in a record time o 1 minute, 59 and ⅖ seconds.

(Opposite page) *Enthusiastic spectators cheer on their favorite horses at Churchill Downs.*

***Mint Julep***

Don your fancy hat and enjoy a refreshing mint julep on Derby day!

2 cups water
2 cups sugar
sprigs of fresh mint
crushed ice
Kentucky bourbon

Boil sugar in water until dissolved, about five minutes. Combine with six to eight sprigs of fresh mint and refrigerate, covered, overnight, to create a mint syrup. Fill each glass with crushed ice, one tablespoon of the mint syrup, and two ounces of bourbon. Stir, and garnish with an extra sprig of fresh mint.

The mint julep is traditionally served in a chilled silver cup, but any festive glass is acceptable. Chill cups in the freezer for 30 minutes beforehand to attain the preferred frosty effect.

1875
2005

# Beale Street

The neighborhood surrounding Beale Street might be quiet, with the trolley that runs along Main Street creating the only significant sound. But when you arrive at the southern doorstep of downtown Memphis, the quiet gives way to the raucous neon-and-brick music clubs that line Beale Street.

Beale Street is not just a spectacle for the eyes, it's also an experience for the taste buds. Pots of gumbo and red beans and rice simmer at every corner. However, the smells and tastes of Beale Street are just side dishes: The main course is the music. Blues, soul, and rock 'n' roll claim the perfectly imperfect city of Memphis as their birthplace. And all three get people dancing on Beale Street every night.

*Memphis is home to Sun Records, the label that signed Elvis Presley to his first recording contract in 1954.*

*Memphis touts itself as the "Birthplace of Rock 'n' Roll," and it's got a strong case for the title. In the mid-1950s, Memphis's blues legacy fused with country music, creating a new sound that found fans across the country. Beale Street has remained the heart and soul of music in Memphis.*

Beale Street has long been a feast for the senses. In the early 20th century, it was one of the busiest markets in the South, with European immigrants selling goods of all kinds to a largely African-American clientele. In the 1980s, Beale Street was redeveloped into an open-air, pedestrian-only center for music, nightlife, and more music. And it's caught on—now the old marketplace hosts musicians, dancers, and sellers every night of the week.

As the neon on the Rum Boogie Cafe advises: "Eat. Drink. Boogie. Repeat."

# Grand Ole Opry

he Grand Ole Opry in Nashville, Tennessee, is a ıltural phenomenon. At its heart, it's a radio pro- am that showcases American country music. It's ıe longest-running live radio program in the nited States. But country music is just the arting point. The Opry is the centerpiece of )pryland, a resort and convention center that overs everything from golf to shopping to, of ourse, country music.

It all began back in 1925 when a brand-new Jashville radio station, WSM, hired a former Memphis newspaper reporter named George Hay to host a weekly program called the "WSM Barn Dance." In 1927, the show was renamed the "Grand Ole Opry," and its popularity snowballed. By 1932, WSM's new 50,000-watt transmitter blasted the program across the country and even to parts of Canada. Over the years, the Grand Ole Opry has become home to the "Who's Who" of American country music.

*Shows at the Grand Ole Opry are magical to the performers and audience alike.*

The six-foot circle of dark oak wood at the Opry House Stage is magical for the performers and audience. The section was cut from the Opry's former home, Ryman Auditorium, and today's performers feel a connection with the country legends who first sang there. From April through December, the Opry hosts Tuesday Night Opry shows—a perfect way to take in the heart and soul of country music.

# Graceland

In his youthful heyday, Elvis Presley was the personification of American cool. He bought Graceland mansion in Memphis's Whitehaven neighborhood in 1957 when he was just 22 years old. He paid $102,500 for the property, an 18-room mansion on nearly 14 acres of country estate surrounded by towering oak trees.

Presley never thought he would see much money in his life. He was born in a sharecropper's shack in Tupelo, Mississippi. But after becoming an international superstar, Presley was rich enough to buy Graceland. Depending on whom you ask, the estate was named for the original owner's wife's aunt, Grace Toof. Presley bought the estate as much for his parents—especially his mother Gladys—as for himself. But Gladys died in 1958 and never got to enjoy the house to the extent Elvis had hoped. The King of Rock 'n' Roll lived in the mansion for most of the second half of his life.

Graceland is strikingly modest, especially by modern standards. Built in 1939, it's a manageable mansion, smaller than most celebrity homes. The house is not unlike a traditional luxury home in the suburbs—except for the King's famously extravagant touches, of course.

Corinthian columns and a limestone facade mark the exterior of the instantly recognizable home. The interior has been preserved as it

*Visitors to Graceland pay their respects to Elvis Presley at his grave in the Meditation Garden.*

vas at the time of Elvis's death in 1977. Like a ›ug in amber, Graceland captures the 1970s :ra in all of its possibilities. Elvis's legendary aste included his so-called "Jungle Room," eplete with an in-wall waterfall and green hag carpeting on the floor and ceiling; his :clectic billiards parlor, plastered in yards of ›rnately patterned fabric; and his TV room, vith a yellow, white, and blue color scheme ınd three television sets Presley watched simultaneously. Outside are the pool, his :ather Vernon's office (next to Elvis's firing :ange), and a building with a racquetball court, which now houses the King's gold records and other awards.

When visiting Graceland, take the audio tour to learn about the history of Elvis. Then you can pay your respects to Presley, who is buried alongside his parents and his grandmother behind the mansion in the serene Meditation Garden. Beyond the mansion and estate, take a peek at the automobile museum housing the King's cars (Elvis's 1955 pink Cadillac and 1956 purple Cadillac convertible are on display), a pair of his private planes, and restaurants and gift shops that sell Elvis souvenirs of every imaginable variety.

Graceland is now on the National Register of Historic Places, and it's become a magnet for Elvis fans everywhere. Fan clubs from as far away as Asia and Europe regularly send flowers and tributes to his grave. The enduring appeal of Elvis and his music is perhaps the most amazing thing about Graceland. His house attracts upward of 750,000 fans a year more than 30 years after his death—a testament to Elvis's lasting popularity.

*The music gates were added after Elvis bought the mansion in 1957.*

## Quick Fact

***Top Ten Sites at Graceland***

1. **Music gates**—these were not part of the property when Elvis purchased it in 1957, but they were added later that year.
2. **Hall of Gold**—located in the Trophy Room just behind Graceland mansion, the Hall of Gold contains gold records and honors that Elvis received as a performing artist.
3. **Firearms collection**—on display in the Trophy Room are Elvis's 37 firearms, including pistols, machine guns, and a sawed-off shotgun.
4. **Badge collection**—also on display in the Trophy Room are the badges Elvis collected from law enforcement and security agencies across the country.
5. **Elvis's record collection**—this exhibit, called Sincerely Elvis, is across the street from Graceland and features Elvis's diverse taste in music.
6. **RCA display**—With 111 titles certified as gold, platinum, or multiplatinum, Elvis's collection is the largest presentation of gold and platinum records in history.
7. **Meditation Garden**—this small garden at Graceland is now the final resting place for Elvis and his immediate family.
8. **Elvis's jet, the *Lisa Marie***—purchased by Elvis in 1975, the jet named after his daughter is now on display at Graceland.
9. **The pink Cadillac Elvis bought for his mother**—this 1955 Cadillac, along with some of Elvis's other trademark cars, is on display at the Auto Museum.
10. **Wedding dress and suit**—Elvis's black paisley brocade jacket, matching vest, and plain black trousers and Priscilla's white silk organza dress are on display in the Sincerely Elvis exhibit.

# Great Smoky Mountains National Park

Shrouded in thick deciduous forest, the Great Smoky Mountains are the United States' highest range east of South Dakota's Black Hills. They are also one of the oldest mountain ranges on the planet. The park's highest point is the 6,643-foot peak of Clingman's Dome, which is just across the North Carolina state line in Tennessee. On clear days, you can see as far as 100 miles from the peak. A cool, damp, coniferous rain forest covers much of the mountain.

The mountains are made of primeval rock and are considerably older than their rough, craggy counterparts out West. Today, the Great Smoky Mountains are protected as a national park but perhaps loved too much—more than nine million visitors take their toll each year.

The Smokies' vast forest is also one of the oldest on the continent. The park often feels like a vestige of an ancient era when trees ruled the planet. Today, over 100 species of trees and 1,300 varieties of flowering plants grow in the park. The respiration of this plant life produces the gauzy haze that gives the mountains their 'smoky' moniker.

*The ridges of the Great Smoky Mountains trail off into the humid air.*

# Biltmore Estate

The Walled Garden on the Biltmore Estate blooms with a progression of color from spring through summer.

'he largest home in the United States is the enterpiece of an immaculate 8,000-acre state that includes lush gardens, active vine-ards, and a luxury inn. Originally the country etreat of the Vanderbilt family, Biltmore has volved into a swanky tourist attraction with a ascinating historical pedigree.

Biltmore mansion is the estate's distin-uishing feature. It was the vision of George V. Vanderbilt. In the late 1880s, he purchased 125,000 acres in the Blue Ridge Mountains near Asheville, North Carolina, for the estate. He commissioned his friend, architect Richard Morris Hunt, to design the mansion.

Construction began in 1889 and lasted six years, requiring the labors of more than 1,000 workers. The fruit of their labor was this 250-room French Renaissance château. It was one of the most technologically advanced buildings of its time. Biltmore had indoor plumbing, electricity, elevators, and some of the first lightbulbs and telephones. There are 65 fireplaces, an indoor pool, a bowling alley, and numerous antiques. The gardens, designed by landscape architect Frederick Law Olm-sted, are similarly superlative.

# Cape Hatteras

Cape Hatteras is a largely untamed string of barrier islands about 70 miles long. This natural wonder has a distinct culture and fascinating history. The dunes, marshes, and woodlands that mark the thin strand of land between North Carolina's coastal sounds and the Atlantic Ocean are a diverse ecosystem defined by the wind and the sea. Nearly 400 species of birds have been sighted in the Cape Hatteras area. Hawks, shorebirds, and songbirds are common in spring and fall; terns and herons populate Cape Hatteras in the summer; and ducks and geese make the area home in winter.

Countless shipwrecks have earned Cape Hatteras a treacherous reputation and the nickname "The Graveyard of the Atlantic." The navigational dangers led to the construction of several lighthouses, including Cape Hatteras Lighthouse and Ocracoke Lighthouse (built in 1823, it's the oldest operating lighthouse in North Carolina).

While crowds are few and far between, Cape Hatteras is a popular recreational destination. Try the waters on either side of the island—they are considered some of the best on the entire East Coast for surfing. The cape is also excellent for surf, sound, and pier fishing.

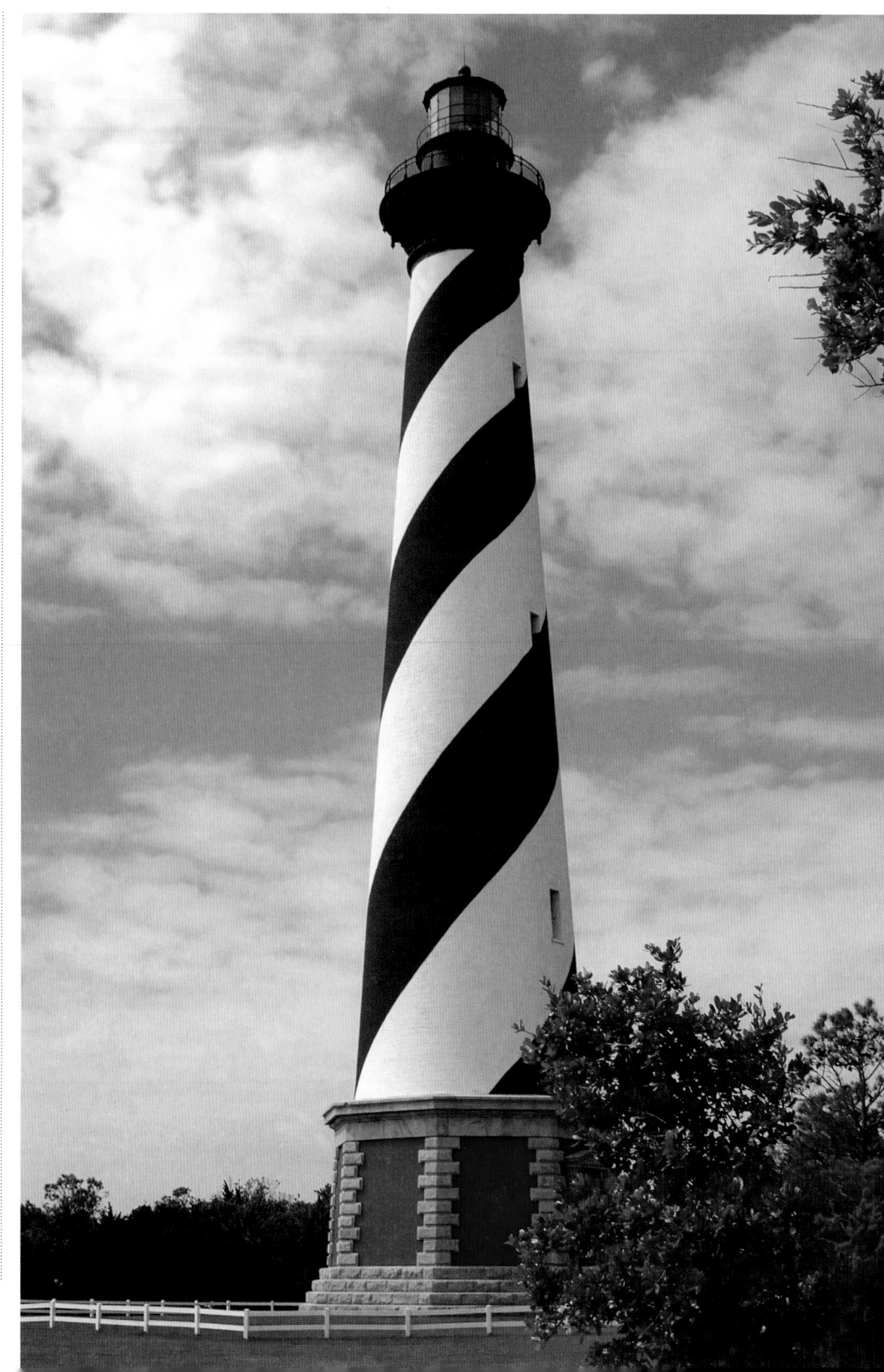

*The 208-foot-tall Cape Hatteras Lighthouse is the tallest in the United States. Visitors may climb the 268 steps to its top for a commanding view of the shoreline.*

# Roanoke Island

1587, Sir Walter Raleigh of England sent expedition to the New World to Roanoke and, a 27-acre isle in Croatan Sound off at is now the North Carolina coast. About 5 settlers, mostly families, sailed across the lantic Ocean and established a village there. t they arrived too late in the year to plant ps, and their leader, John White, returned England for supplies.

Because of tensions between England and ain, White couldn't return to Roanoke nd until 1590. When he arrived, the village

(Above) *Roanoke Island is a fishing community and home to shopkeepers and artists.*

low) Elizabeth II, *docked at Manteo rbor, is a composite design modeled after original* Elizabeth, *one of the ships that led to the New World in 1585.*

was deserted. Roanoke became known as the "Lost Colony." The mystery remains unsolved to this day.

Modern Roanoke Island is home to a historic park that tells this story and others through living-history demonstrations, a replica of a 16th-century sailing ship, and an interactive museum. A walk along the boardwalks and nature trails reveals native wildflowers and protected maritime forest. There's also an outdoor pavilion that hosts a performing arts series.

# Blue Ridge Parkway

The Blue Ridge Parkway glides along the ridgetops of the southern Appalachian mountainside. The peaks are more than 6,000 feet above sea level, offering remarkable views of the verdant fields and country towns far below.

Construction crews began building the parkway in the 1930s to link Shenandoah National Park in Virginia to the Great Smoky Mountains National Park in North Carolina and Tennessee. Construction was paused during World War II.

By 1968, all that remained unfinished was a rugged stretch around North Carolina's Grandfather Mountain. But connecting the dots took nearly 20 more years and required building the Linn Cove Viaduct, a 1,200-foot suspended section of roadway. Considered an engineeri marvel, it remains one of the most success unions of road and landscape on the contine

The Blue Ridge Parkway was officia dedicated in 1987, a full 52 years after co struction began. It now offers a portal in the history, culture, and natural wonder southern Appalachia.

*"America's Favorite Drive" winds 469 miles from Shenandoah National Park to Great Smoky Mountains National Park.*

# Myrtle Beach

outh Carolina's Grand Strand, Myrtle Beach, as been a favorite sun-and-sand destination or more than a century. The beach is named or the numerous wax myrtle trees growing

*Sand and surf are prime attractions at Myrtle Beach. Apache Pier,* (left), *is the longest pier on the East Coast.*

long the shore. The Seaside Inn, which pened in 1901, became the first of many ncreasingly sophisticated resorts that have nade this one of the top tourist areas on the ast Coast.

Myrtle Beach shares its name with the adja-ent city. The beach itself bustles with all sorts f activity. Parasailers fly above the ocean, surf-rs hang ten on the tide, and divers explore he depths below. Pushcarts stocked with rozen lemonade and shops overflowing with -shirts and bright beachwear are always close t hand, as are plenty of children. Myrtle Beach s known for its great family atmosphere, hanks to a lively boardwalk and numerous vaterfront tourist attractions, including an musement park.

# Hilton Head Island

Hilton Head Island is one of the premier beach getaway destinations in the Southeast. The foot-shape barrier island off the coast of South Carolina is only 42 square miles. But the semitropical paradise of white-sand beaches; salt marshes; lagoons; and lush forests of mossy oaks, palmettos, magnolia, and pine is irresistible.

*The Harbour Town Yacht Basin is a favorite attraction on Hilton Head Island.*

The island's pristine natural environment is balanced with the graceful aesthetics of some of the finest resorts and golf courses. The combination is a magnet for visitors: Though the year-round population is just 31,000 people, Hilton Head Island sees more than 2.5 million tourists each year. They come not only for the lush scenery, posh resorts, and great golf, but also for many deep breaths of fresh coastal air, abundant peace and quiet, and those beautiful sunsets that play out over the mainland on the western horizon.

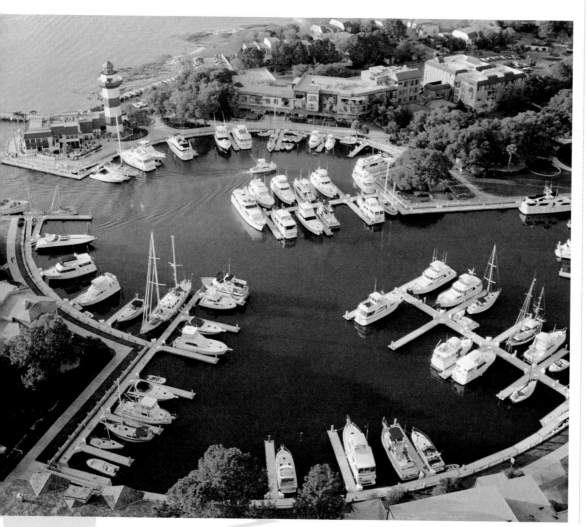

*Hilton Head Island is known for its world-class golf courses, some of which are ranked among the top 100 in the nation.*

# Fort Sumter National Monument

t 4:30 A.M. on April 12, 1861, a 10-inch mortar tore through the air at Fort Sumter, located off the South Carolina coast near Charleston. The fort—then controlled by Union troops—was besieged when the Confederate Army launched a naval offensive. The event was the fuse that lit the Civil War.

South Carolina delegates had voted to secede from the United States the previous year in protest of the election of President Abraham Lincoln. Tensions had been running high leading up to the siege of Fort Sumter, and its bombardment marked the official beginning of the Civil War.

After 34 hours of bombardment, the Union soldiers defending Fort Sumter surrendered to the Confederacy on April 13, 1861, and the fort was controlled by the South until the end of the war in 1865. Reconstruction of Fort Sumter began in the 1870s.

Today, the perfectly preserved fort is a national monument and a symbol of Southern pride. Visitors can see the original cannons and brickwork at the fort. The inside of the battery has been converted to a Civil War museum. And from the upper level of the fort, take in the panoramic view of Charleston and its harbor.

*rt Sumter was restored after being severely damaged during the Civil War. It became a U.S. National Monument in 1948.*

# Martin Luther King, Jr., National Historic Site

Martin Luther King, Jr., was born in a modest, comfortable, Queen Anne–style home in the heart of Atlanta's "Sweet Auburn" district (the city's prosperous African-American downtown in segregated days). Visitors to the Martin Luther King, Jr., National Historic Site in Atlanta, Georgia, are reminded that the great civil rights leader could have lived a cozy, middle-class life as a respected man—and never risked his life for his beliefs. Instead, King spent the 11 years from 1957 to 1968 traveling over six million miles and speaking more than 2,500 times in support of civil rights for all Americans. He took part in protests, most notably the peaceful march on Washington, D.C., where he delivered his moving "I Have a Dream" speech.

The historic site evokes the memory of King's dreams. The visitor center has a helpful video and exhibits aimed at young visitors. The King Center, established by King's widow Coretta Scott King, in 1968, features exhibits on King, Coretta Scott King, and Mahatma Gandhi. The center is the site of King and his wife's graves. He is entombed beside an eternal flame, but King's real eternal fire lives on in those who hear his message.

*The King Center is a memorial to and final resting place of Martin Luther King, Jr.*

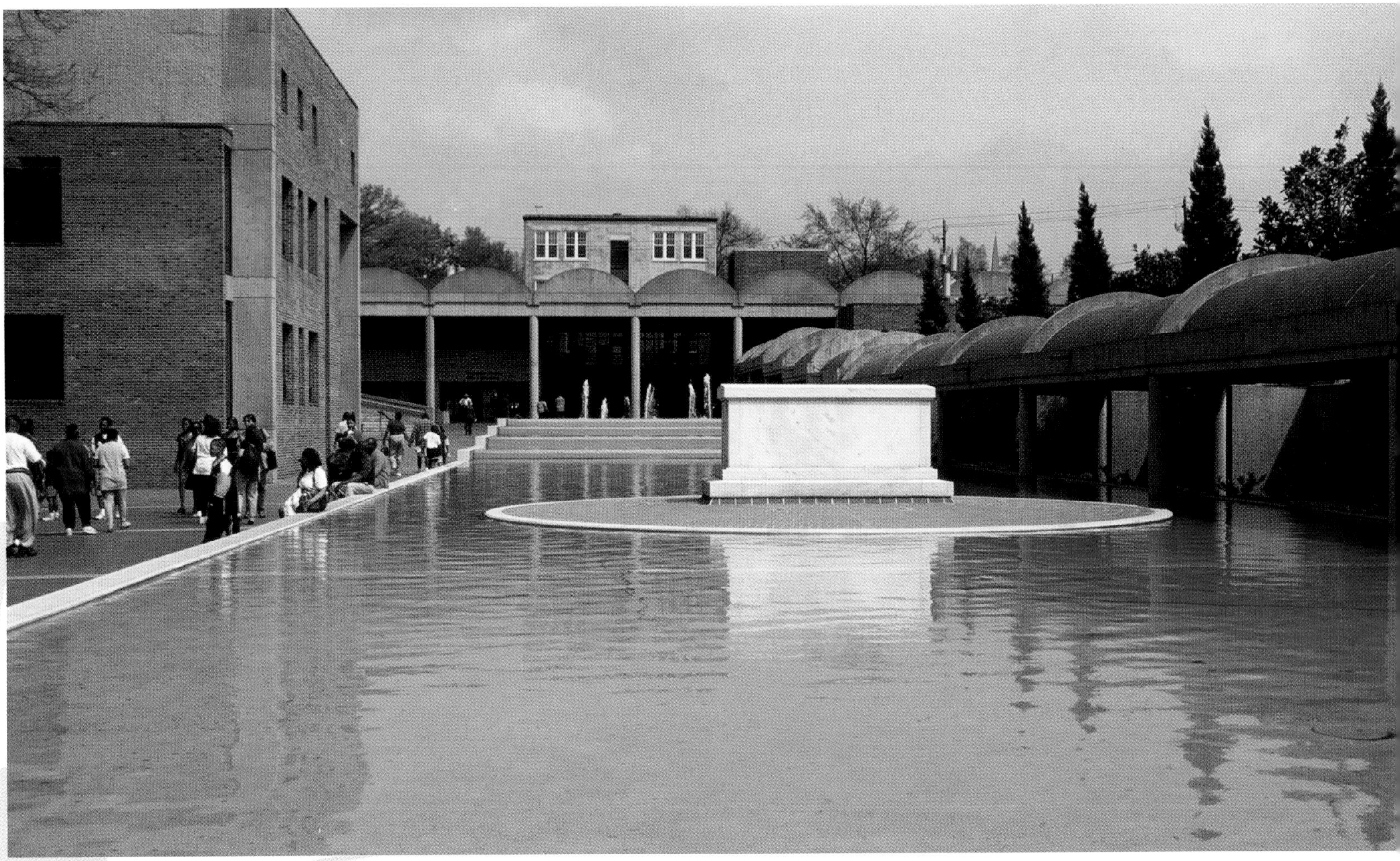

# Cumberland Island National Seashore

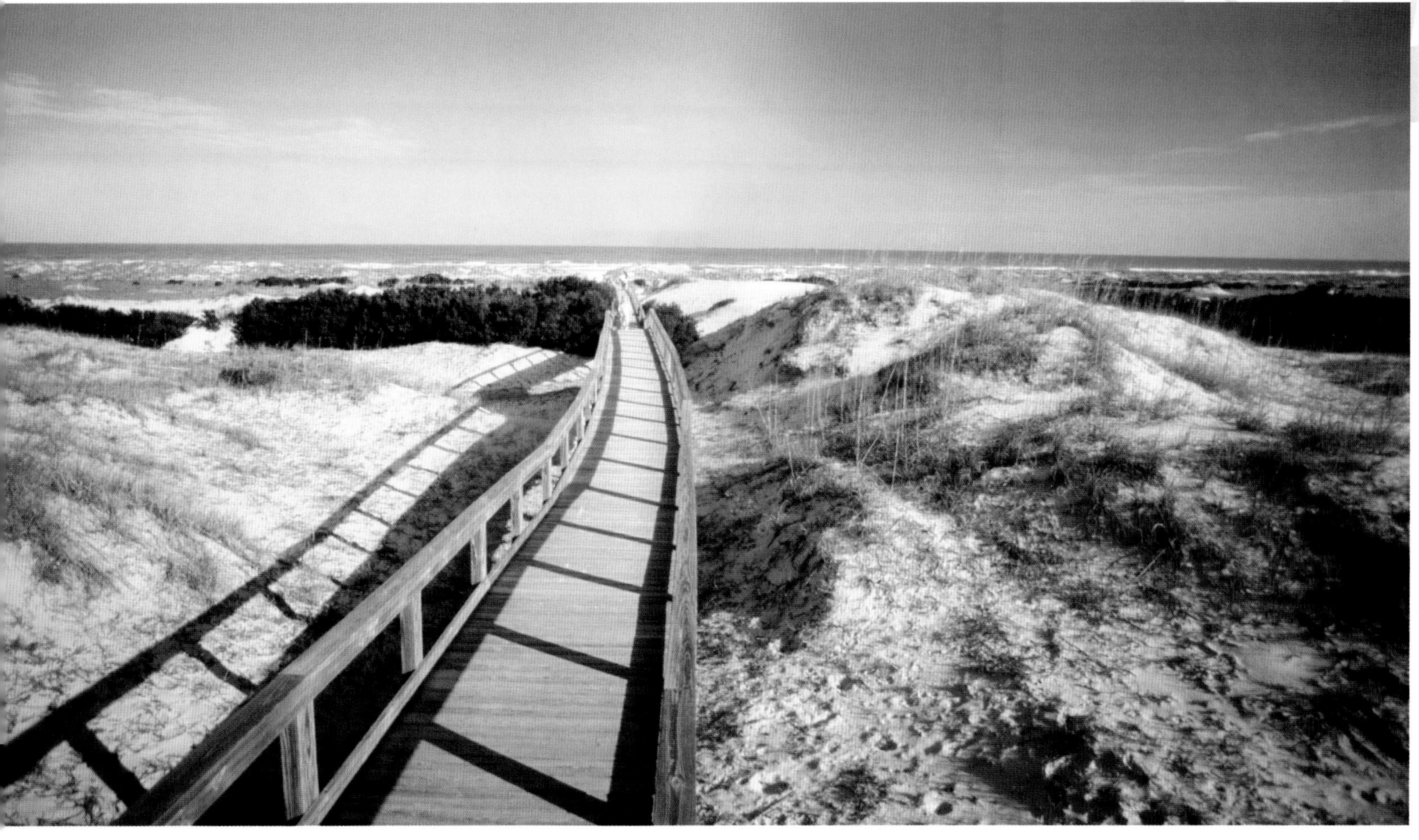

*Cumberland Island is covered by white-sand beaches, dunes, and saltwater marshes.*

ou may have to make an effort to visit beau-ful, mysterious Cumberland Island National eashore. This is due to a policy that permits maximum of 300 visitors per day and has ıly one developed campsite, Sea Camp (res-vations can be made up to six months in lvance). But a trip to the remote island is orth the hurdles.

The lucky few who make it have Cumber-nd Island seemingly to themselves. The island three miles wide ringed by a beach almost 18 miles long. It's covered by acres of marsh, tidal creeks, sand dunes, blinding white sand, and historic ruins and museums that compel admiration and amazement. And this doesn't even take into account the island wildlife. Georgia's southernmost barrier island is a sanctuary for gigantic loggerhead sea turtles. Herds of wild horses roam here, too. It's said they were left behind by Spanish explorers in the 16th century. Cumberland Island's maritime forest of oaks and palmettos, draped with Spanish moss, envelop the island's trails. Summer tanagers, yellow-throated warblers, and pileated woodpeckers as well as armadillos and bull alligators thrive here.

Cumberland Island is dotted with picturesque, haunting ruins. To help make sense of them, the Ice House Museum covers island history dating back to its first inhabitants.

# Chippewa Square, Savannah

Savannah, Georgia, is America's first planned city. General James Edward Oglethorpe (who had previously founded the colony of Georgia) founded Savannah in 1733. He designed his new capital as a series of neighborhoods centered around 24 squares. His layout remains intact today: Twenty-one squares still exist in Savannah. Each has a distinctive architecture, history, and folklore.

Johnson Square, laid out in 1733, was the first Savannah square. Oglethorpe Square, which was called "Upper New Square," was laid out in 1742 by General Oglethorpe. And Orleans Square was built in 1815 in memory of the heroes of the War of 1812.

Chippewa Square is at the center of the downtown historic district between Hull Street and Perry Street. At the square's heart, a statue of Oglethorpe commemorates the founding of Georgia. Excerpts from the original Georgia charter are inscribed on the pedestal, designed by Henry Bacon.

Built in 1815, the square gets its name from the Battle of Chippewa in the War of 1812. By the 1820s, Chippewa Square became Savannah's nightlife center, in part because the Savannah Theatre is just one block north. The showbiz tradition continues to this day: The square served as the backdrop for the famed park-bench scene in *Forrest Gump*.

*A statue of General James Edward Oglethorpe stands at the center of Chippewa Square in Savannah, Georgia.*

# Tybee Island

ighteen miles east of Savannah, Georgia, ybee Island is an exclusive beach getaway vith plenty of opportunities to relax and ightsee. This barrier island's three-mile beach backed by mesmerizing sand dunes. Tybee neans "salt" to some Native Americans, but isitors to the island enjoy far more than just he ocean.

Tybee is a laid-back resort town where you an choose to stay at luxury hotels, deluxe ondominiums, quaint cottages, or bed-and-reakfasts. More than 30 restaurants on the sland serve up fabulous food: Some have lishes with a Caribbean kick, and some fea-ure chef specialties of seafood dishes, such as rab, oysters, shrimp, or fish.

Enjoy boat cruises, fishing trips, or kayak-ng. Venture into the salt marshes to go bird-vatching. Or check out local marine life on lisplay at the Tybee Island Marine Science Center—exhibits feature species from the narsh, shoreline, and reef. There are also bik-ng and hiking trails across the island.

If you have a passion for history, visit Tybee's historic sites. Fort Screven was a for-mer coastal artillery fort, and Fort Pulaski played a vital part in the Civil War. And at 154 feet, the Tybee Island Lighthouse is the oldest and tallest lighthouse in Georgia.

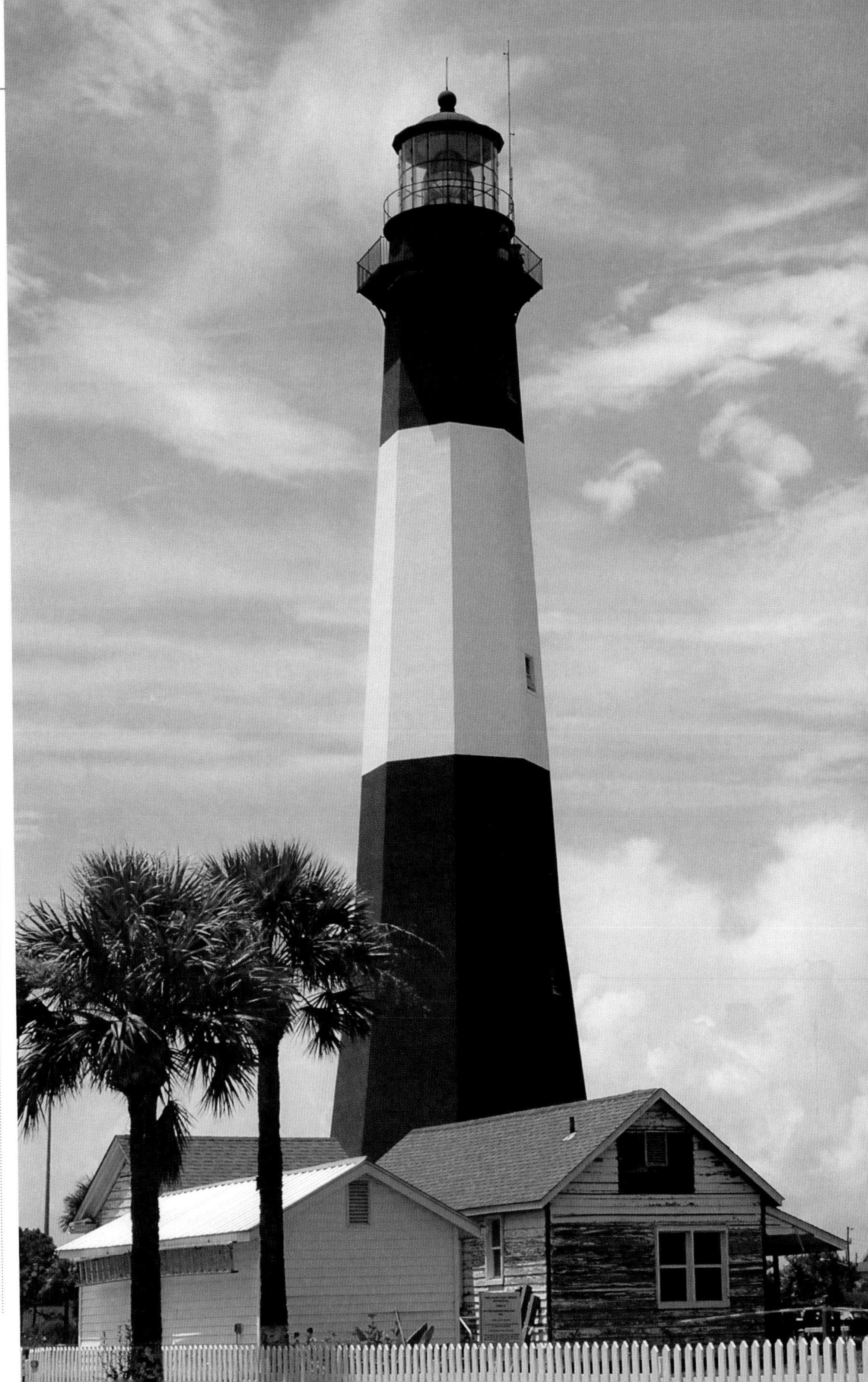

*Since 1736, the Tybee Island Lighthouse has guided mariners. Over the years, it has been rebuilt and repainted with various striped patterns.*

# Stone Mountain

*The massive Confederate Memorial Carving honors Confederate Civil War heroes Jefferson Davis, Robert E. Lee, and "Stonewall" Jackson.*

Stone Mountain, Georgia, is the world's largest exposed piece of granite—7.5 billion cubic feet of rock. This immense, bulging monolith is just a half-hour drive from Atlanta.

But it's not just the size of the mountain that drives people to visit. Stone Mountain's outstanding feature is the Confederate Memorial Carving. Three southern heroes from the Civil War have been carved into the rock: Confederate President Jefferson Davis, General Robert E. Lee, and General Thomas J. "Stonewall" Jackson. The relief is massive, spanning 90 by 190 feet, and is surrounded by a carved surface that covers three acres. While planning for the sculpture began in 1915, it was not completed until 1972.

Stone Mountain can be visited by taking a cable-car ride up the north face. Intrepid visitors can hike along various trails to get closer to the amazing mountain. A visit to the top reveals rock pools and views of a downtown Atlanta that seems close enough to touch.

Located just outside the park's west gate Historic Stone Mountain Village. The villag was established in 1839 and offers more tha 50 specialty shops and restaurants. Visito can browse through quaint antique stores well as shop for art and jewelry created b local artisans.

# Jekyll Island

Jekyll Island is one of Georgia's Golden Isles. It is Georgia's smallest barrier island and lies off the coast midway between Savannah, Georgia, and Jacksonville, Florida. But this small island has a fascinating history and an assortment of relaxing activities for modern-day visitors.

In 1886, a group of famous entrepreneurs including William Rockefeller, Joseph Pulitzer, and J. P. Morgan founded the Jekyll Island Club. The island became a winter retreat for some of America's most elite families. In addition to soaking up some sun during the winter months, the men also met for discussions and dinners. "Secret" meetings at the club are rumored to have led to the creation of the Federal Reserve System and helped William McKinley be reelected to his second term as president. But the blows of the Great Depression and World War II brought about an end to the club. In 1947, the state of Georgia bought the island and turned it into a state park.

*The Jekyll Island Club Hotel is both a historic landmark and elegant resort on Jekyll Island.*

Today tourists can visit the many mansions built by club members (they referred to the homes as merely "cottages"). You can feel like a billionaire for a day at least when you take a carriage ride through the historic district.

The island also has three 18-hole golf courses. For outdoors types, there are ten miles of pristine beach waiting to be explored. Year-round guided nature walks explain Georgia's coastal life. The saltwater marsh, freshwater rivers, and ocean are all great for fishing. And if you feel adventurous, try sailing, sea kayaking, or canoeing.

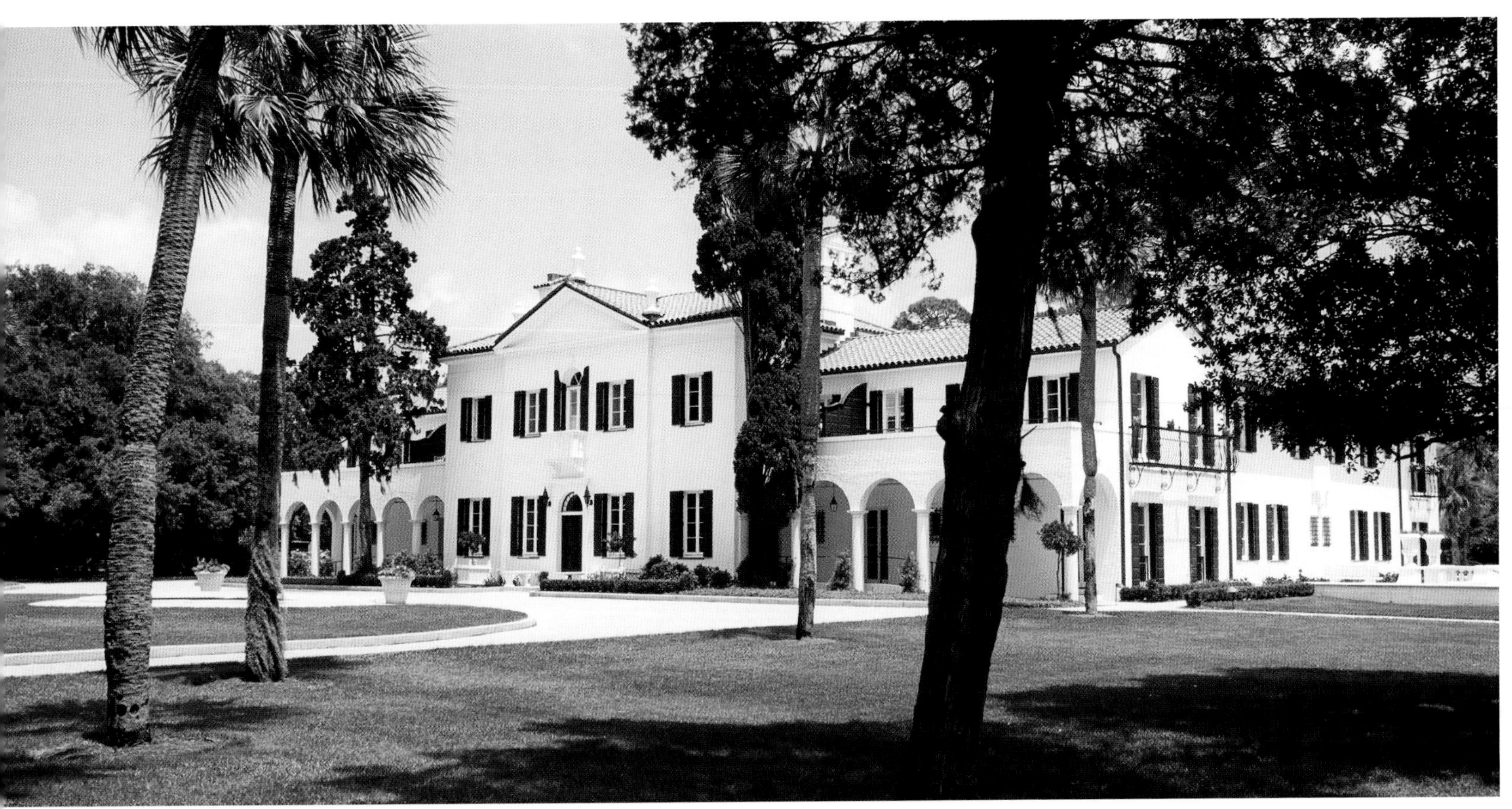

# Amicalola Falls

A hiker's paradise unfolds at Amicalola Falls State Park in northern Georgia. Twelve miles of trails weave through the picturesque Appalachian Mountains. Daring adventurers can brave the eight-mile approach from the park to Springer Mountain. This path is an access point for the 2,150-mile Appalachian Trail that winds all the way up to Maine. It passes through the Amicalola Watershed to Amicalola Falls.

At 729 feet, this is the tallest waterfall east of the Mississippi River. Its name means "Tumbling Waters" in Cherokee. Amicalola Falls is one of Georgia's Seven Natural Wonders (the others being Okefenokee Swamp, Stone Mountain, Providence Canyon, Tallulah Gorge, Warm Springs, and Radium Springs).

Visitors can stay at the modern lodge near the falls, which has 57 rooms. The visitor center has scales where hikers can weigh their packs before departing. Travelers can also stay at the remote Len Foote Hike Inn, accessible by a five-mile hike along the Hike Inn Trail. The secluded inn's 20 rooms are arranged around a two-story lobby. The rustic inn provides many gorgeous panoramas of oak and hickory forests with mountain laurel and rhododendron. It also is an access point for winding mountainside trails where you can catch a glimpse of warblers, vireos, white-tailed deer, rabbits, raccoons, and bears.

*Amicalola Falls, seen here from the crossover bridge, is the tallest cascading waterfall east of the Mississippi River.*

# World of Coca-Cola

*The World of Coca-Cola in Atlanta, Georgia, houses the world's largest collection of Coca-Cola memorabilia.*

oca-Cola was invented in Atlanta in 1886, nd it quickly became a favorite beverage cross the world. The Coca-Cola Company's owcase museum, the World of Coca-Cola in tlanta, Georgia, is a tribute to the brand. As ne scholar wrote, "If Coca-Cola is a super-ar, then the World of Coca-Cola is Coke's raceland: the institutionalization of that iperstardom. Or, to use another metaphor, it the Vatican of Coca-Cola." So if you've ever njoyed a cold Coke on a hot day—whether in Cleveland or Cairo, Atlanta or Athens, Virginia City or the Vatican—the World of Coca-Cola might be just the tonic for you. If you are one of countless hard-core Coke collectors, the place is a must-see.

The three-story museum traces Coke from its early days, when it was rumored to be a mix of kola nuts and cocaine, to the drink's triumph as a beverage of global reach. The exhibition begins with "Creating a Classic," a collection of memorabilia from 1886 to 1926 with interactive video stations. The second gallery, "The Pause That Refreshes," comprises a replica 1930s soda fountain with a real "soda jerk." The museum goes on from there until visitors reach the real objective for many of them: Club Coca-Cola, where they may sample all the soft drinks they wish.

# Everglades National Park

It's a bright day, and you're walking on a boardwalk a few feet above water. The heavy woods thin out into sawgrass, and the water below deepens and clears. You hear a cuckoo and see an anhinga bird with dark, furry-looking feathers and a hooked bill. A cormorant plunges into the water and eats a fish, then settles on the rail just ahead of you. You look down into the water and see a large, primitive-looking garfish and what appears to be a bass. An alligator surfaces; first its broad back appears, then its head and tail. In the distance, past a shimmering purple gallinule bird, a coral snake uncoils around a branch. The cormorant flaps its wings and flies away.

These exotic species and more inhabit Everglades National Park at the southern tip of Florida. Scarcely more than a 90-minute drive from Miami, the park is home to gorgeous fish, turtles, otters, lizards, and birds including great blue herons, ibis, wood stor and red-cockaded woodpeckers. There a plenty of alligators and crocodiles lurking the freshwater and saltwater swamps. And you are *very* lucky, you might even spot a ra Florida panther.

*The Everglades are a diverse ecosystem of swamps and marshes where freshwater and saltwater meet. This unique environment is home to animals including the American alligator* (inset).

*The cypress groves in Everglades National Park are home to many species of waterfowl. More than 350 species of birds have been sighted in the park.*

Just four miles from the park entrance near Homestead, the Anhinga Trail at the Royal Palm Visitor Center is one of the world's most amazing boardwalks. The walkway is built above Taylor Slough, one of the park's many ecosystems. The freshwater slough is something like a stream in the middle of a marsh, where the water moves about 100 feet per day. Other Everglades trails take you through freshwater marl prairie, pinelands, hardwood hammocks, cypress groves, mangrove forests, marine estuaries, and more. Near the Anhinga Trail, the Gumbo-Limbo Trail (which is a quarter-mile long and wheelchair accessible) takes you through a dense hammock of royal palms and gumbo-limbo trees.

The Everglades is a limestone shelf spilling toward the ocean. In the northwestern Everglades and Big Cypress National Preserve, freshwater from as far away as Orlando flows over the Tamiami Formation (limestone formed eons ago by the sand, silt, and calcium of an ancient sea) and mixes with saltwater as it flows into the ocean. The result is a splendid but fragile environment.

Everglades National Park, which covers 1.5 million acres and is the third-largest national park in the continental United States, has five entrances. Most adventurers start at the Ernest F. Coe Visitor Center by the main entrance on the eastern edge of the park. The Royal Palm Center is about four miles west. The Flamingo Visitor Center, 38 miles southwest from the main entrance, takes travelers deep into the park for hiking and canoeing; some areas are bike- and wheelchair-accessible, too. The territory near the center of the park is the preferred place for croc-watching, and Eco Pond, one mile past the Flamingo Visitor Center, is prime gator habitat. (The Everglades is the only place on Earth naturally occupied by both crocodiles and alligators.) In the park's northwest corner, The Gulf Coast Visitor Center lies across the water from the 10,000 Islands, a haven for fishing in the scenic backwaters. And the Shark Valley Visitor Center, on the Tamiami Trail (Highway 41) on the park's northern border, is an outpost on Florida's "River of Grass."

Novelist Marjory Stoneman Douglas founded Friends of the Everglades in 1969. "There are no other Everglades in the world," she wrote. "They are, they have always been, one of the unique regions of the earth; remote, never wholly known. Nothing anywhere else is like them"—not that visitors to this precious preserve need to be reminded.

# Ringling Estate, Sarasota Bay

In its time, the Ringling Bros. and Barnum & Bailey Circus was the greatest show on earth. It became the world's most successful and enduring circus, formed in 1919 when the Ringling Bros. (led by John Ringling) and Barnum & Bailey circuses merged.

John Ringling had a passion for art, collecting works while touring Europe. In 1924, he and his wife, Mable, began building their Italian Renaissance-style mansion on Sarasota Bay, Florida. The building was called Cà d'Zan, meaning "House of John" in Venetian dialect. The mansion is a work of art. The building is capped by a 60-foot tower that was illuminated when the Ringlings were home. Its living room (called the Court) is two-and-a-half stories high. An impressive 8,000-square-foot marble terrace offers awe-inspiring views of Sarasota Bay.

In 1927, the Ringlings began building the John and Mable Ringling Museum of Art (now also known as the State Art Museum of Florida). The Ringlings wanted to share their love of and collection of art with the people of Florida. Their art treasures include more than 10,000 paintings, sculptures, drawings, prints, photographs, and decorative arts. The museum holds the largest private collection of paintings and drawings by Peter Paul Rubens as well as masterworks by Lucas Cranach the Elder, Nicolas Poussin, Frans Hals, and Anthony Van Dyck. All in all, there are 21 galleries of European paintings (including more then 700 Old Masters), antiques, Asian art, American paintings, and contemporary art.

The Circus Museum was added to the estate in 1948. Visitors can relive the magic of the circus through exhibits of costumes, wagons, performance equipment, and other memorabilia that convey its history. Among the attractions is a scale model of the Ringling Bros. and Barnum & Bailey Circus as it was from 1919 to 1938.

*The elegant Cà d'Zan is 200 feet long, with 32 rooms and 15 baths.*

# Miami's South Beach

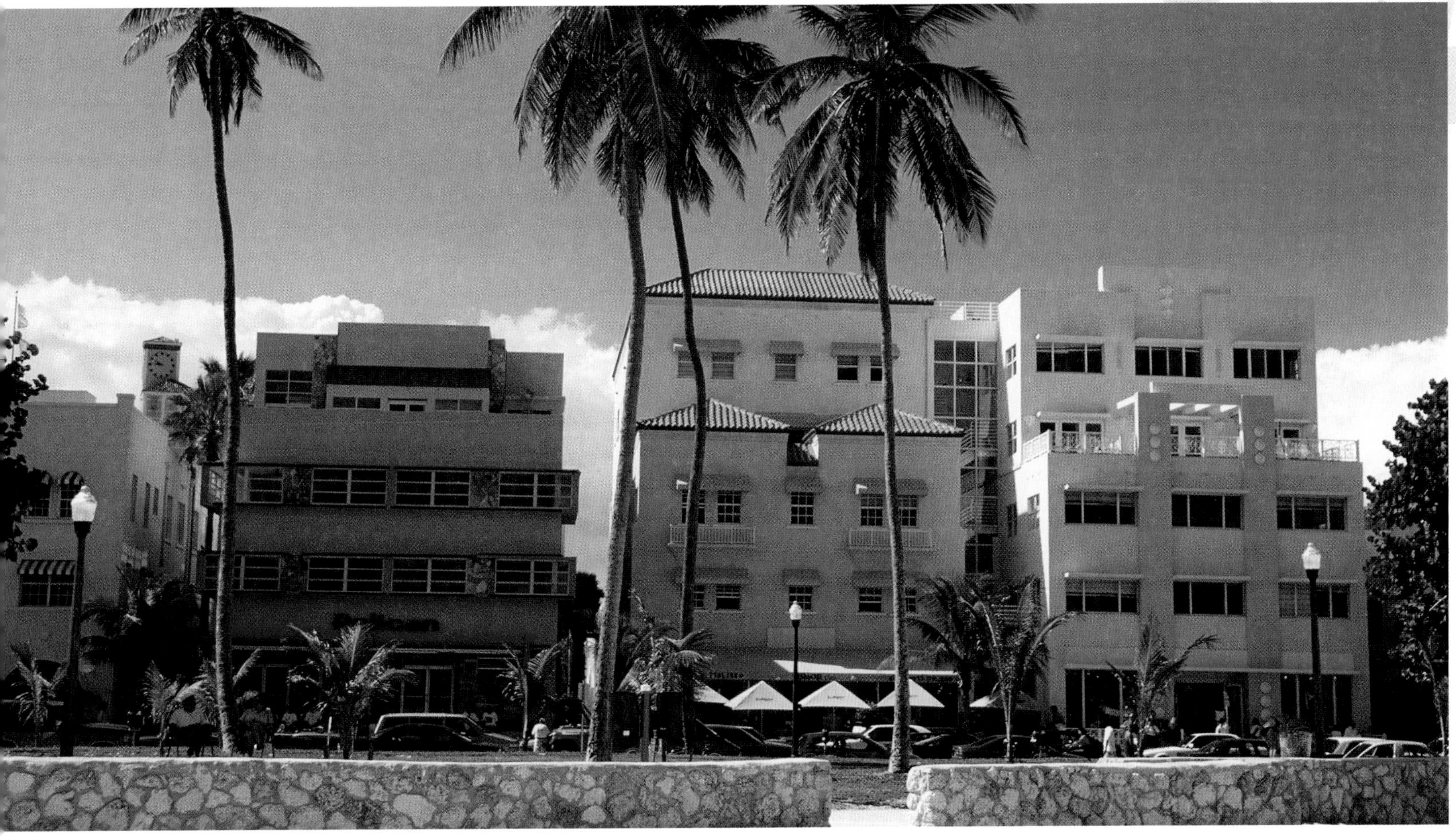

*Buildings in the Art Deco District of South Beach have a distinct whimsical flare.*

South Beach, a section of Miami Beach, is an arts, entertainment, and recreation center of global scope. South Beach is the southernmost 23 blocks of Miami Beach. This district has exquisite restaurants, hip nightclubs, and luxurious oceanfront hotels. Topless sunbathing is common on some beaches.

It is also home to the historic Art Deco District. Most of the hotels and apartment buildings here were built in the 1930s and have the rounded corners and geometric highlights of Art Deco architecture.

The district has spawned smaller, hipper neighborhoods. One such is SoFi, short for South of Fifth Street, a laid-back neighborhood with sizzling spots such as Opium Garden and Nikki Beach. SoFi is also home to the Bass Museum of Art which houses a collection ranging from Botticelli and Rubens to Miami Beach architectural photographs.

South Beach was recognized when its first bar, Mac's Club Deuce, opened in 1906. Today, some diehards consider Club Deuce the last real bar in South Beach. It's now surrounded by a kaleidoscope of glitzy, trendy nightclubs that regularly change names or owners in search of the latest craze. All of this razzle-dazzle begs the question: Has South Beach replaced Los Angeles and the Big Apple as America's hottest nightspot? You decide.

# Cape Canaveral

Cape Canaveral is a barrier island off the east coast of Florida that's spacious enough to include the 58,000-acre Canaveral National Seashore, John F. Kennedy Space Center, and Cape Canaveral Air Force Station. Its 220 square miles are covered by marshes and many miles of shimmering beach.

Visitors are welcome at the Kennedy Space Center, whose tours give an in-depth behind-the-scenes look at NASA, including visits to launch pads and rockets. Outer space may be the island's main attraction, but Cape Canaveral proves that Earth has its share of beauty and mystery, too. The space center borders the Merritt Island National Wildlife Refuge. There, manatees graze underwater in the shadow of a launch pad, and endangered sea turtles swim to shore to lay their eggs in the silence of the night.

The cape is home to many exotic wildlife species. Canaveral National Seashore records indicate there are 1,045 plant species and 310 bird species in the park, including endangered creatures such as the peregrine falcon, the West Indian manatee, the southern bald eagle, and the eastern indigo snake. The park's 24 miles of undeveloped beach comprise the longest stretch on the east coast of Florida.

*The Rocket Garden at the John F. Kennedy Space Center gives visitors an up-close look at the rockets and capsules that first launched NASA astronauts into space.*

# Key West

Key West, Florida, has long been famous as one of America's top destinations for fun-and-sun vacations. Key West has retained its charm, remoteness, intriguing history, natural beauty, and idyllic weather (once the hurricane season subsides) since the 1920s. About the same number of people live there now as then. Its small-town feeling exudes all the characteristics necessary to lure visitors back every year.

Located at the southernmost tip of the Florida Keys, Key West's average temperature is a temperate 77.8 degrees Fahrenheit. Storms aside, Key West has few highs or lows—just steady sunshine. A daily treat, Key West's Mallory Square hosts the Sunset Celebration each evening, with food vendors, fire-eaters, tightrope walkers, and arts and crafts exhibits.

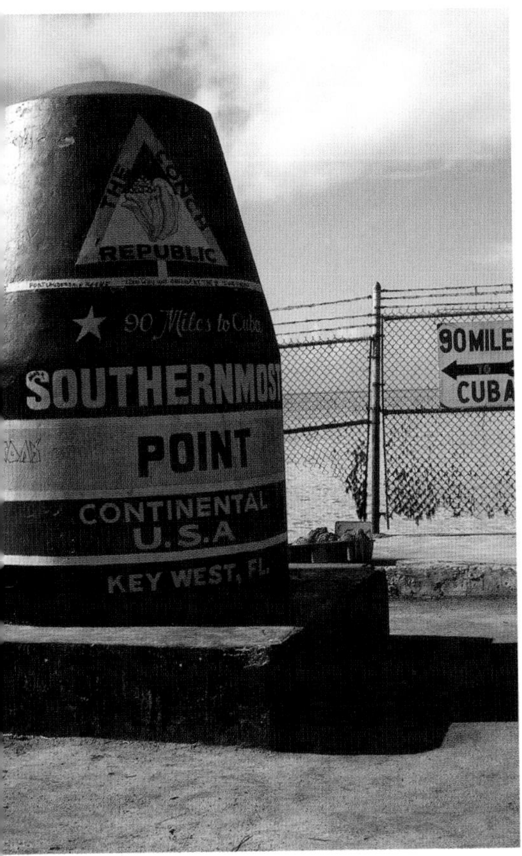


*Tropical Key West is home to the southernmost point in the continental United States.*

Key West, which has also been called "Margaritaville" or the "Conch Republic," didn't always have a reputation for laid-back sun and fun. The name "Key West" is in fact a corruption of *Cayo Hueso,* meaning "Island of Bones." This haunting name was bestowed by early Spanish explorers impressed by the human remains left on the beach.

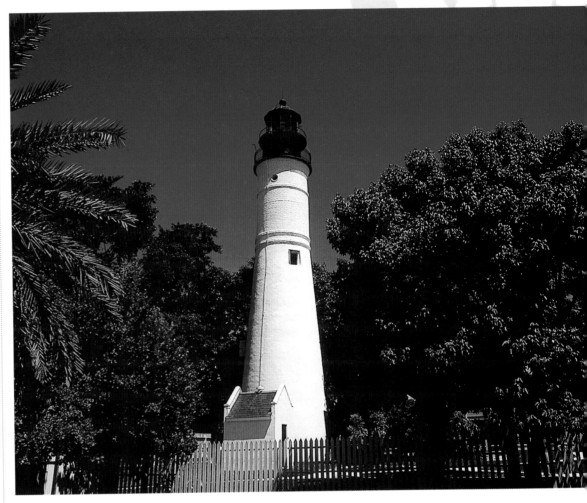

*The Key West Lighthouse, built in 1847, offers spectacular views.*

Key West has become known for its most famous visitors, including artists Winslow Homer and John James Audubon, actor Cary Grant, President Harry Truman, and novelist Ernest Hemingway. Hemingway wrote many of his best works while on the island, and today Hemingway House is Key West's top tourist attraction.

# Castillo de San Marcos, St. Augustine

Castillo de San Marcos and its 25 acres of old parade grounds are a St. Augustine must-see. The fortress, built by Spaniards between 1672 and 1695, is a marvel of a relic constructed to defend the conquistadores' treasure routes against British attacks from the north. The fort is star-shape to provide a maximum view of, but minimum exposure to, an approaching enemy. It includes a 40-foot moat and double drawbridge. The walls are made from coquina, a limestone formed from compacted shells and coral, which is quite durable and could shrug off cannon fire. The fort's upper level, with its watchtowers and cannon, gives visitors a long view out to sea.

St. Augustine's Old City and Castillo de San Marcos reflect Florida's successive historic developments like tree rings. In 1513, after sailing with Columbus on his second voyag to the New World, Juan Ponce de León (he o the Fountain of Youth) was the first explore to set foot in Florida. He landed just south o St. Augustine.

King Philip II of Spain established St Augustine in 1565 as the sword and shiel for the American outpost of his great empire He commissioned Admiral Pedro Menénde

*Castillo de San Marcos has served a number of nations in its history, but it was never taken by military force—control was passed by treaty.*

*Watchtowers on the fort's bastions gave its occupiers time to prepare for incoming attacks.*

de Avilés to remove the French from Florida. Avilés defeated a French fleet of five ships in Matanzas Bay and founded St. Augustine. The settlement joined the Spanish Empire (said to be the *first* empire upon which the sun never set), which stretched from Manila to Mexico City and back to Madrid.

Yet, the sun did set on the Spanish Empire, and the king's fort in St. Augustine passed to the British, then back to Spain. Later it belonged to the United States, then the Confederate States, then the United States again. All this back-and-forth resulted in an unclassifiable Old City that is southern with Spanish and Moroccan accents, definite Britishisms, reminders of 18th- and 19th-century America, and echoes of the ages before that.

In 1738, Fort Mose, just north of the city, became the first settlement created for free African-Americans. This makes St. Augustine the oldest continuously occupied European and African-American settlement in the United States (excluding Puerto Rico). In that spirit, visit St. Augustine's Lincolnville Historic District. Founded in 1866 by freed slaves, and a bastion of the Civil Rights Movement of the 1950s and 1960s, the district is now noted for its Victorian architecture and Gothic churches. Its Yallaha Plantation House, built in 1800, is one of the oldest in Florida. (The oldest home of all is the Old City's Gonzalez–Alvarez House, which was built shortly after the British siege in 1702.)

# Little Havana

The heart of Cuban life in Florida is the vibrant commercial strip in Little Havana called Calle Ocho, or Eighth Street. This bustling neighborhood is southwest of downtown Miami between 12th and 17th avenues.

Calle Ocho is the epicenter of an ethnic explosion that includes immigrant communities from around the world. One of the many highlights is the authentic Cuban cuisine—restaurants serve up seafood paella, succulent marinated pork, and hearty beans and rice. Visitors can also sample the cuisines of Peru, Nicaragua, the Dominican Republic, and myriad other Latin lands. Tourists and locals alike dote on the neighborhood's trademar hand-rolled cigars, merengue and salsa musi and chess and dominoes games.

Then there are the celebrations! The las Friday of each month is known as *Viernes Cu turales,* or Cultural Friday. This Latin stree party showcases Cuban music, dancing, stree performers, food, and local artists. In March the Calle Ocho Festival is one of the world' largest free festivals, drawing more than on million people.

*Residents of Little Havana gather in Maximo Gomez Park to challenge each other to games of dominoe*

*Each year more than one million people gather for the Calle Ocho Festival, which has been called the "world's largest block party."*

# Vulcan Statue

The 56-foot statue of Vulcan in Birmingham, Alabama, is the largest cast-iron statue in the world. The creation of the glorious sculpture is tied closely to the roots of the city.

Birmingham began as a mining town for coal, limestone, and iron ore, which were forged to make steel. By the 20th century, it was a formidable industrial power, and the city's business leaders sought to promote Birmingham. Their audacious answer was to have Italian sculptor Giuseppe Moretti create a cast-iron sculpture of Vulcan, the Roman god of fire, volcanoes, and the forge. The sculpture was unveiled at the 1904 St. Louis World's Fair, where it was a hit and won the mining and metallurgy exhibition grand prize.

Unfortunately when the statue was moved back to Birmingham, its arms were reassembled improperly. The statue was neglected and became a three-dimensional billboard, cradling giant-size Heinz pickle jars and even sporting painted-on jeans. In 1939, Vulcan was finally moved to his proper place on Birmingham's Red Mountain. Restoration of the statue was completed in 2004, and Vulcan Park reopened for the statue's centennial. Today the statue and its panoramic view come closest to fulfilling Moretti's original vision of a brawny, ambitious Birmingham.

*The cast-iron Vulcan Statue in Birmingham has been restored to symbolize the town's steel history.*

# Natchez Trace

*Natchez Trace, which runs from Mississippi to Tennessee, began as a series of tribal trading routes worn into the earth.*

Natchez Trace originated thousands of years ago. Big animals such as deer and bison were the first to tramp along what became the Old Natchez Trace. Then the Choctaw and Chickasaw connected the paths, and the trail became the region's premiere trade route. Arriving Europeans grasped its potential, and by the late 1700s the Natchez Trace bustled with boaters. They would sell their cargo and flatboats or keelboats for lumber in Natchez or New Orleans and then travel back north to Nashville and beyond. The boaters carried their money in gold and silver coins, and the Natchez Trace became legendary for its cut-throat gangs. In 1801, the United States signed a treaty with the Choctaw allowing roads to be built along the route.

Today, Natchez Trace has many meanings. It is the 444-mile Natchez Trace Parkway, which follows the road from Natchez, Mississippi, to just outside Nashville, Tennessee. The parkway's one visitor center is located near Tupelo, Mississippi, birthplace of Elvis Presley. Four sections of trails along the parkway make up the Natchez Trace National Scenic Trail. Crimson clover, butterweed, Japanese honeysuckle, ground ivy, and many other species of wildflowers dot the scenery along the parkway. Adventurers can enjoy numerous hiking trails, picnic sites, and campgrounds, too.

# Gulf Islands National Seashore

From above, the Gulf Islands National Seashore looks like a sandy string of pearls off the coasts of Florida and Mississippi. Along the water are miles of snow-white beaches, bayous, saltwater marshes, maritime forests, barrier islands, and nature trails. Of the more than 135,000 acres of national seashore, 80 percent of the park is underwater.

The environment is diverse, but visitors to the seashore usually focus on the beach. Miles and miles of white powdery sand extend through the sparkling water. Especially intriguing are the barrier islands, notably the Horn Island and Petit Bois Island wilderness areas, each about ten miles out from the Mississippi coast. Camping is permitted anywhere on the islands.

A sub-specialty of Gulf Islands National Seashore is the 19th-century forts. Four of them are on the Florida panhandle side of the park. They were built after the War of 1812 to defend Pensacola Bay. The largest, Fort Pickens, was completed in 1834. Today the fort doubles as one of the park's most popular beach areas. Along with Perdido Key, Okaloosa, and Davis Bayou (on the Mississippi side), it ranks among the most popular beaches in the area.

But the barrier islands are still a buffer to protect the mainland—the park has been bruised by storms such as Hurricane Ivan in 2004. Check for closures before you go.

*The white sand of Gulf Islands National Seashore is believed to have eroded from rocky areas to the north.*

# Delta Blues Festival

*Performers entertain the crowd at Greenville's big annual event.*

The Mississippi Delta Blues Festival is the king of blues festivals. Founded in 1978, the Greenville-based blues festival is the second-oldest continuously operating festival of its kind in the country.

The festival is Mississippi's largest single-day event. Perhaps it has earned its regal status because of the way it was born—from the heart and passion of the state's civil rights and antipoverty movements. The blues were born out of a folk culture context drawing elements from work songs, love songs, slow drags, rags, and spirituals. The Mississippi Delta Blues Festival is the flagship of the Delta Arts Project, founded by the Mississippi Action for Community Education Incorporated (MACE). Its mission is to confront the human rights issues that gave birth to the blues and empower African-Americans.

The festival began as a community gathering where locals played traditional blues on acoustic instruments. While it's still seen as a community event, the festival has drawn top-notch blues artists such as B. B. King, Bobby Rush, Albert King, Bobby Blue Bland, John Lee Hooker, Johnny Winter, Muddy Waters, Furry Lewis, and Big Joe Williams.

# Blanchard Springs Caverns

lanchard Springs Caverns in north-central .rkansas is the jewel of the Ozarks. This ıree-level cave system has almost every kind f cave formation: from soda straws to bacon ›rmations to rimstone cave pools. The most ımous formation in these haunting caverns is ıe 70-foot-high joined stalagmite-stalactite alled the Giant Column.

Anthropologists have found evidence of uman visitors in the caverns as early as 900 .D. But it was the pioneering spelunkers and nvironmental activists in the mid-1950s and 960s who led to further exploration. Early xpeditions took adventurers about 1.4 miles ıto the cave. With careful planning, the caverns ave remained a healthy, "living" cave system.

Visitors can choose from three scenic trails ırough Blanchard Springs Caverns. The Dripstone Trail is a one-hour trail around the upper level that is stroller- and wheelchair-accessible. The Discovery Trail is a longer section that winds through the middle level. If you're looking for a challenge, the four-hour Wild Cave Tour is an introduction to spelunking requiring athleticism, endurance, and equipment available only by reservation.

But even the claustrophobic can enjoy the wide-open serenity of the Ozark National Forest. There are campsites and opportunities for fishing, hiking, and watching wildlife. While in the area, tour the Ozark Mountain Folk Center. And if you're craving more caving, there are tours of other caves in the area including Bull Shoals Caverns, Hurricane River Cave, Mystic Caverns, and Cosmic Cavern (the site of the Ozark's largest underground lake).

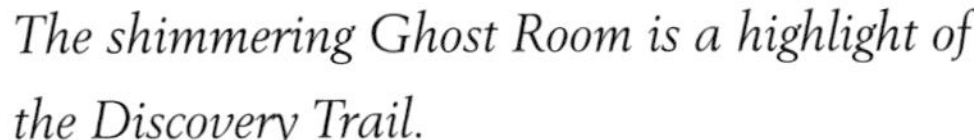

*The shimmering Ghost Room is a highlight of the Discovery Trail.*

*'he cavern's namesake river, Blanchard prings, leaves the cave as a waterfall.*

# Hot Springs National Park

Hot Springs National Park is the smallest and oldest national park in the United States. It is also one of the most unusual. For one thing, much of Hot Springs National Park is a National Historic Landmark District located in downtown Hot Springs, Arkansas. Most important, it contains what some veteran visitors call the world's best hot springs water. About 850,000 gallons of water per day percolate from the side of Hot Springs Mountain at 143 degrees Fahrenheit in 47 hot springs. The popularity of the park has been bubbling, too, rising to about 1.5 million annual visitors.

The importance of preserving these waters was evident to early Americans, and the main mission of the National Parks Service today is to maintain the springs. The Bathhouse Row historic district shows visitors how their predecessors enjoyed the park. The many matchless examples of Gilded Age architecture show how the resort early on earned the title "The American Spa."

*The architectural style and interior details of the Fordyce Bathhouse pay tribute to the "life-giving" waters of the hot springs.*

Yet there's much more to Hot Spring National Park than a relaxing soak. Favorit recreations include hiking, crystal prospecting, camping in Gulpha Gorge Campground and driving or hiking up Hot Springs Mountain to enjoy the 40-mile view from Ho Springs Tower.

# Ouachita National Forest

Ouachita National Forest spans 1.8 million acres in a broad swath north of Hot Springs, Arkansas, that reaches all the way to eastern Oklahoma. The forest is renowned for its glistening streams and pristine lakes. It is the oldest national forest in the South: President Theodore Roosevelt created Ouachita National Forest in 1907.

The Ouachita Mountains first gained praise in 1541 from Hernando DeSoto, and later from French explorers, who named the mountains for the native word for "good hunting ground." The modern motto might be "good fishing": Today the forest contains about 700 acres of fishing ponds and lakes. You can use nonmotorized boats to reach favorite fishing spots. Or if you're water-weary, choose from the extensive trails for hiking, mountain biking, and horseback riding that provide optimum scenic views.

The Ouachita Mountains might be best known around the world, however, as heaven for geology enthusiasts and rock collectors. The mountains were built by orogeny, the folding of the earth's crust. The exposed surface then eroded over time. It has taken millions of years, but the results include astounding finds of diamonds, what many say are the world's finest quartz crystals (especially near Hot Springs and Mount Ida), and ridges made of novaculite flint, a dense, hard rock used for whetstones.

*Autumn foliage heightens the beauty of the riverbanks in Ouachita National Forest.*

# Mardi Gras

Now the biggest annual party in North America, New Orleans's Carnival (also known as "the greatest free show on Earth") is an over-the-top street party that typically attracts more than a million people from all over the world. Carnival culminates with Mardi Gras, or Fat Tuesday, the wild event that turns New Orleans into a center of celebration.

Mardi Gras gives way at midnight to Ash Wednesday, the first day of Lent. While the party has roots in pagan rituals that predate Christianity, it was recognized as a day of celebration by Pope Gregory XIII in 1582 when he placed it on his Gregorian calendar. The Catholic Church in Europe co-opted Mardi Gras as a season of excess before the self-discipline of Lent.

French explorers were the first to celebrate Mardi Gras in the New World, though it's a point of contention whether the first Mardi Gras in America was hosted in Louisiana or Alabama. Some say the first Mardi Gras was celebrated in 1699 on Mardi Gras Island just downstream from present-day New Orleans on the Mississippi River. Others claim the first was in Mobile, Alabama, in 1704.

For the last century or so, however, nobody has thrown a bigger party than the city of New Orleans. Carnival begins with the Feast of Epiphany, on January 6, the twelfth day of Christmas. But because Fat Tuesday falls between February 3 and March 9 every year, most people don't get serious about Carnival until the two-week window before Mardi Gras.

*Visitors crowd Bourbon Street for the annual Mardi Gras parades and celebration.*

The last five days of Carnival—starting with the Friday before Mardi Gras—are the most intense of the celebration. New Orleans's famous French Quarter—in particular, Bourbon Street—becomes a wild party with famous people, frozen cocktails, competition for beads, and tons of fun.

The parades are the flamboyant soul of Carnival. Each parade is organized by a krewe, or group with hereditary membership. There are about 60 krewes in New Orleans. Each krewe selects a king and queen to reign over the parade. The parades put on by the Comus, Rex, and Zulu krewes are among the longest standing and most loved in New Orleans. Elaborate multicolor floats carry krewe members in ornate costumes. They toss trinkets, beads, doubloons, small toys, and candy into the crowds, sometimes in exchange for a wink, a hug, or a flash of flesh.

The parades snake through New Orleans until they reach their destination—a big, bawdy ball. Many of these balls are masquerades where traditional king cake is served to revelers. The king cake is made from roll-like dough brushed with icing. A trinket, usually a bean or tiny plastic baby representing the Christ child, is baked inside. Whoever gets the piece with the trinket is bestowed special status for the remainder of the party.

When the clock strikes midnight on Mardi Gras, the party is officially over. New Orleans

## Quick Fact

### *The French Quarter*

After Hurricane Katrina damaged structures in the French Quarter in 2005, some television personalities questioned whether its unique atmosphere would change. Didn't these experts understand that the French Quarter is eternal?

Here they say, *"Laissez les bons temps rouler"* ("Let the good times roll"), and clearly the good times will return to this famous district. It took months to restore telephone service to New Orleans, but the decision to go ahead with the next Mardi Gras took only weeks. "We've got to have this party," said Blaine Kern, also known as "Mr. Mardi Gras." The French Quarter and Mardi Gras are the heart of New Orleans. Locals and tourists flock to the French Quarter for the crazy party each year, with its parades raining beads, costumes a dozen feet wide, jazz in the streets, and dancing.

While Mardi Gras comes only once a year, the French Quarter has plenty of entertainment to keep visitors delighted year-round. Restaurants serve up some of North America's finest cuisine, with specialties such as po-boys, jambalaya, crawfish etoufée, and shrimp Creole. The French Quarter is also known for its incomparable coffee and Sazerac cocktails.

Stay for a sample of the music that was born in New Orleans. The beats of blues and jazz, stride and boogie-woogie, Dixieland, big band, and rock 'n' roll can be heard in clubs throughout the district.

police officers on horseback clear upper Bourbon Street and send the partiers home. Beginning on Ash Wednesday, many of the city's citizens give up a few pleasures for Lent.

And Mardi Gras will go on, despite—or perhaps to spite—Hurricane Katrina in 2005. This is one party that's impossible to stop.

*The St. Louis Cathedral towers over Jackson Square in the French Quarter.*

# Louisiana State Capitols

Baton Rouge, Louisiana, surprises visitors with not one but two amazing state capitols. Today the Old State Capitol is a museum. Its Gothic-revival architecture is impressive: The building resembles a shiny white medieval castle. The interior is striking, as well: An elaborate central staircase of broad marble steps descends under a kaleidoscopic stained-glass ceiling. However, most of the original furnishings are now gone. Instead, tour the re-creations of old press and government offices and interactive exhibits such as a podium with a TelePrompTer that rolls famous Louisiana speeches. It is notable that Huey Long and Mark Twain—who surely would have agreed on little else—each despised the building and called it ugly.

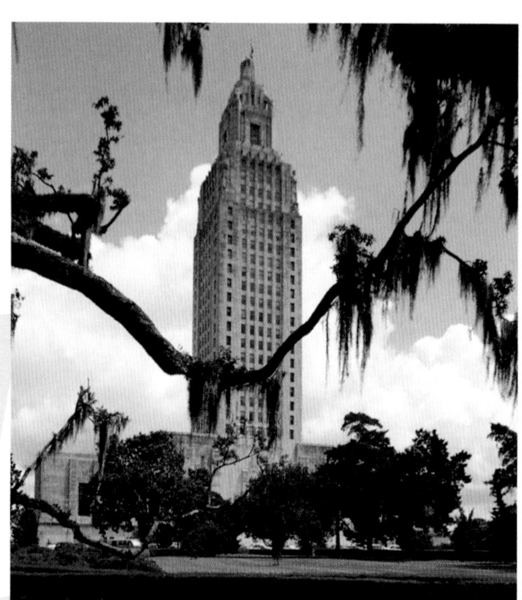

*The new Louisiana State Capitol was dedicated in 1932 after 14 months of construction.*

Long disliked the Old State Capitol enough that he made building a new one part of his first campaign for governor in 1928. Luckily for visitors, the new Art Deco State Capitol is almost as much of an architectural curio as the old one. At 34 stories and 450 feet high, the capitol is the largest U.S. state capitol and the tallest building in Louisiana. The dominating limestone structure defines the Baton Rouge skyline.

In 1935, Long was assassinated in the capitol and is now buried in the center of the Capitol Gardens. Some say the nicks in the walls of the capitol hallway are from the bullets that were fired.

(Above) *The Old State Capitol is one of the premier examples of Gothic-revival architecture in the United States.*

*Checkered floors and a spiral staircase complete the interior of the Old State Capitol.*

# ʼlantation Alley

›uisiana's Great River Road is also known as antation Alley. There, 30 antebellum man-›ns and 10 other ancient properties sit regally bluffs overlooking the Mississippi River. All e open for tours or have been converted into ›tels or bed-and-breakfast inns. Along the reat River Road, they provide a dignified pro-ssion of antebellum architecture surrounded sugarcane fields and pecan groves.

Take in the atmosphere on your way to see e plantations. Start in Baton Rouge and drive uth. Instead of taking I-10 straight to New rleans, travel along the Mississippi River ward Plaquemine, White Castle, and Don-dsonville. Visits to the gracious mansions of e old South still mean magnolia-perfumed ssages through formal gardens and expan-e homes with grand river views.

Nottoway, a gem of Greek Revival architec-re, is one of the largest plantations. The well-own Houmas House was once the center a 20,000-acre sugarcane plantation. This reek Revival mansion is furnished with tiques. It was featured in the novel *North d South* and the movie *Hush, Hush, Sweet harlotte* starring Bette Davis. Oak Alley Plan-tion is a sweeping columned mansion framed live oaks. Oak Alley is probably the most otographed plantation of all. It has been the tting for movies including *Interview with the ampire* and *Primary Colors.* Nearby, Laura antation, with a Creole style and unique ustard facade, is said to be the source of the er Rabbit tales.

*Celina Roman called her home* Bon Sejour *("pleasant sojourn"). But travelers on the Mississippi called it "Oak Alley," impressed by the mighty trees, and the name has stuck to this day.*

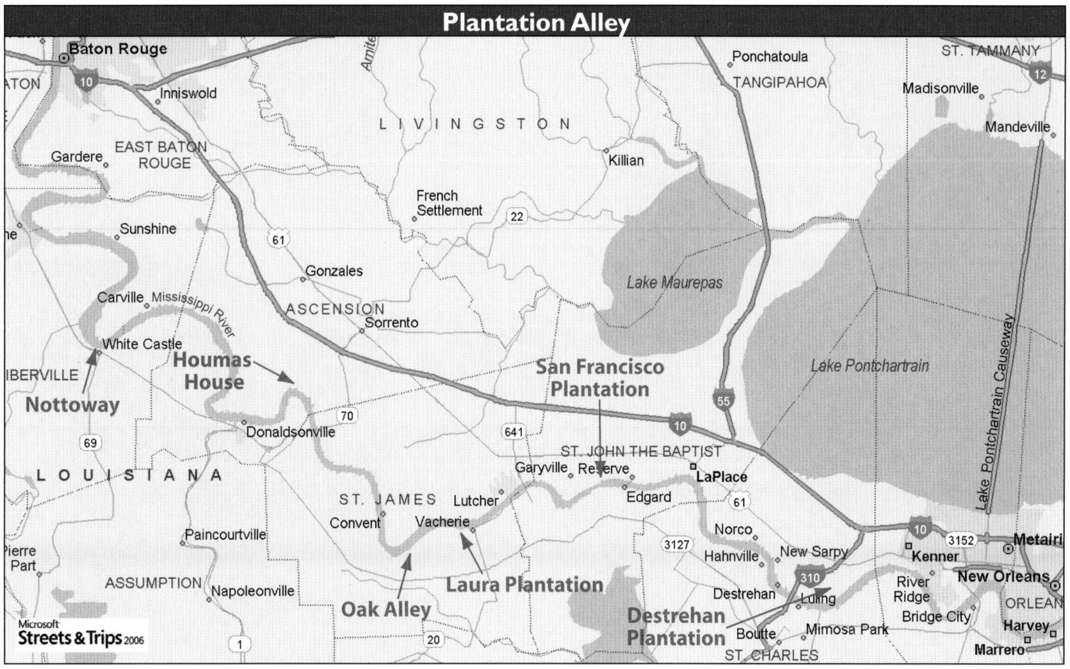

# Rock and Roll Hall of Fame and Museum

Rock 'n' roll lives on today, more than a half-century after its beginning. One reason is Cleveland's Rock and Roll Hall of Fame and Museum. Designed by architect I. M. Pei, the building expresses the raw power of rock music. The geometric and cantilevered forms are often compared to a turntable or pyramid. The striking building and its 162-foot tower anchor Cleveland's North Coast Harbor.

The hall began operation in 1986 with the ceremonial induction of its first class of rock stars: Chuck Berry, Elvis Presley, Little Richard, Sam Cooke, the Everly Brothers, and Buddy Holly, among others. Inside it holds a collection of rock memorabilia and features groundbreaking exhibitions. Broadcasts from the Alan Freed Studio are a fan favorite, as are the exhibitions of Janis Joplin's Porsche, Jim Morrison's Cub Scout shirt, and Ringo Star Sergeant Pepper uniform. The permanent co lection contains rock rarities from pione Louis Jordan to present-day stars. Celebri sightings are frequent, so put on your bl suede shoes and rock, rock, rock!

*The Rock and Roll Hall of Fame is the world's first museum honoring rock music.*

# Professional Football Hall of Fame

n 1920, Canton, Ohio, was home to the Canon Bulldogs, which were then part of the American Professional Football Association. While the team lasted just a few years, its egacy is a permanent part of the Professional Football Hall of Fame. A seven-foot statue of im Thorpe, once a star athlete for the Bulldogs, stands at the Hall of Fame's portal.

Built in 1963, the building has since been expanded three times. Today it measures 83,000 square feet. The Hall of Fame Enshrinement Gallery is the most revered attraction: Each Hall of Famer is commemorated with a bronze bust. The gallery was updated in 2003 to add space and high-tech interactive features. The most innovative attraction is the GameDay Stadium, which shows recordings of professional NFL games in a turntable theater featuring a unique 20- by 42-foot Cinemascope screen.

Once visitors pass the Thorpe statue, they ascend into a rotunda showcasing the 100-year history of the sport, followed by the Pro Football Today display, a history of the NFL's 32 teams. Even if you're just a casual fan, try a game of Hall of Fame Teletrivia or QB-1-Call-the-Play-Theater using the interactive displays. And, of course, no trip would be complete without a stop at the Tailgating Snack Bar.

*Each year, the Professional Football Hall of Fame inducts three to six players, coaches, or sportscasters, who must be retired.*

# The Cincinnati Museum Center

*Originally the Union Terminal train station, the building reopened as the Cincinnati Museum Center in 1990.*

The Cincinnati Museum Center at Union Terminal is an Art Deco masterwork that attracts viewers from around the world who are enticed by its headquarters and gallery building. Like so many other great American buildings, Union Terminal opened during the depths of the Great Depression, in 1933. The building was an architectural icon from the beginning. When it was built, the ten-story Art Deco limestone half-dome was the only building of its kind on the continent. After train travel dwindled, the terminal was declared a National Historic Landmark in 1977 and stood empty for more than a decade.

Today the beautiful terminal is home to five major cultural organizations: the Cincinnati History Museum, the Cinergy Children's Museum, the Museum of Natural History & Science, the Robert D. Lindner Family OMNIMAX Theater, and the Cincinnat Historical Society Library. The Cincinnati History Museum features re-creations of the Cincinnati Public Landing wharf of the mid-1800s including a 94-foot side-wheel steamboat. The Museum of Natural History & Science invite visitors to enter the Ohio Valley ice age o 19,000 years ago in a re-created limestone cave featuring underground waterfalls, streams, and a live bat colony.

# Serpent Mound

Serpent Mound, a winding mound of earth one-quarter mile long and three feet high, remains a mystery despite all the science that has been thrown at it.

There are many Native American mounds in North America, but Serpent Mound State Memorial, near Peebles, Ohio, is the largest prehistoric animal effigy, or image, in the world. Snakes were important in the art and religion of the Maya of Mexico, the Navajo, the Hopi, and other Native American tribes. But what, if anything, that has to do with the mystical Serpent Mound is unknown.

Serpent Mound uncoils in seven curved stages along a bluff over Rush Creek in Ohio and is completed by an oval that appears to represent the head and mouth of the serpent. Some believe that the serpent's head points toward the summer solstice. Park archaeologists say that the builders carefully planned the serpent's form, outlined it with stones, and then covered it with baskets of earth. There are neither signs of burial nor aboriginal civilization. The mystery continues: Serpent Mound was created on a rare raise called a "cryptoexplosion structure"—in other words, a bluff created by a big bang that remains, naturally, a mystery.

*The enigmatic Serpent Mound winds over one-quarter mile.*

# Cuyahoga Valley National Park

Cuyahoga Valley National Park lies between Akron and Cleveland in Ohio. It may be the park service's most urban-friendly environment. The park preserves 33,000 acres along the Cuyahoga River, called "crooked river" by the Mohawk Indians. The forests, plains, streams, and ravines of Cuyahoga Valley National Park contain an astonishing array of fauna, flora, and recreational opportunities.

The park's wetland habitats and woods provide a home to 54 butterfly species, almost 200 bird species (including threatened nonbreeding bald eagles), and 32 mammal species (including the endangered Indiana bat, first discovered in the park in 2002).

A 22-mile stretch of the Cuyahoga River dominates the park, and almost 200 miles of streams course through it. Cuyahoga Valley National Park abounds in marshes and waterfalls, the highest being 65-foot-high Brandywine Falls. Amazing geological features such as the skyscraping Ritchie Ledges are not to be missed. The Beaver Marsh, a beaver dam built along the defunct Ohio & Erie Canal, is a favorite short hike and critical wetlands biosphere.

The park has almost no roads, but you can explore plenty of bike and hiking paths. A perennial favorite is the 20-mile Towpath Trail. Don't miss the cultural exhibits and events such as historic displays and outdoor concerts.

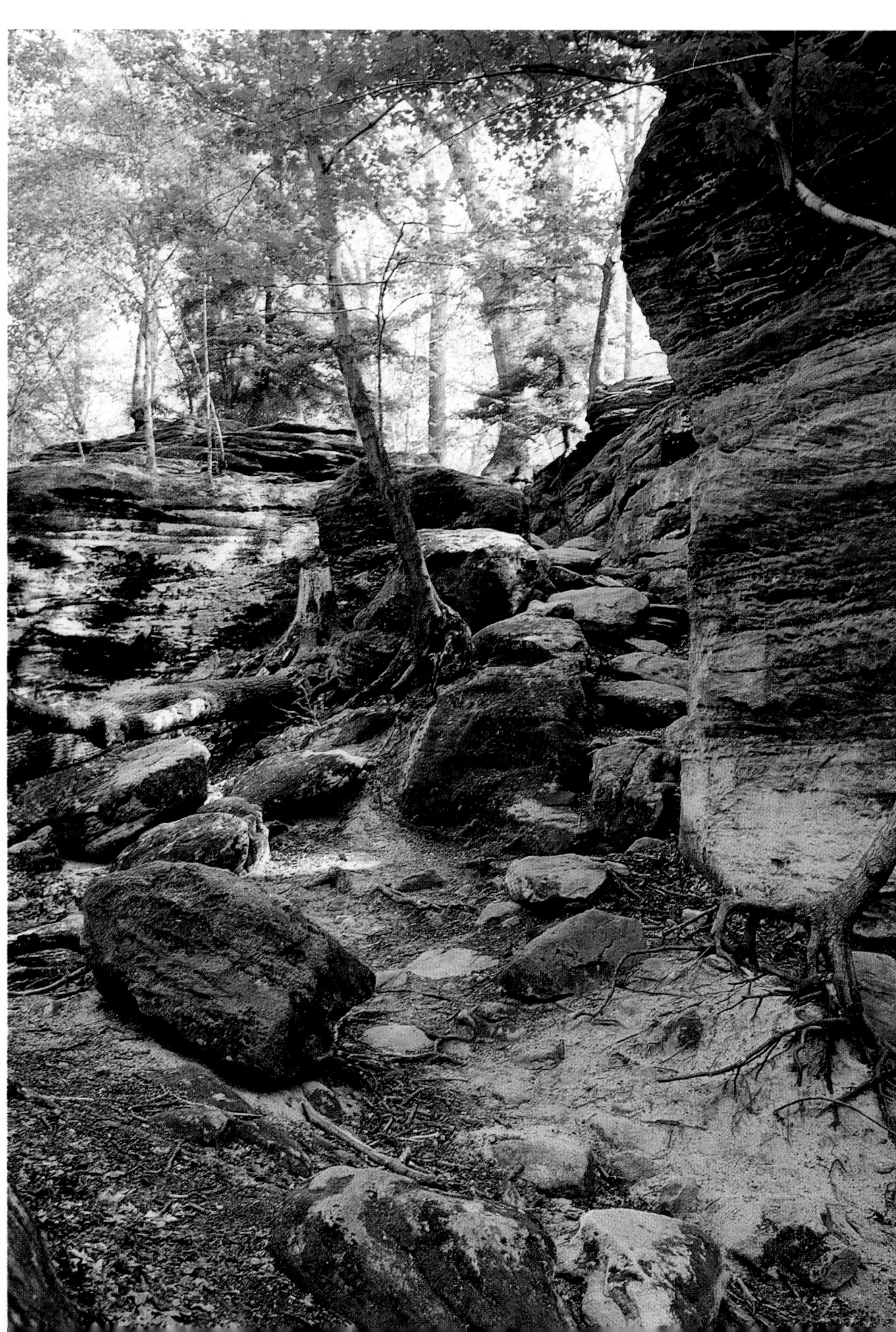

*Cuyahoga Valley National Park is a serene, natural haven amid the urban areas of Ohio.*

# Pictured Rocks National Lakeshore

*Miners Castle is the highlight of a 2.5-mile cruise around Pictured Rocks. Tourists can enjoy a close-up view by hiking to the formation.*

Pictured Rocks National Lakeshore spans 42 miles of Lake Superior shoreline, covering more than 73,000 acres of Michigan's Upper Peninsula. It is a preserve of spectacular scenery and cascading sand dunes. The most photographed location is the five miles of "perched" dunes and sparse jack pine forests of the Grand Sable Dunes. Of the signature sculpted sandstone cliffs, such as Indian Head, Miners Castle, Grand Portal, and Lovers Leap, all but Miners Castle can be viewed only by water. Cruises are a spectacular way to take in these sights.

Despite the remote location, almost 400,000 visitors each year seek out Pictured Rocks for hunting, fishing, hiking, and boating in spring and summer. In fall and winter, snowshoeing, snowmobiling, ice fishing, and cross-country skiing are popular.

You can hike to astonishing waterfalls, including Spray Falls, Alger Falls, Wagner Falls, Chapel Falls, and Laughing Whitefish Falls, with its dramatic 100-foot drop. The 1874 Au Sable Light Station, thought to be the Great Lakes' finest masonry lighthouse, also draws crowds.

# Isle Royale National Park

*The Rock Harbor Lighthouse at the northeast end of Isle Royale was built in 1855.*

Isle Royale, which was carved and compressed by glaciers, is the largest island on Lake Superior: It's 45 miles long and nine miles wide at the widest point. It exists in splendid isolation—you can only get to the island by boat, seaplane, or ferry. Together with numerous smaller islands it makes up Isle Royale National Park, located off of Michigan's Upper Peninsula. (The park is closer to Canada than it is to Michigan.) Only about 20,000 people visit this remote, tranquil setting each year. Those who do often spend at least three days absorbing the peaceful wilderness.

About 85 percent of the park's 850 square miles is water. The island is home to 20 species of mammals, though the mainland has more than 40. Scientists speculate that the moose on the island were brought from the mainland.

There are no roads on the island, but you can choose routes from among the 165 miles of hiking trails. The most striking hike i[s] Greenstone Ridge, a trail more than 40 mile[s] long along a basalt flow that was formed b[y] lava and tinted green by copper. Diving fo[r] shipwrecks is another favorite activity—ther[e] are more than ten major wrecks below th[e] serene water.

# Mackinac Bridge

The mighty Mackinac Bridge straddles the Straits of Mackinac between Lakes Michigan and Huron to connect Michigan's upper and lower peninsulas. Pronounced *MA keh nah,* Mackinac is short for Michilimackinac, which was an Indian territory on what is now Mackinac Island. Measured the conventional way, between towers, Mackinac Bridge is the world's ninth-longest suspension bridge. Measured by impact, it ranks right up there with the Golden Gate Bridge. No wonder Michiganders call it "Mighty Mac."

Ceremonies to celebrate the official beginning of construction were held in 1954; it opened in 1957. The Mackinac Bridge has had a lasting impact on travel in Michigan—on the day it opened, the ferry service to the Upper Peninsula ended. Crossing the seemingly endless bridge can be its own reward, with the added bonus of entering another world: Michigan's incomparable Upper Peninsula.

*The nearly five-mile-long Mackinac Bridge, including approaches, links the upper and lower Michigan peninsulas.*

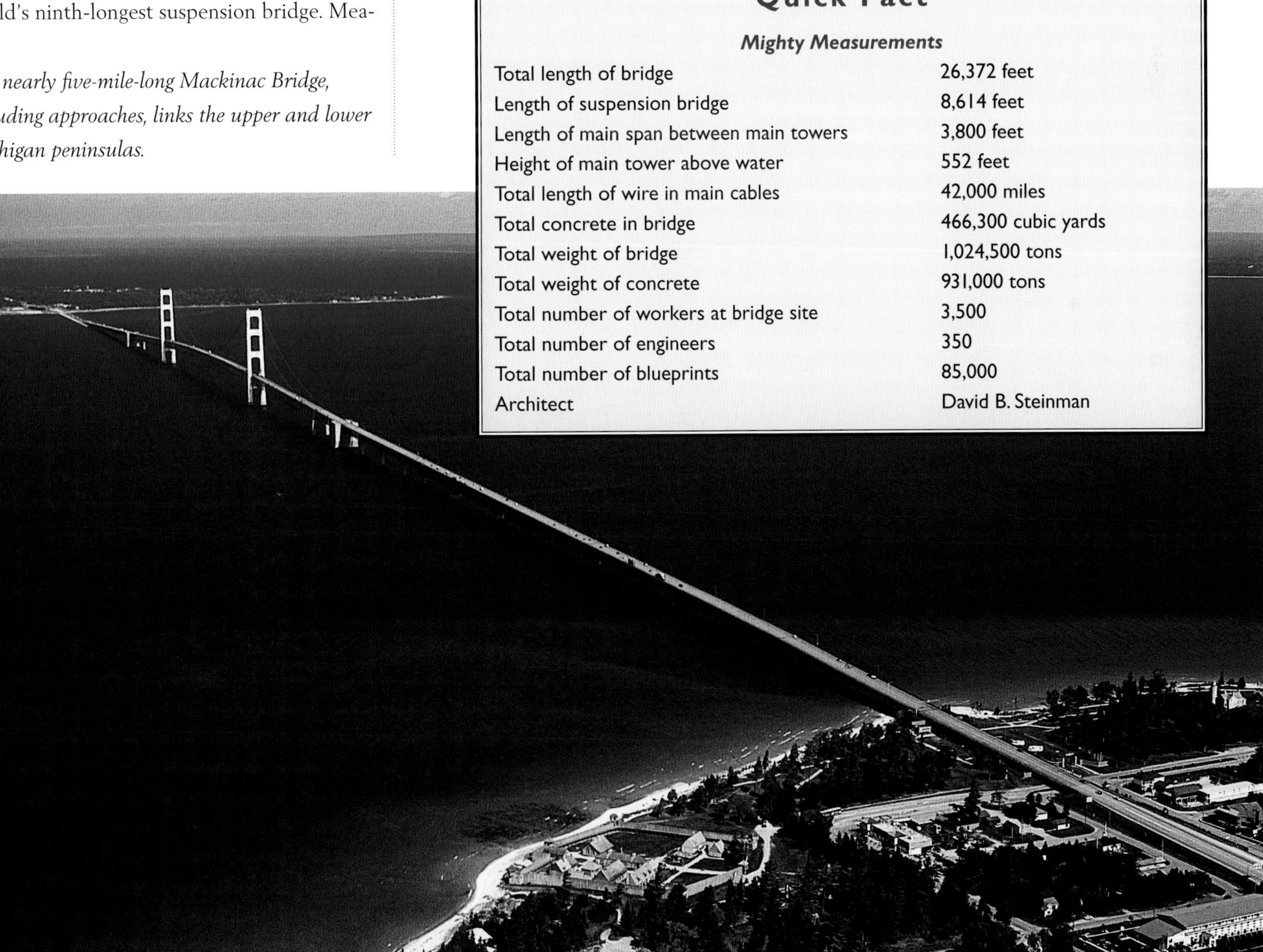

## Quick Fact

***Mighty Measurements***

| | |
|---|---|
| Total length of bridge | 26,372 feet |
| Length of suspension bridge | 8,614 feet |
| Length of main span between main towers | 3,800 feet |
| Height of main tower above water | 552 feet |
| Total length of wire in main cables | 42,000 miles |
| Total concrete in bridge | 466,300 cubic yards |
| Total weight of bridge | 1,024,500 tons |
| Total weight of concrete | 931,000 tons |
| Total number of workers at bridge site | 3,500 |
| Total number of engineers | 350 |
| Total number of blueprints | 85,000 |
| Architect | David B. Steinman |

# Indianapolis 500

Start with four straight sections of asphalt, two long and two short, connected by four turns, each exactly a quarter-mile in length and banked at an angle of 9 degrees and 12 minutes. Mix in 33 of the best cars money can buy and upward of 300,000 fans. Add Memorial Day weekend and nearly a century of tradition, and serve. That's the recipe for the legendary Indianapolis 500.

The race's home is the Indianapolis Motor Speedway, also known as the Brickyard. The speedway first opened in 1909, but numerous poorly attended seasonal races led the owners to focus on one big annual event. That big event was the Indianapolis 500 Mile Race, first held in 1911 on May 30—Memorial Day. It was a breakthrough success for the fledgling track, attracting 80,000 fans who cheered when driver Ray Harroun crossed the finish line first.

*The Indianapolis Motor Speedway, also called the Brickyard, is the famed home of the Indianapolis 500.*

Named for the number of miles covered by circling the 2.5-mile track 200 times, the Indianapolis 500 became an instant rite of spring for the country's racing community. The race has been held at some point during Memorial Day weekend every year since 1911, with the exception of six years during World War I and World War II. Nicknamed "The Greatest Spectacle in Racing," it is one of the longest-standing and richest motorsports events in the world.

The speedway's founders would be hard-pressed to believe how their race and racetrack have evolved. While Harroun averaged 75 miles per hour in his six-and-a-half-hour triumph, modern winners sometimes finish the race in less than three hours. The race now has the largest single-day attendance of any sporting event on the planet.

Many 500-goers are more interested in partying than watching the race. On race day the track's infield hosts a tailgate party of

## Quick Fact

***About the Indy Racing League (IRL) Cars***

- Engines are limited to a 3.0L normally aspirated engine to curb top speeds.
- The engines can produce about 650hp, nearly four times that of an average street car.
- These racing cars get only about two miles per gallon of fuel.
- They can accelerate from 0 to 100 miles per hour in less than three seconds.

*Indy Racing League cars zoom around the 2.5-mile track at top speeds near 220 miles per hour.*

epic proportions. Speedway regulations allow those who park their cars in the infield to fire up barbeques and tap kegs of beer. Deep in the infield, the race is an afterthought evidenced only by the roar of cars speeding down the track's straightaways. The track infield also holds a museum, part of an 18-hole golf course, concert stages, corporate "tent parties," and just about everything else one could shoehorn into a couple hundred acres of former farmland.

Like the logistics inherent in organizing the event, the physics of the race are nothing short of astounding. The cars hit top speeds near 220 miles per hour, meaning the drivers are rocketing through space, covering the length of a football field every second. They're also subjected to g-forces that are four times the earth's normal gravitational pull—in other words, about the same force experienced by the space shuttle's passengers when blasting off from Cape Canaveral.

As for drivers, A. J. Foyt is an all-time legend of the Indianapolis 500. He competed in a record 35 consecutive races. Foyt won four times, the first of only three racers to do so (the others were Rick Mears and Al Unser, Sr.), after which he enjoyed the traditional winner's refreshment: a jug of ice-cold milk.

The Indianapolis 500 is an undeniable testament to America's love affair with cars, speed, and tailgating.

# The College Football Hall of Fame

South Bend, Indiana, with a population just over 107,000, probably would have remained an ordinary college town were it not for Notre Dame's Fighting Irish football team and the countless legends it has engendered. Thus, it seemed logical when the College Football Hall of Fame moved from Ohio to the downtown district of South Bend in 1995.

The Hall of Fame today is highlighted by an unusual architecture of ramps, spirals, and tunnels. The main museum hall is underground. Visitors wind around a giant circular staircase to visit the Hall of Honor. They then branch out to exhibits such as the Great Moments Kiosk and the Pantheon, which showcases recipients of especially prestigious awards; equipment displays; a strategy clinic; and a practice field where visitors can pass, block, and kick. The Pantheon's centerpiece is the Stadium Theater, a re-creation of a live football game that makes visitors feel as if they are on a stadium field among the players, cheerleaders, and 106,000 screaming college football fans.

The first Hall of Fame inductees were selected in 1951. Among the original 54 legends inducted were Walter Camp, Jim Thorpe, and Red Grange. Today more than 900 college football players and coaches are enshrined.

*Some exhibits at the College Football Hall of Fame in South Bend contain sports equipment and artifacts from behind-the-scenes of the game.*

# The Magnificent Mile

Chicago's Magnificent Mile stretches along North Michigan Avenue between Oak Street and the Chicago River. The 100-story John Hancock Center may be the most prominent building on this stretch, but don't overlook the other architectural gems. The Tribune Tower, with its decorative buttresses and gothic design, was once called "the most beautiful and eye-catching building in the world." Park Tower, a 67-story skyscraper, preserves the facade of the landmark 1917 Perkins, Fellows & Hamilton studio. There's also the distinctive Old Water Tower. Built in 1869, the tower was one of the few buildings to survive the Great Chicago Fire of 1871; it has become a symbol of Chicago. Today the tower stands near Water Tower Place, a mall with more than 100 specialty shops.

Which brings us to the truly magnificent part of the Magnificent Mile: Bloomingdale's, Louis Vuitton, Chanel, Gucci, Lalique, Ralph Lauren, Neiman Marcus, Giorgio Armani, Hugo Boss, and Hammacher Schlemmer.

Chicago's Magnificent Mile—bring your credit card.

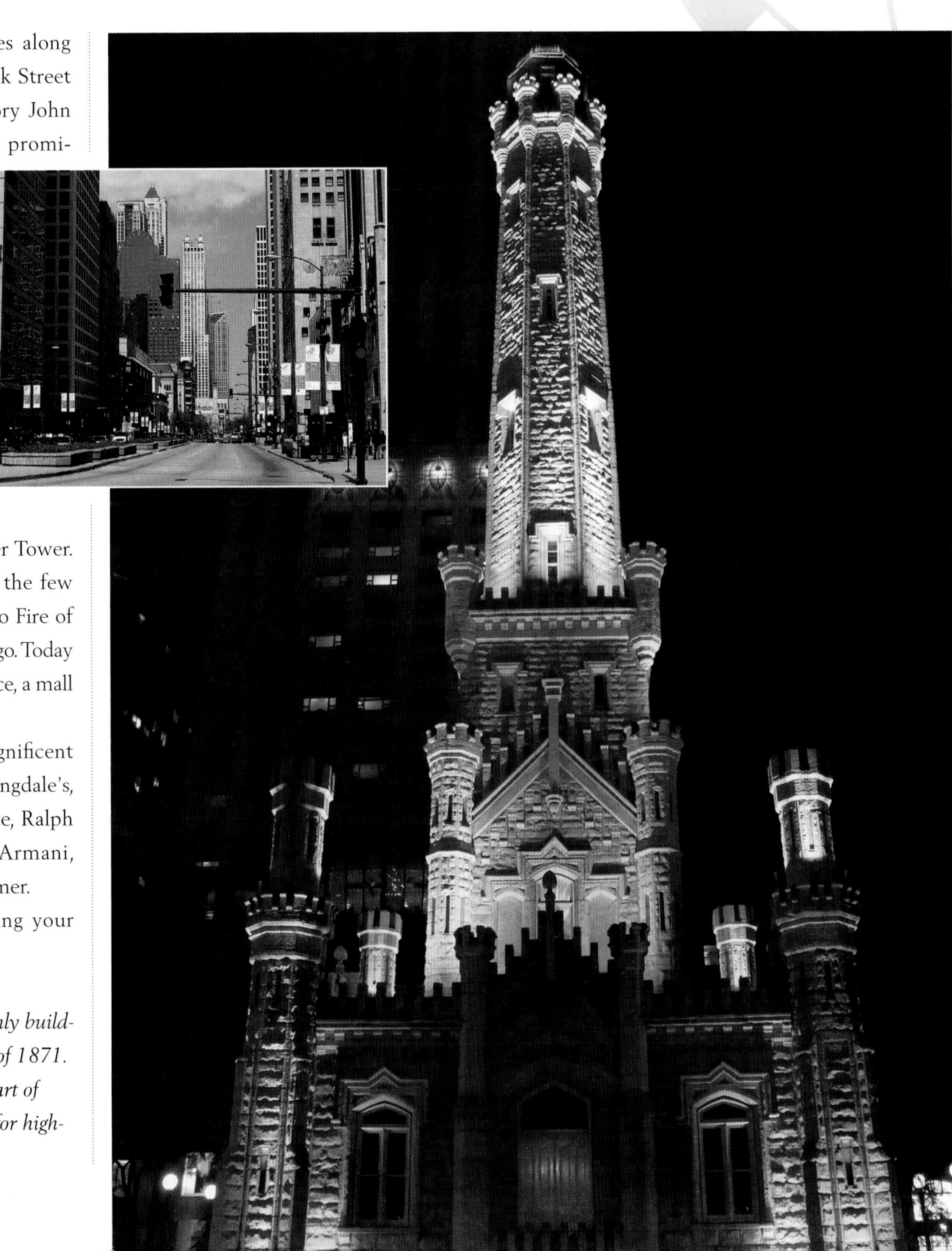

*The Old Water Tower was one of the only buildings to survive the Great Chicago Fire of 1871.* (Inset) *The Magnificent Mile in the heart of downtown Chicago has become a hub for high-end fashion retailers.*

# Chicago Blues

During the 20th century's "Great Migration" of blacks from the American South, many Mississippi Delta blues musicians moved north to the frigid Windy City and found themselves playing in smoky, noisy nightclubs. In the 1930s, blues musicians added electric guitars, electric bass, and drums, and their sound cut through any nightclub's din. By the 1940s, Chi-town blues icons such as Muddy Waters and Howlin' Wolf had created what is now called the Chicago Blues.

One way to sample the Windy City grooves is the Chicago Blues Festival, which features a half-dozen stages and scores of blues acts. The festival takes over Grant Park for four days each June. Or you might prefer to sample the music at the dozens of clubs south of downtown and on the South Side. Well-known clubs such as Buddy Guy's Legends, Lee's Unleaded Blues, Kingston Mines, Frankie's, House of Blues, Checkerboard Lounge, and Rosa's Lounge can be touristy but fun. Don't miss the smaller clubs dotting the Windy City, too—they yield rich musical rewards.

*Crowds are captivated by the soulful melodies and beats at the Chicago Blues Festival.*

# Wrigley Field

*Fans flock to Wrigley to cheer on the Cubs—some even crowd the rooftops of buildings on Sheffield and Waveland avenues.*

Chicago Cubs fans are among the most devoted fans of any sports team. Nowadays, most people worship winners. But the Cubs, a baseball team that has not won a World Series championship since 1908, are the most lovable losers of America's pastime.

Both the Cubs and their fans prize their quaint home ballpark, Wrigley Field. Wrigley was built in 1914 for $250,000 and featured baseball's first permanent concession stand. It's the second-oldest major league park, next to Fenway Park in Boston. And in 1988, it became the last MLB field to host night games when lights were finally added to the park.

The "Friendly Confines" of Wrigley are known for eccentricities. Fickle winds can change the outcome of the game: Watch for home runs when the breeze blows toward Lake Michigan. And hard-hit balls have been getting stuck in the ivy-covered outfield walls since the greenery was planted in 1937.

Wrigley's capacity is relatively small—a mere 41,160 (with new seats added in 2006), plus the apartment rooftops across Sheffield and Waveland avenues. However, any seat will yield a great view of the playing field (the park is well-known for this attribute). Most games are sellouts, but it's worth it to grab a ticket, hot dog, and beer and sit among the famous Bleacher Bums. Afterward, join the untiring Cubs fans at neighborhood bars and restaurants just steps from Wrigley.

# The Art Institute of Chicago

The Art Institute of Chicago boasts more than 300,000 works, including treasured paintings such as Edward Hopper's "Nighthawks," Grant Wood's "American Gothic," and Georges Seurat's "A Sunday on La Grand Jatte." It is one of the most astounding art museums in the world, with an impressive permanent collection and featured exhibits throughout the year. The striking Italian-Renaissance architecture gives the building a distinctive look among the skyscrapers of downtown Chicago.

*This stately lion is one of two that guard the entrance to the Art Institute. "The Bean"* (inset right) *has also become a symbol of Chicago.*

The Art Institute's collections of earl Italian, Dutch, Flemish, and Spanish work include paintings by El Greco, Hals, Rembrandt, and Goya. The comprehensive Impressionist collection features one of th largest collections of Monet's work The museum is also renowned for it arms and armor; Chinese art; print and drawings; and decorative arts such as porcelains, textiles, and glass Then there are the period-furnished rooms and the Thorne Miniature Rooms, tiny reproductions of furnished historic interiors.

If you crave a breath of fresh ai step outside and enjoy the 24.5-acre Millennium Park just across Monroe Street. The park, which opened in 2004, has become a global center for music, art, and architecture Among its most famous attractions are the Jay Pritzker Pavilion, a sophisticated outdoor concert venue designed by Frank Gehry; Ourie Garden; and the popular "Cloud Gate" sculpture more commonly referred to as "The Bean."

## Quick Fact

**Fraternal Twins**

Take a second look—the two magnificent bronze lions that guard the Art Institute's entrance are not identical. The south lion stands in an attitude of defiance, while the north lion is on the prowl.

During the holidays, these proud kitties are adorned with evergreen garlands around their necks.

# Abraham Lincoln Presidential Library and Museum

Abraham Lincoln's wisdom, compassion, and leadership were unmatched in his time. The Abraham Lincoln Presidential Library and Museum in Springfield, Illinois, combines scholarship and showmanship to sweep visitors along from Lincoln's humble beginnings in a log cabin to his presidency during the Civil War. The library opened in 2004, the presidential museum in 2005. Only six months after it opened, the museum welcomed its 400,000th visitor—a record for presidential libraries.

People stream to the Lincoln Library to see books, papers, and artifacts from the life of the Great Emancipator and from the Civil War. Replicas of Lincoln's boyhood home, the Lincoln White House, and his box at Ford's Theatre give an aura of realism to the exhibits.

The Abraham Lincoln Presidential Library and Museum devote 200,000 square feet to telling Lincoln's tale. The 46,000-square-foot space devoted to permanent exhibits is twice the size of the next-largest presidential library.

*Since its opening in 2004, the Lincoln Library has become one of the most popular presidential libraries in history.*

# Lambeau Field

"The Lambeau Field experience" is common knowledge to the citizens of the football-delirious city of Green Bay, Wisconsin. Lambeau Field is one of those magical stadiums where the game experience evokes a rich past. The history of the stadium begins with Vince Lombardi, head coach of the Packers from 1958 to 1967. He was the first to coach the team in the new stadium and was known for sayings like: "If winning isn't everything, why do they keep score?" and "Show me a good loser, and I'll show you a loser."

Lambeau Field was built in 1957 for less than $1 million and was named in 1965 for the Packers' great first coach, Earl L. "Curly" Lambeau, after his death. The stadium was renovated in 2003, but that hasn't diluted the Lambeau Field magic. It seats more than 72,000 people. It has been continuously occupied longer than any other stadium in the National Football League, and it seems t give the Packers a huge home-field advantag Insiders say Lambeau Field also has the NFL nicest fans. Stop by and see if they're right– and don't forget to wear the traditional gear: large cheese-shape hat!

*Despite Wisconsin's often frigid weather, Packers fans cheer on their beloved football team with unmatched zeal.*

# Captain Frederick Pabst Mansion

The front of the Pabst Mansion in Milwaukee is a looming gate reminiscent of a Renaissance fort. The heavy, square architecture was patterned after the 16th-century palaces and fortresses in Flanders, Belgium. Today, Pabst Mansion is called "the Finest Flemish Renaissance Revival Mansion in America."

The magnificent mansion was the 1892 creation of the prolific Frederick Pabst, whose many titles during his lifetime included sea captain, beer baron, real estate mogul, philanthropist, and patron of the arts. Not only does the architecture harken back to the Renaissance, the custom furniture and art do, too. In 2005, 11 paintings that had been part of Pabst's original collection were repurchased and returned to the property.

*In 1889, Milwaukee architect George Bowman Ferry was commissioned to design the Pabst Mansion.*

With 37 rooms, 12 baths, and 14 fireplaces, the mansion lives up to its name. In its time, the house was a high-tech marvel featuring electricity, plumbing for 9 bathrooms, and 16 thermostats. The foyer and massive wood-carved Grand Stair Hall are breathtaking.

# Taliesin

Taliesin is regarded as a prime example of Frank Lloyd Wright's organic architecture. The house is located in Spring Green, Wisconsin, an hour's drive from Madison.

Construction began in 1911, but the project was soon wracked by nightmarish conflicts. In 1914, while Wright was away, a servant murdered seven people, including Wright's mistress, with an ax and set fire to Taliesin. Much of the building was destroyed. Wright fought through his agony and rebuilt the residential wing of the home, naming it Taliesin II. But this wing was again consumed by fire in 1925. The home visitors enjoy today is Taliesin III, which Wright tinkered with until his death in 1959.

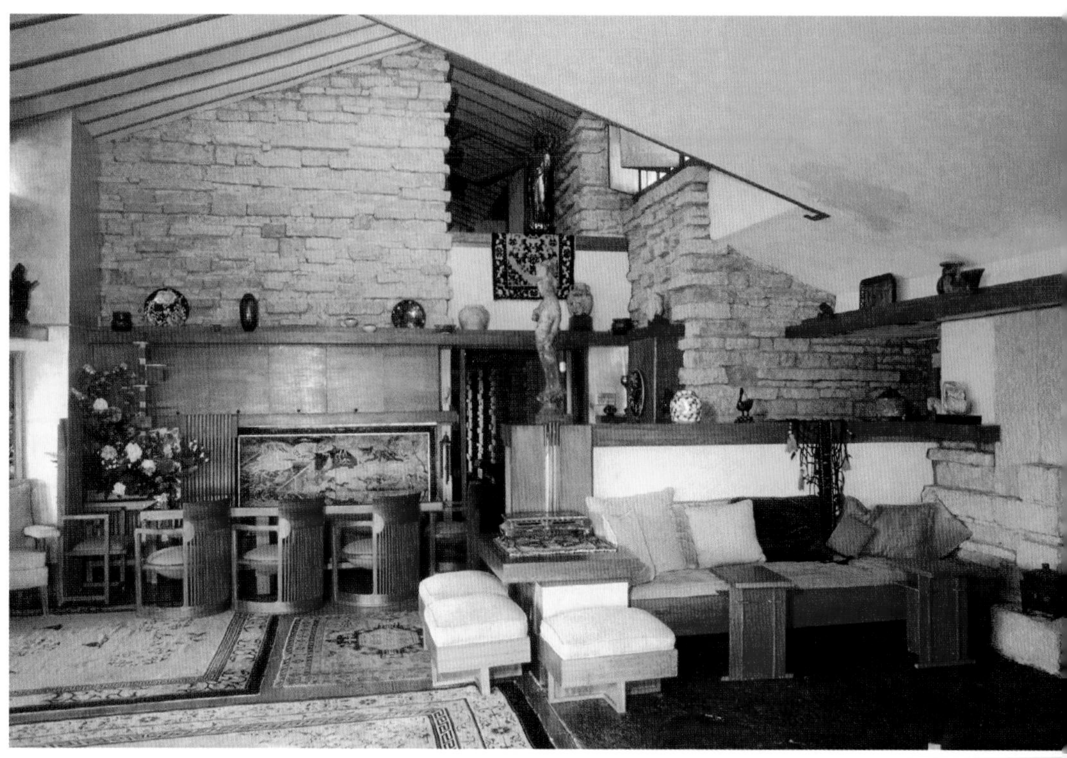

*The spacious interior of Taliesin incorporates local limestone, an aspect of Wright's organic architecture.*

*Taliesin was the start of many experimental ideas that characterized Frank Lloyd Wright's designs.*

Wright built the house in the valley settle by his Welsh ancestors and named it after th Welsh bard Taliesin. The house was originall constructed with local limestone, plaster mad from sand gathered along the Wisconsin Rive cedar, and glass. Wright's technique of buildin the house from native limestone made it loo organic, as though the house was part of th hill on which it was built. In 1976, Taliesin wa recognized as a National Historic Landmark.

Today, tours of Taliesin begin at the Fran Lloyd Wright Visitor Center, the only Wright designed freestanding restaurant. On the tou you'll see many structures Wright built on th 600-acre estate: the Romeo and Juliet Wind mill Tower, Hillside Home School, Tan-y-der and Midway Barns.

# Apostle Islands National Lakeshore

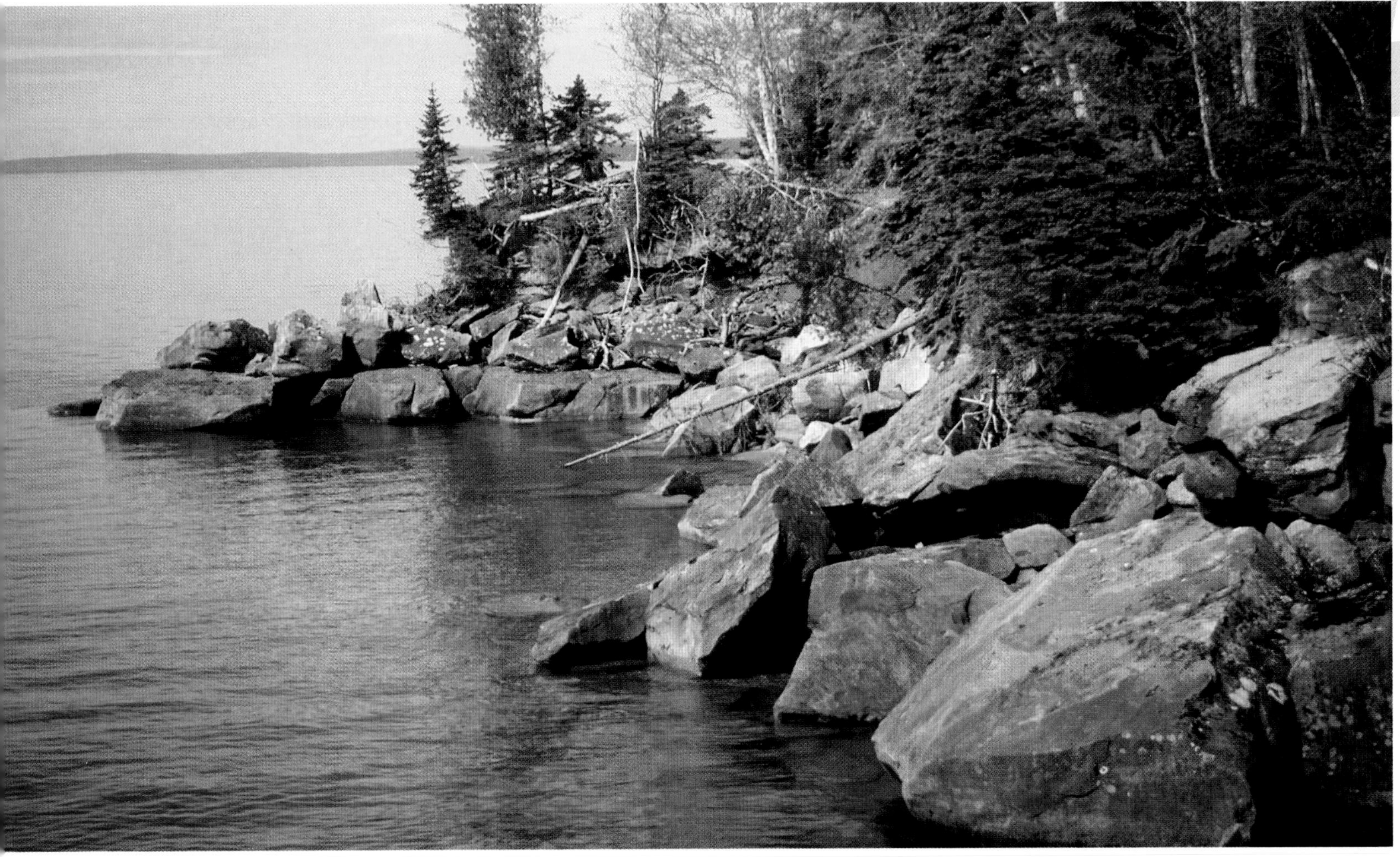

*The cool blue waters of Lake Superior lap at the sandstone rocks along the shores of the Apostle Islands.*

The 21 islands of Apostle Islands National Lakeshore dot the coast of northern Wisconsin just off Bayfield Peninsula. The popular Madeline Island is the largest of the group and the only one that permits commercial growth. Nesting bald eagles at Bay State Park are this island's main attraction.

Winter brings cross-country skiers and ice fishers to the islands. During warmer weather, visitors enjoy hiking, picnicking, scuba diving, swimming, sportfishing, hunting, excursion cruises, kayaking, camping, and sailing.

Once past Madeline Island, take in the beauty of the sandscapes, sea caves, and waterfalls of the lakeshore. There are woods of hemlock; white pine; and northern hardwood and pristine old-growth forests on Devils, Raspberry, Outer, and Sand islands. Deer and beavers are common on the islands, as are black bears, mink, muskrat, otters, red foxes, and snowshoe hares. Fishing has become a favorite pastime, too, with the successful restoration of lake trout. Lake sturgeon, brook trout, lake whitefish, northern pike, smallmouth bass, and many other types of fish are found in these serene waters.

# Milwaukee Art Museum

When you think of Milwaukee, beer, bratwurst, and Brewers baseball come to mind. But while some weren't looking, Milwaukee turned into a sophisticated city with an amazing, world-class art museum.

In 1957, the Milwaukee Art Center opened its Eero Saarinen Building, named after the architect who designed it (he is also the acclaimed architect of the St. Louis Gateway Arch). The building itself is a work of art. It has a floating cruciform shape with four large wings that cantilever in space. The striking building has set the stage for the growth of the museum. It hosts a masterful collection of more than 20,000 works from ancient artifacts to modern masterpieces. Works by Degas, Homer, Monet, O'Keeffe, Picasso, Rodin, Toulouse-Latrec, and Warhol are just some of the treasures.

In 2001, the Quadracci Pavilion, designed by Santiago Calatrava, was added to the building. The prominent pavilion has attracted attention worldwide, and no wonder: It has a light, lacy facade that curves like a sail, despite being built from 20,000 cubic yards of concrete. The addition features a 90-foot-high reception hall enclosed by the Burke Brise Soleil, a sunscreen that can be raised or lowered, making it a moving sculpture. The pavilion expanded gallery space by almost a third.

(Above) *The Milwaukee Art Museum in downtown Milwaukee overlooks Lake Michigan.*

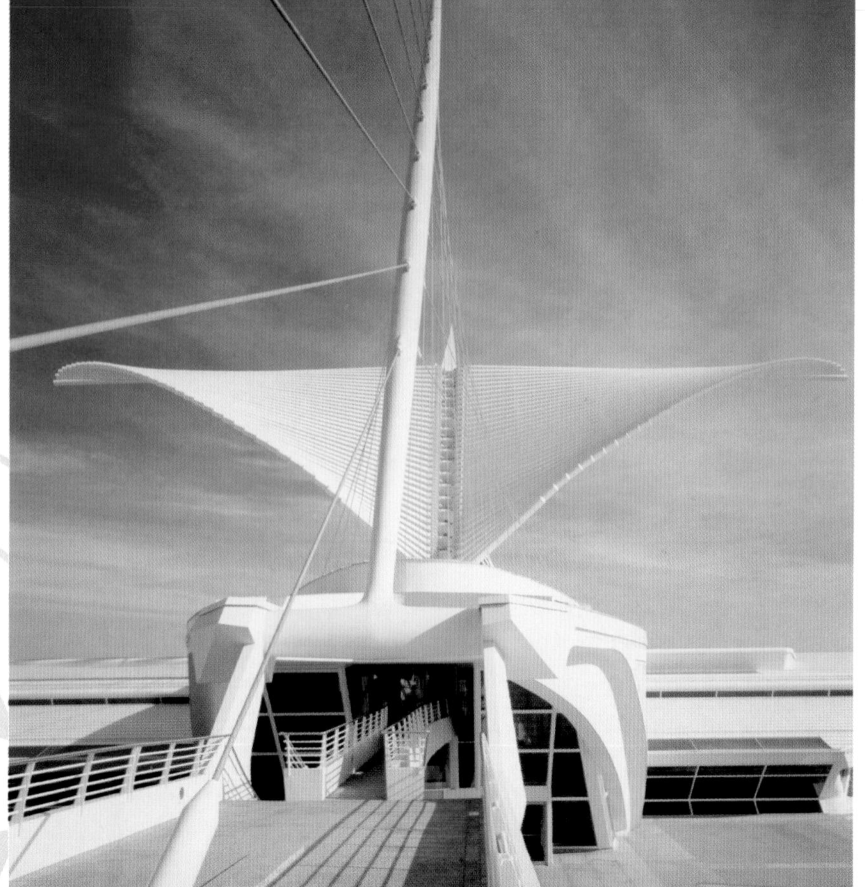

(Right) *The Quadracci Pavilion was the first building designed by Santiago Calatrava to be completed in the United States.*

# Sculpture Garden and Walker Art Center

*Inspired by a novelty item, "Spoonbridge and Cherry" has become a beloved icon. It was designed by Claes Oldenburg and Coosje van Bruggen.*

t's hard to believe, but a hotbed of contemporary art in the United States is a garden in downtown Minneapolis. The Minneapolis Sculpture Garden, along with the Walker Art Center, contains fine examples of modern art.

Especially in warm weather, a lunch hour in the garden can mean eating egg salad on rye beside "Spoonbridge and Cherry," which is a sculpture-bridge of a humongous spoon holding a gigantic cherry. Then take a leisurely stroll over to James Turrell's "Sky Pesher." The installation is approached through an underground tunnel that leads visitors to a room with a 16-square-foot opening at the top of its curved white ceiling. "Sky Pesher" uses lighting to create an illusion that's said to "bring the sky down."

Minneapolis's stellar art institutions have kept pace with the competition. Expansions at the Walker Art Center in 2005 doubled its exhibition space. Later that year, the Sculpture Garden, which was already the largest in the United States, was expanded to 15 acres. The Minneapolis Sculpture Garden now features more than 40 sculptures as well as the all-glass Cowles Conservatory and its displays of orchids, palms, and other native and exotic plants. All of it is framed by the Irene Hixon Whitney Bridge, a stunning pedestrian bridge that spans 16 lanes of highway to link the garden to Loring Park in central Minneapolis.

# Voyageurs National Park

At Voyageurs National Park, it helps to know your way around canoes and other watercraft. Voyageurs is the only national park in the United States that has no roads; if you want to visit, be ready for a voyage—the park is accessible only by waterway. Voyageurs National Park covers nearly 220,000 acres and hosts a quarter-million visitors each year.

The park extends along the southern edge of the great Canadian Shield, also called Laurentian Plateau, an enormous stretch of North America that includes most of Canada and parts of Minnesota, Wisconsin, Michigan, and northern New York. Voyageurs lies in Minnesota close to International Falls. Fifty-five miles of the park run along the U.S.–Canadian border.

The northern parts of the park are tundra; farther south are immense forests of pine, hardwoods, swamps, bogs, lakes, and beaver dams. Four lakes together make up almost 40 percent of Voyageurs: Kebetogama, Namakan, Rainy, and Sand Point.

Rock formations rise in Voyageurs near the edge of the Canadian Shield. These ancient formations of exposed Precambrian rock were scoured by glaciers, which scraped the rocks into rugged shapes. Some areas, including the park's North Woods, are now covered by a thin layer of topsoil sufficient for tree growth. The park' most treasured wooded site is the 75,000-acr Kabetogama Peninsula, a vast forest intersperse with hills, swamps, and small lakes.

Ten millennia ago, the glaciers coverin what is now Voyageurs National Park vanishec and hunters and gatherers began to arrive. Th park currently hosts more than 220 archeo logical sites.

When the Europeans came, the regio became a paradise for trappers. Fur companie

*Vibrant sunsets over the tranquil lakes and bays of Voyageurs are stunning.*

hired "voyageurs" to transport goods between remote spots. These iron men often worked 14 or more hours per day, paddled at a rate of almost a stroke per second when necessary, and portaged 26-foot canoes carrying at least 180 pounds of goods.

Today you can travel to Kabetogama Peninsula and other areas of the park by watercraft in warm weather or by skis, snowshoes, or snowmobiles in winter. How cold are the winters in Voyageurs? They're cold enough that nearby International Falls has been called the "Icebox of the Nation." In fact, automobile makers and other manufacturers test their products against the brutal cold there.

You don't have to be able to portage a canoe to enjoy Voyageurs, because this national park permits motorized watercraft. Boat tours on *The Sight-Sea-Er,* the craft that cruises Lake Kabetogama, are perfect for viewing the park's cormorants, great kingfishers, loons, blue herons, ospreys, eagles, wolves, and coyotes. You also can cruise to the historic Kettle Falls Hotel, a spot on the National Register of Historic Places that can be reached only by boat or seaplane.

***Song of the Voyageurs***

To us the river and clear water
To us, who are no longer lost in their secrets
With us the woods and mysteries
Are where the forests rise
My canoe of fine bark
Rides over the white swells...
My oar is of honest wood.

When the snow masses in the woods
I march through it up to my knees
I take my snowshoe and I drive out
The moose and the caribou
But when the shade of the evening arrives
I have a good bed of fir tree
Sleeping near the jumping flames
I sleep, I dream until the morning.

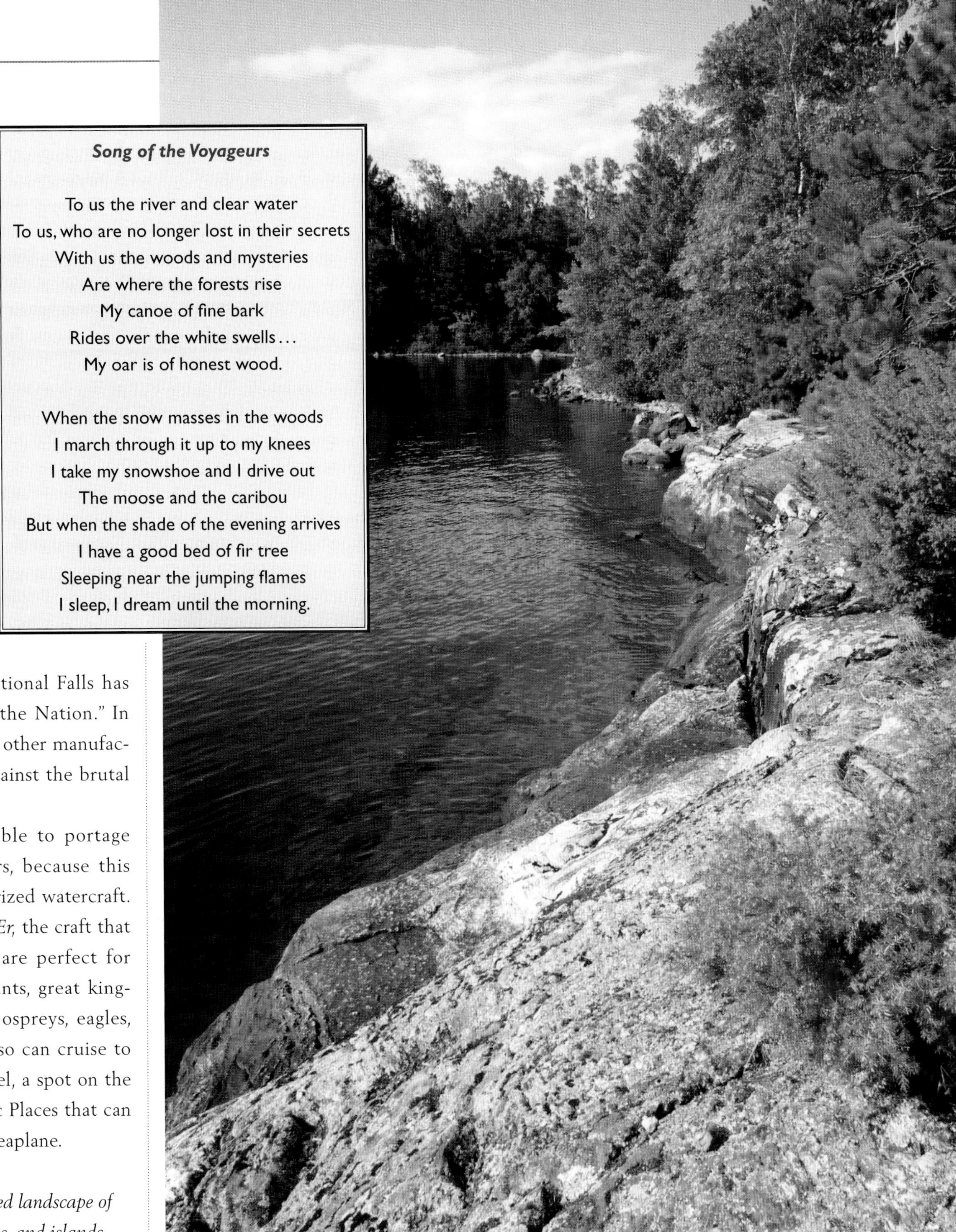

*Carved by glaciation, the rugged landscape of Voyageurs includes ponds, lakes, and islands.*

# Boundary Waters Canoe Area Wilderness

The Boundary Waters Canoe Area Wilderness is the busiest wilderness area in the United States. This may seem like a contradiction, but it isn't: More than 200,000 people visit Boundary Waters each year.

The vast size (over one million acres) of the preserve and its picturesque terrain are a draw for tourists. Some say there are more than 2,000 lakes, but motorized vehicles are only allowed on a handful of these.

The Boundary Waters lie southeast of Voyageurs National Park and stretches along almost 150 miles of the Canadian border. Canada's Quetico Provincial Park lies on the other side of the border. The region is a mass of marshes, lakes, and bogs on terrain once raked by glaciers at the edge of the Canadian Shield. Waterfalls plunge off cliffs, and you can catch a glimpse of native wildlife such as otters, deer, moose, beavers, ducks, loons, osprey, and bald eagles.

*Canoe routes weave through the preserved wilderness of the Boundary Waters.*

*Motorized vehicles are allowed on only a handful of lakes in the Boundary Waters, but canoes can be used throughout the park.*

For recreation, try canoeing, fishing, and camping. Choose from 1,200 miles of canoe routes. Fish for catfish, crappie, sunfish, smallmouth bass, largemouth bass, muskie, walleye, lake trout, panfish, or northern pike that grow to close to 50 pounds. Camping is available by permit on thousands of sites, where you can immerse yourself in this beautiful wilderness.

# St. Paul Winter Carnival

t. Paul, Minnesota, has celebrated the Winter Carnival since 1886, and the freeze-fest has volved over the decades into the cold-weather quivalent of New Orleans' Mardi Gras. The Winter Carnival hosts about 80 events and, in some ears, features a glorious ice palace. Celebratory vents include ice carving (of course!); parades; rt shows; fire-truck rides; skating; softball; winer golf; and searching for a medallion in the now, a tradition that goes back more than half century.

> On a tall hill outlined in vivid glaring green against the wintry sky stood the Ice Palace. It was three stories in the air, with battlements and embrasures and narrow icicle windows, and the innumerable electric lights inside made a gorgeous transparency of the great central hall.... "It's beautiful!" he cried excitedly. "My golly, it's beautiful, isn't it! They haven't had one here since eighty-five!"
>
> —*from* The Ice Palace *by St. Paul native F. Scott Fitzgerald*

Like Mardi Gras, the St. Paul Winter Carival has a creation myth. In this case, it is of ing Boreas, "King of the Winds," and his conict with the Fire King, Vulcanus Rex. When ulcanus triumphs, the carnival concludes.

Historically speaking, the St. Paul Winter Carnival began when a high-handed New York eporter said St. Paul was "another Siberia, nfit for human habitation." Local residents vere determined to prove him wrong—and hey did.

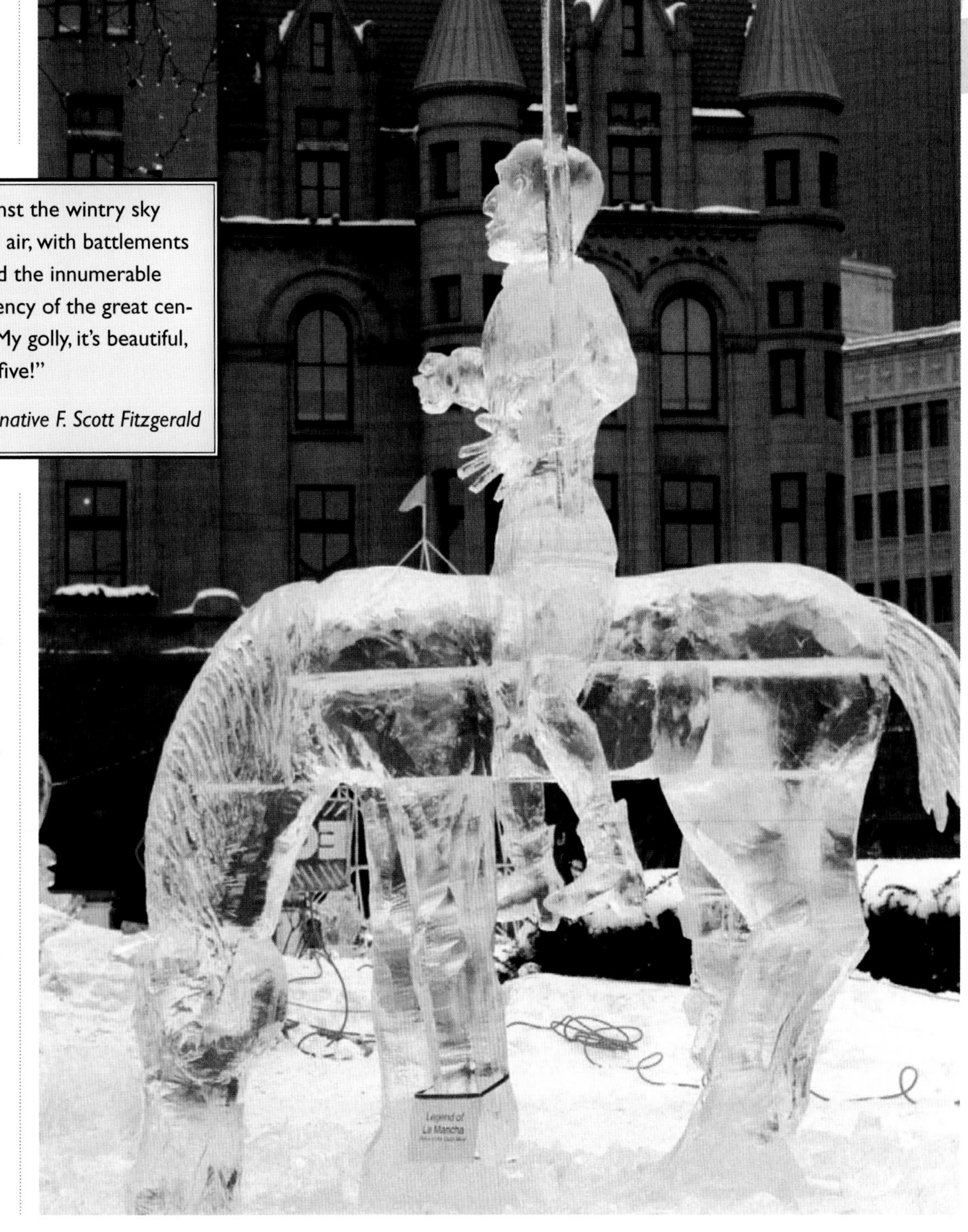

*rtists carve intricate ice sculptures each year r the Winter Carnival.*

# Amana Colonies

America has always had a strong utopian streak, whose sweetest fruit is on display in eastern Iowa's gently rolling hills where you can find the seven communities that make up the Amana Colonies.

The Amana Colonies made up a historic utopian society in Iowa's River Valley. Established shortly before the Civil War by German immigrants of the Community of True Inspiration sect, the colonies today are on the National Park Service National Register of Historic Places.

The Amana communities encompass 20,000 acres and 31 historic places. They were one of the world's longest active communal societies, lasting from 1855 to 1932. Hundreds of buildings were once part of the communities; almost 500 have survived, including the Ox Yoke Inn, the Colony Inn Restaurant, the Amana Woolen Mill, Roger's Anvil/Industrial Machine Shop Museum, the Amana Furniture Shop, and the striking Millstream Brewing Company.

Probably the best place for visitors to start, however, is the Museum of Amana History, which helps explain what the communities' religionists called "the Great Change" away from shared life. The Amana Church remains pivotal in the communities: Residents still attend services and live their lives infused by their faith.

(Above) *Blankets and fabric were produced at the Amana Woolen Mill. Most of its wool came from sheep raised in nearby East Amana.*

(Right) *Many of the Amana Colonies' original buildings have been preserved.*

# 3ridges of Madison County

Iadison County, Iowa, used to be a typical Iidwestern farm area. Less than an hour's rive south of Des Moines, the county was otable as the birthplace of John Wayne, for ie home of the 18-acre Madison County Iistorical Society building, and for its rustic overed bridges. Then Robert James Waller rote *The Bridges of Madison County*, a best-elling novel. Today, Madison County's cov-red bridges have become such a tourist draw that the county now is building reproductions of lost covered bridges.

Madison County at one time had 19 picturesque covered bridges; today just five of the original ones survive: the Cutler-Donahoe Bridge, Hogback Bridge, Holliwell Bridge, Imes Bridge, and Roseman Bridge, all listed on the National Register of Historic Places. A suspected arson fire destroyed Cedar Bridge in 2002. County officials have offered a reward for information leading to the arrest and conviction of the perpetrator. A replica Cedar Bridge was dedicated in 2004.

While Waller's book tells a romantic tale, the bridges' origins were quite practical: The Madison County Board of Supervisors ordered they be covered to preserve their large flooring timbers, which were more expensive than the lumber used to cover the bridges' sides and roofs.

*'he Holliwell Bridge is one of the five original bridges still standing in Madison County.*

# St. Louis Gateway Arch

*Sunlight reflects brilliantly off the stainless-steel-faced St. Louis Gateway Arch.*

The St. Louis Gateway Arch soars 630 feet high and spans 630 feet. This Gateway to the West has been the tallest memorial in the United States since its 1965 unveiling. The arch is actually part of the Jefferson National Expansion Memorial, dedicated to the western pioneering movement.

Architect Eero Saarinen's bold concept of an almost imperceptibly elongated catenary arch with a thinner top was the basis for the design. From afar, the arch seems to be a sculpture of thin light; up close, it's a majestic building. Even at a massive 43,000 tons, the Gateway Arch, miraculously, seems to soar.

A tram to the top of the arch yields glorious panoramas of St. Louis, the Mississippi River, and southern Illinois. At the arch's bottom, the Museum of Westward Expansion commemorates American Indians and 19th-century pioneers, including the Lewis and Clark expedition that departed from that area.

# Branson Strip

oday, most Americans know this once-small own in the Ozarks as the "Branson Strip": The ttle city improbably became one of the enter-ainment capitals of the world.

Branson, Missouri, was a quiet, humble own until the Presley family (no relation to lvis) began performing at Branson's Under-round Theatre (now called Presley's Jubilee Theatre) in 1963. Soon other music acts (country and otherwise) crowded the venues along Highway 76. A building boom followed, and the Branson Strip was born.

The town has a population of just 7,500, but it greets seven million visitors each year. Branson today packs a bundle of top-drawer attractions. Built on a country music foundation, the strip offers acts from country favorites Mel Tillis and the Gatlin Brothers to the Acrobats of China and Russian comic Yakov Smirnov; in all, there are 46 music theaters and more seats than there are on Broadway in New York.

*Developing the Branson Strip brought bright lights and theaters to this once-small town.*

# Dodge City

Wyatt Earp, Bat Masterson, Boot Hill, and Dodge City—to anyone who has ever read Western lore or watched cowboy movies, these are legendary names.

The lawless, gun-slinging reputation of this Kansas frontier town was well deserved. Beginning in the 1860s, Dodge City drew all sorts of people who traveled along the Santa Fe Trail (and later the Atchison, Topeka, and Santa Fe Railroad). Gambling and prostitution ran rampant, and the term "red light district" was coined here after the train masters who would take their red caboose lanterns out with them. With no law in town, disagreements often led to sudden death—and the need for a town cemetery. Boot Hill was born, so-named for the number of men who died in shootings with their footwear still on.

Today Dodge City celebrates its past. Re-creations of Front Street, the Long Branch Saloon, and Boot Hill Cemetery are reminder of the Old West and its colorful history (the buildings represent Dodge City in 1876). There are also tours of Fort Dodge and the Mueller-Schmidt House Museum (built in 1881, the oldest house in Dodge City on the original site).

*Actors reenact famous gunfights along Front Street in downtown Dodge City.*

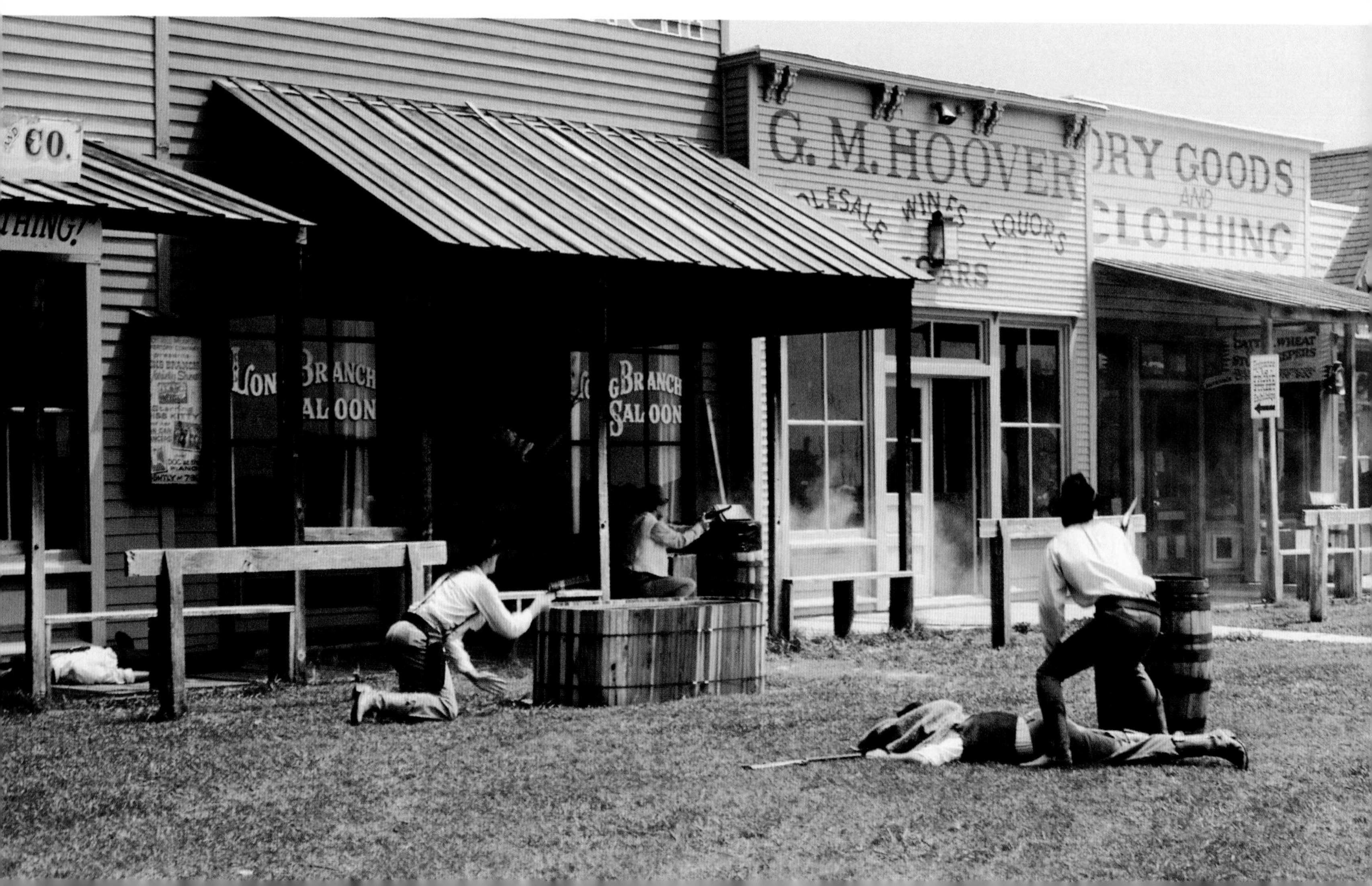

# Carhenge

Jim Reinders and his family arranged old cars, painted gray, to match the configuration of Stonehenge.

n the small town of Alliance, Nebraska, is the unusual sculpture known as Carhenge. Carhenge is a replica of Stonehenge in terms of size and orientation, but the story of its origin is a bit different.

As creator Jim Reinders explained, it was just "something to do at our family reunion." Reinders wasn't kidding: Carhenge was built during a reunion at the family farm in 1987. Reinders and 35 of his relatives grabbed their backhoes, found a forklift, and worked seven 8-hour days to position the 38 cars. Among them, classic Cadillacs, an AMC Gremlin, and a Willys pickup, were stacked in formation and painted battleship gray in accordance with Stonehenge's appearance.

People were immediately drawn to Carhenge. Despite its rather remote location (the closest freeway is 90 miles away), an estimated 40,000 to 80,000 folks visit each year.

# Chimney Rock and Scotts Bluff National Monument

Chimney Rock rises to a spire almost 325 feet above the North Platte River Valley in Nebraska. It can be seen from miles away, so it was the ideal landmark for pioneers traveling the Mormon, California, and Oregon trails. Today, Chimney Rock is a National Historic Site that still marks the place where the plains give way to the Rocky Mountains.

Modern-day visitors often travel the Oregon Trail, today known as US Highway 26, about 45 minutes from Chimney Rock to see Scotts Bluff National Monument, another important three-trail landmark. Especially after a long trip across the prairie, whether by covered wagon or station wagon, the monument is striking for its key features—Scotts Bluff and South Bluff and their dramatic cliffs.

Most of the park is native mixed-grass prairie, which has the virtue of looking as pristine and undisturbed as in the days of the pioneers. Gazing out over the landscape, you can feel a kinship with these brave travelers. The monument also boasts barren badlands between Scotts Bluff and the North Platte River, amounting to an amazing variety of landscape packed into 3,000 acres. A museum on the national monument grounds houses exhibits on the area's history.

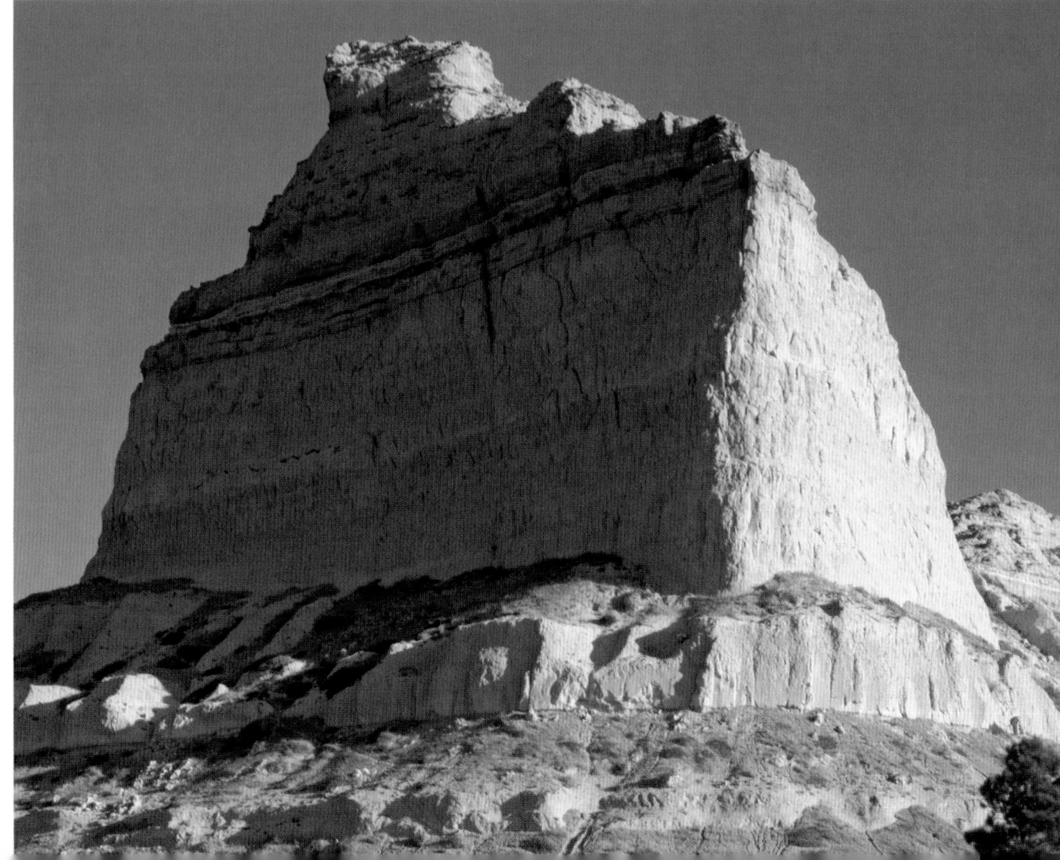

*Chimney Rock* (top) *and Scotts Bluff* (bottom) *are two distinct formations that can still be seen along the historic Oregon Trail.*

# Badlands National Park

Badlands National Park in southwestern South Dakota is 244,000 acres of buttes, pinnacles, and spires. It is the largest mixed grass prairie in the United States and resembles miles and miles of ethereal moonscape.

Strange shapes carved into soft sedimentary rock and volcanic ash dot the landscape of Badlands National Park. Because the land is so dry, wind and water cause rapid erosion (an average of one inch per year) of the sprawling rock formations. The result is a rugged terrain unlike any other in the United States.

Despite the area's forbidding name, American Indians hunted there for 11,000 years and camped in secluded valleys that had fresh water and game. More than a century ago, seven tribes of the Great Sioux Nation roamed the area. Today, visitors are likely to encounter fossil hunters—the Badlands have been a trove for paleontologists since the 1840s.

The park is about 80 miles east of Rapid City, South Dakota, and is divided into two separate sections of four units. The most visited unit is the Cedar Pass Area, near Interior, South Dakota. Try to visit the Badlands Wilderness Area Sage Creek Unit, a primitive camping area, as well.

*Rapid erosion of the plateaus of soft sediment and volcanic ash etched the Dakota Badlands.*

# Mount Rushmore

Four faces, each 60 feet high—the visages of United States Presidents George Washington, Thomas Jefferson, Theodore Roosevelt, and Abraham Lincoln—look out over South Dakota.

From Grand View Terrace, you can pose for photos and gape at the formidable scope of these massive granite busts. Chosen for their accomplishments and leadership, the four men immortalized on Mount Rushmore are Washington, the Revolutionary War hero and stoic first president; Jefferson, who penned the Declaration of Independence and negotiated the Louisiana Purchase; Roosevelt, the conservationist who set the wheels in motion for the country's national park system and ensured construction of the Panama Canal; and Lincoln, who led the country through the bloody Civil War and the abolition of slavery.

Mount Rushmore's immense scale is integral to the artist's message—sculptor Gutzon Borglum insisted that the dimensions of the monument reflect the importance of the events it commemorated.

Besides the available space, Borglum had several reasons for choosing this mountain in the Black Hills of South Dakota. He liked the granite because it was smooth, homogenous, and durable, eroding just an inch every 10,000 years. He liked the mountain because it dominated the surrounding landscape. He also liked that Mount Rushmore faced southeast, so sunlight would illuminate his masterpiece as much as possible.

Building Mount Rushmore has been one of the most monumental public art projects in U.S. history. From 1927 to 1941, Borglum led a team of 400 men and women, who would climb a 700-step staircase every workday just to get to the punch clock. Then they would spend the day jackhammering granite, setting off dynamite (the tool that shaped 90 percent of the mountain), or chiseling while strapped into a chair on the mountain's face, held aloft by a rope. The work was hard, but it was the Great Depression, and jobs were scarce.

Gutzon Borglum masterminded the operation until he died unexpectedly in March 1941. Under the direction of his son, Lincoln, the team labored for seven more months until funding ran dry. Lincoln lobbied Congress for more money to complete his father's vision—Gutzon Borglum originally had envisioned a grand "Hall of Records" carved in the canyon behind Lincoln's face—but with World War II on the horizon, federal funds were scarce.

In some ways, Mount Rushmore has remained a work-in-progress since October 1941, and, strangely enough, it wasn't officially dedicated until 1991. However, Gutzon's vision came to a fruition of sorts in 1998 when the National Park Service installed a titanium time capsule, a variation on the Hall of Records, in the canyon behind Lincoln.

There have been suggestions to add a fifth president on Mount Rushmore. A few recent calls were for Ronald Reagan's visage to be immortalized. Others have campaigned for Franklin D. Roosevelt, Dwight Eisenhower, and John F. Kennedy.

But it's extremely unlikely that a fifth face will ever grace the mountain: It would not only require an act of Congress and the president's signature, but it would also require different geology. With Gutzon Borglum's design for four presidents, there simply isn't enough fault-free granite left on the mountain for another 60-foot bust.

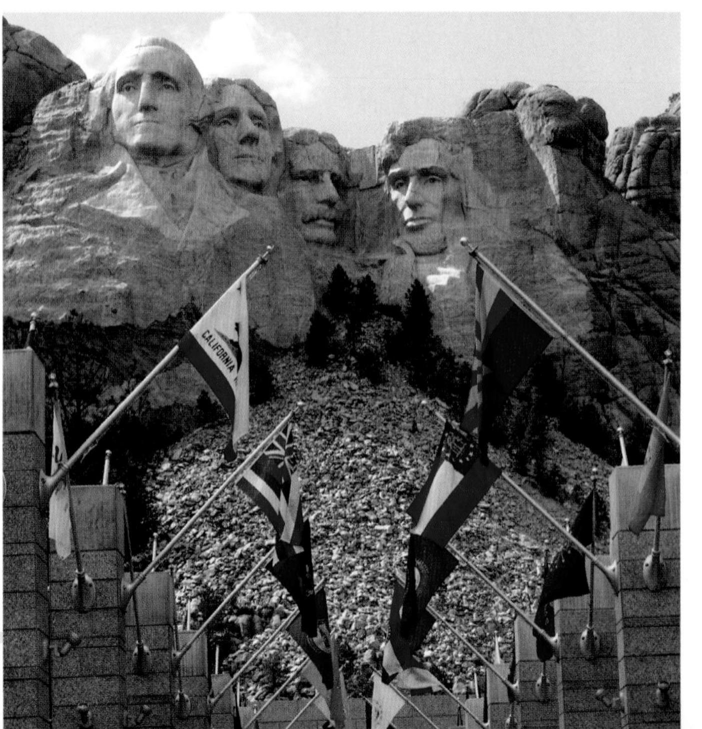


(Opposite page) *George Washington, Thomas Jefferson, Theodore Roosevelt, and Abraham Lincoln gaze over South Dakota.* (Left) *The Avenue of Flags displays the 56 flags of the states and territories of the United States.*

# Crazy Horse Memorial

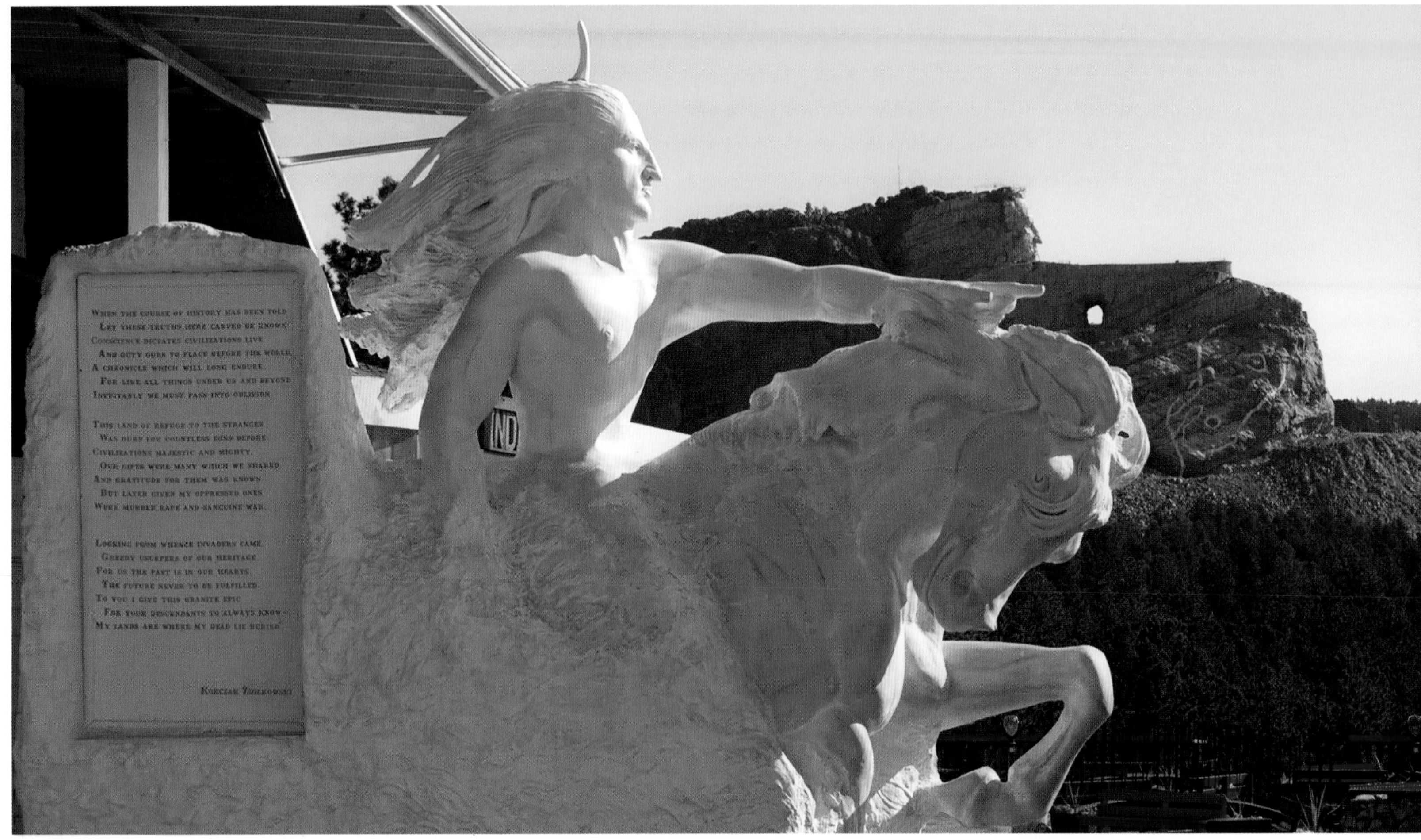


Crazy Horse was a fierce chief who fought to preserve the Lakota Indians' way of life. His magic has lasted to the present day. For proof, go see the magnificent Crazy Horse Memorial near Rapid City, South Dakota.

Both the Crazy Horse Memorial's story and its sheer size are amazing. The memorial's completed face of Crazy Horse—87 feet, 6 inches high—is taller than the entire Mount Rushmore. When the statue is completed, it will be larger than the Sphinx in Egypt and taller than the Washington Monument. Its outstretched arm will be longer than three football fields.

The memorial's story began in 1939. A group of Lakota Sioux chiefs, insulted by Mount Rushmore, asked sculptor Koczak Ziolkowski to create Crazy Horse. The artist studied Crazy Horse for years and began the mammoth project in 1946, first sculpting a marble Crazy Horse, scaled 1-to-300 to the final product.

*Only the face of the colossal memorial to Crazy Horse* (background), *modeled after Ziolkowski's sculpture* (foreground), *has been completed.*

Ziolkowski died in 1982, but his family has carried on his vision, finishing Crazy Horse's face in 1998. The sculpture has been privately financed and will be completed . . . someday.

Because Crazy Horse Memorial is incomplete, some visitors don't grasp its full impact, but most are properly awed.

# Sturgis

or 51 weeks of the year, Sturgis, South akota, is a sleepy town of about 6,000. But r one week in August, it hosts one of the ggest and best parties on the North Ameri- n continent.

The Sturgis motorcycle legacy began 1936 when local merchant J. Clarence 'appy" Hoel purchased a franchise from e Indian Motorcycle Company. His shop

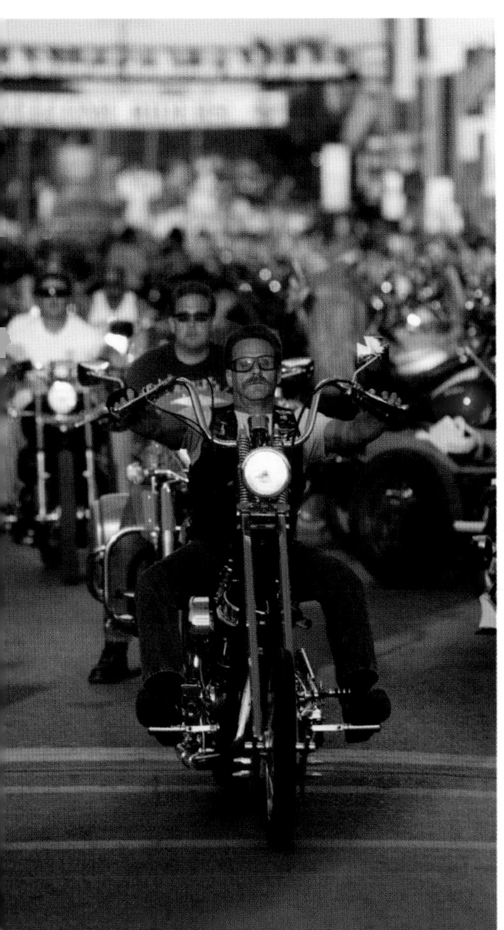

lotorcyclists from across the country gather for e Sturgis Rally each August.

*Bikers line up their motorcycles in downtown Sturgis.*

became the leading Indian dealership (per capita) in the nation. The first rally was launched in 1938. The event has always involved touring cycling shows, races and competitions, and a couple of beers afterward. The rally attracts enthusiasts from hard-core bikers to doctors, lawyers, soldiers, police officers, and philanthropists, all dedicated to having a good time. The rally customarily begins with an enormous pancake breakfast and goes on to motorcycle demos, cycle exhibits, vendors selling motorcycle-theme art, parades, concerts, mobile malls, light shows, and a lot of happy local Sturgis merchants.

**Hog Heaven**

"A sea of humanity and chrome-laden hogs greeted us at the Mecca of Motorcycling—the Sturgis Motorcycle Rally—in the Black Hills of South Dakota. Nowhere in America can you find such a collection of seasoned riders, rank amateurs, and wonderful women..."

—*attendee, 2005 Sturgis Motorcycle Rally*

# Fort Abraham Lincoln and Fort Mandan

Fort Abraham Lincoln's Web site proclaims: "Welcome to 1875, enjoy your visit." And a trip to this picturesque frontier fort and national historic park on the upper Missouri River will indeed take you back to another century, to the time when this fort was the largest and most important on the Northern Plains.

Visitors are invited into the home of General George A. Custer, appointed exactly as it was in 1875 before he rode off to meet his destiny at Little Bighorn, and into the barracks of the 7th Cavalry (decorated with the biographies of the men of Company I).

The fort also contains the remains of the Mandan Indian settlement On-a-Slant Village, discovered by explorers Lewis and Clark in 1804. The settlement was abandoned and collapsing by the time Lewis and Clark found it, so they canoed north to find shelter for the winter. They encountered a Mandan trading town. Today, that location is Fort Mandan National Historic Park—it's a 70-minute drive from Fort Lincoln. When visiting Fort Mandan, see the fascinating Lewis and Clark Interpretive Center. And don't forget Knife River Indian Villages National Historic Site and Fort Union Trading Post National Historic Site; both are located nearby.

*The Fort McKeen Blockhouse once protected the infantry at Fort Abraham Lincoln* (top). *Visitors can learn about Lewis and Clark's expeditions at the replica of Fort Mandan* (bottom).

# Theodore Roosevelt National Park

*This rugged landscape inspired Theodore Roosevelt's conservationist drive.*

Part of the expansive North Dakota badlands, Theodore Roosevelt National Park commemorates the conservation policies of the 26th U.S. President. The park covers more than 70,000 acres, of which 30,000 are wilderness.

The park is divided into three units: The South Unit (the most-visited area), Elkhorn Ranch (Theodore Roosevelt's ranch), and the North Unit (70 miles north of the South Unit near the headwaters of the Little Missouri River). Roosevelt first visited the badlands in 1883 to hunt buffalo and returned there over the next few years. While there, he grew alarmed at the overhunting of the buffalo and destruction of their habitat due to farming and ranching. This fueled his desire to enter politics, and he became known as a conservationist. While in office, he established 150 national forests, 51 wildlife refuges, 18 national monuments, and 5 national parks.

If you hike or ride horseback through the park today, you can spend days out of sight of civilization. Take a leisurely drive and stop at the overlooks to view the ragged landscape or tour the nearby restored cowtown of Medora. Or, hike the half-mile Wind Canyon Trail to see a remarkable view of the strangely beautiful badlands and the Little Missouri River.

# North Dakota State Capitol

The North Dakota State Capitol, a 19-story building known as "The Skyscraper on the Prairie," towers over Bismark. In this city of 50,000, the skyscraper is startling, especially in spring when the front lawn of the building is decorated with some 5,000 petunias that spell out "North Dakota." While the capitol stands only 241 feet, 8 inches tall, in winter, its upper stories often disappear in low-hanging clouds.

Like the Empire State and Chrysler Buildings, North Dakota's capitol is an Art Deco gem with an interesting story. And like the two Manhattan skyscrapers, it was completed in 1934 during the Great Depression. But to save money, the builders simplified the building's exterior, canceling plans to etch stylized decorations on the steel panels and cornice stones. The result was exemplary of the Art Deco International Style—a stripped-down offshoot of the Bauhaus School.

The capitol's grounds have become the site for many memorials and museums in the years since it was built. Enjoy the North Dakota State Heritage Center Museum and Fountain Garden, the capitol's Judicial Wing, the Pioneer Family Statue, the Statue of Sakajawea, and the North Dakota Hall of Fame. Guided tours of the building, including a visit to the 18th-floor observation deck, are also available. If weather permits, take a stroll along the capitol complex's lovely 132 acres.

*This Art Deco skyscraper replaced the original state capitol, which burned down in 1930.*

# nternational Peace Garden

panning the invisible line where North Dakota ecomes Manitoba is the 2,339-acre Interational Peace Garden. Its crux is the longanding goodwill between the United States nd Canada. Officials from both countries edicated the garden in 1932 after selecting n idyllic spot, cradled in the gentle green rinkles of the Turtle Mountains between a sea of wheat to the south and woodland to the north. The garden consists of more than 150,000 flowers, planted annually and shaped into a dramatically beautiful landscape among trees and fountains. Most displays change from year to year, but the traditional arrangements in the shape of the Canadian and United States flags are a permanent feature.

The monuments to peace include girders from the World Trade Center and seven "Peace Poles"—gifts from Japan inscribed with "May Peace Prevail" in 28 languages. At the garden's center, there are two 120-foot towers—one on each side of the border—rising above a chapel whose limestone walls are engraved with words of peace.

wo towers rise above the lush landscape, marking the international border.

*Blossoming flowers and fountains bring the garden to life each spring.*

# San Antonio: The Alamo and Riverwalk

Texas's most visited site, the Alamo, is more modest than its reputation might suggest. But the architecture of this historic mission church now surrounded by modern downtown San Antonio is hard to forget. Violent events nearly two centuries ago made the site legendary. Now, about three million visitors come annually to pay their respects to those who died here.

Spanish missionaries established the Mission San Antonio de Valero in the vicinity of the Alamo in 1718 and worked to convert the local people to Catholicism. They began building the Alamo in 1724 after a hurricane destroyed the original site. The Spanish secularized the mission in 1793. However, it was abandoned before the legendary battle of 1836 broke out.

Today, the missionaries' onetime living quarters, the Long Barrack, have been turned into a museum that recounts Texas's turbulent past, emphasizing the memorable two-week Battle of the Alamo. Visitors can watch a film on the Alamo here. The famed church displays artifacts from the battle, as well. Also onsite are the serene Alamo Gardens, which provide a good spot to rest and reflect.

The church and the Long Barrack are the only two structures from 1836 that are still standing. But people hungry for more Alamo history need only look beyond today's modern urban backdrop: Much of the fighting took place in Alamo Plaza, which still approximates the boundaries once marked by the old fort's walls. Visitors can also see the original founda tion stones of the Low Barrack, which was th fort entrance before serving as Jim Bowie's li ing quarters, near the stairway leading down the Riverwalk to the west.

The popular Riverwalk, also known as Pase del Rio, makes a vibrant circle around dow town San Antonio. Named b Spanish missionaries in the la 17th century, the San Antoni River has a long, rich histor After the HemisFair expositic in San Antonio in 1968, con mercial development along th Riverwalk boomed, and hote galleries, restaurants, café and boutiques now crowd th river's banks. The river bustl with activity; there are holida boat parades, and river taxis a available every day of the wee Visitors can also take narrate tours along the river, which la about 35 to 40 minutes and a available daily. Nearby them parks, museums, theaters, an nightlife and entertainme options are a few of the oth gems San Antonio has to offer

(Opposite page) *Rivercenter Mall is a hub for shops and restaurants on the Riverwalk.*

## Quick Fact

***"Remember the Alamo!"***

The Alamo is an American and Texan icon, an emblem of a series of events that's often misinterpreted, and the subject of numerous books and movies. In March 1836, General Antonio López de Santa Anna's Mexican troops crushed the resistance led by Jim Bowie, Davy Crockett, and William Travis, killing all 189 Texas troops and volunteers who had fought to defend the Alamo. About 600 Mexican soldiers were killed or wounded in the battle.

"Remember the Alamo!" became an instant rallying cry for all of Texas. Six weeks later, General Sam Houston's army defeated Santa Anna at the Battle of San Jacinto, ending the Mexican rule in what is now the Lone Star State. The Republic of Texas was born, beginning another chapter in Texas's stormy history. This era of sovereignty, however, proved short-lived. It ended less than a decade later: In 1845, Texas became the 28th state, though its disputed southern border led in part to the Mexican War one year later.

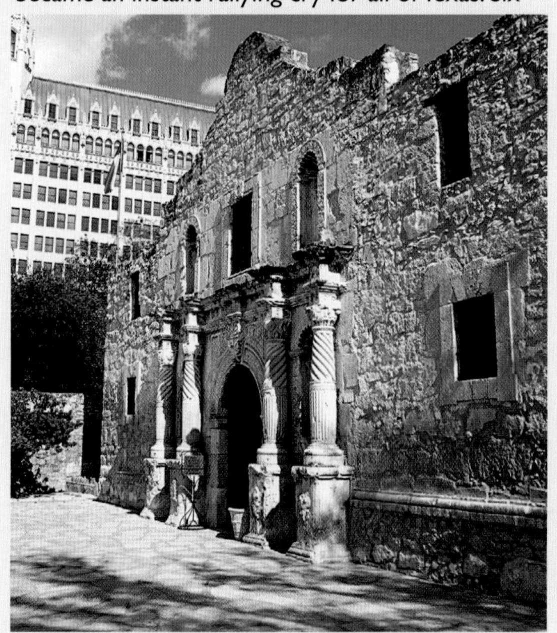

*The Alamo remains an icon and reminder of Texas's struggle for independence.*

Rio Taxi
RIVER SHUTTLE

# Big Bend National Park

Nicknamed "the last American frontier," Big Bend National Park is in the middle of nowhere—and that's a good thing.

The park is named for the turn of the Rio Grande along the park's southern boundary. Surrounded by beautiful, gnarled desert, the heart of Big Bend is the Chisos Mountain Range. Some peaks in the Chisos soar to nearly 8,000 feet in elevation. Cloaked in green forest, the lush mountains are a sharp contrast to the arid surroundings.

While the Chisos are the prime destination for Big Bend's visitors, they're just the tip of the iceberg, so to speak. The Rio Grande has carved three of the continent's most striking canyons—Boquillas, Mariscal, and Santa Elena—with elevations as low as 1,800 fee along the river. Rafters are drawn to travel th river, and hikers climb trails that wind throug the mountains, with the desert acting as a gate way to the north.

Despite the harsh topography, there is a abundance of wildlife in Big Bend. Snake scorpions, birds, bats, tarantulas, deer, an javelinas, the wild pigs of the Southwest, al thrive here.

*The chasms chiseled by the Rio Grande draw adventurous rafters to explore Big Bend National Park.*

# Presidio County Courthouse

*The Presidio County Courthouse regained its original splendor after a 2001 restoration. The gray dome is topped with a statue of Lady Justice.*

Texas is home to some of the United States' most majestic courthouses, and the Presidio County Courthouse in the small west Texas town of Marfa is the state's crown jewel. The 1887 Victorian courthouse, clad in pink stucco and capped with an ornate gray dome, dominates the horizon for miles and is a work of art inside and out. The observation deck on the fifth floor is open to the public and offers a sublime view of Marfa, which is known for its cattle, minimalist art, and starring role as the setting for the classic film *Giant*.

Legend has it that in the 1890s a convicted outlaw managed to shake free of his captors and fire off a shot at Lady Justice, perched atop the courthouse's dome. His bullet took out the scales that were in the statue's hands as he cried, "There is no justice in this country!"

The Presidio County Courthouse was thoroughly restored in 2001. The price tag for the job: $2.5 million, or about 40 times the original budget of $60,000 to build it. The only thing that wasn't refurbished was Lady Justice's still-missing set of scales.

# Austin

*The Congress Avenue Bridge spans the Colorado River in downtown Austin.*

Austin stands out from most Texan metropolises. With more than 650,000 people, this is no small town (though it's certainly much smaller than Dallas and Houston). Austin has a Bohemian aura, due in part to the University of Texas campus. And politics prevail here: Austin is Texas's capital city, and its capitol is the largest in the country.

The aroma of barbecue and Tex-Mex cuisine hangs in the air, and the nightclub-lined Sixth Street is one of the best spots for live music in the entire world. Then there are the 1.5 million Mexican free-tailed bats that hang from the downtown Congress Avenue Bridge which spans the Colorado River. Crowd gather from March through November to watch them emerge en masse at sunset.

It's hard to capture the city's laid-back vibe in words. Maybe the city's unofficial slogan seen on T-shirts and Volkswagen bumpers all over town, says it best: "Keep Austin Weird."

# Texas Gulf Coast

The Texas Gulf Coast is in many ways the United States' forgotten coast, lacking the hype of the East and West coasts. However, its numerous assets run the gamut from remote islands to charming Victorian ports.

Galveston Island was once the state's commercial center, but after it was devastated by a massive hurricane in 1900, many businesses moved to Houston. While the population boomed inland, Galveston recovered and evolved into a resort area. The Strand National Historic Landmark District lies at the cultural center of Galveston. Once known as the "Wall Street of the Southwest," it is now chock-full of antique stores, restaurants, and art galleries, and its buildings feature abundantly delightful architecture.

(Above) *The USS* Lexington, *a World War II Essex Class aircraft carrier, was decommissioned in 1991 and converted to a naval aviation museum in Corpus Christi.*

To the south, Corpus Christi hosts beautiful beaches and the Texas State Aquarium. About 43 miles to the southeast, North Padre Island, designated a national seashore in 1962, is said to be the longest remaining stretch of undeveloped barrier island on the planet. Subtropical South Padre Island is more developed and has been called the "Tip of Texas." It is host to many resorts, a thriving sport-fishing industry, and idyllic beaches.

(Above left) *Warm water from the Gulf of Mexico laps at the shores of South Padre Island.* (Below left) *Sunsets on the harbors of the Texas Gulf Coast streak the sky with violet.*

# Guadalupe Mountains National Park

At the tip of the Trans-Pecos region (the far west Texas panhandle bordered to the north by New Mexico, the south by the Rio Grande, and the east by the Pecos River) and just southwest of New Mexico's Carlsbad Caverns, the Guadalupe Mountains loom over the surroundings like mighty centurians. The rocky cliffs that define the park developed long ago when today's desert was an ancient ocean. The now lofty mountains were once a reef. As the water receded, it left fossil records of Cambrian sea life on today's craggy peaks.

The modern park contains both Guadalupe Peak, which at 8,749 feet above sea level is the highest point in Texas, and McKittrick Canyon, believed by many to be the prettiest spot in the state. The former is a backpacker's dream: The summit offers sublime views of the surrounding desert. The latter is a vestige of the last ice age that explodes with color in the fall.

At first glance, the desert surrounding the Guadalupe Mountains appears dry and barren. However, the park supports several different ecosystems—from the harsh Chihuahuan desert to streamside woodlands, rock canyons and mountaintop pine forests. Coyotes, rattlesnakes, mule deer, black bears, and elk can al[so] be spotted within the park's limits.

It's easy to get away from it all here—Guadalupe Mountains is one of the least visited national parks.

*Rising to 8,085 feet above sea level, the impressive El Capitán soars over the rugged landscape of Guadalupe Mountains National Park.*

# Big Thicket National Preserve

East Texas's Big Thicket National Preserve is 97,000 acres of biological crossroads. This is where the sultry swamps of the South, the verdant forests of the East, and the seemingly endless savannah of the Great Plains meet and mingle. Meadows are scarce, as flora thrives in the rich soil and wet climate.

The unique environment translates into a habitat for all sorts of wildlife. In Big Thicket's diverse biosphere, desert roadrunners live alongside swamp critters such as alligators and frogs, not to mention deer, mountain lions, and 300 species of nesting and migratory birds. This is the only place on the planet where many of these species live side by side. The presence of all these animals in the same low-land forest have earned Big Thicket the nick-name "the American Ark."

*Big Thicket provides a unique habitat of rich wetlands and thick forests that harbors diverse plant life.*

The range of plant life in Big Thicket is even broader: Cacti grow alongside hickory, cypress, and pine trees. And the swampland allows 20 types of orchids and four species of insect-eating plants to thrive, as well.

# Space Center Houston

As the official visitor center for NASA's Johnson Space Center, Space Center Houston gives visitors an in-depth look at the United States' space program. The visitor center is a museum of space science and NASA history, with exhibits including the Kids Space Place and the Astronaut and Starship galleries. The giant-screen theater shows films on space exploration, and interactive simulators allow lay people to get a feel for space travel.

The fascinating behind-the-scenes tram tour is the best way to observe the nuts and bolts of NASA. The tram makes stops at hangars throughout the operational Johnson Space Center, historic Johnson Mission Control, and the International Space Station Assembly Building. The tram tour has been known to stop at the facilities where astronauts train—allowing visitors to peek at how they prepare for a space flight.

(Right) *Pete Conrad's spacesuit from the Apollo 12 mission to the moon is part of the Astronaut Gallery at Space Center Houston.* (Inset above) *Visitors can explore the outdoor Rocket Park, a collection of rockets from NASA's early days.*

# Houston Livestock Show and Rodeo

First held in 1932, the Houston Livestock Show and Rodeo takes over most of the city each year in February and March—it's the largest livestock show and rodeo in the world.

It's also home of the World Championship Bar-B-Que Contest, where more than 300 chefs test their mettle—and brisket—against one another. The cooking competition is held three days before the rodeo.

Beyond the rodeo, the show, and the savory barbecue, music concerts take center stage after nightfall. Elvis Presley performed there in 1970 and 1974, and Alicia Keys sang to a record crowd in 2005.

This event keeps getting bigger and better. In 2006, with attendance nudging two million, it was the most-profitable show of its kind in history. Competitions for 4-H and FFA expanded; attendees could witness calves being born at the Barnyard Babies Birthing Center; and the "old-fashion" Ferris wheel and mechanical bulls still got hearts pumping.

*The rodeo showcases seven events: bareback bronc riding* (inset above), *barrel racing, bull riding* (right), *saddle bronc riding, steer wrestling, team roping, and tie-down roping.*

# Lake Amistad

Lake Amistad is an oasis in the Texas badlands. This confluence of the Rio Grande, Devils, and Pecos rivers on the United States–Mexico border has been alive with human activity for thousands of years. The limestone canyons of the Lower Pecos region have been trafficked by people for more than 10,000 years. In their travels, these people left behind one of the world's most spectacular collections of rock art. The artifacts are scattered throughout nearly 250 known sites that include some of North America's largest multihued rock paintings. In 1969, the rivers were dammed here, creating Lake Amistad. The 67,000-acre reservoir extends up the Rio Grande for 74 miles, Devils River for 24 miles, and Pecos for 14 miles.

(Right) *The Pecos Bridge spans the Pecos River near where it feeds into Lake Amistad.*

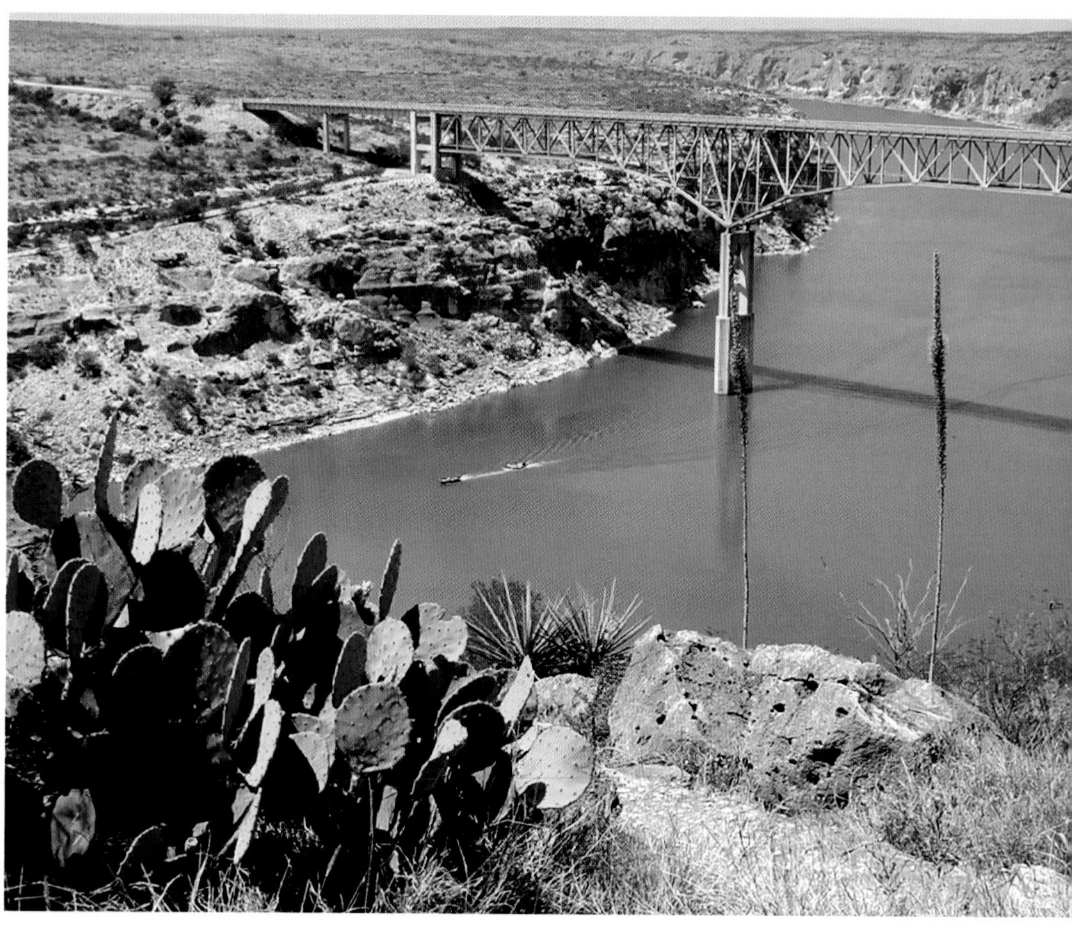

The shoreline wraps around 850 miles, and many people are enticed by the striking blue water, which is extraordinarily clear due to the lack of loose soil. Visitors can traverse the lake on watercraft of all kinds. Many people enjoy fishing for behemoth catfish and bass, swimming, and scuba diving.

Atop the six-mile Amistad Dam is a bridge that connects the United States to Mexico. Its center is marked by a pair of eagle statues, one on each side of the official border.

(Left) *An overlook reveals the dazzling Pecos River below.*

# National Cowboy & Western Heritage Museum

When the founders of the National Cowboy & Western Heritage Museum put their heads together back in 1955, they envisioned creating a tribute to cowboys and people living on the frontier. Today the museum's mission statement, adopted in 1997, is "to preserve and interpret the heritage of the American West for the enrichment of the public."

It took a decade to find a site, construct the building, and amass a collection befitting the museum's mission. In 1965, the facility, located on top of Persimmon Hill in Oklahoma City, opened its doors. By 2005, the museum had evolved into a world-class, 200,000-square-foot complex showcasing one of the United States' top collections of Western art, with works by such legends of the genre as Charles Russell and Albert Bierstadt. "Canyon Princess" is one of the famous sculptures on display at the museum. The 16,000-pound white marble cougar by sculptor Gerald Balciar guards the entrance to the Gaylord Exhibition Wing.

In addition to the incomparable art, the museum has also fulfilled its mission with a re-created early-1900s cattle town; a research center; and galleries dedicated to firearms, Western performers, cowboys, and rodeos.

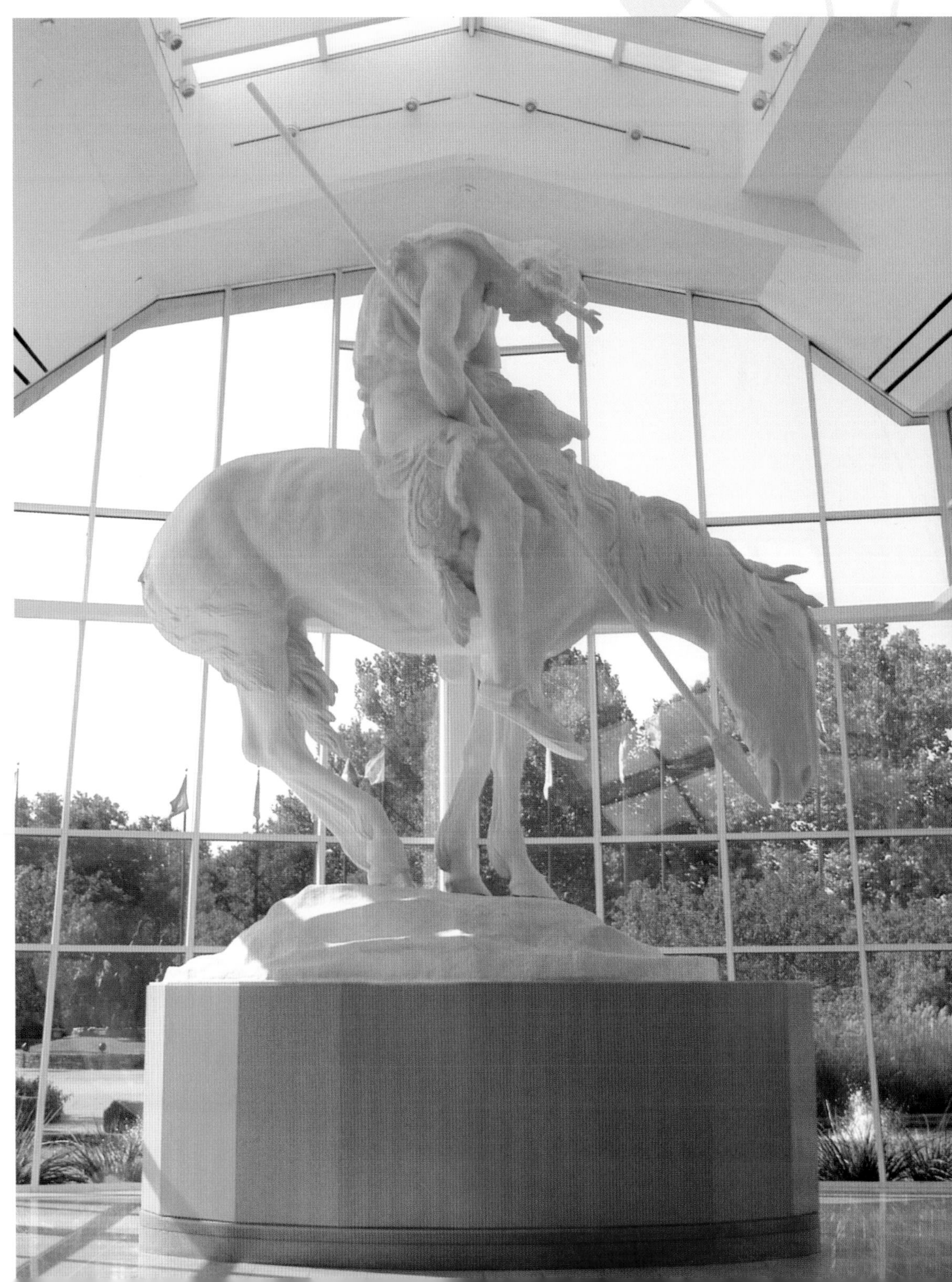

*The statue titled "The End of the Trail" was put on display at the museum in 1994. It was created in 1915 and stood outside in Visalia, California's Mooney Grove Park, for 50 years before the museum acquired it.*

# Woody Guthrie Folk Festival

Bob Dylan's self-described "last hero," Woody Guthrie, is an American icon, not only as a musician but also as a champion of the working class.

While Guthrie's most recognizable musical legacy is probably "This Land Is Your Land," he built a national following with protest songs that focused on class inequality. He became known as a folk musician during the 1930s in California, and his popularity broadened in 1940 when he adopted New York City as his new home. After touring, recording albums, and writing his autobiography in the early '40s, Guthrie's health began to deteriorate due to Huntington's Chorea. He was institutionalized in 1954 and was in and out of hospital treatment centers until his 1967 passing at the age of 55.

Woody's legacy is celebrated the week of his birthday, July 14, in his hometown of Okemah, Oklahoma. The five-day festival is marked by performances by dozens of top-notch folk musicians (regional favorites and nationally recognized touring musicians), a songwriting contest, and a deep reverence for the late, great Woody Guthrie.

*Arlo* (left) *and Abe* (right) *Guthrie, son and grandson of folk legend Woody Guthrie, performed at the 2004 festival.*

# Oklahoma City National Memorial

At this peaceful plaza in the quiet downtown of Oklahoma City, the east gate is inscribed with the time 9:01, the west gate 9:03. The first time represents the moment innocence was lost; the second one the time healing began. On the morning of April 19, 1995, a terrorist's bomb took the lives of 168 people at the Alfred P. Murrah Federal Building in downtown Oklahoma City.

The stark gates frame 168 forever-empty chairs, representing the lives lost that tragic morning. The chairs surround a single American elm, the Survivor Tree. The site is a stirring, visceral reminder of the damage done by violence and the resilience of the human spirit.

A visit here evokes the spirit of hope in America that can rise from tragedy. Across the country, people supported each other to face the coming days with optimism. The memorial in Oklahoma City ensures that those who suffered here will never be forgotten.

*The Memorial Mission Statement guided the memorial's meaning, design, and development.*

*The "Gates of Time" at the memorial are inscribed with the times immediately before and after the bombing.*

*Designers Hans and Torrey Butzer created the concept for the memorial chairs honoring the 168 people who were killed.*

# Roswell

On July 4, 1947, many residents of the sleepy agricultural town of Roswell, New Mexico, reported seeing an unidentified flying object streaking across the night sky. Other locals reported a loud explosion.

The next week, the local newspaper, the *Roswell Daily Record*, reported that the authorities at Roswell Army Air Field had found the remains of a flying saucer that crash-landed in the vicinity. The story was based on the only military or federal disclosure of a possible UFO in history. The facts, however, quickly shifted: Officials recanted the initial account within days and said it was a weather-balloon experiment gone awry.

Nevertheless, the events of July 4, 1947, have been hotly debated ever since, with scads of conspiracy theorists and skeptics dissecting the facts and eyewitness accounts. Conspiracy buffs have cried that this was a government cover-up, alleging that the spacecraft and the bodies of its extraterrestrial passengers were taken to Area 51 in Nevada for top-secret research and experimentation. The skeptics, on the other hand, say the whole thing is hooey and that the UFO in question was indeed a weather balloon. Visitors flock to Roswell's International UFO Museum and Research Center to judge for themselves.

(Above) *The Roswell Museum features New Mexico art and provides studio classes.*

(Right) *The International UFO Museum and Research Center at Roswell is dedicated to collecting and preserving materials and information relevant to the 1947 Roswell incident and other unexplained phenomena.*

# New Mexico Missions

In 1598, Spanish conquistador Don Juan de Oñate crossed the Rio Grande near the city limits of modern-day El Paso, Texas. De Oñate led his party north past Franciscan missionaries along the Rio Grande's banks to its intersection with the Chama River. Here he established the San Gabriel Mission, New Mexico's second Spanish capital, in 1600—a full seven years before the English settled in Jamestown, Virginia.

This first Spanish mission in modern-day New Mexico set the stage for many more to come. Many of the state's 17th-century churches are still standing, and active, to this day. In 1610, the Spanish capital moved to Santa Fe, where San Miguel Mission, now considered the oldest operational church in the United States, was established. Another nicely preserved church from this early era is the Mission of San José at Laguna Pueblo (1699), 45 miles west of Albuquerque. About 25 miles to the southwest is the Mission of San Esteban del Rey at Acoma Pueblo, perched majestically on a 367-foot sandstone mesa since 1626. To the southeast are the ruins of four more 17th-century missions that were abandoned before 1700 and now comprise Salinas Pueblo Missions National Monument.

## Quick Fact

### *Acoma Pueblo*

Nicknamed "Sky City" for its lofty locale atop a sandstone mesa that rises 367 feet above the surrounding desert, Acoma Pueblo is the oldest continuously inhabited city in the United States. It was established prior to 900 A.D.

The 70-acre site was chosen because of its defensible location. Regardless, Sky City was battered during the Spanish colonial period in the 1500s. In fact, Acoma Pueblo was nearly destroyed in 1598 when Don Juan de Oñate led a group of 70 men up the sheer sandstone and took vengeance on the Acomans for an earlier quarrel.

The Spanish took control of the Pueblo and organized mass Catholic conversions and the construction of the Mission of San Esteban del Rey between 1629 and 1640. Fewer than 50 Acomans live year-round in the pueblo today; about 3,000 more live in nearby villages.

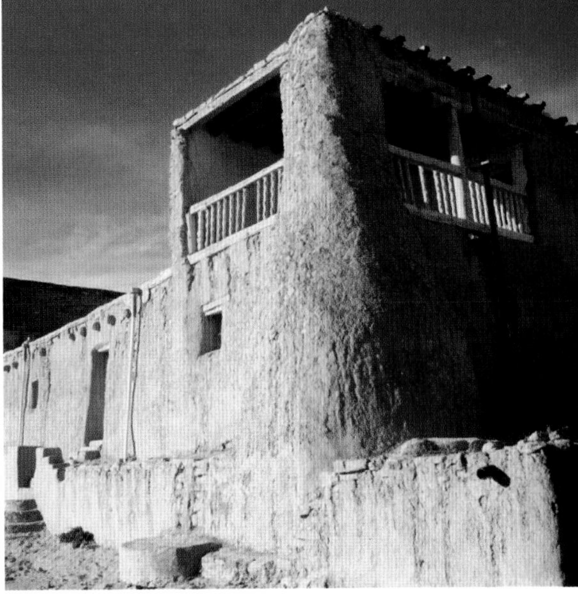

(Above) *Builders carried the stones and beams up the 367-foot mesa to construct San Esteban del Rey (side view shown here).*

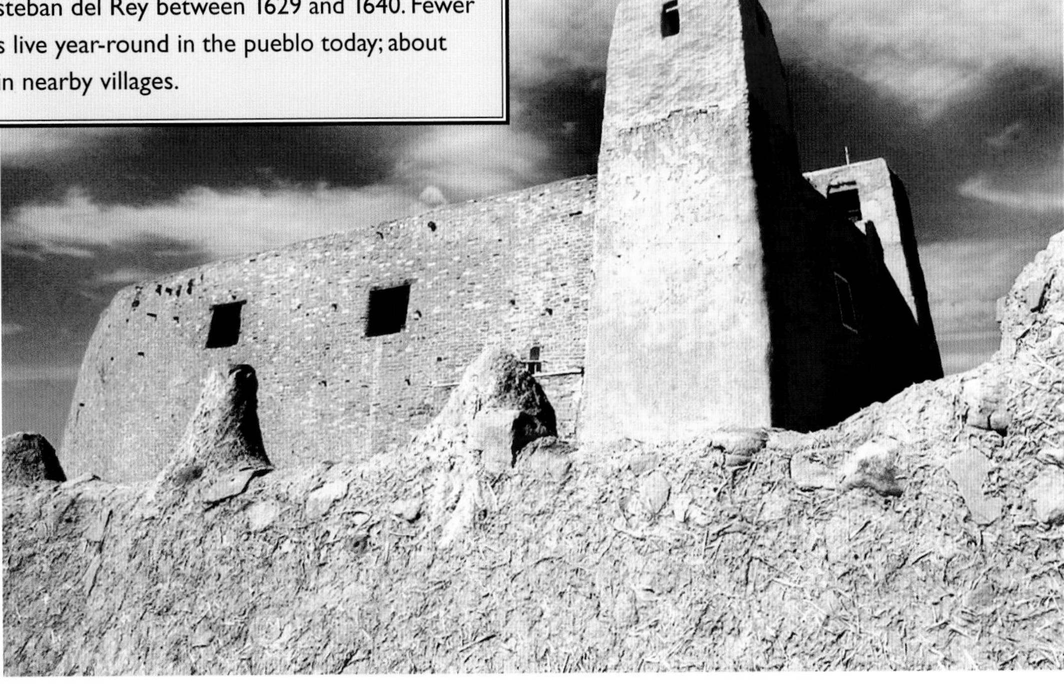

(Right) *San Esteban del Rey was the mission built from 1629 to 1640 at Acoma Pueblo.*

# Santa Fe Plaza

The Santa Fe Plaza has been a bustling outdoor market since the early 1600s. This bazaar featuring all things Southwestern is an amazing place where history, chic, and kitsch comfortably coexist.

When the Spanish came to Santa Fe in 1607, they adopted the native Pueblo's concept of building a central plaza surrounded by walls that could be defended easily. But what was designed for defense was also a good fit for commerce. Intercultural trading began soon after construction started. Because the southeast corner of the plaza was the official endpoint of the heavily traveled Santa Fe Trail (a conduit to and from the Old World), it soon became a thriving market. The original Santa Fe Plaza was more than twice its current size.

Dominating the north side of the Santa Fe Plaza is the Palace of the Governors, the oldest government building in the United States. Merchants display their wares in front of the hotels, shops, and restaurants now occupying the surrounding structures. The central area is open, and what once was used for town meetings and livestock grazing is now ideal for people-watching. Today the architecture of the plaza's buildings represents its diverse history as a crossroads of Pueblo and Spanish culture.

*The marble obelisk in the central plaza has been a source of controversy: It commemorates the Confederate occupation of the city in 1862 and the city's defenses against American Indians.*

# Taos

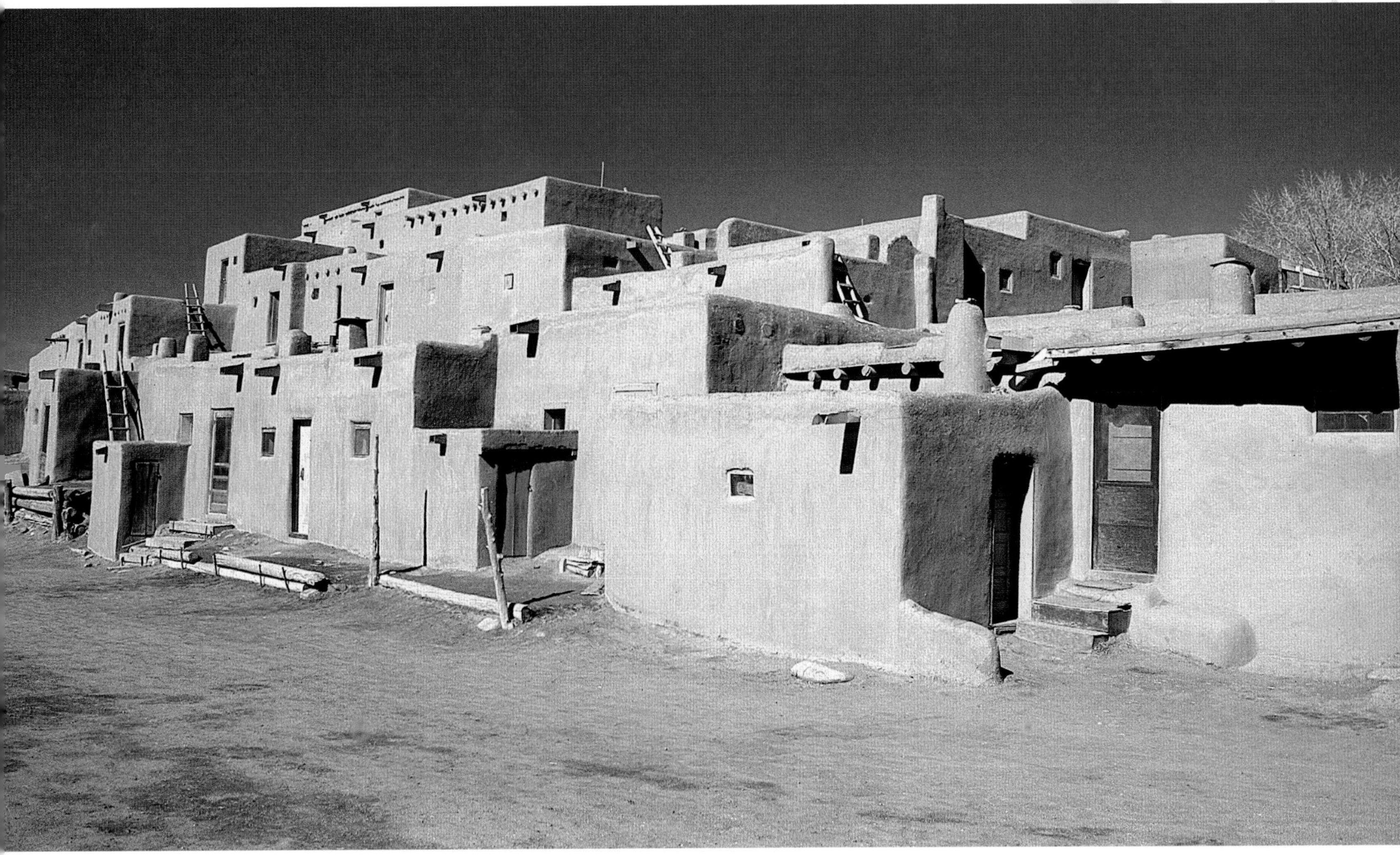

The Taos Valley, cradled amidst the 14,000-foot peaks of the Sangre de Cristo (Spanish for "Blood of Christ") Mountains, has a rich and fascinating history. The first permanent settlement here was a pueblo built in the 10th century, and the present village of Taos was developed in the 14th century. In the 1600s, the Spanish came and built missions, converting as many natives as they could.

But it was an accidental visit in 1898 that shaped modern-day Taos perhaps more than the Franciscan missionaries did. Artists Bert Phillips and Ernest Blumenschein came to town to have a wagon wheel repaired, but they became enchanted by the surroundings and ended up settling in Taos. They invited other artists to the valley, and word of its beauty spread quickly. By the 1920s, Taos was one of the world's most vibrant and renowned artist communities.

In 1955, the Taos Ski Valley opened, marking another seminal moment in Taos's history. Today people come to Taos for its history, culture, galleries, and slopes.

*Taos Pueblo is made from adobe—a mix of sun-dried earth and straw.*

# Carlsbad Caverns National Park

Carlsbad Caverns National Park in southeast New Mexico was established in 1930 to protect Carlsbad Cavern and more than 100 other caves inside a Permian-age fossil reef. The park offers a glimpse into the delicate subterranean plumbing that creates a limestone cavern.

The winged wildlife is a prime attraction at Carlsbad. Every nightfall between May and October, as many as 250,000 Mexican free-tailed bats emerge from the caverns to dive-bomb insects at speeds up to 25 miles per hour. The bats have inhabited the caverns for the past 5,000 years. However, DDT (an agricultural pesticide that was banned in the United States in the 1970s because of adverse environmental effects) nearly crushed the park's bat population; in 2005 it was about 10 percent of what it had been in 1930.

Carlsbad Caverns National Park includes Carlsbad Cavern, which is highly accessible to visitors, as well as the United States' deepest limestone cavern, Lechuguilla Cave, which snakes down to 1,567 feet below the New Mexican desert. Spelunkers must take extreme care: Many of the park's "living" features have been irrevocably damaged by human hands.

## Quick Facts

### *Spelunker's Glossary*

Many beautiful and delicate geological formations can be found in the limestone caves of Carlsbad Caverns.

**columns**—formed when a stalactite and stalagmite join.

**helictites**—curving formations that curl, sometimes appearing to defy gravity. They are very delicate, and geologists are unsure of what causes them to curl.

**soda straws**—hollow mineral tubes formed when water leeches through cracks in the rocks.

**stalactites**—deposits of calcium carbonate resembling icicles that form when water drips from the ceiling.

**stalagmites**—deposits of calcium carbonate formed by water that drips onto the floor.

*Tiny stalactites called soda straws form Dolls Theater, part of the Big Room in Carlsbad Cavern.*

# Canyon de Chelly National Monument

anyon de Chelly in northeastern Arizona ends archaeology, history, and geology.

The canyon was carved by eons of runoff om spring storms and has been inhabited y humans for about 2,000 years. The cliff wellings are spectacular structures with perctly preserved specimens and ruins set in deep caves at the base of vivid red and yellow sandstone walls. The caves are surrounded by an incredible vista of cottonwood trees, green pastures, and fields of maize.

But unlike most of the national parks in the United States, Canyon de Chelly is also part of the Navajo Nation and home to a living community of people who consider the canyon sacred ground. Likewise, visitors to Canyon de Chelly should treat the canyon as such and tread lightly on its floor.

*The red sandstone monolith Spider Rock towers 800 feet above the floor of Canyon de Chelly.*

## Quick Fact

***Spider Rock***

One of the most striking attractions in Canyon de Chelly is Spider Rock.

According to Diné (Navajo) lore, Spider Woman made her home perched at the top of the rock. She was an important and revered deity and is said to have taught the Diné the art of weaving on a loom.

Children were often told if they did not behave, Spider Woman would scurry down her web ladder, snatch them up, and bring them back to the top to devour them. Some said that the top of Spider Rock was white from the bleached bones of Diné children who had misbehaved.

# Grand Canyon National Park

The Great Wall of China, the Great Pyramids of Cheops, the Grand Canyon—all are places only superlatives serve to name.

More than four million visitors come to Arizona's Grand Canyon each year. They explore the canyon by helicopter, raft, mule, car, bus, or boat. Why are so many drawn to this place? What makes it so compelling? Perhaps it was best expressed by John Wesley Powell, the first explorer to navigate the Colorado River through the great canyon, who said, "The wonders of the Grand Canyon cannot be adequately represented in symbols of speech, nor by speech itself."

So there it is—awe. You must go see it for yourself. If you still aren't convinced, you might want to know the Grand Canyon has been named one of the Seven Natural Wonders of the World, and it's the only one in the United States. Take a moment to imagine the Grand Canyon: Most tourists view the canyon from the South Rim's Grand Canyon Village Historic District, where the canyon extends ten miles across and one mile down (though if you're hiking from rim to river, the trail is seven miles long). The Grand Canyon trails descend as much as 800 feet in places, and the canyon itself stretches as much as 18 miles wide. That is some serious real estate!

Apart from its sheer size, Powell noted another aspect of the profound beauty of the Grand Canyon: Its geology displays sequences of Kaibab limestone, thick Coconino sandstone, Hermit shale, and Supai formatio shales and sandstones, creating a sense of orde on an almost unimaginable scale.

The path of the Colorado River throug the Grand Canyon is 277 miles long. Th canyon is not the deepest in the world (Hel Canyon in Idaho, for instance, at 8,000 fee deep is nearly ten times deeper), but it is a immense natural spectacle deserving of it name. The Grand Canyon is the crown jew of the Colorado River, whose labors also cre ated Arches National Park, Canyonland National Park, and Lake Powell in the Gle

*Wind and water eroded the canyon's rocky landscape, revealing colorful layers of limestone sandstone, and shale.*

Views from the Grand Canyon's overlooks reveal the multihued, sculpted chasms.

Canyon National Recreation Area (all of which are located in Utah). The canyon borders the Havasupai, Navajo, and Hualapai Indian reservations.

There are countless spectacular spots for gazing across the canyon or peering into the riverbed below, and each view will seem more amazing than the last. Visitors choose from four park entrances, and a trip from the rim to the riverbed is an overnight hike from any entrance. To get to the park, most take the route north from regional hub Flagstaff, Arizona, to the South Rim and view the canyon from the popular Mather Point overlook or from Hermit Road. Or they take the nearby east entrance, home to the dramatic 70-foot-high stone Watchtower at Desert View. To the north of the South Rim, some enter through the Hualapai Indian Reservation. Adventurous tourists enter the park from the remote North Rim, which is 1,000 feet higher than the South Rim. Roads leading to the North Rim are closed by heavy snows from late October to mid-May.

There are no words to adequately describe the canyon, and even one visit is not enough to truly grasp it. As Powell said, "You cannot see the Grand Canyon in one view, as if it were a changeless spectacle from which a curtain might be lifted."

# Sedona

At the base of the Mogollon Rim and its lofty formations of vibrant red sandstone lies Sedona, Arizona. While only 110 miles north of Phoenix, it seems a world away. Sedona is a small town of just more than 10,000 residents, but its brilliant scenery and lively culture attract more than four million tourists each year.

Atop the Mogollon Rim, many of the wondrous sandstone formations that tower over Sedona are named after objects they appear to mimic, such as Cathedral Rock; Coffeepot Rock; and even Snoopy Rock, named for the beloved beagle from th comic strip *Peanuts.*

Sedona is nestled beneath these dominat ing formations. Boutiques and art galleries ar common along the cobblestone roads. An visitors can enjoy intimate restaurants, friendl local cafés, and quaint bed-and-breakfasts dur ing their stay.

### Quick Fact

Beyond the dramatic natural surroundings, Sedona has attracted attention from the New Age community and UFO watchers. The area has become known as a hot-spot for vortex meditation sites that are believed to aid spiritual development. This reputation has attracted an array of mystics, healers, yoga gurus, and other metaphysical specialists.

*The view of Cathedral Rock from Red Rock Crossing at sunset is unforgettable.*

# Sabino Canyon

he hiking trail leading up Sabino Canyon on e outskirts of Tucson, Arizona, is among the ost beautiful in the United States. The steep d walls, dotted with saguaro, mesquite, and otillo, plummet to the canyon floor, where a aved trail beckons hikers and bikers. There is so a tram to deliver passengers to the top ithout breaking a sweat.

Due to rainy seasons in summer and winter, Sabino Canyon is surprisingly green for a desert, providing habitat for roadrunners, deer, rattlesnakes, mountain lions, and the collared peccaries known as javelinas. Seasonal storms replenish Sabino Creek, which runs down the canyon, and a number of pools that lie along the creek bed.

*The 3.8-mile paved road through the canyon crosses nine stone bridges over Sabino Creek.*

Beyond the paved trail taken by the tram, a more primitive trail leads to the spectacular terminus of Bear Canyon and the cold splash of water known as Seven Falls, which cuts through the untouched desert.

# Taliesin West

*The organic design of Taliesin West blends perfectly with the surrounding arid landscape.*

Once the winter home of Frank Lloyd Wright, Taliesin West is a visionary architectural achievement. In the late 1930s, Wright designed and built the complex in Scottsdale, Arizona, as the winter counterpart to his original Taliesin in Spring Green, Wisconsin. Each site included his living quarters, studio, and campus for his schools of architecture.

Taliesin West covers 600 acres of rugged Sonoran Desert at the foot of McDowell Mountain. The landscape is an integral part of the site: Wright employed rocks and sand on the property as key ingredients in his masterpiece. He didn't limit himself to native materials, however; he also used plastics, canvas, and concrete in innovative ways.

Despite its historic status, Taliesin West i no museum. Since 1940, the vibrant comple has been the headquarters of the Frank Lloy Wright Foundation. The foundation strives t preserve Wright's contributions to architec ture and to promote organic architecture tha blends with its natural environment, of whic Taliesin West is a dazzling example.

# Petrified Forest National Park

Some 225 million years ago, the arid desert of north-central Arizona was a lush, tropical forest dominated by towering conifers. This era ended when catastrophic floods devastated the area, uprooting tree after tree and casting them into the rivers. The rivers carried the forest trees to the middle of the floodplain and left them for dead.

Over millions and millions of years, layers of silt, mud, and volcanic ash covered the spent trees and slowed the process of decay. Silica from the ash gradually penetrated the wood and turned to quartz. Minerals streaked the former wood with every color of the rainbow, resulting in wet-looking "logs" spanning the spectrum from bright red to lime green, navy blue to deep purple.

These unearthly looking specimens proved alluring to pioneers, who shipped them back East where they fetched a high price. To protect the petrified wood in its natural environment, President Theodore Roosevelt created Petrified Forest National Monument in 1906; it became a national park in 1962. Beyond the magnificent petrified wood, the park also contains one of the best fossil records from the Late Triassic period, including aquatic phytosaurs; armored aetosaurs; sharp-toothed rauisuchians; and crocodylomorphs, the ancestors of today's crocodiles.

*Over millions of years, ancient trees in Arizona were streaked with minerals and preserved as shimmering petrified wood.*

# Window Rock

Window Rock is both a community and a geological masterstroke. It is the capital of the Navajo Nation, the largest Native American government in the United States, and home to about 3,000 people. It is also a natural landmark—the city took its name from the wondrous pothole arch. Over millions of years, sunlight, wind, water, and chemical exfoliation formed the distinctive window. These elements slowly peeled away layer after layer of red sandstone, leaving a nearly perfect circular hole in its place.

*Chemical and thermal exfoliation of Entrada sandstone created the astonishing arch known as Window Rock.*

The formation is known as *Tségháhoodzání*, which in Navajo means Perforated Rock. Window Rock has long been a sacred place in the Water Way Ceremony, or *Tóhee*. The 200-foot formation has traditionally been one of four sources for the water Navajo medicine men use in the ceremony performed to ask the gods for rain.

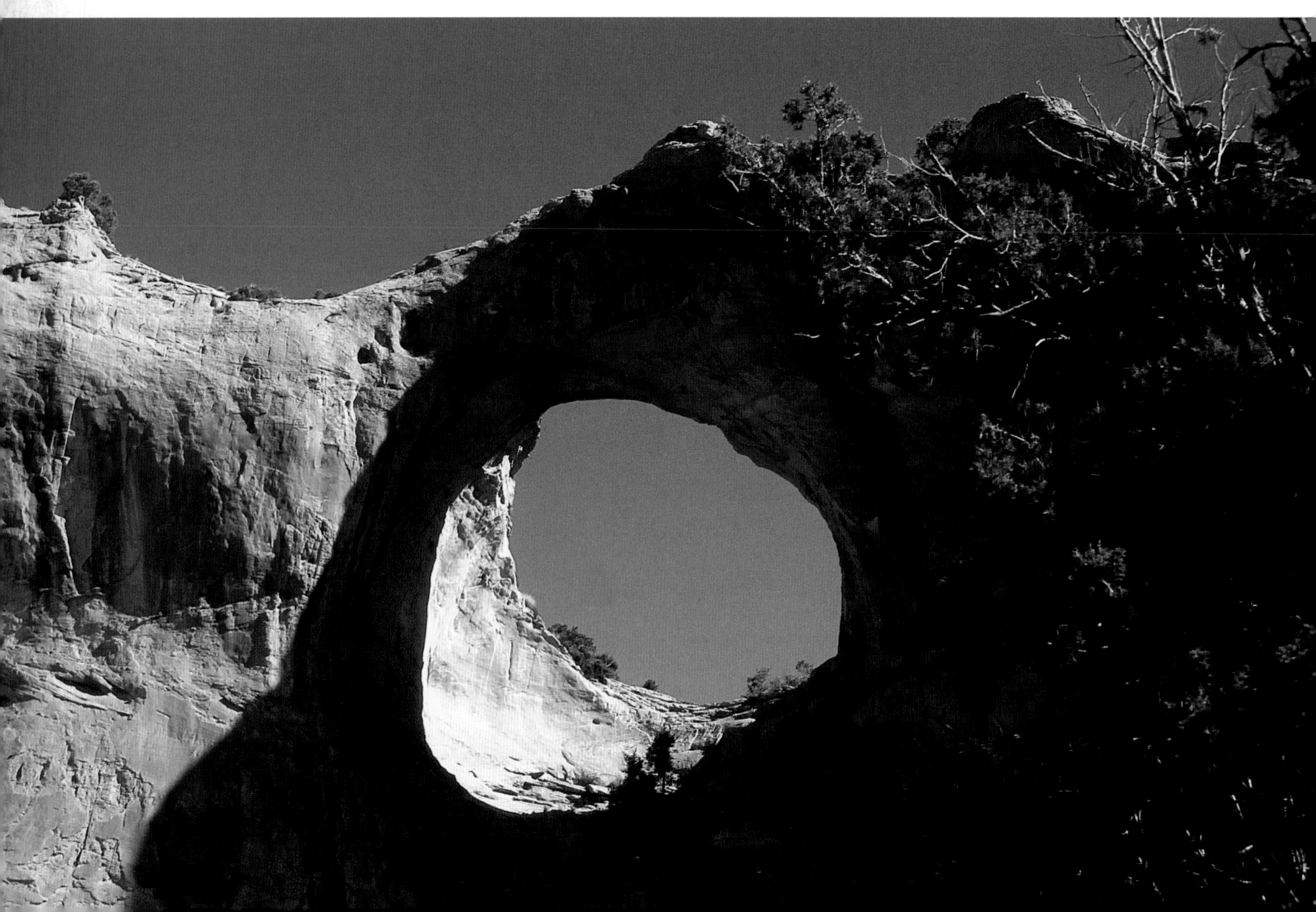

# Great Basin National Park

*Nevada's second-tallest mountain, Wheeler Peak, reaches an elevation of 13,063 feet.*

Amidst the lonely desert that unfolds between the Rockies and the Sierras, a rugged landscape rises into the beautiful blue sky of eastern Nevada. Cut by glaciers from a Pleistocene ice age, forested mountains tower a mile above the flatlands below. Great Basin has been a national park since 1986 and is defined by the Snake Range, which has 13 peaks more than 11,000 feet high and close to 100 valleys snaking among the soaring summits. Alpine lakes cascade into rollicking streams and rivers, and the bristlecone pine forest opens into lush meadows dotted with wildflowers. A labyrinth of limestone caverns winds underground.

Wheeler Peak is the centerpiece of the park. The main park road climbs to 10,000 feet above sea level; a trail leads the adventurous up an additional 3,063 feet to the peak. From this perch, hikers have plenty of space and fresh air to take in the incredible views of the ruggedly idyllic country.

# Las Vegas Strip

The Las Vegas Strip originated in 1938, seven years after gambling was legalized in Nevada. Bucking the trend of the downtown casino, an entrepreneur opened a gambling hall four miles south of Las Vegas's city center on US Highway 91.

What is now known as the Las Vegas Strip began to form a few years later. In 1941, the Hotel El Rancho Vegas resort opened at the corner of San Francisco Avenue and US 91. But this was no mere casino—Hotel El Rancho Vegas offered its guests an unprecedented slate of facilities and activities, including hotel rooms, restaurants, live entertainment, shops, a travel agency, horseback riding, and, of course, a swimming pool. Gambling, nonetheless, remained the top draw.

Downtown remained the prime gambling destination in Las Vegas, however, for many years. And, while the Hotel El Rancho Vegas was innovative and exquisite, its opening was poorly timed, as just eight months later the United States entered World War II. The hotel later had trouble competing against bigger and better resorts that sprang up in the surrounding desert in its wake, and finally succumbed to a catastrophic fire in 1960.

*This neon sign at the south end of the Strip greets travelers who arrive via Las Vegas Boulevard.*

But the trailblazing concept of a comprehensive Las Vegas casino-resort was clearly the vision of the future. Today, Hotel El Rancho Vegas's legacy is unmistakable. Straddling the cities of Las Vegas and Paradise, the Strip dwarfs the downtown areas when the cityscape first comes into view. The ornate palaces of South Las Vegas Boulevard and their endless ribbons of neon make it one of the few stretches of road that's more scenic after the sun goes down.

Amazingly, 16 of the 20 largest hotels in the world are right there on one four-mile slice of real estate in the middle of the Nevada desert. A visitor could walk from one end of the Strip to the other in a couple of hours and see everything from replicas of the Eiffel Tower and the New York skyline to dazzling water fountains and the Little Church of the West he setting for many celebrity weddings. ig-name performers take to the stages here ightly, entertaining the vacationing masses ith comedy, magic, music, and dance.

While casinos still dominate the resorts, the trip has grown increasingly diverse, cultured, nd family-friendly over the years. The MGM Grand, the Strip's largest hotel (with more nan 5,000 rooms), has a lion habitat that's ome to descendants of the very lion that roars efore the title sequence of many MGM films. The Bellagio has a world-class art gallery. New York–New York features a roller coaster on its rooftop. Mandalay Bay has a synthetic beach. There are also museums, music venues, malls, and much, much more.

Nothing is permanent here; the Strip is one of the most dynamic environments on the planet. As the resorts try to capture more market share and more tourist dollars, they constantly expand their facilities and activities, rebuilding and reshaping to keep up with the times. A prime example—in 2005, the $2.7-billion Wynn Las Vegas opened on the former site of the Desert Inn, outdoing the competition with a garden atrium out front, the forested "Lake of Dreams" out back, and a Ferrari dealership inside.

More often than not, the minds behind the opulent resorts lining the Strip hit the mark: The number of visitors flocking to Las Vegas doubled between 1989 and 2004, when an astounding 37 million tourists dropped in on Sin City.

*Glamorous resort-casinos on the Vegas Strip bring the city to life each night with flashing lights and extravagant decor.*

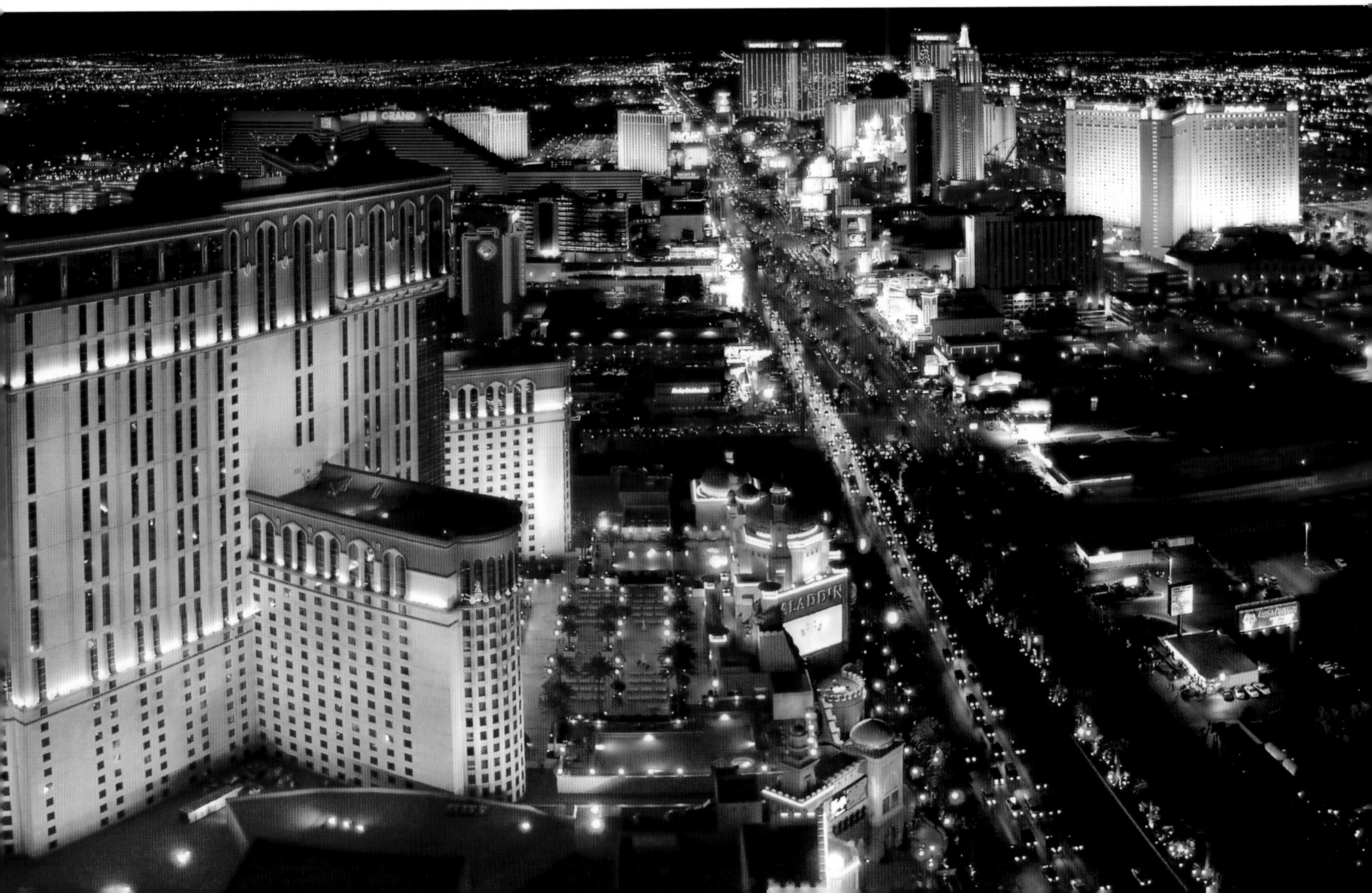

# Hoover Dam

In the Black Canyon of the Colorado River, just 30 miles south of fabulous Las Vegas, Nevada, sits the engineering marvel known as Hoover Dam. The dam was constructed between 1931 and 1935 and consists of 3.25 million cubic yards of concrete, enough to pave a road from New York to San Francisco. The dam widens the Colorado into the vast waters of Lake Mead, a year-round recreation destination that attracts millions of visitors each year for swimming, boating, waterskiing, and fishing.

About 20,000 laborers built the Hoover Dam, which was the largest dam in the world when it was completed. While no longer the world's biggest, Hoover Dam stands as a symbol of the United States' progress during the adversity of the Great Depression. It is a National Historic Landmark and was named a Monument of the Millennium by the American Society of Civil Engineers.

## Quick Facts

***Hoover Dam***

- Height—726.4 feet
- Weight—6.6 million tons
- Can store up to 9.2 trillion gallons of the Colorado River in its reservoir, Lake Meade. That's nearly two years of the average "flow" of the river.
- Has a power-generating capacity of 2.8 million kilowatts.
- Is part of a system that provides water to more than 25 million people in the southwest United States.

*Hoover Dam harnesses the power of the mighty Colorado River, generating power and providing water for millions in the Southwest.*

# Pyramid Lake

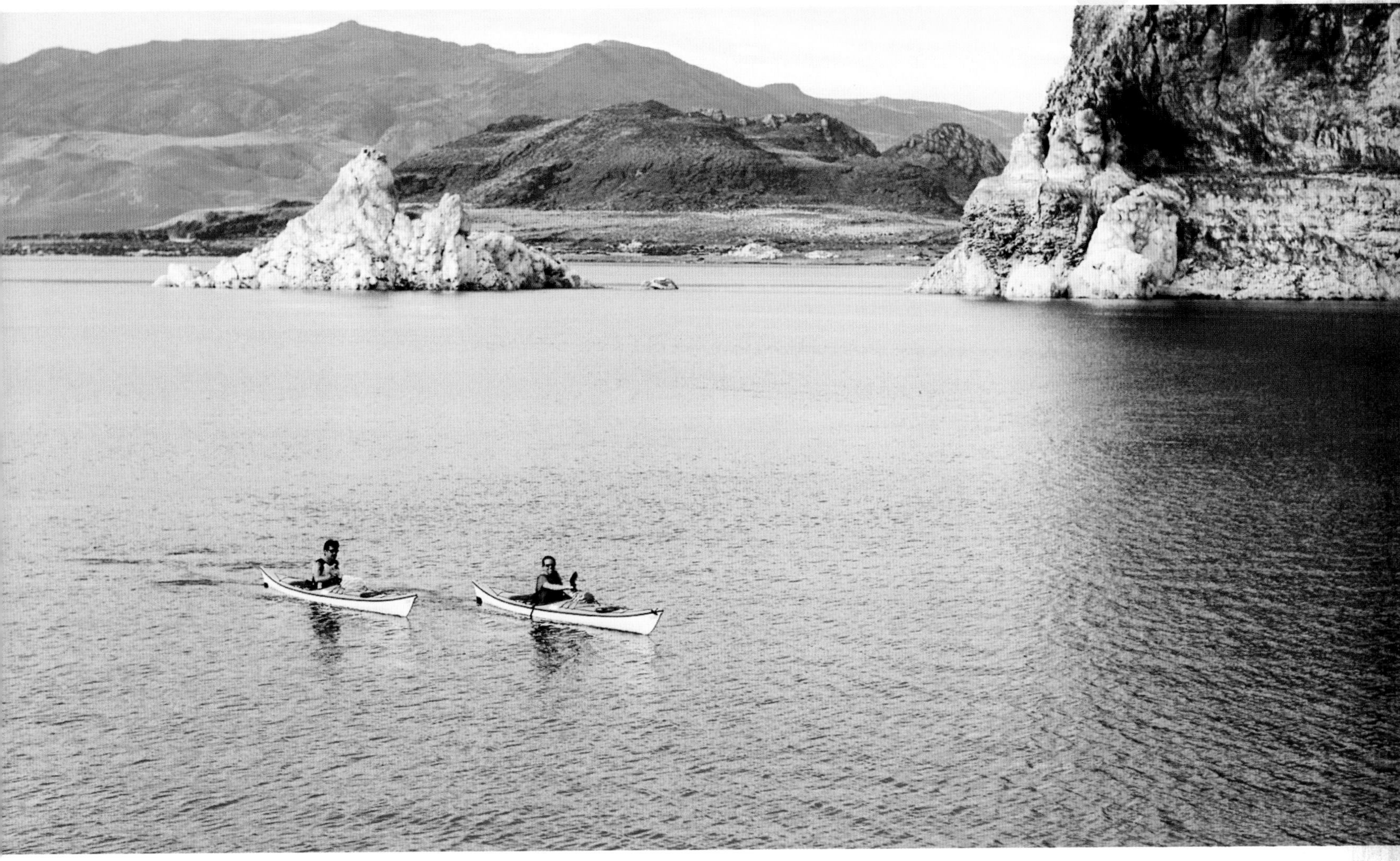

Named for the distinctive 400-foot rock near its eastern shore, Pyramid Lake is a striking contrast to its rugged, arid surroundings in northwestern Nevada. The lake is one of the largest desert lakes in the world and is famous for its tufa rock formations. Its surface vacillates from turquoise to dark blue. Across the lake, views of the mountains, streaked with gray and pink, are unforgettable.

In 1844, John C. Fremont, said to be the first Anglo to gaze at the lake, put a fitting description to paper after this vast oasis punctuated his journey through the desert: "A defile between the mountains descended rapidly about two thousand feet; and, filling up all the lower space, was a sheet of green water, some twenty miles broad. It broke upon our eyes like the ocean."

*Visitors can kayak across idyllic Pyramid Lake or swim or fish in its waters.*

Located on the Paiute Indian Reservation, Pyramid Lake's warm, shallow waters are a magnet for anglers and swimmers. The world-record cutthroat trout—a 41-pound whopper—was pulled from these electric blue waters in 1925.

# Pikes Peak

Lieutenant Zebulon Pike first spied this 14,110-foot mountain along Colorado's Front Range in November 1806. But his attempt to scale the mountain that now bears his name was foiled by heavy snow, and Pike said the rocky pinnacle would never be reached.

Never say never: In 1820, a party led by Major Stephen Long reached the top of Pikes Peak in two days. They were the first to see the commanding views from the mountaintop.

Today, more than half a million people make it to the summit house each year. Of course, nowadays reaching the peak of the mountain is less daunting. Visitors can hike the 13-mile trail to a height of 7,000 feet, or they can avoid breaking a sweat and take the cog railway (since 1889) or highway (since 1916) to the top. In fact, "America's Mountain" is the most visited mountain in North America. Only Japan's Mount Fuji has more visitors each year.

*The snow-capped majesty of Pikes Peak looms over the red rock formations of Garden of Gods in Colorado Springs.*

Pikes Peak plays host to several annual events, including celebratory fireworks displays, a marathon, and the second-oldest car race in the United States: the Pikes Peak Hill Climb, featuring 156 twists and turns on its 12.4-mile route.

# Telluride

Telluride, Colorado, is one of the most alluring towns in the West. This picture-perfect boomtown is nestled in a snug box canyon and surrounded by forested peaks and idyllic waterfalls. It is the perfect blend of ski resort and historic community. According to local legend, Telluride derived its name from a contraction of "to hell you ride," due to the difficulty of reaching the town in the 19th century.

*Tucked among the snow-capped Rockies, Telluride is a skier's paradise.*

Telluride's beginning years in the late 1800s were marked by ambition. The silver veins in the surrounding mountains proved exceptionally rich. The newfound wealth of the town lured outlaws such as Butch Cassidy and the Sundance Kid—Butch's first bank robbery was at the San Miguel Valley Bank in downtown Telluride. The town became one of the world's first electric communities, boasting electric lighting even before Paris, the "City of Lights."

But Telluride's mining economy faltered after World War I, beginning a long, slow period of decline. The United States Postal Service gave up on the town, and the population dropped to 600. Downtown lots sold for as little as $100, and many structures began to deteriorate. But in 1972, the Telluride Ski Resort was born, and the population of miners gave way to Bohemians. The town's destiny—which at one point appeared to be total abandonment—changed suddenly. The entire town has been a National Landmark Historic District since 1964, and this status has kept its lovely character intact.

# Mesa Verde National Park

About 700 years ago people now called the Anasazi lived in communities clinging to the cliffsides of the American Southwest. The name Anasazi originally meant "enemy ancestors" in Navajo but has come to mean "ancient people" or "ancient ones." These ancient people were the ancestors of today's Pueblo Indians, about 20 tribes including the Hopi and Zuni. They left a most remarkable legacy in what is now Mesa Verde ("green table" in Spanish) National Park, which comprises more than 4,000 archaeological sites, including 600 cliff dwellings, in southwest Colorado.

Visitors can see a handful of the most spectacular of these uncanny ruins on tours led by park rangers, and trails to mesa tops are open to hikers. Some tourists balk at the regimentation of the guided tours, but regulation, or overregulation (as some believe), is the price today's travelers pay for the damage done by visitors before them. Pillaging Mesa Verde is nothing new: An 1889 "pottery sale" of stolen artifacts is a notable early example.

Still, Mesa Verde is spellbinding. An anonymous architect said it held "timeless forms and abiding mystery." Others such as author Evan S. Connell have written about the captivating shadows, sunlight, and transcendental aura of the ancient civilization.

*The nicely shaded cliff dwellings in Mesa Verde National Park were home to the Anasazi people who abandoned them about 700 years ago.*

The Mesa Verde cliff dwellings were abandoned for about 700 years. The area's Ute Indians refused to go near the Two-Story Cliff House, believing it was sacred and occupied by spirits of the dead. They were reluctant even to show the ruins to their white friends.

Despite modern amenities, visitors should ake no mistake that the park is part of the ıgged American West. iking at an altitude of 400 feet with next to ɔ humidity is a great ay to enjoy Mesa Verde -be sure to include lots f water, sunblock, and ɔur best hiking boots.

If you're planning a ·enic trip to Mesa Verde, rst fly to Albuquerque, ew Mexico, then drive ɔrth along US 550. Take ɔur time visiting Pueblo ıins on the way at sig- ificant excavations such Chaco Canyon, Hov- ıweep National Monu- ent, Bandelier National Ionument, Yucca House ational Monument, and ztec Ruins National Ionument.

Many Mesa Verde vis- ors stay in nearby Cor- ez or Mancos, Colorado, or in Durango, which about 20 miles east of the park and the site f the historic Strater, Rochester, and General almer hotels. On-site accommodations are vailable at the only hotel inside the park, the ar View Lodge, near the heart of the myster- es of the ancient ones.

## Quick Fact

***Magnificent Ruins***

In 1874, explorer-photographer William Henry Jackson discovered Two-Story Cliff House and other small cliff dwellings in what is now Ute Mountain Tribal Park. In 1888, two ranchers searching for a stray herd discovered the greatest of all the cliff communities, the Cliff Palace complex, which has 150 individual rooms, 23 underground kivas (ceremonial rooms), and towers rising four stories high.

Mesa Verde's fame spread quickly to an astonished world. "The edge of the deep canyon in the opposite cliff sheltered by a huge, massive vault of rock... laid before their astonished eyes a whole town with towers and walls, rising out of a heap of ruins... ruins so magnificent that they surpass anything of the kind known in the United States," wrote Gustaf Nordenskiöld in *The Cliff Dwellers of the Mesa Verde* in 1893.

*'he ruins of Mesa Verde are some of the best reserved archaeological sites in the Southwest.*

# Great Sand Dunes National Park and Preserve

Stretching across 8,000 square miles at an average elevation of 7,500 feet, southwestern Colorado's vast San Luis Valley is the world's largest alpine valley. It's full of mysteries and surprises, from UFO lore to alligator farms to potato farms.

But the most incredible surprise here may be the Great Sand Dunes, sculpted by wind, water, and time. In the shadow of the Sangre de Cristo ("Blood of Christ") Mountains, these are the tallest dunes in North America, reaching as much as 750 feet in height.

The dunes have formed here because the wind blows abundantly from multiple directions. Winds from the southwest and northeast shake loose available sand, blowing it into one of three deposits in the valley: the densely packed sabkha (or salt flat), the outer sheet of fine sand, or the inner dune field—the domain of the biggest dunes. Nearby creeks carry san from the dune field's north and east borde back to where the wind can blow it into th heart of the dunes.

The scale is striking: The dunes contai nearly five billion cubic meters of sand. Th best way to get a feel for this ever-changin landscape is to lace up your hiking boots an work your way up to the summit of Hig Dune—the view from the top gazing acros the sandy dunes is sublime.

*Masterworks of wind, water, and earth, the Great Sand Dunes reach heights of up to 750 feet.*

# Red Rocks Park and Amphitheatre

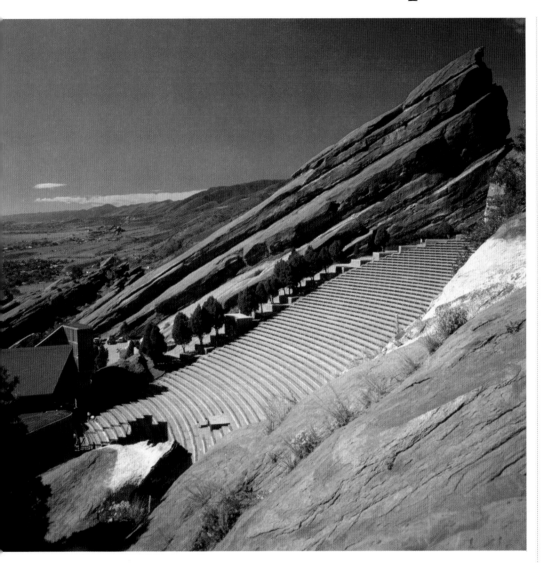

*The giant Creation Rock and Ship Rock frame Red Rocks Amphitheatre.*

n Morrison, Colorado, Red Rocks Park and mphitheatre is nestled in the stunning ountainside and natural red rocks. Its acous- cs are superb, perhaps rivaled only by the eauty of its spectacular surroundings. The orth and south sides of the amphitheatre re 300-foot geological masterstrokes named reation Rock and Ship Rock, respectively. The seats stretch across the steep slope between the two.

In the early 20th century, John Brisben Walker hatched a plan to develop a world-class performance venue here. He went as far as building a temporary platform where he staged numerous concerts featuring leading stars of the East Coast opera scene. But Walker's vision wasn't fully realized until decades later. In the 1920s, the city of Denver bought the land and enlisted the help of the federal government. Red Rocks Amphitheatre was completed in 1947; the venue's first annual Easter Sunrise Service, a tradition that continues to this day, occurred that first year.

A "Who's Who" of the music world has taken the stage here, including Willie Nelson, the Beatles, Jimi Hendrix, and the Grateful Dead. Concert industry trade journal *Pollstar* named Red Rocks its "Best Outdoor Venue" every year from 1989 to 1993 and its "Best Small Outdoor Venue" every year from 1995 to 1999. It then dropped the amphitheatre from consideration—and named the small outdoor venue award after Red Rocks.

*The dramatic red rock formations that give the amphitheatre its name are both visually striking and accoustically ideal.*

# Rocky Mountain National Park

Perched atop the Continental Divide, Colorado's Rocky Mountain National Park is archetypal high country, offering a jaw-dropping panorama of daunting summits and alpine tundra. There are 60 peaks in the park that reach 12,000 feet above sea level. The highest, Longs Peak, scrapes the sky 14,259 feet above sea level.

Based on these lofty numbers, it should come as no surprise that the park has the highest average elevation of any U.S. national park, including those in Alaska. It's even been nicknamed "America's Switzerland." A good portion of Rocky Mountain National Park is above the area's 11,500-foot timberline. A stretch of Trail Ridge Road, the highest continuous road in the United States, climbs above the timberline to a height of 12,183 feet. But the meadows below are starkly different from the harsh landscape of the mountaintops, especially after the wildflowers push through the ground in spring.

More than three million people visit th park each year. The drive along Trail Ridg Road from Estes Park on the east side to Gran Lake, its western gateway, reveals picturesqu scenes. The park's bountiful backcountry is world-class destination for climbing, fishin hiking, and cross-country skiing.

*Crystalline lakes refilled by annual snowmelt are nestled at the feet of Rocky Mountain National Park's awe-inspiring peaks.*

# 'he Great Stupa of Dharmakaya, hambhala Mountain Center

dled in the pine-clad mountains near Red :her Lakes, Colorado, the Great Stupa of rmakaya is the largest stupa (monument great Buddhist teacher) in the West- Hemisphere. It is also the largest and t elaborate example of Buddhist sacred itecture in North America.

'he monument was built in honor of the t Buddhist teacher Chögyam Trungpa poche (1939–1987), the founder of the mbhala movement and one of the key fig- who helped introduce Tibetan Buddhism he United States. He established more 100-meditation centers across the United es and founded the first Buddhist-inspired versity in the country, Naropa University in lder, Colorado. His skull is encased in the e statue of Buddha in the chamber at the a's base, called the heart center.

Construction on the Great Stupa of Dhar- aya began in 1988, and the monument consecrated in 2001. The 108-foot mas- iece is a mesmerizing work of ornate art, n with meaningful symbolism and built ast a millennium. (The engineers behind it l reinforced concrete to maximize the stu- durability.) Stupas in the West have come epresent the contrast between modern and ient world views. The interior of the Great pa of Dharmakaya is spacious. Its design artwork reflect the connection between nese aesthetics and Shambhala teachings.

*The largest stupa in the Western Hemisphere is a monument to Chögyam Trungpa Rinpoche, the founder of the Shambhala movement.*

# Yellowstone National Park

Yellowstone was not only the first national park in the United States—it was the first national park in the entire world. At 2.2 million acres, it is one of North America's largest areas of protected wilderness. These distinctions have preserved Yellowstone's wild nature and made it a model for other parks, whose managers have benefited from the lessons learned, and mistakes made, at Yellowstone.

One striking aspect of Yellowstone is the volcanic plumbing below Earth's surface that powers geothermal features, including dramatic geysers such as Old Faithful, steaming fumaroles (holes in volcanic regions that issue vapors and hot gasses), bubbling hot pools, and belching mud pots. While strolling on the boardwalks that provide close-up views of these superheated attractions, keep in mind that Yellowstone is one of only two intact geyser basins on the planet. (The other, on the Kamchatka Peninsula in Russia, is much less accessible.) Dozens of others have been developed into spas, tapped for energy, or otherwise used and abused by humans.

Geysers are scattered throughout the pa and they dominate the landscape in the a near Old Faithful. A quarter of the worl geysers are located on the hillsides and r erbanks near the Upper, Midway, and Lov Geyser basins.

Yellowstone's wildlife is every bit astounding as its thermal features. The Lan Valley, in the park's northeastern corner,

*Yellowstone is a natural patchwork of pine for ests, glacial lakes, and imposing mountains.*

## Quick Fact

In 1878, journalist Edwin J. Stanley wrote about Upper Geyser Basin in his travelogue *Rambles in Wonderland.* His colorful description remains fitting to this day:

> Just imagine the steam coming up from a thousand orifices, the transparent element spouting forth from a dozen cauldrons at once, and the whole scene, beautiful and strange within itself, bathed with the bright sunlight pouring down from a cloudless sky, softening and blending the variegated hues of the groundwork and arching every column of steam with a halo of brilliant colors! Is it not enough to bewilder and overwhelm the curiosity-seeking tourist and lover of the wonderful?

*The lakeside thermal features at West Thumb are among the many spectacular sights in the park.*

nown as "The Serengeti of North America." here are more large mammals here—deer, noose, elk, bison, bears, and wolves—than in ny other ecosystem on the continent. During he spring, this diverse menagerie is on display s animals graze, scavenge, and hunt.

Yellowstone's wealth doesn't begin and end vith the geysers and the animals. The park is trove of aquatic wonders, especially Yellowtone Lake (the largest high-altitude lake in he continental United States, at 7,733 feet bove sea level) and the spectacular geothermal heatrics on its shores at West Thumb. There s also the Grand Canyon of the Yellowstone River, a geological masterwork punctuated by wo dramatic waterfalls, 109-foot Upper Falls nd 308-foot Lower Falls.

The subtle yet striking beauty of Yellowtone is transitory. The volcanism that powers he geysers is close to Earth's surface under the aldera, which is the heart of the park. The Yellowstone Caldera is still active and has erupted three times in the last two million years, at an average interval of once every 600,000 years. The last eruption—whose force was equivalent to about 10,000 times that of the 1980 Mount St. Helens eruption—occurred about 600,000 years ago. Do the math: The result is a reminder that nature's masterworks are constant works in progress, and some are more temporary than others.

# Cody

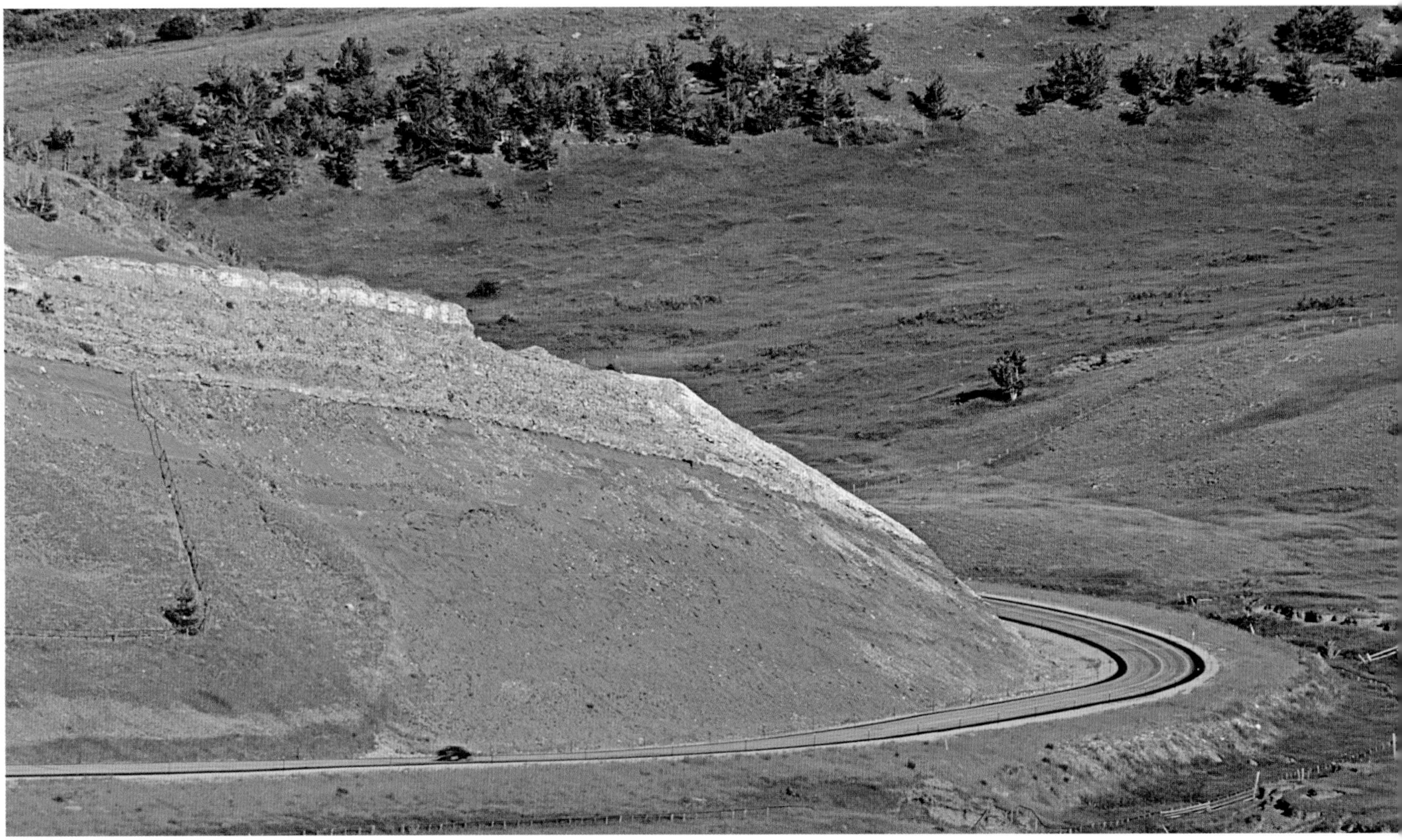

*The terrain around Cody, Wyoming, is remarkably varied, running the gamut from rolling hills to red rocks to evergreen-laden mountains.*

Named for its founder, William "Buffalo Bill" Cody, this is one town in the country where the West lives on. Cody, Wyoming, is a bit of a bug in amber, with wooden boardwalks fronting its historic storefronts on Sheridan Avenue, the city's main drag. Sure, minivans have replaced horse-drawn wagons, and modern development has not passed over Cody entirely, but the culture here still smacks of the Old West in many ways. The city bills itself as the "Rodeo Capital of the World," and it's tough to argue. It's the only city in the country that has a rodeo every night of the week, all summer long: the Cody Nite Rodeo.

With a population of about 9,000 people, Cody is not a big city by any means, but it shines in comparison with its similarly sized peers. The 300,000-square-foot Buffalo Bill Historical Center, for instance, is a world-clas museum with five distinct wings dedicated t Native Americans, natural history, Wester art, firearms, and "Buffalo Bill" Cody himsel Outdoor recreation is also big in these parts The Shoshone River runs right through town and there are mountainous destinations in it backyard, including Yellowstone National Par just 52 miles to the west.

# Grand Teton National Park

The beauty of the Teton Range in northwestern Wyoming is rapturous. It's difficult to take a picture in Grand Teton National Park without capturing these awe-inspiring peaks. The summit of Grand Teton, perhaps the most recognizable mountain in the United States, is 13,770 feet above sea level, and it shoots a mile-and-a-half straight up from the valley floor below. This precipitous rise is nothing short of breathtaking.

Grand Teton National Park is situated in Jackson Hole, the famed valley bounded by Yellowstone to the north and the Tetons to the west. Grand Teton, Mount Owen, and Teewinot are collectively known as the Cathedral Group, and the view of these mountains from the northeast is astounding. Atop the Tetons, the granite is more than three billion years old, making it some of the oldest rock on the continent. The mountains themselves, however, are among the youngest in the Rockies—they formed about ten million years ago.

Farther north, the colossal 12,605-foot Mount Moran rises alone beyond Jackson Lake, the largest of seven crystalline lakes at the foot of the mountain. From there, one can see the Snake River. It follows a 30-mile course through the park, a scenic stretch of wilderness favored by moose, cutthroat trout, and bald eagles.

*Looming above Jackson Hole, the Cathedral Group of the Grand Tetons comprises Grand Teton, Mount Owen, and Teewinot.*

# Devils Tower National Monument

The igneous spire now known as Devils Tower, which in 1906 became the United States' first national monument, had many other names before earning its current moniker. Long before the United States was a country, the Lakota people called the tower *Mato Tipila*, or "bear lodge." The Cheyenne dubbed it *Na Kovea*, meaning "bear's tepee." Both tribes hold it sacred to this day.

The origins of Devils Tower date back 60 million years, when columns of molten magma cooled underground, a full mile-and-a-half below Earth's crust. After eons of erosion, the soft sedimentary layers that once covered the spire disappeared, and the tower now reaches 867 feet from its base into the sky. Its honeycombed columns, cracked on the south side and smooth on the north (due to the sun), are nothing short of bewildering.

Wildlife is abundant near the tower: More than 100 species of birds circle in the sky; chipmunks scurry on the tower; and the forested base is alive with rabbits, deer, and porcupines. Above, the sky holds the promise of unidentified flying objects: Like the Lakota and the Cheyenne, sci-fi fans have long held Devils Tower sacred, thanks to its star turn as the setting for the climactic scene of Steven Spielberg's *Close Encounters of the Third Kind.*

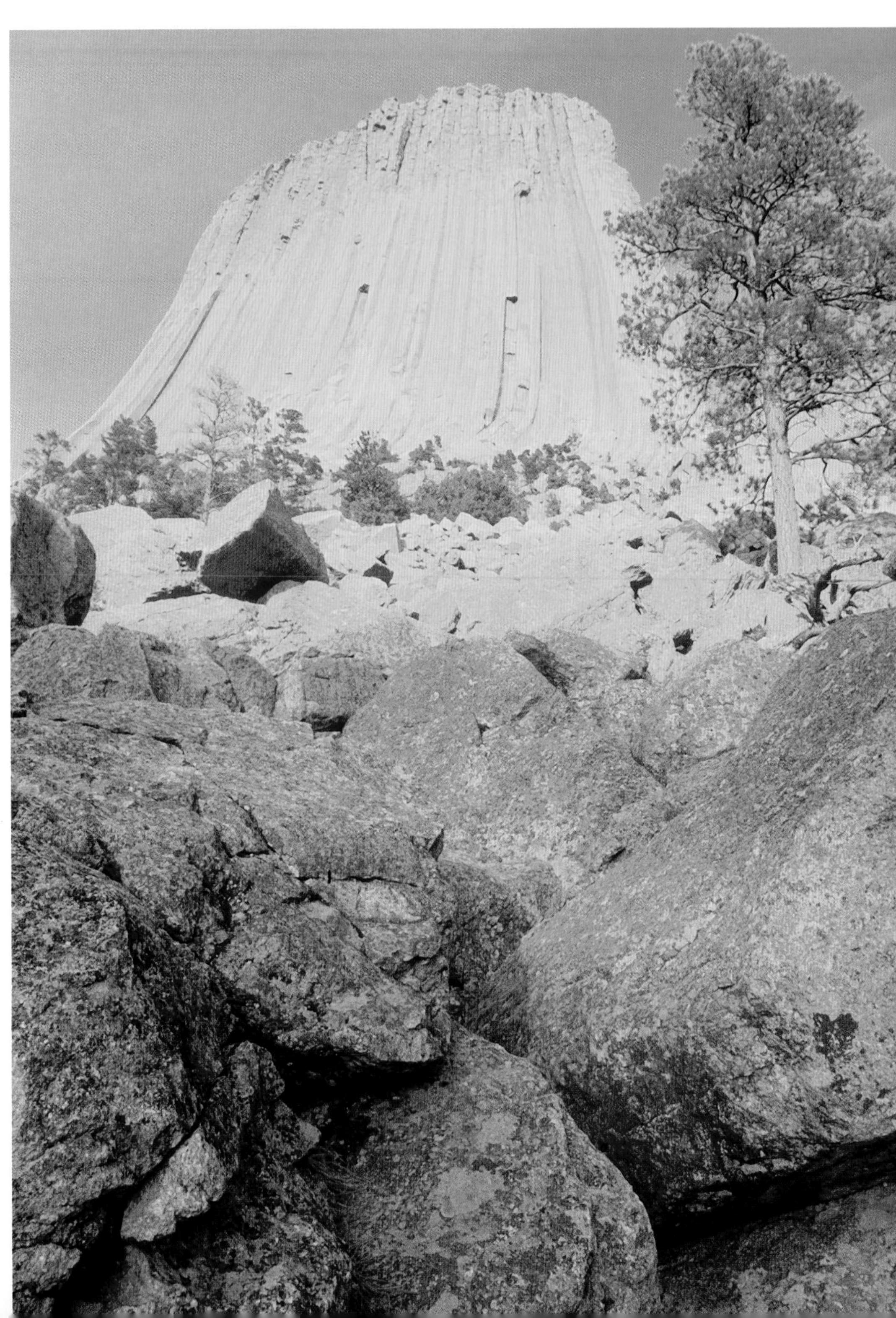

*The pillar of igneous rock that is now Devils Tower was buried until wind and water swept away the layers of sedimentary rock millions of years ago, revealing the columnar tower.*

# Cheyenne Frontier Days

Cheyenne Frontier Days is the world's larg-st outdoor rodeo, earning the nickname "The Daddy of 'em All." But it's not just a rodeo, not by a long shot. It's a midsummer celebra-tion of Western heritage, food, art, and music. There's even a carnival midway and much, much more.

The main event, of course, is the rodeo. Bronco riding, steer roping, wild-horse racing, team roping, and barrel racing are standards—but bull riding is the main attraction and grand finale. The appeal and lofty status of bull riding in the rodeo world today is due in large part to Cheyenne Frontier Days. The bulls weren't reliably ornery until livestock contractors bred a Brahma bull from India into the mix for the event in the 1920s. These beasts weighed more than 1,500 pounds each and were perfectly angry and ferocious buck-ers, making way for their widespread accep-tance in the sport ever since.

The first Frontier Days was staged in 1897. The event began as a plan hatched to revital-ize the economy after the silver bust of 1893. Since its beginning, Frontier Days has been a volunteer operation, and its success is due to the thousands of hospitable Wyoming resi-dents who make the event possible each year. In fact, they feed more than 30,000 rodeo fans a free pancake breakfast every year.

(Right) *Beyond its myriad rodeos and stock shows, Cheyenne Frontier Days features concerts and a carnival midway.*

(Above) *The "Daddy of 'em All" features a cattle drive to the fairgrounds.*

# Medicine Wheel National Historic Landmark

Wyoming's Medicine Wheel is located in a remote area of the Bighorn National Forest at an elevation of 9,642 feet on Medicine Mountain. It is one of the oldest active religious sites on the planet: For 7,000 years, this mountain has been sacred.

Medicine Wheel is part of a larger system of interrelated religious sites, altars, sweat lodge sites, and other ceremonial venues, and it is still in use. In recent years, members of dozens of Indian nations have held ceremonies here, including the Arapaho, Cheyenne, and Crow.

*Measuring 75 feet across, Medicine Wheel in northern Wyoming has been an active religious site for thousands of years.*

The lasting artifact at the site is the actual Medicine Wheel, which is 75 feet in diameter and composed of 28 "spokes" of rocks intersecting in a central rocky cairn. Originally built several hundred years ago, it is now a National Historic Landmark enclosed by a simple fence of rope. It is considered one of the best-preserved sites of its kind.

# Zion National Park

The Colorado Plateau, the Great Basin, and the Mojave Desert converge in Zion National Park. The name Zion, which was given by Mormon pioneers, is Hebrew for "sanctuary." Although the park was established in 1909 as Mukuntuweap National Monument, it became Zion National Park in 1919.

The sheer, vibrantly colored cliff and canyon landscape of Zion stretches across 229 square miles in southwestern Utah. Nine distinct layers of rock can be found throughout the park. The colors of the rocks are accented by traces of iron, creating an array of reds, pinks, whites, and yellows as well as flashes of black, green, and purple.

More than 200 million years ago, the land here was a sea basin, but tectonic forces thrust the land up, and rivers and wind carved the winding canyons. Fossils of seashells, fish, trees, snails, and bones have been found embedded in the rocks. The highest point in the park, atop Horse Ranch Mountain, reaches 8,726 feet. Along the north fork of the Virgin River is a spectacular gorge where the walls of the canyon rise 2,000 to 3,000 feet.

Zion has the richest diversity of plants in all of Utah—in all there are more than 800 plant species, including larkspurs, junipers, pinyon pines, sand buttercups, violets, columbine, asters, and sunflowers. Wildlife is abundant, and you may even catch a rare glimpse of a mountain lion or ring-tailed cat.

There's much more to do at the park than just sight-see: Outdoor activities such as biking, backpacking, hiking, camping, climbing, horseback riding, and swimming are readily available. And bold travelers may even choose to brave the famous Narrows Trail, a 15-mile hike that involves wading upstream through a river, providing breathtaking views of the canyon walls that jut 2,500 feet into the sky.

*The entrance to Zion National Park is a gateway to some of the most visually stunning geological formations on the planet.*

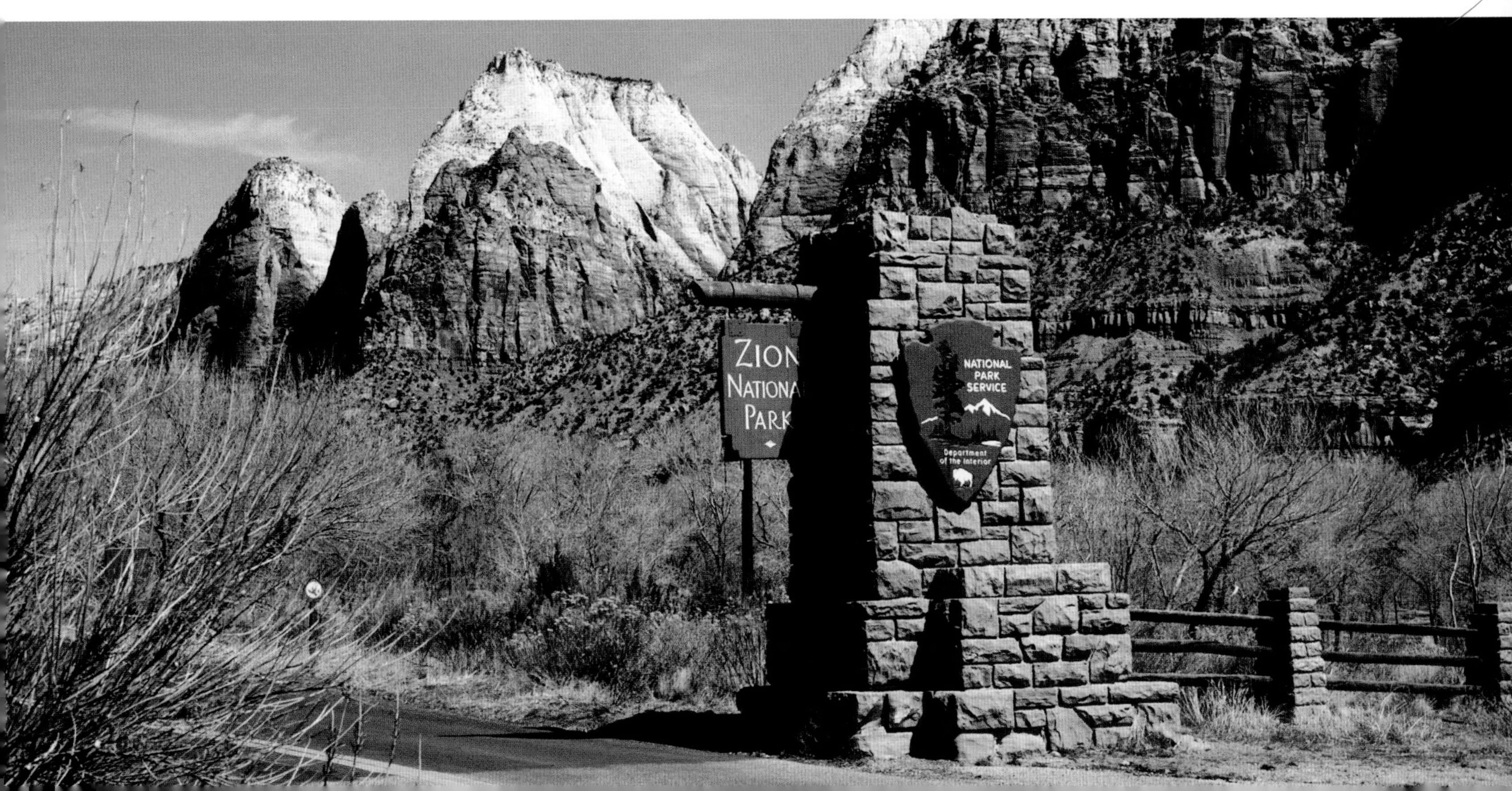

# Arches National Park

Arches National Park in eastern Utah defies the imagination. Sandstone has eroded and been whittled into an astonishing landscape of color, shape, and texture. The definitive features in the park are, of course, the arches of its namesake. The park is home to the densest concentration of these rocky masterworks on the entire planet—there are more than 2,000 in all.

The size of the park's arches range from three feet in diameter to the massive 306-foot Landscape Arch (the world's longest arch). This arch is one of eight along the two-mile-long Devils Garden Trail. The park's best known attraction is Delicate Arch, which stands picturesque against a dazzling panorama of infinite sandstone.

Although these dramatic sandstone portals are the stars of the park, Arches is home to a rich and unusual ecosystem. It sits atop the Colorado Plateau, a high desert region that unfolds from western Colorado into Utah, New Mexico, and Arizona. Other geological wonders are found throughout the park, including balanced rocks; spires; slick-looking domes; and "Park Avenue," a series of bright red fins that loom over the vivid desert like Manhattan skyscrapers.

This rocky, arid landscape is surprisingly rife with flora and fauna. Arches' soil is actually

*Utah's Arches National Park has more natural arches than any other tract of land on Earth—there are more than 2,000 total.*

(Left) *Delicate Arch is a natural masterpiece of sculpted red sandstone.*

## Quick Fact

### *A Geological Primer*

The sandstone here was adjacent to a great inland sea hundreds of millions of years ago. Over time the sea vanished and left behind a salt bed thousands of feet thick in places. Wind carried dust from the adjacent coastal plain, which buried the salt under layers of sediment that compacted into rock over time. This sandstone crust was once more than a mile thick, but it cracked and buckled as the salt gave way under the rock's immense weight. This era left behind a landscape of domes and vertical cracks and set the stage for the formation of the arches seen today.

Water flooded the gaps in the sandstone and, along with the wind, it wore away layers of rock. This left behind a series of "fins" that were further wracked when ice formed on their walls. Sometimes ice would expand in indentations during cold periods and create openings that would allow daylight, wind, and water through. Many of the fins collapsed, but others had the perfect symmetrical blend of durability and steadiness to survive—as arches.

ive: Much of the park is sheathed in a roundcover of multicolored lichens that support an array of desert plant life. Yucca and acti thrive year-round, and there are pockets f willows and ferns in the park's few soggy spots. In spring, the sandy red washes come alive with wildflowers.

Many animals, such as lizards, kangaroo rats, bobcats, mountain lions, and owls, live in the park. Rainwater collects in natural basins in the sandstone (better known as "potholes") that support seasonal populations of hardy amphibians and insects.

Arches National Park also has numerous petroglyphs and tool-making sites, signs of a long and storied human history. Nomadic hunter-gatherers started frequenting the vicinity of the modern park at the end of the last ice age, about 10,000 years ago. Up until about 700 years ago, the Fremont and Pueblo people inhabited the region, and they were followed by the Ute, Paiute, and Shoshone, who still lived in the region when Europeans began exploring it in the 18th and 19th centuries.

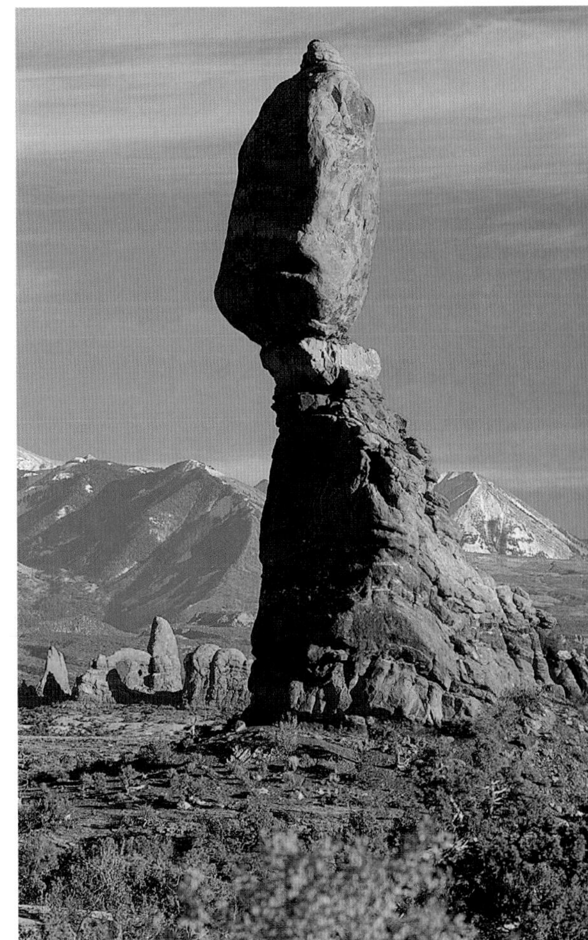

(Above) *Beyond the park's namesake arches is a diverse array of stunning geology, including Balanced Rock in the Windows area.*

# Temple Square

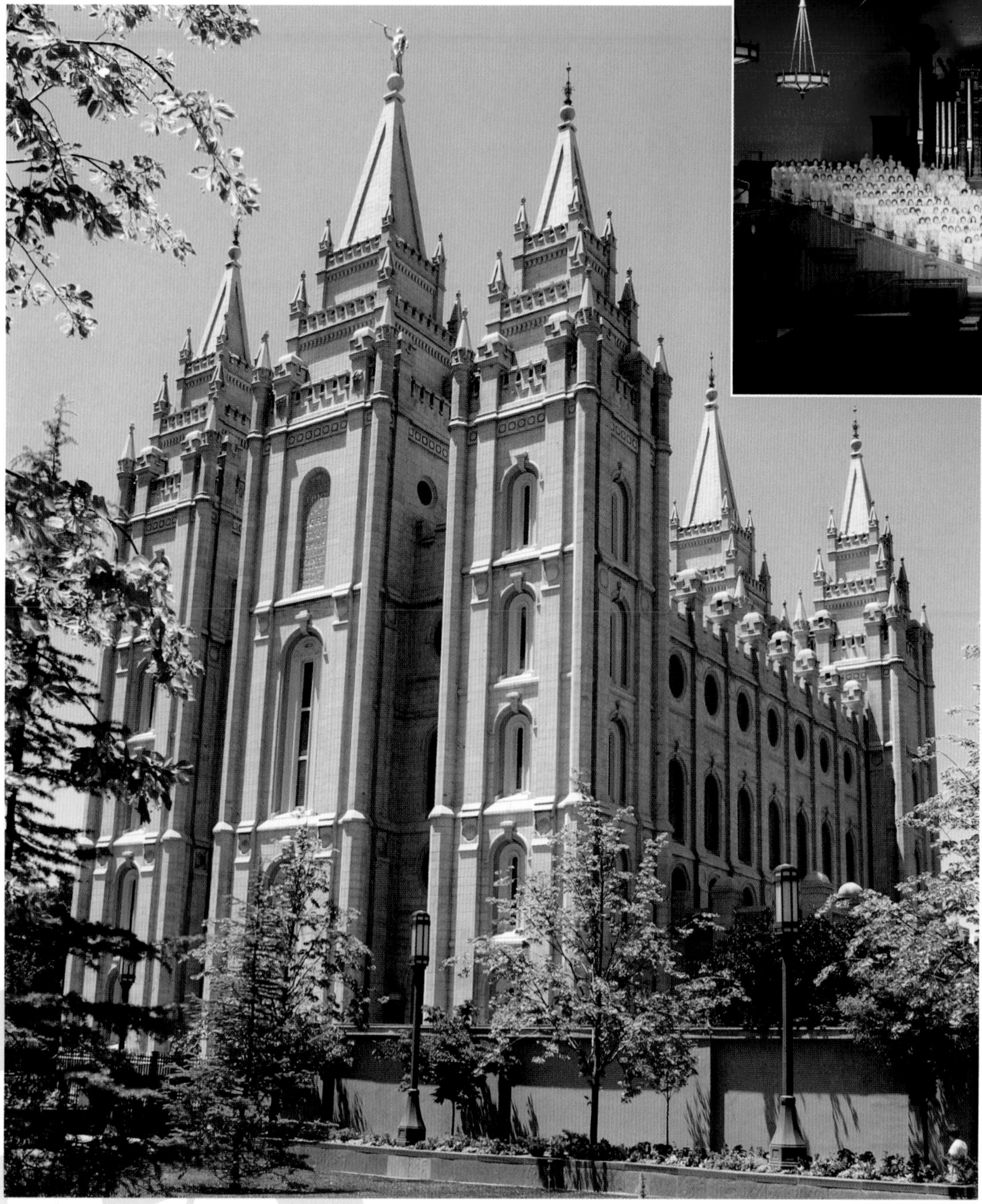

(Above) *The stunning spires of the Salt Lake Temple are the result of four decades of labor.* (Inset) *Temple Square is home to the world-renowned Mormon Tabernacle Choir and the site of one of the largest pipe organs in the world.*

Temple Square is the most visited site in Uta The striking Salt Lake Temple is at its cent This architectural wonder is a living legacy 40 years of hard work and perseverance.

Work on the Salt Lake Temple began 1853, six years after Brigham Young led tho sands of Mormons to the Great Salt Lake escape persecution in Nauvoo, Illinois. Durin the next four decades, workers painstaking carved granite blocks from the walls of Litt Cottonwood Canyon—now the home of tw renowned ski resorts—about 20 miles sout east of Temple Square. Weighing in excess of ton and sometimes as much as 5,600 pounc each block was transported by ox-draw wagon or railroad to the construction sit Master stonecutters then fit the blocks pe fectly into place, without the aid of mortar.

Brigham Young did not live to see th Temple's completion in 1893. But he certain would have approved of the majestic buil ing, capped with six towering spires, which h directed to be built to last an eternity.

# Great Salt Lake

Utah's Great Salt Lake is the largest lake in the United States west of the Mississippi. It covers about 1,700 square miles in the shadows of the grand Wasatch Range. The lake is a remnant of a prehistoric inland sea called Lake Bonneville that was at one time ten times as big as it is now.

The water of the Great Salt Lake is much saltier than the oceans'. Because of the high salinity, the lake supports no fish, but provides habitat for brine shrimp, brine flies, and flocks of migratory birds. Early European explorers believed that the lake was the tip of a Pacific fjord or fed by a river from the ocean.

(Right) *The rocky shoreline of the Great Salt Lake contrasts with the water's still surface and the surrounding salt flats.*

(Left) *The remnant of a once-vast inland sea, the Great Salt Lake has a higher salinity than the Pacific Ocean.*

Today, people boat and swim in its waters and sunbathe on white sand beaches. If you're planning to boat, nonmotorized crafts such as kayaks or sailboats are a better choice—the salty water is corrosive to metal. There are also trails for hiking and mountain biking on Antelope Island, a Utah State Park, as well as other stretches of shoreline. A luminescent sunset over the Great Salt Lake—clouds and sky streaked with vivid hues of orange and red—is unforgettable.

# Monument Valley

Mythic-looking monoliths of red sandstone loom over the sandy desert floor of Monument Valley in Utah and Arizona. Monument Valley is a Navajo Nation Tribal Park. It offers some of the most enduring images in the West. The valley's striking formations have been photographed countless times for Hollywood Westerns, postcards, and advertisements of all kinds—for good reason.

Little has changed since John Ford directed John Wayne here in *Stagecoach* in 1939. Many of the formations in Monument Valley (known as *Tsé Bii'Ndzisgaii* in Navajo, or "Valley of the Rocks") straddle the Utah–Arizona border. They were pushed through Earth's surface by geological upheaval, then carved by wind and rivers. The rock is stratified in three principal layers, with siltstone atop sandstone atop shale.

*Two of the most recognizable formations in Monument Valley are the aptly named East Mitten and West Mitten buttes.*

Among the most recognizable formations in Monument Valley are the 300-foot-tall, precariously narrow Totem Pole; the arch known as Ear of the Wind; and the East Mitten and West Mitten buttes.

# Canyonlands National Park

The wide-open wilderness of sandstone canyons in Canyonlands National Park is the remarkable product of millions of years of rushing water. The Colorado and the Green rivers have shaped this landscape of precipitous chasms and vividly painted mesas, pinnacles, and buttes.

Writer Edward Abbey described Canyonlands as a savage, barren region of Utah. He downplayed the elegance and intense beauty of this rugged land to try to keep people away and preserve its undisturbed wonder.

At the amazing confluence in the heart of Canyonlands, the rivers meet, merge, and divide the park into four distinct sections. In the north is the Island in the Sky, a mesa that rises more than 1,000 feet above the rivers. East of the confluence is the Needles, a landscape of grassy valleys dominated by banded pinnacles. The isolated western area of the park is The Maze, so named for its labyrinth of canyons. The final section, Horseshoe Canyon, is known for its rock art and spring wildflowers. And the rivers themselves provide a habitat that is in many ways the polar opposite of the surrounding arid desert.

*The Y-shape confluence of the Colorado and Green rivers is the heart of Canyonlands National Park.*

# Lake Powell

*With a labyrinth shoreline totalling almost 2,000 miles, Lake Powell is a boating and fishing paradise.*

Beyond the Glen Canyon Dam, the Colorado River widens into Lake Powell. The lake stretches from Lee's Ferry in Arizona to Utah's Orange Cliffs. There are two sides to the story of the reservoir—it has been beloved by some and reviled by others.

Lake Powell is a mecca for outdoors buffs of every stripe, from anglers and boaters to hikers and mountain bikers. The spectacular 187-mile body of water is vast and nestled in the blissful surroundings of red rock. Many vacationers spend their entire trip on the water itself in a rented houseboat. Lake Powell's shoreline stretches nearly 2,000 miles, which is longer than that of the entire Pacific Coast of the contiguous United States.

The construction of Glen Canyon Dam in the 1950s and 1960s remains controversial to this day. Many people opposed building the dam and the submersion of Glen Canyon. After it was built, the dam became a rallying point for environmentalists, who in recent years have called for draining Lake Powell and restoring Glen Canyon.

# Bryce Canyon National Park

ryce Canyon is a spectacular display of geo-
ogical formations in southern Utah. It is the
culpted side of the Paunsaugunt Plateau that
a fantasyland covered by thousands of red
nd orange hoodoos (rock columns). These
andstone towers were left behind when lay-
rs of the surrounding rock eroded.

The seeds for Bryce Canyon's dense forest of hoodoos were planted 60 million years ago, when inland seas and lakes covered southwestern Utah. Over eons, sediment collected on the lake's floor and congealed into rock. Later movements in the Earth's crust pushed the Paunsaugunt Plateau skyward, leaving its eastern edge exposed to the ravages of wind and water. The resulting multihued hoodoos are awe-inspiring.

Bryce Canyon is dynamic. The Colorado River whittles Bryce's rim away at a rate of two to four feet every 100 years—amazingly fast by geological standards.

*n intricately carved collection of vibrantly colored hoodoos populates the unforgettable landscape of Bryce Canyon National Park.*

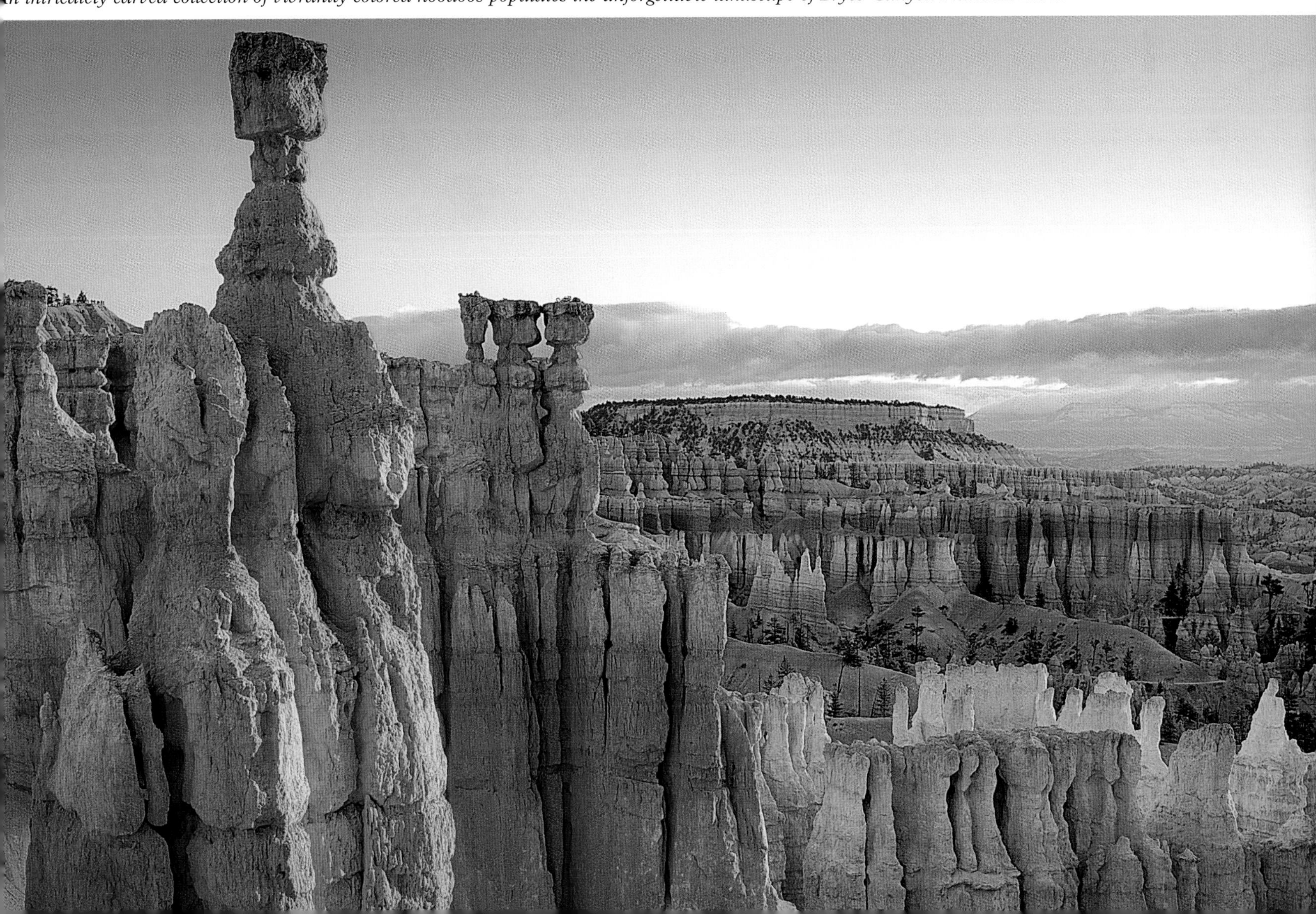

# Capitol Reef National Park

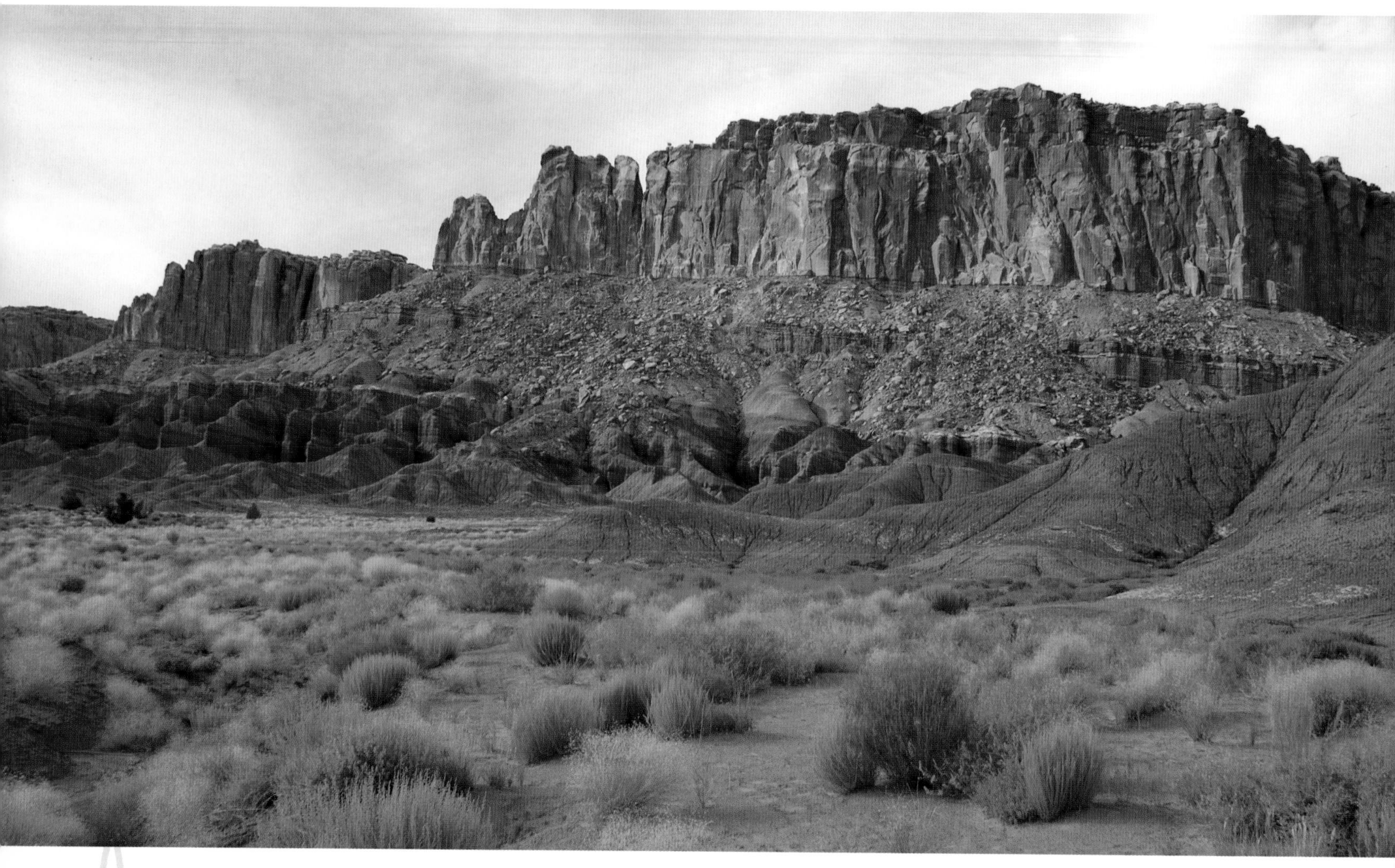

Capitol Reef is not actually a reef, but an area of towering limestone that was indeed underwater millions of years ago. It is actually a monoclinal, what geologists call a wrinkle in Earth's crust.

This wrinkle is known as the Waterpocket Fold, which rises in ridges for 100 miles across southern Utah. Capitol Reef, with sheer cliffs rising 1,000 feet in some places, is the most scenic segment of the fold. The 19th-century pioneers who named it were inspired by the white domes of sandstone that crown it, resembling stately rotundas from afar.

Capitol Reef was known to the native Navajo as "The Land of the Sleeping Rainbow" due to the broad color spectrum adorning the rock walls. It is home to numerous unique formations, including the looming Castle.

*Capitol Reef is the most photogenic stretch of the Waterpocket Fold, a 100-mile-long wrinkle in the earth of southern Utah.*

The Temple of the Sun and the Temple of the Moon are opposing twin monoliths in the spectacular Cathedral Valley near the park's northern border. These sandstone giants were carved by erosion.

# Little Bighorn Battlefield National Monument

As the U.S. government encouraged westward expansion after the Civil War, rapid development threatened the way of life of the Cheyenne and Lakota peoples. In the early 1870s, violence between native warriors and U.S. soldiers escalated, and Lieutenant Colonel George Custer was dispatched to lead 12 companies of the 7th Cavalry in defense of national interests in the Wild West.

At a ridge above the Little Bighorn River near Hardin, Montana, Custer's party was taken by surprise and overwhelmed by a far larger Sioux and Cheyenne war party on June 25 and 26, 1876, during what is now known as "Custer's Last Stand." Custer and more than 200 soldiers under his command perished in the battle, as did at least 60 Cheyenne and Lakota (the exact number is unknown). Despite the outcome, Custer's Last Stand marked the end for the Cheyenne and Lakota peoples' nomadic way of life in the West.

In 1879, the battlefield became a national cemetery for the fallen U.S. Army soldiers. In 2003, a corresponding Indian Memorial—a striking sculpture garden named "Peace Through Unity"—was dedicated. These memorials honor all who fought here, whether for their country, for land, or to preserve their way of life. The solemnity of the battlefield inspires quiet reverence.

*The memorial on Last Stand Hill was built over the mass grave of 7th Cavalry soldiers, U.S. Indian scouts, and others who died here.*

# Glacier National Park

Etched over eons, the perfect geometry scoring the sides of the canyons, valleys, cirques, and mountains of Montana's Glacier National Park is the majestic work of nearly extinct glaciers. Over the last 60 million years, these glaciers have melted, contracted, receded, and shaped vast areas of rock and earth.

Nearly parallel grooves worn into the rocks are a timeless testament to the dogged power of the ice that was once massive enough to pulverize mountainsides and move boulders. Glaciers once dominated the landscape, but after creating the perfectly etched lines on the canyon walls, many melted and became long deep blue lakes. Smaller glaciers can be seen on north-facing walls and other cool alcoves shaded from sunlight.

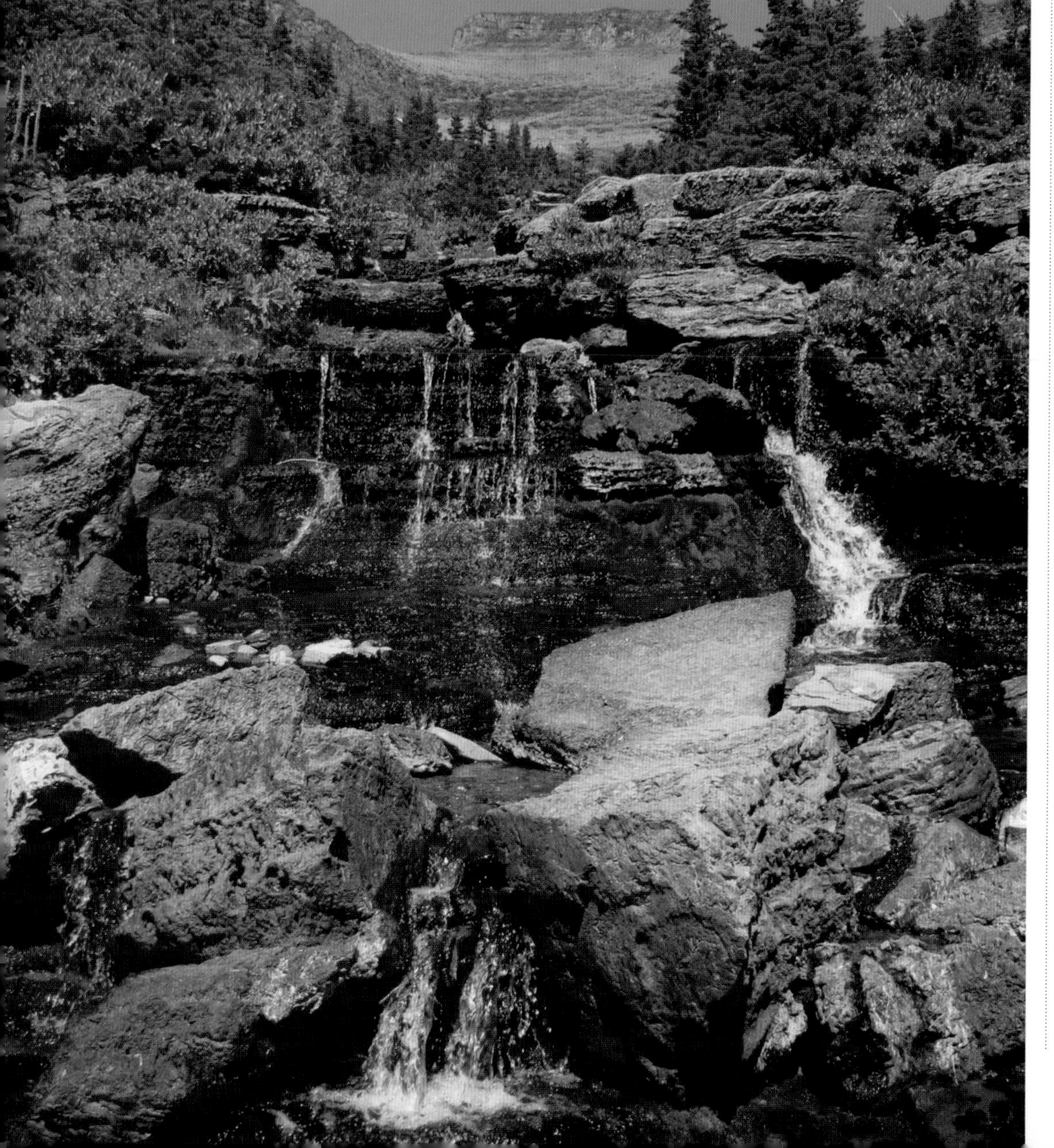

But this is still a land of water, wind, and ice, with a long, determined winter. Six hundred and fifty-three lakes and 1,000 miles of rivers and streams are shoehorned into roughly 1,600 square miles (about the size of Delaware). Cutting over Logan Pass through some of North America's most sublime scenery is Going-to-the-Sun Road, completed in 1932. The trail system covering the rugged terrain is a hiker's paradise.

The creation of Glacier and all of its perfect lines boggles the mind. Renowned naturalist John Muir dubbed it "the best care-killing scenery on the continent." Considering the amount of time and slow, stubborn power required to carve the park's unmistakable scenery makes day-to-day calendars and troubles seem small, short-lived, and self-centered—which for many is a good thing.

The origins of this geological masterpiece are the Lewis and Livingston Mountain Ranges that are at the park's heart. Most of the telltale glacial scars marking the park's scenery follow parallel lines down mountain slopes where

*The park's glaciers are the source of water for countless scenic waterfalls.*

## Quick Fact

***Flathead Lake***

Flathead Lake, which lies just southwest of Glacier National Park, is the largest natural freshwater lake west of the Mississippi River. It is the defining feature of the valley of the same name and a prime habitat for a wide range of wildlife. It is 28 miles long and 15 miles across at its widest point.

Flathead Lake is surrounded by forested mountains. It contains Wild Horse Island, one of the largest inland islands in the entire United States, which is home to wildlife including bighorn sheep, black bears, and bald eagles. Legend has it that the island's name comes from the Salish-Kootnai Indians, who kept their horses on the island to prevent them from being stolen.

Many visitors come to fish in the lake, which is known for its trophy trout. Scenic cruises are also popular. There are plenty of cultural amenities near the shore, including the theater and restaurants in the charming village of Bigfork and the Mission Mountain Winery on the southwestern lakefront.

Flathead Lake is 370 feet deep at its deepest point, which has helped fuel legends of a prehistoric sea creature lurking in its depths. Sightings of a whalelike beast have been reported for more than a century.

gravity pulled the glaciers across the rock. Then there are occasional lines that avert from the parallel slant, where the rock withstood the ice, causing the glacier to veer off course, slightly changing its trajectory though never stopping or reversing it.

Viewed from the plains east of Glacier National Park, the Rocky Mountains are stunning. They abruptly rise from 4,000 feet in elevation to more than 10,000 atop the highest peaks, then just as precipitously drop off to about 3,000 feet at Lake McDonald in the park's southwestern quarter. To the north, Glacier connects with Waterton National Park in Alberta, Canada, and the two make up International Peace Park, a World Heritage Site.

Atop Glacier's alpine passes, bighorns munch on the hardy plants that speckle the rocky cliffs. This is also the domain of black bears and grizzly bears, which were driven to the high country when their natural habitat of the plains was developed for agriculture.

The glaciers here are receding quickly. With global temperatures on the rise, the number of ice shelves has dwindled from historical highs by 50 percent in recent years, and climatologists believe the glaciers might be gone in the next century. Regardless of their fate, the glaciers of northwestern Montana have left a lasting mark on the land—come wintertime, snow beautifully frosts the thousands of hypnotic grooves one by one.

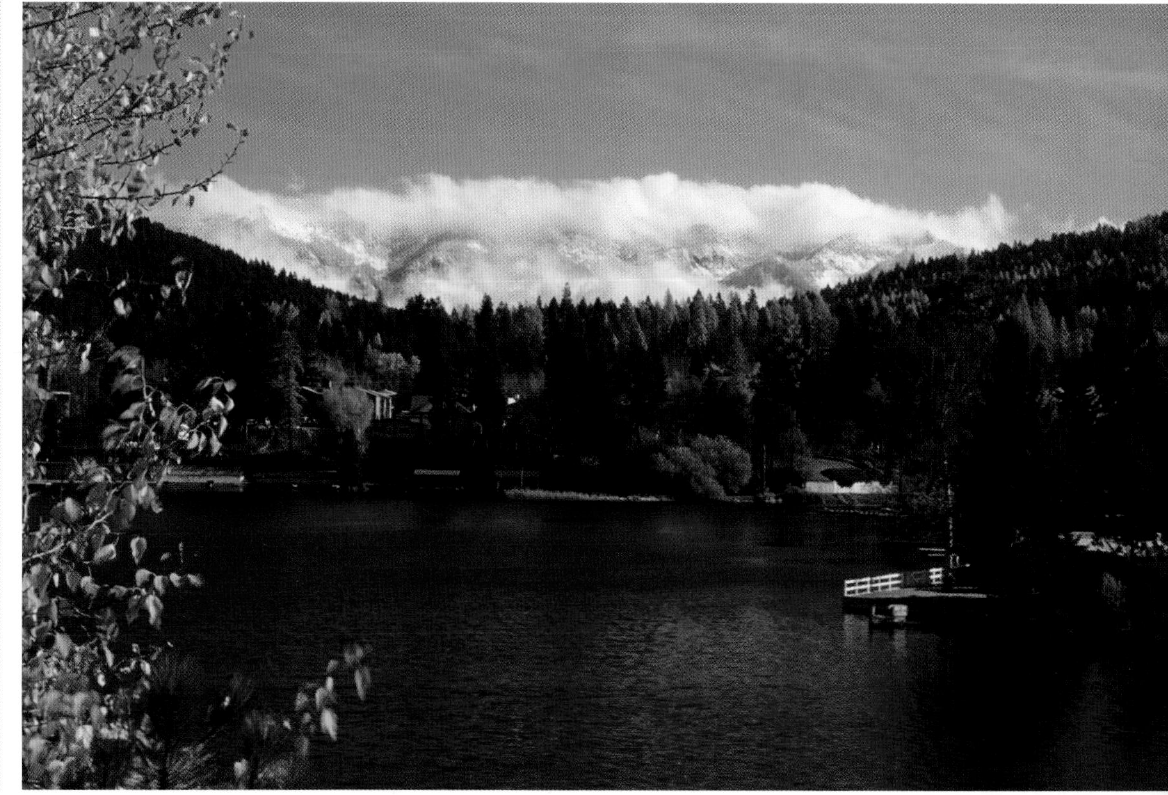

*Just southwest of Glacier National Park, Flathead Lake is another terrific Montana destination—and allegedly home to a secretive monster.*

# Museum of the Rockies

Long before grizzlies and bighorn sheep roamed the Rockies, Montana's claim to fame was wildlife of a different kind—dinosaurs. About 60 million years ago, the region was tropical. Local dinosaurs included the *Tyrannosaurus rex*, *Apatosaurus*, and *Triceratops*, all of which thrived until a shift in climate wiped them out.

This rich prehistory is told at Bozeman's Museum of the Rockies, home to the largest collection of American dinosaur bones in the world, nearly all of which were discovered in Montana. Under the umbrella of Montana State University, the museum gives insight into a world-class dinosaur research center. The museum is in large part the brainchild of Dr. Jack Horner, a celebrated paleontologist and consultant to the *Jurassic Park* films.

*The world-class dinosaur exhibits at the Museum of the Rockies in Bozeman, Montana, include the skull of a* T. rex*—and its jagged smile.*

*Outside the museum, a living-history farm offers a peek back in time into the lives of the Gallatin Valley's pioneers.*

Visitors begin with a crash course on th history of the Rockies, starting with the Bi Bang theory. Then they explore the dinosau exhibits. Some displays showcase casts, an others hold real fossils, including the larg est dinosaur skull in the world (a nine-foo torosaurus noggin) and a *T. rex* femur tha amazingly revealed soft tissues that had bee preserved inside for 68 million years. Th Museum of the Rockies provides comprehen sive displays that go well beyond the typica dusty collection of giant skeletons. The exhib its dig into dinosaur biology and behavior, a well as the science and research that goes int fossil recovery and paleontology.

# ʌakoshika State Park

*ıe bleak but beautiful badlands of Makoshika State Park in Glendive, Montana, sit in stark contrast to the surrounding plains.*

ome 65 million years ago, the plains in east-n Montana were vast, lush, and green. For geological split second, dinosaurs thrived in e area. Then they became extinct, the sea ceded, the mud dried, and the first of several e ages hit. After the last ice age 11,000 years go, the ancient glacial marks left here were ıried under layers of silt.

But wind and weather wore the silt away, revealing layers of red sandstone atop layers of gray mudstone atop layers of dark shale; hoodoos, caprocks, and other geological anomalies; and an otherworldly badlands landscape the Lakota dubbed Makoshika, or "bad earth."

Besides exposing Makoshika's rugged beauty, erosion also helped unearth fossils hundreds of millions of years old, including a remarkable triceratops skull, excavated in 1991. It, along with other fossils discovered here, is now on display in the park's visitor center. There is also an exhibit on one prehistoric area resident that didn't go the way of the dinosaur: the paddlefish, which still swims in the depths of the nearby Yellowstone River.

# Craters of the Moon National Monument and Preserve

The eerie landscape of Craters of the Moon National Monument and Preserve does not look like it belongs in southern Idaho. In fact, it doesn't even look like it belongs on this planet—thus the lunar moniker.

The area owes its mysterious appearance to its volcanic past. The craters are actually pocks

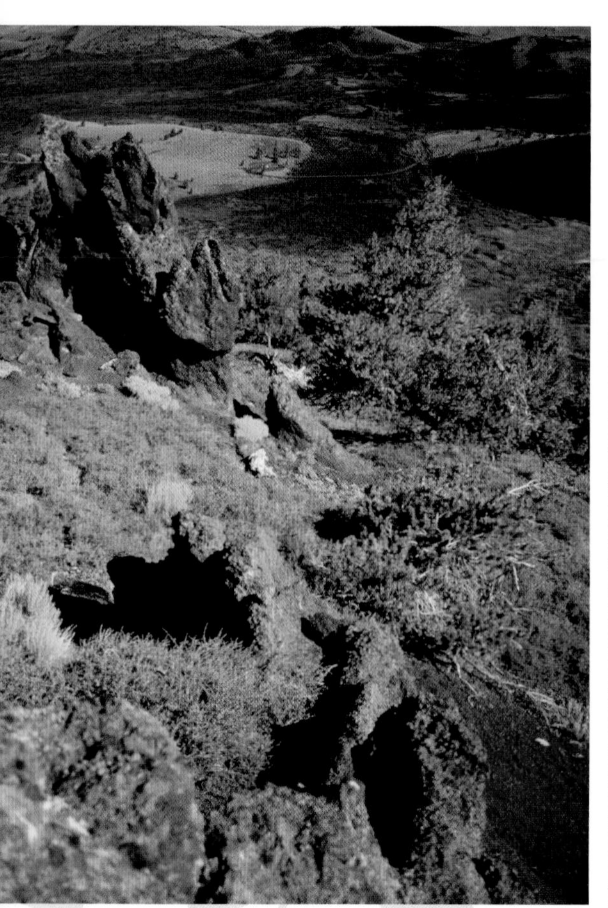

*Unusual igneous rock formations dot the varied landscape at Craters of the Moon National Monument.*

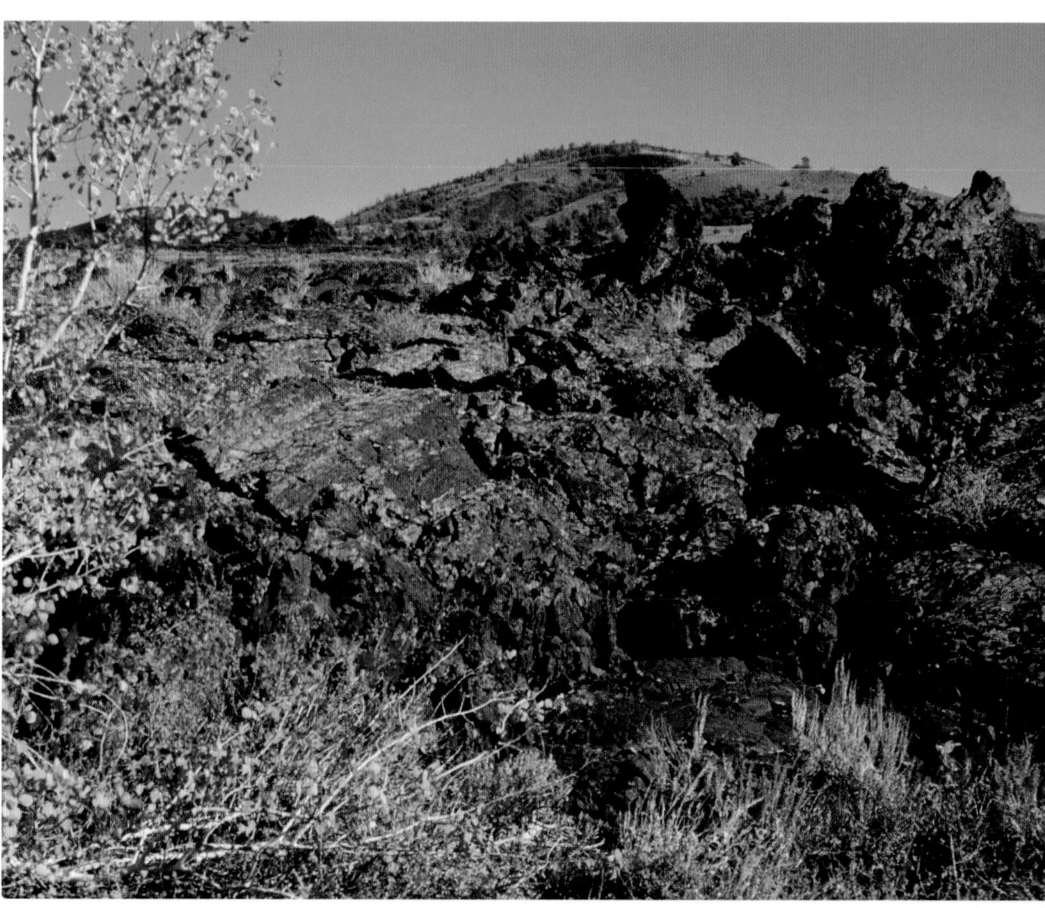

*The otherworldly landscape is a result of a violent volcanic epoch that lasted from 15,000 years ago to 2,000 years ago.*

in several lava fields dotted with sagebrush and cinder cones. The eruptions that created the terrain took place between 15,000 and 2,000 years ago, leaving behind a sheet of hardened lava 60 miles wide and more than 10,000 feet deep at its deepest point.

Craters of the Moon is home to all sorts of interesting features forged by once red-hot magma, such as unusual-looking splatter cones an cavelike lava tubes. The tallest cinder cone, B Cinder Butte, rises more than 700 feet abov the surrounding plain, and there are 19 othe at least 100 feet high. Many scientists think th volcanic zone—called the Great Rift—that cre ated the monument is due for another explo sion in the next few centuries.

# Hells Canyon of the Snake River

A huge lake once covered the area now bisected by the Oregon–Idaho state line. The rocky bulge of the Owyhee Mountains kept the Snake and Columbia rivers separate until giving way roughly a million years ago. Then the Snake rapidly cut its way through as much as ten miles of igneous rock to join with the Columbia, chiseling out the chasm now known as the Hells Canyon of the Snake River.

*The view of the Snake River from the rim of Hells Canyon is nothing short of spectacular.*

Today, Hells Canyon is one of the continent's most dramatic landscapes. The adjacent mountain ridges rise an average of more than a mile above the canyon floor, towering over the white water below. The pinnacle of He Devil Mountain is almost 8,000 feet higher than the river, making for the deepest gorge in the United States.

The oldest rocks in the canyon originated from underwater volcanoes when Hells Canyon was part of a Pacific island chain. Rivers eroded some of the lava, carrying it downstream, and the Seven Devils and Eagle Cap Mountains were pushed skyward. The result is the spectacular Hells Canyon.

# Redwood National and State Parks

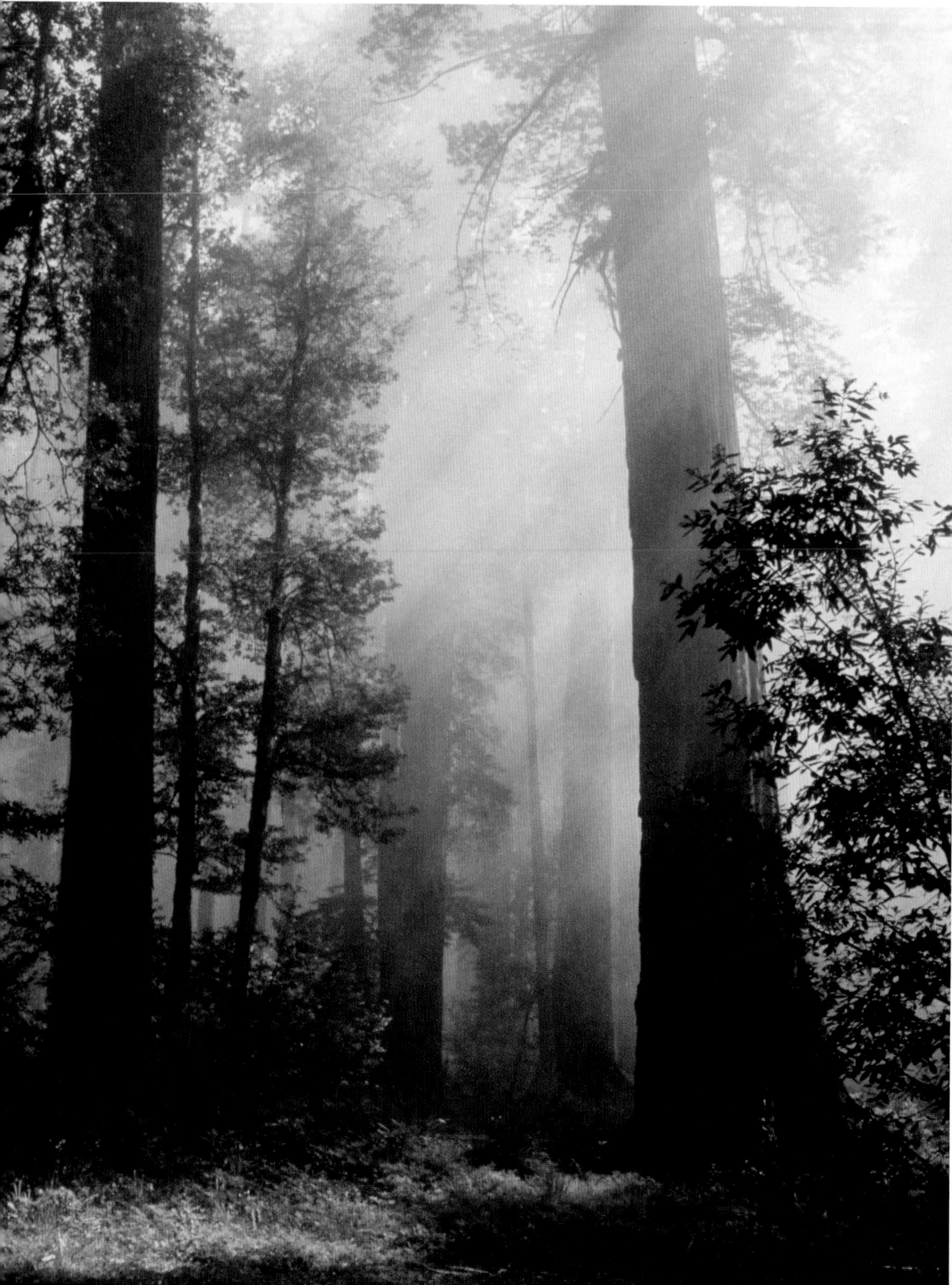

Near remote stretches of northern California's oceanfront, the water, soil, and sun blend perfectly for redwood growth. The results are the redwood forests, which are nothing short of astounding. Walking through the old-growth redwood forest may make you feel as though you've ingested the same potion Alice swallowed after she tumbled down the rabbit's hole into Wonderland.

More than 100,000 acres of soul-stirring forest are protected under the auspices of Redwood National and State Parks, but the ecosystem has been threatened by the logging industry for years. These kings of the conifers once grew elsewhere in North America, but this is the last spot where they thrive in such size and number. Beyond the towering trees, the cool coastal climate is ideal for hiking and taking in the Jurassic-looking scene.

Imagine this: The tallest redwood in the parks is more than twice as tall as the Statue of Liberty. The parks' tallest trees, located in the aptly named Tall Trees Grove, measure about 360 feet from base to treetop, heights that have taken more than 600 years to attain. The first branches of these trees begin 100 to 200 feet above the spongy forest floor, a result of higher branches blocking sunlight as their pinnacles inched skyward.

The number of trees growing today is a mere fraction of those that once blanketed the

*The forest is on a larger scale than any other, affording visitors a brand-new perspective.*

## Quick Fact

### *Tall Tree Tales*

The coast redwood, *Sequoia sempervirens,* is the tallest known plant species in the world. Standing among these giants, it's easy to imagine ancient dinosaurs traipsing through the foliage. Fossil records have shown that this type of redwood thrived during the Jurassic era 160 million years ago and has changed little since then.

- The oldest specimen of coast redwood was logged in 1933—it was 2,200 years old.
- Coast redwoods can reach heights of more than 360 feet, which is as tall as a 35-story skyscraper.
- The tallest known redwood, called the "Tall Tree," was measured at 367.8 feet in 1963. The tree still stands on the Redwood Creek in the park, but its top broke off in the 1980s. It is thought to be 600 years old.
- The diameter at the base of a redwood can be as much as 22 feet.
- These redwoods can weigh up to 1.6 million pounds.
- The bark can be up to 12 inches thick.

*Fallen redwoods become the base for all sorts of new vegetation in the damp climate.*

egion. In the late 1700s, the redwood forest in California and Oregon covered an estimated wo million acres. A century later, loggers had pushed into the region and decimated mile after mile of pristine, primeval forests.

By 1965, the redwood forest had been whittled down to 300,000 acres, and Congress passed legislation in 1968 for about 50,000 acres of it to be protected in national and state parks. In 1978, Congress added another 48,000 acres, including 39,000 logged acres that one park official described as resembling an active war zone. Today, the clear-cut area has been reclaimed for redwood trees, but officials estimate that it will take 50 years for the logging scars to disappear and another 250 years for the new redwoods to grow to modest size.

Despite the redwood's dominance over the scenery, the complex ecosystem of the forest relies on much more than just the trees. The cycles of tree growth and rot supply nutrients to a host of plants and fungi. The lush greenery makes a great habitat for small creatures, such as voles and banana slugs, and large animals, including a sizable elk herd. Marine mammals, including gray whales during their annual migrations, are also visible near the parks in the Pacific Ocean.

Many also believe this area to be the home of the legendary Sasquatch, and hiking through the dense forest and its oversize underbrush makes the existence of Bigfoot seem possible. In these rugged, nearly impenetrable woods, it's conceivable that an entire species could remain hidden for as long as it wished—provided the trees remain protected from the logger's ax.

# Point Reyes National Seashore

The peaceful, pastoral Point Reyes Peninsula is a world apart from San Francisco, just 22 miles to the south. From its eastern boundary, Inverness Ridge, to the Pacific Ocean, the peninsula is a land of windswept beaches, grasslands, and forest. It's the windiest spot on the West Coast.

The entire Point Reyes Peninsula is in perpetual motion—it's moving northwest at approximately two inches a year. The peninsula lies on the Pacific Plate along the San Andreas Fault. Along the fault, pressure builds up gradually when the plates shift, and the fault eventually gives way—in other words, an earthquake occurs. The biggest earthquake was in 1906, when the entire peninsula sho
20 feet northwest in an instant.

Point Reyes National Seashore is rich wit human history, dating back to the Coasta Miwok Indians, who inhabited the peninsul circa 3000 B.C. It is currently a mixed-use uni of the National Park Service, complete wit active dairy operations, an oyster farm, and historic lighthouse.

*Bordered on three sides by the Pacific Ocean, the picturesque Point Reyes has recorded more than 490 bird species.*

# Napa Valley Vineyards

Napa Valley is only five miles across at its widest point and 30 miles long, but its reputation stretches around the world. Located 50 miles north of San Francisco, the valley is home to 110,000 people, five incorporated cities, and 200 wineries.

In the late 1800s, there were more than 500 wineries in the valley. The longstanding success of the local wine industry is a result of the climate and soil, which are ideal for growing grapes. The soil is especially diverse: Fully half of the varieties of soil on the planet are found within the confines of Napa Valley. Stringent county policies limit development outside the cities in Napa Valley, leaving the agricultural land wide open and pastoral.

Napa Valley was carved by the Napa River, which flows directly into San Francisco Bay and attracts anglers and paddlers. But most visitors come for fresh air, good food, and, of course, great wine. The "crush" that accompanies the fall harvest is one of the valley's busiest times.

*In Napa, it's all about quality, not quantity. The verdant 30-mile-long valley contributes only a fraction of California's total wine production.*

# Golden Gate Bridge

The Golden Gate Bridge does for the West Coast what the Statue of Liberty does for the East: It welcomes newcomers while proclaiming the strength, determination, and promise of the United States.

The Golden Gate Bridge also introduces visitors to the sumptuous San Francisco Bay Area. According to Mayor Gavin Newsom, "San Franciscans know we live in the most beautiful city in the world, a jewel on the edge of the Golden Gate."

The bridge opened in 1937 with a celebration in which 200,000 jubilant pedestrians crossed it. During its 50th-anniversary celebration, 300,000 pedestrians walked across which is one terrific way to visit the bridge i you're in shape.

The Golden Gate Bridge, which is paintec orange vermilion (more commonly callec "international orange"), is golden in every other respect.

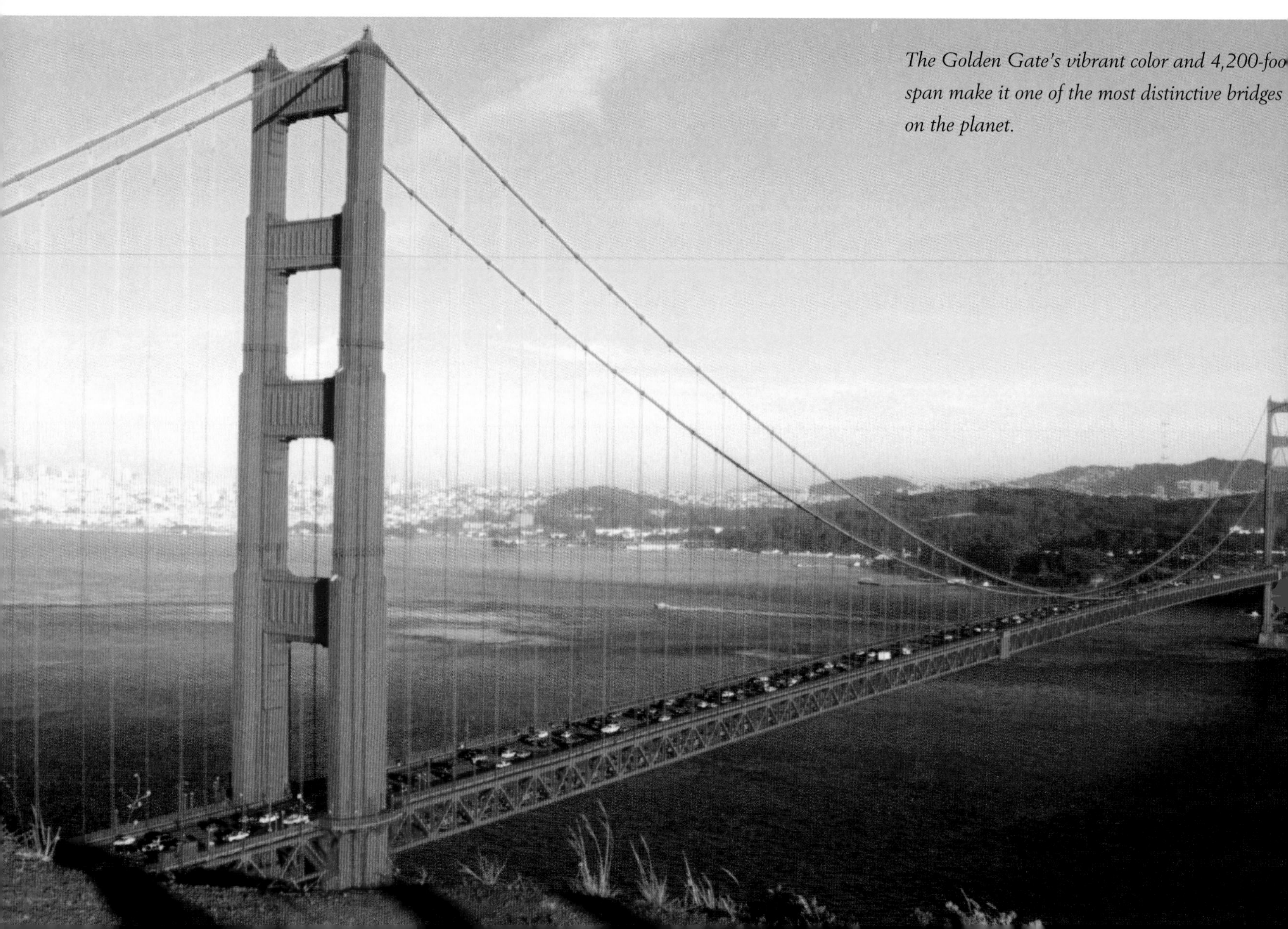

*The Golden Gate's vibrant color and 4,200-foo span make it one of the most distinctive bridges on the planet.*

The bridge was named not for its color but because it spans the Golden Gate Strait, named by explorer John C. Fremont. In 1919, architect Irving Morrow wrote, the strait "is loveliest at the cool end of the day when, for a few breathless moments, faint afterglows transfigure the gray line of hills." Years later, Morrow was responsible for the bridge's stylized Art Deco embellishments as well as its famous color. Some opponents argued that only steel gray or carbon black paint could protect the bridge; the U.S. Navy wanted it painted yellow with black stripes. Morrow insisted paint could be invented to protect and burnish the bridge's graceful, sinewy architecture as well as increase its visibility in fog while blending with its natural surroundings. He was right: The bridge didn't require an overall repainting for 27 years.

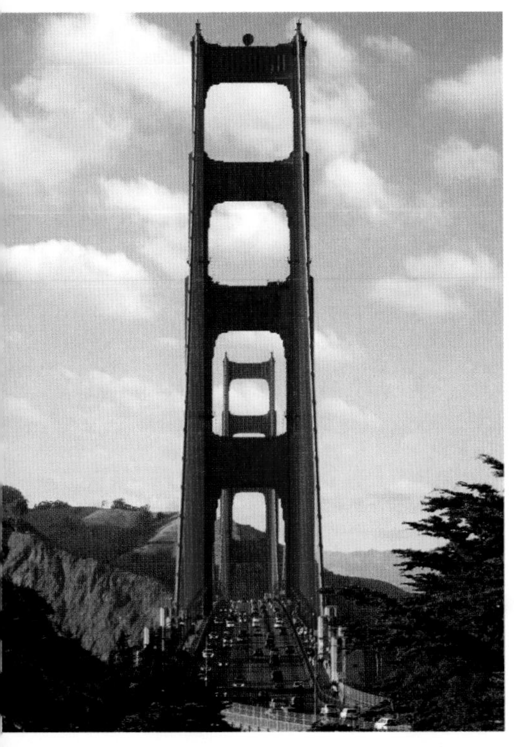

## Quick Fact

### *Alcatraz Island*

Legendary tales of convicts' daring escape attempts surround Alcatraz Island, also known as "The Rock." One of the first escape attempts occurred on January 13, 1939. Five prisoners attempted to flee the island, but they were all captured or killed in the process. The spot now called Barker Beach marks where Arthur "Doc" Barker was shot dead during this prison break.

Alcatraz was an official federal penitentiary from 1934 through 1963, though military prison materials date from 1859 to 1934. While it was initially a military fort built to protect San Francisco Bay, its isolation made Alcatraz the perfect sentencing spot for dangerous convicts. In its years as a prison, no one ever escaped The Rock.

The Golden Gate Bridge saved San Francisco from its isolation on a peninsula. The bridge—which, at 4,200 feet from tower to tower, reigned as the world's longest suspension bridge for 27 years—heralded an era in which suspension bridges defined modernism. So striking and beautiful is its sculptural design, the bridge forged the way for a generation of graceful, buoyant Art Deco architecture in the midst of the Great Depression.

The beautiful bridge is also the centerpiece of the Golden Gate National Recreation Area (though the bridge and recreation area are managed by different agencies). Golden Gate is one of the most popular destinations in the national parks system, with more than 14 million visitors each year. The 74,000-acre expanse includes favorite destinations such as China Beach, Muir Beach, Fort Mason, and Alcatraz Island. It also includes the Presidio of San Francisco, which was established by the Spanish in 1776 and has become the oldest continuously operating U.S. military base.

The park provides panoramas of the Golden Gate Bridge that have been made famous over the years, mainly by Hollywood. The memorable scene in Hitchcock's *Vertigo*, which emphasized the bridge's overwhelming scale and sweep, was filmed under it, on the San Francisco side near Fort Point. It's definitely a view to see firsthand. From across the bay, check out the bridge's magnificence from Fort Baker, located in Marin County. You can find another picture-perfect vantage point across the bridge on its northern side at Marin Headlands, best reached by bus or car. The views from high on the San Francisco side are breathtaking as well, and don't forget the bracing scene from Alcatraz Island!

*Motorists are prohibited from changing tires on the Golden Gate Bridge.*

# Chinatown and Chinese New Year

For 15 days during Chinese New Year, San Francisco's Chinatown neighborhood bustles with sound and color—even more than it usually does. This is the largest Chinatown on the continent, and it pulls out all the stops for the annual festivities. The Chinese New Year begins on the first day of the first moon of the lunar calendar, which usually falls between late January and mid-February.

The Chinese New Year Parade (a San Francisco tradition since just after the 1849 Gold Rush) is now the biggest illuminated nighttime parade in North America. In fact, it's the largest event of its kind on any continent except Asia. Participants take the year's theme and run with it, crafting gorgeous floats that range from purely aesthetic to political. Dancers and stilt-walkers entertain the crowds, and others light firecrackers, pass out "funny money," and do their best to bring good luck to the New Year. The parade culminates with Gum Lung, the Golden Dragon—an ornate, human-powered 200-foot silk, gauze, and velvet beast with a bamboo skeleton.

Year-round, Chinatown is one of the Bay Area's most visited tourist hotspots, with plenty of eateries, bars, and shops. But it also serves as an authentic neighborhood where people live, work, and play.

*San Francisco's vibrant Chinatown is the most populous neighborhood of its kind in North America and a must-see stop on any visit to the City by the Bay.*

# Winchester Mystery House

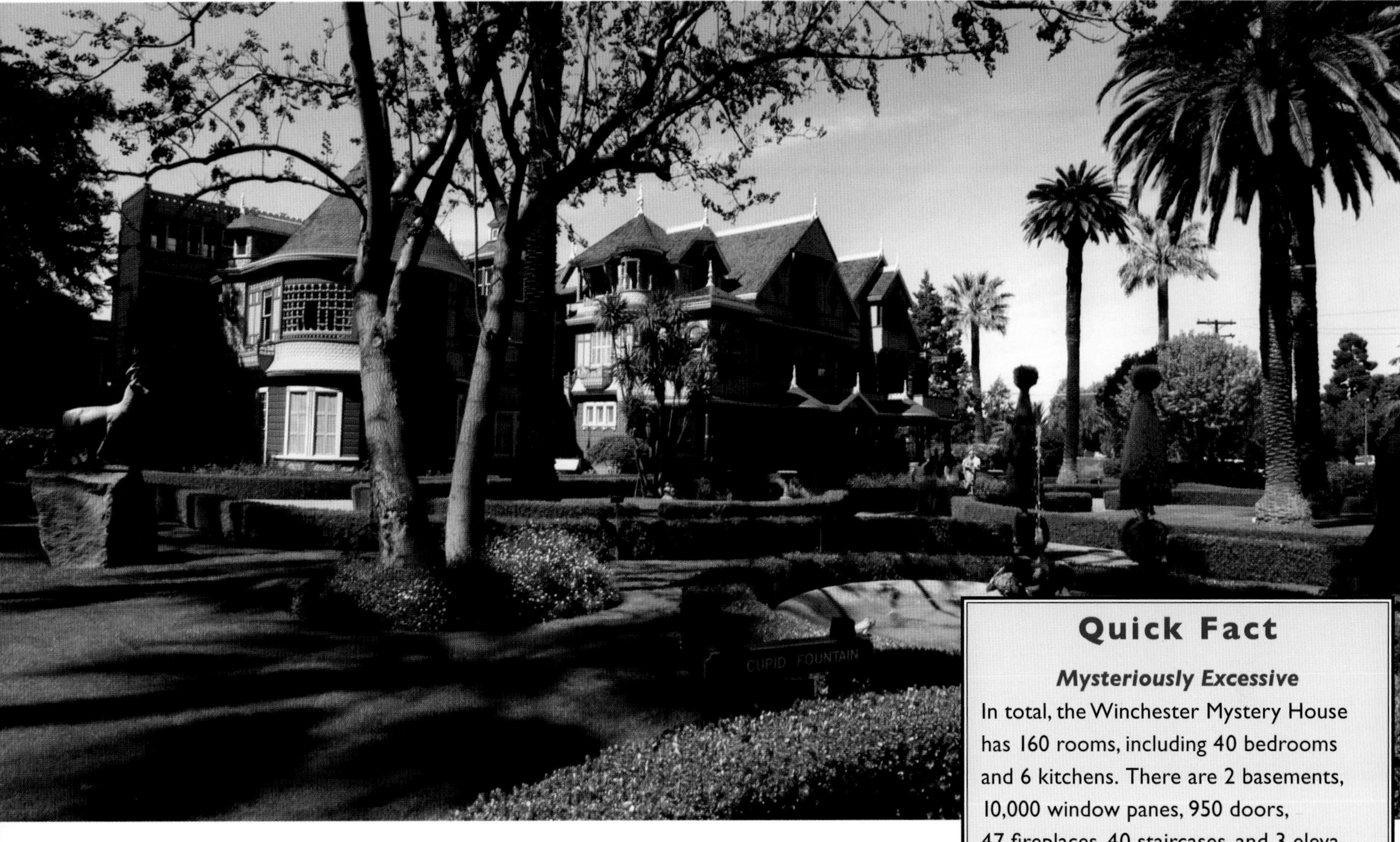


**Quick Fact**

***Mysteriously Excessive***

In total, the Winchester Mystery House has 160 rooms, including 40 bedrooms and 6 kitchens. There are 2 basements, 10,000 window panes, 950 doors, 47 fireplaces, 40 staircases, and 3 elevators. The enormous house required more than 20,000 gallons of paint in all.

n 1884, Sarah Winchester, heiress to the Win-hester Rifle Company, visited a soothsayer fter the death of her husband and baby daugh-er. The medium told her that her fate was ied to her house: Continuous building would ppease the evil spirits and help her attain eter-al life. Winchester took the premonition very eriously. She continued building her San José, alifornia, mansion for the ensuing 38 years, pending the bulk of her multimillion-dollar nheritance in the process.

*Sarah Winchester's superstitions resulted in an oddity of a mansion that was under continuous construction for almost four decades.*

When the hammering finally stopped after Winchester's passing in 1922, there were 160 rooms. But there's more than just sheer size at work here: Winchester chose designs to ward off the evil spirits that she believed plagued her every move. Some stairways and doors lead nowhere, and the stained glass seems to be inspired by a disturbing spider web. A plethora of features are tied to a certain number. The number of palms lining the driveway? The number of hooks in the séance room? The number of lights in the chandeliers? The answer to all three questions is 13, a further sign of Sarah Winchester's superstitions.

# Yosemite Valley

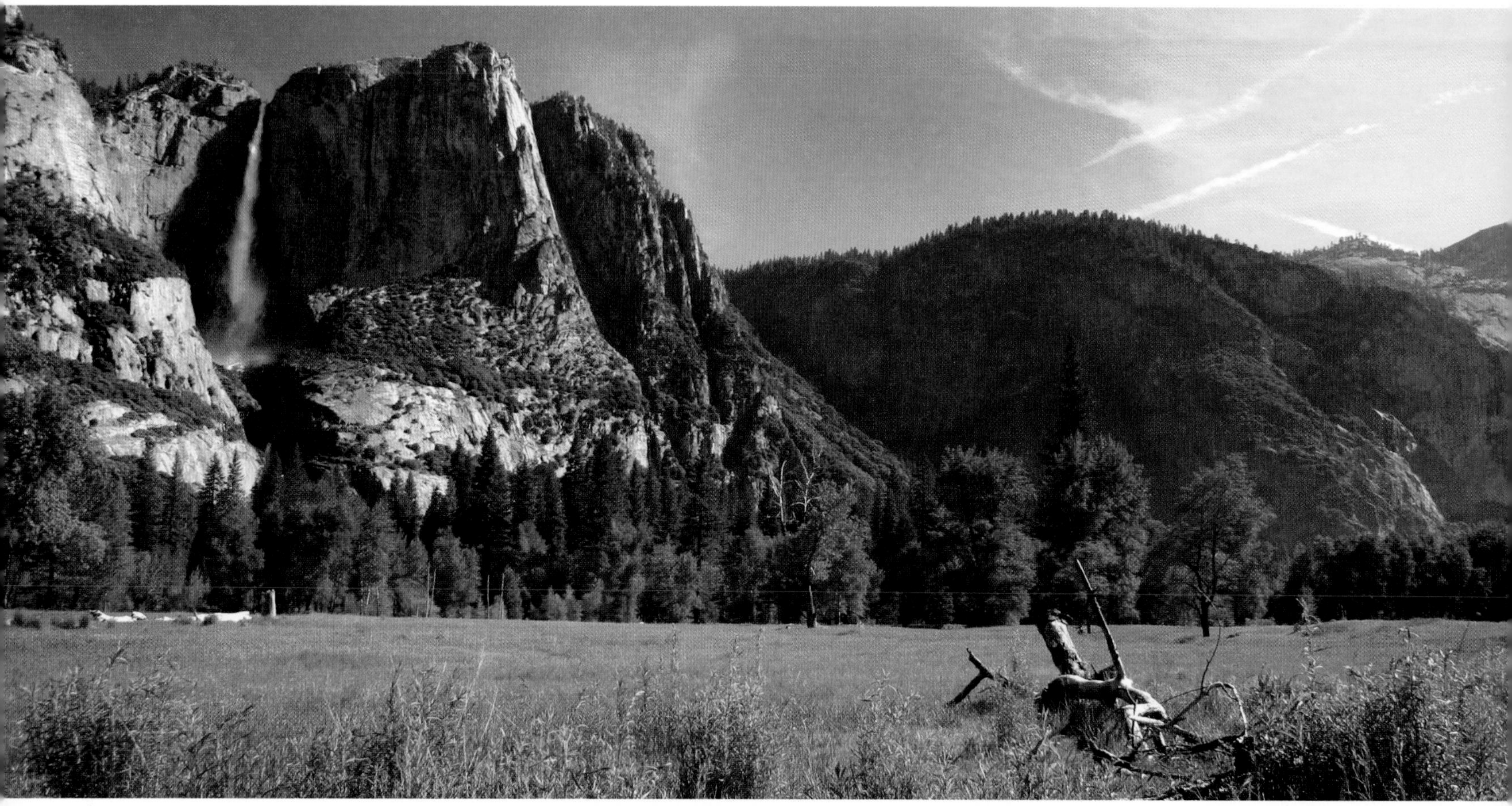

The bearded father of the conservation movement, John Muir, loved central California's Yosemite Valley. One glimpse and it's easy to see why: The unmistakable panorama reveals a dazzling wonderland of granite sculpted over eons by ice, wind, and water. Waterfalls cascade down the granite cliffs, the most famous of which is Yosemite Falls, at 2,425 feet the tallest waterfall in North America—the equivalent of 13 Niagaras. And that's just scratching the surface.

Yosemite Valley is bookended by two famous geologic masterworks. These hulking, distinct formations are known worldwide: Half Dome rises 4,800 feet above the eastern end of the valley, while the 3,600-foot El Capitán (Spanish for "the captain") stands sentry at the western entrance, fronted by one of the sheerest cliffs in the world. As any visitor to Yosemite quickly learns, it's difficult to take a photograph in Yosemite Valley without framing this handsome pair.

Yosemite Valley is undoubtedly one of nature's most awe-inspiring creations, and Muir eloquently described its wonders time and time again. "Nearly all the upper basin of the Merced was displayed, with its sublime domes and cañons, dark upsweeping forests and glorious array of white peaks deep in the sky, every feature glowing, radiating beauty that pours into our flesh and bones like heat rays from fire," he wrote of a view he enjoyed from Yosemite's high country. "Never before

*The 2,425-foot ribbon of water known as Yosemite Falls is just one of many superlative sites visitors gawk at from the valley floor.*

had I seen so glorious a landscape, so boundless an affluence of sublime mountain beauty."

The peaks and meadows of today's landscape in Yosemite Valley are the work of glaciers. The slow-moving sheets of ice carved this masterpiece over the course of the last three million years, expanding and contracting and tearing granite asunder.

Another valley lies to the north: Hetch Hetchy is Yosemite's counterpart in both scale and aesthetics. But in 1913, Congress passed legislation to dam the Tuolumne River, flooding Hetch Hetchy. Muir led the fight against this action, but Congress sided with the city of San Francisco, whose sudden growth called for more and more water.

The transcendent scenery, sheer beauty, and untamed nature of Yosemite Valley draw a crowd. With more than three million visitors each year, the summer traffic can get quite thick. At times, the valley's population exceeds 20,000, making it the center of activity for the entire Sierra Nevada region. Crowds form at the developed areas, the hotels, and the various eateries throughout the valley, but there's still plenty of room to roam. Yosemite National Park is about 750,000 acres in all. And though Yosemite Valley is a mere fraction of that total, even John Muir couldn't investigate every last nook and cranny in his 76 years.

*The landmark granite formation Half Dome was once considered impossible to climb.*

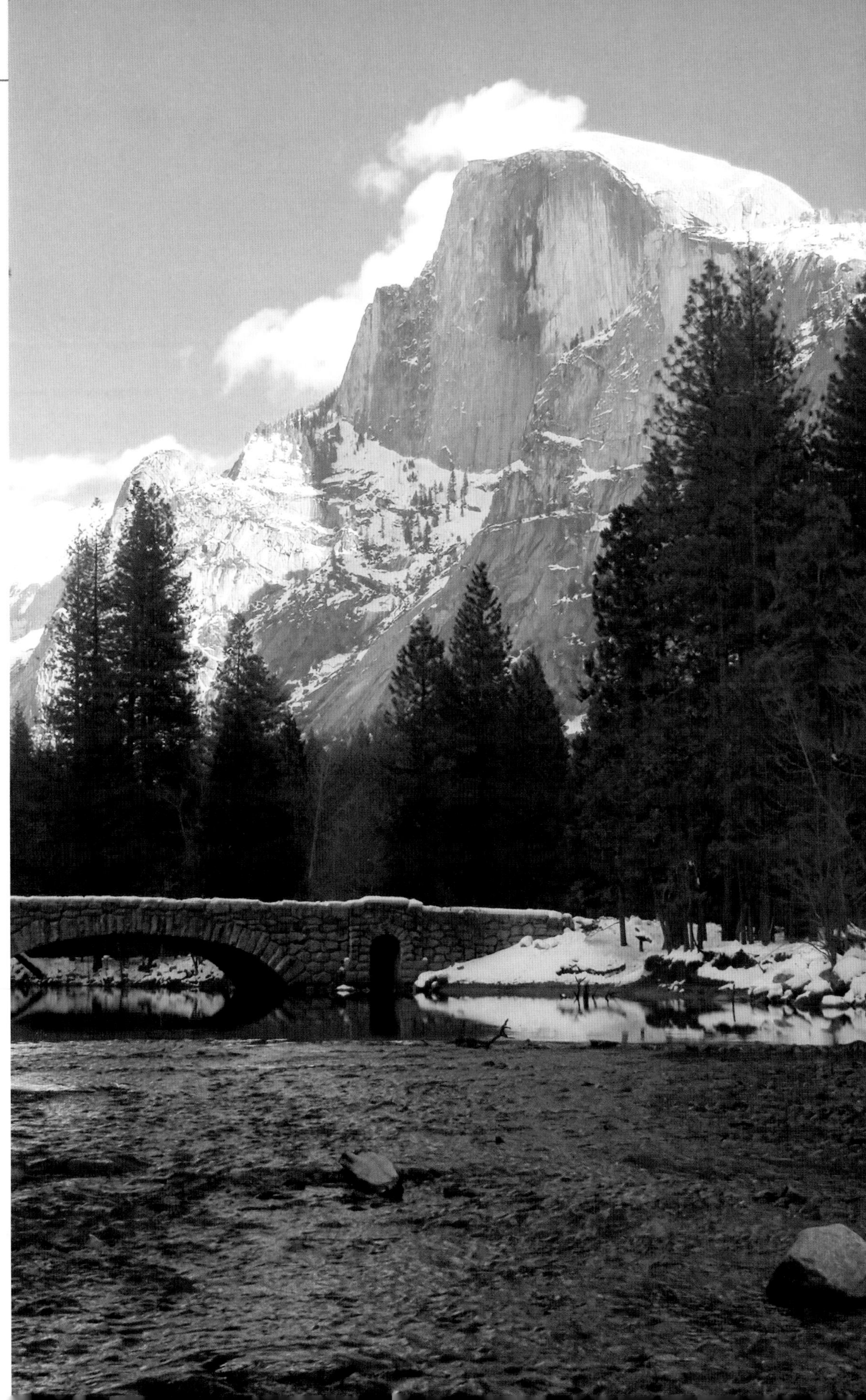

# Monterey Bay Aquarium

One of the finest aquariums in the United States—and quite possibly the world—the Monterey Bay Aquarium attracts almost two million visitors a year, and it's easy to see why.

The aquarium is located in the converted former Hovden Cannery, which canned squid and sardines until the early 1970s on Monterey's legendary Cannery Row. The aquarium opened in 1984 after seven years of planning and construction. In the 1990s, an expansion doubled its size. Today, the aquarium is home to more than 30,000 aquatic creatures, with everything from jellyfish to sharks. The many residents range from large (dolphins, sea turtles, sea otters, sharks) to small (anchovies, barnacles, zooplankton).

The aquarium's exhibits are fed by water that comes directly from Monterey Bay, which hosts one of the most diverse marine ecosystems on the planet. The mudflats, kelp forests, and nutrient-rich water support all sorts of sea life in the confines of the bay.

*Monterey Bay Aquarium is home to a diverse population of sea creatures, including the leopard shark* (top right) *and pelagic sting ray* (bottom right). (Above) *A diver swims to the depths of the aquarium's three-story kelp forest.*

# Death Valley National Park

## Quick Fact

***Death Valley Gold***

A different chapter of the park's history comes in the form of Scotty's Castle, a Mediterranean mansion that's part of the intriguingly odd tale of "Death Valley Scotty." In 1902, Walter E. Scott swindled investors into supporting a nonexistent gold mine. The Castle was actually built and owned by one of his patrons, though Scotty often referred to it as "my castle."

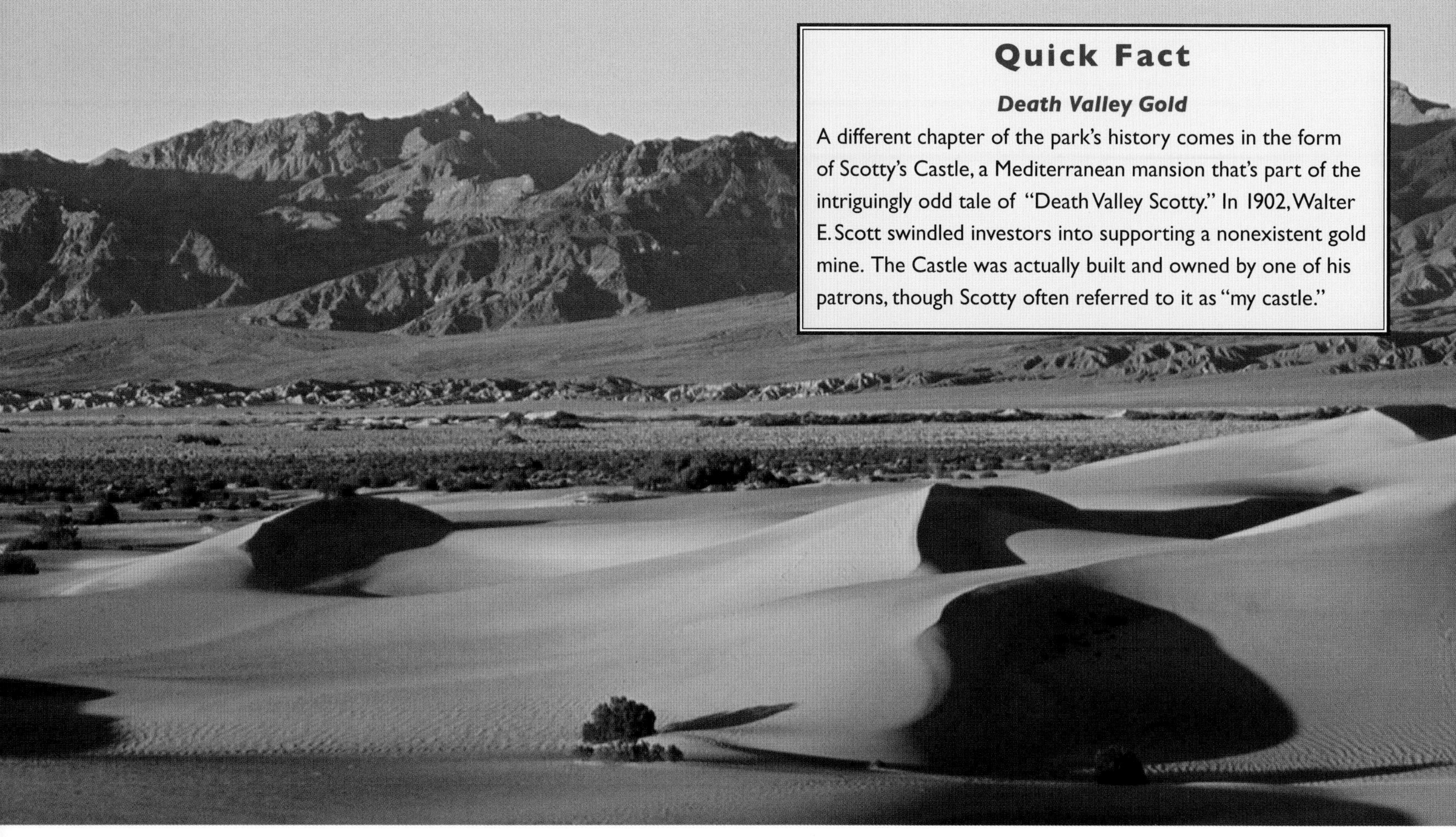

*Generally accepted as the hottest, driest, and lowest place in North America, Death Valley is a land of extremes. It is known for its precipitous peaks surrounded by the ever-shifting dune fields.*

A brutally beautiful land of extremes, Death Valley holds the record for the highest temperature ever recorded in the Western Hemisphere—134 degrees Fahrenheit. The average annual rainfall is less than two inches, making Death Valley the driest spot on the continent. It also contains the lowest point in the hemisphere—near Badwater, the surface is 282 feet below sea level. But the park ventures to other extremes as well, such as Telescope Peak, with an elevation of 11,049 feet and plenty of snow in wintertime. Pacific storms occasionally roar in, causing flash floods that wash out roads, trails, and campgrounds.

At 3.3 million acres, Death Valley is the largest U.S. national park outside Alaska. The vast and varied landscape includes seemingly endless salt and alkaline flats, swaths of ever-shifting sand dunes, and colorful rock cliffs and ridges. The park also includes its share of human history: The Timbisha Shoshone people have called the region home for thousands of years, and a few members still live in the park year-round.

# Hearst Castle

Today, Hearst Castle is a popular tourist attraction on the Golden State's central coast. It remains a tribute to wealth and power beyond almost anybody's wildest dreams.

Over the course of nearly three decades, newspaper baron William Randolph Hearst built this luxurious and legendary home on the 250,000-acre San Simeon ranch he inherited in 1919. An opulent example of Mediterranean Revival architecture, the estate's prime attraction is Casa Grande, the 60,645-square-foot main house. Its more than 100 rooms are the setting for Hearst's priceless collection of European art and antiques. The estate includes a trio of guest abodes (smaller than Casa Grande but still over-the-top and oozing with luxury) and some of the most magnificent swimming pools in all of California, including the stunning marble Neptune Pool.

Providing inspiration for Orson Welles' Xanadu in *Citizen Kane*, Hearst Castle is now property of the California State Park system (the Hearst Corporation donated it to the state in 1957). It is one of the largest historic house museums in the United States. Visitors can choose from five different tours, each revealing sections of the estate from the upper floors and library to the north wing and guest rooms to the gardens and wine cellar.

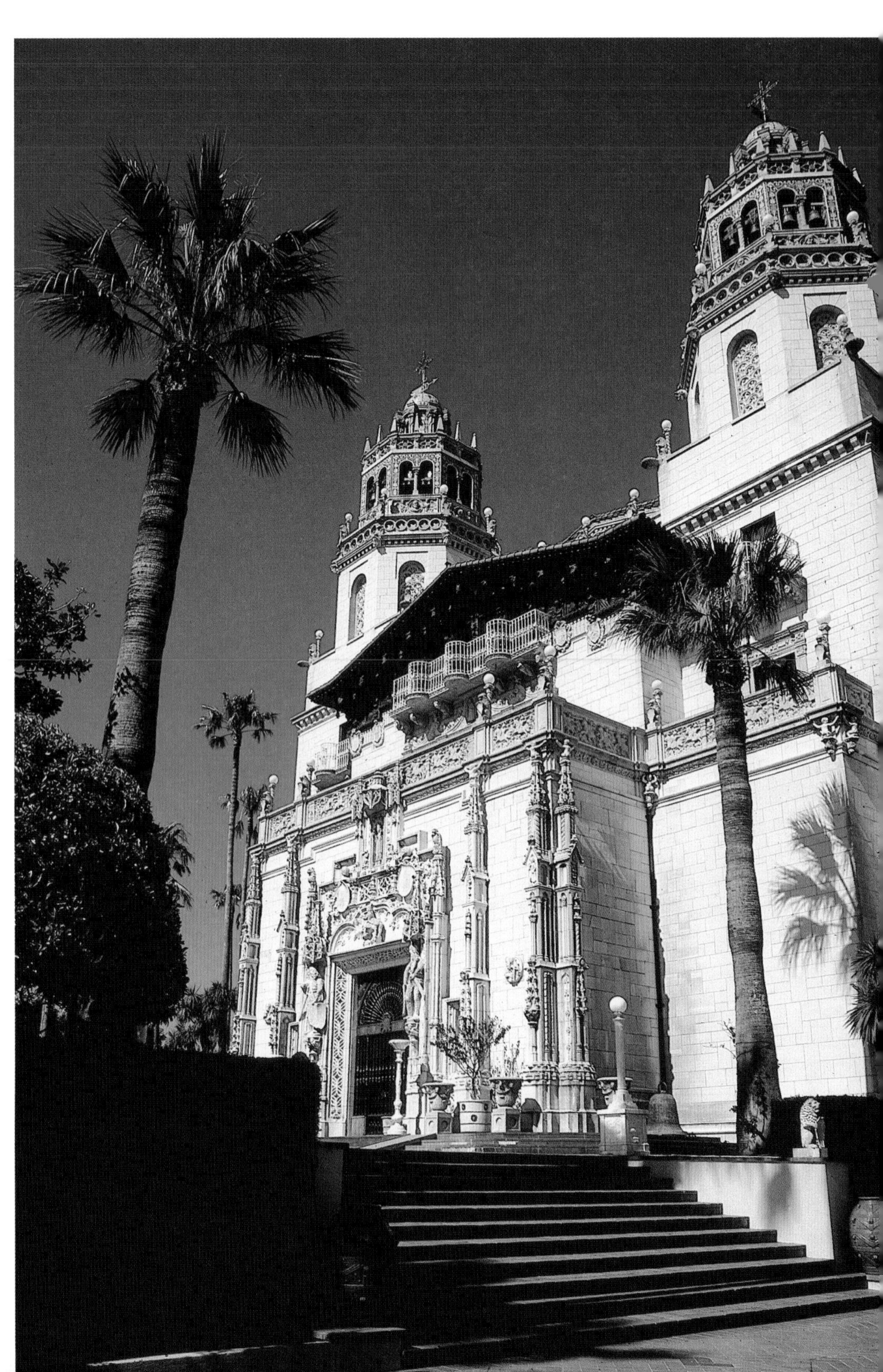

*Currently a state historical monument, the former domicile of newspaper baron William Randolph Hearst is one of the most opulent estates in the country.*

# Hollywood

Hollywood is not just a place. In certain contexts, Hollywood is shorthand for America's film industry. In others, it's the destination for every aspiring actor, director, or screenwriter. It's also the setting for so many legends and rumors it's hard to keep them straight.

Regardless, Hollywood is amazing. The rolling Hollywood Hills, clad in a lush layer of greenery, cradle neighborhoods of all kinds and feature the one-of-a-kind American icon, the Hollywood sign. At first, the sign was a real-estate promotion that read "Hollywoodland." But by 1973, it was in tatters—one O had toppled, and a vandal had set an *L* on fire. This led to its $250,000 reconstruction in 1978.

Down below, on Hollywood Boulevard, the sidewalk sports 2,000 terrazzo-and-brass stars that immortalize giants of the entertainment industry. The street is a colorful spot for people-watching and is the address of Mann's Chinese Theatre, perhaps the most famous cinema in the world. The unmistakable theater has two enormous red columns out front, a bronze roof, and authentic furnishings imported from China. Cast in the cement of the forecourt are the footprints, handprints, and hoofprints of past and present movie stars.

*Nine 50-foot letters comprise one of the most recognizable signs in the world.*

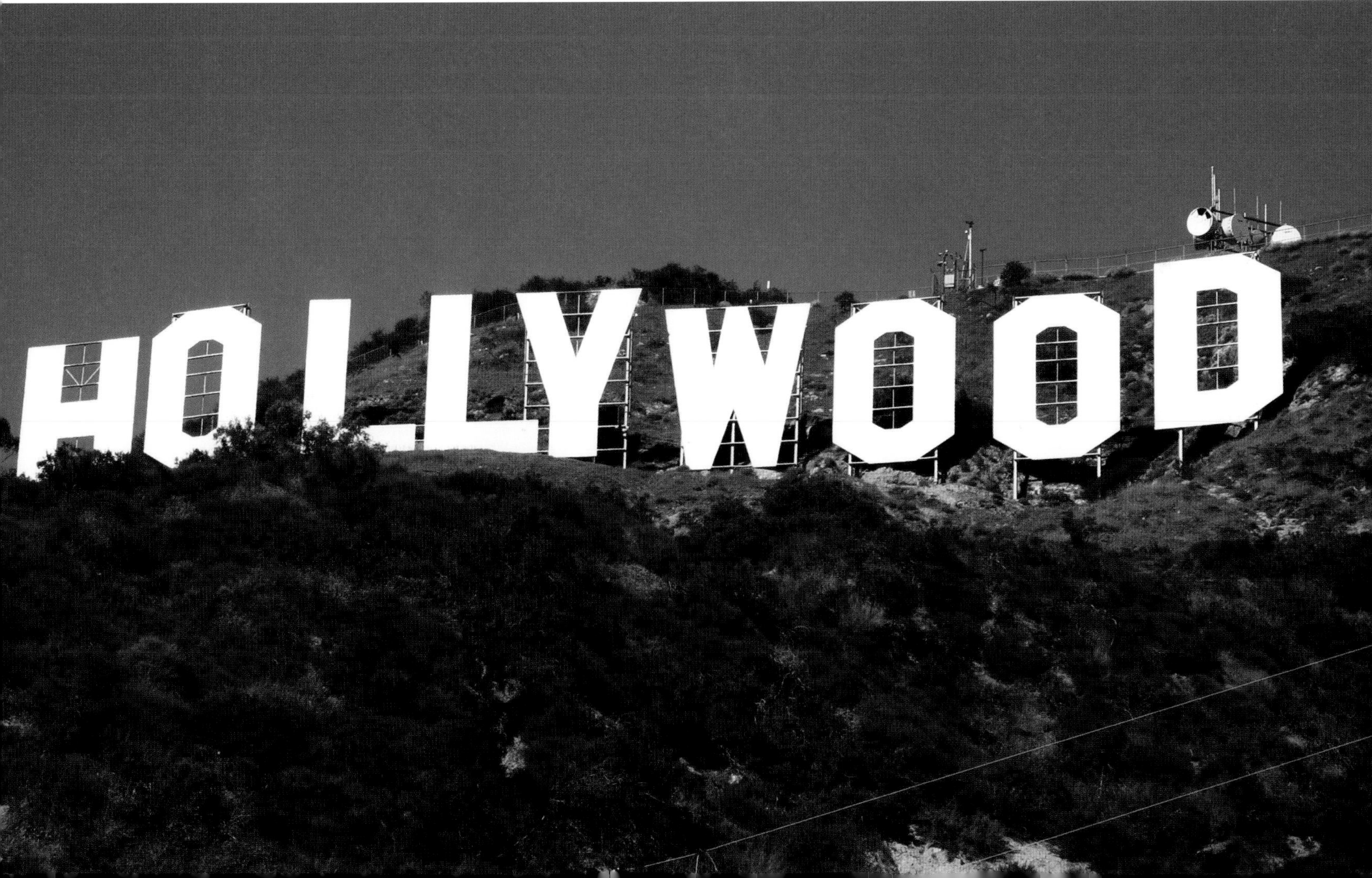

# Venice Beach

The Los Angeles neighborhood of Venice and its fabulous beach were once home to a Coney Island-like amusement pier that attracted throngs of fun-seekers. Although the park went out of business in the 1960s, Venice Beach has remained a people magnet.

Venice was founded in 1905 as Ocean Park, but the name changed in 1911 to reflect the fact the city was modeled after Italy's Venice. Its three-mile beach is in many ways an afterthought. A few people come for the sand and surf, but many more come to shop, talk, or just wander and people-watch. The beach's boardwalk is the heart and soul of California cool, with merchants hocking an array of eclectic art, cheap sunglasses, souvenir T-shirts, and much, much more. Venice Beach has been called the "Roller Skating Capital of the World"; it's fronted by a skating and bicycling path that runs along California's coastline, uninterrupted for 22 miles. There's also Gold's Gym, the famous outdoor weightlifting hotspot commonly called "Muscle Beach."

*Developers modeled the area after Venice, Italy—canals crisscross the residential neighborhoods in the area around Venice Beach.*

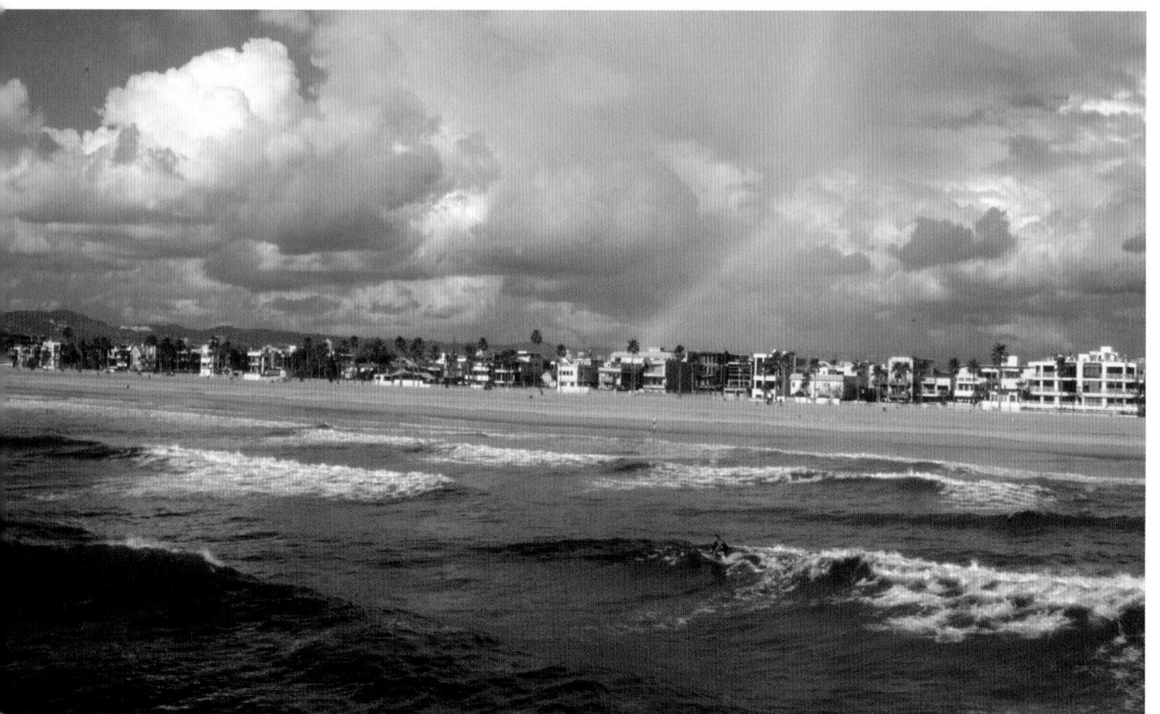

*Venice Beach is the epicenter of California cool; visitors are drawn to its lively, carefree shores.*

Perhaps Mike Bonin, a staff member for the Los Angeles City Council, put it best: "There's lots special about Venice. It is internationally recognized as a place of free expression, diversity, tolerance, and incredible artistic talent. Not to mention funky weirdness."

# La Brea Tar Pits

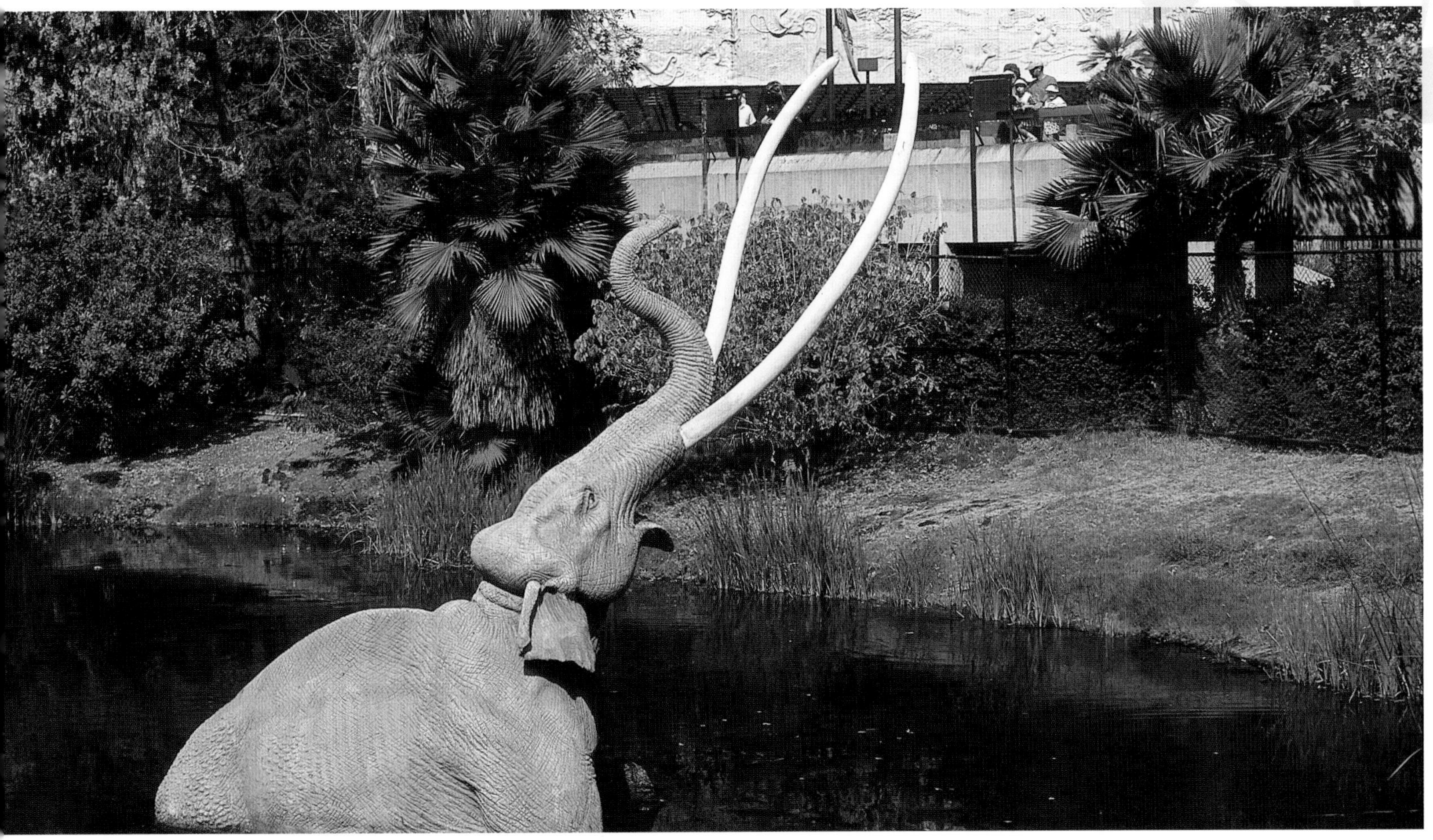

Rancho La Brea is in the heart of urban Los Angeles, thick with traffic and skyscrapers. It's hard to imagine that millions of years ago it was submerged in the ocean, teeming with sea life. When the Pacific Ocean receded about 100,000 years ago, sediment sheathed the area and fossil fuels formed below the surface.

About 40,000 years ago, oil began to seep through the labyrinth of fissures and permeable rock, creating what are now known as the La Brea Tar Pits. Back then, dire wolves, saber-tooth tigers, mastodons, mammoths, and giant sloths (all of which are now extinct) roamed across what would become Los Angeles. The tar pits were an especially dangerous place for these animals. Called "asphalt seeps" by geologists, the oily pits captured and trapped many animals one by one.

*An anomaly in downtown Los Angeles, the La Brea Tar Pits remain an archaeological treasure trove of fossils from thousands of years ago.*

Today, these animals' unfortunate fate translates into an exceptional fossil record preserved in the pits. Archaeologists have unearthed an entire prehistoric ecosystem here, from plants to insects to camels and bison. Today, the La Brea Tar Pits remain an active archaeological site and research facility. Pit 91, the most active area, is excavated during a few months each year in the summer. More than 1,000 fossil samples are discovered here annually.

# Tournament of Roses Parade

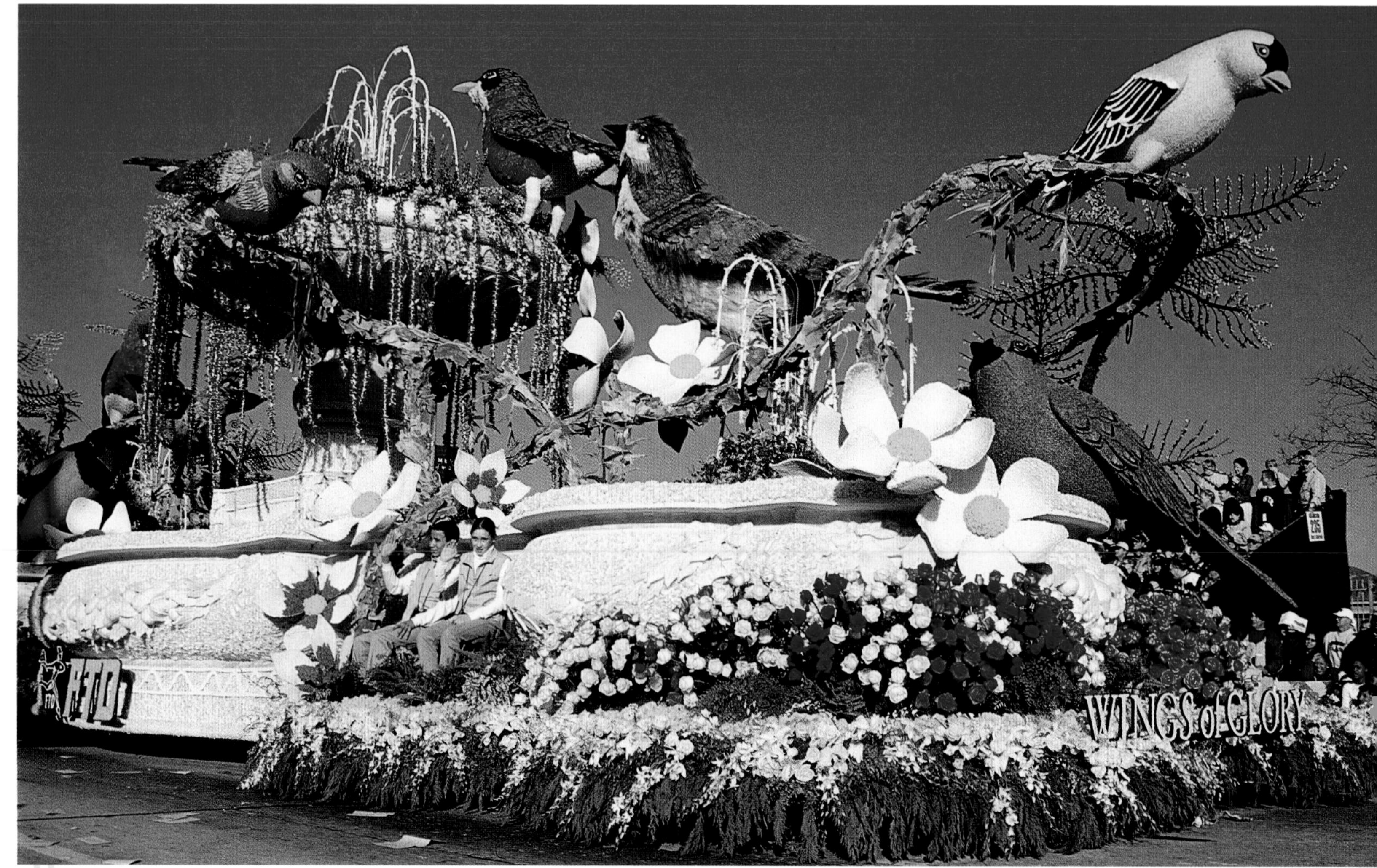


In the late 1880s, Pasadena's Valley Hunt Club hatched a plan. The club's members (transplants from points east) wanted to flaunt the balmy Southern California climate. "In New York, people are buried in snow," said Professor Charles Holder at one of the club's meetings. "Here our flowers are blooming and our oranges are about to bear. Let's hold a festival to tell the world about our paradise."

*The floats in the Tournament of Roses Parade are ornate—albeit temporary—works of movable art.*

With that, the first Tournament of Roses Parade hit the streets of Pasadena on New Year's Day 1890. Flower-adorned carriages cruised down the street in front of a crowd of some 2,000 onlookers. Polo matches, footraces, and tug-of-war contests followed the parade. The event grew more elaborate each year. In 1902, the first Rose Bowl was held. It was the first postseason collegiate football game and is now known as "The Grandaddy of Them All." The modern Tournament of Roses Parade features multimillion-dollar floats, every last square inch of which must be covered in flowers, seeds, bark, or other plant material.

# San Diego Zoo

On 100 acres in Balboa Park, just north of downtown San Diego, is a community with 4,000 full-time residents. Some are quiet and some noisy; others keep to themselves. Some rise at the break of dawn, and some are night owls—literally. There are meat-eaters, vegetarians, and still others who aren't picky at all.

These residents have one thing in common: None of them is human. These animals represent the 800 non-*Homo sapiens* species that make their home in the San Diego Zoo. Among the most famous residents are the giant pandas on loan from the Chinese government, but the entire animal kingdom is well represented, from honeybees to California condors, koalas to Komodo dragons.

The zoo has won many awards for its innovative enclosures and conservation efforts since its founding in 1916. Beyond the animals, the zoo's breathtaking gardens include an amazing 700,000 plants.

*The African black rhino is one of the 800 animal species that call the San Diego Zoo home.*

# Pioneer Courthouse Square

Pioneer Courthouse Square in Portland, Oregon, is nicknamed "Portland's Living Room." And like every good living room, the square offers entertainment and plenty of seating. The two amphitheaters host more than 300 events each year, including concerts and cultural festivals. Those with a flare for art enjoy the fountain; pillars; sculptures; and an astounding Weather Machine, an innovative creation with three symbols that each represent an element of Portland's climate. There's even a signpost that shows how far it is to places as distant as Red Square in Russia.

The square has taken on many forms throughout history. A shoemaker named Elijah Hill bought the block for $24 and a pair of boots in 1849, two years before the city of Portland was officially established. James Field sold it to the fledgling Portland School Board less than a decade later, and it built a schoolhouse on the spot. In 1883, the schoolhouse was relocated to make way for the ritzy Portland Hotel, which remained open until 1951. The spot became a two-level parking structure for about 30 years, until the city acquired the land and transformed it into one of the nation's most vibrant public commons. Today, the square attracts millions of people each year to its special events, including the annual midsummer Festival of Flowers.

*Now serving as "Portland's Living Room," Pioneer Courthouse Square is decorated with colorful swashes and greenery.*

# Crater Lake National Park

The intense blue of Crater Lake is striking. The vivid color is due in part to the depth of this freshwater lake. At its deepest, the lake's floor plunges 1,932 feet below the surface, making it the deepest lake in the United States.

The lake was created centuries ago when rain and snowmelt filled a caldera, a huge bowl that was the remnant of a volcano. During some years, the lake is replenished by wintertime snowfalls of 50 feet or more. Because no water flows through the lake, its water remains pure and tranquil.

Scientists have discovered evidence of hydrothermal vents near Crater Lake's floor, which may play an important role in the lake's ecology. Green algae grows at a record depth of 725 feet below the surface, indicating that sunlight may penetrate deeper into Crater Lake than any other body of water in the world.

In the lake, the remarkable Phantom Ship is an island created by cooled lava, with 160-foot-high ridges and peaks that resemble a ship. Wizard Island is a volcanic cone that rises 700 feet above the impossibly blue surface.

*The vivid blue, perfectly still surface of Crater Lake hides the deepest lake in the United States, which bottoms out nearly 2,000 feet below.*

# Mount Hood

Picture-perfect Mount Hood is a visual reminder to Portland's city dwellers that the great outdoors is just a short drive away—47 miles east, to be exact. At 11,239 feet above sea level, the peak is the fourth-highest in the Cascade Range.

Like all of its Cascade brethren, Mount Hood is a volcano, and an active one at that. It erupted twice in the mid-1800s and has had at least four eruptive periods in the last 15,000 years. The volcanic cone atop the mountain is dominated by snow and ice, with glaciers and snowfields shrouding it year-round.

Mount Hood is a recreational paradise, with popular ski resorts, hiking routes, and backcountry trails. The historic Timberline Lodge is perched at 6,000 feet above sea level and fills to capacity during ski season—which sometimes lasts all year long.

*Oregon's Mount Hood is one of the few mountains where skiers can hit the slopes in the middle of summer.*

# Newberry National Volcanic Monument

In the heart of central Oregon's Deschutes National Forest, Newberry National Volcanic Monument sits atop an active geothermal hotspot. The crux of this hotspot is Newberry Volcano, one of the most massive volcanoes in the United States. Newberry's last eruption, about 1,300 years ago, created a devastatingly beautiful caldera. Located at the summit of the volcano nearly 8,000 feet above sea level, the nearly 20-square-mile Newberry Caldera has two idyllic alpine lakes, one of which drains into a magnificent waterfall.

The volcano's hardened lava flanks are dotted by hundreds of cinder cones and fissure vents. One especially massive cinder cone, Lava Butte, rises 500 feet above its surroundings and was the source of the lava that flowed over this entire area 7,000 years ago. Today, the once-red-hot landscape can be explored via the Trail of the Molten Land.

*The striking boundary between spared forest and volcanic devastation in Newberry National Monument is unmistakable.*

# Multnomah Falls

Ancient Multnomah Falls is a sight to behold. Cascading from its origin on Larch Mountain, it highlights the picturesque Columbia River Gorge in central Oregon. At 620 feet, some claim it's the second-tallest year-round waterfall in the nation. The falls are fed by an underground spring that provides a continuous flow of crystal-clear water that's enhanced by seasonal snowmelt and spring rainstorms. On rare occasions, unusually frosty weather rolls into the gorge and transforms Multnomah Falls into a massive icicle, and the flow of water slows to a slight trickle.

Many visitors take the foot trail up to Benson Bridge (built in 1914 under the direction of Simon Benson). Some believe it's the best spot to view the falls: Look up to see the thin ribbon of the upper falls, or peer down to see the powerful lower cascade as it empties into the Columbia River. From the bridge, a mile-long trail leads to Larch Mountain Lookout at the top of the upper falls, providing a commanding view of the Columbia River Gorge.

Beyond the scenic highway that leads to Multnomah Falls, the gorge is full of beautiful overlooks, excellent hiking trails, and pristine wilderness areas. There are numerous waterfalls beyond Multnomah; the trail to its mouth connects to a network that provides views of eight others nearby.

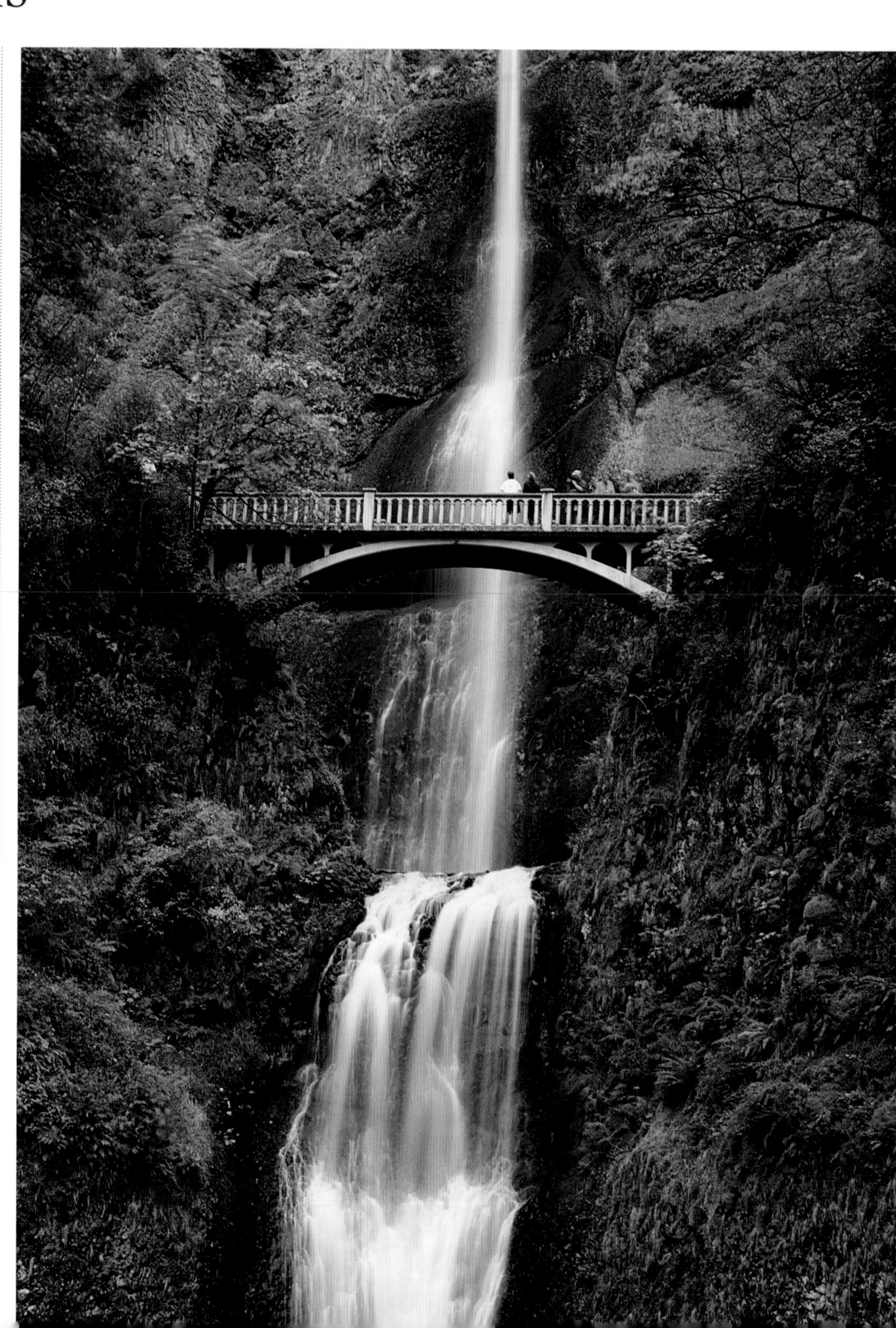

*At 620 feet tall, Multnomah Falls is one of the scenic highlights of the Columbia River Gorge in Oregon's heartland.*

# Astoria–Megler Bridge

Critics call it "The Bridge to Nowhere," and the Astoria–Megler Bridge in northwestern Oregon often appears as just that: a bridge snaking into a soggy fogbank, with miles of water on all sides. It spans four miles across the mouth of the Columbia near where it empties into the Pacific Ocean.

The bridge connects Astoria, Oregon, to Point Ellice, Washington. Opened in 1966, it replaced the congested ferry system that had previously linked the communities. Despite the "Bridge to Nowhere" nickname, the Astoria–Megler Bridge has been a success. It carried a quarter-million vehicles in its first full year and was the last link in US Highway 101 connecting Mexico to Canada.

The Astoria–Megler Bridge is the world's longest continuous truss bridge. It was built to withstand some of the most treacherous conditions on the Pacific Coast. The concrete piers that support the bridge can survive wind gusts up to 150 miles per hour and raging floodwaters that can uproot trees and reach a velocity of nine miles per hour.

*The Astoria–Megler Bridge spans the four-mile mouth of the Columbia River.*

# Seattle Space Needle

Seattle's Space Needle is the most popular tourist attraction in the city, receiving more than a million visitors each year. Originally built for the 1962 World's Fair and still the defining feature on this Emerald City's skyline, the 605-foot Space Needle was the tallest building west of the Mississippi when it was completed in late 1961.

The futuristic blueprints for the Space Needle evolved from artist Edward E. Carlson's visionary doodle on a placemat. Collaboration with architect John Graham resulted in a prototype space-age design that looks a bit like a flying saucer balanced on three giant supports.

But appearances can be deceiving—the Space Needle isn't going anywhere. Anchored to its foundation by dozens of 30-foot bolts, the structure was built to withstand winds of up to 200 miles per hour. Wind does cause the needle to sway, but the top house has only closed once—for an hour and a half in 1993 due to 90-mile-per-hour winds.

The elevators travel at about ten miles per hour, making the trip from the ground to the observation deck in 41 seconds. Once you're at the top, take in the unbeatable views of Seattle and Puget Sound, then partake in a drink at the bar or a meal in the world's second-oldest revolving restaurant.

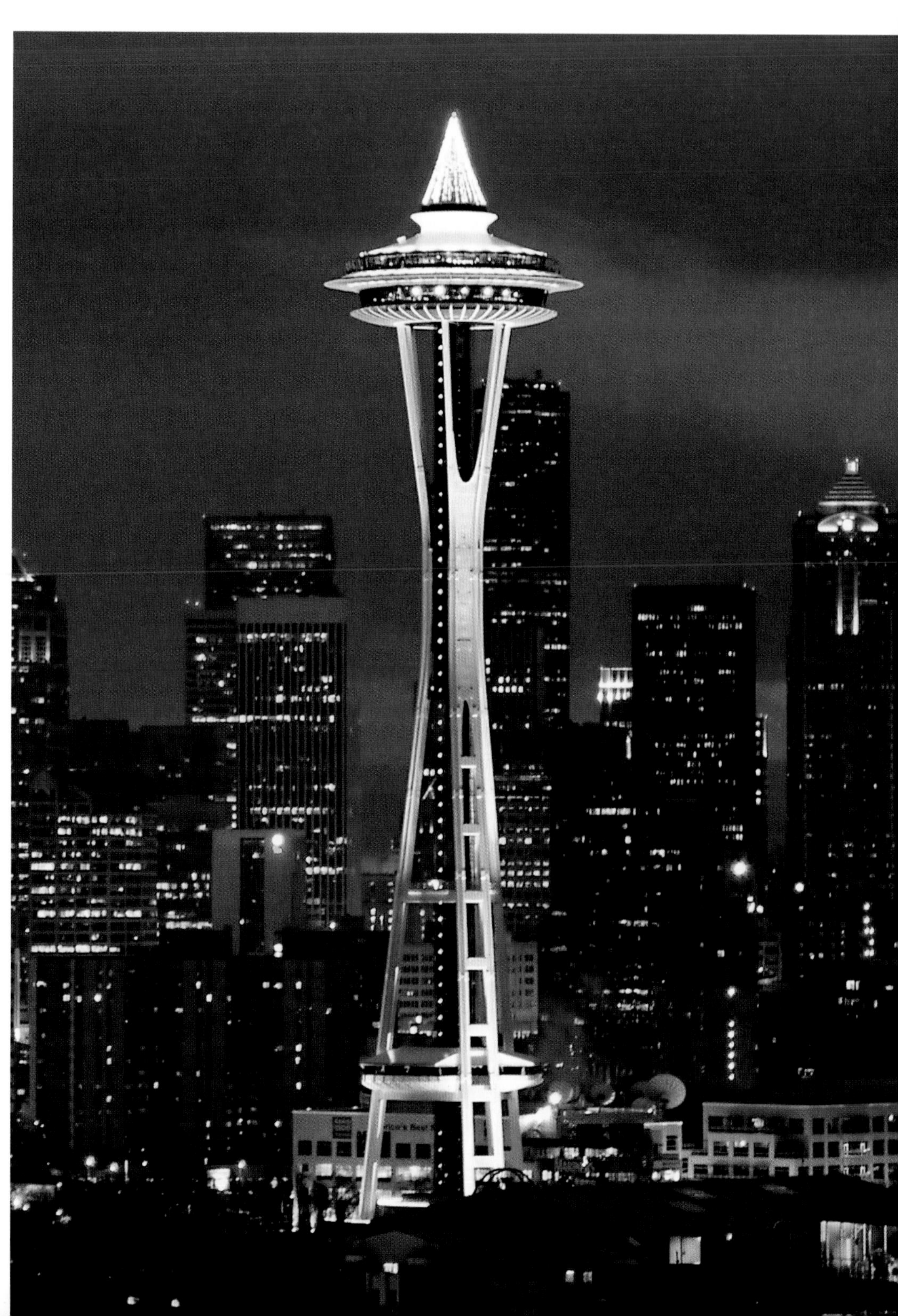

*Seattle's most recognizable structure is the futuristic Seattle Space Needle. It was the premier attraction at the 1962 World's Fair, whose theme was Century 21.*

# Olympic National Park

Olympic National Park, in northwestern Washington, is home to one of the most lush, impenetrable rainforests on the planet. Climate conditions are perfect for the forest to thrive. Moisture is plentiful and the temperature mild, thanks to the Pacific Ocean. Some areas in the park get up to 167 inches of rain a year—more than any other spot in the continental United States. The rain supports a landscape covered by moss, lichen, and fern, giving the forest a vibrant green glow.

But the beauty of Olympic National Park doesn't end with the rainforest. It is one of the most diverse national parks in the United States. The untouched Pacific coastline is ruggedly beautiful, and the majestic Olympic Mountains rise from the heart of the peninsula. While the western side of the park is deluged by rain, the eastern side is just the opposite—it's one of the most parched spots on the West Coast north of Los Angeles.

*Remarkably diverse, Olympic National Park is home to isolated beaches* (below) *and dense rainforests* (right).

# Mount Rainier National Park

*Exceeding 14,000 feet, Mount Rainier is a majestic peak with an icy coat and fiery interior.*

The world of snow and ice atop Mount Rainier, 14,410 feet above sea level, never thaws. At times, the annual snowfall exceeds 90 feet on the mountain's slopes.

But below Mount Rainier's frosty covering, conditions are the polar opposite: Inside, the mountain is an active volcano. Mount Rainier is the tallest mountain in the volcanic Cascade Range. This range also includes Mount St. Helens, which last erupted in 1980 but has shown signs of activity since 2004, and Lassen Peak in California, which blew its top numerous times between 1914 and 1921.

Mount Rainier last erupted in the mid-19th century, leaving a small crater near the peak. While the mountain has been quiet for more than a century, many scientists believe Mount Rainier is due for an eruption any day now—give or take a few thousand years. Mudflows from past eruptions snaked right through what is now downtown Seattle.

Mount Rainier is about one million years old, which is much younger than the mountains over which it towers. (The surrounding mountains, with peaks about 6,000 feet above sea level, are nearly 12 million years old.) Its abrupt growth is a result of its volcanic activity. In its infancy, Rainier was just a volcanic vent atop a slab of solidified lava; thousands of eruptions created the immense mountain.

The frigid climate at Rainier's peak fuels a number of glaciers. In winter, snow and ice accumulate, and the summer warmth then melts some of the ice. The glaciers currently cover 36 square miles on Mount Rainier, amounting to about a cubic mile of ice and snow. It has more glacier cover than any other mountain in the continental United States.

Like the magma below the surface, Mount Rainier's glaciers are a dynamic phenomenon. During the last ice age, about 20,000 years ago, glaciers covered most of the park, whereas today that figure is about 10 percent.

More recently, until about 1850, many of the glaciers on Mount Rainier experienced gains in mass during a 500-year period known as the Little Ice Age. During the Little Ice Age, Rainier's Nisqually Glacier advanced 150 feet, and other glaciers grew, merged, and began to retake land lost in warmer years.

Between the apex of the Little Ice Age and 1950, Mount Rainier's glaciers lost about [illegible] percent of their length, with melting accelerating significantly after 1920. Then, from 1950 through the early 1980s, most of the glaciers grew again, thanks to a mid-century cold spell and heavy snowfall. In the early 1980s, however, the climate shifted, and the glaciers receded once again.

All of this water feeds the vibrant wildflowers. Come summertime, Rainier's subalpine meadows explode with color as lupines, monkeyflowers, asters, and myriad other species bloom. The kaleidoscope of multihued flora is a startling contrast to the stark blue and white of the looming peak.

About 70 miles away from Seattle, Mount Rainier is a distant but singular symbol of the world beyond the city. The mountain is either "out," meaning not obscured by clouds, or it isn't. Most days it isn't, but on clear, summer days the perfect majesty of Rainier beckons the entire city to the great outdoors.

*Mount Rainier's glaciers melt during the warmer months, fueling a labyrinthine network of rivers and streams that flow down the mountain in every direction.*

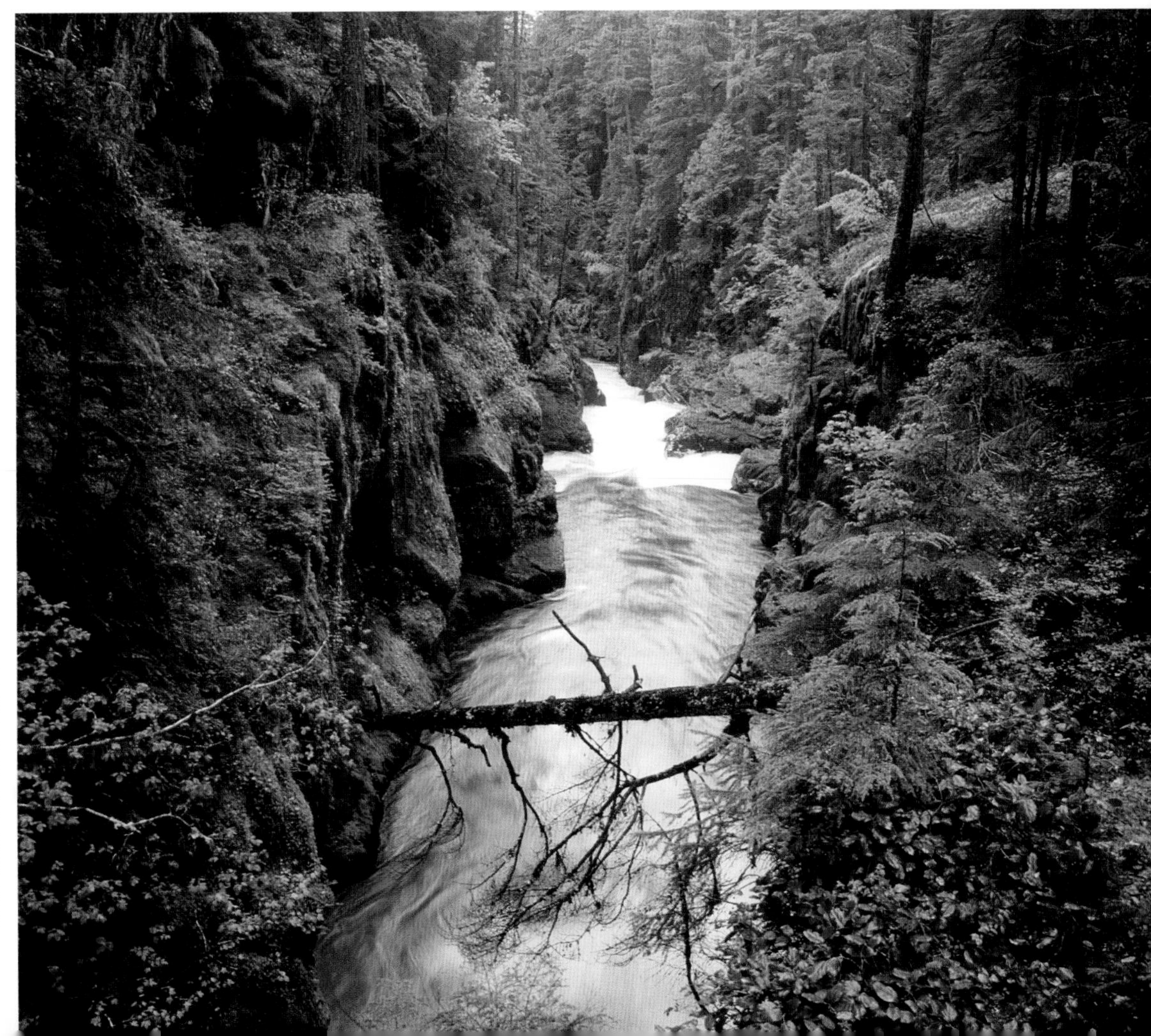

# Mount St. Helens

Washington's Mount St. Helens is perhaps the most famous volcano in the United States. It earned its reputation the morning of May 18, 1980. The mountain shook, and its north face cascaded into a debris avalanche, which created a towering mushroom column of ash that blotted out the sun and drifted into Idaho and beyond. The eruption continued through the evening, lasting about nine hours.

Two years later, President Ronald Reagan signed a bill making Mount St. Helens a National Volcanic Monument, allowing the ecosystem to respond naturally to the eruption. Mount St. Helens National Volcanic Monument attracts scientists who use it a living laboratory as well as hikers and ot outdoors buffs.

The volcano is part of the Cascade Ran which also includes Mount Rainier and L sen Peak. In recent years, Mount St. Hel has shown new signs of activity, with a l dome growing under the crater left from t 1980 eruption.

*The infamous North American volcano Mount St. Helens showed signs of activity starting in 2004 after a mostly quiet quarter-century.*

# Museum of Glass

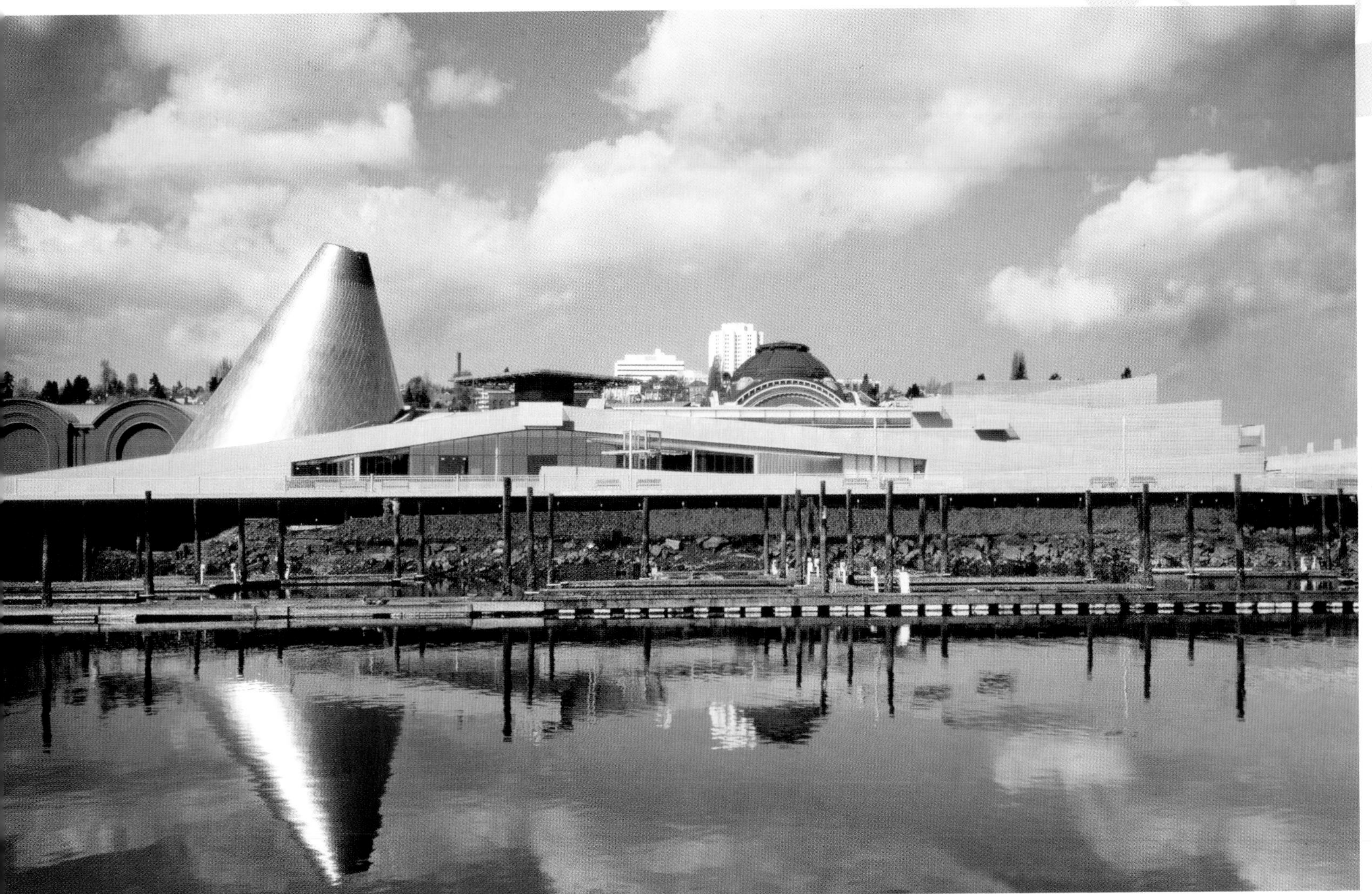

*Tacoma's Museum of Glass is a work of architectural art adorning the waterfront.*

The Museum of Glass is Tacoma, Washington's splashy contribution to the contemporary art world. Its wide array of works in different media have one thing in common: They all incorporate glass. The museum opened in 2002 and has been an architectural landmark along the city's waterfront ever since.

Inside the museum, visitors can browse permanent and temporary exhibitions of all kinds of contemporary glass art. The museum's Visiting Artist Collection is permanent, featuring works created on-site in the Hot Shop Amphitheater. The Hot Shop has hot and cold glass studios and seating for 138 visitors.

The Chihuly Bridge of Glass connects the museum to downtown Tacoma. The 500-foot steel-and-glass pedestrian bridge is adorned with colorful glass spires. It serves as not only a walkway but as a display providing a preview of the stunning glass art masterworks in the museum.

# Pike Place Market

Seattle's Pike Place Market is legendary. The nine-acre spot in downtown Seattle has served as a prime place of commerce since the early 20th century.

Pike Place Market came about because of a 1,000 percent spike in the price of onions in 1906 and 1907. Seattle City Councilman Thomas Revelle offered a solution: a public street market that would cut out greedy intermediaries and allow citizens to buy their produce directly from farmers. The next summer, Pike Place Market opened to the public at the corner of Pike Street and First Avenue. Thousands of customers crowded the corner: They cleared out the eight attending farmers in a matter of a few hours.

From that early success, the market snowballed into its modern incarnation: the foremost farmer's market in the United States. It now has space for 120 farmers and even more craftspeople, as well as 200 other year-round businesses. There are also street performers and the occasional flying salmon—launched by the boisterous staff of Pike Place Fish.

*The goods at the bustling Pike Place Fish Market are fresh from the water.*

# Glacier Bay National Park and Preserve

Glacier Bay is Alaska's southernmost national park. It is also a living laboratory where scientists study glacial recession. The ice in and around Glacier Bay is melting at a remarkable pace; in fact, the phenomenon is the fastest glacial retreat on record.

When Captain George Vancouver first charted these waters in 1794, what is now the bay was little more than an indention in a vast sheet of ice that extended for hundreds of miles. Over the next 200 years, the glaciers receded more than 60 miles, revealing the islands and shorelines visible today and creating a masterpiece of rock, ice, and water.

Today, 16 massive glaciers and majestic mountains, some of which have peaks 15,000 feet above sea level, ring Glacier Bay. The bay is also a critical wildlife habitat, sustaining humpback whales, orcas, porpoises, seals, and sea otters in its waters and moose, black bears, brown bears, wolves, and deer on the surrounding shore.

*Ringed by massive cliffs of cracked rock and ice, Glacier Bay is home to 16 glaciers that are retreating at a rate faster than any other glaciers on record.*

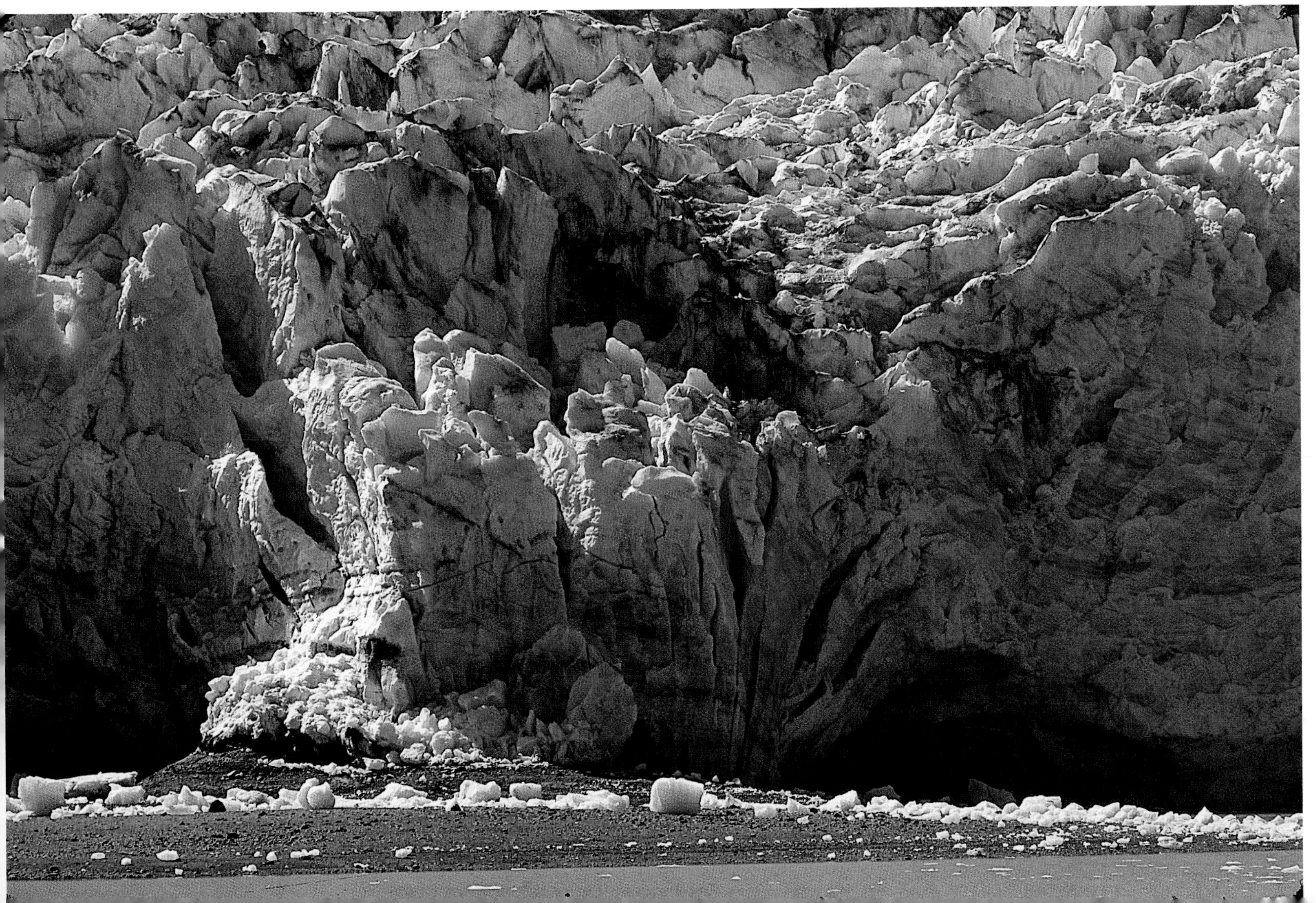

# Denali National Park and Preserve

Denali means "The High One" in the native Athabascan tongue. It's an apt moniker, considering that the 20,320-foot-tall mountain—also known as Mount McKinley—is North America's highest peak. It's also one of the most striking mountains in the world—when it's visible from the surrounding subarctic plateau. Due to clouds, visitors are generally more likely to see a grizzly bear on the plateau than they are to see the top of the mountain. The clouds cooperate about half the time in summer, and when they do, Denali is an awe-inspiring sight. The mountain's sheer bulk, not to mention the precipitous rise of its eternally frosted summit, is overwhelming. At 18,000 feet from base to summit, Denali is home to some of the longest mountainsides in the world.

Because the park is so far north—about 240 miles north of Anchorage—its mountains are not forested like the Rockies and the Sierra Nevada. The timberline falls between 2,000 and 3,000 feet at Denali's northern latitude. Below the rugged high country are tundra-

### Quick Fact

**A Sweet Mountaintop Picnic**

The first successful expedition up Denali's 19,470-foot North Peak was accomplished by a group of local residents in 1910. Amazingly, they enjoyed hot chocolate and donuts at the summit.

*The staggering beauty of Denali on a clear day is a rarity: Clouds usually obscure its peak, 20,320 feet above sea level.*

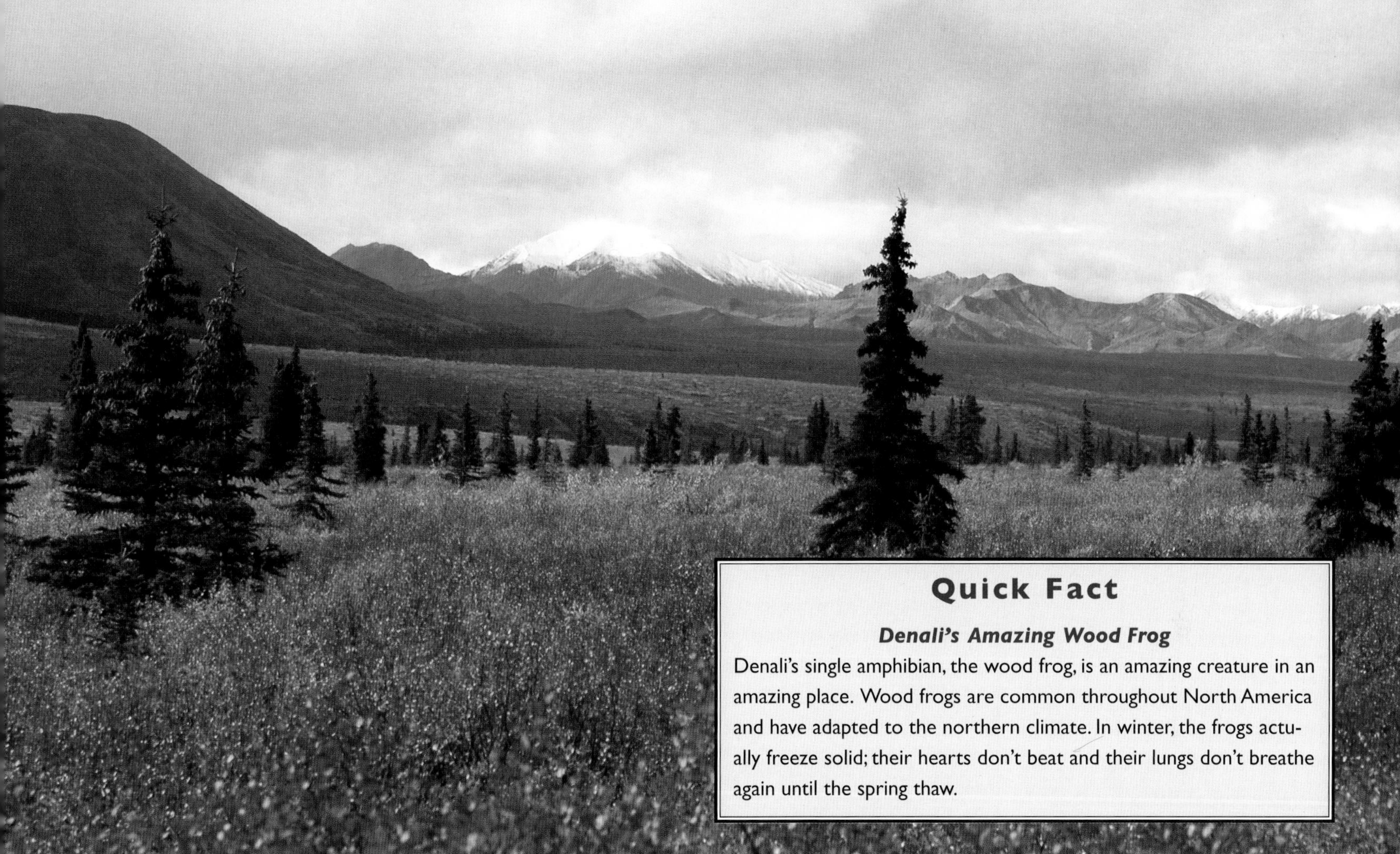

**Quick Fact**

***Denali's Amazing Wood Frog***

Denali's single amphibian, the wood frog, is an amazing creature in an amazing place. Wood frogs are common throughout North America and have adapted to the northern climate. In winter, the frogs actually freeze solid; their hearts don't beat and their lungs don't breathe again until the spring thaw.

*Denali National Park is not just the centerpiece peak—it also includes the surrounding subarctic plateau, an area larger than some states.*

covered lowlands. Immense glaciers connect the two, creeping down Denali and the neighboring peaks.

The park that encompasses Denali and the adjacent mountains of the Alaska Range is a vast, pristine wilderness larger than Massachusetts. Possibly more of a lure than the actual mountain, wild animals attract many of the park's visitors. Denali has earned the nickname "The Subarctic Serengeti" for its thriving wildlife population. Denali's "big five" mammals are grizzly bears, gray wolves, caribou, Dall's sheep, and moose. Peregrine falcons, golden eagles, and other birds soar above; but there are no reptiles in the park, and only one amphibian, the wood frog.

More than 300,000 people visit Denali each year, making it Alaska's most popular park. Compared to other national parks in the state such as Katmai, Kobuk Valley, and Lake Clark, it is more civilized and more easily accessible. The Anchorage–Fairbanks Highway runs right up to the park's eastern border, and the Alaska Railroad makes regular stops at Denali station.

Denali National Park is free of traffic problems; there's just one 90-mile gravel road in its boundaries, and only park buses are allowed to drive to its interior endpoint at Wonder Lake. The absence of cars allows the wild animals to behave more naturally. And, unlike their brethren in Yellowstone and Glacier National Parks, Denali's grizzlies aren't conditioned by the constant flow of traffic.

Visitors naturally tend to focus their wildlife watching near this one road. En route to Wonder Lake, it crosses five river valleys and four mountain passes—in other words, plenty of great habitat for the aforementioned "big five." More ambitious park-goers get off the bus to hike and backpack through the rugged terrain. The primary route into these mountains is Muldrow Glacier, which is literally a river of ice fed by several other glaciers.

# Saxman Native Totem Park

This is the world's largest totem park, consisting of two dozen ornate totem poles in Saxman, near Ketchikan in southeast Alaska. Most of the poles are not dated and were reclaimed from abandoned Tlingit villages in the 1930s by the Civilian Conservation Corps and the United States Forest Service. The poles were relocated to Saxman from villages on Cape Fox and Tongass, Cat, and Pennock islands.

Each totem pole at Saxman Native Totem Park is unique. The colorful carvings share the stories of their makers and the stories of the villages where they once stood.

Among the fascinating totems in the park are the "Sea-Bear Pole," which has a bear-figure base capped by the long fin of a killer whale; a memorial pole to a man who died while fishing for octopus, which has an eagle at its top and a rock oyster at its bottom; and a totem that relates to the Tlingit legend "The Princess and the Frog Clan People." Master carvers create new poles for museums, corporations, and private collectors on-site using traditional techniques.

### Quick Fact

**_The Low Man on the Totem Pole_**

While the expression "the low man on the totem pole" has been interpreted as the least important person, it's actually incorrect. On true totems, the lowest figure (which could be a man, woman, animal, or supernatural being) was actually the *most* important.

Totems were carved to help remember and share stories. Often a chief carver and several apprentices would together carve one totem. The chief would personally carve the lower ten feet of the pole, so that the part that was eye level with viewers was the most intricate. Less experienced apprentices carved the top portion, where the story thinned out.

*This totem is one of more than 20 ornately carved and painted poles on display at Saxman Native Totem Park.*

# Iditarod

"The Last Great Race on Earth," the Iditarod is the equivalent of the Super Bowl, World Series, and Kentucky Derby wrapped into one for the world of dogsledding.

Since 1973, mushers have led teams of 12 to 16 sled dogs from Anchorage to Nome beginning the first Saturday of March. They usually cross the finish line a little more than a week later—but sometimes the race takes nearly a month. On the way to Nome, participants cross two mountain ranges on alternating routes that follow the Yukon River and then cross the frozen Norton Sound. The distance covered is more than 1,000 miles, through some of North America's most spectacular terrain.

The race grew out of Alaska's rich history: In the 19th century, dogsled teams brought mail and supplies to the interior mining camps and took gold out to Anchorage. After a pair of 25-mile commemorative races in the 1960s, the first full-fledged Iditarod—a native word for "clear water" or "distant place"—took place in 1973. Nearly 100 teams typically enter the modern race, making for more than 1,200 dogs.

*Starting in Anchorage and ending in Nome, the Iditarod is among the most grueling competitions for both dogs and humans.*

# Mauna Loa

Part of Hawaiian Volcanoes National Park, Mauna Loa (meaning "Long Mountain") rises 13,677 feet above the blue surface of the Pacific Ocean. It is second in height (in Hawaii) only to Mauna Kea, a quieter volcano. Although many mountain peaks rise higher than Mauna Loa, its actual size is nothing short of astonishing. Measured from its base, which is 18,000 feet underwater, Mauna Loa exceeds even Mount Everest in height—by a full 2,000 feet. And the sea floor, compressed by the sheer bulk of the mountain, has sunk nearly another 30,000 feet. This makes Mauna Loa the world's most massive single mountain, with a bulk more than 100 times that of Washington's Mount Rainier.

Atop the summit of Mauna Loa, a caldera called Mokuaweoweo features a number of craters that have previously erupted. The caldera floor is covered with lava contorted into otherworldly formations, daunting pits, and towering cinder cones. Current-day eruptions within the crater of the volcano are relatively harmless. Volcanologists have been able to reliably predict activity. Because of this, an impending eruption typically draws thousands of people to the crater's rim.

*Predictable eruptions of Mauna Loa draw crowds to view the impressive fireworks display.*

# Haleakala National Park

As legend has it, a long time ago the god Maui captured the sun in a great mountain's summit basin on a Hawaiian island. The mountain came to be known as Haleakala, Hawaiian for "House of the Sun."

Haleakala is actually an enormous volcano that—although dormant since 1790—is a striking reminder of the power seething below the Earth's surface. Impressive cinder cones and lava sculptures on the upper slopes of Haleakala are lasting remnants of furious, tumultuous moments in its past.

The massive crater on Haleakala is not, however, a child of all this volcanism. A climactic shift led to massive rainfall here long ago, and the cascading water eroded the mountainsides into valleys. The crater was created when two valleys became one as the floodwaters wore away the ridge between them.

*While Haleakala is a dormant volcano, the otherworldly valley at its peak was shaped by a flood of water, not lava.*

At the base of Haleakala, the lush, green Kipahulu Valley unravels to the coast. This tropical ecosystem is a distant memory from the volcano's 10,000-foot summit: Guava trees and ferns below give way to yellow brush known as mamane and the silversword plant, unique to the volcano.

# Hanakapi'ai Falls

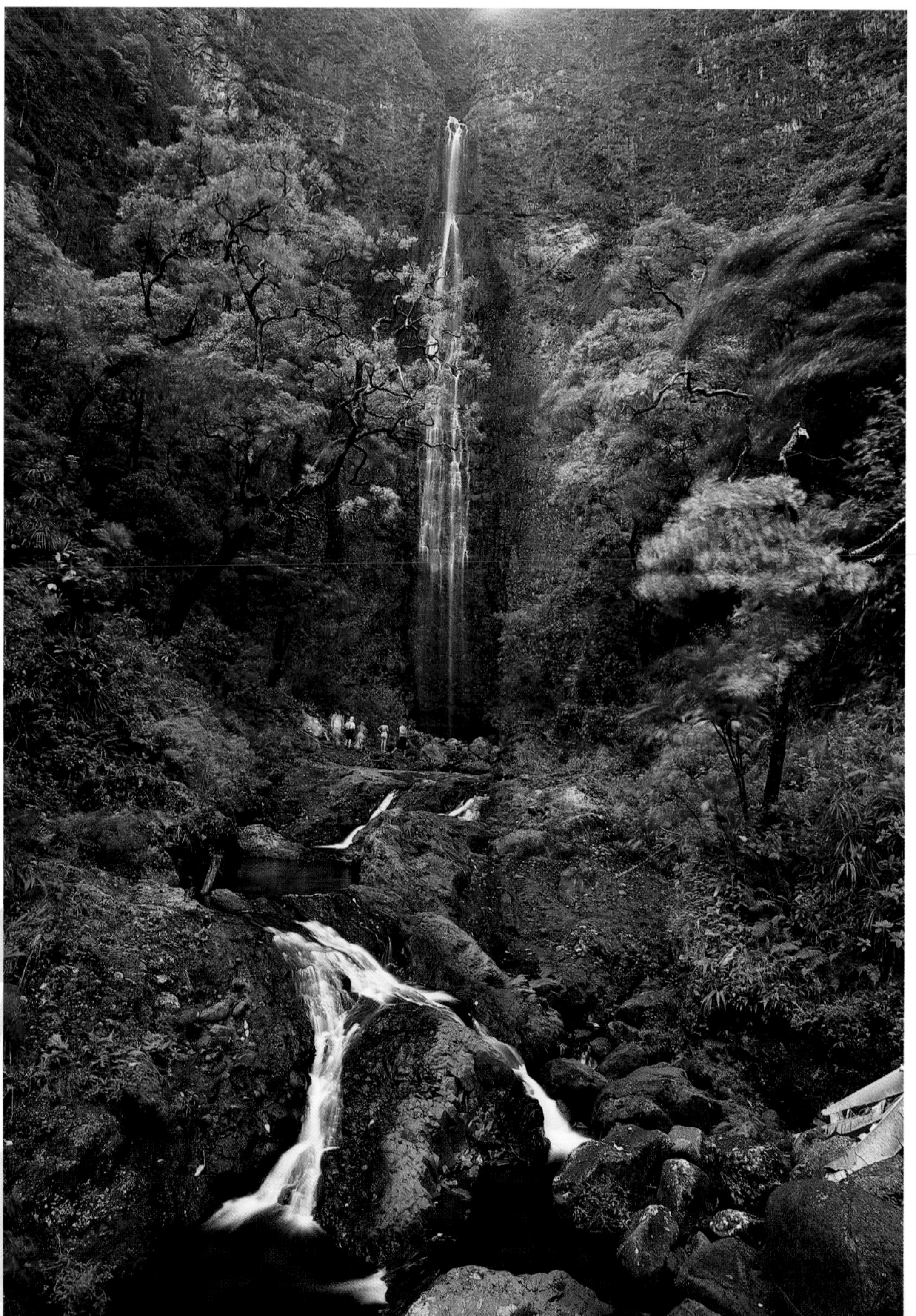

Named for a Hawaiian princess, Hanakapi'ai Falls on the northwestern side of the island of Kauai is the picture of tropical paradise. The beautiful, 300-foot ribbon of water delicately cascades down a rugged volcanic wall, tumbling into an idyllic pool. There are many waterfalls and pools on Kauai, but this is perhaps the most sublime; perfect for swimming, and set amidst a thick rain forest that's teeming with life.

The falls are a popular destination for experienced hikers. The Kalalua Trail, which leads to Hanakapi'ai Falls, begins at Ke'e Beach. This strenuous hike is about four miles long. Be prepared to spend a full day hiking to the falls and back, and be sure to wear sturdy hiking boots and to bring water, food, insect repellent, and sunscreen.

From Ke'e Beach, follow the trail upslope to the Hanakapi'ai Valley, a lush cradle of greenery dotted with a vibrant array of wildflowers. From there the trail continues down to the secluded Hanakapi'ai Beach and the start of the final two-mile leg to Hanakapi'ai Falls. The first leg of the trail from Ke'e Beach is a necessity—the only other ways to get to Hanakapi'ai Falls involve parachutes or boats. But once you reach the falls, you'll be rewarded with breathtaking views and a relaxing swim in its tranquil pools.

*A perfect tropical paradise, Hanakapi'ai Falls is a popular day destination for swimmers and hikers on the Hawaiian island of Kauai.*

# USS *Arizona* Memorial

Dn the morning of December 7, 1941, the quiet of Honolulu's Pearl Harbor was shat-ered by the sounds of gunfire and bombs exploding. The surprise air attack by the mperial Japanese Navy left the United States' Pacific Fleet in tatters and claimed the lives of 2,390 Americans. Of those victims, 1,177 died on the USS *Arizona*, the battleship that sank to the harbor floor less than nine minutes after it was hit by an armor-piercing bomb.

*The solemn memorial spans the middle of the unken USS* Arizona, *commemorating the lives ost when the ship sank on December 7, 1941.*

Twenty years later, the memorial now spanning the middle of the USS *Arizona* was finished. It was dedicated in 1962 to honor those killed during the attack. The memorial is divided into three areas: the first is the entry and assembly rooms, the central section is for ceremonies, and then there's a shrine with the names of all 1,177 victims engraved on the walls. The memorial can be accessed only by boat. Its location in the heart of the harbor provides a serene setting to honor those who died there during the attack that spurred the United States' entry into World War II.

# Cozumel

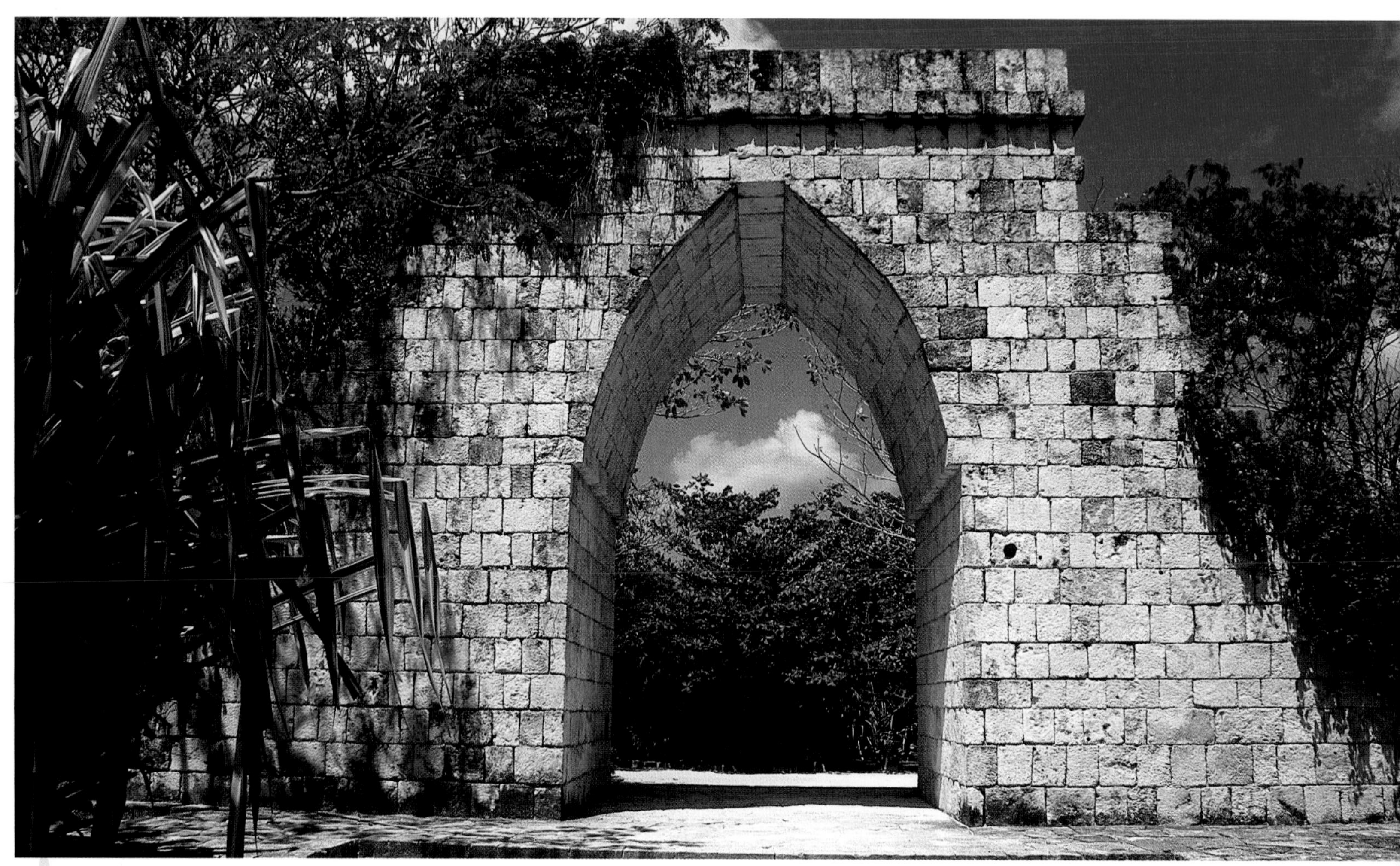

*Cozumel is a trove of natural and historic treasures, including ancient Mayan ruins.*

Cozumel is the island pearl of the Mexican Caribbean. This magnet for sun worshippers and scuba divers lies just 12 miles off the coast of Mexico, not far from the gaudy resort of Cancún. Only about 5 percent of the island is developed.

The island is a world apart, especially for travelers preferring a more relaxed atmosphere than the mainland resorts offer. Cozumel hides countless coves, anonymous beaches, and secret reefs waiting to be explored. Diving, deep-sea fishing, snorkeling, and kayaking are favorite activities. The beaches along the eastern shore are excellent for surfing and swimming, while the land along the west is more developed, and the water is calm for snorkeling or scuba diving.

Chankanaab National Park is among Mexico's oldest marine parks. It features a lagoon, a Mayan cenoté (or well), a pond that links to the ocean through underwater caves, peerless coral reefs, and replicas of Mayan buildings. At the center of the island, you can view real Mayan ruins amidst the jungle and swampy lagoons. Cozumel's San Gervasio is an extensive complex of ruins dating from 100 B.C. to A.D. 1600, when Spanish explorers arrived.

# Guadalajara

an altitude of almost a mile high, Guadalaa is a city of monuments, parks, and historic e-lined streets. The city has been dubbed "City of Roses," Mexico's Pearl of the West. e height of Spanish colonial art and architure is evident throughout the city. Sterling amples include the University of Guadaara, founded in 1792, and the historic disct. At the city's heart is its Centro Histórico, here visitors can get acquainted with local story and colonial architecture. There's o the Catédral Metropolitana de Guadalajara, the city's Metropolitan Cathedral. Begun in 1561 and completed more than a century later, the cathedral is capped by distinctive twin yellow-tiled steeples. Nearby is Plaza Tapatía, Guadalajara's largest plaza, which covers seven square blocks. It's best traveled by foot or *calandria*, traditional horse-drawn touring carriages.

Although Guadalajara is not a resort town, there is plenty of golf, tennis, shopping, and restaurants for tourists to enjoy. There's also a zoo, a children's amusement park (Selva Mágica), bullfights at Plaza de Toros Nuevo Progresso, and rodeos at Lienzo Charro de Jalisco. The city is blessed with a mild mountain climate, and its culture and history draw people from all over the world. Guadalajara is also known by some as the birthplace of mariachi music and the Mexican hat dance.

*The "City of Roses" is built around Centro Histórico, which features the striking colonial architecture of landmarks such as Catédral Metropolitana de Guadalajara.*

# Chichén Itzá

Chichén Itzá is the largest and most-restored archaeological site in Mexico. It lies 75 miles from Mérida, which was probably the most important Mayan city in its time. The ancient relics are anything but ordinary, and many visitors take day-long bus tours to see the ancient cities that make up Chichén Itzá.

The cenotés, or wells, are a highlight of the tour. Some of these wells still yield skeletal remains. Visitors today are told lurid tales of the sacrifices of virgins, children, and the elderly tossed down the wells. These tales are true, though scholars say human sacrifices probably numbered far fewer than some people believe.

Chichén Itzá's four-plus square miles consist of three regions. The Toltecs made the area their capital in the late 10th century A.D. They continued building the stone city until the 12th century, when it declined and the local residents stopped building great structures.

The central wonder of Chichén Itzá is the Kukulcán Pyramid, called El Castillo del Serpiente Emplumada, which means "The Castle of the Feathered Snake." The astonishing city unfolds at the base of the pyramid. Near the

*The amazing Kukulcán Pyramid is the defining feature of Chichén Itzá.*

Temple of the Warriors is the Group of th Thousand Columns, a forest of columns tha proceeds into the jungle. Then there are th Temple of the Jaguar complex and Caraco known as the Mayan Observatory.

About one football field's distance from th Kukulcán Pyramid is the Great Ballcourt o Chichén Itzá. It is 545 feet long and 225 fee wide, open to the sky, and a whisper at on end can be heard clearly at the other. This i

## Quick Fact

### *The Kukulcán Pyramid*

The massive Kukulcán Pyramid was built between A.D. 900 and A.D. 1100. Its base spans one acre, and the giant steps rise 80 feet to the top, offering an unforgettable view of the ruined city. The breathtaking pyramid is capped by a 20-foot-high temple that stands as a monument to the feathered-serpent god Kukulcán (also known as Quetzacoatl and other names in various Mesoamerican tongues). The pyramid is designed to reflect the Mayan calendar: It has four staircases of 91 steps each, or 364 steps, plus the top platform, for 365 steps—one for each day of the year.

The ancient pyramid remains full of mysteries. From some points, echoes of the jungle's resplendent quetzal birds can be heard. On the equinoxes, the setting sun shimmers so that the steps' snakehead sculptures appear to wriggle down the stone. Ordinary conversations at the top of the structure can be heard clearly at the bottom. And if you stand at the foot of the temple and shout, the echo returns as a scream.

where the Mayans played their sacred game of *pok ta pok,* in which teams tried to put a natural rubber ball through a stone hoop without the use of their hands. The losing captain was sacrificed, either by decapitation or by removing the heart.

Before you go, take into consideration that Mayan prophecy holds that on December 22, 2012, Kukulcán will rise from the ground beneath the Great Ballcourt and destroy the world. So you might want to plan around that.

*Reclining amid a forest of columns, this statue of the Toltec god Chaac-Mool atop the Temple of the Warrior was the altar on which ritual sacrifices were placed.*

# Sierra Tarahumara

The Sierra Tarahumara is an immense area of linked canyons and forested plateaus in the northern Mexico state of Chihuahua. The extensive canyon system is the largest in North America and is nearly four times the size of the Grand Canyon. There are six major canyons that wind through the region. Of these, four are about as deep as the Grand Canyon: Urique Canyon is 6,136 feet deep, Sinforosa and Batopilas canyons are each more than 5,900 feet deep, and Copper Canyon is almost 5,800 feet deep.

The canyons are a hiker's paradise and paradox. Most trails are not marked or mapped, and novice hikers are advised to stay near the outskirts or hire local guides. The climate is temperate along the mile-high canyon rims, with cold winters and mild summers. Summer is the rainy season, and wildflowers flourish from the end of September through October. Rivers wind along the bottom of the canyons: Many are impassable due to great boulders and massive waterfalls. The climate is tropical along the bottoms of the canyons, providing a habitat for many threatened animal species, including jaguarundis, jaguars, and ocelots.

The area is home to Mexico's Tarahumara Indians. They call themselves Rarámuri, which translates to "the Runners," and are known for their supreme endurance when chasing game and traveling throughout the canyons. The Tarahumara have maintained many tribal customs and traditions living in remote parts of the Sierra Tarahumara.

> "Overwhelming. That is perhaps the word that best describes the impact on one's senses, on seeing the Sierra Tarahumara for the first time . . ."
>
> —*Bernard L. Fontana,* Tarahumara: Where Night Is the Day of the Moon

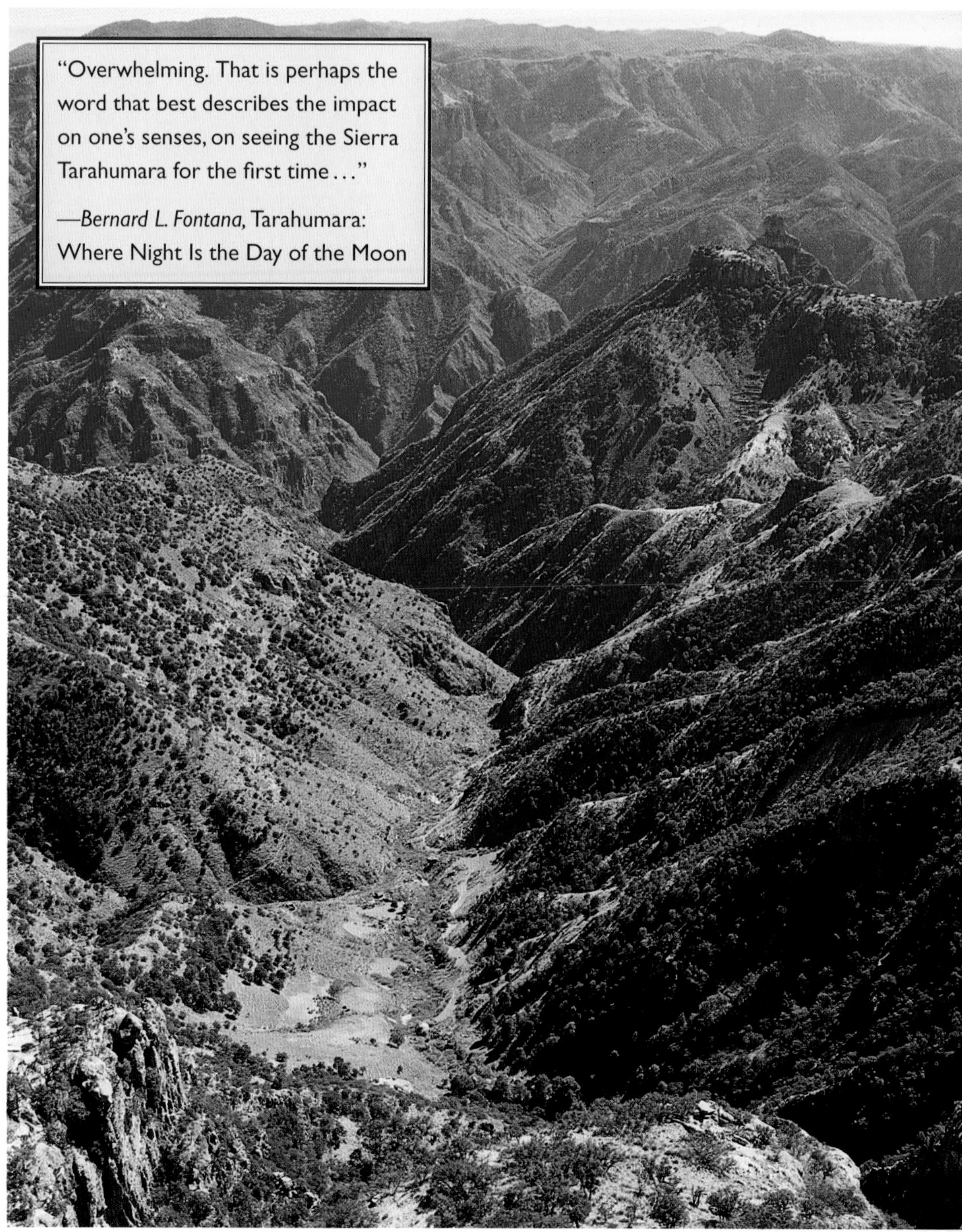

*The Copper Canyon of the Sierra Tarahumara is one of four Grand Canyon-size crevasses in the area, bottoming out almost 5,800 feet below the rims.*

# Plaza de Toros Monumental and Estadio Azteca

Mexico City is as sports-crazed as many cities in the United States. However, the sports that have endured here are bullfighting and *fútbol* (or soccer, if you prefer).

Bullfighting is one of the few remaining bloodsports, and fights in Mexico City combine ritual and pageantry. The height of the bullfighting season is November through March. Brave matadors duel 1,800-pound bulls in Plaza de Toros Monumental. This is possibly the largest bullring in the world (some argue that the bullring in Madrid is larger), with seating for 41,262 and a capacity of 45,000, including standing room. The stadium opened in 1946 and was acclaimed from the start for its monumental architecture, spectator comfort, and exhibitions of bullfighting talent.

Mexico City's other world-class stadium is the three-tiered, 144,600-seat Estadio Azteca. It is the only stadium to host two World Cup finals (1970 and 1986), and it has also hosted the Olympic Games (1968). The stadium is positioned so that as the sun passes overhead from east to west, it isn't a disadvantage for either team. The name of the stadium is an homage to the ancient Aztecs, who once inhabited the land where Mexico City now stands.

## Quick Fact

**Corrida de Toros**

An afternoon at the Plaza de Toros Monumental in Mexico City may be shocking for some. The ritual and drama of a *corrida de toros,* or bullfight, have long been a tradition in Mexican culture.

At the fight, three matadors will each fight two bulls. When each bull is released, the bullfighter's assistant, or *torero,* will take a few passes of the bull with his cape. Then the *picadores,* or horse riders armed with lances, enter the ring and jab the bull to weaken it. Next, the matador proceeds to dominate the bull through precise movements of his cape. At the opportune moment, the matador kills the bull. The traditional and ritualistic way to do this is by plunging the sword deep into the bull's back. However, if the move is not executed perfectly, great shame is brought to the matador.

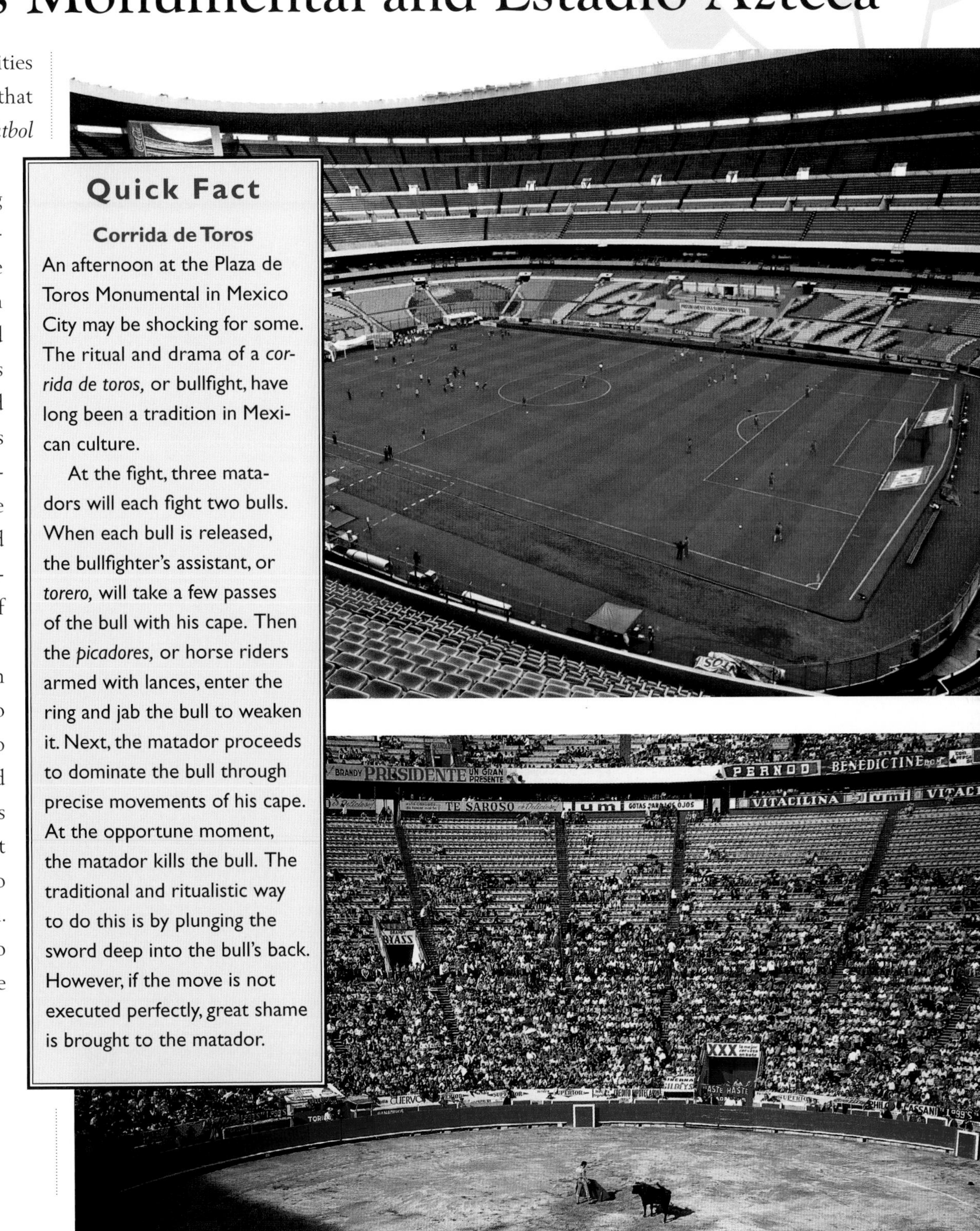


*Mexico City's two landmark stadiums, Estadio Azteca* (top) *and Plaza de Toros Monumental* (bottom), *can together seat nearly 200,000 people.*

# Banff

Banff, Alberta, is about 80 miles from Calgary. Perched at the gateway to the Canadian Rockies, the little town of Banff (population 8,200) is known to some as the hiking, horseback riding, skiing, mineral springs–soaking, snowboarding capital of Canada. At an elevation of 4,537 feet, Banff is the highest town in Canada. The spectacular region rewards visitors with ice walks, snowshoeing, snowmobiling, dogsledding, and sleigh rides in the winter and hiking and rafting in the summer. The pleasing alpine village is crisscrossed with trails (about 1,000 miles in all in the region) an provides opportunities to spot local wildlif and view the stunning peaks of Mount Rundl and Cascade Mountain.

The town marks the entry to Banf National Park, Canada's first national park

*Banff, Alberta, is known as a gateway to the majestic Canadian Rockies, where myriad picturesque mountain lakes are nestled in glacial valleys.*

## Quick Fact

***Lake Louise***

The stunning and serene waters of Lake Louise are just 35 miles from Banff. Sometimes called the "Diamond in the Wilderness," it was first named Emerald Lake for its turquoise-hued waters. The panorama of the lake and sweeping views of Mount Temple, Mount Whyte, and Mount Niblock are breathtaking.

One of the gems of Lake Louise is the Fairmont Château Lake Louise, a spectacular five-star resort hotel nestled in this unique wilderness. The neon nightlife and celebrity glitz common at some mountain resorts are absent from the nearby village of Lake Louise, where the scenery, wildlife, and skiing take center stage.

*The remarkably reflective surface of Lake Louise offers a second chance to see the beautiful mountain scenery, or at least its mirror image.*

Mount Forbes is a spectacle here, reaching 11,850 feet into the sky. More than four million people visit each year: The mild summers make July and August prime time for tourists. In the northwest corner of Banff is Castle Guard Cave, part of the longest cave system in Canada.

Banff National Park is a UNESCO (United Nations Educational, Scientific, and Cultural Organization) World Heritage site. It is also home to the legendary Fairmont Banff Springs Hotel, which rises like a Gothic fortress out of a landscape of boundless mountain forests. Here you can enjoy fine food, golf, skiing, a wine bar, and a spa.

# Vancouver

Vancouver—Canada's third-largest city—is the urban cornerstone of British Columbia and the nation's gateway to the Pacific Rim. The city glistens where the mountains seem to vanish into the coastline and then rise again on Bowen and Vancouver islands. From a distance, the city can look like a diamond cluster rising from the Strait of Georgia to the rolling Coast Mountains and the Fraser Valley beyond.

*Known as one of the most progressive cities on the continent, Vancouver is considered a model city by urban planners around the world.*

As Canada's west coast counterculture capital, Vancouver is an urban explosion with an environmental-minded style. The metro area has more than two million residents. The city is also known for its urbane thrills, its acceptance of alternative lifestyles, and a vigorous club scene.

Great green forests surrounding Vancouver lead to getaways up the fjords and rivers to adventures in Pemberton, up the Chilliwack River, in Cypress Provincial Park, and in the Skagit Valley Recreation Area. There are three ski resorts within a half-hour drive of downtown—Mount Seymour, Grouse Mountain, and Cypress Mountain. And the Capilano River, Seymour River, and Lynn Creek provide white-water thrills come spring meltdown.

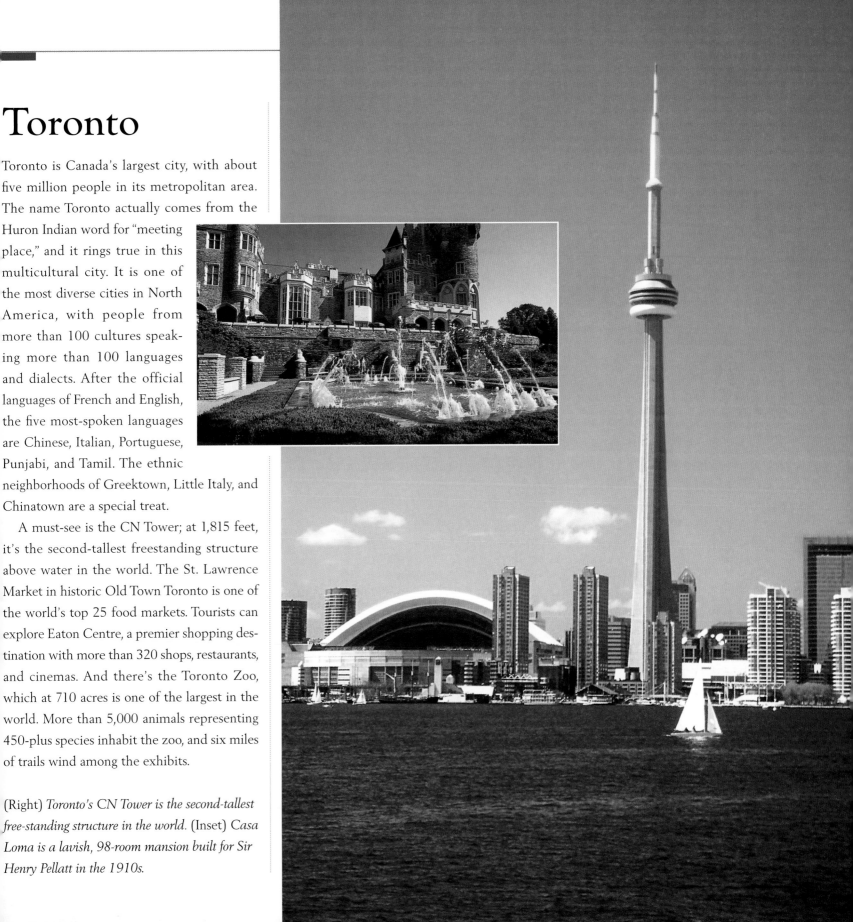

# Toronto

Toronto is Canada's largest city, with about five million people in its metropolitan area. The name Toronto actually comes from the Huron Indian word for "meeting place," and it rings true in this multicultural city. It is one of the most diverse cities in North America, with people from more than 100 cultures speaking more than 100 languages and dialects. After the official languages of French and English, the five most-spoken languages are Chinese, Italian, Portuguese, Punjabi, and Tamil. The ethnic neighborhoods of Greektown, Little Italy, and Chinatown are a special treat.

A must-see is the CN Tower; at 1,815 feet, it's the second-tallest freestanding structure above water in the world. The St. Lawrence Market in historic Old Town Toronto is one of the world's top 25 food markets. Tourists can explore Eaton Centre, a premier shopping destination with more than 320 shops, restaurants, and cinemas. And there's the Toronto Zoo, which at 710 acres is one of the largest in the world. More than 5,000 animals representing 450-plus species inhabit the zoo, and six miles of trails wind among the exhibits.

(Right) *Toronto's CN Tower is the second-tallest free-standing structure in the world.* (Inset) *Casa Loma is a lavish, 98-room mansion built for Sir Henry Pellatt in the 1910s.*

# Yukon

The population of the Yukon Territory is 30,000, give or take a few hardy souls. More than 23,000 of those people live in the capital city of Whitehorse, which was known as a prospector's paradise during the Klondike gold rush of the late 19th century. While once the source for legends and lore, Whitehorse is now home to the SS *Klondike,* the preserved sternwheeler boat that once ferried goods and people along the Yukon River.

Dawson City is a town of just 2,000 people, but nearly 60,000 visitors come each year to see the literary shrines, including the cabins of Jack London and Robert Service. London wrote more than 50 books based on his experiences in the Yukon, Alaska, California, and at sea. Service was the author of volumes of verse, such as *The Spell of the Yukon.* He wrote of the northern land where he found, "The snows that are older than history/The woods where the weird shadows slant/The stillness, the moonlight, the mystery."

The fabled high mountains, vast ice fields, and lush valleys of Kluane National Park and Reserve in southwest Yukon are astounding. The park has one of the most extensive non-polar ice fields in the world. It's also home to Canada's highest summit, Mount Logan, at 19,545 feet. Ivvavik National Park in the northwestern part of the territory is known for its migratory herds of porcupine caribou. The mountains there were never covered by glaciers, and V-shape valleys and isolated conical hills are part of the frigid landscape.

*The harsh climate has taken its toll on the Yukon; weathered remnants of the Klondike gold rush of the late 1800s dot the countryside.*

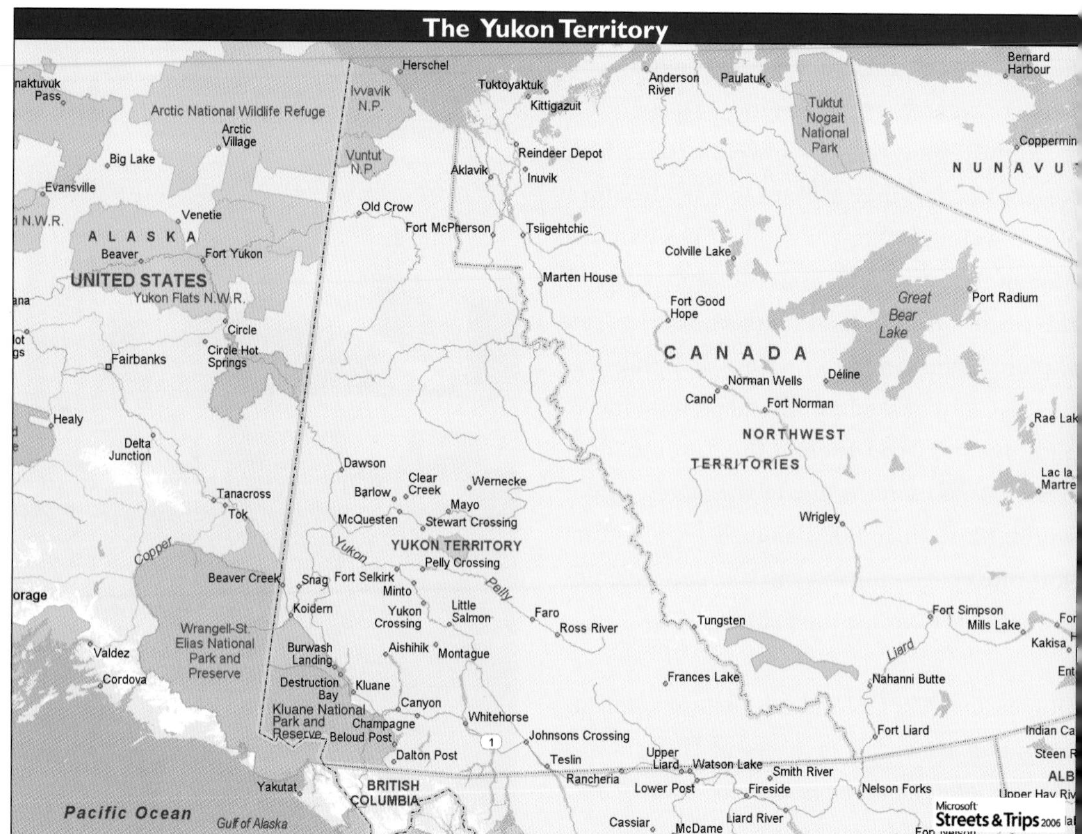

# Montreal

Montreal is one of the largest French-speaking metropolises in the world. Following Québec's laws, all signs are posted in French, but services are available in English in the parts of the city most visited by tourists.

Many visitors start in Old Montreal, the Vieux-Port, which contains a collection of historic buildings that rival most cities in North America. The cobblestone streets lead to the great square, Place Jacques-Cartier. A promenade along quaint shops and fine restaurants takes you past Montreal City Hall. The Château Ramezay, built in the 1700s for the governor and now a museum, lies along rue Notre-Dame, the oldest street in the city. Nearby, don't miss the Place D'Armes square.

The Notre-Dame Basilica is one of the most stunning buildings in Montreal. The Neogothic-style church was built in 1829. The interior is lavishly beautiful, featuring stained glass windows, an elaborate altarpiece, a Casavant organ, and the largest bell on the continent, le Gros Bourdon.

Visitors seeking outdoor recreation are in luck. Montreal's Mount Royal Park sits on a dormant volcano. (The mountain is the origin for the city's name: Jacques Cartier referred to Mont Royal on his voyage there in 1535. At that time, *réal* was a variation of *royal*, and the contraction yielded Montreal.) At 761 feet, the overlook gives a dazzling view of the city.

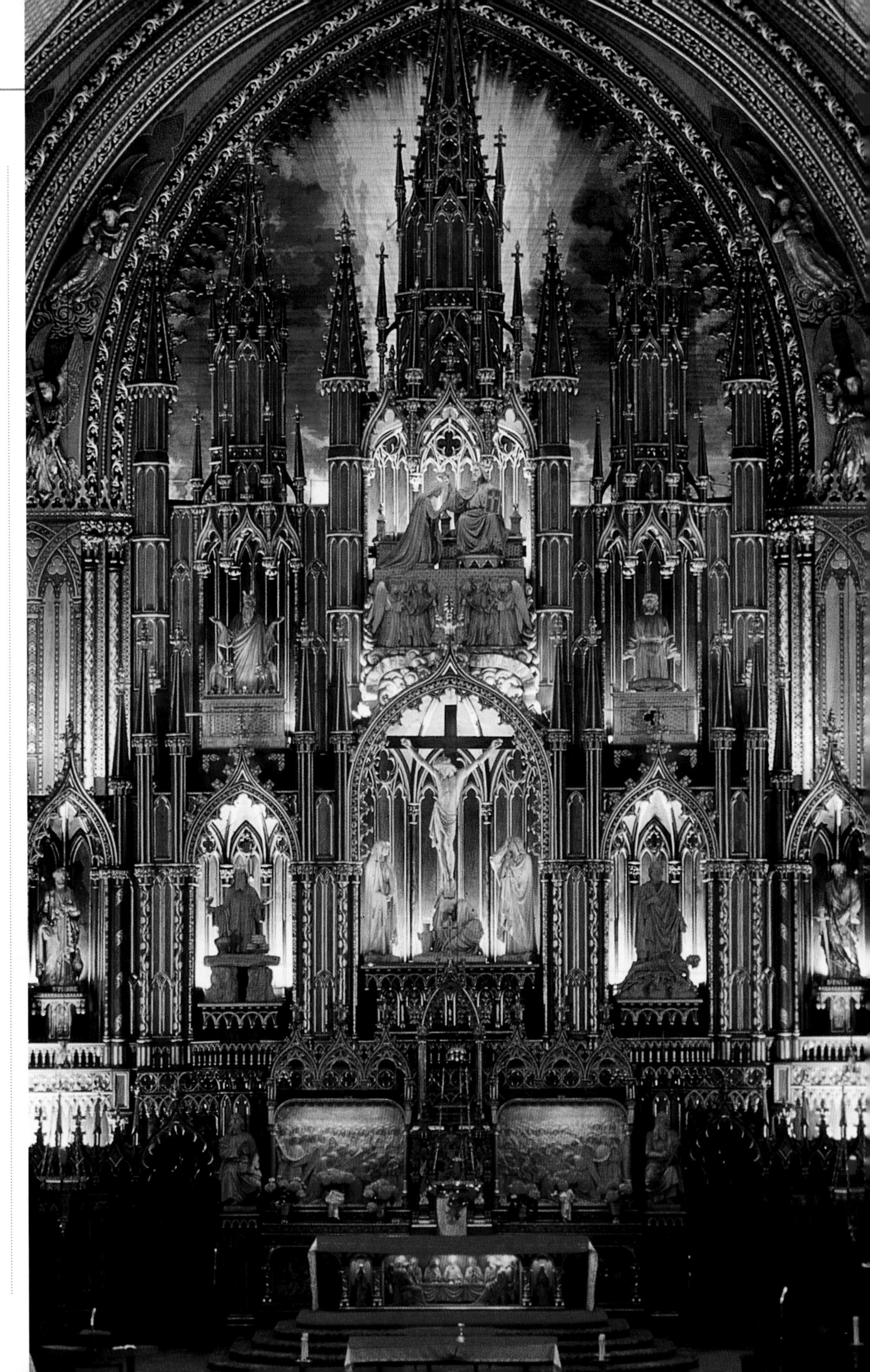

*The ornate altarpiece is a defining feature of the Notre-Dame Basilica in Montreal.*

# Québec City

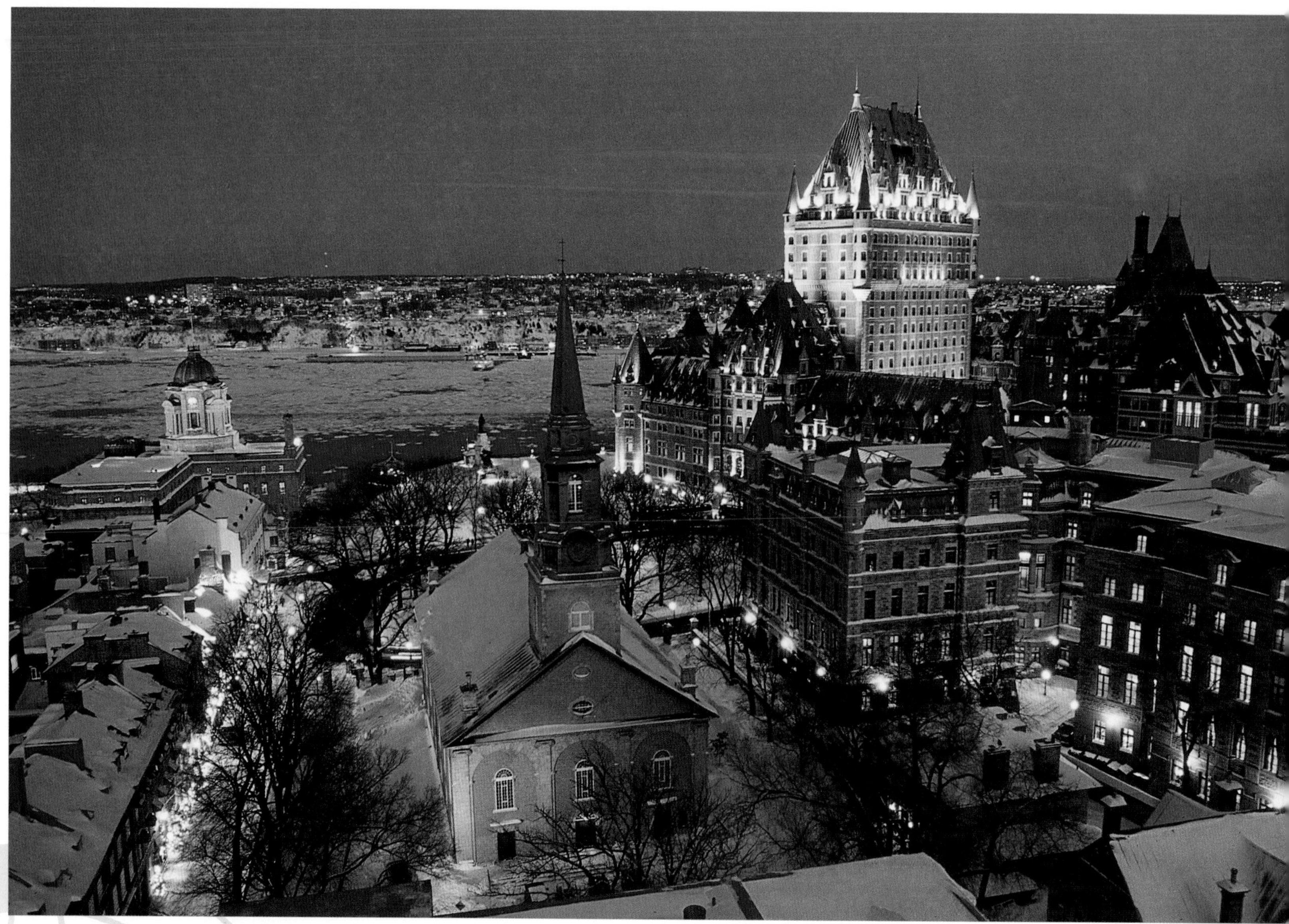

Founded by Samuel de Champlain in 1608, Old Québec City is the cradle of French civilization in North America. The land was settled because of its strategic cliffs: The great stone city rises abruptly atop Cap Diamant. Fort Saint-Louis provided further protection.

Now the Old City offers a giant slice of history in a French-Canadian neighborhood replete with restaurants, bistros, bakeries, and bars. In Lower Town, the Place-Royale marketplace remains one of the most visited spots. Upper Town is the hotspot for fine dining and luxury hotels, most notably Le Château Frontenac. This historic hotel, which opened in 1893, overlooks the St. Lawrence River.

*Le Château Frontenac rises above the Victorian skyline of Upper Town in Québec City.*

# The Calgary Exhibition & Stampede

About 50 miles east of the Canadian Rocky Mountains, where prairie meets foothills, Calgary, Alberta, puts on one of the world's biggest Old West shows. The Calgary Exhibition & Stampede calls itself "The Greatest Outdoor Show on Earth"—and for good reason.

The Calgary Stampede was born back in 1912, when Guy Weadick, a cowboy from Rochester, New York, rode into town with a vision for a Wild West Extravaganza. Weadick talked the "Big Four" well-to-do Calgarians into ponying up $100,000 in all, and Calgary held its first Stampede—an immediate smash success, as it has been ever since.

For ten days each July, the city takes on the atmosphere of the Old West, as residents become cowboys, cowgirls, or lone gunslingers. Townsfolk decorate their homes and businesses in Western style, too. The Calgary Stampede gathers rodeo cowboys and Indians, calf ropers, and beauty queens. It features the Stampede Midway, the Stampede Indian Village, and the daily Grandstand Show, including the traditional Chuckwagon Races and live music acts, such as the famed Young Canadians. Spring sales and auctions (for example, the Calgary Bull Sale) lead up to animal and agricultural events, with contests including the World Championship Blacksmith Competition. More than one million Stampede attendees come to Calgary to soak up the rootin', tootin' action.

*The Calgary Exhibition & Stampede sees all sorts of horseplay—even Canadian Mounties get in on the act.*

# Niagara Falls

*American Falls* (pictured) *and Bridal Veil Falls are in the United States, but the largest of Niagara's three waterfalls, Horseshoe Falls, is in Ontario, Canada.*

Niagara Falls is the best-known group of waterfalls in North America, and quite possibly the world. Tourists have flocked here for more than a century, taking in the overpowering sights and sounds of water in motion as it courses over ancient rock.

Niagara Falls is where Lake Erie drains into the Niagara River, Lake Ontario, and beyond. The falls were born about 10,000 years ago when a slow-moving glacier dammed the river's route and forced it over the low point in the area, a north-facing cliff.

Niagara Falls actually consists of three splendid waterfalls on the Niagara River: Horseshoe Falls in southeastern Ontario (also called Canadian Falls), American Falls in northwestern New York, and Bridal Veil Falls, also in New York. Horseshoe Falls is the largest of the three, at about 177 feet in height. However, this doesn't make it all that tall of a waterfall—Yosemite Falls is more than 13 times taller. But Horseshoe Falls is notably wide—2,200 feet. In fact, more than six million cubic feet of water pour over these falls every minute, making for the most powerful group of waterfalls in North America.

Like all things, Niagara Falls is temporary. The falls have moved several miles southward over the last 200 years due to erosion, and a rockslide in 1954 altered the flow of the American Falls forever.

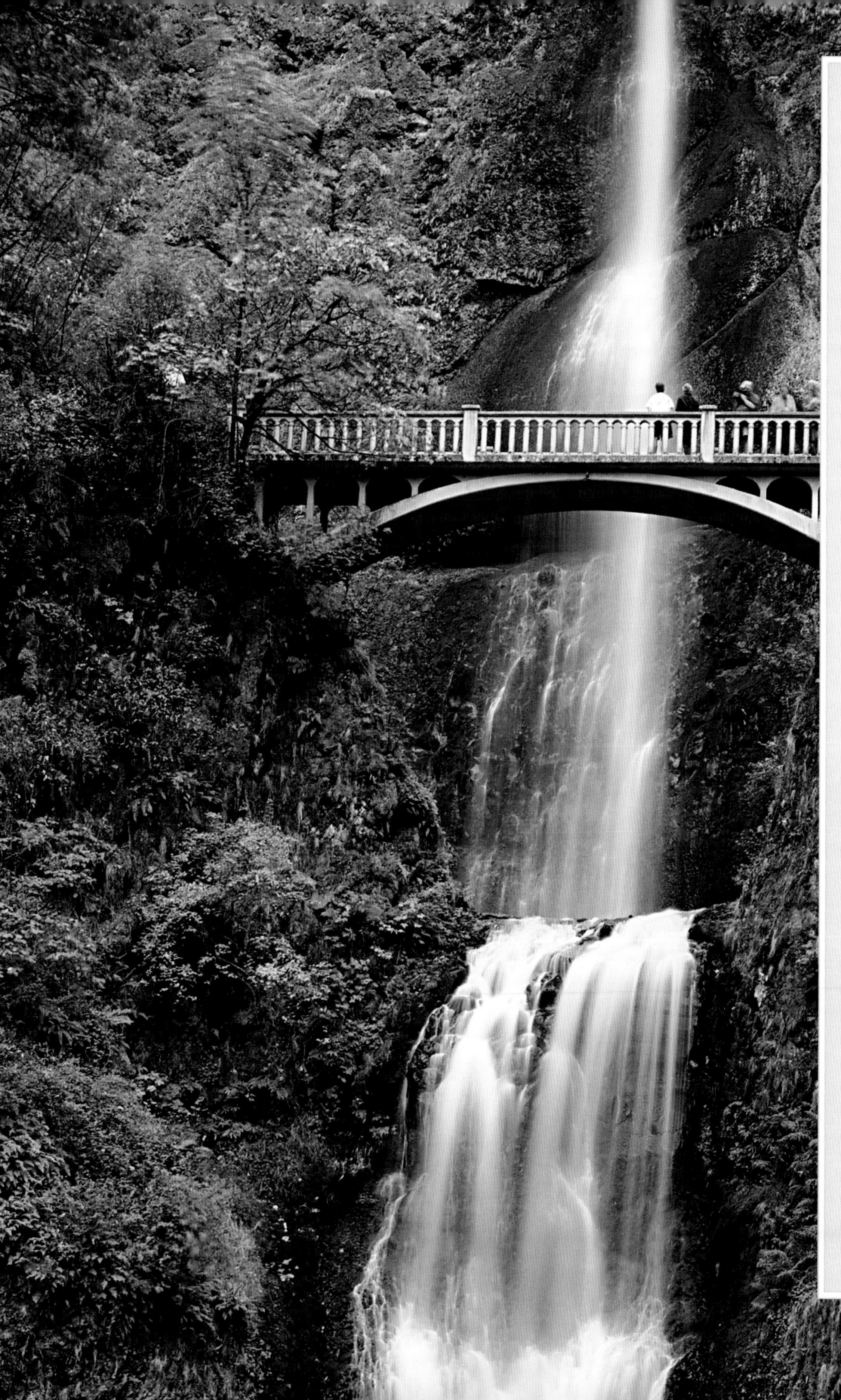

# West Coast

From Hawaii to Alaska, the Pacific Northwest to California, this chapter covers America's remarkably diverse West Coast. Drivers along this region's awe-inspiring scenic routes will encounter icy glaciers and ancient volcanoes, arid deserts and crystalline lakes, urban parklands and remote campgrounds, white sand beaches and cool redwood forests. Oregon's Rogue–Umpqua Scenic Byway follows thundering rivers through narrow canyons. California's Big Sur Coast Highway hugs steep sea cliffs as it twists and turns high above the crashing Pacific. Washington's Mountains to Sound Greenway links Puget Sound and Seattle to the soaring peaks of the Cascades. And all along the way, stopovers provide ready access to the multitude of recreational and cultural bounties lying just beyond the byways.

*Multnomah Falls on Oregon's Historic Columbia River Highway is the fifth-largest falls in the United States; the waters plummet a total of 620 feet.*

# North Shore Oahu/Kamehameha Highway

*Ambling along Oahu's tropical and rustic North Shore, the sun-drenched Kamehameha Highway provides a taste of the Hawaii that once was, as well as easy access to some of the world's top surfing beaches.*

Away from the urban bustle of Honolulu and the crowds of Waikiki, the road that traverses Oahu's North Shore is a study in pastoral tranquility and rural charm, set against the backdrop of the blue Pacific. The Kamehameha Highway (Route 83)—named for King Kamehameha the Great, who conquered and unified all the Hawaiian islands in the late 18th and early 19th centuries—hugs the Pacific Ocean from the eastern (windward) side of the island going north and then west until it dips south toward Pearl Harbor at the town of Haleiwa. Along the way, it passes a succession of small coves and bays and miles of white-sand beaches, some nearly deserted. In summer, the ocean waters tend to be fairly calm and good for swimming. In winter, the waves at Waimea Bay and Sunset Beach may hit 25 to 30 feet or more—the largest surfable waves in the world.

Those who travel Oahu's unspoiled North Shore will soon feel as though they have escaped to the Hawaii of old. Roadside vendors peddle local delicacies such as coconuts, fresh pineapple (the Dole Plantation is farther down Kamehameha Highway to the south), Kahuku sweet corn, and cold shrimp. General stores and food stands offer up some of the islands' most refreshing shaved ice, the exceptionally tasty Hawaiian version of the snow cone; tropical flavors include pineapple, coconut, and passion fruit, and are often served over ice cream or azuki beans. The historic resort town of Haleiwa, the "surf capital of the world," features old-fashioned eateries, intriguing shops, and, of course, the ever-inviting Pacific surf.

*Kualoa Ranch, a historic 4,000-acre working cattle ranch, spreads from steep mountain rises to the sparkling ocean waters.*

As beautiful as the drive is, it's hard to resist stopping at one of the many beaches along the North Shore. Sunset Beach, Ehukai Beach, and Waimea Bay are world famous for their monster waves and surfing competitions. Malaekahana State Recreation Area has terrific swimming and body surfing. Other beaches, such as Shark's Cove at Pupukea Beach Park, are known for their tide pools and snorkeling. Kawela Bay and Kuilima Cove are uncrowded sandy beaches with safe swimming and snorkeling year-round. In winter, beachgoers might spot humpback whales offshore, migrating south from Alaska to mate.

## Quick Facts

**Length:** 31 miles.

**Time:** One hour.

**Considerations:** The road is open year-round, with pleasant temperatures throughout. Water temperatures are 75 to 80 degrees Fahrenheit year-round, but the surf can be very high and the undertow strong and hazardous for swimming in winter. Winter is also the season for spotting migrating whales.

## Highlights

For those who approach from the eastern (windward) side of Oahu, the North Shore drive begins at Kualoa Point, at the northern end of Kaneohe Bay, which overlooks the conical-shape island known as Chinaman's Hat and is the site of Kualoa Beach Park. (Those who approach from the western or lee ward side, almost due north from Pearl Harbor, will begin the North Shore drive at Haleiwa, so simply reverse the order given here.)

**Kualoa Ranch:** Kualoa Ranch, a 4,000-acre working ranch just beyond Kualoa Beach Park, has both seafront and a backdrop of steep green mountain cliffs. It offers horseback riding, ranch tours, and other outdoor activities.

**Sacred Falls State Park:** The highway continues north directly along the windward shore, past Kaaawa Beach, Kahana Bay, and the small resort area of Punaluu.

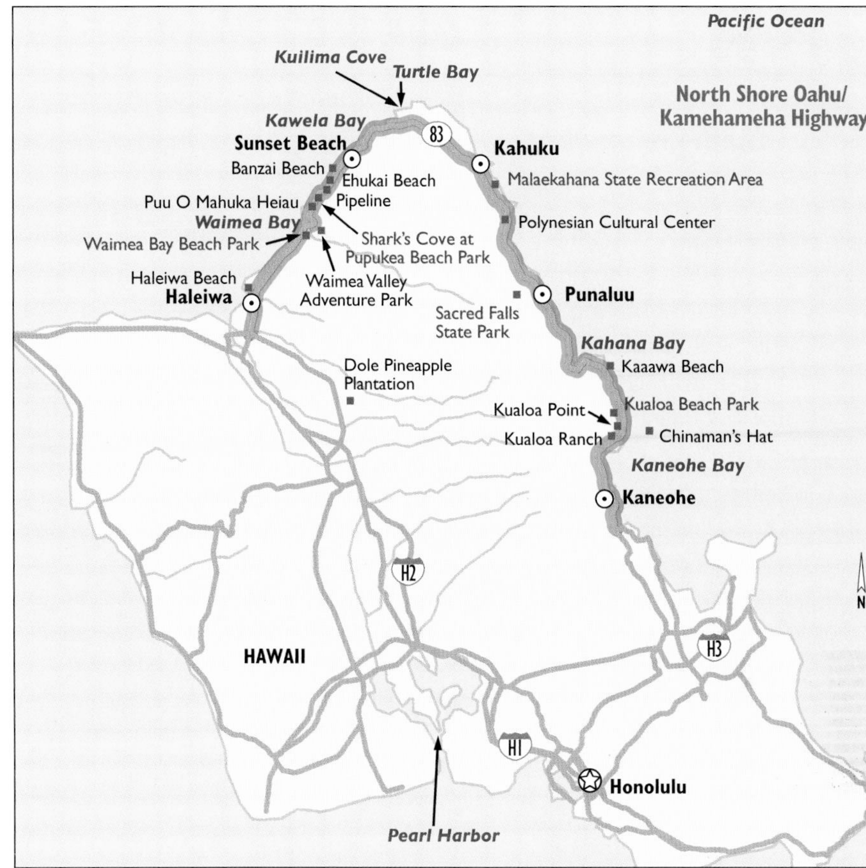


ıst beyond Punaluu Beach is acred Falls State Park, where two-mile hiking trail leads ırough a canyon to the falls, onsidered Oahu's most beauti-ıl. The trail was closed in 1999, owever, due to dangerous rock-ides. Check at the entrance for urrent status.

**olynesian Cultural Center:** A bit ırther north up the coast in Laie is ne Polynesian Cultural Center, said o be Hawaii's most popular paid ttraction, which depicts life in acific island cultures from Hawaii o Fiji and the Marquesas. Evening ıaus and other entertainment are lso offered.

**ahuku:** Near the northernmost oint on the island (Kahuku Point) the historic sugar plantation own of Kahuku, site of an old ugar mill.

**urtle Bay:** As the road dips south-west, an isolated promontory leads o Turtle Bay, surrounded by two rotected swimming coves, Kawela Bay and Kuilima Cove. Besides miles of isolated beaches, Turtle Bay is known for winter whale watching and the North Shore's major resort hotel.

**Sunset Beach, Ehukai Beach, Pipeline, Banzai Beach, and Pupukea Beach Park:** A bit farther west comes a quick succession of world-famous surfing beaches—Sunset Beach, Ehukai Beach, Pipeline, and Banzai Beach—where waves are most powerful in winter. These present the best views of what's called the Banzai Pipeline, where surfers disappear inside the tube-shape barrel of a "perfect wave" and emerge seconds later when it breaks. (*Banzai*, a Japanese war cry, refers to the courage to surf there.) Professional surfing competitions are held on these beaches in winter. Just down the road is Pupukea Beach Park, known for its tide pools, snorkeling, and diving.

**Puu O Mahuka Heiau:** Across from Waimea Bay, take a left turn down Pupukea Road to the Puu O Mahuka Heiau—Oahu's largest *heiau* (sacred temple)—an 18th-century historic landmark perched on a ridge with a spectacular view of Waimea Valley.

**Waimea Valley Adventure Park:** The next left off the highway, Waimea Valley Road, leads to the 1,800-acre Waimea Valley Adventure Park, which has a botanical garden with thousands of species of tropical plants, a 45-foot waterfall, cliff divers, hula demonstrations, a kids' area, and more.

**Waimea Bay Beach Park:** Back on Kamehameha Highway, the surf's up again at Waimea Bay Beach Park, where the waves may reach 30 feet or higher in the winter months. In summer, you can swim in calm turquoise waters.

**Haleiwa:** At the end of this North Shore drive is Haleiwa, established in 1832 on Waialua Bay by Protestant missionaries. The missionaries' original church and the remains of their adobe home still stand, and much of the town has a rustic, early 1900s feel, complete with *paniolo* (Hawaiian cowboy) architecture. Old general stores coexist with modern boutiques, art galleries, eateries, and the North Shore's largest marina.

*Vith calm waters in the summer, the waves at Waimea Bay can reach as high s 30 feet in the winter months.*

# Alaska's Marine Highway

*Alaska's Marine Highway is like no other scenic "highway" in America. Riding ferryboats rather than cars, sightseers encounter magnificent views of fjords, glaciers, mountains, islands, waterfalls, and whales—all from the water.*

Alaska is best seen from a ferry. The only byway of its kind, Alaska's Marine Highway lets you leave the driving to someone else as you travel scenic coastal routes totaling more than 8,000 miles. From the southern terminus in Bellingham, Washington, the ferries ply waters lined with the lush, green rain forests of British Columbia and Alaska's Inside Passage. Voyagers pass glaciers and fjords in Prince William Sound and the windswept Aleutian Islands, rich in cultural, archaeological, and seismic history.

In southeastern Alaska, northbound travelers can end their sail in Haines or Skagway to connect to the Yukon or other Alaska scenic highways, such as the Haines Highway and the Taylor/Top of the World Highway. The mainline vessels are the *Taku, Matanuska, Malaspina, Kennicott,* and *Columbia.* These workhorses of the Inside Passage travel from Bellingham, Washington; Prince Rupert, British Columbia; and southeastern Alaska coastal communities.

Ferryboats travel routes in southcentral Alaska and Prince William Sound. The *Tustumena* travels the Gulf of Alaska and the Aleutian Islands. During the summer, the state's newest ferry, the *M/V Kennicott,* provides several Gulf of Alaska crossings to the southcentral communities of Valdez and Seward.

## Intrinsic Qualities

**Archaeological:** Although you may not see much archaeology from the ferry, stops along the way offer a look at some of Alaska's most intriguing sites. Much of the archaeological evidence left behind is the work of native Alaskans, but some sites along the byway are of Russian and American origin.

Petroglyphs can be found on the byway near Kodiak, near Petersburg in the Tongass National Forest, and in Sitka. In Wrangell, visitors will be delighted to find Petroglyph State Historic Park, where beautiful circles and designs are carved into large stones. A short hike from the ferry landing takes explorers to a collection of more than 40 petroglyphs from an unknown time and culture, even though the native Tlingit people could be descendants of the artists. Archaeologists have made guesses about the significance of the designs on the boulders, but the petroglyphs could be anything from artwork to a record of the past.

In Ketchikan, archaeology and today's cultures come together at the Totem Bight State Historic Park. When native people left their villages to find work in the new towns in Alaska, they also left behind collections of totem poles. During the 1930s, the Civilian Conservation Corps (CCC) came to salvage what was left of these totem poles and re-create what had been lost.

An even more recent archaeological excavation began at Sitka in 1995 to uncover Baranof Castle, built in 1837.

### Quick Facts

**Length:** 8,834 miles.

**Time to Allow:** One month.

**Considerations:** Summer is the busiest season, so make reservations early. During the winter months, the frequency of trips to some communities is reduced. Keep in mind that fees vary from less than $50 to hundreds of dollars depending on how far you go and whether you are bringing your car.

**Cultural:** Alaska's native cultures have been joined over the years by Russian and American cultures to create a rich history and a thriving present.

The lives of residents, along with the industries that allow them to survive in the Land of the Midnight Sun, are around every corner as you enjoy the decks of the ferry or the streets of one of Alaska's towns. Alaska's Marine Highway takes you through fishing villages and historic towns.

Nearly every stop on the byway reveals more history of the native Alaskans who have lived here for centuries. The native people celebrate festivals and wear authentic clothing. Feasts and festivals that

*Prince William Sound along Alaska's Marine Highway is situated in the coastal arc of the Chugach Mountain Range.*

involve dancing, singing, arts, and crafts traditionally occur during the winter, when all the work of the summer has been done. Many of the festivals are held in honor of animal spirits. The festivals and traditions you witness on the byway may be the most memorable part of your trip.

**Historical:** The history of coastal Alaska dates back to unrecorded times, when the first native Alaskans were just getting used to the beautiful, yet extreme, territory in which they lived. Over many centuries, Alaska has come to be appreciated by different cultures that wanted to stake a claim in the area. As you travel along Alaska's Marine Highway, each port unravels more of the past.

Kodiak Island was the site of the first permanent Russian colony in 1784. The same Russian trappers who were willing to brave the elements in Siberia were also willing to settle the land across the Bering Strait if it meant finding more furs. As settlement progressed, a Russian Orthodox mission was established to keep peace between native peoples and the Russians until the parcel of land was sold to the United States. Today, towns such as Sitka, Unalaska, Seldovia, and many others display pieces of Russian history and influence in Alaska.

Development in Alaska really began in 1867 when "Seward's Icebox" became a U.S. territory. News of gold in the Arctic spread like wildfire, and prospectors gathered in mining communities to try their luck. Ketchikan became the gateway to the Klondike Gold Rush, and Skagway became the destination. Skagway still maintains its reputation as a gold rush town with the Klondike Gold Rush National Historic Park. All through the Inside Passage and into southcentral Alaska, miners established communities in places that promised wealth. Some were successful, and many were not, but stories of Alaska were told far and wide in the lower states.

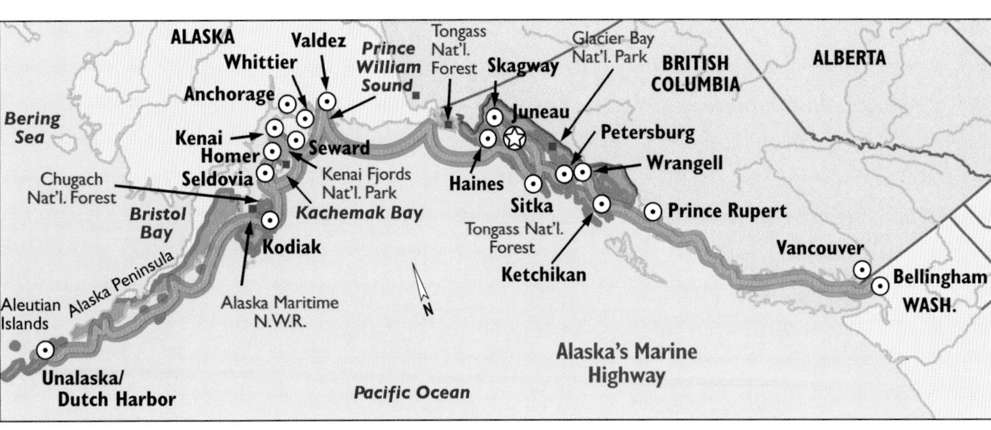


The first tourists to Alaska usually took a steamship on a route developed along Alaska's Inside Passage to see the mystical northern territory and its glaciers and dense forests. Traveling along the coastline remains one of the favorite ways to see Alaska, and Alaska's Marine Highway has preserved the sightseeing tactics of the first Alaskan tourists.

**Natural:** Some of the unique wonders of the world are clustered in the northern corner—a very large corner—known as Alaska. Filled with majestic sea creatures, geological movements, and land overrun with glaciers and forests, Alaska's scenic coastline abounds with natural beauties. In the daylight, you may see a whale as it splashes its tail against the water. At night, the Northern Lights may fill the sky.

As you travel along the shores of Alaska, you observe the unspoiled natural features of the north. Alaska's Marine Highway travels through the Tongass National Forest and along the Chugach National Forest, allowing you to get a good look at both the land and the sea. These beautiful water passageways display rock outcroppings, forest-covered mountainsides, and glaciers. The state has about 100,000 glaciers, most located on the coast. Also notice the smoldering islands along the Alaska Peninsula. These islands are part of the Pacific "Ring of Fire," where underwater volcanoes create island volcanoes that can be seen from the ferry.

Few byways offer a view of such fascinating sea creatures. Whales, seals, fish, and seabirds are all an integral part of an experience on Alaska's Marine Highway. Stop in Seward to visit the Alaska SeaLife Center, where interactive displays tell all about Alaska's wildlife. Both baleen whales and killer whales can be spotted at Glacier Bay National Park and Preserve. At Kodiak Island, nearly two million seabirds live along the shores, while brown bears roam the spruce forests.

**Recreational:** Recreation and adventure go hand in hand, and what is more adventurous than an ocean voyage? From the decks of the ships to the streets of each town to the trails of the forests, you'll find plenty of places to explore along Alaska's Marine Highway. Nearly 98 percent of the land along the byway is publicly owned, which makes wilderness experiences and recreational opportunities virtually endless. While you ride the ferry, you can dine, lounge, and even camp on the decks.

One of the benefits of traveling Alaska's Marine Highway is being able to take your favorite recreational activities with you—mountain biking, kayaking, hiking, or whatever other activities beckon along the coast. At each community, you'll find opportunities to get out and explore, with miles of trails, plenty of parks, and places to stay available at every stop.

**Scenic:** Be sure to bring enough film for your camera. Visiting the coastline of Alaska is like visiting the shores of a fantasy land. Traveling the coast by Alaska's Marine Highway transforms the adventure to a sea voyage, where the wonders of the North are waiting to be discovered. From volcanoes to glaciers, a collection of natural wonders is visible from the decks. You'll see evergreen islands and majestic fjords. Overshadowing a peaceful fishing village, glacier-carved mountains rise up from the shoreline.

Each stop on the route takes you to towns and villages with displays of history and culture. Parts of the scenery on the byway are found in the Russian Orthodox churches and the remnants of booming gold rush towns. Snowcapped mountains in the background and the crisp Alaskan atmosphere only heighten the appeal of each place along the way. And within each city, you are likely to find rivers, trails, or bays where eagles soar and seals still gather.



## Highlights

Alaska's Marine Highway takes you through a variety of towns (listed here from east to west) along the southern Alaskan coastline.

**Ketchikan:** Ketchikan is known as the Gateway to Alaska and is the state's salmon capital. The community is known for its historic Creek Street district and timber industry.

**Petersburg:** This town is known as Little Norway because of its Scandinavian roots. It has several festivals to celebrate the heritage of its residents.

**Sitka:** Numerous volcanic mountains rise out of the ocean and provide a stunning backdrop for this fishing community. Sitka was the Russian capital of North America in the 19th century, as well as the first state capital of Alaska. The community is also a center for Tlingit native culture.

**Juneau:** Juneau is the capital of Alaska and is a historic community with a range of tourism-oriented services and cultural events. The community was settled as a gold mining district and is now the service hub for southeastern Alaska. It is also the gateway to Glacier Bay National Park.

**Skagway:** Skagway is a community with a rich history that includes the Klondike Gold Rush. The history of that period is displayed by a National Historic Park site and by the city's historic architecture. The White Pass and Yukon Route historic railway traverses the 3,000-foot mountain pass to the Yukon, Canada.

**Haines:** Haines is a popular port community. The town is also known for its bald eagle population in the autumn. In October, the world's largest number of bald eagles gather in Haines to take advantage of the late salmon run. This amazing gathering of eagles is the basis of the Chilkat Bald Eagle Preserve and annual Alaska Bald Eagle Festival held in their honor.

**Valdez:** Valdez is the terminus of the Trans-Alaskan Pipeline and the Richardson State Scenic Byway. The area is home to the World Extreme Skiing Competitions as well as many other outstanding winter activities. Don't miss the scenic walking trail.

*Nestled on the west side of Baranof Island, Sitka is flanked on the east by majestic snowcapped mountains and on the west by the Pacific Ocean.*

**Whittier:** Located at the head of Passage Canal, a breathtaking fjord of Prince Williams Sound, Whittier is an important hub connecting the Marine Highway to the Alaska Railroad and to the rest of Alaska.

**Seward:** If you hear names such as Resurrection Bay and Marathon Mountain, you are probably in the romantic town of Seward. The town was named to honor William H. Seward, who helped the United States purchase Alaska from Russia. Near Seward, you'll find Kenai Fjords National Park and the Chugach National Forest headquarters. While in Seward, don't miss a visit to the Alaska SeaLife Center.

**Homer:** Homer is the homeport for a large fleet of halibut charter operators fishing the rich and scenic waters of Kachemak Bay. Both commercial fishing boats and leisure fishers gather at The Spit for boating and fishing. Also located in Homer is the Alaska Maritime National Wildlife Refuge. The refuge is home to seabirds, which find a habitat in the rocks and reefs of Alaskan islands.

**Kodiak:** Kodiak, which is the nation's largest commercial fishing port, was once the capital of Russian America. The community is located on Kodiak Island, a national wildlife preserve.

**Unalaska/Dutch Harbor:** Located in the Aleutian Islands, Unalaska/Dutch Harbor was the first Russian-American community in Alaska.

# Glenn Highway 

*This far-north highway provides passage to a land of native cultures and rugged landscapes as it winds its way from Anchorage toward mountains, rivers, and tundra. Count on long summer days and starry winter nights.*

The Glenn Highway is a place where geology, culture, and scenery come together to create a majestic and rugged landscape that can be seen only in Alaska. Winters bring the fascinating Northern Lights among snow-capped mountains. In the spring, hawks, eagles, and falcons can be seen gliding over the Glenn Highway. Summers bring endless days of wildflowers and green forests along the Matanuska River Canyon that runs between the Chugach and Talkeetna Mountains, creating beautiful views all the way.

Among the mountains and the unforgettable seasons lives a distinct Alaskan culture that has been developing for centuries—beginning with the native Alaskan culture that was altered so much with the arrival of Russian fur traders and, later, gold miners from the lower states. The history of all of Alaska's cultures can be seen along the byway in museums and historic places.

## Intrinsic Qualities

**Archaeological:** Although pieces of archaeology can be found all over the ancient lands along the Glenn Highway, many of them are so delicate that few people know about them. In Knik, south of Wasilla, archaeologists are uncovering a village and many artifacts. The Knik town site became a Euro-American trading and supply post in the late 1800s. Archaeologists have uncovered an old blacksmith shop, an assayer's house, and tools used for refining gold. As the town site is excavated, the discoveries and artifacts are put on display in the Knik Museum in Wasilla.

As you travel the Glenn Highway, you may also want to explore Anthracite Ridge near Sutton. The ridge was formed when a warmer climate existed on the lands that are now Alaska. Ginkgo trees and other warm vegetation were buried here to create the coal resources and fossils that attract both miners and paleontologists. Bones from a dinosaur known as the hadrosaur were also found near the byway at Gunsight Mountain in the Talkeetna Mountains. The dinosaur has been affectionately dubbed "Lizzie."

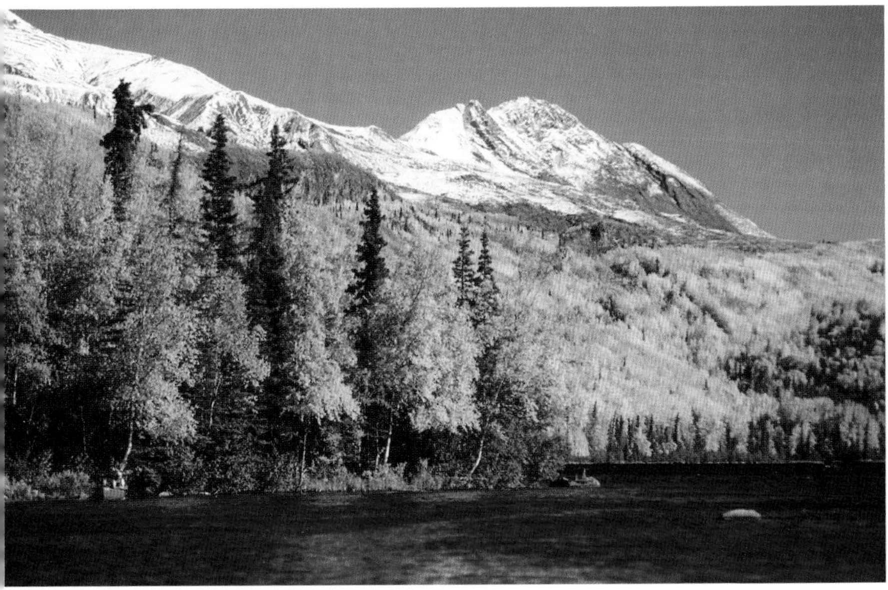

*The Mat-Su Valley was shaped by Ice Age glaciers. Today the valley is covered by beautiful trees, here exhibiting vibrant autumn colors, and by tundra spotted with lakes.*

**Cultural:** Cultures from all over the world have combined along the Glenn Highway. Museums, architecture, and historic districts celebrate the unique history of each culture. To discover the original cultures of Alaska, visit the Anchorage Museum of History and Art or the Alaska Native Heritage Center.

Native society was structured around the family unit. Families hunted together, and when fishing, hunting, or trapping was good, the entire family experienced prosperity. But survival in the Arctic was always a challenge. This way of life remained unchanged for many years, until a new culture emerged during the late 1700s.

When people from Russia began to come to Alaska, they brought their religion with them. Their goal was to introduce the native people of Alaska to Christianity, and one of the rules was that the people could accept the religion only of their own free will. Because of this, the Russian priests who lived in Alaska were extremely dedicated to supporting their parishes during the 100 years they were in Alaska. Yet native Alaskans often combined cultural beliefs: Native people who converted to Orthodoxy would bury the remains of their dead, but also build a small "spirit house" above the grave.

### Quick Facts

**Length:** 135 miles.

**Time to Allow:** Eight hours.

**Considerations:** The Glenn Highway is subject to avalanches; when traveling during winter, check road and weather information prior to the trip, and carry appropriate winter gear. Pull-offs are plowed and available for viewing in the winter.

An economic culture began to grow in Alaska during the 1870s. Rumors of coal, timber, and especially gold brought another significant culture to the land. Mining towns sprung up all over, and Alaska embarked on another great change. Many of those mining towns became the central cities of Alaska; descendants of gold miners became coal miners. Today, Independence Mine State Historical Park allows visitors to explore the lifestyle of the early gold miners in Alaska.

During the 20th century, people continued to gather in Alaska for relief from the Depression or for military strategy during World War II. It was during wartime that the Glenn Highway was constructed as an attempt to better connect Alaska with the lower 48 states.

**Historical:** Alaska is a romanticized land with a history of gold camps, dogsled races, and native Alaskans. Native people with the courage and endurance to establish their culture in this rugged territory settled here nearly 35,000 years ago. Since then, Alaska has maintained its pristine wildernesses, unique wildlife, and exotic atmosphere.

A people known as the Athabascans came from Asia and were the first inhabitants in the lands where the Glenn Highway is now located. The village of Eklutna is a settlement that has been inhabited since the late 1600s by these people. It was not until the 1700s that the land and its people were recorded by Europeans. Explorers James Cook and Vitus Bering opened up European trade between native people in Alaska and their own countries. After the Russian-American Company began to establish missions, trade, and government here in the late 1790s, the people of Russia and Alaska interacted for nearly 100 years, for better or for worse, until another country began to take interest in Alaska.

In 1867, the United States purchased Alaska from Russia and caused a scandal among the American people. They were mortified at the $7.2 million price that the government was willing to pay for a frozen wasteland. But with the continued wealth achieved from fur trapping and gold discovered in Alaska, the area's reputation improved in the eyes of Americans, and people from the lower states began to flock to the territory. The need for roads in Alaska came with the expanding population of miners and trappers; during World War II, Alaska's strategic position also made it a candidate for improved roads. As Alaska's roads improved, communities grew up and were able to have contact with each other. In fact, the Glenn Highway is known for connecting Alaska's history and culture.

**Natural:** Dramatic natural events formed the landscape along the Glenn Highway, and many of these events continue today. Earthquakes and the movement of Earth's plates thousands of years ago created the Chugach and the Talkeetna Mountain ranges, and the rich minerals found in the mountains have been drawing people to Alaska for more than 100 years. It was just off the Glenn Highway where some of Alaska's first gold was discovered. Today, mining is still occurring in the mountains, as geologists search the sediment for fossils and other geological remnants. Rivers, wind, and ice all have played a role in the formation of the mountains, moving the rich sediment from one end of the landscape to the other.

Although the Glenn Highway runs through the tundra, this ecosystem is far from a frozen wasteland. You may see salmon and trout swimming in the rivers while moose wander by the riverside. Flowers, trees, bushes, and meadow grasses are an array of colors. Accumulated meltwater forms wetlands and marshes where birds and waterfowl gather. And when all the land is blanketed with snow, spruce, aspen, and other trees create a winter wonderland.

**Recreational:** Getting a good dose of nature isn't difficult when you visit the Glenn Highway. Chugach State Park is accessible from the byway, and places such as the Palmer Hay Flats and the Matanuska Glacier provide opportunities to spot wildlife or get a closer look at a glacier. With the Chugach and Talkeetna Mountains surrounding the byway, you have many opportunities for hiking and exploring these ancient landforms.

In a place where winter engulfs a large part of the year, winter recreation has been perfected. The lodges and roadhouses along the

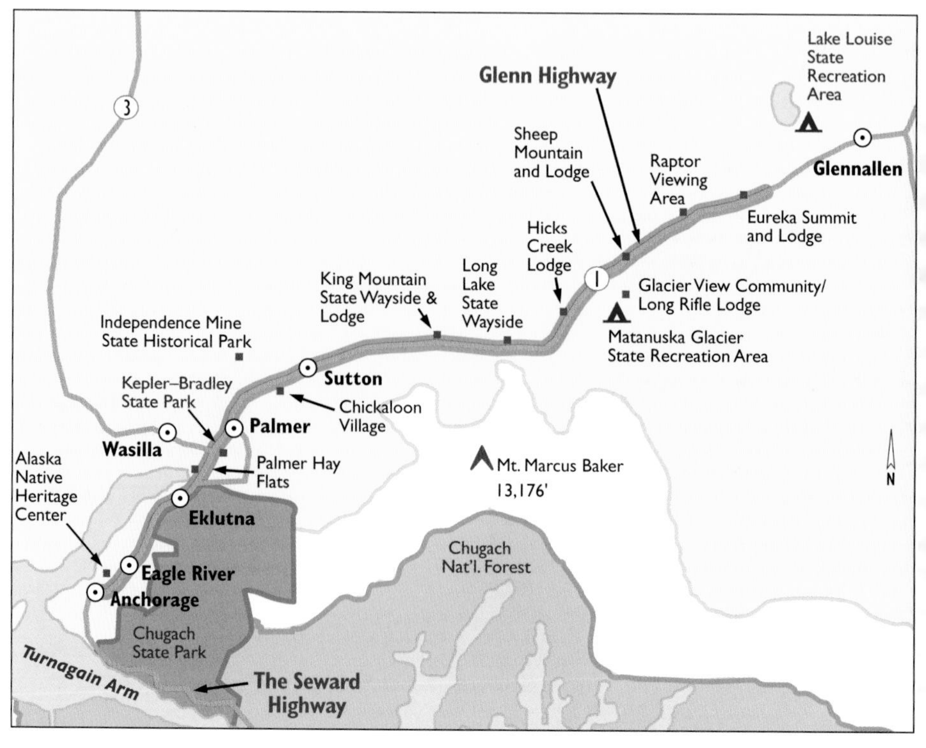

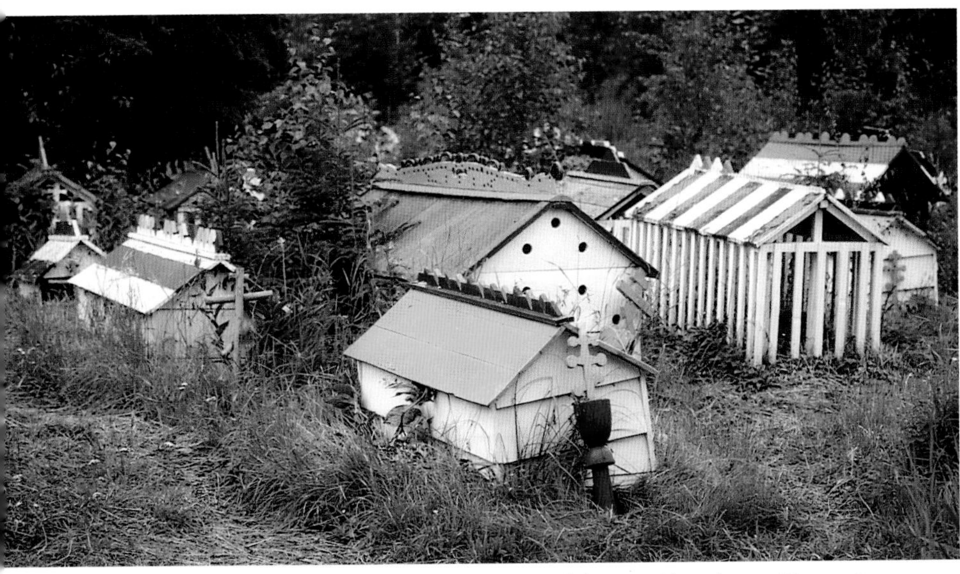

The Eklutna Cemetery has "spirit houses" over the graves of deceased loved ones. The custom comes from a combination of native Alaskan and Russian Orthodox beliefs.

Glenn Highway are perfect places to stop in the winter and enjoy cross-country skiing, snowmobiling, and snowshoeing. You can hardly help enjoying a winter night in Alaska, where the short days lead to extra-long nights. You may want to do some stargazing here or watch for the Northern Lights.

But even in Alaska, the snow melts and summer activities become available to travelers and residents. Alaska is the Land of the Midnight Sun, where, in summer, the long, sunny days make up for the nights of winter. Many people come just to see the wildflowers and watch for wildlife. During March, April, and early May, the air is filled with birds, migrating and moving. A stop at milepost 118 provides an excellent opportunity for viewing birds of prey. The melting rivers and streams are another source of activity. Of course, the fishing in Alaska is superb, but anglers aren't the only ones who enjoy the rivers; rafters and kayakers find places on Alaska rivers to test their skills. In Anchorage, a biking trail is located along the byway for cyclists and in-line skaters to make their way from Anchorage to Chugiak.

**Scenic:** Glenn Highway is bordered by the Chugach Mountain Range from beginning to end. Majestic rock formations rise in between the glaciers that are so prevalent in this area. When the day is clear, you can look to the north and catch a glimpse of Mount McKinley, the highest mountain in the United States. Just past Palmer, the Chugach Mountains are joined by the Talkeetna Mountains. Fields of wild irises decorate the Palmer Hay Flats and follow the Knik River back to a glacier of the same name. Knik Glacier is located in the shadow of Mount Marcus Baker, one of the highest peaks in the Chugach Mountains.

You can see the Matanuska Glacier from the road. This huge mass of slow-melting ice displays the blue, gray, and white colors it has collected over the hundreds of years it has been retreating. When glaciers retreat, they leave streams and lakes behind: The Matanuska River is a collection of melted glacier water that runs among a bed of gray silt, creating a braided appearance. In summer, you can see where meltwater goes.

Glacial meltwater brings entire fields of wildflowers in the late spring and summer. Wetland areas such as the Palmer Hay Flats create views of marshy reeds and willows, where a tundra swan or a Canada goose may be swimming. All along the byway, sights of moose or Dall sheep are reminders that this land still belongs to nature.

## Highlights

The Glenn Highway takes you through several Alaskan towns (listed here from west to east).

**Anchorage:** The city of Anchorage began as a ramshackle community of rail workers living in tents. The community, settled in 1915, has grown and evolved into the largest city in Alaska, with 260,000 people. For a look at Alaskan culture, explore the Anchorage Museum of History and Art or the Alaska Native Heritage Center.

**Eagle River:** This community, within the municipality of Anchorage, is nestled in the foothills of the Chugach Mountains and provides access to the Old Glenn Highway.

**Eklutna:** The Athabascan village of Eklutna has a museum, a Russian Orthodox church, and a cemetery with "spirit houses."

**Palmer:** Palmer is the seat of government for the Matanuska-Susitna Borough, the home of the Alaska State Fair, the center of colonial history, and the heart of Alaska's breadbasket.

**Chickaloon:** This native community is nestled above the confluence of Moose Creek and the Matanuska River in the Talkeetna Mountains. It is the home of Alaska's first native-maintained school and Katie's Wall, built 60 years ago by Katie Wade to stop the cut slope from eroding. Many of the perennial shrubs she planted are still alive today.

**Sutton:** This quaint residential community is located in the Talkeetna Mountains. The Alpine Heritage and Cultural Center provides a look into Sutton's past.

**Glacier View Community:** The Glacier View Community provides several views of the Matanuska Glacier. Matanuska Glacier State Recreation Area lets you walk up next to—or even onto—the glacier.

# Seward Highway 

*Linking Seward to Anchorage, this byway offers vistas of snowcapped mountains, shimmering fjords, alpine valleys, ice-blue glaciers—and glimpses of wildlife, waterfalls, or wildflowers around almost every turn.*

The Seward Highway, linking Anchorage with Seward, passes through some of the most spectacular scenery in the country. For 127 miles, the road winds through a land of remarkable beauty, a land of saltwater bays, frigid blue glaciers, knife-edged ridges, and alpine valleys. From the reflective waters of Turnagain Arm, you rapidly ascend 1,000 feet above sea level to an alpine meadow. Within the hour, you find yourself back at sea level surrounded by fjords, having just passed through a district of rivers and lakes.

## Intrinsic Qualities

**Historical:** The route from Resurrection Bay to Alaska's interior has been in existence for thousands of years; even Russian explorers searched the area for gold and fur in the 1700s. Following the same early routes used by native Alaskans, the Seward Highway has evolved into a modern transportation system.

Natives first used an area along the Seward Highway 9,000 years ago as a hunting camp. In this area, now known as Beluga Point on Turnagain Arm, Tanaina Indians also discovered abundant game in the region more than 8,000 years after the first natives inhabited the area. The region finally received its name in 1778 when shallow water forced James Cook to turn around in his quest for the Northwest Passage, he christened the sound Turnagain River. South of Anchorage, Highway 1 now follows the shore of Turnagain Arm.

In 1895, prospectors discovered gold in Hope in the Kenai Peninsula, and the rush began. Suddenly, the tiny towns of Hope and Sunrise grew into booming gold-mining towns. Sunrise was even considered as a potential state capital. Scattered findings of gold all over the Kenai Mountains established the need for improved transportation routes from the ice-free port of Seward to Turnagain Arm.

By 1910, most miners had left the area in order to follow prospects of gold farther north. Sunrise dwindled into nothing more than a few residences, and mining activity in Hope almost came to a standstill. However, Cooper Landing's economy was soon influenced not by mining but by interest in big game hunting and fishing.

Today, the mining legacy of the Kenai Peninsula lives on through stories, museum photos, and weathered wood remains scattered throughout the Kenai Mountains. The privately owned town site of Sunrise is a historic archaeological district. The Hope Historical Society operates a small museum that displays items from the gold rush.

*Turnagain Pass abloom with lupine is contrasted with the Chugach Mountains.*

### Quick Facts

**Length:**
127 miles.

**Time to Allow:**
Three to five hours.

**Considerations:** From May to mid-October, salmon fishing is at its peak, and you can see whales along the shore and sheep on the mountainsides. Avalanches may cause the road to be closed for short periods throughout the winter, an average of five times a year for approximately four hours each time.

**Natural:** Along the highway, you may hear the honking of Canada geese in the wetlands, the whistle of hoary marmots in the alpine valleys, and the cry of bald eagles in the dense coastal forests. Along Turnagain Arm, you may spot Dall sheep as they scale rugged mountainsides or bring their young near the highway to forage. Moose, bears, mountain goats, salmon, and a variety of birds thrive along the highway as well. Many species of wildflowers help beautify the road corridor.

**Recreational:** The section of the Seward Highway next to Turnagain Arm provides scenic vistas across to the Kenai Mountains. Most of the lands above the highway are within Chugach State Park and provide you with a collection of things to see and ways to see them: windsurfing on Turnagain Arm, rock climbing on roadside rock cuts, rafting or canoeing on rivers, kite flying at Beluga Point, angling at creeks, and bicycling on the highway. Two hundred miles of trails are in the forest alone.

Once a mining town, Girdwood is now home to a world-famous ski resort that offers excellent scenery and plenty of challenges. This town combines the best of today's recreation with classic activities of the past, such as panning for gold. Other byway towns, including Hope and Cooper Landing, offer havens for fishing. In Anchorage, you can browse in shops or visitor centers.

**Scenic:** The trip from Anchorage to Seward is one of the most scenic drives you can take. Frequent pull-offs offer vistas of snowcapped mountains, glaciers, wildlife, and wildflowers at almost every turn, and side trips and hiking trails beckon adventurous explorers.

The road up Portage Valley leads into the 5.8-million-acre Chugach National Forest and past three hanging glaciers that are perched in the cleavage of mountain canyons. Portage Glacier pokes its nose through the mountains at the head of a valley that it cut a long time ago. Since 1890, it has receded one mile and will be out of view by 2020, so don't procrastinate taking a trip to see it. Now, only a few bergs float in water that was once brimming with ice. The visitor center offers excellent descriptive displays of glaciers and the best chance to see ice worms, pin-size critters that burrow into glaciers and eat algae. Temperatures above freezing can kill them.

You can take a day cruise along the rugged coast of Kenai Fjords National Park to see wildlife and tidewater glaciers that calve into the sea. Along the way, you may see orcas breach boatside or a humpback whale with young swimming placidly along. At Chiswall Islands, thousands of puffins and kittiwakes circle the boat. Just when you think you've seen the best, the boat stops at the foot of Holgate Glacier. With the engines cut, the cracking and popping of the 500-foot wall of aquamarine ice thunders through the frigid air. A slab of ice silently slips from the face of the glacier and crashes into the water. Seconds later, the blast reaches your ears. This is no dainty wildflower beside a trickling stream; you're witnessing the raw power of nature that carves valleys through mountains and determines the weather of the entire planet.

## Highlights

The Seward Highway is in a richly varied and highly diverse area of Alaska. Over the length of its route, the character of the byway continually changes with its proximity to water, mountains, and towns.

**Seward:** The Seward Highway begins in the town of Seward nestled among the fjords surrounding Resurrection Bay. Nearby Kenai Fjords National Park offers the chance to see puffins, otters, eagles, arctic terns, whales, seals, and other marine life.

**Ptarmigan Creek Recreation Site:** Traveling north, the landscape surrounding the byway becomes one of alpine meadows dotted with rivers and lakes. During late July and early August, Ptarmigan Creek Recreation Site, 23 miles from Seward, is an excellent place to stop and watch the incredible salmon run, when thousands of red salmon head upstream to spawn.

**Portage Glacier:** Another few miles along the byway is Portage Glacier. Portage Glacier provides an incredible opportunity to watch glacial action on fast forward. One-hour boat tours are available to better witness the action.

**Twentymile Flats:** Farther north is Twentymile Flats, an expanse of lowlands and intertidal mudflats where three river valleys empty their silt-laden waters into Turnagain Arm and provide unobstructed views of the surrounding mountain peaks and glaciers.

**Turnagain Arm:** Turnagain Arm experiences the second-highest tides in the world, often up to a 38-foot change in water level. Bore tides, a rare natural phenomenon in which the front of an incoming tide is a moving wall of water from three to five feet high, can be witnessed during extremely low tide here.

**Anchorage:** Anchorage offers a wealth of historic and cultural sites that you can enjoy.

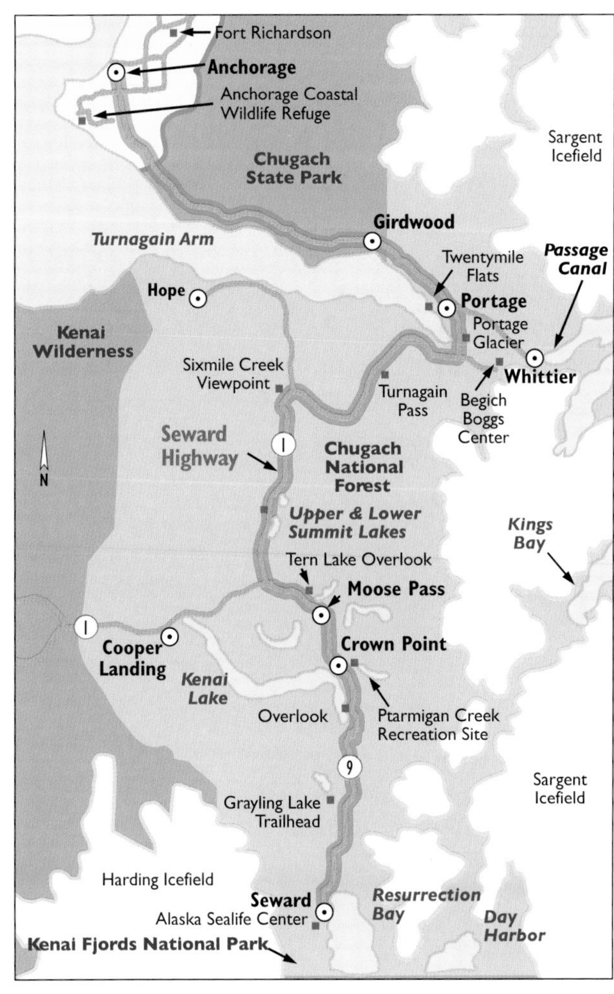

# Chinook Scenic Byway

*Glacier-covered Mount Rainier is the star attraction of this scenic corridor through the Cascades. Ride to a summer playground or winter wonderland, or just stop to gaze along the way at the regal 14,400-foot volcano.*

The Chinook Scenic Byway (also known as the Mather Memorial Parkway) is possibly the most scenic route crossing the Cascade Mountain Range, and it is the most accessible road for viewing Mount Rainier.

The route has a uniquely varied landscape. Traveling east, the route climbs through a closed canopy of Douglas fir. At Chinook Pass, the roadway descends dramatically through the Wenatchee National Forest and along the American River. The road also passes the unique basalt flows of the Columbia Plateau. The byway ends near the fertile agricultural valleys of Yakima County.



## Intrinsic Qualities

**Archaeological:** Even though only about 3.5 percent of the park has been systematically surveyed for archaeological remains, there are 79 known sites in the park, of which 75 have been fully documented and recorded.

One prehistoric site dates between 2,300 and 4,500 years ago. Sites just outside of the park hint at much earlier occupation, perhaps as much as 8,000 years, but most prehistoric archaeological sites are approximately 1,000 years old.

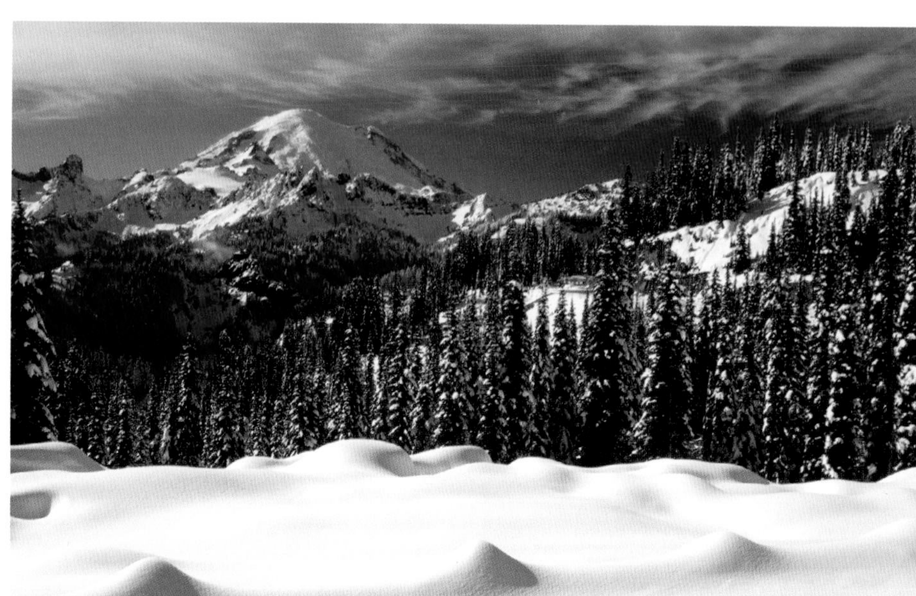

*Just east of Mount Rainier, Chinook Pass is buried under as much as 50 feet of snow during the winter months.*

Later, the area was used on a seasonal basis by lowland Native Americans for hunting and gathering and for spiritual and ceremonial events. A few sites were hunting camps, where cedar bark was stripped from trees, rock shelters created, and stone for tools procured.

In more modern centuries, five principal Native American nations (specifically the Nisqually, Puyallup, Muckleshoot, Yakama, and Taidnapam) came to the park in the summer and early fall to hunt and to collect resources. These American Indians continued to come even after the park was officially designated in 1899. Sites that were used by them are littered with broken weapon points.

Sites from European settlements in the late 19th and early 20th centuries confirm mining, recreation, and early park development. Specifically, sites reveal old campsites, trash dumps, collapsed structures, mineshafts, and other debris.

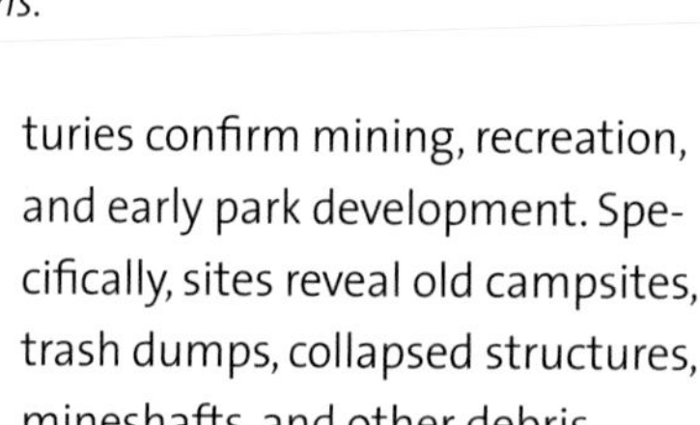

**Historical:** Part of this byway has a unique historic designation: that of a National Historic Landmark District. This district, called the Mount Rainier National Historic Landmark District, was designated so because it is one of the nation's finest collections of "national park rustic" architecture, both in the park's road system and in its historically developed areas.

In the 1920s, the park developed a plan—the Mount Rainier National Park's Master Plan—that is historically significant because it was the first and most complete national park plan developed by the National Park Service Landscape Division.

**Natural:** This byway's wide range of plants and animals live relatively undisturbed and can, therefore, exist in greater abundance (some 50 species of mammals and 130 species of birds live here) and can attain greater longevity. For example, some of the highest alpine stands are up to 1,000 years old.

In addition, extraordinary geological processes have created this absolutely magnificent landscape: Rainier's 25 glaciers form the largest single-peak glacier system in

### Quick Facts

**Length:** 85 miles.

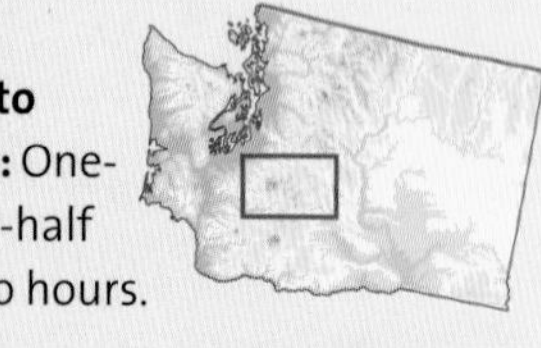

**Time to Allow:** One-and-a-half to two hours.

**Considerations:** The park segment of the road is typically closed during the winter. Autumn and spring access along the byway is weather dependent.

he United States outside of Alaska; he glacier-carved canyon of the ainier fork of the American River s geologically rare; and mountain arks (lush subalpine meadows ncircling the mountain between ,000 and 7,000 feet) are without arallel in the Cascades or Pacific olcano system.

Along the byway and in Mount ainier National Park are four dis- inct life, or vegetation, zones.

In the lowland forest zone, a anopy of stately giants allows little unlight to filter down to the forest loor. Deer, hawks, owls, and bald agles all thrive in these forests.

The montane zone is a bit arther up the mountainside and little wetter and colder. The lelicate and elusive calypso orchid looms here in the spring, and atches of huckleberry bushes bound. Black bears, which really ke huckleberries, are one of this rea's large predators, although ou'll probably never encounter a lack bear.

The subalpine zone is typified y tree "islands" mixed with open neadows. The snow lasts longer among the sheltering trees of this zone. By late July, a rainbow of wildflowers carpets the meadow. A special feature in the subalpine zone are the krummholz, trees that are strikingly twisted and stunted lue to the severe winds and snow. Trees only three feet tall may be centuries old.

The last and highest zone is the alpine zone. It is found above the timberline and is a world of extremes. On a summer day, the sun can shine warm and bright, but in just moments clouds can bring a sudden snow or lightning storm. During storms, the wind knifes across the tundra because there are no trees to break up the wind. Consequently, most alpine plants grow to be only a few inches tall.

**Recreational:** The area surrounding the Chinook Scenic Byway is rife with recreational activities. There are great opportunities for fishing, hunting, hiking, biking, and rafting. Snow sports also abound, given that Mount Rainier and its surrounding area is one of the snowiest places on Earth. Skiing and snowshoeing are the most popular activities.

**Scenic:** The Chinook Scenic Byway takes you through picturesque mountain towns and historical sites and guides you past 14,411-foot Mount Rainier, "the shining jewel of the Northwest." Rainier is the tallest volcano in the 48 contiguous states and is the largest mountain in the Cascade chain of volcanoes extending from California to the Canadian border. At the numerous developed viewpoints along the roadside, you can enjoy its deep, shadowy forests; misty waterfalls; sparkling streams; towering peaks; and snowy, rocky ridges. Stands of old-growth Douglas fir found in few other places are available at every turn.

## Highlights

Chinook Scenic Byway takes you through a variety of sites (listed here from east to west).

**Boulder Cave National Recreation Trail and Norse Peak:** After passing through Cliffdell, the road continues to the Boulder Cave National Recreation Trail and Norse Peak, both known for their beauty and recreational value. Both are within the Mount Baker–Snoqalmie National Forest.

**Fifes Peak and Union Creek Waterfall:** Here, the road changes to a southwesterly course and passes through the old-growth environment that surrounds Fifes Peak. Union Creek Waterfall is also located in this area.

**Edgar Rock Chinook Pass Historic CCC Work Camp, Tipsoo Lake, Chinook Pass Overlook, and Crystal Mountain Ski Resort:** Edgar Rock Chinook Pass Historic CCC Work Camp is located at Chinook Pass, where the parkway resumes its northwestern direction. Tipsoo Lake is on the eastern side of the parkway shortly after the pass, followed by the Chinook Pass Overlook and Crystal Mountain Ski Resort.

**Mount Rainier National Park:** Soon after Chinook Pass, you enter Mount Rainier National Park. This national park is known for its recreational, scenic, and natural resources. Goats, chipmunks, and marmots are some wildlife you might see here.

**Skookum Flats Trail:** Leaving Mount Rainier National Park, the parkway continues through the national forest to the Skookum Flats Trail found at the edge of the forest. A popular viewpoint for Mount Rainier is also located here. The parkway travels through the town of Greenwater and the Federation Forest State Park before continuing on to Enumclaw, where the parkway ends.

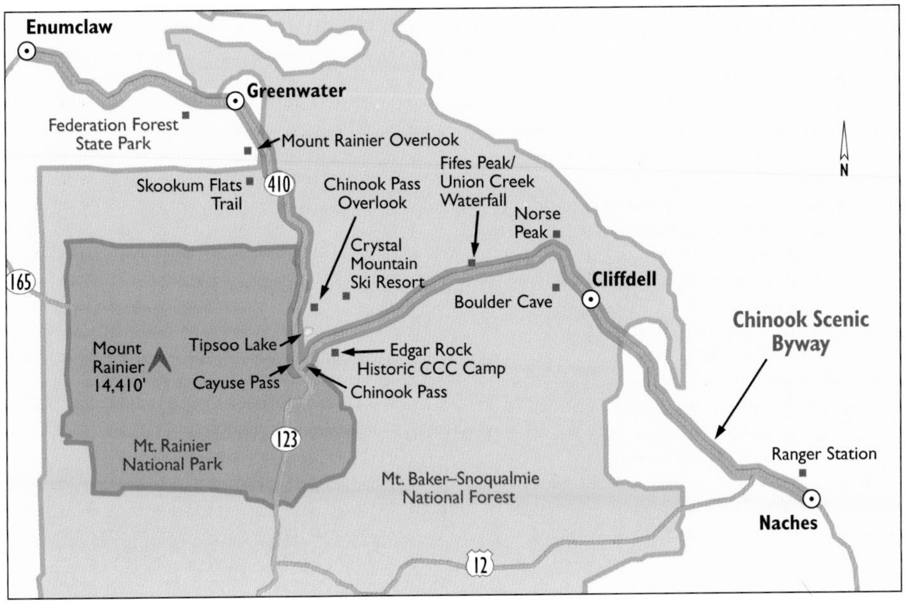

# Mountains to Sound Greenway (I-90)

*A blanket of thick forests puts the "green" in this interstate greenway, which climbs from Seattle's Puget Sound into the Cascades. Hiking trails and sublime views abound along the voyage.*

*The Alpine Lakes Wilderness Area includes approximately 394,000 acres accessed by 47 trailheads and 615 miles of trails.*

Interstate 90 is the primary east/west highway in Washington. It begins at the historic Seattle waterfront and travels east over the Cascade Mountains to the dry plateaus of eastern Washington. As you travel east along this 100-mile byway, you experience lush green forests, the marine beauty of Puget Sound, pastoral valleys, and a dramatic mountain landscape. You also pass through a complete change in climate, geology, and hometown style.

Each year, more than 20 million vehicles travel this route, making I-90 a popular gateway between Washington's largest city and its diverse and striking landscapes.



## Intrinsic Qualities

**Historical:** The byway's historic sites demonstrate different eras of modern history. Some sites possess the soul of the Old West, some seem to still embrace the spirit of early industry, and some retain the more obvious past of the last few decades.

The soul of the Old West is possessed in locations such as Fort Tilton, (the site of an 1850s fort and a wildlife wetland), and Meadowbrook Farm (a historic landscape in the dramatic shadow of towering Mount Si). Meadowbrook Farm was the site of a Native American village that became the world's largest hop ranch at the turn of the 19th century. The Klondike Gold Rush Museum, located in the historic Pioneer Square district, houses photos and memorabilia from Seattle's turn-of-the-19th-century boom days. And what would the Old West be without a few mining operations? Catch a glimpse of a 19th-century coal-mining town at Roslyn. The town hasn't changed much in all these years, except for sprucing up the main street for the 1990s TV series *Northern Exposure*. Roslyn also has a museum with photos, mining tools, and historical information; the historic graveyard is divided into ethnic zones reflecting the many nations that sent miners here.

The spirit of early industry is still embraced in places such as Preston, a turn-of-the-19th-century Scandinavian mill town. Presently, Preston consists of the remnants of a small northwoods logging town along a river, including a number of historic homes and a church. The Historic Thorp Grist Mill, built in 1883, is the oldest industrial artifact in Kittias County. The mill houses a remarkable collection of handmade wooden mill machinery and is open to the public. In addition, Fall City Waterfront was the final upstream landing for early steamboats on the Snoqualmie River, Reinig Road Sycamore Corridor was the tree-lined main street of a former company town, and Mill Pond was the Snoqualmie Mill's former log-holding pond (and is now home to a variety of fish and wildlife).

**Natural:** The western flanks of the Cascade Mountains, through which the greenway passes, are some of the best conifer tree-growing lands in the world. The combination of temperate climate and ample rainfall produces record growth of Douglas fir, western red cedar, and western hemlock. Lumber was Washington state's first industry, and trees from this region helped build San Francisco and many other 19th-century cities. You can still find remnants of the massive trees that once grew here: Spend an hour in a beautiful old-growth forest just a

### Quick Facts

**Length:** 100 miles.

**Time to Allow:** One-and-a-half to two hours.

**Considerations:** Road conditions vary during the winter season; however, the greenway is plowed throughout the winter, and pull-offs allow you to place chains on your tires.

mile from the interstate at exit 47 on the Asahel Curtis Nature Trail. Named for Asahel Curtis, a naturalist, photographer, conservation leader, and a founder of the Mountaineers, the trail provides an excellent glimpse of the ancient forest that once existed. You are surrounded by towering old-growth cedar, pine, and fir trees, as well as underbrush that ranges from devil's club to Canadian dogwood. The atmosphere is completed by rustling streams crossed by log bridges.

**Recreational:** Thousands of miles of recreational trails head from the byway. Most of these trails support hiking, but some of the trails are also great for biking and horseback riding. These trails range in length and difficulty. Some are great for day trips, and others take you deep into the backcountry. Walkers and bicyclists can begin a journey into the mountains from the heart of Seattle on the separated I-90 trail that has its own tunnel and crosses the scenic Lake Washington floating bridge. A series of regional trails lead to the John Wayne Pioneer Trail just south of North Bend (about 40 miles from Seattle). This converted rail/trail crosses the mountains on a wide and gentle slope and includes a two-mile tunnel under the Snoqualmie Summit on its way to the Columbia River. Another of the more frequented hiking areas is the Burke Gilman Trail, which begins in Seattle and goes to the suburban towns of Bothell, Woodinville, and Redmond and passes farmland before arriving at Marymoore Park in the shadow of the Microsoft campus. At the Snoqualmie Summit, exit 52, you can gain access to the Pacific Crest Trail that runs from Mexico to Canada. By taking the trail northward from this exit, you enter the Alpine Lakes Wilderness Area and spectacular high alpine country, dotted with hundreds of small lakes and profuse displays of wildflowers.

Another popular hiking area is in the Cougar Mountain Regional Wildland Park, at 4,000 acres, the largest wild park in an urban area in America. This network through wetland and forest passes 19th-century coal-mining shafts and concrete foundations. Another park, the Squak Mountain State Park, offers excellent hiking because its 2,000 wooded acres are a first-rate wildlife habitat. The Tiger Mountain State Forest has the state's most heavily used trails. This web of trails for hikers, mountain bikers, and equestrians winds through 13,000 acres of working forest and conservation area. The two access points are just minutes from Seattle suburbs.

At 4,190 feet, Mount Si towers over the town of North Bend and is a favorite hiking destination with its strenuous eight-mile round-trip trail to the summit or its five-mile round-trip trail to Little Si. Also, the Rattlesnake Ledge Trail climbs steeply (1,175 feet in 1 mile) from Rattlesnake Lake through classic western Washington forests to rock outcrops that provide sweeping views of the Central Cascades and Snoqualmie Valley. The Middle Fork Snoqualmie River Valley, on the edge of the Alpine Lakes Wilderness, has a variety of trails that wind among more than 100,000 acres of both ancient and recently harvested forests. The valley is minutes from North Bend but is lightly visited. An unpaved 12-mile road leads to a footbridge, the access to many miles of backcountry trails. Other great places to hike around this byway are Twin Falls State Park, the Asahel Curtis/Annette Lake Trail, the trail to Denny Creek and Franklin Falls, Snoqualmie Pass Summit, the John Wayne/Iron Horse Trail and Snoqualmie Tunnel, and the Coal Mines Trail.

**Scenic:** In 100 miles, the Mountains to Sound Greenway starts in the bustle of a major port city, passes through a suburban town where the interstate highway itself won a national award for highway design, and quickly enters dense forests. The front range of the Cascade Mountains looms over the flat, pastoral Snoqualmie Valley at North Bend and from there, looking eastward, dramatic mountain peaks are continuously visible. From the Snoqualmie Summit eastward, Interstate 90 passes two large lakes, which provide both recreational opportunities and irrigation water for the drier lands of central Washington. At the end of the 100-mile byway, you can leave the interstate, drive north a few miles through the historic town of Thorp, and circle back westward on old Highway 10, a dramatic geologic landscape carved and eroded by the Yakima River. Highway 10 rejoins I-90 east of Cle Elum, where you can head east or west.

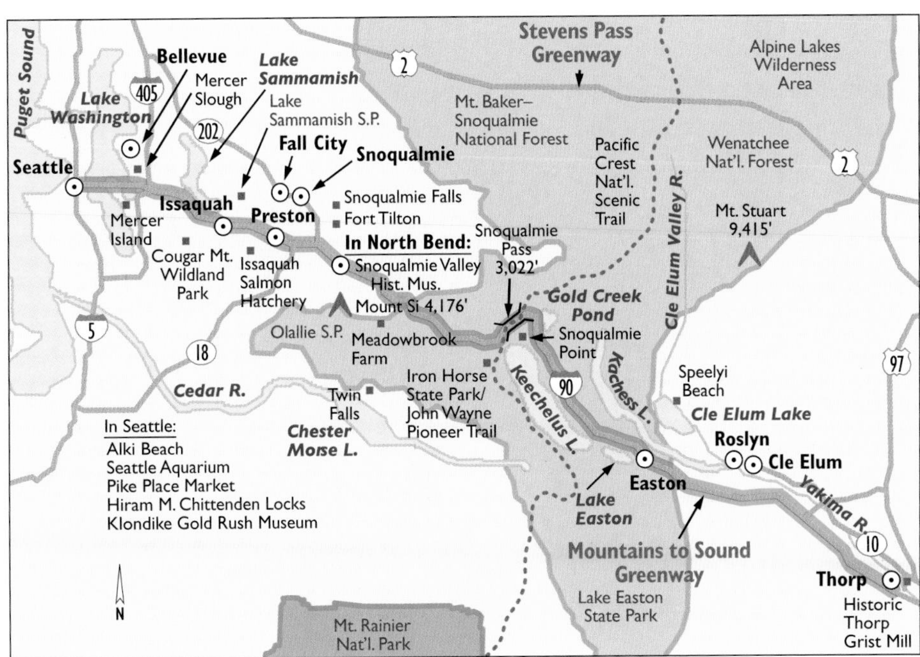

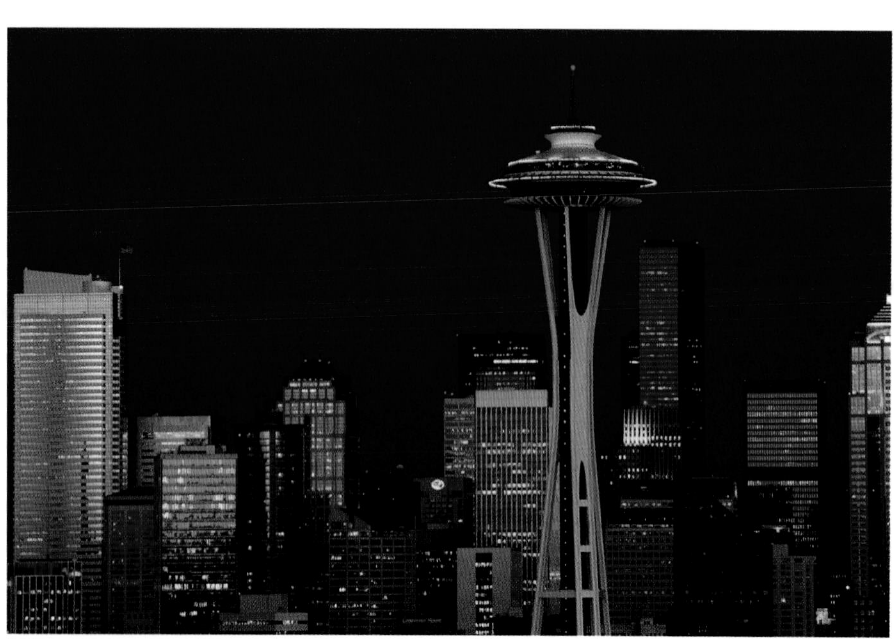

*The original setting of the Seattle World's Fair, including the landmark Space Needle, has been transformed into a center for heritage, arts, and culture.*

All the views along the drive are splendid; however, only a handful of travelers know about an especially magnificent viewpoint. Just west of Snoqualmie Pass, a spot exists where the corridor's diverse richness is most visible. The view extends from the rocky mountaintops of the Cascades to the flourishing green valleys of the Puget Sound lowlands. A little farther west, the view from Snoqualmie Point, a promontory just south of I-90, becomes panoramic—take exit 27, go right up the hill, and park at the gate. A short walk leads to a view that encompasses Mount Si towering nearby; Mount Baker is visible in the far distance on a clear day. The view follows the curve of the corridor past North Bend and on into alpine zones sheathed in silvery snow.

The term "greenway" is particularly applicable to this specific scenic byway. A sizable portion of this byway passes through national forests, enabling you to experience the grandeur of many varieties of trees. A blanket of thick forests of Douglas fir, true fir, hemlock, and cedar make this road truly a greenway. Two kinds of trees that can reach enormous proportions are cedars and Sitka spruce. Many of the old cedars were logged, and you can see their disintegrating stumps dotting the landscape around the forests that have since grown in. With a bit of looking and luck, you may find patches of the old trees, which had diameters of more than 15 feet.

## Highlights

Mountains to Sound Greenway takes you through a variety of towns (they are listed here from west to east).

**Seattle:** Start your drive in Seattle, located on Puget Sound. Along the lively waterfront, ferries leave for outlying islands. Seattle is also home to the famous Pike Place Market near the waterfront; the Pioneer Square District (Seattle's original downtown), which includes the Klondike Gold Rush Museum; and the 1962 World's Fair site, featuring the Space Needle and the Monorail. Alki Beach is a favorite of sunbathers, joggers, and divers, and Discovery Park is an in-city wildlife sanctuary and nature preserve. Also not to be missed are the Seattle Art Museum, with collections of Native American art and contemporary art, and the Museum of Flight, which showcases air and space exhibits.

**Snoqualmie Falls:** Head east on I-90 to 268-foot-high Snoqualmie Falls, just before the town of North Bend. A trail leads to the bottom of the falls.

**Snoqualmie Valley Historical Museum and Mount Si:** In the town of North Bend, the Snoqualmie Valley Historical Museum has displays of pioneer life from the 1890s and other exhibits (open April to October, Thursday to Sunday). Mount Si (4,190 feet) towers over North Bend and features a strenuous eight-mile round-trip hiking trail to its summit.

**Snoqualmie Point:** As the road continues east there are some excellent viewpoints that look out over the Cascades and even to Puget Sound on a clear day. One is Snoqualmie Point, a promontory with a view to nearby Mount Si and beyond. Take exit 27 off I-90, go right up the hill, park at the gate, and walk a short way to the overlook.

**Snoqualmie Pass:** East of North Bend is 3,022-foot Snoqualmie Pass. In winter, it features downhill skiing and snowboarding, while groomed cross-country trails lead off into the backcountry. (Chains or other traction devices are often needed to get over the pass in winter.)

**Lake Easton State Park:** Farther east, near the town of Easton, comes Lake Easton State Park, a good place to camp, with access to hiking and backpacking trails and to cross-country skiing in winter.

**Alpine Lakes Wilderness Area:** Those seeking more solitude can head to the Alpine Lakes Wilderness Area north of the byway, where miles of hiking and backpacking trails head off amid hundreds of small lakes. (The Pacific Crest National Scenic Trail, which runs from Canada to Mexico, passes through here.) To reach the area, get off I-90 at exits 80 or 84 and go north through the town of Roslyn, following Cle Elum Valley Road.

**Thorp:** At the far eastern end of the greenway is the town of Thorp, home of the Thorp Grist Mill. Built in 1883, the mill is the only one of its kind in the country with its machinery completely intact.

# Strait of Juan de Fuca Highway (SR 112)

*Following the shores of a glacial fjord on the remote, rocky coastline of the far Northwest, this byway offers an uncommon sightseeing journey, complete with rugged cliffs, sea stacks, eagles, whales, and windy, white beaches.*

Reaching farther out into the cold waters of the North Pacific than any other point of mainland in the lower 48 states, this byway is a remote stretch of coastline with rugged cliffs and forests. The Strait of Juan de Fuca Highway follows the shoreline of a glacial fjord that connects Puget Sound to the Pacific Ocean. Natural wonders that are rare and exciting events in other places of the world are everyday occurrences here. For example, eagles search for food among intertidal rocks, and gray whales feed in the Strait of Juan de Fuca.

The communities along the highway provide pleasant starting points for exploring the surrounding natural landscape. A boardwalk system provides access to remote shorelines, where Pacific Ocean waves crash against sea stacks—erosion-resistant rock separated from the land by a bit of sea—and rocky cliffs.

*The rugged coastline of Cape Flattery is the northwesternmost point in the contiguous United States.*

## Intrinsic Qualities

**Archaeological:** Native American artifacts are unearthed with relative frequency in this area. The many American Indian remains found here have been gathered into one of the nation's most significant displays, the byway's own Makah Cultural & Research Center, which sits on the Makah Indian Reservation. This center features artifacts from two ancient Native American villages that have been unearthed here in recent years. An Ozette village was discovered in 1966; also, a Makah fishing village, estimated to be nearly 3,000 years old, was excavated in the 1980s.

**Cultural:** The longtime residency of Native Americans gives distinctive seasoning to this area's already unique culture. The still-thriving Makah nation contributes particular savor because it resides, continuing in its traditions, at the western end of the byway. The Makah Cultural & Research Center tells the story of the Makah and other American Indian groups, such as the Klallam and the Quileutes. The Klallam were especially influential; by the late 1700s, they had established 17 villages between Discovery and Clallam Bays and numbered about 2,000 people. The Makah and Ozette, headquartered near Neah Bay and Lake Ozette, also numbered about 2,000 people each. Evidence of the effect of these people is prevalent in the overwhelming number of artifacts that have been found.

**Historical:** This byway's communities have taken care to renovate the buildings that tell the stories of its modern history. For instance, the restored train depot serves as the Joyce Museum, which recounts the area's logging history. Another well-preserved building is the Joyce General Store (it was originally a hotel in the town of Crescent Beach). The West Clallam Schoolhouse is a finely crafted wooden building, built by one of the region's early timber companies. Efforts are also being made to restore the warning horn of the Slip Point Lighthouse Tender's Residence.

**Natural:** It's no surprise that the Strait of Juan de Fuca's many gorgeous variations—its rocky shorelines, snow-covered mountains, and nationally featured tide pools—support a wide range of remarkable and unique flora and fauna. You need only to walk on the beach or take a sea kayak

### Quick Facts

**Length:** 61 miles.

**Time to Allow:** Two to eight hours.

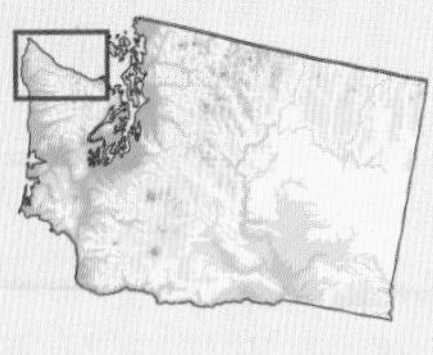

**Considerations:** Gas is available at Joyce, Clallam Bay, and Neah Bay. Pets are not allowed on the trails at Lake Ozette. When on the Makah Indian Reservation, follow their request to "take only pictures; leave only footprints." Flooding and/or landslides occasionally occur. The only fee along the byway is a nominal one at the Makah Cultural & Research Center.

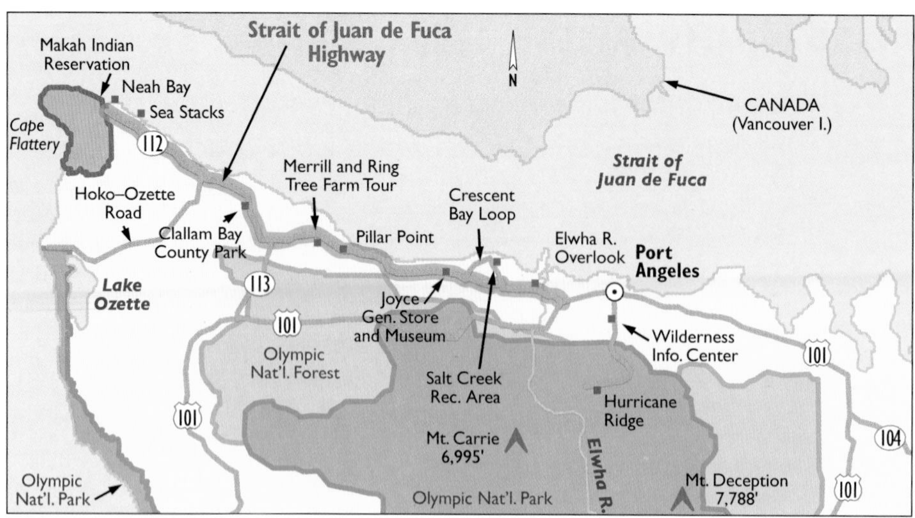


out on the waters to see and feel a kinship with these plants and animals. Olympic National Park offers wild and remote beaches that are yours to discover and are lined with nationally significant old-growth rain forests. Birds and sea mammals crowd around the sea stacks and rocky cliffs off Cape Flattery.

These nearly mythic wonders continue as you travel farther inland. The glacier water and deep gorge of the Elwha River were once home to a legendary run of chinook salmon, fish that were large enough that Native Americans used single skins as ceremonial robes. Unfortunately, these fish no longer exist in this river because populations have been in decline ever since the development of hydroelectric dams. In fact, no type of salmon has been able to negotiate the dams, but funding has been allocated to begin removing the dams.

The byway's tree-covered hillsides have been managed for timber production for more than 100 years, meaning that the length of time from harvest to "green-up" is minimal. These forests, consequently, are a dynamic mosaic of newly harvested areas and mature woodlands. Part of the mature woodlands is an area of dense bald eagle nesting, roosting, and feeding. In fact, when the eagle population is at its peak in the spring and fall, it is common to see a dozen eagles in one day.

**Recreational:** Salmon fishers have come here from throughout the country for decades, one of which was the nation's most famous sportsman, Eddie Bauer (of retail and catalog fame); he even had a fishing cabin along this route. Visitors love to fish for mighty Pacific halibut, several kinds of rockfish, resident blackmouth salmon, beautiful coho salmon, and giant chinook salmon.

Kayaking and scuba diving are thrilling ways to immerse yourself in the marine life of the area. The Strait of Juan de Fuca from Pillar Point to Cape Flattery offers several places where you can launch and kayak through kelp forests and offshore sea stacks. There are both freshwater and saltwater kayaking opportunities in the area. For a different kind of adventure, consider scuba diving. The Strait of Juan de Fuca and the Olympic Coast National Marine Sanctuary offer world-class diving. Rocky reefs and kelp forests enable you to catch views of large and colorful invertebrates, including fish-eating anemones, giant mussels, and the world's largest kind of octopus.

The surrounding area is incredibly diverse. The shores of the Strait of Juan de Fuca and adjacent forests accommodate more than 200 species of birds, many of which may easily be sighted during the spring and fall migration periods. In addition, expect the excitement of shores crowded with bald eagles in the winter months. Swimming in the waters below are a variety of whales. Other marine life will likely catch your eye, including sea lions, porpoises, dolphins, and seals.

**Scenic:** The beaches of the Strait of Juan de Fuca are complex and diverse, ranging from rocky coastlines to sandy white beaches. Immense sea stacks tower offshore. Tide pools abundant in brightly colored marine life dot the rocky shores of this byway.

A look to the other side of the byway brings into focus the mountain knolls and flowering alpine meadows. One of the world's only coniferous rain forests is near the highway. The world's largest specimens of western red cedar and Sitka spruce stalk the terrain, with moss hanging like drapery from their branches.

## Highlights

This tour takes you through some of the highlights of this byway (from east to west).

**Joyce General Store:** After ten miles of enjoying the scenic drive from just west of the city of Port Angeles, you'll come upon Joyce General Store, which was built in the early 1900s; it still maintains its old-time charm.

**Joyce Museum:** Adjacent to the store is the Joyce Museum. This former railroad station displays early area history; it has general store items from the 1920s through the 1940s.

**Pillar Point:** Twenty miles west is Pillar Point, where you'll find an imposing profile of Pillar Point and a view of the Pysht River estuary.

**Clallam Bay County Park:** About 15 miles west of the Point is Clallam Bay County Park, a gorgeous saltwater agate-strewn beach. You can wade and picnic here and see Seiku Point and Vancouver Island.

**Lake Ozette:** A few miles west of there is Hoko–Ozette Road. Take this road for about ten miles to the southwest to get to Lake Ozette, a large lake around which you can hike, bird-watch, and picnic.

# Cascade Lakes Scenic Byway 

*On a route once forged by mountain explorers, this scenic byway offers a passport to panoramic views of snowcapped peaks and alpine lakes. Hiking, rock climbing, and even late-spring skiing adventures await off-road.*

The towering Cascade Mountains provide the backdrop for this scenic drive. These ıountains also offer fabulous iking and challenging rock climbıg. The byway climbs into the eschutes National Forest, where shing, hiking, rafting, and other utdoor sports are plentiful. This rea is also a winter playground; ɔr example, Mount Bachelor Ski nd Summer Resort is filled with now through June.

As you drive by many bodies of vater along the route, it is easy o see why this route was named fter the Cascade Lakes. Some f the lakes that you encounter ıclude Todd Lake, Sparks Lake, ultus Lake, and Crane Prairie eservoir. As you can imagine, this s an angler's paradise. Anglers can pend hours at the banks of these akes, fishing for Atlantic salmon nd other freshwater fish. Waterowl and many species of plants hrive here, as well.

## Intrinsic Qualities

**Archaeological:** The history of how this area was formed is preserved at the High Desert Museum, along with displays and artifacts of the area's Native Americans and original cowboys. Also on display are recreations of prehistoric dwellings.

**Historical:** This same scenic drive was once traveled by early mountain explorers Kit Carson, John C. Frémont, and Nathaniel J. Wyeth. In the days of horse and buggy, this was a well-worn 100-mile dirt road called the Century Drive.

The Lava River Cave, Oregon's longest uncollapsed lava tube, tells the tale of the area's once-active volcanic past. However, it is closed during winter months, and warm clothing is advised when touring the other times of the year. The Lava Lands Visitor Center and Lava Butte also supply good sources of information on volcanic cones and formations.

**Natural:** The geology of the Cascade Lakes Scenic Byway is especially significant. The volcanic Cascade Mountains (unique to the Pacific Northwest) are part of the Ring of Fire volcanic mountain chain that borders the Pacific Ocean. Nowhere else in the country (and possibly in the world) is there ready access to such a great diversity of volcanic features.

You can see stratovolcanoes, shield volcanoes, cinder cones, sheets of pumice and ash, sheets of ashflow tuffs, maars, caves, and several kinds of lava flows and domes. Volcanism and glaciation formed more than 150 small and large lakes for which this region is well known.

This area is also featured in geology textbooks and was used as a training ground for the Apollo moon missions in the 1960s. In 1971, astronaut Jim Irwin (aboard *Apollo 15*) placed a rock from Devil's Lake (a lake along this byway) on the lunar surface—the only Earth rock on the moon!

The route also traverses the drier forests that include lodgepole pine and older ponderosa pine. And 262 species of birds and animals reside here, including two threatened species: the bald eagle and the northern spotted owl.

**Recreational:** You'll find many recreational activities along the Cascade Lakes Scenic Byway. Due to elevation differences and compact geography, six months out of the year you can ski in the morning and hike, fish, bicycle, or kayak in the afternoon.

Within the Deschutes National Forest and the Three Sisters Wilderness Area, you'll find snow-

### Quick Facts

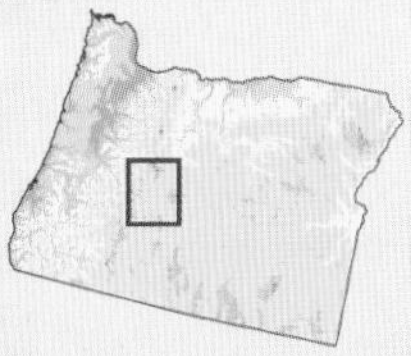

**Length:** 66 miles.

**Time to Allow:** Three to five hours.

**Considerations:** The best time of year to drive this byway is from June through October. Winter snowfall closes a portion of the byway from mid-November until late May each year. When parking for more than a few hours near trailhead markers, expect to obtain a permit and pay parking fees.

*wo extinct volcanoes in the Three Sisters Wilderness Area reflect in the beautiful Sparks Lake.*

capped peaks, more than 150 lakes, and a river. With its dependable, dry powder snow and 3,300 foot elevation drop, Mount Bachelor offers the best downhill skiing in the Northwest. The same snow conditions also provide great cross-country skiing, snowmobiling, and dog sledding.

Excellent camping, fishing, boating, bicycling, hiking, backpacking, mountain climbing, and horseback riding are also available. You can also white-water raft on the Deschutes River.

**Scenic:** As you drive along the byway, dramatic snowcapped peaks tower over you. These peaks are most often mirrored in crystal clear alpine lakes.

The Summit Express lift can take you to the 9,065-foot peak of Mount Bachelor in the summer. The dramatic 360-degree view sweeps a volcanic mountain skyline. You can see for hundreds of miles—from Mount Adams in Washington to Mount Shasta in California.

The area of Sparks Lake and Meadow has been chosen as the site to commemorate Ray Atkeson, Oregon's photographer laureate.

## Highlights

The following scenic tour gives you a chance to enjoy the highlights of this byway.

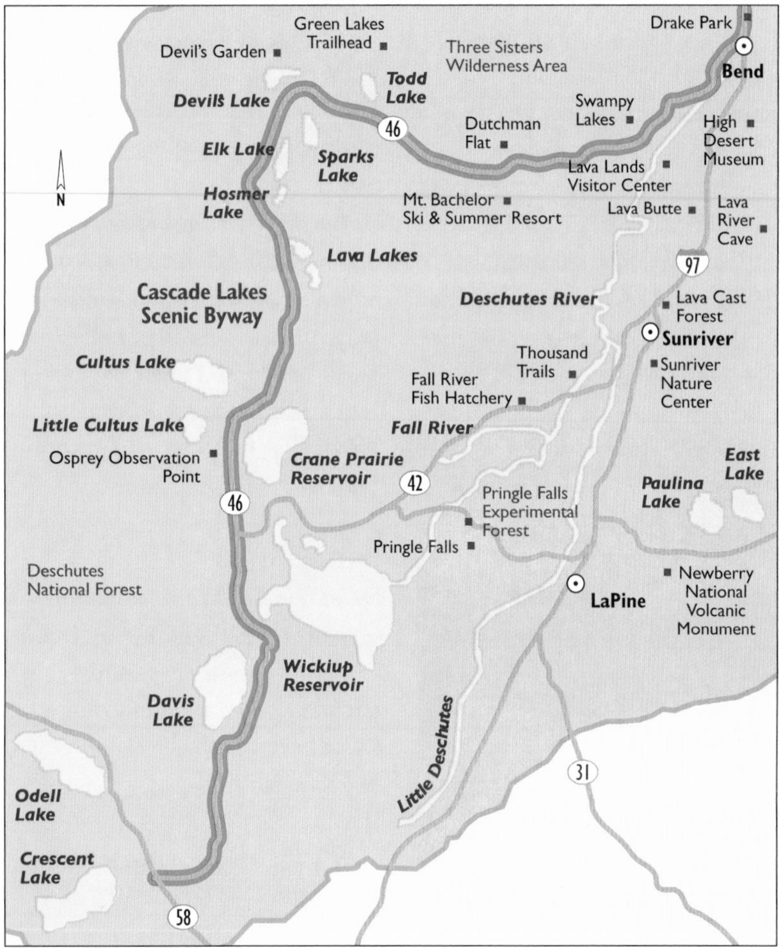

**Drake Park:** Starting from Bend and traveling the Cascade Lakes Scenic Byway, you come across Drake Park, at the Highway 97 and Franklin Avenue intersection. Park in Mirror Pond Parking Lot (just west of the Franklin and Wall intersection), and explore the charming downtown area. The original site of Bend was selected around this area because it was an easy location for early travelers to cross the Deschutes River.

**Swampy Lakes:** Fifteen miles west of Bend on the Cascade Lakes Highway are hiking, mountain biking, and cross-country skiing opportunities at the Swampy Lakes area. From the trailhead at the north end of the parking lot, you can enjoy a variety of marked skiing and hiking trails from two to ten miles in length. The area provides five shelters that are usually stocked with wood in the winter.

**Mount Bachelor Ski and Summer Resort:** Mount Bachelor Ski and Summer Resort is west of the Swampy Lakes, an area where you can spend a whole day relaxing, skiing, or fishing.

**Dutchman Flat:** Just west of the entrance to Mount Bachelor, a whole new scenic landscape beckons to be enjoyed and appreciated. By some quirk of nature, the small pumice desert, called Dutchman Flat, has not accumulated enough soil nutrients to sustain the growth of many plants. Pusspaws with pink blooms and sulfur flowers with yellow blooms are a few of the hardy plants that grow in this unique area.

**Todd Lake, Sparks Lake, Green Lakes Trailhead, and Devil's Garden:** On the byway, you pass Todd Lake, Sparks Lake, and Green Lakes Trailhead, all worthy stops. Continue on west of the Green Lakes Trailhead to a small but scenic area with several springs surfacing from the edge of a huge lava flow, creating a little meadow. Along with the lush meadow grass, you'll find moss, blue lupines, and Native American pictographs. The pictographs are painted on the face of a large dacite boulder, which indicate an ancient trail. This place is called Devil's Garden; while here, you can learn the legends of the area and explore a bit of the ancient American Indian trail.

**Osprey Observation Point:** Continue on the byway to pass picturesque Devil's Lake, Elk Lake, Hosmer Lake, Lava Lakes, Cultus Lake, and Little Cultus Lake until you come to the Osprey Observation Point. Constructed in 1929, it has become an outstanding fishing area and a breeding ground for the osprey (fish hawk), identified in 1969 as a potentially endangered species. From the parking lot, a short walk takes you to an observation area on the west side of the reservoir. Here, you can view snags and artificial nesting poles inhabited by the birds. Many visitors are entertained as osprey dive for fish from more than 100 feet above the water. Continue south to come to the end of the byway.

# Hells Canyon Scenic Byway

*This Oregon trail is a feast for the senses and opens up endless opportunities for four-season recreation, both tranquil and thrilling. Come along as the byway loops through a landscape dramatically sculpted by nature's artistry.*

Leave the fast pace and fenced-in views of Interstate 84, and follow the contours of the land into slower times and wilder places. Travel this 218-mile journey from river's edge to mountaintop and down to valley floor. Share a canyon road with a cattle drive. Pass through lush valleys rimmed by the snow-tipped Wallowa Mountains. Savor the scent of pine. Enjoy panoramic views of rugged basalt cliffs and grassy open ridges. Stand next to the majestic Snake River as it begins its tumbling course through North America's deepest canyon. Place your hand in the weathered track of a wagon wheel. This is a journey you won't forget.

## Quick Facts

**Length:** 218 miles.

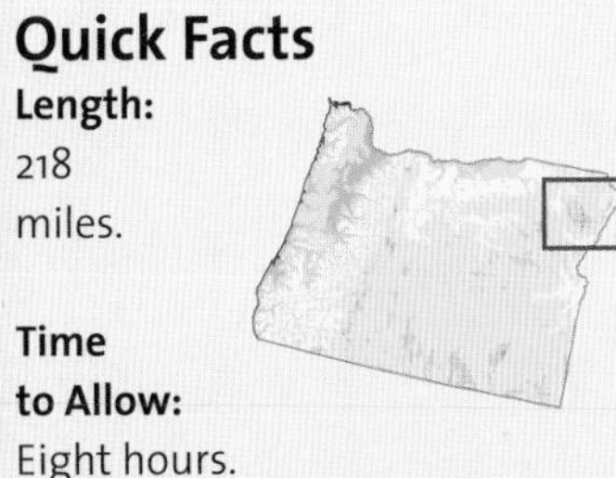

**Time to Allow:** Eight hours.

**Considerations:** You won't find any services beyond Joseph so make sure you have plenty of gas before leaving Baker City or La Grande. Take notice of the travel times as well as mileage between stops, and keep your fuel tank as full as possible. Be prepared for temperatures that vary as much as 50 degrees.

## Intrinsic Qualities

**Archaeological:** Extremes in the land have dictated the course of the area's natural and cultural history. Relatively mild winters and abundant wildlife drew people to the canyon more than 7,000 years ago. Archaeological evidence, ranging from rock art to winter "pithouse" villages, can be found in the Snake River corridor. Pictographs and petroglyphs are scattered along the river where Native Americans spent their winters.

**Cultural:** On the map, northeastern Oregon looks far removed from metropolitan area amenities. However, you may be surprised by the availability of arts and culture. Musical events along the byway range from old-time fiddling to blues to Beethoven. Plays, concerts, and living-history productions can be enjoyed in Baker City. The small town of Joseph has earned a national reputation for its bronze foundries and galleries. Eastern Oregon University, located in La Grande, offers theatrical productions and concerts, including a full season of music from the Grande Ronde Symphony Orchestra. The Historic Elgin Opera House in Elgin is also a crowd-pleaser for concerts, movies, and plays.

**Historical:** For many centuries, the Grande Ronde Valley was used seasonally by Native Americans. Covered largely by wetlands, the beautiful valley was lush with grass and alive with game. Herds of elk summered in the surrounding high country and wintered in the milder valley. Mule deer, pronghorn antelope, and bighorn sheep browsed the hills and meadows. This bountiful scene was a neutral meeting place for members of the Umatilla, Yakima, Shoshone, Cayuse, and Bannock nations, who came to enjoy the hot springs, hunt, graze their horses, and gather plants for food. The picturesque Wallowa Valley was the beloved home of the Nez Perce Indians. By winter of 1877, settlement conflicts drove young Chief Joseph to make a harrowing attempt to reach Canada with a group of 250 men, women, and children. They struggled to within 24 miles of safety before being captured in Montana. They were then sent to reservations.

*Moccasin Lake in the Eagle Cap Wilderness Area is a premier choice for fishers, boaters, or those who simply want to enjoy the inspiring scenery.*

This area remains a significant religious and cultural center for the Nez Perce, Umatilla, and Cayuse Indians.

**Natural:** Millions of years ago, the Wallowa Mountains formed the coast of what would eventually be called Oregon. Uplifted layers of limestone on the peaks harbor fossilized shells that once sat at the bottom of the ocean. Eons of volcanic action and faulting pushed the masses of rock upward while new land formed to the west. The Coast Range, Cascade Mountains, and upland desert of central Oregon now separate the Wallowas from the ocean by hundreds of miles. Flows of pla-

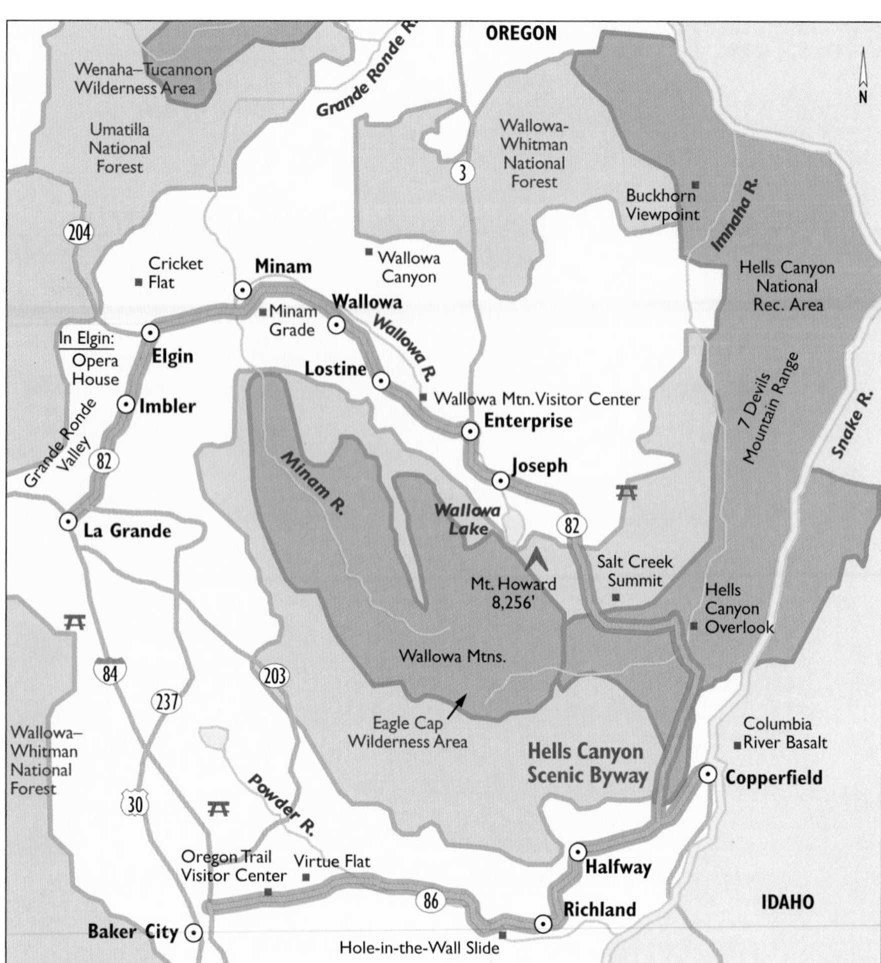




teau basalt, batholiths of granite, and layers of shale were buckled and folded to form the mountain range. Raging rivers and gigantic glaciers carved the peaks and canyons. In short, nature took a long time to sculpt the dramatic beauty you see along the byway.

**Recreational:** Recreational opportunities along the Hells Canyon Scenic Byway are seemingly endless and range from tranquil to thrilling. Four distinct seasons alter the scenery and determine the activities.

Spring and summer are great times to fish for steelhead or trout on the Grande Ronde, Minam, Wallowa, and Imnaha Rivers.

The Wallowa–Whitman National Forest, along with county and state parks departments, operates numerous campgrounds, trail systems, viewpoints, and picnic facilities along or near the route. Hike or mountain bike into the high country. Hire a private outfitter to experience horseback riding and pack trips, rafting, parasailing, or jet boat adventures. Watch hang gliders and hot air balloonists catch the breeze high above the Wallowa and Grande Ronde Valleys.

In autumn, watch and listen for Canada geese filling the air with melancholy calls. Hunt for deer, elk, bear, cougar, and bighorn sheep, or capture them on film. Fall is also the time for cattle drives, harvesting, and blue-sky days crisp with the smell of winter.

Winter's dry, powdery snow adorns area ski resorts and turns backcountry side trips and hiking trails into a giant playground for adventurers. The FS Road 39 section of the byway between Joseph and Halfway is closed to auto and truck traffic in winter, when it becomes an especially popular route for snowmobilers. You can also enjoy winter raptor viewing in Minam and Hells Canyons, a horse-drawn sleigh ride in Joseph, or ice fishing on Wallowa Lake.

**Scenic:** Travel this byway, and see much of the majesty and mystery of the West within a 218-mile corridor. The magnificent Snake River twists and churns over boulders and past towering cliffs. Pungent sagebrush and bunch grasses cover the flats and crouch at the feet of dramatic rock formations. Sparkling streams tumble through thick forests of pine and mixed conifers. Lush valleys lie at the feet of magnificent mountain ranges with peaks that tower to nearly 10,000 feet. Fields of hay, wheat, grass, mint, and canola color the valley floor. Cattle, sheep, and horses graze on a menu of sweet clover and timothy. The historic barns and houses bring human warmth and scale to the dramatic scenery.

## Highlights

The following scenic tour gives you a chance to enjoy the highlights of this byway (from west to east).

**Wallowa Mountains Visitor Center:** Start your summer tour at midday so you can go to the Wallowa Mountains Visitor Center (about half a mile northwest of Enterprise) to get current and detailed information about camps and hikes in the area. Spend the night camping in the Wallowa Mountains or beside the Imnaha River.

**Wallowa Lake:** Visit Wallowa Lake (about six miles south of Joseph), and relax for a few hours of swimming, fishing, boating, or hiking. You can also take a tram from here to the peak of Mount Howard and enjoy wonderful views.

**Hells Canyon Overlook:** Next, visit the Hells Canyon Overlook. The overlook is about 30 miles along the byway from the lake. This is a staggering view, 5,400 feet above the canyon floor.

**Snake River:** In Copperfield (about 15 miles south), secure a jet boat tour on the Snake River. You can also rent rafts and such here.

**Hole-in-the-Wall Slide:** After a few hours of enjoying the Snake River, end your day at the Hole-in-the-Wall Slide. The geographically intriguing slide is about 30 miles southwest of Copperfield.

# Historic Columbia River Highway 

*Designed to offer incomparable views as it sweeps through the Columbia River Gorge past waterfalls and wildflowers, this engineering marvel is both a scenic highway and historic landmark.*

The Historic Columbia River Highway is exquisite: Drive through the Columbia iver Gorge for nearly 50 miles, nd sweep past majestic water-alls, including Multnomah Falls. his byway also travels through a pectacular river canyon that you an often view from the tops of liffs more than 900 feet above he river. During the spring, you xperience magnificent wildflower isplays, including many plants hat exist only in this area.

This is the first scenic highway n the United States to gain the istinction of National Historic andmark. (To give you an idea of vhat this means, less than 3 per-ent of the sites on the National Register of Historic Places become landmarks.) This highway's construction was considered one of the greatest engineering feats of the modern age. Its engineer, Samuel C. Lancaster, tried not to mar the existing landscape. It was designed from 1913 to 1914 to take advantage of the area's many waterfalls and other beautiful spots.

Make sure to travel the well-known western section of the byway from Troutdale to Dodson and the less-traveled eastern section from Mosier to The Dalles. The difference in vegetation zones and views is amazing.

## Intrinsic Qualities

**Historical:** The Historic Columbia River Highway has many nationally significant historic features on the National Register of Historic Places—one of which is the highway itself. It is also a National Historic Civil Engineering Landmark that includes 23 unique bridges. The historic district includes not only the highway, but also the Portland Women's Forum State Scenic Viewpoint, Crown Point and Vista House, Multnomah Falls Lodge and Recreation Site, Eagle Creek Recreation Area, and several other waterfall areas.

**Natural:** The Columbia River Gorge is a spectacular river canyon, 80 miles long and up to 4,000 feet deep, cutting the only sea-level route through the Cascade Mountain Range. The gorge includes 16 endemic plant species (those that exist only within the gorge) and more than 150 rare plant species. Bald eagles, peregrine falcons, Snake River salmon, and Larch Mountain salamanders also reside here. Wildflower tours of this route are common in the spring.

*The Columbia River Gorge is an impressive river canyon carving the only sea-level route through the Cascade Mountain Range.*

### Quick Facts

**Length:** 70 miles.

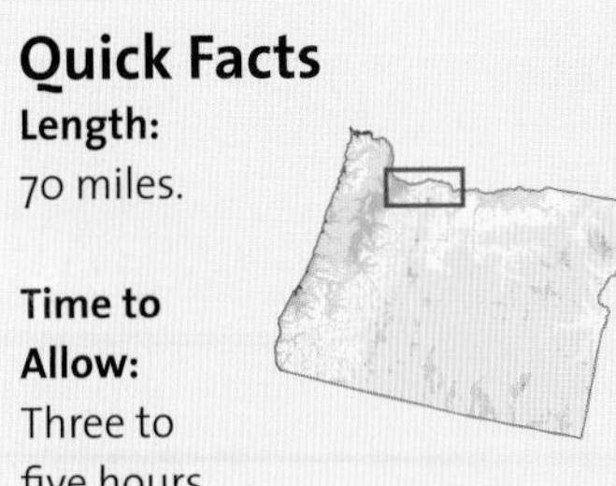

**Time to Allow:** Three to five hours.

**Considerations:** Midweek sees the fewest crowds along the byway. Fall has the best weather; spring provides the best time to view the waterfalls. Some attractions are closed in the winter. Also, the byway is narrow and winding, so you may want to consider traveling in a car instead of an RV.

**Recreational:** Recreational facilities in the Columbia River Gorge National Scenic Area are also of national significance, including the three major highways (Historic Columbia River Highway, I-84, and Washington State Route 14) that are used extensively for pleasure driving. The highways provide access to many hiking trails, windsurfing sites, and the Mount Hood Railroad, a scenic and historic passenger and freight route up the Hood River Valley.

**Scenic:** The Historic Columbia River Highway leaves the Sandy River and climbs to the top of the cliffs, offering spectacular views of the landscape. The byway was designed to take advantage of the

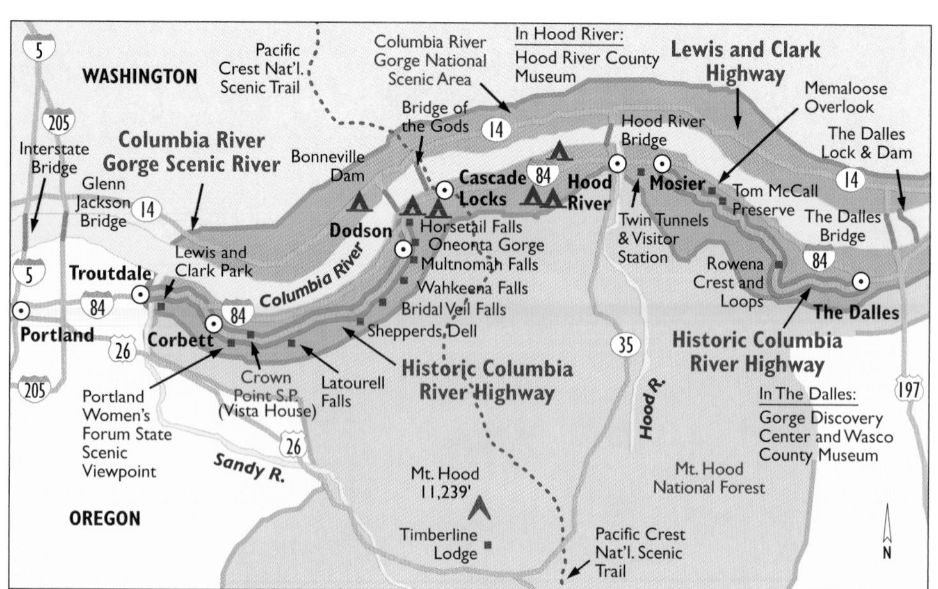


many waterfalls and other attractive sites along the route. The corridor contains some of the most dramatic views available anywhere in the country, including the Columbia River, with basalt cliffs and canyon walls; Multnomah Falls, a 620-foot, two-tiered waterfall that is the most visited natural attraction in the state of Oregon; the largest aggregation of high waterfalls outside of Yosemite, including Multnomah Falls, Horsetail Falls, Latourell Falls, Bridal Veil Falls, and Wahkeena Falls, plus numerous small falls; and giant basalt cliffs and monoliths, including Beacon Rock, Rooster Rock, Crown Point (a National Natural Landmark), and Oneonta Bluff.

## Highlights

Begin your must-see tour in Troutdale, the western entry point to the Historic Columbia River Highway. The attractive setting, unique shopping district, and convenient distance from the interstate make this small town a perfect start to your tour of the highway.

**Sandy River:** The first stop along the tour is Sandy River. An old iron bridge crosses the river at this point. You can even take a side trip to the north to visit Lewis and Clark Park, but be sure to return to the byway to continue your journey east.

**Portland Women's Forum State Scenic Viewpoint:** If you want a stunning scenic vista, you must stop for a look at Portland Women's Forum State Scenic Viewpoint. It is located about ten minutes from Troutdale.

**Crown Point and Vista House:** Crown Point and historic Vista House are next, about a mile farther east. Take a stroll around the point (carefully—the road curves around the building here), and enjoy yet another wonderful view of the river and the Columbia River Gorge.

**Multnomah Falls:** Scattered throughout the next few miles are many waterfalls, each with its own history and qualities. Latourell Falls, Shepherd's Dell, Wahkeena Falls, and Bridal Veil Falls each whet your appetite for the most visited waterfall on the byway: Multnomah Falls. This beautiful double-cascade falls more than 620 feet. Stop and take the hike up to the bridge crossing the waterfall for an up-close view.

**Oneonta Gorge:** Back on the highway, you soon encounter Oneonta Gorge. This narrow canyon and its associated stream offer a terrific environment for a cool, dark, and shady hike. To enjoy it fully, follow the path to the river crossing, take off your shoes, and wade in the chilly stream.

**Bridge of the Gods at Cascade Locks:** Continuing east, you rejoin the interstate for a while. The Bridge of the Gods at Cascade Locks connects Oregon to Washington.

**Hood River:** The city of Hood River, at the confluence of the Hood River and the Columbia River, is the windsurfing capital of the world. Stop and watch expert wind-surfers from the riverside or from vantage points at hotels and viewpoints along the river. Or visit the downtown historic district, and stop by the Hood River County Museum.

**State Trail:** Take time to leave your car and walk a portion of the Historic Columbia River Highway between Hood River and Mosier that has been converted to a state trail. Remnants of the original aut highway and railings may still be seen. Or, if you continue in your ca along the main highway instead, look for tunnels and roadbed high above you—a visible clue to a tremendous engineering feat.

**Memaloose Overlook:** As you leav the rain forest of the gorge and enter the drier, wide rolling plains west of Rowena and The Dalles, stop a moment at the Memaloose Overlook near the Tom McCall Preserve. Below you, the highway twists in the hairpin turns of the Rowena Loops. This engineering achievement remains remarkable even by today's standards.

**Gorge Discovery Center and Wasco County Museum:** After you navigate the switchbacks of the Rowena Loops, catch your breath with a stop at the Gorge Discovery Center and Wasco County Museum. Opened in 1997, this museum offers interpretive exhibits about the human and natural history of the Columbia River Gorge.

**The Dalles:** End your trip on the Historic Columbia River Highway at The Dalles. You can view the nearby Dalles Lock and Dam or tour the historic district of this city

# McKenzie Pass–Santiam Pass Scenic Byway

*Black lava, white snow, blue lakes, green forests—this vivid loop through two high-mountain passes offers some of the most thrilling close-ups of snowcapped volcanoes in America.*

Experience dramatic views of the most beautiful of the High Cascade Peaks. The panorama of lava fields and six Cascade peaks, as viewed from the McKenzie Pass summit, is made even more striking by the contrast between the black lava and white snow. The mountains are mirrored in crystal-clear lakes, and the byway passes amazing waterfalls.

## Intrinsic Qualities

**Archaeological:** Sahalie Falls and Koosah Falls are located on the old Clear Lake Cutoff on Highway 126. *Sahalie* (meaning "heaven") and *Koosah* (meaning "sky") are Chinook Jargon words—part of a rudimentary trade language that allowed people to exchange news and goods in the area. The Kalapuya, Molala, Sahaptain, and Chinook peoples traveled and traded here, perhaps on their way to obtain obsidian in the high Cascades for tools or to gather huckleberries. Connecting the two waterfalls is a loop trail that offers views of foaming white water pouring over 3,000-year-old lava flows.

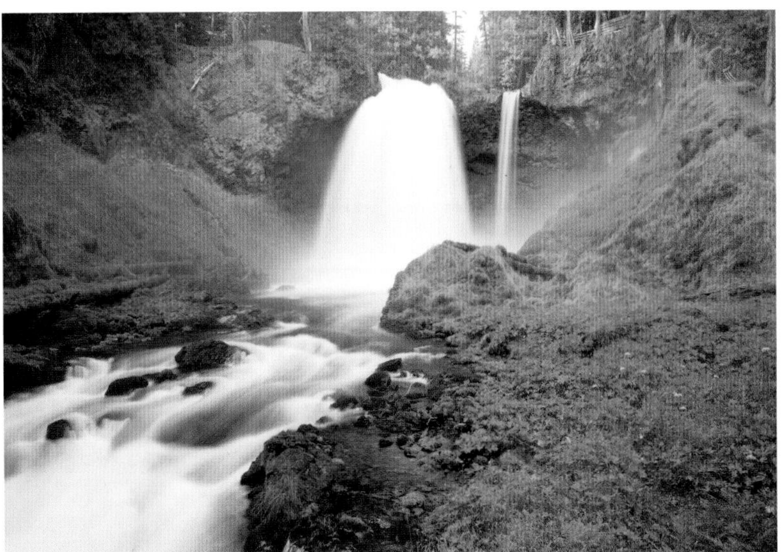

*Lush greenery surrounds the tumbling waters of the Sahalie Falls in Oregon's Willamette National Forest.*

**Quick Facts**

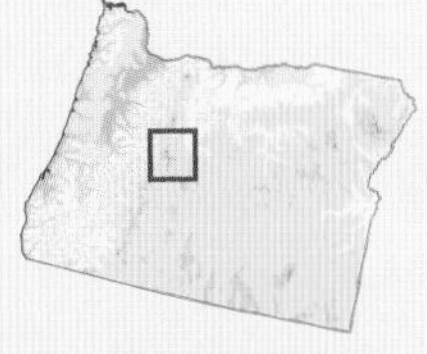

**Length:** 82 miles.

**Time to Allow:** Three to five hours.

**Considerations:** Services are available in the town of McKenzie Bridge. Because of snow, Highway 242 is closed from mid-November to mid-June. Nearly the entire byway is in a snow zone so chains on cars are sometimes required during the winter. Also, due to extremely sharp curves and narrow road width, Highway 242 over McKenzie Pass is closed to vehicles longer than 35 feet. Trailers are discouraged. Parking passes can be purchased from the ranger station, allowing you to park along this byway.

**Cultural:** Communities that reflect rural Western charm anchor the McKenzie Pass–Santiam Pass Scenic Byway and lead you to a variety of cultural events on both sides of the mountains. The town of Sisters, especially, recalls the Old West with a sophisticated town center. The town of McKenzie Bridge, known as Strawberry Flat back in 1902, is a small river settlement located on Highway 126 on the east end of the loop.

The annual John Craig Memorial Race commemorates mail carrier John Craig's journeys across the McKenzie Pass. Craig (1832–1877) died carrying the Christmas mail over this route. Today, Nordic skiers endure winter rain, sleet, hail, and snow to race over historic Highway 242, which is closed in the winter.

**Historical:** The Santiam Pass was discovered in 1859 by Andrew Wiley and was named for the Santiam Indians, a Kalapooian nation living near the Santiam River. The byway crosses the route of the Willamette Valley Cascade Mountain Wagon Road, later known as the Santiam Wagon Road. A portion of the original railroad grade of the Hogg Railroad, constructed as early as 1888, is visible from Santiam Pass near Hogg Rock.

In Oregon during the 1930s, the Civilian Conservation Corps (CCC) enhanced numerous recreational opportunities along the McKenzie Pass–Santiam Pass Scenic Byway, including building the lava rock structure at the top of McKenzie Pass and naming it after the group's foreman, Dee Wright. Since its completion in 1935, the observatory has been a popular attraction.

**Natural:** The natural qualities of the McKenzie Pass–Santiam Pass Scenic Byway are of national significance. You can find outstanding examples of both ancient and recent volcanoes, cinder cones, lava flows, and deep, glaciated canyons. Forests along the byway contain rare old-growth fir and ponderosa pine and are home to a great variety of fish and wildlife, including several threatened species, such as the bald eagle, northern spotted owl, steelhead, and bull trout.

**Recreational:** The McKenzie Pass–Santiam Pass Scenic Byway area offers three wilderness areas, two national trails, several lakes, many snowcapped volcanoes, two rivers, and a major resort. The Pacific Crest Scenic Trail provides an opportunity that is unique in the country: to hike the crest of a major volcanic mountain range. If you're a boater, you can choose lakes or white-water rafting and kayaking on the McKenzie River. Anglers come from all over the United States to fly-fish for wild trout and to fish for trout, salmon, and steelhead on the rivers near the byway. During the winter, you can downhill ski at the Hoodoo Ski Area and snowmobile and cross-country ski on miles of marked trails.

**Scenic:** The view of the Three Sisters and Broken Top Mountains represents the greatest concentration of snowcapped volcanoes with glaciers in the lower 48 states. In addition, the panoramic view of lava fields, six Cascade peaks, and lakes from the summit of McKenzie Pass is breathtaking.

## Highlights

If you're heading east from Eugene/Springfield, begin the byway at the junction of historic Highway 242 and Highway 126. If you're arriving from the east, access the byway from Sisters, a lively town chock-full of arts and crafts offerings and special events.

**Junction Highway 126 and 242:** Turn right to travel to 242, the McKenzie Pass Route. The forest along the byway on this portion is dark green, characterized by water-loving species such as hemlocks, cedars, and firs. The climb eastward is through a thickly vegetated, narrow corridor. Here, the road meanders, and travel is slow.

**Proxy Falls Trailhead:** To take in the beauty of both falls, spend about an hour to hike the $1^{1}/_{4}$-mile trail into the Three Sisters Wilderness.

**Scott Road Historical Marker/ Pull-Off:** Open views of the Three Sisters Mountains—originally named Faith, Hope, and Charity in the 1840s—lie to the east. The Scott Road was really a settler trail named after Felix Scott, Jr. (1829–1879), who pioneered a wagon trail/road over the Cascades northeast of McKenzie Bridge. This route, part of which is a maintained trail into the Three Sisters Wilderness, proved to be almost impassible for wagons.

**Belknap Crater Viewpoint:** View Big Belknap Crater and the smaller cone of Little Belknap Crater here. Little Belknap was the origin of the immense lava fields in the foreground. Use caution when walking out onto the lava.

**Dee Wright Observatory:** Plan on an hour to tour the observatory and walk the half-mile Lava River Trail.

**Windy Point Viewpoint:** At an elevation of 4,909 feet, Windy Point offers a picturesque view of the lava flows and volcanic peaks. Although little vegetation grows on the lava fields, as you make your descent from the summit of the McKenzie Pass, a mixed conifer forest returns, eventually giving way to ponderosa pines at the lower elevation.

### Santiam Wagon Road

The Santiam Wagon Road, which once served as a dominant access route over the Cascade Mountains to the Willamette Valley, operated from 1865 until 1939. A segment of this road traverses the Fish Lake Historic Remount Depot on Highway 126, an early roadhouse for wagon road travelers, where lodging, food, and hay were purchased for less than one dollar in 1890. Today, vintage pre-1940 vehicles and horse-drawn wagons can travel from here to Tombstone Pass by permit.

**East Portal and Sisters:** The Santiam Pass Route begins at the Sisters Portal, heading north at the junction of Highway 126/20 and 242.

**Black Butte:** Black Butte is the prominent composite cone north of the highway. Black Butte is older than many of the dissected High Cascade peaks. The U.S. Forest Service still operates a lookout on the top.

**Mount Washington Viewpoint:** For a quick stop, this roadside pull-off offers a spectacular view of the volcanic peak and basin.

**Sahalie Falls and Koosah Falls:** The McKenzie River surges over a 70-foot-high basalt cliff called Koosah Falls. From here you can hike for an hour on the Waterfalls Loop trail that connects this site with Sahalie Falls (or drive to the site).

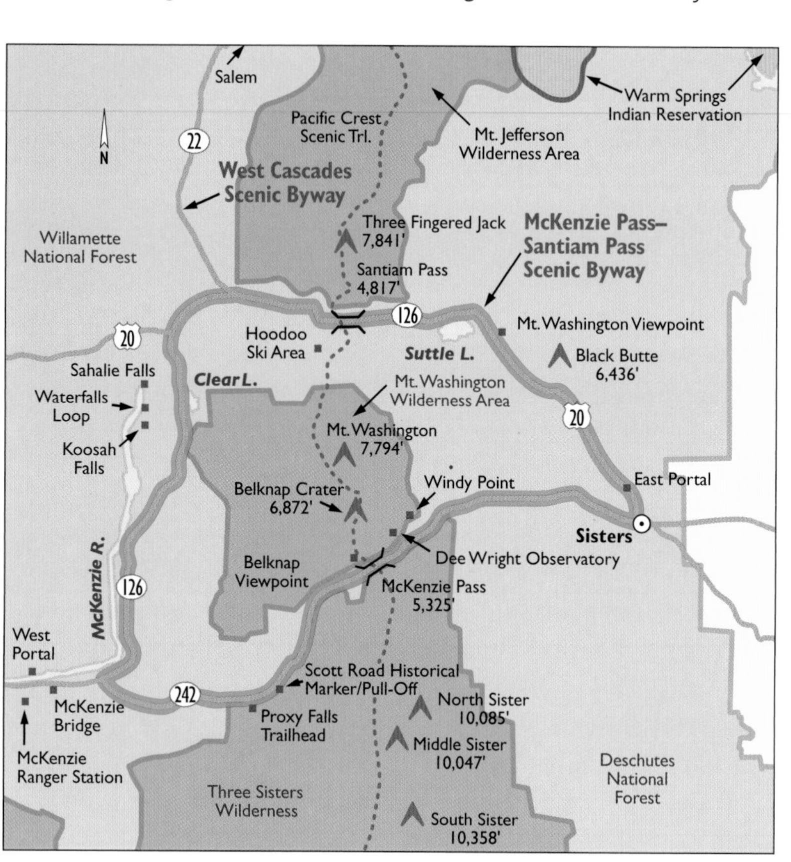

# OUTBACK SCENIC BYWAY

*Rambling through Oregon's rugged, remote backcountry, the Outback Scenic Byway attracts such diverse devotees as photographers, bird-watchers, hang gliders, archaeology buffs—and drivers who long to escape the beaten path.*

This area of Oregon is rugged and remote; in fact, *outback* means "isolated rural country." This byway takes you through Oregon's outback, where the agricultural and timber industries employ many of the residents, where the landscape ranges from lush green forests to arid desert, and where the people who live here seek independence yet know each other by their first names.

## Intrinsic Qualities

**Archaeological:** The Outback Scenic Byway transects the Fort Rock Cave National Register Site, the Picture Rock Pass National Register Site, and the Lake Abert National Register District. All these sites contain significant historic and prehistoric cultural values. The districts have one of the highest cultural site densities in the Great Basin Region, and several archaeological papers and reports of regional and national significance have been published regarding the rock art found here.

**Cultural:** Some of the Outback Scenic Byway's cultural flavor can be seen in the buildings along the byway, which reflect the influence of the Old West.

**Natural:** Among the many natural attributes, the Fort Rock State Natural Area is listed as a National Natural Landmark. Fort Rock is a volcanic maar formation that homesteading families of long ago appropriately named for its four-sided towering walls. This ideal natural fort is colored orange-brown.

Abert Rim, another natural attraction, is one of the nation's longest and most continuous fault escarpments. This rim rises more than 2,000 feet above the highway.

The Summer Lake State Wildlife Area is 18,000 acres in size and home to more than 250 species of birds. The marshlike area, located in the high desert, is strategically important for habitat and nesting. Regionally, it is one of the most important stops for migrating birds that use the Pacific Flyway. Many sensitive, threatened, or endangered species—such as bald eagles, American peregrine falcons, western snowy plovers, greater sandhill cranes, and trumpeter swans—can be seen using this habitat. More than 15,000 bird-watchers flock here annually.

*Abert Rim, dominating the horizon, is a 30-mile-long fault escarpment rising more than 2,000 feet above the desert floor.*

### Quick Facts

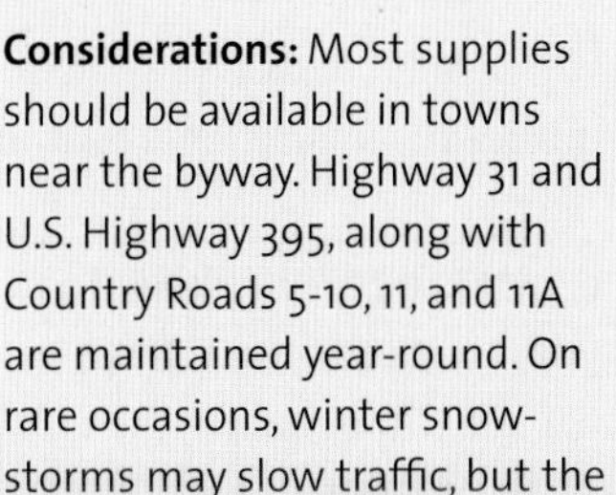

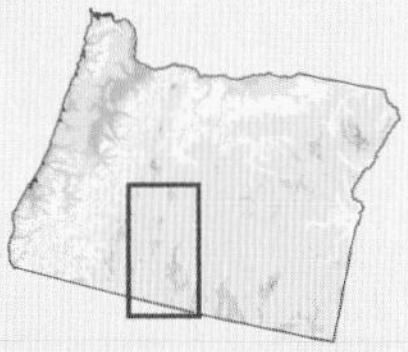

**Length:** 171 miles.

**Time to Allow:** Four to five hours.

**Considerations:** Most supplies should be available in towns near the byway. Highway 31 and U.S. Highway 395, along with Country Roads 5-10, 11, and 11A are maintained year-round. On rare occasions, winter snowstorms may slow traffic, but the roads are almost never closed.

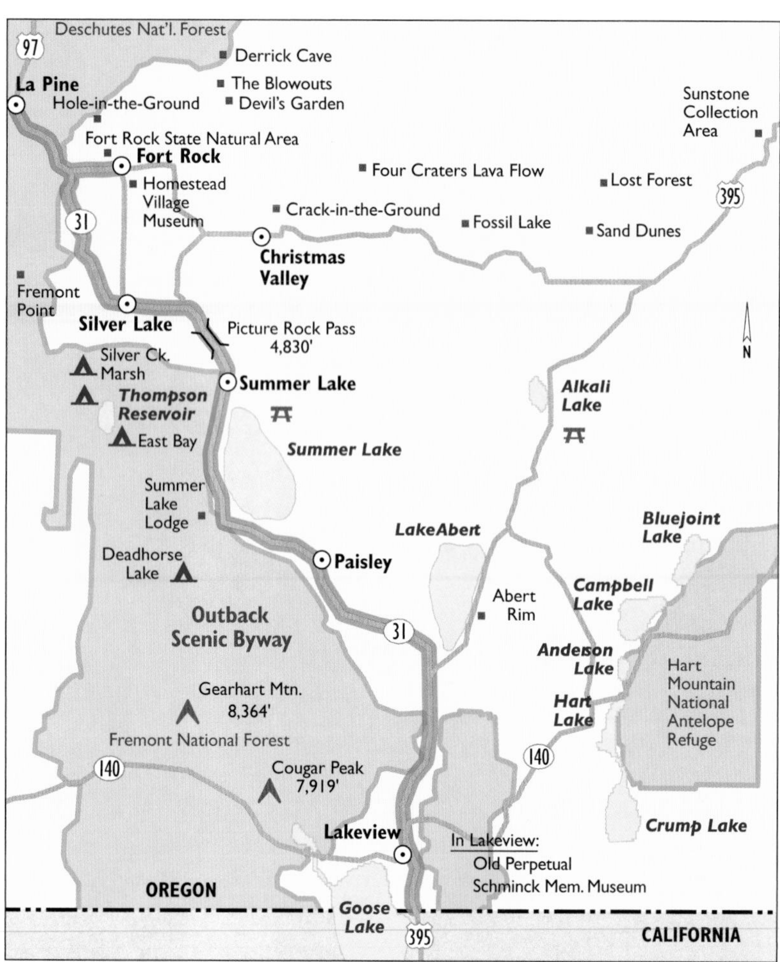


**Recreational:** The thermal updrafts that are created from the warming of the valley and the mountains make the Lakeview area ideal for hang gliding. In fact, Lakeview has been named the hang gliding capital of the West by many hang gliding and sports magazines. An annual hang gliding festival around the Fourth of July attracts hundreds of pilots, making it one of the unique recreational events in Oregon. The U.S. Hang Gliding Association has held two national championships in the Lakeview area. Pilots from around the world come to catch the thermals.

The byway brings those who travel it in close proximity to six national designations, including the Gearhart Mountain Wilderness, the Christmas Valley National Back Country Byway, the Lake Abert and the Warner Wetlands Areas of Critical Environmental Concern, the Hart Mountain National Antelope Refuge, and the Lakeview to Steens Back Country Byway.

**Scenic:** The Outback Scenic Byway is one of the most scenic routes in the Great Basin Region. You pass through different environments as you drive along this road, and the changes among environments are quite dramatic. The different environments include old-growth ponderosa and lodgepole pine stands found in the Eastern Cascades, the sagebrush steppe, the wetlands, and the other high-desert ecosystems.

One of the most striking scenic features along this byway is the sweeping view of Winter and Abert Rims. These rims are 2,000-foot fault escarpment blocks that tower above the byway. Abert Rim is Oregon's longest, most dramatic, and most photographed fault escarpment. This rim is also considered one of the most continuous fault escarpments in the United States.

## Highlights

Starting at the southern end of the byway coming out of California on U.S. Highway 395, you'll see the following sites. If you start on the other end of the byway, begin at the bottom of this list and make your way up.

**Lakeview:** Lakeview is the hang gliding capital of the West. One mile north of Lakeview is the only active geyser in the West, called Old Perpetual. Bring your camera to take a picture of the geyser, which erupts every 90 seconds.

**Lake Abert, Paisley, and Summer Lake:** Continue north on the byway, and if you have an extra 30 to 60 minutes, head east on U.S. Highway 395 to the Abert Rim drive and Lake Abert. If you don't have that much time, continue north on Highway 31 to the town of Paisley and the annual Mosquito Festival that occurs there every July. Continue on past the Summer Lake Lodge and wilderness area; if you have a day to spend in the woods, the area is excellent for fishing and hiking.

**Picture Rock Pass:** Just north of Summer Lake is Picture Rock Pass, an area named for the ancient Native American petroglyphs that decorate rock within walking distance of the highway.

**Fort Rock:** Continue your drive on Highway 31 to Fort Rock. While there, visit the remnants of an ancient volcano at Fort Rock State Natural Area, just seven miles off the byway. Nearby is the Homestead Village Museum, which take from 30 to 60 minutes to explore. From Fort Rock, continue on Highway 31, where the byway ends as it meets U.S. Highway 97.

**Hole-in-the-Ground, Devil's Garden, The Blowouts, and Derrick Cave volcanic formations:** If you have extra time to see additional points of interest, from Fort Rock you can travel Country Road 5-12 past Cougar Mountain to many volcanic formations, such as Hole-in-the-Ground, Devil's Garden, The Blowouts, and Derrick Cave. If you have even more time, from Country Road 5-12, head east to Country Road 5-12B and then south on BLM Road 6109C to Four Craters Lava Flow and Crack-in-the-Ground. Keep heading south to Christmas Valley, head east on Country Road 5-14, and then go north on Country Road 5-14D to the Sand Dunes and the Lost Forest.

# Pacific Coast Scenic Byway 

*As it travels the length of the Oregon coast, this byway by the sea passes fishing ports, oceanfront resorts, rugged cliffs, sandy beaches, dairy farms, windswept dunes, and the occasional migrating whale.*

This byway trots along the full length of the Oregon coast. The northern end starts in the shadow of the impressive Astoria–Megler Bridge, where the mouth of the Columbia River gapes wide (Astoria is the oldest U.S. settlement west of the Rockies). Shining beaches and temperate rain forests govern the following dozens of miles. Paralleling the Lewis and Clark Trail, the route stops by attractive places, such as the resort town of Seaside, famous for its two-mile beachfront promenade, and the busy Garibaldi fishing port on Tillamook Bay.

The southern portion of the byway changes a little because it is dominated by rugged cliffs, farms, and sandy beaches. This segment contains some of the most photographed areas in Oregon; photographers often capture Siletz and Depoe Bays, the colorful Oregon skies, lots of dairy land, and the city of Tillamook (where the famous brand of cheese is produced).

## Intrinsic Qualities

**Archaeological:** The relics and structures located in this area indicate that people have lived and prospered here for several millennia. This byway's archaeological residue fits into two main categories: relics of a native people that reveal a paradiselike past (such as ancient campsites) and evidence of the activities of a more recent people. Of the ancient people, scientists have found remnants of spears, knives, and other hunting equipment.

Discoveries of bones near campsites indicate the type of food these people ate: fish, large animals (elk and deer), and some birds. The people were largely industrious and thrived in this area for thousands of years.

The sites from more recent people are mostly historic bridges and lighthouses such as Yaquina Head's 125-year-old lighthouse, the 125-foot Astoria Column in Astoria, and the occasional shipwreck, such as the one known as Peter Iredale at Fort Stevens State Park. Some of these impressive structures still stand as landmarks to help guide travelers, while others function as attractions for tourists.

*Continuing action of storms and ocean waves and years of build-up have left Oregon Dunes National Recreation Area with dunes as far inland as 2½ miles.*

**Cultural:** Appreciate this area more by taking part in everyday activities to familiarize yourself with the culture. For instance, go to Lincoln City to soar a colorful kite alongside the locals; after that, visit some of Lincoln City's many art galleries. Another popular destination is Bandon, a charming town famous for its lighthouse, giant sea stacks, cheese factory, and cranberry harvest.

You might stop in Tillamook and see Oregon's largest cheese factory for a taste-testing tour: something even residents like to do every now and then. This impressive factory has been around for more than 100 years.

### Quick Facts

**Length:** 363 miles.

**Time to Allow:** 10 to 12 hours.

**Considerations:** Services may be several miles apart or closed at night. Slides and floods caused by extreme weather conditions sometimes temporarily disrupt access. Temperatures are comfortably in the 60s and 70s in the summer and rarely drop below freezing in the winter. Be prepared for fog, drizzle, or rain showers any time of year, but mainly in the winter and spring. Steady breezes are common most of the year. However, winter storms occasionally bring gusts above 50 mph. At the Oregon Dunes National Recreation Area, temperatures are at their highest and winds are at their lowest during the early fall. Be prepared for rapidly changing weather conditions.

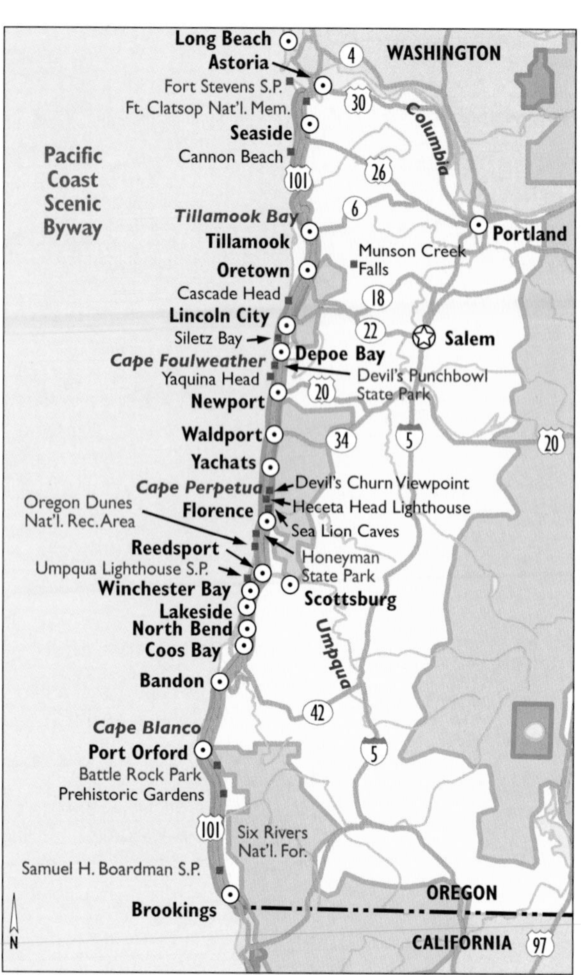




It boasts of continuing to use the time-tested recipe that has made its cheese famous. Other areas of note include North Bend and Coos Bay, cities that comprise the coast's largest urban area; here, you can find cultural activities galore, such as fantastic symphonies, art galleries, and restaurants.

**Historical:** The gorgeous and rich Oregon coast has drawn and sustained native people for centuries, and it has done likewise for sightseers and settlers ever since Lewis and Clark praised the area. Each new wave of people who came to live around the route added a new facet of culture and history to it and left their mark through historical and archaeological remains.

These remains, shadows of the past, are waiting in places such as Astoria. Other important historical sites on the byway include Fort Clatsop National Memorial, a life-size replica of Lewis and Clark's 1805–1806 winter outpost; historic Battle Rock Park in Port Orford, one of Oregon's oldest incorporated towns; and Yaquina Head's lighthouse, a testament to the area's historical shipping industry. The area's history is also evidenced in the many Victorian homes that scale the hillside, the 1883 Flavel House, and the shipwreck of the Peter Iredale at Fort Stevens State Park.

**Natural:** The byway runs along the coastline, bringing highway travelers to the sea and away again, winding by estuarine marshes, clinging to exposed seaside cliffs, passing through gentle agricultural valleys, and brushing against wind-sculpted dunes. Travelers encounter the scenic splendor of sea-stack rock formations that are eroding under constant surf, as well as a plethora of unusual plants and animals that provide natural wonder.

The highest waterfall in the Coast Range is an easy side trip from the byway. To find this waterfall, go seven miles south of Tillamook, and then watch for a small sign to Munson Creek Falls. Follow the narrow road 1$^1/_2$ miles to the parking area. A short stroll takes you to the base of this 266-foot cataract.

Many travelers enjoy watching water wildlife along this byway. Waysides and state parks along the coast make excellent vantage points for observing gray whales that migrate between December and May.

**Recreational:** Beaches along the byway are open to public use. In addition, many state parks can be found on the byway and provide public access to beaches. An abundance of public campsites, motel rooms, beach houses, and eateries along the byway corridor ensure a delightful extended stay along Oregon's Pacific Coast Scenic Byway.

Florence is the gateway to the Oregon Dunes National Recreation Area, a 47-mile sandbox with areas designated for bird-watching and dune riding. Honeyman State Park is a popular place to water ski and camp. As you travel on through the dunes, take a side trip to the Dean Creek Elk Viewing Area at Reedsport. The Oregon Dunes National Recreation Area has more than 31,000 acres. Visitors can camp, arrange a tour, take an exhilarating off-highway vehicle ride, or just walk along tranquil lakes, forest trails, and beaches.

Tucked in among some of the highest coastal dunes in the world, you'll find plenty of fishing and boating opportunities in small communities such as Winchester Bay and Lakeside. The dunes end near the cities of North Bend and Coos Bay, the coast's largest urban area. As Oregon's deepest natural harbor, Coos Bay has long been a major shipping port for the timber industry and a haven for sport-fishing enthusiasts.

Depoe Bay also offers fishing and whale-watching excursions from the world's smallest navigable harbor.

Flying large, beautiful kites is a common practice all along the coast and is especially popular in Lincoln City, which was recognized by *KiteLines* magazine as one of the best places to fly a kite in North America. Annual spring and fall kite festivals draw kite enthusiasts from all over. Get out your kite, and watch with the crowds as the delicate crafts are lofted up into the sky by the strong coastal winds.

**Scenic:** Keep your camera handy so that you can capture the coast's most photographed seascape, Cape Foulweather and the churning waves at Devil's Punchbowl. The superb scenery continues through Waldport and Yachats to Cape Perpetua. Here, you can watch the waves rush in and out of Devil's Churn, or you can hike on trails high above it. As the rugged cliffs give ay to graceful sand dunes, you'll rrive in Florence, a city that xplodes with wild rhododendrons the spring. The drive into Brookngs saves some of the best scenery or last. For example, Samuel H. oardman State Park shows off ine miles of rocky viewpoints and uiet beaches. The Pacific Coast cenic Byway ends in redwood ountry at the California border.

## ighlights

onsider taking the Pacific Coast cenic Byway's must-see tour.

**storia:** You will pass through ong Beach and go on to the city of storia, the oldest American settlenent west of the Rockies. Astoria ffers more points of historical nterest than any other place on he Oregon coast.

**ort Clatsop National Memorial:** or a glimpse into life on one of the nost important expeditions in the ation's history, travel three miles ast on Alternate (Old) 101 to Fort latsop Road and follow signs to he memorial. It is operated by the National Park Service on the site vhere the Lewis and Clark Expediion spent the winter of 1805–1806.

**easide:** Next you will reach the ity of Seaside, which was Oregon's irst seashore resort. The Turnaround there is the location of the tatue designating the end of the ewis and Clark Trail. At the south nd of the Promenade, you will ind the Lewis and Clark Salt Cairn, vhere members of the expedition nade salt from seawater.

**Cannon Beach:** Cannon Beach is the site of the famous annual Sandcastle Building Contest in early June. The beach was named for the wreckage that washed ashore in 1846 after the wreck of the schooner *Shark*.

**Lincoln City:** Lincoln City has miles of ocean beaches known for fine agates and other minerals. There are also ocean cruises and whale-watching trips out of Depoe Bay and Newport. Lincoln City also has Oregon's first factory outlet shopping center.

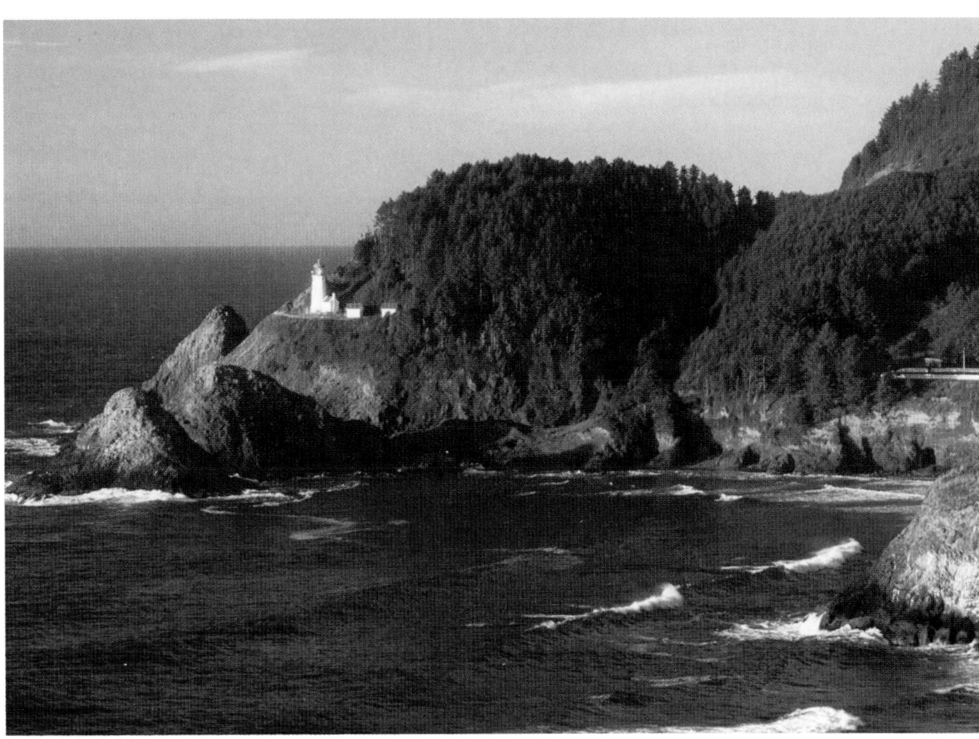

*The beacon at the Heceta Head Lighthouse can be seen 21 miles from land and is rated as the strongest on the Oregon coast.*

**Yaquina Head Lighthouse:** The lighthouse has a museum.

**Devil's Churn:** The basalt that forms the shore here is penetrated by a split in the rock that narrows to a few feet before finally disappearing into the cliff. Fascinating in summer, it is awe-inspiring during winter storms and is an excellent spot for photographers.

**Cape Perpetua Viewpoint:** Just south of Devil's Churn you'll find a road going inland. At the branch in the road, turn left and continue climbing sharply to the Cape Perpetua Viewpoint. There is a fine view of the coast both north and south.

**Heceta Head State Park (and Devil's Elbow State Park):** This pretty little cove is the place to see Heceta Head Lighthouse State Scenic Viewpoint up close. Just walk up the trail to the former assistant lighthouse keeper's home, Heceta House, and continue on to the lighthouse.

**Sea Lion Caves:** These natural caves are home to Steller's sea cows.

**Florence:** There are many delightful shops, restaurants, and galleries near the Siuslaw River in this town.

**Oregon Dunes National Recreation Area (NRA):** The Oregon Dunes NRA extends from Florence to North Bend with many access points off the byway.

**Umpqua River:** The Umpqua River Bridge is one of the historic coast bridges. The Umpqua is a major river in Oregon and is navigable by fairly large vessels upstream as far as Scottsburg.

**Cape Blanco:** Five miles west of the byway, Cape Blanco was discovered by the Spanish explorer Martin de Aguilar in 1603. The lighthouse is located at the westernmost point in Oregon.

**Prehistoric Gardens:** In the rain forest atmosphere of the Oregon coast, the developers of Prehistoric Gardens have created life-size replicas of dinosaurs.

# Rogue–Umpqua Scenic Byway 

*Known as the Highway of Waterfalls and framed by volcanic peaks, this spectacular byway cuts through canyons coursing with wild and scenic rivers. Raft, fish, camp, hike, or ski at many stops along the way.*

The Rogue–Umpqua Scenic Byway ventures deep into the Cascades. About 18 miles east of Roseburg, the North Umpqua River meets with the Little River at Colliding Rivers, one of the few places in the world where this head-on phenomenon occurs. The North Umpqua provides white-water thrills and superb steelhead runs as it tumbles through the Umpqua National Forest.

Whether you're learning about the rich history of the Native Americans, stretching in front of a tranquil lake, or experiencing the rush of white-water rafting on the river known as the "emerald jewel" of Oregon, the Rogue–Umpqua Scenic Byway shares one of the state's best-loved areas with you.

## Intrinsic Qualities

**Archaeological:** The North Umpqua and Rogue Rivers flow through this valley that was inhabited by prehistoric people for more than 8,000 years. Many dating techniques, such as radiocarbon and stratigraphic dating, indicate prehistoric occupations prior to the eruption of the volcano Mount Mazama, approximately 6,800 years ago. The presence of time-sensitive artifacts shows that occupation may go as far back as 12,500 years.

The route encompasses lands once occupied by the ancestors of the Upland Takelma, Southern Molalla, Klamath, and Cow Creek Bands of the Umpqua and Upper Umpqua Rivers. Along the route, interpretative panels are offered at the Colliding Rivers site at Glide, representing an Upper Umpqua village site. There is also a recorded prehistoric fishing locality that is located at the Narrows near Idleyld Park. The Susan Creek Recreation Sites contain cairns, which represent vision questing. A trail provides access, and an interpretive panel gives information on the sites.

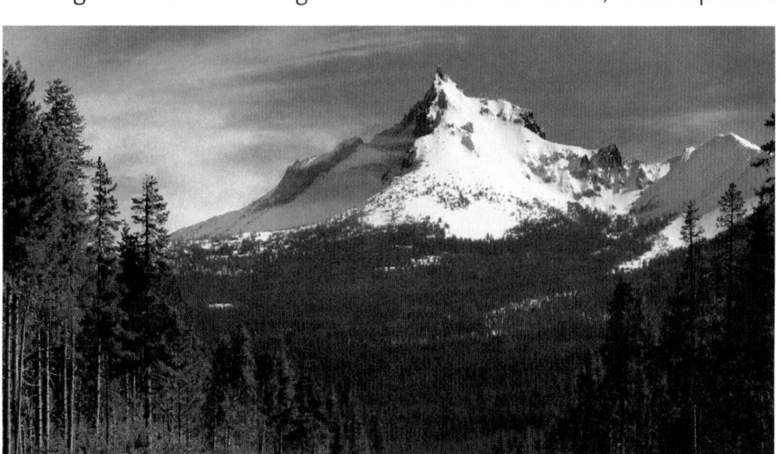

*At 9,182 feet above sea level, the soaring spire of Mount Thielsen is known as "the lightning rod of the Cascades."*

The nature and habitation of the valley changed with the eruption of Mount Mazama. When the volcano erupted, the Upper North Umpqua and Rogue River drainages were covered with a layer of airborne ash as far downstream as Dry Creek on the Umpqua and Elk Creek on the Rogue. A cloud of superheated gas and ash flowed across Diamond Lake and down the North Umpqua River to the Toketee Falls area and down the Rogue River toward Prospect, denuding the forest and destroying whatever plant and animal life happened to be in the way. Subsequent floods carried ash and pumice farther downstream, blanketing terraces. Drainages were choked with ash, and their gravel beds became silted over, altering fish habitat. This cataclysmic event forced early inhabitants to adapt to their new surroundings, and archaeological sites within the Rogue and Umpqua corridors preserve a record of these adaptations, including alterations in clothing, food, and hunting techniques.

**Historical:** Early settlers to the Rogue–Umpqua Scenic Byway laid a foundation for life in this rugged landscape. The Fort Klamath military wagon road made its way over the formidable Cascades to the settlement of Union Creek. The city doesn't remain today, but the wagon trail was an important road to get settlers and supplies over the mountains. In the 1850s, the Siskiyou Mountains in the Rogue River National Forest became home to many prospectors who were searching for gold. In the early days of the byway, American Indians, trappers, traders, explorers, and settlers all made their way into the surrounding area and worked or settled there.

The Civilian Conservation Corps (CCC) further developed the area surrounding the byway during the 1930s. This organization provided work for thousands of people during a time of low employment.

### Quick Facts

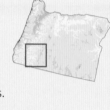

**Length:** 172 miles.

**Time to Allow:** Seven to eight hours.

**Considerations:** It's best to drive this byway during the summer and fall; fall colors are particularly spectacular along this byway. Check your car's fuel level often. Gas stations are few and far between. Also, during the winter months, the roads may be dangerous.

ne CCC was responsible for a ariety of projects, including ›forestation, fire prevention, soil onservation, and development of ecreational areas. Many structures nat stand today along the byway re a legacy of the CCC.

Stretching across the river ear Steamboat is the historic Aott Bridge, a recognized Oregon istoric Civil Engineering Land- ıark. Constructed by the CCC in 935–1936, the Mott Bridge is the nly surviving example of three uch structures built at that time ı the Pacific Northwest. The CCC lso built Diamond Lake's Visitor enter and guard station, as well as ıe ranger house at Colliding Rivers. oth of the historic structures at iamond Lake and Colliding Rivers erve as visitor centers today.

**latural:** Fisheries play an impor- ant role in the ecosystem. The pring-fed rivers flow large mounts of freshwater and sup- ort nationally significant fisher- es of steelhead and salmon. The pper Rogue and North Umpqua ivers sustain critical habitats for variety of resident and migrat- ıg fish species, including summer nd winter steelhead, fall and pring chinook, coho, and sea-run utthroat. These rivers and oth- rs provide large and consistent umbers of native (non-hatchery) sh in the run. In 1997, following he listing of the Umpqua River utthroat trout as an endangered pecies, fishing for trout in the nainstream Umpqua and tributar- es was prohibited. Additionally, all vild steelhead and coho salmon caught in the North Umpqua River must be released.

Two fish hatcheries are also associated with the Rogue–Umpqua Scenic Byway. Located at the base of Lost Creek Dam on the Rogue River, the Cole M. Rivers Fish Hatchery is the largest hatchery on the West Coast, built in 1973 to mitigate the loss of a spawning area when three dams were constructed in the Rogue Valley. The Rock Creek Fish Hatchery, built in lower Rock Creek and a half mile from Highway 138, was constructed in the late 1800s. It still operates to supplement the summer steelhead, spring chinook, and coho fisheries of the Umpqua, the North Umpqua, and South Umpqua Rivers.

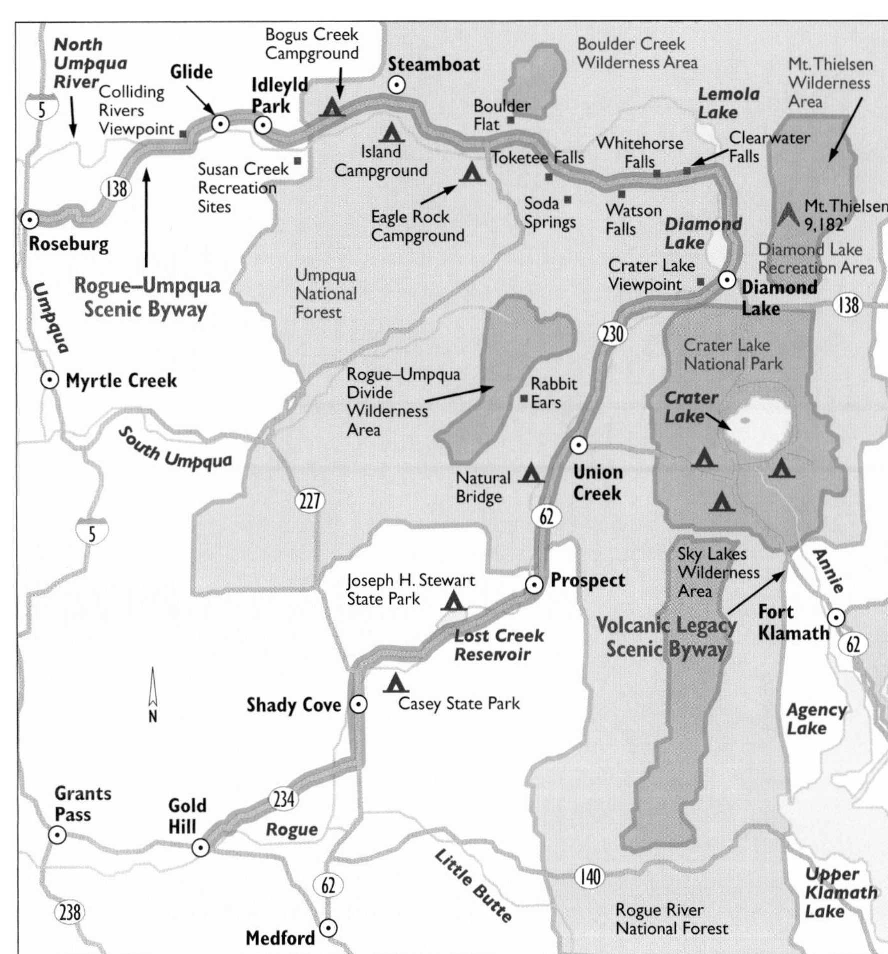


**Recreational:** Many come to fish, hike, camp, bike, and soak in the sites. However, the recreational opportunity that's most popular here is white-water rafting, an exhilarating experience that brings people back each year because of its world-class fun. The 33.8-mile North Umpqua River recreation area offers white-water thrills, including rapids of intermediate to advanced experience levels.

For the days not spent braving the rapids, Joseph H. Stewart State Park on Lost Creek Reservoir is a water paradise, providing 151 campsites with electrical hook-ups; 50 tent sites with water; two group tent camping areas with the amenities of flush toilets, showers, and volleyball and horseshoe pits; and day-use picnic areas. The boating facilities include a marina with a store and café, moorage facility, boat launch, boat rentals, and fish-cleaning facilities. You can also find several other recreation sites on the 30 miles of shoreline created by Lost Creek Reservoir, including McGregor Park, a visitor center called Spirit of the Rogue Nature Center, Takelma Recreation Area, and the Cole M. Rivers Fish Hatchery.

**Scenic:** The tremendous diversity of geologic and volcanic formations, coupled with 15 waterfalls, make the Rogue–Umpqua Scenic Byway a photographer's paradise. Famous artists and photographers have come from all over the world to capture awe-inspiring images here. Nearly every stretch of the route provides serene places to enjoy the beauty of nature.

Volcanic activity ravaged this area, creating many distinctive and stunning landscapes. In the Diamond Lake area, the route is characterized by unique High Cascades volcanic remnants. Some of these include Crater Lake Rim and impressive peaks, such as Mount Thielsen (elevation 9,182 feet) and others.

The Umpqua Rocks Geologic Area parallels Highway 138 from Marsters Bridge to Soda Springs. Along the Upper Rogue River, the highway is built on pumice and ash flows, which were part of the cataclysmic Mount Mazama eruption. The ash flows overlay 1.25-million-year-old lava flows. The river flows through lava tubes above and below the surface at the Rogue Gorge and Natural Bridge interpretive sites. Sedimentary and marine deposits are evident as the highway enters the Rogue Valley, with the exception of the notable Upper and Lower Table Rocks, which are remnants of High Cascades Province lava flows.

You'll find notable waterfalls along this byway, ranging in size and accessibility. One of the most popular is the Watson Falls, the third highest in Oregon. The water tumbles down 272 feet, which causes a cool mist to refresh you on a searing day.



### Diamond and Crater Lakes

After passing more than a half dozen waterfalls, the byway reaches sparkling Diamond Lake, a year-round playground at the base of Mount Thielsen. The paved 11-mile path around the lake is one of the nicest family bike rides anywhere. From here, you're only moments away from Crater Lake's north entrance, which is usually open from June through October; Crater Lake has attracted people from around the world to view its unusual beauty. Scientists from many places come here to study the environment. In winter, you can swing through Highway 230 and Highway 62 to the south entrance, which is open year-round.

## Highlights

Beginning at the northern end of the byway, take this tour. If you start on the other end of the byway, begin at the bottom of this list and make your way up.

**Roseburg:** Start your trip in Roseburg, which lies along both I-5 and the historic Applegate Trail, the southern route of the Oregon Trail. The Douglas County Museum near Roseburg has exhibits on the Applegate Trail and the Umpqua River. Several wineries are nearby.

**Colliding Rivers Viewpoint:** Head east on Highway 138 for about 18 miles to Glide, site of the Colliding Rivers Viewpoint and visitor center. Views are especially spectacular with higher river flows during the wet season. There is also a short nature trail here.

**North Umpqua River:** The byway next heads through a narrow canyon, following the wild and scenic North Umpqua River. There are places along the river where you can stop for hiking, fly-fishing, white-water rafting, and kayaking.

**Toketee and Watson Falls:** Continuing east through the Umpqua National Forest, the byway passes distinctively shaped volcanic rock formations as well as well-marked hiking trails to Toketee Falls and 272-foot-high Watson Falls. The latter is at Milepost 61 along Highway 138.

**Diamond Lake:** Stop next at beautiful Diamond Lake, which has camping, fishing, and an 11-mile paved bike path around the lake. (During the winter, the path becomes a cross-country ski trail.) The visitor center is opposite the campground entrance. Wilderness areas adjoin the lake, and 9,000-foot volcanic peaks form a backdrop.

*The scenic Umpqua River runs through the Umpqua National Forest. Fly-fishing is an especially popular pastime in the waters of the Umpqua.*

**Crater Lake National Park:** The byway now follows Route 230 south. However, the continuation of Highway 138 leads to a worthwhile scenic detour: the nearby north entrance of Crater Lake National Park. The park is the site of Crater Lake, the deepest lake in America, formed within an ancient volcanic caldera. The 33-mile-long Rim Drive, usually open July through mid-October (or the first snowfall), circles the lake; a visitor center is open June to September at Rim Village. A variety of hiking trails lead to panoramic views. (From late fall to late spring, the park's year-round south entrance may be accessed via Routes 230 and 62.) Return to the byway via Route 62 west, which meets up with Route 230 just north of Union Creek.

**Rogue River and Natural Bridge:** South of Diamond Lake, the byway runs alongside the thundering Rogue River, with more opportunities for white-water rafting and camping. Route 230 merges with Route 62 just north of Union Creek. Stop at the Natural Bridge interpretive site, just south of Union Creek, where the river rushes underground into a volcanic channel.

**Joseph H. Stewart Recreation Area:** A bit farther south is Joseph H. Stewart Recreation Area, overlooking Lost Creek Reservoir. It's popular for boating, camping, and fishing.

**Shady Cove:** The byway continues to Shady Cove, where hiking trails lead off into wilderness areas. It is also known as a place for excellent fishing.

**Gold Hill:** The final part of the byway leads west along Route 234 into the town of Gold Hill, where the Rogue River appears once again.

# Volcanic Legacy Scenic Byway

*This remarkably varied volcano-to-volcano route spans two states as it leads to lava fields, snowcapped peaks, mountain lakes, historic towns, wildlife refuges, forest vistas, and year-round recreation.*

Part of a multistate byway; it also runs through California.

The Volcanic Legacy Scenic Byway stretches from California's Mount Lassen to Oregon's Crater Lake, making this byway America's volcano-to-volcano highway. The volcanic activity of the past has created unique geological formations, such as wavy lava flows and lava tube caves. Surrounding this volcanic landscape is a wide diversity of scenery. The byway travels through or near dense forests, broad wetlands and habitat areas, pastoral grasslands, farms and ranches, and well-managed timber resource lands.

As the byway passes the 90,000 surface-acre Upper Klamath Lake, you can see more than one million birds during peak migrations in the fall. The Klamath Basin is the largest freshwater ecosystem west of the Great Lakes. Six national wildlife refuges in these wetlands were favorite fishing spots of President Theodore Roosevelt.

You can also visit the same Pelican Bay where John Muir (naturalist, writer, conservationist, and founder of the Sierra Club) wrote *The Story of My Boyhood and Youth* in 1908.

*Mount Shasta, a dormant volcanic cone, is the second-highest volcano in the United States and a major peak in the Cascade Range.*

## Intrinsic Qualities

**Archaeological:** This byway was (and still is) littered with ancient Native American artifacts. Most of the artifacts that have been discovered along this route are displayed among the 100,000 artifacts in the byway's own Favell Museum of Western Art and Indian Artifacts. This museum focuses on the area's Native Americans but also spotlights nations across the country. It covers 12,000 years of history in its collections of basketry, beadwork, stone tools, and pottery.

**Cultural:** The Klamath nations (more specifically, the Klamaths, Modocs, and Yahooskin) are an integral part of the communities along the byway because they lived here before anyone can remember. Also, the determination and grit they have demonstrated to survive the changes of years, famine, and new settlers have affected positively the attitudes of other groups who have lived in the area, including the groups who caused their setbacks.

The Klamath nations have worked hard to maintain their own culture in spite of difficult circumstances. When the Klamath nations were forced on to reservations in the 1860s, they turned to cattle ranching and made a profitable living. And even though the nations were not federally recognized for about 30 years and had to work without supplemental human services on their reservation land, they have sustained the economy of Klamath County for decades; they contribute $12 million per year to the Klamath County economy. They have also instituted training schools to make their enterprises more competitive.

**Historical:** Much of the historical significance of the Volcanic Legacy Scenic Byway arises from its Native American roots, and the byway is dotted with historic mining and logging towns. Many features along the byway are listed as historical landmarks.

Captain Jack's Stronghold, a national monument located in the Lava Beds National Monument, is historically significant because it was the site of the Modoc War. During the Modoc War of 1872–1873, the Modoc nation took advantage of the unique geogra-

## Quick Facts

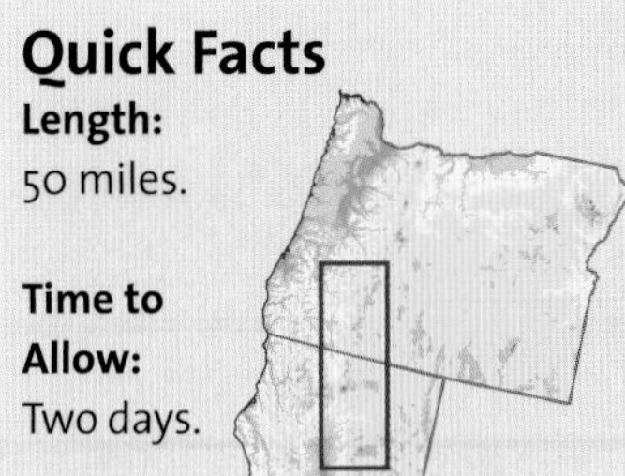

**Length:** 50 miles.

**Time to Allow:** Two days.

**Considerations:** The portion of the route from the south rim of Crater Lake to the North Park Entrance is closed from mid-October to mid-June each year due to snow. The roadway within Lassen Volcanic National Park is typically closed from November through June. The opening of Rim Drive each year is a locally celebrated event that signals the beginning of summer. Views of Crater Lake are available year-round at the south rim near the visitor facilities. The geometry of the byway makes it restrictive with respect to large vehicles, including RVs and tour buses.

phy of their homelands. Under the guidance of their leader, Kintuashk, who came to be known as Captain Jack, the Modoc people took refuge in a natural lava fortress. The site of the fortress is now known as Captain Jack's Stronghold. From this secure base, Captain Jack and his group of 53 fighting men and their families held off U.S. Army forces, which numbered up to ten times more than Kintuashk's nation. However, the nation was still able to hold off the Army forces for five months.

Mount Shasta is another site of historical significance along this byway. The major history of the mountain lies in its geological greatness. It also has a spiritual history. Native Americans of the area believed Mount Shasta to be the abode of the Great Spirit. Out of respect, the natives never ascended past the timberline. A long history of mythology surrounds the mountain, including legends of Lemurians, Atlanteans, secret commonwealth citizens, dwarfs, fairies, Bigfoot, and space beings that materialize at will. Mount Shasta draws visitors from all over the world, some seeking spiritual insight, others searching for the experience of the beauty and wonders that nature has to offer here in this unique alpine region. The upper elevation of Mount Shasta Wilderness was designated in 1976 as a National Natural Historic Landmark.

The Volcanic Legacy Scenic Byway is dotted with historic towns, many of which began as logging communities. McCloud is one example, being a company-built mill town, still revealing its colorful railroad and logging history. The Heritage Junction Museum in the city offers exhibits displaying 100 years' worth of historical artifacts and photographs depicting the region. The still functioning McCloud Railway is also evidence of the logging history of the town. Likewise, the town of Weed was also a logging town, built in 1897. The Weed Historic Lumber Town Museum helps to reveal the part Weed played in the logging industry of the time. Other historical towns along the byway include Westwood, one of the largest company towns in the West during the early to mid-1900s, and Mount Shasta. Also, the Collier State Park and Logging Museum can give you an overview of the area's logging history.

Fort Klamath also tells an important story of early settlement. The fort was built in 1863 to protect Oregon Trail pioneers and southern emigrant trains from the nearby Modoc and Klamath nations who were inclined to attack on occasion. Two notable events happened at this fort: one was when Captain Jack was executed at the fort along with three other Modoc warriors in late 1873 (their graves are at the fort); the second was when the fort played an important part in the 1864 Council Grove peace treaty.

Crater Lake Lodge's historical guest register shows what a popular vacation spot Crater Lake has always been: The location has hosted important visitors, such as First Lady Eleanor Roosevelt and author Jack London. It is listed on the National Register of Historic Places.

Unfortunately, not all of the history along the byway is bright. The Tule Lake Relocation Center was one of ten American internment camps established during World War II to incarcerate 110,000 persons of Japanese ancestry. The majority of these people were American citizens. A large monument of basalt rock and concrete along the north side of State Highway 139 commemorates the relocation center. The monument, dedicated in 1979, incorporates multiple levels of rock walls, a concrete apron, and a state historical marker. The Tule Lake Relocation Center is located off the byway about ten miles from the town of Tulelake. The new Tulelake Museum in the town of Tulelake has a restored camp building and watch tower on display, as well as information about the relocation center.

**Natural:** This byway sustains masses of wildlife in its several wildlife refuge areas, bulky mountains, and unique geological formations. Six national wildlife refuges have been established in the area: Lower Klamath, Tule Lake, Clear Lake, Bear Valley, Upper Klamath, and Klamath Marsh. These refuges are diverse; they include freshwater marshes, open waters, grassy meadows, coniferous forests, sagebrush, juniper grasslands,

*Crater Lake is widely known for its brilliant blue color and magnificent views.*

agricultural lands, rock cliffs, and slopes. More than 400 different species have been identified in the refuges. In the spring, more than one million birds retreat there. This number is added to in the summer, as ducks and Canada geese join the throng. In the fall, the birds (ducks, geese, swans, and green-winged teal) number in the millions. In addition, the Klamath Basin is home to the largest concentration of wintering bald eagles in the lower 48 states.

The Volcanic Legacy Scenic Byway takes you around magnificent Mount Shasta, a solitary peak rising to a height of 14,162 feet. The byway allows you to experience the effects of the geological and volcanic history of the region. It traverses two major geological areas. Lassen Volcanic National Park is located in the southern portion of the byway. The park contains Lassen Peak, one of the largest plug dome volcanoes in the world. Lassen Peak was a major source of the many geological formations of the area. Lava Beds National Monument, located along the northern part of the byway, near California's border with Oregon, is the site of the largest concentration of lava tube caves in the United States. To finish this exciting volcano-to-volcano journey, continue north on Highway 97 to Crater Lake National Park.

Crater Lake, Oregon's only national park, is not only a place for wildlife to refuge, but also is one of the nation's favorite places to retreat. The deepest lake in the United States, it was formed inside the collapsed peak of an ancient volcano, Mount Mazama, that erupted 8,000 years ago. The eruptions were 42 times greater than those of Mount St. Helens in 1980, and the ash spewed over eight states and three Canadian provinces. One of the finest and most accessible examples of a young caldera (a certain kind of volcanic crater) in the world, Crater Lake is recognized worldwide as a scenic wonder.

**Recreational:** The Volcanic Legacy Scenic Byway's length and vast diversity of landscapes provide a wide variety of year-round recreational opportunities. In the summer, you can fish, camp, visit a horse and cattle ranch, whitewater raft, or hike. You can tour a lighted lava tube or spelunk on your own at Lava Beds National Monument, see bubbling mud pots and steam vents at Lassen Volcanic National Park, or drive to an elevation of 7,900 feet on Mount Shasta to view the surrounding landscape. You can also tour the scenic shores of the Upper Klamath Canoe Trail by canoe. Crater Lake National Park is especially good for camping and hiking. Lake of the Woods is popular for any kind of summer activity and is also great for winter activities, such as cross-country skiing (although cross-country skiing is exceptional in many other areas along the byway, as well). Willamette Ski Lodge and Diamond Lake Resort are particularly good for downhill skiing.

**Scenic:** The volcanic landscape of the Volcanic Legacy Scenic Byway includes distinctive features of mountain lakes and streams, three volcanoes (all nationally recognized), lava flows, and lava tube caves. You can experience these volcanic features through attractions at Crater Lake National Park (in Oregon), Lava Beds National Monument, and Lassen Volcanic National Park. However, the volcanic landscape is visible throughout the entire byway. The byway offers extended views of majestic volcano peaks, an abundance of beautiful forest vistas, and up-close views of crisp mountain lakes and streams.

Perhaps the most captivating of the Volcanic Legacy Scenic Byway's qualities are its vast volcano mountain peaks. Mount Shasta is the tallest of the peaks. Others include Lassen Peak and Mount Scott on the rim of Crater Lake. The immensity of the peaks allows them to be viewed from hundreds of miles away. The byway circles around Mount Shasta, providing views from every angle. The majority of peaks along the byway are above the timberline and provide views of broad snowfields and craggy rock outcroppings. At lower elevations, broad grassy meadows with extensive wildflowers offer

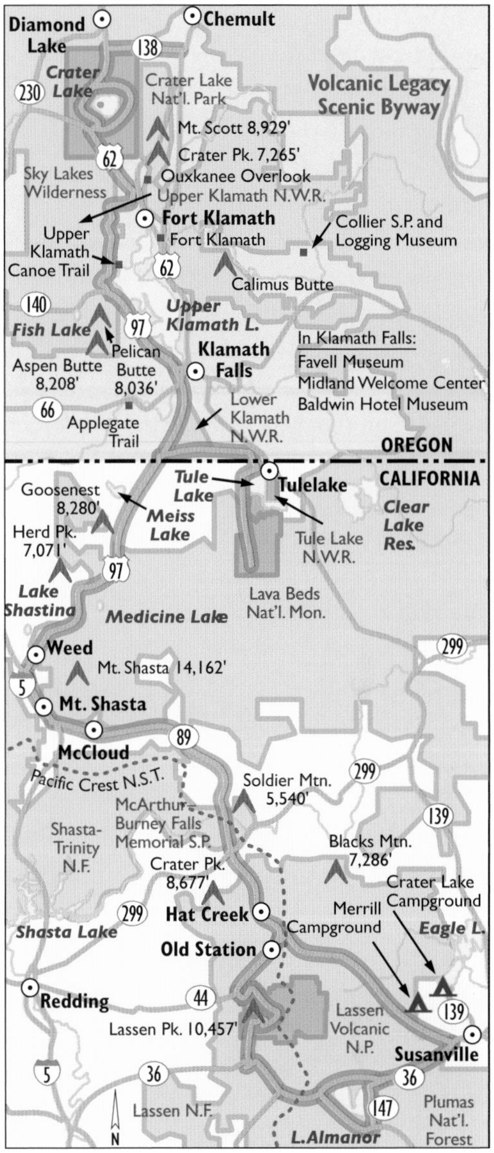


outstanding foreground settings for views of the more distant peaks.

## Highlights

When traveling the byway from north to south, consider following this scenic viewpoints tour. If you're starting from the south, simply read this list from the bottom up.

**Walker Mountain:** The view from the fire lookout near Chemult extends from Mount Jefferson in central Oregon to Mount Shasta in northern California. There, you're surrounded by a sea of forest land. The mountain is accessible by high-clearance vehicle only.

**Crater Lake National Park:** Located 65 miles north of Klamath Falls on Highways 97 and 62, here are the world-renowned views you've seen on postcards and in magazines. Many viewpoints are accessible by wheelchair; some are found at the ends of hiking trails.

**Ouxkanee Overlook:** A short drive off Highway 97 leads to a picnic area with a stunning overlook of the Williamson River Valley and the surrounding landscape. Scan the horizon as far as Mount Shasta in northern California.

**Calimus Butte:** This historic, cupola-style lookout was built by the Bureau of Indian Affairs in 1920 and overlooks the scene of the 48-square-mile Lone Pine fire in 1992, as well as Klamath Marsh and Sprague River Valley. It is accessible by high-clearance vehicle only.

**Pelican Butte:** The summit offers breathtaking views of Upper Klamath Lake and Sky Lakes Wilderness. Old-growth timber lines the narrow, rough road to the top, which takes about an hour and is accessible only by high-clearance vehicle and by foot.

**Herd Peak:** A gravel road off Highway 97 leads to Herd Peak, where a fire lookout is staffed during the summer months and is open to the public. The summit offers breathtaking views of Mount Shasta and the surrounding area.

**Klamath Basin National Wildlife Refuges:** Straddling Oregon and California are the Klamath Basin National Wildlife Refuges, home to a remarkable array of birdlife. Those making this drive in October to November can watch for skies filled with geese and ducks; from mid-December to February, for hundreds of bald eagles; and in springtime, for huge flocks of waterfowl and shorebirds. The Lower Klamath and Tule Lake Refuges both have self-guided auto trails. To reach the visitor center from Highway 97 at the Oregon–California border, follow Route 161 east to Hill Road, then Hill Road south four miles.

**Lava Beds National Monument:** Lava Beds National Monument, south of Tule Lake National Wildlife Refuge, has weird-shaped lava formations, cinder and spatter cones, and undulating beds of volcanic rock, and is honeycombed with nearly 400 lava tube caves (two dozen of which are easily accessible to visitors). Captain Jack's Stronghold, a natural lava fortress where the Modoc Indians held off the U.S. Army during the Modoc War in the early 1870s, is also within the park. There's no gasoline available, however, so fill up before entering. From Highway 97, take Route 161 east at the California border to Route 139, which heads south past the town of Tulelake into Lava Beds.

**Mount Shasta:** Now double back to Highway 97. Vistas on the route south are dominated by mighty Mount Shasta, a 14,162-foot snowcapped volcano. At the town of Mount Shasta (where the byway has briefly joined with I-5), consider a side trip east on the Everitt Memorial Highway. It leads halfway up the mountain.

**McCloud:** Just south of the town of Mount Shasta, take Highway 89 south to the historic town of McCloud, which has a colorful railroad and logging history.

**McArthur–Burney Falls Memorial State Park:** Continue south on Highway 89. Six miles north of the intersection with Route 299, watch for signs for McArthur–Burney Falls Memorial State Park, site of Burney Falls, which Theodore Roosevelt called the "Eighth Wonder of the World." Two cascades spill 100 million gallons of water a day into a deep emerald pool. A one-mile nature trail loops around the park, where there are campgrounds, picnic areas, and a lake for fishing.

**Lassen Volcanic National Park:** Highway 89 leads farther south to Lassen Volcanic National Park. Though the alpine scenery rivals that of Yosemite, it's far less crowded. Don't miss Bumpass Hell, where boardwalk trails lead past bubbling mudpots. Climbers find a challenging five-mile-roundtrip trail to the summit of Lassen Peak, which towers over the park at almost 10,500 feet. The trail gains 2,000 feet elevation and has 40 steep switchbacks.

**Lake Almanor:** Twenty miles southeast of Lassen Park along Highway 89 lies Lake Almanor, a good place to relax with fishing, skiing, and several resorts.

*The waters of Burney Falls tumble 129 feet to create a lovely mist-filled basin. The falls are named for a local pioneer settler from the 1850s.*

# West Cascades Scenic Byway 

*For those who aren't in a rush, here's the slow-paced, scenic alternative to Oregon's north–south interstate. The reward for patience is a breathtaking journey through the Western Cascades.*

The West Cascades Scenic Byway isn't the shortest route between Portland and Eugene, but this 220-mile scenic alternative offers some of the best views of thundering waterfalls, lush ancient forests, rushing white water, and placid lakes. The byway ends near the timber towns of Westfir and Oakridge.

The northernmost access to the byway begins in the historic logging and hydropower city of Estacada, located only 40 minutes from Portland. From the very start, you're immersed in old-growth forest, skimming the edge of the breathtaking Clackamas River. From here, the byway winds through the Western Cascades and its beautiful snowcapped volcanic peaks.

Although two segments of the byway—Forest Roads 19 and 46—are closed in the winter due to snow, the rest of the byway offers access to a range of winter sports. These winter sport facilities range from the most rustic, primitive facilities to highly developed, full-service facilities.

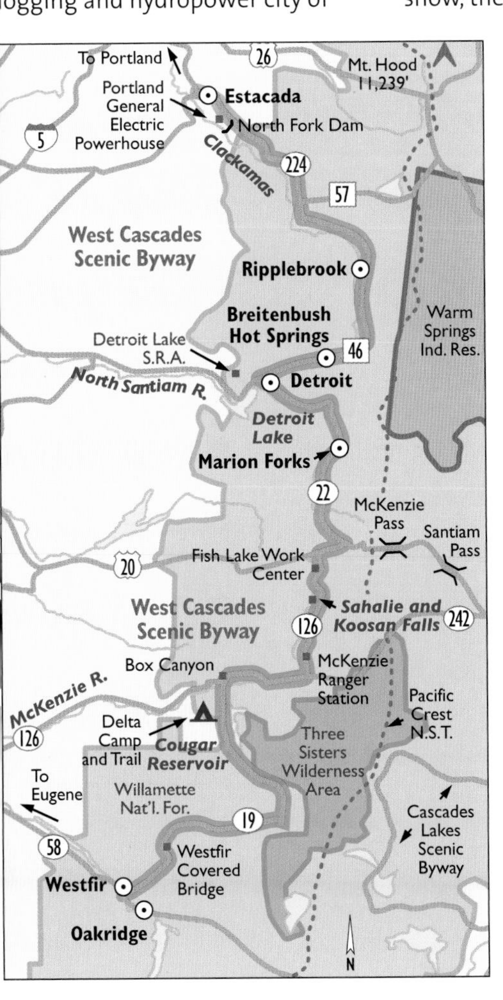


## Intrinsic Qualities

**Archaeological:** Archaeological evidence confirm humans used these lands 10,000 years ago. Previous native inhabitants include the Molalla, Kalapuya, Tenino, and Northern Paiute peoples. Even though the byway has relatively few archaeological artifacts, the story of early inhabitants is told well through the byway's more soft archaeology: rich written and oral histories intertwined with scattered discoveries of tool caches.

For example, a famous oral history is tied with an old trail that formed a natural pass up the Santiam River. The legend says that a fierce battle between the Molalla (of the west hills) and the Paiutes (from the east side) took place on this trail. After the battle was over, the souls of the dead warriors waited to make war on old enemies along both sides of the trail. When settlers began to use the pass, they noticed that the Native Americans bypassed gorges along this trail where these souls were believed to be waiting.

Harder archaeological evidence shows that Native Americans hunted, fished, and gathered huckleberries and wild plants in the Santiam Basin at least 10,000 years ago. They gathered obsidian for their tools from the local Obsidian Cliffs. The tools they made (spear points and scraping tools) have been discovered in caches throughout the three major river basins.

**Historical:** Early industrial companies and the Civilian Conservation Corps (CCC) both helped shape the byway as it is today. One such early industrial company that built structures along the route was the Portland General Electric Company (PGEC); the PGEC built a train bed in the 1920s that now serves as a portion of Highway 224. Also, the logging and power companies practically built the city of Estacada, and they specifically left what is now Estacada's Timber Park, featuring a dam that boasts the longest fish tunnel in the Pacific Northwest. Another company built the Hogg Railroad (now listed in the National Register of Historic Places) in the early 1900s, in an effort to connect the Willamette Valley with Eastern Oregon over the Santiam Pass.

In the 1930s, the CCC built many of the structures that are still used for recreation, education, and

## Quick Facts

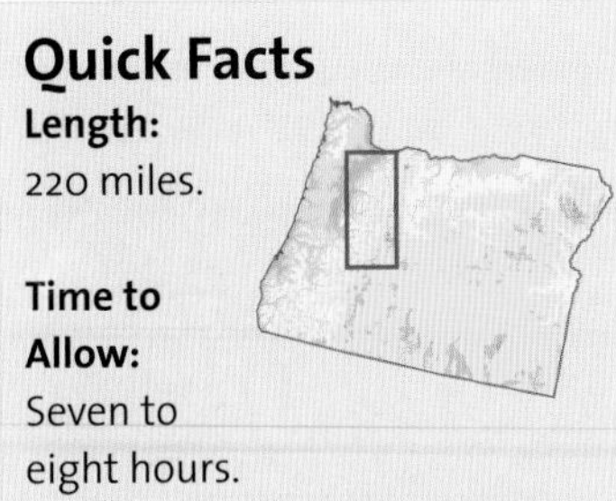

**Length:** 220 miles.

**Time to Allow:** Seven to eight hours.

**Considerations:** Even though Forest Roads 19 and 46 are closed in the winter due to snow (from approximately November 15 to April 30), the rest of the route is open during winter months and provides access to cross-country skiing, snowmobiling, snowshoeing, and winter-only cabin rentals at Fish Lake Remount Depot. You need to buy a $5 day pass to access some of the park.

*A unique feature of the Westfir Covered Bridge, the longest in Oregon, is a covered walkway at the side of the bridge, separate from the roadway.*

administration. Some specific places they developed are Camp Belknap (where the CCC workers actually stayed), Clear Lake Cutoff, Clear Lake Shelter, Paradise Campground, and the McKenzie Campgrounds. They also worked to develop the Willamette Valley Cascade Mountain Wagon Road (known today as the Santiam Wagon Road), which now serves as part of Highway 126.

**Natural:** This byway's systems of mountains, vegetation, rivers, and wildlife support one another vitally. Wildlife thrives in the volcanic peaks and unique geologic formations of the High Cascades; it also flourishes in the Western Cascades' jagged lava flows and smooth glacial valleys. These ranges' old-growth forests of Douglas fir and western red cedar are excellent habitats for the northern spotted owl and the bald eagle (both endangered) and also for the pine marten, pileated woodpecker, Roosevelt elk, black-tailed deer, and mule deer.

The mountains' heavy snow and rain percolate through porous volcanic rocks and reappear as hundreds of springs that feed the byway's numerous rivers and lakes. These rivers support a number of rare and threatened species of fish, including spring chinook, winter and summer steelhead, bull trout, and a rare species of cutthroat trout. This abundant moisture has allowed the development of dense, lush old-growth forests: Some trees measure more than six feet in diameter and are more than 180 feet tall.

**Recreational:** A broad range of recreational activities is available along this byway. Summer brings horseback riding, picnicking, primitive and rustic camping, and fishing. You can also enjoy practically any water and watercraft activity: drift and motor boating, canoeing, jet skiing, sailing, water-skiing, kayaking, rafting, and swimming. The hiking here is especially good because the U.S. Forest Service maintains the byway's three national recreation trails to the highest standard. Hundreds of miles of other trails are also accessed from the byway. In the winter, you can snowmobile, sled, snowshoe, and downhill and cross-country ski.

**Scenic:** As you travel this scenic alternative to I-5, you absorb immaculate mountainscapes, peer into plush forests, watch the mesmerizing flow of pure waters, and scrutinize each shade of autumn's slow-motion explosion. Spectacular views of snowcapped mountains (Jefferson, Washington, Three Fingered Jack, and the Three Sisters) are omnipresent as you skirt the Cascade Mountain Range and travel through the Mount Hood and Willamette National Forests.

Three rivers thread along sections of the byway. These rivers are associated with other enchanting accumulations of water: glossy lakes, silken pools, rushing white water, coarse waterfalls, one-of-a-kind geologic formations, and glacier-carved canyons. One of the most striking and popular of these waters is 120-foot-deep Clear Lake, which is nationally known for its startling clarity.

## Highlights

This tour shares the highlights of the West Cascades Scenic Byway.

**Westfir:** Start your tour at Westfir, which is the southern end of the byway. Near Westfir, take in the Westfir Covered Bridge. At 180 feet long, this unique bridge is the longest covered bridge in the state.

**Cougar Reservoir:** Just a few miles north of the bridge is the Cougar Reservoir, which is a good place to get out and stretch your legs. The dam at the north end of the reservoir is the tallest rock-filled dam in Oregon.

**Delta Campground and Nature Trail:** Right near the reservoir is the Delta Campground and Nature Trail. Ancient western red cedar and Douglas fir stretch up to 180 feet here. Walk under them along the nature trail.

**Box Canyon:** End your tour with a picnic lunch at Box Canyon, which is adjacent (to the north) to the Delta Campground and Nature Trail, right along the McKenzie River.

# Arroyo Seco Historic Parkway (Route 110) 

*The West's first freeway cuts through a canyon from Los Angeles to Pasadena, serving as an eye-pleasing urban gateway to an area rich in history, art, architecture, parklands, and multiethnic culture.*

Dedicated on December 30, 1940, the Arroyo Seco Historic Parkway connects Los Angeles and Pasadena through the historic Arts and Crafts landscape of the Arroyo Seco. The studios and workshops of these turn-of-the-19th-century artists and crafters dotted the banks of this intermittent river. Today, the area's natural and built environment form a seamless cultural landscape, strongly associated with the Arts and Crafts era, that continues to inspire generations.

Conceived in the parkway tradition with its gentle curves, lush landscape, and scenic vistas, the parkway also incorporated modern elements that laid the groundwork for the California freeway system. Combining ideas reminiscent of the older parkway tradition with those of modern freeway design, the Arroyo Seco Parkway (also called the Pasadena Freeway or State Route 110) was the first divided-lane, high-speed, limited-access road in the urban western United States. The parkway was envisioned both as a scenic pleasure road traversing the Arroyo Seco and as a vital traffic conduit linking the expanding cities of Pasadena and Los Angeles.

## Intrinsic Qualities

**Cultural:** The Arroyo Seco was the center for the Arts and Crafts movement on the West Coast and is one of four internationally recognized centers of the movement in America. The Arts and Crafts movement started in the United Kingdom between the late 1850s and early 1860s and was characterized by a disregard for industrialization. Followers of the movement built their own houses out of as many natural materials as possible and handcrafted as much of their environment as possible.

By the late 1890s, the movement had worked its way to America, having significant influence on the Arroyo culture throughout the first two decades of the 20th century. The movement gave rise to thriving enterprises, including furniture design and manufacturing, home plans and kits, ceramics, glasswork, metalwork, and textiles. The influence of the Arts and Crafts movement on the Arroyo Seco culture is most evident in the architecture of many of the structures along the byway. Bungalows along the byway are built of all-natural materials and feature wide porches and long roof overhangs. Additionally, almost all of the buildings feature native Arroyo cobblestone trim, collected from the river of the valley.

*Downtown Pasadena's Plaza Las Fuentes features such notables as a bronze sculpture shaped like a giant dragonfly and Pasadena City Hall, a soaring Italian Renaissance-inspired building.*

### Quick Facts

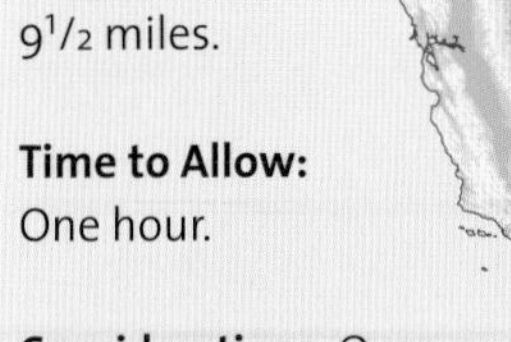

**Length:**
9½ miles.

**Time to Allow:**
One hour.

**Considerations:** Oversize vehicles are prohibited on the byway. Instead of continuous shoulders, the highway has intermittent "turn-out pockets" for disabled vehicles.

**Historical:** The Arroyo Seco Historic Parkway was the prototype of the world-famous Los Angeles freeway system. Its significance in California's highway history is highlighted by its designation as an American Civil Engineering Landmark. The Arroyo Seco Historic Parkway is also California's first and only state historic parkway and is nationally recognized as one of the most significant roadways of the 20th century.

The megalopolis of Los Angeles actually began as just a small settlement of a colony of settlers from Mexico. The Arroyo Seco Historic Parkway lies nearly adjacent to that original settlement, El Pueblo de Nuestra Señora, La Reina de Los Angeles. The site contains more than 20 historic buildings, many of which can be viewed or are now museums.

**Natural:** While located in the second-largest city in the United States, the Arroyo Seco Historic Parkway is an urban oasis with natural areas, diverse parklands, and views of the Angeles National Forest in the snow-peaked San Gabriel Mountains to the north.

*Arroyo Seco*, Spanish for "dry stream," is geographically the most prominent feature of the northeastern Los Angeles landscape. The great, long canyon of the Arroyo Seco extends from the foot of the San Gabriel Mountains north of Pasadena, southward along the western edge of South Pasadena. The canyon then continues south through Highland Park until it joins the Los Angeles River not far from Elysian Park.

**Recreational:** In the 1920s, under the urging of Charles Lummis, Pasadena and Los Angeles recognized the opportunities of the Arroyo Seco to provide recreational access to a growing metropolitan area. Active recreation—such as hiking, swimming, horseback riding, bicycling, fishing, tennis, and golf—is matched by more passive pursuits like bird-watching, painting, and stargazing.

The Arroyo Seco lies in the heart of Los Angeles, a recreational melting pot. The byway itself features Dodger Stadium, allowing you to partake of America's favorite pastime. For golfers, courses are abundant in the area, including Arroyo Seco's own course. Downtown Los Angeles, only a block from the byway, has days' worth of activities, from basketball or exhibits at the Staples Center to provocative contemplation at the Museum of Contemporary Art.

## Highlights

While there's much to appreciate on the drive along the parkway itself, much of the richness of the Arroyo Seco culture is to be found among the historic houses, museums, and outdoor recreational areas found just beyond its exits.

**El Pueblo de Los Angeles Historic Monument, Olvera Street, and Chinatown:** The parkway's southern end is in downtown Los Angeles. Before starting your drive, take time to explore El Pueblo de Los Angeles Historic Monument, where the city was born in 1781. Among the more than two dozen historic adobes and other structures is the oldest surviving house in L.A. Don't miss Olvera Street, a festive pedestrian-only Hispanic marketplace and dining area. Nearby is Chinatown, another fascinating ethnic neighborhood to explore.

**Elysian Park:** Now follow the parkway north, soon passing Dodger Stadium (home of the L.A. Dodgers baseball team) located near 600-acre Elysian Park, the oldest public park in L.A., filled with hiking trails, scenic vistas, and picnic grounds.

**Los Angeles River Center and Gardens:** A bit farther north is the Los Angeles River Center and Gardens, situated at the confluence of the Los Angeles River and the Arroyo Seco. Along with landscaped courtyards and river gardens, there's a bicycle "staging area" where cyclists can handle vehicle maintenance and rest or picnic along several area bike routes.

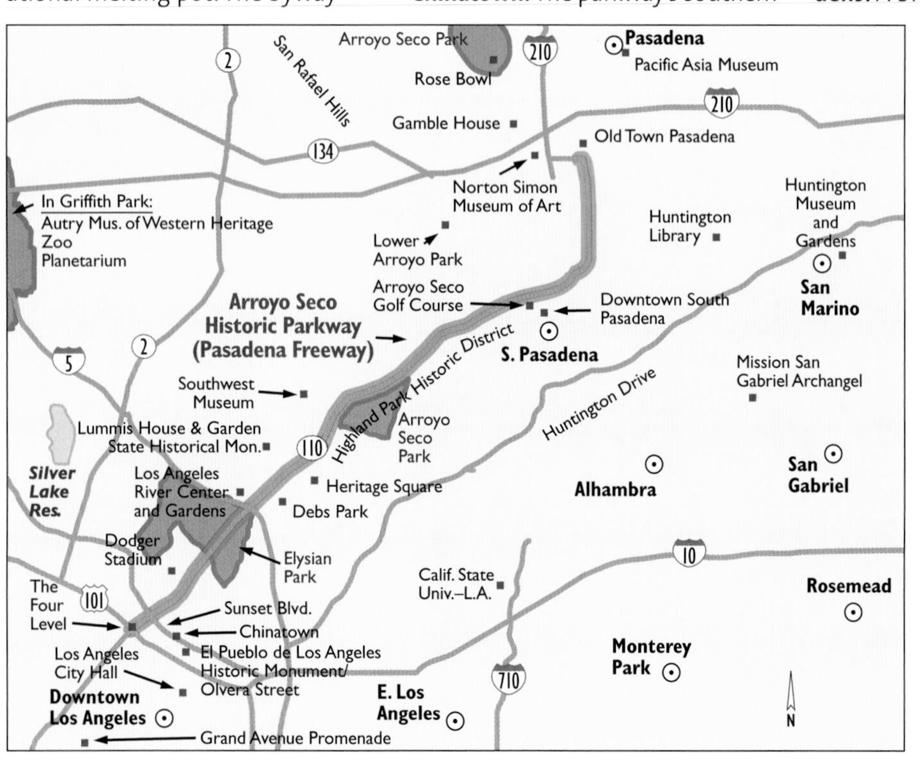


**Lummis House and Garden State Historical Monument:** Just beyond is the Lummis House and Garden State Historical Monument (El Alisal). This was the residence of Charles Lummis, father of the Arroyo Seco cultural movement of the early 20th century. The home, which is built of arroyo rock, includes original furnishings and native gardens.

**Highland Park Historic District:** Prominently visible from the parkway is the Southwest Museum, L.A.'s first museum (dating from 1907), perched in the hills above the arroyo. It's a treasure trove of Native American artifacts, collected by Charles Lummis throughout the Southwest. It's located in the Highland Park Historic District, which is rich in early 20th-century Craftsman-style architecture.

**Pasadena:** When reaching Pasadena, you'll have your choice of several outstanding attractions to tour. Old Town Pasadena, the historic core of the city, is located on Colorado Boulevard between Pasadena Avenue and the Arroyo Parkway. The Gamble House on Westmoreland Place is a landmark example of the Craftsman architectural style and is open for tours. Among Pasadena's premier museums are the Norton Simon Museum of Art; the Pacific Asia Museum; and, in adjacent San Marino, the Huntington Museum and Gardens, a repository of invaluable artworks, manuscripts, and exotic flora from around the world. Pasadena is also the site of the Rose Bowl, home of UCLA Bruins football and of the annual New Year's Day Rose Bowl game.

# Big Sur Coast Highway (Route 1)

*With soaring redwoods, windswept cypresses, plunging waterfalls, fog-shrouded cliffs, and barking sea lions, this highway inspires awe and wonder as it winds along the California coast high above the crashing Pacific.*

Route 1 from Carmel south to the San Luis Obispo County line follows some of he most spectacular and highly cenic shoreline found along California's coast. Views include ugged canyons and steep sea liffs, granite shorelines, sea lions nd other marine life, windswept ypress trees, and majestic red-vood forests.

## ntrinsic Qualities

**Cultural:** The Big Sur is a great example of an area whose culture s largely shaped by the region's geography. The awe-inspiring sce-nic beauty of the Big Sur has lured nd inspired countless artists, uthors, and poets.

The Carmel area and the Sali-nas Valley, less rugged but no less cenic or inspiring, have also had vital role to play in the area's culture. The area has been home to many artists, none more famous han John Steinbeck, whose novels vividly describe life in the fertile Salinas Valley.

**Historical:** Written histories regarding the region now known as the Big Sur began to appear in the mid-1500s, when a Portuguese ship passed by the area's coastline. New groups of European explorers approached the area throughout the late 1500s and early 1600s, many anchoring for a time in Monterey Bay. However, it wasn't until 1770 that the first perma-nent settlement was established, when a Spanish group started a mission in Carmel. The Spaniards first called the area south of the Carmel settlement *El Pais Grande del Sur*, or "the Big Country of the South." These same Spanish settlers were quick to introduce themselves and their culture to the area natives, who had lived in the region for centuries.

Before the Europeans arrived at the Big Sur, the Esselen Indians had thrived in the area as hunters and gathers. By the early 18th century, other Spanish missions followed the Carmel Mission. In the late 1700s, the Spanish missionaries and soldiers forced many of the Esselen and other native peoples to leave their villages and move into the missions. Smallpox, cholera, and other European diseases from foreign settlers almost completely wiped out the Esselen people. Those who were left mixed with other natives in the missions so that they ceased to maintain a separate existence. As a result, very little is known today about Esselen people's way of life.

Until the late 1800s, a small, rough trail served as the best overland route to Monterey from the Big Sur. Eventually, the trail widened into a road of sorts, which was still frequently lost in landslides. This widening allowed the journey to Monterey to be made in just 11 hours, as opposed to the three or four days it had taken previously. After many years of difficult passage over poor roads between the Big Sur and the rest of central California, Route 1 was completed in 1937. By its comple-tion, 15 years of labor and $9 mil-lion had been expended.

**Natural:** The allure of the Big Sur Coast Highway comes not just from the sea and the mountains but also from the convergence of the sea with the mountains. The ocean has helped to carve out the tantalizing craggy rock inlets along the corridor.

The byway enables you to experience the Pacific Ocean in a natural, prehistoric state. The endless blue horizon, as seen from the byway, is most often void of any floating vessels, unlike most other coastlines. Travelers are more likely, in fact, to witness a massive

*The Bixby Bridge, built in 1932, is an engineering marvel known for its environmental sensitivity and esthetically pleasing design.*

### Quick Facts

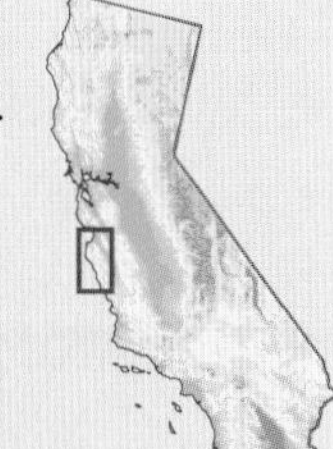

**Length:** 72 miles.

**Time to Allow:** Three to five hours.

**Considerations:** There are occasional mudslides dur-ing severe rainstorms. Also, fill your gas tank in Carmel before heading south or in San Simeon before heading north on Route 1 because you'll encounter few gas stations along the way. The road is narrow and curvy, and in some places it has narrow shoulders and sharp drop-offs to the ocean far below.

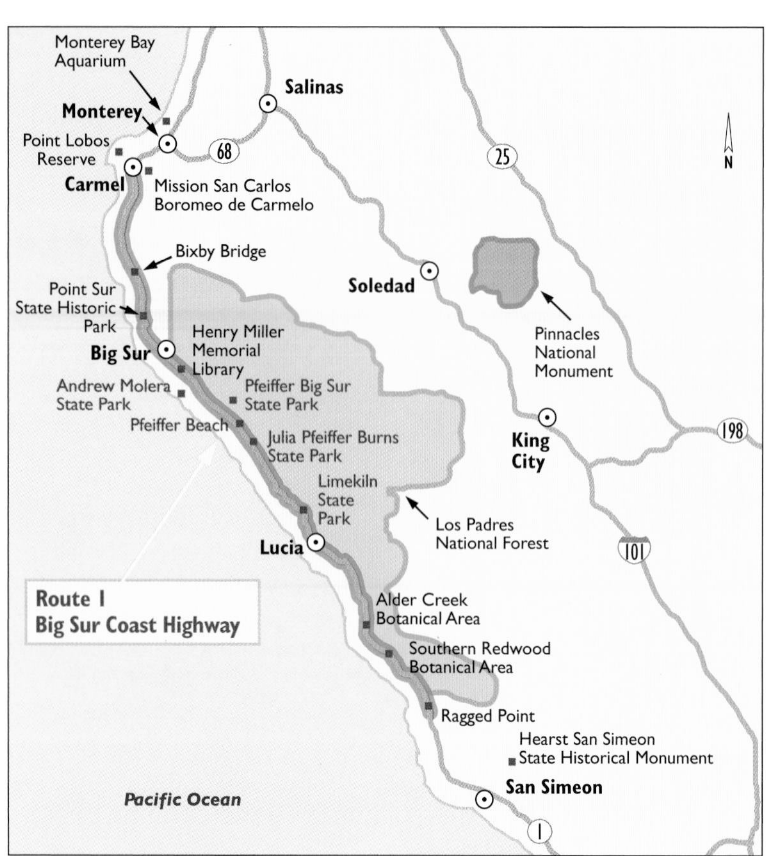


whale surfacing for air or some sea otters playing than to see a freighter waiting to dock.

The San Lucia coastal mountain, on the other side of the highway, is a paradise of cypress and redwood forests, waterfalls, and meadows full of colorful wildflowers, such as lupines and poppies. The mountains also host one of the byway's unique natural elements: the giant redwood tree. Redwood trees thrive in the specific climate along this area and are not native to any other region in the world. Many of the oldest trees are around 2,000 years old. The tallest redwoods have reached heights of 350 feet. Such heights require solid foundations, with many of the giant trees' diameters spanning 10 to 15 feet.

**Recreational:** The Big Sur's beaches offer a wide variety of recreational possibilities. Even during the summer, beaches are subject to generally cool weather. Sunny days are sporadic because a blanket of seasonal fog often hugs the coastline, dropping the temperature in the process. To be prepared, bring a pair of sturdy shoes—getting to the Big Sur's beaches requires at least a short hike.

Several state park and U.S. Forest Service beaches are open to the public year-round. These beaches are recommended due to easy access and breathtaking scenery.

**Scenic:** The Big Sur Coast Highway affords you fantastic views of one of the nation's most scenic coastlines. At certain points along the byway, the only way to get any closer to the Pacific is to get in it! Luckily, scenic overlooks are plentiful along the byway, providing you with breathtaking views from safe pull-offs.

If the vast blue waters of the Pacific aren't enough for you, direct your eyes inland, taking in the beautiful coastal hills and breathtaking mountains.

## Highlights

The Big Sur Coast Highway runs along Route 1 from northwest of San Simeon to Carmel.

**Ragged Point:** On a promontory 400 feet above the Pacific, Ragged Point has incredible ocean views; a waterfall; a steep trail to a secluded beach; and a restaurant, gas station, and motor inn complex.

**Lucia:** Northwest of Ragged Point is the tiny hamlet of Lucia. Lucia has an incredible vantage point looking out over the Pacific.

**Limekiln State Park:** Not far after Ragged Point, the byway enters Los Padres National Forest, traveling north to Limekiln State Park, which has campsites in the redwoods and wonderful coastal views.

**Julia Pfeiffer Burns State Park:** Julia Pfeiffer Burns State Park has trails through the redwoods and a short trail to a spectacular waterfall that plunges 80 feet into the Pacific.

**Pfeiffer Beach:** Secluded Pfeiffer Beach is one popular stop for those who can find it. Watch for paved and ungated but unmarked Sycamore Canyon Road, located on the western side of Route 1 one mile south of Pfeiffer Big Sur State Park. The road leads 2.5 miles to gloriously golden sand.

**Pfeiffer Big Sur State Park:** Pfeiffer Big Sur State Park makes a good central base for exploring the area. The park has a lodge and campgrounds in the redwoods, while hiking trails follow the Big Sur River to an inland waterfall.

**Andrew Molera State Park and Point Sur State Historic Park:** Next up is Andrew Molera State Park, the largest park along the Big Sur Coast, where a mile-long trail crosses rugged headlands to a stretch of wild beach. Just north is Point Sur State Historic Park, site of the historic Point Sur Light Station.

**Bixby Bridge:** The Bixby Bridge follows Point Sur. Built in 1932 and spanning a 100-foot-wide canyon, it's one of the ten-highest single-span bridges in the world at 260 feet above the sea.

**Carmel:** In addition to a picture-perfect beach and intriguing shops, the resort town of Carmel is known for its beautiful Spanish-style mission, founded in 1770 by Father Junípero Serra.

**Point Lobos Reserve:** Often called the "crown jewel" of the state park system, Point Lobos has rocky headlands to hike, hidden coves, and rich marine life, including sea otters and sea lions.

# DEATH VALLEY SCENIC BYWAY

*The surprising splendors of the desert—from spring wildflowers to towering cacti, "painted" rocks to windswept dunes—come alive on this fascinating drive through historic Death Valley National Park.*

Death Valley National Park contains the hottest, driest, lowest point in North merica. It has 3.3 million acres of pectacular desert scenery, intersting and rare desert wildlife, omplex geology, undisturbed vilderness, and sites of historical nd cultural interest.

Located in one of the most emote parts of California, travelrs from all over the world use the eath Valley Scenic Byway (Route 90) as the gateway to Death Valley. nternational visitors see Death 'alley as part of the grand tour of alifornia—more than 75 percent f the summer visitors in this area ome from abroad. Even scientists nd researchers come to study and xplore the park's unique resources.

## Intrinsic Qualities

**Archaeological:** Archaeologists have found traces of distinct prehistoric cultures in Death Valley National Park. The first known inhabitants of Death Valley lived there some 7,000 years ago and were known as the Nevares Spring Culture. After another 6,000 years and many climactic changes, a new group of people entered the valley. This group came to be known as the Desert Shoshone and has been in the valley ever since.

The Desert Shoshone were distinguished by their production of superior arrowheads as well as their pottery-making skills. Their ingenuity led to constructing pits for storing mesquite beans, which were later ground and processed for the seed. The Desert Shoshone moved about the Death Valley region, hunting sheep, deer, and rabbits when the animals were abundant. During other seasons, the people harvested plants and seeds. The Desert Shoshone had this wilderness to themselves until 1849, when emigrants from the east began to arrive.

**Historical:** A tale of the valley's history must include one brief but important period that started when some of the '49ers, who were heading for the California gold fields, took an ill-advised detour through Death Valley. This began the boom-and-bust era of Death Valley, a period that involved more bust than boom. Borax, the "white gold of the desert," was the only significant "gold" found in Death Valley.

Eventually, the prospectors lost hope of finding gold in the desert. Likewise, the miners eventually deserted their borax mines. In the 1870s, for example, Darwin was a thriving mining town. Now, the historical city has but a few residences, a post office, and a phone booth. Rhyolite, once the largest town in the Death Valley area during the mining boom, is now home to a train depot, a jail, a two-story schoolhouse, the ruins of a three-story bank building, and a house built completely of bottles. Skidoo was one of the last gold-mining camps in Death Valley. This ghost town is a marvel of mining engineering that existed from 1906 to 1922. Additionally, Twenty Mule Team Canyon displays a variety of old prospectors' tunnels.

*n Death Valley, the lowest elevation in the Western Hemisphere is contrasted with mountain idges rising from the valley.*

### Quick Facts

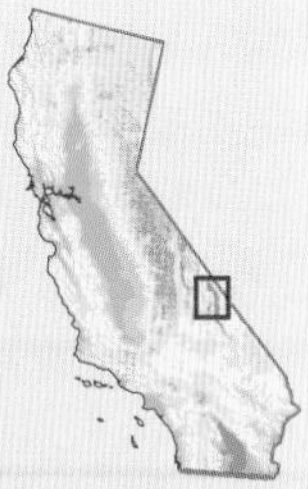

**Length:**
81 1/2 miles.

**Time to Allow:**
Three hours.

**Considerations:** The best times to drive this route are in the winter and spring, spring being the busiest. Be aware of extreme heat, lack of water, and occasional flash floods. Gas is available at Panamint Springs, Stovepipe Wells, and Furnace Creek. Access to Death Valley National Park can be limited by winter snowstorms when traveling from the west over the Sierra Nevada in California on Routes 108 and 120 and on Route 160 from Las Vegas to the east in Nevada. Death Valley National Park charges an entrance fee, but it is good for an entire week.

**Natural:** Death Valley Scenic Byway is one of the most uncommon and dramatic routes in the western United States. Death Valley is the nation's largest park unit outside of Alaska. Because of the faulting in Death Valley, the vertical rise from the lowest point to the top of Telescope Peak is one of the greatest (11,049 feet) in the United States. Traveling on Route 190 from the west end of the park from Towne Pass to some 282 feet below sea level (the lowest spot in North America), this trip is highlighted by rugged natural beauty. You're afforded 80-mile views that include bare mountain slopes towering above huge alluvial fans. Other highlights along the byway are salt-encrusted salinas created by evaporated water basins that accumulate salts, borates, and other minerals. Windswept sands across the valley floor form ever-changing patterns. Desert varnish, shiny black iron, and manganese oxide, which cover the cobbles, make an interesting mosaic of pavement.

With an average of $1^1/_2$ inches of rain a year and average high temperatures nearing 120 degrees Fahrenheit during the summer, this region is one of the driest and hottest environments in the Western Hemisphere. Passing from the lowest point to the highest summit, you traverse four major plant zones, each determined by climate and elevation. The diversity of plants along this drive ranges from Piñon pine and juniper in the upper elevations to the valley's mesquite, desert holly, and cacti. This complex ecosystem includes kangaroo rats, sidewinder rattlesnakes, burrowing owls, and bighorn sheep. Thousands of years of adaptation in the plant and animal species make this drive a fascinating experience.

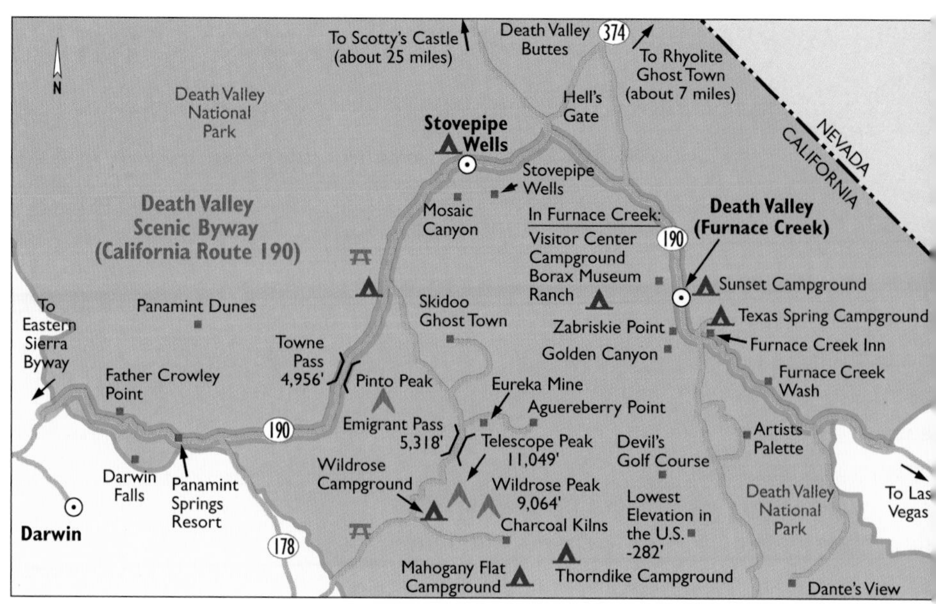


**Recreational:** One of the best ways to discover Death Valley National Park is to get out of the car and take a hike. Due to the extreme elevation changes and climate, however, many of the hikes within Death Valley may be too difficult for the average visitor, but several very easy to moderate hikes are accessible to just about everyone. When you do go for a hike, remember to drink two quarts of water. Sunglasses and a hat will help, too, because the sun often glares throughout the park.

**Scenic:** Death Valley Scenic Byway is a dynamic route. Death Valley National Park's scenic diversity includes deep rugged canyons, sand dunes, and, surprisingly, even fragile wetlands. The desert is also surrounded by high rising mountain ranges, adding dramatic contrast to the scenic variety.

Toward the western end of the byway, you climb to the pull-off for Father Crowley Point at the top of the Argus Mountain Range. The short drive to this observation point provides spectacular views overlooking the Panamint Valley and the complex geology of the Panamint Mountain Range. This observation point is the perfect location to view the setting sun on Telescope Peak. You can also peer down into Rainbow Canyon.

## Highlights

Consider taking this scenic tour of Death Valley, beginning in the early morning from the east.

**Death Valley National Park:** Enter Death Valley National Park on Route 190 about three miles northwest of Death Valley Junction.

**Furnace Creek Wash:** Traveling north along Route 190, you'll notice that you're following along the Furnace Creek Wash. There may or may not be any water, but watch for thunderstorms—water rises fast in this area!

**Furnace Creek:** When you stop at Zabriskie Point, about eight miles past the entrance, you'll enter the heart of Death Valley—Furnace Creek. This area is full of history and is a recommended base camp for visiting Death Valley. Stop at the Furnace Creek Visitor Center to orient yourself to the park.

**Stovepipe Wells:** After spending the heat of the day indoors, take an afternoon drive farther north along Route 190 to Harmony Borax Works and Salt Creek. Catch the sunset near the sand dunes, and then head back into Furnace Creek or on to Stovepipe Wells, where a hotel and campground are available.

**Charcoal Kilns or Scotty's Castle:** Take a day to explore the southern end of the park, including Devil's Golf Course, Artists Palette, and Golden Canyon. In the summer, take a detour through Emigrant Pass and on up the road to see the Charcoal Kilns. Parts of the roads to these sites are not paved, so a four-wheel-drive, high-clearance vehicle is recommended. Or head north to Scotty's Castle for a great tour.

# San Luis Obispo North Coast Byway (Route 1)

*Pastoral countryside, golden beaches, rocky coves, serene hills, clean air, the blue Pacific, even an American castle in the sky—this California coastal byway is an enchanted pathway for daydreamers and nature lovers.*

A continuation of the Big Sur Coast Highway.

Route 1 in north San Luis Obispo County winds past and through some of the inest views in the western United tates. The byway blends the rural eauty associated with much of oute 1 in the northern portion f the state with the convenience nd amenities found in the more eavily populated southern sec- ions of California.

## ntrinsic Qualities

**Historical:** The city of San Luis Obispo had its beginnings in the 772 founding of the Mission San uis Obispo de Tolosa by Father unípero Serra; it was named for he Franciscan saint known as ouis, Bishop of Toulouse (France). Built on a knoll beside a sparkling reek, the mission became the ub of a growing settlement, erving as the center of both he community and the county.

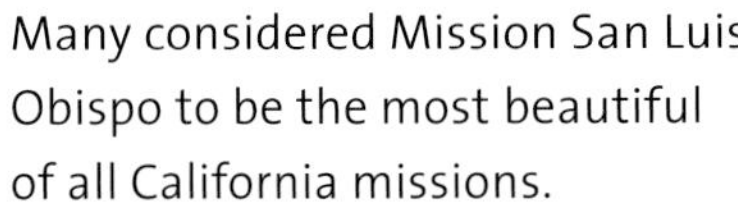

Many considered Mission San Luis Obispo to be the most beautiful of all California missions.

During the 1880s, the Southern Pacific Railroad built a railroad south from San Jose. After a five-year delay, the railroad came to San Luis Obispo in 1894. Construction of the railroad helped bring both industry and variety to the small community and changed the face of the city.

Hearst Castle, or the Hearst San Simeon State Historical Monument, is just off the byway. The castle, a living monument to the area's early 20th-century history, was built by publisher William Randolph Hearst, who entertained the rich and famous there. He intended it to be an elaborate getaway, complete with fine art and architecture. This historic treasure now provides a look into the windows of the past; it is one of the most heavily visited facilities in the California State Park System.

**Natural:** The San Luis Obispo North Coast Byway's prominent resource is the ocean, including its sea life and nationally recognized bays: Morro Bay and Morro Bay National Estuary. The bays and ocean along the route often afford travelers views of otters, seals, sea lions, and whales. Morro Bay National Estuary serves a critical environmental function of the Pacific Coast by supporting many species of migratory birds protected by international treaties.

*Bird-watching, golfing, sailing, and hiking are just some of the recreational opportunities you can enjoy at Morro Bay.*

One of the most remarkable recent activities along this stretch of Route 1 is the establishment of breeding colonies of elephant seals near Piedras Blancas Point. As you drive, elephant seal colonies are easily viewed from the byway. In addition, the California Department of Transportation, working closely with Hearst Ranch Corporation, has provided excellent vista points and informational kiosks about the seals, which are the largest of all pinnipeds and can exceed two tons in weight and ten feet in length. Like many marine mammals, elephant seals were hunted to near extinction in the 19th century, and, until recently, the huge seals lived in isolated areas far from humans. Then, in 1990, they started colonizing the unspoiled beaches and coves just south of Point Piedras Blancas.

The San Luis Obispo North Coast Byway also bisects lush valleys and rural farmland. The byway skirts the Morro Peaks and the Santa Lucia coastal mountain range and goes through the state's southernmost native Monterey pine forest. Equally important is the fertile land of the area, a significant natural resource for farming, which is one of the important industries of California.

**Recreational:** The San Luis Obispo corridor is blessed with pristine opportunities for outdoor recreation. Visitors may hike, cycle, surf, ride horses, watch birds, windsurf, hang glide, kayak, and fly kites, among many other activities. The excellent climate of the area allows for year-round recreation.

## Quick Facts

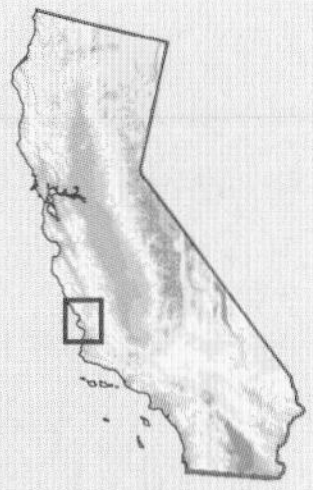

**Length:** 57 miles.

**Time to Allow:** Two hours or more.

**Considerations:** Temporary seasonal closures are expected each year north of San Luis Obispo County. These closures occur most often along the rugged Big Sur Coast during heavy rainfall months.

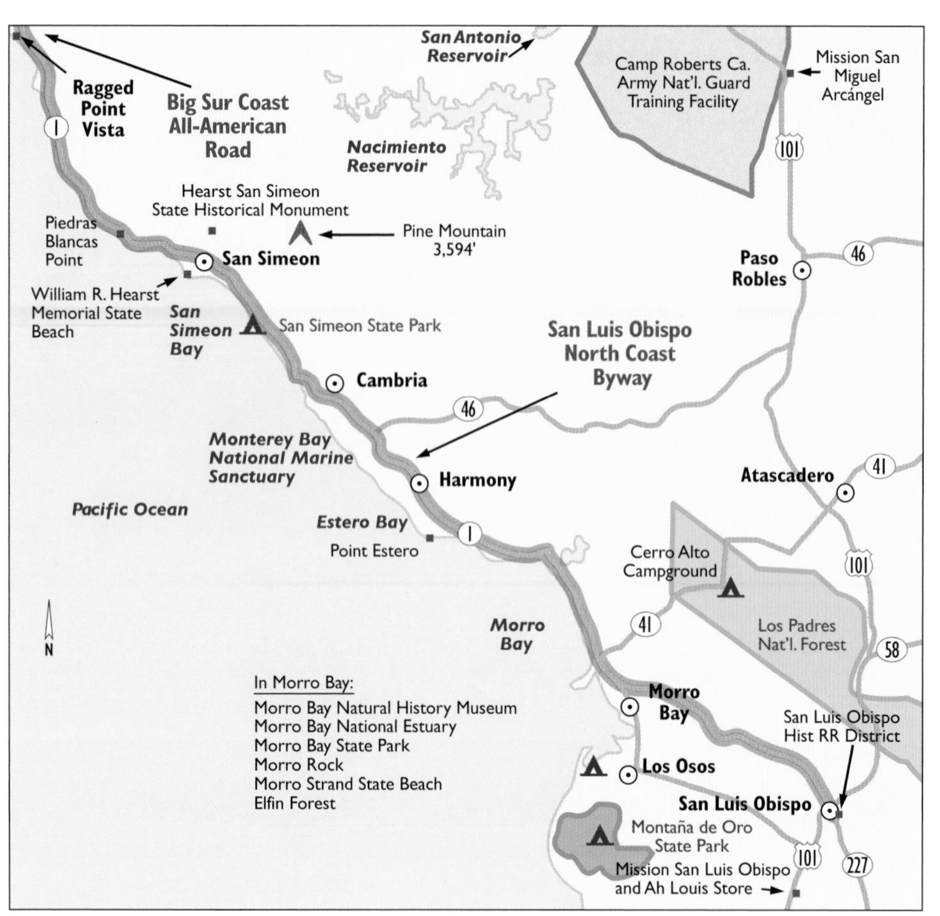


The byway's close proximity to countless cycling routes makes it a desirable destination for cyclists. The highway itself generally has generous shoulders and makes for a great bike ride.

Perhaps the best way to take in the immense scenic opportunities of the byway is to hike or ride horses right along the coastline. Coastal access adjacent to the southern boundary of the Monterey Bay National Marine Sanctuary, for example, gives you the opportunity to experience the magnificence of the Pacific Ocean.

The Harmony Coast contains unique opportunities to explore rocky coastal inlets by kayak. Just north of the California beach community of Cayucos on rural Route 1, rocky sections support some of the state's richest and most extensive tide pool habitat areas. Kayaking allows for in-depth exploration of these intriguing natural habitats.

**Scenic:** The harbors and bays found along the byway have undoubtedly served as inspiration for artistic seascape paintings. Morro Bay, a working fishing village and a protected harbor, is also home to the Morro Bay National Estuary and Morro Rock. Morro Rock, abruptly rising more than 500 feet above the bay, provides a dreamy backdrop for activities in the clean harbor. Other scenic bays along the route include Estero Bay, San Simeon Bay, and the southern portion of part of the Monterey Bay National Marine Sanctuary.

The spectacular shoreline of the San Luis Obispo North Coast Byway is backed by a series of coastal terraces that rise to the foothills and then to the high ridges of the Santa Lucia Range. The land is covered with open rangelands, including coastal prairie grasslands, oak savannas, pine forest meadows, and grassland-covered upland slopes. In spring, these areas are mantled in the lush green of new growth, followed by vibrant displays of orange California poppy, purple lupine, and other colorful native wildflowers. Later in the year, these same grasslands are toasted to a golden brown, providing rich contrast to the somber and dark evergreen forests around Cambria. Softly sculptured hills ring the city, with a series of steep, conical peaks, called *morros*. Morros are the remains of ancient volcanoes jutting up from the valley floor.

## Highlights

Begin your tour at the Mission San Luis Obispo de Tolosa, and end at Hearst San Simeon State Historical Monument.

**Mission San Luis Obispo de Tolosa and Ah Louis Store:** Starting at the southern end of the route in San Luis Obispo, visit the 1772 Mission San Luis Obispo de Tolosa, the fifth of California's historic Franciscan missions. Just up the street is the Ah Louis Store, a center of San Luis Obispo's 19th-century Chinese community.

**Montaña de Oro State Park:** Montaña de Oro State Park is a spectacular stretch of coastline and mountain parkland that includes beaches, tide pools, hiking trails, and camping. It's eight miles south of Morro Bay via Los Osos Valley Road.

**Morro Bay:** Morro Bay is home to an estuary and 576-foot dome-shape Morro Rock, known as the "Gibraltar of the Pacific." Drive to its base to watch the many seabirds that congregate there. Nearby is Morro Bay State Park, popular for boating, fishing, picnicking, and camping.

**Cambria:** Continuing north from Morro Bay on Route 1, consider stopping at the pretty little town of Cambria to shop, eat, or spend the night.

**Hearst San Simeon State Historical Monument:** Farther north on the route is Hearst San Simeon State Historical Monument, better known as Hearst Castle. The fabulous estate has 165 rooms and 127 acres of gardens, terraces, walkways, and pools. Several different tours are available.

# Tioga Road/Big Oak Flat Road 

*California's highest-elevation automobile pass slices through Yosemite National Park's dramatic Sierra Nevada high country, complete with vistas of granite peaks, pristine mountain lakes, wildflower-covered meadows, and lush evergreen forests.*

Tioga Road/Big Oak Flat Road offers one of the most spectacular passages over he Sierra Nevada, making it the ighest automobile pass in Caliornia, with an elevation change f more than one mile from west o east. Along the route, views nclude towering peaks, exquisite akes, vibrant meadows, and lush orests with giant sequoia groves. uolumne Meadows offers visiors a chance to see how ancient laciers created this serene and ugged landscape.

The byway provides motorists vith an opportunity to experience his scenery from a vehicle. For hiking enthusiasts, it offers some of the most beautiful High Sierra backcountry trails.

## Intrinsic Qualities

**Historical:** The area now encompassed by Yosemite National Park was once home to various nations of Native Americans. By the mid-1800s, when American explorers first caught sight of the area, the natives were primarily of Southern Miwok ancestry and called themselves the Ahwaneechee. The word *Yosemite* is in fact derived from the Ahwaneechee word for grizzly bear, *uzumati*. These earliest inhabitants of Yosemite soon found themselves at odds with the new settlers of the area. The Gold Rush of 1849 brought thousands of settlers to Yosemite, many crossing over the Sierra Nevada in search of their dreams.

Conflict between the natives and the new settlers followed, and eventually California authorized the organization of the Mariposa Battalion to gather the Ahwaneechee and relocate them to various other places in the state. Thus the Yosemite valley opened for tourism, which today brings more than three million visitors annually.

The many new visitors to the beautiful area did not come without impact, so citizens began a campaign to preserve the area. On June 30, 1864, President Abraham Lincoln signed a bill granting Yosemite Valley and the Mariposa Grove of Giant Sequoias to the state of California as an inalienable public trust. This marked the first time in history that the federal government set aside scenic lands simply to protect them and to allow for their enjoyment by all people. This act also paved the way for the establishment of the nation's first national park, Yellowstone, in 1872. Later, a concerned and energetic conservationist, John Muir, brought about the creation of Yosemite National Park on October 1, 1890.

**Natural:** The Tioga Road crosses right through the middle of an area known worldwide for its unique natural features. Yosemite National Park includes three major natural features: forested mountains and bald granite domes, mountain meadows, and Earth's largest living thing—the giant sequoia tree. Two hundred miles of roads help travelers enjoy all these features, whether by car or by the free shuttle buses

### Quick Facts

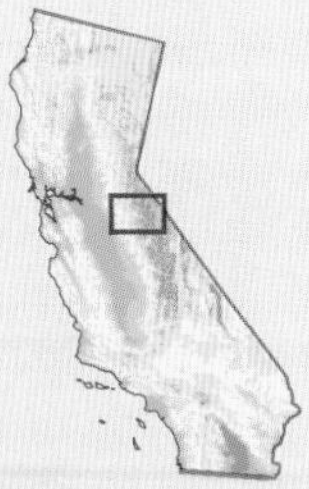

**Length:** 64 miles.

**Time to Allow:** Three hours.

**Considerations:** Tioga Road is closed during the winter from Crane Flat Junction to Lee Vining due to snowfall. The maximum speed limit is 45 mph along the byway. You'll find limited fueling opportunities. Yosemite National Park charges an entrance fee.

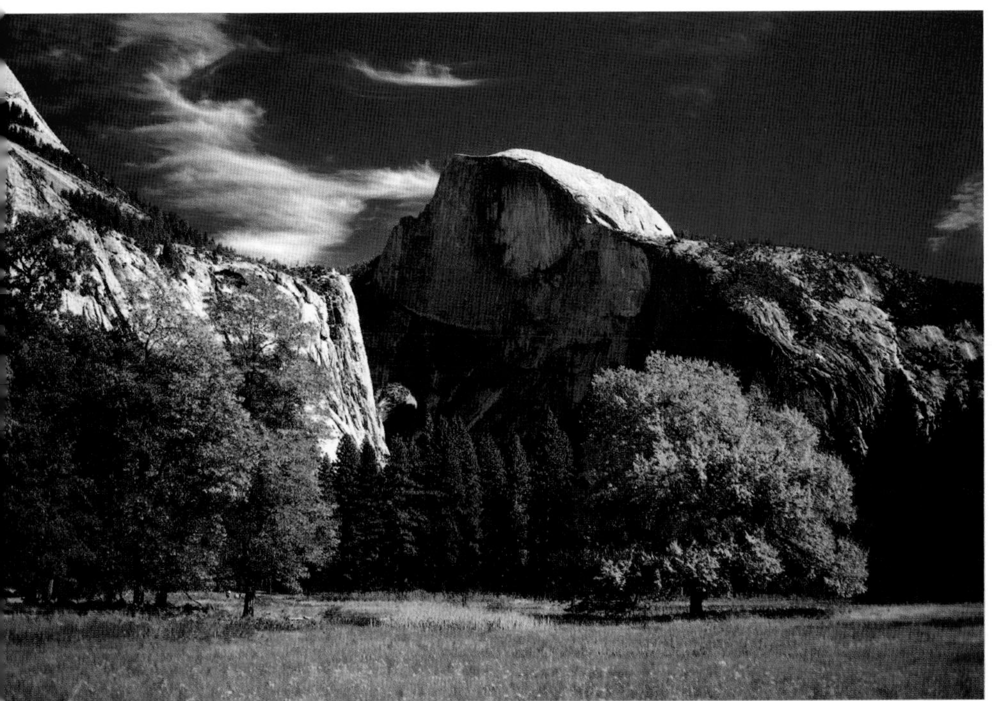

*The missing half of Half Dome in Yosemite National Park is assumed to have been sheered off during the Ice Age when glaciers passed through the area.*

offered in some areas. To get to know the real Yosemite, however, you must leave your car and take a few steps on a trail.

The mountains and granite domes of the Sierra Nevada began to take shape about 500 million years ago, when the region lay beneath an ancient sea. The seabed consisted of thick layers of sediment, which eventually were folded, twisted, and thrust above sea level. At the same time, molten rock welled up from the earth and slowly cooled beneath the layers of sediment, forming granite. Over millions of years, erosion wore away most of the overlying rock, exposing the granite. While this continued, water and then glaciers shaped and carved the face of Yosemite, leaving massive peaks and bare granite domes. Today, the park ranges from 2,000 feet to more than 13,000 feet above sea level.

The meadows of Yosemite are natural wonders in their own right. They are the most diverse parts of Yosemite's ecosystem, providing food and shelter for nearly all the wildlife living in the park. In the summer, the meadows and lakes are busy with life, as the plants and animals take advantage of the short warm season to grow, reproduce, and store food. The meadows are also unique because they are immense fields of bliss recessed and secluded in the middle of towering granite mountains. The more popular and accessible meadows are found in Yosemite Valley, Tuolumne Meadows, and Wawona. The middle and upper elevations of the park also contain secluded, perfect mountain meadows.

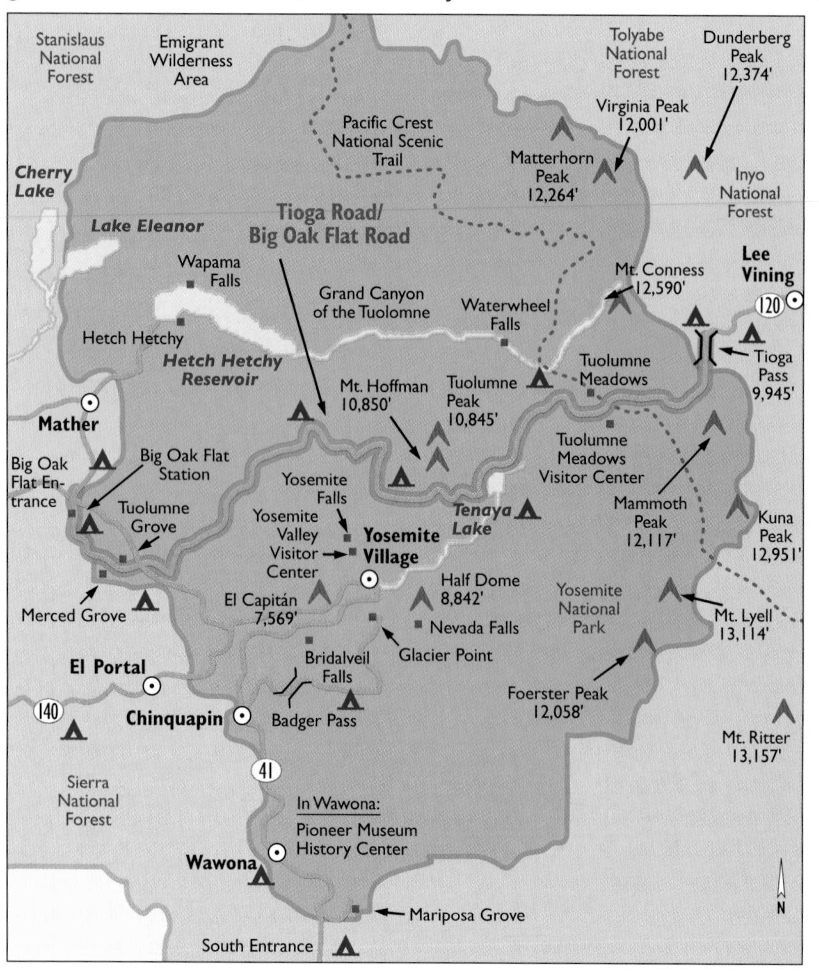


The mighty sequoia is the largest living thing on Earth. Yosemite is one of the few locations where the sequoias can be found, growing in any of three sequoia groves. Mariposa Grove of Giant Sequoias, 35 miles south of Yosemite Valley, is the largest of the groves. The oldest of the sequoia trees have been dated at more than 2,700 years old. The greatest of the trees have trunk diameters of more than 30 feet! Although the more slender redwood trees along California's coast surpass the sequoia in height, the much more robust sequoia is no shorty, with the highest measuring more than 300 feet tall.

**Recreational:** For more than a century, Yosemite National Park has been a premier destination for recreation. Its unique natural qualities and breathtaking scenery provide the perfect backdrop for outdoor recreational activities. Put hiking on top of your to-do list because just a bit of hiking can take you to places more rewarding than sites just off the highway.

The summer season, although short along the Sierra Nevada, offers the most accommodating environment for recreation. Hiking, fishing, camping, wildlife viewing, mountain and rock climbing, backpacking, and photography are some activities available in the park. Yosemite's wilderness presents experiences for both seasoned hikers and novices. About 800 miles of trails offer a variety of climate, elevation, and spectacular scenery.

In the winter, Yosemite's high country is a serene, white wonderland. The land is covered by deep, undisturbed snow, creating a landscape far different from the summer's. The winter months in Yosemite are seeing increased numbers of mountaineering activities. Meanwhile, cross-country skiing and snowshoeing have grown in popularity and opened up a new world for backpackers. Whether you visit in the winter or summer, Yosemite National Park offers an unparalleled chance to get away from it all.

**Scenic:** The Tioga Road traverses an area in which the most memorable features are remembered not only for their superb natural beauty but also for their unmatched size. Massive granite domes and cliffs take your breath away. Sequoia trees have branches that are larger than the largest of other tree species, while the park's famous waterfalls are remembered for their size and spectacle. For ages, Yosemite has lured and inspired painters, photographers, and writers. Yet most find that no work of art can adequately provide the sense of amazement and serenity granted to Yosemite's visitors.

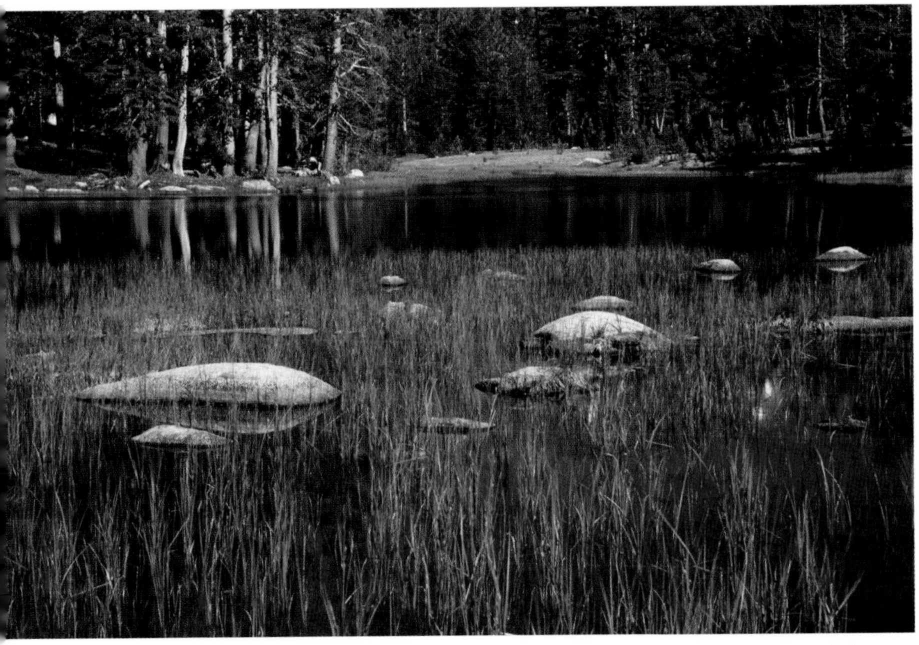

*'isitors see tall grass in up-close views of the wetlands of Tuolumne Meadows. Beyond this )hoto are magnificent vistas of the mountains in the distance.*

Spring provides the best time o see Yosemite's waterfalls, as he spring thaw brings with it an bundance of runoff water to fall rom cliffs and peaks. Peak runoff ypically occurs in May or June, vith some waterfalls (including 'osemite Falls) often dwindling o only a trickle or even becoming ompletely dry by August. Yosemite alls are the highest in the park at ,425 feet and are the fifth-highest alls in the world. From here, you an walk to Lower Yosemite Fall 320 feet) in just a few minutes. A nike to the top of Upper Yosemte Fall (1,430 feet) is a strenuous, all-day hike. Other famous falls nclude the Bridalveil Falls (620 feet), Nevada Falls (594 feet), Ribbon Falls (1,612 feet), Staircase Falls (1,300 feet), and Horsetail Falls (1,000 feet). Horsetail Falls, on the east side of El Capitán, is famous for appearing to be on fire when it reflects the orange glow of sunset in mid-February.

The Tioga Road passes through an area of rugged mountain scenery mixed with sublime mountain meadows. The road continues through an area featuring sparkling mountain lakes; bare granite domes; and lofty, forested mountain peaks. Some of the best views are available on the many scenic overlooks along the road, while hiking is sometimes necessary to view that perfect mountainscape.

## Highlights

Consider taking this tour of Yosemite National Park, beginning on the east end by ascending the Tioga Pass and entering the park.

**Tuolumne Meadows:** Enjoy the drive as you approach Tuolumne Meadows. Expect to spend several hours learning and exploring through tours and tram rides. You can also take advantage of the concessions offered by the park.

**Tenaya Lake:** Fifteen to twenty miles past Tuolumne Meadows, look to the south and notice Tenaya Lake. Look up to the north, and you see the towering peaks of Mount Hoffmann and Tuolumne Peak. One of these peaks is just five feet shorter than the other; can you tell which one is which? Continue along the Tioga Road throughout most of the park, a fantastic drive.

**Tuolumne and Merced Groves:** As you approach the junction of the Tioga and Big Oak Flat roads, chances are you'll want to get out and enjoy the sights. The Junction at Crane Flat is a good stopping place. To the north is Tuolumne Grove, a short hike onto a pretty grove of sequoia trees with a self-guided nature trail. A little down the road and to the south is Merced Grove. The trail into Merced is more difficult than at Tuolumne but just as enjoyable.

**Big Oak Flat Station:** As you near the end of the byway at the Big Oak Flat Station, be sure to stop and gather information about Yosemite. As you exit the park, you may wish to turn to the north and take a side trip up to Hetch Hetchy Reservoir. This is an especially great idea if you like the outdoors and backcountry trails. Fishing is available at the reservoir.

**Yosemite Valley:** After a visit to the reservoir, turn back toward Big Oak Flat Road and head down into the Yosemite Valley, about 40 miles to the south. Stop at the visitor center for up-to-date information about activities and sights, including the famous Half Dome, El Capitán, and Bridalveil Falls. Hotels and restaurants are plentiful here, which makes the area an excellent place to stay the night.

**Wawona:** Continue south along Highway 41 (Wawona Road) into Wawona. Although smaller than Yosemite Valley, plenty of amenities are still to be found here, including the Pioneer Museum History Center. If you visit in the summer, hop on the free shuttle bus at the Wawona store, which will take you seven miles away to the Mariposa Grove. The grove is famous for the "drive through trees," the giant sequoias. Although cars no longer drive through these trees, feel free to explore by foot or tram (for a fee). Toward the top of the grove, a small museum and gift shop help orient you.

**Sierra National Forest:** The tour ends as you head south and out the South Entrance toward Fish Camp and into the Sierra National Forest, which is a whole new treasure to discover.

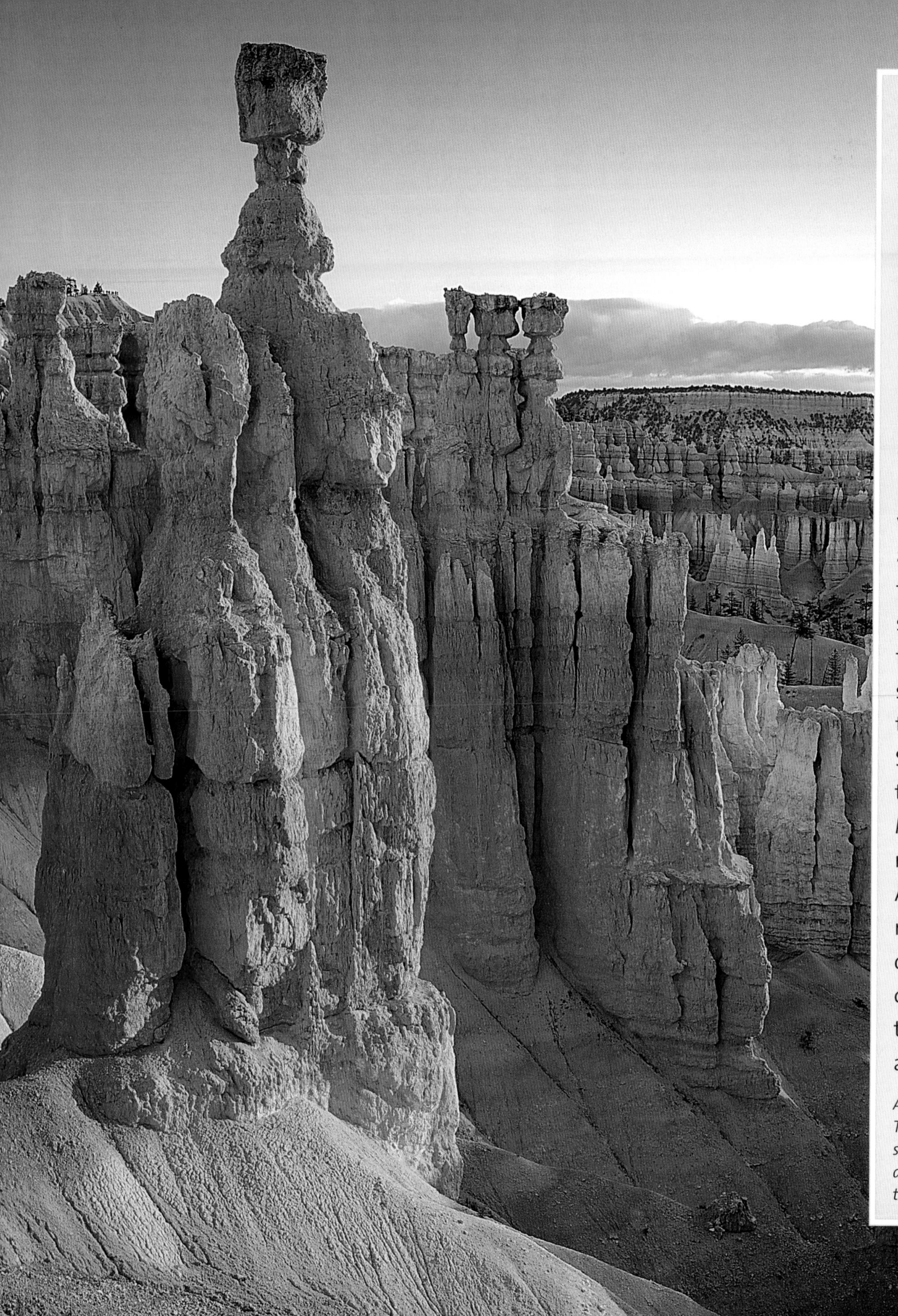

# MOUNTAIN

From Idaho's green forests south to Arizona's high deserts, the vast mountain region spans the Old West of America's history and imagination. The area's landscapes range from rugged to serene, but for drivers along its most scenic byways, one theme unites them all: the allure of wide-open spaces, punctuated by snowcapped mountain peaks and adorned by sparkling rivers, amazing rock formations, and a frontier spirit mirrored in the small towns and cities. Colorado's San Juan Skyway journeys to the top of the world. New Mexico's Billy the Kid Trail rides through outlaw country. And Idaho's Pend Oreille Scenic Byway is a water-lover's dream. Enjoy the drives, but don't forget to stop and savor the views and diversions along the way.

*At Utah's Bryce Canyon, on A Journey Through Time Scenic Byway, erosion has shaped colorful limestones, sandstones, and mudstones into whimsical formations known as hoodoos.*

# Beartooth Highway 

*With the rugged peaks of the glacier-flanked Beartooth Range as a backdrop, this stunning highway travels through three national forests to Yellowstone National Park, luring vacationers year-round.*

Part of a multistate byway; it also runs through Wyoming.

From its beginning at the border of the Custer National Forest to its termi-us near the northeast entrance o Yellowstone National Park, he Beartooth Highway (U.S. 212) ffers travelers the ultimate high ountry experience. It travels hrough the Custer, Shoshone, nd Gallatin National Forests.

Since its completion in 1936, the ighway has provided millions of isitors with a rare opportunity o see the transition from a lush orest ecosystem to alpine tundra n the space of a few miles. The eartooth Range is one of the highest and most rugged areas in the lower 48 states, with 20 peaks higher than 12,000 feet in elevation. Glaciers are found on the north flank of nearly every mountain peak higher than 11,500 feet in this range.

*rooks Lake in Wyoming's Shoshone National Forest has fishing, campgrounds, railheads, and commanding views of the Absaroka Range.*

## Intrinsic Qualities

**Archaeological:** Archaeologists have found numerous small, limited-use camps here that offer isolated finds and resource extraction sites. Because of the specimens found in the camps, the location of the camps, and even the frequency of the camps, archaeologists believe the area was used for spiritual purposes rather than primarily for food (which was previously thought).

Even though Native Americans dwelt in various places throughout present-day Montana and Wyoming, archaeological evidence from the Beartooth Mountains is somewhat limited. The high elevation most likely restricted living there on a permanent basis. There is only a short time during the summer to hunt and gather plants specially adapted to high elevations before the cold returns. The rest of the year, deadly weather conditions contribute to making it a hostile environment. Coming here, rather than staying in the fertile plains in the low country, can mean only that the steep mountains held deep significance for Native Americans.

**Cultural:** The Beartooth Highway's most important cultural value is the chance to appreciate some of the activities that flourish in natural environments. After understanding the people's occupations and interests in this part of Montana and Wyoming, visitors often leave with a longing to return to the simple yet strenuous life found in this area.

Some of the locals' occupations include ranchers, lumberjacks, sports enthusiasts, and anglers.

### Quick Facts

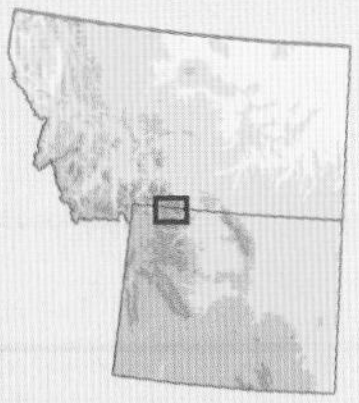

**Length:**
54 miles.

**Time to Allow:**
Three hours.

**Considerations:**
Driving from Red Lodge to Cooke City (east to west) in the morning and west to east in the afternoon reduces glare. The alpine climate is rigorous, and severe weather conditions can occur any month of the year. Summer temperatures range from the 70s on sunny days to below freezing during sudden snowstorms. Snow conditions might close sections of the drive.

These and other similar activities thrive today along the Beartooth Highway, continuing a long tradition of using the natural resources of these public lands.

**Historical:** The first recorded travel across the Beartooth Pass area occurred in 1882, when General Sheridan with a force of 129 soldiers and scouts (and 104 horses and 157 mules) pioneered and marked a route across the mountains from Cooke City to Billings. A year later, Van Dyke, a packer, modified the trail and located a route off the Beartooth Plateau into Rock Creek and Red Lodge. Van Dyke's trail was the only direct route between Red Lodge and

Cooke City until the Beartooth Highway was constructed in 1934 and 1935. Remnants of Van Dyke's trail are visible from the Rock Creek Overlook parking lot, appearing as a Z on the mountain.

Doctor Siegfriet and other visionaries from the Bearcreek and Red Lodge communities foresaw, in the early 1900s, the value of a scenic route over the mountains to connect to Yellowstone Park. These men spent many years promoting the construction of a road over the mountains and even began the construction of a road using hand tools and horse-drawn implements.

Other routes were surveyed from 1920 to 1925, and in 1931 President Herbert Hoover signed the Park Approach Act, which was the forerunner to the funding of the road now known as the Beartooth Highway.

**Natural:** A variety of theories exist on the formation of the Beartooth Mountains, but geologists generally agree that the mountains resulted from an uplifting of an Archean block of metamorphic rocks that were eroded, flooded with volcanic lava on the southwest corner, and covered with glaciers. Seventy million years of formation went into making this section of the Rocky Mountains.

The Palisades that stretch along the Beartooth Front were first sedimentary rocks deposited as flat-lying beds in an ancient sea. Thrust skyward, they have become conspicuous spires. Pilot and Index Peaks are the remainders of an extensive volcanic field that came into existence 50 million years ago.

Yellowstone National Park has been an active volcanic center for more than 15 million years.

Erosional forces are still at work. Glaciers have shaped the mountains into the range they comprise today. The glaciers edged their way down just 10,000 years ago. Younger rocks are the sources of coal exploited by the early settlers of Red Lodge.

The Stillwater Complex, a body of igneous magma formed along the northern edge of the mountain range 2.7 million years ago, is one of the rarest and least understood geologic occurrences in the world. It is the site of the only source of the platinum group of metals in the United States.

**Recreational:** Recreational opportunities are abundant in the area traversed by the Beartooth Highway. You can cross-country ski on the snowfields in June and July or hike across the broad plateaus and on Forest Service trails (some of which are National Recreation Trails). Camp, picnic, or fish for trout in the streams and lakes adjacent to the highway. View and photograph nature at its finest, including wildflowers and wildlife (moose, Rocky Mountain goats, mule deer, black bears, grizzly bears, marmots, and pikas). You can even visit a guest ranch, take a guided horseback trip from Cooke City, bicycle, and downhill ski on the headwalls.

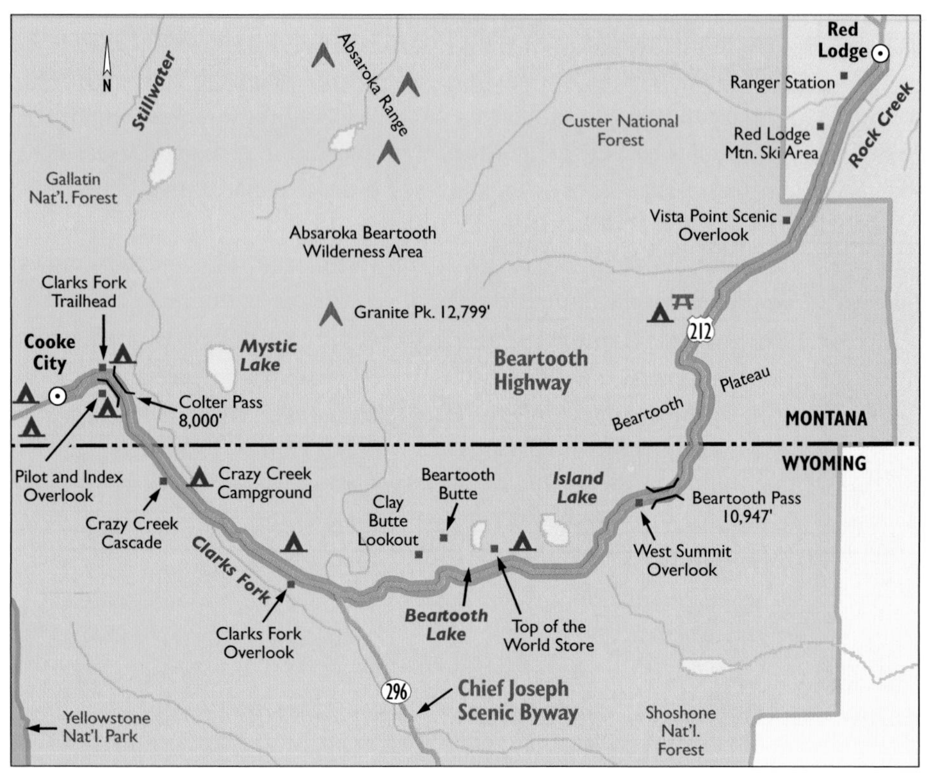


If you enjoy skiing, each summer in June and July, the Red Lodge International Ski Race Camp is conducted on the north side of the East Summit on the Twin Lakes Headwall. This camp is for aspiring Olympic-caliber skiers and provides a viewing opportunity for highway travelers.

Each summer, the Red Lodge Chamber of Commerce sponsors a one-day, unannounced "Top of the World Bar" in a snowbank at or near the West Summit and provides complimentary nonalcoholic beverages, horse rides, photos at the bar, and on occasion even a look at a live pink elephant.

**Scenic:** The spire known as the Bears Tooth at Beartooth Pass was carved in the shape of a large tooth by glacial ice gnawing inward and downward against a single high part of a rocky crest. Beartooth Butte is a remnant of sedimentary deposits that once covered the entire Beartooth Plateau. The red-stained rock outcrop near the top of Beartooth Butte was a stream channel some 375 million years ago, so fossils are found in abundance in the rocks of Beartooth Butte.

In these treeless areas, near or above timberline, vegetation is often small—a characteristic that is vital to the survival of the plants at this elevation. Wildflowers, many of which are as tiny as a quarter-inch across, create a carpet of color during the 45-day-or-shorter growing season.

In contrast, the common flowers found below the timberline in wet meadows are Indian paintbrush,

*Overlooks give interpretive information, as well as awe-inspiring views of the valley below in this beautiful mountainous area of Montana.*

monkeyflower, senecio, and buttercups, and in drier areas are lupine, beardtongue, arrowleaf balsamroot, and forget-me-nots. Mid-July is generally the optimum time for wildflower viewing.

Wildlife varies from the largest American land mammal, the moose, to the smallest land mammal, the shrew. Other animals commonly seen are mule deer, white-tail deer, marmots, elk, and pine squirrels. Birds include the golden eagle, raven, Clark's nutcracker, Steller's jay, robin, mountain bluebird, finch, hawk, and falcon. Watch for water ouzel darting in and out of streams.

The snowbanks often remain until August near Beartooth Pass, and remnants of some drifts may remain all summer. A pink color often appears on the snow later in the summer, which is caused by the decay of a microscopic plant that grows on the surface of the snowbank. When the plant dies, it turns red and colors the snow pink.

## Highlights

Consider using the following itinerary as you travel the Beartooth Scenic Byway.

**Red Lodge:** Red Lodge is an 1880s coal-mining and ranching town that is lined with turn-of-the-19th-century red brick storefronts and hotels that cater mainly to skiers and visitors to Yellowstone. Visit the Beartooth Nature Center, which exhibits native wildlife, at the north end of Red Lodge. The road follows Rock Creek into the mountains, winding through grassy hills that soon give way to heavily forested mountains. Rocky outcrops interrupt evergreen forests, and an occasional spire juts over the trees. About 13 miles from Red Lodge, the road climbs away from the creek, and suddenly the vista opens up toward the 1,800-foot cliffs that bend around the head of the valley in a tight semicircle.

**Vista Point Scenic Overlook:** After five miles of dramatic switchbacks, stop at the Vista Point Scenic Overlook. Here, at 9,200 feet, a short path leads to the tip of a promontory with phenomenal views across Rock Creek Canyon to the high rolling country of the Beartooth Plateau. As you continue on U.S. 212, the trees give out entirely, and you begin crossing a landscape of low, rounded hills covered with grasses, sedges, and lavish wildflowers in summer. Soon, the road cuts back to the rim of the canyon, and from the narrow turnouts, you can see a chain of glacial lakes 1,000 feet below. Even in July, enough snow accumulates against the headwall here to draw skiers.

**Beartooth Plateau:** As you travel farther on the byway from the north on U.S. 212, the Beartooth Plateau looms over the surrounding prairie foothills as a hulking mass of black, rounded mountains.

**Absaroka Range:** As you pass the ski lift, the Absaroka Range breaks over the western horizon in a row of jagged volcanic peaks. Wildflower meadows lead to the west summit of Beartooth Pass, at an exalted 10,947 feet. From the pass, you descend to a forest of lodgepole and whitebark pines toward 10,514-foot Beartooth Butte. Soon, you pass Beartooth Lake.

**Clay Butte Lookout:** In another mile, follow the gravel road to Clay Butte Lookout, a fire tower with a smashing view of some of Montana's highest mountains.

**Crazy Creek Campground:** Continue 5½ miles to an unmarked bridge over Lake Creek, and take the short path back to a powerful waterfall thundering through a narrow chasm. A completely different sort of cascade fans out over a broad ram of granite in the trees above Crazy Creek Campground, 2½ miles farther.

**Pilot and Index Overlook:** At the Pilot and Index Overlook, you're looking at the northern edge of the Absaroka Range, an eroded mass of lava, ash, and mudflows that began forming 50 million years ago.

**Cooke City:** From here, the road follows the Clarks Fork River through what is left of a centuries-old forest. Unfortunately, much of this forest fell victim to the great Yellowstone fires of 1988. Soon, the road passes through the tiny tourist crossroads of Cooke City, begun as a 19th-century mining camp. Four miles beyond, the drive ends at the northeast entrance to Yellowstone National Park.

# Northwest Passage Scenic Byway

*In the spirit of Lewis, Clark, and Sacagawea, this modern-day Northwest Passage follows the historic route of the Nez Perce Indians through canyons, valleys, and evergreen forests, past wild rivers and Native American cultural sites.*

Follow the footsteps of Meriwether Lewis and William Clark as they searched for the Northwest Passage—a link between the Missouri River and the Columbia River through the unexplored Rocky Mountains. Lewis and Clark's arduous journey proved that no easy route existed; however, they were led by Sacagawea to the trail through the mountains that had been used by generations of Nez Perce Indians. Along this byway, you will see numerous Nez Perce cultural sites and Lewis and Clark campsites.

## Intrinsic Qualities

**Archaeological:** At Big Eddy, evidence of early native occupation has been discovered. In Eimers Park, the remains of mammoths and an extinct species of bison were discovered at the bottom of Tolo Lake in 1994. During the excavation, archaeologists determined that the bones exhumed were only a fraction of what is actually at the bottom of Tolo Lake.

**Cultural:** Although a conglomeration of cultures and people make up the Northwest Passage, none of the cultures has preserved its heritage like the Nez Perce. Agriculture and industry fostered by the coming of homesteaders and gold miners exist side by side with the customs of the Nez Perce. Experience one of their powwows, or see the Nez Perce National Historic Park, where local arts and crafts are displayed.

**Historical:** Before the Northwest Passage became a nationally recognized corridor, the route was home to the Nez Perce, and it remains their home even today. For thousands of years, this native culture built villages and camps along the Clearwater River. The Northwest Passage was a main route for the Nez Perce as they traveled through the mountains and forests of what is now northern Idaho. The society of the Nez Perce met the society of European culture when Lewis and Clark traveled through the area in 1805 and 1806.

After the coming of the Lewis and Clark Expedition, new visitors wanted to do more than explore. Trappers, missionaries, and miners soon followed, and they interacted with the Nez Perce. For a time, people gathered in the area in hopes of discovering gold. The mining districts from this period in history eventually became the towns that are now on the byway.

In the 1870s, conflict mounted between the Nez Perce and the U.S. government. The battle ended with many of the Nez Perce dead; the rest were moved to reservations. Today, the byway travels along the Nez Perce Indian Reservation and passes Nez Perce National Historic Park in Spalding and Kamiah.

**Natural:** Although many of the valleys are now green agricultural fields, the mountainsides are covered in trees, and the sights and smells of the forest still have an overwhelming presence on the byway. Canyons and valleys appear along the byway to display the varied topography of the area. Rocks exposed along the byway are part of basalt lava flows from the

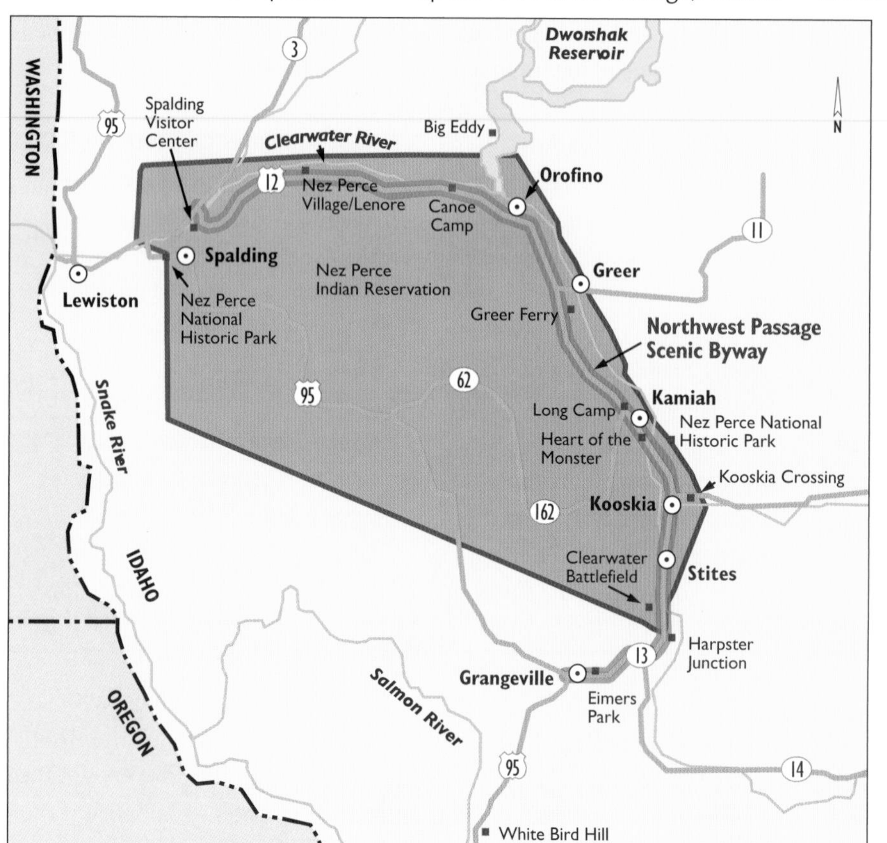


### Quick facts

**Length:** 90 miles.

**Time to Allow:** Three hours to three days.

**Considerations:** U.S. 12 above Kooskia is a winding, two-lane road with occasional passing lanes and slow vehicle turnouts.

Columbia Plateau that formed millions of years ago.

In addition to the scenery, wildlife also thrives here. The rivers are filled with fish, such as steelhead trout and Chinook salmon, and the forests are home to deer, elk, and other species. The variety of tree and plant life that grows along the byway creates a habitat for all these creatures.

**Recreational:** If you like water, you'll love that this road is surrounded by rivers. Along the byway, travelers can hardly escape the allure of the Clearwater River and its forks. Nearby, you will also find the Snake and Salmon rivers. And whether you choose to enjoy what's in the water or the water itself, you won't be disappointed. Chinook salmon swim in the waters, and fly-fishing for steelhead trout is one reason people return to the Northwest Passage. White-water rafting on one of the byway rivers is also irresistible.

If you get enough of the water, a walk in the woods may entice you. Many travelers take trails through mountains for the sweeping vistas they can enjoy along the way. National forests, wilderness areas, and even state parks give you the opportunity to find trails and go exploring.

**Scenic:** Four different landscapes can be found on the Northwest Passage: open canyon, closed canyon, valleys, and panoramic views. From Spalding to Orofino, enjoy the sights of an open canyon, where the water moves along the canyon's flat bottom between sloping hills. From the hillsides, you will see panoramic views of the river and surrounding land. Near Orofino and Harpster, a closed canyon dominates the landscape with steep canyon walls and dense forests of ponderosa pine and Douglas fir. The closed canyon is where the river moves faster around corners and down hills through the trees. Sometimes, a glimpse of the water is enough to make visitors want to stop and explore this beautiful area. In the closed canyon area, rocky outcroppings add to the rugged mountain atmosphere.

The valley landscape from Kamiah to Stites is characterized by a much calmer river and agricultural fields of green. From Harpster to Eimers, the view from the road is broad and sweeping. National forest lands are perennially beautiful, and the nearby pastoral fields change with the seasons, just as the Clearwater River does.

## Highlights

Begin your trip at the byway's western end at the town of Spalding.

**Nez Perce National Historic Park:** The Nez Perce National Historic Park in Spalding is located on U.S. 95, the best place to get an overview of the park. The Nez Perce National Historic Park is spread across 38 separate sites in four states; several of the sites lie along this byway. Learn the history of the Nez Perce people at one of the sites.

**Nez Perce Village:** The highway rest stop at Lenore contains interpretive signs about a Nez Perce village that used to stand here. The site was believed to have been occupied for some 8,000 years.

**Canoe Camp:** Four miles west of Orofino comes Canoe Camp, where Lewis and Clark built five dugout canoes in 1805 so they could continue their expedition down the rivers. It's a good spot for fishing or bird-watching.

**Big Eddy:** Northeast of there, on the Dworshak Reservoir, is Big Eddy, where you can picnic, swim, canoe, fish, hike, or camp.

**Long Camp:** One mile west of the town of Kamiah is the site of the Lewis and Clark Long Camp, part of the Nez Perce National Historic Park in Kamiah.

**Heart of the Monster:** In East Kamiah, two miles upstream from the Clearwater River bridge in Kamiah and the point at which the Nez Perce forded the river in 1877, is the Heart of the Monster, a rock formation and source of one of the Nez Perce nation's oldest legends. (The legend has it that a coyote saved the Nez Perce, as well as all animal life, from being swallowed by the monster.)

**Clearwater Battlefield:** Two miles south of Stites, watch for a pull-off on the west side of the road that marks the Clearwater Battlefield; the Nez Perce were pursued here in 1877. The site can be viewed from the highway.

**White Bird Hill:** The byway ends at Grangeville. South of Grangeville stands White Bird Hill, site of the famous battle of the Nez Perce wars. From the hill, view the wheat- and wildflower-filled prairie, as well as canyons and mountains.

*The first battle of the Nez Perce War was fought at White Bird Battlefield in the summer of 1877. The historic site is about 15 miles south of Grangeville.*

# Payette River Scenic Byway 

*As the pulsating white water of the Payette River rushes alongside, this byway cuts through pine forests and a picturesque valley dotted with resort towns and is framed by jagged mountain peaks.*

A drive along the Payette River Scenic Byway can be distracting for motorists. Rather than watching the road, they may be more inclined to watch the river as it crashes and tumbles its way over rocks and through the narrow river valley. Be sure to take advantage of the occasional pull-offs that allow you to view wilder parts of the river and treat your senses to the sights, sounds, smells, and rhythms of Idaho's famous white water.

Enjoy the scenic drive along the river through the Boise and Payette National Forests before arriving in the high, picturesque mountain valley dotted with the resort towns of Cascade, McCall, and New Meadows. Between the thunderous roll of the white water and the quiet serenity of the valley landscapes, you will find a thrilling adventure as you travel this mountain byway.

## Intrinsic Qualities

**Historical:** The people and events associated with this Idaho river stretch thousands of years back in time, creating generational ties between the past and present and between old-timers and new arrivals in Idaho. But most of the recorded history of this area started only a couple hundred years ago. Fur trappers of the early 1800s, working for Hudson's Bay Company, named the Payette River in honor of their comrade, Francois Payette, a French-Canadian who explored much of southwestern Idaho. After explorers mapped the territory, pioneers began to settle the area.

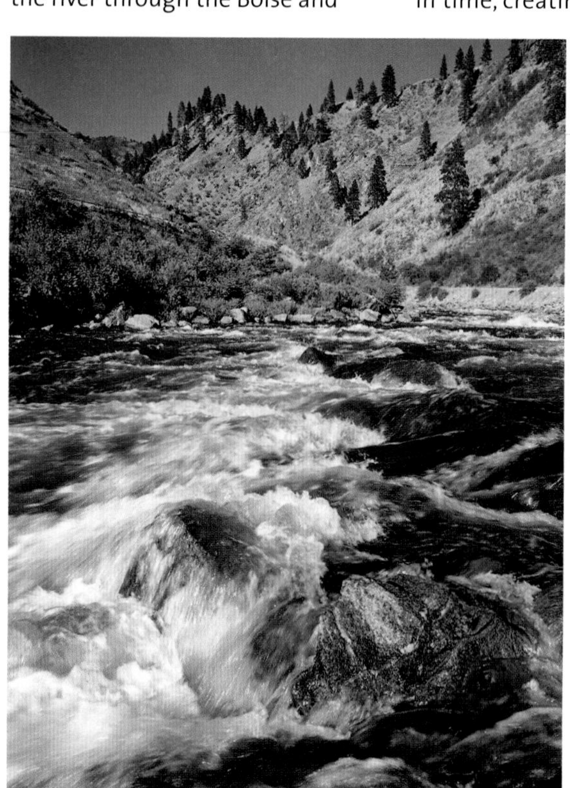

*Although serene in some places, the Payette River is known for its challenging and exhilarating white water.*

Later, people began the construction of a bridge now called the North Fork Bridge, although locals refer to it as the Rainbow Bridge because of its arch. It crosses the North Fork of the Payette River north of Smiths Ferry. Built in 1938, the bridge displays an open-spandrel design introduced to Idaho in the 1920s. Unlike other bridges of this type, the North Fork Bridge has not been altered over the years and is listed on the National Register of Historic Places.

**Natural:** Along the Payette River Scenic Byway rests the Idaho batholith, which offers a wealth of knowledge for geologists, as well as precious samples for gemologists. This unique geological feature covers much of the area and is primarily made up of granite. A lot of this batholith formation began millions of years ago, when magma pushed up Earth's crust and created many of the Idaho mountains. The magma eventually hardened below the surface and is now known as the batholith; through erosion, you can see the cooled rock today. Yet much has happened to the land in the last 12,000 years, making Idaho a geologically active place. Quite recently (relatively speaking), magma oozed out of Earth's crust in many places and has also shot out of volcanoes, warping the land and changing the environment.

> **Quick Facts**
>
> 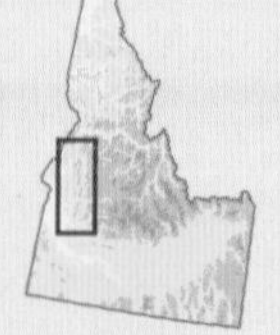
>
> **Length:** 112 miles.
>
> 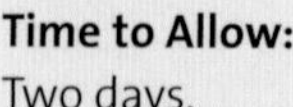
>
> **Time to Allow:** Two days.
>
> **Considerations:** The roadway is a narrow, winding, two-lane road with occasional passing lanes and slow vehicle turnouts.

Due to differences in the magma's cooling times and conditions the Idaho batholith contains many rare and valuable minerals, including the star garnet, jasper, and opal, making Idaho an ideal place for gemologists to collect gems. (Idaho is, after all, known as the Gem State.) The area also boasts many gold, silver, copper, and zinc veins.

This Idaho batholith created a unique landscape that interests sightseers, as well as geologists. There are mountains made out of solid granite and valleys carved out of this hard mineral. And because many areas near Payette River Scenic Byway are still quite new (geologically speaking), several rugged peaks have not bowed down to the effects of gravity. Furthermore, people can see the races of glaciers, as these, too, ave not yet disappeared.

**ecreational:** Of all the activities vailable here, white-water rafting anks perhaps as the most popular. eople find braving the rapids on he Payette River especially enjoy- ble. There is an abundance of vhite water along the byway, and afters rarely experience a boring noment. The rapids range in size, o rafters with less adventuresome pirits can usually avoid the more ommanding waves. As you raft n the Payette River, you'll witness parkling clean water and gor- eous, jagged peaks looming high bove the canyon.

Other than rafting, you can find umerous places to settle down or a relaxing picnic, enjoy world- lass trout fishing, and hike or bike the plentiful mountain trails. Many enjoy viewing wildlife in the vetlands around this area, which ttract bald eagles, ospreys, and Canada geese. During the cold vinter months, snowmobiling eplaces rafting as the most popu- ar activity, although skiing and nowshoeing follow close behind.

**cenic:** The scenic beauty found long the Payette River Scenic Byway is one of the road's strongest features, an aspect most people remember years after traveling here. Travelers are lulled by the flow of the Payette River.

Cascade Reservoir, with its calm serenity and abundant wildlife, can be glimpsed around the corners of the mountains and through the valley surrounding it. Visitors can pull off into access areas, watch the trout anglers, and gaze at bald eagles and ospreys flying overhead. Several picnic grounds also offer you clean mountain air and an opportunity to soak up the natural scenery. Nestled among mountains and trees is a spectacular view of Payette Lake.

Not all scenic features along the byway are natural, however; constructed features such as the Old Tate Barn are reminiscent of old-time America. The agricultural and Finnish culture of the area is preserved on Farm-to-Market Road and Elo Road. An old Finnish church, with a cemetery next to it, gives a glimpse of what the area was once like.

## Highlights

The byway's southern end begins in Boise, the Idaho state capital. Start here, and end in Ponderosa State Park.

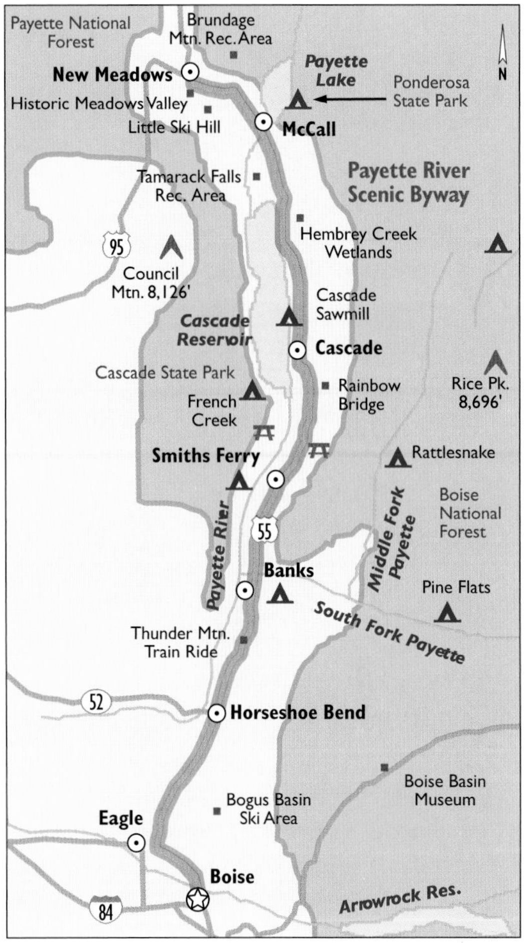


**Boise:** Boise is the home of the Basque Museum and Cultural Center, with exhibits about the local Basque community, the largest in the United States; the Idaho Botanical Gardens; the Idaho State Historical Museum (with exhibits on fur trading, ranching, mining, and other historical aspects of Idaho and the Pacific Northwest); and nearby 1,100-foot-tall Table Rock.

**Payette River:** Take Route 55 north to the old mining town of Horseshoe Bend on the Payette River. Between Horseshoe Bend and the town of Banks to the north, the Payette River offers white-water rapids of moderate difficulty, with several easy access points. There are also good swimming beaches south of Banks.

**Rainbow Bridge:** North of the town of Smiths Ferry is the Rainbow Bridge, built in 1938. Also called the North Fork Bridge, it forms a 410-foot span across the North Fork of the Payette.

**Cascade State Park:** Continue north to Cascade State Park on Cascade Reservoir, which is popular for fishing, boating, swimming, camping, and wildlife viewing.

**McCall:** Farther north is McCall. McCall was settled in the 1820s as a timber town, but it is now a resort town on the shore of Payette Lake. You can find good boating, sandy beaches, and mountain scenery here.

**Ponderosa State Park:** Near McCall, Ponderosa State Park occupies a peninsula that juts into Payette Lake. Besides scenic overlooks of the lake, the park has boating, swimming, hiking, biking, camping, and winter skiing amid ponderosa pines and Douglas firs.

### McCall

The city of McCall, built by early settlers, is well worth a visit. Much of the city's history is on display at the Central Idaho Cultural Center. This center occupies the original Southern Idaho Timber Protective Association (SITPA) buildings. The SITPA was a cooperative fire organization established in 1919 to oversee private, state, and federal lands. These buildings were constructed by troops stationed in McCall during the 1930s. Hollywood discovered McCall in 1938. The famous movie *Northwest Passage*, starring Robert Young and Spencer Tracy, was filmed on the shores of Payette Lake and on the North Fork of the Payette River.

# Pend Oreille Scenic Byway

*A water-lover's dream, this byway hugs the northern shores of Idaho's largest lake and follows a sparkling, splashing river to the Montana border—with fishing, hiking, bird-watching, and even moose-spotting along the way.*

Visit the Pend Oreille Scenic Byway, and discover a water-lover's paradise! The byway follows the shore of Lake Pend Oreille (pronounced OH-ray) for the majority of the length of the byway and then winds alongside the Clark Fork River to the Montana state line. You'll find yourself beneath towering mountains that are reflected in the many miles of water along the byway.

The area is largely undeveloped, ensuring that you will be treated to the serene outdoors of Idaho by viewing waterfowl, other species of wildlife, and a variety of plants. Be sure to take advantage of the many pull-offs along the road to experience an uninhibited view of this majestic area.



These days, there's never a dull moment with Lake Pend Oreille and the Clark Fork River nearby. You can go boating, fishing, sailing, canoeing, kayaking, and swimming in the lake, rivers, and streams that line the byway. If water sports aren't your thing, go camping, hiking, biking, horseback riding, or golfing. In the wintertime, hit the slopes at Schweitzer Mountain Ski Resort.

*Clark Fork River offers many opportunities to view wildlife, enjoy canoeing or kayaking, and simply rest and relax in this natural setting.*

## Quick Facts

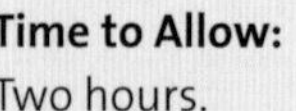

**Length:** 33 miles.

**Time to Allow:** Two hours.

**Considerations:** Idaho 200 is a two-lane road with no passing lanes. It can be icy during winter months, so drive with caution. Also remember that the Pend Oreille Scenic Byway and most of northern Idaho is in the Pacific time zone.

## Intrinsic Qualities

**Historical:** Lake Pend Oreille and the Clark Fork River have been important in the development of the area that is now the Pend Oreille Scenic Byway. Before humans had an impact on the environment, however, glacial Lake Missoula had a significant effect on the land. Subsequent glacial cycles caused cataclysmic flooding, which began in the area of Cabinet Gorge, near the Idaho–Montana border, and then spread across Oregon and Washington before reaching the Pacific Ocean. This tremendous phenomenon created many of the geological formations seen in the area today.

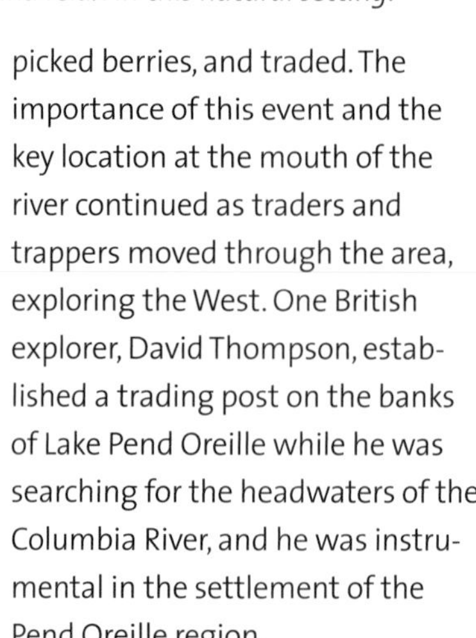

After the glacial ice abated, the land became habitable, and the native Kalispel people lived in the area. The Clark Fork River was an important aspect of their existence, and the Kalispels hosted an annual regional gathering at the mouth of the river. There, they hunted, fished, picked berries, and traded. The importance of this event and the key location at the mouth of the river continued as traders and trappers moved through the area, exploring the West. One British explorer, David Thompson, established a trading post on the banks of Lake Pend Oreille while he was searching for the headwaters of the Columbia River, and he was instrumental in the settlement of the Pend Oreille region.

As traffic through the West and Northwest continued to grow, new routes of transportation were needed. With the creation of the steamboat, the waterways in the area of the Pend Oreille Scenic Byway became connected, enabling people to travel efficiently from one place to another. When the Northern Pacific Railroad was being built in the Pend Oreille section, many structures, such as bridges, were built to span the many areas of water. The wooden bridge built to cross the Pack River was the longest structure in the entire transcontinental system.

**Recreational:** With unspoiled landscapes and clean country air, it is no wonder that Idaho is known for its many outdoor activities. Pend Oreille Scenic Byway is no exception, and with more than 100 miles of shoreline along Lake Pend Oreille, water recreational opportunities are never far away. Boating, fishing, sailing, and other water sports are all available along the byway. The water is clean and pure, and it draws visitors from around the world. In addition to the scenic and recreational Lake Pend Oreille, two rivers are accessible along the byway. The Clark Fork River stretches across two miles of delta and wetland; the river itself s a popular place to go fishing. The ack River does not create such a ast delta, but it provides wonderul opportunities for canoeing and ayaking. The byway is located in Bonner County, which accounts or 20 percent of the total surface vater in Idaho's 44 counties, and ollows either a lake or river for its ntire length.

Water sports may dominate he recreational scene, but a look oward the forests to the sides of the lake reveals an area rich in other recreational opportunities. A number of trails are accessible hrough the Kaniksu National Forest, affording you the chance to go hiking, biking, or horseback riding. Hunting, berry picking, and snowmobiling are additional activities hat you can enjoy.

The abundance of water along he byway makes this an ideal route to travel for bird-watching. The delta area at the confluence of the Clark Fork River provides prime opportunity to see different waterfowl up close in the marshes and wetlands. A variety of fish can also be found in the lake and rivers of the byway, and 20-plus-pound rainbow or Mackinaw trout can be caught during week-long fishing derbies that begin in May and end in November. You may also spot deer and moose all along the byway and near the water.

**Scenic:** With more than 100 miles of shoreline, Lake Pend Oreille dominates the area. Glassy water reflects the mountains, sunsets, and farming scenes, and the water draws wildlife to its shores. Crashing waterfalls and tranquil lake and river scenes await you along the byway.

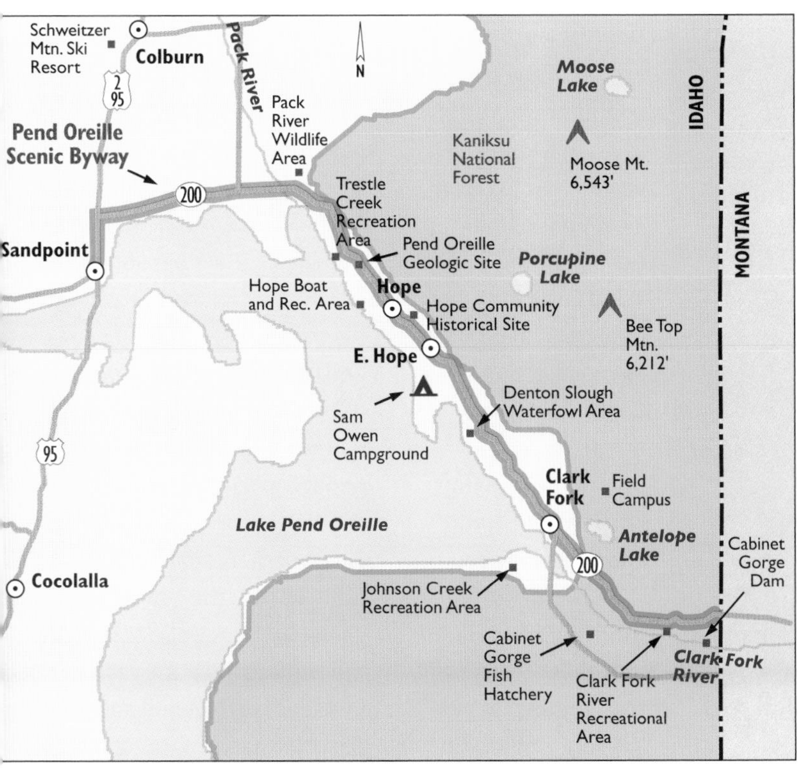


## Highlights

Start at the resort town of Sandpoint, and end at the Cabinet Gorge Dam.

**Sandpoint:** Sandpoint has a public beach with swimming and boat access to Lake Pend Oreille, as well as plenty of places to shop, eat, and stay.

**Schweitzer Mountain Ski Resort:** If it's winter, skiers can detour a short distance north from Sandpoint on Routes 2/95 to Schweitzer Mountain Ski Resort, Idaho's second largest, with six chairlifts. In summer, the chairlifts operate for scenic rides and to ferry hikers and mountain bikers up to the top.

**Lake Pend Oreille:** Head south and then go east on the Pend Oreille Scenic Byway, as the road hugs the northern shores of Lake Pend Oreille, Idaho's largest lake with more than 100 miles of shoreline. Pull-offs allow chances for boating, kayaking, fishing (for some of the world's largest trout), swimming, camping, and picnicking.

**Pack River Wildlife Area:** Next, go to the Pack River Wildlife Area, a river delta system that's a haven for waterfowl and other wildlife. (Watch for moose along the shores.) There's primitive access for canoes and kayaks here.

**Trestle Creek Recreation Area:** When the Trestle Creek Bridge crosses the Pack River, watch for the Trestle Creek Recreation Area, which provides open access to the lake and hiking trails. You might spot eagles in winter.

**Pend Oreille Geologic Site:** A turnout along the roadside marks the Pend Oreille Geologic Site, where there are panoramic views of the lake and its major islands.

**Hope:** The tiny town of Hope was the site of a settlement in 1809 by British explorer David Thompson, who built the first fur-trading post in the Pacific Northwest. Hope is also a boating and swimming access area, with boat ramps and docks on Lake Pend Oreille.

**Clark Fork River:** As soon as Lake Pend Oreille ends, the Clark Fork River begins. Consider doing some fishing, or bird-watch for blue herons, ospreys, swans, and grebes. The Johnson Creek Recreation Area, close to the Clark Fork River, and the Denton Slough Waterfowl Area, a bay near the river, are good spots.

**Clark Fork River Recreation Area:** The Clark Fork River Recreation Area offers river access for those who want to float down the peaceful Clark Fork River, as well as primitive campsites.

**Cabinet Gorge Dam:** The byway ends at the Idaho–Montana state line. Watch for the privately owned Cabinet Gorge Dam. Cabinet Gorge is the historic location of the face of the ice dam that created ancient glacial Lake Missoula. When the dam burst some 15,000 years ago, the rushing waters formed Lake Pend Oreille.

# Wyoming Centennial Scenic Byway

*Crossing the Continental Divide and a high mountain pass, the Wyoming Centennial Scenic Byway offers stunning mountain views, access to several national parks and forests, and chances to spot wildlife along the way.*

Wyoming Centennial Scenic Byway is one of the most beautiful drives in the West, passing through some of the continent's most wild and spectacular country. The landscape changes dramatically along the way, from high desert badlands to alpine conifer forests and sage-covered hills. The byway begins nearly 7,000 feet above sea level, then climbs even higher, crossing the Continental Divide at the 9,658-foot Togwotee Pass. Before it reaches the pass, the byway offers a series of stunning views, including the Upper Wind River Valley, two mountain ranges, and strikingly shaped cliffs and rock formations. The descent into Grand Teton National Park is equally dramatic, with wonderful views of the jagged-peaked Grand Teton range as the road plunges down into Jackson Hole Valley.

The route provides access not just to Grand Teton, but to Yellowstone National Park to the north and the Jackson resort area to the south. Recreational opportunities are available all along the way, including two national forests with campgrounds and hiking trails, rivers and lakes popular for fishing and boating, and, in winter, venues for skiing and snowmobiling. Chances to spot wildlife—including elk (which spend their winters in the National Elk Refuge near Jackson and their summers in Grand Teton and Yellowstone National Parks)—are abundant.

## Quick facts

**Length:** 55 miles.

**Time:** One to two hours.

**Considerations:** The Togwotee Pass sometimes closes in winter due to snow and inclement weather. Try to make this drive in early morning, when wildlife is more visible and the morning sun glints off the Teton range.

## Highlights

You are encouraged to take this enjoyable tour of the Wyoming Centennial Scenic Byway.

*The varied landscape of the Shoshone National Forest includes breathtaking rivers, meadows, and mountains.*

**Dubois:** The southern tip of the byway begins at the rustic town of Dubois, elevation 6,917 feet, a center for trout fishing on the Upper Wind River. In Dubois, the National Bighorn Sheep Interpretive Center has educational exhibits and information on bighorn sheep habitat and conservation. Dubois is also home to the Wind River Historical Center, which features displays on the settlement and history of the Upper Wind River Valley as well as the geology and natural history of the region.

**Shoshone National Forest:** Take U.S. 26/287 northwest, which parallels the Wind River as it travels past the Wind River Range and the volcanic Absaroka Range; watch for the nearly 12,000-foot Ramshorn Peak. The 2.4-million-acre Shoshone National Forest, which blankets the land both to the east and west of the road, is thick with aspens, evergreens, spruce, and willows and is home to 236 peaks and 156 glaciers.

**Tie Hack Memorial:** About 17 miles from Dubois, the byway passes the Tie Hack Memorial, dedicated to the early 20th-century lumberjacks (mostly from Sweden and other Scandinavian countries) who cut

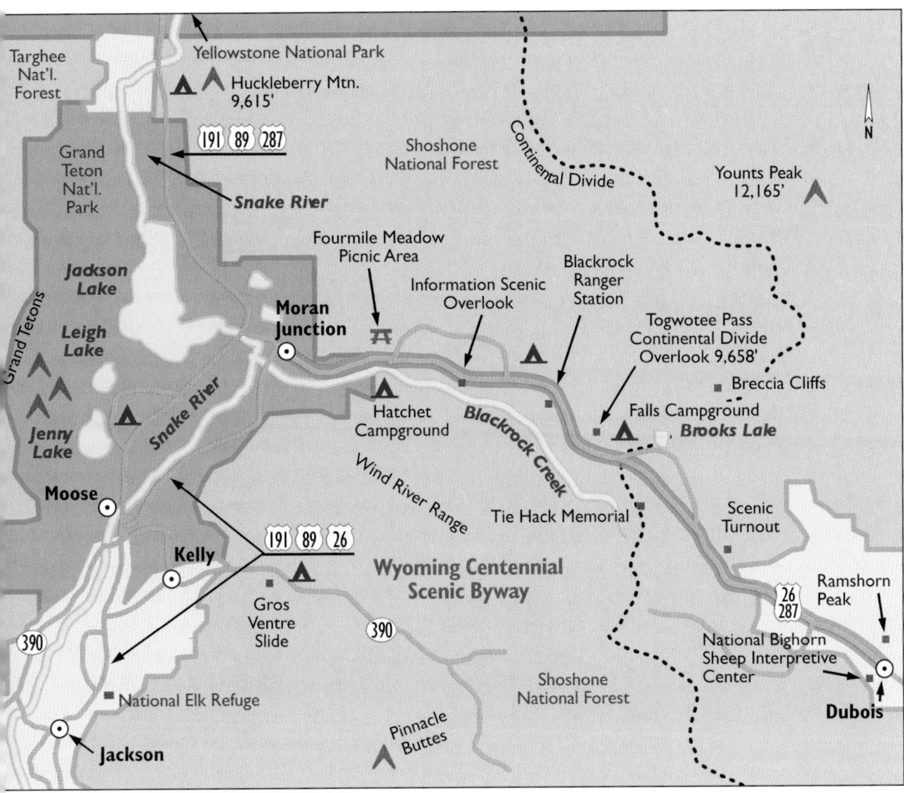


and shaped railroad ties by hand from local forests, for use in building the transcontinental railroad. Each man could hack about 30 ties per day, earning 10 cents per tie.

**Breccia Cliffs, Pinnacle Buttes, and Falls Campground:** Next, watch for the castlelike rock formations known as the Breccia Cliffs and the Pinnacle Buttes in the Teton Wilderness. Stop at Falls Campground to follow the short trail to Brooks Falls, or hike farther to Wind River Lake. In the meadows, watch for wildlife such as elk, moose, deer, and even grizzlies.

**Togwotee Pass:** The road rises to Togwotee Pass, elevation 9,658 feet, which marks the Continental Divide. Snow can be heavy in winter and often lingers by the roadside into July. Stop at the overlook for a great view.

**Grand Tetons:** The road then descends, steeply at points. Soon coming into view are the Grand Tetons, the jagged, glacially carved string of snowcapped peaks that rise like skyscrapers out of the valley and are the most recognizable mountains in Wyoming. Be sure to stop at the overlook, which provides one of the best views of the range, including 13,770-foot Grand Teton and seven other peaks topping 12,000 feet. There are also campgrounds and picnic areas as the road levels off into a valley.

**Grand Teton National Park:** When the byway reaches beautiful Grand Teton National Park, there are continuing views of the Tetons, framed by sagebrush, forests, lakes, and the Snake River. Float trips are offered on the Snake River. Hiking, camping, mountain climbing, boating, and kayaking are all popular in the park, which is also a favorite of photographers.

**Yellowstone National Park or Jackson:** At Moran Junction, the end of the byway, drivers face a tough choice. The largest park in the lower 48 states, Yellowstone National Park lies 27 miles to the north via the Rockefeller Parkway. Route 26, meanwhile, turns south toward the resort area of Jackson, passing the 25,000-acre National Elk Refuge on the way. About 7,500 elk call the refuge home each winter. In summer, watch for elk in Grand Teton National Park or in Yellowstone.

*The jagged peaks of the Grand Tetons are reflected in one of the sparkling lakes in Grand Teton National Park.*

# LAKE TAHOE–EASTSHORE DRIVE

*The eastern shore of America's highest alpine lake is the scenic centerpiece of this resort-lined roadway. Four-season recreation abounds, from swimming in crystalline waters to skiing down snowcapped peaks or even rolling the dice.*

Called the most beautiful drive in America, the 28-mile Lake Tahoe–Eastshore Drive affords breathtaking views of spectacularly clear Lake Tahoe. The pristine alpine lake is surrounded by the snowcapped mountains of the Sierras. The byway is mostly undeveloped, except for the excellent recreational opportunities offered by the lake, including the Zephyr Cove Resort, stables, campgrounds, the Tahoe Rim Trail, ski resorts, hotels, casinos, and fabulous golf courses. As part of the Pony Express Trail and home to the historic sacred grounds of the Washoe Indians, Lake Tahoe's eastern shore offers a wide variety of activities during every season. The Lake Tahoe–Eastshore Drive is one of the most beautiful winter byways in the country, with the draw of an alpine climate and the ever-crystalline lake. Throughout the year, visitors come from miles around to enjoy Lake Tahoe.

## Quick Facts

**Length:** 28 miles.

**Time to Allow:** One hour.

**Considerations:** The busiest season is July through September and the last week of December. There are occasional brief road closures during snowstorms.

## Intrinsic Qualities

**Cultural:** Lake Tahoe is well known for its diverse and interesting culture of both recreation and arts. Events take place through the year that attract visitors for reasons ranging from high drama to downhill ski relays. During the summer months, artists gather at Lake Tahoe for exhibitions and workshops, making the area one of the best places to find cutting-edge and classic artwork. While Tahoe's art is a sight to behold, don't miss out on any of the many festivals that take place throughout the year. The festivals themselves are works of art.

Perhaps Lake Tahoe's best-known summer festival is the Lake Tahoe Shakespeare Festival at Sand Harbor, which takes place every year. Imagine relaxing on a beautiful sand beach while enjoying your favorite Shakespearean drama. Enjoy the first-class performance near crystal blue waters, set against the stately backdrop of the Sierra Nevada, under a thousand glittering stars. The Lake Tahoe Shakespeare Festival's theater was recently rebuilt and is magnificent. Bring a jacket, a blanket, and some edibles, and then sit back, relax, and enjoy high drama in one of the most stunning locations imaginable.

Lake Tahoe offers a variety of winter festivals, as well. Winter begins early here with the Native American Festival and Snow Dance. During the Snow Dance, a two-day event held the first weekend in October, Native Americans dance in full regalia and pray for snow to ensure an abundantly snowy winter. Lake Tahoe also heralds the arrival of winter with other festivals, such as the Northern Lights Winter Festival and Snow Fest.

*Crystal-clear Lake Tahoe provides a variety of recreational choices including sailing, fishing, and swimming, all with the snowcapped Sierras as a backdrop.*

**Historical:** Lake Tahoe was originally a peaceful, earthy place, connected to the rest of the world by narrow trails over high mountain passes. Native Americans would gather in the summer to fish, hunt, and harvest nuts and berries for the long winter spent in Nevada's high desert. The American Indians called their special place *Da ow aga*, meaning "the edge of the lake." It is believed that Tahoe got its name from the European settlers' mispronunciation of the first two syllables. Tahoe remains a gathering place for people hoping to enjoy the outdoors.

While on an expedition in search of the mythical Buenaentura River in 1844, explorers it Carson and John C. Frémont nstead stumbled on Lake Tahoe, etting out the secret that had ong been kept from the outside vorld. Frémont's accurate accounts f his High Sierra travels led other urious explorers to the mountain ake. Soon after, gold and silver rospectors flocked to Lake Tahoe, ut their explorations were in ain. However, in 1859, rich silver eposits in nearby Virginia City egan a logging boom. While the omstock Lode opened the area o big business, it nearly stripped he Lake Basin of its first growth of rees because its lumber was used or timber supports in the underround mines.

As more people laid eyes on he natural treasure, word of the vondrous lake spread through he land. Among these proclaimrs was humorist Mark Twain, vho described the area as wholeome and pure. Stagecoach stops ver the Sierra exposed visitors to ahoe's scenic beauty and tranuility. Many were lured to stay ecause they felt that they had ound paradise.

Westerners began to develop ake Tahoe's shore in the early 900s as a summer retreat for an Francisco's elite. Plush hotels prang up, and guests amused hemselves at Lucky Baldwin's allac House and Casino, known oday as the Tallac Historic Site at outh Shore. Gambling was illegal n the California side of the lake, ut enforcement was sporadic, nd arrangements with cooperative authorities were routine. Raiding law enforcers often found patrons playing nothing more objectionable than pinochle and canasta. By 1941, the *Tahoe Tattler* was reporting that Tahoe's number two industry was nightlife, a close second to the resorts. Each weekend, an estimated 3,000 people would flock to the bars, casinos, and dance halls and spend anywhere from 25 cents for a glass of beer to $50,000 for an expensive game of chance.

A boom of another kind was soon occurring at Lake Tahoe. Using Nevada's advantageous tax laws as bait, an enterprising businessman named Norman Blitz convinced more than 80 of the nation's most rich and famous to make Lake Tahoe their home. This effort sparked the development of thriving real estate and construction industries at the lake.

**Natural:** Lake Tahoe is a masterpiece of nature. Surrounded by mountains, Lake Tahoe is the highest lake in the United States, the third-deepest lake in North America, and the tenth-deepest lake in the world. The lake holds more than 39 trillion gallons of water. Lake Tahoe is incredibly blue because the thin, clear mountain air allows the lake's pure, crystal-clear water to reflect the blue sky above. For this reason, the lake also appears a dramatic red during sunsets and reflects a somber, churning gray during storms. The spectacular shoreline is 71 miles long, 29 miles of which are on the Nevada side. Beautiful vegetation and numerous kinds of wildlife inhabit the area in and around Lake Tahoe.

Lake Tahoe was created millions of years ago through the shifting of geological faults. Immense forces began the process with the tilting of the Sierra Nevada block. As a result, two parallel faults were developed: One margin created the Carson Range and the other the Sierra Nevada. About two million years ago, volcanic activity reshaped the entire landscape of the region. Lava formed a barrier across the basin's northeastern outlet, creating a natural dam and, eventually, Lake Tahoe. Next, vast glaciers developed in the surrounding mountains. These gradually moved down the V-shape canyons on the western side of the lake. The massive glaciers scoured away any loose rock, and the canyons were reshaped into the wide, U-shape valleys of Emerald Bay, Fallen Leaf Lake, and Cascade Lake.

Lake Tahoe has a variety of unique plant and animal life that makes hikes and walks an exciting experience. One particularly striking plant, a fairly common sight when the snow is melting, is the snow plant. This member of the wintergreen family is an asparaguslike plant that doesn't photosynthesize; instead, it receives nourishment from the roots of neighboring plants and decaying organic matter. Despite its somewhat disturbing means of survival, the plant is extremely lovely, rare, and (fortunately) protected by law. Another beautiful flower is the crimson columbine, a well-known flower that grows in moist areas and is appreciated for its delicate features. The lupine is also easily recognized by the palmate leaf, resembling the fingers of a hand, and striking blue flowers.

While the Lake Tahoe area is full of a variety of animal life, from coyotes to bears, you will most often likely see various kinds of birds. The western tanager is a beautiful bird and one of the most colorful

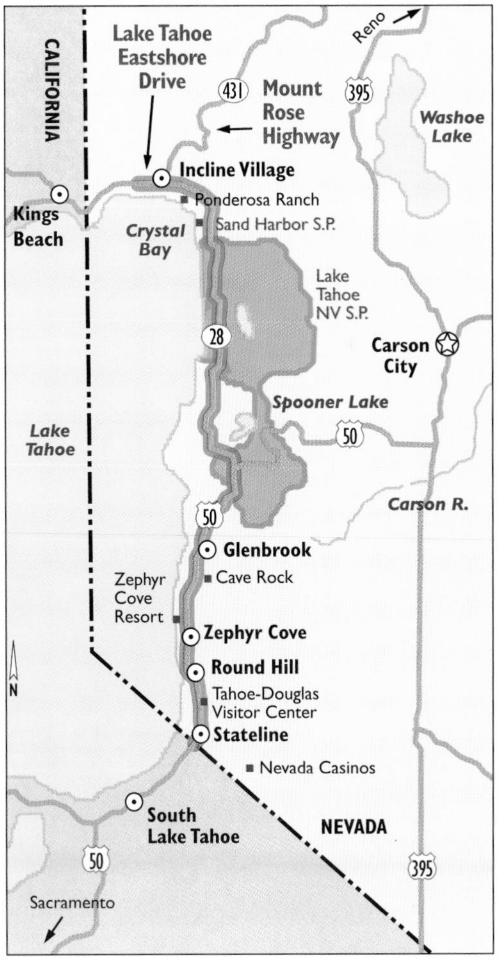

in the Lake Tahoe Basin, with a red head and a bright yellow body and black markings on its back, wings, and tail. Another bird in the area is the mountain chickadee, the most common bird in the Tahoe Basin. This bird is small with a black cap, a black bib, and a white line over each eye. It is acrobatic and swings from branches as it hunts for insects and seeds; it also makes a distinctive three-note whistle.

**Recreational:** When it comes to winter activities, Lake Tahoe has it covered. Tahoe has more snow (averaging about 400 inches per season), more variety, and more ways to play than just about any other place. Lake Tahoe has the largest concentration of ski resorts in North America, including six world-class resorts you won't want to miss. The terrain ranges from leisurely bowls to steep hills that make your heart thump. However, excellent skiing and snowboarding are not all that Lake Tahoe has to offer. Snowmobiling, snowshoe excursions, snow tubing, and cross-country treks open up the millions of acres of national forest land waiting to be explored. Ice skating, sleigh rides, and sledding are fun activities close to the byway. Lake Tahoe also hosts numerous special events all winter long, including Snow Fest.

If you prefer warmer weather, Lake Tahoe's links are second to none. Extra altitude makes even the worst golfer feel like a pro, and the breathtaking backdrops and outstanding course architecture will make bogeys seem a little less burdensome. The Lake Tahoe region boasts more than a dozen courses at all levels of play.

### Snow Fest

During Snow Fest, a ten-day festival with a huge variety of events, you can take part in ice-carving competitions, snow sculpture contests, parades, and a polar bear swim in the frigid Lake Tahoe. Snow Fest's opening-night ceremonies feature activities such as a torchlight parade of skiers, fireworks, a bonfire, and music. The events are not to be missed and include downhill finals, the largest cross-country ski races in the western United States, and celebrity races. The closing weekend has included the nationally televised Incredible Snow Dog Challenge, which features snow competitions of the canine variety, such as freestyle flying disk, agility, search and rescue, and dog sledding.

Surrounded by national forest lands, wilderness, and state parks, Lake Tahoe possesses some of the country's most spectacular scenery. With almost 300 miles of trails, hikers have plenty of room to roam. Backcountry buffs can trek up waterfall trails, hike along wildflower-carpeted meadows, or visit serene alpine lakes and stunning overlooks of Lake Tahoe. There are flat, moderate, and steep trails to suit every ability. Looping its way around the lake, the Tahoe Rim Trail, with paths for hiking and horseback riding, offers 165 miles of trail, with elevations ranging from 6,300 feet to 9,400 feet. This trail is generally moderate in difficulty, with a 10 percent average grade, and provides views of Lake Tahoe, the high desert, and snowcapped peaks of the Sierra Nevada. Trailheads accessible along the byway include Tahoe Meadows Trailhead to Tunnel Creek Road (Highway 431), Spooner Summit Trailhead (Highway 50), and Spooner Summit South to Kingsbury Grade. The Tunnel Creek Station Road Trail starts at Highway 28 across from Hidden Beach about one mile past Ponderosa Ranch (there's no sign, so look for the gate). This is a steep trail road, about 1½ miles each way, located at the ruins of the western portal of the old log flume tunnel. There is limited parking along Highway 28. The Marlette Lake Trail starts near the Spooner Lake Picnic Area at the junction of Highway 28 and 50 at the green metal gate on the east side of Highway 28. This trail is about five miles each way to the lake and passes through mostly mild terrain.

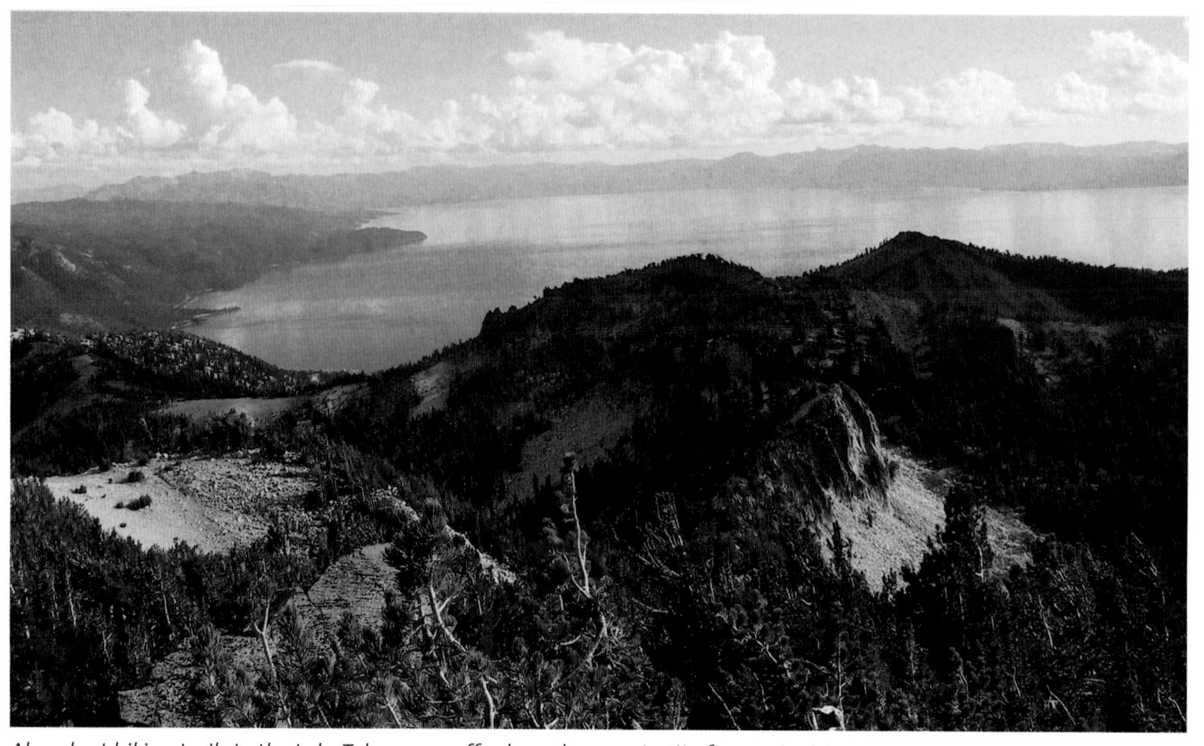

*Abundant hiking trails in the Lake Tahoe area afford ample opportunity for scenic vistas.*

A combination of one of the ʋorld's top single-track trails, pectacular views, and miles of pen backcountry beckons bikers rom around the world to the Lake ahoe basin. The best-known Tahoe ike trail is the spectacular Flume rail, carved out of the edge of a nountain some 2,000 feet above he lake's stunning east shore. The lume Trail follows a precarious oute dug out of the granite cliffs nore than a century ago by labor-rs developing a water supply and umber transport for the mines of he Comstock Lode. Today, the 14-nile Flume Trail offers a challeng-ng ride with a 1,000-foot elevation ain and sweeping views, all within Nevada's Lake Tahoe State Park. he common starting point for this rail is Spooner Lake, which fea-ures parking and trail information. ocated at the junction of high-ways 28 and 50, Spooner Lake is a 5-minute drive south from Incline Village. Groves of aspen trees, tow-ring peaks, old-growth pine, and igh mountain lakes greet bikers along the Flume Trail. After a quick urn onto a small outlet creek, the rail suddenly clings to a slope overlooking the azure Lake Tahoe. The northern terminus of the trail can take the rider to either Sand Harbor or the Ponderosa Ranch. For the ambitious rider, a loop via Tunnel Creek Road, Red House, and Hobart Lake creates a 25-mile loop back to Marlette Lake, as well as a stunning downhill ride to Spooner.

**Scenic:** Lake Tahoe–Eastshore Drive has rightly been called the most beautiful drive in America. Many people find they don't have words to describe its exquisite beauty and often rely upon writers, such as Mark Twain, for well-worded acclaim and praise. Painters find their brushes inadequate to capture the deep pines crowding the craggy cliffs, the crimson sunsets burnishing the skies, and the clear aquamarine waters reflecting the Sierra Nevada Range swathed in icy snow. Weather cooperates while visitors take in the splendor of their surroundings, and the sun shines an average of 307 days a year. And while the pristine silence of the lake that others from the past once enjoyed has been replaced by happy tourists, the majesty of Lake Tahoe still affords solitude and a purely heavenly ambience.

## Highlights

To hit the highlights of the Lake Tahoe–Eastshore Drive, consider following this itinerary.

**Crystal Bay:** You may want to begin traveling the byway at the northern terminus at Crystal Bay along the California–Nevada border. There are several casinos in this area to enjoy.

**Incline Village:** The highway winds toward Incline Village, one of Tahoe's finest communities. A side trip up Mount Rose Highway, approximately four miles, leads to a lookout that provides a view of the entire Tahoe Basin.

**Ponderosa Ranch:** Back on Highway 28, the Ponderosa Ranch is the location of TV's legendary *Bonanza* series that made Lake Tahoe famous worldwide. The Ponderosa offers Cartwright Ranch House tours, an Old West town with shops and memorabilia, summer hay-wagon breakfasts, and more.

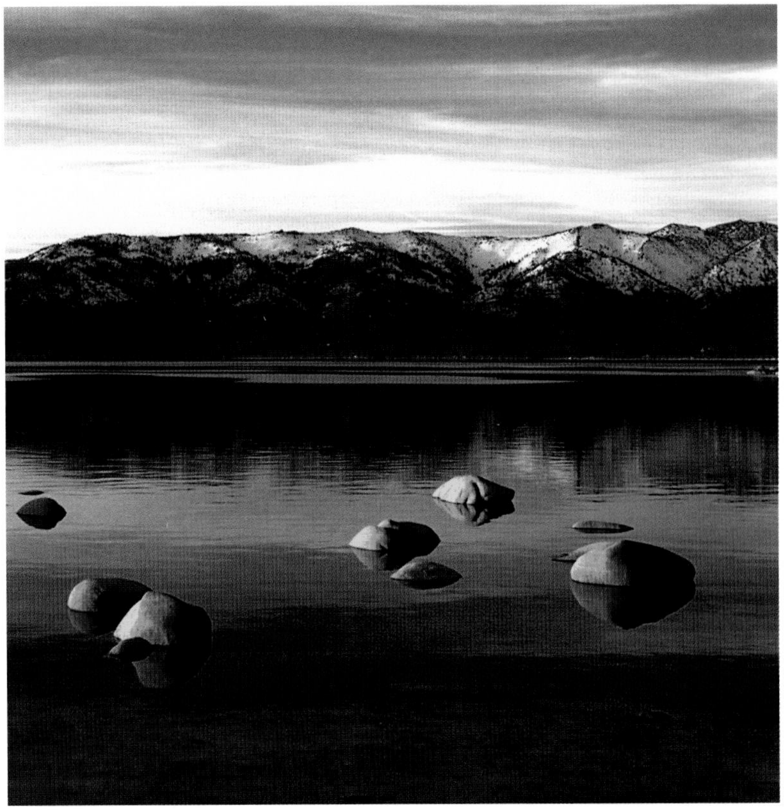

*Recreational opportunities abound at Incline Village. Private beaches with picnic areas and world-renowned golf courses can be enjoyed here.*

**Sand Harbor, Spooner Lake, and Glenbrook:** The byway continues south down the east shore. One of Tahoe's most beautiful beaches, Sand Harbor is located here in the Lake Tahoe Nevada State Park. Following the bouldered Nevada shore, the highway continues south through forests of pine and fir. Stop at Spooner Lake for wooded picnic areas and a walk along the water. Turn right at the intersection of Highway 50, and head south past historic Glenbrook, once a busy logging town and now an exclusive community and golf course.

**Cave Rock and Zephyr Cove:** Your next landmark is Cave Rock, where the highway passes through 25 yards of solid stone. This is a holy spot for the native Washoe Indians who put their deceased to rest in the cold waters below the outcropping. Farther along is Zephyr Cove with its beautiful old lodge, beach, and tour boats.

**Stateline:** The tour now returns you to South Lake Tahoe and the high-rise hotel/casinos in the Stateline area, a perfect place to stop at a restaurant or lounge, take in a show, or try your luck in the casinos.

# Las Vegas Strip 

*The most glittering, neon-lit drive in America explodes with visual delights as it leads past exotic and lavish casino resorts. It's the only byway in the country that's more scenic by night than by day.*

Often referred to as the Jewel of the Desert, Las Vegas has long been recognized as the entertainment vacation capital of the country. The Las Vegas Strip—at the heart of this playland—sparkles like no other place on Earth. More than 35 million visitors from around the world are drawn to the lights of the strip each year to experience its unique blend of exciting entertainment, scenic beauty, and lavishly landscaped resorts.

Gambling is only the beginning for many of the resorts along the Las Vegas Strip. These outrageous destinations transport their visitors through time and place, and offer much more than slot machines.

The Las Vegas Strip hosts thousands of motorists a week; after you arrive on the strip, however, you may be surprised to find that it's also a very enjoyable walking environment. The strip is the only byway that is more scenic at night than during the day. In fact, 365 days of the year, 24 hours a day, the Neon Trail offers a fascinating foray past spectacular resorts featuring a variety of visual delights. Whether it's pirates plundering, fiery volcanoes spouting, or tropical gardens luring the weary, the Las Vegas Strip offers a variety of fascinating visual experiences that enchant and mesmerize visitors of all ages. The many facets of this corridor make it truly a one-of-a-kind destination.

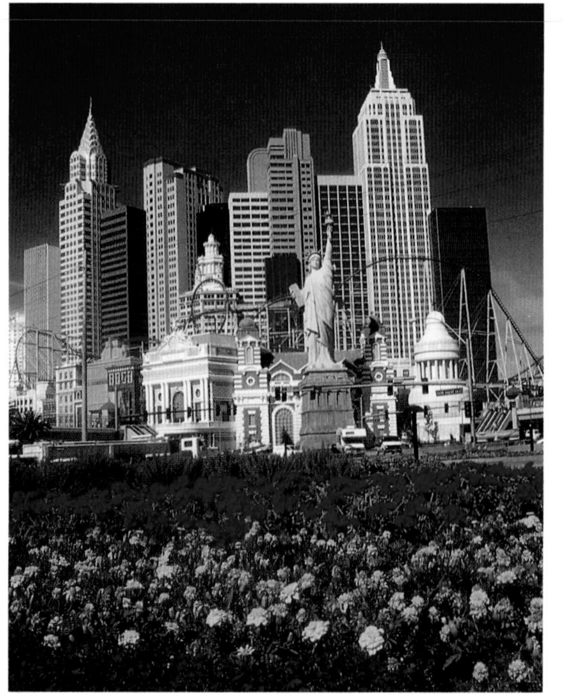

*New York–New York Casino is one of the famous gaming attractions in Las Vegas, Nevada.*

## Intrinsic Qualities

**Cultural:** While Las Vegas is perhaps best known for its gaming culture—the popularity and influence of which have spread to cities all over the world—the Las Vegas Strip possesses many other outstanding cultural amenities. The diversity and magnificence of the architecture of the hotels and resorts along the strip are certainly worth noting. Some of the world's most talented architects have created complex fantasylands all along the strip. Just a few of the more recent projects include reproductions of the streets of New York, a bayside Tuscan village, the canals of Venice, and a replica of the Eiffel Tower and the Arc de Triomphe.

Many of the resorts on the Las Vegas Strip also feature world-class art galleries that are full of paintings by world-renowned artists, such as Renoir, Monet, and van Gogh. Other resorts hold galleries of unique items, such as antique automobiles or wax figures. The Guinness World of Records Museum offers an interesting array of the unusual, and the World of Coca-Cola Las Vegas features an interactive storytelling theater.

Various hotels on the Las Vegas Strip feature a variety of top-caliber theatrical and dance shows. Several hotels and casinos host world-class sporting events and concerts featuring top-name entertainers. And no matter where you go on the strip, you are bound to run into the dazzling light displays that permeate the area. The magical re-creations found along the byway are the symbols of our society's most fantastic dreams of luxury.

### Quick Facts

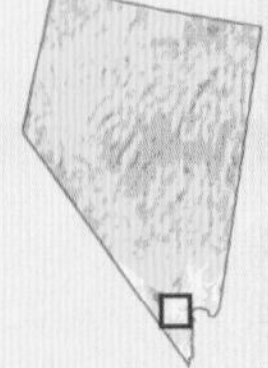

**Length:** $4\frac{1}{2}$ miles.

**Time to Allow:** From half an hour to several hours.

**Considerations:** The strip is usually fairly crowded and congested. Nighttime is busier than daytime, and holidays are especially busy. This is an environment that is full of pedestrians, so be on alert when driving. Consider driving the byway once each direction. This way, you will be able to view all the sites that line both sides of the street and catch some that you may have missed.

**Historical:** The Las Vegas Strip, world-renowned for its neon glitter, possesses an equally colorful historical past. The unique history of Las Vegas is undeniably entwined with the culture of gaming. Gambling was legalized in Nevada in 1931, and the first casino opened downtown that same year. Competition was intense, and casino builders soon were looking at land outside the city limits just south of downtown along Highway 91 (the Old Los Angeles Highway), which is now known as the Las Vegas Strip.

Most of the Las Vegas Strip is not really located within the Las

Vegas city limits, but along a corridor of South Las Vegas Boulevard located in unincorporated Clark County. The area was sparsely developed until 1938, when the first resort property was built four miles south of downtown Las Vegas at the corner of San Francisco Avenue (now Sahara) and Highway 91 (South Las Vegas Boulevard). Reportedly, city officials had denied licenses to certain businesspeople with questionable connections who had applied to build a casino in the downtown area. Undaunted, they decided to build outside the city limits, just south of the downtown district.

In 1940, construction began on El Rancho Vegas resort at the corner of San Francisco Avenue and Highway 91. The original El Rancho Vegas introduced a new style of recreation and entertainment to the Nevada desert by combining lodging, gambling, restaurants, entertainment, shops, a travel agency, horseback riding, and swimming in one resort. El Rancho Vegas was followed a year later by the Last Frontier Resort Hotel and Casino. The famous Little Church of the West was originally constructed in the resort's Frontier Village. Listed on the National Register of Historic Places, the small chapel has survived four moves on the strip.

One of the strip's more colorful (and infamous) characters, Ben "Bugsy" Siegel (reputed hit man for New York mobster Lucky Luciano) oversaw the construction of the fabulous Flamingo Hotel, the third major (and most extravagant) resort to be built on the strip. Although Siegel met his unfortunate demise soon after the resort's 1946 opening, his prophecies for the future of Las Vegas came true. This new popular playground of Hollywood stars prospered, with the Flamingo setting the stage for the many luxurious resorts yet to be imagined.

As the 1950s began, only four major resorts stood along the strip, but three more major players were about to hit the scene. The Desert Inn, the Sahara, and the Sands all arrived on the strip in the early 1950s, further enhancing the strip's image as a self-contained playground by featuring elaborate tennis courts, an 18-hole golf course, larger casinos, and fabulous showrooms with Broadway's and Hollywood's brightest stars. Las Vegas has continued to build on this legacy, developing newer and more elaborate resorts often to make certain that Las Vegas retains the image of the most fabulous playground on Earth.

**Recreational:** The simplest and easiest recreation on the strip is strolling and sightseeing along the boulevard. Intriguing arrays of fantasylands in lush surroundings welcome you to the strip. But the excitement only begins with sightseeing. From comfortable and plush hotels to exciting displays of lights and fountains, Las Vegas creates a dreamlike environment with color, sound, and light all combined to make the experience on the strip memorable.

For the more adventuresome, roller coasters featured at several hotels provide rides that twist, loop, and turn for your delight. Other resorts provide 3-D ride films appealing to the senses of sight, sound, and motion. Many of these rides feature the latest technologies for extra thrills. Most of the resorts along the strip offer displays of grandeur for every visitor to enjoy. Anyone driving the byway can stop to see erupting volcanoes, dueling ships, dancing fountains, circus acts, and lush tropical gardens.

In addition to a variety of theatrical and dance shows, the resorts have varied spectator sports, such as boxing matches. There isn't a resort on the strip that doesn't offer visitors every amenity imaginable. World-class spas, pools, and exercise rooms are as enticing as the casinos. When you aren't searching for slot machines, you may choose to browse through the many stores and boutiques each resort has to offer. You will find everything from designer fashion to specialty candies to Las Vegas souvenirs. Whatever you choose to do, you can find it in Las Vegas.

**Scenic:** As one of the most geographically isolated major cities in the continental United States, Las Vegas provides you with an extraordinary visual experience. The matchless Las Vegas Strip serves as the gateway to a host of memorable experiences that are distinctly

Las Vegas. The strip's incredible array of resorts are constructed around themes that transport visitors to different exotic realms, including a medieval castle, the Parisian Eiffel Tower, a lakeside Italian village, and a pyramid in ancient Egypt. Day or night, the Neon Trail provides a fascinating foray past spectacular resorts that offer a variety of visual delights to pedestrians and motorists alike.

## Highlights

The Southern Las Vegas Strip Walking Tour begins at Las Vegas Boulevard and Russell Road, although you can go the opposite way by reading this list from the bottom up.

**Little Church of the West:** The famous "Welcome to Fabulous Las Vegas" sign announces that you're on the right track. On the east side of the strip, you see the Little Church of the West, the site of many celebrity weddings and a favorite place today to have a memorable wedding.



**Mandalay Bay:** Park the car at the free parking garage at Mandalay Bay (most of the large hotels offer plenty of covered free parking). Explore the tropical-themed hotel, including a fun sand and surf beach. Mandalay Bay is one of the newer hotels on the strip (built in 1999), and that makes it a popular attraction.

**Luxor:** From Mandalay Bay, you can walk north to Luxor, the great black glass pyramid. (If you prefer, hop on the tram that takes you right to the front doors of Luxor—you may want to save your energy for later in the trip.) While at Luxor, don't miss the King Tut Tomb exhibit, an exact replica of the ancient Egyptian pharaoh's tomb. A rotating IMAX film experience is also a popular attraction here. This unique hotel is amazing and has one of the largest atriums in the world.

**Excalibur:** After spending time at Luxor, hop on the tram that takes you over to Excalibur. This is the place for an exciting dinner and show. The majestic castle offers adventure at its Fantasy Faire Midway, an arena of games appropriate for everyone in the family.

*The Bellagio Hotel and Casino in Las Vegas is accented by Lake Bellagio and the spectacular Fountains of Bellagio.*

**New York–New York:** After spending time at the medieval castle, cross the over-street walkway into 1930s- and '40s-inspired New York–New York. Billed as "the Greatest City in Las Vegas," New York–New York has attractions that are all themed to the New York life. Park Avenue shopping, a fast-paced Manhattan roller coaster, and Greenwich Village eateries help keep the theme intact.

**Monte Carlo:** It's not time to stop yet. The Monte Carlo, just north of New York–New York, is just as classy, but with a purely European twist.

**Bellagio:** After a jaunt to Monte Carlo, walk farther north, getting close to the halfway point. The big lake and fantastic fountains are part of Bellagio, a hotel that strives for utter perfection. Check out the art gallery here; it houses some fantastic pieces. The gallery has original paintings by van Gogh, Monet, Renoir, Cezanne, and other masters.

**Paris:** Now, at Flamingo Road, cross the street to the east—over to Paris. This is the midpoint of the tour, and this area is full of places to sit and rest or to grab a bite to eat. While at Paris, tour the Eiffel Tower. This is an exact replica, in half scale, of the original in France. The plans for the original were lent to the developers of the hotel so they could be as accurate as possible. There's also a two-thirds-scale replica of the Arc de Triomphe near the hotel entrance—complete with Napoleon's victories inscribed on it.

**MGM Grand:** Head south to the next stop on this tour, the MGM Grand. This very large hotel strives to make visitors feel like stars. Elegance abounds at this hotel. Don't miss the Lion Habitat here: a walk-through tour that showcases beautiful lions, some of which are descendants of Metro, the MGM marquee lion. The only thing separating you and the lions is a glass wall on both sides.

**Tropicana:** Just south of the MGM Grand is the famous Tropicana, home to the longest-running show on the strip: *Folies Bergere*.

**Glass Pool Inn:** After the Tropicana, cross the street again and take the tram from Excalibur to Mandalay Bay. At Mandalay Bay, get back in your car and cross the street to see the Glass Pool Inn. This motel was originally called Mirage Motel but sold the rights to its name to the much larger entity many years ago. The motel features an unusual above-ground pool with portal windows that has been featured in many movies.

**Southern Las Vegas Strip:** Finish off the tour of the Southern Las Vegas Strip by driving north back past the Tropicana and MGM Grand and beyond. The drive provides amazing views that you may have missed on the walk.

# Pyramid Lake Scenic Byway

*Shimmering like a blue jewel in the desert north of Reno, ancient Pyramid Lake is a haven for migrating waterfowl and home to striking rock formations. This byway offers enchanting views of its natural treasures.*

Pyramid Lake is a bright jewel in the arid Nevada landscape. Fish, animal, and plant life are sustained by its 300-foot-deep waters and by the fresh water flowing in the Truckee River. In addition to the cui-ui fish, an indigenous species found only in Pyramid Lake, the lake is known for the Lahontan cutthroat trout that the Native Americans manage through their fisheries program. The mountains surrounding the lake support deer, antelope, and bighorn sheep. The lake is also a resting place for a variety of migrating waterfowl. Anaho Island, a National Wildlife Refuge, is the breeding ground for a large colony of American white pelicans. It is also home to a variety of other shorebirds. The tufa formations found at this lake are some of the lake's most distinctive natural features. These formations are calcium carbonate deposits formed by precipitation over hot springs. They include the Pyramid (which gives the lake its name) and the Needles.

## Quick Facts

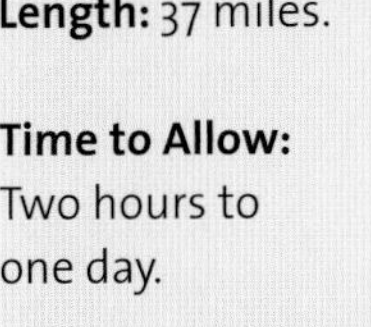

**Length:** 37 miles.

**Time to Allow:** Two hours to one day.

**Considerations:** Many of the road shoulders are sandy, and vehicles can get stuck easily. The best place to fill up with gasoline is in Wadsworth, near I-80.

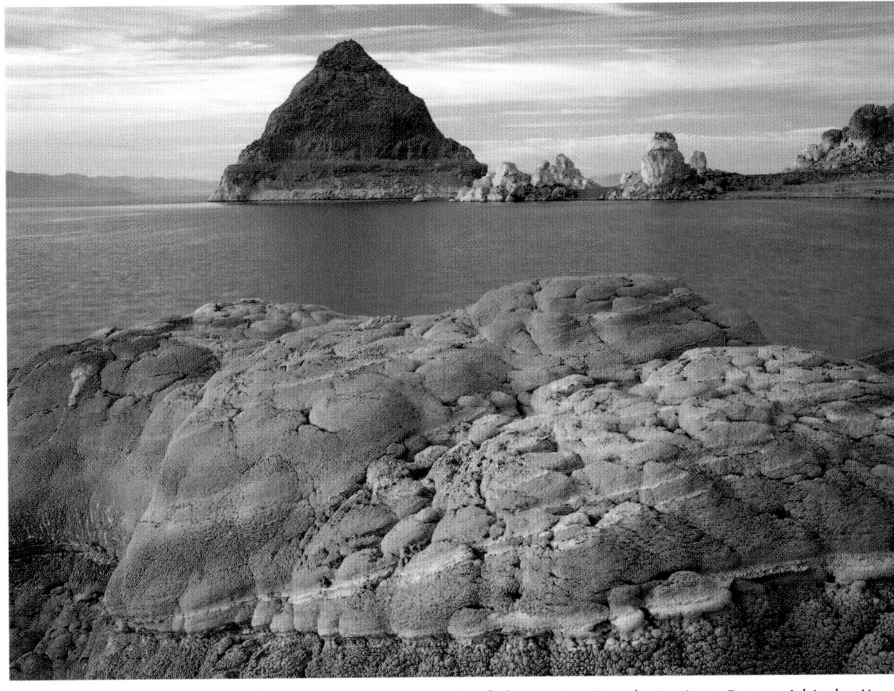

*The unusual stone pyramid shape rising up out of the water is what gives Pyramid Lake its name. Other interesting rock formations can be found here as well.*

## Intrinsic Qualities

**Archaeological:** Since time immemorial, the Northern Paiute people comprised many bands that occupied northwestern Nevada and southeastern Oregon. By roaming in small, family-centered groups, these remarkable people adapted their way of life in order to be comfortable living in a high desert environment. One band centered its territory around Pyramid Lake and were called *Kuyuidokado*, or cui-ui eaters.

On display at the Pyramid Lake Visitor Center are tools and artifacts that reflect the ancient culture that was essential to these peoples' survival. Much of the collection has established a time line for archaeologists in determining when these tools were used.

**Cultural:** The Pyramid Lake Paiute nation is governed by ten council members who are elected biannually in December and on staggered two-year terms. The majority of enrolled members, numbering around 1,700, reside on the Pyramid Lake Indian Reservation, and approximately 12 percent of this membership live in other areas throughout the western United States.

There are strong cultural ties between the lake and the Kuyuidokado. Unfortunately, the cui-ui fish are endangered. So are the Lahontan cutthroat trout, which are also indigenous to Pyramid Lake and Truckee River. The Kuyuidokado feel it is their duty to save these two fish species because they consider themselves the keepers of the lake.

**Historical:** Hundreds of years before settlers traveled through Nevada, the Paiute Indians lived near Pyramid Lake, then called Coo-yu-ee Pah. Their traditional culture was centered around the lake. The Paiute depended on the cui-ui fish to survive. Unfortunately, in 1859, the Paiute Indian Reservation was formed, giving only a fraction of the land to the Paiute people. They continued to live as they had been and create a culture rich in history and family.

The present name of the lake was given by John C. Frémont in January 1844. The first band of explorers stumbled upon the lake after a difficult journey through the harsh desert that lasted several weeks. They pitched their camp near a striking 400-foot-high rock island outcropping. Frémont wrote in his journal on January 14 and suggested a name for the fascinating lake: Pyramid Lake. The explorers were also captivated by the stone needles, pinnacles, and steaming sulfur springs, which the Paiute people still hold sacred today.

**Natural:** The present-day vision of Pyramid Lake took millions of years to form. It is the remnant of an inland sea, Lake Lahontan, which covered more than 8,000 square miles about 11 million years ago. Today, Pyramid Lake is 26 miles long, 4 to 11 miles wide, and 350 feet deep at its deepest point. It has been called the world's most beautiful desert lake and presents a range of colors from turquoise to emerald green to deep blue. Because Pyramid Lake used to be part of an inland sea, it is a very alkaline lake, the type found in semiarid or arid environments. Visiting the lake is almost like going to the beach. Unlike the beach, however, Pyramid Lake has a number of interesting formations scattered around and throughout its waters. The lake is also home to a variety of wildlife that visitors usually don't see at the beach.

Tufa needs just the right kind of conditions to form, and Pyramid Lake is the world's largest producer of tufa rock. It is created when the following environment is present: a stable lake, a source of calcium, high water temperatures, and a stable bedrock or substrate. When all of these conditions are present, all that is necessary is a branch or rock around which the carbonate can form. Pyramid Lake demonstrates its age through the tufa formations. Changes in color and texture of the rock, as well as primary silt level changes, also indicate what kinds of weather Pyramid Lake has survived, including winds, droughts, floods, and glacial activity.

Other tufa formations attract attention, too. The primary area, the Needles, is located at the northwest end of the lake, in the hot springs area. This area of continuing geothermal activity contains more tufa deposits than anywhere else in the world. Other types of formations exist around the lake, such as the Stone Mother and her basket. The basket is actually a rounded, hollowed rock, but a legend exists about the Stone Mother that goes like this: In the ancient days, a mother had four sons. They could not get along and were forced to leave. Their mother, in terrible grief, sat in the middle of the desert and cried so many tears that they filled the lake. She was in such despair she just dropped her basket beside her, and then the mother and her basket turned to stone.

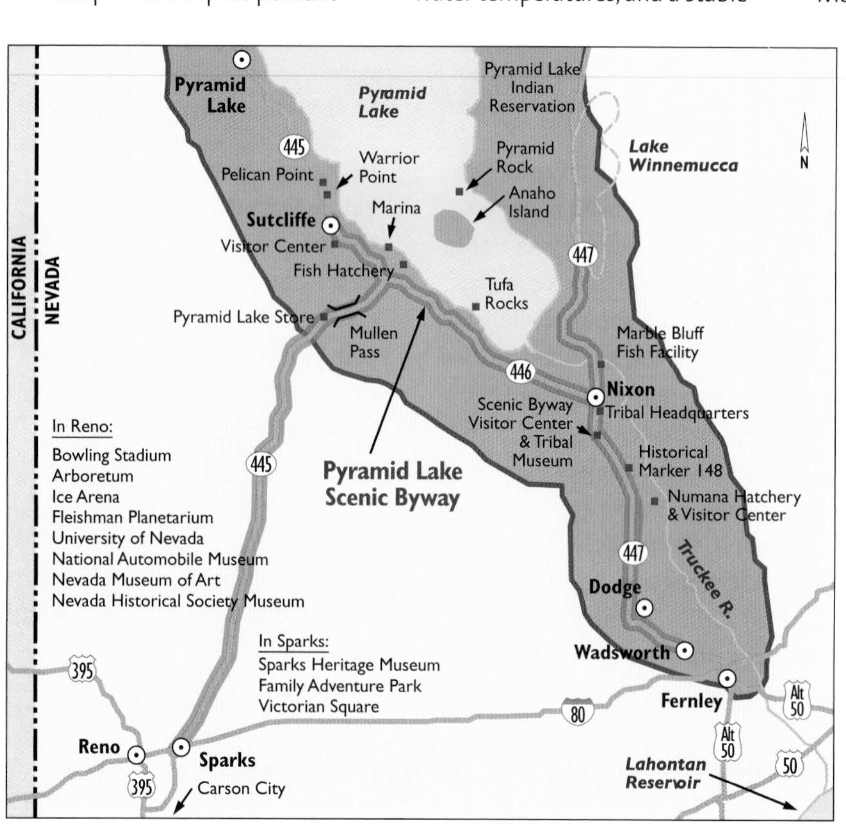


Anaho Island, located in Pyramid Lake, is a National Wildlife Refuge that is one of only eight nesting grounds for white pelicans in North America. As many as 9,500 pelicans nest on the island in the spring, so both the federal government and the Paiute people carefully protect the island from intruding boats or visitors. The best place to view the pelicans is from the southeastern or southwestern shores with binoculars, and the best time of year to see them is March through October. Numerous other types of birds—including double-crested cormorants, California gulls, blue herons, golden and bald eagles, rock wrens, owls, falcons, snowy egrets, and California quail—draw bird-watchers.

Because the nature of the lake is so well protected and preserved by the Paiute, an uncommon amount of wildlife lives undisturbed at Pyramid Lake. Not only do many birds live here, but also burros, bighorn sheep, bobcats, wild horses, mountain lions, pronghorn antelope, coyotes, and jackrabbits. There are few spots in the country where visitors can see such a range of wildlife.

**Recreational:** Pyramid Lake offers all kinds of opportunities to enjoy the surrounding nature. You can hike, rock climb, ride horseback, backpack, and so much more. And, after a full day of activity, hot springs at the north end of the lake among the needle rocks allow you to relax while enjoying Pyramid Lake's famous tufa formations. The lake itself draws the most recreationists; it is a favorite of anglers, who throughout the history of the lake have gone from fishing as a means of survival to fishing as a business venture to fishing for sport.

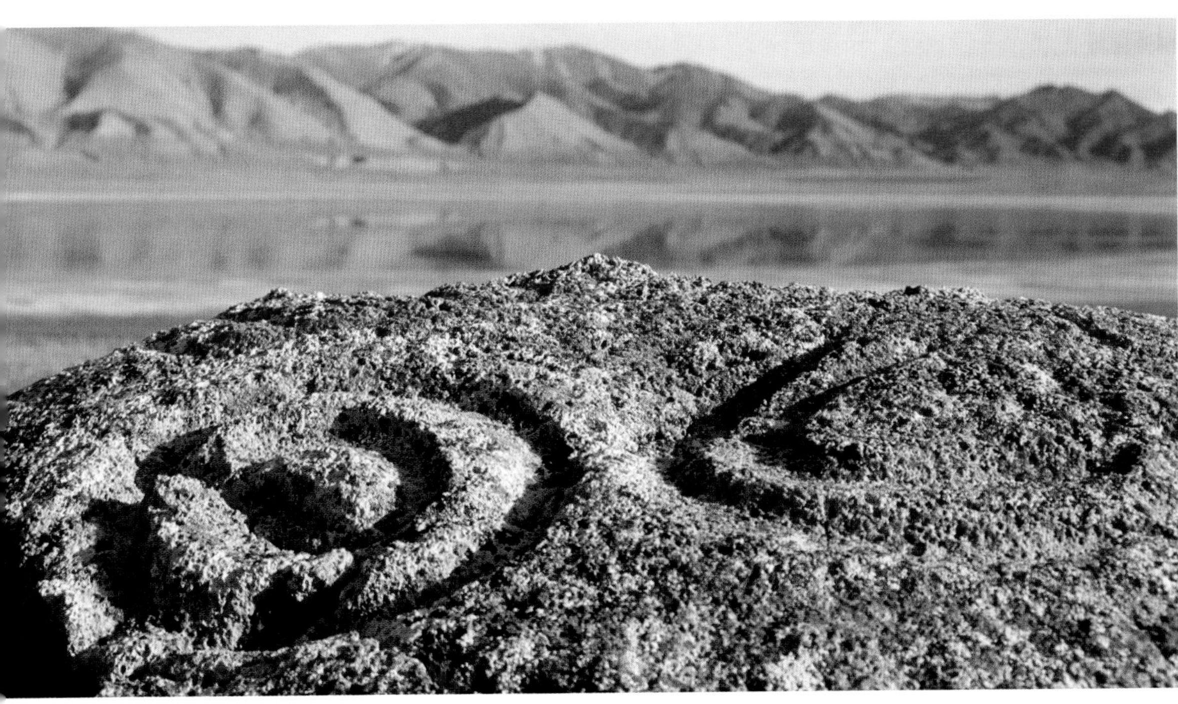

*Petroglyphs like this one at Lake Winnemucca can be found on the byway.*

Fishing at Pyramid Lake is an experience all its own. The water is unlike most lake water and is a startling pastel blue. The surroundings are pure desert, with little vegetation. After some practice, many fishers have discovered that the best way to catch fish in Pyramid Lake is from the top of a five-foot ladder or other tall object. The fish come into the shallows, and the added altitude gives anglers a better view, as well as a longer casting range. Be careful, though. While you can see the fish, the fish can also see you. Fish often roam the edges of the lake near a series of ledges or drop-offs. If you stand on a tall object and wear polarizing lenses, you can actually see the fish take the fly ten feet away. Pyramid Lake has also been known for the size of its fish, especially the cutthroat trout. In 1925, a Paiute named Johnny Skimmerhorn caught the world's record cutthroat—a 41-pounder. Photographs from the '20s and '30s show celebrities such as Clark Gable struggling to hold up a pair of massive cutthroat. Another photograph shows a group of Nevadans peeking out from behind a line of shimmering fish that stretches eight feet long from a day's catch. Unfortunately, the fish are no longer as large because of extensive fishing, but five- to ten-pounders are not uncommon.

**Scenic:** Travelers driving to Pyramid Lake for the first time may be surprised by the scenic beauty that a cold, blue lake offers in the middle of the desert. The lake is situated in a valley amid distant hills and snowcapped mountains. It is an unexpected oasis in the middle of the dry landscape of Nevada.

A drive around Pyramid Lake offers an enchanting view of this remnant of an ancient inland sea that changes from green to turquoise to deep blue. The sunset casts a red glow on the lake and surrounding formations that you can behold at scenic turnouts. During the day, just the sight of the deep blue waters of Pyramid Lake is a refreshing experience for hot travelers.

## Highlights

On this Pyramid Lake must-see tour, you can start in either Sparks or Wadsworth because the driving directions given here start and end in the Reno/Sparks area.

**Numana Hatchery and Visitor Center:** Start your trip in Wadsworth, and then drive north along Route 447, following the course of the Truckee River. You can stop at the Numana Hatchery and Visitor Center to learn about the area's natural history and the Native American fisheries program or take a walk along the wetlands nature trail, where you experience the unique habitats of the river valley.

**Scenic Byway Visitor Center and Tribal Museum:** As you continue to drive north, you will come over a rise and see the lake spread out before you. Just ahead is the Scenic Byway Visitor Center and Tribal Museum. From here, you can take a side trip north on Route 447 into the town of Nixon, site of the Tribal Headquarters, and beyond to Marble Bluff Fish Facility and Lake Winnemucca.

**Pyramid Lake:** You can also head west on Route 446 toward Sutcliffe. Route 446 follows the west shore of Pyramid Lake, with plenty of beaches for swimming, fishing, or enjoying a picnic lunch. In Sutcliffe, you'll find the Pyramid Lake Marina, with a visitor center and museum, as well as stores and visitor services. North of Sutcliffe are more beaches, especially at Pelican Point and Warrior Point.

**Mullen Pass:** Returning south from Sutcliffe, take Route 445 south toward Sparks. As you drive up toward Mullen Pass, you can stop at the pull-off on the left for a scenic vista of the lake. If you get a chance to visit here as the sun sets, the Pyramid, Anaho Island, and the slopes of the Lake Range may be bathed in a red glow, offering a dramatic counterpoint to the urban glitter awaiting you as you return to Reno.

# Dinosaur Diamond Prehistoric Highway

*Following this diamond-shape byway is like taking a trip to prehistory. Dinosaur bones, Native American rock art, and geological wonders await—along with current-day hiking and biking trails, desert festivals, and wide-open spaces.*

Part of a Multistate Byway; it also runs through Colorado.

The Dinosaur Diamond Prehistoric Highway provides a unique and unparalleled opportunity to experience the thrilling story of dinosaurs and the science and history of discovery behind them. The route combines opportunities to witness dinosaur bones still in the ground being excavated and to see dinosaur bones prepared by paleontologists for museums. Museums all along the byway display both reconstructed skeletons and fleshed-out re-creations of dinosaurs found in the area. Between and sometimes overlapping the dinosaur sites are areas of major archaeological interest. The prehistoric Native Americans who occupied this area saw its many rock cliffs as ideal surfaces for their petroglyphs and pictographs. Some of the finest examples and densest concentrations of this rock art in North America are located along or near the byway.

Along with unique red, gray, and green rock formations, you can enjoy forested mountain passes, canyons, cliffs, rivers, and plateaus along the Dinosaur Diamond Prehistoric Highway. Wide-open spaces and miles of unobstructed views are the reward for those who travel this byway.

## Intrinsic Qualities

**Archaeological:** The Dinosaur Diamond Prehistoric Highway showcases the desert lifestyle of about 1,000 years ago, when Native American cultures lived and hunted in the area. These cultures maintained their way of life in the desert. The best evidence of these ancient people is the abundance of petroglyphs and pictographs in the area. (Petroglyphs are pictures that are pecked into rock surfaces by using harder rocks, often made into tools; pictographs are pictures painted onto the rocks.)

Hundreds of rock surfaces in the Moab area display rock art that was created by the Paleo-Indian, Fremont, and Anasazi cultures. The Golf Course Rock Art site near Moab Golf Course is a large area covered with human and animal figures. Within Arches National Park, Courthouse Wash has both petroglyphs and pictographs on a panel that is 19 feet high and 52 feet long. Also in Arches, Ute rock art can be seen at the Wolfe Ranch near the Delicate Arch Trailhead.

Between Wellington and Myton is Nine Mile Canyon, the greatest concentration of rock art in the United States and the premier site of the archaic culture of the Fremont Indians. The canyon also has examples of dwellings that have been untouched for hundreds of years. Nine Mile Canyon is well preserved because of the dry climate and isolation from large population centers. Because of this preservation, the canyon is home to more than 1,000 rock art sites.

**Cultural:** Eastern Utah has been and continues to be home to many ranches and cattle. In celebration of this culture, rodeos are held periodically throughout the area. In Vernal, the Dinosaur Roundup Rodeo is one of the largest rodeos in the world. In Price, the Black Diamond Stampede Rodeo is held every year. In Moab, Butch Cassidy Days celebrate the history of the area's most famous outlaws. The San Rafael Swell was a favorite hideout for Butch Cassidy and the Sundance Kid and their gang. The Outlaw Trail went from the wild country of Robber's Roost down by Hanksville, up through the San Rafael Swell and either Nine Mile Canyon or along the

*Arches National Park preserves more than 2,000 natural sandstone arches, including the world-famous Delicate Arch.*

### Quick Facts

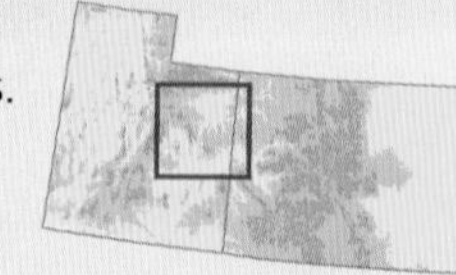

**Length:** 512 miles.

**Time to Allow:** 11 1/2 hours to several days.

**Considerations:** The mountain passes at Reservation Ridge on U.S. 191 and Douglas Pass on CO 139 can be treacherous during winter storms. These roads are rarely officially closed, but there can be delays of up to a few hours. Cleveland Lloyd Dinosaur Quarry is at the end of 13 miles of gravel road that is accessible to sedans in all weather except deep snow; it is closed during the winter months. The Mill Canyon Dinosaur Trail and Copper Ridge Dinosaur Trackway are reached by a couple of miles of dirt road that is accessible to two-wheel-drive automobiles in good weather but are not advisable in wet conditions. Dinosaur trackways are difficult to see under snow cover.

anyons of the Green River into he Uinta Basin. It then either ontinued along the Green or up nd over the eastern Uintas to rown's Park in the tri-state area of Wyoming, Colorado, and Utah. Matt Warner, a former outlaw in he gang, was elected marshal in rice for a number of years. Today, he Outlaw Trail Festival is held every summer in Vernal in honor of hese famous outlaws. Josie Moris, an old friend of Cassidy's, built small cabin in Cub Creek, part of Dinosaur National Monument. It s preserved and stabilized so that visitors can experience what it was ike to rough it in the Old West.

Moab is known as the mountain bike capital of the world, but it is also home to many different festivals and celebrations. Every year in the early spring, participants from all over gather for the Jeep Safari. The slick red rock and warming temperatures in the desert at that time of the year make it a perfect location for extreme driving. If you have more traditional events in mind, the Moab Film Festival showcases the work of independent filmmakers, and Moab hosts an outdoor music festival, as well.

Stroll by Colorado's largest and most diverse outdoor sculpture exhibit, which is on display along Grand Junction's downtown shopping park. The exhibit, entitled *Art on the Corner,* highlights a unique variety of work created by local artists. The nearly 25-year-old ongoing event introduces visitors to many distinct artistic approaches.

**Historical:** The first recorded venture of Europeans into the area was the Escalante–Dominguez Expedition in 1776. This expedition began in Santa Fe and attempted to blaze a trail to California in order to access the missions located there; however, their journey was unsuccessful due to the barriers formed by the western Utah deserts. The expedition was led by Father Silvestre Velez de Escalante and Father Francisco Dominguez, accompanied by Captain Bernardo de Miera y Pacheco, a retired military engineer. They explored Canyon Pintado from Douglas Pass toward what is now Rangely, Colorado; crossed the Green River near Jensen, Utah; and traveled as far west as Spanish Fork before turning back south to return to Santa Fe.

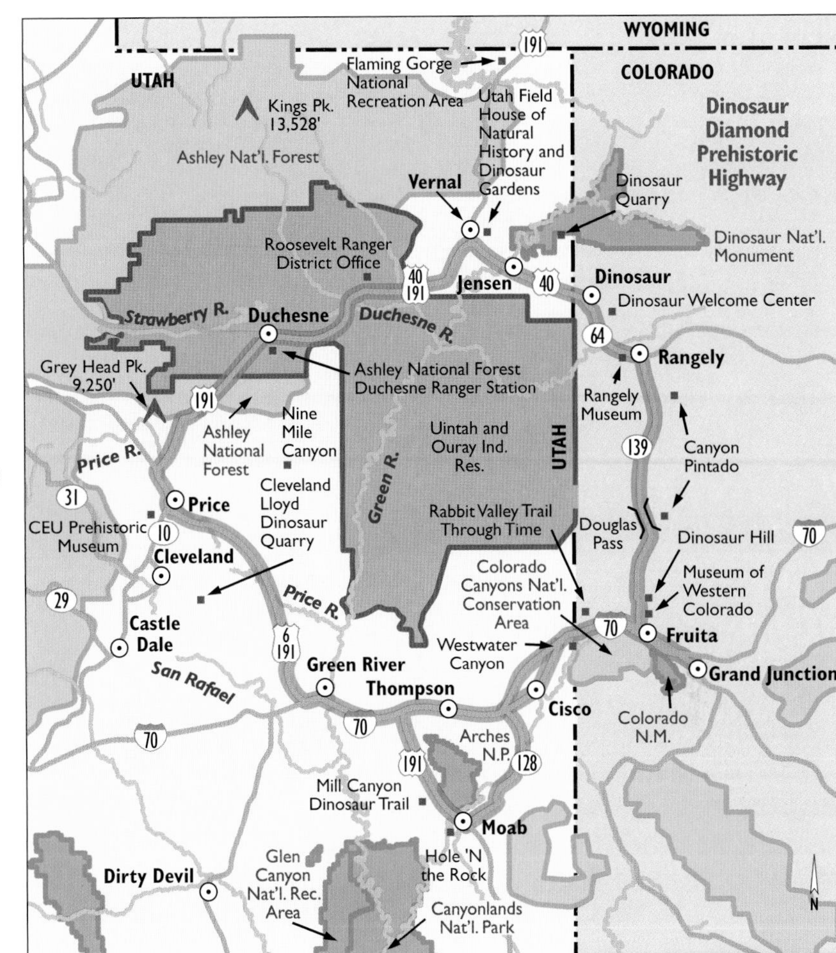


While Escalante and Dominguez came to the area in search of another route west, others have been drawn to eastern Utah because of scientific exploration. Beginning with John C. Frémont in the early 1840s, reports of the majesty of the mountains, the roaring rivers, the expanse and austerity of the deserts, the abundance of game, and the clues to vast mineral resources have enticed adventurers to the intermountain west of the United States. John Wesley Powell, Clarence King, and Ferdinand V. Hayden led extensive geological surveys that helped quantify these resources. Their reports tempted paleontologists with a vast array of undescribed fossils, particularly dinosaurs and prehistoric mammals.

Settlement in the area inevitably brought about great changes to the landscape, such as mining. In the Uinta Basin, Gilsonite was the first hydrocarbon to be mined, bringing a small, narrow-gauge railroad (the Uinta Railroad) into the southeastern edge of the basin near Dragon. Although several attempts were made to build more railroads into the basin, none was successful. As a result, the Uinta Basin remains one of the largest areas of the United States to be undeveloped by railroads. After World War II, petroleum development and phosphate mining became integral to the rural economy. The railroad from Grand Junction, Colorado, to Price, Utah, brought the development of the coal resources in Carbon and Emery counties. As a result of this mining industry, an influx of some 18 different ethnic groups from across southern and eastern Europe and Asia came to work in the mines.

**Natural:** The area encompassed by this diamond-shape byway is the best place in the world to see dinosaurs in a variety of ways: models and bones on display in museums, bones still in the ground at the sites where they were discovered, bones currently being

*Island in the Sky area of Canyonlands National Park rests 1,000 feet above the surrounding terrain. Green River Overlook gives visitors a sweeping view.*

excavated by paleontologists, and trackways preserved in rocks.

Today, the bones and tracks of dinosaurs can be seen at various sites along the byway. Many of these sites are located in their natural settings, which makes this byway one of a kind. Actual dinosaur quarries, which are areas where dinosaur bones are excavated, are along the byway, especially near Moab, Vernal, and Price.

The only two enclosed dinosaur quarries in America are located on the Dinosaur Diamond: one at Dinosaur National Monument and the other at the Cleveland Lloyd Dinosaur Quarry. The bones discovered at Dinosaur National Monument in 1909 by Earl Douglass date from the Jurassic Period (about 145 million years ago) and were preserved in a riverbed that has been quarried for fossils. Portions of more than 300 individual dinosaurs have been recovered, making the site one of the most prolific dinosaur quarries in the world. The Cleveland Lloyd Dinosaur Quarry has the densest concentration of Jurassic dinosaur bones in the world. The quarry is so dense because, about 145 million years ago, dinosaurs were trapped in a muddy bog. Area ranchers found the jumbled remains of these bones, and the quarry has provided dinosaur mounts in more museums around the world than any other in existence. At this quarry, 44 *Allosaurus* specimens have been excavated; appropriately, Utah made the *Allosaurus* the state fossil in 1988. In nearby Price, dinosaur skeletons, tracks, and fossils are on display at the College of Eastern Utah Prehistoric Museum. These exhibits invite visitors to learn more about not only the history of the area but also about the effect of dinosaurs on eastern Utah.

**Recreational:** River rafting is a popular sport to participate in along the byway. Both calm-water and white-water trips are available through companies out of Vernal, Moab, and Green River. The white-water sections can be frightening even for experienced river runners during the high water levels of spring melt, yet some stretches of both the Green and Colorado rivers have flatwater that can be enjoyable in canoes. Grand scenery waits around every bend in the river. In fact, the Green River in Desolation Canyon has cliffs higher than the Grand Canyon in Arizona.

Hiking opportunities are everywhere along the byway. The terrain is varied, giving visitors a feel for the many aspects of the landscape along this route. In the mountains, numerous spectacular peaks and lakes are accessible to hikers. The Uintas Mountain Range, the largest east–west mountain range in the 48 contiguous United States, includes the highest point in Utah—Kings Peak—at 13,528 feet. The desert, particularly near Moab, is another popular place to hike and is an entirely different experience from alpine hiking. The red slickrock around Moab provides the perfect surface for hiking while looking for dinosaur trackways or arches. All of the national parks and monuments along the byway are outstanding places for hiking and camping, as well. Outfitters are available all along the byway for visitors who want guides, horses, or even llamas to help with the load. Hunting and fishing are also popular recreational activities in the area.

Moab has world-famous mountain biking trails to challenge expert riders and to lure beginners. The city has quickly become a mountain bikers' paradise, with trails traveling over many miles, often on slickrock. The Slickrock Bike Trail is located east of Moab in the Sand Flats Recreation Area. The Poison Spider Mesa Trail is another popular trail for both jeeps and bikes and is located on the Potash Road. This trail offers spectacular views of the area surrounding Moab and the Colorado River. Fruita also has excellent mountain biking trails.

Winter sports are also popular along this byway. Snowshoeing, cross-country skiing, snowmobiling, and ice fishing can be enjoyed in the high country, while hiking (without the summer heat) is a popular activity in the southern desert areas.

**Scenic:** The Dinosaur Diamond Prehistoric Highway's many scenic views capture the expansive area of land surrounding the byway. Wide vistas are normal in this desert country, with the horizon stretching on for miles. On hot summer days, the blue sky seems like an endless expanse, and sunsets—going on forever—are magnified because of the open sky. Vistas can include features that are more than 100 miles away.

Canyons with walls of red, green, beige, purple, gray, and white greet you. These scenes are intermingled with forested mountain passes and snowcapped mountains. As you travel winding roads out of canyons, sweeping views of the valleys below open up before you. Along the northern acet of the Dinosaur Diamond, ne Uintas Mountains cut the sky-ne. Ancient faults and tectonics ontrolled the development of this naverick mountain range.

## Highlights

ou can start anywhere along this rcular byway, which loops through ortheastern Utah and northwest-rn Colorado. For purposes of this our, start in the southeastern Utah ortion of the loop.

**Hole 'N the Rock:** At Cisco, Utah, ust off I-70, follow Route 128 south o Moab, home of the Hole 'N the ock, a 5,000-square-foot dwelling arved into huge sandstone rock. Moab sits at the foot of a mini-oop at the bottom of the larger yway loop.

**Arches National Park:** From Moab, ollow U.S. 191 a short distance orth to the visitor center for rches National Park, a spectacu-ar outdoor museum and site of he greatest concentration of atural stone arches and bridges in the world. Once the bed of an ancient sea, Arches National Park has more than 2,000 giant stone arches, as well as pinnacles and spires. Dinosaur tracks and American Indian rock art are also preserved here. You can hike, back-pack, camp, or sightsee along 24 miles of paved roads.

**Cleveland Lloyd Dinosaur Quarry:** Now follow U.S. 191 (which tempo-rarily joins with U.S. 6) as it heads west and then north along the large byway loop. The Cleveland Lloyd Dinosaur Quarry lies south of the town of Price not far from the byway. The quarry contains one of the densest concentrations of Jurassic dinosaur bones ever found (12,000, from 70 different dino-saurs), supplying museums around the world. There are picnic areas and hiking trails here.

**Flaming Gorge Recreation Area:** Continue on U.S. 191, which now loops northeast toward Vernal. If you'd like to cool off or fish at a lake, the Flaming Gorge Recreation Area lies north of Vernal along U.S. 191, surrounding 91-mile-long Flaming Gorge Reservoir and 500-foot-high Flaming Gorge Dam. The reservoir extends north into Wyoming.

*The Fremont Culture of prehistoric American Indians left petroglyphs and pictographs along the walls of Nine Mile Canyon.*

**Dinosaur National Monument:** From Vernal, the byway follows U.S. 40 east toward Colorado. At the junction of U.S. 40 and State Route 49, 13 miles east of Vernal in Jen-sen, go north on State Route 49 to an entrance for Dinosaur National Monument. More skeletons, skulls, and bones of Jurassic dinosaurs have been found here than in any other dig in the world.

**Dinosaur Quarry:** Jensen is the site of the Dinosaur Quarry, a remark-able fossil deposit with an exhibit of 150-million-year-old dinosaur remains. The byway now continues east along U.S. 40 into Colorado.

**Douglas Pass and Canyon Pintado:** Enter Colorado via U.S. 40, which leads to the town of Dinosaur. Drive south on State Route 64 to Rangely. Continue south on Route 139, which travels through the 8,268-foot Douglas Pass. Along the route is Canyon Pintado, which has signifi-cant examples of Fremont Indian rock art. Watch for roadside displays.

**Museum of Western Colo-rado and Dinosaur Hill:** Grand Junction is home to the Museum of Western Colorado, which has exhibits about dinosaurs and regional nature and history. Dinosaur Hill has a self-guided walking trail that leads around a quarry with paleontological excavations.

**Colorado National Monument:** Route 139 meets U.S. 6 just north of Fruita. Follow U.S. 6 southeast to the town of Grand Junction. Rim Rock Drive, which can be accessed either from Fruita or from Grand Junction, leads 23 miles along canyon rims in Colorado National Monument. Deep canyons, rounded domes, towering monoliths, and other geological features are located within the monument.

**Rabbit Valley Trail Through Time:** Now double back north on U.S. 6 to I-70, which leads west toward Utah. Just before reaching the Utah state line on I-70, the Rabbit Valley Trail Through Time offers a one-mile walking trail through fossilized flora and fauna from the Jurassic Age.

**Colorado Canyons National Conser-vation Area:** A bit off the Dinosaur Diamond Prehistoric Highway southwest of U.S. 191 (via route 131) is Colorado Canyons National Con-servation Area, which holds more spectacular rock formations, includ-ing arches, spires, and canyons. The huge, largely undeveloped park also has Native American picto-graphs and Puebloan ruins, desert flora, and portions of the Green and Colorado rivers, where you can arrange white-water trips. Some park roads are safe only for high-clearance four-wheel-drive vehicles. The byway then continues its loop into Utah.

# The Energy Loop: Huntington and Eccles Canyons Scenic Byways

*As this two-byway loop winds through the canyons and valleys of Utah's backyard, the legacies of coal mining, ancient cultures, and prehistoric creatures come alive at every stop.*

Situated amid mountainous terrain and pine forests, the Energy Loop runs through Utah's beautiful backyard. Travelers come from miles away to fish the trout-filled waters along the route or to enjoy a picnic in the beautiful forest surroundings. You can also see signs of red rock country.

Deriving its name from the rich coal-mining history of the area, the Energy Loop combines two of Utah's byways: the Huntington Canyon Scenic Byway and the Eccles Canyon Scenic Byway. Along the way, you can see early Mormon settlements in Sanpete Valley or visit unique museums in the byway communities. Towns from Scofield to Huntington revere the days when coal mining was the livelihood of so many of their ancestors. As you pass today's mines, note the harmony between the environment and industrial development.

## Intrinsic Qualities

**Archaeological:** The Energy Loop and the surrounding areas in central Utah offer an archaeological menagerie for visitors of any knowledge level. As you pass places on the byway, informational kiosks offer stories and facts about the archaeological past of the area. Huntington Reservoir is especially notable for its excavation of the 27-foot mammoth skeleton that was found in 1988. Other excavations in the area have yielded a short-faced bear, a giant ground sloth, a saber-toothed tiger, and a camel, all from an ice age long ago. Examples and casts of these archaeological finds can be seen in museums on and near the byway, the most significant being the College of Eastern Utah Prehistoric Museum.

Although the Energy Loop is most famous for the mammoth skeleton that was found at the Huntington Reservoir, other treasures await visitors, as well. Museums in the area—such as the Fairview Museum, the Museum of the San Rafael in Castle Dale, and the College of Eastern Utah Prehistoric Museum—feature artifacts of human inhabitants from the recent past of the pioneers to the more distant past of the Fremont Indian culture. Near the byway, you can travel through Nine Mile Canyon, a place that has more than 1,000 sites of pictographs and petroglyphs left on the rocks by an ancient people.

You will also find tributes to dinosaurs in many of the area museums. Not only have ice-age mammals been found, but the area also holds an extensive dinosaur quarry. East of Huntington, the Cleveland Lloyd Dinosaur Quarry is where 145-million-year-old bones and fossils from the Jurassic Period are uncovered by paleontologists. The reconstructed skeletons and exhibits in the visitor center and area museums provide a vast amount of information about these creatures of the past. From millions of years ago to just hundreds of years ago, the Energy Loop and its surrounding areas have much to offer in the way of archaeological exploration.

**Cultural:** The cultural patchwork of the area begins with the Fremont Indians. These people moved into the area sometime between A.D. 300 and 500. Although they were a primitive people, they left behind artifacts of a culture in their rock art, baskets, and figurines. The Fremont Indians usually lived in pit houses made of wood and mud that people entered through an opening in the roof. The weapons and tools of this culture were much different than neighboring American Indian cultures, indicating the unique existence of the Fremonts. By the time European settlers reached the area, the Fremont Indian culture had disappeared.

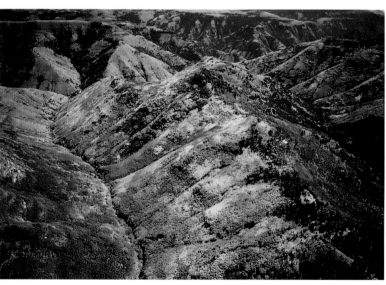

*Fairview Canyon, east of the town of Fairview, is a favorite of snowmobilers and those seeking rugged beauty any time of the year.*

### Quick Facts

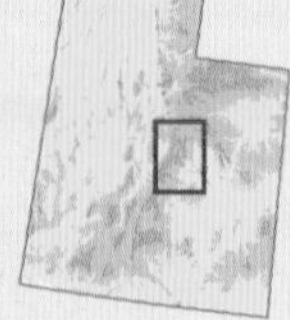

**Length:** 86 miles.

**Time to Allow:** 1½ to 4 hours.

**Considerations:** Because sections of this byway climb to altitudes above 10,000 feet, dress warmly during all seasons. Certain roads may be closed in winter due to heavy snowfall.

Settlers who came to the area in the early 1800s found an untamed wilderness with many resources. Ranchers found meadows with grass that was perfect for grazing livestock. Coal was one of the most important resources found in the area, and as a result, coal-mining towns sprang up all around. The coal-mining culture was a society of hardworking men, women, and children who worked in and around the mines—often at the peril of their own lives. Their story can be found in places like the Scofield Cemetery and several deserted towns. Coal mining, power plants, and hydroelectric power harnessed in the reservoirs are all still present today. These all play a direct part in the name of this byway—the Energy Loop.

**Historical:** Few areas in the United States can boast of undiscovered and diverse historical resources the way the area surrounding the Energy Loop can. Travelers along the route see a variety of important historical landmarks, including Native American historical sites, Spanish exploration routes, and the early Mormon settlements that have grown into towns. You are in for a diverse historical experience not likely to be matched as you visit the historic coal-mining and railroad industries that have deep roots in the area, along with the small-town museums in the byway communities.

**Natural:** The Energy Loop abounds with natural resources that make it the scenic and productive area that it is. All along the byway, you see evidence of energy—harnessed or unharnessed—on the Energy Loop. Places like the Skyline Mine and the Huntington Power Plant bring natural fuels to the surface, while canyons and wildflowers bring scenic nature to the surface. With these natural qualities combined, the Wasatch Plateau is a thriving habitat for both wildlife and people.

Through ancient fault lines and geological uplifts, the canyons and valleys along the byway present a unique topography and beautiful places to stop or pass. Red rocks of sandstone line the walls of Huntington Canyon, while Eccles Canyon takes drivers through forested ridges and grassy meadows. Because of the thick forests of maple, aspen, and oak, the fall is a colorful time in the canyons of the Energy Loop.

For the same reasons that this area is rich with prehistoric fossils, it is also rich with coal. The coal in this area was formed nearly 100 million years ago, when plants were covered by land or water. The plant matter was compressed by sediment and hardened into the carbon substance we call coal. Although you may not see any coal, its presence is one of the unique natural qualities of the byway.

As you drive the byway, the natural splendor that surrounds the road is impossible to ignore. Streams rush by with trout hiding just near the banks. Mature forests of aspen and pine create a lush habitat for wildlife that lives on the byway. You may catch a glimpse of a fox or a badger. The wetlands of the Fairview Lakes are the best place on the byway to observe waterfowl or perhaps a bald eagle. The meadows, streams, and forests all combine to create the perfect habitat for creatures great and small. On the mountaintops, birds of prey circle near the clouds while chipmunks scurry through open fields. And in the spring and early summer, wildflowers dot the road and paint the ridgetops.

**Recreational:** All along the byway, cars are stopped at the sides of the roads, but the drivers are nowhere to be seen unless you check the river. Anglers come from all around to fish for the trout that swim in the waters of Huntington Creek. Fly fishers have their pick of cutthroat, brown, and rainbow trout when fishing the streams and rivers on the byway. Fishing in the six reservoirs along the byway is a common recreational activity.

Hiking and biking are activities worth trying along the Energy Loop. The rocks and cliffs of Huntington Canyon are an enticing invitation to explorers ready to hike along such diverse terrain. Tie Fork Canyon offers a hike among trees and wildflowers of every kind. Joes Valley is a stop that offers options for anglers and hikers.

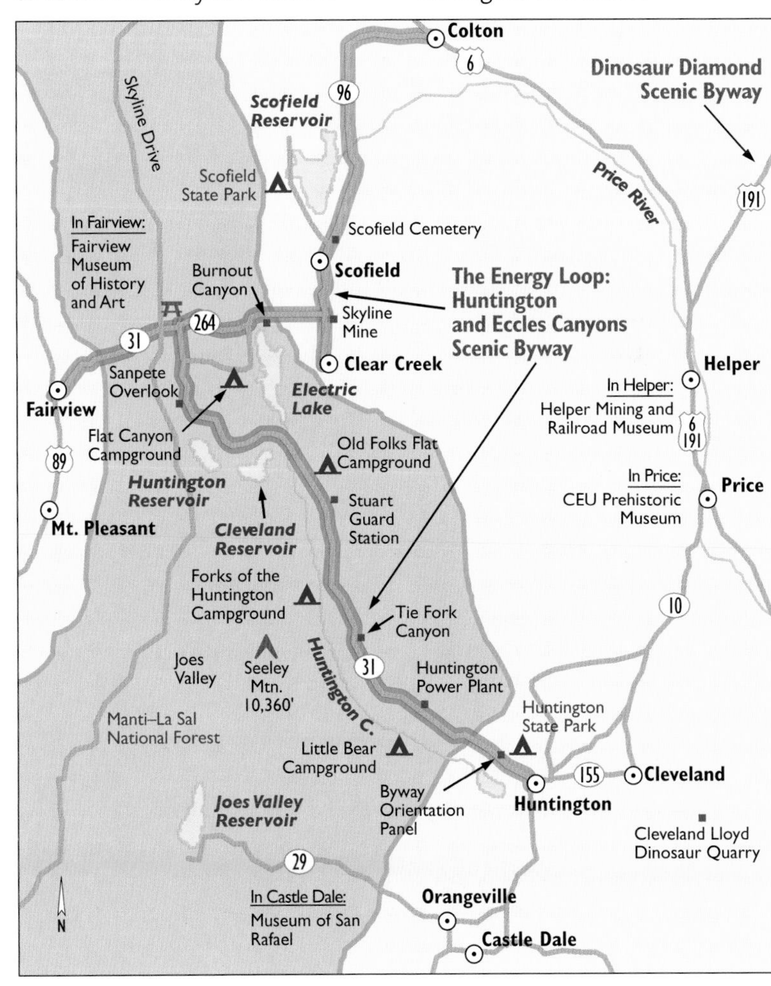

**Scenic:** Wherever the starting point is on the Energy Loop, the road takes travelers through contrasting terrain that changes abruptly. The landscape of the Energy Loop is made up of different areas known as the San Rafael Swell and the Wasatch Plateau. As you drive through these areas, notice the interplay between vegetation and terrain as it creates a scenic view. In some places, mountains are covered in pine and aspen, creating lush, forested canyons. In others, the vegetation is sparse among the red rock formations along the plateaus.

Driving through the beautiful stands of mature trees of the Manti–La Sal National Forest, you will notice mountain streams and winding inclines. The shades of light and dark clash directly with the pine and the aspen on the mountaintops of Eccles Canyon. The long grass in the meadows lines the banks of Huntington Creek, with some of the blades dipping down into the scurrying water below. In the distance, you may catch a glimpse of an old log cabin or, perhaps, a bluebird perched on an old fence. Grass and sagebrush appear among the aspen at the tops of the mountains, and a stop at Sanpete Overlook offers a view of the sprawling mountains and valleys beyond overshadowed by clouds.

Tucked away on the corners of the Energy Loop are small communities and historic mining towns. These present a break in the route and an opportunity to drive the streets of the communities to see old buildings and cemeteries. Many of the towns like Scofield and Fairview offer informational kiosks or museums for exploration.

The alluring wilderness begins to appear at the south end of the byway in a swift transition from pine-forested mountains to rocky, red cliffs. Unique yellow and red rock formations with holes, crevasses, and trees scattered throughout are the results of an erratic art form of nature. Some of the rocks appear in vertical slabs wedged together to form a cliff. Others have pockmarks so distinct that, from a distance, they could be mistaken for an archaic language. Scenic turnouts are irresistible for photographing a rock formation against the sky or a river rushing through the canyons.

The scenic qualities of the Energy Loop are diverse and breathtaking. The byway stretches across the Wasatch Plateau, rising high through steep canyons and down into pristine valleys. Castle Valley is located on the eastern side of the byway at the edge of the dramatic San Rafael Swell near Huntington. This desert valley is gorgeous and in stark contrast with the forested canyons found between Huntington and Fairview.

The byway makes its way up Huntington Canyon, over a high summit, and down into Fairview Canyon, where you are treated to extraordinary views of mountain slopes and the Sanpete Valley below. Streams, lakes, and reservoirs are abundant on the byway. At the higher elevations where the Huntington and Eccles Canyons intersect, you'll see U-shape glacial valleys with rounded peaks and cirques cut by ancient glaciers.

*Joes Valley Reservoir, a 1,200-acre lake, is a popular destination for fishing and water skiing.*

## Highlights

Traveling from Fairview, this tour suggests scenic vistas that will make your visit to the Energy Loop a fulfilling one.

**Electric Lake and Burnout Canyon:** Beginning in Fairview, take UT 31 approximately ten miles to its junction with Highway 264. Follow 264 for about another ten miles, and you will come upon a turnout, along with a view of Burnout Canyon and Electric Lake. Electric Lake was constructed to provide power for the Huntington Power Plant. At the bottom of the lake lay old mines and kilns.

**Scofield:** Twelve miles past the Electric Lake Overlook on Highway 264, you will meet State Highway 96. Travel north for five miles to the historic town of Scofield, once the largest town in all of Carbon County. On May 1, 1900, one of the worst mining accidents in U.S. history claimed the lives of hundreds of miners. Visit the old cemetery to see the gravestones of the miners lost on that tragic day. A little farther north, Highway 96 runs beside Scofield State Park and Reservoir, which provides good trout fishing.

**Sanpete Valley Overlook:** Leave the Scofield area by heading south on Highway 96, following the road you came in on. Drive back to the junction of Highways 264 and UT 31, and follow UT 31 southeast toward the town of Huntington. Approximately seven miles from the junction, you will find another turnout that shows an impressive view of the Sanpete Valley.

**Joes Valley Overlook:** Continue traveling south for around eight miles on UT 31 to another scenic overlook. This turnout provides a view of Joes Valley below, a popular recreation area for locals.

# Flaming Gorge–Uintas Scenic Byway 

*Utah's highest mountains, its favorite outdoor playground, and the real Jurassic Park lie along this colorful desert byway, where Butch Cassidy once rode with his gang; a reservoir promises cool fun on the water.*

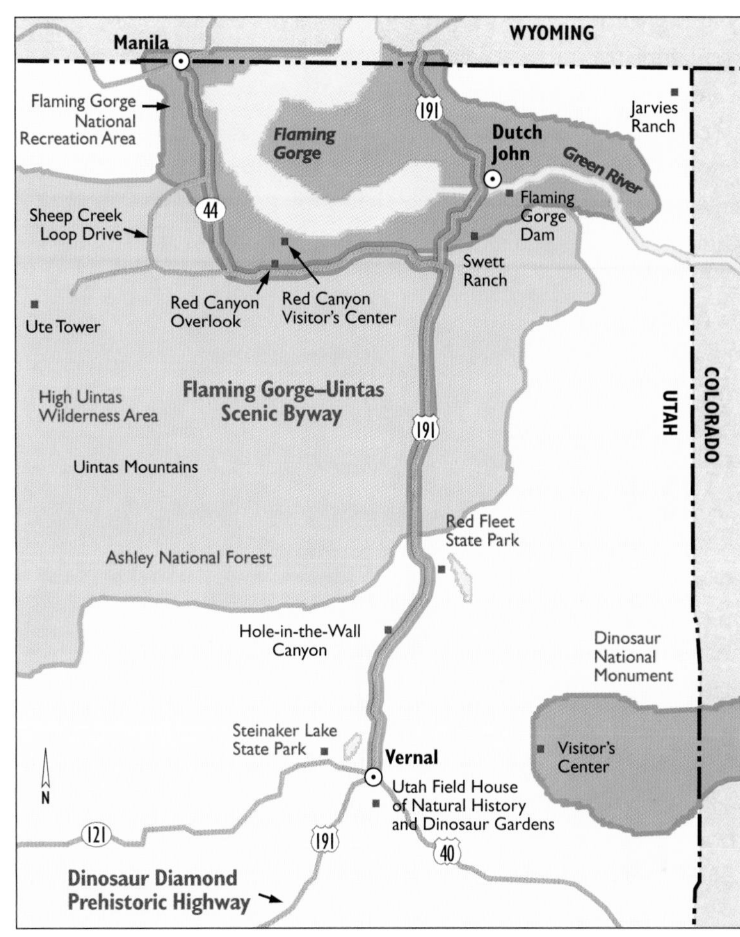


As one of the most aptly named landscapes in the country, Flaming Gorge ɔrovides the kind of scenic vistas hat refuse to fit in the viewfinder ɔf your camera and must be elived in your memory after you eturn home. Driving this byway, 'ou get to watch Flaming Gorge ınd the Uintas Mountains unfold 'rom several different perspectives.

## ntrinsic Qualities

**rchaeological:** Beyond its obviɔus scenic beauty, Flaming Gorge–Uintas Scenic Byway has ɔieces of stored ancient history within its grounds and cliff sides. 'ictographs and petroglyphs are hought to have been left behind ɔy the Fremont Indians many ıundreds of years ago. Ancient rock art can also be found near Dinosaur National Monument on one of the nature trails.

But ancient history goes back even further on this byway, and one of the main reasons people travel to this area is to see the largest quarry of Jurassic dinosaur skeletons in the country. Dinosaur National Monument is a must-see on the Flaming Gorge–Uintas Scenic Byway. Discovered in 1909, the quarry has yielded 11 dinosaur species, plus more than 1,600 bones. Here, you can see bones in and out of the quarry and all the places they have to go in between.

**Historical:** The route along the Flaming Gorge–Uintas Scenic Byway is rich in history and culture. The first European explorers were Fathers Dominguez and Escalante. Wesley Powell explored the Green River and named many of the byway's geographic sites, including Flaming Gorge. General William H. Ashley explored the area and established several trading posts. He organized the first Mountain Man Rendezvous in 1825 near Manila.

The byway parallels the Outlaw Trail that Butch Cassidy and members of the Wild Bunch used. Two turn-of-the-19th-century homesteads on the byway, Swett Ranch and Jarvies Ranch, are presently managed and interpreted by the Forest Service and Bureau of Land Management. The town of Vernal celebrates Outlaw Days with an outdoor theater depicting sagas of the Wild Bunch, a ride along the Outlaw trail, and other community events. The influence of Mormon settlers is also evident in the Manila and Vernal areas.

**Natural:** The Flaming Gorge–Uintas Scenic Byway winds over the eastern flank of the Uintas Mountains and through the Flaming Gorge National Recreation Area, leading you through diverse plant communities that provide a great habitat for more than 390 species of birds, mammals, reptiles, amphibians, and fish. You'll have access to several developed viewing platforms, overlooks, displays, and signs that interpret the different wildlife species. This byway is one of the few areas in the United States where visitors have the chance to

### Quick Facts

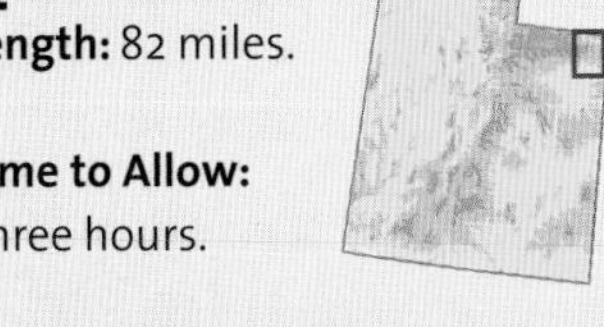

**Length:** 82 miles.

**Time to Allow:** Three hours.

**Considerations:** Because the public lands along the byway are managed under the Multiple Use Concept, you may have the opportunity to encounter a real western cattle drive along the roadway during the spring and fall months. Sections of the mountain highway are occasionally closed due to extreme snowfall during the winter.

see large herds of deer, elk, moose, and pronghorn antelopes on any given day. The seasonal weather changes complement the wildlife migration patterns, which means that you may encounter Rocky Mountain bighorn sheep, river otters, yellow-bellied marmots, kokanee salmon, red-tailed hawks, mountain bluebirds, golden eagles, bald eagles, and ospreys. Additionally, thousands of sandhill cranes migrate through the Vernal area in April and October.

This landscape is the basic setting for the real Jurassic Park, not only for dinosaurs but also for other prehistoric creatures, such as sharks, squid, and turtles. The Utah Field House of Natural History and Dinosaur Gardens serves as an orientation center for the byway. Dinosaur National Monument features the largest working dinosaur quarry in the world; the world-class displays of dinosaurs and interpretive exhibits provide you with a greater appreciation for the geologic and prehistoric features found along the byway.

**Recreational:** Flaming Gorge Reservoir is the most popular recreation spot in Utah. It offers highly developed facilities for camping, hiking, riding, skiing, snowmobiling, and other activities on a year-round basis. The visitor center, gift shops, restaurants, outfitters, guides, boat rentals, and other retailers work together as partners to make this a quality experience.

Flaming Gorge Reservoir is surrounded by 367 shoreline miles, creating an angler's paradise. World-record brown trout exceeding 30 pounds and lake trout more than 50 pounds have been caught here. People from all over the world visit the Green River for premier blue-ribbon fly-fishing experiences. The nearby High Uintas Wilderness Area (Utah's largest) offers hundreds of miles of hiking trails and numerous camping sites; it also boasts of hundreds of high-elevation lakes with great fishing opportunities.

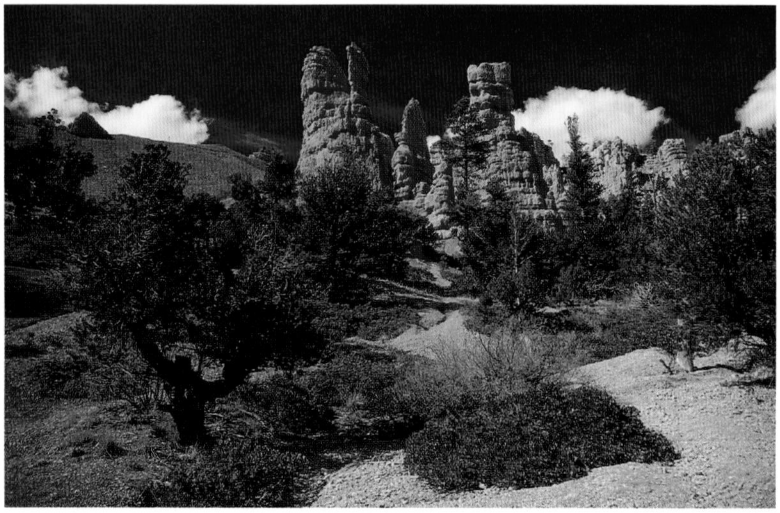

*Hoodoos and other unique geological structures make Red Canyon especially distinctive. These interesting formations become more common as Red Canyon comes closer to Bryce Canyon National Park.*

**Scenic:** One of the most beautiful sights as you drive this byway is to watch the sun as it reflects off the water of the 91-mile Flaming Gorge Reservoir. The most famous scenic view of the gorge, however, is of Red Canyon just below the Flaming Gorge Dam. The canyon walls on both sides of the water create an image of a lake clinging to the mountainsides. Half of the byway follows Flaming Gorge as it curves into the Green River. The red plateaus sloping into Sheep Creek Bay look like abandoned sinking ships as the water laps at the edges.

The mountains that surround the gorge itself are densely forested. Traveling through Ashley National Forest, the byway gives you an excellent opportunity to enjoy the eastern edge of the Uintas mountain range, which is the only major east–west range in the United States. As Utah's tallest mountain range, the Uintas are an inviting sight as the peaks tower to the sky. The forest is home to wildlife and beautiful scenery consisting of red rocky mountains and majestic peaks. The crags and geological formations along the drive add immensely to the unique views that make Flaming Gorge memorable.

## Highlights

While visiting the Flaming Gorge–Uintas Scenic Byway, you can take the following self-guided tour.

**Utah Field House of Natural History and Dinosaur Gardens:** Driving on the byway from Vernal, you don't want to miss the Utah Field House of Natural History and Dinosaur Gardens on the north side of Main Street near Vernal. See life-size dinosaurs and Fremont and Ute Indian artifacts.

**Dinosaur National Monument:** If you have the time, take a side trip, following U.S. 40 and traveling 20 miles east of Vernal to visit the Dinosaur National Monument.

**Flaming Gorge Dam:** If you're making a quick trip, continue on U.S. 191 to the Flaming Gorge Dam, six miles from the Greendale Junction (U.S. 191 and UT 44). There you'll find picnic sites and other visitor facilities. Be sure to take the guided tour through the dam.

**Swett Ranch:** Make a U-turn back on U.S. 191 to travel west on UT 44. If you have time for a longer visit, you could stop at the Swett Ranch and partake of pioneer history.

**Red Canyon Overlook and Visitor's Center:** Continue on your way to the Red Canyon Overlook and Visitor's Center in the Flaming Gorge National Recreation Area, about five miles off of UT 44. The caves and ledges of this scenic wonder offer glimpses into the ancient history of this area.

**Sheep Creek Loop Drive:** If you have some extra time, continue on UT 44 and turn left onto the Sheep Creek Loop Drive to the Ute Tower.

# A Journey Through Time Scenic Byway—Highway 12

*As it passes through rugged and colorful canyons lying between two national parks, this byway showcases a land of ancient cultures, pioneers, and explorers—with a piece of history beckoning around every turn.*

As you drive the byway that connects Bryce Canyon National Park and Capitol Reef National Park, you are treated to enticing views and stops, along with a kaleidoscope of color. Byway towns in between offer the flavor of a simple life in the middle of a fantastic wilderness. Historic stops and pull-offs provide stories for curious byway travelers. Ancient ruins and artwork can be found throughout the canyons and rock faces that line this byway.

## Intrinsic Qualities

**Archaeological:** Driving this road through some of Utah's most unusual landscapes, the climate and topography seem all too fantastic for human beings to dwell there. Nevertheless, evidence of ancient civilization is around every corner and within almost every crevasse of the canyons along Highway 12. The Anasazi, Fremont, and Utes all left their mark on the rugged and challenging land. Their occupation has been preserved in the sandstone of the plateaus and under the sands and soils of the valleys.

The structures that the Anasazi left behind astound travelers and archaeologists alike. Alcoves high in the rocks hold ancient stone granaries where this hunting-and-gathering culture would store the food they had collected. The granaries reside in grooves within the cliff side and consist of rocks stacked like bricks with a small hole in the center near the bottom of the structure. It is not known how the people of so long ago would have reached these heights.

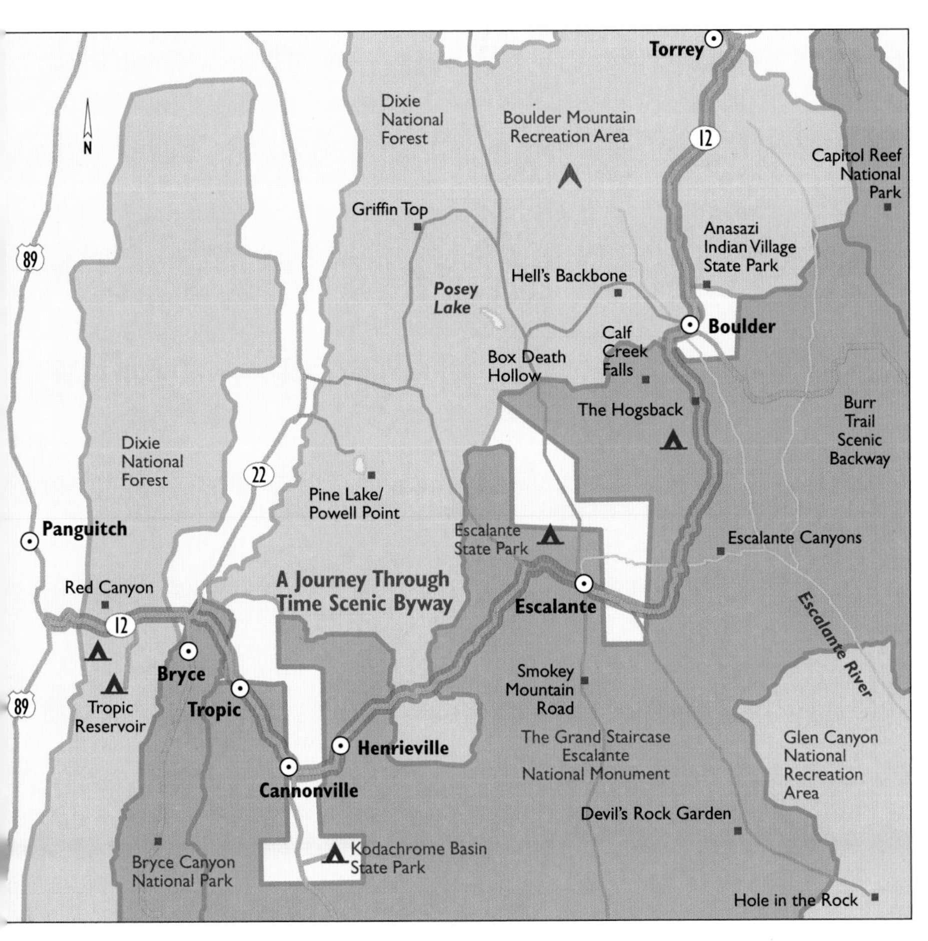


Farther along the byway, a remarkable display of an excavated Anasazi village is located on the byway in the community of Boulder. The Anasazi Indian Village State Park Visitor Center is located at the site of a village that once held 200 people. Walls of homes and structures of pit houses are displayed there.

Some of the most impressive examples of rock art can be seen at Capitol Reef National Park as images of ancient people and animals line the red rock face of nearby Highway 24 and the Fremont River.

**Cultural:** The archaeological remains and artwork of the Fremont Indians and the Anasazi enable modern-day experts and visitors to speculate about what these people must have been like. These cultures had a belief system of legends and histories that explained the landforms that surrounded them. One thing is certain: The cultures of the Anasazi, Fremont, and Paiute

## Quick Facts

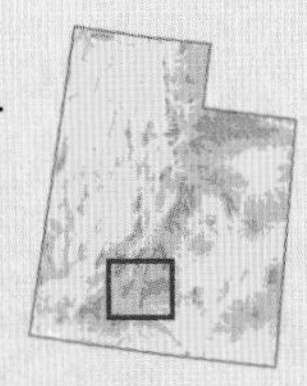

**Length:** 124 miles.

**Time to Allow:** One to three days.

**Considerations:** Several stretches of this road are quite isolated and rugged, some with 12 percent grades. The road climbs to 8,000 feet as it crosses Boulder Mountain, rising and falling in steep switchbacks through Escalante Canyons and Boulder Mountain. The Aquarius Plateau/Boulder Mountain segment receives heavy accumulations of winter snow and may be closed temporarily during heavy snowstorms. Please also note that the Hogsback is high and narrow and can be windy. High-profile vehicles should be prepared.

*The Escalante, the final river in the continental United States to be named, ambles slowly between towering canyon walls.*

revered the land of Highway 12 as a special land.

Mormon pioneers established communities more than a century ago whose presence today has brought a new collection of stories and histories. The communities that visitors will observe display the classical elements of a Mormon settlement. Mormons would gather in a town and spread their farms all around the town.

**Historical:** The first explorers were Spanish and claimed the land for Spain in 1776. The name of the town Escalante comes from one of the priests who was on the expedition, Silvestre Velez de Escalante. John Wesley Powell more thoroughly explored the land nearly 100 years later in 1869 on a treacherous journey on which he lost several of his company. By the time he explored the area, Mormon pioneers had already begun to inhabit the region.

The town of Panguitch was the first place the pioneers attempted to settle. Because of conflicts with the Native Americans, they abandoned the settlement until 1871. A string of other towns, including Tropic and Boulder, retain a western town appearance with wood storefronts, stone walls, and old-fashioned architecture.

**Natural:** Red Canyon, Bryce Canyon, and Kodachrome Basin offer some of the strangest geological sites. The walls of Bryce Canyon are lined with singular, humanlike pinnacles that protrude from the rock. The irregular shapes of the rocks in Bryce Canyon were formed when ancient rivers carved exposed layers of the earth. The meandering of these rivers must have been erratic, for there are thousands of paths through the pinnacles. Red Canyon displays a range of orange and red colors in the rock. Take a hike to discover all the natural arches there. In Kodachrome Basin, evidence of another natural wonder from millions of years ago is in the strange pinnacles of stone. Kodachrome used to be a geyser basin not unlike the kind found in Yellowstone National Park today. Geologists believe that the towers of stone there are actually fossilized geysers. Their vivid colors are evident from a distance.

**Recreational:** Some of the most captivating hikes in Utah are located just off A Journey Through Time Scenic Byway in the slot canyons of the Grand Staircase or near one of the byway's state parks. Red Canyon and its accompanying canyons offer trails for hikers, bikers, horseback riders, and ATV enthusiasts.

**Scenic:** Spanning a route of more than 120 miles, this byway travels through some of the most diverse and ruggedly beautiful landscapes in the country. The surrounding red rock formations, slickrock canyons, pine and aspen forests, alpine mountains, national and state parks, and quaint rural towns all contribute in making Highway 12 a unique route well worth traveling.

## Highlights

This tour starts in the vicinity of Bryce Canyon on the western end of the byway.

**Bryce Canyon National Park:** Follow Highway 12 east from the intersection of U.S. 89. At State Route 63, and then turn south into Bryce Canyon National Park, a 56-square-mile area filled with colorful, fantastic cliffs and pinnacles created by millions of years of erosion.

**Kodachrome Basin State Park:** Highway 12 then leads east to Kodachrome Basin State Park, which contains strange, vividly colored stone pinnacles, believed to be ancient fossilized geysers.

**Escalante State Park:** Continuing east on Highway 12, the next stop is Escalante State Park, a petrified forest with mineralized wood and dinosaur bones. The park also has a reservoir for swimming, fishing, and boating (with ramps), as well as hiking trails, picnicking, birdwatching, and camping.

**Anasazi Indian Village State Park:** Highway 12 now swings north toward the town of Boulder. Near Boulder is the Anasazi Indian Village State Park, including a partially excavated village with museum. Probably occupied by Fremont and Kayenta Anasazi Indians from 1050 to 1200, it was one of the largest ancient communities west of the Colorado River. Picnic areas are available.

**Capitol Reef National Park:** Off the northeastern end of the byway is 378-square-mile Capitol Reef National Park (the visitor center is located along State Route 24, which leads east off Highway 12). Here, red sandstone cliffs are capped with domes of white sandstone. A 25-mile round-trip scenic drive leads through the park

# Logan Canyon Scenic Byway 

*With its mountain peaks, sparkling river, inland lakes, and colorful rock formations, this canyon byway entrances not just sightseers but rock climbers, hikers, cyclists, picnickers, anglers, boaters, and skiers.*

Beautiful mountains that tower over the city of Logan and the turquoise waters of Bear Lake captivate visitors and residents year-round. You'll be enchanted by inland seas, a dramatic landscape surrounding this byway formed by great earthquakes and mountains that tower over the road on both sides. Driving the Logan Canyon Scenic Byway is like entering a new world where the mountains, trees, and river together reveal the undying patterns of nature.

*Contrary to the name, Ricks Spring is not a wholesome natural spring, but rather a diversion of Logan River.*

## Intrinsic Qualities

**Cultural:** From mountain men to mountain climbers, Logan Canyon has fostered a variety of cultures from its earliest days. As cultures have shifted and evolved over the last few centuries in this corner of northern Utah, memories of the past are still in place. Cultural influences of mountain men and Native Americans still surface from time to time in the modern cultures of agriculture and industry.

The Shoshone and Bannock nations had been living in the areas near Cache Valley and Bear Lake for many years before their lands were forever changed by the coming of fur trappers and, later, settlers. Local nations still gather to practice beautiful cultural dances and songs; their artwork can be seen in summer fairs and festivals. Mountain men are also honored with festivals and activities.

The coming of the Mormon pioneers made a significant impact on the area's culture. Settlers from the Church of Jesus Christ of Latter-day Saints (LDS) developed an agricultural society that still thrives in Cache Valley. The Mormon pioneers also brought with them an appreciation for family and heritage.

Today, because they live so close to a perfect wilderness, most everyone in Cache Valley and Bear Lake has a personal attachment to at least one aspect of Logan Canyon. From exploring nature trails to fishing and canoeing, the skills and pastimes of the first people in Logan Canyon remain with today's residents.

**Historical:** Although most of the places in Logan Canyon were named in the last 150 years, influences from an earlier past can still be found in places along the byway. Guinavah–Malibu Campground carries the Shoshone word for "bird water," which was the earliest name for the Logan River. A mountain man named Jim Bridger gave his name to the region that encompasses the canyon known as Bridgerland. Cache Valley, at the west end of the canyon, was named for the caches that trappers made in the area to store their furs. As Mormon pioneers entered the area in the mid-1800s, they established Temple Fork, where they procured the materials they would need to build their temple and tabernacle. And many of the names in the canyon came from the days of the Civilian Conservation Corps (CCC). Most notable of their achievements is the amphitheater at the Guinavah–Malibu Campground.

Stories of highfalutin families at Tony Grove or an 11-foot-tall bear named Ephraim can be found in places all along the way. One of the best places to find out about Logan Canyon history is at the mouth of the canyon in Logan. Lady Bird Overlook is a location that carries history of its own. It was named for President Lyndon Johnson's wife, Lady Bird Johnson, who initiated the highway beautification plan in the 1960s. At the overlook, you can discover the story of a 1,000-year-old tree and find out why one of

### Quick Facts

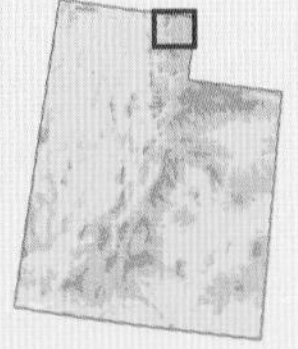

**Length:** 41 miles.

**Time to Allow:** One hour.

**Considerations:** Please note that Logan Canyon Scenic Byway is a two-lane highway. Although the byway has more passing zones on the upgrade than the downgrade, you'll find only five to eight passing zones. Also, because winter weather can be severe, the highway patrol may require that vehicles carry tire chains.

the most beautiful spots on the byway is called China Row.

Logan Canyon was in the land of the Shoshone and the Bannock. Later, Logan Canyon saw the days of mountain men trapping animals for their fur. When the Mormon pioneers arrived, the wild land of Logan Canyon was forever changed. Civilization came to the byway to explore it and discover the wonders of the canyon in the same way that travelers do today.

**Natural:** In Logan Canyon, wilderness waits at the doorstep of the Cache Valley community. The canyon is alive with wildflowers, shrubs, and trees of every kind.

Although the mountains seem high, they were once covered with the water of an inland sea called Lake Bonneville. Many of the rock formations that visitors enjoy in the canyon were caused by erosion from Lake Bonneville. Outcroppings, such as the one called the China Row, are simply ancient beaches where the sediment has become solid and provides a perfect place for activities like rock climbing. Just looking up at these mammoth walls of nature is a mesmerizing experience; knowing that they were once ancient beaches makes them even more exotic.

The enchanting Tony Grove Lake, formerly a glacier, is a favorite natural feature in the canyon. Covered with wildflowers in the spring, the shorelines of the lake are partly a mountainside and partly a forest of pine trees. Water has carved numerous caves through the limestone of the canyon, including Logan Cave and Ricks Spring.

The Logan River is the heart of Logan Canyon, its rhythm changing with the seasons. During the spring, the river rages with snowmelt runoff, reaching high velocities. In summer, the river slows, fed by delayed runoff from groundwater storage and augmented by the many springs and tributaries that flow into it. The river surface begins to freeze in the fall, and by midwinter the river forms ragged sheets of ice. When the weather is fair, visitors on the shores of Second Dam watch fish jumping and beavers swimming across the water to their dams. In the winter, deer step lightly on the mountainside and pause by the river for a drink.

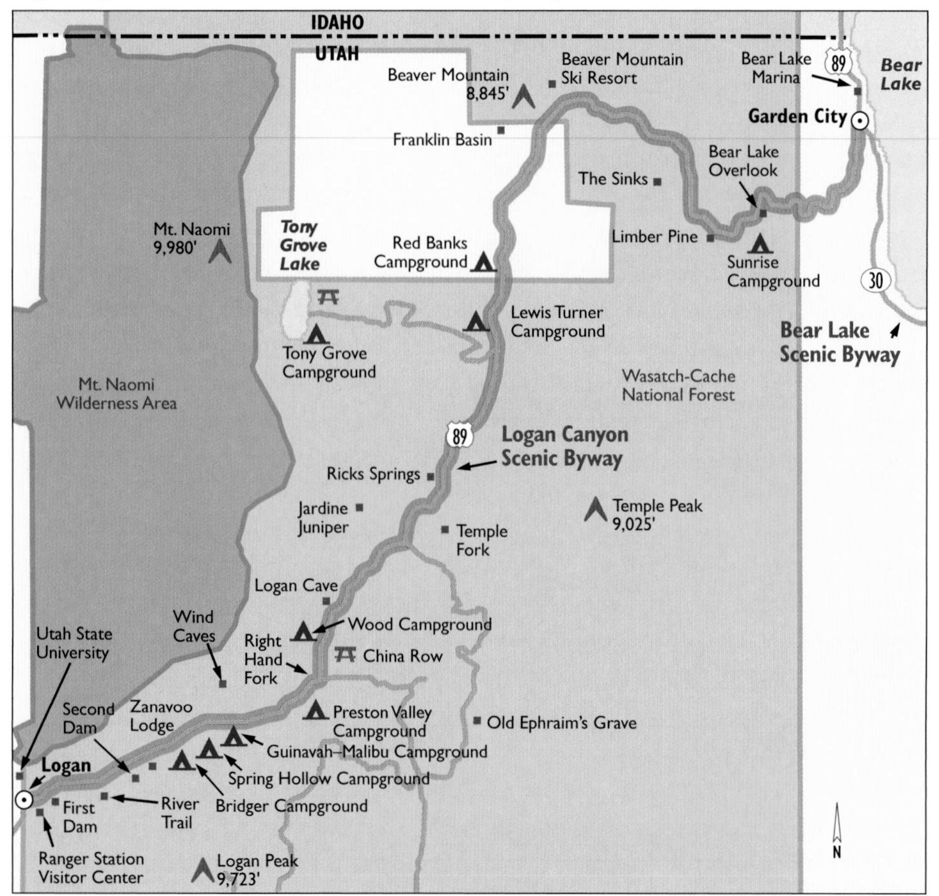


**Recreational:** Logan Canyon recreation is one of the main reasons people come to Cache Valley to visit and to stay. After a short drive into the mountains, you'll find a garden of recreational opportunities—some relaxing and others extreme. From a serene early morning hike to rock climbing, Logan Canyon is the best place for miles around to unwind.

Logan Canyon's limestone outcroppings are calling for you to climb them. Rock climbers gather from spring through fall to challenge the million-year-old mountainsides. Most of the climbs are bolt-protected sport climbs. In winter, climbers can be found making their way up a frozen waterfall. Another mountainside challenge is offered within the crisp winter air at Beaver Mountain, where skiers and snowboarders gather to test skills of balance and coordination.

Although they might be the most exciting of mountain sports, skiing and climbing aren't the only activities available in Logan Canyon. With 300 miles of hiking trails, Logan Canyon is also a hiker's paradise. Trails lead to every kind of destination, from an ancient juniper tree to a pristine mountain lake. Runners and cyclists especially love the Logan River Trail starting at Red Bridge. On summer mornings, the air is cool and green leaves hang over the trail, creating a scenic place to exercise.

Roads available at Temple Fork and Right Hand Fork provide opportunities for ATVs and motorcyclists to enjoy the exciting back roads to the canyon. During the winter, trailers carrying snowmobiles can be seen entering Logan Canyon. They might be heading to Franklin Basin or The Sinks, where valleys between the trees offer the perfect places to traverse the snow.

When all the snow melts, water sports reach their heights in Logan Canyon, whether you are

*There are many trails and many caves in Utah. One of the most memorable trails is the one up to Wind Caves with its spectacular view of the canyon below.*

boating or fishing. Logan Canyon is home to the Logan River and Bear Lake, where many travelers take boats and jet skis during the summer for an exhilarating run across its mesmerizing waters. Visitors can also fish for the Bonneville Cisco, which is only found in Bear Lake. The Logan River is famous for fly-fishing, but anglers of every kind and age gather at Second and Third Dam to try their luck with a pole. A careful observer will be able to see groups of trout as they gather underneath a bridge nearby, but scuba divers at the east end of Bear Lake have the best view of the local fish. A more secluded setting is found at Tony Grove Lake, where the most popular activity—besides fishing—is the peaceful paddling of canoeing.

**Scenic:** Logan residents climb the canyon road year-round for recreation, a chance to enjoy the great outdoors, and the exhilaration that Logan Canyon scenery provides. They have favorites, such as Tony Grove Lake, Second Dam, or China Row, where an atmosphere of shady trees, mossy banks, and clear water feeds the imagination. Visitors to Logan Canyon find themselves in an undiscovered wilderness, an enchanted forest, or in the mountains of a distant country. From the mouth of the canyon at First Dam to the captivating overlook at Bear Lake, Logan Canyon scenery draws audiences that come back to see the performance change.

As you begin your ascent to the summit of Logan Canyon Scenic Byway, you'll find yourself overshadowed by the towering mountains, the tops of which are one mile above the road. Just below the road, the Logan River flows over a rocky bed through a series of dams. Each dam has its own inviting qualities. Ducks swimming among cattails and reeds set a tranquil scene for anglers at Third Dam and Spring Hollow. A collection of shady picnic tables along the water's edge at Second Dam entices visitors for a lunchtime stop. Later on the drive, the mountains pull apart, revealing grassy meadows on either side of the byway.

Evergreen pine and juniper intermingled with deciduous maples and aspen provide a contrast of color that makes Logan Canyon a superb road in the fall. Strips of deep red run in the crevasses of the mountainsides where a cluster of maples is growing. Perhaps one of the best times to enjoy the late fall is just after a rainstorm, when low-lying clouds float just above the road and every tree and leaf displays rich browns, oranges, and reds.

You may have trouble naming the most beautiful scenic highlight on the byway or even pinpointing what makes the byway beautiful. It's the way rocky precipices jut out of the mountainside; the way the mountainside slopes upward, taking a forest of trees with it; the way the trees become brilliant red in the fall; and the way the road winds through it all that make the Logan Canyon Scenic Byway one of the most enchanting drives in the country.

## Highlights

For your own memorable Logan Canyon tour, consider following this itinerary.

**Second Dam:** From summer to spring, Second Dam is one of the most popular fishing spots on the byway. Just a short drive up the canyon, Second Dam is a wilderness getaway with mountains on all sides and shady picnic areas.

**Wind Caves:** Years of wind and water have worn a delicate triple arch and natural cave into the limestone outcropping at the top of this two-mile trail. Also known as the Witch's Castle, this fascinating formation provides a clear view of China Row.

**Logan Cave:** This used to be a popular cave to explore, but because of vandalism in 1998, the Forest Service gated and locked the cave entrance. The upside is that by keeping people out of the cave, the native bat population will likely thrive. Nevertheless, curious travelers still make short hikes to the mouth of the cave to peer into its dark recesses.

**Ricks Springs:** Ricks Springs has been a wayside stop for a long time. Early settlers drank the water here and experienced discomfort because the water does not come from a natural spring.

**Tony Grove Lake and Mount Naomi Wilderness Area:** A seven-mile paved road climbs to a height of 8,050 feet to reach Tony Grove Lake and the Mount Naomi Wilderness Area. The area around this glacial lake explodes into wildflowers in the early summer. The campground features 37 popular sites. A popular 0.8-mile trail takes visitors around part of the lake.

**Bear Lake Overlook:** On a clear day, Bear Lake sparkles an unusually clear turquoise blue. A display explains the history and geology of the lake and surrounding area.

# NEBO LOOP SCENIC BYWAY

*Lakes, forests, rocky overlooks, wildflowers, and fiery displays of fall color line the popular Nebo Loop as it makes its way into the Wasatch Mountains. Take it slow, and enjoy one of nature's grandest shows.*

This byway begins in the quiet community of Payson and ascends back and forth through a canyon of deep, fresh forest that turns to visual fire in the fall. The route continues alongside a cold, rocky creek that drops off into intermittent miniature waterfalls; fishers sit aside this creek in the cool of dusk, listening to a cricket symphony and the birds' sonata.

By degrees, the landscape changes into a high-mountain wilderness. Only fields of crisp, bright wildflowers interrupt the thick stands of aspen. Incredibly high overlooks show the Wasatch Mountains sitting loosely below you like a pile of ribbon. From these overlooks, you can also see the byway's namesake, 11,877-foot Mount Nebo.

This area is so well liked that more than one million people visit annually, and a good percentage of them reserve campsites a year in advance. During the summer, most people like to fish at the glass-smooth lakes, such as Payson, or hike on the many trails, such as Loafer Mountain Trail.

## Quick Facts

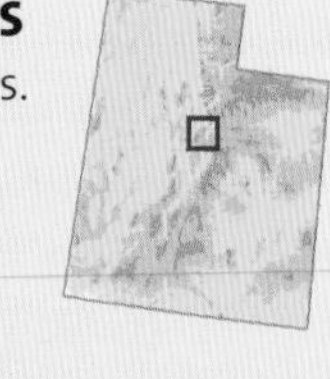

**Length:** 37 miles.

**Time to Allow:** One hour.

**Considerations:** Most of the route is somewhat narrow and winding. This means that you won't have much opportunity to pass slower vehicles, and speed limits average 30 mph. Plan to sit in the front seat of your vehicle if you are susceptible to carsickness. A 200-foot-long section of the route consists of hairpin curves, so you must slow to about 15 mph in order to get around the 90-degree turns safely. Heavy snowfall in the winter necessitates the closure of the Nebo Loop Scenic Byway to passenger vehicles from October to the first of June each year. However, Utah State Park employees groom the road for winter use.

*Mount Nebo in the Uinta National Forest is the highest peak in the Wasatch Range, reaching 11,877 feet at its summit.*

## Intrinsic Qualities

**Archaeological:** Archaeological sites in the area show that this valley had one of the largest Native American populations in the Great Basin. In fact, if you had gone to the byway's Utah Valley Overlook in about 1500, you would have seen smoke curling up from several large villages. This byway now retains two archaeological sites.

The first, the Nephi Mounds, was a site used by the Fremont Indians around 1300. The Nephi Mounds archaeological site is agricultural in nature, as opposed to most of the mounds in the United States, which are ritualistic or artistic in nature. As one of the primary sites for the Fremont Indian farming, Nephi Mounds was discovered by modern peoples when a farmer uncovered American Indian relics in his field.

The second is Walker Flat, a favorite camping spot of the Ute Indians, who liked to spend their summers in these mountains. Walker Flat is also where the Walker War broke out between the Utes and Mormon settlers. The historic Peteetneet Academy displays information about Ute Chief Walker and his followers, the protagonists of the Walker War.

**Cultural:** Settled by Mormon pioneers in 1850, the area surrounding the byway took on the culture of the farmer and the frontiersman, with pieces of the native cultures mixed in. Although towns such as Payson and Nephi were established nearby, Mount Nebo and its surrounding landscape were preserved even after a road was placed through these backwoods areas. Proud of their pioneer and native heritage and the legacy of the Nebo Loop, today's residents of Payson, Nephi, and surrounding communities fully enjoy the rivers, lakes, and forest.

The byway covers two counties, and as you continue south, the communities become smaller. The city now known as Payson was once called Peteetneet, named for Chief Peteetneet of the Ute Tribe. Peteetneet, which means "little waters," is now the name of the academy that exhibits art and museum pieces. Visitors stop at the Peteetneet Academy on their way to the natural wonders of the ebo Loop. And like any communities with traditions, the byway ommunities host unique festials throughout the year. Over abor Day weekend, for example, ayson hosts the Golden Onion Days celebration.

As you drive the byway, you may vant to follow the examples of he local residents and grab your ent and a fishing pole to camp our way along the Nebo Loop. top by some of the orchards long the way that have been a nain supply of food and income or Nebo's communities for nearly wo centuries. By stopping at mall communities along the way, you get to see what's in store eyond Mount Nebo.

**Historical:** The road that became he Nebo Loop had been used for centuries by Native Americans and, later, by explorers and sawmill companies. The road was then built by the Civilian Conservation Corps (CCC) and enhanced by the addition of recreational facilities.

People have inhabited the byway and its surrounding areas for unrecorded amounts of time. The elusive Fremont Indians made their home here before the Utes, who played a part as settlers arrived in Utah. The Walker War, one of two significant wars between Utah Utes and the Mormon settlers, took place on the northern end of the byway.

Important explorers, such as Father Francisco Dominguez and Father Silvestre Velez de Escalante (1776), Jedediah Smith (1826), and John C. Frémont (1843), investigated the area and found it attractive. Mountainman Daniel Potts, who came in 1827, said that the Utah Valley was beautiful. The Mormon Battalion also used the road in 1848 on their way back from California and the Mexican War, and the 49ers used it to go west for gold.

Early pioneer settlement is marked by places such as the Winward Reservoir. Payson farmers built the reservoir between 1890 and 1907 with horse teams and drags and named it after the city's first water master. Later in the mid-1930s, the CCC made great contributions to the development of the byway and its components. For example, the CCC's rockwork allowed both the paved byway road and the stream to occupy the narrow space that it does.

The old Loafer Ski Area and the Maple Dell Scout Camp demonstrate the longtime popularity of this byway for recreation. The Loafer Ski Area was a popular place to relax from 1947 to the mid-1950s. The old slope, whose concrete slab foundations you can still see, had a 930-foot-long towrope and a 284-foot elevation drop. The ski area was rudimentarily furnished: a simple shelter, a toilet, and an outdoor picnic area. The Maple Dell Scout Camp has produced vivid memories for Utah scouts since 1947. Continual improvements have been made at the camp; one of the most notable was the construction of a large lodge in 1960. Later, a dance hall, cottages, and a swimming pool filled with water from a nearby icy spring were added.

By preserving the Nebo Loop as it is today, visitors are able to see this beautiful wilderness as it was 100 or 200 years ago. Its more recent history is preserved in its museums and exhibits and in structures and buildings all along the byway.

**Natural:** The Nebo Loop Scenic Byway takes you into the Wasatch mountain range, where you overlook the Utah Valley. The range was formed from great movements of the earth's crust and an uplift of sedimentary layers. Viewing the topography from the byway gives you a sense of Utah's place in the Rocky Mountains.

Some favorite places for travelers on the byway are the Payson Lakes Recreation Area and Devil's Kitchen. Climbing the byway toward the lakes, you'll pass Payson Creek running through the forest. When you reach the peaceful lakes, you'll find them to be a mountain retreat perfect for fishing, picnicking, or just enjoying the serenity of the gently lapping waters. The Devil's Kitchen has been compared to Bryce Canyon: Red rock and strange pillars of rock called hoodoos decorate this part of the byway. This is where Utah's sandstone sculptures begin.

The byway travels through the Uinta National Forest full of cottonwoods, maples, pines, and aspen. The forest springs up on either side of the road, shading it with millions of leaves. You may also notice the change in plant life as you ascend the byway; views of sagebrush are soon overtaken by pine and spruce trees. Among the trees live elk, deer, and bobcats. On a very rare occasion, a bear or cougar comes into view, but these

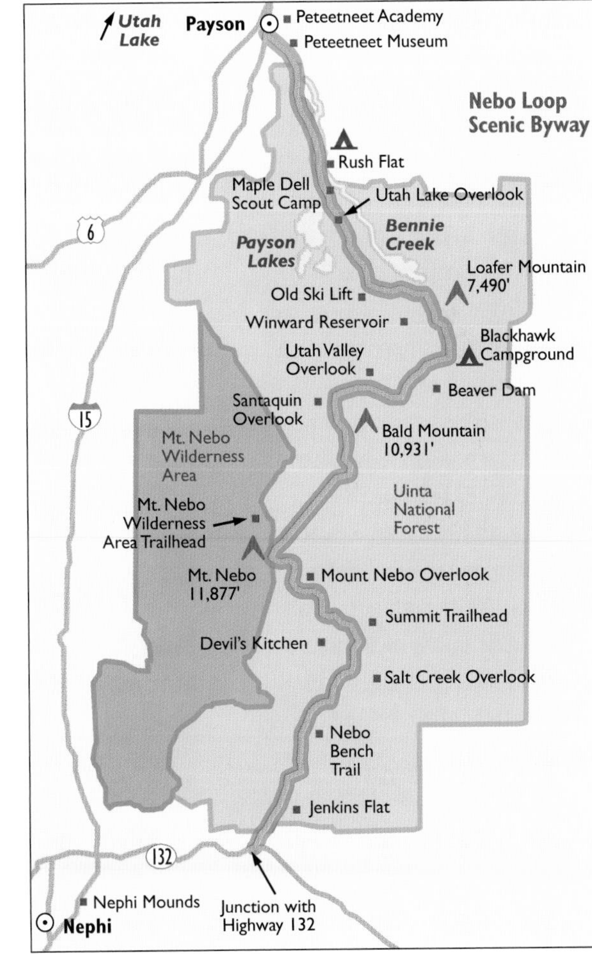

creatures spend time in the most secluded places.

From lush forests to sandstone basins, the Nebo Loop offers a compact view of some of Utah's unique terrains. Be sure to explore realms of the Nebo Loop Scenic Byway—all created by nature.

**Recreational:** All the typical outdoor recreational activities can be done here, and some activities, such as hunting and horseback riding, that are rarely allowed in other urban forests are allowed here. Nebo Loop is also a popular area for watching wildlife; specific viewpoints have been designed for observing deer, elk, moose, and bears.

Because the byway is so popular, reservations must be made at least a year in advance for Blackhawk and Payson Lakes Campground; the typical weekend occupancy rate is 95 percent during the camping season. Payson Lakes Campground is the most popular because it offers swimming, canoeing, hiking, fishing, a fully accessible nature trail, and fishing piers for people with disabilities. Few scenic byways offer so much recreation while showing so little evidence of use.

Although the byway attracts more than one million visitors each year, the design of the facilities makes them almost fade into the woods, keeping them fairly invisible to a driver. Payson Lakes Campground illustrates this fact by offering a myriad of recreational activities that remain hidden from the byway, yet the road is only a few hundred feet away. In the midst of the typical camping experiences is the Mount Nebo Wilderness Area, which offers primitive, roadless recreation for the adventurer. In the winter, byway recreation includes ice climbing, snowmobiling, snowshoeing, and cross-country skiing.

**Scenic:** A rare spectrum of crisp, vibrant views is packed into this relatively short byway, where jagged, frozen mountains are infused with vigorous colors. The diversity spreads across the byway's flat bottomlands, mid-elevation scrub oak, high alpine fir and aspen, snow-covered peaks, red rock formations, gray sandstone cliffs, and salt flats. Devil's Kitchen typifies this diversity: The short trail to Devil's Kitchen is towered over by dark green pine, but just a short walk later, the green disappears, and the huge red rock spires that are Devil's Kitchen jab into the deep blue sky.

The byway is an essay in color: Wildflowers paint blossom mosaics in the spring, and trees explode with color in the fall. If you get up onto one of the byway's many overlooks, you can view other diverse scenes, such as the urban sprawl of the Wasatch Front and the Utah Lake, the largest body of fresh water in the region.

## Highlights

As you travel the Nebo Loop Scenic Byway from Payson, consider following this itinerary.

**Peteetneet Academy:** The school was built in 1901 by well-known architect Richard C. Watkins and consists of a three-story building with a bell tower and a red sandstone accent on brick walls. Peteetneet is still used for classes in the fine arts and public meetings and events.

*Peteetneet Academy, which was named in honor of a local Ute Indian chief, served as an elementary school until 1988. It is now a cultural arts learning center and museum.*

**Maple Dell Scout Camp:** Since 1947, this camp has given scouts a chance to take in vivid scenery and participate in outdoor recreation. In 1960, a large lodge was constructed, along with a dance hall, cottages, and a swimming pool.

**Payson Lakes:** Payson Lakes has trailer camping and disabled-accessible sites and features, a shoreline nature trail, two beaches, and a universal access pier.

**Blackhawk Campground:** This popular campground has group and individual campsites, as well as a horse camping facility. The area accommodates equestrian users by featuring tie racks, double-wide camping spurs, and easy access to the trails.

**Mount Nebo Overlook:** Much of the geologic base of Mount Nebo is derived from the Oquirrh formation, which includes quartzite, limestone, and sandstone. The multiple advances and retreats of mountain glaciers formed cirque-shape basins predominantly found in Bald Mountain and Mount Nebo. Many legends are associated with Mount Nebo and its Native American history.

**Devil's Kitchen:** Devil's Kitchen is one of the highlights of the byway. Eroded layers of red-tinted river gravel and silt form spires and sharp ridges. Visitors viewing this unique feature will marvel at its brilliant contrast to the surrounding mountain greenery. There is a restroom and a disabled-accessible picnic area.

# Frontier Pathways Scenic and Historic Byway 

*In a land of high-country homesteads and in the shadow of 14,000-foot peaks, this byway threads mountain passes, valleys, and canyons. Historic walking tours and mountain biking trails are just two of the enticing diversions.*

During the winter of 1806, Lieutenant Zebulon Pike nearly froze to death in he Wet Mountain Valley within ight of the peak bearing his ıame. Nevertheless, this valley and ts mountain became a beacon to 9th-century settlers, who came o take advantage of the good oil and climate. Today, the valley ›oasts one of the state's finest :ollections of historic ranches and armsteads (some dating to the 840s), trading posts, and stage- :oach stops. Also, this pastoral ›aradise contrasts with the severe- ooking Hardscrabble Canyon, the vhite-capped Sangre de Cristos, ınd the sharp mesas and hogbacks :hat flank the Arkansas River.

## Intrinsic Qualities

**Cultural:** This byway chronicles the joys and sorrows that its early residents experienced while breaking in the land. It is a living showcase of the evolution of architecture, transportation, and agriculture that you can experience by visiting the Frontier Pathway's old homesteads, cabins, barns, stagecoach stops, and settlements. This landscape hasn't changed much in the last 100 years, so you can still see how different groups of people used their ingenuity to harness the land. Evidence of their resourcefulness is found in the area's nationally important high-country homesteading.

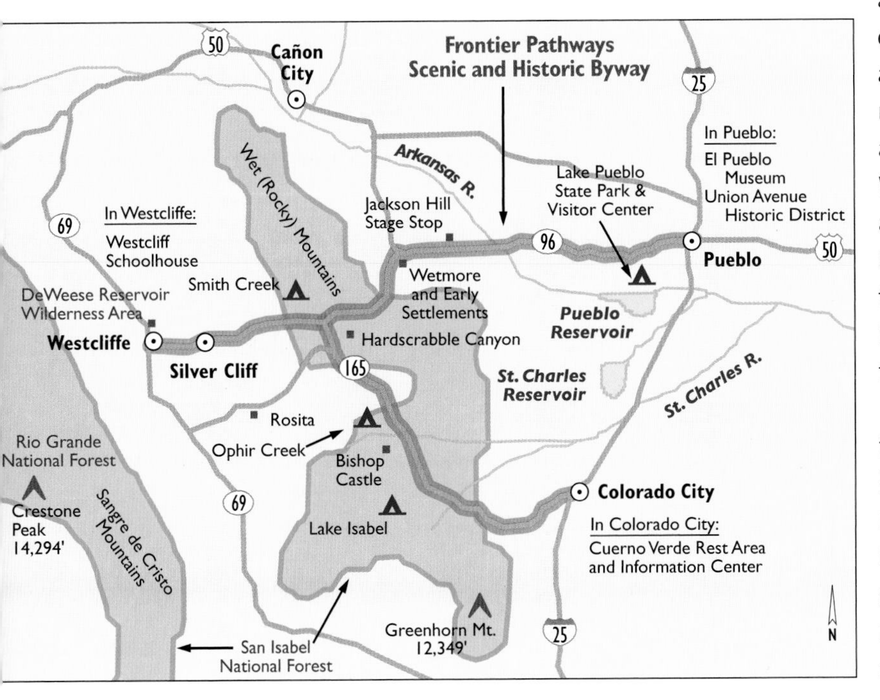


**Historical:** The Frontier Pathways Scenic and Historic Byway is seeping with nationally significant history. For example, some of the first high-country homesteads, ranches, and farms were developed here. In 1779, the Spanish Governor De Anza, with the help of the Utes, defeated Comanche Chief Cuerno Verde (Greenhorn) right in this very valley. Also, German and English colonists settled here in the mid-1800s, and their heritage still pervades this area.

**Natural:** The Wet Mountains and Greenhorn Valleys are not well known, even to long-time Coloradoans, making this byway an excellent getaway. Home to a remarkable number of diverse species of plants and animals, this area attracts naturalists, nature lovers, and botanists. (Note that the Wet Mountains are neither an extension of Colorado's Front Range—the mountains immediately west of Denver—nor are they part of the Continental Divide.)

As the only trout native to Colorado, the greenback cutthroat trout was believed to be extinct until it was rediscovered in a stream near the Frontier Pathways and successfully reintroduced statewide.

### Quick Facts

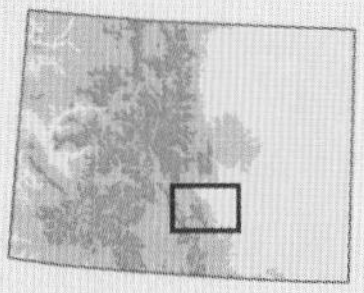

**Length:** 103 miles.

**Time to Allow:** Four hours.

**Considerations:** Be aware that wildfires are an ever-present danger in the dry summer months; follow all posted signs regarding campfires, and do not throw cigarettes out the car window. Abandoned mines are extremely dangerous—look and take pictures but do not explore. This byway traverses high mountain passes; be prepared for all types of weather. High altitudes bring increased sun exposure and reduced oxygen, so wear sunscreen and sunglasses and don't overexert yourself.

**Recreational:** Year-round opportunities at this recreational mecca include climbing 14,294-foot-high Crestone Peak, shopping and dining in Pueblo's Union Avenue Historic District, and playing in the Wet Mountain Wilderness. You can also fish for trout on the banks of Lake Isabel, backpack on the nationally renowned Rainbow Trail south of Westcliffe, and hike the Sangre de Cristos Mountains or Greenhorn Wilderness.

While the summer sun is out, you may enjoy fishing for trout in streams, mountain biking, and horseback riding. You can also get

*Just four miles north of the little burg of Westcliffe, the DeWeese Reservoir Wilderness Area is a beautiful location for wildlife photography opportunities.*



in some sailing, power boating, or water-skiing at the Lake Pueblo State Park. Consider taking time to discover Pueblo Mountain Park, which is on the National Register of Historic Places. During the winter, be sure to cross-country ski, downhill ski, or ice fish on the Pueblo Reservoir.

**Scenic:** Photographers will need to long-focus their cameras in order to capture a sliver of the 100-mile-long Sangre de Cristos Range. As the backbone of the Rocky Mountains, the Sangre de Cristos' many grand peaks jut into the clear blue sky; seven peaks reach higher than 14,000 feet.

You can also discover other intriguing photographic subjects among the shops and streets of Pueblo's Union Avenue Historic District or during your descent into dramatic Hardscrabble Canyon.

## Highlights

To take in the highlights of the Frontier Pathways Scenic and Historic Byway, consider this must-see tour.

**El Pueblo Museum:** This museum, located in the town of Pueblo, gives you an opportunity to learn about the interaction of several different cultures: American Indian, Mexican, and American. It is a full-size replica of Old Fort Pueblo, which was used by fur traders and other settlers from 1842 to 1855. Fascinating artifacts, colorful murals, and interesting stories bring the history of the Pueblo area to life.

**Wetmore and Early Settlements:** More than 150 years ago, buckskin-clad French traders, scrappy American farmers, and fur traders lived in nearby settlements. In the 1830s, three French trappers built a fort on Adobe Creek to facilitate trade with the Ute Indians. It was called Buzzard's Roost, or Maurice's Fort, after Maurice LeDuc. Later settlements in the area included Hardscrabble in 1844 and Wetmore in the late 1870s.

**Sangre de Cristos Mountains (west of Silver Cliff):** Miners, ranchers, and modern-day motorists have all marveled at this breathtaking view of the Sangre de Cristos. This 50-mile stretch of mountains includes 22 peaks that are more than 13,000 feet in elevation.

**Westcliff Schoolhouse:** This schoolhouse, located in the town of Westcliffe, was built in 1891. No one knows why the school name, still visible above the front doors as "Westcliff," was spelled without the e.

# Gold Belt Tour Scenic and Historic Byway

*Following historic railroad and stagecoach routes through the Rockies, the splendid Gold Belt Tour leads to atmospheric mining towns, world-class fossil sites, dramatic Royal Gorge, and memorable views of Pikes Peak.*

On the Gold Belt Tour, the roads themselves are part of the personality f the byway. The byway follows istoric railroad and stagecoach outes, leading you to North merica's greatest gold camp, hree world-class fossil sites, nd numerous historical sites. he Shelf and Phantom Canyon oads offer adventurous driving xperiences along unpaved routes hrough winding canyons. Paved oads wind through the gently olling mountain parklands of the ligh Park route, where Colorado's ighest mountain ranges rise in he distance. Teller 1 (a county oad) travels through the pastoral lorissant Valley, with Pikes Peak n the background.

The five byway communities invite you to share in their rich history. In Cripple Creek, the historical hub of the mining district and a National Historic Landmark, visitors enjoy the variety and beauty of the early 1900s architectural styles in the downtown district. The area's mining heritage continues in Victor, the City of Mines. Surrounded by hundreds of historic mines, Victor is the headquarters for a modern gold mine. Victor's downtown district, a National Historic District, includes beautifully restored buildings. To the south, you can enjoy the Royal Gorge, as well as restaurants, museums, and historic sites in Cañon City and Florence. Florissant, the byway's northern gateway, offers the Florissant Heritage Museum to interpret the area's numerous historic sites and Ute cultural sites.

Also located along the byway are the Garden Park Fossil Area, the Florissant Fossil Beds National Monument, and the Indian Springs Trace. These sites form an internationally important area for paleontological discovery and research. The Florissant Fossil Beds Visitor Center, Dinosaur Depot Museum, wayside exhibits, and trails offer visitors the opportunity to experience these wonders.

## Quick Facts

**Length:**
135 miles.

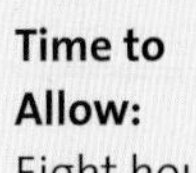

**Time to Allow:**
Eight hours.

**Considerations:** The Phantom Canyon and Shelf Roads have rough, gravel surfaces so it is better to avoid them in wet weather. A four-mile segment of the Shelf Road becomes soft and slippery during wet periods and is not recommended for two-wheel-drive vehicles. A four-wheel-drive vehicle is recommended on the Shelf Road. Please note that vehicles more than 25 feet long are not permitted to travel the Phantom Canyon Road. RVs are not suitable for Shelf Road or Phantom Canyon Road.

## Intrinsic Qualities

**Archaeological:** Archaeological sites can be found throughout the byway and provide a comprehensive look at the past and the creatures that lived in this area millions of years ago. With three fossil beds along the byway, gold was clearly not the only treasure to be found within the mountains and hills of this section of Colorado. When settlers were done digging for gold, many excavations of the fossil beds in the area began, and the discovery and search for fossils on the byway continues today. What has been found is one of the most diverse and complete collections of fossils on the continent.

For millions of years, creatures have been preserved in the rock and stone along the Gold Belt Tour; in fact, 460-million-year-old tracks of arthropods have been found at Indian Springs Trace. This discovery led scientists and even visitors to conjecture about the way the world was so many ages ago, and scientists use these fossils to explore new ideas in evolution. The Florissant Fossil Beds include imprints and fossils of creatures and their environment from 35

*ikes Peak, the inspiration for the song "America the Beautiful," is one of the sights that isitors travel Colorado's Gold Belt Tour Scenic and Historic Byway to see.*

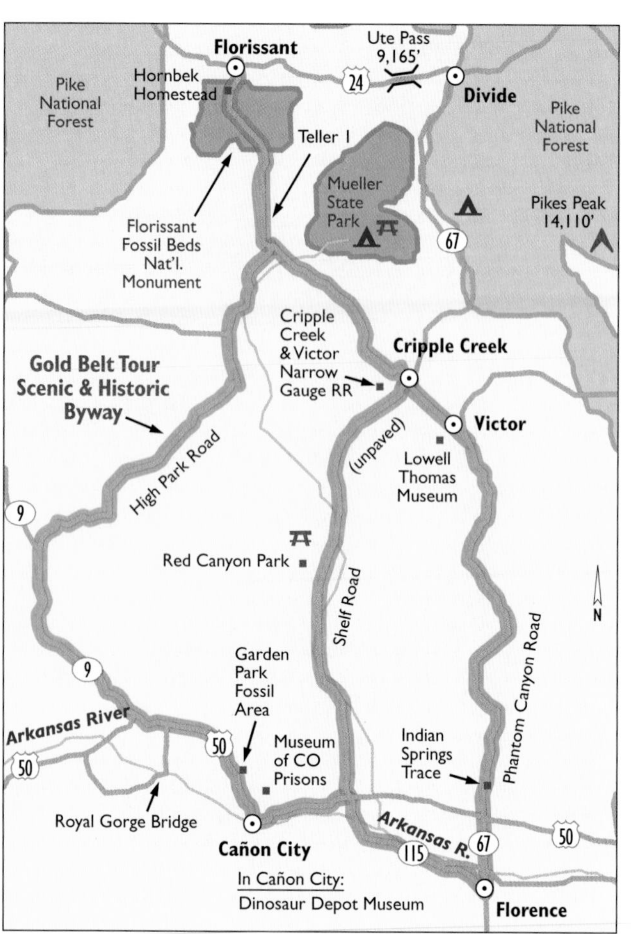


million years ago. Garden Park Fossil Area holds bones of many favorite dinosaurs, including *Brachiosaurus* and *Stegosaurus*. Exploration of the fossil beds along the Gold Belt Tour gives you a glimpse of Earth's age and fascinating history. Although fossil hunting is prohibited for visitors at these places, in areas outside these parks, you may find a fossil of a prehistoric plant or insect.

**Cultural:** The Gold Belt Tour once sported a classic culture of the Wild West. Gold miners, saloons, and the untamed land of the Rocky Mountains are all part of the cultural past of this byway. Although you probably won't experience a gunfight in the streets of a byway town, the towns along the Gold Belt Tour are fiercely proud of their heritage and bring pieces of the past to the surface for visitors throughout the year.

The mining culture was not the first culture to inhabit the mountains of the Gold Belt Tour. Many native cultures, including the Ute, lived here and developed their own unique way of life. The area was a prime hunting spot and a good place to spend the winter because of its relatively mild climate. The history of these cultures has faded to only a few stories and archaeological artifacts.

In the 1800s, a new culture came to the Gold Belt Tour. Settlers from the east brought with them a new organization of towns, roads, and mines, coupled with all the lawlessness of gunfights and hangings. Respect for the land by the area's predecessors was replaced by a way of life that used up the resources around the people. When the gold boom subsided, however, the communities of the area decreased to smaller sizes, allowing the surrounding regions to continue in their natural beauty.

Now, the culture of the byway is one that appreciates the natural wonders of the byway while still remembering the days of miners and cowboys. Many of the towns that exist today along the byway hold festivals and events throughout the year that both visitors and residents attend.

**Historical:** The three roads that constitute the Gold Belt Tour are the historic routes that connected the Cripple Creek Mining District to the communities to the north and south. The historic communities of Cripple Creek, Victor, Cañon City, Florissant, and Florence along with the byway played important roles in what was the most productive gold-mining district in North America.

Cripple Creek was the center of the Gold Boom. Bob Womack discovered gold in 1890, setting off a gold rush that brought people from all over the country and put Cripple Creek on the map. By 1900, three railroads, two electric tram lines, modern water and sewer systems, and many other conveniences separated Cripple Creek from the average western mining camp. Cripple Creek became the financial and commercial center of what is known as the Cripple Creek Mining District. Today, many of the historic buildings that played such a prominent role in the days of gold have been restored, and the entire downtown area of Cripple Creek is a National Historic Landmark.

Victor, which lies just southeast of Cripple Creek, was historically the home of the miners and their families. The downtown area of the city boasts several buildings that are on the National Register of Historic Places, and Victor's downtown itself is a National Historic District.

Florissant is north of the Cripple Creek Mining District. It stands at the crossroads of two important Ute Indian trails. It was a stopover for American Indians, trappers, traders, and mountain men long before silver and gold were discovered in the mountains to the west. In 1886, the railroad came through Florissant and was the closest rail connection to the mining district in the early years of the gold boom.

South of the Cripple Creek Mining District lies the Arkansas River Valley and two more communities that have historical significance. Cañon City and Florence both sought the overflow of wealth coming out of Cripple Creek during the golden years. Both cities were established in the second half of the 1800s and have a rich historical past. In Cañon City, visitors can enjoy a tour of some early railroad depots that have been restored.

Along with the communities found on the Gold Belt Tour, the routes themselves have historical significance. Phantom Canyon Road follows the abandoned railroad grade of the Florence and Cripple Creek Railroad, the first railroad to reach the gold mines.

Today, travelers on Phantom Canyon Road go through tunnels, drive over bridges, and see past remnants of train stations used by the railroad back in the 1890s. Shelf Road was constructed in 1892 and was the first direct route from Cripple Creek to the Arkansas River Valley. Today, travelers experience the shelf—a narrow, winding section of road perched high above Fourmile Creek—much the same way that people experienced it in the 1890s.

After you reach the outskirts of Cripple Creek, you will pass several historic mines and mills. High Park Road goes through a high-elevation park that is home to cattle ranchers. This land along High Park Road represents 150 years of ranching history. Historic ranch buildings, such as the Fourmile Community building, lie along the byway route. Other roads such as Skyline Drive near Cañon City provide beautiful views and interesting historical background.

**Natural:** Located in the Rocky Mountains, the Gold Belt Tour is a worthwhile visit for anyone who enjoys outdoor splendor. The landscape along the byway resulted from multiple alternating periods of mountain building and flooding by an inland sea; you can see sandstone formations and limestone cliffs that were formed as a result of this geological history. The remains of ancient plants and animals deposited during the flooding produced the rich coal and oil fields in the Arkansas Valley near Florence. It also created fossil beds at Garden Park Fossil Area and Indian Springs Trace.

In addition to its unique collection of fossil beds, the Gold Belt Tour is a land with a volcanic history. In the areas of Cripple Creek and Victor, volcanic activity that occurred six million years ago formed the terrain. One volcanic cone was nearly 15 miles wide and rose 6,000 feet above surrounding hills. This volcanic activity is the reason the byway is called the Gold Belt Tour today; it influenced the formation of the gold that was discovered in the 1800s.

Visitors here can see a wide variety of fossils, from those of insects to petrified trees. The fossils offer insights into the environment of 34 million years ago. Garden Park Fossil Area, located along Shelf Road, has provided the world with many unique and complete dinosaur skeletons. The first major discoveries of large, plant-eating dinosaurs were made here in the 1870s, while the best example of a complete *Stegosaurus* skeleton was found in 1992. You can take a guided tour and view the fossil quarries where these miraculous discoveries were made. Adjacent to Phantom Canyon Road lies Indian Springs Trace, which contains portions of an ancient seafloor and was designated a National Natural Landmark in 1979.

The Cripple Creek Caldera, a 24-square-mile basin, is the site of the most productive gold-mining area in North America. The caldera formed when a volcanic center collapsed. The collapse shattered the rocks around its edges, and volcanic activity later filled the cracks in the rocks with rich mineral deposits. As you travel the Gold Belt Tour, you can learn about and view the Cripple Creek Caldera at the Cripple Creek overlook.

**Recreational:** Although it is no more the gold-mining district it once was, the Gold Belt Tour is still the road to riches as far as recreation is concerned. Camping is available in several places throughout the area, allowing you to camp your way through the Gold Belt Tour. In addition to outdoor recreation areas, you'll likely be pleased with the historic museums and fossil parks along the route.

The Royal Gorge Park, owned by Cañon City, is one of Colorado's top tourist destinations. The impressive chasm of the Royal Gorge is spanned by the world's highest suspension bridge. At the bridge, a concessionaire operates an incline railway, aerial tram, and other attractions for visitors. Hiking trails and picnic areas can be found throughout the park. Beginning at Cañon City, the Royal Gorge Route leaves on a scenic train ride through the bottom of the gorge. Not only are you treated to a view of the natural wonders in the gorge, but you also catch glimpses of history in ruins from the Royal Gorge War. Cañon City also provides you with opportunities to explore prehistoric creatures at the Garden Park Fossil Area or the Dinosaur Depot Museum.

A portion of the Arkansas Headwaters Recreation Area is located along the byway. Colorado's Arkansas River between Leadville and Cañon City is among the nation's most popular white-water rafting destinations, hosting more than 300,000 boaters annually. The river also offers some of Colorado's best fly-fishing.

Shelf Road Recreation Area attracts rock climbers from around the world. The limestone cliffs offer short but extremely difficult climbs in some places. In other spots, they are more than 100 feet high and are enticing even to expert climbers. An extensive trail network along the cliffs provides

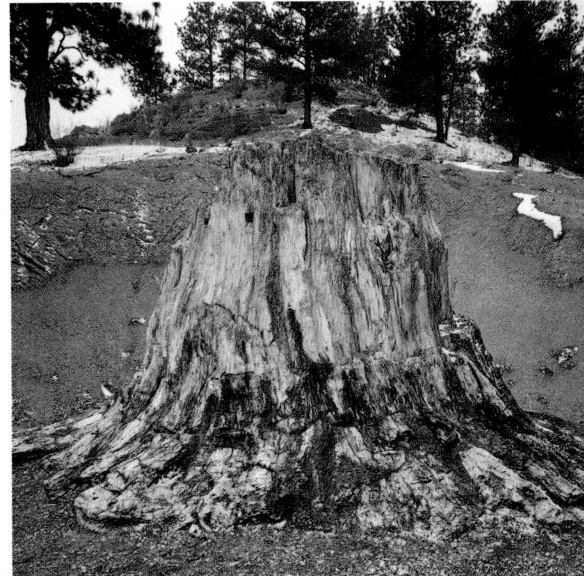

*A petrified Sequoia tree stump is just one of the wonders visitors will see at Florissant Fossil Beds National Monument.*

hiking opportunities for climbers and nonclimbers alike. On Shelf Road, climbers can picnic at Red Canyon Park. Camping and hiking are also excellent pastimes at Red Canyon Park. Additionally, many travelers enjoy picnicking along Phantom Canyon Road after a drive through the forested areas.

**Scenic:** From majestic Pikes Peak to the depths of the Royal Gorge, the Gold Belt Tour is a scenery lover's delight. The dramatic changes in terrain and the majestic Rocky Mountains are the elements that give this byway its unique flavor. The territory echoes with the Old West and the days when gold miners filled the countryside. Historic buildings, scenic roads, and natural splendor give the Gold Belt Tour even more scenic qualities.

Red Canyon Park, along Shelf Road, is filled with spires, windows, and other amazing rock formations eroded from red sandstone monoliths. The park roads provide easy access to a variety of scenic viewpoints. Skyline Drive, located on the western edge of Cañon City, climbs a 600-foot-high tilted sandstone ridge called a hogback. It offers a panoramic view of Cañon City and the lower Arkansas River Valley. The Royal Gorge, located along the High Park segment of the byway, is one of Colorado's most famous tourist destinations: You can cross the bridge in a car or on foot or take the incline railway to the bottom of the gorge.

Historic buildings and museums are part of the picturesque towns you drive through along the Gold Belt Tour. You might drive past an old homestead framed against a Colorado grassland and imagine yourself in the days when gold glittered in the hills and the railroad brought new and interesting people every day.

Plains and grasslands characterize the southern portion of the byway near Cañon City. Phantom Canyon and Shelf Roads climb out of the valley to the high country, following creeks or clinging to canyon walls hundreds of feet above the canyon floor. As you make your way up the canyons, the plains give way to the forest. As the road nears Cripple Creek and Victor, the scenery opens up to a view of high mountain ranges and majestic Pikes Peak. The area is covered with subalpine forests of Engelmann spruce, subalpine fir, and quaking aspen. Travelers driving through this area are very likely to catch a glimpse of some of the best wildlife the Gold Belt Tour has to offer. In addition, High Park Road and Teller 1 travel through rolling mountain parkland, offering awe-inspiring views of two of Colorado's highest mountain ranges: the Wasatch and Sangre de Cristos ranges.

*The world's highest suspension bridge, the Royal Gorge Bridge spans the chasm, crossing 1,053 feet above the Arkansas River.*

## Highlights

As you travel the Gold Belt Tour, consider following this itinerary.

**Royal Gorge Bridge:** The first place you'll want to stop is the Royal Gorge Bridge. Travel west out of Cañon City on High Park Road for about eight miles, turn right, and you'll come to the bridge (and the park) in about half a mile.

**Dinosaur Depot Museum and Garden Park Fossil Area:** As you drive back through Cañon City, take time to stop at Dinosaur Depot Museum on Royal Gorge Boulevard. Dinosaur Depot Museum shows some the fossils found at the Garden Park Fossil Area. You can take a guided tour of the museum that includes an informative video showing the removal of famous dinosaur fossils. This is also the place to set up a tour of Garden Park Fossil Area, located just north of Cañon City. Garden Park Fossil Area has been the location of the some of the most important discoveries of dinosaur fossils in North America. Tours should be made in advance; self-guided trails and exhibits are also available at the Garden Park Fossil Area.

**View of Pikes Peak:** As you travel Shelf Road north to Cripple Creek, you will be treated to a beautiful vista of the west slope of Pikes Peak, named for explorer Zebulon Pike. Pikes Peak towers 14,110 feet.

**Cripple Creek:** Take U.S. 50 west and then Shelf Road north 26 miles to historic Cripple Creek, the center of the Cripple Creek Mining District. Cripple Creek is a National Historic Landmark, and many of the buildings that were built during the early 1900s have been restored.

**Florissant Fossil Beds National Monument:** From Cripple Creek, travel west on Bennett Avenue to Teller 1. Seventeen miles from the junction on Teller 1, stop at Florissant Fossil Beds National Monument, which offers walking and guided tours. The fossils found here are renowned for their variety of species: More than 80,000 fossilized specimens of tree stumps, insects, seeds, and leaves have been catalogued. The historic Hornbek Homestead is also located here. Picnic areas, a visitor's center, and hiking trails are available.

# Grand Mesa Scenic and Historic Byway

*The Grand Mesa Scenic and Historic Byway looks out over lakes, valleys, mountains, and forests from 11,000 feet above sea level. Lingering at scenic overlooks is the top pastime.*

The Utes called the Grand Mesa "Thunder Mountain." This name is fitting because, when standing at the Lands End Observatory, the Grand Valley unfolds more than a mile below, and you can imagine yourself as Zeus, ready to hurl thunderbolts. The 63-mile route is transcendent as it climbs through the dusty canyon of Plateau Creek to the cool evergreen forests of the mesa top.

Many scenic overlooks along the byway allow you to glimpse the extraordinary landscape below. The Lands End Road follows the rim of the mesa for much of the way. From here, you may be able to see the peaks of the LaSal Mountains 60 miles to the west in Utah and may even see the San Juan Mountains in Colorado 90 miles to the south.

## Intrinsic Qualities

**Historical:** The first Europeans known to have come to the Grand Mesa were members of the famous Dominguez–Escalante expedition. In 1776, Ute guides led them over Grand Mesa because the expedition couldn't find a good land route to California on their own. More Europeans came as fur traders in the mid-1800s.

Early treaties "gave" this land to the Utes, but as settlers moved to Colorado, the U.S. government made a series of treaties with the Utes that reduced the territory by degrees. In the early 1880s, the Utes were moved to reservations in Utah and southwestern Colorado, and cattle and sheep ranchers soon dominated the area.

Since 1881, the valley floor has been home to farmers, who rely on water from the Grand Mesa for their crops and orchards. Beginning in the late 1800s, numerous water storage and irrigation projects were initiated to bring the water from the mesa. These water conservation systems continue to operate today.

Fishing has been promoted since 1893, when the Mesa Resort Company was established. The company built several lodges and more than 300 summer homes. Skiing on the mesa dates back to 1939, with the construction of the Mesa Creek Ski Area. Relocated in 1964, it is now The Powderhorn Ski Resort.

Touring the scenic Grand Mesa began with horse and buggy trips that lasted several days. Access was improved in 1895 with the completion of the first road through Plateau Canyon. A stage line and freight wagons regularly traveled the route. The road was improved with convict labor in 1911 and later became part of the Pikes Peak Ocean-to-Ocean Highway.

A second access route to the top of the mesa was constructed in 1933 by ex-servicemen on a Civilian Conservation Corps (CCC) crew. The twisting, rocky road was then known as the Veteran Road in their honor. It is now called Lands End Road. With the advent of better roads and automobiles, the popularity of Grand Mesa touring has continued to expand.

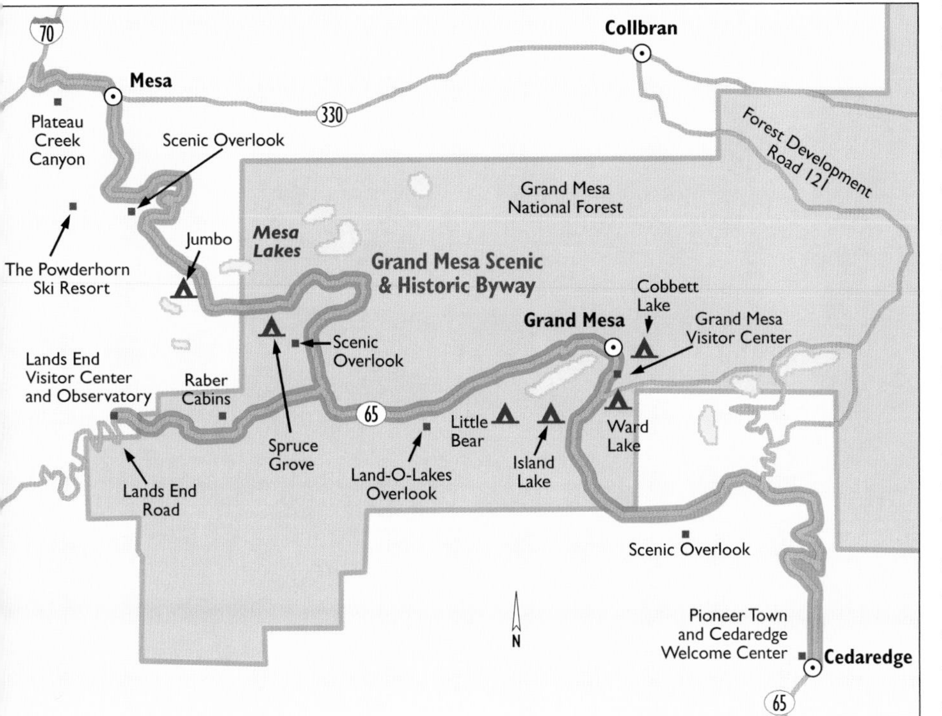


## Quick Facts

**Length:** 63 miles.

**Time to Allow:** Two hours.

**Considerations:** There are no services between Cedaredge and Mesa. In the dry summer months, wildfires are an ever-present danger; follow all posted signs regarding campfires, and do not throw cigarettes out the car window. Abandoned mines are extremely dangerous—look and take pictures but do not explore. This byway traverses high mountain passes; be prepared for all types of weather. High altitudes bring increased sun exposure and reduced oxygen.

**Natural:** Geologically, the Grand Mesa is a lava-capped plateau. Lava flows occurred in ancient river valleys about ten million years ago. However, unlike many lava flows, no volcanic cone or crater was associated with the Grand Mesa flows. Instead, these flows rose through fissures in the earth's surface on the eastern part of the mesa.

Erosion over the last ten million years has removed the hills that were composed of softer rocks. These rocks surrounded the harder lava-filled valleys, leaving the lava-capped terrain as a high plateau. During the Wisconsin Ice Age that occurred 50,000 to 100,000 years ago, glaciers formed on Grand Mesa. Some of these glaciers flowed down the north side of the mesa, over the area where The Powderhorn Ski Resort is now located and into the valley of Plateau Creek. The town of Mesa is built upon glacial gravels, and many of the lava boulders in Plateau Canyon were deposited by a glacial river that was much larger than the present-day Plateau Creek.

The drive along the Grand Mesa Scenic and Historic Byway takes you up through numerous ecological transitions that you would normally have to travel a much longer route to see. The ecology includes 5,000-foot elevation piñon-juniper desert canyons, aspen foothills, lily ponds, and alpine forest at 11,000 feet. The animal life found in each zone changes with the seasons. During the summer, elk and deer roam the alpine forests, while winter snow depths of five feet or more drive them to the lower elevations. There is a great change in temperature as the elevation changes, too. Even though it can be hot and dry on the valley floor, the mesa's top may have enough snow for a snowball fight.

*The Grand Mesa is the world's tallest flat-top mountain. From the top, you will see breathtaking views of the vibrant valley and the spectacular mountain ranges.*

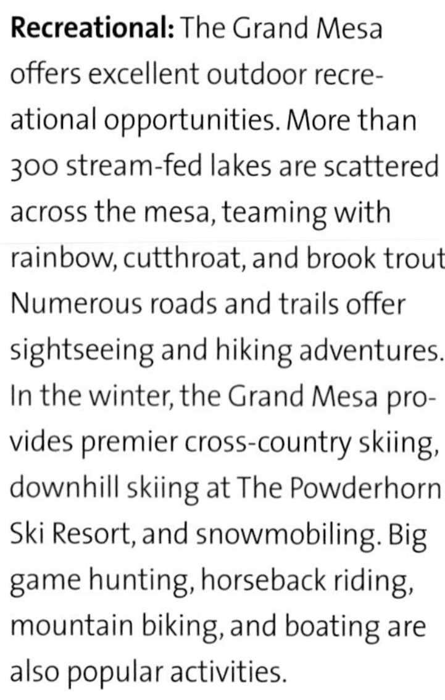

**Recreational:** The Grand Mesa offers excellent outdoor recreational opportunities. More than 300 stream-fed lakes are scattered across the mesa, teaming with rainbow, cutthroat, and brook trout. Numerous roads and trails offer sightseeing and hiking adventures. In the winter, the Grand Mesa provides premier cross-country skiing, downhill skiing at The Powderhorn Ski Resort, and snowmobiling. Big game hunting, horseback riding, mountain biking, and boating are also popular activities.

**Scenic:** The byway offers a unique experience to travelers seeking an alternative to the typical fast-paced travel routes. Highway 65 provides for safe, comfortable year-round passage along this nationally designated byway. Lands End Road provides a safe travel experience seasonally, offering magnificent vistas from a 10,000-foot elevation. The byway passes through shimmering aspen and aromatic pine forests, by meadows of wildflowers, and among endless sparkling lakes. You have the opportunity to observe major changes and diversity in the landscape, from desertlike approaches to dense forests atop the Grand Mesa. Scenic overlooks, rest areas, trails, and picnic areas are clearly marked along the byway.

## Highlights

You can begin this Grand Mesa must-see tour in the Lands End Observatory and proceed south.

**Lands End Observatory:** This spur of the byway ends at the spectacular views around the Lands End Observatory. This structure, which is listed on the Register of Historic Sites, was built in the late 1930s as a public-works project. It is perched on the edge of Grand Mesa and offers views of the valley 6,000 feet below and the LaSal Mountains in Utah to the west.

**Land-O-Lakes Overlook:** When you return to Highway 65, proceed south to the sign for the Land-O-Lakes Overlook. Due to the area's geology, the Grand Mesa is dotted with more than 300 streams and reservoirs. A 100-yard trail to this overlook provides a great view that displays many lakes and the West Elk Mountains in the east.

**Grand Mesa Visitor Center:** This beautiful log structure is located at the intersection of Highway 65 and Forest Development Road 121. The Grand Mesa Visitor Center provides information and an interpretive hiking trail.

**Pioneer Town and Cedaredge Welcome Center:** These facilities are located together in the town of Cedaredge. Exhibits are open to the public daily, Memorial Day to late September. The facilities provide visitor information, exhibits, and a tour of a reconstructed town that depicts the lives of pioneers in the area.

# San Juan Skyway

*Mountain passes, cliff dwellings, spring waterfalls, winter skiing, and fall splendor mark this "Million Dollar Highway" as it journeys to the top of the world and back in time.*

Discover history and new heights on the San Juan Skyway. This loop trip hrough the San Juan Mountains of outhwest Colorado follows more han 200 miles of state-maintained ighways on a journey from towerng mountains and alpine forests to he rolling vistas and ancient ruins f Native American country.

On this byway, you can drive hrough the heart of five million cres of the San Juan and Uncomahgre National Forests. The kyway takes you over mountain asses and through quaint towns.

## ntrinsic Qualities

**rchaeological:** Among this yway's many archaeological sites, Mesa Verde (located in Mesa Verde National Park) is arguably the most outstanding one. Mesa Verde (Spanish for "green table") offers an unparalleled opportunity to see and experience a unique cultural and physical landscape. The culture represented at Mesa Verde reflects more than 700 years of history. From approximately 600 through 1300, people lived and flourished in communities throughout the area. They eventually constructed elaborate stone villages, now called cliff dwellings, in the sheltered alcoves of the canyon walls. In the late 1200s and within only one or two generations, they left their homes and moved away.

The archaeological sites found in Mesa Verde National Park are some of the most notable and best preserved in the United States. Mesa Verde National Park offers visitors a spectacular look into the lives of the ancestral Pueblo. Scientists study the ancient dwellings of Mesa Verde in part by making comparisons between the ancestral Pueblo and their descendants who live in the Southwest today—24 Native American nations in the Southwest have an ancestral affiliation with the sites at Mesa Verde.

**Historical:** The discovery of precious metals led to the exploration and settlement of areas along the San Juan Skyway during the late 19th century. Narrow-gauge railroads played an important role during the mining era and in the history of southwest Colorado as a whole.

With their rails set three feet apart as opposed to the standard gauge of nearly five feet, the narrow-gauge lines made it possible for trains to operate in mountainous country with tight turns and steep grades. Evidence of these defunct, narrow-gauge lines is manifested by the water tanks, bridges, trestles, and sections of railroad bed found along the byway. One narrow-gauge railroad, the Durango and

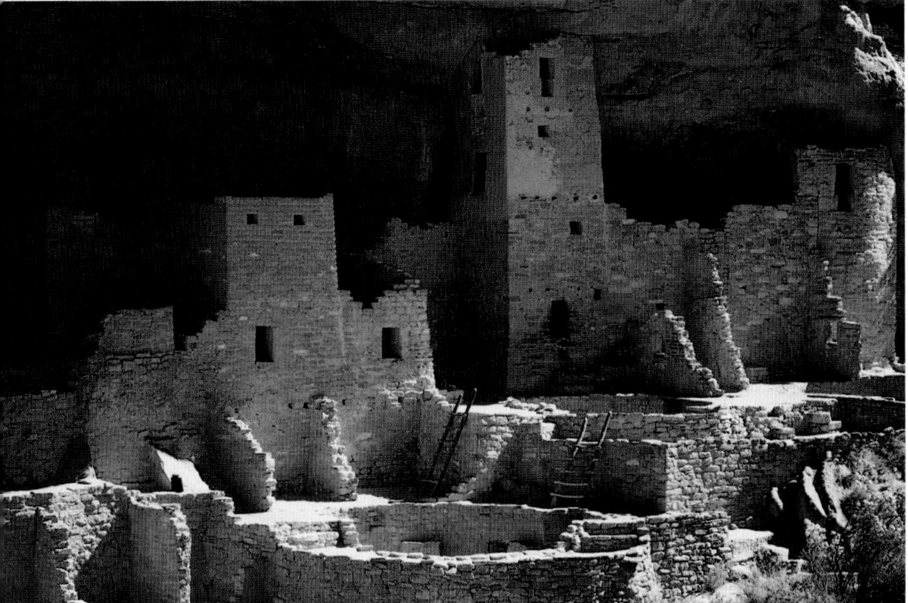

*Aesa Verde National Park offers visitors an outstanding view into the lives of the ancient ueblo people who once inhabited these cliff dwellings.*

### Quick Facts

**Length:**
233 miles.

**Time to Allow:**
One to two days.

**Considerations:** The country along the San Juan Skyway is exciting to explore, but safety should always be a major concern. Old and unstable mills, mines, and timber structures may be decaying and hazardous. Be prepared for changing weather both while driving and while hiking. If you are not accustomed to high altitudes, get plenty of rest and resist overdoing activities during your first two days in the area. Mountain passes are sometimes closed for an hour or two (sometimes even a day or two) in the case of heavy snowstorms or slides during the winter. The two-lane road between Ouray and Silverton has incredibly beautiful views; it is also narrow and steep, has many hairpin switchbacks and a tunnel, includes tremendous drop-offs with no railings or shoulders, and offers few places to pass. Some curves are signed at 10 mph.

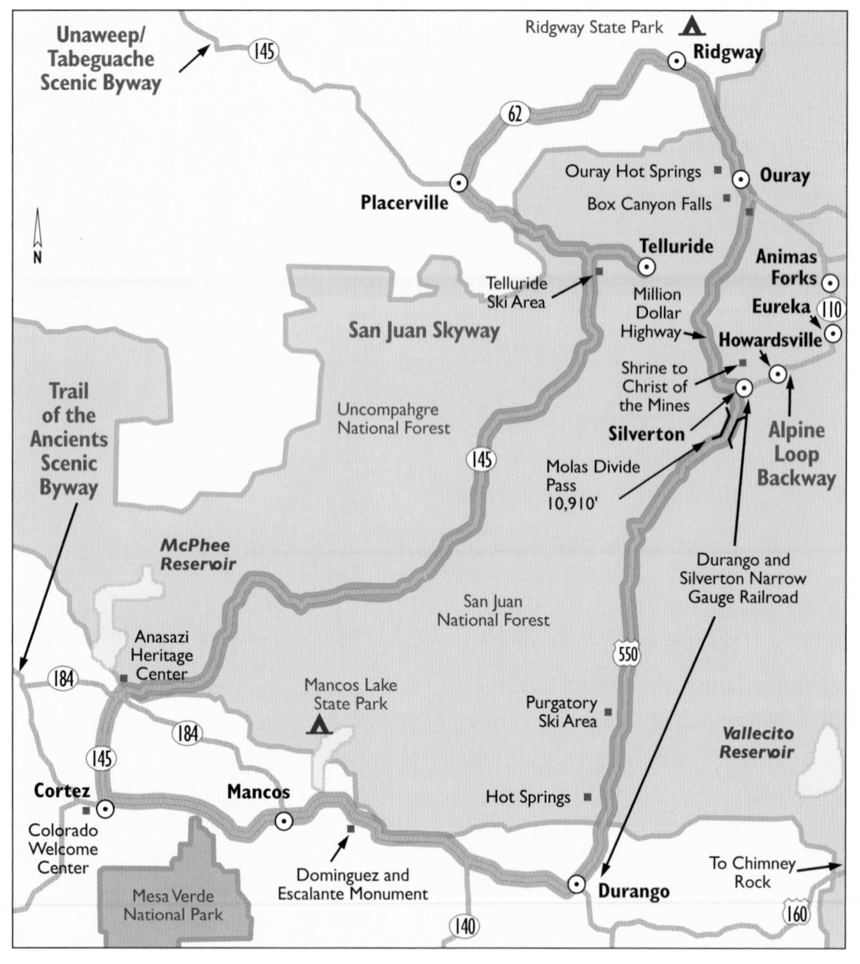


Silverton, continues to operate as a tourist line. It was constructed from 1881 to 1882 by the Denver and Rio Grande Railroad to haul ore and provisions, and in 1968 the line was designated a National Historic Civil Engineering Landmark. As it travels along the Animas River amidst majestic mountains, the Durango and Silverton Narrow Gauge Railroad offers scenic vistas and the experience of riding an authentic coal-fired, steam-powered railroad. It is one of southwest Colorado's major attractions and carries more than 200,000 passengers a year.

**Natural:** The already spectacular San Juan Skyway takes on especially vibrant beauty in the fall. The lush green of deciduous vegetation on the mountainsides is transformed into shades of gold, red, bronze, and purple, with evergreens adding their contrasting blues and greens.

The aspen trees are the first to turn shades of gold and rosy red. With their shimmering leaves, the aspen groves glow when the sun shines through them. The cottonwood trees, located along rivers and creeks, are next to turn gold, and a variety of shrubs complement the scene with their fall hues of red, purple, bronze, and orange.

Autumn is a favorite time for locals and tourists alike to enjoy the warm days, cool and crisp nights, and breathtakingly beautiful scenery of the San Juan Skyway.

**Recreational:** Summer activities include hiking, mountain biking, kayaking, four wheeling, hunting, and fishing. Winter activities include snowshoeing, snowmobiling, and skiing.

Durango Mountain Resort at Purgatory offers downhill skiing and a Nordic center with a groomed track. In summer, the lift takes visitors up the mountain for sightseeing and wildflower viewing. The lift is also a way to get to the top of the mountain biking trail system and to the top of the tobogganlike Alpine Slide.

**Scenic:** The brawny and pine-furrowed Rockies lounge around this byway, and their uneven ridges yield to tree-packed forests, flashing streams, and slate blue lakes. The scene extends into stretches of breezy grasslands divided occasionally by hand-hewn weathered fences. This byway is known as the Million Dollar Highway not only for its connection to gold and silver mining, but also for its first-class scenery.

## Highlights

The following tour begins in Mesa Verde National Park and ends in the town of Ouray. If you are beginning the tour from Ouray, simply begin at the bottom of the list and work your way up.

**Mesa Verde National Park:** At this park, explore cliff dwellings made by the Anasazi Indians. These dwellings were mysteriously abandoned by the Anasazi approximately 200 years before Columbus discovered America.

**Durango:** This authentic Old West town, founded in 1880, still retains its Victorian charm. Restored historic landmarks line downtown streets, while nearby ski resorts beckon to adventurous winter travelers.

**Silverton:** This remote mining community can be reached either by taking the historic Durango and Silverton Narrow Gauge Railroad or by driving over the 10,910-foot Molas Divide Pass. Many of the beautiful Victorian buildings in Silverton are registered as National Historical Sites.

**Ghost towns:** The ghost towns of Howardsville, Eureka, and Animas Forks are all located within 14 miles of Silverton. At Animas Forks, you can walk through the remnants of a 19th-century mining town or wander through beautiful meadows of wildflowers.

**Million Dollar Highway:** The section of highway from Silverton to Ouray has been named the Million Dollar Highway because of the immense amounts of silver and gold that were carted through these passes. This road is quite possibly the most beautiful section of byway anywhere in the country and is not to be missed.

# Santa Fe Trail Scenic and Historic Byway 

*Paralleling a historic corridor to the West, modern-day travelers on Colorado's Santa Fe Trail retrace the routes of pioneers, Native Americans, traders, ranchers, and miners. All would still recognize this timeless landscape.*

Part of a multistate byway; see also New Mexico.

The Santa Fe Trail Scenic and Historic Byway is a rich legacy of the many people vho made their way across south-astern Colorado. This transpor-ation route served as a corridor ɔ the West and resulted in the neshing of many cultures and raditions. Today along the byway, estivals and museums honor the nany men and women who left distinctive mark on the area, ncluding early Native Americans, nilitary personnel, ranchers, min-rs, and railroad passengers.

## ntrinsic Qualities

**rchaeological:** Early people left igns of habitation along this yway in many forms, including ock art, Native American tepee ings and fire circles, and other vidence of prehistoric and ettlement-era activities.

Southeastern Colorado has nany sites that have both petro-glyphs and pictographs. These images speak of days long past, and part of the enjoyment of viewing rock art is hypothesiz-ing about what the images may mean. Perhaps these symbols were religious in meaning, were used as calendars, or conveyed information about natural resources.

Visitors to the Santa Fe Trail Scenic and Historic Byway will find sites where this rock art is located. Archaeological sites exist at Picket Wire Canyonlands and Comanche National Grassland. A 1997 archaeological survey documented more than 70 sites in the Timpas Creek (Comanche National Grassland) area alone. Loudon–Henritzie Archaeological Museum in Trinidad features exhibits on the area's geology, fossils, and archaeology.

**Cultural:** Southeastern Colorado is embedded with Mexican culture; the area was a Mexican territory longer than it has been a part of the United States. Even after the United States acquired Mexico's northern provinces in 1848, the Santa Fe Trail served as a conduit for exchange among Spanish, Native American, and American cultures. Communities along the byway continue to celebrate the diverse inhabitants through traditional celebrations, culturally representative architecture (such as adobe structures), religious folk art, and Hispanic culture at Trinidad's Baca House Museum (located in the Trinidad History Museum) and other museums. Large murals depicting the Santa Fe Trail and Western history are painted on the exterior of commercial buildings as reminders of cultural contributions.

**Historical:** The Santa Fe Trail Scenic and Historic Byway parallels the Santa Fe Trail, which served as a trade route between Missouri and the Mexican frontiers from 1821 to 1880. Traders, miners, military, and settlers all used this route. Even during the Civil War, the area saw action as Colorado volunteers fought against Confederate troops. With the coming of the railroad, the Santa Fe Trail entered a new phase of its history.

The Santa Fe Trail extended for 900 miles from Missouri to Santa Fe and was instrumental in carrying people and goods across the land. The Mountain Route of the Santa Fe Trail was traveled by caravans of traders, often journeying four horses abreast. Although the Mountain Route was 100 miles longer than the Cimarron Route and included the difficult climb over Raton Pass, the Mountain Route was preferred because water was more accessible and the area was less vulnerable to attacks from Native Americans.

Travel on the trail was beneficial but dangerous for those making the journey. In 1834, Charles and William Bent and Ceran St. Vrain built a fort to protect trading activities among the Americans,

*During much of the original adobe fort's 16-year history, Bent's Old Fort was the only major permanent pioneer settlement on the Santa Fe Trail.*

### Quick Facts

**Length:** 188 miles.

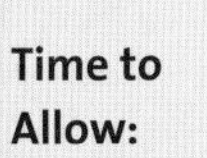

**Time to Allow:** Four hours.

**Considerations:** The best time of year to drive this byway is early spring through late fall.

Mexicans, and Native Americans. Visitors can go to Bent's Old Fort today and see what fort life was like. Miners heading to California in search of gold often chose the shorter, although more dangerous, route of the Santa Fe Trail rather than the Oregon Trail.

After the railroad came through the area, the nature of the Santa Fe Trail changed, and in 1861, the Barlow–Sanderson stage line was established with Trinidad as a major stop. With America embroiled in the Civil War, the Colorado Territory also saw an increase in military traffic.

Visitors traveling the route today can view existing historic sites, including trading posts (Bent's Old Fort), stage stops, visible wagon ruts, graves, ruins of Trail-era ranches, and statues commemorating pioneers.

**Natural:** The Santa Fe Trail corridor provides an opportunity to discover an undisturbed, pristine landscape while observing the wide diversity of wildlife habitats. Southeastern Colorado varies from prime agricultural land to expanses of native grassland; four state wildlife areas in the corridor cover more than 10,000 acres. Rivers have carved canyons and valleys, where striking geology and unusual rock formations can be found.

The wildlife consists of free-ranging antelope, mule deer, bighorn sheep, bobcats, foxes, coyotes, and mountain lions, as well as small mammals, amphibians, reptiles, fish, and birds.

The Comanche National Grassland offers an area of rich natural qualities. The features of this landscape vary from short and midgrass prairies to deep canyons and arroyos, or waterways. This area was once the site of a sea, and today fossils of prehistoric sea creatures have been found in the Comanche National Grassland. In addition to these fossils, there is a set of dinosaur tracks south of La Junta that is the longest set of tracks in North America.

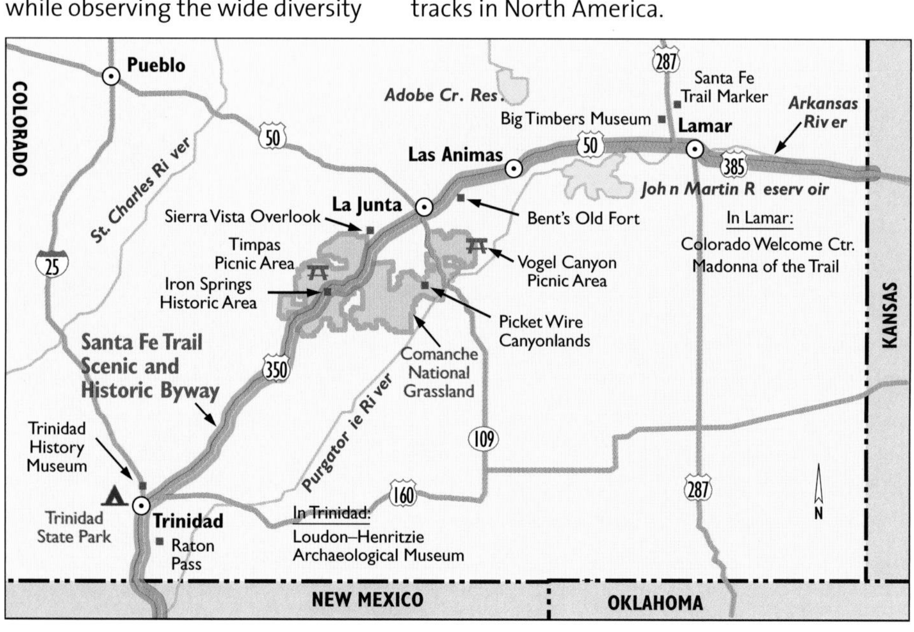


**Recreational:** The Santa Fe Trail Scenic and Historic Byway offers more than 30,000 acres of public land that supports a variety of recreational activities.

The Arkansas River follows the byway for a good portion of the route, providing many opportunities to enjoy the riverbanks. In addition, the John Martin Reservoir's blue waters give you a chance to enjoy a fun day of swimming, picnicking, camping, boating, water-skiing, sailing, or windsurfing. Fishing is another popular activity both on the lake and in nearby rivers.

An abundance of other wildlife is located along the byway. Desert bighorn sheep, eagles, cranes, pelicans, lesser prairie chickens, and hummingbirds can often be spotted in the area. Hunters come to this area of southeastern Colorado for prime hunting opportunities; in fact, Prowers County is known as the goose-hunting capital of the nation.

**Scenic:** Scenic qualities along the byway range from panoramic vistas of the Spanish Peaks, Fisher Peak, and Raton Pass to the verdant, irrigated croplands of Colorado's high plains. Picturesque windmills and evidence of homesteads provide travelers with a glimpse of life as a settler. In addition, the byway passes through communities that are scenic in their own right, from the Corazon de Trinidad National Historic District to quaint rural farm towns.

## Highlights

The Santa Fe Trail historical tour begins at Bent's Old Fort and follows the trail toward Trinidad.

**Bent's Old Fort:** This National Historical Site is a reconstruction of Bent's Fort, which was built in the 1830s. The fort played an important role as a trading post for trappers and the Plains Indians and also as a supply depot during the Mexican–American War.

**Sierra Vista Overlook:** For Santa Fe Trail travelers heading south, the changing horizon from plains to mountains was a major milestone on their journey. One of their guiding landmarks was the distant Spanish Peaks, which came into view along this section of the trail. A short walk up the side of a bluff gives you an excellent view of the Rocky Mountains and surrounding prairie, much like what early travelers saw. To reach this overlook, drive southwest from La Junta on Highway 350 for 13 miles. Turn right (north) at Highway 71 for a half-mile, and then turn left (west) to the parking lot.

**Trinidad History Museum:** This museum complex, operated by the Colorado Historical Society, houses five attractions in one location. Visitors to the site can visit the Santa Fe Trail Museum, the Baca House, the Bloom Mansion, the Historic Gardens, or the bookstore.

# Top of the Rockies Scenic Byway 

*The Continental Divide and the country's highest-elevation community both lie along this awe-inspiring scenic byway, which cruises the mountaintops amid startling close-ups of 14,000-foot peaks.*

The cool mountain air and fresh scent of pine trees beckons you to the Top of the Rockies Scenic Byway. Towering peaks flank the highways, and open lowlands give you a rest from steep mountain passes. However, don't be fooled by these "lowlands" because Leadville, the hub of the byway, is the highest incorporated community in the United States, located 10,200 feet above sea level. Mount Elbert (14,433 feet) and Mount Massive (14,421 feet)—the highest and second-highest mountains in Colorado—stand just outside of Leadville.

## Intrinsic Qualities

**Historical:** Mining shaped a way of life along the Top of the Rockies many years ago. The rich mines of the area led to the growth of communities such as Twin Lakes, Minturn, Leadville, and Red Cliff. The military presence of the 10th Mountain Division at Camp Hale added another distinct chapter in the history of the byway.

In 1860, the mountains and hills came alive as gold was discovered in California Gulch. Soon, silver was also discovered in the area, bringing individuals such as Horace Tabor, David May, J. J. and Margaret Brown, the Guggenheims, and the Boettchers. Fortunes were made, and communities soon developed to meet the needs of the growing mining populations. Many of these towns, such as Kokomo, Recen, and Robinson, are now nonexistent, having been destroyed by fires or other natural disasters.

While mining brought many people to the area, when fortunes were harder to come by, many residents turned to farming, and thus the boomtowns remained lively communities. Leadville today maintains the Victorian charm and influence that kept people in town after the mining boom was over.

Other factors contributed to this area's historical development. The 10th Mountain Division, which trained at Camp Hale, fought in the military campaign in Italy during World War II. Camp Hale was the training site of the Invisible Men on Skis. The troops used the high elevation, steep slopes, and winter conditions to train for mountain and winter warfare in the Apennine Mountains of Italy. The 10th Mountain Division saw action during the war, and a memorial to those who lost their lives in this campaign stands at the entrance to Ski Cooper.

*The last fields of wildflowers flourish before yielding to the timberline and the majestic peaks of the Rockies.*

**Natural:** The many impressive peaks along the Top of the Rockies Scenic Byway combined with the national forests in the area give the byway a wealth of natural features. The byway threads through three national forests: the Pike National Forest, the San Isabel National Forest, and White River National Forest. In all, six wilderness areas cover about 900 square miles, which are being protected to ensure that future generations will be able to explore and experience this rugged and pristine wilderness.

The Mount Massive Wilderness Area in San Isabel National Forest covers 18,000 acres and is characterized by Mount Massive. The processes of uplift, warping, buckling, and to a lesser extent, glaciation have given shape to the peaks in the Sawatch Mountain range and created hidden lakes. The Rocky Mountains and Continental Divide are higher here than anywhere else between the Arctic Ocean and the Isthmus of Panama.

### Quick Facts

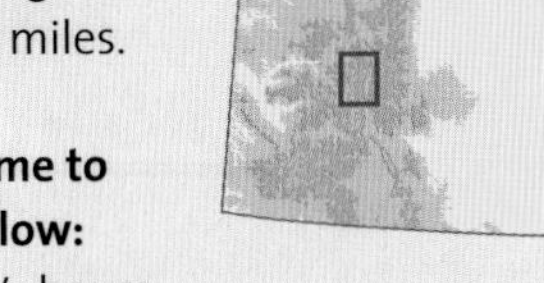

**Length:** 75 miles.

**Time to Allow:** 2½ hours to 1 day.

**Considerations:** The only part of this byway that ever closes is the Vail Pass segment of I-70; bypass it by taking Highways 24 and 91, which take a little more time. Wildfires are an ever-present danger in the summer months; follow posted signs regarding campfires, and do not throw cigarettes out the car window. Abandoned mines are extremely dangerous—look but do not explore. High altitudes bring increased sun exposure and reduced oxygen so wear sunscreen and sunglasses and don't overexert yourself.

**Recreational:** Recreation along the Top of the Rockies is both diverse and abundant. The many lakes and streams provide rafting and fishing adventures, while the high Rocky Mountains lend themselves to camping, hiking, skiing, or mountain biking. Popular four-wheel-drive-vehicle trails take you off the beaten track to various destinations. Mount Massive Golf Course outside of Leadville claims the distinction of being the highest golf course on the continent.

The Arkansas and Colorado rivers give you a chance to enjoy rafting; from high water rapids to float trips, the area has something for everyone. These same rivers boast outstanding fishing. Twin Lakes and Turquoise Lake afford opportunities to fish, camp, and boat along the tranquil shores of the mountain lakes.

These lakes and rivers are set among and near some of the highest mountains in the Rocky Mountains. Near Leadville, the Sawatch Mountain Range has two peaks higher than 14,000 feet, and the Colorado and Continental Divide trails provide many opportunities for hiking. Numerous mountain biking trails are also in the area. Wilderness areas are the perfect place for extensive rugged outdoor adventure, such as backpacking, camping, hunting, horseback riding, four-wheeling, and climbing. You can visit more than 300 miles of hut-to-hut trails associated with the 10th Mountain Hut and Trail System, one of the most extensive backcountry hut-to-hut systems in North America.

World-class skiing facilities along the byway also make this one of the major recreational draws for the area. Both Copper Mountain Ski Resort and Ski Cooper provide opportunities to ski. Other wintertime activities include backcountry skiing, cross-country skiing, and snowmobiling.

**Scenic:** Driving the Top of the Rockies Scenic Byway is an adventure set among some of the highest country in Colorado. With Leadville located at just more than 10,000 feet and Mount Elbert and Mount Massive both more than 14,000 feet, you are literally at the top of the Rocky Mountains. Both Tennessee Pass (10,424 feet) and Fremont Pass (11,318 feet) take you over the tops of these grand mountains, offering never-ending views of mountaintops and deep canyons. Cool air, even in the summer months, provides a perfect environment for exploring the many attractions along the byway.

Every turn on highways 91 and 24 going to Leadville yields another view of a peak jutting into the sky. The forested mountainsides offer you a chance to witness the many shades of green that can be seen within the forests. Within each of the four national forests, woodland creatures, such as deer, may be spotted alongside the road. Clear mountain lakes and tumbling streams are easily accessible and seen from the road.

The open valley around Leadville is flanked on the west side by the Sawatch Mountain Range, with Mount Elbert and Mount Massive standing guard over the valley. Colorado's largest glacial lake, Twin Lakes, is set at the base of Twin Peaks and offers a peaceful and tranquil setting for the byway traveler.

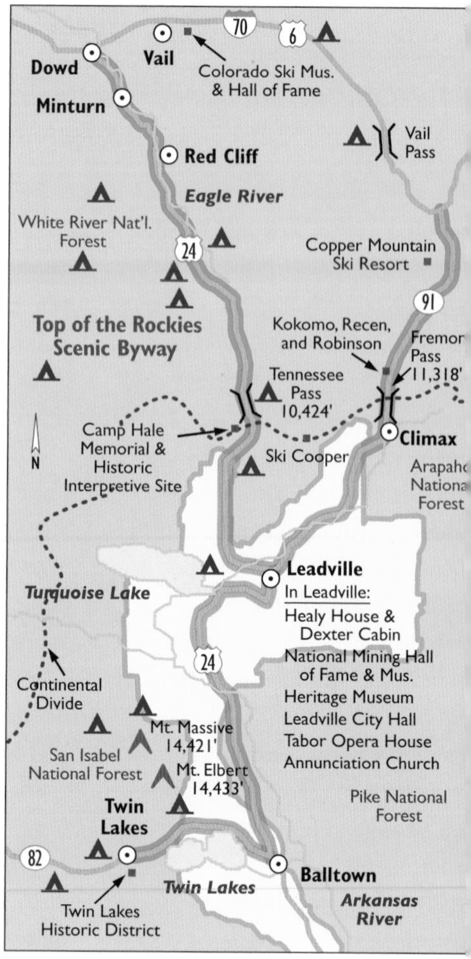

## Highlights

The Top of the Rockies historical tour begins in the town of Dowd, which is about five miles west of Vail along Interstate 70. If you're beginning the tour from Leadville, simply start at the bottom of the list and work your way up.

**Dowd and Minturn:** The byway passes briefly through these small mountain communities and then quickly gains elevation as it winds its way up and over rugged mountain passes. Be sure to bring a camera because views from the road to the valleys below are incredible, especially in the fall.

**Camp Hale Memorial and Historic Interpretive Site:** This site is located on the byway near milepost 160 and features several plaques detailing the history of the 10th Mountain Division that trained here before serving in Europe in World War II.

**National Mining Hall of Fame and Museum:** Located in Leadville, visitors can see displays of hundreds of fine specimens of gold, silver, ore, and minerals, including spectacular examples loaned from the Smithsonian Institution and the Harvard Mineralogical Museum.

**Tabor Opera House:** When it opened in 1879, the Tabor Opera House was said to be the finest theater between St. Louis and San Francisco. This building is one of only a few Tabor-associated buildings still standing in Colorado.

**Annunciation Church:** Started in 1879, this historic church in Leadville was dedicated on New Year's Day, 1880. The church's steeple has become a prominent landmark of this area. It houses a 3,000-plus-pound bell.

# Trail Ridge Road/Beaver Meadow Road

*The highest continuous paved road in the United States, this byway on the roof of the Rockies offers stirring vistas at every overlook as it climbs through Rocky Mountain National Park.*

Sitting in a national park encompassed by national forests, the Trail Ridge Road/Beaver Meadow Road is one of the most beautiful byways in Colorado. The overarching characteristic of the byway is its many overlooks, all of which bestow stirring vistas of 415 square miles of the towering (14,000-plus feet) southern Rockies.

The clear atmosphere of this alpine tundra makes seeing the night sky from one of the overlooks incomparable. Constellations, planets, meteor showers, and phases of the moon seem brighter than ever and just beyond arm's reach.

Because this is such a protected area, elk, deer, mountain sheep, coyotes, moose, beavers, ptarmigans, marmots, pikas, eagles, and peregrine falcons can be seen more often than in other (unprotected) areas of Colorado and the nation. Also, the tender tundra wildflowers, which generally peak in July, are an exceptional treat.

*Rocky Mountain National Park encompasses nearly all of the Trail Ridge Road/Beaver Meadow Road and gives a rare opportunity to see up-close alpine tundra.*

## Intrinsic Qualities

**Historical:** The first Europeans to see this area were French fur traders. In 1859, Joel Estes and his son, Milton, rode into the valley that now bears their name. A few others had settled in this rugged county by 1909 when Enos Mills—a naturalist, writer, and conservationist—began to campaign for preservation of the pristine area, a portion of which became the Rocky Mountain National Park in 1915.

**Natural:** One-third of the park is above the treeline, and the harsh, fragile alpine tundra predominates. The uniqueness of this area is a major reason it has been set aside as a national park. Just below that, at the upper edges of the tree line, the trees are twisted and grotesque and hug the ground. More than one-quarter of the plants found here are also found in the Arctic.

Just below that, forests of Engelmann spruce and subalpine fir take over in a subalpine ecosystem. Openings in these cool, dark forests expose wildflower gardens of rare beauty and luxuriance in which the blue Colorado columbine reigns. And in the foothills, open stands of ponderosa pine and juniper grow on the slopes facing the sun; on cooler north slopes Douglas fir grow.

**Recreational:** The recreational opportunities on this route are varied and excellent. For example, you can enjoy horseback riding, camping, fishing, rock climbing, and numerous winter activities.

Several campgrounds beckon, some of which are open year-round. The Rocky Mountain National Park maintains more than 260 miles of trails for private and commercial horse riders. Hire horses and guides at two locations on the east side of the park or from a number of liveries outside the park boundaries during the summer season.

Four species of trout live in the mountain streams and lakes of Rocky Mountain National Park: German brown, rainbow, brook, and cutthroat trout. These cold waters may not produce large fish, but you do get to enjoy the superb mountain scenery as you fish. Rocky Mountain National Park also offers a variety of challenging

### Quick Facts

**Length:**
53 miles.

**Time to Allow:**
Two hours or more.

**Considerations:** This route is open to through traffic Memorial Day to mid- or late October; closed by snow the rest of the year. You can't get fuel inside Rocky Mountain National Park so you'll have to fill up in Estes Park or Grand Lake. Beware of vapor lock, a common occurrence for vehicles from low altitudes. Speed limits are generally 35 mph. Park entrance fees are required: $20 per carload for seven days, $10 per pedestrian, bicyclist, or motorcyclist for seven days; commercial bus fees vary.

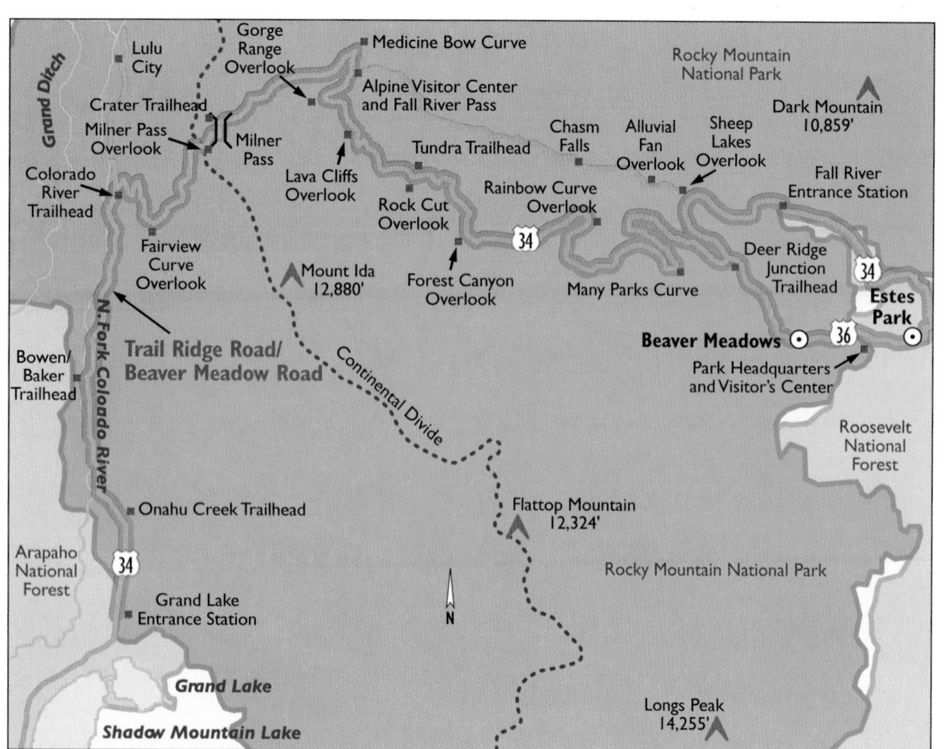


ascents throughout the year for climbers. The Colorado Mountain School is the park's concessionaire, operating a climbing school and guide service.

Winter brings cross-country skiing in the lower valleys and winter mountaineering in the high country. Access roads from the east are kept open and provide you with a panorama of the high mountains.

**Scenic:** The highest continuous paved road in the United States, this route affords an almost-too-rapid sequence of scenic overlooks as it skips along the roofs of some of the tallest Rockies (more than 12,000 feet). From these wind-scoured peaks, you can gaze out to the dark masses of other Rockies, posed like hands of cards in the distance. The land adjacent to the route is otherworldly; the tundra's twisted, ground-creeping trees; crusted snow; and hard-faced boulders seem like they belong to a colder, more distant world.

## Highlights

While visiting the Trail Ridge Road/Beaver Meadow Road, you can take a self-guided tour of the route. If you enter the park from the east (either the Fall River or Beaver Meadows entrance), start at the beginning and move down the list.

**Rainbow Curve Overlook:** At 10,829 feet, this overlook is more than two vertical miles above sea level. At this elevation, every exposed tree is blasted by wind, ice, and grit into distinctive flag shapes. Tree branches here survive only on the downwind side of tree trunks. Higher still, trees survive only where the severely pruned shrubs are covered and protected by winter snowdrifts.

**Forest Canyon Overlook:** Here, the erosive force of glacial ice is unmistakable. Although the ice did not reach as high as the overlook, it still lay more than 1,500 feet thick in a V-shape stream valley. With the grinding of a giant rasp, the ice scoured the valley into the distinctive U-shape of today.

**Rock Cut Overlook:** Here on the roof of the Rockies, the climate is rigorous. Severe weather can come at any time. Periods of drought may occur in both summer and winter, and winter blizzards are frequent. Temperatures remain below freezing all winter, and they frequently drop below freezing in summer. Wind speeds here can exceed 150 miles per hou in either summer or winter, and ultraviolet radiation is twice what it is at sea level. Sunlight is 50 percent more intense.

**Alpine Visitor Center and Fall Rive Pass:** Beside the visitor center, there is a gift shop and a short tra to an overlook at 12,003 feet.

**Milner Pass:** Here, Trail Ridge Road crosses the Continental Divide. At this point, waters enter either the Atlantic or Pacific drainages. The Rockies divide these two great watersheds, but the Continental Divide may be a mountaintop, a ridge, or a pass. From this point, a short trail leads past Poudre Lake, headwaters of the Cache La Poudre River, and up to Old Fall River Road. This road was the original road over the Continental Divide. The trail then connects with another trail leading to Mount Ida, at 12,880 feet. This is a 4 1/2-mile hike.

*Travelers can catch a glimpse of Longs Peak at several locations along the climb to the top of Trail Ridge Road.*

# Kaibab Plateau–North Rim Parkway

*Crossing over a gorgeous high plateau and flanked by rivers and forests, this parkway forms a scenic passage to the North Rim of the Grand Canyon, nature's unsurpassed scenic wonder.*



This route crosses over the gorgeous Kaibab Plateau and travels through two forests: the Kaibab National Forest and Grand Canyon National Park. Along the route, you'll find plenty of places to hike and camp. Groves of golden aspen, flowery meadows, ponds, outcrops of limestone, and steep slopes on all sides break up the dominance of the regal coniferous forest. Also, the Colorado River flows right around the byway, so opportunities for water sports abound.

*An awe-inspiring chasm formed over the millennia, the Grand Canyon provides ample opportunity to explore its amazing natural wonders.*

## Intrinsic Qualities

**Archaeological:** People have occupied the Kaibab Plateau for at least 8,000 years. The earliest people inhabiting this region were hunter-gatherers who utilized the plateau extensively for its big game opportunities and for plant and mineral resources. These people, referred to as the Archaic people, were highly nomadic. Between 500 B.C. and 300 B.C., the life and methods of the people using the Grand Canyon area began to change. The first evidence of plant domestication is linked to this period. Archaeologists refer to the people of this era as the Basket Maker people. Although they still depended heavily on hunting and gathering, they were slowly incorporating horticulture into their lifestyle. The Basket Maker period lasted until around A.D. 800.

Toward the end of the Basket Maker period, pottery was made and people became less mobile. Over time, it is believed that the Basket Maker culture transitioned into what is now known as the Pueblo culture. The Pueblo people relied more heavily on farming than the Basket Maker people; they also built more permanent village sites that included upright masonry structures and cliff dwellings known as pueblos. They developed beautiful painted pottery styles. The Pueblo people abandoned the area by the late 1200s. Archaeologists are unsure why they left; they suspect that prolonged drought and increased population levels forced the Pueblos to leave.

The Paiute people moved into the area shortly after the Pueblo people left. These people continue to live in the area today. The Paiute people were hunters and gatherers who used the Kaibab Plateau for its wild plant and animal resources. While some of the Paiute farmed in historic times, they were not originally a farming people. As with the earlier archaic cultures, the Paiute were highly nomadic. Unlike the Pueblo people, who built masonry pueblo structures, the Paiute lived in temporary brush structures called wikiups. This form of housing allowed them to move their camps on a regular basis to where resources were seasonably available. The Paiutes gave the region the name we still use today; Kaibab is a Paiute term meaning "mountain lying down." Today, the Paiute live on the Kaibab Paiute Indian Reservation located near Fredonia. They continue to use the Kaibab Plateau for traditional cultural practices.

**Cultural:** The rich cultural diversity of Arizona is proudly displayed on the Kaibab Plateau–North Rim Parkway. Here, you find a diverse cross section of Native Americans and pioneer stock. Visit the local towns of Kanab and Fredonia to see the rich heritage that is still

### Quick Facts

**Length:** 42 miles.

**Time to Allow:** One hour or more.

**Considerations:** All roads are winding and steep. Arizona's climate is dry and hot, so be sure to carry plenty of water. Wear proper footwear to minimize the risk of serious injury. There is also the danger of fires, lightning, and flash floods. Most roads are not maintained during the winter.

maintained today. From good old country fairs to the vibrant Western Legends Round Up, everyone is sure to have a good time.

**Historical:** The Kaibab Plateau is rich with the history of preservation and conservation. In 1893, the Grand Canyon Forest Reserve was created, and in the first decade of the 20th century, national forests were designated. Then, in 1906, President Theodore Roosevelt created the Grand Canyon National Game Preserve to protect the Kaibab mule deer, and in 1908, the Grand Canyon Forest Reserve became the Kaibab National Forest.

The historic Jacob Lake Ranger Station was built in 1910 to help administer lands that included what is now Grand Canyon National Park. The ranger station is located along the road that originally led to the North Rim of the Grand Canyon. Eventually, the road to Grand Canyon National Park was moved to its present location, but the Jacob Lake Ranger Station continued to be used to administer Kaibab National Forest lands. It is one of the oldest remaining ranger stations in the country and is now an interpretive site presenting the life of a forest ranger. It can be accessed from Highway 67.

After a devastating wildfire in 1910 burned through much of the Idaho panhandle and parts of western Montana, the United States ushered in an era of fire suppression. Prior to that time, little was done to suppress fires. However, after 1910, fire lookouts and trail systems were developed in earnest throughout the national forest system. The earliest fire lookouts on the Kaibab Plateau consisted of platforms built at the tops of tall trees that were accessed by ladders. Eventually, lookout buildings and towers were built, including the Jacob Lake Fire Lookout Tower in 1934. The tower is located on the east side of Highway 67 and can be viewed from the Kaibab Plateau–North Rim Parkway.

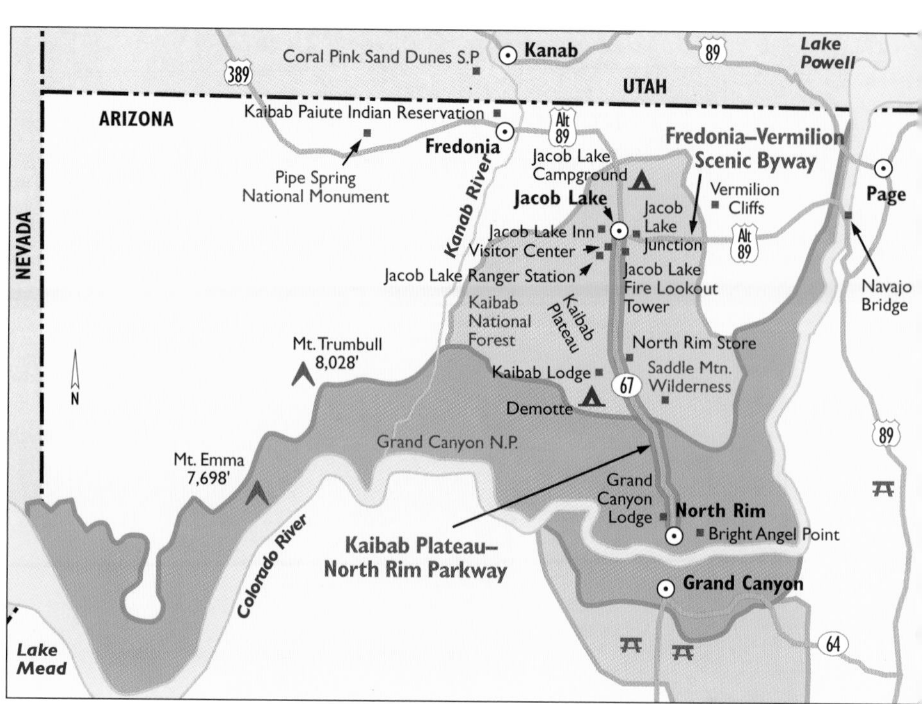


Today, the Jacob Lake Ranger Station and Fire Lookout Tower are on the National Register of Historic Places, and the Jacob Lake Fire Lookout Tower is on the National Register of Fire Lookouts.

**Natural:** The Kaibab Plateau could be called an island of forest; sage and grass cover the lower elevations that surround it. The plateau is bordered on the south by the Grand Canyon and on the east and west by the Colorado River, sometimes reaching elevations of 9,000 feet. Some of the trees found at its higher elevations include ponderosa pine, Engelmann spruce, aspen, blue spruce, oak, piñon, pine, and juniper. At lower elevations, you'll find bitterbrush, Gambel oak, sagebrush, and cliffrose.

Within the forest are irregular areas entirely free of tree growth. These parks are found in canyon bottoms, dry southern exposures, and ridge tops near the forest's exterior limits. Naturally occurring water is scarce in the North Kaibab Ranger District. Melting snow seeps through the gravelly soil to emerge as springs several hundred feet below the plateau rim.

The Vermilion Cliffs are spectacular because of their brilliant colors. It is also thrilling to watch the Grand Canyon walls change color as the sun sets; watching the morning sun hit the canyon is just as unforgettable.

The Grand Canyon stands alone as the world's most awesome natural wonder, and the surrounding Kaibab National Forest offers plenty of native forest wildlife. Keep an eye open for large, soaring birds; the endangered California condor was recently introduced to this area.

**Recreational:** Nonmotorized and motorized trails are maintained for hikers, walkers, bikers, equestrians, cross-country skiers, four-wheel drivers, and snowmobilers. Fifty miles of the cross-state nonmotorized Arizona Trail traverse the district, providing opportunities for day hiking or multinight trips. Many miles of closed roads provide outstanding mountain biking opportunities for all rider levels. (Remember that wilderness areas do not allow mountain bikes.) Spring and fall are the best seasons for enjoying both the wilderness and the Grand Canyon National Park trails due to extreme summer temperatures and winter inaccessibility. If you plan to stay overnight below the rim of the Grand Canyon, purchase a permit from the Grand Canyon National Park Backcountry Office.

For hunters, the Kaibab Plateau is famous for producing record-class mule deer, with established seasons for bow, black powder, and ifle hunting. Game birds, such as he chukar partridge and Merriam's turkey, also have established seasons. The Arizona Game and Fish Department sets the hunt dates and numbers, and hunters are selected by drawings.

The winter season on the Kaibab Plateau is a unique experience. Lodging is available on the plateau at Jacob Lake and Kaibab Lodge. Nordic skiing and snowmobiling are the most popular activities on the plateau in the winter. The area east of Highway 67 is open only to nonmotorized activities. The North Rim is also open only to nonmotorized activities, with no facilities or services during the winter season. All areas west of Highway 67 are open to motorized and nonmotorized activities. Winter conditions are surprisingly severe on the Kaibab Plateau. Be prepared for four to eight feet of snow, along with cold and windy weather.

On national forest lands, camping is not limited to campgrounds; instead, camping is permissible off of any dirt road or out of the sight of a paved highway at no charge. Backcountry camping is prohibited within a quarter-mile of water to allow wildlife undisturbed access. Backcountry campers also must stay at least a half-mile from a developed campground or other facility. Campers are also asked to stay out of meadows, due to the fragile environment.

Jacob Lake area campgrounds open in early May and close in late October. Forest Service and National Park Service campgrounds have water and toilets, but no RV hook-ups. Private campgrounds at Jacob Lake or off the plateau do have full RV hook-ups, however. Tents and RVs are welcome at all campgrounds. Demotte Park is not suitable for large RVs; all other campgrounds can handle any size. Group campsites are available by reservation at Jacob Lake and the North Rim. The Forest Service campgrounds operate on a first-come, first-served basis, and reservations can be made at the North Rim and private campgrounds. The free Jacob Lake picnic area is open May 1 to November 1 during daytime hours. No fee is charged for camping at Indian Hollow Campground, but camping is primitive, and water is not available.

**Scenic:** In many areas along the Kaibab Plateau–North Rim Parkway, you can get out, stretch your legs, and take one of the trails to scenic overlooks in the Grand Canyon. The golden glow of the red rocks and the lonely sound of the wind in the early morning are enough to inspire the most inexperienced of poets. Be sure to bring a journal and a camera.

## Highlights

While visiting the Kaibab Plateau–North Rim Parkway, you can take the following self-guided tour of the byway.

**Jacob Lake Junction:** The Jacob Lake Junction is at highway marker 579 or the junction of Highway 67 and State Highway 89A. The Kaibab Plateau Visitor Center offers information and interpretive displays about the natural and cultural resources of the plateau. The visitor center also has books, videos, postcards, and other interpretive sales items through the Public Lands Interpretive Association. Jacob Lake Inn is a historic lodge offering accommodations, a restaurant/café, and a gift shop. At Jacob Lake Campground, you'll find family sites and group sites available.

**Jacob Lake Fire Lookout Tower:** Get to Jacob Lake Fire Lookout Tower on highway marker 580.3 or one mile south of the Jacob Lake Junction/Highway 67 and State Highway 89A. Visit this historic tower, and find out how fires are detected. Views of the Grand Staircase are visible from the tower. The tower is usually staffed during the day and may be closed for two days during the week; check in at the visitor center for current openings.

**Demotte Park Overlook:** Find this overlook at highway marker 604 or 22 miles south of the Jacob Lake Junction on the byway. Demotte Park is one of the largest meadows on the Kaibab Plateau, and it's filled with deer, coyotes, and numerous species of birds. Wildflower enthusiasts will also enjoy the diversity and abundance in this meadow. Near this stop is the historic Kaibab Lodge. Rustic cabins and a restaurant, gift shop, gas station, and convenience store are available.

**Grand Canyon National Park–North Rim:** Forty-four miles south on Highway 67, the end of this scenic parkway leads to a spectacular view of the North Rim of the Grand Canyon. Several hiking trails are located at or near the rim. The North Rim Visitor Center is open seven days a week 8:00 A.M. to 6:00 P.M. Information, interpretation, and interpretive sale items are available. The North Rim's Historic Lodge offers accommodations, restaurant, and mule rides.

*The Kaibab Plateau provides spectacular views that can be enjoyed by photographers, bird-watchers, hikers, campers, and others.*

# BILLY THE KID TRAIL

*Infused with the romance of the Wild West, this route through Billy the Kid country rides the trails of outlaws, sheriffs, and cowboys. Bring the kids.*

The Lincoln County area surrounding the Billy the Kid Trail is rich in history. It has been home to Billy the Kid, the Lincoln County War, the Mescalero Apache nation, Kit Carson, "Black Jack" Pershing, the Buffalo Soldiers, the world's richest quarter horse race, and Smokey Bear.

## Intrinsic Qualities

**Archaeological:** A fingerprint, carbon-dated to be roughly 28,000 years old, was discovered in a cave 70 miles south of Ruidoso. It is the earliest known evidence of human's presence in North America. Members of the Paleo-Indian cultures converged in the area between 9000 B.C. and 6000 B.C. to hunt the woolly mammoth and now-extinct species of bison that roamed the area.

**Cultural:** Although many people consider Santa Fe the cultural capital of New Mexico, Lincoln County is more than willing to rival this claim. Spectacular annual events showcase the route's cultural dynamics.

Some of the best art in New Mexico can be found in Ruidoso. The Harris Poll has recognized the Ruidoso Art Festival, held each year in late July, as one of the most outstanding juried art shows in the Southwest. The cool pines create a beautiful mountain setting for spectacular art from more than 125 accomplished, professional artists.

Held at Ruidoso Downs the second weekend of October, the Lincoln County Cowboy Symposium gathers the world's finest cowboy poets, musicians, chuck wagon cooks, and artisans.

For a better glimpse at the real West and American Indian cultures, be sure to see the Mescalero Apache Ceremonial Dances. Held during the first week of July, these ceremonial dances celebrate the Apache Spirit.

Any description of the cultural qualities of Lincoln County would be incomplete without mentioning the Spencer Theater for the Performing Arts. Opened in 1997, the Spencer Theater creates a year-round venue for world-class performances in theater, music, and dance. An aristocrat among theaters, the $22 million structure is splendid and elegant, yet intimate and welcoming.

*Sierra Blanca in the Lincoln National Forest takes on a mystical appearance in stormy weather.*

### Quick Facts

**Length:** 84 miles.

**Time to Allow:** Two hours.

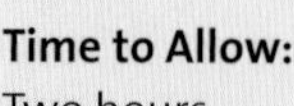

**Considerations:** The altitude along this byway ranges from 6,500 to 7,000 feet above sea level, but there are few, if any, seasonal limitations. All of the roadways are paved, and snow is cleared in the wintertime when there is significant accumulation.

**Historical:** Henry McCarty, better known as Bonney or Billy the Kid, is the most well-known person from this area. He is believed to have been born in New York City sometime in 1859 or 1860. His family moved to Indiana and then to Wichita, Kansas. In 1874, his mother died, and Billy the Kid was placed in foster homes. He soon ran into trouble with the law and was sent to jail, only to escape through the chimney. Billy the Kid wandered from ranch to ranch and eventually wound up in trouble with the law again when he killed a man at a saloon in Arizona.

When Billy the Kid returned to New Mexico, he and his gang of rustlers became embroiled with the feud going on among James Dolan, John Tunstall, and Alex McSween. Billy the Kid started on Dolan's side, but when he was thrown in jail, he made a deal with Tunstall and became a part of the Regulators, a group that took the law into their own hands after some of their men had been killed. After the Lincoln County War, Billy the Kid made his living by gambling and rustling cattle. He spent his time eluding the law, usually from Pat Garrett, whose job was to hunt for Billy the Kid. After being arrested by Garrett and escaping from jail, Billy the Kid was killed by Garrett in Pete Maxwell's bedroom on July 14, 1881.

One small ferrotype is the only existing authentic photograph of Billy the Kid. Taken by an unknown itinerant photographer outside Beaver Smith's saloon in Old Fort Sumner in 1879, it reveals a young and handsome man. The rumpled hat and layers of utilitarian clothing immediately clash with Hollywood's images of the outlaw. In the photo, he wears a gambler's pinkie ring on his left hand that means he may have cheated at cards. His colt pistol jaunts from his right hip.

**Natural:** A drive along the Billy the Kid Trail not only provides byway enthusiasts with glimpses into New Mexico's desperado past but also offers grand views of the region's natural treasures.

The Lincoln National Forest is host to two prominent mountain ranges, the Sacramento Mountains to the south and the Capitan Mountains to the north. These ranges surround the Billy the Kid Trail and provide natural views guaranteed to beat the house. Each of these mountainous ranges features towering peaks in an otherwise flat and arid region. Capitan Peak (10,083 feet) and Sierra Blanca (11,973 feet) provide stunning views and are solid bets for viewing wildlife.

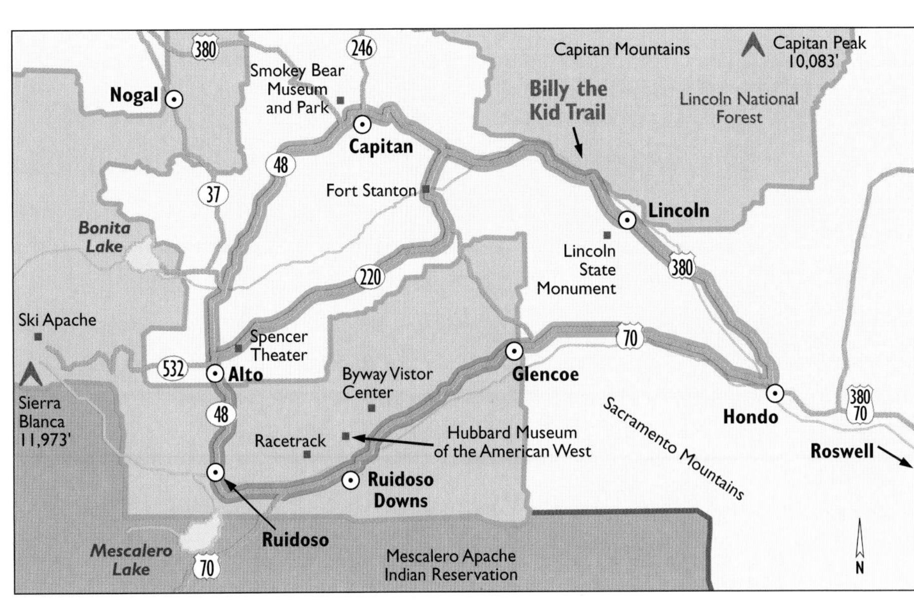


**Recreational:** The Billy the Kid Trail features many recreational opportunities. The historic district of Lincoln, the Hubbard Museum of the American West, Fort Stanton, the Spencer Theater for the Performing Arts, the Ruidoso Downs Racetrack, the Smokey Bear Museum and Park in Capitan, and Ski Apache all lend appeal to the area.

As wild as the West (and kids) can be, the whole family will enjoy the hands-on displays at the Hubbard Museum of the American West.

**Scenic:** The Billy the Kid Trail travels through a region marked by exceptional beauty and diversity. From grassy plains to dense pine forests, the region is known for its stunning views and cool mountain climate. Teeming with fish and wildlife, this area beckons hunters, anglers, skiers, and photographers from around the country. Visually, it is breathtakingly different from the arid desert that surrounds it.

## Highlights

Consider taking the following historic tour of Billy the Kid country.

**Byway Visitor Center:** Begin your tour at the Byway Visitor Center located on U.S. Highway 70, and view the exhibits.

**Hubbard Museum of the American West:** Right next door to the visitor center is the Hubbard Museum of the American West. Here, exhibits, artifacts, and fine art tell of the special history of the area.

**Ruidoso:** Heading west on U.S. Highway 70, you pass through the village of Ruidoso, and then turn north on NM Highway 48. Traveling about 26 miles along NM Highway 48, notice the beautiful Sierra Blanca to the west.

**Capitan:** The next stop of the tour is in Capitan. Here, the Smokey Bear Museum and State Park is a must-see; Smokey is actually buried here. The museum offers exhibits, games, and films about fire safety. There is also a documentary film about Smokey's life.

**Fort Stanton:** Travel southeast to Fort Stanton. The fort itself is not accessible; however, be sure to stop at the Fort Stanton Post Office and speak with Willie Mae Hobbs, an expert about the Fort Stanton area. The Fort Stanton Cemetery and Cave are definite stops along the tour.

**Lincoln:** After Fort Stanton, drive northeast on U.S. 220 and then southeast U.S. 380 until you arrive in Lincoln. The Lincoln County War started here, and this is also where Billy the Kid made his last escape. Museums and markers are all over this village, which looks almost exactly as it did in the 1850s.

# El Camino Real

*First carved by Spanish explorers, the historic "Royal Highway" follows the Rio Grande from the Mexican border to Santa Fe. Along the way are soaring peaks, American Indian pueblos, and the city of Albuquerque.*

One of the most important of the historic trails of New Mexico, El Camino Real is not only the first European road in what is now the United States, but for many years it was also the longest road in North America. The northern portions of El Camino Real followed the Rio Grande Pueblo Indian Trail, which existed for centuries before the Spanish explorers arrived. The land along El Camino Real has been a meeting ground of peoples and a haven of cultural diversity through the centuries.

El Camino Real follows the Rio Grande River from the U.S.–Mexico border to Santa Fe. It traverses a land rich in history and culture. The scenic beauty of El Camino Real is as varied and colorful as its culture, history, and people. From the low-lying flatlands of the south to the soaring peaks of the northern mountains, the terrain climbs 10,000 feet in altitude, creating a landscape of dramatic contrasts.

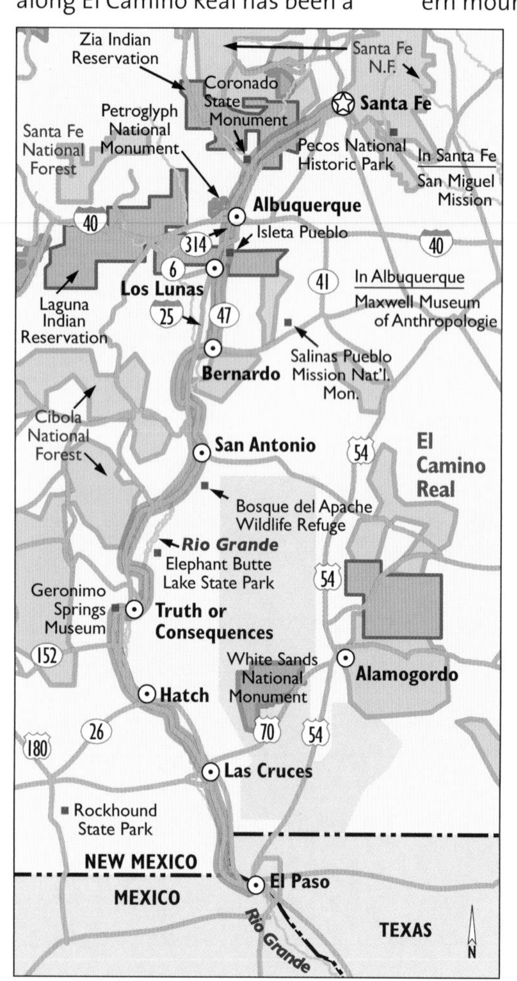


## Intrinsic Qualities

**Archaeological:** Many archaeological attractions are found along El Camino Real in New Mexico. Kuana Pueblo was one of the Rio Grande Valley villages visited by Francisco Vasquez de Coronado in 1540. He called this region the Tiquex Province because its inhabitants spoke a common language, Tiwa. Abandoned before the 1680 Pueblo Revolt against Spanish rule, this large and important site, called the Coronado State Monument, has been excavated and partially restored.

The San Miguel Mission in Santa Fe was established in the early 1600s. Records of its early history were destroyed during the Pueblo Revolt, but the adobe walls were left unharmed. In the early 1700s, the mission walls were reinforced with stone buttresses. An audio presentation is available for visitors.

More than 15,000 petroglyphs have been carved into the lava rock that covers the mesa west of the Rio Grande. The earliest of these rock drawings were made by prehistoric inhabitants almost 3,000 years ago. Many others were added by Pueblo peoples, and more were added later by Spanish explorers and settlers. This gallery of ancient art is interpreted at Petroglyph National Monument.

**Cultural:** The cultural landscape along El Camino Real includes a rich variety of people and places. A number of American Indian Pueblos played a significant role in the history of El Camino Real, particularly in establishing trade routes before the arrival of the Spanish. Some pueblos are open to the public year-round and encourage tourism and recreation. Others are open only by invitation during special events (such as feast day celebrations and dances). In addition, the cultural history of New Mexico and El Camino Real can be enjoyed at a number of museums throughout the byway, including the Maxwell Museum of Anthropology in Albuquerque and the Geronimo Springs Museum in Truth or Consequences.

**Historical:** El Camino Real, also called the Royal Highway of the Interior Lands, linked New Mexico with New Spain (Mexico) in the Spanish colonial period (1598–1821), the Mexico national period (1821–1848), and the U.S. Territorial period (1848–1912). El Camino Real ran from Mexico City to Chihuahua City, then crossed the desert to El Paso del Norte on what is now the U.S.–Mexico border. After reaching El Paso del Norte, it more or less paralleled the Rio Grande (called Rio Bravo del Norte) as far as Santa Fe in northern New Mexico.

## Quick Facts

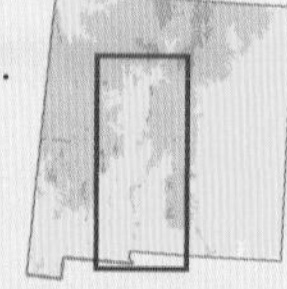

**Length:** 299 miles.

**Time to Allow:** Nine hours.

**Considerations:** During the winter, there are frequent snowstorms. An especially dangerous area during a snowstorm is La Bajada, located south of Santa Fe en route to Albuquerque. As you travel farther south and the elevation decreases, the temperature increases on a year-round trend.

El Camino Real is one of the most important historic trails in New Mexico. The northern portions of El Camino Real followed the Rio Grande Pueblo Indian Trail, which existed for centuries before the Spanish explorers arrived. This route allowed the Pueblo Indians of New Mexico to have interregional trade with the pre-Columbian Indian civilizations of Mesoamerica. Throughout the byway, you'll discover many historic places to visit.

**Natural:** The Lower Sonoran life zone covers much of the southern quarter of El Camino Real. At an altitude below 4,500 feet, these arid flatlands support cholla; prickly pear; creosote; and yucca; and cottonwood, olive, and cedar trees. The Upper Sonoran life zone, ranging in elevation from 4,500 to 6,500 feet, encompasses the northern two-thirds of New Mexico. As in the Lower Sonoran, cacti and desert grasses thrive, but piñon and oak trees replace the yucca and creosote. In Santa Fe, the Transition zone (6,500 to 8,500 feet) consists of ponderosa pine, oak, juniper, spruce, and Douglas fir.

You'll find many natural features along El Camino Real, including the Sandia Mountains and other mountain ranges, many national forests, and several national wildlife refuges.

**Recreational:** El Camino Real provides a wealth of recreational sites and facilities for visitors to enjoy. Recreational sites lure many outdoor enthusiasts to the Land of Enchantment. Elephant Butte Lake State Park, the largest lake and park in New Mexico, hosts more than a million visitors every year. It has more than 200 miles of shoreline.

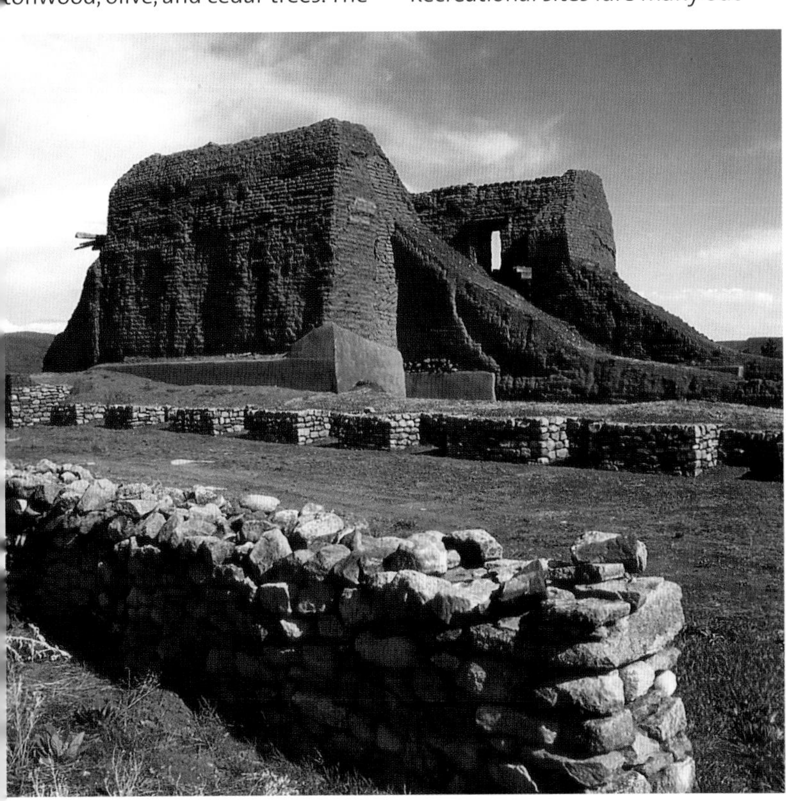

*Pecos National Historical Park preserves nearly 10,000 years of history, including fascinating mission ruins.*

**Scenic:** The scenic beauty of El Camino Real is as diverse and colorful as its culture, history, and people. From the low-lying flatlands of the south to the soaring peaks of the northern mountains, the terrain climbs 10,000 feet in altitude, creating a landscape of dramatic contrasts.

## Highlights

This El Camino Real must-see tour begins in Pecos National Historic Park and continues south to Las Cruces. If you're traveling in the other direction, simply start at the bottom of the list and work your way up.

**Pecos National Historic Park:** A visit to Pecos National Historic Park just south of Santa Fe is a great stop to learn about 10,000 years of history, including the ancient Pueblo of Pecos, two Spanish colonial missions, and the site of the Civil War battle of Glorieta Pass.

**Santa Fe:** The town of Santa Fe offers a bevy of sights, sounds, foods, and festivals. Stop for an hour or a week—you'll never tire of the offerings here.

**Coronado State Monument and Petroglyph National Monument:** Visit two archaeological must-sees before reaching Albuquerque: Coronado State Monument and Petroglyph National Monument. The visitor center in Coronado State Monument offers information on the Southwest. Hiking trails are available at Petroglyph National Monument.

**Isleta Pueblo:** Just south of Albuquerque, stop at the Isleta Pueblo. Take time to examine the amazing art produced there, a treat best appreciated in person.

**Salinas Pueblo Missions National Monument:** A small side trip will bring a great afternoon at the Salinas Pueblo Missions National Monument in Abo. Surrounding the ruins here are exhibits, trails, and picnic areas.

**Truth or Consequences:** Stop in the town of Truth or Consequences (T or C, for short). This town has many recreational opportunities. And don't forget the Geronimo Springs Museum in downtown T or C.

**White Sands National Monument:** Back on El Camino Real, head south toward Las Cruces. On Interstate 10, head east toward Alamogordo, where a real treat awaits you at White Sands National Monument. Be sure to pick a day when missiles are not being tested, though: The highway is often closed during times of testing. Scheduling information is available by calling the monument. Spending an evening in Las Cruces is a perfect end to the exploration of El Camino Real.

# Historic Route 66 

*Although much of this icon of American folklore has been absorbed by newer roads, drivers can still get their kicks on parts of Route 66, a blacktop ribbon of adventure across northern New Mexico.*

Many of the early curiosities that made Route 66 intriguing to travelers have fallen victim to interstate highways, but you can still see much of the route's character if you leave the beaten path, both around Albuquerque and on other parts of Historic Route 66. On Albuquerque's eastern edge, you can pick up parts of Route 66 at Tijeras Canyon, where a serene and rural atmosphere allows you to leave the big city behind. Other parts of Historic Route 66 lead you to quaint and historic sites, enabling you to catch a glimpse into the past.

## Intrinsic Qualities

**Archaeological:** Petroglyph National Monument along Albuquerque's West Mesa gives you the chance to see amazing images carved by native people and early Spanish settlers. With five volcanic cones, hundreds of archaeological sites, and an estimated 25,000 images carved by native pueblo indians and early Spanish settlers, the monument protects part of the early culture and history of the area for generations to come.

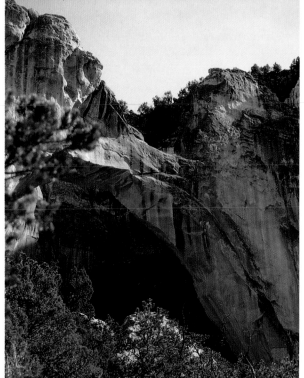

*La Ventana is a large natural arch in the sandstone bluffs on the eastside of El Malpais National Monument.*

Covering a 17-mile stretch, the Petroglyph National Monument allows the past to come alive; images on the rocks tell the stories of natives and settlers in carvings of animals, people, spirals, stars, and geometric shapes. Perhaps the most famous symbol found at the Petroglyph National Monument is that of Kokopelli, a depiction of a humpbacked flute player.

Although no one knows the exact dates the carvings were made, archaeologists have compared the petroglyphs with other artwork of a known date. Some carvings are thought to have been created between 1300 and 1650; others are closer to 3,000 years old. The most recent are thought to have been created by Spanish settlers during the Spanish colonial period.

**Cultural:** Museums and abandoned pueblos featuring ancient artwork and dress provide byway travelers with reminders of the early culture that thrived for centuries. The Apache, the Navajo, and some nomadic nations all inhabited the desert land; some lived in permanent mud-brick settlements near waterways that were called pueblos when first encountered by Spaniards. The word *pueblo* also refers to a Native American culture that is unique to the Southwest and not to a particular Native American group. Even though they share many common elements, each pueblo has its own government, social order, religious practices, and language.

The Pueblo people are further distinguished by their art. Each group's jewelry, pottery, weavings, and other art have a different style. Black-on-black matte pottery, for example, is unique to the San Ildefonso pueblo. Geometric black and white pots are particular to the Acoma. Other non-Pueblo Indians, such as the Navajo and Apaches, are known for their unique and beautiful artwork, as well: the Navajos for their weaving and silverwork; the Apaches for their basket weaving.

Many Native American nations have cultural centers, where contemporary artists' work can be viewed and purchased. The byway's museums display ancient artifacts that bring past cultures a little closer. Visitors are also often

### Quick Facts

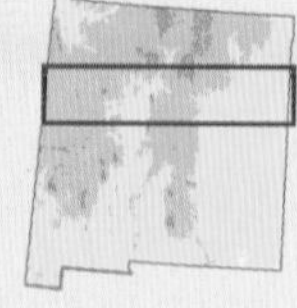

**Length:** 604 miles.

**Time to Allow:** 16 hours.

**Considerations:** The busiest seasons are summer and winter. In areas of higher altitude, wearing sweaters and jackets is recommended, even in warmer months.

llowed on American Indian land o tour trading posts, cultural enters, and shops.

Spanish conquest is much ngrained in early New Mexico's ulture. Explorers from Spain in earch of riches happened upon he New Mexico area in the early 540s. Although they didn't find heir sought-after gold, they lid find thousands of potential Catholic converts. By 1680, Spansh priests had set up more than 30 missions in the area. Although nuch of the colonization was peaceful, the Spanish culture and Catholic religion imposed on some American Indian nations led to he Pueblo Revolt of 1680. Native Americans from all over the area overthrew the settlers, burned churches, and killed priests. The Spanish returned 12 years later and were more attuned to native cultures and religions.

Today's culture is a blend of the Spanish and Native American cultures: Catholicism and indigenous religions, along with festivals and architecture that reflect both cultures. Spanish and Native American art, architecture, and music meshed to create a blend that today is known simply as Southwestern. Mariachi music, pottery, and adobe buildings are cultural reflections of the Southwest that result from a fascinating mixture of many civilizations.

**Historical:** When incumbent governor A. T. Hannett lost the 1926 New Mexico gubernatorial election to Richard Dillon, he was infuriated over the loss and what he felt was a betrayal by his own party. So he exited with a flamboyant farewell gesture, sending orders to E. B. Bail, the district highway engineer, to assemble all road-building equipment north of U.S. 60 and cut a new road between Santa Rosa and Moriarty before the year (and Hannett's term) ended. Historic Route 66 as we know it today was created.

Hannett, in his 1964 book *Sagebrush Lawyer,* recounts that he conceived of the idea of a shorter route by laying a ruler on the map between Santa Rosa and Gallup. Of course, the idea was protested not only by chamber of commerce members in Santa Fe (who led a fight to enlarge and straighten a northern route), but also by delegations from the small towns along U.S. 60, a highway that passed through Vaughn, Encino, Mountainair, and Socorro before heading north to Albuquerque. Business leaders in those towns knew that U.S. 60 would have to compete with the new road, but Hannett prevailed because the new shortcut would almost halve the distance from Santa Rosa to Albuquerque.

Plunging ahead, Bail, the district highway engineer, realized the near impossibility of the order. Assembling equipment and organizing road crews would take the rest of November, which meant that the actual construction of 69 miles had to be accomplished in just 31 days. The new cutoff would connect the road seven miles west of Santa Rosa to an existing highway from Moriarty on into Duke City, reducing the distance from 195 miles to 114.

Bail's account of the adventure, first published in 1952 and later appended in *Sagebrush Lawyer,* credits the road crews with marshaling the motley collection of surplus World War I Caterpillars, tractors, and graders. They did battle against the blowing snow and dense piñon forests. Irate citizens along the southern and northern routes, upset by the impact that reduced traffic would have on their vital tourist business, tried to sabotage the project. Workers found sugar in gas tanks and sand in their engines. Bail brought in blankets so that the workers could sleep next to their equipment at night. Ironically, no one troubled with the most logical way to put a hitch in the project—by fighting it with a lawsuit.

The road was not quite completed by the end of the year so, immediately after taking the oath of office on January 1, 1927, the new governor, Richard Dillon, dispatched an engineer from Santa Fe to halt the venture. However, inclement weather prevented his arrival at the job site before January 3. By then "Hannett's Joke" was complete, and cars drove across the new road. (Hannett denied that his method for accomplishing the project originated as a joke.)

Hannett, whose home base had been Gallup, moved to Albuquerque, practiced law from an office in the Sunshine Building, and wrote a daily column for the *Albuquerque Journal*. Although no monument credits him with the golden thread that helped Albuquerque develop into a metropolitan center, one of the city's streets is named Hannett.

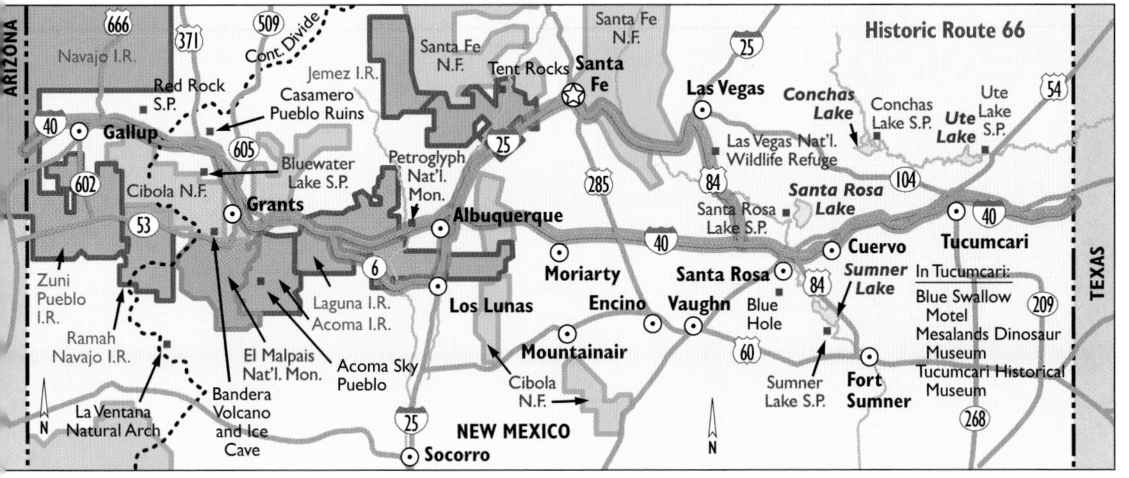


**Natural:** Historic Route 66 is full of natural caves and geological formations. One of the most fascinating natural formations is La Ventana, a large natural arch in the sandstone bluffs on the east side of El Malpais National Monument and Conservation Area near Grants. Established in 1987, this monument preserves 114,277 acres, of which 109,260 acres are federal lands. El Malpais means "the badlands," but contrary to its name, this unique area holds many surprises. Volcanic features such as lava flows, cinder cones, pressure ridges, and complex lava tube systems dominate the landscape. Sandstone bluffs and mesas border the eastern side, providing access to vast wilderness.

Another famous and exciting place to visit in El Malpais is the Bandera Volcano and Ice Cave. Nicknamed the Land of Fire and Ice, the two features offer contrasting phenomena: an ancient lava trail winding toward an ice cave on one fork and an erupted volcano on the other. In the ice cave, layers of blue-green ice are up to 20 feet thick and sit in part of a collapsed lava tube, and the temperature never rises above 31 degrees Fahrenheit. The Bandera Volcano is 800 feet deep and erupted more than 10,000 years ago, leaving a 23-mile lava flow.

*The people of the Acoma Pueblo Village live much like their ancestors did. They reside in the original historic pueblo buildings, and there is no electricity or running water.*

**Recreational:** Evidence of New Mexico's diversity in culture, climate, and landscape is everywhere, making the area surrounding Historic Route 66 the perfect place to find any type of recreation imaginable.

No trip to the area would be complete without dining in one of the authentic Mexican restaurants. Famous for its fiery-hot chili peppers, New Mexican cuisine is an adventure in itself.

The climate of central New Mexico makes outdoor recreation possible year-round. Summers lend themselves to hiking, camping, biking, and fishing, while New Mexico's winters delight both downhill and cross-country skiers with trails and runs across the state.

The Sandia Mountains, located near Albuquerque, provide exciting recreational opportunities. Travelers enjoy hiking and biking beginner to advanced trails in the summer and skiing the 200 acres of terrain of the Sandia Peak Ski Area in the winter. The ski area's tramway whisks you and your skis or bike to the top of the mountain year-round; just one reason the Sandia Mountains are an excellent place for outdoor adventure.

The geography of the area is unlike any other place. Lush forests, clear lakes, and sporadic mountains break up the desert landscape. Natural caves and rock formations in El Malpais National Monument and Conservation Area are open for tourists to view. Erupted volcanoes, bat caves, and sandstone cliffs and mesas dot the beautiful area, providing a truly rare chance to see one of the world's most fascinating regions.

If urban entertainment is what you are looking for, New Mexico has that, too. You may want to catch a symphony, attend a hockey game, or shop in unique outdoor markets. The nightlife heats up as the temperatures cool down after dark. Dance clubs, bars, and live music venues around the larger cities come alive at night.

**Scenic:** Historic Route 66 is unique in that it embodies plains, grasslands, vistas, mountains, deserts, and virtually every kind of terrain available in New Mexico. The beautiful and varied desert landscape along the byway, coupled with unique Southwestern architecture, provides an exceptionally scenic drive. The sunsets and sunrises on the byway are spectacular, and you can see for miles in any direction in most places along the route.

Historic Route 66 is a truly amazing visual experience. Orange rock dotted with green plantlife rests dramatically against a turquoise-blue sky in summer, creating a postcardlike desert scene. Yet, a few miles down the road, a forest surrounds a bright blue lake, with a waterfall cascading down the dark rock. You'll often find this contrast in this unique geological area: Six of the seven life zones identified on Earth are found in New Mexico.

As you approach cities, you'll notice that the distinctive architecture of the cities also embodies Southwestern flavor. The stucco and brick buildings are often colorful and particular to the pueblo style. This style is apparent in the downtown shops, outdoor markets, and residential areas. Even new construction keeps the traditional style alive with colorful buildings of stucco and landscape of cacti and yucca.

## Highlights

Because Historic Route 66 is more than 600 miles long, the following must-see tour of the byway is split into two sections: one starting near Grants and heading westward into Gallup; the other starting east of Tucumcari and heading westward into Santa Rosa.

### Western Must-See Tour

**Acoma Sky Pueblo:** The first stop along this section is just south of McCarty's, off of exit 96. The Acoma Sky Pueblo offers a unique view worth seeing—a city atop a 400-foot mesa. The people of the Acoma Pueblo ask that visitors respect the posted warnings and signs and be respectful of residents. Always ask permission to take photos. Also, if you are fortunate to visit on a celebration day or during a dance, remember that dances are prayers and require concentration. Please do not talk to the dancers, walk on the dance plaza, or applaud when a dance ends.

**El Malpais National Monument:** The next stop along Route 66 is El Malpais National Monument near Grants. The monument can serve as a central post while visiting several other sites, including La Ventana Natural Arch and Bandera Volcano and Ice Cave.

**Bluewater Lake State Park and Casamero Pueblo Ruins:** North of Grants, Bluewater Lake State Park offers a relaxing afternoon of hiking and fishing. The Casamero Pueblo Ruins near McKinley County Road 19 offers a unique view of the area's history. Casamero Pueblo was first recorded by an archaeologist in the mid-1960s. A portion of the site and many smaller sites were reported to have been vandalized prior

*The Blue Hole is a natural artesian spring delivering 3,000 gallons of water a minute. At more than 80 feet deep, the pool is amazingly clear nearly to the bottom when undisturbed.*

to this time. Between 1966 and 1975, most of Casamero Pueblo was excavated by archaeologists. In 1976 and 1977, they stabilized the ruins to help prevent deterioration of the walls. Interpretive signs were placed at the site describing the cultural history of the Chacoan Anasazi and the features present at Casamero. The Bureau of Land Management restabilized Casamero Pueblo in 1986, replacing eroded mortar and loose stones. The Casamero Pueblo Ruins is fenced to keep livestock and vehicles from disturbing the site. A parking lot is provided along McKinley County Road 19 for visitors.

**Gallup:** The Route 66 Drive-In in Gallup makes a great stop for lunch in keeping with the theme of the drive. Don't forget the Red Rock Museum at Red Rock State Park, just east of Gallup. Also, while in Gallup, finish your trip along western Route 66 by inquiring about ongoing activities at the Gallup McKinley County Chamber of Commerce.

### Eastern Must-See Tour

**I-40:** The modern Route 66 is essentially Interstate 40, although it detours slightly through Tucumcari and Santa Rosa. This section caused quite a lot of trouble back in the early days of Route 66, when the road was narrow and dangerous. This 40-mile stretch of road heading into Tucumcari was poorly maintained and was full of potholes. Driving long hours through this flat countryside often caused motorists to doze off; hitting an unexpected pothole would cause them to lose control. Many people died in collisions on this narrow road. In fact, some of the older residents in the area will tell you that there were "only six inches and a cigarette paper between you and death on 66." Today, I-40 is wider, safer, and well maintained.

**Tucumcari:** Once in Tucumcari, take exit 335 into town. Historic Route 66 continues along Tucumcari Boulevard. While in Tucumcari, you can easily spend the day shopping or visiting the Blue Swallow Motel (one of the oldest motels in town and one of the most famous along Route 66), Mesalands Dinosaur Museum, and Tucumcari Historical Museum.

**Conchas Lake State Park:** At the end of Tucumcari Boulevard, you can choose one of two routes. This tour takes you north on Route 54 toward Conchas home to Conchas Lake State Park, one of New Mexico's largest lakes. The park has a wide variety of water activities, and onshore exploring offers the potential of finding ancient rock formations and American Indian dwellings.

**Santa Rosa:** Heading farther west along I-40, you pass through Cuervo, and head on to Santa Rosa. The Route 66 Auto Museum is a must-stop for anyone taking in the true spirit of Route 66. The more adventurous will most likely enjoy a dip at Blue Hole, an 81-foot deep clear, natural artesian spring famous for its scuba diving opportunities. A stop at nearby Santa Rosa Lake State Park and Sumner Lake State Park will give the recreationally minded plenty of choices.

# JEMEZ MOUNTAIN TRAIL

*Ghost towns, volcanic rocks, hot springs, American Indian pueblos, campgrounds, and forests—the Jemez Mountain Trail beckons explorers to a land rich in history, geology, culture, and outdoor recreation.*

North of Albuquerque, at the unspoiled village of San Ysidro, begins one of New Mexico's most spectacular scenic drives: the Jemez (pronounced HAY-mez or HAY-mus) Mountain Trail. San Ysidro is a village where you can find the work of local artisans and view the restored Spanish adobe church.

## Intrinsic Qualities

**Cultural:** The greater Santa Fe area is extremely culturally diverse due to strong Native American and Spanish influences. Of the 19 Native American communities located in New Mexico, eight are in the greater Santa Fe area. All eight are Pueblo Indian nations, and their communities are referred to as pueblos. Many of these pueblos were established centuries ago; the Taos Pueblo, for example, is thought to have been continuously occupied for close to 1,000 years. Each pueblo has its own government, traditions, and ceremonies and is a sovereign and separate entity. The pueblos typically welcome visitors, especially during specific dances and feast days.

A people of great faith, the early Spanish settlers arrived in 1607 with scores of Catholic priests. Just as the Spanish created houses of worship from an adobe mix of mud and straw, they built villages and towns in the same architectural fashion.

Like adobe architecture, art forms practiced by early Spanish settlers were shaped largely from resources they found in their natural environment. Using native aspen and pine, paints derived from natural pigments, and other local materials, they created utilitarian goods and religious objects to adorn their homes and churches. At first, the work echoed the traditional artworks and motifs they had carried with them to the New World from Mexico and Spain. But in time, native artisans developed styles and techniques that were unique to New Mexico alone. Ranging from santos (carved images of saints), furniture, and textiles to works in tin, iron, silver, and straw, the art of the Spanish colonial era remains the art of many Santa Fe-area families. Meanwhile, other artists have carried their ancestors' legacy to new levels of excellence by working in more modern media, including sculpture, photography, painting, jewelry, and literature.

**Historical:** Jemez State Monument and Bandelier National Monument are popular places to discover more about the history of the area. Both monuments have exhibits and self- and ranger-guided tours.

**Natural:** You'll find many wonders along the Jemez Mountain Trail. For example, the history of the Jemez Mountains goes back one million years to a volcano's eruption. The eruption created an area of mountains, mesas, and canyons the size of a small eastern state.

Dominating the western half of the Santa Fe National Forest, the Jemez Mountains resemble a wagon wheel on a topographic map. The hub is formed by the giant Valles Caldera (a crater created by the volcano's violent explosion), and the spokes are made by the mesas built of volcanic tuft. Elevations in the Jemez Mountains range from 6,000 to 11,000 feet. One of the legacies of the volcano is the canyons' Swiss cheeselike rock cliffs and strange cone-shape tent rocks.

The towering volcanic plug of Cabezon (meaning big head) is famous in Navajo folklore. The volcano has a trail leading to its 8,000-foot summit. In addition, one mile north of the Jemez State Monument at Soda Dam is an unusual geological formation

*Soda Dam is a large mound of calcium carbonate deposited over millions of years by hot springs bubbling from Earth's interior.*

### Quick Facts

**Length:** 132 miles.

**Time to Allow:** Three hours.

**Considerations:** Highway 126 is not paved and is generally closed in the winter due to snow. Different sections of the trail have various accessibility and safety issues. Travelers should be aware of several fire precautions. Call any U.S. Forest Service Office for hazard updates.

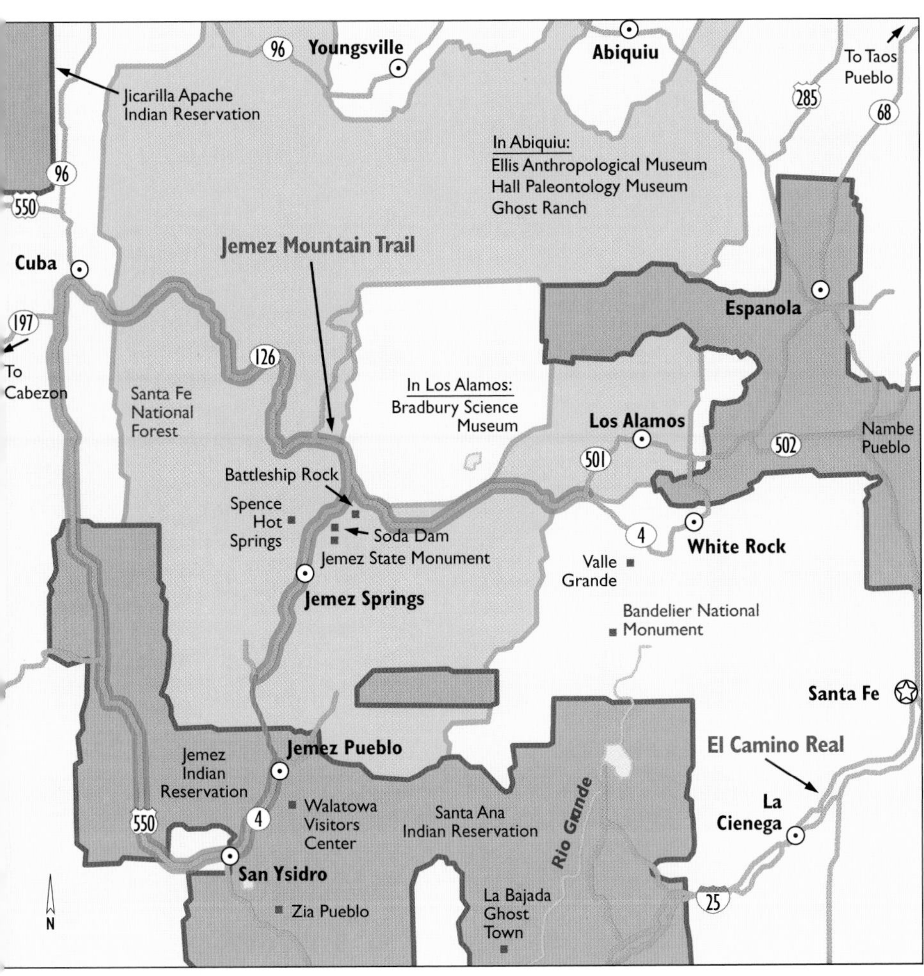


where, over thousands of years, minerals from a natural spring have created a dam that blocks the Jemez River. The river pours through a hole in the dam, forming a waterfall. Soda Dam has become one of the most popular swimming holes in the Jemez Mountains. Also along the byway is Battleship Rock, a sheer cliff that rises suddenly above the river like the prow of a ship. A few miles past Battleship Rock is the parking lot for Spence Hot Springs, an accessible and scenic place for a long soak in hot mineral waters.

**Recreational:** The Jemez Mountain Trail offers all sorts of outdoor recreation. Travelers enjoy hiking trails of varying degrees of difficulty, biking trails, fishing, and several camping locations. The unique geological features also allow for outdoor adventures; you can visit caves and tunnels.

For the adventurous, Battleship Rock in the Jemez Mountains provides challenging terrain and an intriguing landscape: The trail is covered in shiny black obsidian created from volcanic eruptions five million years ago.

If you enjoy biking, the Jemez Mountain Trail provides several trails. Advanced bikers may want to explore Guacamalla and Paliza canyons, a steep terrain that offers excellent views of green meadows.

**Scenic:** In all seasons, the Jemez Mountains offer some magnificent scenery. Visitors enjoy escaping to a quieter, more relaxing way of life.

## Highlights

As you travel the Jemez Mountain Trail, consider using this itinerary.

**Los Alamos:** Your trip through the Jemez Mountains begins in Los Alamos, famous as the home of the Los Alamos National Laboratory for its work and historic role in the Manhattan Project and the development of the atomic bomb. The Bradbury Science Museum offers a great deal of information.

**Valle Grande:** After that, travel east and follow the signs to Valle Grande, the remains of a volcano that erupted 1.4 million years ago. Hot springs and recreational opportunities abound here.

**Cuba:** After Valle Grande, continue north to Highway 126. This road, all the way to Cuba, is not paved but is well traveled. However, a four-wheel-drive vehicle is recommended for better safety.

**Cabezon:** After a rest in Cuba, travel south along Interstate 550. A quick detour off of the byway heading west on 197 will take you to Cabezon, a ghost town that was a flourishing city until the 1940s. Back on Interstate 550, head south through the national forest and down toward the many American Indian pueblos. The Zia and Jemez pueblos have wonderful opportunities for learning and adventure. (Note that the Jemez Pueblo is not open to the public, except on festival days.)

**Spence Hot Springs:** The Jemez State Monument is a perfect getaway in the late afternoon and is highlighted by a dip in the Spence Hot Springs.

**Bandelier National Monument and Ghost Ranch:** Bandelier National Monument, near the Rio Grande, is a wonderful place to see the ruins of many cliff houses and pueblo-style dwellings of 13th-century Pueblo Indians. A little to the north of Los Alamos, in Abiquiu, a cluster of fantastic museums at Ghost Ranch is a trip not to be missed.

### Jemez Pueblo

Jemez Pueblo, about five miles from San Ysidro, is located at the gateway of the majestic Cañon de San Diego. There are more than 3,000 Native Americans here, most of whom reside in a single Puebloan village known as *walatowa*—the Towa word meaning "this is the place." Enjoy traditional Jemez foods and arts and crafts available at roadside stands in the beautiful Red Rocks area. Jemez Pueblo also offers recreation areas where you can picnic, fish, and enjoy the great outdoors.

# SANTA FE TRAIL 

*Ride the historic Santa Fe Trail in the footsteps of Western pioneers, Spanish missionaries, and American Indian traders. Start in Santa Fe, and enjoy prairie vistas, rugged landscapes, and the other Las Vegas along the way.*

PART OF A MULTISTATE BYWAY; SEE ALSO COLORADO.

The Santa Fe Trail was the first of America's great trans-Mississippi routes. The trail, including the Mountain and Cimarron routes, traversed more than 1,200 miles from Franklin, Missouri, to Santa Fe, New Mexico. From 1821 to 1880, it was an important two-way avenue for commerce and cultural exchange among Spanish, American Indian, and American cultures.

The area around the Santa Fe Trail boasts more than 20 historic districts and 30 individual sites that are recorded on the National Register of Historic Places.

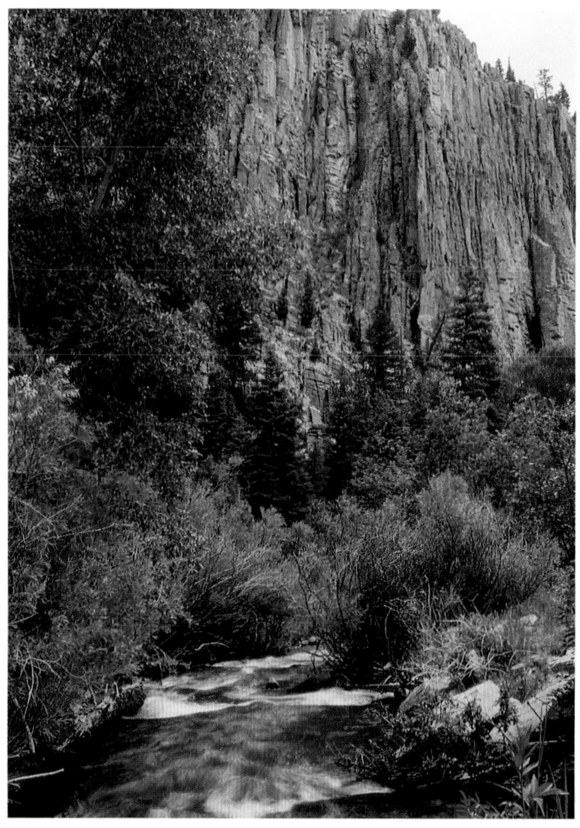

*In New Mexico's high country, Cimarron Canyon State Park features the Cimarron River and granite cliffs as dominant aspects of the landscape.*

## Intrinsic Qualities

**Archaeological:** The Santa Fe Trail offers many archaeological sites, including some with early excavations. From 1915 to 1927, Pecos was the subject of one of the first organized excavations of a Southwestern ruin. Pioneer American archaeologist Alfred V. Kidder analyzed the stratigraphy (the sequence in which the archaeological remains of the pueblo were deposited). He noted changes in the artifacts, especially the pottery, from the lower, older layers of occupation through the upper, younger layers. Kidder used the relative ages of the pottery remains to establish relative dates of occupation at Pecos. Based on that information, he and his colleagues devised the Pecos Classification, a sequence of eight prehistoric cultural periods that applied to sites throughout the Southwest.

In 1965, Congress and the president authorized the establishment of Pecos National Monument. In the summer of 1966, National Park Service archaeologists began excavation of the church and convent; their findings not only cast new light on the history of the Southwest but also substantiated reports of 17th-century writers whose words had been held suspect.

Both the church and the convent were puzzling. The 17th-century ecclesiastics had described the church as being large, splendid, magnificent, and of unusual design, but the remaining adobe walls are of a church that had none of those characteristics. However, it was discovered that the convent was much larger than a church of modest size.

In the summer of 1967, the project archaeologist discovered stone foundations resting on bedrock and fragments of burned adobe walls. Under and around the ruins of the known church, further excavations uncovered the foundations of an earlier church that was nearly 170 feet long, 90 feet wide at the transept, and 39 feet wide inside the nave. The building was typical of the fortress churches of Mexico. It had bastioned nave walls and subsidiary chapels in thick-walled, cruciformlike (cross-shaped) arms near the sanctuary. Only 18 such structures were known in the Americas until the Pecos find, and none was north of Mexico City.

It is now clear that the large church and convent were constructed in the 1620s and later destroyed during the Pueblo Revolt of 1680. The convent was then reconstructed, and a new church was built following the Reconquest, probably in the early 1700s.

The archaeological survey now in progress is designed to locate small sites showing evidence of activities on which the Pecos livelihood was based. Evidence of agriculture field systems, including check dams, farming terraces, and overnight houses, has been uncovered. Rock art and hunting camps have also been identified, including Apache tipi ring sites that verify historical reports of Apache

### Quick Facts

**Length:** 381 miles.

**Time to Allow:** Eight hours.

**Considerations:** The best time to drive this route is in the early spring through late fall.

ncampments for trade with the Pecos people. Some evidence uggests that the Pecos area may ave been at least a marginal site or human occupation for several housand years.

Excavations have uncovered two arge semi-subterranean houses n the grassy flats south and west f monument headquarters. These ithouses, the first to be reported rom the Upper Pecos River area, vere built in the 9th century. They vere probably part of a village hat may have been occupied on a easonal basis. The architecture is imilar to that of both the Anasazi eople of the Rio Grande Valley nd the Mogollon of southern New Mexico.

**Cultural:** The Santa Fe Trail was the first trail of commerce between the Southwest and the United States. From 1821 to 1880, the Santa Fe Trail was an important two-way avenue for commerce and cultural exchange among Spanish, Native American, and American cultures. You can see evidence of this abounding culture in many of the events and activities on the byway.

**Historical:** The Santa Fe Trail was the first international trade route, carrying needed materials from Missouri to northern Mexico and taking back silver, furs, mules, and wood to Missouri.

As early as the 1700s, Pueblo and Plains Indian trade fairs at Pecos and Taos introduced Spanish residents to native products. Yet trade between New Mexico and other settlements throughout the West was banned because New Mexico was a colony of Spain and could trade only with the mother country. Beginning in 1810 and succeeding in 1821, uprisings in Mexico gave New Mexico freedom to trade with anyone. November 16, 1821, is recognized as the start of legal international trade between New Mexico and the United States; this date also marks the beginning of the Santa Fe Trail.

The Santa Fe Trail passed through the territories and ranges of many Native American nations, including the Pawnee, Arapaho, Cheyenne, Comanche, and the Kiowa, so American Indian traders used it as a commercial route. After the Mexican War (1846–1848), the Jicarillas, Comanches, Kiowas, and other nations became increasingly threatened by the traffic on the trail. With the American promise to the people of New Mexico to subdue the various American Indian nations, an intermittent war began that ended in the mid-1870s. The American Indian nations of New Mexico were then confined to reservations.

After the Mexican War (and with New Mexico a U.S. Territory), the trail became mainly a military road. It supplied goods to the large contingent of troops in the Southwest, and mercantile goods were still carried into Mexico and New Mexico. After the Civil War, railroads began laying tracks to the West. By 1879, the first locomotive reached Las Vegas, New Mexico, and in 1880, the railroad reached Lamy, essentially ending wagon traffic across the 900 miles of plains.

**Natural:** The Santa Fe Trail offers an array of flora and fauna. Vegetation ranges from small pockets of tall grass prairies to the buffalo and blue grama grass found on the short grass plains east of the Sangre de Cristos Mountains. South and east of Las Vegas, the trail enters the piñon pine and juniper vegetation zones as the elevation increases in the mountains. Antelopes, coyotes, elks, and bears are prevalent in the area. Bird life is profuse, including small mountain bluebirds, hawks, bald eagles, and golden eagles. Many species of reptiles also inhabit the area, including the prairie rattlesnake and the western diamondback rattlesnake.

From its easternmost point at Old Franklin, Missouri, the trail traveled west to Cimarron, Kansas, where it split into two routes. The original trail, the Cimarron Route, headed southwest across Colorado, Oklahoma, and New Mexico.



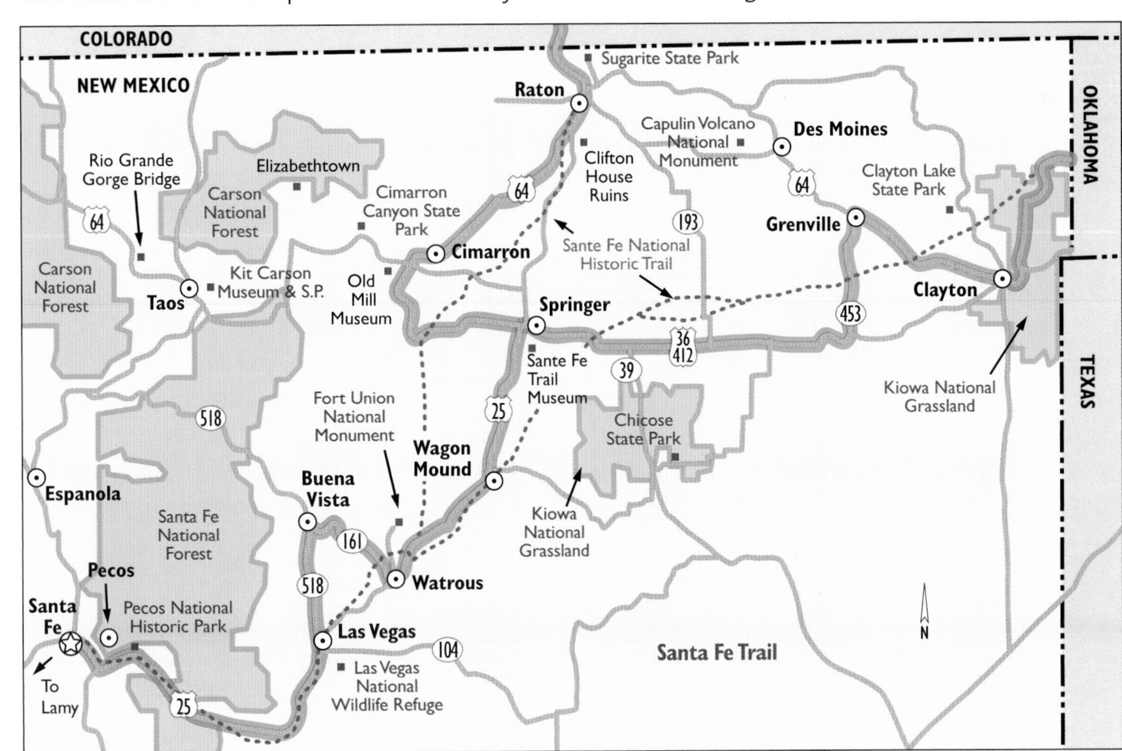

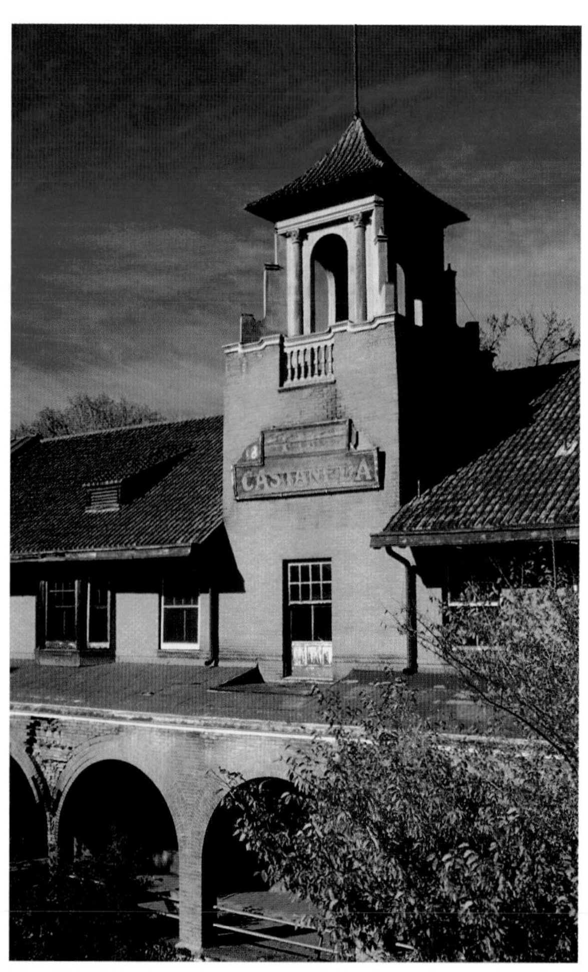


*The Hotel Castaneda was one of the finest luxury hotels of the Fred Harvey chain built along the Santa Fe Railway.*



The Mountain Route headed west into Colorado and then went south to New Mexico. The routes joined again at Watrous.

The Cimarron National Grassland near Elkhart, Kansas, contains 23 miles of the trail's Cimarron Route, the longest trail segment on public land. A 19-mile companion trail, a mowed swath across the prairie, parallels the actual trail route. Point of Rocks, a large outcropping of rock that rises above the prairie, was visible for long distances from both directions along the trail. Today, you can drive to the top to enjoy this view.

A short distance east of Point of Rocks is Middle Springs, a small oasis on the prairie where water rises from an ever-flowing artesian spring. It was the only reliable watering spot for 30 miles each way along the trail. This welcome resting spot along the trail now has a picnic area and walking trail for your enjoyment.

The winding ribbon of the Cimarron Route crosses the Kiowa National Grassland 15 miles north of Clayton, off Highway 406. Time, weather, and erosion have not erased the deep wagon ruts stretching across two miles of this grassland.

The Mountain Route coursed northwest after splitting from the main trail at Cimarron, Kansas. Along its length, it unraveled the Aubry Cutoff a few miles east of the Kansas/Colorado line and the Granada Fort Union Road just west of the state line.

As it continued its westward path, the Mountain Route curved to the north, tracing what is now Route 50. Here, the changing horizon from plains to mountains was a major milestone on the journey, surely causing great excitement among the travelers. The mountains may have also produced apprehension as travelers anticipated having to climb with heavily laden wagons.

**Recreational:** You'll find many recreational activities along the Santa Fe Trail, including fishing, camping, skiing, mountain biking, and hiking. Several state parks and recreational areas are located in northeastern New Mexico. As a matter of fact, outdoor recreation is one of the top four reasons people visit New Mexico.

**Scenic:** The Santa Fe Trail has some spectacular and rugged scenery. For example, amid the surrounding Fort Union Ranch at Fort Union National Monument, wagon ruts can be seen in the distance. Nearby, travelers visit Fort La Junta (built in 1851) and the 1863 fort and supply depot.

There are also many different plants found along the Santa Fe Trail. For example, the flowering plants along the trail are the result of volcanic activity from long ago. Also, six miles of the Santa Fe National Forest embrace the trail between the villages of Glorieta (atop the 7,432-foot-high Glorieta Pass) and Canoncito. Ponderosa pine, golden aspen, auburn scrub oak, piñon pine, and juniper are all found here.

## Highlights

This Santa Fe Trail tour begins in Santa Fe and heads east to Clayton. With a little backtracking, the trail goes north and enters Colorado over the Raton Pass.

**Pecos National Historic Park:** Your first stop will be at Pecos National Historic Park, where you'll want to spend some time learning about the ruins of a 14th-century American Indian pueblo and two 17th-century Franciscan missions.

**Las Vegas:** Your next stop should be in Las Vegas, New Mexico. It has a great wildlife refuge.

**Fort Union National Monument:** Going north, still on I-25, you'll pass Buena Vista and come into Fort Union National Monument. The remains of this star-shape fort are a fantastic sight.

**Springer and Clayton:** The Santa Fe Trail Museum should be your next stop as you approach the town of Springer and the major highway junction. Enjoy the Kiowa National Grassland as you drive east to the border and the town of Clayton. While here, don't forget to stop and enjoy Clayton Lake State Park, a great place to camp.

**Raton:** Next, leaving the byway for a few miles, take Highway 64 up to Raton for a fun experience at the Sugarite Canyon State Park. Then, back on the byway, hop on Highway 64 going south through Cimarron. This drive is fantastic and takes you through the Cimarron Canyon State Park. At this point, you may choose to head over to Taos or back to Santa Fe.

# Turquoise Trail 

*Leave the freeway behind to travel the backcountry Turquoise Trail into a four-season mountain wilderness. Then gaze down from the top of a crest to savor some of America's most stunning views.*

Back roads often lead to glorious scenery and great discovery, and so it is with the Turquoise Trail. When you leave the freeway and venture onto the scenic and historic Turquoise Trail, you get a chance to see 15,000 square miles of central New Mexico from a bird's-eye view atop Sandia Peak, the magnificent summit of the Sandia Mountains that rises 10,378 feet. From here, you can venture into Sandia Mountain Wilderness and hike through aspen glades and across flowering meadows, coming upon one spectacular view after another.

You can also visit the ghost mining towns of Golden, Madrid, and Cerrillos, towns now with great arts, crafts, theater, music, museums, and restaurants. In addition, the Museum of Archaeology and Material Culture in Cedar Crest exhibits a 12,000-year timeline that tells the story of North America's earliest inhabitants and goes chronologically through history until the Battle of Wounded Knee in 1890.

## Quick Facts

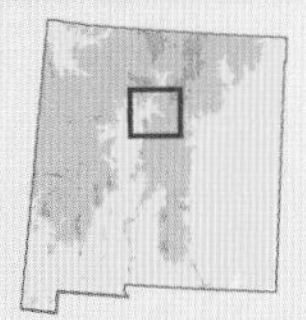

**Length:** 61 miles.

**Time to Allow:** Three hours.

**Considerations:** If you're venturing into the mountains, take a coat or jacket. Snow may cause a chain rule and/or four-wheel-drive requirements to be in effect between October and March.

## Intrinsic Qualities

**Archaeological:** Over thousands of years, many people have inhabited the area along the Turquoise Trail. Pottery shards, ancient mining quarries, and pueblos are just some of the evidence ancient inhabitants left behind. Prehistoric Native Americans relied on many features of the area for their economy, such as the rich deposits of turquoise and local lead, which were used for decoration and glazes in their pottery.

The Tijeras Pueblo, an archaeological site located near the ranger station of the Cibola National Forest, once housed several hundred people. These people lived in the area more than 600 years ago. The San Marcos Pueblo offers limited tours (by appointment) and serves as a research site that provides archaeological field experience for students at the University of New Mexico. Many adobe and masonry pueblo structures remain intact at the San Marcos site, and estimates are that the pueblo had between 3,000 and 5,000 rooms. During the 1300s and mid-1400s, the pueblo was also a center for pottery making.

One of the oldest dwellings in the area may be Sandia Cave.

*Hundreds of balloons paint a fanciful rainbow of colors in the sky over Albuquerque during the annual International Hot Air Balloon Festival.*

Evidence surrounding the cave's earliest occupants remains controversial, but excavations from the cave suggest that people lived in the cave during three different time periods. Pre-Colombian Pueblo-style artifacts; hearths and tools of nomadic hunters; and Folsom spear points used on bison, giant sloths, and horses have all been found in the cave.

The early pueblo inhabitants of the area surrounding what is known today as Cerrillos Hills Historic Park worked on many turquoise pits, quarries, lead (galena) mines, refining areas, workshops, hearths, and campsites. Most of the activity here occurred between 1375 and 1500, but grooved axes, mauls, picks, and American Indian pottery are all that is left. These mines were critically important to the people in the area because they supplied valuable turquoise that allowed decoration of pottery, jewelry, and other items.

**Cultural:** New Mexico's vibrant history has permeated modern society and left cultural treasures throughout the area. Retaining the flavor of the Southwest, local artisans have saved several of the region's ghost towns and transformed them into artistic communities. Along the byway, you will find shops and galleries filled with paintings, sculpture, pottery, leather goods, jewelry, furniture, beadwork, toys, art wear, and antiques. Some of the old company stores and houses have also been

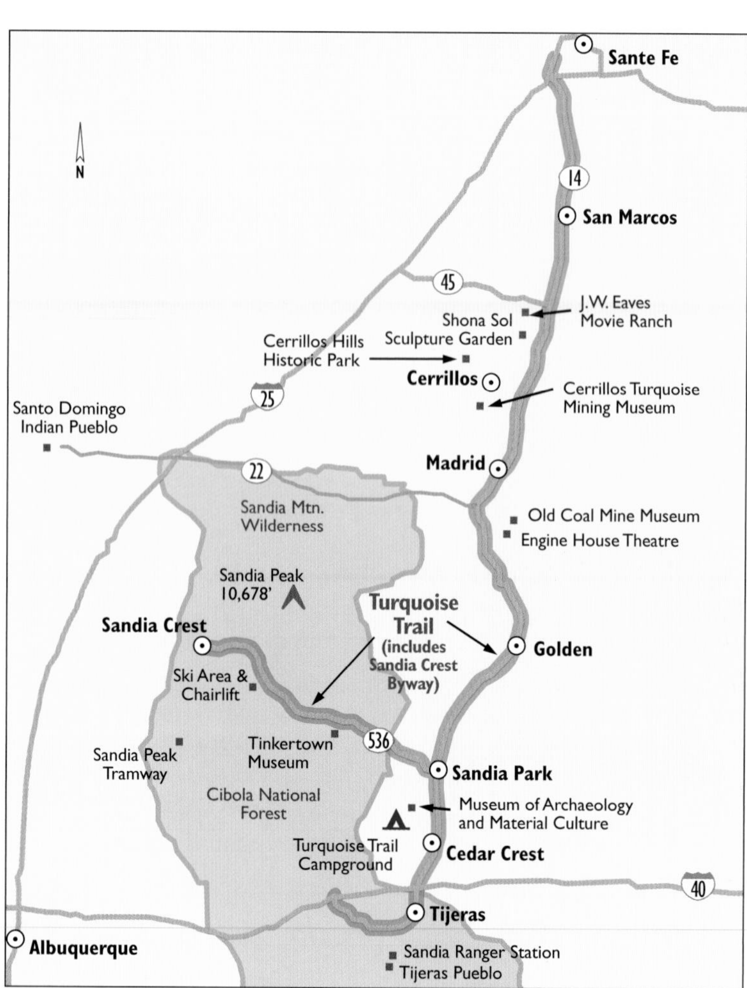




refurbished as restaurants and bed-and-breakfasts.

**Historical:** Native Americans were the first people to extract gold, silver, lead, zinc, and turquoise from the hills. Indeed, the turquoise found near the Turquoise Trail is considered by some to be the finest in the world. Usually sky blue to light-greenish blue, turquoise can also be white, dark blue, jade green, reddish brown, and even violet. In the early 1900s, Tiffany's of New York helped to popularize the shade known as robin's egg blue.

When the Native Americans began their mining efforts, the mineral deposits were in pure veins. Early digging implements included stone hammers, chisels, and files. After the minerals had been removed, the native miners would carry the ore and rock outside the mine in reed baskets or buckets made of hide. Spanish explorers estimated that native miners had removed 100,000 tons of rock, based on huge tailing piles and 400-year-old piñon trees growing from the piles.

Although some mining occurred during Spain's (and later Mexico's) ownership of the land, the majority of mining appears to have been done during the territorial expansion of the United States.

Golden began with humble beginnings during the 1825 gold rush, the first gold rush to occur west of the Mississippi. Here, two mining camps were created to mine placer gold (gold extracted from streams or rivers). In 1880, several mining companies moved into the area and renamed the two camps "Golden" to match their high hopes of profiting. However, these hopes faded by 1884, and the population of Golden steadily decreased.

Another popular New Mexico mining community, Cerrillos, hit its peak in the 1880s, due in part to the arrival of the railroad. The early 1880s quickly expanded the local mines, with more than 2,000 land claims filed on only a few square miles of land. Soon, Cerrillos swelled to accommodate 21 saloons and 4 hotels. Sadly, prosperity abandoned Cerrillos within the decade. Today, the Cerrillos Hills Historic Park and the immediately adjacent lands contain approximately 90 vertical or near-vertical shafts, with depths exceeding six feet.

Madrid was founded in the oldest coal-mining region of the state and gradually grew to become the center of the coal-mining industry for the region. Under the direction of the superintendent of mines, employees were to donate from 50 cents to $1 a month for community causes and were also required to participate in town events such as the Fourth of July celebrations and Christmas light displays. In fact, Madrid became famous for its Christmas light displays. However, the town's Christmas celebrations ended in 1941 with the start of World War II. Eventually, people began choosing natural gas over coal, and the mines near Madrid closed in the early 1950s. The mines were the town's economic backbone, and once they closed, the town was abandoned.

**Natural:** Proud of its natural legacy, New Mexico has preserved many vibrant natural wonders that can be easily accessed along the Turquoise Trail. In the byway's short length of 61 miles, you're whisked through forests and mountains that are home to a dazzling array of wildlife. Depending on the terrain, you can observe desert wildlife or woodland creatures. Many of these animals make their homes among the juniper, pine, and spruce-fir forests.

But the natural treasures on the Turquoise Trail began forming millions of years before roads were constructed anywhere in the area. Between 24 and 34 million years ago, the Cerrillos and Ortiz Mountains along the Turquoise Trail were dikes, or branches, of magma that solidified thousands of feet underground. By the time early Native Americans began to settle these areas, these dikes were exposed and began to crack. This erosion process soon made the area famous for its rich supply of minerals, including gold, silver, lead, zinc, coal, and a wide assortment of turquoise. Today, fossil hunters sift through the outcroppings of shale, hoping to find one of the many fossils of prehistoric life hidden there.

Part of the byway travels into the Cibola National Forest. Here, the climate varies with elevation, which ranges from 5,000 to more than 11,300 feet. Snow can be found in the timberline until June, and some of the higher elevations become very cold at night.

The high points of a visit to the Turquoise Trail, however, are Sandia Peak and the Sandia Mountain Wilderness, which offer a view of the sublime. Long considered sacred by some Native Americans, they provide a welcomed respite.

**Recreational:** The Turquoise Trail has numerous opportunities to enjoy recreation.

Built in 1966, the Sandia Peak Tramway is the longest continuous jigback tram in the world, which means it has one car going up while another is coming down, and it has the third-longest clear span in the world. It is the only place in the United States where visitors traveling on an artificial transportation system are virtually surrounded by a nationally designated wilderness area.

The pristine Sandia Mountain Wilderness is a natural, scenic, and recreational wonderland located adjacent to metropolitan Albuquerque. More than 100 miles of recreational trails in the wilder-ness area offer a wide variety of terrain.

**Scenic:** The Turquoise Trail offers many miles of unspoiled natural beauty. Mesas, deserts, and grasslands are packed with wildlife and provide a home for horses, cattle, and even an occasional llama or ostrich.

A unique quality of this byway is the weather. The arid desert climate makes the scenic drive possible in all four seasons. During the summer months on the byway, you see fast-moving clouds and hundreds of lightning bolts electrifying the sky. In contrast to these wild storms, you may be inspired by the multicolored sunsets in a calm evening sky.

*Sandia Crest, the summit of the Sandia Mountains, gives a bird's-eye view of the magnificent landscape below.*

Some of the most enjoyable scenery found along the byway was created by humans. You can view tailings from historic coal mines, representing the only location in the nation where both anthracite and bituminous coal were found.

## Highlights

The best way to experience the nature of the Turquoise Trail is to stop at the small towns along the byway and speak with the folks who live there. Here's a sampling of places you may want to stop.

**Tijeras Pueblo:** Between 1948 and 1976, excavations in this area helped scientists learn about the Tijeras Pueblo, a large nation believed to have been in existence between 1300 and 1600. Many remains are on display at the Maxwell Museum of Anthropology at the University of New Mexico in Albuquerque. The pueblo itself includes 200 rooms, a dozen small buildings, and a kiva. After excavation was done, the area was covered again with soil to preserve it.

**Sandia Ranger Station:** The first stop along the trail is at the Sandia Ranger Station on NM 337. This is a nice way to learn the early history of the area. Inquire about road conditions here, as well as about special activities that may be planned.

**Sandia Peak Tramway:** Continue north on 14 out of Tijeras, and turn left on Highway 536 heading toward Sandia Peak. While at Sandia Peak, be sure to stop at the Museum of Archaeology and Material Culture and the Tinkertown Museum. Continue on to the Sandia Peak Tramway. After the tram, continue to the highpoint of the road and take a quick tour of the Sandia Cave—with your flashlight!

**Madrid:** Head back down Highway 536, turn left, and continue north on Highway 14. Drive toward Madrid. Expect to spend some time here enjoying the Old Coal Mine Museum and the Engine House Theatre. This town, after being deserted due to a mine shutdown, was listed for sale in the *Wall Street Journal* in 1954 for $250,000. No one bought it, but the town has been revived since the 1970s by artisans.

**Cerrillos:** Just north of Madrid and before Cerrillos, be on the lookout for a unique art display. Animal bones and glass are the tools of artist Tammy Jean Lange. A few miles up the road is Cerrillos. Thomas Edison is reported to have stayed here briefly while conducting studies with the area's minerals. The Cerrillos Turquoise Mining Museum is a special feature of the town. Don't leave Cerrillos without a stop at the What Not Shop.

**Shona Sol Sculpture Garden and J. W. Eaves Movie Ranch:** Five miles past Cerrillos, look for the Shona Sol Sculpture Garden, a gallery of African sculpture. Finally, make a stop at the J. W. Eaves Movie Ranch, home to many famous movies, including *Silverado*.

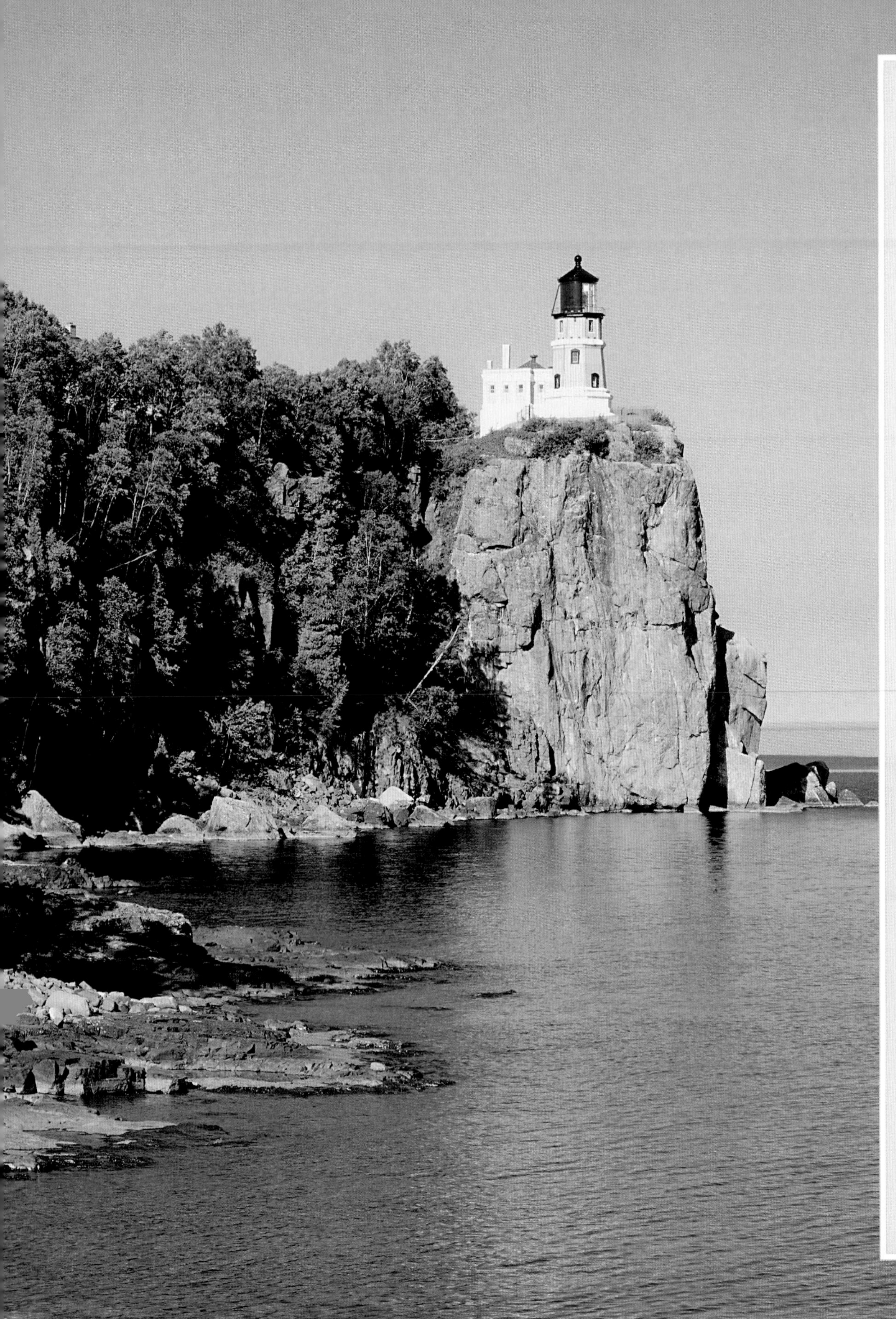

# MIDWEST

One-of-a-kind geologic formations, centuries-old historic monuments, and more await travelers along the byways of the Midwest. Follow the Edge of the Wilderness to not only find rustic charm, but to also discover the breathtaking beauty of the Minnesota North Woods. Experience a different kind of seclusion while traveling through the mountainous Peter Norbeck Scenic Byway in South Dakota. Eclectic urban beauty welcomes visitors on byways such as Woodward Avenue in Detroit. Several states in the Midwest tell the tale of a road of a different kind, The Great River Road, roaming side-by-side with the waters of the mighty Mississippi River. The Native American voice is heard throughout Midwestern byways, most notably along South Dakota's Native American Scenic Byway, which actually traverses Sioux lands.

*North Shore Scenic Byway's Split Rock Lighthouse has been restored to its 1920s appearance.*

# SHEYENNE RIVER VALLEY SCENIC BYWAY

*The relatively new history of the rugged homesteaders and the ancient history of the Native Americans who first inhabited this area give this byway unique cultural diversity mixed with pastoral scenic attractions.*

The Sheyenne River Valley Scenic Byway is distinguished by its small-town ospitality and a mixture of scenic ills and grassy flatlands. Pastoral cenery catches travelers' atten-on, featuring wildflowers, wild rasses, quaint farms, grassy hills, nd wildlife. Old prairie churches, ne-room schoolhouses, quaint rms, and historic towns allow ne traveler to experience a little of ne old frontier.

## ntrinsic Qualities

**rchaeological:** Archaeological tudies show that the Sheyenne iver Valley may have been inter-nittently occupied for more than ,000 years.

*anoramic pastoral scenery abounds in the Sheyenne River Valley. The outstand-ng views are endless here.*

Located in Valley City, Medicine Wheel Park includes a reproduction of a medicine wheel (a stone solar calendar) and an extensive Native American burial mound complex dating around 15,000 years ago. The Standing Rock, which is known as *Inyun Bosndata* by the Sioux Indians, who consider it sacred, is also found at the park. The four-foot-tall Standing Rock is an inverted cone shape that sits on a complex of prehistoric burial mounds.

Hosting the Viking sculpture at Fort Ransom, Pyramid Hill measures 650 feet long, 520 feet wide, approximately 100 feet high, and is level on top, with the north, west, and south sides of uniform shape. Although geologists consider this to be a natural geologic formation, some think that humans made about one-third of the mound, which was built an estimated 5,000 to 9,000 years ago by an ancient civilization. Native American tradition holds this site to be a place of emergence.

**Cultural:** The cultural heritage of the Sheyenne River Valley Scenic Byway has been strongly influenced by a mixture of customs and traditions passed on from the region's first settlers. The unaltered natural settings and rustic outdoor facilities of the region's most remote areas are a short distance from modern and sophisticated art centers, museums, restaurants, and hotels.

The cultural patchwork found in the Sheyenne River Valley Scenic Byway corridor is a result of this surprising diversity and contrast, as well as the number of cultural attractions and events. Among these cultural attractions are pioneer cemeteries, historic churches, antique shops, guest inns, museums, monuments, and community concerts and theaters. Cultural events include farmers' markets, horse shows and rodeos, county fairs, community days, antique and art shows, vintage tractor and car shows, and ethnic festivals.

## Quick Facts

**Length:** 63 miles.

**Time to Allow:** Nine hours.

**Considerations:** Part of the road from Kathryn to Lisbon is a gravel surface (about 15 miles). The byway contains a total of about 26 miles of gravel roads. During the growing season, you may encounter minor changes in travel speeds when meeting or passing agricultural equipment. Spring sometimes brings closures due to flooding and excessive rainfall.

**Historical:** About 15,000 years ago Native Americans began to filter from the north and west into the area east of the Rocky Mountains, foraging for food. The region's earliest inhabitants were members of these prehistoric cultures. The first written records of the region surrounding the Sheyenne River Valley came from the explorers Joseph Nicolas Nicollet and John C. Frémont, who noted the landmark Standing Rock on their maps during their exploration of 1839. They also recorded their experiences with the local Native Americans while camping in the area now known as Clausen Springs. The next written account from the area does not take place until James L. Fisk passed through, leading an emigrant train to the gold fields of Montana in 1862 and 1863. In 1867, the Fort Ransom military post was established on the Fort Abercrombie to Fort Totten Trail, to protect wagon trains on their way to the gold fields of Montana and to guard pioneer settlers and railroad workers passing through the area. Today, the Fort Ransom Historic Site recalls the importance of the original outpost.

With the advance of the Northern Pacific Railroad in 1872 came the first permanent European settlers to the area. The Great Dakota Boom, beginning in 1878, marked the influx of a stream of mostly Norwegian immigrants.

Dramatic changes to the Sheyenne River Valley landscape resulted from the agricultural activities, urban development, and construction of transportation routes that accompanied the region's settlement. Sections of the river were dammed for mills, water supply regulation, pollution abatement during low-flow periods, and recreational purposes; and dikes were constructed to reduce flooding in river valleys. But through it all, the Sheyenne River Valley, its many historical structures, and its citizens have continued to share the valley's rich history and to provide visitors with memorable experiences.

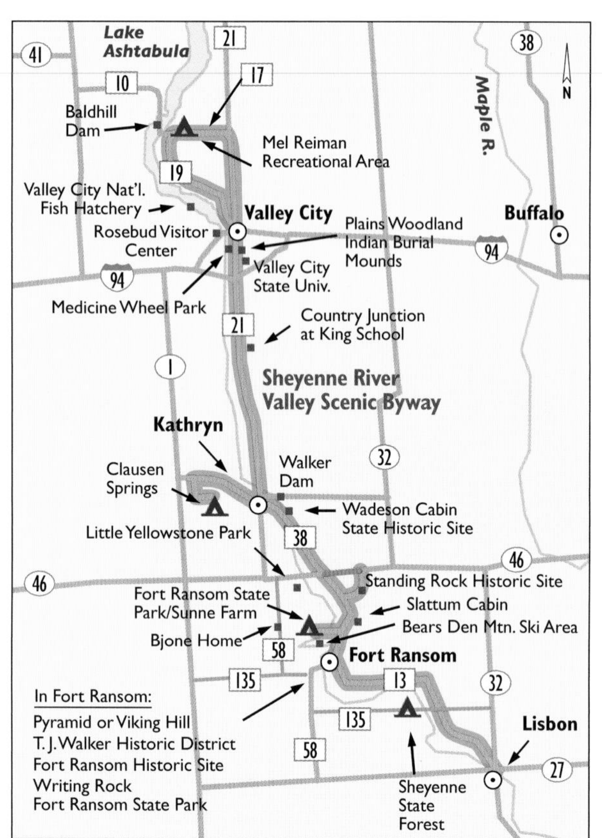


**Natural:** Much of the Sheyenne River Valley's uniqueness can be attributed to the oak savannah riparian forest, a zone whose wide variety of vegetation supports the existing wildlife diversity. This rolling sand-dune landscape of oak savannah along the Sheyenne River is perhaps the most remarkable scenic quality of the area. Other unique areas include Clausen Springs Recreational Area, Little Yellowstone Park, Mooringstone Pond at the Writing Rock site, and Sheyenne State Forest. For the angler, the Sheyenne River offers an abundance of game fish, from catfish to walleye. The river contains about 50 different fish species.

Although forests and the river are the defining features along the byway, the traveler longing to see undisturbed prairie lands will not be disappointed. A fine sample can be found within the boundaries of Fort Ransom State Park, a 900-acre site with a 1½-mile segment of certified North Country Scenic Trail. If that's not enough, the Sheyenne National Grassland area is only about ten miles east of the byway and represents some of the most pristine, untouched grasslands in the nation.

**Recreational:** Activities include hiking, biking, and horseback riding all along the byway in spring, summer, and fall. The area's river and lake provide great opportunities for canoeing, boating, and kayaking. In the winter, cross-country and downhill skiing, snowshoeing, and snow-mobiling are popular. Fishing is a year-round pastime that can be enjoyed all along the corridor, as is bird-watching. The byway is also a great location for hunting, whether it be for waterfowl, upland bird, deer, moose, or fur-bearing species.

Standing out on the basically lakeless landscapes of the North Dakota plains, Lake Ashtabula in the Sheyenne River Valley has several resort areas located along its 27-mile length, providing a plethora of recreational opportunities. There are resorts, camping areas, swimming areas,restaurants fish-cleaning stations, boat-rental locations, and cabin rentals.

Fort Ransom State Park provides a wealth of outdoor activities, including educational programs, camping, fishing, picnicking, horseback riding, canoeing, cross-country skiing, hiking, birding, and nature photography. Amenities include an outdoor amphitheater, canoe landing, campsites, nature trails, playground, picnic shelters, visitor center, and horse corrals. There is also a farm that demonstrates pioneer farming methods. It's called the Sunne Farm and is home to the Fort Ransom Sodbusters Association.

A ski resort, Bears Den Mountain, is not something you would expect to see on the flat plains of North Dakota, but you can find it at Fort Ransom. This site offers a chairlift and T-bar, two beginner rope tows, snowmaking, grooming, a cafeteria, and rental equipment. The 285-mile Sheyenne Valley Snowmobile Trail system has a wide variety of riding areas, such as flat ditches, shelterbelts, national grasslands, and the Sheyenne River bottom.

**Scenic:** Viewing the fall colors of native prairie and hardwood forests in the Sheyenne River Valley is one of the most popular attractions for travelers. Seasonal changes provide for a pleasant drive at any time of the year. This beautifully forested river valley with its associated panoramic views; tumbling, spring-fed creeks;

The picturesque Fort Ransom Valley is located in Fort Ransom State Park.

and resident wildlife make this a truly scenic byway. The river is lined with riparian forests of basswood, American elm, green ash, and bur oak, which are home to several rare species of plants and animals.

In addition to remarkable natural features, human activities are important components of the scenery of the Sheyenne River Valley. Picturesque farmsteads nestle in the valley, while historic churches, one-room schoolhouses, and pioneer cemeteries dot the countryside. The Highline Bridge is 3,860 feet long and hangs 162 feet above the riverbed. It is one of the highest and longest single-track railroad bridges in the nation—not something you would expect to see on the plains of North Dakota.

## Highlights

One of the fascinating things about the Sheyenne River Valley Scenic Byway is the array of attractions that offer a glimpse into how various groups have interacted with the land over the years. The following itinerary suggests some highlights of those attractions.

**Baldhill Dam and Lake Ashtabula:** Operated by the U.S. Army Corps of Engineers, Lake Ashtabula includes eight recreational areas with ample year-round opportunities. Stop by the Corps of Engineers office on the west side of the dam for maps and information.

**Valley City National Fish Hatchery:** Ashtabula means "fish river" in the local Native American dialect. In keeping with that, eggs are harvested from the lake for use in the fish hatchery operated by the U.S. Fish and Wildlife Service, with a subunit just south of the dam and the main hatchery a bit farther south at Valley City. The Valley City National Fish Hatchery is a popular area for hiking, fishing, and picnicking. The goose pond is a fishing pond for kids and an exclusive area attraction.

**Historic Bridges Tour:** As you continue your journey south along the byway, Valley City is your next stop. One of the interesting highlights of the city is the Historic Bridges Tour, featuring eight bridges with a variety of architectural styles, history, and interpretive signage.

**Rosebud Visitor Center:** For maps, information, and a bit of railroad history, stop at the Rosebud Visitor Center, located on the I-94 business loop between exits 290 and 294. The building houses an 1881 railcar that is one of only eight of its type that were built. The railcar, known as "Rosebud," is the only one known to have its artifacts still intact. The Rosebud Visitor Center provides information about the entire Sheyenne River Valley.

**Medicine Wheel Park:** Another point of interest in Valley City and certainly not to be missed is the distinctive Medicine Wheel Park. The wheel, 68 feet in diameter with 28 spokes radiating from the middle, is on the campus of Valley City State University and is intended to pay homage to the spirit and purpose of the original Indian medicine wheels used for centuries by Native Americans of the Great Plains.

**Plains Woodland Indian Burial Mounds:** Just to the east of the Medicine Wheel are the Plains Woodland Indian Burial Mounds. These Sheyenne River mounds were used for centuries but were first charted in 1883.

**Fort Ransom State Park:** Continuing south 34 miles along the path traveled for centuries, first by Native Americans and then by fur traders and pioneers, your next stop will be Fort Ransom State Park. Though the fort itself was abandoned in 1872, Fort Ransom State Park offers ample recreational opportunities for history lovers, as well as for outdoor sports enthusiasts of all kinds.

**Bjone Home and Sunne Farm:** Fort Ransom State Park features two historic homesteads that reflect the life and times of the Norwegian homesteaders who settled this area. The Bjone Home is used as the visitor center and houses exhibits highlighting local tradition and Norwegian legends. The Sunne Farm is a living-history farm used each year during the second full weekend in July and the weekend after Labor Day, for Sodbuster Days, to demonstrate homesteading and ethnic heritage.

**Fort Ransom:** Fort Ransom is specifically known for having some of the best bird-watching in the state. Canoeing on the Sheyenne River is popular, and canoe and kayak rentals are available at the park. Also offered are hiking and snowmobile trails and horse trails and corrals, as well as some excellent fishing.

# Edge of the Wilderness 

*Rustic seclusion, breathtaking views, and a multitude of natural recreational opportunities greet travelers on the Edge of the Wilderness.*

Celebrate northern hospitality, hometown pride, and the treasures of our natural heritage. Minnesota, midway between America's east and west coasts, is home to 12,000 lakes. It is filled with beautiful country and all the pleasures of the four seasons. The Edge of the Wilderness is the rustic slice of this great state, with more than 1,000 lakes and one mighty river, the Mississippi, all in landscapes of remarkable natural beauty.

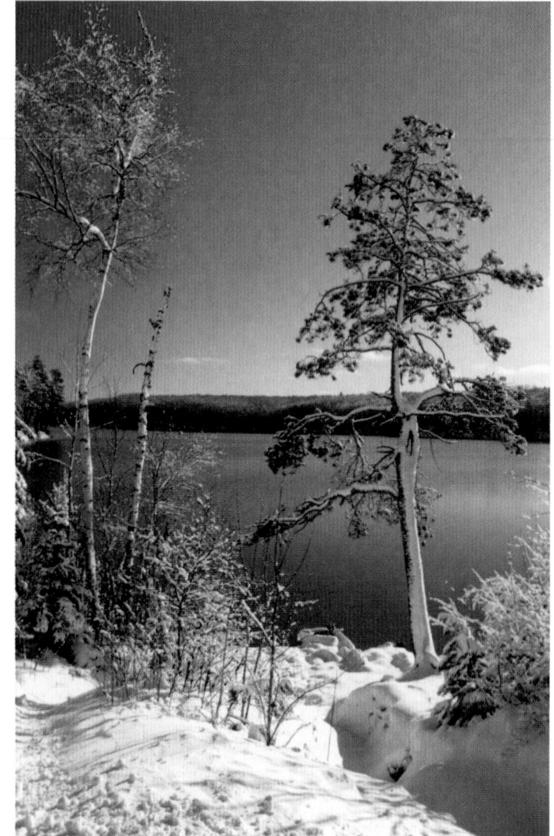

*The winter months frost the trees that stand vigil on the banks of North Star Lake.*

There are still more trees than people here, offering classic North Woods seclusion.

The Edge of the Wilderness begins in Grand Rapids with meadows and lakes, then winds through mixed hardwoods and stands of conifers and aspens in the Chippewa National Forest. Rounding bends and cresting hills, you will find breathtaking views that, during the fall, are ablaze with the brilliant red of sugar maples, the glowing gold of aspen and birch, and the deep bronze of oak.

The Edge of the Wilderness route offers some of Minnesota's most popular sporting and resorting opportunities in its unique environment of clear lakes, vast shorelines, and hills blanketed in hardwood forests and northern pines. Recreation seekers will find hiking, camping, fishing, cross-country skiing, and snowmobiling within the byway corridor. You will find that you are really living on the "edge."

## Intrinsic Qualities

**Historical:** At the height of the Great Depression, President Franklin D. Roosevelt formed the Civilian Conservation Corps (CCC) to provide jobs and restore the environment. CCC camp crews often were called the Tree Army. They were responsible for planting more than two billion trees across the United States in nine years. Other tasks included road construction; site preparation; surveys of lakes, wildlife, and streams; and even rodent control.

The Day Lake CCC Camp was one of 20 camps established in Minnesota during the Great Depression. Day Lake was the only camp in the forest to host African-Americans in the segregated CCC program, and was one of only six that lasted past the CCC era; it became one of four camps in the Chippewa National Forest that housed German prisoners of war during World War II (1943–1945).

Today, on the west side of Highway 38 are the remains of a concrete shower. East of the highway and up the hill are the outside stone stairway and a chimney that are remnants of the camp mess hall. Many old camp foundations and sites are also visible. After its closing, much of the Day Lake CCC Camp was replanted with red pine, hiding many of the signs of its history.

### Quick Facts

**Length:** 47 miles.

**Time to Allow:** Three hours.

**Considerations:** The best time to drive this route is during the fall foliage season (end of September, beginning of October). High season includes July and August. Highway 38 courses up and down and curves often—that's part of its charm. Locals named it Highway Loop-de-Loop in the early days. As you drive the byway, be aware of the lower speed limits, other traffic on the highway, and weather conditions. This is a working roadway, with trucks carrying logs and other local products.

**Natural:** Aspen, birch, pines, balsam fir, and maples blanket the rolling uplands of the forest along the Edge of the Wilderness. In between these trees, water is abundant, with more than 1,000 lakes, 920 miles of rivers and streams, and 150,000 acres of wetlands. The forest landscape is a reminder of the glaciers that covered northern Minnesota some 10,000 years ago. From the silent flutter of butterflies to the noisy squeal of wood ducks, and from the graceful turn of deer to the busy work of raccoons and beavers, this place of peace is bustling with activity. Many travelers try to dentify the laugh of the loon, the onk of the goose, and the chorus of sparrows, red-winged blackbirds, goldfinches, and crickets.

Look skyward to glimpse an eagle, turkey vulture, or osprey. There are more bald eagles on the Edge of the Wilderness than any other part of the lower 48 states. An eagle nest may measure up to ten feet in diameter and weigh 1,000 pounds.

Minnesota has the greatest number of timber wolves in the lower 48 states, as well. (They are considered a threatened but not an endangered species in Minnesota.) Less often seen but still present in the area are coyotes, bears, and moose. White-tail deer, ruffed grouse, and waterfowl offer good hunting and wildlife viewing opportunities, too.

During the autumn and spring, woody white stands of birch lace the forest floor along the byway. If you are a longtime resident or resort vacationer, you may no longer notice this phenomenon. But to newcomers, the question arises, "What happened to make all these trees fall to the ground?"

Paper birch trees, which live only 40 to 80 years, are found throughout Minnesota's northern woodlands. As late as the 1900s, Chippewa nations in the north built birch bark canoes. They also used birch to create torches. Early settlers prepared birch for railroad ties for the trains that edged northward. In today's economy, birch is used as lumber and firewood and for veneers. Birch also contributes nutrients to the forest floor and has served as food for various insects. Stands of birch often begin to grow after a fire, windstorm, or timber harvest. Another reason so many birch trees lay on the ground is that birch loses out to the taller-growing aspen as both sun-loving species compete. Along the Highway 38 corridor, you can see how birch trees topple due to competition from other trees, disease, and insects, as well as from northern Minnesota's light soils.

**Recreational:** Following World War II, northern Minnesota's tourist and resort industry grew rapidly. Itasca County had a peak of about 300 resorts in the 1940s and 1950s. Today, there are approximately 100 resorts and vacation sites in the area, many vacationers returning year after year. North Star Lake—at more than three miles long and about a half-mile wide—is considered one of the best fishing and recreational lakes in the area. It is representative of many of the lakes on the Edge of the Wilderness, with its scenic beauty, islands and bays, clear waters, and recreational offerings. The still-visible remnants of the railroad trestle provide a good habitat for the lake's many fish. The lake is 90 feet deep and is managed for muskie. Visitors also catch walleye (the state fish of Minnesota), northern pike, largemouth bass, smallmouth bass, bluegills, and crappies.

With a wingspan of more than six feet, keen vision, and white head and tail feathers, the bald eagle is truly a magnificent bird. People often make a special trip to

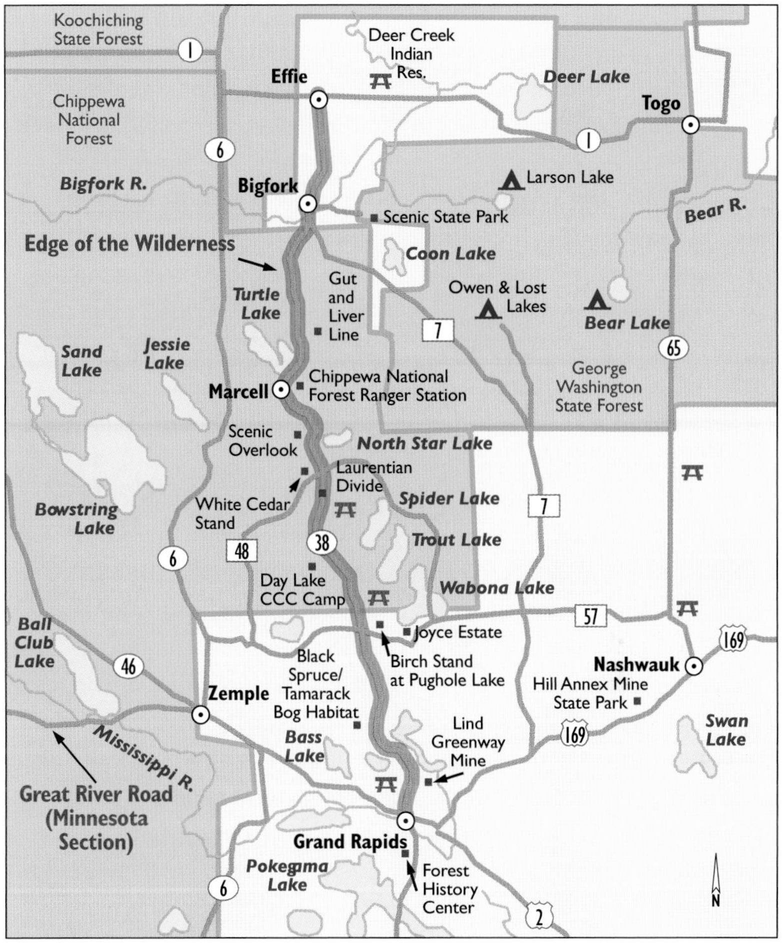


the Chippewa National Forest just to observe bald eagles. Spending time along the shorelines of the forest's larger lakes is the best way to treat yourself to the sight of an eagle in flight. Large, fertile lakes; towering red and white pines; and remote areas provide ideal nesting and feeding habitat for bald eagles. Nesting birds return in late February and early March, though a few birds spend the entire winter in the forest. Eggs are laid in early April, and the young eagles leave their lofty nests in mid-July. Eagles occupy their breeding areas until the lakes freeze over.

The best opportunity for viewing bald eagles is from a boat; in fact, one of the best opportunities to see eagles is to canoe down the Mississippi River. You can search the lakeshore with binoculars to spot eagles that are eating fish on the beaches. These birds of prey often perch in trees found around the larger lakes, such as Bowstring. The Bigfork River is also a favorite eagle area. However, if you do not have a boat, you can simply find an area along the beach with a good panoramic view of the lake. Campgrounds, picnic areas, and boat landings are good places to visit.

**Scenic:** What makes the Edge of the Wilderness unique is its rich and wide variety of upper Minnesota terrain, vegetation, wildlife, and history. While some elements are fairly common in other areas, no other route exposes travelers to so much variety in such a short distance along such a beautiful and accessible corridor. The Edge of the Wilderness is definitely a road to take slowly in order to enjoy the scenery of forests and meadows.

On the outskirts of Grand Rapids, the corridor begins to hint at the landscape to come. At first, the route is flat and flanked by mixed lowland meadows, swamps, and lakes. Very quickly, however, the corridor leaves most signs of the city and begins its rolling journey through mixed hardwoods and stands of conifers with aspen. With so many curves and hills, the corridor hides from view many memorable scenes until the traveler is upon them. Seemingly mundane turns in the road yield eye-popping surprises. The terrain continues in this way for half its length until the town of Marcell, where the terrain flattens slightly and offers more conifers. Between Bigfork and Effie, the corridor's terminus, the landscape introduces lowland wetlands, a flatter landscape that served as the bed of glacial Lake Agassiz thousands of years ago. Surrounding forests continue to contain aspen and lowland conifers such as jack pine and spruce.

A visitor to the Edge of the Wilderness could simply travel the route without stopping to take advantage of its recreational and interpretive opportunities, yet still leave with many vivid memories of the corridor. The byway hugs the terrain, rising above lakes and then sloping down to meet their shores before rising up again through the trees and down into wetlands. Throughout the southern half of the route, maples, paper birch, and quaking aspen branches provide a canopy that envelops travelers in the lush forest. During the fall color season, the corridor displays bright red sugar maples, warm gold birch and aspens, and maroon red oaks. After the leaves have fallen and the ground is covered with snow, the forest opens up and offers new opportunities to see the terrain and spy on wildlife.



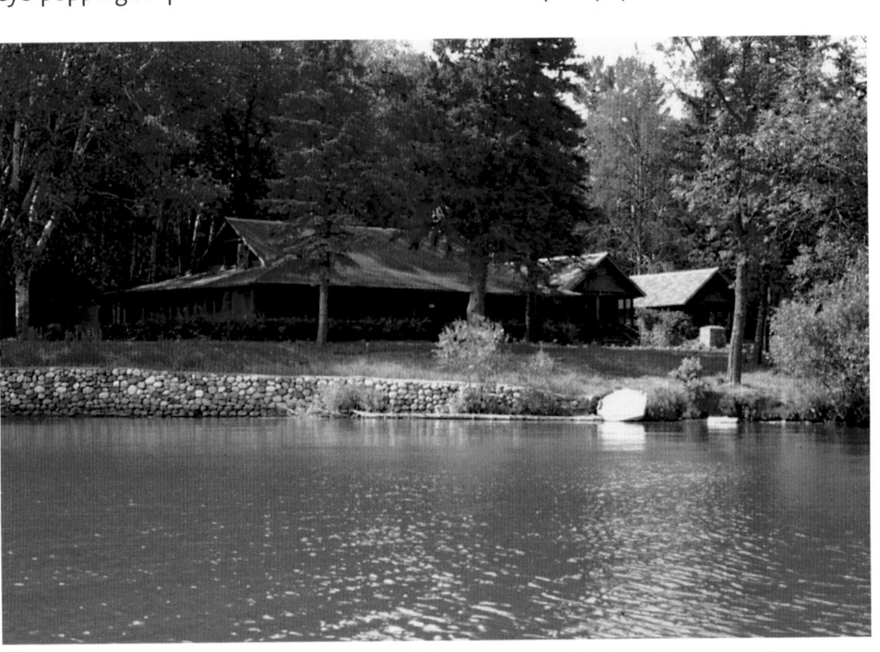

*Visitors can tour the grounds of Trout Lake's historic Joyce Estate and examine the rustic log architecture of the hunting resort's buildings.*

## Highlights

The Edge of the Wilderness officially begins in Grand Rapids, Minnesota. The byway proceeds north with sites of interest marked consecutively as follows.

**Grand Rapids:** Grand Rapids is in a historic logging and papermaking region. It is named for its strong rapids on the Mississippi River. Other waterways, including lakes, and forests help make Grand Rapids recreational opportunities great.

**Lind Greenway Mine:** The Lind Greenway Mine is a historic iron mine. Here you can find a mountain-size tailing of rock, soil, and iron ore fragments, reaching some 200 feet in the air.

**Black Spruce/Tamarack Bog Habitat:** Black Spruce/Tamarack Bog Habitat is one of the largest and most mature bogs in the area. It began forming here some 16,000 years ago when the last of four glaciers covered this part of Minnesota.

**Trout Lake and Joyce Estate:** The Trout Lake area offers 11 lakes for outdoor enthusiasts. While fishing, visitors are likely to see loons, herons, and beavers. Joyce Estate is an impressive 1920s estate in the Trout Lake area.

**Day Lake CCC Camp:** Day Lake CCC Camp has a long and varied history of use as both a Depression-era work camp and a German POW camp during World War II.

**Laurentian Divide:** On the north side of this site, the divide directs the waters to empty into Hudson Bay and on to the Arctic Ocean. On the south, water flows into the Mississippi River and eventually into the Gulf of Mexico.

**Scenic Overlook at North Star Lake:** Years ago, loggers cut down trees around this potato-shape lake during winter then floated them downstream when the temperature rose.

**Chippewa National Forest Ranger Station:** The Chippewa National Forest encompasses 1.6 million acres of forest and lakes, providing ample opportunities for the outdoor adventurer.

**Gut and Liver Line:** Make a stop here to view the remnants of old lumbering operations. Locals share legends and tales about this line on the Minneapolis and Rainy River Railroad.

# Grand Rounds Scenic Byway

*Home to such diverse sites as St. Anthony Falls, the only natural falls along the Mississippi River, and an artistic rendering of a giant spoon capturing an enormous cherry, the Grand Rounds Scenic Byway is a unique urban journey.*

Offering a unique byway experience, the Grand Rounds Scenic Byway is a ontinuous course of paved pathays. It encompasses more than miles of parks, parkways, bike aths, and pedestrian paths that ncircle the byway's host city, inneapolis. The scenic system ncludes the Chain of Lakes, Lake okomis, Lake Hiawatha, and the Iississippi River, as well as Minehaha Creek.

Parks, recreation centers, historic istricts, and lakes are all defing characteristics of the Grand ounds Scenic Byway. Depending n the season, you interact with a ndscape encompassing combinaons of natural areas, historical eatures, and cultural amenities.

**Quick Facts**

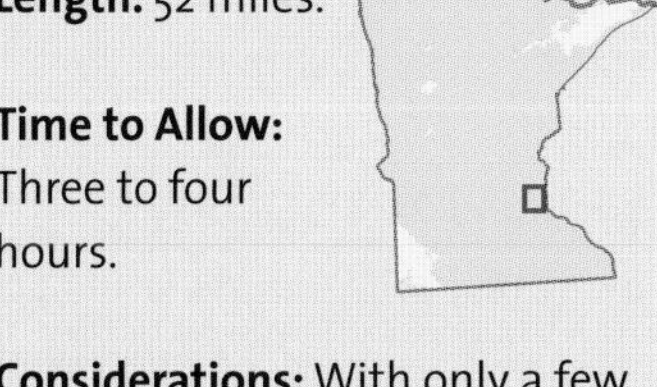

**Length:** 52 miles.

**Time to Allow:** Three to four hours.

**Considerations:** With only a few exceptions, the route is generally above local flood plains. During the winter, in addition to the roadway surfaces, a single paved trail is plowed throughout the system for shared use by pedestrians and cyclists. Truck traffic is prohibited from using all but several short segments of the byway.

The Grand Rounds Scenic Byway has been the crème de la crème of urban byways for more than a century, being the longest continuous system of public urban parkways and providing motorists with access to an unprecedented combination of intrinsic qualities of the highest caliber.

*The new bandshell on Lake Harriet has architectural features that harken to the area's historic past.*

## Intrinsic Qualities

**Archaeological:** Recent archaeological digs in the old milling district of Minneapolis have revealed artifacts from the time when Minneapolis was a milling capital. Visitors can explore the way life used to be in Minneapolis at the newly constructed Mill Ruins Park. This park is a restoration of original walls, canals, and buildings of the West Side Milling District. Another of the archaeological features along the Grand Rounds Scenic Byway is the Winchell Trail. Located on the Mississippi River, this trail preserves an original Native American trail that linked two celebration sites.

**Cultural:** An urbanized culture originating in the early 1800s is what visitors to the Grand Rounds Scenic Byway will experience. However, amid this urban culture is a prominent appreciation for nature and the arts. This can be seen in the beautiful parkways, lakes, and parks on the Grand Rounds. Hiawatha Avenue and Minnehaha Park are examples of remnants of a culture that held a great respect for the waters of Minnesota.

Architectural styles ranging from fine to functional exist all along the byway. Unique bridges hold views to the old milling district of the city, where settlers made a living working in the sawmills. Modern art can be found in the uptown area of the byway and in the lakeside areas. This art is one contribution of a culture that has evolved from all the previous inhabitants of the Minneapolis area.

**Historical:** The Grand Rounds Scenic Byway is one of the nation's longest and oldest connected parkway systems owned entirely by an independent park board. This road has many historical qualities. For example, the Stone Arch Bridge found along the byway is a National Civil Engineering Historical Landmark Site. Minnehaha Falls, also found along the byway, is immortalized in Longfellow's epic poem "The Song of Hiawatha." Master crafting is a significant element of the beauty of the Grand Rounds Scenic Byway, while other forms of architecture are being brought to the surface again. The St. Anthony Falls Heritage Trail offers a wide-ranging perspective on Minneapolis, exploring many highlights of the city's history.

**Natural:** With the Mississippi running through it and lakes scattered all around it, it's no wonder the Grand Rounds is a scenic attraction for nature lovers. In very few other urban places in the world is nature so artfully integrated with the city. St. Anthony Falls is the only natural waterfall and gorge along the entire 2,350-mile course of the Mississippi River; Minnehaha Park contains one of the most enchanting waterfalls in the nation; and the Chain of Lakes is a place on the byway to enjoy the lakeshore or sail a boat onto the water. All in all, the Grand Rounds Scenic Byway connects nine lakes, three streams, two waterfalls, the Mississippi River, and surrounding nature to travelers.

At the Eloise Butler Wildflower Garden, you will find hundreds of plants and flowers native to Minnesota. The garden has expanded into a preserve that is also home to many birds. A rose garden is located on Lake Harriet Parkway, while at Minnehaha Park, the Pergola Garden displays native wildflowers. Theodore Wirth Park includes a section known as Quaking Bog. This five-acre bog is covered in moss and tamarack trees. Exploring these parks and gardens will give you a taste of the best of nature.

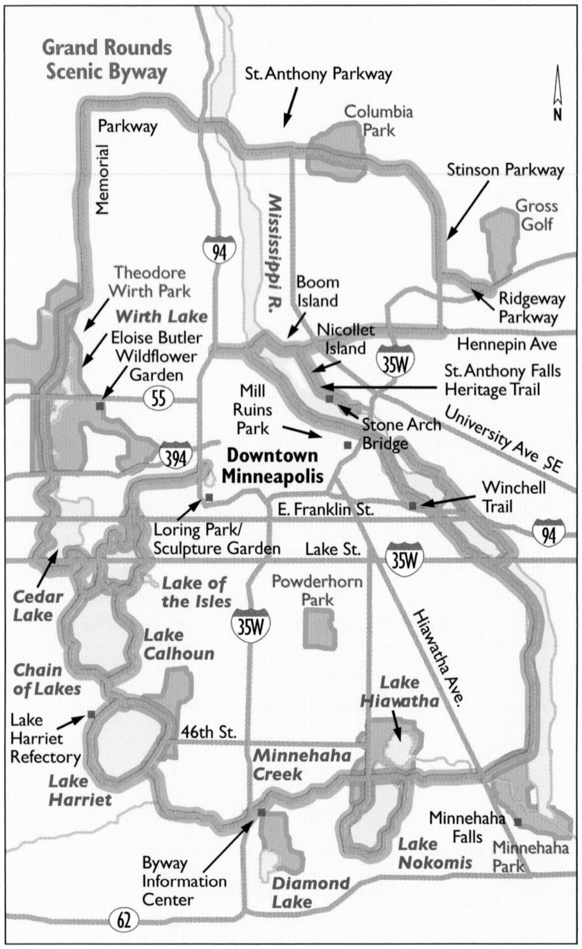

**Recreational:** With such widely varied attractions in one city, you'll find many places to see and different activities to do at each of those places. Outdoor recreation is not out of reach, while touring historical buildings and parks is a possibility, as well. Sailboats and canoes are seen every day on the Chain of Lakes, while bikers and hikers have miles of roads to enjoy. The Grand Rounds is one of the nation's first park systems to create separated walking and biking paths. The byway is also host to many national running events; for example, the Twin Cities Marathon on the Grand Rounds was named "the Most Beautiful Urban Marathon in the Country."

**Scenic:** The scenes of the Grand Rounds vary greatly, but they represent the city of Minneapolis at its finest. The architecturally diverse Minneapolis skyline is visible from nearly every portion of the Grand Rounds Scenic Byway. Watch the buildings sparkle in the daylight or see them silhouetted by a Minnesota sunset. The familiar view of the Stone Arch Bridge leads travelers to the historic district of Minneapolis with brick streets and flour mills. The sight of Minnehaha Falls is also a view linked directly to the ideals that embody Minneapolis.

The Grand Rounds Scenic Byway also includes outdoor sculptures, fountains, and public gardens that have been created by world-renowned artists. Where else can you find a creative rendition of a giant cherry captured by an equally enormous spoon? The fountains and sculptures of Minneapolis are the jewels of the city that set it apart from other urban sections of the country.

## Highlights

Drive the Grand Rounds Scenic Byway and you will see virtually all of the following sites.

**Theodore Wirth Park:** Beginning at the northeastern terminus of the Grand Rounds on Highway 35 W, travel west and follow the byway as it winds around to Theodore Wirth Park. This park is well worth the visit and includes the Eloise Butler Wildflower Garden, with its spectacular display of wildflowers and other flowering plants.

**Loring Park/Sculpture Garden:** Returning to the byway, follow it around Cedar Lake to Lake Calhoun. Here, turn northeast and travel around Lake of the Isles to Loring Park, home of the well-known Sculpture Garden. With its impressive display of sculpture and fanciful artwork, the Sculpture Garden is one of the highlights of the Grand Rounds.

**Lake Harriet Refectory:** Return in the direction you came, only continue to wind around Lake Calhoun to Lake Harriet to visit the Lake Harriet Refectory, another popular site along the Grand Rounds Scenic Byway.

**Minnehaha Park and Lake Hiawatha:** Continue following the byway as it turns and travels east to Minnehaha Park, where you can view the falls, and Lake Hiawatha.

**Nicollet and Boom islands:** From here, follow the byway north to its terminus at Nicollet Island and Boom Island. Both offer historic and recreational opportunities in downtown Minneapolis.

# Great River Road 

*The source of the mighty Mississippi River is a must-see and is on the Minnesota section of the Great River Road. Don't forget to look for legendary Paul Bunyan and his blue ox, Babe, along the way.*

PART OF A MULTISTATE BYWAY; SEE ALSO ILLINOIS, IOWA, AND WISCONSIN.

The Great River Road offers the best of Minnesota. The route encompasses the anks of the Mississippi River, o,000 lakes, beautiful bluff lands, nd a variety of outdoor recreation nd wildlife. Brilliant wildflowers, vergreen forests, colored autumn eaves, rainbows, snowflakes, nigrating birds, and waving fields of grain make this byway a photographer's paradise.

Recreational spots have taken ver the land of the lumberjack, vhere Paul Bunyan and his blue x, Babe, roamed freely in stories. State parks and lakeside resorts are all part of the fun that visitors will find on the Great River Road today. And then there is the river itself. Minnesota is where the mighty Mississippi begins. Its meanderings make up a trail of cultural, historical, natural, recreational, and scenic sites. Whether camping in the forested areas of the north or relaxing in a Minneapolis hotel, you will find accommodations in the perfect setting.

The Great River Road is an adventure along a myriad of quaint towns and urban cities. The Twin Cities metropolitan area offers the hustle and bustle of a city that is rich in history, culture, and recreational opportunities. Deep wilderness surrounds the river towns of Minnesota and offers relaxation and privacy.

eap the 15 or so stones that cross the Mississippi iver at its headwaters in Lake Itasca.

## Intrinsic Qualities

**Cultural:** The Great River Road in Minnesota takes you along the southeast end of the state, providing a look at the culture that began and continued on the banks of the Mississippi. This is where you find the Great River and the source of the development of civilization in Minnesota. It began with the American Indian nations of the Sioux and Chippewa, who lived in the area for many years before they began to interact with the Europeans in fur trade. When wildlife grew scarce, new settlers began an industry of logging, which forced native nations out of the area so that logging could proceed.

Although many people initially came to the area for jobs in the logging industry, tourism also blossomed as people traveled to see the beautiful Minnesota forests. In the 1930s, people began to restore the once-great forests of giant red and white pines. An appreciation of nature is still part of the byway culture today.

Cultures of the past have left their traces. Native American languages can still be found in names like Lake Winnibigoshish and Ah-Gwah-Ching (Leech Lake), while the heritage of the European settlers resounds in the names of communities all along the road. You will also find more recent pieces of American culture in Lindbergh State Park and the Lindbergh home, a memorial and a glimpse at the boyhood of the famous pilot Charles Lindbergh.

The Great River Road communities in Minnesota offer many festivals that celebrate the legends, products, immigrant culture, and art found along the byway. For example, as you travel from Itasca to Bemidji, you can experience the Annual Ozawindib Walk, the Annual International Snowsnake Games, and the Lake Itasca Region Pioneer Farmers' Reunion and Show. You can also enjoy the Annual Winter Bird Count, Art in the Park in July, and the People's Art Festival in November. Finally, you can visit the Paul Bunyan and Babe the Blue Ox statues that were erected in 1937 for a winter carnival.

In the Minneapolis to St. Paul area of the byway, you can experience 1840s food, dining, and preparation. Special events include Children's Day, Historic Mendota Days, the Mill City Blues Festival,

### Quick Facts

**Length:** 575 miles.

**Time to Allow:** Two days or longer.

**Considerations:** Several portions of the northern part of the road have a gravel surface. The speed limit on the byway varies, but generally it is 55 mph in the country and 30 mph through towns. During winter, you may find some icy patches in the rural parts of the roadway.

the Capital City Celebration, and a New Year's Eve party. Also, visit the Taste of Minnesota, the Minneapolis Aquatennial, the St. Paul Winter Carnival, and La Fete de Saint Jean-Baptiste. From Red Wing to Winona, stop and visit the Red Wing Shoe Museum. Some of the fun events that occur along this part of the byway include a Music Festival, a powwow, River City Days, and an Antique and Classic Boat Rendezvous.

**Historical:** When Henry Rowe Schoolcraft identified the true source of the Mississippi as the crystal-clear waters that flow from Lake Itasca, the final boundaries of the Louisiana Purchase were set. The Mississippi River, however, was important to Native Americans centuries before the Europeans arrived. In fact, the name Mississippi was an Algonquin name that, when applied to rivers, meant Great River (hence the name Great River Road). During the 1820s and 1830s, Fort Snelling and Grand Portage (on Lake Superior) were the focal points of Euro-American activity in the region. Strategically located at the confluence of the Mississippi and Minnesota Rivers, Fort Snelling served as the first U.S. military outpost in the area.

The Great River Road traces the river through the Chippewa National Forest, created by Congress in 1902. Although originally only small areas of pines were preserved, now more than 600,000 acres of land are managed by the National Forest Service. In this forest is historic Sugar Point on Leech Lake, another of the Mississippi River reservoirs. You can also visit Battleground State Forest, the site of the last recorded American Indian battle with the U.S. government, and Federal Dam, one of six dams constructed in the area between 1884 and 1912 to stabilize water levels on the Mississippi downstream. The legacies of the great pine forests along the Mississippi live in the majestic trees that remain. In Bemidji, the most recognizable landmark is the 1937 colossal statues of Paul Bunyan and Babe the Blue Ox, located on the shore of Lake Bemidji. The legend of the giant lumberjack illustrates the importance of the lumber industry for many northern Minnesota towns.

Due to its closeness to the river, St. Paul became a transportation hub, opening up the upper Midwest. It also became Minnesota's state capital, and Minneapolis became the nation's main flour-milling district. St. Anthony Falls in Minneapolis and the city's locks and dams provide testimony to people's success at harnessing the power of the river to create a thriving urban center. Flour, beer, textiles, and lumber were produced and successfully transported to the nation and the world through the lock-and-dam system that begins here. In the early 1900s through the 1930s, the Cuyuna Iron Range produced more than 100 million tons of ore that was used to build the U.S. military machines of the great world wars. In Crosby, travelers visit the Croft Mine Historical

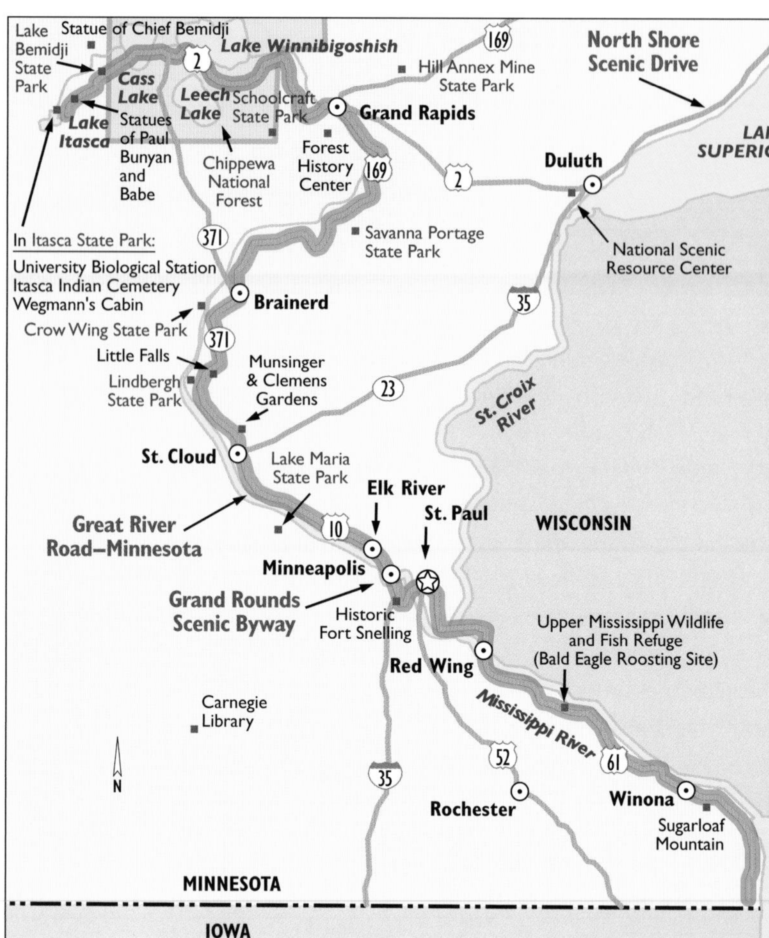


Park; this mine operated between 1916 and 1934 and produced the richest ore found on the Cuyuna Range, with a composition of 55 percent iron. Portsmouth Lake in Crosby, once the largest open pit mine on the Cuyuna Range, is now one of the deepest lakes in Minnesota at 480 feet.

Camp Ripley, a Minnesota National Guard facility, tells two stories: the history of Minnesota soldiers from the Civil War to the present and the development of the weapons of war.

In Little Falls, the Great River Road follows Lindbergh Drive to the boyhood home of Charles Lindbergh, pilot of the first solo flight across the Atlantic Ocean. The evolution of the United States can be traced along the Great River Road on the Ox Cart Trail, still visible though Schoolcraft and Crow Wing State Parks. Across the river from the Great River Road, Elk River's most noted resident, Oliver H. Kelley, founded the Patrons of Husbandry (popularly known as the Grange), a group that evolved into the Democratic Farmer Laborer, or DFL, party. Today, the Oliver H. Kelley Farm is a 189-acre living-history farm operated by the Minnesota Historical Society. This historic site explores the life and lifestyle of the Kelleys, who lived here in the late 1800s. Byway travelers also learn through excellent interpretation about the historic importance of the Great River Road and the river as transportation routes and vital links among Mississippi River communities.

**Natural:** One of the most naturally diverse sections of the Great River Road can be found in Minnesota. Travelers are beckoned to the Great River Road to enjoy a multitude of lakes, native wildlife, and rugged river bluffs. If you seek outdoor beauty, you will find what remains of the once-abundant pine forests that have been drawing travelers to Minnesota for more than 100 years. Visitors never tire of seeing the lakes along the Great River Road in Minnesota, and there are plenty to see. Nearly every town has its own lake along the road, and when the lakes end, the vastness of the Mississippi River is just beginning. Natural wildlife abounds in the marshes and prairies along the road. Visitors will pass a major roosting site for bald eagles and wildlife habitats for deer, waterfowl, turkeys, and pheasants.

Between the many lakes, streams and rivers flow, urging travelers on. The landscape along the route is the handiwork of a crowd of glaciers that meandered through the area, leaving pockets and creases for rivers and lakes. Large hills were smoothed into the rolling landforms that visitors can see along the road. The great Mississippi River bluffs are present on the byway, evidence of a notable geological past. This past combined with a present of hardwood forests, lakes, and wildlife creates a beautiful natural setting that will tempt you to leave your car throughout your journey on the Great River Road.

**Recreational:** From the headwaters to the Iowa border, Minnesota's portion of the Great River Road allows visitors to partake in a vast variety of recreational opportunities. No matter what the itinerary or expectation, there is something to suit every taste on the Great River Road. And the fun and adventure continues throughout all four of Minnesota's very distinct seasons.

The water itself creates a large amount of the recreational draw to the Great River Road. A taste of the recreational possibilities that are available on the water include swimming, sunning, fishing, boating, sailing, canoeing, kayaking, and waterskiing—just to name a few. Strung along the edge of the river are plenty of things to do, as well—particularly for outdoor enthusiasts. One of six state parks may be the perfect stop after a drive on the byway. At places like Itasca State Park, visitors can enjoy hiking or biking the trails, picnicking, or even bird-watching. The northern part of the byway provides a haven for hunters and anglers. The wilderness in this area is home to a great deal of wildlife.

Winter weather is no excuse to stay indoors in Minnesota. Several places along the byway offer miles of cross-country skiing and snowmobiling. Visitors also find places for downhill skiing. But if moving through the snow doesn't sound appealing, perhaps drilling through the ice does. Ice fishing is a popular pastime for visitors to the Great River Road; ice-fishing resorts, services, and house rentals can be found from one end of the Great River Road to the other. And large catches from the icy waters of Minnesota's many lakes are not uncommon and are a well-known secret among residents of the state.

**Scenic:** As you travel along the Great River Road, you can look upon pristine lakes, virgin pine forests, quaint river towns, and a vibrant metropolis. You can view eagles, loons, and deer, as well as blazing hardwood forests and hillsides fluttering with apple blossoms. Experience the awesome power of locks and dams, imagine life on a barge as other barges glide past, recall Mark Twain's time on paddle wheelers, feel the wind that pushes the sailboats, and watch water-skiers relive the sport's Mississippi birth.

Travelers along the Great River Road are witnesses to a river that is constantly changing. It first evolves from a clear, shallow stream into a meandering, serpentine watercourse. It then changes into vast marshes and later becomes a canoe route. After this, the waterway becomes a rolling river that powers dams and mills as it squeezes its way past the only gorge on the river. It then passes over large waterfalls, through the first locks, past tall sandstone bluffs, and finally into a mile-wide river that is surrounded by a vast and fruitful valley.

*Humble Lake Itasca in the pine forest of Minnesota is the source of the Mighty Mississippi River.*

*Nine thousand years of human history and archaeological importance have made Mille Lacs Kathio State Park a National Historic Landmark.*

## Highlights

The following must-see tour of the Great River Road's northern section gives you a sample itinerary to follow, if you so choose.

**Itasca State Park:** Covering about 32,000 acres, Itasca State Park embraces the headwaters of the Mississippi River and 157 lakes, the foremost of which is Lake Itasca, the source of the great river. Site of the University Biological Station, the park has stands of virgin Norway pine and specimens of nearly every kind of wild animal, tree, and plant native to the state. Camping and hiking, as well as historic sites, are abundant here. Itasca Indian Cemetery and Wegmann's Cabin are important landmarks in the area.

**Lake Bemidji State Park:** Leaving Itasca State Park, the Great River Road heads northeast toward the Chippewa National Forest and Lake Bemidji State Park. Just 31 miles north of Itasca State Park along Highway 371, the Bemidji area is rich in diverse activities. Stopping at Lake Bemidji State Park provides a lot of fun, including the two-mile Bog Walk, a self-guided nature trail. A small fee per car (per day) applies when visiting Lake Bemidji State Park.

**Paul Bunyan, Babe, and Carnegie Library Building:** Outside the park, along the shores of Lake Bemidji, lie several historic sites, including the famous statues of Paul Bunyan and Babe the Blue Ox, and of Chief Bemidji. The Carnegie Library Building, on the National Register of Historic Places, is also located here. You'll find many campgrounds and resorts in the area for staying the night.

**Cass Lake:** Cass Lake is the next stop along the tour of the Great River Road. It's a popular spot for fishing and camping. This lake is unique: Star Island, in Cass Lake, is an attractive recreation area because it contains an entire lake within itself. Other fabulous lakes in the area are worth visiting, too.

**Grand Rapids:** Enjoy the scenery of northern Minnesota as you follow the signs into the city of Grand Rapids. The city offers many activities, including the Forest History Center, a logging camp that highlights the logging culture of Minnesota.

**Savanna Portage State Park:** Heading south out of Grand Rapids, follow the signs toward Brainerd. On the way to Brainerd, be sure to stop at Savanna Portage State Park, with its 15,818 acres of hills, lakes, and bogs. The Continental Divide marks the great division of water—where water to the west flows into the Mississippi River and water to the east runs into Lake Superior. Be sure to walk along the Savanna Portage Trail, too, a historic trail traveled by fur traders, Dakota and Chippewa Indians, and explorers more than 200 years ago. A small fee per car (per day) applies when visiting the park.

**Brainerd and Lindbergh State Park:** The town of Brainerd is a great place to stop for lunch. Many lake resorts nearby offer camping, hiking, and fishing. After Brainerd and south of Little Falls, just off of Highway 371, is Lindbergh State Park. Look for bald eagles here when visiting in the spring or fall. During your visit, stop in at the historic boyhood home of Charles Lindbergh, the famous aviator. The home is operated by the Minnesota Historical Society and is adjacent to the park. A small fee per car (per day) applies when visiting.

**Munsinger and Clemens Gardens:** Once in the city of St. Cloud, the Munsinger and Clemens Gardens offer a relaxing end to this portion of the Great River Road. The nationally known gardens are located near Riverside Drive and Michigan Avenue, right in town. One treat of the gardens is the display of antique horse troughs filled with unique flowers. The gardens are popular but spacious, so they're hardly ever noticeably crowded. The southern tour continues from this point all the way through Minneapolis and St. Paul and along the Mississippi River and Wisconsin border, down to the border of Minnesota and Iowa.

# Historic Bluff Country Scenic Byway 

*The geology of the Historic Bluff Country Scenic Byway yields unique habitats including caves, underground streams, and the Sinkhole Capital of the United States.*

Follow the panoramic Root River Valley to the Mississippi River. The scenery along the estern end of the byway showases Minnesota's rich and rolling rmland, while the eastern part of e route winds toward the Great iver Road along a beautiful trout ream and canoe route through pectacular tree-covered bluffs aturing limestone palisades and ch hardwoods.

This valley was untouched by e glaciers, and has weathered gradually over time to create a magnificent pastoral setting dotted with small towns, quaint and historic lodgings, and a recreational bike and hiking trail.

*raditional Midwestern farms punctuate the landscape and rovide nostalgic scenery along the byway.*

## Intrinsic Qualities

**Archaeological:** The Huta Wakpa and the Cahheomonah people who were native to the Driftless Area along the byway realized its virtues as they found good hunting ground and resources for making tools. As a result, many Native American sites were once located all along the byway. Now, many of these sites have been lost by time and nature. Still in existence is the Grand Meadow Quarry Site. This natural bed of chert provided materials for Native American arrowheads and tools for 10,000 years. Archaeological interpretation for visitors is limited to stories of the past and the occasional piece of chert that might be discovered in the forest.

**Cultural:** Among the small Minnesota communities of the Historic Bluff area, a trail to the past defines today's cultures. Some of these cultures, such as the Old Order Amish population, have changed little since first settling here. Others have evolved and yet keep a firm hold on their heritage. The descendants of Norwegians and Germans still celebrate many of the same events that their ancestors did 150 years ago.

Little is left, however, of the Native American culture that once dominated the lands along the byway. At one time, the Winnebago and the Dakota developed celebrations and rituals around the Root River. The few nations that survive appreciate cultural sites and sacred places in Bluff Country, and archaeological sites provide a look at places that were important to these cultures.

The settlers who built the towns in Bluff Country were industrious. Towns flourished, and their downtown sections contained splendid architecture that can be observed today. The attitude of growth amid small-town life is still present in byway towns. Meanwhile, the past is alive in Amish communities, where people live without electricity, automobiles, and many of the cultural ideals that most Americans hold. Amish buggies can be seen near Harmony, Preston, and Lanesboro. Furniture created by Amish craftspeople can be found at shops in byway towns.

### Quick Facts

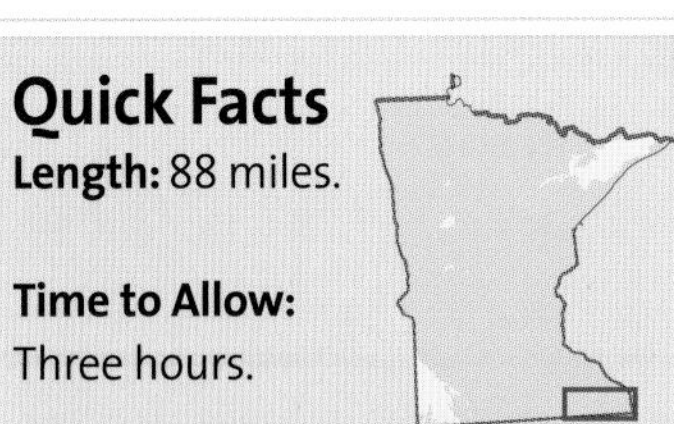

**Length:** 88 miles.

**Time to Allow:** Three hours.

**Considerations:** An extremely scenic route through the Yucatan Valley, the segment between Houston and Caledonia to the south curves frequently and climbs many steep grades in response to the area's topography. When traveling the Bluff Country, be careful of the wildlife inhabiting the area. Rattlesnakes are occasionally found on rock outcrops and on river bottoms.

**Historical:** When southeastern Minnesota was settled, little towns sprang up as the centers of agricultural trade and social activity. Farmers congregated to sell their crops and buy supplies, while grain was stored in silos or grain elevators such as the one in Preston, which once belonged to the Milwaukee Elevator Company. This grain elevator is now a rest stop for travelers along the Root River Trail. The towns profited from

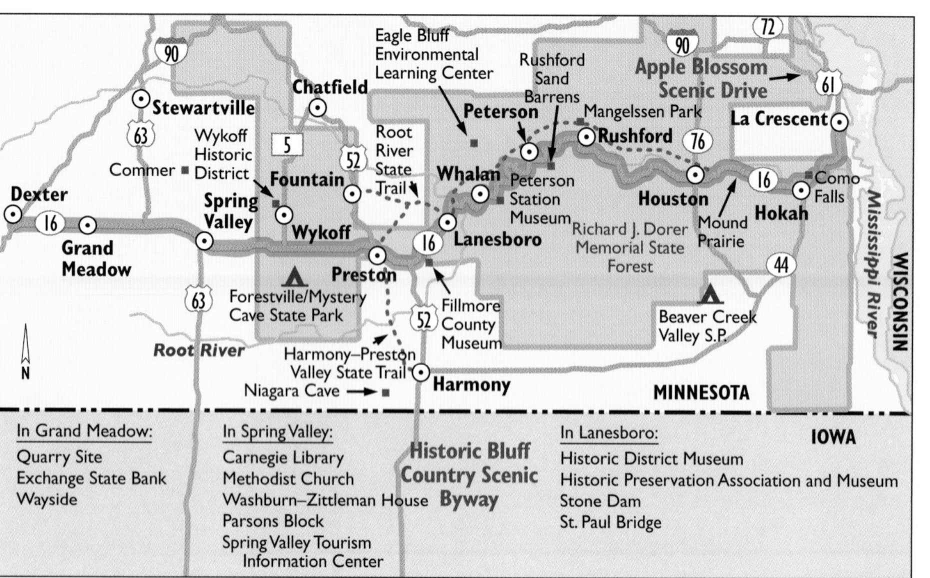


agricultural success, and now many of them display historic districts and buildings with elaborate architecture. Many of the buildings, including churches, libraries, and banks, are available to travelers as they explore history on the byway.

As a result of the successful farming industry, mills began to appear in Bluff Country. In Lanesboro, a dam on the river provided power for three flour mills. The commercial district thrived there from the 1860s through the 1920s, and visitors today can tour these brick buildings and the shops and restaurants inside them. Towns along the byway also benefited from the coming of the railroad. The entire town of Wykoff was platted and settled when the railroad passed through. The old Southern Minnesota Depot in Rushford now serves as a trail center. When the railroad left, the tracks lay in disrepair for many years until they were converted to the Root River Trail.

**Natural:** Deep river valleys, sinkholes, caves, and bluffs are all natural features of the byway that travelers will want to explore. The Root River flows along the byway, calling to explorers from a tree-lined bank. The byway celebrates its natural qualities with trails, parks, and places to stop and learn more about byway surroundings.

Unique habitats are found throughout. Labeled as Scientific and Natural Areas, these places support unusual plant and animal species because some natural features of the land remain unchanged while the rest of the state has been changed by glaciers.

The caves and underground streams along the byway are a result of karst terrain, which is created when rainwater is absorbed into the ground and dissolves the calcite limestone that lies beneath. As this thick layer of limestone weakens, sinkholes form. Streams that continue to flow through the dissolved limestone create caves and caverns. The Mystery Cave and Niagara Cave are two places where you can see the results of a few streams and a little rainwater. You may also want a good look at a sinkhole. The nearby city of Fountain is known as the Sinkhole Capital of the United States.

If you'd like to get out of the caves and enjoy nature above ground, the byway offers forests, rivers, and bluffs. The Root River and the Richard J. Dorer Memorial State Forest provide places to enjoy the greenery of trees and the sunlight as it sparkles on moving water. Maple, oak, and birch create a setting for bird-watching, and in the fall, their colors draw audiences from miles around. As the Root River flows along the byway and separates into two branches, canoe access points allow you to get a closer look.

**Recreational:** The forests, the trails, and the river are the central places for recreation on the byway. And because most of the byway goes through these places, recreation is never far away. State parks and natural areas provide places for hiking, camping, and exploring. With two caves within the byway vicinity, spelunking is a skill that every traveler will want to develop.

Most travelers like to explore places with unique names and histories. The Forestville/Mystery Cave State Park has both. Not only do visitors have the opportunity to go spelunking in the Mystery Cave but they also are able to explore the site of one of Minnesota's oldest communities, Forestville.

Two state trails on the byway are the perfect place for bikers, hikers, and, in wintertime, cross-country skiers. The Root River State Trail and the Harmony–Preston Valley State Trail connect to provide miles of scenic trail for visitors to enjoy. Along the way, signs give information about the surrounding area.

Perhaps the most inviting trail on the byway is one made of water. The Root River is perfect for an afternoon or a day in a canoe. The Root River is not just a waterway, but also home to a population of trout. Anglers enjoy the wooded atmosphere of the Root River as they try to tempt a prizewinning fish. The Root River is central to many of the activities along the byway, but even if you stray from the riverside, you'll be sure to find something to do.

**Scenic:** Bluff Country is a land of rolling hills, pastoral fields, and scenic rivers. Several places along the way highlight the beauty of a river valley or a hardwood forest. The colors of the landscape change with each season to provide rich greens, beautiful golds, and a winter white. Each season has its own spin on the scenery, but you'll find the same scenic place whenever you drive the byway. And when you aren't enjoying the scenery from your car, you can be out on the byway experiencing it.

Historic buildings, bridges, and walls along the byway only enhance the scenery, making it one of the most picturesque corners of the country. As civilization has developed in this natural prairie, industrious cultures and families have left churches, homes, and parks for future generations to enjoy. Their efforts create an added sense of pastoral perfection as the fields and forests are accented with classic buildings that stand the test of time.

## Highlights

Use this itinerary to enjoy some of the distinctive geologic attractions on and near the byway.

**Spring Valley Tourism Information Center:** Begin your journey near the western edge of the byway at the Spring Valley Tourism Information Center. Here you will be able to pick up maps and additional information about area attractions, including historic sites, recreation, state parks and forests, lodging, and dining.

**Mystery Cave:** Mystery Cave is the longest cave in Minnesota, with more than 12 miles of passageways in two rock layers, and is the state's best example of karst features. In dry years the entire South Branch of the Root River sinks into the cave through gravel crevices in the river bottom. Mystery Cave is a constant 48 degrees Fahrenheit, so be sure to bring a jacket.

**Forestville:** While at the Forestville/Mystery Cave State Park, be sure to also tour the vestiges of historic Forestville. All eight of the remaining buildings are listed on the National Register of Historic Places, and historians will guide you through the experience, explaining in authentic real-time what life was like for the original settlers of the area.

**Fountain:** The town of Fountain is known as The Sinkhole Capital of the United States. A sinkhole can be seen at the entrance to Fountain near the welcome sign, and there is a viewing platform near the Root River State Trail. Sinkholes are common throughout the Historic Bluff Country, as evidence of the ground water percolating through the geography, dissolving away carbonate rock, limestone, and salt beds.

**Niagara Cave:** Well worth the detour off the byway, is Niagara Cave. From Fountain follow Highway 52 south (it will join the byway road of Highway 16 briefly) beyond the byway about four miles to the town of Harmony. At Harmony take county Highway 139 south 2½ miles to Highway 30. Turn west on Highway 30 for approximately 2½ miles, and follow signs for Niagara Cave. It is one of the largest caves in the Midwest, with a 130-foot rock-vaulted dome, a 60-foot waterfall viewable from a bridge 70 feet in the air, a wishing well, and a wedding chapel.

**Harmony:** On your way back to the byway, be sure to stop in Harmony. At the Visitor Information Center near the picturesque Village Green in downtown Harmony you can pick up a free 32-page Visitor's Guide and abundant information about Historic Bluff Country; tours of the area's Amish culture; regional bike trails; and arts, entertainment, dining, and shopping venues.

**Mangelssen Park:** Just before entering Rushford on the north side of Highway 16 is Mangelssen Park, which sits atop a bluff, offering a sweeping panorama of the city of Rushford and the Root River Valley. Mature trees, including a bur oak estimated to be 175 to 200 years old, outline scenic views.

**Rushford:** After returning to the byway on Highway 16, enjoy the southeastern Minnesota scenery as you head east toward Rushford. About 2½ miles before you arrive in Rushford, within the Richard J. Dorer Memorial State Forest, is the Rushford Sand Barrens, a distinctive Scientific Natural Area. Thirteen rare plant species reside here, with a dry-sand oak savanna and a jack pine savanna as dominant features of this environment.

**Como Falls:** Inspired by the bluffs and steep sides of the Root River Valley, continue east to the last of this sampling of geologic formations of southeastern Minnesota. Como Falls is a peaceful part of the quiet village of Hokah near the eastern edge of the byway. Located in Como Falls Park at the east end of Falls Street just off of Main Street, Como Falls is on Thompson Creek. Signage explains the history of the falls, Thompson Creek, and Edward Thompson, the town founder who established a dam and a mill there. The forces of time and erosion are clearly visible at the falls.

*The Root River Trail follows along the Root River, providing hikers and bicyclists an opportunity to view the Bluff Country from a different vantage point.*

# Minnesota River Valley Scenic Byway

*The Green Giant Company began in the village of Le Sueur along the Minnesota River Valley Scenic Byway where agriculture from both the past and the present wait to be explored.*

The Minnesota River flows gently between ribbons of oak, elm, maple, and cottonwood trees. The Minnesota River Valley Scenic Byway, which follows the river, wanders past rich farmland and through towns steeped in Minnesota history. Passing through rolling farmland and woodlands bordering the river between Belle Plaine and Browns Valley—300 miles of highways and gravel roads—is a scenic, historical, and cultural experience.

## Intrinsic Qualities

**Cultural:** The Minnesota River Valley is a productive land, and as a result, people have been living here for hundreds of years. They thrive on the land and develop rich cultures to complement their successful lifestyle along the Minnesota River. In every town and stop along the byway, travelers have the opportunity to discover the industrious society that has made this land thrive.

The Dakota people share their regional history and thriving modern-day culture through festivals, museums, restaurants, hotels, casinos, and trading posts. European pioneers left their mark, as well, and their strong ties to their European heritage remain and are celebrated today. Residents of New Ulm welcome visitors to numerous celebrations, shops, restaurants, and lodging, all of which focus on their German heritage. Milan residents are likewise proud of their Norwegian heritage, and their community festivals focus on the food, crafts, and traditions of their ancestors. Many other communities on or near the byway demonstrate their proud heritage through festivals, events, and museums.

*The Minnesota River offers an impressive visual treasure for visitors as it meanders across the state before joining the waters of the Mississippi River.*

**Historical:** Once a wild and untamed river valley, the land of the Minnesota River Valley Scenic Byway used to belong solely to the Dakotas. The land was rich and fertile and seemed ripe for the picking, yet struggles erupted during the same years that the Civil War was raging. In 1862, the largest and bloodiest Native American war in the history of the United States occurred. For ten years, the land was divided between the Dakota people and new settlers. The first reservations were developed, but the Dakotas eventually wanted their land and their way of life back. The result was a six-week war in which many settlers and Dakotas were killed. When the war was over, Abraham Lincoln pardoned many of the more than 300 Dakota men who were going to be hanged. The remaining 38 men became part of the largest mass execution in U.S. history.

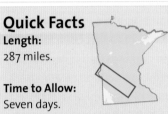

**Natural:** When you aren't driving through enchanting towns and pastoral fields, you see that the land is overtaken by nature and the wilderness that's native to Minnesota. Prairies and woodlands combine to form natural areas full of plants and animals. These pristine areas are perfect places to see the Minnesota River Valley's natural ecosystems.

The Minnesota River is now gentle and calm. However, the river valley was once filled by the Glacial River Warren. The glacial river carved the valley down into ancient bedrock and exposed outcrops of gneiss. The valley topography varies from one to five miles in width and from 75 to 200 feet deep. The Minnesota River flows from the Hudson/Mississippi Continental Divide in Browns Valley through the steep bluffs and low floodplain area that characterize one of the most impressive landscapes in Minnesota.

The array of landscapes in the river valley boasts a large variety of wildlife and plant life. Wooded slopes and floodplains of willow,

### Quick Facts

**Length:**
287 miles.

**Time to Allow:**
Seven days.

**Considerations:** The best time to drive this route is in the fall, due to changing leaf colors.

cottonwood, American elm, bur oak, and green ash rise into upland bluffs of red cedar and remnant tall grass where preserved tracts of prairie remain for public use and appreciation. Prairie chickens, turkeys, white-tailed deer, coyotes, foxes, beavers, and many species of fish and birds live here, as do bald eagles.

**Recreational:** The Minnesota River is one of the great tributaries of the Mississippi River. It provides some of the best recreational opportunities in the upper Midwest. Outdoor recreation abounds, including bird-watching, canoeing, hiking, trail riding, fishing, hunting, camping, boating, snowmobiling, cross-country skiing, and golfing. State parks and recreation areas combine outdoor recreation with opportunities to discover history.

All of these activities can be found along the byway at the six state parks, at scientific and natural areas, at wildlife-management areas, or at the local parks or waysides. Camping along the byway is one of the best ways to experience the nature of the river valley. Spending time near the river, you can better enjoy the beautiful scenery at one of the byway's lakes or take a stroll along the Minnesota River itself.

**Scenic:** The Minnesota River Valley showcases a variety of scenic elements. The byway brings travelers along the river and through prairies, farmland, cities, woodlands, and wetlands. Vistas from high upon the bluffs of the river let your eyes wander over the landscape, just as bald eagles, which are so commonly seen here, would do. Some roads along the river bottom bring you right up to the river, where your senses enjoy the sights, sounds, and smells of the river valley. Along the way, you'll find magnificent farmsteads of today and yesterday, bustling communities, tremendous historical sites, wildlife, and some of the most unspoiled prairie in the Midwest—all of which entice you to stop and enjoy them.

## Highlights

The following itinerary is suggested to explore some of the offerings of New Ulm. It is a unique city with a distinctly German–American heritage and much to offer the visitor.

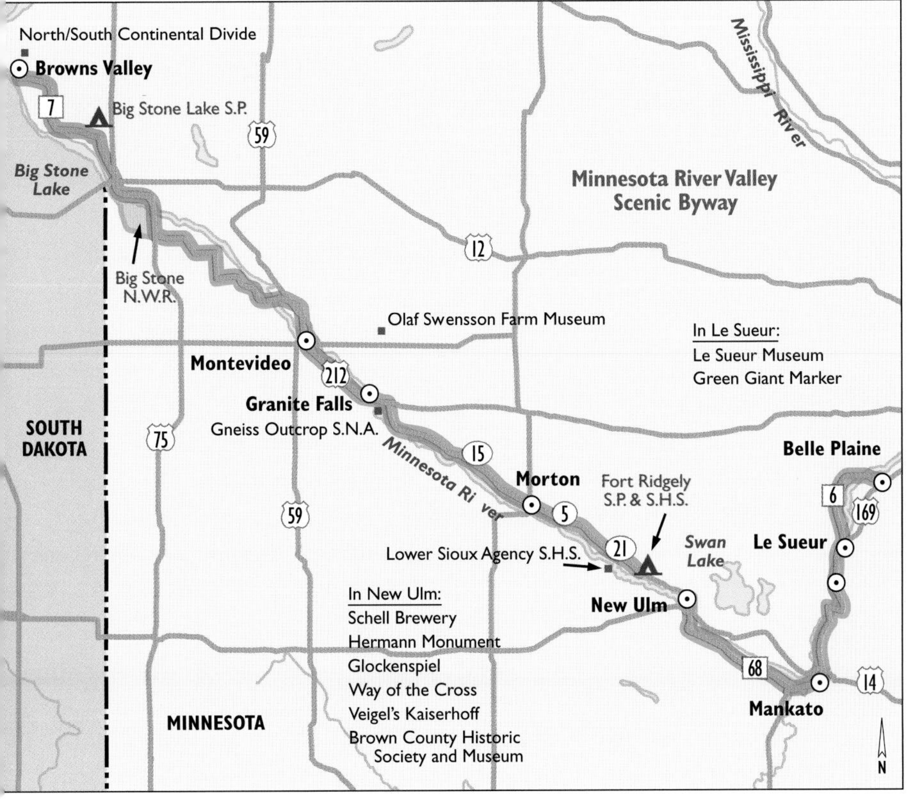


**Schell Brewery:** Coming into town from Mankato, turn west on 18th South. Your first stop will be the Schell Brewery, New Ulm's oldest industry and the second-oldest family-owned and managed brewery in the country.

**Brown County Historical Society and Museum:** The Brown County Historical Society and Museum is located at the corner of Center and Broadway streets. Giving an excellent overview of the area, this German Renaissance building was built in 1910 for use as the New Ulm Post Office.

**Hermann Monument:** At Center and Monument streets is the Hermann Monument, giving a nod to local German heritage by paying homage to a Teutonic hero, Hermann. Designed by architect Julius Berndt and dedicated in 1897, the 102-foot-tall monument can be climbed for a commanding view of New Ulm and the Minnesota River Valley.

**Glockenspiel:** At 4th North and Minnesota streets in Schonlau Park is the Glockenspiel, a rare freestanding 45-foot-tall carillon clock tower. At noon, 3:00 P.M., and 5:00 P.M., animated figurines revolve to show the history of New Ulm.

**Way of the Cross:** About halfway up the 5th North Street hill is the Way of the Cross, behind the New Ulm Medical Center. This unique outdoor Catholic shrine was built into the hillside in 1903 and 1904. The Sisters of the Order of the Poor Handmaids of Jesus Christ pushed wheelbarrows up the hill, hauling cobblestones to build the Stations of the Cross, rock walls, and paths. The statuary was crafted in Bavaria.

**Veigel's Kaiserhoff:** After visiting these sites that have a German flavor, complete your trip to New Ulm by enjoying lunch or dinner at Veigel's Kaiserhoff, New Ulm's oldest restaurant, located on Minnesota Street. It offers excellent German cuisine.

# North Shore Scenic Drive

*The North Shore Scenic Drive is home to the Superior Hiking Trail, a 200-mile recreation trail connecting all eight of Minnesota's state parks.*

The North Shore of Lake Superior, the world's largest freshwater lake, is 154 miles of scenic beauty and natural wonders. It has what no other place in the Midwest can offer—an inland sea, a mountain backdrop, and an unspoiled wilderness.

## Intrinsic Qualities

**Historical:** It is believed that the first people to settle the North Shore region arrived about 10,000 years ago. These Native Americans entered the region during the final retreat of the Wisconsin glaciation.

The first Europeans, French explorers, and fur traders reached Lake Superior country around 1620. By 1780, the Europeans had established fur-trading posts at the mouth of the St. Louis River and at Grand Portage.

The late 1800s saw a rise in commercial fishing along the North Shore. Some of the small towns along the North Shore, such as Grand Marais and Little Marais, were first settled during this period. Many of the small towns still have fish smokehouses.

Lumber barons moved into the region between 1890 and 1910, and millions of feet of red and white pine were cut from the hills along the North Shore. Temporary railroads transported the logs to the shore, where they were shipped to sawmills in Duluth, Minnesota, and Superior, Bayfield, and Ashland, Wisconsin. Today, many of those old railroad grades are still visible, and some of the trails still follow these grades.

Miners digging for high-grade ore from the Iron Ranges in northeastern Minnesota established shipping ports such as Two Harbors in 1884. With the rise of taconite in the 1950s, they developed shipping ports at Silver Bay and Taconite Harbors along Superior's shores. These harbors are still in use, and visitors driving the route may see large 1,000-foot-long ore carriers being loaded or resting close to shore. The shipping history and Lake Superior's unpredictable storms have left the lake bottom dotted with shipwrecks, which now provide popular scuba diving destinations.

*The Gooseberry River tumbles over five falls on its way to Lake Superior. Gooseberry Falls State Park is considered to be a gateway to the North Shore.*

**Natural:** The North Shore Scenic Drive follows the shoreline of the world's largest freshwater lake, Lake Superior, which contains 10 percent of the world's freshwater supply. This byway is a marvelous road to travel, never running too far from the lakeside and at times opening onto splendid views down the bluffs and over the water.

The Sawtooth Mountains, which frame the North Shore, are remnants of ancient volcanoes. The glaciers that descended from Canada 25,000 years ago scoured the volcanic rock into its current configuration. Cascading rivers coming down from the highlands into Lake Superior continue to reshape the landscape today. Northeastern Minnesota is the only part of the United States where the expansive northern boreal forests dip into the lower 48 states. The Lake Superior Highlands have been identified to be of great importance for biodiversity protection by the Minnesota Natural Heritage Program and the Nature Conservancy.

The environment along the corridor supports a number of wildlife species, including beaver, otter, timber wolf, white-tailed deer, coyote, red fox, black bear, and moose. Federally listed threatened species of bald eagle, gray wolf, and peregrine falcon also have populations here. Northeastern Minnesota is recognized as one of the better areas in the nation for viewing rare birds. Diversity of habitat, geography, and proximity to Lake Superior combine to attract a variety of avian life that draws

### Quick Facts

**Length:**
154 miles.

**Time to Allow:**
One day.

**Considerations:** The weather along the shore can be quite cool at times, so a jacket is recommended, even in summer. At times in winter, snowfall is heavy. However, because homes and businesses exist along the route, the plowing of this road is a priority.

ird-watchers from around the vorld. In the fall, hawks migrating long the shore of Lake Superior umber in the tens of thousands. Vinter is an excellent time to ee northern owls, woodpeckers, nches, and unusual waterbirds.

**ecreational:** The North Shore is ne of the primary destinations or recreational activities in the Aidwest, with facilities for outdoor ctivities, including camping, hikng, biking, skiing, snowmobiling, ishing, and canoeing. The impresive natural beauty of the North hore has been an attraction since he completion of Highway 61 in he early 1900s.

When you're ready for a break rom outdoor excitement, try ouring some of the classic hisorical sites in the area. The Minesota Historical Society takes are of the Split Rock Lighthouse and provides interpretive programs. The Lake County Historical Museum, which is housed in the old Duluth & Iron Range Railway Depot, contains excellent exhibts on the region's history. In Two Harbors, you can tour an operating ighthouse and the *Edna G.,* which was the last steam tug to work he Great Lakes.

**Scenic:** The North Shore Scenic Drive offers splendid vistas of Lake Superior and its rugged shoreline, as well as views of the expansive North Woods. The road crosses gorges carved out by cascading rivers, offering views of waterfalls and adding diversity to the landscape. The falls at Gooseberry Falls State Park make this the most visited state park in Minnesota.

A few charming towns dot the shoreline. Most started out as small fishing and harbor towns, shipping ore and timber. For many travelers, the quaint town of Grand Marais is as far as they will go; however, the scenery becomes even more spectacular as you continue driving north toward the Canadian border. The byway ends at Grand Portage. Here, a national monument marks the beginning of a historic nine-mile portage trod by American Indians and Voyageurs. At Grand Portage State Park, you can view the High Falls. At 120 feet, these are the highest waterfalls in Minnesota. The falls' magnificence is a fitting end to a trip up the North Shore.

## Highlights

Here are some highlights of the North Shore Scenic Drive.

**Canal Park:** Begin your experience in Canal Park in Duluth. Follow Canal Park Drive over Interstate 35 to Superior Street.

**Fitger's Brewery Complex:** Located in historic downtown Duluth, the refurbished Fitger's Brewery Complex offers many fine shops and restaurants.

**Rose Garden:** To continue along the byway, take a right onto London Road. Follow London Road for the next 5½ miles, to Leif Erikson Park, which contains the Rose Garden, a popular attraction for visitors.

**Two Harbors:** Connect with the byway loop in downtown Two Harbors by turning right onto Highway 61 west of town. You can see steam-powered boats and other attractions in Two Harbors. Follow Highway 61 to 6th Street (Waterfront Drive), where you take a right and pick up the byway once again.

**Burlington Bay:** Continue on the route by taking a left onto 1st Street (Park Road) and following it to Highway 61. Here, hiking trails line the shore of Burlington Bay. Taking a right on Highway 61 and continuing on that route will lead you along the remainder of the drive, which ends about 122 miles later at the Canadian border.

**3M Museum:** Follow 6th Street to South Avenue, where you will take a left. Prior to taking a left, be sure to stop at the 3M Museum. The 3M Museum is the only museum in the world dedicated to sandpaper. As you drive down South Avenue, you can begin to see the massive ore docks that extend from the waterfront.

# Great River Road 

*The Wisconsin Great River Road corridor incorporates four nationally recognized, naturally significant areas and more than a dozen state-recognized scientific areas.*

Part of a multistate byway; see also Illinois, Iowa, and Minnesota.

Wisconsin's Great River Road flanks the majestic and magnificent Mississippi River as it winds its way along 250 miles of Wisconsin's western border. The road is nestled between the river on one side and towering bluffs on the other. Most of the time, the road parallels the river, but when the road does meander a short way from the river, it treats its guests to vistas of rolling farmland, as well as beautiful forested valleys and coulees.

## Intrinsic Qualities

**Archaeological:** Nearly 12,000 years ago, Wisconsin was inhabited by people who hunted prehistoric animals such as mammoths and mastodons. The primitive cultures of the corridor left many artifacts and monuments to the past—not the least of which were the great mounds of grand designs and animal shapes. Today, Wisconsin archaeologists research these ancient cultures, as well as the cultures of the first explorers and traders who came to settle along the Wisconsin Great River Road.

### Quick Facts

**Length:**
250 miles.

**Time to Allow:**
Ten hours.

**Considerations:** Fuel stations and food services are available in the 33 river towns along the byway. These towns are found on average every ten miles.

The Wisconsin Great River Road runs through a place called the Driftless Area because it was not covered by glaciers during the last ice age. Because of this, many exposed rocks gave ancient inhabitants of the area an opportunity to create rock art that is still being discovered today. In caves and outcroppings, petroglyphs and pictographs have been found that depict an ancient way of life.

Archaeological displays can be found in many local museums. You can view mound groups and village sites at Wyalusing State Park, Diamond Bluff, La Crosse, Prairie du Chien, along Lake Pepin, and at Trempealeau in Perrot State Park. In the city of La Crosse, archaeological enthusiasts can view displays at the Riverside Museum that catalog Wisconsin from the earliest times to the present. As the headquarters for the Mississippi Valley Archaeology Center, the University of Wisconsin–La Crosse Archaeology Center offers an opportunity to view displays explaining techniques and prehistory.

There are 33 archaeological sites along the corridor that are listed in the National Register of Historic Places. Excavations of these sites have revealed pottery, ceramics, arrowheads, and tools, while burial mounds are prevalent throughout the corridor. In Onalaska, an entire prehistoric village has been uncovered, revealing structures and artifacts that indicate the lifestyle of the earliest inhabitants of the area. At Trempealeau in Perrot State Park, you'll find ancient mounds in the shapes of animals.

*The bluffs above the unique village of Alma offer sweeping views of the Mississippi River.*

**Cultural:** The varied past and present cultures of the corridor are recorded and revealed in the 33 river towns, the many state historical markers, and the archaeological sites found along the byway. The residents of the corridor take pride in preserving their heritage, as evidenced by the many festivals. Some of these festivals include La Crosse's Riverfest and Oktoberfest, Villa Louis's Carriage Classic, Prairie du Chien's Fur Trade Rendezvous, Alma's Mark Twain Days, and Pepin's Laura Ingalls Wilder Days.

Well-maintained early homes and storefronts are evident throughout the corridor, as well. Architecture from the 19th and 20th centuries is scattered throughout the towns and cities of the byway; many of them reflect the varied architectural trends of the early days of settlement. As you watch for unique architecture, you will also want to notice the mail-order houses that were constructed in a matter of days after arriving by train. Today, unique buildings and art forms continue to surface on the Great River Road. At Prairie Moon Sculpture Garden in Cochrane, for example, a unique form of art typical of the Midwest is displayed.

**Historical:** American Indians were the first people to live in this region, as evidenced by artifacts from archaeological sites and the presence of burial mounds. Thousands of mounds can be found throughout the area that display the culture of the Hopewell Indians who once lived here. The culture of this people evolved over the years, and they began to establish large, permanent villages. Known as the Oneota people, they were able to farm the river valley using hoes made from bison shoulder blades. By the time the first Europeans arrived, this culture had disappeared, replaced by a group of Sioux.

French missionary Jacques Marquette and explorer Louis Jolliet were the first Europeans to come through the area. They were searching for a waterway that would connect the Atlantic Ocean and the Gulf of Mexico. Later, French forts were established, and commerce and trade between the European and native cultures ensued. The area changed hands from the American Indians to the French to the British and finally to the Americans, but not without struggle. From the beginning, Native Americans fought to retain their ancestral lands, but to no avail. Settlement began in Wisconsin soon after the Black Hawk War between the Sauk Indians and American troops. In 1848, Wisconsin became a state.

Wisconsin thrived as a state for lumbering and sawmills. Because the Mississippi flows along its western border, Wisconsin was in a good position for the steamboat industry to develop. Steamboat races and wrecks were as legendary then as they are today. Remnants of 19th century Mississippi culture can be seen along the Great River Road: Abandoned quarries and old building ruins are just some of the things you may spot that remind you of an earlier day.

**Natural:** A number of nationally recognized natural wonders are found along this byway. For example, the Mississippi River/Wisconsin Great River Road corridor features the Upper Mississippi River National Wildlife and Fish Refuge, the Trempealeau National Wildlife Refuge, and the Genoa National Fish Hatchery. There are also 12 state-recognized natural areas featuring state parks and wildlife areas. In addition, many state-designated scientific areas are located along the corridor.

**Recreational:** Every season offers spectacular recreational opportunities on the Upper Mississippi River along the Wisconsin Great River Road. The Upper Mississippi provides excellent boating and sailing, and there are more than 50 local parks, beaches, recreational areas, and water access sites along the route. On Lake Pepin, a huge lake in the Mississippi River, boaters have access to numerous boat landings, marinas, and docking sites. Fishing is a favorite activity because of the variety of fish species, ranging from catfish to walleye. The sandbars along the river provide places for public camping, picnicking, or just getting off the road.

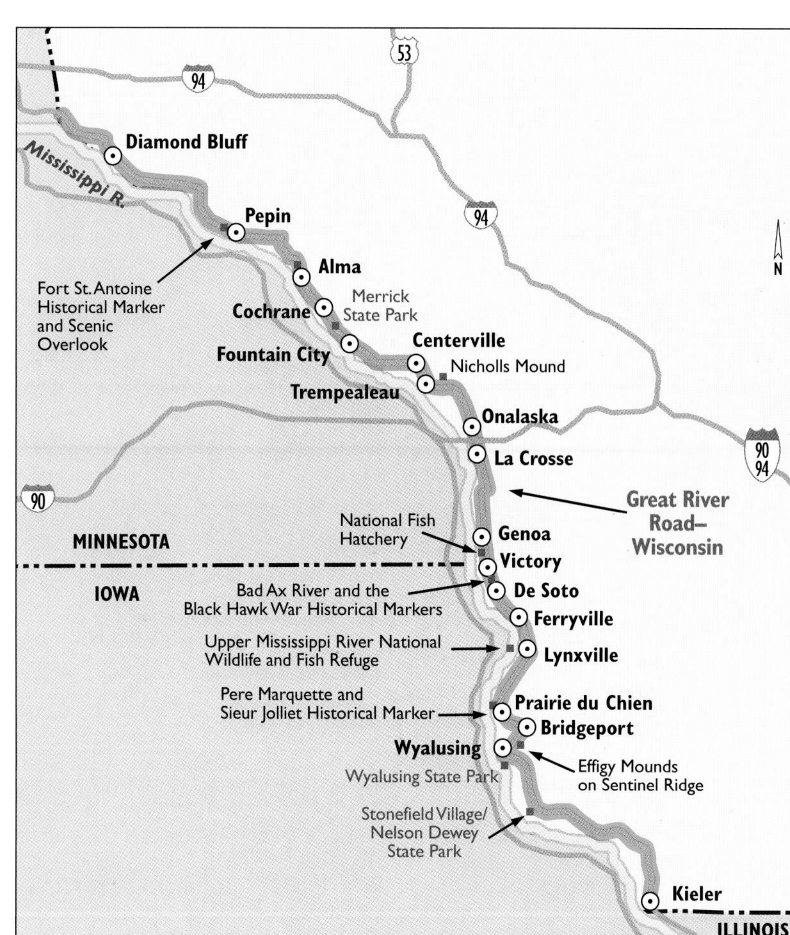


Bird-watchers enjoy seeing bald eagles as the magnificent birds catch their dinners. Berry-picking and mushroom-hunting are also popular activities, and many travelers choose to experience a farm vacation by milking a cow. Shopping and antique hunting in quaint river towns may be of interest to shoppers, while golfers will find enticing, scenic golf courses.

The Wisconsin Great River Road provides safe accommodations for bikers—with alternate choices of separate bike trails and local roads or streets. Depending on the cyclist's preference and skills, the rider has a choice of touring the Great River Road on-road or off-road. Canoe and bike rentals are available so that every visitor may enjoy these forms of recreation.

Winter in Wisconsin provides ice fishing and wind sailing on the river. Many travelers prefer cross-country or downhill skiing, snowshoeing, and snowmobiling

*The Wisconsin River meets the waters of the Mississippi near Prairie du Chien.*

through deep valleys and scenic bluffs. Summertime is excellent for dinner cruises on the river, or you can rent a houseboat and explore on your own. The river valley features hiking and biking trails, picnic areas, and camping opportunities in the numerous parks and campgrounds along the byway.

**Scenic:** Wisconsin's Great River Road meanders through the Mississippi River corridor. This corridor forms the southern half of the state's western border. The corridor's dramatic and beautiful landscape was created by melting glaciers, which carved the magnificent river valley.

Many segments of the Wisconsin Great River Road parallel the Mississippi River, some of which gracefully snuggle between the bluffs and the river. You're afforded numerous vistas of the mighty Mississippi and its valley and vast backwaters. You are also accommodated by more than 20 waysides, scenic overlooks, and pullout areas. Travel the Great River Road during all four seasons to experience its year-round splendors.

## Highlights

The following is an itinerary for the Victory to Bridgeport section—which is only one portion of Wisconsin's Great River Road.

**Victory:** Begin your tour in Victory. This small settlement along the Great River Road has a picturesque setting: snuggled next to the river on one side, with bluffs acting as a backdrop on the other. Five settlers laid out this village in 1852 and named it Victory to commemorate the final battle of the Black Hawk War fought south of the village 20 years earlier. Victory prospered during the wheat boom of the 1850s, but today, it is only a remnant of its past.

**De Soto:** The village of De Soto is four miles south of Victory. This river town has the distinction of being named after the famous Spanish explorer Fernando de Soto, the first European to see the Mississippi River. It was platted in 1854 on the site of a small outpost of the American Fur Company. Today, this community is a shadow of its past, when it peaked with sawmills, grain dealers, blacksmiths, dressmakers, breweries, and hotels. Learn from the locals how the wing dams constructed in the Mississippi diverted the river closer to their community.

**Ferryville:** Eight miles south of De Soto lies Ferryville. This little town clings to the bluffs along the river and is the longest one-street village in the world. It was first called Humble Bush but was renamed Ferryville when platted in 1858. The name reflects the founder's intentions to establish ferry service across the Mississippi to Iowa. Ferryville still clings to the bluffs and portrays a true river-town experience.

**Lynxville:** Your next stop, Lynxville, is eight miles past Ferryville. Because of the stable depth of the river at Lynxville, it was a reliable and popular landing during the steamboat era of the mid- to late-1800s. Although the steamboats are gone, this quaint little river town remains as the host community to Lock and Dam 9 and some apple orchards.

**Prairie du Chien:** With about 6,000 residents, Prairie du Chien is the largest town on your tour. Stop at the Wisconsin Tourist Information Center to find out about the many area attractions of this second-oldest settlement in Wisconsin. It became a trade center as early as the 1670s with the arrival of Marquette and Jolliet. Hercules Dousman built Villa Louis, an opulent 1870s estate with one of the nation's finest collections of Victorian decorative arts, that is now owned and operated by the State Historical Society. The Villa Louis Historical Marker at this site provides an overview of the origin and history of this luxurious mansion. Artifacts of medical history from the 1800s and an exhibit of medical quackery are displayed at the Fort Crawford Medical Museum. Some warehouses built in the early 19th century by the American Fur Company survive on historic St. Feriole Island, as do remnants of the old American fort built to protect this outpost. Tour the town in a horse and carriage or view the Mississippi River aboard a boat.

**Bridgeport:** Driving seven miles southeast of Prairie du Chien, you arrive in Bridgeport. The name of this village is most fitting. In the late 1800s, a ferry carried grain and other farm products across the Mississippi River to waiting railroad cars in Minnesota. Today, Bridgeport is near the highway bridge crossing the Wisconsin National Scenic River and the gateway to Wyalusing State Park and Sentinel Ridge, where the Woodland Indians left behind hundreds of earthen mounds.

# Woodward Avenue (M-1) 

*In Motor City, activities and history focus on the automobile, but downtown Detroit is also home to the International Freedom Festival in July, the largest fireworks display in America.*

The Motor City put the world on wheels, so welcome to Detroit's main drag: Woodward Avenue. Stretching out from the base of Detroit at the Detroit River, Woodward follows the pathway of growth from the heart of the city. Lined with history, cultural institutions, and beautiful architecture, Woodward Avenue travels through downtown Detroit and the Boston Edison neighborhood; past Highland Park, the Detroit Zoo, the delightful city of Birmingham, and the Cranbrook Educational Community in Bloomfield Hills; and into the city of Pontiac. Nearly every mile has historical sites that have shaped the industrial life of our nation.

Woodward Avenue includes both landmarks of the past and monuments to the future. You can find one of the largest public libraries in the nation, as well as one of the five largest art museums. From the Freedom Fireworks Display on the Detroit River to the annual Thanksgiving Day Parade to the phenomenal Woodward Dream Cruise, it's as if this street were meant to blend memories with the future.

*The heart of Detroit's vibrant downtown can be viewed from the Detroit River. The river is the most traveled border between Canada and the United States.*

## Intrinsic Qualities

**Cultural:** Much of the culture in southeast Michigan stems from the development of the automobile. When visiting museums such as the Detroit Institute of Arts (DIA) and the Detroit Historical Museum, the impact of the automobile is evident. Your first steps into the DIA will take you to huge two-story murals painted by Diego Rivera that depict life on the assembly line.

The Woodward corridor is one of six areas comprising the Automobile National Heritage Area (under the jurisdiction of the National Park Service). Woodward Avenue is home to other major cultural institutions, as well, including the Cranbrook Educational Community; Orchestra Hall; and the Detroit Public Library, which is among the ten largest libraries in the nation.

The region's culture can also be defined by its faith. Traveling from Detroit to Pontiac, you pass by more than 50 churches, many of which are on national or state historic registers. Prominent among these is the National Shrine of the Little Flower in Royal Oak.

**Historical:** Detroit is known internationally as the Motor City because of its role in the development of the automobile. This is the birthplace of the assembly line (Ford's 1913 Model T Plant on Woodward), a major technological innovation that made the automobile affordable to most families. The assembly line had a major impact on American society and in the development of urban areas.

The first people who may come to mind when talking about the automobile industry are the Fords, Chryslers, and Durants. But you should also remember the thousands of auto workers who established the industry and carry on to this day—the United Automobile Workers (UAW). Henry Ford's five-dollar-a-day wage attracted thousands to his factories, but the working conditions were brutal—this was true of all auto plants. In the late 1930s, the UAW was born and, with fair wages and better working conditions, auto workers and their families now enjoy a decent quality of life. Some of the former homes of early auto barons are located in Detroit's historic neighborhoods, such as the Boston Edison Historic District.

**Recreational:** The city of Detroit and neighboring communities have worked hard and invested a lot of energy to develop safe, fun activities that the whole family can enjoy. Some of the highlights

### Quick Facts

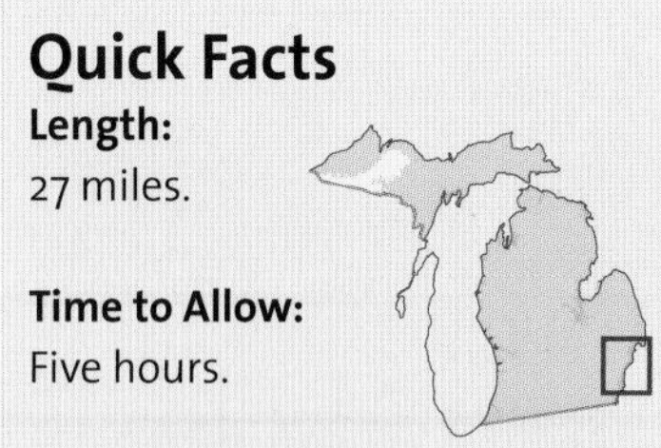

**Length:**
27 miles.

**Time to Allow:**
Five hours.

**Considerations:** The busiest months are August because of the Woodward Dream Cruise and November because of America's Thanksgiving Day Parade. Because this byway passes through downtown Detroit, avoid driving it during rush hour.

found along this byway include watching animals at the world-class Detroit Zoo, attending the Woodward Dream Cruise (where thousands from around the world gather to view classic cars from around the country), touring historic homes and mansions, making maple syrup at the festival in Cranbrook, standing on the sidewalk during the famous America's Thanksgiving Day Parade, or watching the largest fireworks display in the nation explode over the shimmering Detroit River.

**Scenic:** A unique quality of Woodward Avenue and the region is the geographic location of Detroit at the Canadian border. Driving southeast on Woodward from Pontiac, you conclude your journey at Hart Plaza, located on the Detroit River in Detroit's central business district. Approaching the plaza, the Windsor, Ontario, skyline unfolds in front of you. Noticeable at a closer distance are Belle Isle to the east and the Ambassador Bridge to the west. The Detroit/Windsor border is the only geographic location along the American–Canadian border (of the contiguous states) where the United States is north of Canada.

If you visit during the International Freedom Festival in July, you will notice hundreds of sail and power boats. This fun-filled family event has a million people celebrating our nation's heritage, watching hundreds of exploding shells reflect off the glass of the high-rise office buildings and the river.

## Highlights

This byway begins in Pontiac and ends in Detroit, where you can take the following downtown Detroit historical tour.

**Detroit River:** The tour begins just south of Woodward Avenue at the Detroit River, a designated American Heritage River. It is the most frequently traveled major boundary between Canada and the United States. It is also a major national and international waterway for the movement of freight and other commodities from the United States to foreign markets. In 1701, French explorer Antoine De la Mothe Cadillac founded Detroit at the foot of the present-day Woodward Avenue at the Detroit River. Detroit celebrated its 300th birthday in 2001.

**Campus Martius:** Located at the intersection of Michigan, Monroe, Cadillac Square, and Fort Street on Woodward Avenue, Campus Martius was part of the historic 1807 plan of Detroit by Judge Woodward. Today, it has been rebuilt as a public park and home to new office developments. This site includes the Michigan Soldiers' and Sailors' Monument of 1872.

**Lower Woodward Historic District:** The Lower Woodward Historic District is on Woodward north of State Street and south of Clifford. This district contains many former retail and office buildings constructed from 1886 to 1936. Significant loft development activity is underway in these buildings.

**Woodward East Historic District:** Woodward East Historic District (Brush Park) is located east of Woodward, bounded by Watson and Alfred Streets within the Brush Park neighborhood. Known for its high-Victorian-style residences constructed for Detroit's elite in the late 1800s, it is the location of a major urban townhome development.

**Peterboro–Charlotte Historic District:** The Peterboro–Charlotte Historic District is located on Peterboro at Woodward Avenue. The architecture represents a study in late 19th-century middle-class single-family dwellings and early 20th-century apartment buildings.

**Charles Wright Museum of African-American History:** Located in Detroit's Cultural Center on Warren, the Charles Wright Museum of African-American History offers one of the United States' largest collections of African-American history and culture.

**Detroit Historical Museum:** The final stop, the Detroit Historical Museum, is located on Woodward in Detroit's Cultural Center. The museum specializes in telling the history of the Detroit area from its founding in 1701 to the present, and includes permanent exhibits, temporary exhibitions, programs, and events. It is especially noted for its Streets of Old Detroit exhibit.

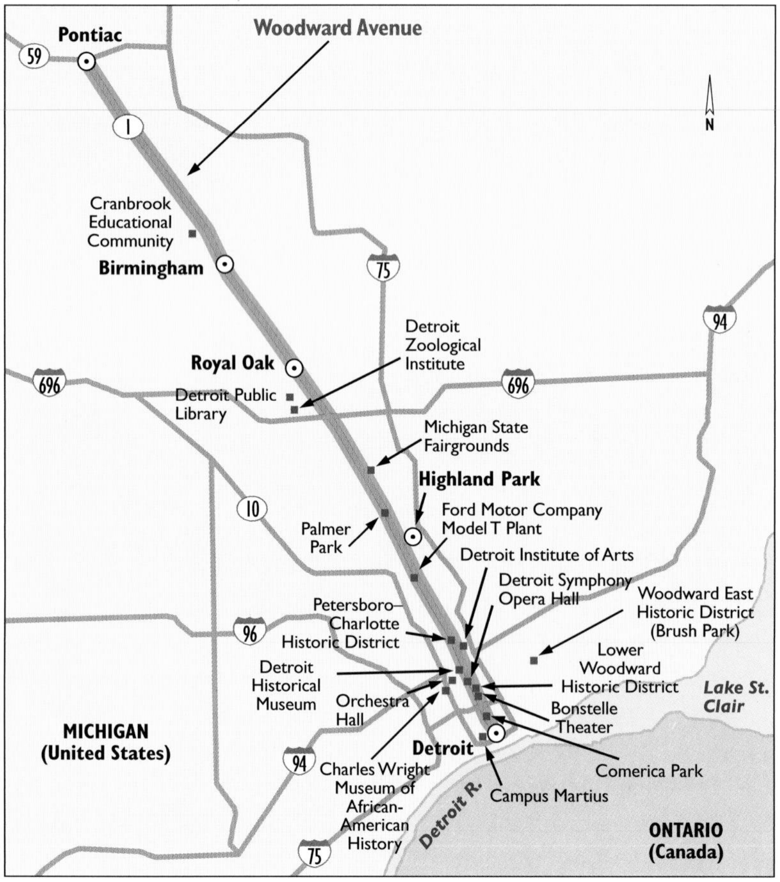

# NATIVE AMERICAN SCENIC BYWAY 

*Watch for excellent interpretive signage and natural wonders as you travel through Sioux tribal lands. Buffalo and other native animals truly do roam free here.*

Along this byway, the lakes and streams of the Great Plains tell the story of the oux's connection with the land. urney through the Crow Creek nd Lower Brule Indian Reser- ations, and view their unique ultures firsthand. Buffalo roam on ne high plains that sharply con- ast the nearby bottomlands and ne bluffs along the river. The Big end of the Missouri River features rominently in the geography of ne area. Dams created Lake Fran- s Case and Lake Sharpe, which re excellent recreational areas, as ell as places of beauty.

## ntrinsic Qualities

**rchaeological:** A significant num- er of archaeological studies are eing conducted along the Native merican Scenic Byway. One of the najor interpretive sites along the yway, the Crow Creek Massacre te near the southern border of the Crow Creek Indian Reservation, is a well-known archaeological landmark. In 1978, archaeologists from the University of South Dakota and the Smithsonian Institution uncovered the remains of nearly 500 people, victims of the largest prehistoric mas- sacre known in North America. The event occurred around 1325. Archaeologists have several ideas about what happened at the Crow Creek site. One theory is that there were too many people for the land to support and that village farm- ers got involved in battles over the land.

he Oahe Dam is the world's second-largest earth-filled dam. It provides flood ontrol for the powerful Missouri River.

**Cultural:** Travel through the grounds of one of the most sig- nificant Native American nations in the country. You encounter two Sioux reservations as you drive the byway: the Crow Creek Indian Reservation and the Lower Brule Indian Reservation.

When Lewis and Clark traveled through this part of the country, they came with the intention of forming a peaceful relationship with the people there. Remnants of that journey remain today, as travelers explore a new landscape and a new culture.

The Native American Scenic Byway is a journey through the heart of the Sioux nation. Excel- lent cultural interpretive sites give you an in-depth, educational, and entertaining experience with Native American culture.

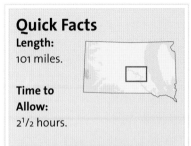

**Historical:** The history of the Sioux and other indigenous peoples who preceded them is an important part of Native American culture. A major change in the Sioux culture was initiated by their contact with Lewis and Clark, who went up the Missouri River in 1804 and returned in 1806. Their voyage of discovery is one of the major interpretive themes of this byway. In this area, Lewis and Clark first observed mule deer, coyotes, antelopes, jackrabbits, magpies, and several other animals, plants, and birds. Lewis and Clark were followed by fur traders, who in turn were followed by steamboats, which were followed by settlers. Fur-trading posts were converted into military posts, and the great Sioux Reservation was reduced to its present size. Communities were built, and the river was dammed. Through it all, the land remains, giv- ing evidence of the past.

### Quick Facts

**Length:** 101 miles.

**Time to Allow:** $2^1/2$ hours.

**Considerations:** Because most tourist traffic occurs during the summer months, several of the interpretive sites (those with trained staff and living-history interpreters) are closed during the off-season. The speed limit along the byway is 55 mph, and gasoline is available in Oacoma, Chamberlain, Fort Thompson, and Fort Pierre.

**Natural:** One of the prominent natural features of the byway is the buffalo that roam the area. The traditional Sioux culture was dependent upon the buffalo—it provided food, shelter, and imple- ments. The elimination of the buf- falo almost eliminated the Sioux culture, but buffalo are now being returned to the reservations.

Another prominent natural feature of the byway is the Missouri River, the main route of commerce through central North America for hundreds of years. The Big Bend of the Missouri is one of the best- known geographic features of the continent. Native plants are also an integral part of Native American ceremony and lifestyle.

**Recreational:** The damming of the river along this byway created Lake Francis Case and Lake Sharpe. These impounded waters provide excellent recreational opportunities. All types of water sports are available, and the fishing is among the best in the country. The recreational facilities along the lakes are managed by the U.S. Army Corps of Engineers, and nice camping facilities are also available. The communities at either end of the byway offer biking, hiking, and nature trails. In addition, both Sioux reservations have well-managed hunting and fishing programs that are available to the public.

**Scenic:** The scenery along the byway is spectacular. The hills and bluffs along the river are rugged and prominent. The bottomlands where creeks and streams enter the river are characterized by woodlands and wetlands. The high plains have a unique appeal of openness and freedom. Visitors often have the opportunity to view wildlife along the byway.



## Highlights

This itinerary takes you the entire length of the byway, from north to south. If you're traveling in the other direction, read this list from the bottom and work your way up.

**Oahe Dam:** You can begin traveling the Native American Scenic Byway at the Oahe Dam, the world's second-largest earth-filled dam. Originally built to control flooding from the Missouri River, today the dam is a popular site for water recreation activities of all sorts.

**Pierre:** Six miles southeast is the north terminus, at South Dakota's capital, Pierre. While in Pierre, tour the Cultural Heritage Center, which showcases South Dakota history. Also in Pierre is the state capitol, one of the most fully restored U.S. capitols.

**Missouri River:** The Missouri River runs parallel to the byway. You can enjoy numerous water recreational activities, including swimming, camping, boating, and fishing, at many points along the byway.

**Farm Island Recreation Area:** Located four miles southeast of Pierre is the Farm Island Recreation Area. The park is nestled along the shores of the Missouri River and provides a great place for a variety of outdoor recreation activities. Camping, boating, and fishing are popular here. Swimmers enjoy the beach of the Missouri River.

**Fort Pierre National Grassland:** Traveling south of Pierre, you pass through the Fort Pierre National Grassland. The land is publicly owned and administered by the U.S. Forest Service. The grassland is noted for crop fields of sorghum, wheat, and sunflowers.

**Lower Brule Indian Reservation:** Only 30 miles southeast of Pierre begins the Lower Brule Indian Reservation. Visitors to the reservation enjoy the tribal casino, as well as visits to Lake Sharpe and the Big Bend Dam.

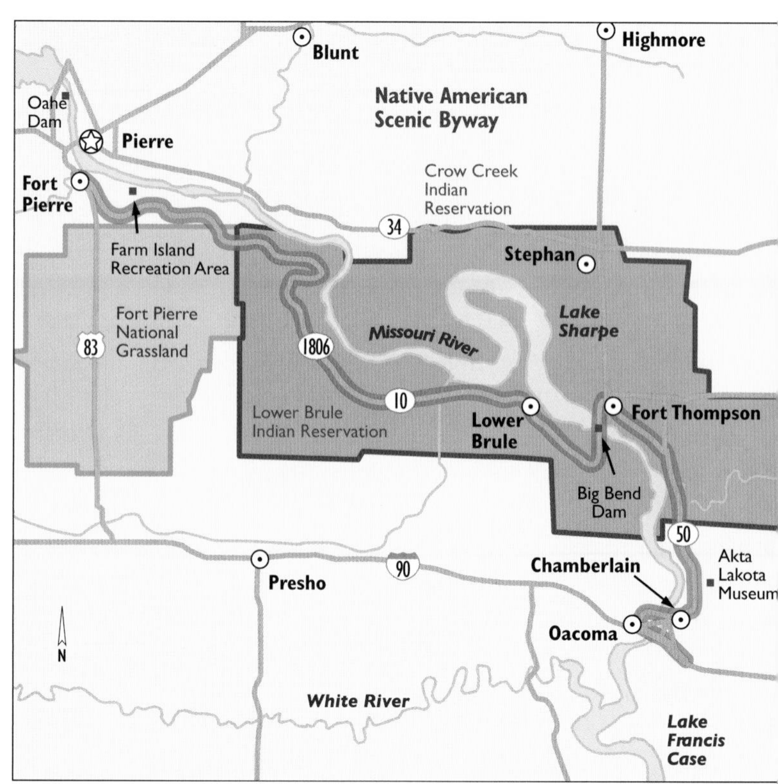


**Crow Creek Indian Reservation:** The Crow Creek Indian Reservation begins near Big Bend and continues until the southern terminus of the Native American Scenic Byway. Casinos, water sports, fishing, entertainment, and hunting are available on the reservation.

**Lake Sharpe:** Lake Sharpe stretches some 80 miles from the Oahe Dam in the north to the Big Bend Dam in Fort Thompson. It is easily accessed at the West Bend State Recreation area 50 miles east of Pierre on the byway.

**Big Bend Dam:** Big Bend Dam is located approximately 50 miles southeast of Pierre. Built to control flooding of the Missouri River and to provide hydroelectric power, the dam has created vast reservoirs that today provide ample opportunity for fishing and water recreation. Swimming, sailing, scuba diving, and fishing are popular activities in the area. Take the tour of the powerhouse to learn about the engineering feat of creating the dam. One-hour tours of Big Bend Powerhouse are available at no charge. Picnic areas, docks, and marinas are available. A visitor center is located at the dam.

**Akta Lakota Museum:** The Akta Lakota Museum is located in Chamberlain and is devoted to preserving and promoting Sioux culture. The museum is located at the St. Joseph's Indian School for Native American Youth.

# PETER NORBECK SCENIC BYWAY 

*Not only home to beloved American landmark Mount Rushmore, the Peter Norbeck Scenic Byway also fascinates visitors with ghost tours from 1800s gold-rush days, amazing geological formations, and the occasional mountain goat.*

This 68-mile scenic route honors a South Dakota conservationist, governor, and U.S. senator. Peter Norbeck first saw the Black Hills in 1905 after crossing the prairie on rugged, unimproved roads. His first visit began a lifelong love affair with the hills. Norbeck Overlook, Norbeck Wildlife Preserve, and now the Peter Norbeck Scenic Byway all bear his name and memorialize his conservation achievements.

## Intrinsic Qualities

**Cultural:** The earliest modern inhabitants of the Black Hills were the Crow Indians. Not much is known about these residents, except that they were forced to move west by the Cheyenne Indians. Ironically, the Cheyenne held the Black Hills for only a few decades. Westward-expanding Sioux Indians reached the hills around 1775 and quickly defeated the Cheyenne nation. The Sioux reigned over the High Plains for nearly a century.

In 1876, following the discovery of gold in the Black Hills, the Sioux War broke out. After several defeats by the U.S. Cavalry, the Sioux, with neighboring nations in Wyoming and Montana, united to battle General George Custer's troops. Custer and his troops were massacred in the Battle of Little Bighorn, and the Sioux emerged victorious. However, as more U.S. troops arrived on the plains, most American Indians were disarmed and forced onto reservations. The government bought the Black Hills from the Sioux. Tension between the Sioux and the settlers remained high. The government built Fort Meade to permanently house soldiers who would protect the settlers. Hundreds of Sioux people died at Wounded Knee Creek when a minor melee triggered nervous troops to open fire. The Wounded Knee incident of 1890 marked the end of bloodshed between Native Americans and settlers.

*Sylvan Lake, located in Custer State Park, is the oldest reservoir in the Black Hills of South Dakota.*

**Historical:** In 1905, Peter Norbeck traveled to the Black Hills from his home on the eastern Dakota prairies. He soon became the unlikely steward of the Black Hills and a nationally prominent conservationist and legislator.

One of Norbeck's greatest concerns was creating a great state park befitting the extraordinary beauty and diversity of the Black Hills. He envisioned a preserve that would encompass features such as the Needles, Harney Peak, and the Sylvan Lake area. His tireless efforts led to the establishment of Custer State Park in 1919 and the Norbeck Wildlife Preserve in 1920.

In 1919, work began on the Needles Highway, following a route through rugged terrain that was often impassable on horseback. Norbeck supplied 150,000 pounds of dynamite to one of the engineers who said he would need it to build the road. By 1921, the Needles Highway was completed.

### Quick Facts

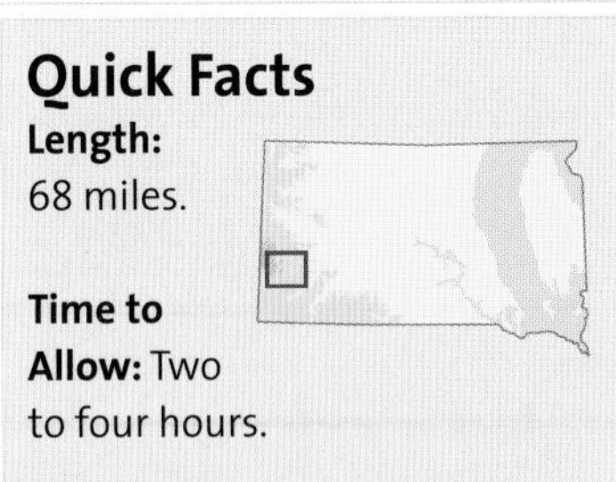

**Length:** 68 miles.

**Time to Allow:** Two to four hours.

**Considerations:** Portions of the byway have steep grades, sharp curves, and tunnels with height and width restrictions, with speed limits ranging from 20 to 45 mph. Custer State Park and Mount Rushmore are fee sites. Portions of Highways 16A south of Mount Rushmore and Highway 87 east of Sylvan Lake are closed during the winter.

**Natural:** The Peter Norbeck Scenic Byway lies predominately within the crystalline (or granite) core of the central Black Hills. For the most part, sedimentary formations have eroded away from this range, often exposing massive granite mountainsides, outcrops, and spires. At lower elevations, meadows interrupt stands of ponderosa pine and aspen, while narrow streams lined with grasses or hardwoods, such as bur oak and willow, tumble through parklike settings.

Some of the prominent peaks near the byway include Harney Peak (7,242 feet) and the Needles

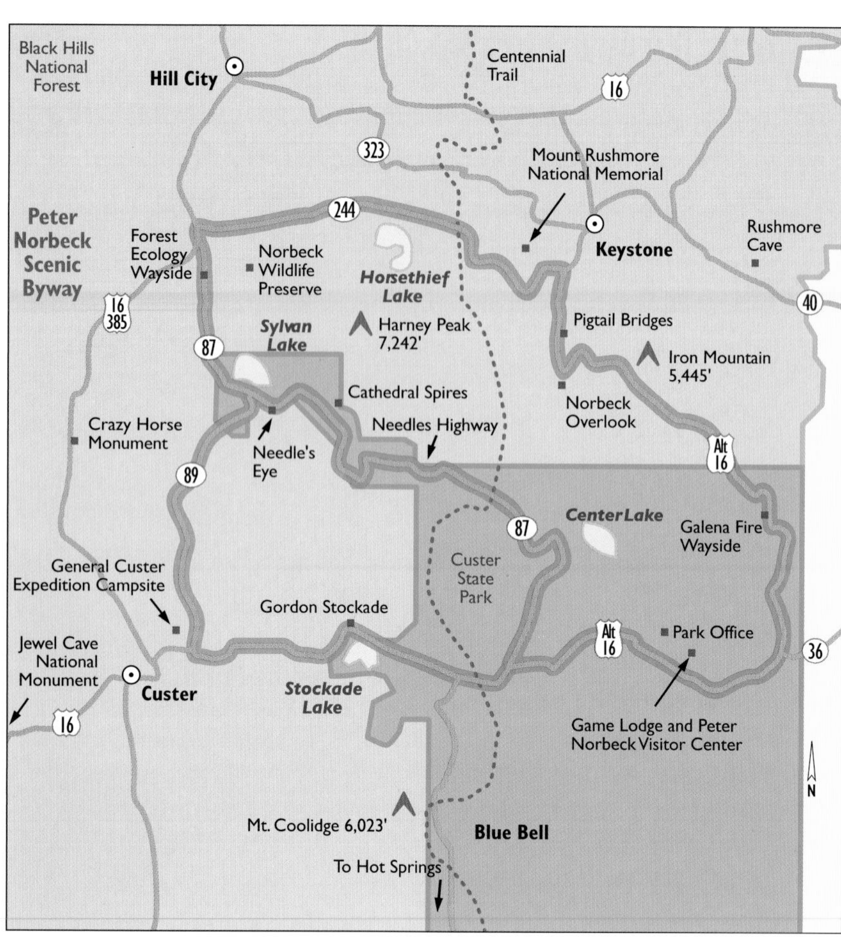




area of granite spire, Mount Coolidge (6,023 feet), Iron Mountain (5,445 feet), and Mount Rushmore (5,725 feet).

**Recreational:** One of the best ways to see the Peter Norbeck Scenic Byway is to see it as Peter Norbeck did—on foot. Trails wind throughout Custer State Park and the Black Hills National Forest. For cyclists and hikers, Centennial Trail runs into backcountry areas.

Many visitors travel the byway for the sole purpose of seeing a national landmark. Roads with names like the Needles Highway are just waiting to be explored. The Needles Highway is a natural attraction for scenic drivers, and rock climbers find the granite spires of the area irresistible.

**Scenic:** The byway passes a handful of lakes that are perfect for shoreline picnics or a little fishing. Piles of giant granite boulders make Sylvan Lake unique, and its inviting shoreline makes it a perfect place to stop and rest on the hike to Harney Peak. On calm days, the lake reflects the boulders above it. At the edge of Horsethief Lake, you will find towering ponderosa forests, perfect for an afternoon of hiking and exploring.

## Highlights

Please be aware that portions of the Peter Norbeck Scenic Byway have steep grades, sharp curves, tunnels, and bridges.

**General Custer Expedition Campsite:** General Custer Expedition Campsite was the base camp for the 1874 Custer Expedition that explored and mapped the Black Hills and discovered gold here.

**Gordon Stockade and Stockade Lake:** The Gordon Stockade is a replica of the 1874 structure built by the first settlers in the hills. Also in the area is Stockade Lake, where you can camp or picnic.

**Needles Highway:** Continuing farther east along the byway, turn left onto Highway 87 heading north to the Needles Highway. Along this highway, you should notice the Cathedral Spires, a spectacular rock formation in the 1.7-billion-year-old Harney Peak granite. Also in the area is the Needle's Eye, a unique erosion feature reaching 30 to 40 feet in the air.

**Sylvan Lake:** Sylvan Lake is the oldest reservoir in the Black Hills, constructed in 1898. Take time to swim, fish, hike, camp, or rock climb in the area.

**Forest Ecology Wayside:** Next up is the Forest Ecology Wayside, which conveys the natural history of the Black Hills forests and fire.

**Norbeck Wildlife Preserve:** This preserve is home to deer, elk, mountain goats, bighorn sheep, and many bird species.

**Horsethief Lake:** Horsethief Lake is a favorite spot for camping and for hiking into the backcountry.

**Mount Rushmore:** Mount Rushmore was carved by Gutzon Borglum between 1927 and 1941 and stands as a memorial to significant figures of America's government.

**Pigtail Bridges:** These unique bridges, designed by Norbeck and built by the Civilian Conservation Corps in the 1930s, span steep climbs in short distances. The bridges consist of a series of spiral curves, like the shape of a pig's tail.

**Norbeck Overlook:** Stop at the overlook to view the panoramic scenes of Harney Peak and the outcrops of ancient granite.

**Galena Fire Wayside:** The Galena Fire Wayside area focuses on the 1988 wildfire that burned more than 16,000 acres.

**Game Lodge and Peter Norbeck Visitor Center:** Game Lodge was built as the gamekeeper's residence and later served as the 1927 Coolidge summer White House. Only a short distance from Game Lodge is the Peter Norbeck Visitor Center, offering information on Norbeck's life and area history.

**Park Office:** West of the lodge is the Park Office. You can continue west once again to where the tour began.

# Great River Road 

*ʾrehistoric Native American mounds are common from the prairies of the Midwest to the Eastern Seaboard, but the Effigy Mounds National Monument along Iowa's section of the Great River Road is the only place in America where the large mounds are shaped in the lifelike outlines of mammals, birds, and reptiles.*

Part of a multistate byway; see also Illinois, Minnesota, and Wisconsin.

Join travelers from around the world to discover dramatic vistas of Old Man River during ll seasons. View soaring eagles nd 100,000 migrating geese nd ducks. Experience Midwest ospitality on the main streets f river towns and cities, or visit acred sites and landscape effigies f Native Americans. You can also xperience the Mississippi River on teamboats, commercial barges, nd recreational crafts.

The byway's story begins with he landscape: Abrupt and dramatic imestone bluffs cut by glacial neltwater in the north contrast vith broad sandy floodplains in he south. For thousands of years, Native Americans knew the impor- ance of the continent's largest river. ater, its meandering course marked he political boundaries of territo- ies, towns, cities, states, and counties of the advancing society. Today, the Upper Mississippi River and the Great River Road are national repositories of geological wonders, unparalleled scenic beauty, wildlife, native vegetation, and the miracles of hydrology. The river and road are also milestones to the expansion and development of the United States and the Midwest.

**Quick Facts**

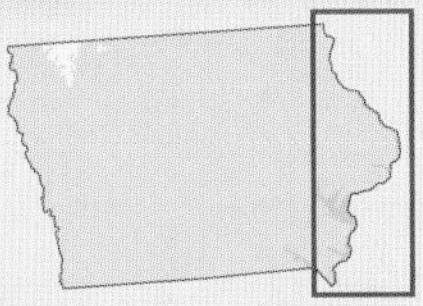

**Length:** 326 miles.

**Time to Allow:** Two days.

**Considerations:** Short portions of the road may be closed once every few years due to winter snowstorms. Such interruptions usually last less than 36 hours.

## Intrinsic Qualities

**Archaeological:** A primary site on the Great River Road is the Effigy Mounds National Monument, the site of 195 mounds. Of these 195 mounds, 31 are effigy outlines of mammals, birds, or reptiles. Eastern Woodland Indians built these sites between 500 B.C. and A.D. 1300. They are preserved and interpreted for the public. Additional property is being added to the monument site to expand its protection of these unique resources. Other important sites are found at the Mines of Spain State Recreation Area and the Toolesboro Indian Mounds National Historic Landmark.

**Historical:** Although most of Iowa was settled in the mid-1800s, the Mississippi River made it an accessible territory long before the United States became a nation. Native Americans and explorers alike saw the raw, unharnessed power of this beautiful passageway. One of the first outposts was Fort Madison, where history is re-created today. Like much of the United States, the Great River Road was under Spanish and French rule until the time of the Louisiana Purchase in 1803.

*Effigy Mounds National Monument contains 195 prehistoric mounds. Eastern Woodland Indians built the mounds with 31 being in the shape of effigies.*

Soon after, settlers and industry came to Iowa. Bustling river towns created cultural landmarks such as Snake Alley—the curviest road in the United States. Little towns along the road grew and became the cities they are today. During the booming days of river trade, writer Samuel Langhorne Clemens (better known as Mark Twain) captured the atmosphere and the time period in his novels.

When the Civil War came to Iowa, most of the people living there fought for the Union. Civil War memorials are now found in several of the towns on the byway.

**Natural:** Geology, the hydrologic cycle, and erosion are among the big stories that the Mississippi River and the Great River Road tell in Iowa. The forces of nature can be seen in the way the river has cut a deep channel in ancient limestone layers in the northern reaches. The ever-changing channel of the river, the deposition of sediments, and the broad floodplain of the Mississippi River in the southern part of the state speak of a different natural dynamic. The Upper Mississippi River National Wildlife and Fish Refuge is the state's oldest and most popular wildlife refuge. Many other state, county, and city parks provide opportunities for spotting and watching wildlife.

**Recreational:** Recreational opportunities abound along the Iowa Great River Road. Water activities include boating, sailing, fishing, waterfowl hunting, and swimming. For decades, the Iowa Great River Road and its side roads have been popular pleasure routes for sightseeing. Numerous multipurpose trails and support facilities are available along the road.

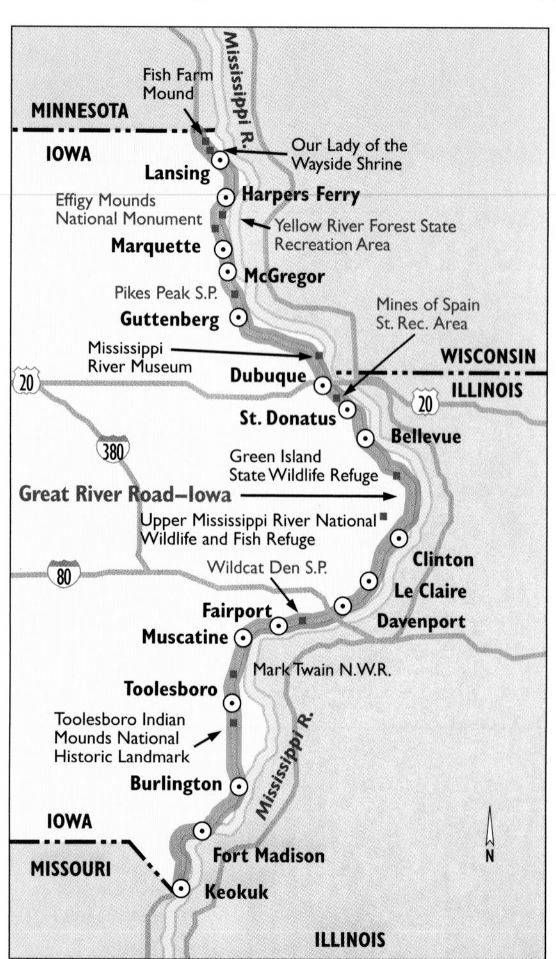


**Scenic:** The magnificent scenery of the Great River Road is centered around the Mississippi River. The river is almost continuously visible from the Great River Road (or is within a few miles of the byway). Dams along the river create large pools of open water upstream. Along the northern part of the river, steep limestone bluffs descend directly to the banks. Downstream, the floodplain opens to afford long, uninterrupted views of the valley. Roadside spots, shady parks, and locks and dams of the Mississippi River offer places for you to stop and take in the scenic beauty of the Great River Road and the Mississippi River.

The four seasons provide dynamic backgrounds and changes in the vegetation and activity on the water. The rural landscape offers a multitude of settings for small farms, protected wetlands, streams and rivers, and woodlots and forests. The residential and main street architecture of small towns and river cities offers much interest and contrast to the rural images. Many efforts exist to protect the countryside landscape character.

## Highlights

Not sure where to begin? Consider taking this Lansing-to-Guttenberg tour of Iowa's Great River Road.

**Lansing:** The tour begins in Lansing, home of Mount Hosmer Park. Also of interest is the Fish Farm Mound (an Indian burial site) and the nearby Our Lady of the Wayside Shrine.

**Harpers Ferry:** The next stop, Harpers Ferry, is 15 miles past Lansing. The town is built on a concentrated area of Native American mounds and was an important river town after the introduction of the steamboat. The Mississippi backwaters behind the town still attract hunters, trappers, and commercial fishers.

**Yellow River Forest State Recreation Area:** Just south of Harpers Ferry lies the Yellow River Forest State Recreation Area. This 8,000-acre forest contains some of Iowa's greatest terrain, with high scenic bluffs and cold streams. The Iowa Department of Natural Resources harvests the Yellow River Forest timber for use all over the state. The Paint Creek section of the forest houses most recreational opportunities, including camping, canoeing, snowmobiling, hunting and fishing, and hiking trails.

**Effigy Mounds National Monument:** Effigy Mounds National Monument, the next stop, is just two miles south of Yellow River Forest. Prehistoric mounds are common from the plains of the Midwest to the Atlantic seaboard, but only in this area were some of them constructed in an effigy outline of mammals, birds, or reptiles. Eastern Woodland Indian cultures built these mounds from about 500 B.C. to A.D. 1300. Natural features in the monument include forests, tallgrass prairies, wetlands and rivers.

**Marquette:** The Effigy Mounds National Monument Visitor Center located in Marquette, includes displays of local Woodland and Mississippian cultures, artifacts, and a herbarium. Riverboat casino gambling is available on the *Miss Marquette* Riverboat Casino.

**Pikes Peak State Park:** Pikes Peak State Park is five miles south of Marquette. This park boasts one of Iowa's most spectacular views across the Mississippi, on the highest bluff along the river. It was named for Zebulon Pike, who was sent in 1805 to scout placement of military posts along the river. A fort was never built on this land, and it went into private ownership. Because settlers were not able to build on this property, the peak remains as Zebulon Pike saw it 200 years ago.

**Guttenberg:** The tour terminates in Guttenberg, 15 miles south of Pikes Peak State Park. Guttenberg boasts two scenic overlooks and a mile-long landscaped park along the river. A copy of the Gutenberg Bible is on display at the local newspaper. The city offers blocks and blocks of historic buildings.

# Loess Hills Scenic Byway 

*The Lewis and Clark Trail, Oregon Trail, Mormon Trail, and California Trail all traverse the Loess Hills Scenic Byway. Some of the natural features on the byway are only found here and one other place on the planet—on the opposite side of the world, in China.*

The Loess Hills Scenic Byway weaves through a landform of windblown silt deposits along the eastern edge of the Missouri River Valley. This unique American treasure possesses natural features that are found in only two places in the world: western Iowa and the Yellow River Valley of China. Travelers are intrigued by the extraordinary landscape of prairies and forest-covered bluffs.

The *loess* (pronounced LUSS) soil deposits were initially left by glacial melt waters on the floodplain of the Missouri River. These deposits were then blown upward by strong winds. The steep, sharply ridged topography of this area was formed over thousands of years by the deposition and erosion of the windblown silt. The rugged landscape and strong local contrasts in weather and soil conditions provide refuge for a number of rare plants and animals.

As you drive the western edge of Iowa, you pass through dozens of prairie towns. Larger cities such as Council Bluffs and Sioux City offer venues of recreation, culture, and history.

You will want to enjoy the many nature areas along the way, as well. The Dorothy Pecaut Nature Center, the Hitchcock Nature Area, and the Loess Hills State Forest are just a few of the many places on the byway that are dedicated to preserving and restoring the native prairies of western Iowa.

*Soil deposits left by glacial melt waters in the floodplain of the Missouri River, wind-blown and eroded over thousands of years, formed the unique Loess Hills.*

## Intrinsic Qualities

**Archaeological:** Archaeological studies reveal places in the Loess Hills that have been continuously occupied for 12,000 years. Cultures from 12,000 years ago until recent times have been studied and cataloged in order to provide an idea of what human existence has been like in the Loess Hills. Hints of past civilizations are enough to make the Loess Hills an archaeologically significant area.

Evidence of a nomadic culture of hunters and gatherers was found in Turin (which is on the byway) in the middle of the 20th century. The site yielded some of the oldest human remains in North America. The bones date back nearly 8,000 years and provide an inside look into life during that time period. In the city of Glenwood, stop at the Mills County Historical Museum to explore a reconstructed earth lodge and artifacts that were discovered in the area. You may also want to stop at Blood Run National Historic Landmark, where there was once a center of commerce and society for the Oneota Indians. During the period of 1200 to 1700, these people constructed buildings, homes, and effigy mounds in the area. The collection of resources from Loess Hills is informative to archaeologists and visitors to the byway.

### Quick Facts

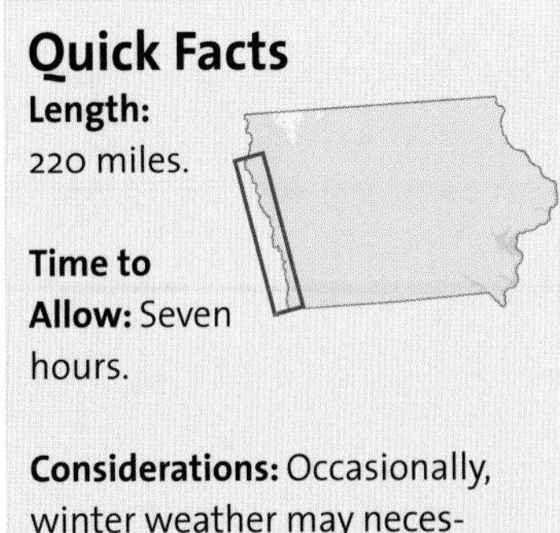

**Length:** 220 miles.

**Time to Allow:** Seven hours.

**Considerations:** Occasionally, winter weather may necessitate a slower rate of travel. Also, the gravel roads on some of the excursion loops may also become somewhat degraded during periods of high rainfall.

**Cultural:** Many of the first European settlers of the Loess Hills of Iowa came from Danish, German, or Swedish cultures that settled in the United States nearly 200 years ago to create a unique heritage. These people learned to live among each other, creating a diverse culture characteristic of the United States.

The byway culture today is a blend of the old and new living side-by-side. Urban centers such as Sioux City and Council Bluffs give way to hidden corners of agricultural hamlets.

From cities to villages, cultural events occur regularly on the byway. While some visitors may choose to attend theatrical events and tour museums, others may want to taste some of the local flavor at a farmer's market, county

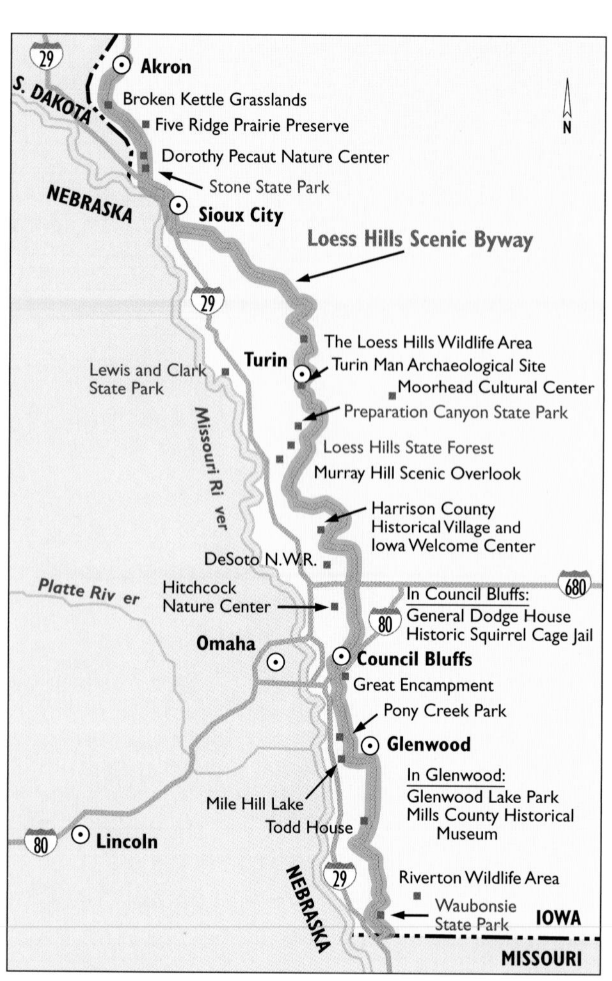


fair, or heritage celebration. When travelers come to the Loess Hills Scenic Byway, many of them take part in activities such as the rodeo or apple harvest festivals. To learn more about the people of the Loess Hills, visit the Moorhead Cultural Center, which has displays and activities that tell the story of people and culture on the byway.

**Historical:** The history of human settlement in the Loess Hills has left many stories behind in old buildings and sacred places. A home and hunting ground to some of the continent's earliest people, human habitation in the Loess Hills has been developing for many years. The people native to this land had a great respect for the Loess Hills. The land was greatly honored until the early 1800s; when explorers began to wind their way through this land in the 1700s, it was the end of an old way of life around the Loess Hills.

Historical treasures remain within the Loess Hills from the period of European settlement, as well. To see pieces of this history, follow the Lewis and Clark Trail north and south along the hills or prepare for a trip along one of the many trails that traveled to the West. The Oregon Trail, Mormon Trail, and California Trail all traversed the Loess Hills in their route westward. In fact, the Mormon Trail had a stopover point in the hills called the Great Encampment that was used during the winter months. At this point, permanent settlement in the Loess Hills became an option for pioneers crossing the plains.

The places left behind are protected as designated historic sites. You will find National Historic Landmarks, places on the National Register of Historic Places, and National Historic Trails. Museums and information centers along the byway allow visitors to study the history that surrounds the hills. Buildings such as the General Dodge House and the Woodbury County Courthouse display styles of architecture from another time. Many sites in the Loess Hills were also used on the Underground Railroad to transport escaped slaves to the north. And you will find monuments to the first explorers, including Sergeant Floyd of the Lewis and Clark expedition, who was the only explorer to die during the journey. Museums cover everything from Civil War history to prehistoric life in this part of Iowa.

**Natural:** Along the Loess Hills Scenic Byway, the rare kind of soil known as loess has been formed into hills that allow a unique kind of ecosystem to develop. This ecosystem features plants and animals that are rarely found anywhere else. Not only do the hills represent a rare kind of soil, but they are also a slice of the once vast prairie lands of the United States. The hills contain most of Iowa's remaining native prairie, making the byway a site that preserves natural history.

The area of the Loess Hills has been dubbed a National Natural Landmark in order to further promote its protection. There are also four Iowa State Preserves in the Loess Hills, including Five Ridge Prairie Preserve, where you can observe the untouched habitat of the prairie. When you drive through places such as Broken Kettle Grasslands on the byway, you may see unique plants like the ten-petal blazing star.

Because many of the creatures along the byway are threatened or endangered, you will also find wildlife refuges along the byway. The DeSoto National Wildlife Refuge is maintained by the U.S. Fish and Wildlife Service; you may be able to glimpse migratory waterfowl nesting and feeding in the area. About 500,000 snow geese stop here in the fall as they travel south. Many other species of birds and geese stop and stay at the wildlife refuge.

The Dorothy Pecaut Nature Center is an excellent place to find out more about the habitat and ecosystem of the Loess Hills. The center provides many engaging exhibits, including live animal displays and a butterfly garden. Other preserves and parks along the byway have their own information centers where visitors can find out more about a particular place or part of the Loess Hills. After you have stopped at the centers and preserves, you'll have a true appreciation for the area's unique traits.

**Recreational:** During a drive on the Loess Hills Scenic Byway, you will want to get out of the car and stretch. And there are several places along the byway that are perfect for more than just stretching. Opportunities for outdoor recreation are around every corner.

between preserves and state parks, you will have an excellent chance to view unique wildlife. DeSoto National Wildlife Refuge is a home and hotel to many waterfowl and migratory birds. Wildlife watching is a popular activity on the byway's four preserves. At Stone State Park, try camping or tour the trails in your own way. Whether you love hiking, biking, or horseback riding, all these modes of transportation are welcomed. Even snowmobilers ride through these wooded trails onto the white prairie in the wintertime. Stop at an orchard or farm to pick your own apples.

If outdoor recreation isn't a priority, try touring historical sites and monuments. Historical museums are located throughout the byway, along with many unusual buildings and historic districts. Gaming is also a popular activity on the byway at the casinos in the byway communities. Visitors will find slot machines, table games, and nightlife. In addition, the best antique shopping in Iowa is rumored to be found in the communities along the byway. Cross the river from Council Bluffs to Omaha, Nebraska, to explore this busy city full of distractions. Or simply settle down at a quiet restaurant for a bite to eat and time to look at the map.

**Scenic:** The rolling hills created by the loess soil of the Loess Hills make driving this byway a pleasant experience from any angle. The hills themselves are in the setting of the Missouri River Flood Plain. Visitors who drive the Loess Hills Scenic Byway enjoy the scenic overlooks and the sight of the hills rolling on and on. Viewing the unique formations of the Loess Hills creates a sensation of continuity as you see the prairie as a whole. Because of the unique properties of loess soil, you can enjoy "cat steps" in the hills where the loess has slumped off, creating a unified ledge. In the distance, you may catch a glimpse of the Missouri River.

*DeSoto National Wildlife Refuge preserves habitat for migratory waterfowl, and presents interpretive displays on the historic development of the Missouri River basin.*

Throughout the year, the prairie rolls through the seasons. Fall is one of the favorites of travelers who come to see the hardwood forests and prairie vegetation change to rich hues of red and orange. Pieces of an agricultural lifestyle form a patchwork of fields and historic communities along the byway. Pioneer cemeteries next to country churches tell the stories of earlier settlers who came through this place and the hardships they had to face. Travelers also experience the sights of the cities on the byway, such as Sioux City and Council Bluffs, which remain great stopping points at any time of year. Parks, museums, and historic buildings offer a taste of the byway cities.

## Highlights

When driving this byway, consider using this Loess Hills prairie tour as your itinerary.

**Broken Kettle Grasslands:** The tour starts in the Broken Kettle Grasslands, just south of Akron. The preserve constitutes the largest remaining section of the vast prairie that once covered most of Iowa. It contains some flora and fauna not found in any other part of the Loess Hills to the south or the state of Iowa, including the prairie rattlesnake and the ten-petal blazing star.

**Five Ridge Prairie Preserve:** Five Ridge Prairie Preserve, located on the Ridge Road Loop, about five miles south of Broken Kettle Grasslands, is a combination of prairie and woodlands. This is one of the best sites of unbroken prairie remnants in Iowa. You'll notice the climate changes between open grasslands, which are warmed by the sun and dry prairie breezes, and the shadowy woods, which remain cooler and more humid. Expect to find more than a few rugged hiking trails at this site.

**Dorothy Pecaut Nature Center:** The Dorothy Pecaut Nature Center is on the Stone Park Loop just south of the Highway 12 entrance to Stone State Park. The center is devoted wholly to Iowa's Loess Hills. The center has live animal displays, hands-on exhibits, a butterfly garden, and a walk-through exhibit showing life under the prairie.

**Stone State Park:** Your final stop, Stone State Park, is located on Sioux City's interpretive northwest side. It has 1,069 acres of prairie-topped ridges and dense woodlands. Dakota Point and Elk Point provide scenic overlooks of Nebraska, South Dakota, and Iowa. The multiuse trails handle hikers, bicyclists, horseback riders, and snowmobilers. Campsites with showers are available. This park is a site on the Lewis and Clark National Historic Trail.

# GREAT RIVER ROAD 

*The Illinois section of the Great River Road gives an overview of the complete timeline of American history. From the Underground Railroad to the westward movement of the Mormons, this section of the byway tells it all.*

PART OF A MULTISTATE BYWAY; SEE ALSO IOWA, MINNESOTA, AND WISCONSIN.

Experiencing the Mississippi River for the first time is a memory few can forget. The awe that many people feel toward this river may come from the power of a flood or the beauty of a golden sunset that reflects off the still winter waters, turning graceful steel bridges into shimmering lines of color.

Looking out over the river, it is almost impossible to comprehend the complex layers of history that have been acted out along its banks. From the large communities of the Hopewell Indian culture (the most complex society in North America that existed from approximately A.D. 700 to 1400) and early French colonial settlements and fortifications to the frightened, cautious, and optimistic slaves who sought freedom on the Underground Railroad, this corridor has played a role in many of this continent's most dramatic hours. Today, 15 percent of the nation's shipping passes through the river's complex system of locks and dams, yet such commercial activity occurs under the spreading wings of the newly thriving American bald eagle.

It is from the Great River Road that most visitors and residents understand and define their relationship with the Mississippi. It is from this road that the historic sites and cultural artifacts of the area can be accessed, from Native American mounds to the Mormon (Church of Jesus Christ of Latter-Day Saints) temple. The beautiful Mississippi bluffs tower over the byway as permanent sentinels for the great river. Whether directly along the banks of the river or winding through the vast flood plain miles from the water, the Great River Road links resources, people, and history.

## Quick Facts

**Length:** 557 miles.

**Time to Allow:** Four or five days.

**Considerations:** Generally, the entire route of Illinois' portion of the Great River Road is within the 100-year flood plain. While flooding does not occur regularly, roads are closed and detours are marked when flooded.

## Intrinsic Qualities

**Archaeological:** A little-known treasure trove of archaeological sites, the Illinois Great River Road has several places for visitors to discover pieces of the past. Among the archaeological qualities that can be found along this road are burial mounds of Native Americans who lived along the river. The mounds, many of which were built more than 2,000 years ago, are representative of Native American religious practices and reverence for their ancestors. Cahokia Mounds State Historic Site near East St. Louis and Collinsville has been designated as a United Nations World Heritage Site. Among the most fascinating of the archaeological structures on the Great River Road is Monk's Mound, a 100-foot-tall, four-tiered platform that took 300 years to build.

In addition to Native American sites, many villages on the byway offer a taste of archaeology in their preservation of the not-so-distant past. Many villages, such as Maeystown, Galena, and Nauvoo, are listed on the National Register of Historic Places. These villages often re-create the lifestyles of the first settlers along the Great River Road for visitors who want to know more about the nation's past. With both Native American heritage sites and historic sites of the earliest European settlers, the Great River Road offers opportunities for you to discover America's archaeology all along the way.

*This Italianate home was a gift to the Ulysses S. Grant family by a group of Galena citizens upon the General's triumphant return from the Civil War.*

**Cultural:** Some of the first people to settle along the banks of the Mississippi River were Native Americans. These nations were embedded in a culture that held the utmost respect for nature and the resources of the land. Their inextricable connection to the land can be seen in the burial mounds they left behind, as well as in museums and monuments.

Since the habitation of the first cultures in the area, several other cultures have passed through the Illinois Great River Road area, and some have stayed permanently. During the 1800s, the now-historic communities along the Great River Road were settled for reasons that ranged from gold rushes to religious freedom. The people who live in these communities maintain a distinct place on the byway, with their styles of architecture and inventiveness. Today, the culture of the Great River Road embodies the relaxed hometown pace. The towns and villages along the byway offer you a change of scenery and a chance to slow down. These towns are often small and full of rich historical detail that influences cultures even today.

**Historical:** As an area that has enraptured American Indians, explorers, and settlers, the Illinois Great River Road holds pieces of the past that are intriguing to today's visitors. Since 1938, the road has been protected and enhanced in order to preserve its scenic and historical qualities. The heritage of the native nations of the Sauk and Fox Indians remains prevalent in many places along the byway.

You can find historic architecture in several of the towns along the road: Nauvoo, Quincy, Alton, Belleville, and Cairo allow you to experience the Great River Road as the settlers of nearly 200 years ago did. These cities all have their share of historic places and buildings that are full of pioneer stories and Civil War tales. As a passage on the Underground Railroad, the river represents a piece of African-American history, as well. The river itself holds a story of steamboats chugging up the river. It represents the ingenuity of inventors and engineers in the earliest days of travel. The river is the lifeblood of the area that has drawn so many people to its shores.

**Natural:** Among the bluffs and rolling hills of the Illinois Great River Road area, you can observe wildlife and nature at its fullest. The lands surrounding the byway are home to white-tailed deer, wild turkeys, ducks, and geese. Supported by the rich natural resources that abound in the river area, these creatures can be seen throughout the drive. During the fall, the trees along the byway exhibit a beautiful spectrum of color, providing a fringe of brightness along the river. By the time winter sets in, there is a new visitor to the Great River Road. The American bald eagle arrives in late November, and by late December, hundreds of these magnificent birds are roosting in the rocky walls of the bluffs overlooking the river. Travelers come from miles around to watch the eagles dive and soar in the air above the bluffs.

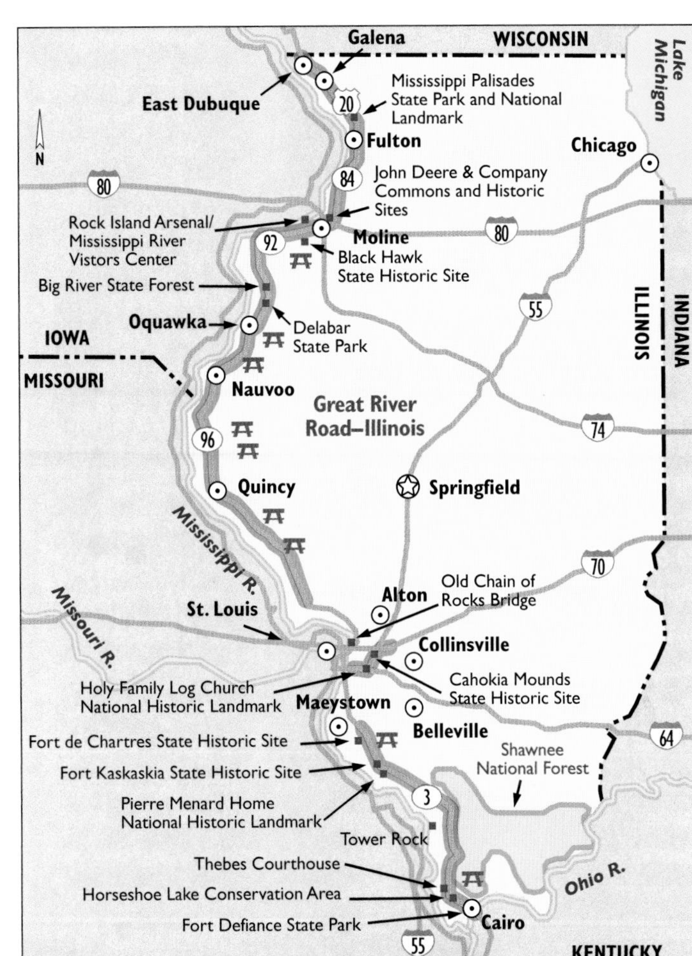


All along the banks and bluffs of the river, you will enjoy many interesting sights. At one point on the Illinois Great River Road, you will see a formation known as Tower Rock. This formation is an isolated mass of limestone that divides the river in half. In the areas surrounding the river, you'll also find lakes, wetlands, and swamps that provide their own style of natural beauty.

**Recreational:** On and around the river, you have places to go and different ways to get there. Hikers and bikers find riverside trails attractive, while other travelers may prefer to enjoy a pleasant afternoon on a riverboat. Ferries, canoes, and even old-fashioned steamboats give you a closer view of the greatest river in the nation. To see more of the communities on the byway, you may enjoy a trolley tour or a park area, as well as museums and historical buildings. Museums and monuments to the past are sprinkled along the road to give you a sense of what came before on the Great River Road.

Other forms of fun can be found on the byway, too. More than 75 golf courses help you track your progress along the byway by greens. Travelers who would like to test their luck can try a riverboat casino. Communities all along the byway offer numerous stops for antique shoppers who are looking for a piece of Illinois' past to take home with them, and if antiques aren't enough, plenty of novelty shops and gift shops abound. For the hungry traveler, many restaurants along the byway are sure to suit your fancy. Entertainment is an element of the byway's recreational offerings, too. Many towns host musicals, dinner shows, and old-fashioned theater experiences.

Chances to enjoy the outdoors along the Great River Road come often. In addition to the Shawnee National Forest, 29 state recreation and/or conservation areas are available along the route of the Great River Road. The Mississippi Palisades State Park and National Landmark offers phenomenal views to and from the bluffs (palisades) along the Mississippi River. The facilities for tent and trailer camping, fishing, cross-country skiing, and ice fishing are top notch.

The Big River State Forest is a 2,900-acre facility dedicated to demonstrating sound forestry practices. Firebreaks and a fire tower afford breathtaking views and hikes. Nearby, camping, hiking, and river and lake fishing are available at Delabar State Park. In the south, Horseshoe Lake Conservation Area is one of the loveliest places to hike, camp, hunt, and boat. Horseshoe Lake is a quiet, shallow lake lined with cypress and tupelo gum and wild lotus. You can find places for bird-watching and exploring wetlands, and canoeing along the river is a popular recreational pursuit all along the byway.

**Scenic:** The Mississippi River itself is a natural phenomenon that few visitors will forget. This body of moving water presents a picture of the forces of nature at work with their surroundings. Perhaps one of the prettiest sights you will see along the byway is the great waters of the Mississippi River flanked by the glacier-carved bluffs at the river's edge. Along the byway, observe scenic vistas and bluffs that overlook the river: Erosion from glacial movement has left unique formations of rock in the riverside topography. Feast your eyes on the rich architecture that has been a part of this area's history. From grand courthouses to historic bridges, sights all along the byway complement the natural beauty of the Great River Road. In the summer, the fields along the byway are adorned with wildflowers. During the fall, several communities host festivals celebrating the season, and the drive along the byway becomes even more scenic with every leaf that dons its fall color. And keep in mind that a sunset on the Mississippi River is a sight not to be missed.

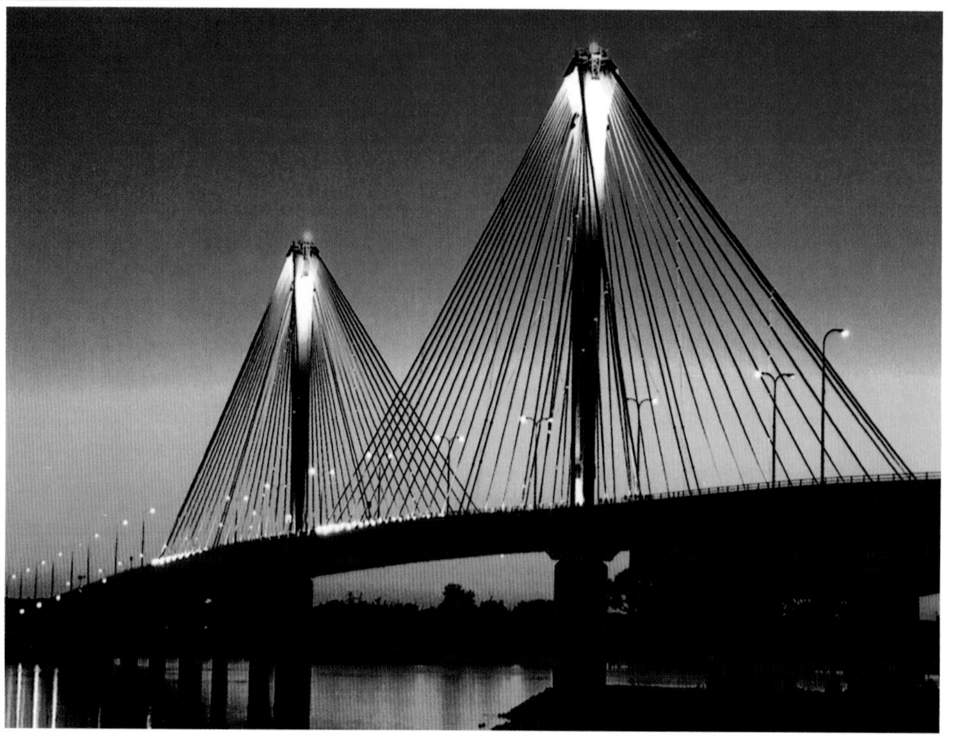

*The 4,500-foot-cable Clark Bridge connects Alton, Illinois, with St. Louis, Missouri.*

## Highlights

When traveling the Moline-to-Nauvoo section of the Illinois Great River Road, consider using the following itinerary.

**Moline:** Both the past and present of the world-famous John Deere & Company operations are centered in Moline, where you begin your tour. At the John Deere & Company Commons, catch historic trolleys to other Deere sites, tour the John Deere Pavilion with interactive displays of historic and modern farm equipment, and visit the John Deere Store. The Deere Administrative Center, Deere corporate headquarters, lies on the outskirts of Moline. This building, designed by Eero Saarinen, and grounds are widely regarded as masterworks of architecture and landscape architecture. The Deere-Wiman House and Butterworth Center are mansions built in the late 1800s by Charles Deere. Guided tours of the homes and gardens are available.

**Rock Island Arsenal:** Rock Island Arsenal lies on spectacular Rock Island in the Mississippi River directly in front of the John Deere & Company Commons. Visitors to the island can visit Historic Fort Armstrong (1816–1817), the Rock Island Arsenal Museum (with exhibits of military equipment and small firearms), and other historic structures. The Rock Island Arsenal is the largest weapons manufacturing arsenal in the country. Located next to Lock and Dam 15, the largest roller dam in the world, the U.S. Army Corps of Engineers

*Tower Rock, blanketed by stands of upland forest, is a small limestone island carved by the powerful forces of the Mississippi River.*

Mississippi River Visitors Center features an observation deck for towboats and birds. The visitors center has displays about Upper Mississippi geography, ecology, and the lock-and-dam system. It is also a designated Great River Road interpretive center.

**Black Hawk State Historic Site:** Two miles south of Rock Island lies the next stop on the tour, Black Hawk State Historic Site—a wooded, steeply rolling 208-acre tract. American Indians and 19th-century settlers made their homes here, but the area is most closely identified with the Sauk nation and the warrior-leader whose name it bears—Black Hawk. The site, which is also noted for its many natural features, is managed by the Illinois Historic Preservation Agency. The Hauberg Indian Museum, located in the lodge constructed by the Civilian Conservation Corps, interprets the culture of the Sauk and the Mesquackie. Nearly 175 species of birds and 30 species of wildflowers, as well as a prairie restoration, can be observed here. Dickson Pioneer Cemetery is where many early settlers are buried. Picnicking and hiking are also available.

**Big River State Forest:** Following the byway along the Mississippi River for another 50 miles, you arrive at the 2,900-acre Big River State Forest. The forest lies in Henderson County, six miles north of Oquawka, where gas and food are available. The area's oldest pine plantation, the Milroy Plantation, with towering red, white, and jack pines lies within. The forest is a remnant of a vast prairie woodland border area that once covered much of Illinois. Two endangered plants, penstemon and Patterson's bindweed, are found here. A prominent landmark in the forest is its fire tower, located at the headquarters area and accessible to the public at nonemergency times. Sixty miles of firebreaks interlace Big River State Forest, which are used by hikers, horseback riders, and snowmobilers. Tent, trailer, and equestrian camping sites, boat launch, picnic areas, hunting, stables, and scenic drives are available.

**Delabar State Park:** Located on the Mississippi River about $4\frac{1}{2}$ miles south of Big River State Forest and $1\frac{1}{2}$ miles north of Oquawka, the 89-acre Delabar State Park offers quality outdoor experiences for anglers, hikers, campers, and picnickers. More than 50 species of birds have been sighted in the park, making it a destination for bird-watching, too. Picnic areas, playground facilities, tent and trailer camping, trailer dumping, hiking trails, river and lake fishing, boat launching, ice fishing, and ice skating are available in the area.

**Nauvoo:** This tour of a short section of the byway terminates about 45 miles south of Delabar State Park in Nauvoo. The town is located at a picturesque bend in the river at Hancock County. Nauvoo was settled by Joseph Smith and members of the Church of Jesus Christ of Latter-Day Saints (LDS) and served as the religious, governmental, and cultural center of the church from 1839 until Joseph Smith's death in 1844. Two visitor centers interpret the remaining town sites. The LDS Visitor Center features costumed hosts, interpretive displays, a sculpture garden, and tours of 25 Nauvoo town sites. The Joseph Smith Visitor Center, run by the Reorganized Church of Jesus Christ of Latter-Day Saints (RLDS), features displays, an informative video, and access to the grave site and homes of Joseph Smith and family. In late 1999, the LDS church began rebuilding the historic limestone temple destroyed in the late 19th century. Nearby Nauvoo State Park features recreational opportunities. The wine and cheese traditions of the French Icarians, who came to Nauvoo after the LDS church, are still pursued.

# Historic National Road

*Along the Historic National Road visitors will have a chance to view bridges that are engineering marvels. But be sure to also look for Monk's Mound, a Native American engineering marvel. It took 300 years to build and is now a United Nations World Heritage Site.*

Part of a multistate byway; see also Indiana, Maryland, Ohio, Pennsylvania, and West Virginia.

The route of the Historic National Road is a road of history. Nineteenth-century river transportation and commerce, along with historic cemeteries, tell of the struggles of the early settlers on the western frontier. County fairs and main street storefronts speak of small towns where you can still find soda fountains, one-room schools, and old hotels.

Small and large museums, a National Register Historic District, and National Register Historic Sites are found all along the byway. Prehistoric Native American life is evident here, as well, along with giant earthwork mounds that took 300 years to build. The atmosphere of old-fashioned travel is stored in the little shops and lodgings in towns along the way. The western end of the byway takes you to Eads Bridge and the gateway to the West.

## Quick Facts

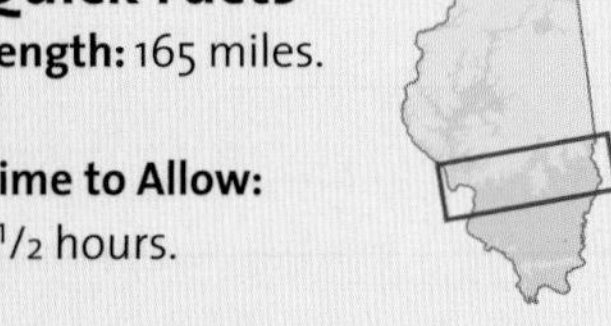

**Length:** 165 miles.

**Time to Allow:** 3½ hours.

**Considerations:** High season is during the fall. Some delays may be experienced during severe weather, and seasonal storms may increase driving times.

## Intrinsic Qualities

**Archaeological:** The Cahokia Mounds State Historic Site bisects the Historic National Road. This remarkable World Heritage Archaeological Site consists of the largest mound buildings built by Native Americans on the North American continent. As you pass the site while driving the byway, you see Monk's Mound rising out of the ground on the north side of the byway, covering 14 acres and rising 100 feet into the air. You may also notice a large circle of wooden posts, known as Woodhenge, next to the road. The visitor center is the pride of the Illinois Historic Preservation Agency and provides more information on the site and the people who created it.

*Monk's Mound at Cahokia Mounds State Historic Site is the largest earthen mound built by Native Americans on the North American continent.*

**Historical:** In 1806, Congress appropriated funds to construct a National Road that would run westward from Cumberland, Maryland, to the Mississippi River. The Illinois section was surveyed in 1828 by Joseph Schriver, and construction was started in 1831. The section to Vandalia was completed in 1836. However, the western section was never funded due to high costs and waning interest in road building. With the coming of the Terre Haute–Vandalia–St. Louis Railroad that paralleled the road, the National Road fell into disrepair, only to be resurrected in the early 1920s when it was hard surfaced and designated U.S. 40. Today, most of the original alignment of the 1828 surveyed road is still in place and is in public hands.

On the eastern end of the byway is Marshall, home to Illinois' oldest continuously operating hotel. Also on the eastern end is the village of Greenup, with its unique business section decorated with original overhanging porches. This village was designated as a Historic Business District on the National Register of Historic Places. In the central section is Vandalia, the second capital of Illinois. The Capitol, in which Abraham Lincoln passed his test to practice law, is now a State Historic Site and sits on the Historic National Road.

**Natural:** The Historic National Road in Illinois is dominated at each end of the byway by rivers. The Wabash River is on the east end, and the mighty Mississippi River lies on the west end. Rivers and lakes are scattered throughout the middle area, with flat prairies and hilly landscapes combining to create many natural features along the way. Different species of wildlife make their homes along the route, and fish are plentiful in the many lakes and rivers.

The topography along ne byway was created by laciers that advanced and etreated over the land uring the Pleistocene eriod, leaving behind noraines and glacial eposits that created egions of undulating ndscape in some areas nd flat prairies in other reas. The landscape of the yway is defined by three najor areas: the Embar-ns River Basin on the east ide, the Wabash River asin in the central area, nd the Sinkhole Plain on the west ide (which is contained in the Aississippi River Basin).

The Mississippi River is the hird-largest river in the world. rom flooding to fertile land, the ver has shaped the lives of Native mericans, pioneers, settlers, and urrent residents of the many ties that dot the banks of the ver. More than 400 species of vildlife—including ancient lin-ages of fish—live in and near the Aississippi River.

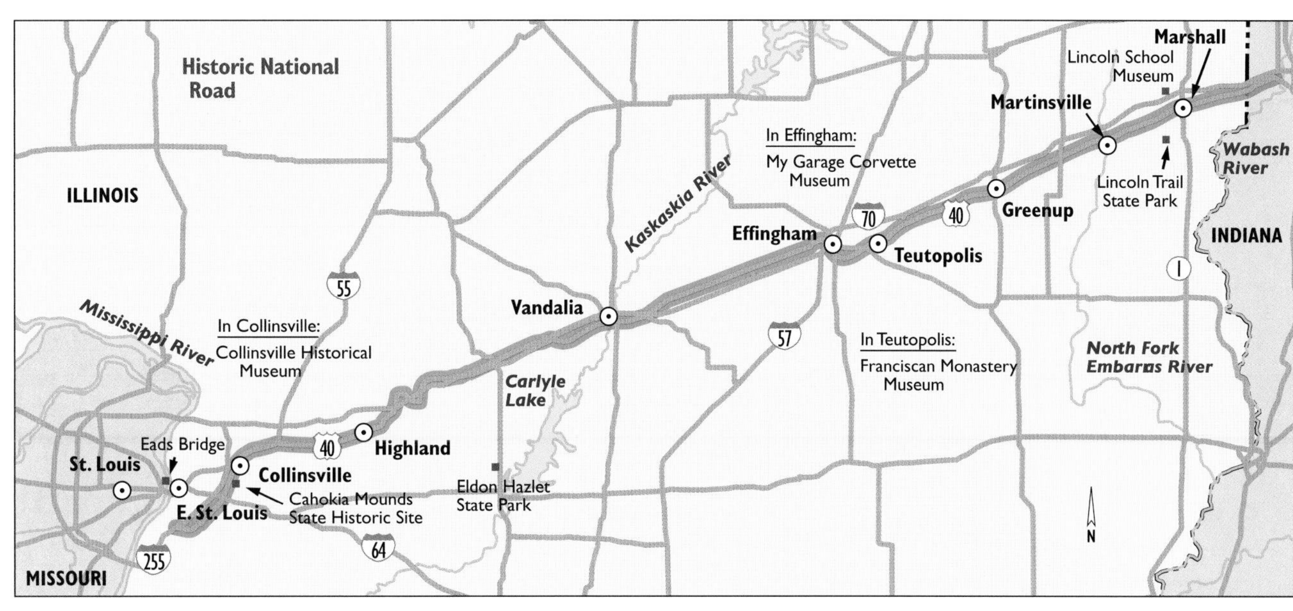


ecreational: The byway offers nany recreational opportunities. ou can bike or hike on the vari-us trails along the way. Numer-us state parks allow you to enjoy he natural characteristics of the yway; many of the towns have arks and recreational facilities.

At Lincoln Trail State Park, you an travel the route Abraham Lin-oln took from Kentucky to Illinois. his park is on part of that route, nd today, it is a place where you can enjoy hiking, fishing, boating, or camping. Summer is not the only time to enjoy this area, how-ever; wintertime sports include ice fishing, ice skating, and cross-country skiing.

Many lakes, rivers, and streams provide recreational opportunities. Carlyle Lake is a 26,000-acre mul-tipurpose lake known for its great fishing and waterfowl hunting. At Eldon Hazlet State Park, controlled pheasant hunting is available, and bird-watching is also a popular activity. Carlyle Lake is well known among sailors, and you can rent a houseboat at the park. Camping and golf courses are available here, as well.

**Scenic:** The landscape of the Historic National Road in Illinois offers many scenic views to the byway traveler. The route is dotted with towns and rural communi-ties, interspersed with rural lands and farms. The large metropolitan area of the western edge of the byway, in Collinsville and East St. Louis, provides a different kind of scene. From historic buildings and bridges to gently rolling hills, this byway exemplifies a scenic drive.

In the east, the rolling hills and interspersed forests provide a dif-ferent view than the flat, unbroken views presented on the western edge of the byway. In between, cultivated fields, distant barns, farmhouses, and grazing livestock all speak of the nature of the land.

## Highlights

The Illinois section of the Historic National Road begins in Martins-ville and goes to Collinsville.

**Lincoln School Museum:** This quality museum is located near Martinsville. The building itself was built in 1888, and the school is open to groups for an interpreta-tion of early pioneer days.

**Franciscan Monastery Museum:** Dating to 1858, this historic mon-astery has a wonderful museum that displays artifacts from early settlers, as well as the Franciscan Fathers. Visitors can view pioneer items such as toys and kitchen utensils, and religious items such as Bibles and vestments. There are also antique legal documents on display, such as marriage licenses. The monastery is located about five miles east of Effing-ham in Teutopolis.

**My Garage Corvette Museum:** This museum, located in Effing-ham, about 30 miles west of Martinsville, is a must for auto-mobile lovers. On display are vintage Corvettes from the 1950s and 1960s.

**Collinsville Historical Museum:** Located about 90 miles west of Effingham in Collinsville, this museum offers visitors a unique glance into the region's residents all the way back to John Cook, the first settler in 1810. Many interest-ing artifacts are on display, includ-ing a variety of Civil War objects and miners' tools.

# Lincoln Highway 

*Transportation might not be the same today without the Lincoln Highway. It was here where they had the idea of paving several one-mile stretches of the formerly dirt roads to create "seedling miles" in an effort to foster a public desire for good roads, thus changing transportation history.*

This historic byway follows the original alignment of the Lincoln Highway, the first paved transcontinental highway in the United States. The 179-mile route crosses the width of northern Illinois, starting in Lynwood on the Indiana border. The route ends in Fulton at the Iowa border. The Illinois portion of the highway, located near the center of the 3,389-mile transcontinental route, was the site of the first seedling mile of paved roadway constructed to demonstrate the superiority of pavement over dirt roads. The Lincoln Highway was also the first instance in which directional signs and urban bypasses were used.

## Intrinsic Qualities

**Cultural:** The culture of the Lincoln Highway centers around its communities, which share a pride in being part of the history and future of transportation. In most of the Lincoln Highway communities, you find at least one defining characteristic. In Dixon, it is the Victory Arch that spans the highway; in Chicago Heights, it is the Arche Fountain commemorating Abraham Lincoln; in Batavia, it is the unique architecture.

**Historical:** In 1912, a core group of automobile industrialists and enthusiasts established an organization to promote the development of "good roads" and conceived a route for a paved, transcontinental road. This group sought to secure private funding to build a road that would serve the needs of industry, particularly the automobile industry. The first seedling mile was completed in Malta, Illinois, just west of DeKalb, in October 1914. Four more seedling miles were constructed in 1915. The stark contrast between these smooth patches of pavement and the bumpy or muddy roads leading up to them created a groundswell of public opinion in favor of good roads.

This clamor for action was directed at local, state, and federal officials and resulted in the passage of the Federal Aid Road Act of 1916, which authorized and appropriated $75 million for the construction of what were called post roads. This amount was to be matched by the states seeking to build the roads, thus starting the practice of federal-state grant matching for road construction. Many parts of the road were constructed by volunteer labor, such as the Mooseheart segment, which was built by area businesspeople, manual laborers, and others to demonstrate their support of their community and of local businesses.

Shortly thereafter, America became involved in World War I, shifting national attention onto the war effort and away from the road-building effort. However, interest in good roads resumed in earnest shortly after the war ended in November 1918. In 1919, Lincoln Highway Association leader Harry Ostermann persuaded the War Department to conduct a transcontinental motor convoy trip from the East Coast to San Francisco on the marked route of the Lincoln Highway. A 69 vehicle convoy combining public and private vehicles took off from the White House on July 7, 1919. The convoy, primarily following the Lincoln Highway route, finally arrived in San Francisco, but not after considerable difficulty on the dirt roads traveled en route. The seedling miles of concrete made a

*An arched footbridge adds to the ambience at the Fabyan Japanese Tea Garden, one of the attractions of Fabyan Forest Preserve.*

### Quick Facts

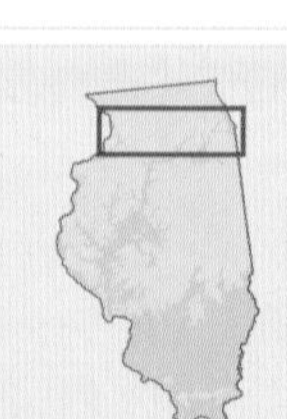

**Length:** 179 miles.

**Time to Allow:** Five to six hours.

**Considerations:** The best time to drive this route is early summer. This byway is long and may be difficult to follow as it winds its way through and around the Illinois interstate system and countryside. To experience all that the Lincoln Highway has to offer, you may want to spend two days driving the route.

trong impression. Among those articipating in the convoy was t. Colonel Dwight D. Eisenhower, who much later applied his expe-iences on the Lincoln Highway, long with his experiences with World War II and the German utobahn system, to conceive of n interstate road system to aid he movement of troops, goods, nd people across the country.

Various aspects of the Lincoln Highway's early development predated and predicted some of he technical and fundamental lements of current U.S. trans-portation policy. They included directional signage, a system of concrete markers designed to ssist travelers determining their ocation along a given roadway. Never before had a consistent road ignage system been employed. Another new concept was the urban bypass: The Lincoln Highway was purposely routed 25–30 miles outh and west of Chicago to avoid congestion and time delays.

Since 1935, much of the original Lincoln Highway has been paved over, bypassed, or con-verted to numbered U.S., state, and county highways or municipal streets. Very few of the 1928 cement markers still exist. How-ever, the name Lincoln is still attached to much of the route in the form of roadway and street names, local Lincoln businesses and brochures, articles, and artifacts preserved in museums and historical societies along the route.

**Recreational:** From the rolling hills of western Illinois and the Mississippi River Valley to the sights and sounds of the Chicago metropolitan area, the Lincoln Highway includes an impressive collection of diverse recreational opportunities. Near Franklin Grove, stop at Franklin Creek State Natural Area to enjoy a picnic by the edge of Franklin Creek. Hiking, skiing, horseback riding, and snowmobiling trails are available there. As you near Chicago, you'll find increased shopping opportunities in places such as Chicago Heights and Joliet. In Geneva, tour the Japanese Gardens or go biking on the Riverwalk. While touring each community, you are sure to come across several enticing activities.

**Scenic:** Although the scenic qualities of the Lincoln Highway may differ from those of other byways, the highway is scenic nonetheless. Several architectural treats await you. Often, this architecture is combined with elements of nature for a scenic effect. Many of the most interesting sites on the byway can be seen from the car, but you will likely want to get out and try some of the biking trails or river walks.

## Highlights

This tour begins north of Aurora and travels west across the state. If you wish to take the tour traveling east, read this list from the bottom and work your way up.

**Mooseheart:** Just north of Aurora on Illinois Route 31, you'll find Mooseheart. This lodge is an important piece of history for the Lincoln Highway because members of the Moose Lodge raised $12,000 to pay for the initial paving of the Lincoln Highway. Members of the lodge from all over the country then traveled to Illinois and helped grade the road using picks and shovels. In appreciation for the efforts of the members of the lodge, the state later paved an extra ten-foot strip, which is still visible today, in front of Mooseheart.

**DeKalb Memorial Park:** Traveling west from Mooseheart on State Route 60, you come to the city of DeKalb. The Memorial Park in DeKalb is famous for its memorial clock called Soldiers and Sailors, which was originally dedicated in 1921. The clock was restored completely in 1996, and in 1999, a community mural was painted on the side of the old Chronicle building, located behind the park.

**First Seedling Mile:** Cement companies donated the cement to pave seedling miles on the highway. The first seedling mile in the country is located west of Malta on State Route 38.

**Railroad Park:** Located in Rochelle, west of Malta, is Railroad Park, one of two X rail crossings in the country. People come from all over the world to watch the rail traffic of the Union Pacific and the Burlington Northern Santa Fe Railroads, the two major rail carriers in the eastern United States.

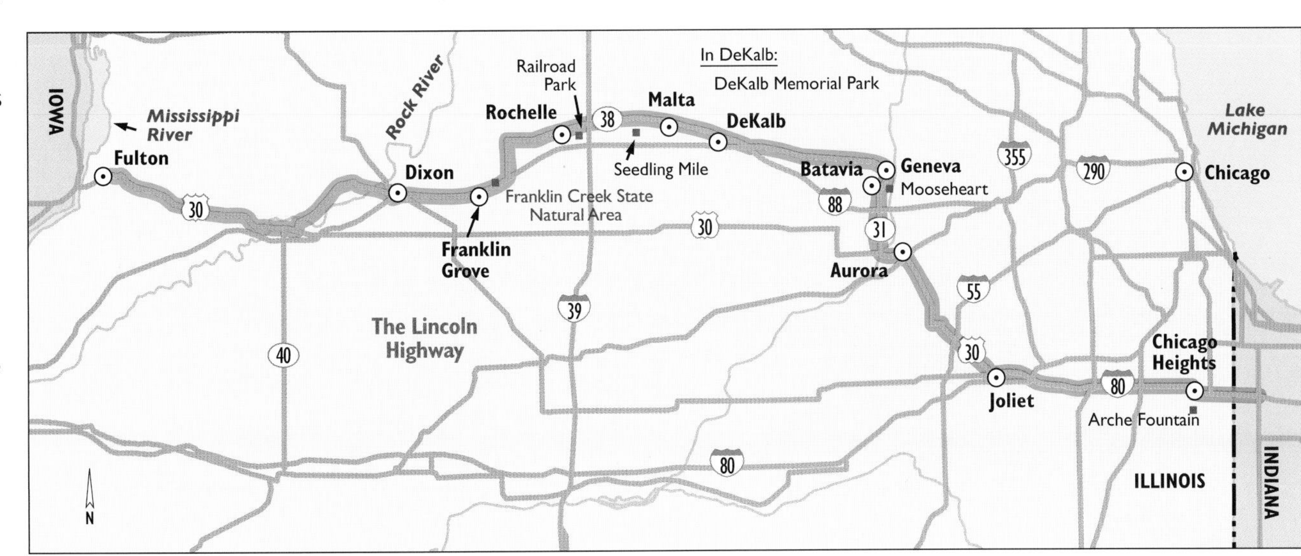

# Meeting of the Great Rivers Scenic Route 

*With the confluence of three major rivers, there is an abundance of activity. Visitors sample peaceful solitude amidst sublime natural features, abundant water recreation, and historical and cultural attractions in genuine river towns that have been gateways for pioneers of all kinds.*

Within a 25-mile expanse, the Mississippi, Missouri, and Illinois Rivers meet to form a 35,000-acre floodplain. This confluence is the backdrop for the Meeting of the Great Rivers Scenic Route. The river systems have been vital transportation routes as long as there has been human habitation, moving people and goods to world markets.

The Meeting of the Great Rivers Scenic Route offers a dramatic composite of the Mississippi River. Beneath white cliffs, the byway runs next to the Mississippi, beginning in an industrial, urban setting and changing to a scenic, natural area. As though moving back through time, expanses of pastoral countryside and stone houses are reminders of a time long ago. Artifacts of the earliest aboriginal people in America reside here, and the byway's rich historical and archaeological qualities unfold. Little towns along the byway seem almost forgotten by time, giving travelers a look at historic architecture and small-town life along the Mississippi River.

*The Pere Marquette Lodge was built in the 1930s and expanded in recent years.*

## Intrinsic Qualities

**Archaeological:** Despite present-day development, archaeological remains are largely intact along the Meeting of the Great Rivers Scenic Route. For example, the Koster Site, located south of Eldred, is world renowned because of the evidence found that shows that humans lived on the site 8,000 years ago. Structures dating back to 4200 B.C. are considered to be the oldest such habitations found in North America, and villages flourished here circa 6000 B.C., 5000 B.C., and 3300 B.C. More than 800 archaeological sites have been inventoried along the route. Experts believe that the Mississippi and Illinois Rivers, known as the Nile of North America, nourished the development of complex and sophisticated Native American cultures. So complete are cultural records that archaeologists term the area "the crossroads of prehistoric America."

**Cultural:** Visitors discover real river towns along this byway. To celebrate each unique aspect of their culture, many of the communities on the byway have established their own museums. In addition, the region displays an appreciation of high culture through orchestras, theaters, galleries, institutions of higher learning, and many diverse festivals that celebrate the arts. Throughout the year, more than 50 festivals and fairs celebrate the history, art, music, and crafts of this region.

**Historical:** The Mississippi River is internationally famous. Father Jacques Marquette and Louis Jolliet first made their expedition down the Mississippi in 1673. Later, when the Illinois Territory was formed, the Missouri River was the gateway to the unexplored West, and the Illinois River led to the Great Lakes and was also a connection to the East. Early American explorers began in the confluence area. Lewis and Clark, for example, embarked from Fort Dubois near the mouth of the Missouri. Eventually, towns were settled on the shores of the rivers, providing a secure way for travel and commerce using the rivers. The buildings that composed these towns still stand, many of them dating to the early 1800s.

As the nation grew and developed, many of the towns along the

### Quick Facts

**Length:** 57 miles.

**Time to Allow:** Two hours.

**Considerations:** One of the only gas stations along the entire byway is located in Grafton. Roads can be closed during the spring due to flooding and during the winter due to ice. When this happens, alternate routes are provided. Also, ferries cannot operate when the river freezes. During these times, use the Joe Paige Bridge at Hardin to connect with Kampsville in Calhoun County.

byway were growing and developing, as well. Although many of the towns that stand today seem to be nestled somewhere in history, some of the byway's communities have been at the edge of new ideas. During pre-Civil War times, the Underground Railroad ran through this area, bringing escaped slaves to the safety of the north. Confederate prison ruins found on the byway are another testament to this corner of Illinois' involvement in the Civil War.

By the late 19th century, Mark Twain's Mississippi River stories had inspired an ideal of Mississippi legends, history, and culture in the minds of Americans. Meanwhile, as the river and its uses were also evolving, paddleboats gave way to barges and tows. River traffic increased as industries grew, and Lock and Dam 26 was built. Today, historic 18th-century river towns, islands, bars, points, and bends create beautiful scenery beneath limestone bluffs, which are covered by forests that extend nearly 20,000 acres. Historical and cul-tural features in the 50-mile corri-dor have received national recognition, with seven sites presently registered on the National Register of Historic Places.

**Natural:** Nature abounds along the Meeting of the Great Rivers Scenic Route. The wetlands from three different waterways, the rock bluffs, and the stately trees all harbor native creatures and provide lovely views along the byway. The palisade cliffs and towering bluffs provide a characteristic drive along the riverside where visitors can see the results of this great channel of water carving its way through post-glacial terrain. You may want to enjoy the nature of the byway from the car, look for hikes along the way, or get out and explore a wildlife refuge.

Located right in the middle of the United States is Piasa country, a bird-watcher's heaven. Migratory flyways using the Mississippi, Illinois, and Missouri Rivers converge within a 25-mile zone from Alton to Grafton. This offers amazing opportunities to see many species of birds that pass through this chokepoint region, from the American bald eagle to the white pelican. Deer, otters, and beavers are present, as well as raccoons, opossums, and squirrels. Fishing enthusiasts will discover many species in the local waters.

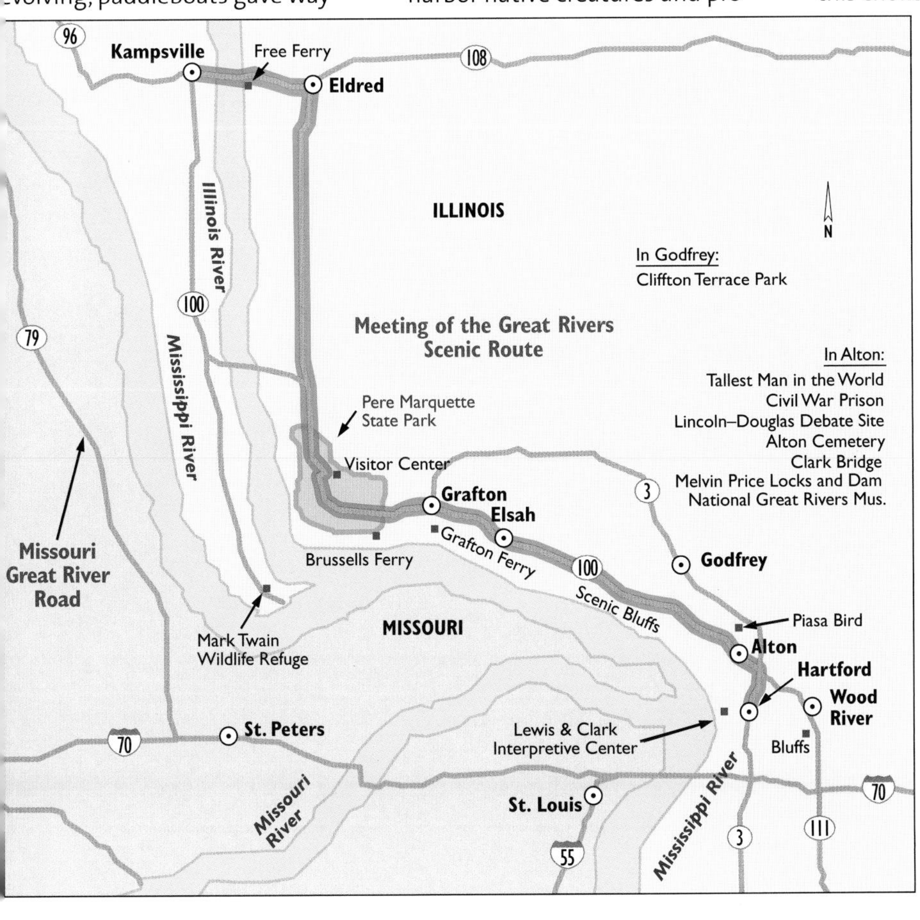


Many natural points of interest dot this byway. For example, Pere Marquette State Park is one of Illinois' largest state parks. It is nestled along the banks of the Illinois River on the byway near Grafton. Here, a myriad of trails take you within the wild forests and up to spectacular viewing areas along the bluff line above.

The Riverlands Environmental Demonstration Area is another natural point of interest. Located near Alton, this U.S. Army Corps of Engineers site provides a fertile wetland that attracts all types of wildlife. Early-morning travelers frequently see wildlife making their way to the river. The Mark Twain Wildlife Refuge is located near Pere Marquette State Park and is often open to the public. The preserve offers sanctuary to rare and endangered migratory birds on their long flights up and down the Mississippi and Illinois Rivers.

All the stunning views that can be enjoyed from a vehicle can also be enjoyed on foot or by bike. The Sam Vadalabene Trail, a bicycle and walking trail, winds more than 25 miles from Alton to Pere Marquette State Park on the byway, making this a byway that encourages and accommodates hikers and bikers.

**Recreational:** After you have seen the sights on the Meeting of the Great Rivers Scenic Route, you may decide to enjoy the surroundings on a closer level. Trails and paths along the byway offer excitement for hikers and bikers. Also, forests that line the roadsides are perfect places for camping, picnicking, or simply enjoying the peaceful solitude that nature affords. Be sure to tour the historic districts of the byway communities and stop at the museums and visitor centers that provide a closer look at the byway and its characteristics.

There is always fun to be found on the Mississippi River. Visitors enjoy the water in every way, from parasailing to jet skiing. Sailboats and riverboats keep the river alive with movement year-round. During the summer, families stop at one of the two water parks along the byway or travel on one of the four free river ferries located in the area. The Meeting of the Great Rivers Scenic Route is one of the most accommodating to bikers, with a bicycle path that goes directly along the byway.

Shopping for crafts and antiques in the historic riverside towns along the byway is a pleasant pastime, and golfers enjoy the ten courses in the region. There's a theater in Wood River and an amphitheater in Grafton for musical productions, stage productions, and other kinds of entertainment. It is hard to miss the Alton Belle Riverboat Casino on a leisurely cruise down the river. In addition to the attractions along the byway, festivals, fairs, and events are always occurring in its communities.



**Scenic:** The Mississippi River is like a chameleon. Depending on weather conditions, sun angles, and the color of the sky, the waters can turn from serene pale blue to dark navy to muddy brown. Insiders' favorite time for viewing the river is early in the morning as the sun is rising. Often, the river is glasslike, creating a mirror of the sky above. The blue is sweet and clear, and the reflections of the bluffs and trees are remarkable. Majestic bluffs tower above the byway, creating a stunning wall of trees, rocky cliffs, and soaring birds. The meandering curves of the river provide amazing views, and you can see up and down the river for miles. The bluffs, which are imposing when immediately adjacent to the road, diminish into the far horizon at several viewing areas.

Note the unusual sunsets around these parts. Most think of the Mississippi as a southbound river that cuts up and down the center of the nation. This is not true here. In Piasa country, the Mississippi River makes a distinct turn and the current flows from west to east. In Alton, Elsah, and Grafton, the sun rises and sets in the long stretch of water. On many evenings at dusk, the fiery reds, yellows, and oranges run nearly the entire length of the river. One of the great pastimes along this byway is celebrating these glorious and unique sunsets.

Along the road to Eldred, the bluffs give way to rolling hills, farms, and forests. Depending on the season, roadside stands with fruits and vegetables may entice you to stop. The apples and peaches in Jersey, Calhoun, and Greene Counties are legendary. In Eldred, an old-fashioned Illinois town full of Americana, most travelers stop for a slice of pie and get out to smell the crisp, fresh air. Moving northward, you see the great Illinois farmlands that bring the bounty of food to both America's and the world's dinner tables. Soon the road branches westward, and the journey ends with another free ferry over the Illinois River into Kampsville.

This byway is a must-see destination during all four seasons. In the spring, the trees and shrubs turn the bluffs and countryside into a wonderful tapestry of colorful buds and blossoms. Summer brings festivals, fairs, and river recreation. Autumn hosts the Fall Color Caravan and some of America's most amazing foliage, accented by the nearby rivers. Finally, the winter brings the American bald eagle by the hundreds to winter along the bluffs and feed along the banks of the rivers. The rivers, majestic bluffs, fantastic trees and wildlife, quaint villages, and rolling farmlands all make this byway a wonderful adventure.

## Highlights

This must-see tour of the Meeting of the Great Rivers Scenic Route begins at the northernmost point (Kampsville) and concludes at the southernmost point (Alton).

**Kampsville:** Kampsville is in Calhoun County on the Illinois River. Take the free ferry ride (drive east on Highway 108 approximately five miles to Eldred), and go to the home of the American Center for Archaeology, which is the site of Old Settlers Days with Lewis and Clark, and Civil War and othe reenactments.

**Eldred:** Eldred is a wonderful village in Greene County at Highway 108 and Blacktop Road. The Eldred Home shows a glimpse of life in the 1800s and 1900s. Turn south onto Blacktop Road. Drive approximately 15 miles to the intersection of Blacktop Road, Highway 100, and Highway 16; continue straight ahead and onto Highway 100 southbound. Drive approximately ten miles south to Pere Marquette State Park.

**Pere Marquette State Park:** This park is in Jersey County on Route 100. This 7,895-acre preserve

*Sights such as this one of the Mississippi River can be seen while driving the Meeting of the Great Rivers Scenic Route.*

## ALTON

The historic town of Alton has a solid Midwestern appeal. Lewis and Clark trained the Corps of Discovery, Lincoln and Douglas had their final debate, and Reverend Elijah Lovejoy was martyred here while defending the freedom of the press and fighting slavery. The tallest man in history, Robert Wadlow, called Alton home. Also, spanning the Mississippi River at Alton is the famous Clark Bridge, a suspension marvel that was featured in a two-hour PBS Nova documentary entitled "Super Bridge." It is a beautiful structure that proves that intelligent and compassionate engineers can marry function and form.

Nearby in Hartford-Wood River, Lewis and Clark built Camp Dubois, assembled the Corps of Discovery, and set off on their monumental expedition. During the Civil War, thousands of Confederate soldiers were held at the Federal Penitentiary; today, a solemn monument and cemetery honors the dead. Alton has fantastic recreational facilities, including golf courses and ball fields that welcome national championship tournaments. The city has unique casual and fine restaurants, bed-and-breakfasts, inns, hotels, an antique shopping district, a shopping mall, parks, riverboat gaming, and other leisure activities throughout the year.

overlooks the Mississippi and Illinois rivers. Outdoor enthusiasts will enjoy the park's nature trails, prehistoric sites, horseback riding, camping, fishing, boating, and hiking. The park also has a wonderful lodge built in the 1930s by the Civilian Conservation Corps. The fireplace alone soars 50 feet into the grand hall, and the great room is rich with massive timber beams and stone. Continue southward out of Pere Marquette State Park onto Highway 100. Drive approximately three miles to Brussells Ferry.

**Brussells Ferry:** Take a free ride on the Brussells Ferry across the Illinois River, and get a feel of the river under the wheels of your vehicle. Nearby is the Mark Twain Wildlife Refuge, the seasonal home for hundreds of thousands of migratory birds including American bald eagles, herons, owls, pelicans, geese, ducks, and many rare species.

**Grafton:** Grafton is on Highway 100 in Jersey County. All but wiped out by the Great Flood of 1993, this amazing river town bounced back and is now considered one of the most important stops on the byway. Bed-and-breakfasts, inns, antiques and specialty shops, casual family dining, riverside entertainment, summer outdoor family amphitheater, a small museum, a visitor center, parasailing, jet skiing, pontoon boats, fishing, hunting, hiking, bike trails, cottages, horseback riding, a mystery dinner theater, and more can be found in Grafton. Festivals abound throughout the spring, summer, and fall. Continue southbound approximately a half-mile to the bluffs running along the Mississippi River.

**Scenic Bluffs:** Without question, the most spectacular view along this route is from just outside Grafton, approximately 15 miles northwest of Alton. The bluffs tower above the river with the byway road between the peaks and the riverbank. The Mississippi is alive with commercial traffic, sailboats, and wildlife, in contrast to the majestic bluffs overhead. Any time is good viewing, but late afternoon and sunset are very rewarding. Be careful: Many people stop along the highway to take pictures of the bluffs and river. Try to remain in your car to photograph the scenery. Also exercise caution because of many bicyclists and fast-moving traffic at all times. Continue eastbound on Highway 100 about five miles from Grafton to Elsah. Be prepared to make an abrupt northward turn.

**Elsah:** Elsah is considered by many national travel writers as the river town that time forgot. This adorable village contains more than two dozen homes built in the 1800s, when Elsah was an important riverboat stop. Because the town has almost no contemporary structures, you immediately feel as if you have been transported back into the mid-1800s. Bed-and-breakfasts and small shops abound. Continue eastbound onto Highway 100 about ten miles to the Cliffton Terrace Park.

**Cliffton Terrace Park:** This roadside park features picnic facilities, seasonal wildlife viewing, and a playground. Continue eastbound onto Highway 100 about five miles to the legendary Piasa Bird. Be alert for an abrupt turn northward as you begin seeing riverside barges along the banks.

**Piasa Bird:** American Indian nations and early European explorers claimed to have seen this mythical bird. Today, a gigantic bluff painting depicts the half-dragon, half-cat creature. Restored from early sketches and photography of the 1800s, the site is being developed into an interpretive park and wetlands area. Continue southeasterly about one mile on Highway 100, and enter Alton.

**Alton:** The community dates to the early 1800s as a major river port just north of St. Louis and can best be summed up by the word *historic*. Continue eastbound on Highway 100, going approximately three miles. Turn north into the Melvin Price Locks and Dam Complex and National Great Rivers Museum site.

**Melvin Price Locks and Dam Complex, National Great Rivers Museum:** About two miles past the Clark Bridge, on Highway 100, is the Melvin Price Locks and Dam Complex and the site of the National Great Rivers Museum. This colossal structure tames the mighty river and aids in flood control and navigation. A wonderful riverfront walkway surrounds the dam and museum. Watch long strings of barges full of fuel and grain pass through the locks to be lowered or raised as the river winds down to the delta. It offers a wonderful view of the Alton skyline and Clark Bridge.

# Ohio River Scenic Byway

*Along the Ohio River Scenic Byway interesting spurs offer must-see natural highlights. For instance, the Cache River Spur takes visitors to an ecosystem designated by the United Nations as a Wetlands of International Importance.*

PART OF A MULTISTATE BYWAY; SEE ALSO INDIANA AND OHIO.

This byway's history is closely tied to the Ohio River, which it follows. Many forts from the Civil War and the French and Indian War were strategically placed along this route, and the Underground Railroad had many stops along this byway. This is where you can find the Cave in Rock, an enormous cave that was once home to river pirates. It is now a great vantage point from which to watch today's river traffic.

## Intrinsic Qualities

**Archaeological:** Digs were conducted at Fort Massac State Park in Metropolis from 1939 to 1942, and again in 1966 and 1970. From these digs, reconstruction of the fort was started. A museum holds artifacts from the excavations.

### Quick Facts

**Length:** 188 miles.

**Time to Allow:**
Eight to ten hours.

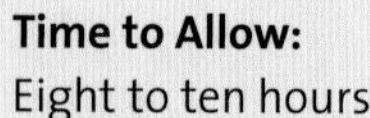

**Considerations:**
During periods of significant flooding, segments of the route may be closed, especially the terminus of the route in Cairo. A narrow and hilly segment of the byway near Tower Rock in Hardin County is not advised for RVs or tour buses. An alternate route has been identified for these vehicles along the roadside.

**Cultural:** The spirit of those who live along the Ohio River can be seen at Fort Defiance Park in the town of Cairo. The park is a beautiful place to watch the constant meeting of the Ohio and Mississippi Rivers that refuse to merge. The Ohio River waters become a blue ribbon, rippling far down the brown Mississippi currents.

Because all this magnificent scenery is found along the Ohio River, there is much evidence in Cairo of the people's desire for beauty. For example, located in the Halliday Park at Washington and Poplar is "The Hewer," a statue that was made in 1906. Sculpted by George Grey Barnard and exhibited at the St. Louis World's Fair, this original bronze statue was declared by Laredo Taft to be one of the finest nudes in America.

**Historical:** Many historical sites are situated along the Ohio River Scenic Byway. These sites cover everything from early Native American cultures to Civil War sites. Kinkaid Mounds, a designated byway site, is a monument to the Native American people who once inhabited this region.

The cities of Old Shawneetown and Golconda have numerous historic structures from the 1820s and 1830s. Cairo, positioned at the confluence of the Ohio and Mississippi Rivers, was a thriving port city and an important strategic site during the Civil War, a history that's alive today in Cairo's many old houses and buildings. Fort Massac State Park in Metropolis is a reconstructed fort from the French and Indian War.

*The earliest written record of Cave in Rock is from a French explorer who visited the cave in 1729.*

The Ohio River has been a river of both opportunity and tragedy during its history. While the state of Illinois possesses many Underground Railroad sites, the byway also passes near the Slave House, where captured fugitive slaves and even freed blacks were incarcerated before being returned to the South. This constituted the little-known Reverse Underground Railroad.

**Natural:** The Ohio Valley in Illinois is home to some of the most dramatic features along the entire Ohio River. The Garden of the Gods in the Shawnee National Forest preserves a grouping of unique limestone features with such names as Camel Rock and the Devil's Smokestack. Nearby Rim Rock and Pounds Hollow are also linked by the byway route. Along the byway, the Spur to Cave-in-Rock State Park is a great limestone cavern on the Ohio River. Farther west, the designated Cache River Spur takes visitors to a rare wetland ecosystem, designated by the United Nations as a Wetlands of International Importance.

The Horseshoe Lake Conservation Area in Miller City, seven miles north of Cairo, has 10,645 acres, including a 2,400-acre lake. The first 49 acres of the park were purchased by the Department of Natural Resources in 1927 for development as a Canada goose sanctuary. Additional tracts of land, including Horseshoe Island, continued to be purchased in order to create the conservation area that greets visitors today. As many as 150,000 Canada geese winter at this site.

**Recreational:** You can enjoy camping in both the Fort Massac State Park and in the Shawnee National Forest. The Shawnee National Forest in Illinois has 338 miles of equestrian/hiking trails, 454 campsites, 16 designated campgrounds, and 27 designated picnic areas. Seven wilderness areas in the Shawnee National Forest are available for wilderness study.

In the tradition of the Mississippi steamships that featured gambling, drinking, and Old West living, a casino steamship still leaves the port of Metropolis. Along the Metropolis riverfront is the Merv Griffin Theater, which presents a range of entertainers on special dates throughout the year.

## Highlights

The Ohio River Scenic Byway must-see tour begins in Cairo and runs to the Indiana border.

**Fort Defiance Park:** Fort Defiance Park is right on the byway. Stop and view the confluence of the Ohio and Mississippi rivers, where you can see tugs working.

**The Hewer, Safford Memorial Library, and U.S. Custom House Museum:** Taking Highway 51 right through Cairo (on Washington Avenue), travel 1½ miles to The Hewer statue in Halliday Park on the corner of Washington and Poplar avenues. About a half-mile later, you can see the Safford Memorial Library, where you can pick up a 50-cent book out of the "treasure bin." Across the street is the U.S. Custom House Museum.

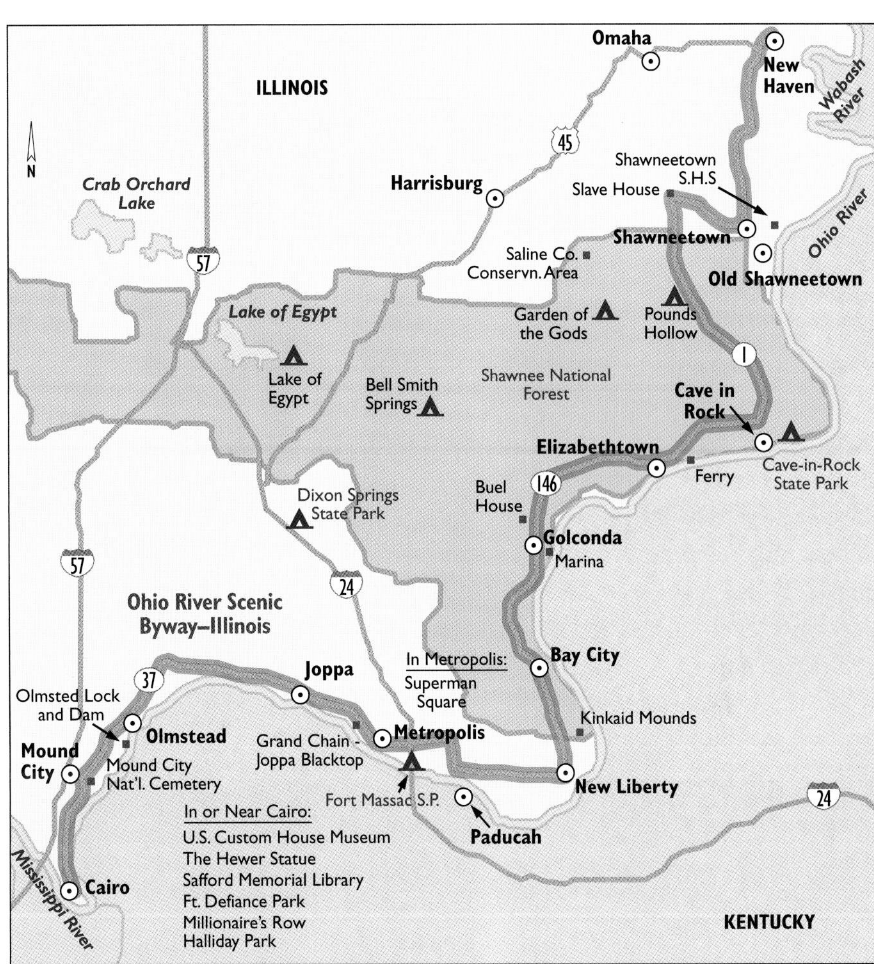


**Millionaire's Row:** Where Highway 51 and Washington Avenue split, take a short detour following Washington Avenue along Millionaire's Row to see turn-of-the-century mansions such as River Lore and Magnolia Manor, which is open for tours. Then turn right on 28th Street to rejoin the byway.

**Mound City National Cemetery:** Heading north out of Cairo is the Mound City National Cemetery. Confederate and Union soldiers are buried side by side here. From Mound City, the byway route goes onto Highway 37.

**Olmstead Lock and Dam:** Traveling north on Highway 37, about five miles later is the Olmstead Lock and Dam project, which offers a lookout pavilion and restrooms. The route then goes up Highway 37 about five miles to the Grand Chain Joppa Blacktop, and then it runs into Highway 45.

**Superman Square:** Highway 45 goes south into Metropolis, where you can see Superman Square in the center of town. A riverside casino is located in Metropolis.

**Fort Massac State Park:** Fort Massac State Park is the next stop (two miles south of Superman Square), located on Highway 45, with picnic tables, a museum, and a variety of events that occur throughout the year. Follow the byway out through Brookport, Unionville, and Liberty up through Bay City to Golconda (about 45 miles from Metropolis), where you will find the Golconda Marina, the Buel House, and many antique and novelty shops.

**Cave-in-Rock State Park:** Continue on Highway 146 and go through Elizabethtown and on to Cave-in-Rock State Park, with a lodge, a restaurant, picnic tables, and trails.

**Garden of the Gods Wilderness Area:** North of Cave-in-Rock State Park, you can stop by Garden of the Gods Wilderness Area in the Shawnee National Forest to enjoy the hiking trails and picnic tables.

# Historic National Road

*Traversing the entire width of the state, the Historic National Road in Indiana gives visitors a relaxing journey through small-town America, pastoral farmland, natural features formed by ancient glaciers, and the high-octane urban offerings of Indianapolis.*

PART OF A MULTISTATE BYWAY; SEE ALSO ILLINOIS AND OHIO.

One of America's earliest roads, the National Road was built between 1828 and 1834 and established a settlement pattern and infrastructure that is still visible today. Nine National Register Districts are found along the route, as are 32 individually designated National Register Sites offering education and entertainment. As you travel Indiana's Historic National Road, you find a landscape that has changed little since the route's heyday in the 1940s.

Historic villages with traditional main streets and leafy residential districts still give way to the productive fields and tranquil pastures that brought Indiana prosperity. From the Federal-style architecture of an early pike town (a town that offered traveling accommodations and little else) to the drive-ins and stainless-steel diners of the 1940s, you can track the westward migration of the nation in the buildings and landscapes that previous generations have left behind.

Along the way, you will find many of the same buildings and towns that were here during the earliest days of westward expansion. A visit to Antique Alley gives you a chance to do some antique shopping and exploring along this historic road. The Indiana Historic National Road is a unique way to experience the preserved pike towns along the route, such as Centerville and Knightstown.

## Quick Facts

**Length:** 156 miles.

**Time to Allow:** Three to nine hours.

**Considerations:** High seasons are spring and fall. In the spring, poppies, irises, and wildflowers are spread along the roadside. Black locusts and redbuds are also in bloom. During September and October, community festivals occur all along the byway.

*To maximize exposure to the National Road, owners built onto the front of their buildings. Archways between rowhouses gave access to backyards.*

## Intrinsic Qualities

**Archaeological:** Eastern Indiana was the home of two groups of Native Americans identified by scholars as the Eastern Woodland Societies, who made their homes in the area following the retreat of the glaciers. One group occupied the area around 7000 to 1000 B.C., the other from approximately 1000 to 700 B.C. Many of their campsites have been found in the area of the Whitewater River Gorge. The Whitewater River Gorge was an important area after glacier movement and activity had stopped in the area. The area was excellent for hunting and fishing, with flowing streams and an abundance of resources.

**Cultural:** The National Road brought the nation to Indiana. The lure of limitless opportunities and the romance of the West drew tens of thousands of pioneers through Indiana between 1834 and 1848. Many stayed and settled in the Hoosier State, thus creating a new culture—the foundation for our national culture. This is because religious and economic groups left the distinctive colonial societies of the eastern seaboard and merged in the Midwest. Settlers to Indiana brought with them their own particular mix of customs, religions, languages, building styles, and farming practices. Quakers, European immigrants, and African-Americans looking for new opportunities all traveled the National Road. Evidence of this mix of cultural influences can be seen along the corridor today in the buildings and landscapes. It can also be learned at the Indiana State Museum's National Road exhibit, and it can be experienced on a Conestoga Wagon at Conner Prairie Living History Museum or at a Civil War encampment along the route.

As the region matured, the culture continued to evolve under the influence of the nation's primary east–west route. Richmond was home of the Starr Piano Company, and later the Starr-Gennet recording studios, where jazz greats such as Hoagy Carmichael and Louis Armstrong made recordings in an early jazz center. The Overbeck sisters, noted for their Arts and Crafts pottery, lived and worked in Cambridge City. The poet James Whitcomb Riley, author of "Little Orphan Annie" and "Raggedy Man," lived in Greenfield. Also, Indianapolis, the largest city on the entire Historic National Road, became an early center for automobile manufacturing. Today, visitors experience such attractions as the Children's Museum of Indianapolis (the largest children's museum in the world) and the Eiteljorg Museum of American Indians and Western Art, as well as a variety of other museums and cultural institutions.

The Historic National Road in Indiana represents one segment of the historic National Road corridor from Maryland to Illinois. The historic and cultural resources within Indiana are intimately tied to traditions and customs from the eastern terminus of the road in Cumberland, Maryland, and are built on goals and expectations of a nation looking west.

**Historical:** The National Road was the first federally funded highway in the United States. Authorized by Thomas Jefferson in 1803, the road ran from Cumberland, Maryland, west to Vandalia, Illinois. Designed to connect with the terminus of the C&O Canal in Cumberland, the National Road gave agricultural goods and raw materials from the interior direct access to the eastern seaboard. It also encouraged Americans to settle in the fertile plains west of the Appalachians. For the first time in the United States, a coordinated interstate effort was organized and financed to survey and construct a road for both transportation purposes and economic development.

Built in Indiana between 1828 and 1834, the National Road established a settlement pattern and infrastructure that is still visible today. The historic structures along the National Road illustrate the transference of ideas and culture from the east as the road brought settlement and commerce to Indiana. The National Road passes through well-preserved, Federal-style pike towns and Victorian streetcar neighborhoods, and it is lined with early automobile-era structures, such as gas stations, diners, and motels.

**Natural:** The topography of Indiana was created by glaciers that advanced and retreated over the land during the Pleistocene Period. Leaving behind moraines and an undulating landscape, the glaciers also helped to create the Whitewater River Gorge, where fragments of limestone, clay, and shale bedrock can be seen. The gorge and surrounding region is known internationally among geologists for its high concentration of Ordovician Period fossils.

**Recreational:** You can find many opportunities for recreation along the Historic National Road in Indiana, as well as in nearby cities. Golf is a popular sport along the highway, as evidenced by the many golf courses. Biking and hiking are other extremely popular sports along the byway. Local park and recreation facilities are often directly accessible from the byway or can be found nearby.

Professional sports can be enjoyed along the byway, as well. White River State Park in Indianapolis offers you an opportunity to enjoy a Triple-A baseball game at Victory Field. Just off the Historic National Road in downtown Indianapolis are the RCA Dome,



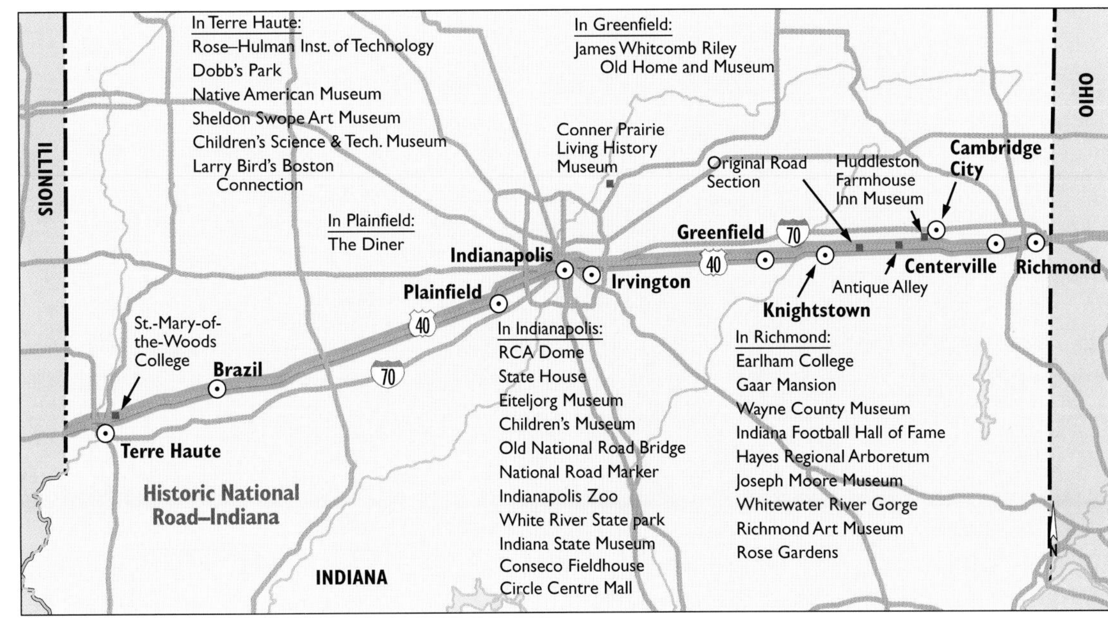

home of the Indianapolis Colts, and Conseco Fieldhouse, home of the Indiana Pacers.

**Scenic:** The Historic National Road is a combination of scenes from rural communities, small towns, and a metropolitan city. This combination makes the byway a scenic tour along one of the most historically important roads in America. Small-town antique shops and old-fashioned gas pumps pop up along the byway, which makes the Historic National Road a relaxing and peaceful journey. Broad views of cultivated fields, distant barns and farmhouses, and grazing livestock dominate the landscape. In other areas, courthouse towers, church steeples, and water towers signal approaching communities that draw you from the open areas into historic settlements. The topography of the land affords vistas down the corridor and glimpses into natural areas that sit mostly hidden in the rural landscape. This repeating pattern of towns and rural landscapes is broken only by metropolitan Indianapolis.



## Highlights

The following are just some of the points of interest available to you when traveling west across the Indiana portion of this byway from the western border of Ohio. If you're traveling east, read this list from the bottom up.

**Historic Richmond:** As one of Indiana's oldest historic towns (founded in 1806), Richmond has one of the Hoosier State's largest intact collections of 19th-century architecture. You can visit four National Register Historic Districts; Hayes Regional Arboretum; a bustling historic downtown full of unique shops and restaurants; and a fascinating collection of local museums, including the Wayne County Museum, the Richmond Art Museum, the Gaar Mansion, the Indiana Football Hall of Fame, the Joseph Moore Museum at Earlham College, and the Rose Gardens located along the road on the city's east side.

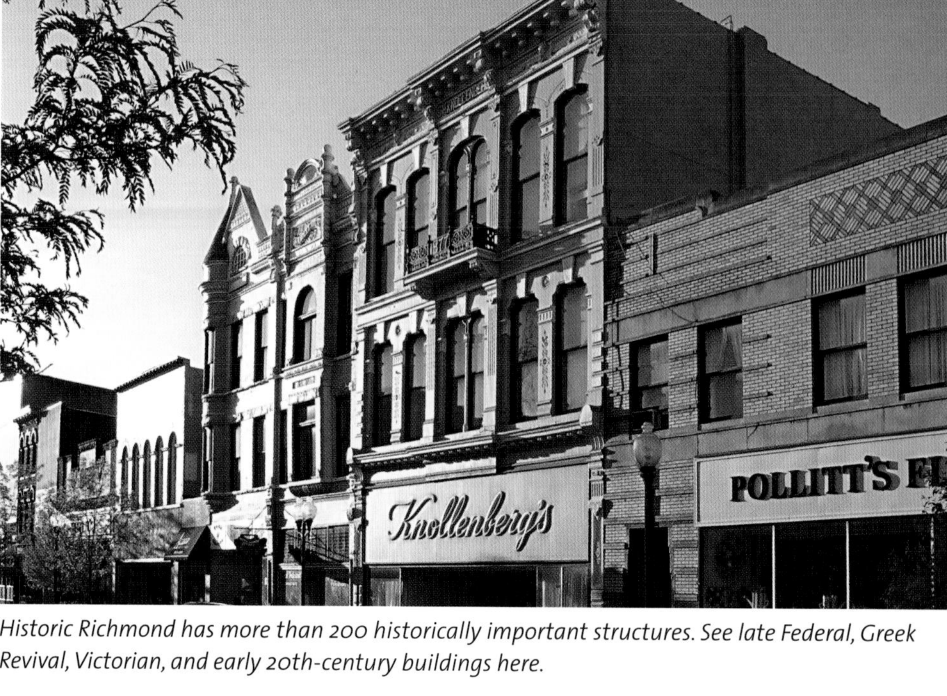


*Historic Richmond has more than 200 historically important structures. See late Federal, Greek Revival, Victorian, and early 20th-century buildings here.*

**Centerville:** One of the historic highway's most intact and quaint National Road-era pike towns is listed in the National Register of Historic Places for its fine collection of architecture. Historic brick houses connected by brick archways characterize the town. Centerville also has a noteworthy collection of small antique and specialty shops and is home to the world's largest antique mall, just several blocks north of the National Road.

**Pike towns and Antique Alley (Richmond to Knightstown):** You can meander along the National Road and enjoy the tranquil agricultural landscape interspersed with pike towns that recall the early years, when travelers needed a place to rest every five miles or so. This route is also heralded as Antique Alley, with more than 900 antique dealers plying their trade in and between every community along the route.

**Huddleston Farmhouse Inn Museum and Cambridge City:** A restored National Road-era inn and farm tells the story of the historic highway and the people who formed communities along its length. The museum is owned and operated by the Historic Landmarks Foundation of Indiana and is the home office of the Indiana National Road Association, the National Scenic Byway management nonprofit group. The museum displays the way of life of an early Hoosier farm family and the experience of westward travelers who stopped for food and shelter. Cambridge City is also listed in the National Register of Historic Places and has unique historic buildings that are home to diverse shops and local eateries.

**Knightstown:** Knightstown grew because of its location on the National Road between Richmond and Indianapolis. The town has retained its significant collection of 19th- and 20th-century architecture; a large section of the town is listed in the National Register of Historic Places. Today, you can visit four antique malls, watch a nationally known coppersmith, and stay in one of two bed-and-breakfasts. Also available is the Big Four Railroad Scenic Tour.

**Greenfield:** The James Whitcomb Riley Old Home and Museum on the National Road in Greenfield tells the story of the Hoosier poet and allows you to experience his life and community with guided tours. The small town also is rich in local flavor, with many shops and restaurants to satisfy you.

**Irvington:** A classic 1870s Indianapolis suburb was developed as a getaway on the city's east side. Irvington has since been swallowed by the city but retains its stately architecture and peaceful winding cul-de-sacs. Listed in the National Register of Historic Places, Irvington recalls turn-of-the-century progressive design principles and allows the modern visitor a glimpse into the city's 19th-century development.

**Indianapolis:** The center of Indiana's National Road is also its state capital. Downtown Indianapolis offers a growing array of activities and amenities, from the state's best shopping at Circle Centre Mall, an unprecedented historic preservation development that incorporates building facades from the city's past into a state-of-the-art mall experience, to gourmet dining and an active nightlife and sports scene. Along Washington Street just east of downtown, you can visit the Indiana Statehouse, the Indianapolis Zoo, the Eiteljorg Museum of American Indians and Western Art, and White River State Park. The Indianapolis Colts play at the RCA Dome, and the Indiana Pacers continue the ritual of "Hoosier Hysteria" at Conseco Fieldhouse downtown.

**Plainfield:** Twentieth-century automobile culture dominates this area. Motels and gas stations remain from the early days and are interspersed with the sprawl and development of the modern city. The Diner, on the east side of Plainfield, is a remnant from the early days of travel, a stainless-steel café with an atmosphere reminiscent of the 1940s, an atmosphere that is quickly disappearing. From Plainfield to Brazil, look for roadside farmers' markets.

**Brazil:** The western extension of the National Road was surveyed through what is now Brazil in 1825; today, its National Register-listed Meridian Street remains a classic example of how the historic highway promoted the growth of communities along its length. The village is also full of curios and collectibles.

**Terre Haute:** The western edge of Indiana's National Road is anchored by Terre Haute, a community offering historic points of interest and cultural experiences of various kinds. Rose–Hulman Institute of Technology on the city's east side was founded in 1874 and is an exceptionally beautiful college campus; just west of the city on State Road 150, the St. Mary-of-the-Woods College campus offers a touch of European elegance in the Indiana forest. Its campus is in a beautiful wooded setting and has several buildings dating to its 1841 founding. You can choose National Road restaurants along the city's Wabash Avenue, located in historic buildings. Dobb's Park, a half-mile south of the highway at the intersection of highways 46 and 42, is home to a nature center and Native American Museum. The Sheldon Swope Art Museum at 25 South 7th Street features 19th- and 20th-century artworks in a 1901 Renaissance Revival-style building with an Art Deco interior. The Children's Science and Technology Museum on Wabash Avenue houses rooms full of hands-on learning displays and special exhibits. Fans of basketball legend Larry Bird can see memorabilia at Larry Bird's Boston Connection and view a museum of his career keepsakes, including his Olympic medal, most valuable player trophies, photographs, and other mementos. Continue on Indiana's Old National Road to the Illinois portion of the road.

*The town of Greenfield is attempting to revitalize its downtown. Historic buildings are being preserved, while new construction is happening.*

# OHIO RIVER SCENIC BYWAY

*Travelers on the Ohio River Scenic Byway in Indiana have the unique opportunity to follow in Abraham Lincoln's boyhood steps, trod the path of freedom seekers on the Underground Railroad, and experience the fascinating history of quaint river towns.*

PART OF A MULTISTATE BYWAY; SEE ALSO ILLINOIS AND OHIO.

This winding, hilly route follows the Ohio River. The route offers a pleasant escape from suburban concerns as it passes villages, well-kept barns, vineyards, and orchards. Historic architecture along the way retains a charm that is often missing from modern development.

Here, tucked away in the very toe of southwestern Indiana, are swamps full of water lilies and rare birds. The most rugged part of this byway features rock outcroppings, forested hills, caves, and scenic waterways. The limestone bluffs (dotted with cave entrances) are abundant with wildlife.

The Lincoln Living Historical Farm is a re-created 1820s homestead with a cabin, outbuildings, split rail fences, animals, and field crops.

## Intrinsic Qualities

**Archaeological:** Angel Mounds State Historic Site is located on the banks of the Ohio River near Evansville. It is one of the best-preserved Native American sites in North America, where an advanced culture lived between A.D. 900 and 1600. These people were named Mississippian by archaeologists. The town served as an important center for religion, politics, and trade. Noted archaeologist Glenn A. Black directed excavation of the site from 1938 until his death in 1964. At the park is an interpretive center, where artifacts are displayed and explained.

**Historical:** In the early days, the Ohio River was the primary way west for early settlers of the frontier. Later, with the coming of the steamboat, the Ohio River became the center of the transportation and industrial revolution. Prior to the Civil War, the river had great significance as the boundary between slave and free states. The river is used today for recreation and to transport coal to generating plants.

Abraham Lincoln's family built a farmstead along Little Pigeon Creek, not far from the Ohio River. At the Lincoln Boyhood National Memorial, you can see and help with the daily chores the Lincoln family performed on the Indiana frontier. Log farm buildings are staffed during the summer months by costumed interpreters.

Corydon was the place where the Indiana State Constitution was drafted in 1816. The Corydon Capitol State Historic Site preserves the state's first capitol, constructed of Indiana limestone.

The Culbertson Mansion State Historic Site in New Albany preserves a 22-room French Second Empire home built in 1869. It was built by a wealthy local merchant.

The Levi Coffin House in Fountain City (which is north of the byway and was back then called Newport) was the place where more than 2,000 freedom seekers found refuge. Levi Coffin, known to many as the President of the Underground Railroad, opened the doors to his home to offer food, shelter, and clothing to runaway slaves on their journey to freedom.

### Quick Facts

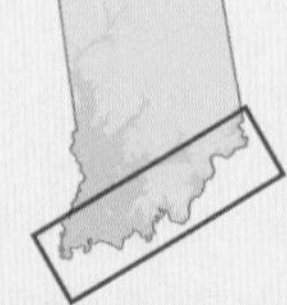

**Length:** 303 miles.

**Time to Allow:** Two days.

**Considerations:** Some areas along this byway are prone to flooding during the fall and spring, causing occasional closures. The road can become slippery in the winter or when it rains. The road is also narrow in some spots, and sometimes it is winding and hilly.

**Natural:** As a traveler of this route, you will enjoy agricultural countryside dotted with well-kept barns, vineyards, and orchards. Vistas of rural villages dominated by church spires and historic courthouses span the byway, and thriving cities with imposing architecture can be seen, as well. Tucked away in southwestern Indiana, you can find cypress swamps, water lilies, and rare birds.

One of the natural features that is found along the Ohio River Scenic Byway is the Hovey Lake tate Fish and Wildlife Area south f Mount Vernon. This area is a ,300-acre wetland. Adjoining the ke is the Twin Swamps Nature reserve, the highest-quality ypress swamp in Indiana.

In Evansville, nature can be ound even in the middle of the ty at the Wesselman Woods ature Preserve, a 200-acre stand f virgin timber. Hoosier National orest offers 193,000 acres of forst, along with four lakes, scenic rives, river overlooks, and Ohio iver access sites.

The Needmore Buffalo Farm in lizabeth southeast of Corydon is ome to a sizable North American ison herd. Visitors can discover ne role of the buffalo in southern ndiana and purchase buffalo meat nd craft items.

**ecreational:** The Hoosier National orest has plenty of opportunities or enjoyment. Falls of the Ohio tate Park in Clarksville offers nany nature hikes where you can ook at fossil beds and various quatic habitats. There are also icnic areas and a museum.

**cenic:** The beauty of the Ohio iver Scenic Byway is unmatched, specially in the fall when the orests surrounding the byway hange to red and golden tones. hese beautiful colors are reflected n the blue serenity of the Ohio iver. You can also take a side trip ff the byway that leads to breathaking views and opportunities or exciting sightseeing in the ational and state forests surounding the byway.

In addition, you don't want to overlook the charm of the Indiana towns with their historic districts that stand proud with regal Victorian homes.

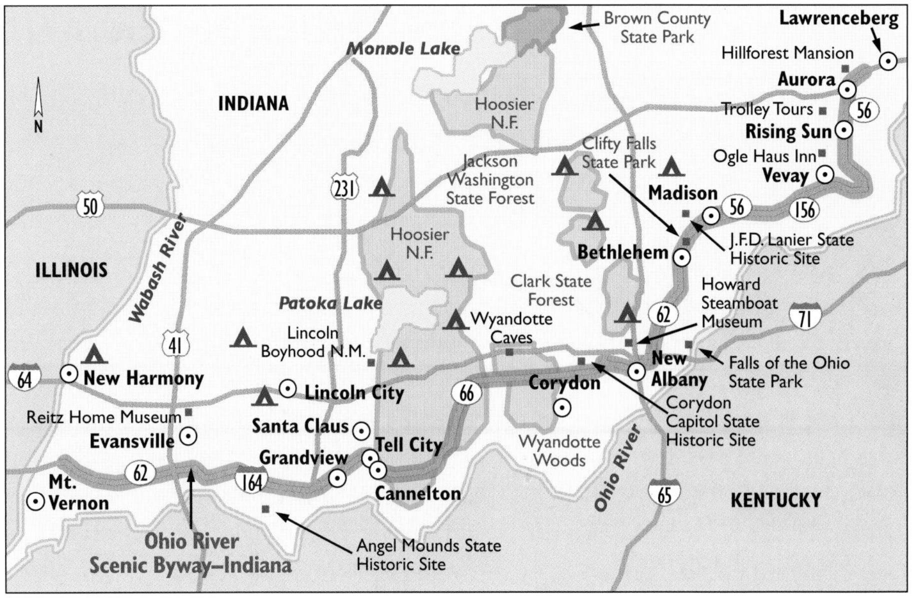


## Highlights

While heading east to west on the byway, consider using the following itinerary.

**Hillforest Mansion:** Begin at Hillforest Mansion in Aurora and sightsee. Travel along Highway 62, and continue on Highway 56 to Madison. This stretch is approximately 60 miles, but it's on very curvy roads and will take longer than you may expect.

**J. F. D. Lanier State Historic Site and Clifty Falls State Park:** The J. F. D. Lanier State Historic Site is located in Madison, and Clifty Falls State Park, with its many trails (some of them rugged), is located just outside the town on Highway 56. The town of Madison also has several historic sites open to the public, as well as a wonderful Main Street.

**Howard Steamboat Museum and Falls of the Ohio State Park:** Follow Highway 56 out of Madison, and head south on Highway 62, just past the town of Hanover. Highway 62 will take you into Jeffersonville, Clarksville, and New Albany. These are also known as the Falls Cities and are directly across the Ohio River from Louisville, Kentucky. The Howard Steamboat Museum and Falls of the Ohio State Park are located here.

**Corydon Capitol State Historic Site:** Continue on Highway 62 out of New Albany to Corydon. This is where the Corydon Capitol State Historic Site is located—Indiana's first state capital. Other historic sites and a Civil War battle memorial are also located in Corydon. Corydon is approximately 20 miles from New Albany.

**Wyandotte Caves and Woods:** About ten miles west of Corydon on Highway 62, you come to the Wyandotte Caves and Wyandotte Woods. A variety of cave tours are available, and Wyandotte Woods offers hiking, camping, and picnic areas. Just past the town of Leavenworth, about eight miles from the Wyandotte area, take Highway 66. Around this area, you'll enter the Hoosier National Forest, where you will find a variety of activities.

**Lincoln Boyhood National Memorial:** Stay on Highway 66 through the Ohio River towns of Cannelton, site of the Cannelton Cotton Mill (a National Register site), Tell City, and Grandview. As a side trip, take U.S. 231 north just past Grandview to Lincoln Boyhood National Memorial. This national park celebrates the life of Abraham Lincoln. He lived in a cabin at this site from the age of 7 to 21.

**Angel Mounds State Historic Site:** Back at Grandview, stay on Highway 66 to Newburgh. Angel Mounds State Historic Site is between Newburgh and Evansville.

**Reitz Home Museum:** The Reitz Home Museum is located in the historic downtown Riverside District of Evansville. This is just a short distance from the Ohio River. Take Highway 62 west out of Evansville. It's about 25 miles to the Illinois border and the end of the Indiana portion of the route.

# Western Trails Scenic and Historic Byway

*Whether ruffians of the Old West capturing their ill-gotten gains or hopeful pioneers on the way to capturing their version of the American dream, their story and more is told on the Western Trails Scenic and Historic Byway.*

Sometimes it was a destination, as in the case of the cattle drives to the railroad town of Ogallala. Other times the towns along the Western Trails Scenic and Historic Byway were simply campsites on the way to the Rocky Mountains and beyond. The natural features of the landscape provided the signposts marking the way along the path, the terrain as rugged as those who traveled it. Today, the Western Trails Scenic and Historic Byway in the panhandle of Nebraska greets visitors with a feast, inviting them to drink in the stark beauty of the Plains; devour the history of the Old West; and consume the wonders of the geology, archaeology, and paleontology that await all who venture here.

Plenty of western trails cut through Ogallala on the eastern edge of the Western Trails Scenic and Historic Byway—including the Oregon Trail, Mormon Trail, Pony Express, Union Pacific, and Texas Trail—providing a wealth of frontier history. Gamblers, cattlemen, and fur traders gathered in the romping, rollicking town of Ogallala in the late 1800s where liquor flowed freely across the bar, riches flowed freely across the gambling tables, and once in awhile a young cowpoke's blood flowed freely across the floor as his luck ran out at the local saloon. Originally an outpost for fur trappers from St. Louis who were able to get along with the nearby Pawnee Indians, pioneers followed as the western trails came through. But it was the coming of the Union Pacific Railroad that dramatically changed the destiny of Ogallala. Massive cattle drives from Texas drove the economy during the summer months in the latter part of the 19th century, with ten to twelve herds, each with 2,500 head of cattle, locating south of town. Various "service" industries came in each summer also, bringing a temporary population of floaters, gamblers, tradespeople, and dance hall hostesses. A less rowdy town now, Ogallala encourages visitors to experience some of the frontier frolics in local attractions and to enjoy spectacular outdoor recreation just outside city limits at Lake McConaughy.

*Chimney Rock was the most recognized and noted landmark along the Oregon Trail. The unique formation now rises 325 feet above the prairie floor.*

As the Western Trails Scenic and Historic Byway travels west, it follows the Oregon and Mormon trails. More than simply pathways to the state of Oregon, they were the only practical routes to the western United States. In a 25-year period more than a half million people went west via this corridor. The wagon ruts of these intrepid voyagers are still visible at Ash Hollow. Natural features of the western Nebraska landscape provided landmarks for Native Americans and pioneers as they traveled these trails. Chimney Rock is the landmark most often noted by the pioneers on the trails and one of the most famous features of the American West. Courthouse and Jail Rocks were landmarks for the pioneers but were also used by Native Americans for sending smoke signals and camping. The story of the people and the places of the past is told at the Oregon Trail Museum at Scotts Bluff National Monument.

Pioneers, rowdy cattlemen, and Native Americans weren't the only

## Quick Facts

**Length:** 144 miles.

**Time to Allow:** 2 1/2 hours.

**Considerations:** Roads are occasionally closed in the winter due to blizzard conditions.

ones to travel along this region of the Great Plains. Western Nebraska has been sustaining life since prehistoric times. Ash Hollow State Historical Park is home to the remains of ancient rhinoceros, mammoths, and mastodons, and Agate Fossil Beds National Monument is an important source for 19.2-million-year-old Miocene mammals with interactive displays for visitors of all ages.

## Highlights

The Western Trails Scenic and Historic Byway has many attractions to share with visitors. The following itinerary is suggested as a sampling of some of the many things to see and do.

**Ogallala:** On the eastern edge of the byway is the town of Ogallala. Since cowboys generally were buried with their boots on, the first cemetery in the area was aptly named Boot Hill. Another must-see in Ogallala is Front Street, a replica of some typical businesses from Ogallala's heyday. Visitor attractions include a museum, saloon, and evening entertainment complete with cowboys and dance hall girls.

**Lake McConaughy:** Known as "Big Mac" to the locals, Lake McConaughy, just outside of Ogallala, is Nebraska's largest reservoir. Camping, boating, surfing, and fishing are popular at this recreation area. And the Bald Eagle Viewing Center below Kingsley Dam, along with the surrounding environs of the lake, attracts one of the largest and most varied bird populations documented in America.

**Ash Hollow State Historical Park:** Just beyond Big Mac is Ash Hollow State Historical Park, a haven for weary travelers for centuries. Prehistoric Native Americans used the area for encampments, and pioneer wagon trains would rest here for a day or two, refreshed by the sweet springwater. Wagon wheel ruts are still visible on the bluffs of Windlass Hill overlooking Ash Hollow. A visitor center and abundant exhibits help visitors learn about the geology, prehistoric animals, ancient Native American nations, and the pioneer trek west at this prairie oasis.

**Courthouse and Jail Rocks:** In the absence of modern road signs to guide their way, early travelers used the natural terrain as guideposts. Courthouse and Jail Rocks, located five miles south of Bridgeport on Highway 88, are two remarkable geological formations, which became landmarks along the Oregon and Mormon trails. They are composed mainly of Brule clay and Gering sandstone, and are the easternmost extension of the Rocky Mountains.

**Chimney Rock National Historic Site:** Outside of the town of Bayard, 1½ miles south of Highway 92 on Chimney Rock Road is Chimney Rock National Historic Site. Once the most recognized landmark on the Oregon Trail, today the visitor center features original maps made from Captain John C. Frémont's exploration of the Oregon Trail in 1842–43.

**Gering:** Gering has several sites and activities for travelers. North Platte Valley Museum has an authentic sod house, log house, and military exhibits. Robidoux Trading Post has been faithfully reconstructed using historical information and 100-year-old hand-hewn logs. Farm and Ranch Museum preserves and interprets the agricultural heritage of the Great Plains.

**Scotts Bluff National Monument:** Continuing west on Highway 92, three miles west of Gering is Scotts Bluff National Monument. Dedicated to preserving the legacy of America's westward movement, this site consists of 3,000 acres of prairie, scenic sandstone bluffs, and the Oregon Trail Museum. Drive or walk to the summit of the majestic natural landmark that was used by countless thousands of Native Americans, fur trappers, and pioneers. The view of the North Platte Valley is truly stunning. Chimney Rock, 25 miles away, is visible in the distance.

**Agate Fossil Beds National Monument:** A scenic drive beyond Scotts Bluff National Monument, Agate Fossil Beds National Monument is an internationally recognized fossil site and was once a part of Captain James Cook's Agate Springs Ranch. The nearby beds are a valuable source for 19.2-million-year-old mammal fossils. Cook entertained Chief Red Cloud and other Sioux Indians, and the monument's Cook Collection reflects years of gifts brought by the Native Americans during visits.

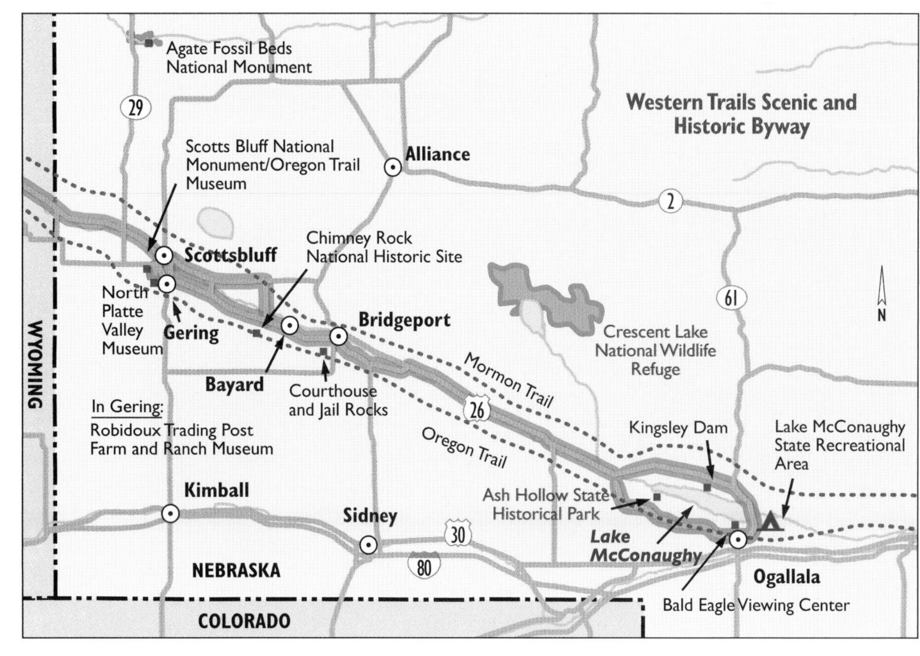

# Amish Country Byway

*Reportedly the largest concentration of Amish in the world is in this part of Ohio. This fascinating people hold true to their rich traditions and heritage, making the Amish Country Byway a trip to their on-going yesteryear.*

In this 21st century of cell phones, computers, fast cars, appointments, and time commitments, there is a community within America that holds steadfast to its traditional beliefs, customs, and slower lifestyle. The Amish people in Holmes County, Ohio, make up the largest concentration of Amish communities in the world, and they provide a unique look at living and adapting traditional culture.

The Amish community is a living reminder of the principles of religious freedom that helped shape America. With a devout sense of community and adherence to beliefs, the Amish Country Byway gives a rare opportunity to witness a different way of life.

## Intrinsic Qualities

**Cultural:** The Amish have established themselves in the Holmes County area, and it is estimated that one in every six Amish in the world live in this area. The Amish choose to live a simple way of life, which is clearly evident by the presence of horses and buggies, handmade quilts, and lack of electricity in Amish homes. Entrepreneurial businesses owned by the Amish add to the friendly atmosphere along the byway while creating a welcome distance from the superstores of commercial America. In the 21st century, the Amish Country Byway is an important example of a multicultural community, as both the Amish and non-Amish traditions are strong in the region. These two cultures have built on similarities while still respecting differences. By working together, they have created a thriving, productive community.

The Amish, as a branch of the Anabaptist people, are traditionally devout and religious. Like so many other immigrants, they came to America in search of religious freedom. In Europe, the Anabaptists had been persecuted for their beliefs, but today Amish beliefs are more accepted and laws have been passed protecting their rights in regard to education, Social Security, and military service. Horses and buggies, plain dress, independence from electricity, homemade quilts, spinning tops, and lots of reading materials are some of the things you might find in an Amish home. A community event, such as a barn raising, helps build relations among neighbors and is an efficient way to get work done.

Another important aspect of the byway is the influence of early Native Americans and Appalachian folklore. The presence of both is felt along the byway, as festivals and parades, such as the Killbuck Early American Days Festival, celebrate these early settlers. Coalfields and stone quarries drew settlers from the east, and today this influence is manifested in the strong mining and manufacturing industries in the area.

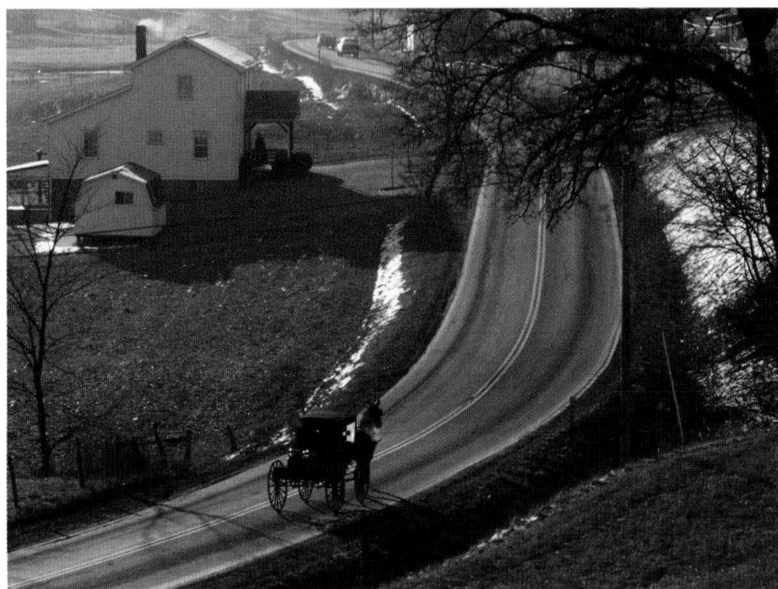

*An Amish horse and buggy travels down a peaceful road in Ohio. Holmes County has the largest concentration of Amish communities in the world.*

### Quick Facts

**Length:** 76 miles.

**Time to Allow:** Four to six hours.

**Considerations:** Early autumn means harvest season (which brings produce stands) and stunning fall foliage. Please respect the privacy and religious beliefs of the Amish and don't take pictures of them. Because of the unique agriculture and culture of Amish Country, you must share the road with Amish buggies, agriculture equipment, cyclists, etc. The two-lane state routes and State Road 62 should be traveled at a somewhat slower pace than most paved roads. Keep in mind that many services are not available on Sundays. Roads are sometimes bad in the winter because of ice or snow. Every ten years or so, spring and summer bring flooding, but rarely are the major highways closed.

Agriculture is the economic heart of Amish Country, and visitors to the area are likely to see rows of haystacks or fields being plowed. Holmes County boasts the second-largest dairy production in the state, the largest local produce auction during the growing season, and weekly livestock auctions in the communities along the byway. The Swiss and German heritage of the early settlers in the county is evident in the many specialty cheese and meat products and delicious Swiss/Amish restaurants. A variety of festivals and local produce stands along the byway allow visitors to taste a part of Amish Country. Agriculture-based auctions are held regularly at the Mount Hope, Farmerstown, and Sugarcreek sale barns, and specialty sales are held throughout the year at various times.

When the Amish settled in the area, most depended on agriculture as their profession, but others who were not farmers worked instead in blacksmith shops, harness shops, or buggy shops. In addition, many specialties sprang up, such as furniture-making. Today, shops are scattered along the byway, specializing in everything from furniture to gazebos.

**Historical:** The story of the Amish Country Byway is the story of the movement and settlement of people. The byway serves as a reminder of why people came to America and the struggles that many had in settling new and uncharted lands. Today, roads forged by the early settlers in the area have been upgraded to highways, and while Amish farmers still use horses and buggies as transportation, the roads have improved their journey. The historic nature of the byway is felt from these roads to the numerous buildings that stand on the National Historic Register.

Long before the Amish came to call Holmes County home, bison herds crisscrossed the state, led by instinct down the valleys and along the terminal moraine. American Indians later used the trails left by the bison. Eventually, these trails became the main paths of the Amish. Today, those paths make up State Route 39, one of the main arteries of the Amish Country Byway. In the 1830s, before the railroad, Amish and non-Amish farmers would drive their fattened pigs along well-worn paths to the Ohio Erie Canal at Port Washington from Millersburg. This walk to the canal was referred to as a three-day drive. Today, along the byway, the Amish and their neighbors continue to work together, making Holmes County an important agricultural, furniture manufacturing, and cheese-producing region of Ohio and the nation.

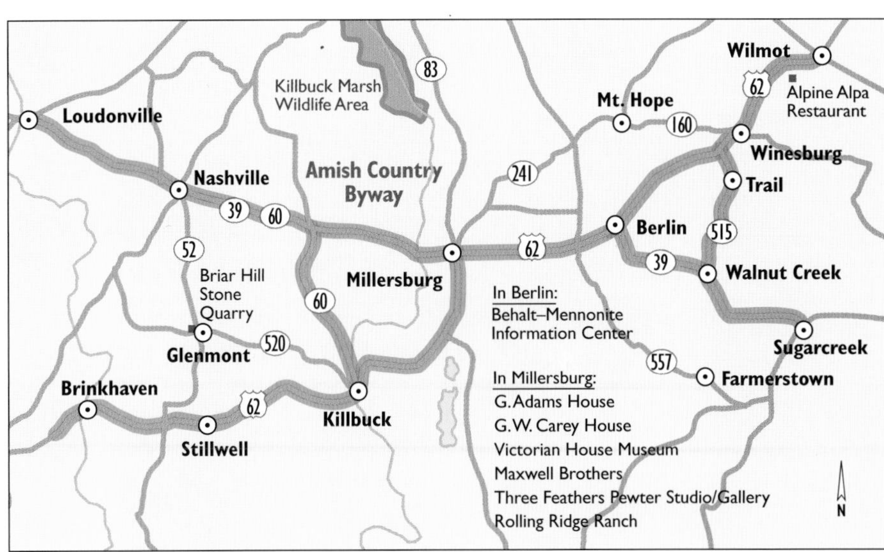


**Natural:** The Amish Country Byway may be known primarily for its distinctive cultural and historical aspects; however, many natural features in the area make this a place where people would naturally choose to settle. The area is diverse in its natural features, and you can enjoy them from your car or by exploring various regions along the byway.

The Amish Country Byway is literally the product of being at the upper edge of the terminal moraine, making it the northwest gateway to Appalachia. (A terminal moraine marks the farthest point to which a glacier has advanced.) Because of this terminal moraine, natural paths developed, one of which has become the byway as it is known today. This activity causes arc- or crescent-shaped ridges to form, and this is what has happened along the byway. The terminal moraine runs west to east, paralleling State Route 39 with visible formations along the road. Large rock cliffs and small, deep lakes in the northwest portion of the Amish Country Byway are the products of this geological process. Briar Hill Stone Quarry is the largest sandstone quarry in operation in the United States and is located just off the byway near Glenmont. This quarry has provided an important natural resource, and many Amish farms and schools have been established in this area.

Another important industry along the byway is drawn from the forests of large oak and cherry trees. Rich soil and available water tables underneath the ground have made this a rich area for timber to grow. There has been an increase in the demand for hardwood over the past few years, and the Amish Country Byway is known for its good timber. The Amish often use this timber as they make their furniture, and you can see the finished products for sale along the byway.

The natural wonders found at the Killbuck Marsh Wildlife Area are mainly the wildlife of the wetland region. This area is home to birds and other wildlife. Most notably, the American bald eagle has roosting nests in the marsh area. Local bird-watchers, especially the Amish, have formed groups and organizations to document the birds and provide educational activities to inform others about the value of birds and wildlife as a resource in the area.

**Recreational:** From leisurely drives to hiking and biking, recreational opportunities exist for everyone traveling the Amish Country Byway. Every season can be enjoyed, with hiking, biking, rodeos, horseback riding, tennis,

*Killbuck Marsh Wildlife Area is noted for being Ohio's largest marshland outside of the Lake Erie region.*

golfing, and hunting in the summer months. You can also enjoy numerous water activities, such as canoeing, swimming, fishing, and boating. Winter can be a memorable experience, with activities such as cross-country skiing and snowmobiling.

The Amish Country Byway is not one for speed demons. By slowing down, you get to experience the many recreational opportunities that are unique to this byway. There are carriage rides, hay rides, and sleigh rides that reflect the agricultural traditions of the area, while unique activities, such as hot air balloon rides and airplane rides, may also be enjoyed. One of the most popular activities is visiting Amish homesteads and farms, antique shops, and museums. In addition, you can find many places to stop and enjoy some good cooking or shopping.

The Holmes County Trail goes through Millersburg and links the byway with the northern part of the county and state. This trail is open to bicycles, hikers, and buggies. The local Amish citizens who sit on the Rails to Trails board provide valuable insight into how to make this a success for the Amish, their non-Amish neighbors, and visitors. This trail travels through beautiful Amish Country and is a good way to get off of the main byway route.

Another way to get off the main byway route is to use the area's river and creek network. These rivers and creeks were critically important to the transportation and commerce of the past, and today they provide a great opportunity for visitors to go canoeing, swimming, boating, or fishing. The Killbuck Creek feeds into Killbuck Marsh Wildlife Area, which also provides excellent bird-watching opportunities. Tucked away on the western edge of the byway, the Mohican River is the basis for making this one of the most popular recreational retreats in the state of Ohio. Canoeing is especially popular along the river; this area has been coined the Camp and Canoe Capital of Ohio.

**Scenic:** The view on the Amish Country Byway is one of rolling hills; undisturbed marshland and forests; beautiful trees and landscapes; well-kept farmhouses, barns, and ponds; neat rows of agricultural crops; brilliant displays of flowers; and bucolic scenes of Amish farmers/laborers with their families and children.

The simple living of the Amish and the gentle hospitality of the residents of Holmes County make the Amish Country Byway a scenic and peaceful trip indeed. The gently rolling farmlands of the byway give you a chance to experience the area's grand agricultural tradition. Bales of hay, freshly plowed fields, barn raisings, and locally grown produce sold at the roadside are some of the scenes that will greet you.

## Highlights

The following itinerary gives you an idea for spending a day on the eastern half of U.S. 62.

**Killbuck Marsh Wildlife Area:** Enjoy the peace of the early morning at the Killbuck Marsh Wildlife Area. Fish or hike while the sun rises. Have a picnic breakfast while enjoying the birds and scenery.

**Millersburg:** Downtown Jackson, Clay, and Washington Streets are a Historic District. There are plenty of National Register of Historic Places homes to see, such as the G. Adams House, the G. W. Carey House, and the Victorian House Museum. There are also a lot of shops downtown, such as Maxwell Brothers and the Three Feathers Pewter Studio/Gallery. Take time to look around and see what else you can discover. You can find plenty of places to eat in Millersburg, so this a perfect place to have lunch before you head off to the Rolling Ridge Ranch.

**Rolling Ridge Ranch:** The Rolling Ridge Ranch is a good place for families to visit. Kids love the petting zoo and playground. You can take wagon rides and see many different kinds of animals at the ranch.

**Behalt–Mennonite Information Center:** Behalt–Mennonite Information Center is an essential next stop because you can learn about the Amish and Mennonites and why they live the way they do. See the historical mural. This is interesting, free education.

**Alpine Alpa Restaurant:** Just about the time you're done at the Information Center, you'll be ready for dinner. The Alpine Alpa Restaurant is just up the road from the Information Center. It's famous not only for its food, but also for the interesting things you can see and buy there. You can also experience a bit of Swiss culture.

# CanalWay Ohio Scenic Byway 

*The story of the immigrant life, industrialization, and American innovation can be told along with that of enduring historic farms still operating along the CanalWay Ohio Scenic Byway.*

The construction of the Ohio and Erie Canal in 1825 drastically changed the people and pace of this region. Many byway visitors travel this route to learn about the development of the pre- and post-canal eras. The route also offers an impressive display of historical sites, along with many opportunities for hiking, biking, and water sports.

## Intrinsic Qualities

**Archaeological:** The CanalWay Ohio Scenic Byway boasts more than 500 archaeological sites; seven are listed on the National Register of Historic Places. One site, Irishtown Bend, is located in Cleveland Flats. This is where an early settlement of Irish canal workers lived. While visitors can't see very much at this site because the house foundations that have been semi-excavated have been covered up for protection, the findings at this site are significant.

**Cultural:** The influences on area culture can be classified into four elements: the resilience of farming communities, life during the canal period, the gumption of immigrants, and the accomplishments of wealthy industrialists.

Farming is still important to area culture, and the strength of past and present farmers is reflected in the sturdiness of the farms themselves: Many farms from the mid-19th century are still standing and working. The village of Zoar, which was founded in 1817 by a German religious sect, the Zoarites, is still working according to many of its old agricultural practices.

The sway of the canal era on area culture is apparent because its flavor is still potent in the historic cities of Clinton, Canal Fulton, Boston, and Peninsula.

The neighborhoods that immigrants developed retain their special foreign flavor, creating small pockets of spice along the byway. These National Register historic neighborhoods near Cleveland are based on Archwood–Dennison Avenue, Broadway Avenue, Ohio City, and Warszawa.

The ambitions of early wealthy industrialists are represented in the homes they built. Some of the more notable are the Stan Hywet Hall (Goodyear Rubber Company founder Frank A. Seiberling's home) and the Anna Dean Farm (Diamond Match founder O. C. Barber's estate).

Replete with continuous high-culture events, the larger cities on the route (Cleveland, Akron, Barberton, and Strongsville) retain several historic and well-known venues. The area's culture is manifested in locally produced festivals and entertainment.

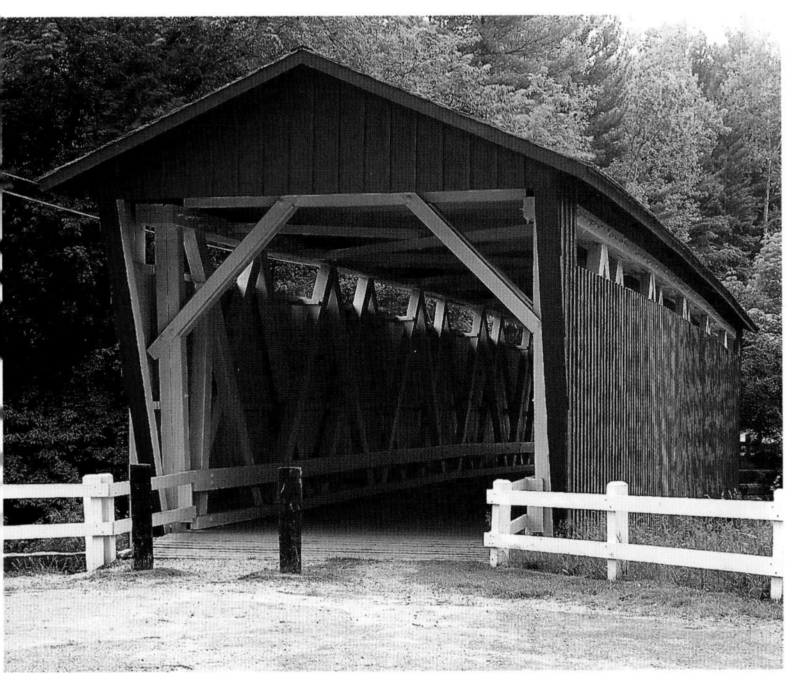

*Covered wooden bridges are a reminder of earlier days and rural travel in Ohio's Cuyahoga Valley.*

### Quick Facts

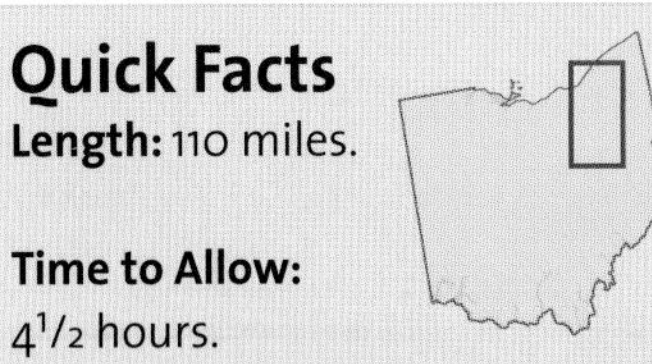

**Length:** 110 miles.

**Time to Allow:** 4 1/2 hours.

**Considerations:** Riverview Road in south Cuyahoga County is occasionally closed due to flooding. This happens only during major storms and does not last for very long. Fort Laurens, Towpath, and Dover Zoar Roads also lie in the flood path.

**Historical:** People have lived in the CanalWay Ohio area for nearly 12,000 years. The area was an important transportation route for American Indians, and it was deemed neutral territory so that all might travel safely from the cold waters of the Great Lakes to warmer southern waters. European explorers and trappers arrived in the 17th century, and immigrants slowly moved in over the centuries to farm. The modern catalyst for area development was the Ohio and Erie Canal, which gave way to the area's industrial era. The CanalWay Ohio Scenic Byway takes you through places that still show evidence of the early inhabitants and the effects of industrial development.

The countryside north of Dover consists of wooded ravines and hillsides. It is separated by tilled croplands and isolated farms. This setup comes from early settlement

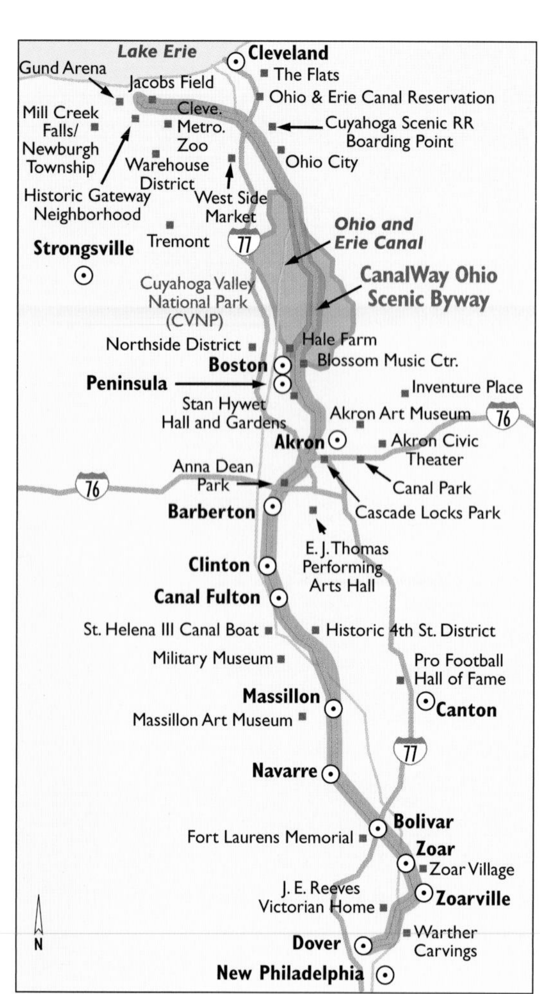


of the Pennsylvania Germans and the Moravians.

The newly constructed Indigo Lake Visitor Shelter is a stop on the old railroad. Here, visitors can fish in the adjacent lake, access the canal towpath, or walk to Hale Farm. This is a 19th-century farm, presented to visitors through a full program of living history.

Towns such as Dover, Bolivar, Navarre, Barberton, Canal Fulton, and Clinton show the influence of the canal with their early 19th-century architecture, original canal-oriented street patterns, locks and spillways, and towpath trails along the historic canal route. Tours on the *St. Helena III Canal Boat* in Canal Fulton give visitors firsthand experience of canal life. The Canal Visitors Center is housed in an 1852 canal tavern.

Waters from the area's lakes provided the cooling needed for the industrial rubber boom, which created the prosperous Akron of the 1920s. Brick factories illustrate life in industrial-era Akron.

**Natural:** The CanalWay Ohio Scenic Byway is a biological crossroad because it transects three regions: lake plains, glaciated plateau, and unglaciated plateau. This results in a great diversity of plants and animals, textbook examples of forest communities and habitats.

The primary trees in the glaciated plateau region are beech-maple (the most common), oak-hickory, and hemlock-beech. Ice Age hemlock-beech forests are found in ravines, while oak-hickories are found atop ridges and in drier areas. The Tinkers Creek Gorge National Landmark has a rare settlement of hemlock-beech on the moist valley floor.

Rolling hills and steep valleys characterize the unglaciated plateau region. Oak-hickory is common in this southern part of the route. Many of these lands are held and preserved by public agencies.

**Recreational:** There is plenty to do along the CanalWay Ohio Scenic Byway. Towpath Trail near the Ohio and Erie Canal is extremely popular—more than three million users enjoy the trail in a typical year. Other recreation includes skiing, golfing, picnicking, hiking, fishing, and boating, and water excursions are available along the rivers, too. In addition, the route passes through several entertainment districts.

**Scenic:** The scenery found along the CanalWay Ohio Scenic Byway is interestingly diverse. It ranges from the heavy industry of the Cleveland Flats (and the resulting immigrant neighborhoods) to rolling hills and farmland. You can also see the remnants of the towns and villages associated with the canal, as well as samples of 200-year-old architecture.

## Highlights

This itinerary takes you through Cuyahoga Valley National Park and into Akron. Although it does not cover the entire distance of the byway, it gives you a taste of how you can drive a portion of this road.

**Cuyahoga Valley National Park:** Start with a dawn picnic breakfast at the Cuyahoga Valley National Park (CVNP). The CVNP is on the byway, and its entrance is about eight miles south of Cleveland. In this gorgeous 33,000-acre region, you can do just about anything outdoorsy (hiking, golfing, bicycling, horseback riding, and so on). Admittance is free. After breakfast, go biking along the Towpath Trail, which runs through the park for about 44 miles; historical structures, canal locks, and wayside exhibits are added features of this trail. Take an hour or two to enjoy a bike ride along any part of the trail.

**Hale Farm:** For another two (or three) hours before lunch, stop at Hale Farm, which is at the southern end of the CVNP. There is an admittance fee for this living-history farm, where you can wander the grounds and talk to the artisans who make the impressive wares for sale there. The glass blowers, candlemakers, potters, and blacksmiths demonstrate the industries of the mid-1800s. The buildings and history here are fascinating. Eat lunch and head south to Akron.

**Akron:** Akron is a buzzing city with much to do. One possibility is to stop at the Akron Art Museum. Admission and parking here are free for visitors, and the museum always has engaging exhibits.

**Cascade Locks Park:** After your visit at the museum, go to the Cascade Locks Park (also in Akron). Admittance is free here, as well. This park has 15 canal locks in a one-mile stretch (all necessary to climb over the Continental Divide), and you can follow them along on a trail; signs along the trail explain the locks and the history of the canal. There are also two historic buildings to visit in this park.

# Historic National Road 

*Time and topography determined the development of the Historic National Road in Ohio as pioneers' wagons gave way to railroads and then to autos, and as travelers will see, steep climbs and deep valleys gave way to gently rolling hills.*

PART OF A MULTISTATE BYWAY; SEE ALSO ILLINOIS AND INDIANA.

The Ohio Historic National Road paved the way west through the newly formed states of Ohio, Indiana, and Illinois and provided a direct connection to the mercantile and political centers of the East Coast, helping to secure the influence and viability of these new settlements. As much as the road's boom times during the early and mid-19th century signified its importance to national expansion, its decline during the late 19th and early 20th centuries reveals the rise of the railroad as the primary means of transport and trade across the nation. Likewise, the renaissance of the National Road in the mid-20th century reflects the growing popularity of the automobile.

Today, the byway is a scenic journey across Ohio. The steep, wooded hills and valleys of the eastern edge of the byway give way to the gently rolling farmland of the western part of the byway. Picturesque farms, hiking trails, craft industries, and historic sites and museums await you along this portion of the Historic National Road.

**Quick Facts**

**Length:** 228 miles.

**Time to Allow:** Four days.

**Considerations:** Excessive and heavy snow or rain falls occasionally in this part of the country. It may impair drivability but does not result in long-lived road closures.

## Intrinsic Qualities

**Archaeological:** Prehistoric civilizations once dominated the land surrounding what is now known as the Historic National Road in Ohio. Remnants of these early people can be found just off of the byway. One important aspect for these early cultures was making tools and weapons. They found flint for these tools at the site of Flint Ridge State Memorial. The Hopewell Culture frequented Flint Ridge because of the quality and beauty of the flint found there. This flint was a very important resource to that culture. Flint from Ohio has been found from the Atlantic seaboard to Louisiana. Flint was so important, in fact, that it has become the state gem of Ohio.

Located near Newark, the Moundbuilders State Memorial and Ohio Indian Art Museum tell about the Hopewell Indian civilization, which is most remembered for the large earthworks they constructed. Exhibits show the artistic achievements of cultures that lived in the area from around 10,000 B.C. to A.D. 1600. The Octagon Earthworks and Wright Earthworks are also located near Newark.

**Cultural:** The Historic National Road in Ohio hosts a rich tradition of culture. Museums, festivals, and other cultural facilities offer a chance to both explore more of the National Road's history and seek diversions from it. Outstanding performing arts venues are well represented along the byway. In addition to these cultural features, the eastern section of the byway is known for its selection of traditional and modern crafts.

*Brick Road, a stretch of the path of the original National Road, gives visitors a glimpse into early 1900s travel.*

**Historical:** The history of the Historic National Road in Ohio highlights the importance of this road in terms of development and settlement that it brought to the Ohio area. The history of the construction of the National Road is significant because it serves as an example of larger events that were transpiring in America simultaneously. Early pioneer settlement gave way to railroads, and finally the automobile became the most frequent traveler along the National Road.

**Natural:** While traveling the Historic National Road in Ohio, you are treated to a diverse byway that traverses steep wooded hills and valleys in the east and gently rolling farmland in the west. This diversity of natural features offers refreshing and contrasting views along the byway. The changing landscape determined how the National Road was constructed, as well as the types of livelihoods settlers engaged in throughout the history of the road.

**Recreational:** A tremendous network of large state parks, regional metropolitan parks, local parks, and privately run facilities provide a bountiful array of outdoor recreational facilities. For the most part, the state parks are located on the eastern half of the byway, and more than 50,000 acres of state parks, forests, and wildlife areas are easily accessible from the byway. Along portions of the byway, you can hike, camp, fish, hunt, and picnic while relishing the various species of local flora and fauna.

**Scenic:** Changing topography and landscapes provide scenic views for travelers of the byway, from hilly ridges to long, unbroken views of the horizon. Small towns, unique and historic architecture, and stone bridges all provide scenes from the past along the byway. Farms, unspoiled scenery, and large urban landscapes give you a sense of the great diversity of this byway.

## Highlights

The Historic National Road is sometimes known as "Main Street of America." While the Historic National Road in Ohio crosses the entire state, this itinerary suggests travelers linger a bit along a few of the quaint main streets and their towns that helped make the Historic National Road legendary.

**Cambridge:** Although Cambridge brand of glass ceased production in 1958, the name remains synonymous with quality glass, and collectors are drawn to this town to visit the Cambridge Glass Museum and the Degenhart Paperweight and Glass Museum, both located on the eastern edge of town on U.S. 22, and the National Museum of Cambridge Glass in downtown Cambridge, one block south of Main Street. Hopalong Cassidy Museum is in the Tenth Street Antique Mall, located just one block over from the National Museum of Cambridge Glass. The museum contains an extensive collection of memorabilia and products endorsed by a star of the western movies, William Boyd, a Cambridge native son who played cowboy hero Hopalong Cassidy. Fans of the old western flicks will enjoy the Hopalong Cassidy Festival held the first weekend in May each year.

**New Concord:** Following U.S. 40 west from downtown Cambridge for about nine miles, tourists come to the village of New Concord. Former U.S. Senator John Glenn, the first U.S. citizen to orbit planet Earth and the oldest human ever to venture into space, grew up in New Concord. The John and Annie Glenn Historic Site and Exploration Center includes Senator Glenn's fully restored boyhood home, as well as plans to expand the site to include additional buildings and educational opportunities in coming years.

**S-Bridge Park:** Also in New Concord on the west edge of town at the intersection of Main Street (U.S. 40) and OH 83, is the S-Bridge Park. The S-bridge was less expensive to build when the road crossed a creek at an angle, and the S-bridge crossing the Fox Creek in New Concord is in excellent condition. Now a footpath, it offers visitors an opportunity to view the bridge up close and from underneath.

**Norwich:** Approximately three miles beyond New Concord turn right onto Norwich Drive. This road, the old route into the burg of Norwich, becomes Main Street. At the end of the street, veer right onto Brick Road. This is a one-mile stretch of the former path of the National Road and is entirely paved with bricks, a popular way to pave during the early part of the 20th century. The road is open to automobiles so visitors can get the feeling of what it was really like to motor along the National Road in the early 1900s. At the end of the Brick Road, turn right to continue heading west on U.S. 40.

**National Road/Zane Grey Museum:** The final stop is the National Road/Zane Grey Museum located outside of Norwich just before I-70. Mile markers, a 136-foot diorama, vehicles, and films come together to tell the tale of the Historic National Road. Additionally the museum has a collection of memorabilia interpreting the life of area native and western novelist, Zane Grey. This particular part of Ohio is known especially for its production of art pottery, and this museum also does a notable job of telling this part of the area's history.

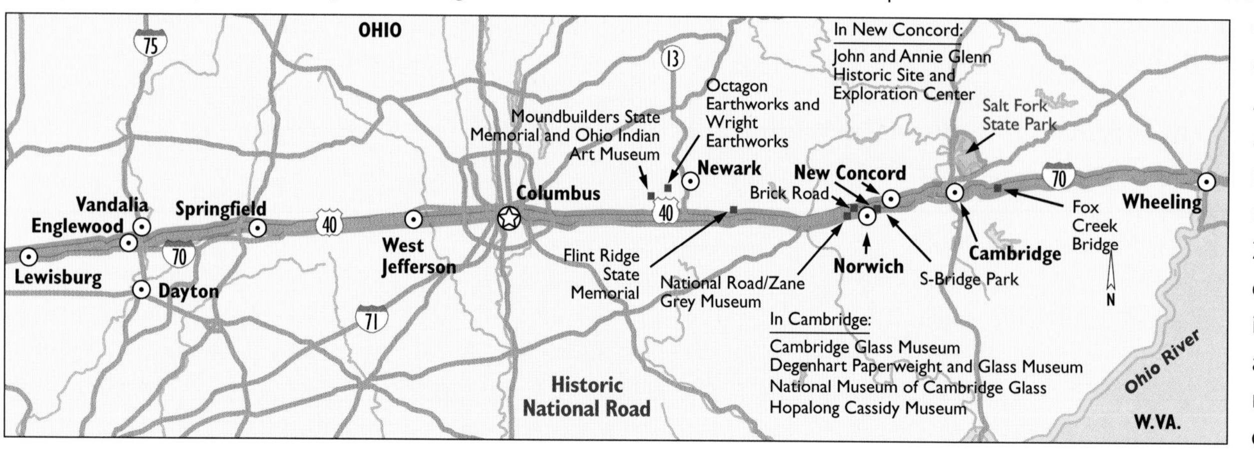

# OHIO RIVER SCENIC BYWAY 

*Including the birthplaces of three U.S. presidents, the Ohio River Scenic Byway is ripe with history and culture, sharing the story of centuries of human activity in the area.*

PART OF A MULTISTATE BYWAY; SEE ALSO ILLINOIS AND INDIANA.

This scenic route follows the Ohio River, so you can enjoy majestic river views for the ntire drive. The Ohio River is a istorical American icon. Native mericans and early European ettlers used it heavily, especially o access the West. It marked the oundary between the North and outh during the slavery era and vas later the gateway to freedom or many slaves. The river was also he means of progress for industri-lists and merchants.

## ntrinsic Qualities

**Archaeological:** Several archaeolog-cal sites and museums are found long the Ohio River Scenic Byway. These include several Native Ameri-an cultural sites in Tiltonsville, as vell as the Mound Cemetery.

The town of Portsmouth, which osts the Southern Ohio Museum nd Cultural Center, is where many travelers learn about the history of this area. There are also Native American cultural sites near here.

**Cultural:** The Ohio River has been a center of human activity for centuries and, therefore, is a cultural hotbed. Academic and historical organizations recognize this fact and have made the river and the immediate area the focus of their cultural studies. One such organization is the University of Kentucky's Ohio River Valley Series. This intercollegiate project specifically studies how the state's history has been affected by the social use of the Ohio River.

**Historical:** The region's rich history includes the migration of people along the river into the states that border it, as well as the those states that are located within the river's basin. The industry and technology of the area were important to the river, too. They changed the river's influence on the region through the development of steamboat travel and shipping, the creation of locks and dams, the establishment of industries such as steel and coal plants and their associated landing docks, and the development of large chemical and electrical power generating facilities.

**Natural:** This byway contains many natural features that surround both the Ohio River and the forests along the byway. Many native animals and plants add to the scenic quality of the byway. Natural sites along the byway include Fernwood State Forest, located near the Mingo Junction on State Route 151; the Quaker Meeting House, located near Mount Pleasant on State Route 647; and Barkcamp State Park. This park has historical significance and is located by a lake just off the byway turning from Bellaire on State Route 149. Campsites are available.

### Quick Facts

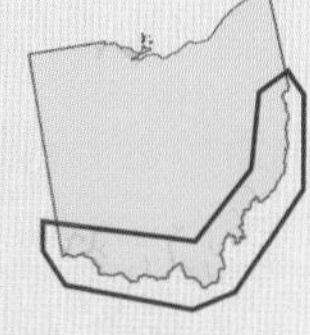

**Length:** 452 miles.

**Time to Allow:** Two days.

**Considerations:** Although flooding along the Ohio River is a rare event, it is most likely to occur between November and April, and the byway route could be affected. In addition, short sections along the route may experience annual or biannual flooding, including the portion of U.S. 52 east of Cincinnati known as Eastern Avenue. Snowstorms are possible, particularly from mid-December through mid-March, and can cause road closures.



**Recreational:** Several state forests and parks along this byway offer opportunities for outdoor recreation. Camping is available at the Barkcamp State Park, in the Forked Run State Park near Belpre, and in the Shawnee State Forest near Portsmouth. The Wayne National Forest begins near the town of Gallipolis and ends near Hanging Rock along the byway. You can camp at the Vesuvius Recreation Area in the forest, as well.

*The John Rankin house sits near the Ohio River. Reverend Rankin was one of the most active "conductors" on the Underground Railroad.*

**Scenic:** This scenic byway leads travelers through the colorful tapestry surrounding the Ohio River and also through many national and state parks. During the fall, the golden leaves of the forests reflect in the shining waters of the Ohio River, giving travelers a sense of serenity as they drive the byway. Families coming in the summer feel the energy of nature's fresh, green growth as their children play along the banks of the Ohio.

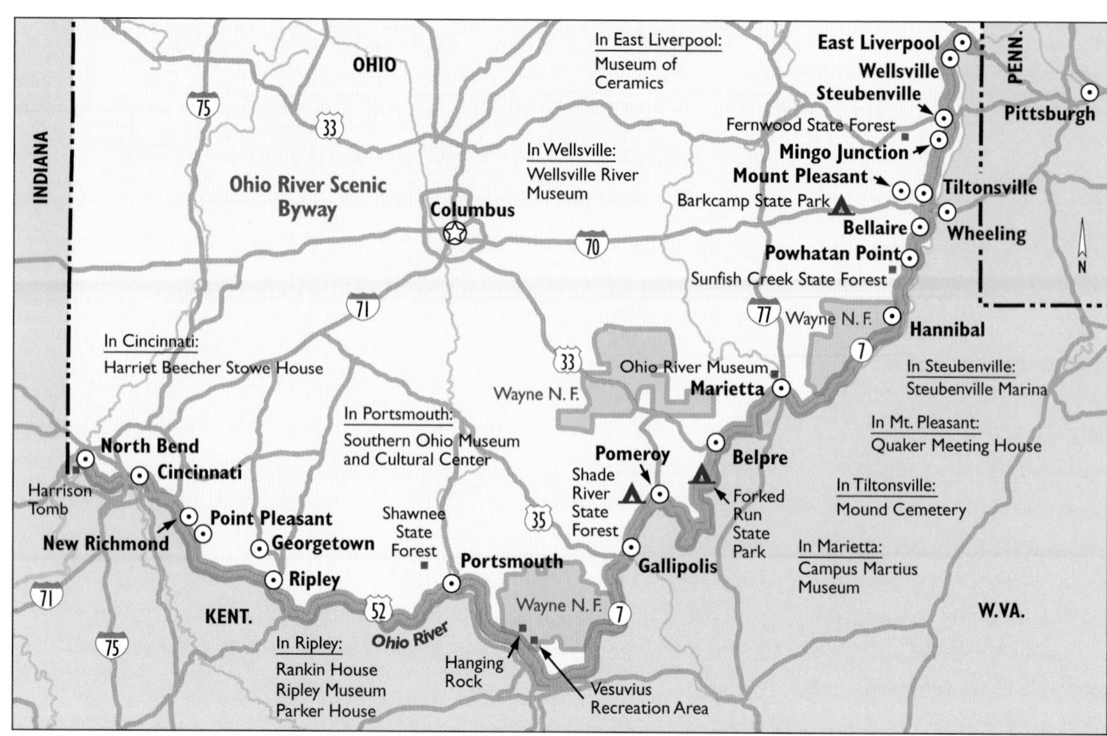


## Highlights

Starting from North Bend, you can travel alongside the Ohio River without flood walls obstructing your view.

**North Bend:** Your first stop is at the nation's great monument, the Harrison Tomb, located off Cliff Road, west of U.S. 50, North Bend. The 60-foot marble obelisk in this 14-acre park pays tribute to William Henry Harrison, the ninth U.S. president.

**Cincinnati:** Continue to Cincinnati, and visit the historic Harriet Beecher Stowe House. It was here that Stowe learned of the injustices of slavery and wrote her famous novel, *Uncle Tom's Cabin*.

**Point Pleasant:** Point Pleasant is the birthplace of the 18th U.S. president, Ulysses S. Grant (U.S. 52 and State Route 232): a one-story, three-room cottage.

**Georgetown:** Follow Grant's life back on U.S. 52, heading north, taking State Route 231 to historic Georgetown, where you can visit Grant's boyhood home on Grant Avenue. From Georgetown, head south again on State Route 68 to State Route 62, back to U.S. 52.

**Ripley:** Stop in the town of Ripley, and visit the Ripley Museum and Rankin House. Abolitionists John and Jean Rankin hid some 2,000 escaped slaves in this way station on the Underground Railroad. The Parker House, also in Ripley, was another home involved in the Underground Railroad.

**Portsmouth:** Continue on U.S. 52 to the town of Portsmouth, a traveler's delight. Here you'll see artistic flood-wall murals that beautify the byway and protect the city from the rising waters of the Ohio River.

**Gallipolis:** Continue to the French Art Colony of Gallipolis. Here, you can learn about the rich history of the local area and state. While traveling through, note the French-style homes along the riverbanks.

**Pomeroy:** The city of Pomeroy has been featured on *Ripley's Believe It or Not* for its unusual courthouse, which is built into the side of a cliff and is accessible on all three levels from the outside.

**Marietta:** The early days of Marietta are remembered at the Campus Martius Museum, which offers displays of riverboats and other antiquities. You can also stop at the Ohio River Museum next to the Campus Martius Museum.

**Steubenville:** Heading north up the river, you run into the town of Steubenville, where you witness the Old Fort Steuben reconstruction. Demonstrations, land office tours, and food are available here. In downtown Steubenville, you'll see murals depicting the 1850s and 1920s city life of the town. The murals are painted on the sides of many of the buildings in the area.

**Wellsville:** Continuing on State Route 7, you come to Wellsville and the Wellsville River Museum, a three-story building constructed in 1870. Period furniture and paddle-wheel displays are featured in the various rooms.

**East Liverpool:** Continue on the byway to the Museum of Ceramics in the town of East Liverpool. The town has been called Crockery City and is known for its artistic place settings. The city's ceramics museum operates out of the former post office. From here, you can continue following the byway into Pennsylvania if you want.

# FLINT HILLS SCENIC BYWAY

*Rare virgin prairie and cowpokes who still wrangle bovines in the spirit of generations past join with Native American and pioneer history to make this an enthralling experience.*

The Flint Hills Scenic Byway is a modern road easily reached from the Kansas Turnpike, I-70, U.S. 50, and U.S. 56, but it is a scenic trip back in time. Panoramic views of now-rare tallgrass prairie, Native American historic sites, the still-visible wagon ruts left by the countless thousands who traversed the Santa Fe Trail, and of course, the stark beauty of the Flint Hills all greet the visitors to this area.

The Flint Hills, as with so much of the Great Plains, became the site of friction between the indigenous people and the European pioneers. Treaties were needed as far back as 1825. Meaningful historic sites all along the Flint Hills Scenic Byway tell the tales of the native people groups, the pioneers who came to homestead in these hills, and those who merely passed through on their way to seek their fortune elsewhere in the Old West.

The geologic time period in the Flint Hills represents the Permian Period, with the area being covered by the shallow Permian Sea some 250 to 290 million years ago. The marine fossils, time, and the effects of nature worked together to create the unique topography of the Flint Hills: flat-topped hills of limestone and flint and verdant valleys, all accented by the preserved tallgrass prairie and cattle ranches that have been operating for generations.

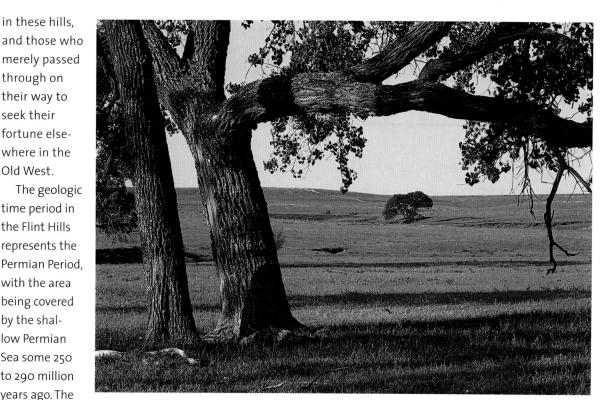

*A precious remnant of prairie, a fraction of the once vast expanse that greeted pioneers, can be found at Tallgrass Prairie National Preserve.*

## Quick Facts

**Length:** 47¼ miles.

**Time to Allow:** One hour.

**Considerations:** During the annual controlled burn of prairie grasses, those with respiratory difficulties will want to apply caution. Winter can be an especially beautiful time to visit, but dangerous with strong winds, cold temperatures, and occasionally ice.

One of America's newest national parks, the Tallgrass Prairie National Preserve has nearly 11,000 acres of virgin, never-plowed prairie safeguarded. The preserve protects a nationally significant example of the once vast tallgrass prairie ecosystem. Of the 400,000 square miles of tallgrass prairie that once covered the North American continent, less than 4 percent remains, primarily in the Flint Hills of Kansas. This makes it one of the rarest and most endangered ecosystems in the world. The preserve has two hiking trails that give visitors the opportunity to experience this exquisite prairie first-hand. It is a treat to stop and listen, perhaps hearing as the pioneers did from their Prairie Schooners, the wafting waves of this grassland ocean as the wind whistles through the bluestem and other native grasses. The beauty that will greet guests is striking and unforgettable.

## Highlights

The Flint Hills Scenic Byway stretches between Council Grove on the northern end at the intersection of U.S. 57 and U.S. 56, and Cassoday on the southern end of the byway at K-177 and I-35. It is a beautiful drive year-round showing off the unique views of the prairie. The following itinerary is suggested to experience some of the highlights along the byway:

**Kaw Mission State Historic Site and Museum:** At the northern end of the byway historic sites are abundant in Council Grove, named for the treaty council held here in 1825 with the Osage natives allowing safe passage of Americans and Mexicans along the Santa Fe Trail. The Kaw Mission State Historic Site and Museum on Mission Street was where 30 Kaw (or Kansa) Indian boys lived and studied from 1851 to 1854. The Kaws, known as "The People of the South Wind," gave the state its name. You can view exhibits that showcase the history and culture of the Kaws and the Santa Fe Trail that passed nearby.

**Council Grove:** Council Grove's early day calaboose is a friendlier place to visit today. Built in 1849 and believed to be the lone jail on the Santa Fe Trail at the time, it used to house desperados, ruffians, robbers, and horse thieves. Other "must-sees" in and around Council Grove include the old bell that was erected in 1866 to warn townsfolk of impending American Indian raids; the still-visible ruts from the Santa Fe Trail; and the Last Chance Store, built in 1857 and truly the "last chance" for trail travelers to buy supplies for their trip to Santa Fe, New Mexico.

### Wagon Train Trip

After traveling the Flint Hills Scenic Byway the modern way, consider spending a weekend traveling it the way the pioneers did. A weekend Wagon Train trip includes hearty outdoor meals cooked over a pit fire; activities based on the work and play of the Kansas homesteading era; songs and sonnets of the Old West; and information about the historic trails, geology, and plant life of this shrinking American Tallgrass Prairie. Voyagers travel in authentic covered wagons.

**Tallgrass Prairie National Preserve:** Farther south the byway passes one of America's newest national parks, Tallgrass Prairie National Preserve. Ranger-guided and self-guided tours are available, as well as hiking and wheelchair-accessible trails with interpretive kiosks. The preserve is also home to Spring Hill Ranch. Original owner, Stephen F. Jones, named his ranch the Spring Hill Ranch in 1881 for the abundant springs on the property. Visitors are welcome to explore the limestone mansion, barn, schoolhouse, and several other remaining outbuildings. Living history interpreters enhance the visit and invite guests to participate in activities.

**Limestone Mansion:** The impressive Limestone Mansion at Spring Hill was built on a hillside with a two-story exposure on the upper side and a three-story on the lower level. The architecture represents a blending of Renaissance influence and Plains Vernacular. Individual building stones are square cut on all bearing surfaces and have a rough-hewn face. The stones are all the same size. The expensive hand-cut stone would be impossible to duplicate today. The massive barn measures 110 feet wide and 60 feet deep. The stone structure that became the Lower Fox Creek Schoolhouse was built in 1882. In 1974, the school was placed on the National Register of Historic Places.

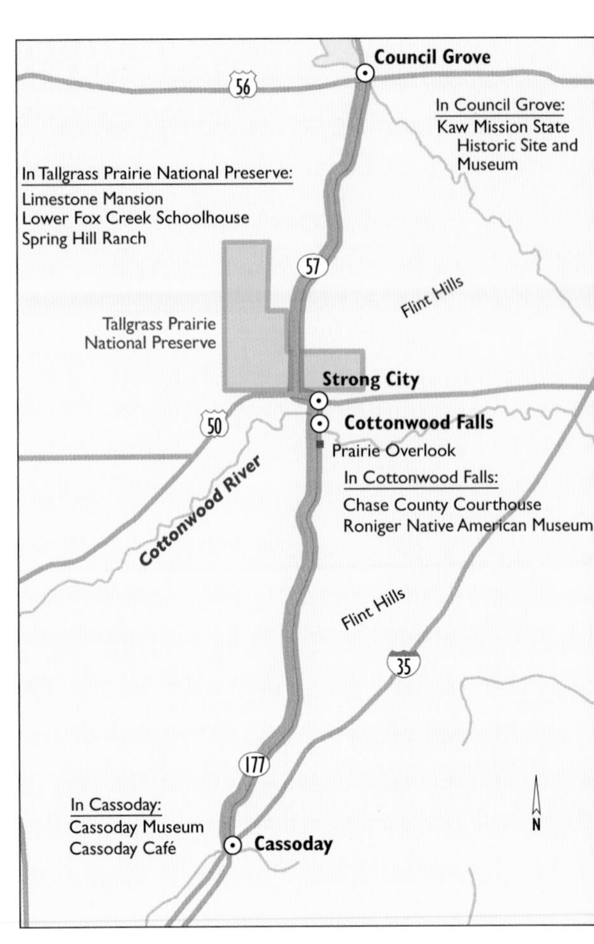


**Cottonwood Falls:** After visiting Tallgrass Prairie National Preserve and Spring Hill Ranch, the Flint Hills Scenic Byway then follows the path through Strong City and a mile later, Cottonwood Falls, site of the Chase County Courthouse, in operation since 1873 (the oldest courthouse in Kansas and the oldest operating courthouse west of the Mississippi). The Roniger Native American Museum is also in Cottonwood Falls and, with a collection of arrowheads, is considered one of the largest individual collections in Kansas.

**Prairie Overlook:** South of Cottonwood Falls, the picturesque highway travels among the hills for grand vistas of the ranches in the area, then eases down to the stream to follow splendid stone walls around farms still in operation. The scenic overlook south of Cottonwood Falls gives you a wonderful view of the vast expanse of the prairie as the pioneers might have seen it.

**Cassoday:** The village of Cassoday, with its tiny population of 130 and its fame as "The Prairie Chicken Capital of the World," is the southern end of the byway where those looking for curios and antiques may find just what they have been looking for. Also visit the Cassoday Museum located in the Old Depot. Whether it's time for a meal or not, the Cassoday Café is an interesting stop where city slickers can see hitching posts out in front used by today's working cowpokes who ride into town for lunch.

# Crowley's Ridge Parkway 

*Pure ocean sand in this landlocked state and the earliest recorded cemetery in the New World are but two of the wonders awaiting visitors to Crowley's Ridge Parkway.*

Part of a multistate byway; see also Arkansas.

Crowley's Ridge, characterized by sand, gravel, and deep gullies, has formed primary route of transport nd commerce for the people of his region for centuries. Various eoples have used the ridge to scape the swamps and wetlands. combination of land travel on he ridge and connecting rivers rovided a means of subsistence ver a vast corridor.

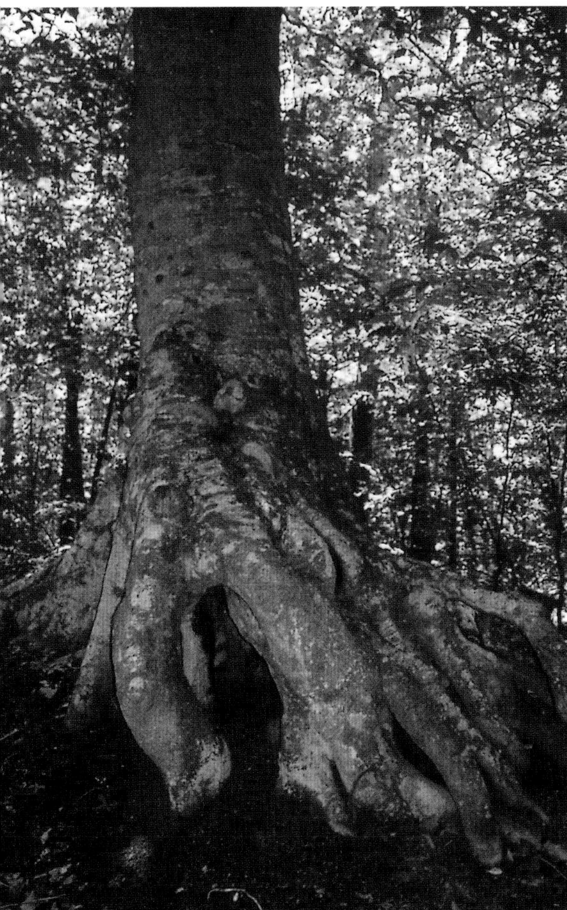

*Morris State Park has 27 types of trees and more than 300 different kinds of plants.*

## Intrinsic Qualities

**Archaeological:** The earliest recorded cemetery in the New World is found in Greene County, Arkansas, on Crowley's Ridge. Excavated in 1974, the Sloan Site was both home and burial ground for a small group of Native Americans who lived here approximately 10,500 years ago. Living in small bands in semi-permanent villages, they established the earliest documented cemetery in North America.

The Mississippian site of Parkin is now the Parkin Archaeological State Park in Cross County, Arkansas, and provides a museum, visitor center, walking tour, and research station. This site features a rectangular planned village of 400 houses, with a plaza surrounding mounds and evidence of a large population that interacted with the de Soto expedition.

**Historical:** Crowley's Ridge, with its heavy clay and gravel, proved to be a focal point for the historical and cultural events that shaped the region around it. From the unique plant life of the ridge to the lowland swamps, this region is a story waiting to be told.

The first known Native Americans were known as the Mound Builders. They date from A.D. 900 to 1500 and were agriculturists who lived in permanent villages. They made ceramic pots and various utensils, some of which remain on and below the surface today. Sizable collections of these artifacts can be found in the small museums throughout this region. Huge collections also exist at Arkansas State University and Southeast Missouri State University. However, these mounds are being challenged by the migration of a rice-planting culture and the disastrous raids of illegal collectors and artifact thieves.

The early European immigrants to this region were German, Scots-Irish, and English. Many of them came from Virginia, Tennessee, Kentucky, and Mississippi, and they brought African-American slaves with them. The byway intersects many of these ethnic islands that have shaped the history and culture of the region. The migration of the cotton culture brought a lifestyle that continues to influence local food, architecture, family values, and religion. Midwestern barns and Southern homes and churches can be found, as well.

There continues to exist in this region what the residents call the Chalk Bluff Trail. This trail extends from Cape Girardeau, Missouri, to Helena, Arkansas, and runs along the high ground of the ridge. The trail was originally used by Native Americans as they moved through the region on hunting expeditions. European settlers used the trail as they migrated to the West: it was the only safe way to travel through the swamps in order to capitalize on the 19th-century opportunities that existed in what is now the great American Southwest. Crowley's Ridge was the only all-weather access for settlers to transport trade items. In the 1850s, a plank road was built from

## Quick Facts

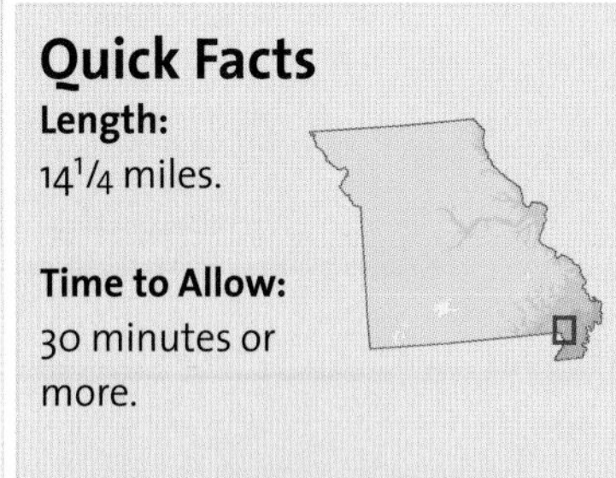

**Length:** $14\frac{1}{4}$ miles.

**Time to Allow:** 30 minutes or more.

**Considerations:** Plenty of services are available along the route for any special needs; however, watch your engine temperature so that you notice if it begins to increase.

Gideon to Portageville, providing the first east-west avenue to Mississippi River ports. The ridge became a vital highway during the Civil War, used by both Union and Confederate troops. On May 1–2, 1863, an engagement known as the Battle of Chalk Bluff occurred on the banks of the St. Francis River where it crosses Crowley's Ridge in a narrow gap. Small by most Civil War measures, the event was nevertheless significant to people in this region. Local cemeteries contain graves of both Union and Confederate soldiers.

Following the Civil War, many changes occurred in this area, including a restructuring of agriculture and technology that provided for increased farm size. New plows, threshers, seeders, and shellers allowed farmers to work more acres and increase yields per acre. This put more pressure on transportation and further

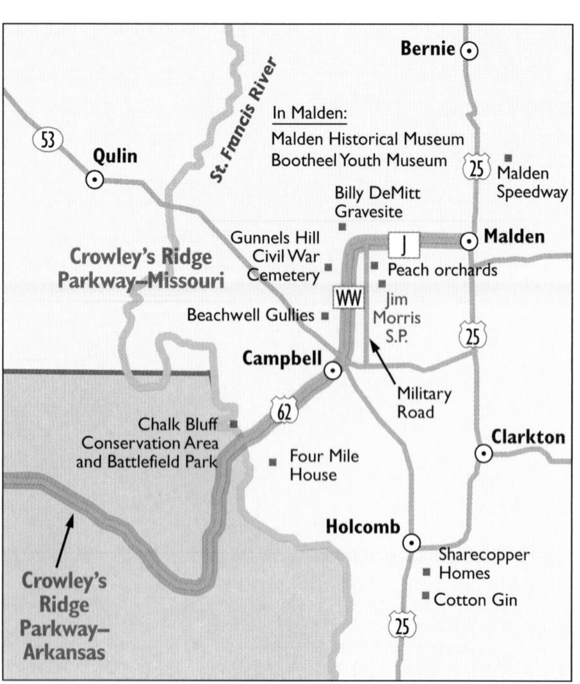


changed the region. The importation of cotton added to the region's transformation. Cotton farmers from the deep South came into the region as they tried to escape the boll weevil, which had temporarily devastated their lands and crops. Droughts in the 1930s withered those crops, however, and brought government programs to the area. In 1933, Congress passed the Agricultural Adjustment Act, which sought to stabilize agriculture. Soil conservation acts also impacted the region and reflected the changing nature of the times. Those benefits that came into the area generally went to the large planters, while little went to the growing number of sharecroppers and tenant farmers.

The land on and around Crowley's Ridge was generally worked well into the 20th century by sharecroppers who lived at the poverty level. The Southern way of life that existed in this area meant that there was little in the way of a middle class. African-Americans in the region were almost entirely in the sharecropper class. This system was widespread across the South in the aftermath of the Civil War, but was especially rigid in the new cotton lands of southeast Missouri. This situation led to one of the greatest stories to come out of Missouri in the 20th century, the story of the sharecropper strike of 1939.

The problems that plagued farmers in this region are still the same today in southeast Missouri. The large farm operator, through increased mechanization, has been able to survive and prosper, while the small farmer (and there are many in this area) has had little economic success. As farms continue to grow larger, owners of small farms have been forced to abandon both their land and their hope. Many have moved to larger cities or taken employment outside the farm. The area around the ridge continues to decline in population while land values increase.

**Natural:** Crowley's Ridge begins south of Cape Girardeau near Commerce, Missouri. It moves west in an arc, coming back to the great river near Helena, Arkansas. The last period of glaciation, some 15,000 years ago, caused massive buildup and melting of the glaciers that resulted in great floodwaters beyond modern imagination and created the Ohio and Mississippi Rivers as marginal ice streams. The Mississippi was west of Crowley's Ridge, the Ohio River to the east. The old route of the Mississippi may have followed the course of what is now the St. Francis River. Following the last ice melt, the Ohio joined the Mississippi River just south of the Thebes Gap at Cairo, Illinois. The narrow band of uplands known as Crowley's Ridge is the only remaining remnant of this story. The current river system moved to the east and left Crowley's Ridge.

Crowley's Ridge is a unique landform that is effectively isolated like an island in the middle of a small ocean of land. Plants and animals that inhabited the ridge were isolated and cut off from their natural migratory patterns, so a number of rare or endangered plants and animals are indigenous to the ridge. Of the various natural communities on the ridge, the rarest are the plants that occur along the seeps, runs, and springs. Nettled chain fern, yellow fringed orchid, umbrella sedge, black chokeberry, and marsh blue violet are some examples of these rare and exquisite plants.

The natural changes that happened in the landscape affected not only plants and animals but also humans. Some historians contend that Hernando de Soto was the first white explorer to reach Crowley's Ridge. If he did so, it remains unclear exactly where he made his first entrance into what is now Missouri. If and when he crossed the Mississippi River above the area that became Memphis, Tennessee, it is likely that he and at least some of his men followed American Indian and animal trails to the high ridge into present-day Dunklin County, Missouri.

As other immigrants from all parts of northern Europe moved west, they generally moved down the Ohio, crossed the Mississippi, and landed on the Missouri shoreline. This landing usually occurred t Norfolk Landing, located south of Cairo, Illinois. From there, immigrants would cross the alluvial prairie" swamps and head to the high ground of Crowley's Ridge. As early as the 1850s, there was discussion and even plans to drain the great wetlands. However, it was not until the early 20th century that the Little River Drainage District was formed and systematic and extensive drainage occurred.

Lumber companies moved into the region after 1913 when the massive log drives on the Mississippi were stopped by the Keokuk Dam. Soon, the region was a timberless, uninhabitable swamp. The Little River Drainage District did the rest. In what is the greatest land transformation in history, southeast Missouri was moved from natural wetland to field and farm in less than half a century.

## Highlights

The following is a suggested itinerary for traveling Crowley's Ridge Parkway in Missouri.

**Malden:** Visit the free Malden Historical Museum, and enjoy the exhibits, which include the history of Malden and the Dennis Collection of Egyptian Antiquities. Or spend some time at Malden's Bootheel Youth Museum, where adults and kids can both enjoy activities that explore the worlds of math, science, the arts, and more. Interactive exhibits include making (and standing inside!) a giant soap bubble, freezing shadows on the wall, and making music on sewer pipes. When you are ready to continue your drive, leave Malden on County Route J to the west. Enjoy the rural scenery. You may even spot the Military Road, but the easiest place to see the Military Road is at the next stop.

**Billy DeMitt Gravesite:** About three miles from the junction of routes J and WW is the famous site where 10-year-old Billy DeMitt was killed during the Civil War for refusing to tell a group of guerrillas where his father was. A marker at the spot commemorates this tragic story, a true legend in southeast Missouri.

**Jim Morris State Park and the Military Road:** Shortly after you turn south on County Route WW, you find Jim Morris State Park. In addition to showcasing many varieties of trees and other vegetation unique to the ridge, the park is the most practical way to see the Military Road. Access the road by the bicycle or pedestrian paths here. This road was used by military troops in the Civil War and by settlers as they moved across the Missouri bootheel. The entire road runs from the intersection of routes J and WW to one mile north of Campbell, with a total length of approximately six miles, and can be reached at various points along the route.

**Peach orchards:** As you drive south on County Route WW, keep an eye out for the more than 800 acres of peach orchards. In the spring, the scent of peach blossoms fills the air. If you are lucky enough to be driving this tour in the summer, be sure to stop at one of the peach stands and buy a tasty treat for the drive ahead.

**Beachwell Gullies:** Near County Route WW are the visible remnants of erosional forces that scoured the ridge about 200 feet deep from the top of the ridge to the bottom of the gully. The sand here is pure ocean sand (in a landlocked state!), and saltwater shells have been found in this area, evidence that this area was once part of a vast ocean. The gullies can be accessed by a pedestrian trail that is approximately one mile long.

**Campbell:** Next, visit the historic city of Campbell, which has roots dating back to before the Civil War. Several buildings in the Historic District, many of which are on the National Historic Register, are open to visitors. Dine in the quaint local restaurants, and visit the antique shops in the Historic District.

**Chalk Bluff Conservation Area:** As you leave Campbell, turn southeast onto U.S. Highway 62. Shortly before the St. Francis River and the Arkansas border, stop and visit the Chalk Bluff Conservation Area. This area is full of Civil War history. The Military Road and trenches from the Civil War can still be seen today, especially along the river. Continue on across into the tip of Arkansas to see a related Civil War historical site, Chalk Bluff Battlefield Park.

**Chalk Bluff Battlefield Park:** This park will be of interest if you are seeking Civil War history. It is located at a Civil War battlefield site where several skirmishes were fought. The history of the area is interpreted on plaques along a walking trail. Picnic tables are available, as well.

*The St. Francis River is the lowest point in the state of Missouri.*

# LITTLE DIXIE HIGHWAY OF THE GREAT RIVER ROAD

*River's edge experiences and bird's-eye views from the bluffs of the Mississippi River give travelers a glimpse of what has inspired others for centuries. The area is a habitat for eagles, including the stately bald eagle.*

The Little Dixie Highway (also called the Mississippi Flyway Byway) is home to a culture expressing a unique Southern flair. Accents of the South are revealed in the area's Victorian-era streetscapes and plantation-era mansions. This touch of the South has earned the region its nickname, Little Dixie.

## Intrinsic Qualities

**Cultural:** As you may expect from a region with such a diverse history, the Little Dixie Highway can boast equally varied and rich cultural qualities. Although the issue of slavery and the Civil War divided the nation, the cultural heritage of the United States proved remarkably resilient. The same can be said about Pike County, where churches and fraternal organizations helped to create a close-knit society that rebuilt itself after the war.

Clarksville's crafters have taken an active role in preserving this town's cultural heritage by restoring its historic commercial district, which is listed on the National Register of Historic Places. Artisans have performed the work necessary for the historically accurate restoration of this Victorian-era commercial district. A network of artists, artisans, and galleries, called the Provenance Project, takes an active role in promoting towns from Clarksville to Hannibal.

**Historical:** Perhaps more than anything else, the Mississippi River has provided this entire nation with stories. Mark Twain probably would have agreed that no single geological feature in the country could claim to be the father of a historical and cultural offspring as rich and colorful as the Mississippi River. During the early 1800s, the river served as the edge of the West, the barrier dividing civilization from the wild frontier. As the young nation continued its growth and expansion, clashes continued between new settlers and the native peoples. Eventually, the river proved no longer to be a barrier to the frontier, but a starting line for settlers' hopes and dreams.

Missouri was a state whose role in the slavery debate proved pivotal. The plantation homes and Southern-style architecture that marks the landscape throughout the length of the byway stands as a testament to that time. As travelers look out over the Mississippi River and see the shores of Illinois just across the mighty river, they are also reminded of the fact that freedom for the slaves always lay tantalizingly close.

The stories of the struggle for justice and freedom soon turned into tales of triumph and renewal. Struggles for a new kind of justice and freedom accompanied the hope ushered in by the Emancipation Proclamation. As the nation attempted to rebuild, so, too, did the residents of Pike County work to repair the damage caused by slavery and the Civil War. The county's buildings provide evidence of the prosperous society that overcame the ravages of division.

*Near the town of Hannibal, the Mississippi River is as inspiring to those who gaze upon it as it was to young local writer Mark Twain.*

### Quick Facts

**Length:** 30 miles.

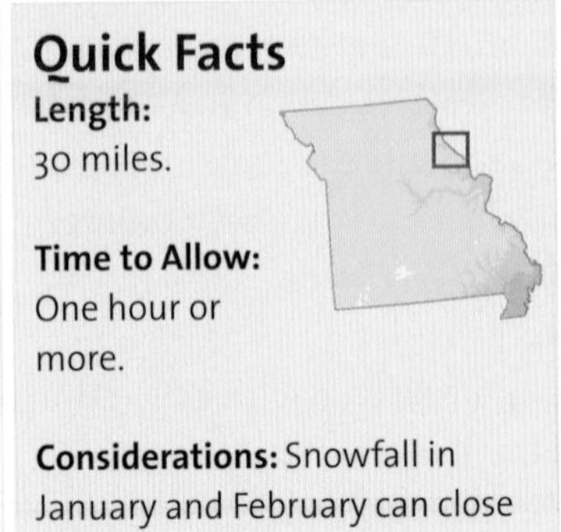

**Time to Allow:** One hour or more.

**Considerations:** Snowfall in January and February can close the highway until snow plowing can occur.

**Natural:** There is nothing quite like strolling along the banks of the Mississippi. The calm waters of the giant stream seem to stretch across for miles and provide habitat for an abundance of plant life and wildlife. This particular region of the river is an important bird habitat.

A flyway is simply a path for migrating birds. The Mississippi River provides a flight corridor for approximately 40 percent of all North American waterfowl, making this a prime spot for birdwatching. In addition, the Missouri Audubon Society has documented about 39 species of migratory shorebirds in the area, such as the killdeer and the sandpiper. As if that weren't enough, the area also serves as habitat for eagles.

**Recreational:** The Little Dixie Highway runs parallel to the area's major source of recreation, the Mississippi River. Recreational opportunities related to the river include some river islands open to the public; great opportunities for fishing, hiking, and cycling; a few wildlife reserves; two boat launches; the Eagle Center in Clarksville; a pair of riverfront municipal parks; Lock and Dam #24 at Clarksville; and a variety of scenic overlooks.

The Mississippi River has long been a prominent source of fish; catfish and crappie are the most common types found in the river. The parks and other points along the byway offer great opportunities to land that 20-pound Mississippi River catfish. The reserves along the byway also offer exceptional fishing. Clarksville and Louisiana each have a boat dock.

**Scenic:** The scenic overlooks from high bluffs north of Louisiana and at the Louisiana Cemetery, in particular, offer a bird's-eye view of the river and of the lush Mississippi Valley. The valley is a deep shade of green most of the time, full of dark, fertile soil that has provided food for Americans for centuries. The Pinnacle, at 850 feet above sea level, is the highest point on the Mississippi River. Barges, other boats, and occasionally even riverboats can be seen from these various overlooks.

## Highlights

Beginning at the southern end of the Little Dixie Highway, this itinerary offers some historic and scenic highlights along the route.

**Clarksville Historic District:** The Clarksville Historic District is noteworthy for the historical accuracy in the extensive restoration efforts. The detail work on the buildings of this quaint riverfront district is evident not only on the edifices themselves but also in the businesses that occupy them. As in the beginning days of the town, today highly skilled craftspeople take up business here.

**Clarksville Eagle Center:** Operated by the World Bird Sanctuary of St. Louis, Missouri, the Eagle Center prepares visitors for the eagle-viewing opportunities along the byway. Overlooking the Mississippi River, the Clarksville Eagle Center provides maps and brochures.

**Lock and Dam #24:** Continuing north from Clarksville along Missouri Highway 79, the byway will first come to Lock and Dam #24, the grounds of Holcum Concrete, Silo Park, and the Clarksville Refuge, all of which afford excellent bird-watching opportunities, especially of bald eagles, and up-close views of the impressive Mississippi River.

**Louisiana Area Historical Museum:** On Georgia Street in the town of Louisiana, Missouri, is the Louisiana Area Historical Museum. The museum, which is open daily from 1:00 P.M. to 4:00 P.M., as well as other attractions in the Georgia Street Historic District make up the most intact Victorian streetscape in the state of Missouri and are listed on the National Register of Historic Places.

**Ted Shanks Conservation Area:** Following Highway 79 north then east on Route TT, nature lovers come to Ted Shanks Conservation Area. This 6,705-acre wetlands area is sanctuary to waterfowl, songbirds, and mammals. In addition to bald eagles, great blue herons, and great egrets, more than 260 species of birds have been documented here. The headquarters contains educational exhibits, displays, and slide shows, and an observation room overlooks the marsh. A self-guided auto tour takes visitors through the area, while hiking, fishing, and hunting are also available.

**DuPont Conservation Area:** Back on Highway 79 and a mile farther north lies the DuPont Conservation Area. The location of a dynamite factory from 1892 to 1932, the land was donated by the DuPonts to the Conservation Commission in 1938. Subsequent land acquisitions brought the area to its current size of 1,328 acres. Rock bluffs provide spectacular views of the Mississippi River. Other activities include nature study, camping, and bird-watching along this natural flyway, along with seasonal hunting and fishing.

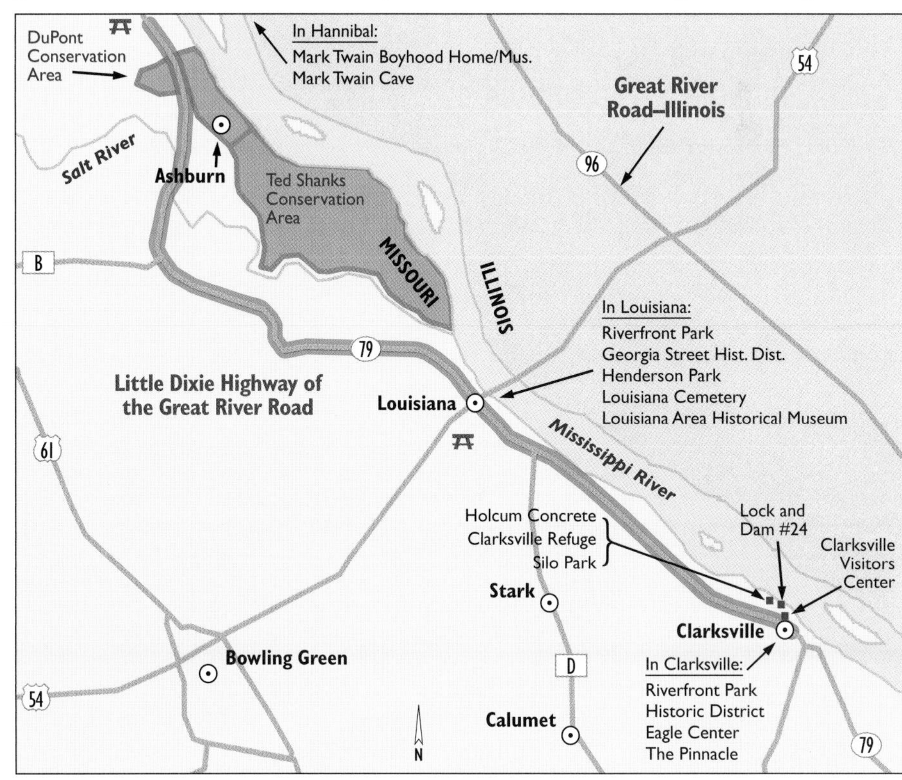

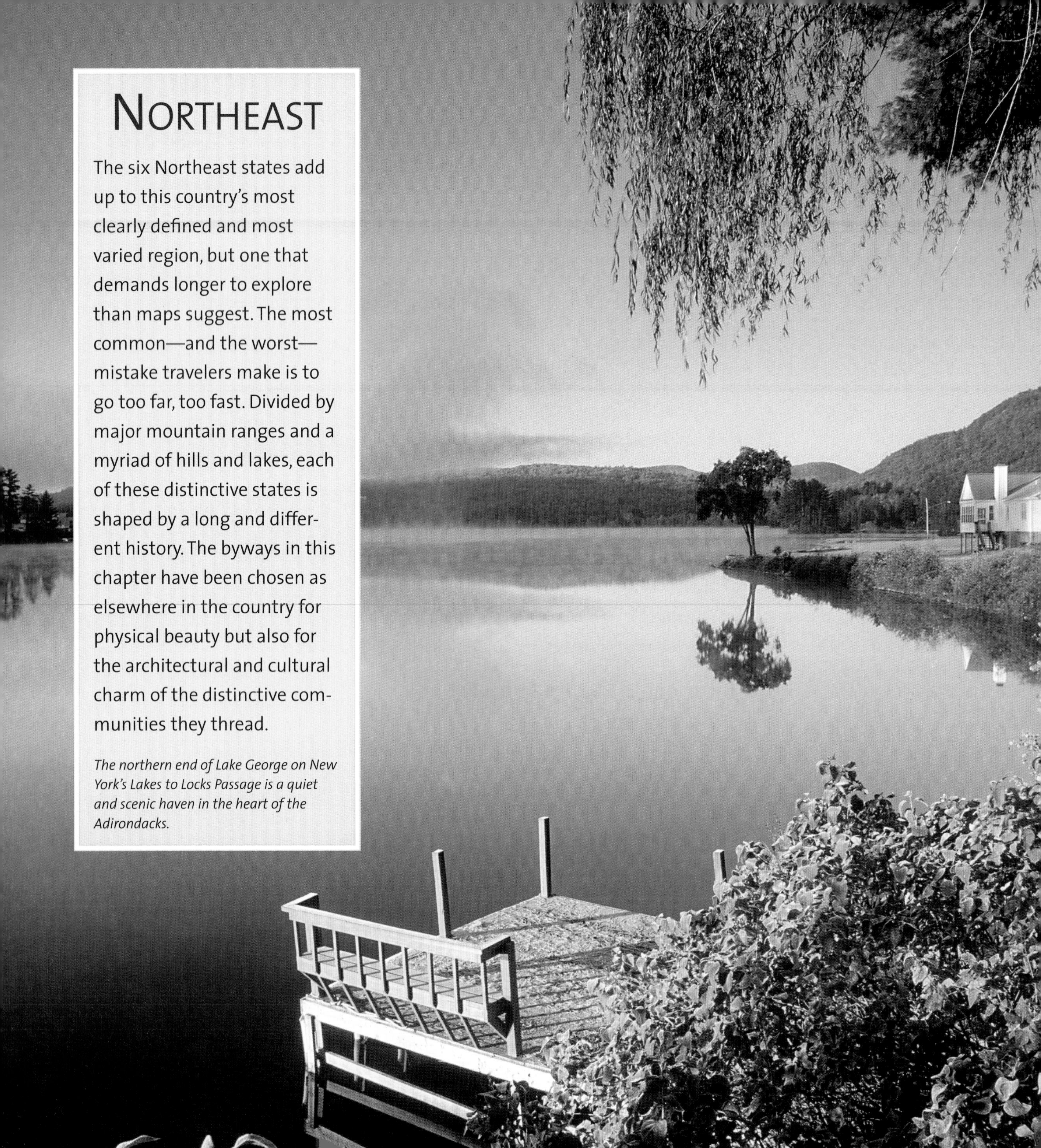

# NORTHEAST

The six Northeast states add up to this country's most clearly defined and most varied region, but one that demands longer to explore than maps suggest. The most common—and the worst—mistake travelers make is to go too far, too fast. Divided by major mountain ranges and a myriad of hills and lakes, each of these distinctive states is shaped by a long and different history. The byways in this chapter have been chosen as elsewhere in the country for physical beauty but also for the architectural and cultural charm of the distinctive communities they thread.

*The northern end of Lake George on New York's Lakes to Locks Passage is a quiet and scenic haven in the heart of the Adirondacks.*

# Acadia Byway 

*Acadia National Park spreads across much of Mount Desert, a mainland-hinged island known for its many rounded mountains rising abruptly from the sea. The Loop Road circles both ocean and shore, accessing hiking trails, bicycle paths, and the top of Cadillac Mountain.*

Fog is a common sight along this byway, muting the landscape with its romantic gray mists. In the midday sun, the sea's bright blue surface is studded with colorful lobster buoys. Seen at sundown from Cadillac Mountain, the sea glows in soft pinks, mauves, and golds.

As the name suggests, the Acadia area was French before it was American. French explorer Samuel de Champlain sailed into Frenchman Bay in 1604, naming the area Mount Desert Island because of its landmark bare top. Today, the National Park Service owns approximately half of the island that makes up Acadia National Park. The island boasts lush forests, tranquil ponds, and granite-capped mountains, where exploring is made easy by an extensive system of carriage roads and hiking trails. This alternate transportation network provides access to all areas of the park for walkers, equestrians, bicyclists, and cross-country skiers.

Villages on Mount Desert Island present a variety of lifestyles. Bar Harbor offers many accommodations and amusements. Northeast Harbor shelters sailboats, both large and small, and a summer colony.

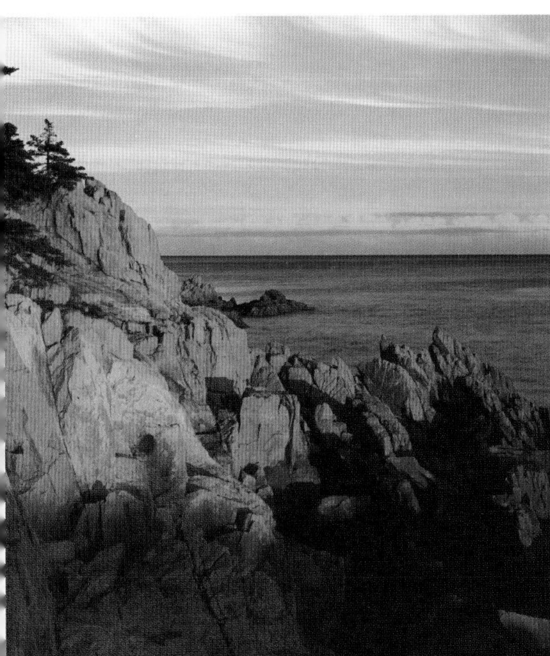

*The rugged cliffs in Acadia National Park give spectacular views of the Atlantic Ocean.*

## Intrinsic Qualities

**Archaeological:** Deep shell heaps suggest Native American encampments dating back 6,000 years in Acadia National Park. The first written descriptions of Maine coast Native Americans were recorded 100 years after European trade contacts began. In these records, Native Americans were described as people who lived off the land by hunting, fishing, collecting shellfish, and gathering plants and berries.

The Wabanaki Indians called Mount Desert Island *Pemetic*, or "the sloping land." They built bark-covered conical shelters and traveled in delicately designed birch bark canoes. Archaeological evidence suggests that the Wabanaki wintered on the coast and summered inland in order to take advantage of salmon runs upstream in the winter and to avoid harsh inland weather.

**Cultural:** While Maine is rich in culture, perhaps the best-known sights along the coast are the lobster traps and colorful buoys. Catching lobster has been a profitable activity in Maine since the 1840s. Today, the sight of a lobster fisher reeling in a trap is common.

The lobster boats are not the same wooden dories originally used, but they are still a unique sight along the waters. They generally have a round bottom and a double wedge hull, ranging from 20 to 40 feet. The actual lobster traps come in various designs. Two of the best known are the parlor trap and the double-header trap, and they're set anywhere from 50 feet to miles apart. During the summer, lobster can be found in shallow waters (60 to 100 feet), but during the winter, lobsters descend to depths of more than 200 feet.

### Quick Facts

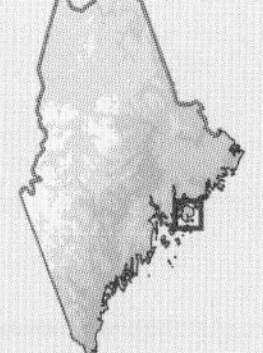

**Length:** 40 miles.

**Time to Allow:** Three hours.

**Considerations:** Mount Desert Island has a free seasonal bus service that visitors are encouraged to use; the central terminal is in downtown Bar Harbor. The buses stop at many of the hotels and campgrounds along the way. They also stop anywhere that offers adequate space to pull over. You can easily flag them down. The Park Loop Road is closed from late November to mid-April. Other roads can be closed during extreme weather conditions. You must pay a car toll to get on Park Loop Road at the national park.

**Historical:** Acadia's long history of settlement and colonization began with Samuel de Champlain, who led the expedition that landed on Mount Desert on September 5, 1604. Because de Champlain, who made the first important contribution to the historical record of Mount Desert Island, visited 16 years before the Pilgrims landed at Plymouth Rock, this land was known as New France before it became New England.

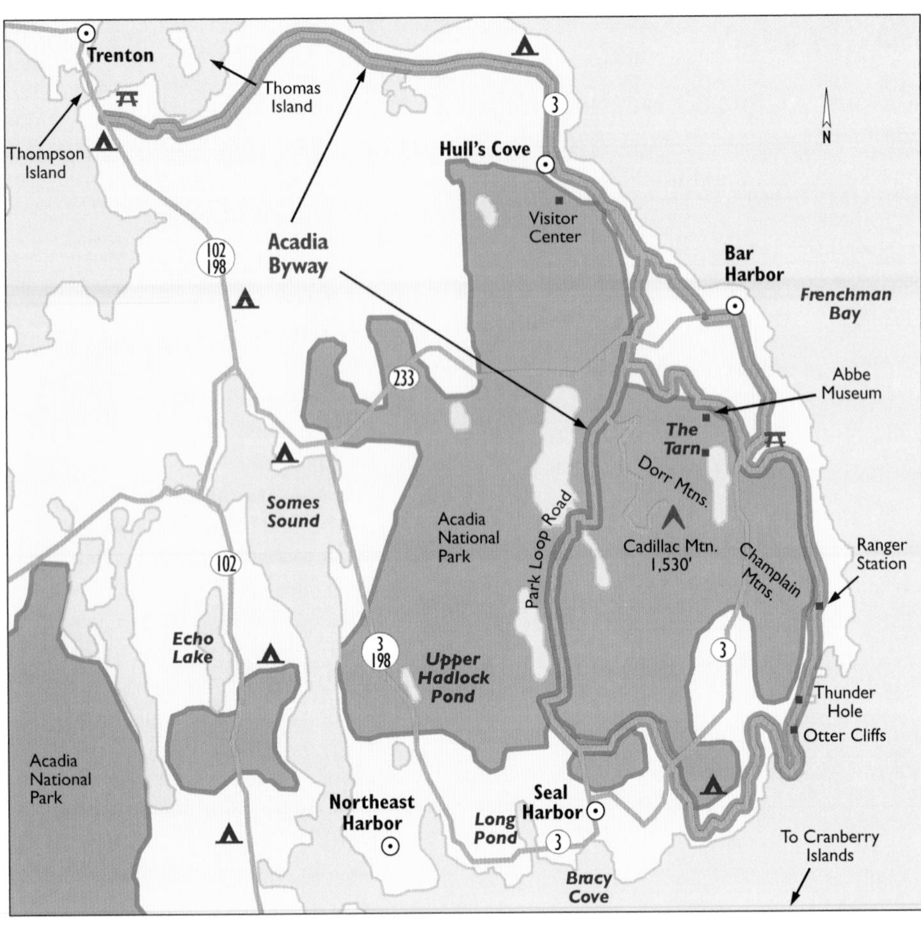




The land was in dispute between the French to the north and the English to the south. After a century and a half of conflict, British troops triumphed at Quebec, ending French dominion in Acadia. Hence, lands along the Maine coast opened for English settlement. Soon, an increasing number of settlers homesteaded on Mount Desert Island. By 1820, farming and lumbering vied with fishing and shipbuilding as major occupations. Outsiders—artists and journalists—revealed and popularized the island to the world in the mid-1800s. Painters, then called rusticators, inspired patrons and friends to flock to the island. Tourism became a major industry.

For a handful of Americans, the 1880s and Gay Nineties meant affluence on a scale without precedent. Mount Desert, still remote from the cities of the east, became a retreat for prominent people of the times. The Rockefellers, Morgans, Fords, Vanderbilts, Carnegies, and Astors chose to spend their summers on the island. They transformed the area with elegant estates, euphemistically called "cottages." For more than 40 years, the wealthy held sway at Mount Desert until the Great Depression, World War II, and the fire of 1947 marked the end of such extravagance.

Although the wealthy came to the island to play, they also helped to preserve the landscape. George B. Dorr, in particular, was a tireless crusader for conservation. Dorr and others established the Hancock County Trustees of Public Reservations. This corporation's sole purpose was to preserve land for the perpetual use of the public, and it acquired some 6,000 acres by 1913. In 1916, the land became the Sieur de Monts National Monument, and in 1919 it became the first national park east of the Mississippi, with Dorr as the first park superintendent. The name changed to Acadia in 1929, and today the park encompasses 35,000 acres of land.

**Natural:** Acadia Byway runs right along Acadia National Park, where the views are outstanding. Acadia is home to a menagerie of wildlife that captivates the most experienced nature-watcher. Whether you yearn to catch a glimpse of whales and seals or native and migratory birds, Acadia offers it all.

A variety of whales can be seen in the Gulf of Maine, with antics that bring a smile, along with a sense of awe. Although finback, minke, and right whales can be seen, humpbacks are among the most playful of the whales. They are known for spy hopping (sticking their heads out of the water to look around), lobe tailing (throwing the lower half of their bodies out of the water), and tail slapping. To witness a humpback whale breaching (jumping completely out of the water) is a particularly amazing sight. Pay attention to the humpback's tail during its aerobatics—each whale's tail is unique.

Acadia is an especially fertile area for bird sightings. In fact, 338 species—some migratory and some native—frequent the area. The peregrine falcon, once nearly extinct, can be seen winging overhead. They seem to circle lazily, but these raptors can attack prey at speeds of more than 100 miles per hour. They are most active at dawn and dusk in open areas. Puffins, also once nearly extinct, are making a comeback on islands along the Maine coast. Visitors may see this clown of the sea during offshore excursions.

**Recreational:** Relatively small at only 13 miles wide and 16 miles long, Acadia National Park offers a multitude of activities. Acadia maintains 45 miles of carriage roads for walking, riding, biking, and skiing and more than 100 miles of trails just for hiking. Situated right along the coast, the area is perfect for boating, sailing, and kayaking.

Hiking is one of the best ways to see all that Acadia has to offer. Trails crisscross the entire island. Take time to steal softly through a still forest, skip along the thundering coast, or meander through a swaying meadow. Up Cadillac

Mountain is a particularly inspiring hike; its summit is the highest point on the Atlantic coast north of Rio de Janeiro. If you reach it before dawn and stand at the summit, you will be the first person in the continental United States to see the sun begin its journey across the sky and witness the beginning of a brand-new day.

Want to see as much of the park as possible? Try cycling. If you prefer paved roads, you'll find Acadia's smooth rides beckoning, while mountain bikers are in for a pleasant surprise: 45 miles of carriage roads wind around rippling lakes, through tunnels of leafy branches, over hills, and under a number of stone bridges.

For water enthusiasts, Acadia offers a number of alternatives. Ocean canoeing and kayaking are drawing new converts every day. The thrill of gliding on the surface of the rolling sea is an experience never to be forgotten. You can immerse yourself more fully in the ocean experience by swimming at one of the beaches, although water temperatures rarely exceed 55 degrees. Echo Lake, a freshwater lake, is somewhat warmer. Take a trip on one of the schooners for a glimpse into sailing experiences of the late 1800s. Relax in the gentle breeze, try your hand at deep-sea fishing, or help the crew with the lines.

**Scenic:** Acadia National Park preserves the natural beauty of Maine's coasts, mountains, and offshore islands. Acadia Byway takes you through a diverse area of scenery, from the seashore to the green vegetation inland. Park Loop Road, constructed specifically to take visitors through the variety of sights that Acadia has to offer, leads you along a path of breathtaking delight. The views from Acadia's mountaintops encompass shadowy forests, gleaming lakes, hushed marshes, bold rocky shores, and coastal islands. The ocean, which surrounds Acadia on all sides, strongly influences the atmosphere of the park.

Travel the byway, and stop to enjoy the tide pools along the beaches. Pockets in the rocky shore trap pools of water as the tide recedes, and remarkable plants and creatures grow and live in them, surviving the inhospitable world between tides. A little farther along, step into part of the woodlands where sunlight filters through the branches of spruce, fir, birch, aspen, and oak. Around another curve, a clear, shimmering freshwater lake appears. At yet another place along the byway, climb through the mountains and enjoy the stark beauty of the cliff faces and numerous plant species.

*Bar Harbor was once known as Eden, and is now known for its Maine lobster and unique ambiance.*

## Highlights

Take your time while traveling this byway. Because this route is on the coast and in a national park, you'll find no end to the brilliant views. Although the byway runs just 40 miles, you can spend several days here.

**Visitor Center:** Pick up some brochures at the visitor's center near Hull's Cove. If you're planning to hike, you'll want to know how difficult each of the hikes is so that you can plan according to your level of expertise. You'll also want to find out the cost of ferries if you plan to go out to the Cranberry Islands or go whale-watching.

**Bar Harbor:** Spend time in the city of Bar Harbor, soaking in the relaxed atmosphere, eating at a fine or charming local-flavor restaurant, and exploring a few of the hundreds of specialty shops. You can seek out plenty of night-life: bars, clubs, concerts, and specialty movie theaters (one is Art Deco; one has couches and pizza). You may even be able to catch one of the two annual music festivals, part of the annual film festival, or an opening night at an art gallery.

**Dorr and Champlain mountains and The Tarn:** Spend the day hiking around Dorr and Champlain mountains and The Tarn. Explore off-road Acadia National Park on a mountain bike; take the 45 miles of carriage roads that are safe, serene, gorgeous, and well maintained.

**Thunder Hole, Otter Cliffs, Otter Point, and Cranberry Islands:** Be sure to hit Thunder Hole (and its associated historical ranger station). Otter Cliffs and the adjoining Otter Point are simply remarkable. You may want to don a jacket as you sit on the rocks and have a picnic lunch. Hop a ferry out to the Cranberry Islands to explore or take a ferry to whale-watch. You can see many other kinds of wildlife while whale-watching: bald eagles, puffins, and peregrine falcons. You can ocean kayak or canoe, deep-sea fish, or take a windjammer cruise. Equipment for all of these activities may be rented, and plenty of guides are available.

# Old Canada Road Scenic Byway 

*U.S. 201 runs north from the long-settled village of Solon along the Kennebec River. Beyond the hydro dam in Bingham it widens into shimmering Wyman Lake, then narrows again, churning through Kennebec Gorge to the delight of white-water rafters. Follow Benedict Arnold's lead, continuing north through Jackman and on to Quebec City.*

Find a snapshot of the past on the Old Canada Road Scenic Byway. Pass through villages and outposts that are much as they were at the turn of the 19th century. Remote and unspoiled, this neck of the Maine woods is a unique and beautiful place, where people live, work, and visit. The byway is in one of the most picturesque roads in the Northeast. It winds right alongside the Kennebec River, Wyman Lake, the Dead River, and vast forests. Rivers dominate the southern half of the route, while forests command the northern section.

The southern half of U.S. 201 is where you will first encounter old-time villages such as Solon and Bingham. Vernacular architecture contributes to the feel of an earlier time. Moscow gives way to the steep shoreline of Wyman Lake.

### Quick Facts

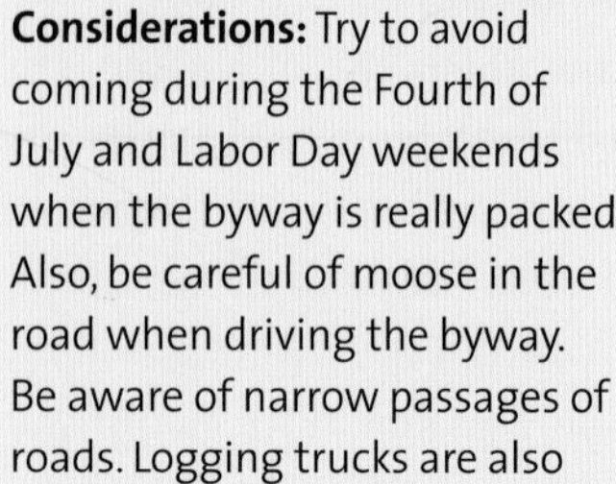

**Length:** 78 miles.

**Time to Allow:** At least $2^1/_2$ hours.

**Considerations:** Try to avoid coming during the Fourth of July and Labor Day weekends when the byway is really packed. Also, be careful of moose in the road when driving the byway. Be aware of narrow passages of roads. Logging trucks are also frequent on the byway.

Your drive hugs the shore, revealing undeveloped ridges on the opposite shore and islands framed by dramatic stands of white birch. North of the West Forks, you'll see mountains and ridges, and an occasional moose or deer.

## Intrinsic Qualities

**Archaeological:** The Maine Historic Preservation Commission reports numerous archaeological sites around the Kennebec River that link Maine Native Americans with other Native Americans. The oldest evidence in this area dates back at least 7,000 years.

The Kennebec River was crucial to the boundaries that were set and reset between the French and English, who were both trying to control this part of North America in the early 1600s. The English established trading posts (and later forts) at Augusta and Waterville. The French sent Jesuit missionaries along the route. Extensive archaeological remains show French and English habitation along the byway.

*The Kennebec River offers a mix of unending scenery, thrilling roller-coasterlike white water, and superb fishing opportunities, all in a remote setting.*

**Cultural:** The Old Canada Road, which runs from the Canadian border to Solon, Maine, is rich in history brought by the French who settled the area in the 1600s. The byway served as a route for loggers, but the area was virtually uninhabited with the exception of a few sporadic villages. Today, evidence of the influence of French and English culture is found in language, music, community celebrations, and food.

The folk culture and regional identity come in part from the immigration of people from French-speaking Canada. This influence is especially strong in the northern portion of the route, where many residents are bilingual. Many occupants of the area speak what is known as "Valley French," which is a combination of French, Quebecois, and English.

Throughout the year, communities along the byway celebrate their culture through festivals that honor French music and traditions. Because many of the French continued south to what is now Louisiana, both old French and Creole music are often celebrated in the area.

Visitors can learn about the area's early history and culture by touring the Jackman–Moose River Historical Museum in Jackman. The museum offers exhibits and memorabilia honoring logging culture and World War II, both of which influenced the present-day culture.

**Historical:** The Canada Road served as the primary link between Lower Canada and Maine from about 1820 to 1860. The various east–west linkages, as well as the southern connections that allowed detours off the Canada Road, permitted migrants to disperse along this route throughout New England.

The road began as settlers from the Kennebec Valley moved northward into Somerset County. The Yankee pioneers found themselves closer to the markets of Quebec City than to those of Boston. In the early 19th century, Quebec was a growing lumber and ship-building port, as well as a military and administrative center, and it needed provisions. So Yankee drovers took livestock north, through the woods on a trail they built between the roads that lay alongside the Kennebec and Chaudière Rivers (the Chaudière River is in Canada). It became obvious that it was to almost everyone's advantage to "close the gap" between these two road systems.

In 1815, the road Chemin de la Chaudière along the northeast shore of the Chaudière River was extended to the fork of the DuLoup River and continued up the northeast shore of the DuLoup to just below the frontier. This 28-mile roadway was almost 18 feet wide and followed the earlier drover's trail.

In 1817, the legislature authorized construction of a "traveled path" to be made suitable for the passage of loaded carts, sleds, and other such conveyances. It was to largely follow the old cattle drover's trail. Almost 25 miles in length, it ran from the north shore of Parlin Pond to the Canadian line. The next year Somerset County had the final 43 miles of road built between Concord and Parlin Pond along the west side of the Kennebec River.

By 1830, the dream of commercial profit finally drove government officials to upgrade the Canada Road into a carriageway that would accommodate drovers, entrepreneurs, government and military officials, laborers, couriers, hikers, sailors, farmers, and their families. Infrastructures began to develop in response to the increase in traffic, as post offices, inns, stage lines, and customs houses were established.

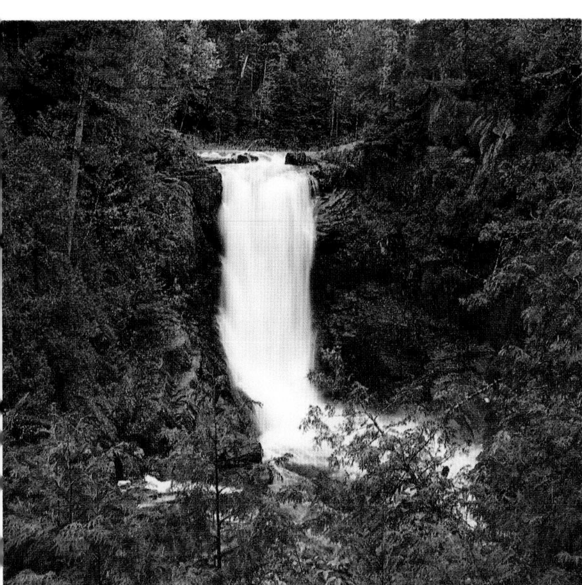

*Moxie Falls is one of the highest falls in Maine. The woods around the falls contain a network of hiking trails.*

**Natural:** Moose are the largest animals that will be seen along the byway. Standing up to seven feet tall, many call the byway home. They are unique in the fact that their legs are so long they need to kneel in order to drink from shallow puddles or lick salt from the roadways, as they often do. Please heed warning signs and enjoy the moose... at a safe distance.

Beavers have had a tremendous impact on the landscape for centuries. Their engineering skills have submerged thousands of acres, creating beneficial habitats for other creatures. Their work often creates enjoyable canoeing, kayaking, and fishing opportunities. Evenings provide the best opportunity for viewing this talented woodland rodent.

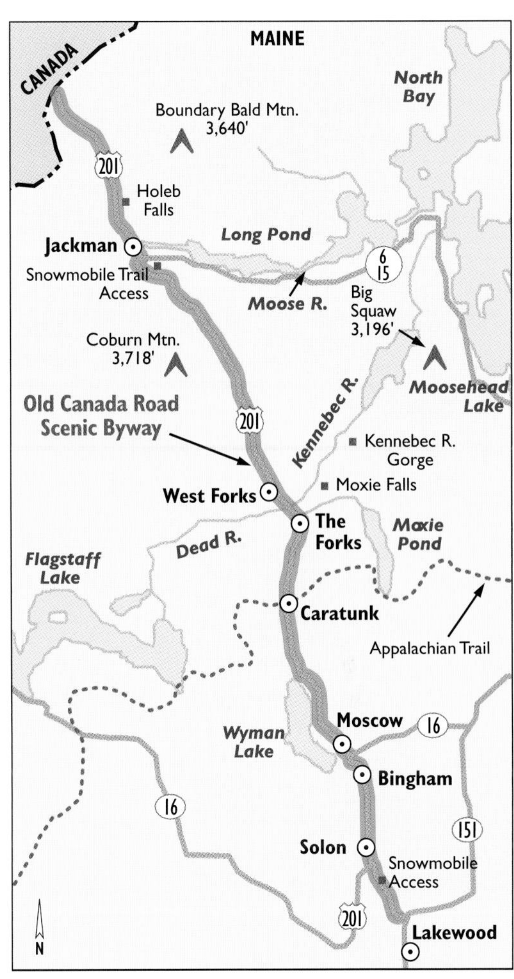


**Recreational:** Hunting, fishing, and camping are the main attractions, but white-water rafting in this area of Maine is a thrill throughout the summer and fall. Winter offers the solace of silent trails or the invigoration of a lengthy snowmobile ride to distant towns and Canada.

Traditional sporting camps are plentiful and provide unique experiences in rustic accommodations. Hotels in Solon, Bingham, Caratunk, The Forks, West Forks, and Jackman provide lodging throughout the year.

Camping is available at a number of isolated public sites and private campgrounds, many near some of Maine's beautiful lakes and ponds. Canoeing is enjoyed on numerous lakes, ponds, bogs, and rivers. Enjoy birding from the serenity of a canoe floating in the lake. Drop your line in the water to lure tasty brook trout. Travel by canoe to untracked shores. For a unique experience to remember, visitors can enjoy the Moose River Bow Trip, a three- or four-day canoe or kayak trip of the Moose River that starts and ends at Attean Pond near Jackman.

The Appalachian Trail, one of the most famous multistate hiking trails in the United States, crosses the byway in Caratunk. The trail's 270-mile terrain throughout Maine is considered some of the most difficult of the 14 states the trail runs through, but the scenery is breathtaking. This rugged trail takes hikers through waist-high bogs, up steep inclines, and across the Kennebec River, which can only be crossed by ferry.

**Scenic:** The northern section of the drive is one of the few places in New England where you can still drive for miles through undeveloped mountains and forest. Look for spectacular mountain views from Attean Overlook in Jackman, where you will see several sparkling lakes at the feet of majestic mountains.

Famous for gorgeous and inspiring fall color, the striking foliage along the byway draws many people. The bright crimson, orange, and gold landscape, worthy to grace a postcard, can be witnessed from early September to October.

Wintertime creates spectacular scenery—icy rivers snake down craggy mountains and through forests blanketed with fluffy white snow, winter birds perch on branches of snowy trees, and hungry moose venture closer to the road in search of food. Visitors may see a number of species of birds as they snowshoe the winter trails along the Kennebec, or happen across untracked forest clearings.

Springtime along the byway is beautiful, but wet. The rainy season brings lush, green plant life, but also muddy trails, so this season is best enjoyed from the road. Visitors may want to kayak the Kennebec and Moose Rivers during this season, because the area is less crowded and the rivers have the most water.

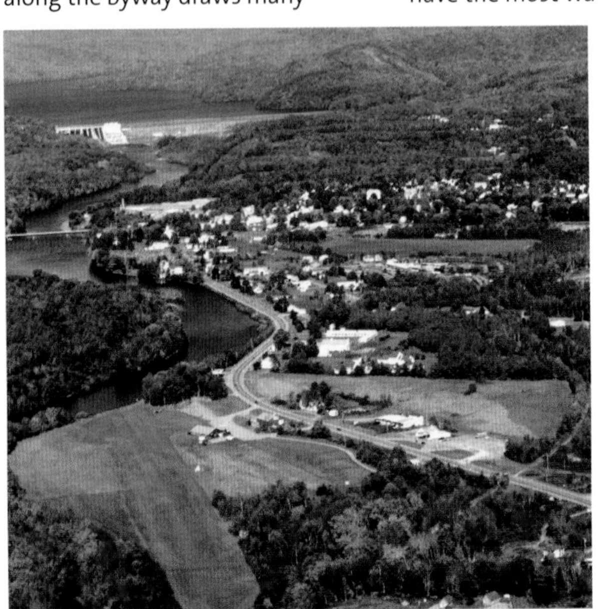

*An eagle's-eye view shows the Old Canada Road snaking its way between the Kennebec River and quaint villages.*

Summer is the busiest travel season along the byway, but not just for the recreational opportunities. Summer provides some of the most spectacular views of the forest and water near the byway. Be sure to visit some of the many crystal-clear lakes, which are full of lively fish this time of year, and hike trails through green forests, which create a lush backdrop for spectacular animal life.

## Highlights

The byway starts where Route 151 intersects with U.S. 201 north of the town of Lakewood and ends near the Canadian border.

**Solon and Bingham:** Drive north on U.S. 201, which passes through two old-time villages, Solon and Bingham. Both are bounded on the west by the Kennebec River. Solon has wintertime snowmobiling trails.

**Wyman Lake:** Just north of Bingham is 13-mile-long Wyman Lake, which is a fishing hot spot for perch, bass, and sunfish. In January, there's ice fishing for landlocked salmon and trout.

**Appalachian Trail:** Farther north, the 2,160-mile-long Appalachian Trail crosses the byway at Caratunk. While the trail runs from Maine all the way to Georgia, day hikes are popular through the rugged terrain here. To cross the Kennebec River at Caratunk, hikers can use a free ferry service that runs from late May to mid-October.

**Kennebec and Dead rivers:** Continuing north, the Kennebec River meets the Dead River at The Forks. Both rivers offer thrilling whitewater rafting. The Kennebec heads through remote wilderness and the beautiful Kennebec River Gorge and produces huge roller-coaster waves, with many class IV or higher rapids along 12-mile runs. Watch for deer, river otters, and eagles along the route. In late spring and early fall, the Dead River has the longest continuous class III–IV white water in New England. It offers milder rapids for much of the summer.

**Moxie Falls:** Also from The Forks, a short drive and less than a mile walk leads through the pines to the 90-foot-high Moxie Falls, which makes a nice picnic spot. From U.S. 201, turn east onto Lake Moxie Road and follow it to the signposted trailhead for the waterfall. There are also hiking trails near Moxie Falls.

**Jackman:** North of The Forks, the Jackman area is a recreational mecca. In winter, a huge network of snowmobile trails includes thousands of miles of groomed crisscrossing trails leading up to Canada and across to New Hampshire. In warmer weather, the scenic Moose River, which runs through Jackman, has only mild rapids and features some of the Northeast's most popular canoeing and kayaking, complete with camping on a 34-mile route. Eagles, ospreys, deer, and moose are some of the watchable wildlife.

**Holeb Falls:** Along the Moose River west of Jackman, stunning Holeb Falls has a long vertical drop into a swimming area at its base. With its mountainous backdrop, this area is known as the Switzerland of Maine.

# Rangeley Lakes Scenic Byway 

*Wind through the western mountains of Maine on the Rangeley Lakes Scenic Byway. Trail your way through richly wooded forests, brisk mountain streams, farm fields, and a chain of lakes and ponds. Nature is all around you!*

The Rangeley Lakes Region, the byway's namesake, was settled by a small number of hardy pioneers in the early 1800s. Rugged and remote, this region grew slowly, while sustaining about a dozen family farms and lumber mills throughout the first half of the century. In the 1860s, the small community began to change when vacationers from cities along the Eastern Seaboard discovered 10- to 12-pound brook trout swimming in the region's pristine waters. As word spread about the unparalleled fishing and the unspoiled beauty of the region, large numbers of anglers and their families began an annual trek to the region. By 1925, the Rangeley region had become a premier destination resort area that attracted visitors, as well as a host of U.S. presidents, from all corners of the nation.

Today the region's cultural history and outstanding scenic, natural, and recreational resources offer local residents and visitors an array of activities that extend throughout the year. During the summer months, treat yourself to a host of festivals, concerts, and museums, as well as boating, hiking, fishing, bicycling, and wildlife watching. When autumn paints the hillsides in red and gold, come enjoy leaf watching, hiking, and hunting in the crisp Maine air. A cup of fresh squeezed cider from the Apple Festival, a tour of the Wilhelm Reich Museum, or a drive along the bronzed byway will round out your autumn day in Rangeley. Winter arrives early, cloaking the region in 12 feet of snow. Between Christmas fairs, concerts, and the annual Snodeo festival, join skiers, snowmobilers, and ice skaters and take to the slopes, trails, and lakes. Then, as temperatures rise and the days increase in length, spring ushers in the annual "ice out contest."

*Excellent fly-fishing attracts people to the scenic Kennebago River. Nearby trails provide ample opportunities for hiking and wildlife viewing.*

## Quick Facts

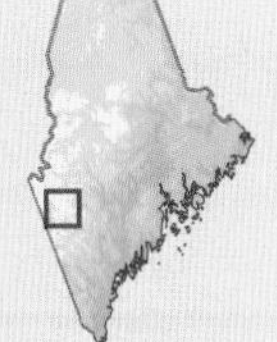

**Length:** 36 miles.

**Time to Allow:** $2^1/2$ hours.

**Considerations:** Located off the beaten path, traffic congestion is never an issue. However, during Rangeley's Snodeo and its Fourth of July celebration, traffic is heavier than normal; please allow for slight delays so that you will not miss these terrific events.

## Intrinsic Qualities

**Archaeological:** The first people known to have inhabited Maine were the Paleo-Indians. They moved from the south or west about 9,000 years ago as the area that is now Maine was recovering from the last glaciation. Typically, they camped on land away from river valleys and were probably the only prehistoric people to have done so. Near the end of the Paleo-Indian era, trees spread across Maine and forced the state's inhabitants to live and travel along coastal areas, lakes, and waterways.

Four types of archaeological sites are found in Maine: habitation and workshop sites, lithic quarries, cemeteries, and rock art. Habitation and workshop sites make up more than 95 percent of the known archaeological sites in Maine. Artifacts found at these sites were used by the Paleo-Indians to procure and process food and to manufacture and maintain tools.

Northwest of the Rangeley Lakes Scenic Byway on the shoreline of Aziscohos Lake is the Vail Site. It is located in a high mountain river valley, and artifacts from this classic Paleo-Indian habitation site date back to 11,000 B.C. Surrounded by smaller habitation sites, the Vail Site includes a stone meat cache and two killing grounds, the first of their kind to be recorded east of the Mississippi River. Professional excavations in eight or nine sites recovered more than 4,000 tools.

Although no bones were found at the Vail killing sites, it has been suggested and supported through other site research that the prehistoric people hunted caribou almost exclusively. One of the most significant finds at the Vail Site was a series of finely crafted fluted points. The points are very sharp and many are thought to have tipped thrusting spears. These discoveries also support the idea that the hunters were aware of the

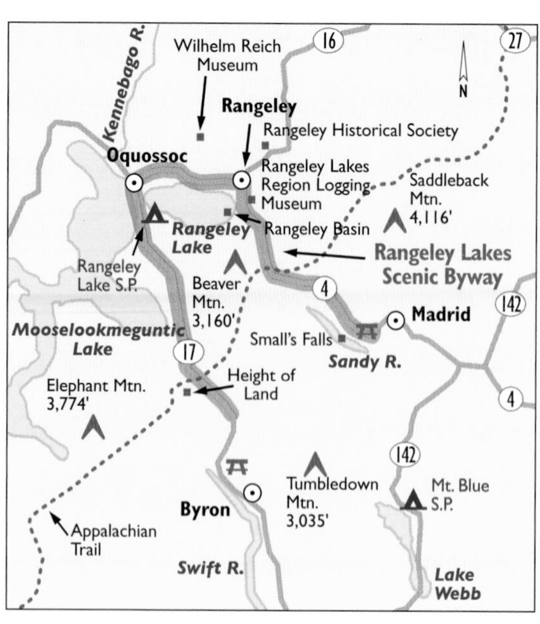


seasonal migration of caribou herds and that they slaughtered hundreds of them en route to their winter habitat.

**Cultural:** Responding to the sudden flood of anglers (or "sports" as they were affectionately called) in the late 1800s, the local residents built rustic sporting cabins along the shores of the region's lakes. Equipped with beds, gas lamps, and fireplaces, these simple but comfortable structures offered a welcome alternative to a lumpy bedroll and canvas tent.

With an intimate knowledge of the lakes, the locals acted as guides, using the famed Rangeley Boat to row their clients to the best fishing holes in the region. Equally adept with a skillet and a campfire, the guides treated the sports to lakeside dinners of fresh trout, locally grown vegetables, and hefty mugs of coffee. The tradition of sporting cabins and guiding continues today, as anglers cast for the "speckled beauties" throughout the spring and summer months.

A dangerous and difficult way to make a living, logging supported many of the local families and contributed to the development of a strong regional identity. For nearly a century, two-person teams used crosscut saws and sturdy pairs of horses or oxen to fell and haul the mighty trees over the snow to the region's frozen lakes. When the ice gave way each spring, the logs were hauled across the lakes by steamship. Finally, dams built to hold back the mighty waters were released, sending cascades of logs downriver to the paper mills.

Over the years, technological advances slowly replaced the handsaws, oxen teams, and axes. As a result, the physical demands of the job were reduced while the overall productivity was increased. Today, the highly advanced mechanical harvester and 18-wheeler have replaced the double-bladed axe and river drive. Two-person crews have replaced the lumber camp and the storytelling, joking, and camaraderie that rose among the fallen trees as the loggers labored through the frigid winter months toward a common goal. Fortunately, this unique story of the industry and the changing cultural landscape has been preserved at the Rangeley Lakes Logging Museum. Open on weekends in the summer, the museum captures the past and brings it forward to the future to be relived a few hours at a time.

**Historical:** Long before settlement of the region by pioneers from the south, two Native American nations made the lakes area their home during the warmest months of the year. The St. Francis nation from the north and the Abenakis from the south hunted game and fished for trout in the many lakes and rivers. Archaeologists have uncovered evidence of campsites and arrowheads near the outlet of Rangeley Lake indicating that this was one of their favorite sites to spend the summer.

The region was first "discovered" by British lieutenant John Montresor in 1760. However, it was not until 1794 that the region, as part of the Commonwealth of Massachusetts, was surveyed and mapped.

In 1796, four investors, including Philadelphian James Rangeley, Sr., purchased nearly 31,000 acres of land in the western mountains for timber and mineral rights. However, it was nearly 26 years before any of the owners set foot on their land. In 1817, Luther Hoar and his family of eight established the region's first substantial and permanent settlement. The following year, two other families settled near the lake. When James Rangeley, Sr., died, his son inherited the land and bought out the remaining partners. James, Jr., and his family decided to make this wild place their home. Only 12 years later, the area was officially renamed Rangeley, and by 1840, the population has increased to 39 families.

The settlement of Rangeley was small, but thriving. Soon, anglers from out of state discovered Indian Rock, where brook trout weighing more than ten pounds could be caught. By 1860, Rangeley had acquired a reputation as a fishing paradise. Local residents were very accommodating to all of the anglers and began building sporting camps, cabins, and hotels to house their guests.

In the 1880s, the region was prominently featured at several National Sporting Expositions, as well as in newspapers up and down the East Coast. As a result, outdoor enthusiasts arrived in throngs, and by 1900, there were more than 200 fishing guides in the area. The state's most famous and first registered Maine guide was Cornelia "Fly Rod" Crosby. Certified by the state in 1898, Crosby was not only a superb angler but he also was the individual who first pioneered and promoted the now fashionable policy of "catch and release" and the adoption of fishing seasons.

By 1909, the population had swollen from a mere 238 in 1860 to nearly 1,400. The region boasted a number of five-star resorts and sporting camps, among them the Mooselookmeguntic House, Rangeley Lake House, and Grant's Kennebago Camps. A number of wealthy and influential families from New York, Philadelphia, and

Boston owned many of the private camps, and the late 1920s and '30s became known as the "Golden Age." Entire families boarded trains to escape the heat and smog of the big cities for a summer of leisure and sport at their favorite resort. Upon arrival they were treated to exquisite dining, ballroom dancing, golf, casino gambling, moonlight boat rides, and a "Boston orchestra."

Following the outbreak of World War II, the travel and leisure habits of the nation changed. Reservations at the grand hotels declined dramatically, and by 1958, the famed Rangeley Lake House was razed. Fortunately, Rangeley is able to adapt to the changing demands of vacationers, and today is an extremely popular summer resort and summer home destination. Several historic sporting camps are still thriving as public resorts for outdoor recreationalists, and the more-than-90-year-old Rangeley Inn (once part of the Rangeley Lake House) continues to stand as a testament to the grand Hotel Era.

**Natural:** The Rangeley Lakes region is a wonderful place to do a little wildlife watching. More than 10,000 acres of land have been preserved, which includes more than 20 miles of lake and river shore, ten islands, and a 4,116-foot mountain. In such a wide range of settings, visitors are likely to see a variety of wildlife. Bird-watching is a particular favorite. In fact, just about any bird that comes to the Northeast can be found here, including rare or endangered breeds.

The best way to see birds, if you are not planning to stay a few seasons, is to tromp through the woods at the Audubon Bird Sanctuary. Canoes and kayaks are the best way to see waterfowl and shore birds. A trip along Kennebago River will often bring views of kingfishers, cranes, and herons. A less strenuous motorboat ride on Rangeley or Mooselookmeguntic Lakes will offer sightings of the common loon.

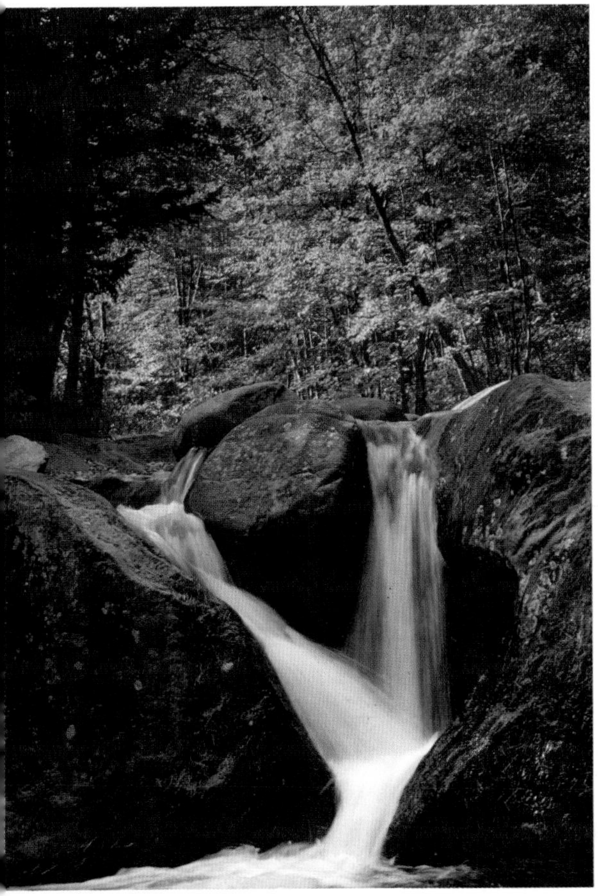

*Water cascading from high ledges and a rest area with hiking trails and picnic tables make Small's Falls popular.*

Rangeley Lakes is a favorite with deer and moose. They are often spotted in the late spring and early summer. Wooded trails are a great place to spot them. Bike rides in the early morning offer a wonderful way to cover more territory without the startling sound of an engine. If you are lucky, you may see bear, deer, rabbits, and coyote. You may even happen across a litter of playful fox pups. If you can stand the bugs, take a quick jaunt down to a bog. These areas are alive with an assortment of life. A quiet night by a pond may offer glimpses of beavers, otters, and a variety of ducks.

**Recreational:** Blessed with an abundance of natural resources, the Rangeley region provides four seasons of recreational treats. During the summer, this region comes alive with activities such as Fourth of July picnics and fireworks, blueberry and logging festivals, auctions, concerts, and stage performances.

Fall attracts many travelers because of the brilliant foliage and is a great time to hike. Since 1933, the famous Appalachian Trail has crossed both Routes 4 and 17 and leads to many of the region's highest peaks. A strenuous, but very rewarding, hike is along the trail northward to the summit of Saddleback Mountain. This hike is ten miles round-trip and offers exceptional scenery along the way. Hikers should be prepared for sudden shifts in weather and high winds that rake the open ridgeline. An easier hike is the one-mile trek to Bald Mountain. The trailhead is a mile south of Haines Landing on Bald Mountain Road in the picturesque village of Oquossoc. A viewing platform at the peak offers spectacular 360-degree views of Mooselookmeguntic Lake, Rangeley Lake, Gull Pond, and Richardson Pond.

Canoeing is also a favorite in the Rangeley Lakes region. Sometimes referred to as a canoeist's paradise, the miles of interconnected waters, dense forests, and looming mountains contribute to the allure. Most of the lakes and ponds have public launches while Rangeley Lake has several: the Rangeley Lakes State Park launch on the south side of the lake, the public landing in the northwest corner of the lake at the intersection of Routes 17 and 4 in Oquossoc, and the town park in downtown Rangeley.

Winter sports include alpine and cross-country skiing, as well as snowmobiling, sled dog racing, and ice fishing. Rangeley has an extensive system of snowmobile trails (more than 125 miles) that link to the Interconnected Trail System (ITS), which allows travel all the way across Maine and into Canada. Nearby Saddleback Ski

Resort has 41 trails and the highest vertical drop in the state while the local cross-country ski club boasts some of the best skiing and grooming in New England.

Spring and winter in Rangeley blend together until mid-April, allowing snow sport enthusiasts to play for a month longer than their neighbors to the south. When the ice finally goes out on the lakes and the green buds begin to swell on the trees, Rangeley's famous fishing season kicks into high gear.

**Scenic:** This area of gleaming lakes and rolling hills is one of the loveliest reaches of Maine's outback. Unlike the area around Maine's coast, the Rangeley region is dense woodland opening up occasionally to make room for lakes, streams, and ponds. Fluid meadows dot the area with wildflowers waving in the wind. The serene quality of the area provides a place of unusual beauty and peace that allows wildlife to roam and thrive. While the best views and experiences can be had out in the open on a walk through nature's majesty, the sights gained at every turn on the byway are equally impressive. Drives lead to striking overlooks of mountains, lakes, and forests.

The scenic vista Height of Land is particularly enchanting in the fall. One of the most dramatic turnouts in the state, Height of Land shines during the fall foliage. It offers a stunning view of the mountain ranges blanketed in dazzling oranges, reds, and yellows. The nearby deep blues of lakes provide a startling contrast.

## Highlights

The byway begins on Route 4 just west of the town of Madrid. Alternatively, you can start at the opposite end of the byway, which starts on Route 17 a few miles north of the town of Byron. If so, simply reverse the order of this itinerary.

**Small's Falls:** Start at Small's Falls, a waterfall and roadside picnic area on Route 4. The 54-foot waterfall has swimming and wading pools at the bottom, with rock waterslides. Other waterfalls are nearby, reached by hiking trails.

**Sandy River:** The cliff-lined Sandy River begins at Small's Falls and runs west alongside the byway, with put-ins for canoes. The section of the river from Small's Falls to Phillips (15 miles) has class I–III rapids, best suited to expert canoeists when water flows high in the spring.

**Appalachian Trail:** The rugged Appalachian Trail, which runs more than 2,000 miles from Maine south to Georgia and provides access to many of the area's mountain peaks, crosses Route 4 near Piazza Rock, an enormous, overhanging ledge. The rock may be accessed via a clearly marked side trail near the Appalachian Trail. Watch for moose along the byway.

**Rangeley Lake:** The byway skirts the eastern shores of Rangeley Lake, which has boat launch sites, camping, and good fishing (for landlocked salmon and brook trout) before entering the lakeside village of Rangeley, a center for outdoor sports.

*Rangeley Village and Haley Pond are in the foreground of this aerial view, while on the far side of the village Rangeley Lake stretches out.*

**Rangeley Lakes Region Logging Museum and Rangeley Historical Society:** The Rangeley Lakes Region Logging Museum displays industry photos, equipment, and artifacts, while the Rangeley Historical Society (open July–August only) has exhibits on Rangeley's history, including vintage hunting and fishing equipment.

**Wilhelm Reich Museum:** About three miles west of Rangeley on Route 4 is the Wilhelm Reich Museum, devoted to the controversial Austrian psychotherapist and scientist who had a home and laboratory here. Besides displays on Reich's life and work, there's an observatory with mountain and lake views.

**Mooselookmeguntic Lake:** At Oquossoc, turn south onto Route 17 and follow it along Mooselookmeguntic Lake (an Indian word meaning "portage to the moose feeding place"), Maine's second largest. The lake is known for fishing, hiking trails, campsites, and great scenery.

**Height of Land:** Just southeast of Mooselookmeguntic is the Height of Land, considered one of the top scenic overlooks in all of New England, with views of the lake, forests, and mountains. The Appalachian Trail crosses the byway again here.

**Swift River:** The byway ends north of Byron. Accessed from Byron, the Swift River offers another good challenge for experienced canoeists (with class I–III white water) and is known for its scenic, natural, and recreational splendor.

# Schoodic Scenic Byway 

*This little-traveled stretch of Route 1 runs along the far, eastern rim of Frenchman Bay, with spectacular views back across the water to Mount Desert's mountains. Follow Frenchman Bay down the Schoodic Peninsula, through Winter Harbor to the open ocean at Schoodic Point, known for a great view of the high waves.*

### Quick Facts

**Length:** 29 miles.

**Time to Allow:** 1 1/2 hours.

**Considerations:** March, April, May, September, and October are excellent because the crowds aren't as heavy. The byway is beautiful in any season. July and August are the most crowded.

Looking for the "real" Maine? Flee tourist attractions and national chains, and come here, to a landscape and lifestyle that residents want to preserve and you will want to experience. Wake from a good night's sleep at a historic bed-and-breakfast and spend the day lobstering, clamming, and picking blueberries, and walking in vast timberland. Stop and browse at small shops and yard sales where local artisans and craftspeople sell their wares.

Nature and scenery along the byway match its cultural heritage for richness and beauty. As you travel this route, look sea- and skyward for glimpses of soaring animal life. Ducks, eagles, and osprey are plentiful near the many lakes, rivers, and coastlines along the byway. View gorgeous landscapes of mountains, islands, fields of blueberries and wildflowers, historic buildings, and lighthouses. Discover one of the last frontiers of the eastern seaboard on the Schoodic Scenic Byway.

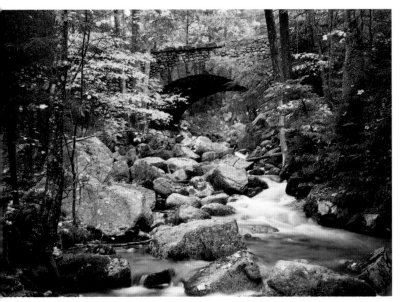

*Mount Desert Island is home to Acadia National Park where this cobblestone arched bridge blends perfectly with the stunning scenery.*

## Intrinsic Qualities

**Archaeological:** The earliest inhabitants of this area were small groups of Native Americans who settled here several thousand years ago. Clams, which could be harvested from mud and sand tidal flats, were a staple of their diet. Because clamshells can take thousands of years to deteriorate, the buried mounds of shells that are revealed by coastal erosion still mark those sites. Most of these sites are on private property, but some exist in the Schoodic section of Acadia National Park.

The first documented visits of European explorers mapped the coast in the early 1500s. These explorers were mostly Portuguese, English, Spanish, and French. Although Native Americans lived in the area of the Schoodic Scenic Byway for thousands of years, there were no European settlements until after the French and Indian War, around 1760. Numerous archaeological sites on the Schoodic Peninsula have been excavated and studied by researchers from the Maine Historic Preservation Commission.

**Cultural:** This region of Maine is unique because of its local Downeast culture. The term *Downeast* has been around for a long time. Years ago, when sailors hauled cargo to the northeast of New England the prevailing wind came from the southwest, pushing their schooners downwind in an easterly direction. While other areas of the state market this idiom, they fail to capture the essence of real Maine living. The true Downeast Maine is an untouched jewel. The people of Maine, true Mainers (pronounced "May-nuhs"), want to keep their treasure a secret. Consequently, only the adventurous have stumbled upon the delights tucked away in the jagged coastline around the Schoodic Peninsula. The people of this area really do make a living off the sea and work primarily as anglers, shipbuilders, seafarers, and tradespeople. They only farm as a supplement to these other businesses and occupations.

The Schoodic Scenic Byway provides visitors with a beautiful way to explore the Downeast countryside. Take time to enjoy the many festivals and activities. Winter Harbor is a busy fishing port where a lobster festival is held every August with lobster boat races and good food. Schoodic Arts for All, a group of local artists and community members, features a number of different activities

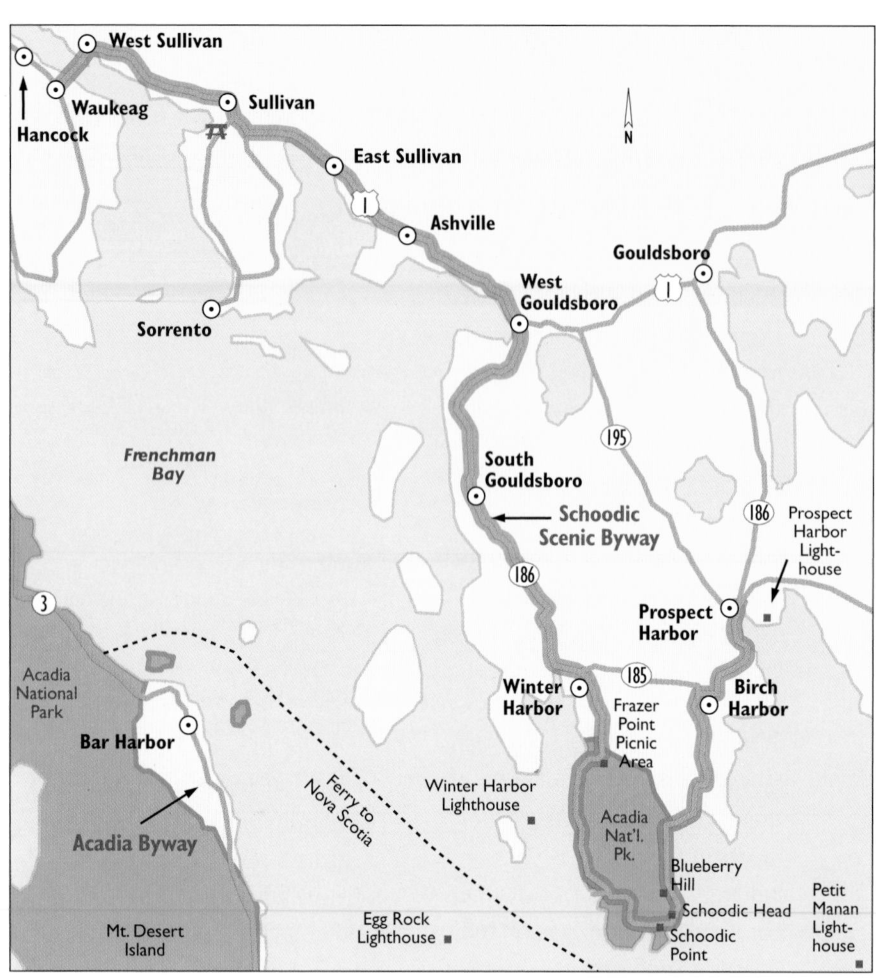




such as the community steel band, traditional old-time string-band music, dancing, and more. Locally produced goods made by artisans and crafters are sold through small shops and yard sales year-round. Downeast clam bakes and lobster festivals are true traditions in this area, as well as summer "coasting" on a schooner.

**Historical:** The earliest Europeans here may have been the Vikings who briefly visited about a thousand years ago. The first documented visits were those of Portuguese, English, Spanish, and French explorers who mapped the coast in the early 1500s. Frenchman Bay, between Mount Desert Island and Gouldsboro Peninsula, got its name when English sailors saw (and avoided) a French man-of-war moored there.

Settlers from southern Maine, New Hampshire, and Massachusetts began moving into this area to harvest trees that were turned into lumber and shipped to Boston. During the 1880s, John G. Moore, a wealthy New Yorker from Steuben, Maine, purchased most of the land on Schoodic. In 1897, he put in a road and welcomed the public to visit. After Moore's death, the land eventually passed to George B. Dorr, a conservationist, who donated it to the Interior Department as an addition to Acadia National Park.

**Natural:** The Schoodic Scenic Byway passes through a land of lobsters, clams, blueberry fields, and timber. The peninsula lures travelers with thundering waves crashing against the peaks, and then unfolds its history. Free from the pressures of every day, the Schoodic Peninsula whispers the stories of nature to its travelers, enticing them to learn more about how it was shaped by glaciers millions of years ago. While contemplating age-old mysteries, if visitors are still, the peninsula and its surrounding islands come alive with a flurry of wildlife and various kinds of rare and uncommon birds wing overhead or scuttle in the brush.

The glorious scenery and natural formations of the peninsula attract wildlife, seabirds, and waterfowl. The best place in Acadia to see seabirds is on the Schoodic Peninsula and its surrounding islands. Petit Manan, in particular, offers a national wildlife refuge that allows visitors to see a variety of birds. While taking a hike along the Shore Trail, travelers will be able to see blue-headed vireos and black-capped chickadees among the scrub and stunted trees. White cedar swamps are home to pine warblers and yellow-shafted flickers. Nesting seabirds are the major attraction, and Petit Manan houses Atlantic puffins; common, Arctic, and endangered roseate terns; razorbills; laughing gulls; and Leach's storm petrels. In addition to seabirds, wading birds and bald eagles also nest on the refuge islands.

**Recreational:** The Schoodic Peninsula has plenty of recreational opportunities. Recreation varies from outdoor activities, such as hiking and walking, to browsing through galleries. There are also three picnic areas along the byway that provide access for sea kayaking and tidal pool combing. Bicycling is very popular around Schoodic Point Road. The drive along the byway is recreation itself, with wonderful views that provide places for sight-seeing and contemplation.

The easygoing Schoodic Head Trail takes travelers through striking landscape. Stands of northern white cedar, red and white spruce, paper birch, and jack pine tower over the rocky terrain. Vibrant green patchworks of a myriad of moss species meander across the pink granite boulders. Lichen patterns of silver and purple adorn rocks along the banks of the stream that parallels the trail. Charming small pools and miniature waterfalls gurgle above the sound of the crashing surf on the point. Schoodic Head Trail brings visitors onto a dirt road that connects with the Alder Trail, a southeasterly trail favored by woodcocks, spruce grouse, chickadees, and many small song birds. The Alder Trail takes travelers back to the Park Loop Road.

The Schoodic Peninsula offers biking enthusiasts an enjoyable 13- to 29-mile ride, depending on how far the visitor wants to go. The loop meanders through picturesque fishing villages and along a dramatic section of rocky shoreline. A short side trip to the fishing village of Corea is only six miles out and well worth the trip. Other side trips include a shorter ride to Lighthouse Point just a half-mile off of the main ride.

**Scenic:** Exploring the Schoodic Peninsula is an unexpected experience. This uncrowded area allows travelers to pass through the stunning scenery with a feeling of solitude and discovery. This byway takes the traveler along the coast through quaint fishing villages, vernacular architecture, and striking, serene Atlantic views.

The views from the byway are captivating and will belong to the visitor alone, rather than a crowd of people. The wind and weather patterns are delightfully dynamic and unpredictable, ranging from clear, brisk, invigorating weather to damp, cool, fog-laden doldrums. On the Schoodic Peninsula, stormy days actually offer fantastic sights. Nature's spectacular play of foamy water pounding upon the rocky coastlines is truly awe-inspiring.

## Highlights

The byway begins at the west end of the Hancock–Sullivan Bridge about eight miles east of the village of Hancock on U.S. 1. It's best to start at this end of the byway because the most scenic stretch, which runs through a section of Acadia National Park, runs one way going west to east.

**Sullivan:** At West Sullivan, follow U.S. 1 east along the upper reaches of Frenchman Bay to Sullivan. Sullivan has Downeast-style architecture set around a central common with outstanding views south to Frenchman Bay and Mount Desert Island (site of the main section of Acadia National Park near Bar Harbor).

**Winter Harbor:** Just west of the town of West Gouldsboro, take Route 186 south, passing through South Gouldsboro and the resort town of Winter Harbor, where there are lodgings and restaurants.

**Acadia National Park:** East of Winter Harbor, go south onto Moore Road, which leads to the Schoodic Peninsula and the mostly undeveloped Schoodic section of Acadia National Park. The one-way Schoodic Drive then leads a bit more than seven miles along the park shoreline. Watch for deer, moose, seals, eagles, ospreys, herons—and bicyclists—along the way.

**Frazer Point Picnic Area:** After entering the park, the first turnout is for the Frazer Point Picnic Area, which features barbecue and picnic facilities with scenic views of Winter Harbor and its nearby islands, coves, and rocky beaches.

**Winter Harbor Lighthouse:** Continuing down the one-way road, watch to the west for Mark Island and the 1856 Winter Harbor Lighthouse. With Mount Desert Island's Cadillac Mountain rising in the background, it's considered the most photogenic lighthouse along the byway. The best pictures are available from turnouts in the first mile after entering the park.

**Schoodic Point:** At Schoodic Point, the southernmost tip of the peninsula, Atlantic Ocean waves crash to the shore against granite rocks. The pounding surf can sometimes reach heights of 50 feet. Watch for rocks on the roadway in this area.

**Blueberry Hill:** A mile northeast of Schoodic Point, stop at Blueberry Hill to picnic, hike, and take pictures of offshore islands. This is one of the best vantage points for viewing 123-foot Petit Manan Lighthouse, Maine's second tallest, which dates from 1817. Watch for puffins in summer; they have a colony on Petit Manan Island, which is a wildlife refuge. (The island is often shrouded in fog, however.)

**Schoodic Head:** A hiking trail (called the Anvil) leads from Blueberry Hill to a steep 180-foot promontory with great views of Little Moose Island. The trail then continues to 440-foot Schoodic Head, which offers incredible vistas back across Frenchman Bay. This is the best spot to view and photograph Egg Rock Lighthouse, built in 1875. On a clear day, Schoodic Head also provides more views of the Petit Manan and Winter Harbor lighthouses.

**Prospect Harbor Lighthouse:** The byway continues north out of the park. At Birch Harbor, rejoin Route 186 as it goes north to the village of Prospect Harbor, where the byway ends. The Prospect Harbor Lighthouse rises on a peninsula directly across from the village harbor. The light keeper's cottage is available for overnight stays by military families, both active and retired.

*The southern tip of Schoodic Point has massive granite outcroppings and pounding surf.*

# KANCAMAGUS SCENIC BYWAY

*An east–west shortcut through the heart of White Mountains National Forest, Kancamagus Scenic Byway accesses otherwise remote waterfalls, swimming holes, hiking trails, and campgrounds.*

Enjoy what many consider one of the top fall-foliage trips in the world when you drive the Kancamagus Scenic Byway. Undoubtedly one of the most scenic routes through the White Mountains of New Hampshire, the "Kanc," as locals call it, climbs to nearly 3,000 feet on the flank of Mount Kancamagus. You can meander through beautiful forests, follow old logging roads, and cross American Indian hunting paths. In the fall, these woods yield a stunning array of colors that underscore the area's great natural beauty. Be sure to take the time to pull off the road and enjoy the hiking trails, waterfalls, and scenic overlooks this byway offers.

On the eastern section of the byway, you can visit the Rocky Gorge Scenic Area, and see where the Swift River has, over time, worn a narrow cleft through solid stone. Here you can appreciate nature's handiwork at its best while you wander through the woods and over the gorge to lovely Falls Pond.

The Kancamagus Scenic Byway was named for an early Indian Chief of the Penacook Confederacy. Called "The Fearless One," Chief Kancamagus tried to keep the peace between his people and the white settlers. However, repeated harassment by the English ended his efforts, bringing war and bloodshed. In the early 1690s, Kancamagus and his followers moved to northern New Hampshire and Canada.

## Quick Facts

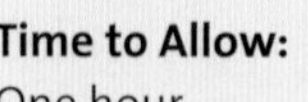

**Length:** 28 miles.

**Time to Allow:** One hour.

**Considerations:** The byway is heavily traveled, especially during the fall foliage season. Visitors should expect delays and crowded parking areas. Also, there are no gas stations along the byway, and the road is very curvy. Moose cross the highway often, so use extreme caution, especially at dusk. A "passport" is required for any vehicle that is left unattended in the National Forest.

## Intrinsic Qualities

**Cultural:** The first thing someone might say when describing this area's culture is that it is simply "New England." It can be generalized that the people of the area are peaceful, high-class, old-fashioned, friendly, and that they savor the simpler pleasures of life. Here are a few details, presented in a chance fashion, as one would discover them if they were actually traveling the byway: The area's people cherish their historic homes that are nestled in the quiet and stately White Mountains; they restore and keep well their whitewashed, clapboard churches and farmhouses; they enjoy their several local festivals and events; and they stroll unhurried on their tree-lined main streets, browsing leisurely among the specialty shops. And, perhaps, after a day of farming or logging (or maybe even after a "hard" day of skiing or backpacking, if they're on holiday), they might stop in to see a show at their town's old-fashioned movie theater, or have a superb meal at one of the old "grand hotels" of which they're so proud. And you really get the feeling while you're on this byway that you're welcomed just like any other returning guest at The Balsams (one of the area's famous and historic "grand hotels"): with a pint of maple syrup and "welcome back" note.

**Historical:** The town of Passaconaway, settled in about 1790, is named after Passaconaway, who, in 1627, united more than 17 central New England nations into the Penacook Confederacy. The byway was named for his grandson, a great chief of this confederacy, Kancamagus. Both Passaconaway and

*The Albany Covered Bridge, built in 1858, is a Paddleford truss style with added arches. It spans the scenic Swift River.*

Kancamagus also have mountains named after them.

More recent history can be found at the Russell–Colbath House, the only remaining 19th-century homestead in the area. (It is now a U.S. Forest Service information center.) The name memorializes the house builders and Ruth Colbath who, on a fall day in 1891, was told by her husband Thomas that he would be going out for a "little while"—which turned out to be 42 years. Every night during those years, Ruth placed a lamp in the window to welcome her husband. When he finally returned in 1933, Ruth had died, and the property had been sold. It is not known why her husband was gone so long.

**Natural:** One of the most exciting aspects of spending time in the White Mountains is the opportunity to see wildlife. The state's moose herd, for example, has made a dramatic recovery since the early days of the 20th century when unregulated hunting and loss of forest habitat to agriculture decimated the herd. Today, in spite of a limited annual hunt, moose are found throughout the state. They're often seen in swampy or wet areas near roads. The Kancamagus Scenic Byway and the northernmost sections of the White Mountains are well-known for viewing these animals. If you do happen to see some moose while driving the byway, keep a respectful distance. Moose are especially unpredictable in their movements, and when threatened may either stand their ground, charge, or run. Because they are more active at dusk and at night, they are difficult to see. Stay alert and brake for these large animals because it could save your life.

Black bears are also common along the Kancamagus Scenic Byway, as are frogs, turtles, and snakes. The Loon Mountain Wildlife Theater in Lincoln is an excellent place to see native New Hampshire animals in a controlled setting.

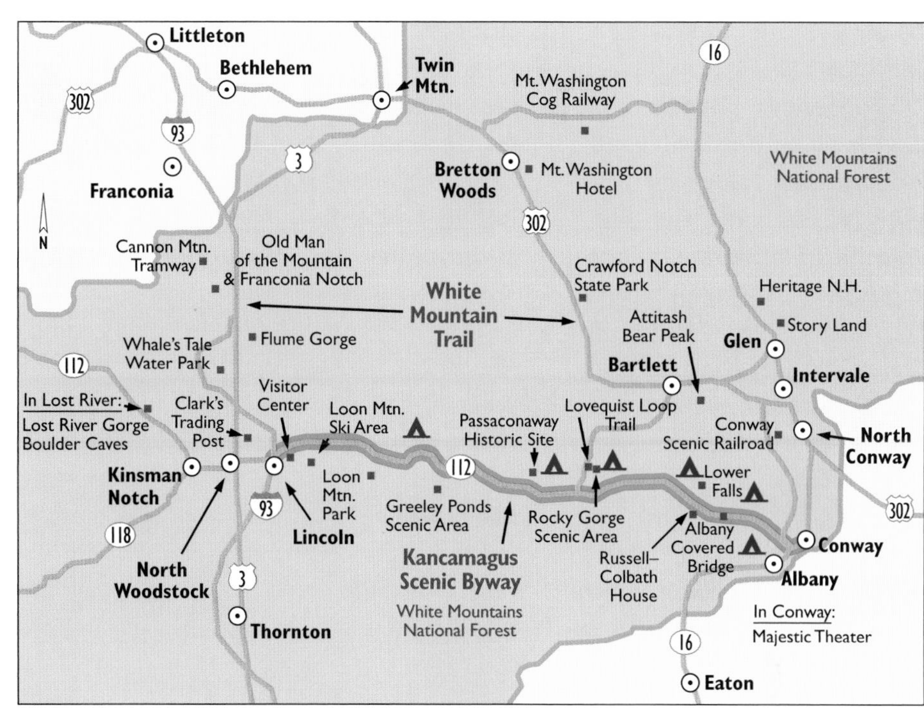


There are approximately 56 species of mammals and 183 species of birds along the byway. These species of birds include 38 year-round species, 35 migrant or winter species, and 110 total species during the summer months. Of special interest along the byway is the peregrine falcon population, an endangered bird that is making a comeback in the area thanks to dedicated reintroduction efforts. Nearly 60 captive-bred falcons have been released from cliff sites in the area, some of which have returned to the cliffs to raise their young. There is even one pair of falcons that has nested along the Swift River since 1989. The state-listed endangered blue-gray gnatcatcher also resides in the area.

Spruce hardwoods, northern hardwoods, and paper birch trees forest the slopes of the White Mountains and the river valleys around the Kancamagus Scenic Byway. This combination of hardwoods and conifers creates a breathtaking tapestry of color during the fall season. Locals and tourists alike spend a great deal of time traveling the byway during the fall as they take in the vibrant scenery.

**Recreational:** Hiking, snowshoeing, backpacking, and cross-country skiing are the most popular activities on this route. This forest's hundreds of miles of such trails range from easy family jaunts to some of the nation's most famous and challenging excursions. Some of these trails have great fishing.

An example of a very easy hike is the Rail 'n' River Trail, which is a flat, one mile round-trip along the river. It is wheelchair and stroller accessible, and you get to it from the Russell–Colbath House. For something a little more difficult, there's the Greeley Ponds Trail, which is about five miles long and features two ponds, the Upper Greeley Pond (dark aqua-green, and surrounded by old growth timber and towering cliffs) and the Lower Greeley Pond (shallow and more typical of a beaver pond). Both ponds offer trout fishing and an enjoyable place to have a picnic lunch. Find the Greeley Ponds trailhead nine miles east of exit 32 on I-93. A difficult hike is the four-mile trail to the summit of 2,660-foot Mount Potash. This trail hikes along somewhat dangerous cliffs, but it affords excellent, panoramic views of the Swift River Valley and the surrounding mountains (the trailhead is 13 miles west of the Saco Ranger Station).

**Scenic:** The Kancamagus Scenic Byway is blessed with some of the most breathtaking scenery in New Hampshire. Located in the White Mountains National Park, the byway is flanked by the White Mountains. Because the byway is surrounded by a mixed forest of coniferous and deciduous hardwoods, it comes alive with color every fall. Locals and tourists all come to the area to see the rare mix of brilliant fall color against the majestic green of evergreen stands. The Kancamagus Scenic Byway is well known for providing some of the most beautiful vistas in the country.

## Highlights

Aside from the incredible scenery of the White Mountains National Forest, this itinerary highlights things to see and do for the entire family along the Kancamagus Scenic Byway.

**Lost River Gorge and Boulder Caves:** Beginning in the town of North Woodstock, the Lost River Gorge and Boulder Caves invites visitors to, indeed, find the Lost River, as it seems to play hide-and-seek, meandering in and out of the granite outcroppings of Kinsman Notch. Boardwalks give easy access into most areas, or slightly more strenuous trails are available to lead adventurers into caves, as well as along the gorge and into the Nature Garden at the end of the self-guided tour. An upper boardwalk is wheelchair accessible.

**Clark's Trading Post:** Clark's Trading Post at the western edge of the Kancamagus Scenic Byway near Lincoln isn't quite what the fur traders of frontier days would recognize, but it has a history and tradition all its own and is certainly a must-see along the byway. Run by the Clark family as a roadside attraction since 1928, highlights of Clark's Trading Post include the trained black bear show, the Seiranian Family Circus, bumper boats, a climbing wall, several historical displays and museums, and the White Mountain Central Railroad.

**Loon Mountain:** Just east of Lincoln, Loon Mountain adventures await. Gondola rides to the summit give a bird's-eye view of the entire area and surrounding mountains. Once at the summit more adventures begin, including exploring glacial caves, hiking an interpreted nature trail, visiting with local artisans as they create their wares, and climbing a four-story observation tower to behold some of the most sublime scenery you will ever experience.

**Passaconaway Historic Site:** The early days of the mountain lifestyle can be studied at the Russell–Colbath House just 12 miles west of Conway at the Passaconaway Historic Site. Built in the early 1800s, it is the area's only remaining 19th-century homestead. Furnished as it would have been in the early days, the home is listed on the National Register of Historic Places. The U.S. Forest Service also has an information center located here, and the Rail 'n' River Hike is an easy half-mile trail that begins at the historic home.

*Rocky Gorge has been managed for the safeguarding of its scenic features ever since its designation as a Natural Scenic Area in 1937.*

**Rocky Gorge Scenic Area and Lovequist Loop Trail:** Three miles east of the Passaconaway Historic Site is Rocky Gorge Scenic Area and Lovequist Loop Trail. The superb scenic quality of Rocky Gorge has been preserved ever since its designation as a National Scenic Area in 1937. An impressive waterfall, the narrow gorge, and an easy walking trail around Falls Pond make this the perfect place to relax and enjoy the natural serenity for a bit before continuing on.

**Conway:** The picturesque village of Conway is home of the Conway Historical Society, headquartered in the Eastman Lord House, the 1818 residence of a Conway mill owner and now listed on the National Register of Historic Places. Seventeen rooms are open to the public with furnishings ranging from 1818 through 1945. Also, you can pick up a map of the walking tour of the historic sites of Conway here, or drop by the Conway Public Library at 15 Main Street, which is one of the interesting stops on the tour.

**Majestic Theater:** At 36 Main Street in Conway is the 400-seat Majestic Theater built in 1936. The Art Deco design and the original velvet stage curtain give a sense of the Golden Age of Hollywood. This combines with current state of the art technology such as Schneider lenses and the only eight-channel Sony digital sound system in northern New England. Though the theater is quite historic in ambiance, current Hollywood hits grace the giant screen and provide a fitting evening's end to a day on the Kancamagus Scenic Byway.

# WHITE MOUNTAIN TRAIL 

*This is the historic tourist trail through the White Mountains, accessing resort towns and a variety of ways to waterfalls, woodland trails, and mountain peaks.*

Take a drive through a landscape unspoiled by overdevelopment when you travel the White Mountain Trail of New Hampshire. Enjoy the uninterrupted mountain and river views, wetlands, and woodlands that captured the imagination of writer Nathaniel Hawthorne and inspired landscape artist Thomas Cole. Despite the passage of time since the days of Hawthorne and Cole, this rural New England area remains beautiful.

## Quick Facts

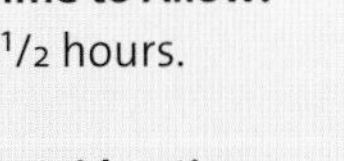

**Length:** 108 miles.

**Time to Allow:** $2^1/2$ hours.

**Considerations:** The White Mountain Trail can safely and conveniently accommodate two-wheel-drive vehicles with standard clearance. It is also safe for tour bus travel. Except for Bear Notch Road, the highway is maintained year-round, including snow plowing during the winter months. There are several safety hazards relating to winter driving conditions due to winter storms, collision of vehicles with moose, and improper parking along the highways. Although moose present one of the most exciting viewing opportunities along the highway, they can cause traffic control and safety problems as people stop to view and take pictures. At some locations along the highway, informal parking can cause hazards.

Take time to discover the history of the White Mountain Trail. Parts of it have been used for centuries, as attested by the charming 18th- and 19th-century buildings you will see along the way. The railroad also helped to shape this area and made possible the lumber industry, which spurred the development of many towns in the region, such as Bartlett, Conway, and North Conway. Be sure to see the amazing Frankenstein Trestle, which supports railroad tracks below the cliff in Crawford Notch.

Toward the beginning of the 20th century, the creation of the national forests coincided with the dawning of the automobile age, assuring Americans an opportunity to vacation a world away from the "citied world," yet within driving distance of the great Eastern cities. Since then, recreational pursuits enjoyed here have grown from hiking, fishing, and sightseeing to include downhill and cross-country skiing, camping, mountain biking, leaf-peeping, and antique hunting. You can also enjoy just about anything "outdoorsy" under these towering granite cliffs and soaring mountains.

## Intrinsic Qualities

**Archaeological:** There are many archaeologically significant sites along this byway. However, in order to preserve these sites, they are kept secret. If you have a serious interest in the locations and work being done at these sites, contact one of the local ranger stations.

*Silver Cascade Falls in Crawford Notch State Park is easily accessible just off Route 302.*

**Cultural:** The influx of tourism and the development of the lumber industry spurred the development of many towns throughout this region. The history of this growth is found in the historic structures that remain in towns such as Bartlett, Conway, and North Conway. Along the trail there are numerous sites that are already on the National Register of Historic Places or are eligible to be placed on this National Register. These sites represent a range of different cultures and time periods. Examples include the Mount Washington Hotel, the Abenaki Indian Shop and Camp, the Crawford House Artist's Studio, and the North Conway Depot and Railroad Yard.

**Historical:** Throughout history, transportation routes have always helped cultures further develop their social and economical systems, and this route is no exception There are many historical events associated with the White Mountain Trail. Some of these include the creation of towns, villages, national forests, resorts, hotels, and the railroad.

The White Mountains were originally home to the Abenakis and other Native Americans. At the beginning of the 19th century, the White Mountains were a place for artists and others. The White Mountain School of Art was a group of landscape painters that included Thomas Cole, Benjamin Champney, and Frank Shapleigh. Also during this era, Nathaniel Hawthorne and Reverend Thomas Starr King captured readers' imaginations with tales of the White Mountains.

By 1891, Crawford Railroad Station stood at the top of Crawford Notch. This railroad was a magnificent feat of engineering, especially considering the region's terrain, climate, and isolation. The Frankenstein Trestle, which supports railroad tracks *below* the cliff in Crawford Notch, still makes observers gasp.

As access to the White Mountains improved, a series of ever-grander inns, hotels, and resorts was constructed to meet the needs of an increasingly affluent clientele. The most elegant of these, the Mount Washington Hotel, was the setting of the historic Bretton Woods Monetary Conference in 1944. It was at this conference where the dollar was set as the standard of international currency, earning the hotel a place on the list of National Historic Landmarks. This event, combined with the hotel's spectacular setting, contributed to its success as a thriving resort and stunning landmark.

The 1923 demise of another grand hotel, the Profile House, and the subsequent sale of its land to the Society for the Protection of the New Hampshire Forests and the State of New Hampshire, resulted in the creation of Franconia Notch State Park. More than 15,000 people, including children, contributed funds to make this purchase possible.

Five sites are listed on the National Register of Historic Places. Eleven individual sites and three historic districts are also eligible for the National Register of Historic Places. These sites represent historic structures used for religion, commerce, transportation, and residential needs.

Logging towns, such as Carrigain in Crawford Notch (1892–1898), appeared and vanished as the harvest swept through the notches, surviving only as the names of mountains, hiking trails, and state historic markers. The movement to conserve tracts of forestland was, in part, a reaction to the large-scale lumber cutting that alarmed early conservationists.

The visible evidence of the preceding ages is now as much a part of the physical landscape as the towering granite cliffs and soaring mountains of the White Mountain Trail.

**Natural:** The White Mountain Trail is surrounded by glaciated mountains, swamps, and lakes. Elevations range from 500 to 4,000 feet, and a few isolated peaks are even higher than 5,000 feet. Summers along the route are warm, and precipitation is evenly distributed throughout the year. However, winter can be very cold. The average length of the frost-free period is about 100 days, and the average annual snowfall is more than 100 inches.

This region is in the transition zone between the spruce-fir forest to the north and the deciduous forest to the south. Valley hardwood forests are composed of sugar maple, yellow birch, beech, and hemlock trees. Low mountain slopes support spruce, fir, maple, beech, and birch trees. Higher on the mountain, you can find pure stands of balsam fir and red spruce that devolve into Krummholz at higher elevations. Alpine meadow (tundralike growth) is found above the timberline on Mount Washington.

The wildlife in this area is the same as the wildlife that is found in both the mixed forest and boreal forest. However, some species are unique to the trail's alpine tundra, such as the long-tail shrew, boreal (southern) redback vole, gray-cheeked thrush, spruce grouse, and gray jay.

**Recreational:** There are plenty of places to hike, fish, sightsee, downhill and cross-country ski, camp, and mountain bike along the White Mountain Trail. Hiking trailheads dominate the roadway on both sides. There are great hiking trails for families, day hikers, and backpackers. The Crawford Path (created in 1819) is the oldest continually maintained footpath in the country. Twenty 4,000-foot mountains are located along this byway, as well.

Fly-fishers can find heaven if they hike a bit to mountain lakes and streams. This wilderness also offers some of the most breathtaking ski slopes in the East.

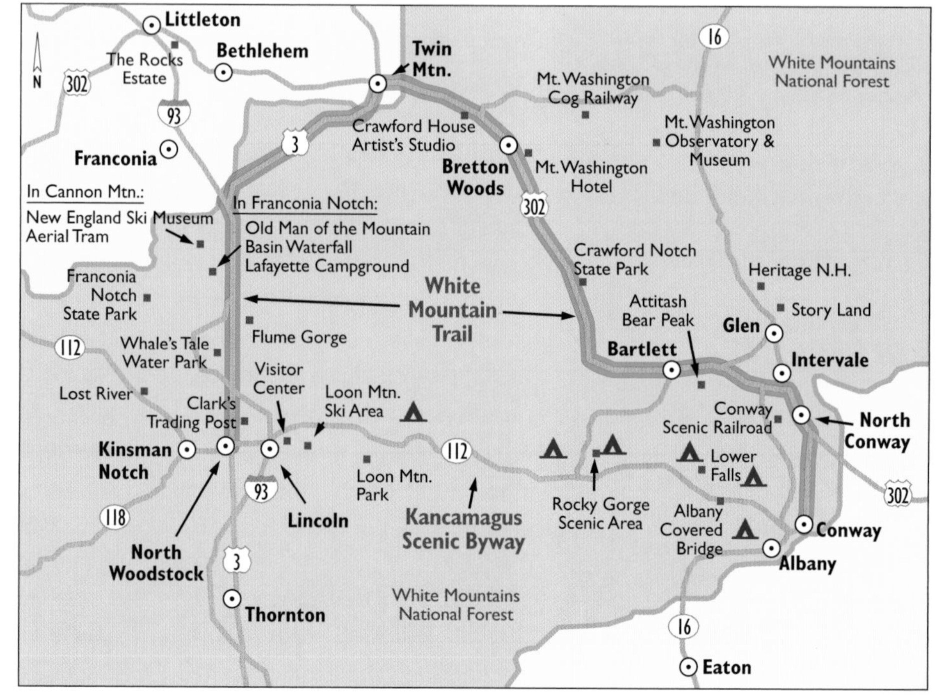

*The steam-powered Mount Washington Cog Railway has been taking passengers to the summit since 1869.*

**Scenic:** The White Mountain Trail winds around mountains and along rivers, offering views of some of the most beautiful scenery in the East. Mount Washington is on the north side of the byway. This is the tallest mountain in the Northeast and is home to some of the world's worst weather.

Notches are unique geographic features found only in New Hampshire and Maine (there are only six total notches). Both Crawford Notch and Franconia Notch are spectacular. Franconia Notch was once home to the Old Man of the Mountain, a profile of a man carved into the stone by glaciers high atop a mountain. This profile was a recognized wonder since the time of the Native Americans who imbued it with spiritual powers. Sadly, the formation succumbed to erosion in May 2003, and its rugged profile was irrevocably damaged.

## Highlights

Rambling through the White Mountains National Forest and connecting at each end of the Kancamagus Scenic Highway, the White Mountain Trail has an abundance of things to see and do, a few of which are highlighted below.

**Clark's Trading Post:** For more than 70 years, the Clark family has entertained visitors at Clark's Trading Post. At this site they have a museum, a fire station, a steam locomotive, and trained black bears.

**Franconia Notch State Park:** Franconia Notch State Park is home of Old Man of the Mountain Historic Site, Cannon Mountain, New England Ski Museum, and Flume Gorge. Also in the park are the Basin waterfall, the Cannon Mountain Aerial Tram taking visitors to the 4,180-foot summit of the mountain, recreation trails, and Lafayette campground. Be sure to stop by the visitor's center at Flume Gorge for a 15-minute film, maps, and interpretive exhibits.

**The Rocks Estate:** Located off Route 302, The Rocks Estate just outside Bethlehem is a historic working Christmas tree farm owned and operated by the Society for the Protection of New Hampshire Forests. Picnic areas, six miles of self-guided scenic and educational trails, and 55,000 Christmas trees make this a unique place to visit year-round.

**Mount Washington Cog Railway:** For a truly unforgettable way to ascend Mount Washington, try the world's first mountain-climbing cog railway. On especially clear days, the vista from the summit allows for glimpses of four states, the Canadian province of Quebec, and the Atlantic Ocean. A round trip on the historic railway takes about three hours and allows for a 20-minute stop at the summit. Bring a jacket, as it can be considerably cooler at the summit than at the base of the mountain. The Mount Washington Cog Railway is located off Route 302 in Bretton Woods.

**Mount Washington Observatory and Museum:** Mount Washington Observatory and Museum, located at the summit of the mountain, is accessible by the Mount Washington Cog Railway, the Mount Washington Auto Road, or via several trails in the area. Definitely a must-see, the museum features displays about the brutal meteorological conditions on Mount Washington, exhibits on the geological history of the Presidential Range, and a unique presentation of alpine flowers that have been preserved in synthetic resin. New to the museum is the Weather Discovery Room, which helps observers explore the weather phenomena of Mount Washington.

**Glen:** The village of Glen has two attractions side-by-side geared to families with young children. Story Land, a vintage theme park, opened in 1954 with a fairy-tale theme. Those who visited as children in the early days of the park are now returning with their kids and grandkids and still finding the theme park as enchanting as they remembered. Heritage–New Hampshire opened in time for the U.S. Bicentennial Celebration in 1976 and takes visitors on a multimedia walk through time with 25 theatrical sets, special effects, live characters, and guides.

**Conway Scenic Railroad:** To view the beautiful White Mountains National Forest from another vantage point, try the Conway Scenic Railroad. Nostalgic trips in historic rail cars on the Valley Train allow guests to travel through the valley past fields and woodlands, rivers and glens, enjoying the ambiance of period wicker seating and rich mahogany woodwork. Or try their Notch Train and travel through Crawford Notch past sheer bluffs, abrupt ravines, babbling brooks and streams, panoramic mountain vistas, and across the Frankenstein Trestle and Willey Brook Bridge. On-board guides tell the history and folklore of the railroad and area, as well as points of interest.

# Smugglers' Notch

*Vermont's most dramatic road winds up from Stowe, the state's most famous resort village, and over a shoulder of Mount Mansfield, its highest mountain. Scenic pull-offs invite access to rock formations and hiking trails.*

Native Americans traced the path over this high pass, but its name dates from use during the War of 1812 as a supply line to the British Army in Canada, which happened to be fighting the U.S. Army at the time. In 1807, President Thomas Jefferson had imposed an embargo against trade from Canada, a hardship for Northern Vermonters for whom Montreal was a prime market. The first carriage road through the pass wasn't opened until 1894, and the present Route 108 dates from 1910. It was improved in 1922 in time for Prohibition, during which "Smugglers' Notch" took on new meaning, this time with contraband flowing south from Canada.

Route 108 links Stowe with a town north of the notch that's called Jeffersonville after President Jefferson. In Stowe, where most travelers begin, it's known as "The Mountain Road."

Smugglers' Notch has been considered a State Scenic Road since 1978 under the Vermont Scenic Roads Law. Breathtaking forests and amazing rock outcroppings beckon visitors to hike through and climb them. Or guests might be just as happy driving and stopping at the numerous pull-offs and just taking in the gorgeous scenery.

Some of the plants along the route are found there and nowhere else in Vermont. Peregrine falcons might also be viewed.

## Highlights

Begin your tour in Stowe, and end in Jeffersonville.

### Quick Facts

**Length:** 18 miles.

**Time to Allow:** One hour.

**Considerations:** The eight-mile stretch within Mount Mansfield State Forest that's officially a state scenic road is closed December through mid-May, when it's reliably snow-covered and popular with cross-country skiers.

*The alpine tundra atop the summit of Mount Mansfield offers a commanding view of Mount Mansfield State Forest.*

**Stowe:** One of Vermont's oldest and most famous ski towns, Stowe, actually attracts more visitors in summer and fall, luring them out of their cars and onto their feet and bicycles. The Stowe Recreation Path parallels the Mountain Road for its first $5^1/_2$ miles, running through cornfields and meadows. There are two Moss Glen Falls in Vermont: One is in Stowe, and the other is near Granville. Be sure to visit the one on this route in Stowe.

**Mount Mansfield:** Since the mid-19th century locals have been enticing visitors up to the heights of Mount Mansfield, a distinctive mountain with a series of peaks resembling the upturned profile of a man's face. Mount Mansfield is the highest point in Vermont. In 1858 an inn was built under "The Nose," along with an amazingly

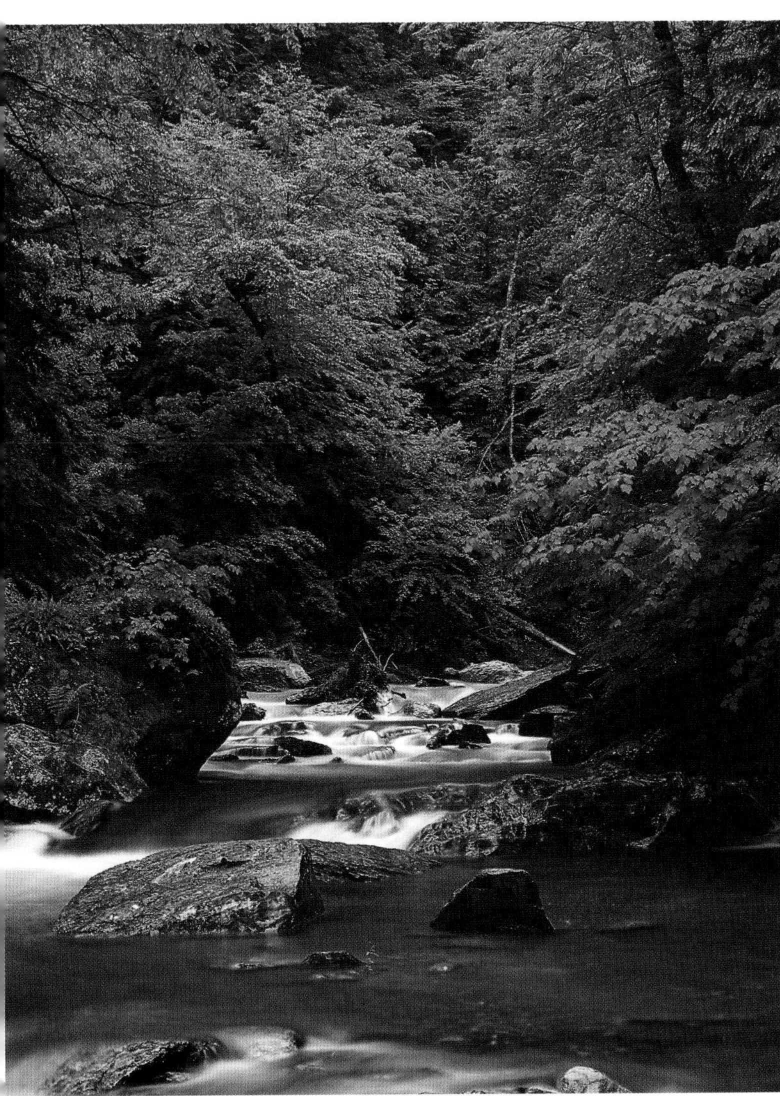

*The stream just below Moss Glen Falls courses over boulders, making its way through Putnam State Forest.*

steep access road (now a ski trail in winter). The inn is long gone, but in summer and fall this toll road is still a local attraction, along with Stowe Mountain Resort's eight-passenger gondola that operates, weather permitting, to the Cliff House, a ski station with a view down the narrow valley to the east. It's still, however, a half-hour trek below "The Chin," a peak that on a clear day offers a truly spectacular view west across the Champlain Valley to the Adirondack Mountains.

**Mount Mansfield State Forest:** For its first seven miles Route 108 is lined with lodging places, shops, and restaurants but beyond the turnoff to the toll road and then the gondola, the road enters the Mount Mansfield State Forest and steepens to an 18 percent grade. Smugglers' Notch State Park offers tent and trailer campsites.

**Big Spring:** Beyond this park the full meaning of "Notch" becomes apparent. Although the road is paved, it winds around boulders and beneath 1,000-foot-high cliffs that hem it down to one-lane. Drive slowly, and sound your horn before turns.

The turnoff beyond the height-of-land (at 2,161 feet)—with an information booth that's usually staffed in summer and fall—is the obvious place to stop. The Big Spring is here, an ideal brookside site for a picnic (there are even grills). Ask about hiking distances to natural rock formations with names like Elephant Head, King Rock, the (amazing) Hunter and His Dog, and Smugglers' Cave.

**Smugglers' Notch Resort:** The road continues to wind on for eight miles, down through more cliffs and boulders and just as it straightens and drops through woodland, motorists are startled by a condominium town rising out of the trees. This is Smugglers' Notch Resort, a self-contained and family-geared village. Route 108 continues spiraling downward, finally leveling in the village of Jeffersonville that is a different place than the resort country south of The Notch. Explore the Lamoille Valley, circling back to Stowe via the villages of Johnson, Hyde Park, and Morrisville. On the other hand, the drive through Smugglers' Notch is an adventure that deserves an encore.

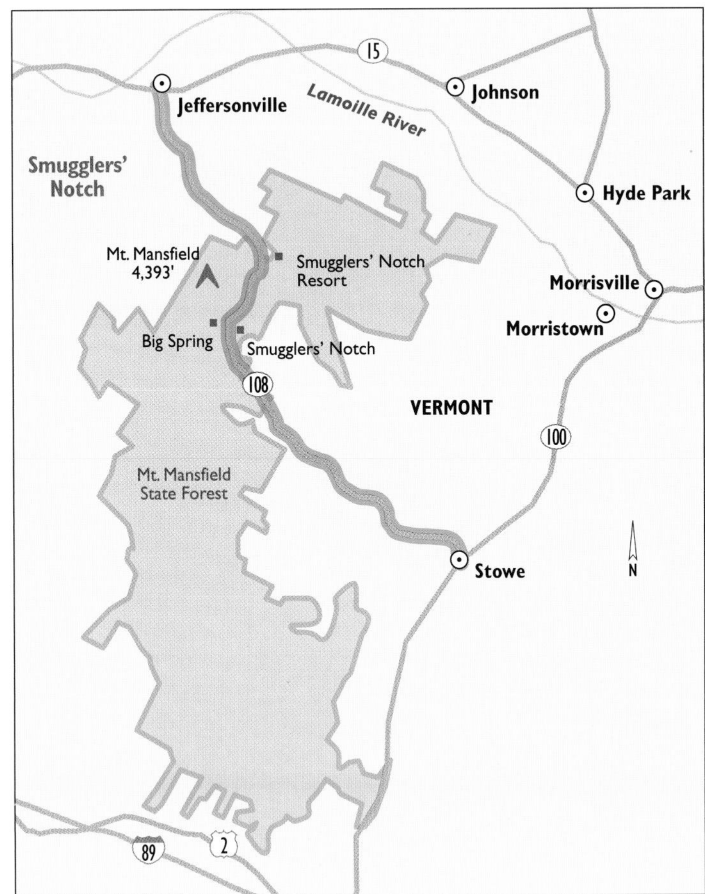

# Middlebury Gap

*Must-stops on the Middlebury Gap Road (Route 125) include Texas Falls and a wooded walk keyed to poems by Robert Frost, who spent 23 summers in a nearby cabin.*

Vermont is a long, narrow state, and most of its highways run north/south or take the low, lazy way along rivers. The exceptions are the high roads that cut east/west across the state, climbing up one side of mountain ranges, then plunging down the other. These high mountain passes are generally known in Vermont as "gaps," and cresting gaps is a bit like surfing. The Middlebury Gap is a fine example. It climbs, levels, and then drops down into the next valley. Look at the right moment, and what you see are mountains that rise on mountains, like waves on waves beyond.

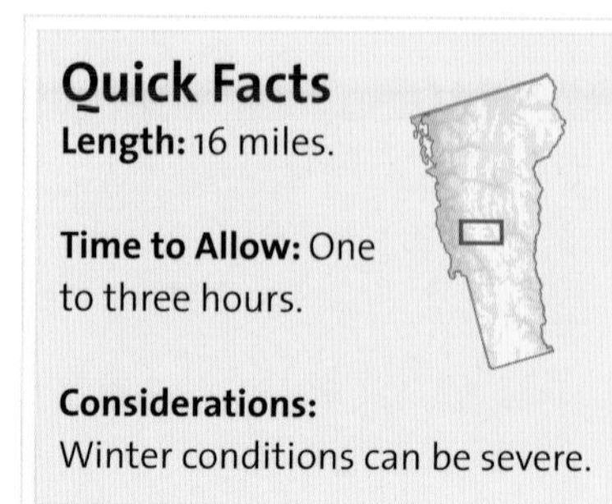

**Quick Facts**

**Length:** 16 miles.

**Time to Allow:** One to three hours.

**Considerations:** Winter conditions can be severe.

*The Green Mountain National Forest follows the backbone of Vermont and is a breathtaking sight no matter what season of the year.*

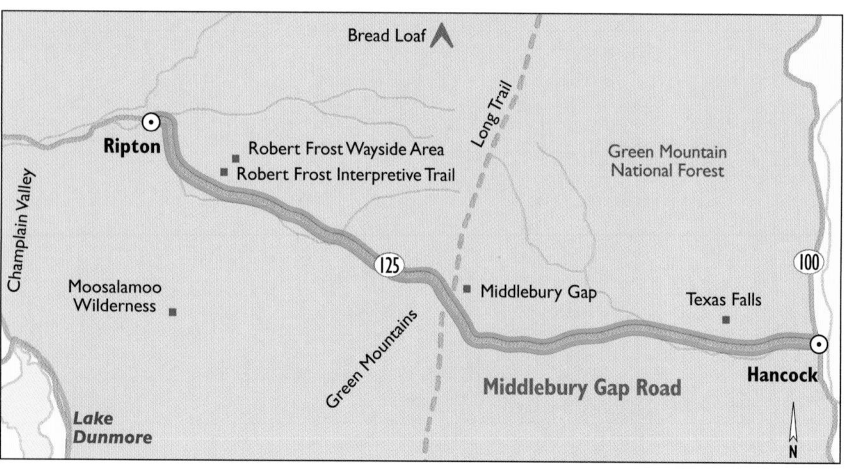


## Highlights

Begin this route in beautiful Texas Falls, and end in the village of Ripton.

**Texas Falls:** Pick up Route 125 at its junction in Hancock with Route 100, the scenic old road that runs up the middle of the state. The turnoff for Texas Falls comes so quickly that you may miss it, but don't. A quarter-mile north of the road a series of shoots and pools is rimmed by interesting rock formations, viewed from footbridges.

**Long Trail:** Route 125 climbs up into Middlebury Gap itself, marked at 2,149 feet in altitude by a sign for the Long Trail, the 255-mile-long trail running high up in the Green Mountains, the spine of the state. You enter the Green Mountain National Forest and seem to be striking deeper into woodland when a big, yellow 1860s hotel suddenly appears. Now owned by Middlebury College, this is the Bread Loaf Conference Center, well known for its summer literary programs. It was here that poet Robert Frost taught, summering in a nearby cabin from 1939 until 1962.

**Robert Frost Wayside Area:** Less than a mile west of Bread Loaf the Robert Frost Wayside Area offers picnic tables, grills, and a map of the neighboring Moosalamoo Wilderness Area with its campsites and mountain-biking trails.

**Robert Frost Interpretive Trail:** A bit farther west, past a classic old Vermont cemetery, is the Robert Frost Interpretive Trail. A path leads across the brook and into the pines. The trail is salted with Frost poems.

**Ripton:** Next comes the small mountain village of Ripton with its white clapboard meetinghouse and post office/general store. Here Route 125 begins its descent, dipping ever-downward along the Middlebury River. Look quickly and for a second or two the Champlain Valley, Lake Champlain, and the Adirondack Mountains are spread below.

# Lakes to Locks Passage 

*Running along Lake Champlain, east of the Adirondacks, the Lakes to Locks Passage transports visitors through a land rich in old history and new adventures. Come by car, but carry your bike, kayak, or hiking boots.*

Driving through the villages and hamlets of Lakes to Locks Passage, travelers are swept into a place of history. State parks and preserves offer hiking trails, lakeside beaches, and wildlife-spotting opportunities. Paralleling Lake Champlain and the Champlain Canal, the byway promises scenic views mixed with plenty of history.

Precolonial history is woven throughout the names of places and historic sites. The French explorer Samuel de Champlain named Lake Champlain in 1609. The struggle between nations and people occurred here among the Huron, Algonquin, and Iroquois. During the French and Indian War, the French and British built settlements and fortifications all along the passage. Since then, many changes have moved through the Lakes to Locks Passage, but the natural beauty remains as a constant appeal to new explorers and visitors.

Explorers along the Lakes to Locks Passage travel the road by car, but those who know a little bit about the area bring a bicycle along, too. Lake Champlain Bikeways are known as some of the best cycling roads in the country. But whether you travel by bicycle, on foot, or in the car, all the routes along the byway offer access to unique points of interest.

## Intrinsic Qualities

**Cultural:** Residents along the Lakes to Locks Passage look at their part of the country as a working land; the seasons harmonize with the agricultural activities that take place along the byway. From sugar in the winter to strawberries in the summer, the land along the passage is continually productive. This productivity began long ago with the Iroquois and Abenaki, who were able to develop strategies of survival there. The culture along the byway today is one that cherishes resources both agricultural and natural.

*The view of Lake Champlain from Fort Ticonderoga gives little wonder why this location was chosen for a strategic military fortress.*

With bountiful harvests of fresh-cut hay and ripening tomatoes and gardens, life along the byway is bright and thriving. The people who live and work here enjoy the lakes, rivers, and forests as much as travelers do. During the Industrial Revolution, the rich iron deposits and the forests of the Adirondacks fueled the country. Later, another resource was discovered. Remember that yellow pencil you chewed on in elementary school? Ticonderoga was the name written on the side of the pencil, and it was made from the rich graphite deposits found along the shores of Lake Champlain and Lake George. In fact, the region is known as the paper and pencil capital of America.

As you travel the Lakes to Locks Passage, check out a few of the places where you'll get a glimpse of the local culture. The Waterford Historical Museum and Cultural Center offers a closer look at the oldest incorporated village in the United States. Many of the exhibits offer insight into colonial farming, and the museum overlooks the Mohawk River. Rogers Island Visitors' Center provides a look at the early cultures that lived in the area, and the Ticonderoga Heritage Museum exhibits the history of industry at Ticonderoga. Many other museums and centers offer a

### Quick Facts

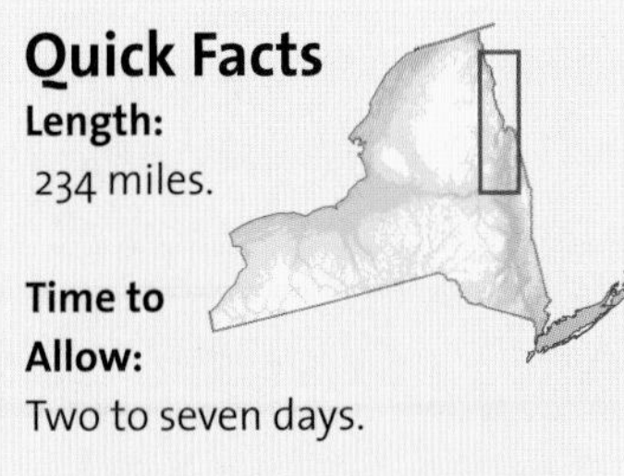

**Length:**
234 miles.

**Time to Allow:**
Two to seven days.

**Considerations:** Many of the ferries crossing from New York to Vermont are closed in the winter.

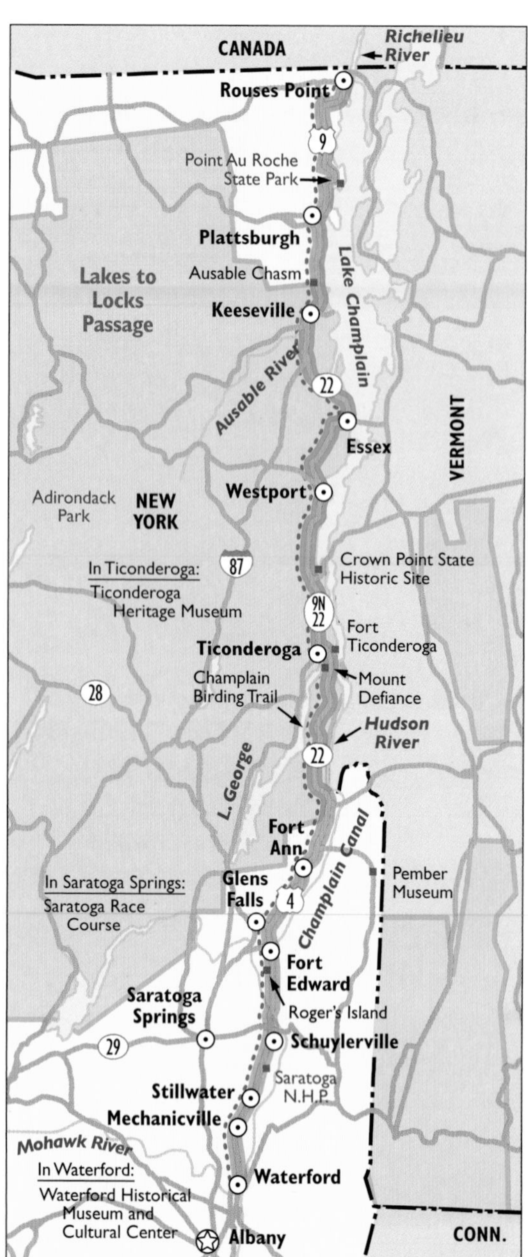


piece of byway culture that allows you to understand the way of life along the Lakes to Locks Passage. You'll find that byway culture enhances your ride and may even give you an inside look at the best things to do along the way.

**Historical:** Lakes to Locks is a passage of early American history. From the first Native Americans to the European explorers to the colonists, the geography and history of the land has played an important part in creating a passageway along the corridor that is now a byway. Expeditions and battles have been carried out on its soil. The growth and development of a new nation has also occurred along the byway, making it the well-known passage that it is today. The many historical sites along the byway are evidence that it has always been a land much sought after.

When Samuel de Champlain arrived in the area in 1609, he found people there who loved the land and who struggled for it. The Iroquois were battling with the Algonquins and Hurons, who were joined by the French. As de Champlain explored the area with the Algonquins and Hurons, they reached a beautiful lake with four islands and mountains in the distance. The lake was beautiful and, being the traditional explorer that he was, de Champlain called it "Lake Champlain." Meanwhile, an English sea captain named Henry Hudson anchored his ship in what is now Albany on his journey to find the legendary Northwest Passage to China. His naming of the upper Hudson River through Lake George and Lake Champlain later influenced trade routes and Dutch settlements in the New World. By 1709, the British had settled the southern end of the passage, while the French had settled the northern end. Eventually, this separation determined the boundary of New York and Canada, but the arrangement would also play a part in the French and Indian War, as several different nations fought for control of the land.

The French and Indian War continued for seven years until 1763, when the French ceded Canada to Great Britain. For 15 years, the passageway that is now the Lakes to Locks Passage was under the control of Great Britain, but another war was about to take place. In 1775, American colonists began the Revolutionary War that changed the country forever. The American Navy gathered at the south end of Lake Champlain to delay British invasion. A year later a victory at Saratoga won French support and further control of the area. The battles at Saratoga are now considered the turning point of the Revolutionary War as the rebels gained control and a new country was formed.

A new country meant new growth, and settlements were founded all along the Hudson and Champlain valleys. But the peace and prosperity were interrupted once again by war. This time, the War of 1812 set the British against the Americans once again. At the end of the war, the border between the United States and Canada was finally drawn, and peace and growth returned to the area. As the nation expanded, road and canal building became important endeavors. The Champlain Canal allowed movement of mineral and timber resources from the Adirondacks throughout New York. As the land was developed and population grew, New York became the influential place that it is today. Drivers can see the history of a nation in the communities, forts, and battlefields all along the Lakes to Locks Passage.

**Natural:** The natural lakes and rivers of the byway flow through a landscape dotted with mountains. Chasms and forests create scenic places for hiking and adventure. The natural qualities of the Lakes to Locks Passage are closely tied to the scenery and the recreational opportunities that abound on the byway. Lake Champlain or one of its connecting waterways is on the east side, while the Adirondack Mountains are on the west side. Open landscape creates scenic views and inviting places to stop along the way.

Glaciers from an ice age created the landscape along the byway. The mountains, lakes, and rivers were all affected by the presence of these great blankets of ice. The mountains were eroded and rounded, the lakes were filled to the brim, and the rivers ran away with the surplus water. The discovery of a whale skeleton on the hores of modern Lake Champlain s an indication of the vastness of he ancient glacial lake. The gorge now known as the Ausable Chasm s sandstone sculpted by the fast-moving Ausable River.

Today, Lake Champlain is one of the largest freshwater lakes in he world, full of many varieties of rout, bass, perch, pike, and other fish. And fish aren't the only kind of wildlife along the byway. Lakes to Locks Passage is host to a natural migration via the Atlantic Flyway. The Champlain Birding Trail allows you to watch for birds of all kinds as they migrate through the area. From Canada geese to red-winged blackbirds, creatures with feathers are well represented on the byway.

**Recreational:** The land that surrounds the Lakes to Locks Passage has been a vacation destination since the early 1800s, when it was part of "The Northern Grand Tour." Artists, writers, and the elite of the time would enjoy the scenery on a train ride or from a canal boat. Today, gazing out the car window is only the beginning. The Lakes to Locks Passage is a place for boating, bird-watching, biking, and diving beneath the surface of Lake Champlain. The waterways are the center of recreation here, but even if you don't like the water, you'll find plenty to do.

Waterways connect Lake Champlain to rivers and canals. Boaters will find access to this beautiful lake by the Champlain Canal, the Hudson River, or the Richelieu River of Quebec. Lake Champlain is the sixth-largest freshwater lake in the United States, and the boating and fishing are superb. Boaters, kayakers, and windsurfers can all find communities with marinas, supplies, and places to relax. And if you don't have a boat, rentals and tours are available all along the lakeshore. Trout, bass, pike, or perch may be the reason you decide to take a boat onto Lake Champlain—fishing Lake Champlain is such a dynamic experience that experts participate in fishing tournaments held there. With 585 miles of shoreline, professional and amateur anglers can fish and enjoy a picnic on the shore of the lake.

The sights beneath the surface of Lake Champlain also interest visitors to the byway. America's best collection of freshwater shipwrecks can be found at the bottom of Lake Champlain, and diving is the best way to see them. You can find diving services and information about which sites are accessible. The Lake Champlain Underwater Historic Preserve and the Submerged Heritage Preserve are the places to start when searching for an exciting dive. Your dive may even include Champ, the legendary Lake Champlain Monster.

A name like Ausable Chasm just calls for adventure, and that is exactly what kayakers and rafters find as they travel down a two-mile stretch of the Ausable River. If you prefer exploring on foot, steel bridges afford a bird's-eye view of the chasm. You can cross from one end of the gorge to the other to observe massive rock formations or walk along the cliffs through a forest. On the edge of the Adirondack Park, this part of the byway is the perfect place for camping, hiking, or cycling. The Champlain Bikeway is one of the best cycling spots in the country. The route is nearly 360 miles long and goes through many parts of the byway and into Quebec. The walkways and bikeways allow you to see the byway and its recreational opportunities from several different perspectives.

**Scenic:** Part of the fun of driving the Lakes to Locks Passage is the variety of landscapes and terrains you pass along the way. Lakesides and forests are accented by historic buildings and quaint towns of America's early days. In the setting of lakes and agricultural countryside, the occasional colonial building or fort can be spotted. Meanwhile, the open valleys and rolling landscape of the passage provide a route for cyclists and visitors who are interested in a scenic walk. The road gently curves past rivers and through bits of northeastern mixed forest to bring you to destinations such as Lake Champlain, Ausable Chasm, and Adirondack Park.

The passage begins in a place where canals and rivers converge, and then it follows the path of the Champlain Canal where visitors and residents are boating and canoeing. You will definitely want to stop at Fort Ticonderoga and,

*The privately owned Ausable Chasm has numerous rapids, waterfalls, and rock formations for visitors to enjoy.*

before you leave, obtain directions to nearby Mount Defiance, where an incredible vista of Lake Champlain, Fort Ticonderoga, and Mount Independence in Vermont are visible. At the north end of Lake Champlain, you can catch glimpses of Valcour Island and drive to Plattsburgh for a historic tour and scenic views of the lake. At Point Au Roche State Park, enjoy the Lake Shore Road that guides you through scenic farmland and views of the northern lake islands in Vermont. To make the journey through the Lakes to Locks Passage even more interesting, information and signs are placed all along the route to provide an extra story or two about the history of the land and the development of the lake, the canal, and its locks.

## Highlights

Begin the Lakes to Locks Passage in Waterford, and make your way north to Plattsburgh and Rouses Point.

**Waterford Historical Museum and Cultural Center:** Head north from Troy on Route 4. At the town of Waterford, stop at the Waterford Historical Museum and Cultural Center, located in an 1830 Greek Revival mansion overlooking the Mohawk River and the old Champlain Canal. The museum has exhibits about Waterford, the oldest continually incorporated village in the United States.

**Saratoga National Historical Park:** About five miles north of the town of Stillwater, watch for Saratoga National Historical Park, site of a 1777 American victory that marked the key turning point of the Revolutionary War. A ten-mile auto tour runs through the battlefield.

**Saratoga Springs:** To visit the historic resort town of Saratoga Springs, take Route 29 west from Route 4 a few miles farther north. Saratoga Springs is the site of the beautiful Saratoga Race Course, the nation's oldest thoroughbred racetrack, and a public spa where the rich and famous have long taken the waters.

**Adirondack Park:** Continue north on Route 4 to Route 22 north. Off to the left are the southeastern fringes of 6.1-million-acre Adirondack Park, the largest park in the lower 48 states. The multi-use park covers much of eastern upstate New York, encompassing dozens of towns, as well as recreational lands that include 46 mountain peaks more than 4,000 feet high, some 1,000 miles of rivers, and more than 2,500 lakes and ponds. The byway passes near the eastern shores of resort-lined Lake George, and then continues north along the eastern edges of the park for much of the rest of the route.

**Fort Ticonderoga and Mount Defiance:** Occupying a strategic location at the outlet of Lake George and above the southern tip of Lake Champlain is Fort Ticonderoga, built in 1755 by the French. Americans later captured it from the British in 1775, the first major victory of the Revolutionary War.

*Both the British and the French claimed Crown Point in their struggle to dominate North America. Much later the Americans gained control of the location.*

Daily ceremonies (May to mid-October) feature fife and drum parades and cannon firings. A scenic road leads from the fort up to the summit of Mount Defiance, featuring great views stretching into Vermont.

**Lake Champlain:** East of the byway lies Lake Champlain, the sixth-largest freshwater lake in the United States. The byway continues along its western shores for most of the rest of the route. The lake is a natural wonderland, ideal for fishing, boating, scuba diving, bird-watching, and bicycling.

**Crown Point State Historic Site:** Farther north just off Route 9N/22 is Crown Point State Historic Site, where the ruins of two Colonial-era forts, St. Frederic and Crown Point, are preserved. They were occupied by a succession of French, British, and American soldiers during the French and Indian and Revolutionary wars.

**Ausable Chasm:** Continue north (following Routes 22 and 9) to Ausable Chasm, a tourist attraction since 1870. The chasm, more than a mile long and up to 50 feet wide and 200 feet deep, was carved by the Ausable River, which plunges in falls and rapids past sandstone cliffs and huge rock formations. Paths and bridges crisscross and line the chasm, and river rafting trips are available.

**Plattsburgh:** Nearing the Canadian border, the city of Plattsburgh is worth a stop. Among the historic homes is the Kent–Delord House Museum, which served as British officers' quarters during the Battle of Plattsburgh in the War of 1812. Ferries leave for Vermont from Cumberland Head north of town, 24 hours a day year-round.

# Seaway Trail 

*Following the shores of two Great Lakes and the St. Lawrence Seaway, the ever-scenic Seaway Trail leads to Niagara Falls, the Thousand Islands, historic lighthouses, intriguing museums, and waterside fun in far upstate New York.*

The Seaway Trail brings the nation's earliest days to life and makes the nation's present days more lively. Follow this 454-mile byway paralleling the St. Lawrence River, Lake Ontario, Niagara River, and Lake Erie and discover historical scenery that is anything but sleepy.

Delight in this drive through naturally scenic landscapes, welcoming harbors, city skylines, and quaint villages. Plan time to pause at fresh fruit and vegetable stands or sample apple pie and the sweetest corn in the country at farmers' markets, country fairs, and u-pick farms. You'll find festivals from Chautauqua's vineyards to Niagara Falls celebrating every season. Beyond the flavor of the rural community, travelers will find high culture in the cities along the byway, as well. Cities such as Rochester and Buffalo offer a myriad of museums and a slew of historic sites.

With some of the world's best year-round sportfishing, anglers looking to catch the big one just may find it along the Seaway Trail. The shores of Lake Ontario and Lake Erie present plenty of options for water recreation. Historic lighthouses also line the trail, creating stops for further exploration. And if you enjoy a picnic in the park, there are many sites to choose from at the state parks lining the byway.

*Though spanning the border of two countries, the misty thundering waters of Niagara Falls are accessible on the American side from Niagara Falls State Park.*

## Intrinsic Qualities

**Cultural:** The state of New York has been developing its culture for hundreds of years. Cities and towns along the Great Lakes and the St. Lawrence River add flavor not only to the Seaway Trail but also to the nation. As you travel this National Scenic Byway, spend a night in a cozy bed-and-breakfast, or tour a historical site from the War of 1812. Whatever you do, you will become acquainted with the culture of the Seaway Trail. It is a culture immersed in history and at the cutting edge of change.

The cultures of the Iroquois and the Mohawk leave an intriguing legacy that reflects an America of the past. These cultures can be rediscovered on the Seaway Trail in places like the Seneca Iroquois National Museum in Salamanca or the Akwesasne Cultural Center in Hogansburg. Businesses all along the trail display the crafting of the past in beautiful beadwork, cornhusk dolls, and silversmithing. The presence of these cultures is also apparent in their seasonal festivals and powwows.

Eventually, these cultures mixed in with the British and the French as they arrived to stake their claim in the New World. The roots of these lasting European influences are commemorated at Old Fort Niagara, as well as at many other historic sites. As the country opened up to other European cultures, Italian and Greek immigrants made their way to New York, too. Their mark can be seen in the Old World architecture and woodcarvings in towns along the way. The cultures of a few religions also have roots on the Seaway Trail. Travelers on the trail will be able to visit Amish farms, remnants of Shaker heritage, or historic sites significant to the Mormon Church. These cultures have been mixing over the years to form the diversity of festivals and monuments along the trail today.

One of the best places to experience the culture of the Seaway Trail is in the local restaurants and bed-and-breakfasts. Here, you will discover an old-fashioned hospitality that has been preserved and handed down from eras that came before. In the towns and the cities on the trail, historic buildings have

### Quick Facts

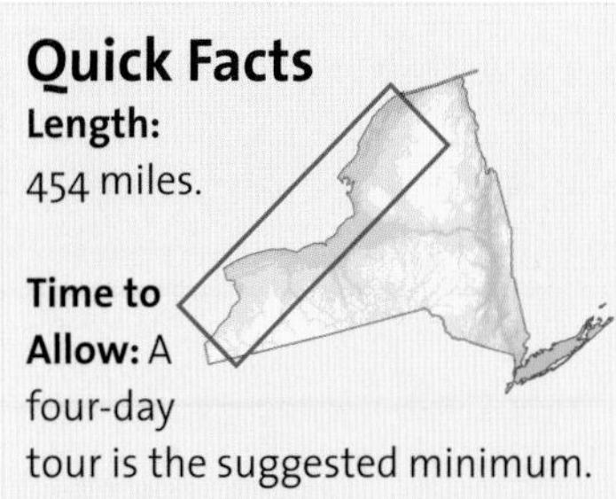

**Length:** 454 miles.

**Time to Allow:** A four-day tour is the suggested minimum.

**Considerations:** Parkway through mid-trail prohibits motor coaches without permits. Bicycling is possible in areas where shoulder width allows use.

been converted to places to rest and enjoy the local cuisine. The people of the Seaway Trail are just waiting to share their heritage in their architecture and their recipes.

Ultimately, the Seaway Trail is a byway where visitors enjoy the diversity that the country has to offer. From festivals to fine dining, the Seaway Trail is sure to have a cultural style that intrigues you.

**Historical:** Sea captains and military captains have created legacies along the Seaway Trail. Their stories are told, sometimes re-created, and sometimes only imagined all along the byway in the 42 different historic sites. Learn about the history of the war that inspired "The Star-Spangled Banner." Many sites from the War of 1812 are located all along the byway and marked for visitor convenience. Quiet towns along the way offer a portal into the past where sea captains built their homes and simple businesspeople lived and worked. Visit America's oldest freshwater port in Oswego, and see if you can spot all 28 lighthouses located along the way. The ghosts of a maritime culture still haunt this byway. The Seaway Trail is full of history and dozens of ways to explore it.

Old forts and battle structures still remain all along the byway, one of which is Old Fort Niagara. This fort is located close to the famous falls of the same name and boasts 300 years of history of being passed from the French to the British and finally to the Americans. As a gateway to the Great Lakes, the St. Lawrence River, and thus, the interior of the country, the fort was situated in an extremely strategic position. As a result, it has a colorful history of battles and wars. Travelers will encounter a different world as they step through the gates of the fort. Soldiers and townspeople "from" 300 years ago are roaming about the area, ready to explain a black-powder rifle or the history of a battle. Historians who choose to live history come here to explain the past to visitors of the present.

*The Rainbow Bridge straddles the Niagara River connecting Canada (on the left of the photo) and the United States (on the right of the photo).*

Other structures along the byway leave more a sensation of mystery than of history. Visit Boldt Castle of the Thousand Island Region for a glimpse of true love and tragedy at the turn of the 20th century. The magnificent stone structures located in this area will transport travelers to another time and country through the architecture that is found only in the castles of Europe. All along the shores of the Great Lakes, lighthouses spring up to lure visitors to get out their cameras to capture their picturesque quality. Among the most significant of the Seaway's lighthouses are Dunkirk Lighthouse, Thirty Mile Point Lighthouse, and Sodus Point Lighthouse. These lighthouses, as well as many of the others, date back to the early 1800s when navigation in bad weather was dependent upon these beacons. Exploring the sites along the byway will only lead to a discovery of more of the abundant history that is embedded along the Seaway Trail.

**Natural:** Bays along the byway's edge sprout cattails, and the rivers and lakes create coves and overhangs of rock from another time. The bluffs that are familiar on the Seaway Trail often hold swallows' nests in the pockmarks in the rock. Because of natural sites that can be seen from the river, canoe trips are perhaps one of the best ways to see the natural world that thrives on the Seaway Trail every day. But whether you paddle or hike, the Seaway Trail offers a look at coexisting wildlife and geology.

Recognized for its bird-watching opportunities on some of America's most well known lakes and rivers, the Seaway Trail offers a natural view of New England. Bird species from waders to warblers flock to the Seaway Trail to enjoy the moderate climate with plenty of freshwater sources. Usually a hiking trail on the byway will take you into the thick of bird country where they can be seen with or without binoculars. From spring to winter, bird-watching remains an activity that can be enjoyed on the byway year-round. In the winter, visitors may catch a glimpse of a snowy owl, and in the spring, birds of prey visit the byway on the Lake Erie shoreline. All along the St. Lawrence River, beavers, ducks, and porcupine continue to make a home as they have for thousands of years.

It would seem that the land itself is alive on the byway. Lakes are lapping, rivers are rushing, and stone is being sculpted ever so slowly. Some of the most prominent geological features on the byway are the Chimney Bluffs. These peaks and spires amid a mixture of clay are found inside a drumlin on Lake Ontario. Traveling down the St. Lawrence River, you'll notice rocks of a pink hue beneath the water's surface and on the shore. This rock is some of the

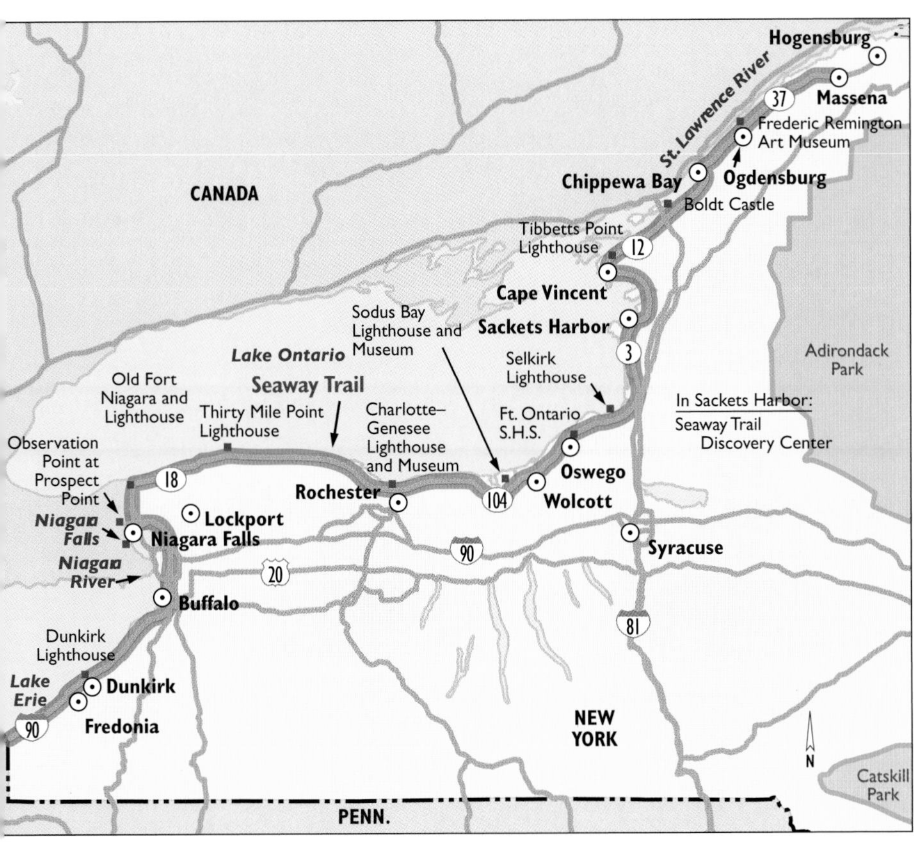


oldest in North America with the same composition as the Adirondacks. A landmark of international fame rests between Lake Ontario and Lake Erie on the Seaway Trail. Every year, visitors come from miles around to witness the power and splendor that belong to Niagara Falls. Water plunges from the upper Niagara River to the channel below to create an effect that has mesmerized humanity for centuries.

**Recreational:** With state parks and bustling cities all along the route, the Seaway Trail is not lacking in the selection of activities it offers visitors. Throughout the year, visitors to the byway enjoy shorelines and waterways with plenty of access. In the winter, when water sports might be less appealing, there is always the draw of both downhill and cross-country skiing. There are more than 30 state parks just along the byway. Detour off the road a bit and you'll find a few more. Little villages and points of interest lure visitors all along the trail. The natural beauty of the Finger Lakes is almost as enticing as the legend behind them. Lighthouse enthusiasts will want to tour all 28 of the historic lighthouses from Lake Erie to the St. Lawrence Seaway. Exciting adventures await among the Thousand Islands Area. A flavor for life by the sea is what visitors will acquire after spending time on this byway.

**Scenic:** The Seaway Trail is a roadway covered in country charm with a twist of the city. Around every corner, visitors are sure to find museums, historic sites, parks, and cemeteries. Cities, apple orchards, wildflowers, and shoreline are all part of the view. There are so many things to see along this byway that a well-planned itinerary is a must for travelers to see everything that suits their fancy. The Seaway Trail is the perfect way to see the best of New York.

As the trail travels the northern edge of New York, drivers and passengers alike will enjoy a view that reveals the waters of Lake Erie, the Niagara River, Lake Ontario, and the St. Lawrence River. State parks, often with campgrounds, dot the shores of these lakes and rivers, providing scenery and relaxation for visitors. There is nothing quite like a gentle breeze from the lake. And the sight of Niagara Falls may be one of the high points of the drive. The falls lie on the channel between Lake Erie and Lake Ontario, and they are a scenic wonder unto themselves. All along the St. Lawrence River, visitors will have the opportunity to experience nature at a closer distance.

Take the time to stop at a few historic homes and cities to walk along harbors or through gardens. This area was the beginning of prosperity for the nation from the earliest times. Between the larger cities, such as Buffalo and Rochester, travelers will also find villages of a slower pace. Full of personality, these places will point visitors in the direction of the most unique points of interest. Visitors will also find 28 lighthouses along the way. Be sure to bring a camera for that perfect moment when the setting sun hits a historic lighthouse at just the right angle. Enjoy the scenery of the Seaway Trail and take the time to tour the scenes that intrigue you on this National Scenic Byway.

## Highlights

Covering both urban and rural, inland and waterfront areas, the Seaway Trail has a plethora of pleasurable places awaiting travelers. This listing of highlights captures just a bit of the flavor of this unique byway.

**Frederic Remington Art Museum:** On the northeast end of the byway in the town of Ogdensburg is the Frederic Remington Art Museum, commemorating the life and work of the famed bronze sculptor and painter of western art. A majority of the museum's vast holdings came as a bequest from Remington's widow upon her death in 1918, and includes not only paintings and bronzes but also sketchbooks, notes, photos, and even the cigars that were in his pocket before he died, giving a personal—as well as professional—view of the great artist.

**Heart Island and Boldt Castle:** Just off Alexandria Bay, Heart Island

and Boldt Castle are intriguing monuments to love, loss, and luxury. Built in the early 1900s as a symbol of love for his wife by the proprietor of New York City's famous Waldorf-Astoria Hotel, George Boldt never returned to the island or to the extravagant Rhineland-style castle after his wife died suddenly in 1904. Acquired and rehabilitated by the Thousand Islands Bridge Authority, the island and its various buildings are now open to the public.

**Seaway Trail Discovery Center:** For an overview of the Seaway Trail and complete information to take with you along your journey, a stop at the Seaway Trail Discovery Center in Sackets Harbor is a great idea. Located in the old Union Hotel in historic downtown along the waterfront, the Discovery Center has nine exhibit rooms featuring a lighthouse video display, animatronic and interactive exhibits, and abundant information about the history of the Seaway Trail.



**Fort Ontario:** On Fourth Street in Oswego is the star-shape Fort Ontario, restored to its mid-1800s appearance. An orientation exhibit tells the history of the fort from its beginnings in 1755, including its use as an emergency refugee center for victims of the World War II Holocaust. Costumed historians re-create the lives of military men, their families, and civilians from the mid-1800s.

**Thirty Mile Point, Selkirk, and Tibbetts Point Lighthouses:** Following along the waters of the Great Lakes, the Seaway Trail has several historic lighthouses, some of which are open to the pubic. And although lighthouses rarely offer overnight accommodations, the Seaway Trail is fortunate to have three lighthouses available for overnight stays: Thirty Mile Point Lighthouse at Golden Hill State Park; Selkirk Lighthouse at the mouth of the Salmon River on Lake Ontario, Port Ontario; and Tibbetts Point Lighthouse Hostel at the mouth of the confluence of the St. Lawrence River and Lake Ontario, Cape Vincent.

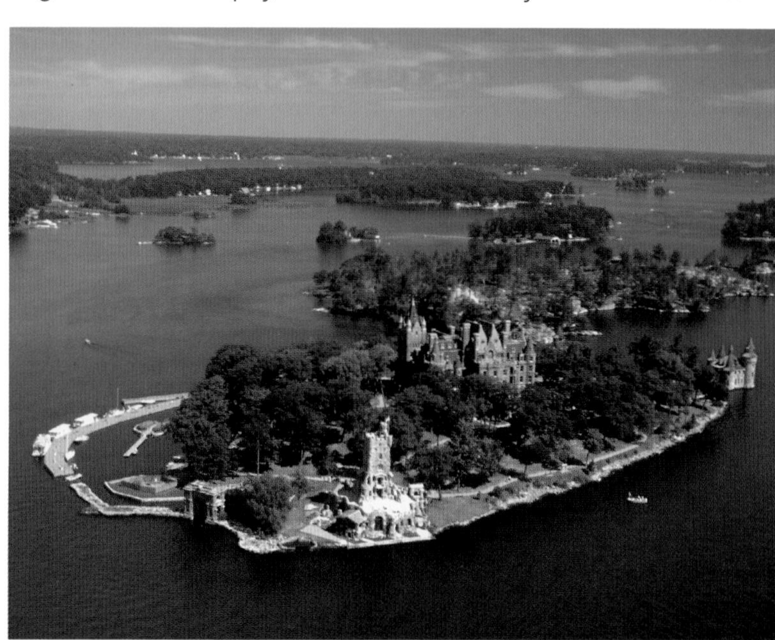

*Built as a tribute to love, Boldt Castle on Heart Island was never occupied by its owner. It is now a major landmark on the St. Lawrence River.*

**Sodus Bay Lighthouse and Museum:** Those lighthouses that do not provide overnight accommodations but do have tours provide wonderful experiences for visitors. One is Sodus Bay Lighthouse and Museum. Multimedia exhibits present the early history of the area, early railroading history at Sodus Point, and fishing here. And of course, a major attraction is the climb to the top of the lighthouse tower, 70 feet above the waters of the lake for a spectacular view.

**Charlotte–Genesee Lighthouse and Museum:** In Rochester is the Charlotte–Genesee Lighthouse and Museum. The keeper's house has exhibits about lighthouse lore, local history, and navigation, while the adjacent building has exhibits focused on the early history of the site. And visitors are welcome to climb the tower.

**Old Fort Niagara:** Old Fort Niagara is a National Historic Landmark belonging to the United States now, but it wasn't always so. With a history reaching back into the 1700s, the fort has been in the hands of the French, the British, and eventually the United States. Visitors can explore 16 points of interest on the self-guided tour, including several buildings, monuments, earthen fortifications, and the lighthouse. Living historians and multimedia displays tell the exciting history of the fort and the people who occupied it.

**Niagara Falls:** The finale to this itinerary is the sublime Niagara Falls, accessible in Niagara Falls State Park. Though the falls straddle the border of the United States and Canada, the U.S. side has retained much of its natural environment while still having plenty for visitors to do. You'll want to begin your journey at the Niagara Gorge Discovery Center, showcasing the natural history of Niagara Falls and the Gorge with interactive displays and a 180-degree multiscreen theater presentation. The geology of the Niagara Gorge is detailed, including information about the ancient rock layers, minerals, fossils and more.

**Observation Tower:** Also at the Niagara Falls State Park, the Observation Tower at Prospect Point gives a commanding view of the American Falls and the churning waters in the gorge below. An elevator ride to the bottom of the Observation Tower takes you to the dock where you can board the *Maid of the Mist* for a boat ride to the swirling basin of the Horseshoe Falls. The Cave of the Winds trek takes you down 175 feet into the Niagara Gorge and within 20 feet of Bridal Veil Falls.

# Mohawk Trail

*The hilliest section of Route 2 runs through the Berkshire Hills in northwestern Massachusetts. Shadowing an ancient Native American path, it has been known as the Mohawk Trail since it was formally declared one of the country's first scenic "auto routes."*

In 1914, the most mountainous miles of the Mohawk Trail were graded and specifically dedicated to "auto touring." This stretch begins in the small city of North Adams and zigzags its way up the "Hairpin Turn" to the western summit of Hoosac Mountain. It runs eastward along heavily wooded ridges, then drops into the long-settled Deerfield Valley, and finally descends into the broad Connecticut River Valley.

In 1914, the fastest way from North Adams to Boston was by rail, via the 4½-mile Hoosac Tunnel, itself considered a wonder when it opened in 1875. By 1914, however, cars were becoming affordable and folks were eager to break away from the dictates of the rails, to stop and go where they wanted. The challenge of driving *over* rather than riding *through* Hoosac Mountain drew families—driving their first cars—from throughout the Northeast. Recognized as a destination in its own right from the 1920s through the 1950s, this initial stretch of the Mohawk Trail sprouted tea shops and motor courts, trading posts and campgrounds, both private and state.

In the 1960s, vacation patterns and highway routes changed. The 1965 opening of the Massachusetts Turnpike (Route 90) knocked an hour off the time it takes to cross the state and further backroaded Route 2. The Mohawk Trail's vintage lookout towers, motor courts, tearooms, and trading posts faded.

Formore than a decade now the tourist tide has once more been turning. White-water rafters on the Deerfield River are filling the old roadside lodging places, and bed-and-breakfasts draw travelers into the surrounding hills. The village of Shelburne Falls, long known for its Bridge of Flowers, has become a showcase for the area's many craftspeople and chefs. Once more the Mohawk Trail is becoming a destination, this time for travelers who appreciate its layerings of history, as well as its natural beauty.

*This site is a ridge above the town of Greenfield, which inspired poet Frederick Goddard Tuckerman, a writer admired by Hawthorne, Tennyson, and Emerson.*

## Quick Facts

**Length:** 38 miles.

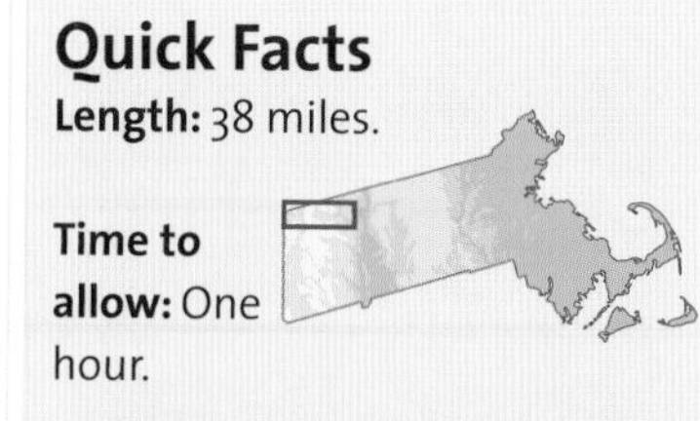

**Time to allow:** One hour.

**Considerations:** From mid-October through early May conditions may be treacherous due to ice and snow, but the road never closes. It's most beautiful late May through mid-October and usually crowded only on weekends during foliage season (late September through early October).

## Highlights

Start in North Adams, and end in Greenfield.

**Massachusetts Museum of Contemporary Art:** North Adams boomed into existence with the construction of the Hoosac Tunnel in the late 19th century, and its mills prospered until the 1970s, a period when much of its fine Victorian-era downtown was razed in the name of urban renewal. Thanks to the Massachusetts Museum of Contemporary Art, which now fills four large former mill buildings with changing exhibits and performances, the state's smallest city once more offers quality lodging and dining.

**Longview Tower Specialty Shops:** The Longview Tower Specialty Shops were opened in 1923 by two sisters. The five-story observation tower was rebuilt of steel in 1952 and is worth the climb, commanding a three-state view of hills in Vermont, New Hampshire, and Massachusetts. You can also see a panorama of the Connecticut River with its flanking farms and the town of Greenfield from the tower.

**Natural Bridge State Park:** The centerpiece of 49-acre Natural Bridge State Park is a white-marble formation bridging a gorge, a tourist attraction since the 1830s, and a popular picnicking and fishing spot.

**Hairpin Turn–Western Summit:** Cars from the 1920s frequently required a stop to cool their radiators at the top of a steep climb, such as the ascent of some 2,000 feet in altitude in the couple miles between North Adams and the Western Summit of Hoosac Mountain. The Wigwam and Western Summit Gift Shop at the top of the Hairpin Turn no longer has its wooden viewing tower but retains its '20s aura. This and a matching "tearoom" at the opposite end of the trail were built by the same two enterprising sisters who opened the Longview Towers Specialty Shops.

**Savoy Mountain State Forest:** The forest's 11,118 acres are largely mountainous and wooded. Within Savoy Mountain State Forest, take a drive to North Pond, which is good for swimming, trout fishing, boating, and camping.

**Whitcomb Summit:** The highest point on the route (2,173 feet) is marked by a steel version of a wooden tower placed here in 1915. It commands an amazing view of waves of hills. The cottages and café here date from the 1920s.

**Tannery Falls:** Be forewarned that this turnoff is unmarked. Just east of the bridge that marks the town line between Savoy and Florida, turn south on Black Brook Road and then on Tannery Road into the Savoy Mountain State Forest. From the parking area a trail follows a narrow stream steeply down to the bottom of a glorious cascade.

**Mohawk Trail State Forest:** This is a 6,457-acre forest with 56 campsites and six log cabins. You can swim in the river or hike one of the extensive trails.

**Zoar Gap:** Zoar Gap is a dramatic gorge best viewed from a whitewater raft on the Deerfield River. Zoar Outdoor, based in a 1750s house on Route 2 in Charlemont, pioneered rafting to take advantage of timed hydro releases on the Deerfield.

**Charlemont:** Here the Deerfield River slows, widens, and turns east, flanked by broad fields that have been farmed, judging from the vintage of the farmhouses, since the 1770s. The hospitable Charlemont Inn has been feeding and housing travelers since the 18th century. The Bissell Covered Bridge spans Mill Brook just north of Route 2, and the white-steepled Federated Church is known for the quality of its acoustics and of the Mohawk Trail Concerts held here in July and August. Also in Charlemont is the Indian Plaza Gift Shop, the site of periodic powwows.

**Mohawk Park:** Mohawk Park in West Charlemont features a bronze statue of a Native American placed here by the Improved Order of Red Men in 1932. The Mohawks seem to have been selected as the namesakes of this trail primarily because people had heard of them. It's true that warrior members of this Upstate New York nation occasionally came this way to raid settlements, but it's likely that the path here was blazed by local nations such as the Pocumtucks.

**Shelburne:** The American Indian trading posts along the Mohawk Trail are historic and have survived only through longtime family ownership. In Shelburne, look for the Big Indian Shop, so named for its 28-foot-tall American Indian guarding the door, and for the Mohawk Trading Post with its fiberglass buffalo outside and authentic wares within.

**Shelburne Falls:** Two bridges, one a pedestrian walkway planted with trees and flowers, span the Deerfield River linking two towns to create a lively village composed of shops and restaurants on either bank. The falls themselves once powered the picturesque Lamson and Goodnow Cutlery Mill, which features an outlet store, and the "Glacial Potholes" at their base are a multicolored and unusually shaped phenomena. The Bridge of Flowers, a former trolley bridge, has been tended by local garden clubs as a war memorial since 1919, and a restored trolley seasonally operates on a piece of track up by the depot. The village is known for its quality crafts cooperatives.

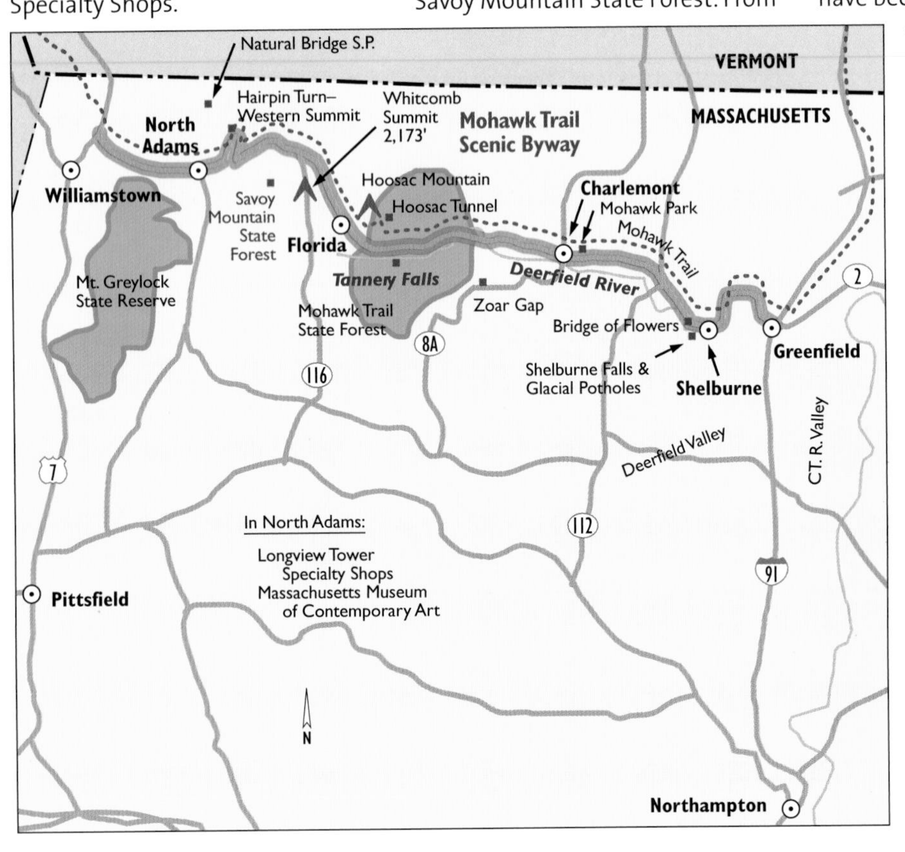

# Connecticut State Route 169

*The Norwich–Woodstock Turnpike, as it was originally known, links 18th century villages in the Quinebaug and Shetucket Rivers Valley, better known as Connecticut's Quiet Corner. State parks and forests abound, along with prep-school campuses and antiques shops.*

Consider everything you know about New England—spectacular autumn color, historic buildings, charming cities—and you will have an idea of what you will find on Connecticut State Route 169. Much has changed over the years on this byway, but the history and traditions of the area are still very much a part of the lives of the people who belong to the communities.

Take the opportunity to experience some of the sights along this historical stretch of road. Visit the beautiful churches in Pomfret that date back to the 1800s. Or find out what life was like for a prosperous family in the mid-19th century at the Roseland Cottage/Bowen House Museum in Woodstock. Or simply explore some of the towns at your leisure, admiring the distinctive architecture and well-kept parks.

As you travel the byway, you will visit many wonderful communities. The route crosses through Lisbon, where the feeling of an early American community is still evident. Explore Canterbury, where Connecticut's interpretation of Georgian architecture is prominent. Then you will find yourself in Pomfret, once known as "the other Newport" for its strong influx of wealthy summer vacationers. Finally, you will pass through Woodstock, with its many architectural surprises clustered around a town common. Traveling this byway, you will sense an area that is moving ahead in the times while still maintaining a sense of pride in its history.

*The salmon-colored Roseland Cottage has stunning original furnishings for the public to view.*

## Intrinsic Qualities

**Cultural:** The historic and cultural significance of this area was spotlighted by its designation as a National Heritage Corridor. The Quinebaug and Shetucket Rivers Valley National Heritage Corridor (Q-S NHC) recognized the great potential for recreation and site interpretation due to the byway's abundance of outstanding 19th-century mills, mill villages, and beautiful landscapes. State Route 169 forms the western edge of the Q-S NHC and is considered an important element in the Heritage Corridor, especially as a means for linking its many diverse historic sites.

In addition to two National Historic Landmarks (Prudence Crandall Museum and Roseland Cottage), there are more than 175 historic sites and districts recognized by local and state surveys and/or the State or National Registers of Historic Places. The National Register of Historic Places lists two districts along State Route 169 (Bush Hill and Brooklyn Green, both in Brooklyn), as well as individual properties. The rich architectural heritage of villages, such as Brooklyn, Pomfret, and Woodstock, is representative of the hill town communities that settled this part of Connecticut and are still very much intact.

### Quick Facts

**Length:** 32 miles.

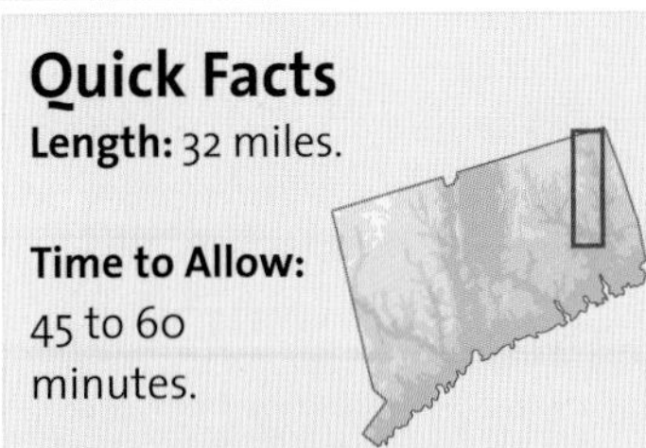

**Time to Allow:** 45 to 60 minutes.

**Considerations:** Watch for children while passing through the small towns located along the byway. Also, autumn is a great time to travel the byway because fall color adds a touch of brilliance to the route.

**Historical:** The history of this ancient road is inextricably tied to the history of the hill towns of northeastern Connecticut. Since prehistoric times, the route has wound its way along, up, and down the spines of age-old hills in a north-south direction. Windham County historian Ellen Larned tells us that a "Nipmuck Trail" ran from Wabbaquasset (i.e., the Woodstock area) to the seashore. If some parts of that trail and today's State Route 169 are not the same, there were undoubtedly footpaths of American Indian origin that took much the same course. On the northern end, it seems certain that John Eliot and Daniel Gookin crossed portions of this route in

1674 as they made their way to what is now Woodstock. During the decade that followed other people made forays into Wabbaquasset territory, burning cornfields and American Indian forts. It is only logical to assume that they used American Indian trails and perhaps some part of what is now State Route 169.

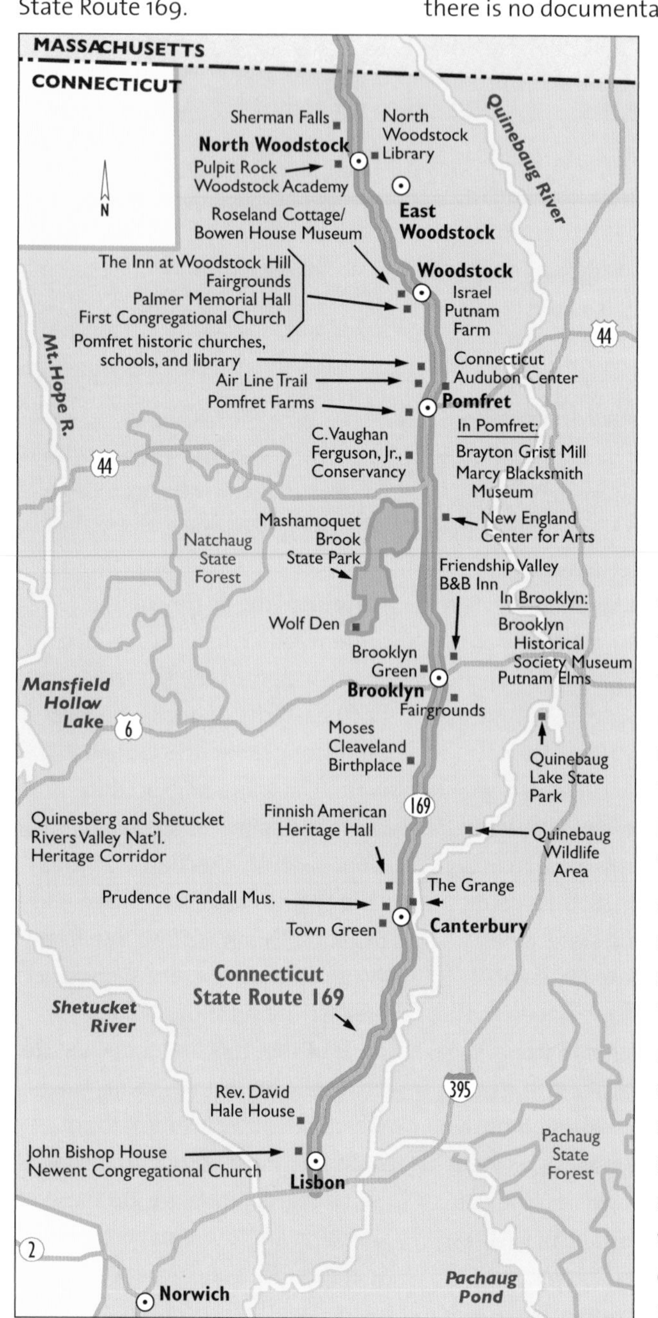


The first improvements by Europeans most likely occurred after the settling of Norwich in 1659; Lisbon was then a part of Norwich. However, the course of the lower portion of the highway was changed sometime after 1854, detaching the most ancient part of the road in that region. At present, there is no documentation for the road at the southern end. At the northern end, the Proprietor's Records of Woodstock record the laying of a road from North Running Brook, north of the village of Woodstock, to Sawmill Brook, in South Woodstock, by the first "Goers" during the summer of 1686. The public right-of-way was eight rods wide in some parts, and six rods wide in others (the rod used was probably 11 feet). This was quite a large width considering it was used primarily for foot traffic, occasional teams of oxen, and riding horses. This width allowed for common lands on either side of an improved, traveled way.

The Woodstock portion of the Norwich and Woodstock Turnpike was made free in 1836, while the rest of the road remained a toll road for another ten years. In 1846, the corporation persuaded the Connecticut assembly to relieve it of its obligations on the grounds that the cost of the road had been more than $14,000 and that no "considerable profit" had ever been realized. Since the operation of the Norwich and Worcester Railroad, the income had not been sufficient to provide for the necessary repairs and no dividends had been paid for six years. Consequently, the railroad was blamed for the demise of the 19th-century turnpike era.

Railroads also had other effects on the hill towns. To Pomfret, where the railroad passed over the highway, it brought summer tourists and a grand way of life; to other towns bypassed in favor of the thriving mill towns along the Quinebaug, it brought a long, slow decline. The period of dormancy is in large part the reason why so much of the path of this historic highway has remained unchanged throughout the years. As for the Norwich and Woodstock Turnpike, it undoubtedly remained much the same until the advent of the automobile and the development of the state highway system in the 20th century, when it was first given the number 93, which was later changed to 169. Early photographs are plentiful, showing portions of the road as a narrow, graded, and crowned dirt road. It has grown somewhat wider through the years, has been blacktopped along its entire length, and in recent years has been very well maintained. Even with all these improvements, one can still feel the bumps and turns of the ancient road, see the horizon ahead disappear and reappear, and feel a continuity through time with all who have traveled this beautiful road.

**Natural:** The spectacular views that travelers are able to witness from State Route 169 are owned by the thousands of individual (and lucky) property owners that live along the corridor. The attractive pattern of land use that has evolved over many centuries is the result of the individual actions of the residents of the five towns that the corridor traverses. State Route 169 traverses the physiographic region of Connecticut known as the "Eastern Uplands." Within the eastern uplands there are three distinct landscape types: Glacial Till Uplands—the ridge tops and side hills, Drumloidal Glacial Till Uplands—the more rounded and oval shaped uplands, and Glacial Outwash Plains—the bottomlands.

These three landscape types form a subtle impression upon the visitor to northeastern Connecticut, and a visit along State Route

*The grounds of Roseland Cottage feature a 150-year-old boxwood parterre garden, bowling alley, and ice house.*

169 traverses all three. Starting from the south, the route parallels the Quinebaug River bottomlands, barely skirting the side hills until just north of Canterbury. Here the road intersects a drumlinelike formation, and then it descends back down into the bottomlands associated with Blackwell Brook. Just north of Brooklyn, the road starts to climb again across glacial till uplands, and then it reaches what is sometimes referred to as the Woodstock Drumlin Field.

The most visible landscape type comes from the view of the immediate roadway environment. This includes the close landscape of the villages, woodlands, and farmsteads adjacent to the road. This intimate setting, often framed by stone walls and mature lines of trees, is the most memorable experience along State Route 169, and this is one of the few areas where this type of southern New England landscape remains intact. The stone walls found along this route are the result of hundreds of years of agricultural development, and in that sense, the walls are irreplaceable.

The network of streams and wetlands found throughout the corridor also add to the beautiful scenery and natural qualities of the byway. Waterways such as the English Neighborhood Brook play throughout the long-distance vistas and the mature tree canopies on the route. Many of the lands and waters that compose this system of wetlands and waterways are already protected by existing floodplain and wetland ordinances, creating a backbone of greenways and open spaces that help to embrace and separate different uses of land.

Within the scenic views along State Route 169 are extensive areas of woodland. Many of these areas have avoided agricultural use to become mature woodland as the agricultural economy has been transformed from farming to manufacturing to a service-sector orientation. These woodlands continue to play an important role in the way both visitors and residents alike perceive the character of the corridor. The highly visible wooded hillsides that provide a particularly attractive setting for the towns and villages along State Route 169 are a main characteristic of the drive. When combined with the attraction of fall color, these wooded hillsides are even more enticing.

**Scenic:** As visitors drive State Route 169, they are taken on a tour of provincial Connecticut with all its natural and cultural charm. The scenic qualities of the road are further enhanced by the extraordinary number of antique 18th- and 19th-century structures that have survived along the whole length of the highway.

Each town and village along the way has its own subtle, unique character in the buildings and people that live there. Between villages, the north/south running ridges of hills provide frequent vistas, sometimes in two directions, and a gentle, undulating path of travel. The natural flora is mingled with a still viable agricultural heritage, delighting the eye with changing patterns. The wooded hills are covered with many varieties of trees and shrubs, including some giant and very old trees of varied species. These trees fade into vast cornfields and occasional wooded areas that come right to the edge of the road to envelop travelers with a sense of deep forest and life. Travelers also see well-groomed hay fields, picturesque apple orchards, rustic farm scenes, and an abundance of wildflowers.

The catalog of delights to be found along the road is endless. Beneath a canopy of tall trees, each village has a significant number of early houses, one or more churches, a library (often in an antique building), a grassy common or green, and all the other features thought of as "New England." In the villages, or along the road, visitors will find graveyards with carved gravestones dating from earliest times. Students of gravestone carvers come from all over the country to see the stones found in this region. Lining the edges of the roads are stone walls of amazing variety and fences and gates. If travelers want to stop and leave their cars, they can see and hear countless species of birds, insects, and other fauna and rare wildflowers. All of these are free for any who come and look. For those who want to shop a bit, there is an assortment of gift shops, good restaurants, and very pleasant bed-and-breakfast accommodations.

One extraordinary feature of this byway is that there is so little intrusion of commerce, industry, or development along the route. Nowhere along the 32 miles is there a stretch more than a half-mile in length that can be said to be dull or unsightly. As of this date, there is not one strip mall, and the only modern office buildings of more than one story are the Woodstock remnants of a defunct college. These are in a lovely, parklike setting that is now owned by Data General. About a mile away, Linemaster Switch, one of the largest employers in Woodstock, has a large frontage property on the road with not a single building in view.

## Highlights

Though only a brief distance, this scenic byway is long on history with charming villages dating back more than 300 years. This itinerary covers some of the natural and historic highlights of your journey along Connecticut State Route 169 as you travel from north to south.

**Roseland Cottage:** Begin at the Roseland Cottage/Bowen House Museum in Woodstock. This home with Gothic Revival architecture was constructed in 1846 and hosted elegant soirees attended by the elite of the day, including numerous presidents. The cottage features original furnishings, bowling alley, and garden. Guided tours are available on the hour.

**Connecticut Audubon Center:** Though Pomfret has many historic churches and homes, it is the natural features of the area that are highlighted at one of northeastern Connecticut's newest attractions. The Connecticut Audubon Center is a nature center that offers educational programs and bird walks. It is also the gateway to the adjoining 700-acre Connecticut Audubon Bafflin Sanctuary.

**Brayton Grist Mill and Marcy Blacksmith Museum:** Just west of Pomfret on Route 44 is the Brayton Grist Mill and Marcy Blacksmith Museum, located at the entrance to the Mashamoquet Brook State Park. It is an 1890s mill with the original equipment. The Marcy Blacksmith Museum has exhibits that detail more than a century of blacksmithing and three generations of the craft.



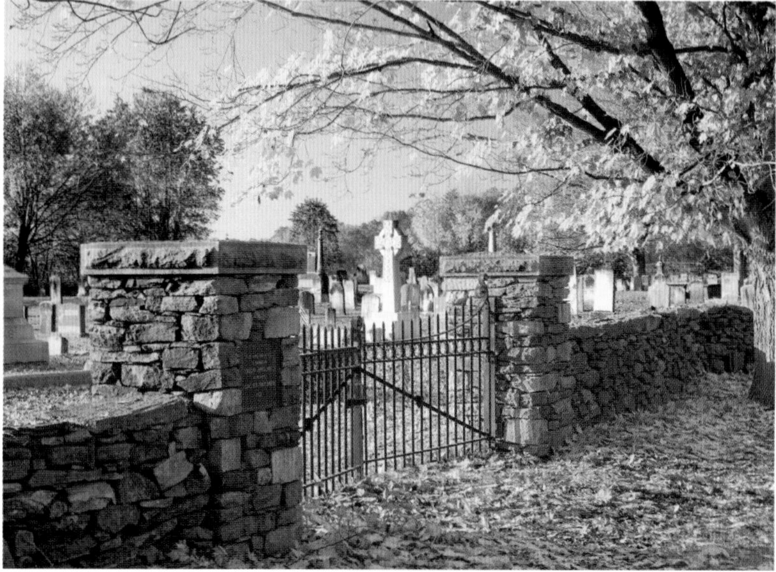

*The Carey Cemetery in Canterbury has headstones dating before 1800.*

**Mashamoquet Brook State Park:** This park offers camping, hiking, and picnicking. The most famous feature is the Wolf Den into which, on a night in 1742, Israel Putnam crept and shot a wolf that for years had preyed upon local sheep and poultry. Putnam later gained fame as a major general in the Continental Army during the Revolutionary War. Near the Wolf Den are the Table Rock and Indian Chair natural stone formations.

**Brooklyn Historical Society Museum:** This museum houses a collection of 18th- and 19th-century artifacts and Brooklyn memorabilia. Additionally it features historic items about the life of Revolutionary War hero Israel Putnam and special annual exhibits. The law office of Putnam's great-grandson, Daniel Putnam Tyler, is also open to the public.

**Putnam Elms:** Yet another Putnam family site is Putnam Elms. Constructed in 1784 by the Putnam family and still maintained by Putnam descendants, the house is open for tours and contains exhibits about the history of Colonel Daniel Putnam and his father, General Israel Putnam.

**Finnish American Heritage Hall:** Built in the 1920s, the Finnish American Heritage Hall in Canterbury is not only a social hall for those whose families immigrated and contributed to the melting pot of America but it is also the site of the Finnish American World War II memorial dedicated to Americans, including all the Finnish Americans, who fought in the war. On April 10, 1998, the Finnish Hall, along with numerous other buildings and residences on the Canterbury Green, was entered onto the National Register of Historic Places.

**Prudence Crandall Museum:** This museum is located on the site of Prudence Crandall's home, the first academy for black women in New England. Crandall's activities were not without controversy. Admitting Sarah Harris, a young black girl, to the women's academy outraged parents and townsfolk and caused an angry mob to ransack the school. Fearing for the safety of her students, Crandall closed the academy. Today this National Historic Landmark features three period rooms, changing exhibits, and a research library.

**John Bishop House:** At the end of the byway is the John Bishop House in Lisbon, which was built in the early 1800s. The structure features doors that are butt-hinged, nails that are machine cut and headed, and a framed ridge in the attic. The house also has seven fireplaces. A shaftway leading from the buttery down to a dug well, where water could be obtained without leaving the house, is a unique feature.

# Merritt Parkway 

*Built with pride in the 1930s as a "Parkway," Merritt Parkway is more sinuous than modern highways, winding its way through parklike landscaping and under Art Deco bridges. Truck-free, it's an alternative to I-95 through Connecticut to New York City.*

The Merritt Parkway is one of the only roads listed on the National Register of Historic Places, a distinction usually reserved for buildings or battlefields. Drive Merritt Parkway, and see for yourself why it inspires both reverence and devotion among fans and supporters, many of whom use it daily or live near its winding path through Connecticut's Fairfield County. Built in the 1930s to cope with America's new fascination with the automobile, this byway is enshrined in the hearts of many as an icon of the automobile age and a model of highway planning.

## Intrinsic Qualities

**Cultural:** As a scenic byway, Merritt Parkway has won national acclaim. From political leaders to talk show hosts, everyone has something to say about this parkway, and it always has something to do with the beautiful scenery visitors will experience on the prettiest drive in Connecticut. The road is nearly 75 years old and is traveled daily by at least 60,000 vehicles, but it remains a perfect combination of nature and industry. Perhaps it is because of the amount of travel that occurs on the road that it has become part of our nation's cultural heritage. Whatever the case, people inside and outside of Connecticut know about the Merritt Parkway.

**Historical:** On July 1, 1934, Oscar Tuthill, the First Selectman of Greenwich, turned a spade of earth at King Street near the Connecticut–New York border to begin construction of the Merritt Parkway, which was among the first parkways in the nation and the first median-divided, limited-access highway in Connecticut. Its name was changed from Merritt Highway to Merritt Parkway one year after construction began. On September 2, 1940, just more than six years later, the final section of the roadway was completed and the entire parkway opened to traffic.

Described by one historian as "one of the most beautiful and best-engineered highways of the time," the parkway was built to solve traffic problems in the state. Before the parkway, local motorists and long-distance travelers were forced to compete for the same highway space. Drivers could move only at slow speeds, and merchants in communities along the route were upset because their customers were unable to find convenient parking.

*Putnam Cottage was originally built in the 18th century. Since then, it has undergone many changes and has recently been restored to its colonial appearance.*

### Quick Facts

**Length:** 37 miles.

**Time to Allow:** A little less than one hour.

**Considerations:** The speed limit on the Merritt Parkway ranges between 45 and 55 mph. Avoid driving the parkway during morning and evening rush hours. There is an eight-foot vehicle height limit due to the many low overpasses on the parkway.

The Merritt Parkway was a direct product of a period in American road-building history when there was a great deal of interest in linking urbanized regions with graceful highways set in natural surroundings. This parkway quickly emerged as a national model. To ensure a natural appearance, long, gradual, vertical curves were designed. Rock cuts were rounded and landscaped to produce a natural setting. The Merritt Parkway's designers attempted to integrate the traveled way into the roadside and its surroundings. The landscaping of the parkway followed closely upon completion, attempting to heal the scars of construction.

In addition to the roadside beauty that can be viewed while

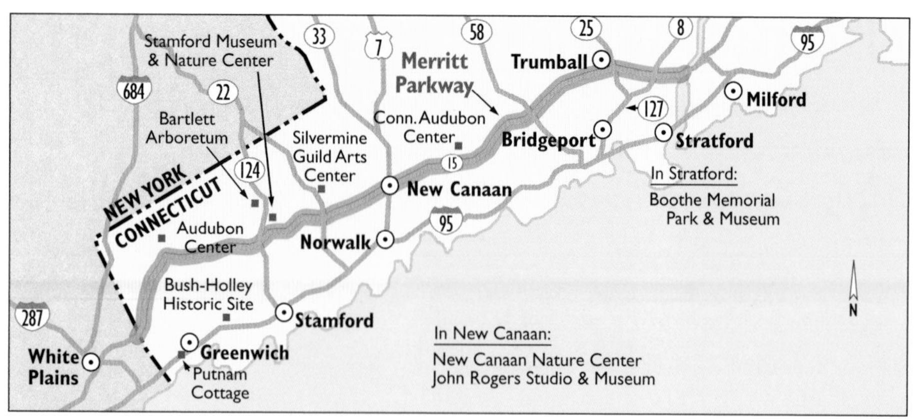


driving along the Merritt Parkway, motorists are also treated to a unique exhibition of ornamental bridges. These structures were the creation of George Dunkelberger, an innovative bridge designer and architect. There were originally 69 bridges, with some carrying the parkway under intersecting roads and railroad tracks and others carrying the parkway over intersecting roads and rivers. These bridges were designed primarily in the Art Moderne and Art Deco styles, with no two alike. In the more than 65 years since the parkway's completion, three of the original bridges have been replaced and a number of others have been altered in response to needed maintenance or repair, but the bridges still remain a scenic element of the byway.

The 37-mile roadway now stretches across Fairfield County from the town of Greenwich to the Housatonic River in the town of Stratford. The stately, neatly landscaped parkway connects the Hutchinson River Parkway at the New York state line with the Wilbur Cross Parkway at Stratford. Together, the Merritt and Wilbur Cross Parkways form part of Route 15 in Connecticut. In 1991, the parkway was listed on the National Register of Historic Places, a statement of its role as a nationally recognized cultural resource, as well as a valued part of Connecticut's heritage. It is also a critical transportation facility for the southwestern part of the state. In early 1992, the parkway was designated as a State Scenic Road, further highlighting its importance to Connecticut's character. Since its creation, millions of motorists from all over the nation have enjoyed the scenic beauty of the parkway, especially its brilliant spring displays and rich autumn foliage.

**Natural:** The bridges of the Merritt Parkway make it unique, but the landscaping plays another important role. The green trees and lawns that surround the parkway in the warmer months of the year are missed in the winter. Each fall, the landscaping reveals its more colorful side, and the Merritt Parkway becomes one of the most popular byways in the country. The landscaping on the parkway avoids being urbanesque by appearing to be the rolling hills of a New England wood.

Over the years, the placement of trees along the parkway has been carefully considered and maintained. When Merritt Parkway was first constructed, landscape architect Weld Thayer Chase selected the exact location for each major new tree. It was the vision of landscape artist Earl Wood to rely on native plant species rather than introduce exotic ones. The landscapers talked the parkway engineers into saving many existing trees along the route and transplanting plants scheduled for removal in temporary nurseries to be reused after construction. The rolling hills along the parkway were also carefully landscaped. The jagged outcrops of stone exposed by blasting were covered with pockets of plant materials, and it helped to retain the natural feel of the parkway.

Dealing with Dunkelberger's bridges presented a special challenge, since some planting was needed to help them blend in. Chase solved the problem of revealing the abutments of the bridges by planting low, spreading shrubs as ground cover near the bridges and larger trees in clusters angling back from the abutments.

The parkway plants continue to grow and flourish today. Current landscape architects still carefully place new trees along the byway to preserve its natural look. So take a leisurely drive along the Merritt Parkway and enjoy nature as you travel from one city to another.

**Recreational:** The Merritt Parkway was designed and built as a driver's road. Efficiency and speed took a back seat to the enjoyment of those who would sit in the front seat, especially the driver. Understandably, the primary form of recreation that is available is simply driving the Merritt Parkway. With an engaging variety of twists and turns; intriguing highway architecture; and lush, native surroundings, the Merritt Parkway has become a popular route for tourists and commuters alike. Due to its popularity, morning and afternoon rush hours are not the most pleasant times to travel the route and should be avoided if possible. At other times, a drive down the Merritt Parkway is a memorable driving experience that anyone can appreciate.

**Scenic:** For many, the 69 original bridges are the heart of the special appeal of the Merritt Parkway. The popular belief is that a different designer made each bridge; however, they are all the work of a single architectural designer, George Dunkelberger.

The Merritt Parkway bridges have no style or icon that threads them together as a result of Dunkelberger's eclectic design ideas. It takes a keen eye to catch what is going on in the metal balustrade of the Merwins Lane Overpass in the town of Fairfield.

This includes small butterflies caught in a stylized metal spider-web that are about to be devoured by the web's builders. The low relief sculpture on the Comstock Hill Road Overpass in Norwalk, the work of Milford sculptor Edward Ferrari, is adorned with the bust of a Pilgrim or Native American, apparent references to New England's colonial past. Not all the bridges are so subtle, however. Some use bold forms as the basis of their design. The Morehouse Highway Bridge, with its series of steplike sections that march down-ward from one side of the cut to the other, is one example. The Lake Avenue Bridge in Greenwich is unusual in that the metal arches are not shrouded in concrete, but span the roadway in two grace-ful segmental arcs bedecked with cast-iron vines.

## Highlights

A scenic alternative to other north-south corridors, the Merritt Parkway gives easy access to some of the activities and attractions listed here.

**Boothe Memorial Park and Museum:** Near the northern end of Merritt Parkway, in the town of Stratford is the Boothe Memorial Park and Museum. The Boothe Family resided on this 32-acre estate from the mid-1600s to 1949. Ten of the 20 historic buildings have been restored at this National Historic Landmark. Displays include early farm equipment, carriages, trolley history, and more. The site also has a beautiful rose garden, an observatory and educational center, picnic facilities, and playground.

**New Canaan Nature Center:** Taking exit 37 off the Merritt Parkway and passing through the center of New Canaan, the New Canaan Nature Center is just a mile north on Route 124. The center has 40 acres of habitat diversity and walking trails, an apple cider house, and a maple sugar shack. The nature center also features a visitor center with natural science exhibits, a Discovery Center, a solar greenhouse, an arboretum, and various gardens. To return to Merritt Parkway, go back through New Canaan.

**John Rogers Studio and Museum:** The John Rogers Studio and Museum was built in 1878 by John Rogers, famous as "the people's sculptor" in the latter half of the 19th century. The studio is now a National Historic Landmark, containing a large collection of Rogers' statuary, much of it sculpted on site. Visitors can also tour the Hanford Silliman House, once an 18th-century tavern and inn.

*The New Canaan Historical Society is a haven for those who love history. You can find preserved items, dating back to 1713, concerning New Canaan.*

**Silvermine Guild Arts Center:** Just outside of town is the Silvermine Guild Arts Center. It began more than a century ago, in 1895, as a colony for artists and writers founded by sculptor Solon Borglum, brother of famed Mount Rushmore sculptor Gutzon Borglum. Today the Silvermine Guild Arts Center features a gallery of changing exhibits with works from both local newcomers and nationally renowned artists.

**Bush–Holley Historic Site:** Connecticut's first art colony was in the town of Greenwich at the southern end of Merritt Parkway. Now a National Historic Landmark from around 1730, the Bush–Holley Historic Site features the Bush–Holley home, an 1805-period visitor's center housed in a former post office, and the Hugh and Clair Vanderbilt Education Center, set in the historic barn and artists' studio. The grounds and gardens have been restored to the appearance they had when the Cos Cob Impressionist Art Colony thrived with more than 200 students here between 1890 and 1920. Tour guides enhance your visit to the house, and you can explore the grounds at your leisure.

**Putnam Cottage:** Known as Knapp's Tavern during the Revolutionary War, Putnam Cottage was a popular gathering place for patriot leaders and ordinary travelers along the Boston Post Road. General Washington was even known to have eaten lunch here. But it gained fame as a hideout for General Israel Putnam when he heroically escaped from the Redcoats. Placed under the care of the local chapter of the Daughters of the American Revolution in 1906, Putnam Cottage is a repository of Colonial artifacts and is open to the public as a historical museum.

# Coastal Rhode Island

*From Narragansett Bay to the Atlantic, this scenic route showcases the Ocean State's coastline, passing through its capital city and its ritziest resort on the way to its beach-lined southern shore.*

The most scenic alternatives to the interstate—specifically I-95—are U.S. 1 and its offshoot 1A. However, they are not the quickest routes for driving through Rhode Island. The smallest state in the Union, just 37 miles wide by 48 miles long, Rhode Island is nonetheless blessed with some 400 miles of coastline, counting its many coves, bays, and islands. Much of the coastline is lined with beaches that are open to the public. Driving U.S. 1 and U.S. 1A—with a side trip over to the resort town of Newport—is the best way to experience the coast, although short side trips are necessary to access many of the beaches and small coastal resort areas.

This route provides a capsule viewing of much of the best of Rhode Island, including the lively capital city of Providence and the tony bayside resort of Newport, where some of America's wealthiest families built mansions on or near the water. It also passes through small, picturesque towns with colonial- or Victorian-era homes and little coastal villages that are a pleasant place to spend a weekend getting away from it all. Historic lighthouses line the route.

As small as Rhode Island may be, this route could easily take several days to explore if you linger in Providence and Newport or in one of the small resort towns or villages along the way.

## Highlights

Begin in Pawtucket, a blue-collar city in the state's Blackstone Valley.

**Slater Mill Historic Site:** Pawtucket is home to the Slater Mill Historic Site, the nation's first water-powered cotton spinning mill, dating from 1793. Its success at spurring mass production effectively ushered in the Industrial Revolution.

**Providence:** Drive south to Providence, the capital city of more than 175,000 people, built along the Providence River and situated on the northern lip of Narragansett Bay. Plan to spend some time in the city enjoying the history, the greenery, and the flourishing music and art scenes. A huge marble dome tops the Rhode Island State House; inside the Capitol is a famous Gilbert Stuart portrait of George Washington. Roger Williams Park has paddleboats and summer concerts in addition to New England's best zoo. Don't miss Benefit Street, with its many houses dating from the 18th and 19th centuries.

**Wickford:** Drive south from Providence on U.S. 1 and 1A to Wickford, where the route once again meets up with Narragansett Bay. Wickford is a pretty village dating from the early 1700s. Explore Main Street for a taste of the waterfront and the town's colonial-era homes.

**Newport:** A few miles south of Wickford, take Route 138 east toward Newport, crossing Narra-

### Quick Facts

**Length:** 92 miles.

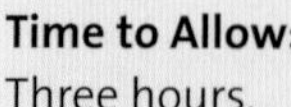

**Time to Allow:** Three hours.

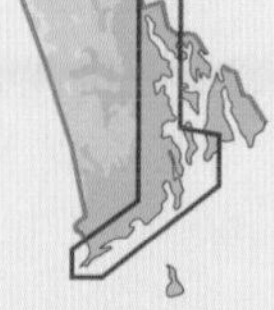

**Considerations:** Summer is prime time for the beaches, but spring and fall may be the prettiest seasons. Snow may make for hazardous road conditions in winter. Signage can sometimes be confusing along the route, and rush-hour traffic may be heavy through the Providence area.

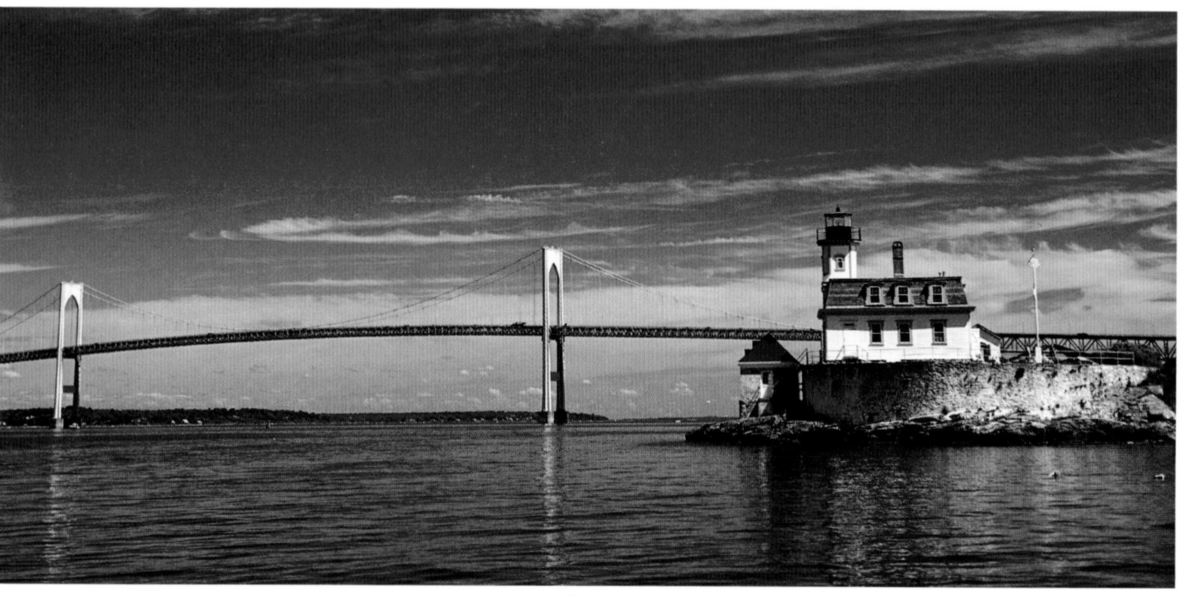

*The Newport Bridge brought an end to the official duties of the Rose Island Lighthouse. But today the lighthouse is active again as part of an environmental education program.*

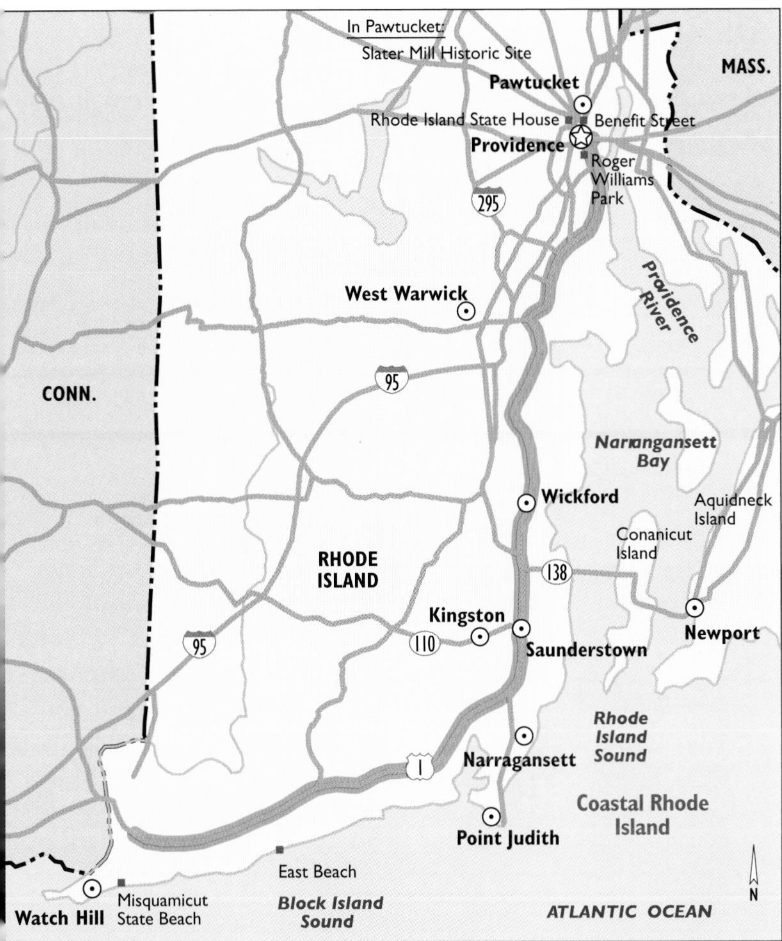


gansett Bay via the Jamestown and Newport bridges and Conanicut Island. After the Newport Bridge, the road enters Aquidneck Island. Reaching Newport, on the southern tip of Aquidneck, follow signs downtown to the waterfront (typically jammed with yachts, sailboats, and other craft). The Long Wharf area is good for lunch. Nearby Bellevue Avenue is lined with "summer cottages" (as the rich called their palatial mansions) built by old-money families in the 1890s, America's Gilded Age. Along Bellevue Avenue are Beechwood (home of the Astors); Rosecliff (used as a set in the film *The Great Gatsby*); and Belcourt Castle, home of the Belmonts. Ochre Point Avenue is the site of the Breakers (the 70-room Vanderbilt "cottage"), while Ocean Drive harbors Hammersmith Farm, where John and Jackie Kennedy were married. Newport also features the International Tennis Hall of Fame and the Museum of Yachting, reflecting Newport's status as sailing capital of the East Coast and longtime host of the America's Cup. It's also the site of the annual summertime Newport Jazz Festival.

**Saunderstown:** Now head back on Route 138 to U.S. 1A, and go south along the coast a short distance to Saunderstown, site of Gilbert Stuart's birthplace (located between U.S. 1 and 1A). Stuart, best known for painting more than 100 portraits of George Washington, lived in the house until age seven. Also the site of the first snuff mill in America, it has been restored and furnished in the mid-18th-century style and contains reproductions of some of Stuart's works.

**Point Judith:** Farther south on 1A is Narragansett, a Victorian-era resort town located at the point where Narragansett Bay meets the Atlantic Ocean. Continue south from there to Point Judith, site of a historic lighthouse at the tip of a peninsula and several beautiful beaches, including Scarborough State Beach, which has a beach-side boardwalk. The village of Galilee on Point Judith is the embarkation point for ferries to Block Island, an unspoiled resort island with wonderful beaches, scenic walking trails, lighthouses, cliffs, and several wildlife refuges, about 12 miles off the coast.

**East Beach and Misquamicut State Beach:** Returning to U.S. 1, head west along South County and Rhode Island's southern coastline. Short side trips south of U.S. 1 lead to salt ponds, piney woodlands, and miles of wide, flat, white-sand beaches. Among the best beaches are East Beach, south of Charlestown, and Misquamicut State Beach, near the western tip of the state. The latter is a two mile-long stretch of sand typically filled with sunbathers and lined with amusements and snack bars.

**Watch Hill:** The drive ends at Watch Hill, the state's westernmost beach resort, rich with Victorian architecture and home to the oldest merry-go-round in America, the Flying Horse Carousel, whose carved wooden steeds have been flying since 1867.

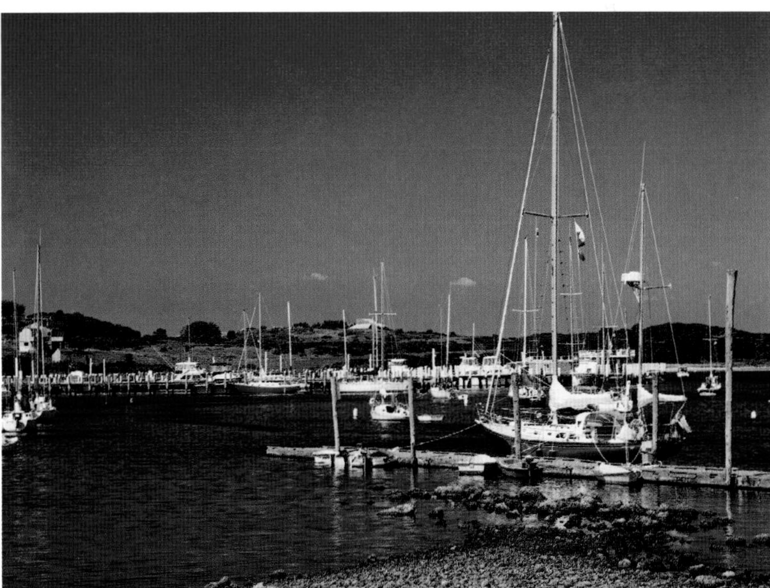

*Accessible by ferry, Block Island offers a laid-back way of life and an escape from everything but fun and relaxation.*

# Historic National Road 

*Follow in the footsteps of George Washington and Daniel Boone over one of the most historic transportation corridors in America. Once a buffalo trace through southwestern Pennsylvania's Laurel Highlands, the National Road became the nation's first interstate route.*

Part of a multistate byway; it also runs through Illinois, Indiana, Maryland, Ohio, and West Virginia.

As America entered the 19th century, the young nation faced one of its first challenges: how to link the people and cities along the Eastern Seaboard to those on the frontiers west of the Allegheny Mountains. Settlers moving west faced perils aggravated by the lack of a well-defined roadway. And easterners were unable to take advantage of the abundant produce and goods from the western frontier without a road to transport them over the Alleghenies. The solution was the National Road, America's first interstate highway, and the only one constructed entirely with federal funds.

Construction began in 1811, and by 1818, the road stretched from Cumberland, Maryland, to what is now Wheeling, West Virginia. In time, the National Road ran the whole way to Vandalia, Illinois, a distance of 600 miles.

For three decades, the history, influence, and heritage of the National Road have been celebrated at the annual National Road Festival, held on the third weekend each May. The festival features memorable festivities and a wagon train that comes into town.

## Intrinsic Qualities

**Cultural:** The National Road was developed from existing Native American pathways and, by the 1840s, was the busiest transportation route in America. Over its miles lumbered stagecoaches, Conestoga wagons with hopeful settlers, and freight wagons pulled by braces of mules, along with peddlers, caravans, carriages, foot travelers, and mounted riders. In response to demand, inns, hostels, taverns, and retail trade sprang up to serve the many who traveled the road. Today, reminders of National Road history are still visible along this corridor, designated as one of Pennsylvania's heritage parks to preserve and interpret history throughout the region.

**Historical:** The first cries for a "national road" were heard before there was even a nation. Such a road would facilitate settlement and help the budding nation expand in order to survive and flourish. Economic considerations weighed heavily in favor of a national road, which would be a two-way street, allowing farmers and traders in the west to send their production east in exchange for manufactured goods and other essentials of life. In May 1820, Congress appropriated funds to lay out the road from Wheeling to the Mississippi. Construction in Ohio did not commence until 1825. Indiana's route was surveyed in 1827, with construction beginning in 1829. By 1834, the road extended across the entire state of Indiana, albeit in various stages of completeness. The road began to inch across Illinois in the early 1830s, but shortages of funds and national will, plus local squabbles about its destination, caused it to end in Vandalia rather than on the shore of the Mississippi River.

The major engineering marvels associated with the National Road may have been the bridges that carried it across rivers and streams. The bridges came in a wide variety of styles and types and were made of stone, wood, iron, and, later, steel. As the bridges indicate, an amazing variety of skills was needed to build the road: Surveyors laid out the path, engineers oversaw construction, carpenters framed bridges, and masons cut and worked stones for bridges and milestones.

**Natural:** By the early 1800s, the National Road was a lifeline, bringing people and prosperity to the regions of the country removed from the East Coast.

*In the highlands of southwestern Pennsylvania is Fallingwater, one of the most famous homes in America, designed by renowned architect Frank Lloyd Wright.*

### Quick Facts

**Length:** 90 miles.

**Time to Allow:** Two hours to one day.

**Considerations:** The colors of fall make it a great time to travel the Historic National Road.

First a Native American trail cutting through the mountains and valleys, and then a primitive wagon trail to the first federal highway, the National Road is surrounded by the views of pristine hardwood forests blanketing rolling hills, vintage homes and barns, historic farmlands, orchards, and hunting grounds.

**Scenic:** The scenic qualities of the Historic National Road can be described as a rich tapestry that changes with the seasons. Obvious reference can be made to the beauty of the budding leaves in the vast mountain woodlands, the lush green look of the trees and fields in summer, or the vibrant colors of autumn. Some of the real beauty, however, arrives with winter, with the starkness of the woods and barren trees.

One of the most amazing sights along the road occurs just after you climb the Summit Mountain traveling west from Farmington and Chalk Hill at the Historic Summit Inn. Just over the crest of that "hill," your eyes fall onto a vast, endless valley, with rolling hills and a lushness that makes you believe you have found the promised land. This breathtaking view beckons you to imagine the sense of jubilation pioneers must have felt after struggling to cross the Appalachians, realizing that the mountains were behind them as they began their final, steep descent down the western side.

## Highlights

This tour begins in picturesque Fallingwater and ends at the lovely Pennsylvania Trolley Museum.

**Fallingwater:** One of the most celebrated buildings of the 20th century, architect Frank Lloyd Wright's Fallingwater perches dramatically above a small waterfall on Bear Run. Completed in 1937 as a vacation retreat for the wealthy Kaufmann family of Pittsburgh, it aptly illustrates Wright's concept of "organic architecture"; that is, it was built to fit into the surrounding landscape of rocky, tree-shaded hillsides. Escorted tours reveal some of Wright's idiosyncrasies; he was short in height, so ceilings are low—he designed to his own personal scale.

**Kentuck Knob:** Near Fallingwater, another wealthy family hired Wright. More modest in scope, their home sits high on a hillside hidden by trees as you drive onto the encircling 80-acre estate. From the outside, the house fits unobtrusively into its woodland setting, lacking the dazzle of Fallingwater. But the visual rewards, the magical spaces, are inside. The living room appears large, a look enhanced by a long wall of floor-to-ceiling windows. The ceiling is of polished wood, which reflects the light. In the evening, the glow is said to be very romantic. Though the house is luxurious, it boasts only a carport, not a garage. Wright, it seems, hated the clutter that a garage often generates.

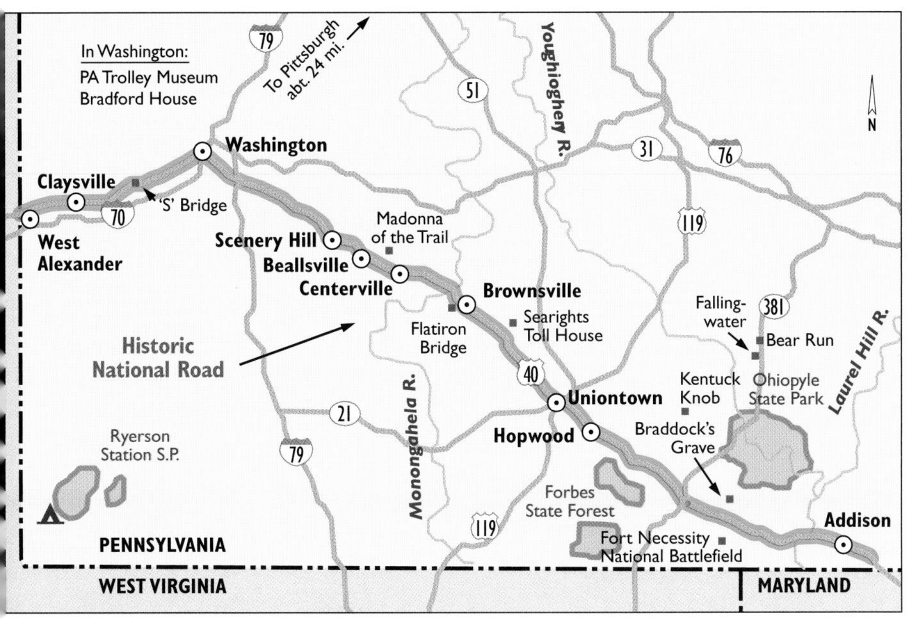


**Ohiopyle State Park:** Just outside Fallingwater, Ohiopyle State Park and the village of Ohiopyle form a center for whitewater rafting and float trips. Several licensed outfitters offer trips of varying degrees of difficulty from gentle floats to daring, white-knuckle challenges. The outings take place on the Youghiogheny River—known as the "Yock"—which winds through the heavily forested state park.

**Fort Necessity National Battlefield:** Fort Necessity is the site of George Washington's only military surrender (during the French and Indian War). Though the rebuilt fort is only a modest ring of stakes thrusting from the earth, it marks an important lesson for Washington that surely must have aided him two decades later in the American Revolution.

**Braddock's Grave:** A simple stone marker at Fort Necessity National Battlefield indicates the presumed gravesite of British General Edward Braddock. At the time of his death, he was commander of all British forces in North America. In 1755, a year after Washington's surrender to the French, Braddock led a snail's pace march against the French, who were instigating Native American attacks on settlers from Britain's American colonies. Failing to heed Washington's advice on wilderness tactics, Braddock was fatally wounded. His army of 1,400 suffered 900 casualties.

**Pennsylvania Trolley Museum:** Preserving some 45 trolleys dating from the 1880s, the Pennsylvania Trolley Museum in Washington re-creates the trolley era on the early 20th century. Visitors can learn about the evolution of transportation and ride the museum's carefully restored trolleys on a four-mile track into the past.

# Revolutionary War Trail: Washington's New Jersey Campaign

*New Jersey's Revolutionary War Trail is a winding path that links four of General George Washington's most important victories in the early years of the Revolutionary War. An unofficial route, it travels some of the state's prettiest scenery, a rumpled green landscape where small streams tumble beneath stone bridges.*

Historians have termed New Jersey the "Cockpit of the American Revolution" because so much of the battle raged within its borders. New Jersey was the front line for much of the war. This 90-mile drive, beginning in Trenton and ending to the east in Freehold, tells an inspiring story. Against all odds, George Washington and his ragged, ill-equipped, and untrained band managed to outwit and outmaneuver their British and Hessian adversaries and ultimately carry the fight for liberty to victory.

As you follow Washington's footsteps, he and his soldiers seem almost to come alive, stepping for the day from the pages of a history textbook. You will visit well-preserved houses where Washington stayed while on the march and where he plotted his risky and desperate strategies. In museum displays, you will see such war-related items as an original war document signed by Washington, the authentic red tunic of one of the Redcoat enemy, and tools and equipment used by citizen soldiers in their daily life.

Beyond the colonial history, you can stroll the trendy streets of historic Lambertville, lined with hip craft shops, contemporary art galleries, and fine antique houses. Take time out to hike a mile or two along the shady towpath of the Delaware and Raritan Canal, a state park. Throughout the Revolutionary War Trail, small cafés, coffee shops, and ice cream parlors are plentiful.

### Quick Facts

**Length:** 90 miles.

**Time to Allow:** Three hours.

**Considerations:** The drive can be undertaken at any time. However, battlefield visitor centers may be closed weekdays during the cold weather months. Check ahead. The parks, however, do remain open year-round, allowing you to walk the scenes of combat.

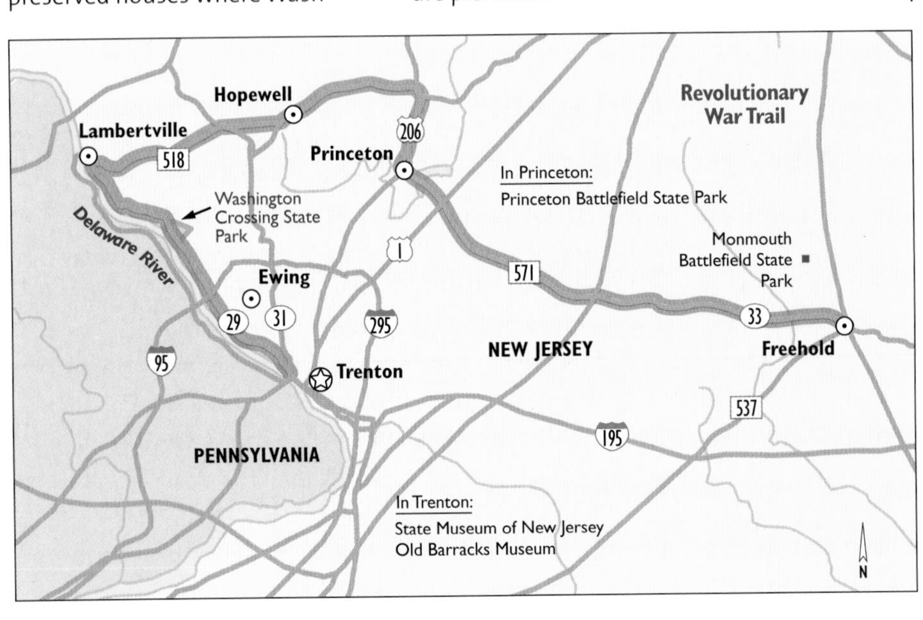


## Highlights

Here are some points of interest you'll want to see along the Revolutionary War Trail: Washington's New Jersey Campaign.

**State Museum of New Jersey:** View a replica of the famed painting *Washington Crossing the Delaware*. Standing in stalwart pose, Washington and his officers are being rowed through storm-tossed waves on the Delaware River to the New Jersey shore. Though of doubtful historical accuracy, it does help you imagine that fateful night.

**Old Barracks Museum:** Costumed interpreters re-create the life and living quarters of British and Hessian troops stationed in Trenton in the early months of the Revolutionary War. The anniversaries of the Battles of Trenton are celebrated the weekend after Christmas each year, and birthday cake is served yearly on Presidents' Day in honor of George Washington.

**Washington Crossing State Park:** Sprawling across 841 acres of fields and woodlands, the park preserves the site at Johnson's Ferry where Washington's troops landed on the New Jersey shore. The Johnson Ferry House, dating to 1740, may have served briefly as Washington's headquarters during the crossing. Across the road, Continental Road, a six-foot wide wooded path, is believed to be the place where Washington's Continental Army began its march to Trenton.

**Lambertville:** Once a major industrial river town, Lambertville has become a chic weekend getaway destination. Visitors browse its well-preserved Victorian-era streets in search of fine antiques and artwork by local painters.

**Hopewell:** A small village settled in the 17th century, Hopewell retains an old-fashioned charm. Large

*This colonial gambrel-roofed house was likely used briefly by General George Washington and other officers at the time of their famous Christmas crossing of the nearby Delaware River.*

white-frame houses, shaded by towering maples, overlook broad expanses of well-tended lawns. Cafés and coffee shops may tempt you to stop. On June 23, 1778, Washington and his officers (including the Marquis de Lafayette) met in Hopewell to plan the Battle of Monmouth.

**Princeton Battlefield State Park:** Part of the Princeton Battlefield is contained within the Princeton Battlefield State Park. Every January, a reenactment of the Battle of Princeton occurs here. The visitor center exhibits detail the American victory here. The center occupies the Thomas Clarke House; he was a Quaker farmer who built the two-story white-frame structure in 1772. During the fight, it served as a hospital for the Americans.

**Princeton:** Famed as the location of Princeton University, it is a pretty city with a cluster of fine shops near the campus. Two sights not to miss are the soaring Princeton Battle Monument, depicting a road-weary Washington on horseback, and the lovely stained-glass windows of the university's chapel. President James Madison, class of 1771, is pictured in the Window of the Law.

**Monmouth Battlefield State Park:** The park encompasses miles of spectacular landscape, a restored farmhouse, and a visitor's center. The visitor's center displays artifacts from the Battle of Monmouth. The exhibits also recall legendary Mary Ludwig Hays, who gained immortality as Molly Pitcher. Troops gave her the name when she carried water to them during the dreadfully hot day of battle. As the legend goes, she took over loading a cannon when her husband dropped from heat exhaustion.

# CHESAPEAKE COUNTRY SCENIC BYWAY

*Find quiet relaxation among serene water views as you ease through the historic port towns of the Chesapeake Bay's eastern shore. Learn about the hardworking waterpeople, whose harvest of crabs and oysters is a staple at picturesque cafés.*

There's a story around every corner of the Chesapeake Country Scenic Byway. As you drive this beautiful route, historic towns and buildings transport you to a new time. Nearly 15,000 years ago, American Indians began to cluster along the coast, thriving on the abundant wildlife. When the settlers from Europe came, many saw the Chesapeake Bay as an ideal spot to colonize.

If you enjoy bird-watching, be prepared for a treat. Rare and endangered species such as the colonial waterbird can be seen in wetlands along the byway. As a significant stop in the Atlantic Flyway, the region provides a tremendous number of critical waterfowl staging areas. Regional bird clubs sponsor a full schedule of bird walks and opportunities to view migrating waterfowl, neotropical birds, hawks, eagles, and vultures. If you enjoy hunting, waterfowl hunting opportunities abound.

## Intrinsic Qualities

**Cultural:** As travelers explore Chesapeake Country, they will notice the relationship that people still have with the waterways that create their environment. More than just recreational areas, the rivers and inlets of the area support a seafood economy, and as early as the 1600s, the settlers of the area were dependent upon the rivers and Chesapeake Bay for transportation. Travelers to the byway will likely see several different forms of watercraft from schooners and sloops to skiffs and canoes.

Not everyone was or is an angler along the byway. The success of Chesapeake's civilization rests on agriculture, as well. Colonial families settled farms on the coastline while more recent farmsteads are located inland on rich soil. Towns formed where farmers would sell their goods and buy supplies. The historic towns of the byway reflect the way life has changed and remained the same in this corner of Chesapeake Bay. Buildings and districts on the National Register of Historic Places remind visitors and residents of the way things once were.

Travelers will not find a lack of places to visit on the byway. Churches and walking tours are found in nearly every town along the way. Museums collect the stories of the past to tell to curious visitors, and the stories of the present are readily available through residents at local festivals or fishing tournaments. The thread that connects the past with the present is the culture that still exists along the Chesapeake Country Scenic Byway.

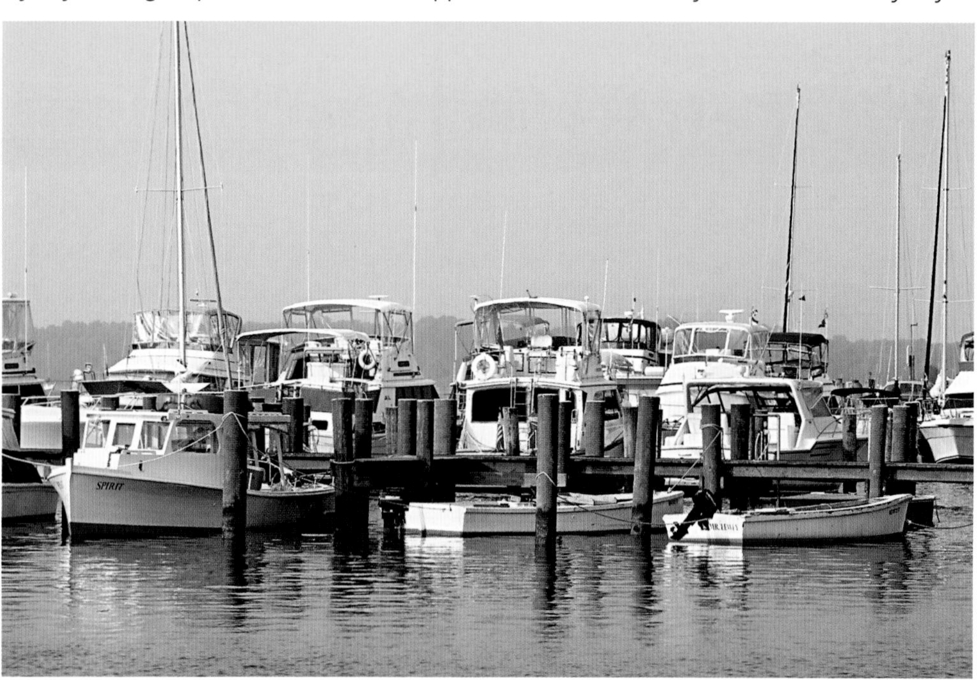

*The Chester River stretches 60 miles across Maryland. It is a hub of activity: boating, fishing, and even serving as a stop for migrating fish and wildlife.*

### Quick Facts

**Length:** 85½ miles.

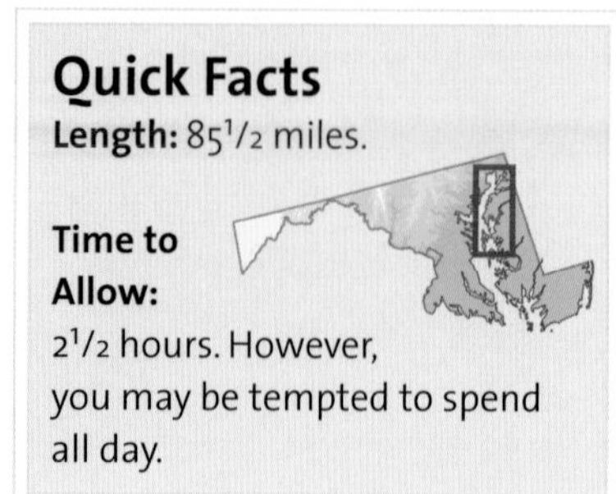

**Time to Allow:** 2½ hours. However, you may be tempted to spend all day.

**Historical:** All along the Chesapeake Country Scenic Byway, towns and buildings from the bustling colonial period still stand with the same charm they had when they were first erected. This corner of Chesapeake Bay has been settled since the 1600s as a major port and commercial area. Central to many of the nation's most significant turning points, the byway can tell stories from the Revolutionary War and the War of 1812.

As travelers study the map of the byway, names such as Queen Anne's County, Georgetown, and Kingstown all reflect the beginnings of British colonialism in the New World. Many of the counties, towns, and buildings along the byway are named for their counterparts in England.

In the mid-1600s, a Dutch mapmaker named Augustine Herman proposed the construction of a waterway that would connect the Delaware River and Chesapeake Bay. The waterway would reduce the time it would take to transfer goods to and from the Chesapeake Bay area. Nearly 200 years later, in 1804, construction on the Chesapeake and Delaware Canal began. The canal is still in operation today—a piece of history that remains an important part of the present. It reduces the water route between Baltimore and Philadelphia by nearly 300 miles and is recognized on the National Register of Historic Places and as an Engineering Landmark.

**Recreational:** If being in a boat on shimmering blue water sounds like fun to you, the Chesapeake Country Scenic Byway has much to offer. Recreation on the byway revolves around its water sources. Chesapeake Bay and all of its inlets provide great places for boating, fishing, or enjoying a sandy beach. If you keep your eyes open, you see that recreational opportunities are available all along the shore.

For sailing, Chesapeake Bay, the Sassafras River, and the Chester River are ideal spots to catch a bit of wind and glide across the water. Marinas and access points are located all along the shores and coasts, providing places for visitors to tie up their boats in the evening to go ashore for the nearest seafood restaurant. Fishing, crabbing, and oystering are a tradition on the Eastern Shore, so whether you participate in the catching or the tasting, it's a great tradition to get involved in. Charters for fishing are arranged in Narrows, Chestertown, and Rock Hall. Fishing from bridges or the shore can be as rewarding as a charter.

Two splendid beaches are available on the byway. Betterton Beach and Rock Hall Beach provide sandy shores and fresher water. Betterton Beach began as a resort area as early as the 1920s. Since then, families vacation there or just come for a day trip. At Rock Hall Beach, visitors are met with a great place for a beach cookout or swimming. But people aren't the only ones who enjoy the shores of the Chesapeake.

At refuges and wetlands along the byway, visitors have the opportunity to catch a glimpse of the waterfowl in the area. At Eastern Neck National Wildlife Refuge, Chesapeake Farms, Horsehead Wetlands Center, and Echo Hill Outdoor School, naturalists can get a taste of the native outdoors in Maryland. And the byway is one of the best ways to get to all of these places. Endangered bird species nest in refuges and the Atlantic Flyway brings many more species to the area. Make sure to bring a pair of binoculars for a closer look at some of the hawks, eagles, and neotropical birds in the wetlands.

**Scenic:** A canvas of pastoral countryside is the perfect background for scenery that includes

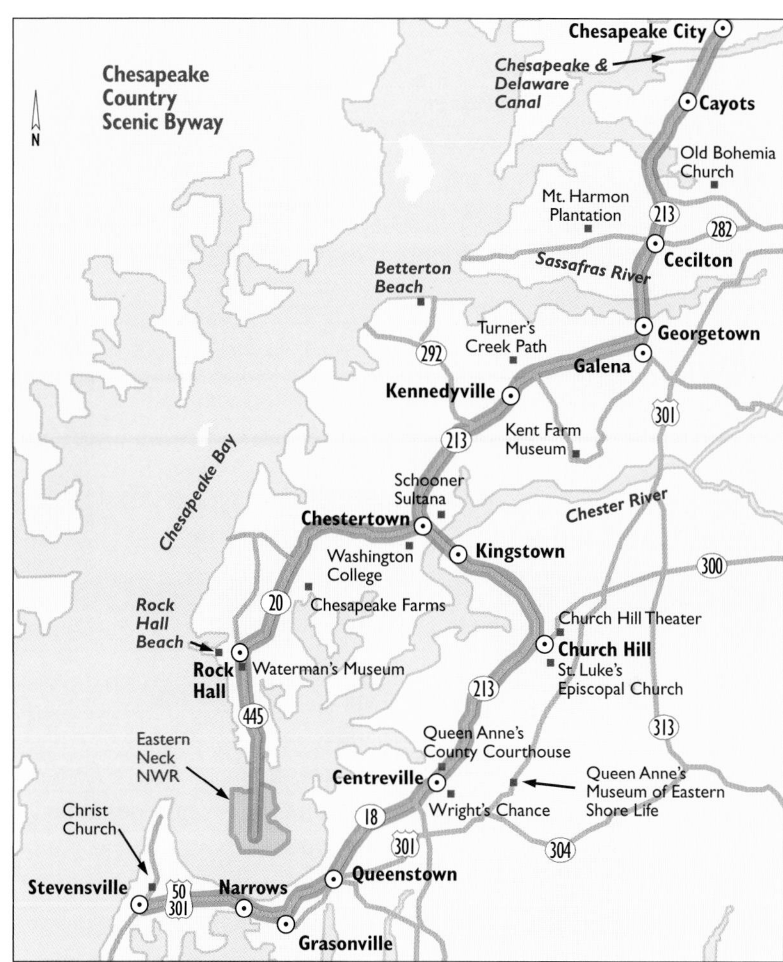


historic churches, bays, beaches, and stylish 18th-century main streets. Painting a picture of the Chesapeake Country Scenic Byway requires only a leisurely drive along some of Maryland's most scenic roads. Travelers will be delighted at the sight of a perfectly situated town among the landscape of the byway. Colors of a grassy field or a windswept shore combine to create a drive for every kind of artist.

Along the byway, sights of rolling farmland with streams that border the fields provide a look at a land that has changed very little over the last two centuries. The fields have been supporting residents for generations. Every so often, there is a break in the farmland and a panoramic view of the Chesapeake Bay appears to delight travelers and entice them to come closer. There is nothing so enchanting as the sight of a schooner gliding along the water. Occasionally on your drive, a flock of birds will fly overhead as an indication that you are entering a marshland area.

## Highlights

There is a mix of pastoral scenery and rural bustle along the Chesapeake Country Scenic Byway that will entice you to stop and tour the tiny villages, browse in unique shops, and enjoy some tasty Maryland crabs freshly harvested from the bay. This itinerary, however, gives the traveler a sampling of the agricultural and water-based heritage that has continued to sustain the area from the beginning.

**Stevensville:** Surrounded by the waters of the Chesapeake Bay, Kent Island is home to the quaint village of Stevensville, where the tour begins. Stevensville's historic district has nearly 100 well-preserved buildings amidst quiet narrow streets. Among the historic structures worth noting are the Stevensville Train Depot, the Cray House, and the distinctly different Christ Church.

**Centreville:** Crossing over onto the Eastern Shore and traveling north on Maryland Route 213, Centreville captures the essence of small-town America with a distinctly colonial flavor. Wright's Chance is an early plantation house, circa 1744. Now home to the Queen Anne's County Historical Society and open to the public, it has an exquisite collection of Chippendale and Hepplewhite furniture and Canton china.

**Queen Anne's Museum of Eastern Shore Life:** Also in Centreville is Queen Anne's Museum of Eastern Shore Life, displaying artifacts that tell the story of the unique life of those who have called this area home. The collection includes antique farm implements, tools, and specialized equipment used to harvest the bounty of the Chesapeake Bay, Native American artifacts, and household items.

**Chestertown:** Farther north on the byway is the port town of Chestertown. Turn left onto Cross Street, and head into the heart of downtown, once a colonial port on the Chester River. In fact, Chestertown was the Eastern Shore's chief port between 1750 and 1790 for shipping both wheat and tobacco. Wealthy merchants and planters built the elegant brick townhouses that dominate the historic district and waterfront. Be sure to stop by the Kent County Office of Tourism for information about Chestertown and Kent County.

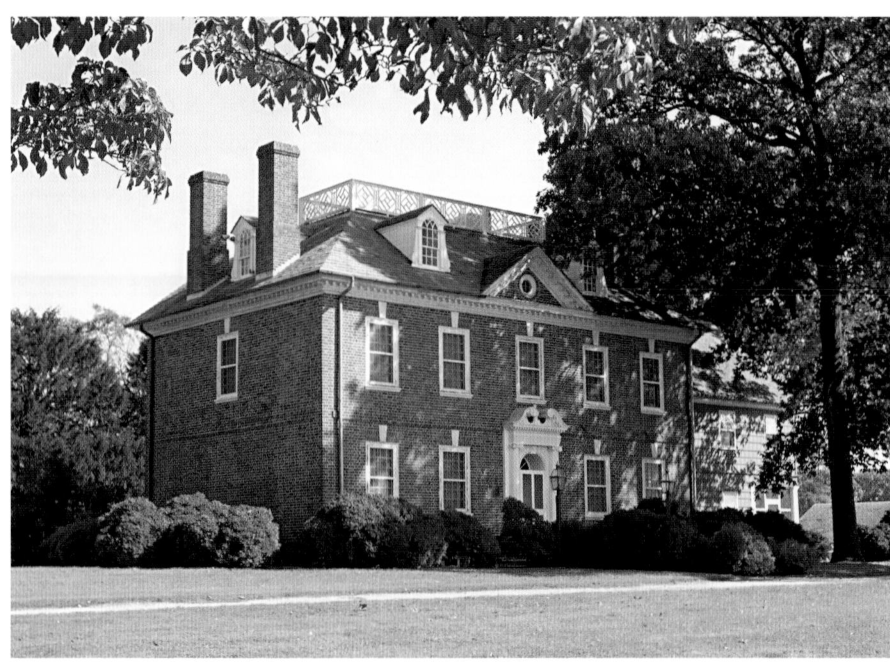

*The manor house, separate kitchen, gardens, tobacco prize house, and wharf are open at Mount Harmon Plantation for tours.*

**Waterman's Museum:** Just past Chestertown, turn left for a brief detour onto Maryland Route 291, then bear right onto Maryland Route 20 West (this will be taking you in a southerly direction). The Waterman's Museum in Rock Hall was created to tell the story of local watermen, a way of life that continues in Chesapeake Country. This unique nautical center of recorded history includes exhibits about oystering, crabbing, and fishing. A reproduction of a shanty house is also on display, along with historical photographs, local carvings, and of course, boats.

**Chesapeake Farms:** Returning back the way you came on Maryland Route 20, turn right on Ricauds Branch Road to visit Chesapeake Farms. Though the history of the Chesapeake Country Scenic Byway dates back to colonial times, the 3,300 acres of Chesapeake Farms is thoroughly modern in its techniques. It is a scientific area devoted to the development, evaluation, and demonstration of new and superior agricultural and wildlife management techniques. An extensive self-guided driving tour of the farm is available.

**Turner's Creek Park:** Return to Maryland Route 20 and back to Maryland Route 213, heading north. From Maryland Route 213 take Maryland Route 298 East to Turner's Creek Road. Turn right and follow the road to Turner's Creek Park. Here visitors can tour historic structures such as the Latham House, circa 1700. Also at the park on the first and third Saturdays of the month, tours are available of Kent Farm Museum, where visitors can view antique farm machinery, a collection of antique implements from a variety of other occupations, and other artifacts of early rural life.

**Mount Harmon Plantation:** Continue north on Maryland Route 213 through villages full of charm and history. Just past the town of Cecilton, turn west on Maryland Route 282, and follow the road to Mount Harmon Plantation. Originally a thriving tobacco plantation shipping its bounty off to England, the manor house dates back to 1730. The property is bordered on three sides by water and offers a superb vista. Visitors can tour the main house, the tobacco house, and outdoor colonial kitchen.

# Historic National Road 

*A gateway to the West for thousands of settlers, the road cuts across Allegheny Mountain ridges dotted with historic communities, each with the look of a century past.*

PART OF A MULTISTATE BYWAY; IT ALSO RUNS THROUGH ILLINOIS, INDIANA, OHIO, PENNSYLVANIA, AND WEST VIRGINIA.

## Quick Facts

**Length:** 170 miles.

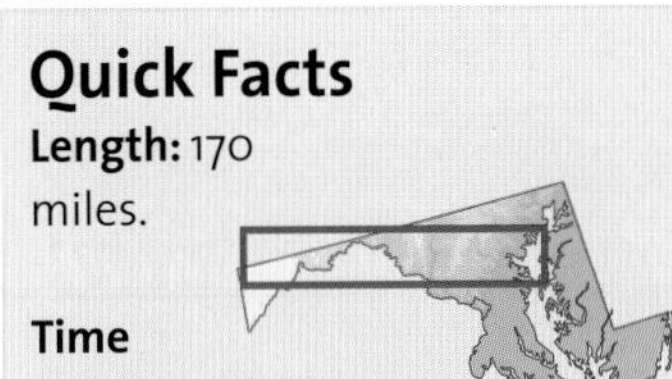

**Time to Allow:** 4½ hours.

**Considerations:** You may want to plan stops for gas and food because this is a long byway. You'll also find numerous historic sites and museums to visit, so you may want to plan additional time to drive the byway.

Many layers of urbanization have modified this historic route, but the diligent traveler still may follow the old Historic National Pike through the streets of Baltimore westward into the historic Maryland countryside. Today, with the construction of new roads, many historic towns and sites originally connected to the Historic National Pike lure modern travelers with rugged charm, including a host of antique shops, specialty shops, and unique restaurants.

## Intrinsic Qualities

**Cultural:** As the first federally funded road, this byway blazed a trail for the emerging nation to follow. Maryland's Baltimore to Cumberland section of the Historic National Road was designated the Historic National Pike. Towns and cities along the pike began to spring up to provide comforts for weary travelers heading west.

Modern travelers of the Historic National Pike will find communities proud of their vibrant heritage. With Interstate 70 bypassing many of the original Historic National Pike cities, they have developed into artistic communities with a passion for diversity.

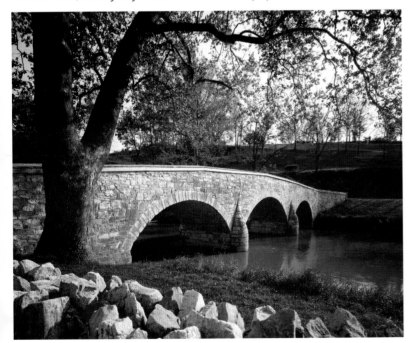

*Burnside Bridge, crossing Antietam Creek, was eventually taken by Union soldiers, in spite of the best efforts of greatly outnumbered Rebel troops.*

**Historical:** In the late 18th century, as the population of the United States began to grow, President Thomas Jefferson encouraged the development of a transportation infrastructure that would connect the Eastern Seaboard with points farther inland. The construction of the National Road westward from Cumberland was the first such investment by the federal government.

**Natural:** From the shores of the Chesapeake Bay to the majestic Negro Mountain, the Historic National Road offers many natural wonders. Many state parks along the byway offer quiet breaks in the long drive. As the byway continues into western Maryland, it passes through many mountain peaks. Before the byway continues into Pennsylvania, it journeys through the city of Cumberland, which is nestled in a small mountain valley. Here, mountains tower 1,000 feet around the city.

The most magnificent feature to note in the byway is the Narrows, located northwest of Cumberland. The Narrows is an unusual geologic formation near Cumberland that provides a pass through the Allegheny Mountains. Wills Creek runs north and south through the Narrows, creating the narrow gorge through Wills Mountain.

**Recreational:** Perhaps the most popular destination in all of Maryland is Baltimore's Inner Harbor, where you'll find outdoor performances, numerous eateries, the National Aquarium and Marine Mammal Pavilion, the Maryland Science Center and Davis Planetarium, the Pier 6 Concert Pavilion, historic ships, Harborplace shops, and much more.

If you love outdoor activity, this byway features fantastic biking, boating, hiking, and rock climbing. You can find numerous places to fish and hunt deer, turkey, grouse, squirrel, rabbit, quail, and waterfowl. If you like to view animals but not necessarily hunt them, you can also find excellent bird-watching areas.

**Scenic:** From the picturesque shores of the Chesapeake Bay to the towering mountains near Cumberland, the Historic National Road delivers breathtaking scenery every step of the way. You will see early stone bridges, Pennsylvania–German back barns with limestone-faced gable ends, and the last tollbooth left on the Maryland part of the Historic National Road.

Views are quite beautiful approaching South Mountain, from the top of the mountain (Washington Monument State Park), and around Middletown. Washington Monument State Park on South Mountain contains a spectacular overlook located approximately one mile from the byway, from which the surrounding Middletown Valley can be admired. The Appalachian Trail crosses by this landmark.

## Highlights

Start your must-see tour in Baltimore at the B & O Railroad Museum.

**B & O Railroad Museum:** The city of Baltimore was instrumental in the birth of passenger train service in 1830, an event commemorated by the B & O Railroad Museum. The museum is a storehouse of railroading lore, boasting a large collection of historic steam engines and restored passenger and freight cars.

**Fort McHenry National Monument and Historic Shrine:** When the wind is calm, U.S. park rangers fly a replica of the giant "Old Glory" that Francis Scott Key saw when he was inspired to write what became America's national anthem. Exhibits at the massive, star-shape fort overlooking Baltimore's harbor tell the story of that fateful dawn in 1814, when the fort's defenders survived an intense British bombardment in the War of 1812.

**National Aquarium:** Two distinctive glass pyramids overlooking Baltimore's harbor house the National Aquarium. As you enter, the stingrays immediately capture your attention. From the pool, you ascend five levels. Level Two traces Maryland's waterways from the mountains to the sea. Level five is a re-created South American rain forest. Most spectacular of all is the descent through a giant circular tank, where sharks slip silently past.

**New Market:** Step back in time in the historic village of New Market, which claims the title of "Antiques Capital of Maryland." Most of the old brick and wood-frame structures along a six-block stretch of Main Street display antiques of all kinds—from inexpensive knickknacks to costly French furniture pieces. Small alleyways lead to more shops and to cornfields and pretty country views.

**National Museum of Civil War Medicine:** In the heart of Frederick, the National Museum of Civil War Medicine tells the story of how medical treatment improved radically in the four years of the war as both sides coped with a flood of ill and wounded soldiers. The use of ambulances and the technique of embalming both emerged from the conflict, exhibits explain. The town of Frederick received many of the Union casualties from the nearby Battle of Antietam.

**Antietam National Battlefield:** Fought on September 17, 1862, as Confederate General Robert E. Lee attempted to invade the North, the Battle of Antietam has entered the history books as the single bloodiest day of the Civil War. More than 23,000 men were killed or wounded—partly as a result of the blunders of their commanders. A 26-minute orientation movie outlines the battle and its aftermath, and the park's museum puts a personal face on the combatants by featuring personal camp gear of two of the participants. An eight-mile drive, bike, or hike trail visits the battle sites.

**Chesapeake and Ohio Canal National Historical Park:** A popular hiking and bicycling route, the towpath of the Chesapeake and Ohio Canal parallels the Potomac River for 184½ miles from Washington, D.C., to Cumberland. Operating from 1828 to 1924, the canal was used primarily to haul coal from western Maryland to the port of Georgetown in Washington. Original structures, including locks, have been preserved, and the towpath is open for recreation for its entire length. At Cumberland, its terminus, you can hike or bike a portion.

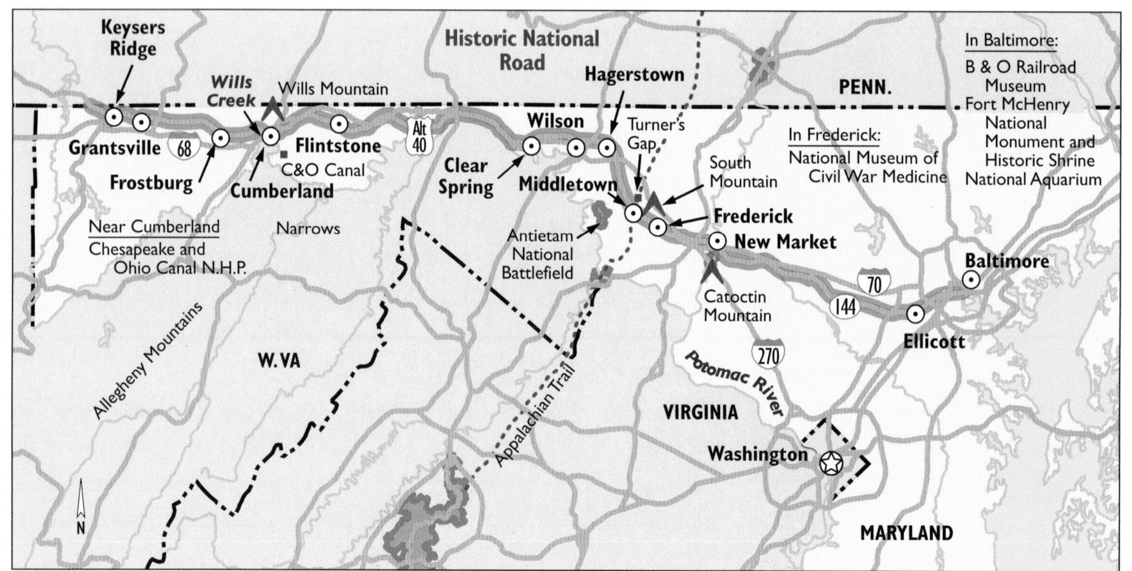

# The Delaware Coast

*From historic Lewes, a 17th-century Dutch colony, south to Fenwick Island, Delaware's Atlantic shore is a nearly nonstop stretch of inviting sandy beaches and popular beach towns with bustling boardwalks.*

Nearly the entire length of this 25-mile drive down Delaware's Atlantic Coast is lined with sandy beaches that draw sun worshippers from all over the region. Twelve miles of beach are located within three state parks. They are quiet, only lightly developed oases between the more commercialized resort town beaches catering to visitors seeking boardwalk amusements and waterside lodging and dining.

Fortunately, the resorts—Lewes, Rehoboth Beach, Bethany Beach, and Fenwick Island—have resisted high-rise growth, and each retains a small-town charm. Victorian in look, they remain a nostalgic throwback to the beach vacations of that earlier time. The state parks preserve the landscape mostly as it might have looked a century or more ago. At dawn, shorebirds of all kinds scamper over the sand seeking breakfast, and majestic grass-topped dunes overlook pine forests and salt marshes.

Summer, of course, is the high season, and you might want to undertake this drive in a bathing suit and sandals. But even in winter, the beaches draw strollers who revel in the views of storm-tossed waves crashing ashore.

## Highlights

This tour starts in the historic small town of Lewes and ends at the beautiful Fenwick Island Lighthouse.

**Cape Henlopen State Park:** A 5,000-acre natural area, the park thrusts between the Atlantic Ocean and Delaware Bay. Boardwalk steps ascend a high dune to reveal a long beach of golden sand. In season, lifeguards are on duty, and restroom and changing facilities are available. In addition to numerous swimming and sunbathing opportunities, Cape Henlopen State Park has many hiking and biking trails. And, in May, shorebirds migrating north from South America pause at

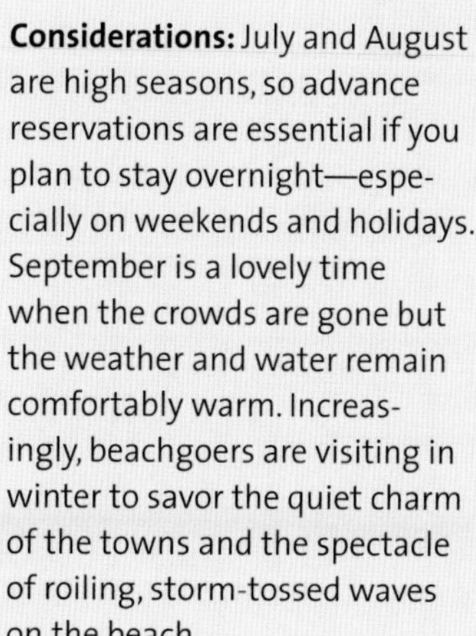

## Quick Facts

**Length:** 25 miles.

**Time to Allow:** 90 minutes.

**Considerations:** July and August are high seasons, so advance reservations are essential if you plan to stay overnight—especially on weekends and holidays. September is a lovely time when the crowds are gone but the weather and water remain comfortably warm. Increasingly, beachgoers are visiting in winter to savor the quiet charm of the towns and the spectacle of roiling, storm-tossed waves on the beach.

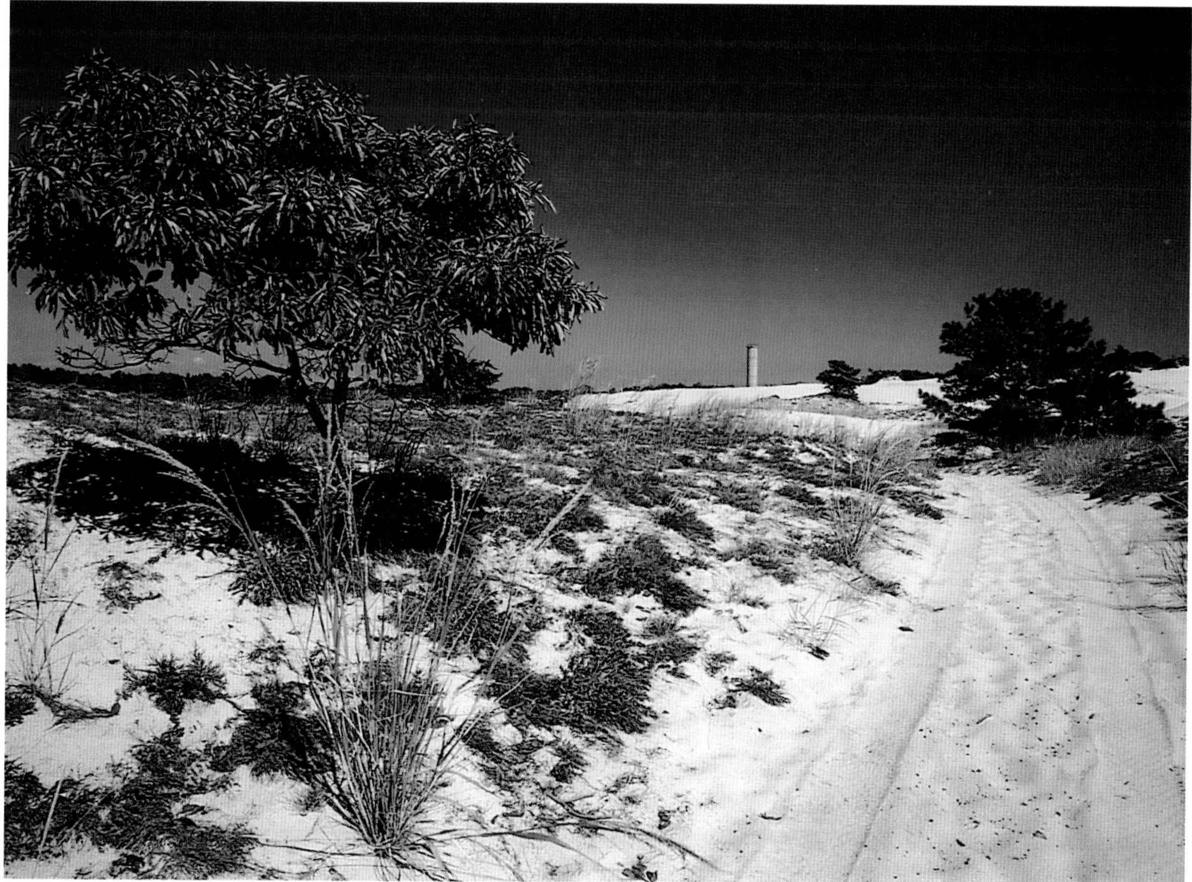

*Rising more than 80 feet above the shoreline, The Great Dune at Cape Henlopen State Park is the highest dune between Cape Cod and Cape Hatteras.*

an isolated point of the park to rest for a few days. Each May, horseshoe crabs come to the shores to mate and lay eggs. The Seaside Nature Center also offers glimpses at wildlife, with several aquarium exhibits.

**Lewes:** Mostly overlooked by summer hordes flocking to Rehoboth Beach, just six miles south, Lewes retains the look and charm of a small town of the past. In fact, it was the first town in Delaware. On Second Street, Lewes' "main" street, visitors can stroll beneath a canopy of giant old trees or sit on a bench and nibble cones from a nearby ice cream shop.

**Zwaanendael Museum:** Looking like a Dutch transplant of the town hall in Hoorn, Holland, the museum details Lewes' early Dutch heritage, recounts its modest role in the War of 1812, and more thoroughly explores its recent past as a headquarters for ship pilots on the Delaware River. Pick up printed walking tours of the town.

**Rehoboth Beach:** Founded by a Methodist church group, Rehobeth is a biblical term meaning "room enough." Rehoboth Beach is a very Victorian-looking town. It is Delaware's largest beach resort, and yet it is still very much a small, though very sophisticated, town. Many vacationers visit this beach from the D.C. area. In fact, Rehoboth Beach is sometimes referred to as the "nation's summer capital." Its shops display stylish beachwear, contemporary crafts, and antiques. Families return year after year, invariably spending part of each day strolling the mile-long wood boardwalk overlooking a wide beach. The boardwalk offers an amusement arcade, French-fry stalls, T-shirt shops, and all the other traditional trimmings of a venerable American beach town.

**Delaware Seashore State Park:** A beachgoer's delight, the 2,825-acre park boasts six miles of ocean and bay shoreline. In season, lifeguards patrol, and restrooms and changing facilities are available. Shallow bay waters make the park a popular sailboarding and sailing destination. Colorful sails glide across the bay in a rainbow dance. Surf fishing on the ocean is a big sport here.

**Bethany Beach:** A pretty little family resort with a boardwalk, Bethany Beach got its start in 1901 as a church retreat. Even though times have changed, the town continues to bill itself as the "quiet" resort. It only recently allowed liquor to be sold, and liquor laws are still pretty strict. An amazing red cedar sculpture called Chief Little Owl, or Whispering Giant, is a landmark of Bethany Beach. This sculpture is a new incarnation of a previous version that was damaged. Both sculptures were created by artist Peter Toth.

**Fenwick Island State Park:** A three-mile-long barrier island with 344 acres of ocean and bay shoreline, Fenwick Island State Park claims description as the "quiet" beach. Here the white sand slopes gradually into the Atlantic Ocean, creating a vast swimming area families can enjoy. In season, lifeguards are on duty, and restrooms and changing facilities are available. A designated surfing area has been established. And at three dune crossings you can surf or fish after purchasing a vehicle permit.

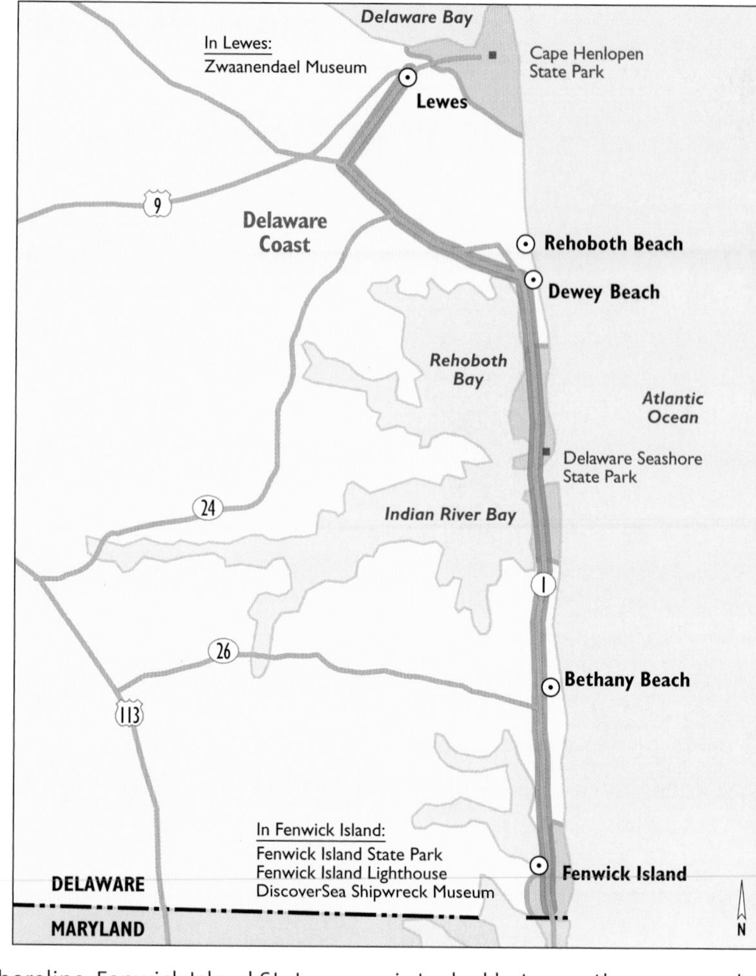


**Fenwick Island:** The southernmost of Delaware's beach resorts, Fenwick—another of the "quiet" towns—claims Delaware's finest beach. About a mile long, the town is tucked between the ocean and the bay. The bay attracts sailboarders and jet skiers. A small museum, DiscoverSea Shipwreck Museum, chronicles coastal shipwrecks.

**Fenwick Island Lighthouse:** Since 1858, the 89-foot-tall lighthouse has warned ships away from Fenwick Shoal. Once it burned whale oil, but today it operates automatically by electricity. You can enter the base, where there is a mini-museum, but climbing to the top is not permitted. The lighthouse sits on the Mason–Dixon Line, and just outside the lighthouse fence is the Maryland state line, which concludes this drive.

# SOUTH

Imagine a scenic roadway that stretches for more than 450 miles without a single stop sign or stoplight. No, this isn't a fantasy. It's the Blue Ridge Parkway, which weaves among the scenic mountain peaks of Virginia and North Carolina. Among America's most beautiful drives, it's only one of many rewarding routes that explore the South's scenic, cultural, and historical attractions. In Virginia, trace the final days of the Civil War in the footsteps of Ulysses S. Grant and Robert E. Lee as their armies raced to a little village called Appomattox that was suddenly thrust onto the pages of history. In Louisiana, meander through a unique world of water, where you might spot an alligator or try your skill at crab fishing. In Alabama, honor the memory of civil rights marchers who helped achieve the right to vote for all Americans.

*The Drayton Hall on Ashley River Road in South Carolina offers a glimpse of the Colonial South.*

# Country Music Highway 

*Tracing the length of eastern Kentucky, the highway unveils the rich musical heritage of a region that produced such country music stars as Loretta Lynn, Wynonna Judd, and Dwight Yoakam.*

## Quick Facts

**Length:** 144 miles.

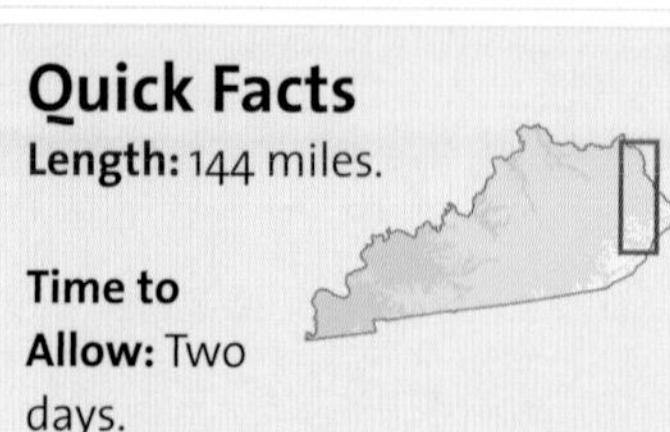

**Time to Allow:** Two days.

**Considerations:** Summer and fall are the best seasons to drive this route. Summer is especially popular for travelers because there are many festivals and entertainment venues open during the summer months.

Running almost the entire length of eastern Kentucky, the Country Music Highway is a byway devoted to the rich heritage and history of the region. You will be immersed in the traditions of eastern Kentucky mountain music since this byway has been home to over a dozen well-known country music stars, including Naomi Judd, Billy Ray Cyrus, Ricky Skaggs, Keith Whitley, Dwight Yoakam, and Patty Loveless.

## Intrinsic Qualities

**Cultural:** The quality of the musical heritage of the byway is exhibited by its famous musicians; however, it is also exhibited through the continued commitment to the arts by current residents. The best evidence of this is at the Mountain Arts Center (MAC) in Prestonsburg. This $7 million facility houses the Kentucky Opry, a nationally recognized group of local musicians who perform regularly and work to preserve the tradition of eastern Kentucky mountain music. In addition to the Opry, the MAC also sponsors a wide variety of country music performances.

And, of course, music can be heard in a variety of venues along the route, including the historic and beautiful Paramount Theater in Ashland and the Mountain Arts Center. Jenny Wiley State Resort Park offers a Broadway performer-staffed summer theater program that features five different shows running concurrently on their outdoor stage, and Appalshop is an award-winning film and music documentary and preservation organization in Whitesburg. In addition to these sites, music can be heard at numerous small venues, such as the coal camps of Seco and Carcassone and at a long list of festivals, such as the Seedtime Festival in Whitesburg and the Apple Festival at the Mountain Home Place in Paintsville.

*Within Jenny Wiley State Resort Park is Dewey Lake, shown here on a misty morning. The lake is a great place to boat and fish.*

**Historical:** Before settlers called eastern Kentucky home, Native Americans lived and hunted in the region. The history of these early American Indians is depicted in the Highlands Museum and Discovery Center in Ashland.

The American Indians' lands were soon encroached upon by early settlers. The life of early pioneers is documented in Paintsville at Mountain Home Place. This facility consists of a reconstructed 19th-century pioneer farm, complete with oxen and an award-winning film on the settlement of eastern Kentucky narrated by local native Richard Thomas (best known for the role of John Boy in *The Waltons*).

The discovery and mining of coal in this region has been influential on the history of eastern Kentucky. The Van Lear Coal Miners' Museum explains the importance and history of this resource. Coal also affected the community by creating rich coal barons. John C. C. Mayo was one such person. The elegant Mayo Mansion and Mayo Church in Paintsville provide visitors with details about Mayo's rags-to-riches story.

A more well-known story from the region exemplifies the influence of these industrial barons who exploited the resources in small areas such as eastern Kentucky. The Hatfield–McCoy feud has become a well-known story about feuding families. The legendary feud from the mid-1800s has no singular cause, rather it developed over several years with real and imagined grievances and very real and tragic events. The Hatfield–McCoy feud is an example of how the Appalachian people sought to deal with outside barons who purchased much of the land in the region and then mined it for coal and lumber for generations without allowing the locals to gain much profit from the enterprise.

**Natural:** The beautiful nature and scenery along the Country Music Highway is evident in the many state parks and rivers. In fact, the Kentucky State Park System's motto is "The Nation's Finest."

Jenny Wiley State Resort Park is the premier state park in this area. The park rests on Dewey Lake and is situated in the heart of the Appalachian Mountains. Because of its location in the mountains, Jenny Wiley State Resort Park was once an area of coal mining. Another park is Yatesville Lake State Park. Yatesville Lake State Park offers visitors another chance to enjoy the unique natural qualities of eastern Kentucky. This mountain reservoir is an impoundment of the Big Sandy River, and here you can find a variety of fish, such as bluegill, bass, crappie, and catfish.

Near the byway is Breaks Interstate Park, one of two multistate state parks in the nation. This site features a 1,600-foot-deep gorge. The area in this park is 250 million years old and was carved by the Russell Fork River.

The Lilley Cornett Woods is another site of natural significance. It is part of the largest stand of old-growth forest with the greatest ecological diversity in the mid-South region.

## Highlights

Music is everywhere along the byway, but there are definitely other must-see attractions. Here are a few of the sites you will want to visit.

**Ashland:** Begin at Ashland, birthplace of country music legends the Judds and Billy Ray Cyrus. Visit the Paramount Arts Center, housed in the historic Paramount Theater in downtown Ashland. The Ashland Paramount Theater was built in 1930 using the design of a model theater created by Paramount Pictures for construction at the Chicago World's Fair of 1932.

**Highlands Museum and Discovery Center:** Also in Ashland is the Highlands Museum and Discovery Center. The Country Music Heritage exhibit and other displays give a wonderful overview of the Country Music Highway.

**Prestonsburg:** The best way to get oriented in Prestonsburg is to first stop by the tourism office for maps and information about not only the town of Prestonsburg but also the surrounding area and attractions, including Loretta Lynn's childhood home in Butcher Hollow between Prestonsburg and Paintsville, the Kentucky Appalachian Artisan Center, and the Samuel May House.

**Middle Creek National Battlefield:** This area was impacted by the Civil War, and Middle Creek National Battlefield outside Prestonsburg tells the story. At the Battle of Middle Creek, an obscure Ohio professor and newly minted colonel in the Union army attacked and defeated the Confederate forces. James Garfield's victory on the battlefield led to a military career that eventually propelled him to the presidency.

**Pikesville:** Pikesville was the boyhood home of singer Dwight Yoakam. Stop at the tourism office for more information, especially for a map of the Hatfield–McCoy Driving Tour.

**Pikesville Cut-Through:** Pikesville Cut-Through is an engineering feat second only to the Panama Canal as the most extensive land-moving project in the Western Hemisphere. The cut is more than 1,300 feet long and 523 feet deep and required the moving of a mountain, major highway, railroad, and river.

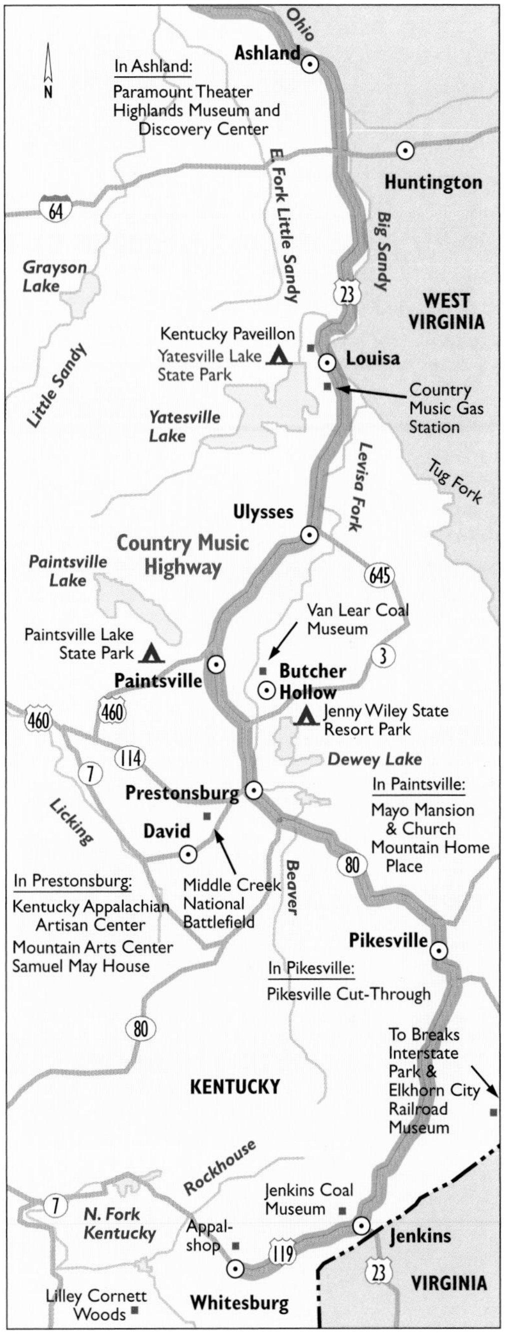

**Breaks Interstate Park:** Comprising 4,500 acres of lush mountain scenery and 13 miles of hiking trails, this park is also home to the deepest gorge east of the Mississippi River. The chasm is named for the break in Pine Mountain caused by the rushing waters of the Russell Fork of the Big Sandy River. Visitor activities and services include a restaurant, museum, gristmill, guided tours, spelunking, horseback riding, and driving and biking trails.

**Elkhorn City:** Elkhorn City was the girlhood hometown of Patty Loveless and home of the Elkhorn City Railroad Museum. More than 1,000 pieces of railroad memorabilia are on display.

# Red River Gorge Scenic Byway

*Following the scenic Red River, the byway through Daniel Boone National Forest enters a rugged landscape of tumbling waterfalls, steep cliffs, rocky crags, and countless natural stone arches.*

Take a journey through magnificent natural wonders on the Red River Gorge Scenic Byway. From the historic Nada Tunnel to the end of the byway in Zachariah, discover more than 100 stone arches, waterfalls, and plenty of natural beauty. Carved over eons by the Red River, today's gorge is now *the* site for outdoor adventures.

## Intrinsic Qualities

**Cultural:** The culture along the byway has been one focused on nature. American Indians resided in this area for thousands of years, living off the land and using the naturally occurring rock shelters as homes. Today, these shelters can be seen along the byway.

The logging industry brought another culture to the area. The land was used as a profit-making resource, and the remnants of that culture survive today at the Gladie Historic Site and the Nada Tunnel.

**Historical:** The most important historical aspect of the Red River Gorge area is the impact and development of the logging industry from 1880 to 1920. Once Kentucky was opened up to settlement, people began building in the area. This development created the need for building supplies, such as timber, and as a result, the forest in the Red River Gorge area became a rich resource.

*Sky Bridge Arch is accessible from a trail that passes over and beneath this interesting rock formation.*

The logging industry enjoyed many prosperous years in the Red River Gorge area, and evidence of that era of history remains today. The Gladie Historic Site celebrates the settlement that evolved around the logging business. Only the cabin exists today, but more than a hundred years ago the area would have been alive with the busy sounds of a thriving logging camp. The Nada Band Mill is another example of the importance of the logging industry in the area. Located in the town of Nada, this mill was run by the Broadhead–Garret Company, a company that conducted the region's largest timbering effort.

As the area developed into a rich logging region, the need arose for a means of transporting the timber out of the area. Logs were floated down streams and shipped to distant markets by railroad. The railroad was most readily available after 1912 with the opening of the Nada Tunnel. Construction of that tunnel had begun in 1910 and 1911, with two crews working from each side using steam-driven jackhammers and carbide lamps.

**Natural:** Rich in natural wonders, the Red River Gorge Scenic Byway is a treasure for those looking for stone formations, plant and animal life, and river and wilderness areas. The Red River Gorge Geological Area, a National Natural Landmark, comprises the majority of the byway. Located within the Daniel Boone National Forest, the Red River Gorge area hosts a unique collection of flora and fauna. This diverse area has endangered, threatened, sensitive, and rare species of both plants and animals because of the location and glacial history of the area. The presence of 90 percent of the native fauna of eastern Kentucky points out the diversity and stability of habitats in the area.

The main attraction of the Red River Gorge Scenic Byway is the abundance of natural stone arches in the gorge. More than 100 natural arches are located in this area. Backdropped by forested slopes, ridges, and cliffs, these arches have been in the making a long time. Around 70 million years of wind and water have made these arches what they are today.

### Quick Facts

**Length:** 46 miles.

**Time to Allow:** Five hours.

**Considerations:** Roads may become icy during winter, so travel with caution. Help preserve the past by not disturbing or collecting historical or archaeological artifacts. There are many cliffs in the Red River Gorge area, so plan accordingly. Watch small children near the edge of cliffs, and avoid camping near the edge of cliffs.

Undeveloped and rugged, the Clifty Wilderness area and the Red River offer you the chance to experience more of the natural landscape of the area. Clifty Wilderness is 12,646 acres of forested slopes, narrow stream valleys, stone arches, rock shelters, and towering cliffs. The Red River is another area that can be enjoyed for its unaltered nature. In fact, the Red River may be inaccessible in some areas because of the natural vegetation, such as hemlocks, or steep cliffs and boulders.

**Recreational:** The Red River Gorge Scenic Byway can be a recreational destination unto itself. The Red River provides you with some stunning views of water tumbling over boulders and through steep cliffs. However, the river is also a prime spot to go canoeing and kayaking. The abundance of rock formations and cliffs make this byway a first-class spot for rock climbing.

The byway travels through a national forest and also Natural Bridge State Resort Park. An extensive trail system, known as the Sheltowee Trace National Recreation Trail, runs through the Daniel Boone National Forest. Trails in the Red River Gorge Geological Area also visit more than 100 stone arches. In addition to this extensive system, within Natural Bridge State Resort Park, there are nine trails. Camping, miniature golf, swimming, and square dancing can also be enjoyed at the resort.

**Scenic:** The byway's forested hills interspersed with rocky cliffs and natural stone bridges offer you a visual treat with every turn. Native trees often tower over the road creating a tunnel-like experience.

Because the byway mostly travels through a gorge that was created by the erosion effects of rivers, the byway is never far from water and wildlife will be more likely to be spotted. If you are in the mood for the unusual spotting of wildlife, at the Gladie Historic Site you can get an up-close view of the resident bison herd.

## Highlights

Use this itinerary as a guideline to catch the highlights of the Red River Gorge Scenic Byway.

**Sky Bridge:** One of the best known and most accessible arches of this area is Sky Bridge, 75 feet long and 23 feet high. Sky Bridge's arch features a magnificent view of Clifty Wilderness.

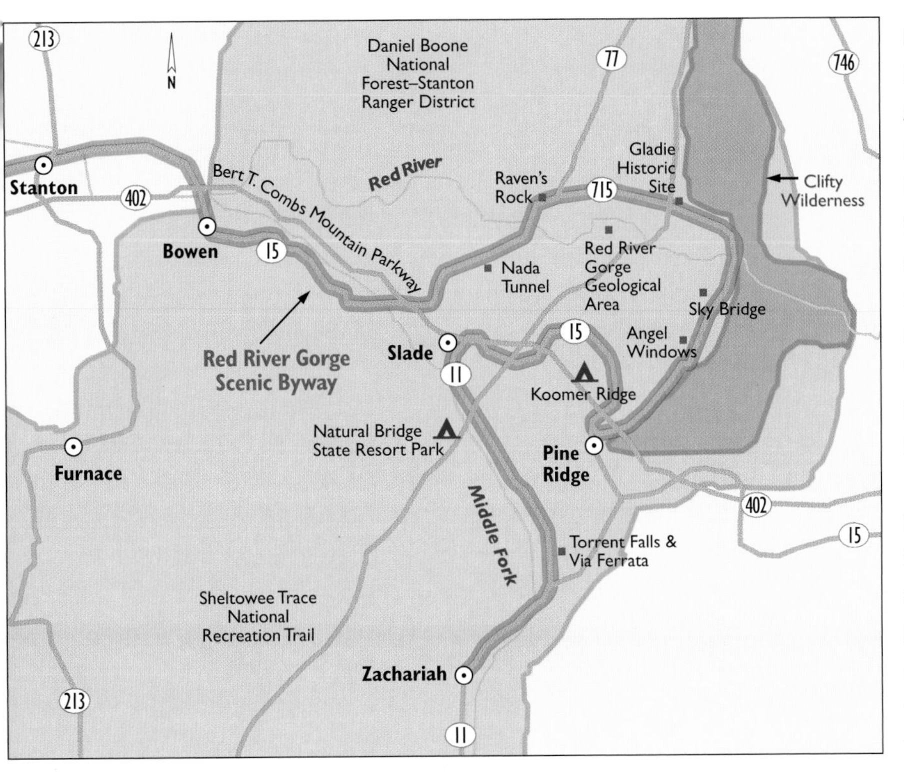


**Nada Tunnel:** Enter the Red River Gorge Geological Area through the 900-foot Nada Tunnel. Open to one-lane traffic only, the tunnel was hand-carved without any modern technology for use by a logging railroad during the early 1900s. The tunnel is listed on the National Register of Historic Places.

**Clifty Wilderness:** Within the gorge is Clifty Wilderness, a hardy and untamed area designated as wilderness by Congress in 1985. This 12,646-acre area features arches, rock shelters, and towering cliffs encircling steep, forested slopes and narrow stream valleys.

**Gladie Historic Site:** Gladie Cabin, a reconstructed log house, is the only structure in the gorge that dates back to the late 19th century.

**Raven's Rock and Angel Windows:** Raven's Rock offers some of the best views of the Red River Gorge. Angel Windows is another of the most easily reached of the arches.

**Natural Bridge State Resort Park:** Standing 65 feet high and 78 feet long, the great natural sandstone arch known as Natural Bridge is located in the Natural Bridge State Resort Park. This park is nestled within the Daniel Boone National Forest and pampers patrons with lodging, dining, a gift shop, meeting rooms, a nature center, swimming pool, fishing, camping, and hiking. For a different view of the Natural Bridge and some spectacular Kentucky scenery, try the Sky Lift. The 22-minute ride carries passengers to within 600 feet of the sandstone formation.

**Torrent Falls and Via Ferrata:** Near the southern end of the byway are Torrent Falls and Via Ferrata. Torrent Falls is actually three waterfalls, the highest being 165 feet high and the tallest in Kentucky. Torrent Falls flows over an immense natural rock house. The Via Ferrata is a European climbing system using iron handgrips and footsteps that are drilled right into the natural rock wall.

# Wilderness Road Heritage Highway

*Daniel Boone marked this trail through the Appalachian Mountain forest that now bears his name. Following his path, tap your toes to the mountain music that echoes in the high ridges and hidden hollows.*

From panoramic views of the Appalachians in Cumberland Gap National Historic Park, to a community culture centered on folk art and mountain music, this byway is packed with reasons to immerse yourself in the woodland culture of the Southeast.

## Intrinsic Qualities

**Cultural:** From music to crafts, this byway is a celebration of the early influence of pioneers. Today, traditional country music and entertainment is alive in Renfro Valley, which hosts performances throughout the year.

In addition to the preservation of traditional music, many communities along the byway promote the making and selling of crafts. Berea is considered the Crafts Capital of Kentucky.



**Historical:** The Wilderness Road Heritage Highway begins at perhaps one of the most historically significant sites in regard to the settlement of the United States. Cumberland Gap National Historic Park celebrates an important corridor, the Cumberland Gap. Native Americans crossed the Appalachians on what they called the Warriors Path, and they relied on this naturally occurring route to provide access to the country across the Appalachian Mountains. Kentucky was seen as a great wilderness for more than 150 years after the initial pilgrims set foot on the eastern seaboard, but soon explorers such as Daniel Boone scouted out the area.

One of the most important pioneers to come through the Cumberland Gap was Dr. Thomas Walker. The Dr. Thomas Walker State Historic Site celebrates the life of this first pioneer to discover the Cumberland Gap and then explore Kentucky. Exploration of the new Kentucky lands opened the area up for settlement, and scores of pioneers followed in Dr. Walker's footsteps.

As America grew, debate turned to war in 1861. Many of the American Civil War battles were fought in Kentucky. The Cumberland Gap was a key transportation route throughout the war. A battle of the Civil War was fought at Camp Wildcat, located along the Wilderness Road Heritage Highway. The reenactment of this battle is a popular event.

**Natural:** Rivers, caves, trails, and forests all combine to give Wilderness Road Heritage Highway visitors a sense of the landscape of Kentucky. Coal is a vital part of industry along the byway. The geological formations of many years have combined to create this environment.

One of these unusual formations is found at the very beginning of the byway. The Pine Mountain geological formation runs along the border of Tennessee and Virginia, and the major opening for this feature is the Cumberland Gap. The Cumberland Gap is an 800-foot naturally occurring break in the rock. The gap was carved by wind and water long ago. The overlooks and trails allow visitors to experience the expansive nature of the outdoors of Kentucky, and within the park itself there are a variety of awe-inspiring features.

Additionally, the Daniel Boone National Forest is a dominant presence along the Wilderness Road Heritage Highway. This forest has many varieties of trees, such as red oak, birch, red maple, hemlock, Virginia pine, and many others. Rocky cliffs can be seen throughout the forest, as well.

Smaller, but still full of natural wonder is the Kentucky Ridge

*Cumberland Gap is the second-largest historical park in the nation and features numerous historical and natural sites of interest.*

### Quick Facts

**Length:** 93 miles.

**Time to Allow:** Two days.

**Considerations:** Summer and fall are the best seasons to drive this byway. Summer is high season. During the fall, the mountains are bright with fall colors.

State Forest, which is mainly accessed by visiting Pine Mountain State Resort Park.

**Recreational:** Whether you are in the mood for hiking, camping, wildlife viewing, biking, fishing, or boating, the Wilderness Road Heritage Highway offers travelers a variety of opportunities. There are numerous rivers, and the byway is near Laurel River Lake, where visitors can boat and fish. The byway travels over some of these rivers, making it a prime spot to view wildlife, both waterfowl and other species of critters. Near the byway you can even spot some elk, which make up the largest herd in the eastern United States.

Cumberland Gap National Historic Park and Pine Mountain State Resort Park offer the majority of the byway's opportunities to find hiking, biking, and horseback riding trails. There is an extensive system of trails in Cumberland Gap National Historic Park, for anything from easy nature hikes to overnight trails. In Daniel Boone National Forest, the Sheltowee Trace National Recreation Trail covers 269 miles.

There is golfing at Pine Mountain State Resort Park and dramatic views in both Cumberland Gap and Pine Mountain. At Pine Mountain State Resort Park, a swimming pool and an amphitheater set in a natural forest cove offer relaxing entertainment and fun while you travel the byway.

**Scenic:** The scenic landscape of the Wilderness Road Heritage Highway is a continuous flow of dramatic views, refreshing small towns, and historically significant features. You will notice a progression in the scenery and land as you move northward along the byway. In the south, the dramatic Cumberland Gap gives you a chance to see a naturally occurring break in a geological formation. The Pine Mountain Range gives way to gentler, rolling hills as you travel northward on the byway. These foothills are home to picturesque small farms, grazing cattle, tobacco fields, and forested hillsides.

## Highlights

This itinerary gives a few of the highlights moving along the Wilderness Road Heritage Highway from north to south.

**Kentucky Music Hall of Fame and Museum:** In Renfro Valley is the Kentucky Music Hall of Fame and Museum, honoring all genres of music and musical artists.

**Levi Jackson Wilderness Road State Park:** Near London is the Levi Jackson Wilderness Road State Park. In the 20 years after 1774, more than 200,000 pioneers traveled over the Wilderness Road and Boone's Trace during the settlement of Kentucky. Today, visitors can walk in the footsteps of the early pioneers on hiking trails that include original portions of these historic paths.

**Colonel Sanders Café and Museum:** Just a bit off the scenic byway but well worth the brief detour is the town of Corbin, home of the Colonel Sanders Café and Museum. First opened in 1940, this is the location of Harland Sanders's first restaurant where he developed his famous chicken recipe.

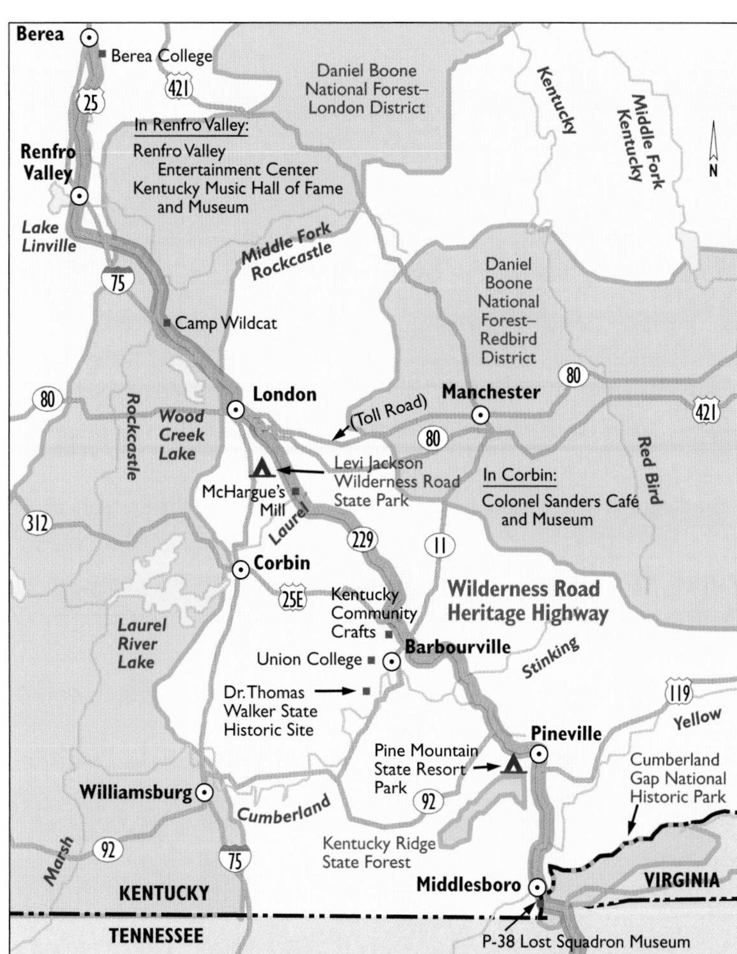


**Dr. Thomas Walker State Historic Site:** Just five miles southwest of Barbourville is Dr. Thomas Walker State Historic Site. Preceding Daniel Boone into Kentucky by 17 years, Dr. Walker led the first exploration into the Cumberland Gap, and a reconstruction of the log cabin he built can be toured.

**Middlesboro:** At the far end of the Wilderness Road Heritage Highway is the town of Middlesboro. A few of the must-sees include the P-38 Lost Squadron Museum, a World War II P-38 Lightning that was recovered from a Greenland ice cap under 268 feet of ice, and the Bell County Coal Museum and Coal House.

**Cumberland Gap National Historic Park:** The climax of the trip is this park, featuring several historic and natural points of interest. Rangers guide visitors on an adventure through majestic cathedral-like Gap Cave. A shuttle transports visitors to the remote Hensley Settlement. And of course a trek to Cumberland Gap itself is a must.

# Coal Heritage Trail 

*Winding mountain roads search out remnants of a one-time coal-mining boom. Step into a coal miner's home and a company store, view a railroad yard, and brave a visit deep inside a former coal mine.*

Experience life in the coal camps on the Coal Heritage Trail in West Virginia. As you wind through the mountains and valleys of the byway, you will see many physical remnants of the coal boom that furthered the industrialization of America.

## Intrinsic Qualities

**Cultural:** Experience the culture of the coalfields that developed from different racial and ethnic groups working and living together. As coal became a primary resource for fuel after the Civil War, southern West Virginia and its coalfields grew quickly. Immigrants from Europe and from the southern states of the nation gathered along the Coal Heritage Trail. Although the byway is a representation of cultural harmony, distinctive ethnic communities, old-world traditions, and festivals are kept alive to enjoy today. Physical elements such as onion-domed Orthodox churches are available for enjoyment, while shops and stores exist that preserve the heritage of the past.

*The New River Gorge Bridge is the longest single-span steel arch bridge in the Western Hemisphere.*

**Historical:** The story of southern West Virginia's coalfields is one of working-class culture, industrial might, and racial and ethnic diversity. The coal mines along the Coal Heritage Trail produced abundant economical fuel that transformed rural America into an industrial land, providing jobs and homes for thousands of people fleeing persecution and oppression. Immense fortunes were made by those who invested in the industry, and a society was produced with a peculiar and fascinating legacy.

What makes the Coal Heritage Trail significant are the physical remnants of the coal boom that remain scattered in the deep valleys of the region. These artifacts provide a wonderful opportunity for understanding the role that West Virginia coalfields played in the industrialization of America.

As mining jobs were lost to mechanization, the people of the coalfields left in search of employment in the cities of the industrial Midwest and beyond. The descendants of these people and other visitors interested in the many facets of heritage and culture represented on the byway are visiting the area. Visitors will see historic structures, including coal mines and railroad structures. Visitors will also experience coal camp life by seeing coal miner houses, company stores, company offices, and similar structures that defined coal camp life.

**Natural:** Amid the Appalachian Mountains, the Coal Heritage Trail makes its way through the Ohio Valley. Before its industrial days, the area along this byway was rugged and undeveloped. With the industrial revolution, a new natural resource was discovered in the Trans-Allegheny Frontier. Deposits of some of the world's best bituminous coal were found throughout southern West Virginia. This type of coal is low in sulfur and high in BTU volatility, and this produces "smokeless coals."

**Recreational:** Visitors to the Coal Heritage Trail enjoy outstanding recreational and natural features. The rugged and beautiful mountains of the coalfields are the physical signature of the region and were instrumental in the development of isolated coal camps that were connected to the outside world only by the railroad that also hauled out coal. Numerous state parks and wilderness

### Quick Facts

**Length:**
97 1/2 miles.

**Time to Allow:**
Three hours.

**Considerations:** Slower speeds are recommended because the road is narrow and has numerous curves. Drivers may also encounter large coal trucks using the road in some areas. There are no seasonal accessibility limitations. However, be sure to allow extra driving time during inclement weather.

areas provide access to recreational areas offering hiking, skiing, canoeing, mountain biking, white-water rafting, and other activities.

**Scenic:** The Coal Heritage Trail is an industrial byway that tells its story through the physical artifacts and cultural traditions that remain. The byway is linked together by the mines, towns, coal camps, and industrial artifacts that are hidden and then revealed by the extreme topography of the landscape.

## Highlights

Not only rich in scenery, this area is rich in heritage, a place where coal reigned supreme. This itinerary gives you a few of the must-see highlights along the way.

**Princeton–Mercer County Chamber of Commerce:** Before entering the Coal Heritage Trail, a stop in Princeton at the Princeton–Mercer County Chamber of Commerce is a good way to begin your trip. Located just off U.S. 460 on Oakvale Road, the Chamber of Commerce has plenty of maps and information about the region and it also is home to the Wiley Cabin and Museum. The 1932 cabin has three exhibit rooms, a library, and a craft shop.

**Bluefield:** From Princeton take U.S. 460 to Bluefield to begin traveling along the Coal Heritage Trail. On Commerce Street is the Eastern Regional Coal Archives and Museum. The facility collects, preserves, and makes available coal-related heritage through photographs, memorabilia, and other artifacts. Also in town is the Bluefield Area Arts Center on Bland Street in the Old City Hall. It is home to an art gallery, the Summit Theatre, a restaurant, and the Mercer County Convention and Visitors Bureau.

**Bramwell:** The historic village of Bramwell was once the wealthiest town per capita in America, home to 14 millionaires who made their fortunes here. A brochure with a walking tour and map of the historic highlights of the luxurious heydays of Bramwell is available at the Bramwell Town Hall and at several of the bed-and-breakfasts that are the former homes of the wealthy coal barons.

**Bank of Bramwell:** The Bank of Bramwell was once so prosperous that the janitor would take heaping mounds of moneybags in a wheelbarrow to the train station each day. Bust by 1933 as a result of the Great Depression, the historic bank building, still oozing with opulence and elegance, was home to the local paper by the turn of the 20th century.

**Bramwell Presbyterian Church:** The Bramwell Presbyterian Church was patterned after a Welsh cathedral and contains such lavish extra touches as local bluestone tiles cut and laid by Italian masons who also came to seek their fortune.

**Welch:** Though a tiny village now, the town of Welch is noted for its four-story granite courthouse and the History in Our Mountains Museum. At the museum visitors can begin with a 25-minute film about the coal industry. A self-guided tour takes guests on a journey through history.

**Beckley:** The city of Beckley awaits visitors at the northern end of the Coal Heritage Trail. In the New River Park in Beckley are two definite must-sees for those eager to experience the coal heritage of the region.

**Mountain Homestead:** The Mountain Homestead is located directly behind the Youth Museum at New River Park and has re-created a typical settlement on the Appalachian frontier. Trained interpreters enhance the visit to each reconstructed historical building, including the two-story log house, weaver's shed, one-room schoolhouse, barn, blacksmith shop, and general store.

**Beckley Exhibition Coal Mine:** This mine gives visitors a realistic glimpse into the world of coal mining as it was in the early 1900s. Tours travel underground through nearly 1,500 feet of passageways in an authentic coal mine 500 feet below the New River Park. Guides are veteran miners and provide vivid details of life in the mines. Visitors can also browse in the coal mining museum.

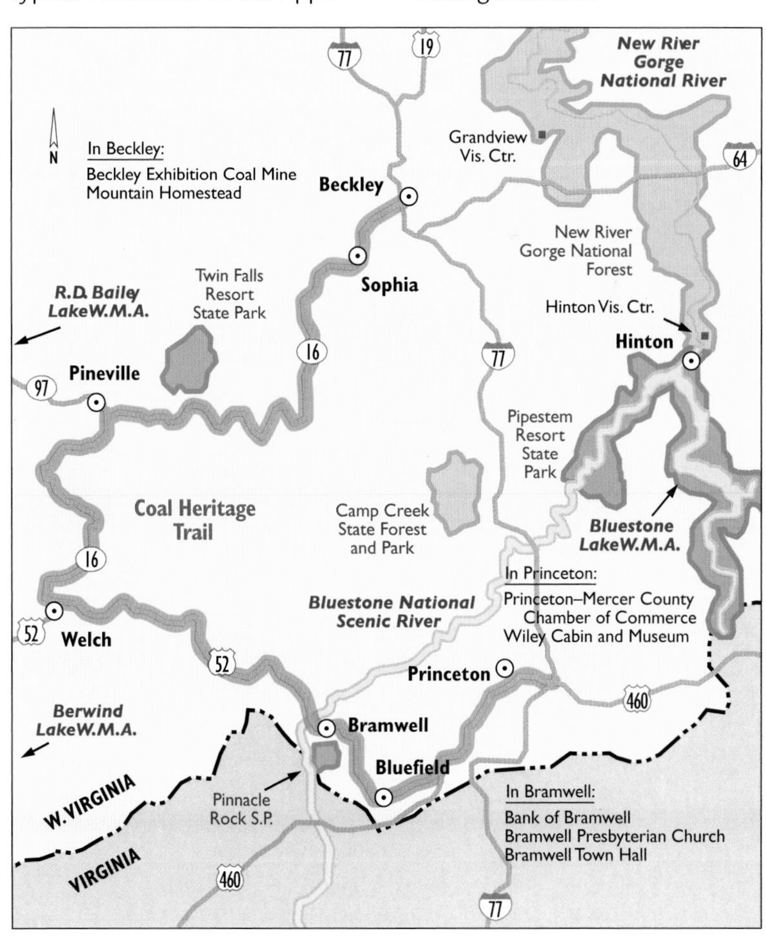

# Highland Scenic Highway

*Nonstop panoramas unfold as you ascend forested mountain slopes in the state's wild Allegheny Highlands. Four scenic overlooks invite you to reflect on the views.*

Travel through a wild and undeveloped portion of the Monongahela National Forest on the Highland Scenic Highway in West Virginia. See rolling, mountainous terrain covered by hardwood forests and capped by dark spruce at higher elevations from one of four overlooks. This view is one you won't want to miss. Hidden within this panoramic view, you'll find plenty of places to visit and things to do.

## Intrinsic Qualities

**Cultural:** As an isolated area with abundant natural resources, the wilderness of the Highland Scenic Highway was an early haven for Americans seeking to avoid the horrors of the Civil War. Families who moved to the area at this time maintained their seclusion for decades.

In the 1960s, the descendants of these families experienced a visit from people researching for the Smithsonian Institution. As the researchers studied and recorded the oral histories of the families in this area, they discovered that the language spoken was still the Elizabethan English of the early U.S. settlers. Tradition and folk tales of the area have been recorded and are a remnant of the mountain cultures of the East.

**Historical:** There are many historical events associated with the Highland Scenic Highway. As intensive logging developed along this road, so did the habitation of the area. In the early 1900s, logging of almost all the timber in the area was done. Due to the lack of transportation possibilities into the area, the land surrounding the Highland Scenic Highway remained relatively unsettled for decades. However, once the area was recognized as a resource, it was not long before a logging culture established there. Remainders of these logging times along the Highland Scenic Highway can still be found today. For example, the Tea Creek Campground was constructed on the site of an old logging camp.

Another important historical event that occurred along this byway was the birth of a famous author, Pearl S. Buck, in Hillsboro.

A darker time in the history of the byway occurred during World War II. East of Cranberry Glades is the site of the former World War II Mill Point Prison Camp. This camp housed federal prisoners of the time, conscientious objectors, and moonshiners.

**Natural:** This region has a great deal to offer in the way of natural phenomena. The byway meanders through the Monongahela National Forest. Part of the byway follows the Williams River as it entices anglers to test their skill.

A region of 750 acres that the Highland Scenic Highway encompasses is rich in acidic wetlands known as bogs. The largest of these wetlands is the Cranberry Glades Botanical Area. It consists of four bogs that are home to some unusual species of plants and animals. The spongy ground of the bog is made up of partially decayed plant material known best as peat. Five species of birds, carnivorous plants, and a species of bog orchids can be found in the Cranberry Glades area. A half-mile boardwalk has been constructed through two of the bogs for visitors to explore the area without disturbing the fragile ecosystem. This forest-covered land was acquired by the U.S. Forest Service in 1934. Since then, it has been a prized area of West Virginia where rivers, mountains, and trees form a spectacular outdoor experience. Several trails wind throughout the area where visitors can travel the wilderness on foot.

The gorge that holds three waterfalls known as the Falls of Hills Creek includes geological points of interest, as well as a wide range of plant life. The falls were formed from the unstable layering of shale and sandstone. This layering is exposed to add to the natural beauty of the area. The

### Quick Facts

**Length:**
43 miles.

**Time to Allow:**
Two to four hours.

**Considerations:** There are no services along the route, and there is no snow removal during the winter. Also, be aware that some of the road is used by large coal trucks.

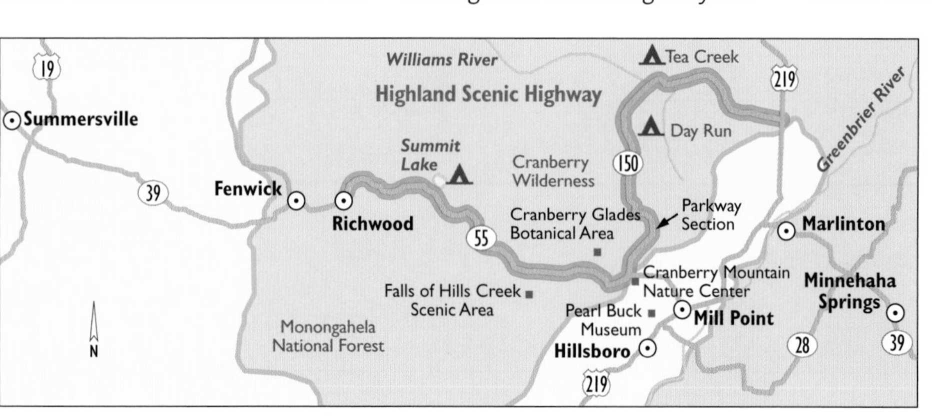

Hills Creek area is also well known for its abundance of wildflowers in the spring.

As visitors hike through the Monongahela National Forest, they may stumble onto natural treasures and views untold. Just recently, unusual honeycomb rock formations were found very near to the byway.

**Recreational:** The Highland Scenic Highway area offers recreational opportunities for travelers who enjoy hunting, fishing, hiking, or camping. For example, along the Cherry, Cranberry, and Williams rivers, you'll find anglers casting for trout. The West Virginia Division of Natural Resources stocks the streams with rainbow, brook, brown, and golden trout. Summit Lake, a beautiful 42-acre reservoir, contains trout, bass, and panfish. Boats with electric trolling motors are allowed on the lake. Hunting is available in the Monongahela National Forest in accordance with West Virginia state regulations.

More than 150 miles of trails are located in the area of the Highland Scenic Highway. The Falls of Hills Creek Scenic Area, the Cranberry Glades, and the Big Spruce Overlook offer three barrier-free trails. For those interested in a backpacking experience, Cranberry Wilderness and the Tea Creek area offer places for camping. Visitors should camp away from trails and streams. Many trails in the area also offer opportunities for horseback riding and are suitable for cross-country skiing in the winter. Mountain biking is permitted on most of the trails located outside of the Cranberry Wilderness.

Three campgrounds are included in the Highland Scenic Highway area. If a stay by the lake sounds appealing to you, Summit Lake Campground is two miles from State Route 39/55. For campsites by the Williams River, Tea Creek Campground is one mile from the parkway portion of the byway, and Day Run Campground is only four miles away.

**Scenic:** In addition to the wetlands, wilderness, and mountainous terrain, the Highland Scenic Highway also offers many scenic points of interest that will enchant visitors. For example, the three waterfalls at the Falls of Hills Creek are 20 feet, 45 feet, and 63 feet in height. Visitors can inspect the falls up close by following a trail three-quarters of a mile.

## Highlights

"Scenic" is the key word when traveling along this route. A natural wonder, the highlights of the trip are listed here.

**Richwood:** Begin your journey in the town of Richwood. Originally known as Cherry Tree Bottoms, it was a "company town" of the Cherry River Boom and Lumber Company. Today, this is the place to find local outfitters and guides to prepare for a rigorous adventure in the Monongahela National Forest or simply to obtain maps.

**Falls of Hills Creek Scenic Area:** The Falls of Hills Creek Scenic Area, a 114-acre area, contains three waterfalls. The first 1,700 feet of trail is a paved, wheelchair-accessible path to the upper falls viewing platform. The rest of the trail is more demanding with stairways and boardwalks leading to the lower falls.

**Cranberry Mountain Nature Center:** This nature center offers information about the Monongahela National Forest and other nearby attractions. An exhibit hall and audiovisual programs provide interpretation of forest ecosystems and local history.

**Cranberry Glades Botanical Area:** Cranberry Glades Botanical Area is an ecological anomaly. The four glades, or bogs, contain plant life normally found 500 miles north. Many of the distinctive plant species found here are descendants of plants that were forced south by the glaciers that covered Canada and the northern United States about 10,000 years ago. The Cranberry Glades is the southernmost part of the migration, making this area biologically unique.

**Cranberry Wilderness:** Not suitable for homesteading but quite appealing to the Cherry River Boom and Lumber Company, the area now known as Cranberry Wilderness was completely logged out by 1930. The U.S. Forest Service purchased the land in 1934. Cranberry Wilderness is 35,864 acres and has approximately 60 miles of trails, many of which follow old railroad grades, logging roads, or Forest Service roads.

*The Falls of Hills Creek includes three falls, with Hells Creek descending a total of 220 feet between the upper and lower falls.*

# HISTORIC NATIONAL ROAD 

*West Virginia's share of this historic corridor crosses the state's slender northern panhandle, edging past Oglebay Resort Park, a beautifully landscaped preserve with many recreational attractions.*

PART OF A MULTISTATE BYWAY; SEE ALSO ILLINOIS, INDIANA, MARYLAND, OHIO, AND PENNSYLVANIA.

West Virginia's Historic National Road takes you on a trip through history. In 1863, West Virginia developed into a new state. The building where the Restored Government of Virginia was established is located along the byway; many important decisions and debates regarding the Civil War took place in this building. You can tour this historic site that has been painstakingly preserved and beautifully restored.

The Historic National Road boasts many impressive museums and art galleries. One of the most popular museums along the byway is the Kruger Street Toy and Train Museum in Wheeling. The byway also features restored mansions, such as the Oglebay Institute Mansion Museum. This 16-mile attraction offers a high level of historic aesthetics and cleanliness. To make this route even more accommodating, you can find bike paths and paved trails through most of the byway's highlights.

## Quick Facts

**Length:**
16 miles.

**Time to Allow:**
Less than one hour.

**Considerations:** The byway is open all year, but many feel it is best to drive during the summer, the high season, when more cultural activities are taking place.

## Intrinsic Qualities

**Cultural:** The cultural qualities of the Historic National Road are many in number and offer diverse experiences. Two of perhaps the most meaningful include music (particularly Jamboree U.S.A.) and religion.

The Capitol Music Hall, located next to the famous Wheeling Suspension Bridge, is home to both Jamboree U.S.A. and the Wheeling Symphony Orchestra. The Jamboree is the second-longest-running live radio program in America's history. Since 1933, famous artists from all over the nation have their shows aired live over the radio each Saturday night. It was founded with the idea of promoting the regional country music that is dear to the South. When the Jamboree first began, fans drove hundreds of miles for this weekly event. This tradition continues today, as many still drive great distances to participate in the yeehawin' fun.

Religion has played a powerful role in shaping the communities along the byway. Places of worship dot this area, some with beautiful aesthetics and architecture. Churches along the route tell the story of the great diversity of those who traveled and settled here. You can view beautiful cemeteries near the churches with many monuments and headstones indicative of the artistry of earlier eras.

*The Bissonnette Gardens at Oglebay Resort Park are enticing. Visitors can walk on the red brick paths and view the seasonal flower displays.*

**Historical:** Without question, the historic qualities are the richest attribute this byway has to offer. With two national historic landmarks, numerous designated historic districts, and National Register structures, the Historic National Road had a great impact on not only West Virginia's past, but on America's, too.

The National Road Corridor Historic District consists of a variety of homes built by Wheeling's wealthy industrial class. It also includes Wheeling Park, Greenwood Cemetery, and Mount Cavalry Cemetery. In 1888, farms outside the city began to be developed as "suburbia." The Woodsdale–Edgewood Neighborhood Historic District is a result of this type of development. The district contains many high-style houses, such as Queen Anne, Colonial Revival, and Shingle styles. As the route descends Wheeling Hill into the city of Wheeling, you enter the North Wheeling Historic District. Ebenezer Zane, the founder of Wheeling, laid out the Victorian district in 1792. The houses include a variety of simple Federal townhouses offset with the high styles of Italianate, Queen Anne, Second Empire, and Classical Revival architecture.

The Wheeling Suspension Bridge crosses the Ohio River to Wheeling Island. The engineering marvel spans 1,010 feet and was the first bridge to cross the Ohio River. Designed by Charles Ellet, Jr., it was the longest single span in the United States at the time of its completion in 1849. You cross the bridge to get to Wheeling Island, one of the largest inhabited river islands in the country. The Wheeling Island Historic District includes a diverse collection of lavish 19th-century residential homes.

**Recreational:** The city of Wheeling has some of the world's fastest canines in the races. This popular event is usually open every day.

Visitors go to Wheeling Downs to watch the races in person. These sleek canines give quite a show as they thunder along at speeds of up to 40 miles per hour. At Wheeling Downs, people can enjoy the luxury of attending the races while eating at a fine diner that overlooks the track.

**Scenic:** Time almost stands still while looking down on the city of Wheeling from Mount Wood Overlook. With careful observation, you can spot restored Victorian homes, as well as other important buildings in the nation's history. This vantage point, resting on top of Wheeling Hill, also overlooks the mighty Ohio River. It's at these heights that the observer starts to appreciate the accomplishment of early Americans who constructed the single-span Wheeling Suspension Bridge across this wide river. As you continue to gaze in the area around Wheeling, more sights become visible. Ancient deciduous forests surround the city and small streams make their way to the grand Ohio River. Maple trees thrive here, and some of the locals harvest the syrup.

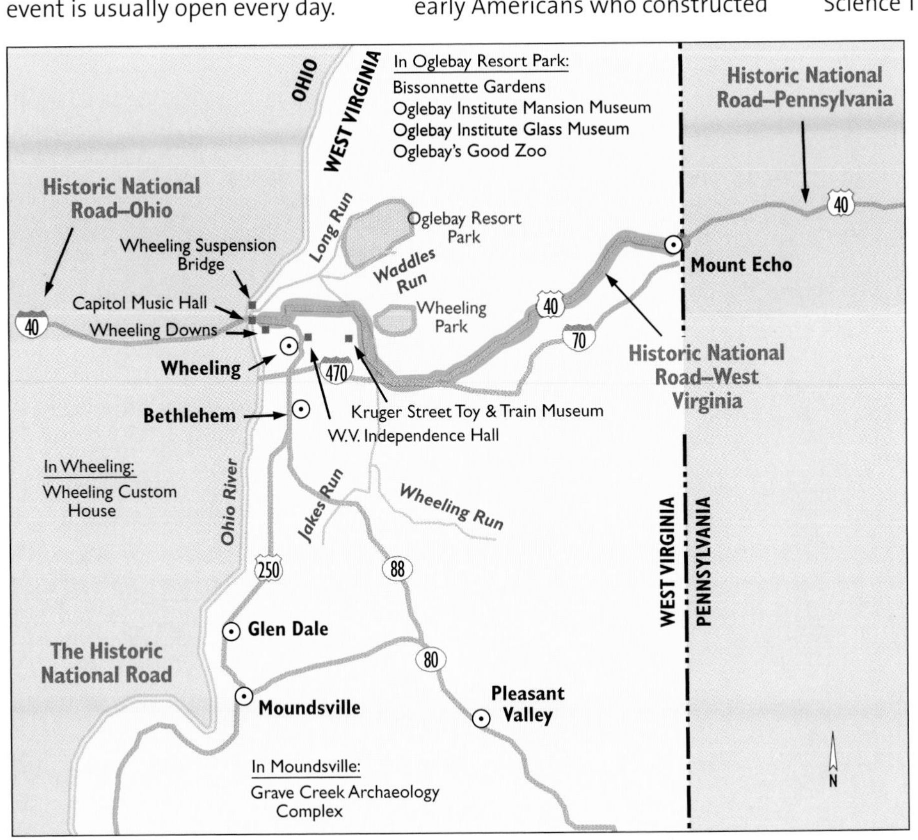


## Highlights

Look to these points of interest for a great tour of West Virginia's Historic National Road.

**Oglebay Resort Park:** Covering 1,650 rolling green acres, Oglebay Resort Park is a major regional recreation center. It features the 30-acre Good Zoo, displaying 80 species of animals; the Benedum Science Theater, offering laser shows; a 1 1/2-mile miniature train ride; 16-acre Bissonnette Gardens, a re-creation of 19th-century gardens; two championship golf courses; two swimming pools; tennis courts; horse stables; and lodging, restaurants, and specialty shops.

**Oglebay Institute Mansion Museum:** Built in 1846 as an eight-room farmhouse, the Greek Revival-style home later was expanded to become a private summer estate. Willed to the city of Wheeling, in 1930 it became a museum, and it displays period antiques.

**Oglebay Institute Glass Museum:** Adjacent to the mansion, the Glass Museum features 3,000 examples of Wheeling glass made from 1829 to 1939. Displays include cut lead crystal, Victorian art glass, carnival glass, and other Ohio Valley glass designs. Of note is the 225-pound Sweeney Punch Bowl, the largest piece of cut lead crystal ever made. It is regarded as a masterpiece of Victorian glass.

**Wheeling Custom House:** Completed at the beginning of the Civil War, the stately Wheeling Custom House has been dubbed "the birthplace of West Virginia." Meeting here in 1861, delegates from Virginia's western counties voted to nullify the state's secession from the Union while creating what became the separate state of West Virginia. It was admitted to the Union in 1863. A video provides details, and a museum displays period artifacts and gives more background on the statehood process.

**Grave Creek Archaeology Complex:** The Adena, a mound-building people who lived in the region from 1000 B.C. to A.D. 700, are represented by the 2,000-year-old Grave Creek Mound. It is the largest of the Adena burial mounds. In the adjacent Delf Norona Museum, exhibits detail the life of the Adena people. The mound was built by hauling 60,000 tons of dirt in basket loads.

# MIDLAND TRAIL 

*Peer into the deep New River Gorge from high above, or sign onto a white-water rafting trip that splashes beneath the soaring cliffs. Beyond the gorge, small towns are reminiscent of a bygone day.*

Travel the Midland Trail, and enter a land of world-class white-water rafting, Civil War remnants, African-American history, and small towns full of country charm. The byway will carry you through areas rich in industrial culture, over hills and through valleys arrayed in scenic beauty, and finally out into rolling farmland settled during the colonial era.

## Intrinsic Qualities

**Cultural:** Part of the cultural heritage of today comes from the history of yesterday. The Midland Trail holds many historical sites significant to the life of Booker T. Washington who played an influential role in African-American education and equality. He is memorialized today at historic buildings and information centers on the byway. People remember the first developments of industry along the byway when Elisha Brooks used 24 kettles to extract salt from the area's brine in 1797.

Although West Virginians have found a significant role in the industry of natural resources, an appreciation for the arts and outdoors has also been cultivated here. Nothing is more revered in today's West Virginia culture than outdoor recreation and adventure. White-water rafting is second to none. The skill and craft of byway residents can be found in the many stores along the way. Quilts are a specialty, and visitors will be able to find quilt shops in Malden, Lookout, Ansted, and several other byway communities. Cabin Creek Quilts in Malden has made quilts for such figures as U.S. presidents, Jackie Kennedy, and Barbra Streisand.

**Historical:** There are many historical events associated with the Midland Trail. As the new country struggled to move westward over the Appalachian Mountains, the Midland Trail was the most direct but most difficult passage from the mid-eastern colonies. Following buffalo and Native American trails, Daniel Boone explored the route. Eventually a combination of land and water routes opened up the land and the natural resources to the nation. Buffalo, American Indians, settlers, and later industrialists sought out the rich salt brines of the Kanawha Valley. The river provided transportation for coal and timber. The battles fought over this route started before the Revolutionary War and continued through the Civil War.

Claudius Crozet was responsible for planning Virginia's road system. He designed and constructed many roads, including the Midland Trail.

These roads became very important during the Civil War. The state provided many troops for battle, and the Midland Trail itself was used as a warpath.

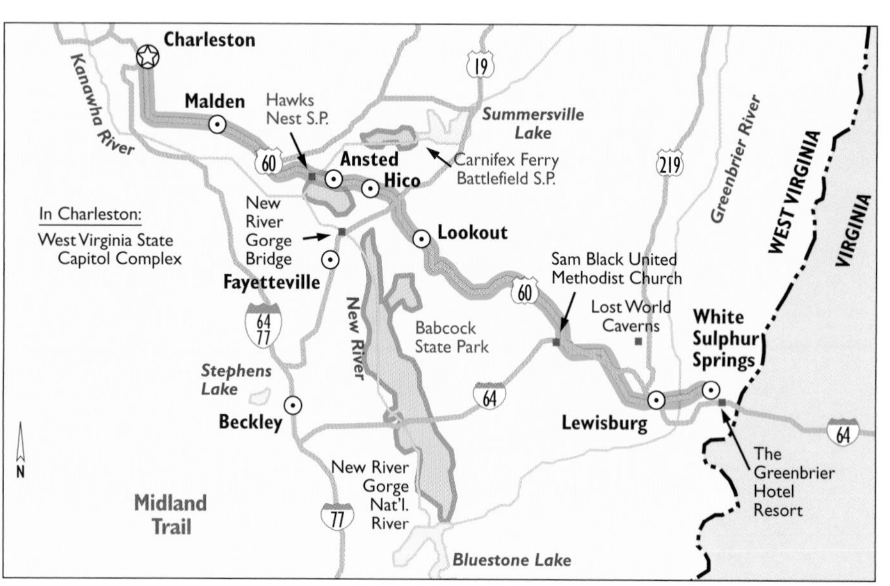


### Quick Facts

**Length:** 117 miles.

**Time to Allow:** Two to eight hours.

**Considerations:** High season occurs from April to October when an abundance of outdoor extreme sports are available. There are a number of quality pull-offs that give visitors the opportunity to enjoy the scenic qualities of the Midland Trail to the fullest extent. There are no planned seasonal closings.

For a time, the Midland Trail was nearly forgotten as people used the railways. Meanwhile, the 20th century began, and the area's resources fueled the industrial development. The slaves who toiled in the salt works and the immigrants who cut the Hawks Nest Hydroelectric Tunnel through silica rock left behind a history of the nation's growing pains. In the mid-20th century America's love affair with the automobile was heightening, and the trail became U.S. 60, the preferred truck route over the mountains. Today, its roadside parks, turnouts, and mom-and-pop businesses still resemble the traveling conditions present after World War II. Yet the road leads to a place of change and history in Charleston, the state's capital.

**Recreational:** World-class white-water rafting and outdoor sports are found along the Midland Trail. The best white water east of the Mississippi annually draws more than 160,000 people to raft the New River, and more than 60,000 people raft the Gauley River during its 22-day fall season. Outdoor adventurers also participate in kayaking, canoeing, fishing, hunting, rock climbing, hiking, and mountain biking. One of the most adrenalizing activities happens once a year on the third Saturday in October. For a thrilling spectacle, watch trained jumpers as they leap from the 876-foot-high New River Gorge Bridge.

Local communities also offer recreational activities. Ansted has an annual street luge competition. The Greenbrier Hotel Resort, a National Historic Landmark, has 54 holes of championship golf, including the golf course called Oakhurst Links. At the 1884 course, golfers must still use 19th-century wooden clubs and equipment, and play by 19th-century rules.

**Scenic:** The Midland Trail is a scenic drive through the rolling farms of Greenbrier County and the mountains of Fayette County. Numerous pull-offs and scenic overlooks provide spectacular vistas in all seasons, from the springtime forests dotted with beautiful dogwood trees to the multicolored foliage of the fall. The scenic beauty of waterfalls and the New River Gorge are classic Appalachia. At the Kanawha County end of the trail, the road follows the river. Here the industrial heritage is visible in many places. At the trail's start, the state capitol and the area around it provide a parklike setting. Its gold dome shining with the fire of the sunset is a picture worth seeing.

## Highlights

Before the interstate system crisscrossed the country, the Midland Trail was a major thoroughfare in West Virginia. Here are some of the highlights.

**Charleston:** Begin your journey at Charleston, the capital of West Virginia. The town is filled to the brim with historic landmarks.

**West Virginia State Capitol Complex:** The complex includes the capitol with its marble rotunda containing a splendid two-ton chandelier. The complex also has several statues and fountains, a veterans' memorial, a museum, the Governor's Mansion, and the antebellum Holly Grove home.

**Hawks Nest State Park:** At Hawks Nest State Park visitors can ride the tram 876 feet to the base of the New River Gorge. The park also features a museum, lodging, scenic dining, and four trails.

**Ansted:** Continuing east on U.S. 60 visitors come to the town of Ansted. Attractions include the gravesite of Julia Neale Jackson, mother of Thomas "Stonewall" Jackson; Halfway House, a former tavern on the Kanawha Turnpike and headquarters of the Chicago Dragoons during the Civil War; and African-American Heritage Family Tree Museum.

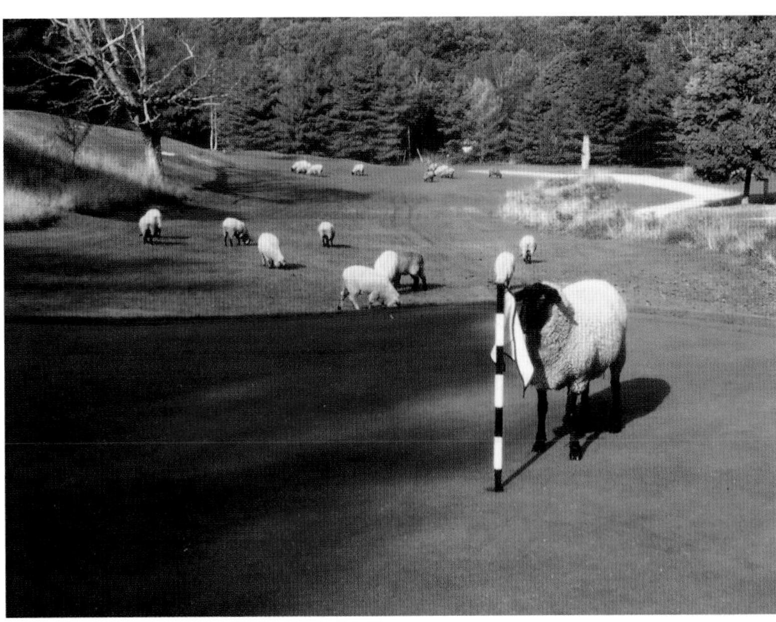

*At Oakhurst Links, the first organized golf club in the United States, the "mowing" flock of sheep adds to the authenticity of the 19th-century experience.*

**Sam Black United Methodist Church:** Farther east near the junction with I-64 is this church, built in 1901. Reverend Sam Black was a Methodist circuit rider for nearly 50 years.

**Lost World Caverns:** North of Lewisburg are the Lost World Caverns, featuring the nation's largest compound stalactite, the 30-ton "Snowy Chandelier." The Lost World Caverns Visitors Center and Natural History Museum features the largest collection of dinosaur and fossil replicas in West Virginia.

**Lewisburg:** The historic town of Lewisburg has enough attractions, including a 235-acre historic downtown district, to keep visitors busy for several days.

**White Sulphur Springs:** The climax of the trip is the resort town of White Sulphur Springs. Among many highlights is the Oakhurst Links. Duffers at Oakhurst play the course just as golfers did in 1884.

**The Greenbrier Hotel Resort:** The Greenbrier Hotel Resort housed a secret until 1992. Buried 720 feet into the hillside specifically to accommodate the U.S. Senate and House of Representatives in case of a nuclear attack is a bunker. Visitors are encouraged to tour the facility. The Greenbrier Hotel Resort offers a multitude of activities and attractions. Guided tours of the elegant interior design and architecture are offered year round; the Presidents Museum details the memorable moments from the visits of 26 U.S. presidents; tours give a glimpse into the history as well as the natural beauty that surrounds the resort.

# Washington Heritage Trail 

*George Washington crisscrossed the state's eastern panhandle, and you can follow in his path. Soak in the mineral waters of the little spa town of Berkeley Springs, as Washington once did.*

Follow the footsteps of America's first president and founding father when you travel the Washington Heritage Trail. So much of George Washington's history is preserved and relived along the byway that you can almost feel his presence. The byway offers a retreat from the hustle and bustle of metropolitan life. Travel through farms and apple orchards and enjoy the scenic beauty of the area as you explore the history of the people and places that shaped this great nation.

## Intrinsic Qualities

**Archaeological:** From archaeological mounds to old cemeteries and towns, the Washington Heritage Trail offers pieces of the past for interested travelers. Visitors will find Green Hill Cemetery as a museum of stone-carver's art. In the same area on the byway, visitors can go to one of the earliest known African-American cemeteries, as well as a Dutch cemetery from the mid-1700s.

Prehistoric archaeological sites dating from as early as 12,000 B.C. can be found in the Heritage Trail area. One prehistoric site that travelers find interesting is the earthen mound at Woods Resort. Artifacts recovered from the mound suggest that it was built between 800 B.C. and 300 B.C.

**Cultural:** Cultural qualities along the Washington Heritage Trail reflect the rich history and diverse culture of West Virginia's heritage, which blends Virginia gentility with mountain hospitality and charm. The panhandle's pioneers are recognized by annual events. Berkeley Springs honors the nation's first president each March with the George Washington's Bathtub Celebration.

In addition, the Belle Boyd House retains extensive historical and genealogical archives. Civil War scholars can immerse themselves in the archives at Shepherdstown's George Tyler Moore Civil War Center.

Far from being confined to history, celebrations along the byway focus on other facets of the eastern panhandle's unique cultural legacy, such as arts and crafts, apples, and drinking water.

**Historical:** Beginning in the days of George Washington, the eastern panhandle of West Virginia has been a pocket of history. It has seen troops of three wars, the growth of a population, the indus-

### Quick Facts

**Length:** 136 miles.

**Time to Allow:** Six to eight hours.

**Considerations:** This byway is long (136 miles) and has a host of historical sights to see. Visitors may want to consider spending an extra day or two in order to experience all that the Washington Heritage Trail has to offer.

*Lined with more than six million bricks, the Paw Paw Tunnel in the C&O Canal National Historic Park is the largest made-by-hand structure on the C&O Canal.*

trialization of a society, and the developments that have allowed the area to achieve national recognition. For example, the eastern panhandle was an important source of quality enlisted officers during the Revolutionary War.

Many of the region's settlements were established during the late 18th century, including Shepherdstown and Martinsburg. Much of the panhandle's early activity occurred around these settlements, and historic structures line the roads of the Washington Heritage Trail.

By urging the establishment of a federal armory at Harpers Ferry, George Washington inadvertently played a role in the tensions that sparked the Civil War. The armory was seized by abolitionist John Brown during his famed 1859 raid, an event that focused the nation's attention on the issue of slavery. The Potomac Valley was the stage for a number of critical Civil War campaigns, one of which culminated in the battle at Antietam, the bloodiest of all Civil War battles.

Also, George Washington's interest in making the Potomac River navigable sowed the seed for what became the Chesapeake and Ohio Canal, which was critical to the movement of goods and people through the Potomac Valley for more than 70 years.

Confederate forces traveled portions of the Washington Heritage Trail in Morgan County during Thomas Jonathan "Stonewall" Jackson's 1861–1862 winter campaign. In Morgan County, nearly 16,000 Union forces camped at Camp Hill Cemetery east of Paw Paw—the same location used by General Edward Braddock's forces during the French and Indian War. Panhandle railroads like the Baltimore and Ohio were strategically important during the war, as well, and Martinsburg's B&O Roundhouse Complex National Register of Historic Places District preserves some of the resources that were targeted by Confederate raiders.

**Natural:** The bountiful natural qualities of the Washington Heritage Trail spring from the unique geomorphology that shaped West Virginia's eastern panhandle. Indeed, the earth's moving crust created the dominant landscape features that are experienced along the byway, including the ridges, valleys, and mineral springs of the eastern Appalachian Mountains.

**Recreational:** Recreational activities are abundant on the Washington Heritage Trail. Sightseeing is one of the most popular activities. In addition to visiting historical sights and passing scenic overlooks, fishing, hunting, boating, golf, and racing are all activities that are available.

Resources for walkers and hikers abound in the eastern panhandle, including everything from historic walking tours of Shepherdstown and Charles Town to many wonderful hiking trails. Shorter hiking trails can be found in the Cacapon Resort State Park and at the Coolfont Resort, and longer hikes exist along the Tuscarora Trail that runs the length of Sleepy Creek Mountain. The 2,100-mile-long Appalachian Trail has its headquarters in Harpers Ferry and can be accessed there. Another great hiking trail, the C&O Canal Trail, is probably the least strenuous and one of the most scenic trails. It can be accessed at Harpers Ferry and Paw Paw.

The network of mountain streams and rivers in the panhandle provides ample opportunities for both fishers and boaters to enjoy the water. River rafting, canoeing, and kayaking trips on the Shenandoah and Potomac rivers can be arranged through outfitters in Harpers Ferry.

Not surprisingly, the Sleepy Creek Public Hunting and Fishing Area remains the largest public area open to hunters. Golfers can enjoy a round or two at public and private courses such as those at the Woods Resort, Locust Hill, and Cacapon Resort State Park. Fans of thoroughbred racing can try their luck on a trifecta wager

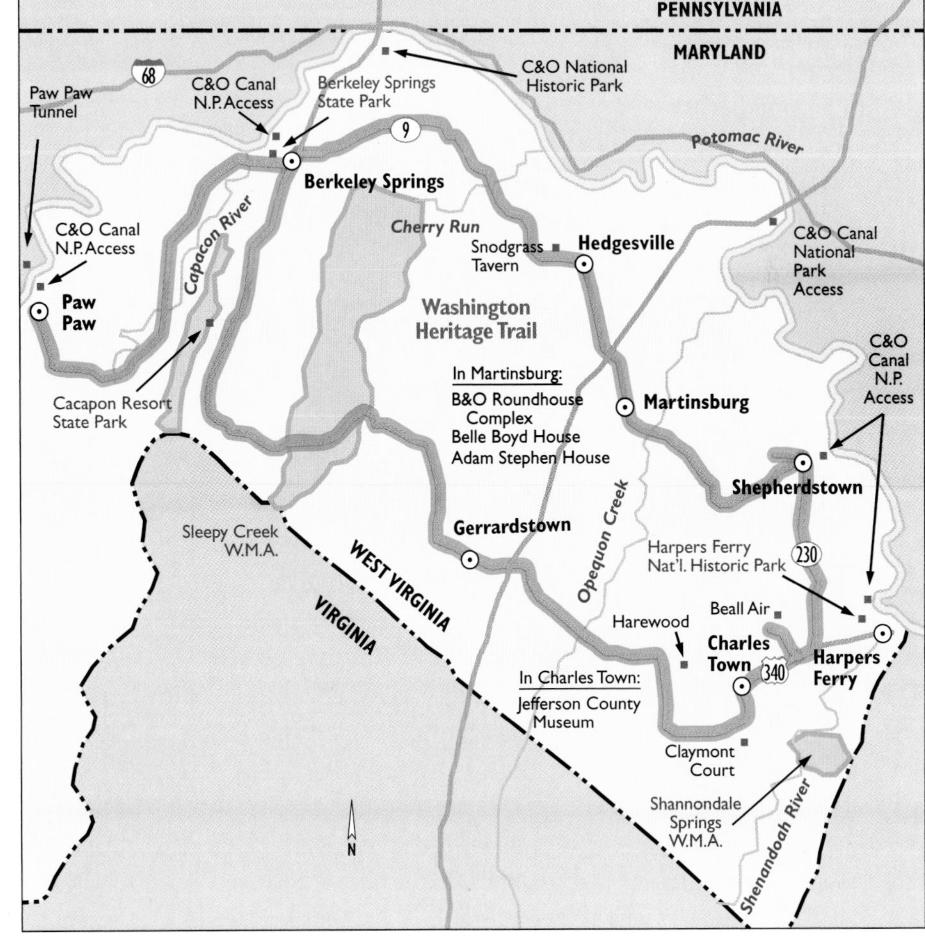

at the Charles Town Race Track. Auto racing enthusiasts can also get their fill at the Summit Point Raceway.

**Scenic:** The positive experience for travelers on the Washington Heritage Trail is often punctuated by spectacular views of the panhandle's topography. Vantage points on the ridges offer sweeping vistas of the valleys between the ridges. Conversely, viewpoints in the valleys demonstrate the grandeur and sheer size of the adjoining mountains.

The aesthetic qualities and characteristics of the hamlets and towns further emphasize the scenery offered along the Washington Heritage Trail with ornate architecture, modest church steeples, and downtown streets.

*The picturesque village of Harpers Ferry is at the confluence of the Shenandoah and Potomac rivers and at the crossroads of major episodes of American history.*

## Highlights

Meandering through the stunning scenery of the West Virginia panhandle, this itinerary highlights some of the fascinating things to see and do along the way.

**Paw Paw Tunnel:** Just a mile north of the town of Paw Paw is the Paw Paw Tunnel in the C&O National Park. Built by the C&O Canal Company in the 1800s, the structure is a 3,118-foot passage through Sorrell Ridge lined with six million bricks.

**Berkeley Springs:** George Washington visited the colonial spa town of Berkeley Springs nearly a dozen times. Several Washington Heritage Trail sites are here, as well as full-service spas, award-winning eateries, antique malls, museums, and more.

**Berkeley Springs State Park:** Berkeley Springs State Park is in the center of town and features the original 74-degree warm mineral springs, including a public tap for free spring water. Two facilities operated by the State of West Virginia offer treatments to the public, including the historic Roman Bath House. Also at the park is George Washington's Bathtub, the only outdoor monument to presidential bathing.

**Belle Boyd House:** The Belle Boyd House in the historic town of Martinsburg houses several noteworthy Civil War history displays. Ms. Boyd was quite a successful Confederate spy during the war.

**Shepherdstown:** Shepherdstown began as a gristmill in 1739 and is the oldest incorporated town in West Virginia. Many 18th- and 19th-century buildings still exist, including the former Entler Hotel.

**Harpers Ferry:** In addition to George Washington, other famous fellows who had key roles in the history of this town include Thomas Jefferson, Meriwether Lewis, and Frederick Douglass. Harpers Ferry National Historic Park interprets the history of this fascinating town with tours, several museums, park exhibits, interpretive signage, special events, and activities.

**Charles Town:** John Brown was tried for treason, convicted, and hanged in the nearby village of Charles Town. Of the three treason trials in U.S. history, two of them have been tried here. The courthouse is open for guided tours.

**Jefferson County Museum:** The Jefferson County Museum in Charles Town has an extensive collection of artifacts, relics, photographs, documents, and more, all detailing the history of this town from Native American days through World War II, including the wagon on which John Brown was taken to the gallows.

# Lee's Retreat: On the Road to Appomattox, The Civil War's Final Days

*Lee's Retreat, an official Virginia Civil War trail, traces the historic route through lush farm country only slightly changed in the decades since.*

In the waning days of the Civil War, Union and Confederate armies raced across the Virginia countryside to the village of Appomattox, where Robert E. Lee ultimately surrendered to Ulysses S. Grant.

Civil War armies traveled mostly by foot, horse, and wagon. Today, motorists with an interest in American history can follow their path in a series of drives recalling the major campaigns in Virginia. You follow the course of action, often on the same roads used by the combatants. Directional signs guide you, and waysides along the route explain what happened. At each stop, you can tune your car radio (AM 1620) to hear more details.

The most poignant of the Civil War drives (because it culminated in the war's end), and the most scenic is Lee's Retreat, a 110-mile driving tour that follows the day-to-day, and sometimes hour-to-hour, progress of the armies west from Petersburg to Appomattox. Perched atop a broad, grass-covered hill, the village where the two armies converged has been preserved as a national historical park. Surrounded by acres of rolling green farmland and pastures, it looks much as it did on the day of Lee's surrender, April 9, 1865.

Essentially a history lesson, the drive provides plenty of opportunities for fun-filled recess. At Farmville, where Lee hoped to find food for his hungry troops, you can lunch in an outdoor café alongside the racing Appomattox River. Just outside Appomattox, little Holliday Lake State Park tempts with a fine sandy swimming beach.

## Quick Facts

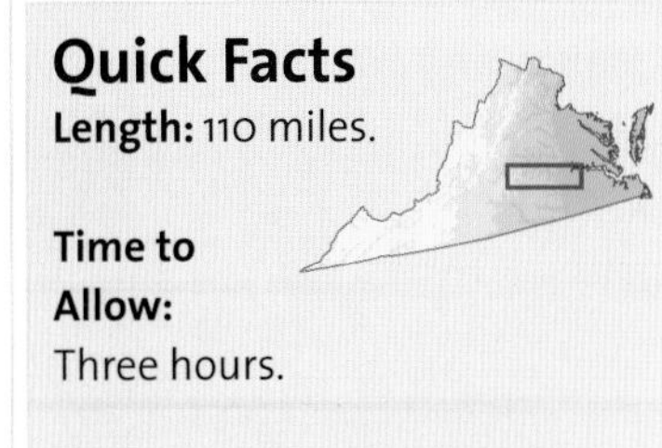

**Length:** 110 miles.

**Time to Allow:** Three hours.

**Considerations:** A brochure detailing the route of Lee's Retreat is available at Virginia tourism information offices and at the Petersburg Battlefield visitor center. The route can be driven year-round, although snow-covered roads are an occasional possibility from December into March.

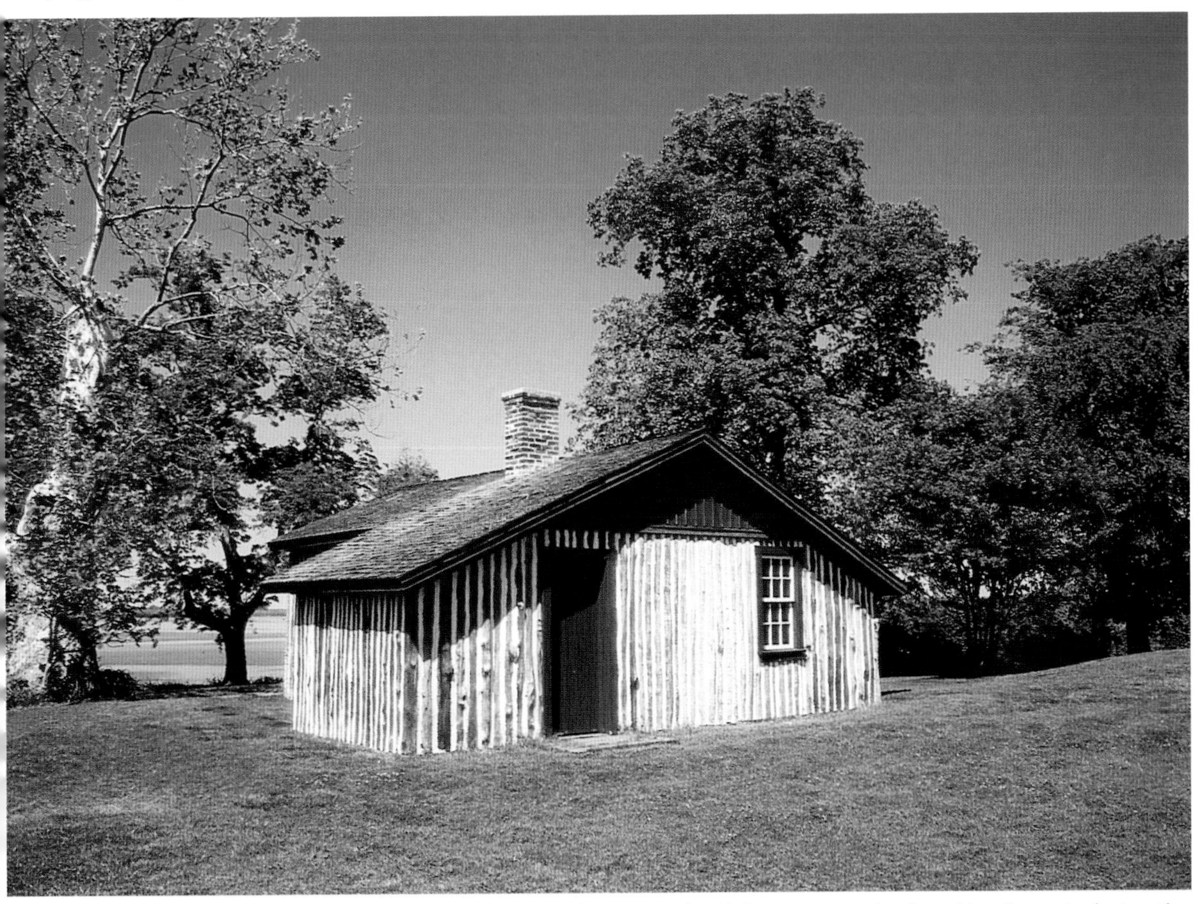

*Small and rustic, General Grant's cabin was meant to simply protect the Union commander from the elements during the long siege of Petersburg.*

## Highlights

Consider using the following itinerary as you travel Lee's Retreat.

**Siege Museum:** The civilian story of the Petersburg siege—the lives of the 18,000 people who endured both hunger and cannon bombardment—is told at the Siege Museum. During Christmas of 1864, exhibits relate, the townsfolk kept up their spirits by staging "starvation balls." Festive music was played, but there was no food on the plates.

**Petersburg National Battlefield:** Site of the nearly ten-month siege, the park's most notable sight is the Crater, symbol both of Union ingenuity and bungled opportunities. Early in the siege, military mining experts devised a plan to dig a nearly 500-foot tunnel under a Confederate fort to blow it up. The blast succeeded, creating a huge hole and leveling 500 yards of Confederate lines. But the Union attack force, stunned by the violent spectacle, delayed its advance, giving defenders a chance to rally.

*The tiny village of Appomattox includes not only the house where General Lee surrendered his Confederate troops to Union General Grant but also several other buildings such as Meek's Store.*



**Pamplin Historical Park and the National Museum of the Civil War Soldier:** Seven galleries re-create the life of the common soldier in camp, on the march, and in battle. The museum is located on the site of a Union attack that breached Lee's defenses shortly before his flight to Appomattox. A one-mile trail explores the battlefield.

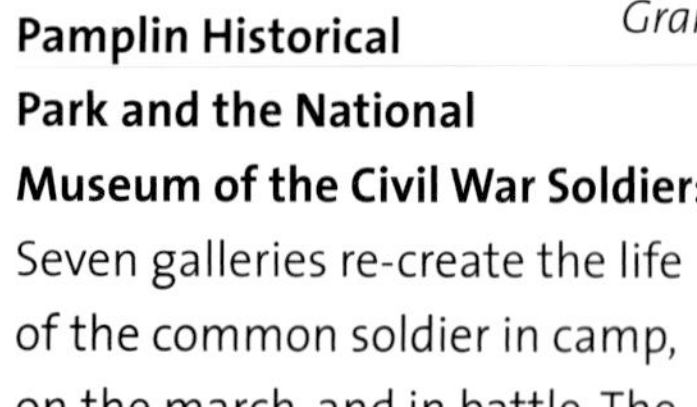


**Sailor's Creek Battlefield Historic State Park:** Fought here on April 6, 1865, dubbed "Black Thursday," the battle resulted in a harsh Confederate defeat. It proved a key in Lee's decision to surrender. His already shrunken army lost 7,700 men, including eight generals.

**Farmville:** A central Virginia commercial hub, Farmville boasts an attractive downtown center where visitors can browse for antiques and enjoy a lunch alongside the Appomattox River. Lee hoped to feed his army here, but the federal cavalry intruded. Just to the south, Twin Lakes State Park operates a swimming beach on Goodwin Lake.

**Appomattox Court House National Historical Park:** Other Civil War parks commemorate the violent clash of armies. Appomattox is a place of peace, a beautiful and quiet memorial to the end of four long years of war. As such, it honors the remarkable dignity and the generosity of the combatants in the final hours of the conflict.

**Holliday Lake State Park:** Ringed by public forest, the park is a recreational antidote to the somber story told on Lee's Retreat. Swimming, fishing, canoeing, rowboats, and paddleboats can be found here.

# Virginia's Skyline Drive

*Virginia's Skyline Drive flows like a stream among the high rocky peaks of the Blue Ridge Mountains in Shenandoah National Park, allowing majestic views of green farm valleys and a famous river far below.*

One of the wonders of America's national parks, the 105-mile-long Skyline Drive was built to show off the Blue Ridge scenery. On both sides of the winding road, tree-covered slopes drop sharply to the valley floor. To the east is the Piedmont, Virginia's rolling foothill country, where green pastures and golden fields form a patchwork quilt. To the west sprawls the broad Shenandoah Valley, where the Shenandoah River, fabled in song and story, makes repeated silvery loops.

From beginning to end, the drive tempts motorists to stop at nearly 80 overlooks, although only the most dedicated of sightseers would try to take in them all. Running north to south, the route parallels a 101-mile segment of the Georgia-to-Maine Appalachian Trail, which it crosses some 32 times. Almost any of these intersections is a good place to stretch the legs on a short stroll on the trail. During fall foliage season, the mountains are ablaze in color.

*Numerous overlooks along Virginia's Skyline Drive offer motorists an opportunity to stop and absorb the dramatic views.*

Deer are plentiful along the drive, so much so that it is wise to keep alert at the wheel. And it is not unusual to spot a startled mama bear and her cubs dashing into the woods to get out of your way. Shenandoah National Park is home to an estimated 300 to 500 bears. Learn along the way of the hardscrabble life of the Appalachian folk who once farmed these lush Blue Ridge slopes and hollows.

## Quick Facts

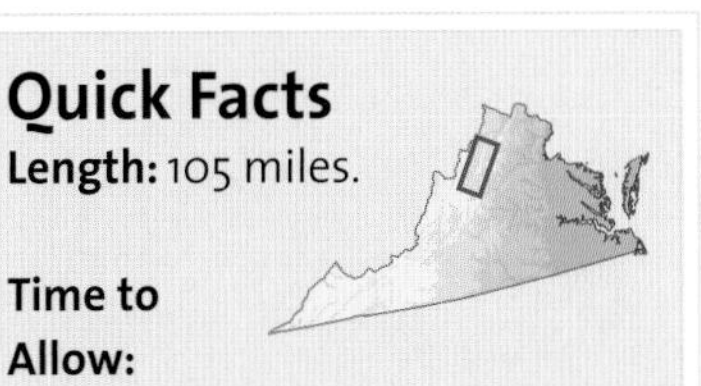

**Length:** 105 miles.

**Time to Allow:** Three to six hours.

**Considerations:** Shenandoah and Skyline Drive are open year-round, but most facilities (lodging, dining, service stations, and campgrounds) are closed from late fall to early spring. Snow, ice, and blinding fog can shut down the road temporarily in winter. The fall foliage show is spectacular, but weekend motorists in October often create near gridlock conditions on Skyline Drive.

## Highlights

Start this beautiful tour in Front Royal, and end in Rockfish Gap.

**Front Royal:** A small city, Front Royal is both a gateway to Shenandoah National Park and Shenandoah Valley. Nearby visit Linden Vineyards; Cedar Creek Battlefield; and Belle Grove with its garden and orchard, maintained by the National Trust for Historic Preservation. At Shenandoah River State Park, go for a three-mile, three-hour tube float (with shuttle service).

**Dickey Ridge Visitor Center:** This rustically appealing old structure straddles the narrow crest of the Blue Ridge, presenting views east and west. Take in the 12-minute introductory slide show, "Gentle Wilderness," and learn about the Appalachian Mountain people who once lived here. Stroll the Fox Hollow Trail to the Fox Family homestead.

**Hogback Overlook:** When a haze doesn't intrude, you can see the South Fork of the Shenandoah River and its many bends.

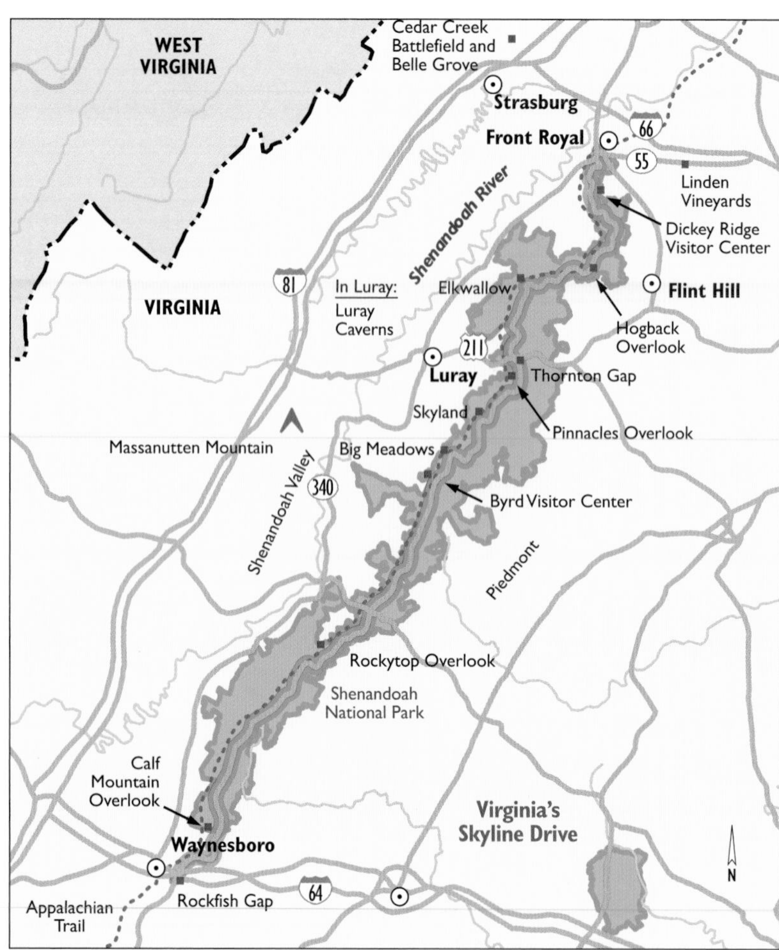




**Elkwallow:** The camp store and service station here are open May through October. The picnic ground is open year-round.

**Thornton Gap:** Panorama Restaurant, a park facility, is open from May through October. From this park entrance, descend west to the town of Luray and Luray Caverns, one of the East's largest commercial caves. It is noted for its "stalacpipe" organ, which produces symphonic serenades from a rock formation.

**Pinnacles Overlook:** Skyline Drive intersects the Appalachian Trail here. Stretch your legs on a short hike north or south. You might run across hikers en route from Georgia to Maine with interesting tales to tell.

**Skyland:** The 177-room lodge with a restaurant is the oldest and largest of Shenandoah's two main lodges. Occupying motel-like wings, the rooms are plain but comfortable. Many have outstanding valley views. You will find the horse stables here.

**Big Meadows:** The park's other major lodge and restaurant, Big Meadows offers 25 rooms in the main building and 72 more rooms in rustic cabins. Built in 1939 of stone cut from nearby Massanutten Mountain, its interior is paneled with native chestnut, a tree now nearly extinct because of the chestnut blight. Learn more about the history of Shenandoah and Skyline Drive at the Byrd Visitor Center.

**Rockytop Overlook:** Take in a good view of the Big Run watershed and its wild canyon country.

**Calf Mountain Overlook:** Before this drive ends, enjoy a stunning 360-degree view.

**Rockfish Gap:** Skyline Drive ends (or begins) here on the outskirts of Waynesboro. Straight ahead is the beginning of the 469-mile Blue Ridge Parkway, another scenic national park route tracing the Blue Ridge south through western Virginia and North Carolina to the entrance to Great Smoky Mountain National Park. Waynesboro is about a 30-minute drive from Charlottesville, home of Thomas Jefferson's Monticello—America's most intriguing presidential residence.

*Luray Caverns are ancient in their origins yet familiar in the names of their formations. Here are the famous "fried eggs."*

# Oklahoma's Little Smokies

*This drive meanders through southeastern Oklahoma, a mountainous landscape of rivers, lakes, and forests that offer plenty of outdoor recreational choices. Along the way, it explores the state's rich Native American heritage.*

Oklahomans call southeastern Oklahoma's rumpled terrain the "Little Smokies." Not so lofty as the Great Smoky Mountains, these rugged green mountains boast an abundance of tall timber, splashing streams, and crystal-clear lakes. This is a drive both for outdoor lovers who simply want to savor the views and for those more active travelers eager to tackle a hiking trail, paddle a canoe, or test their skill at fly-fishing. Swimming beaches at several lakes provide an inviting break from touring.

For much of the way, the north-to-south route traverses sprawling 1.8-million-acre Ouachita National Forest, which drapes across the Ouachita Mountains on the border of Oklahoma and Arkansas. Deer and black bear are abundant—this part of Oklahoma claims to be the "deer capital of the world." Ouachita is the French version of an American Indian word that means "good hunting grounds." Colorful wildflowers carpet the meadows along the road. The fall foliage is renowned as some of the finest.

A part of the forest, called the Winding Stair Mountain National Recreation Area, has been designated primarily for outdoor fun. Trails range in difficulty from the rigorous—for example, the 192-mile Ouachita National Recreation Trail, which intersects this drive—to the comfortably easy. Almost anyone can manage a trio of short, gentle nature trails at the Robert S. Kerr Memorial Arboretum.

Unless you are a resident of the Sooner State, signs that declare this corner of the state Kiamichi Country may puzzle you. The official Oklahoma Travel Guide also uses the phrase. Kiamichi, tourism officials explain, is a French word for a "water bird." French explorers, fur trappers, and traders were early visitors here.

The drive begins among the farmlands and orchards of Spiro, where a dozen ancient mounds display evidence of the people who lived here from 850 to 1450. And it ends in the state's far southeast corner at Idabel, the state's "dogwood capital" and home to the Museum of the Red River. The museum houses what is considered some of the finest art and artifacts from the earliest residents here.

## Quick Facts

**Length:** 130 miles.

**Time to allow:** Six to eight hours.

**Considerations:** The most comfortable seasons for touring are spring, when the dogwoods and other flowering trees and shrubs are in bloom, and in fall for the foliage show. Winter can be damp; summers are hot and humid.

*The Victor Area of Lake Wister State Park offers visitors not only superb scenery, but also such amenities as a boat ramp, picnic area, and playground.*

## Highlights

Begin in the prehistoric Spiro Mounds Archaeological Park. Travel through history to the Museum of the Red River.

**Spiro Mounds Archaeological Park:** An important prehistoric American Indian site, the park harbors 11 grass-topped mounds. They formed a complex that began as a small farming village and grew to become an important trading, religious, and political center flourishing between 850 and 1450. Workers hauling basket loads of dirt constructed the mounds in layers. Initially there were 12 mounds, but a burial mound was excavated haphazardly in the 1930s for its numerous artifacts of stone, copper, shell, basketry, and fabric.

**Robert S. Kerr Museum:** The mansion of former U.S. Senator Robert S. Kerr, who was the state's first native-born governor, is a grand home built of such materials as stone, oak, pine, and cedar. Adjacent to it is a museum of eastern Oklahoma pioneer history.

**Robert S. Kerr Memorial Arboretum and Botanical Area:** An 8,000-acre preserve, the arboretum shelters special plant communities. At the Kerr Nature Center, three short interpretive trails provide an introduction to the region's natural heritage.

**Cavanal Hill:** Dubbed "the world's highest hill," this pine-draped knob rises to 1,999 feet, just 12 inches short of being officially designated a mountain. It stands within the city limits of Poteau, a onetime pioneer outpost—Poteau comes from the French word for "post." Cavanal is visible from almost anywhere in town. A 4½-mile paved road climbs past beautiful new homes edging up its slopes. At the summit, a grand panoramic view of the Poteau River Valley is spread before you.

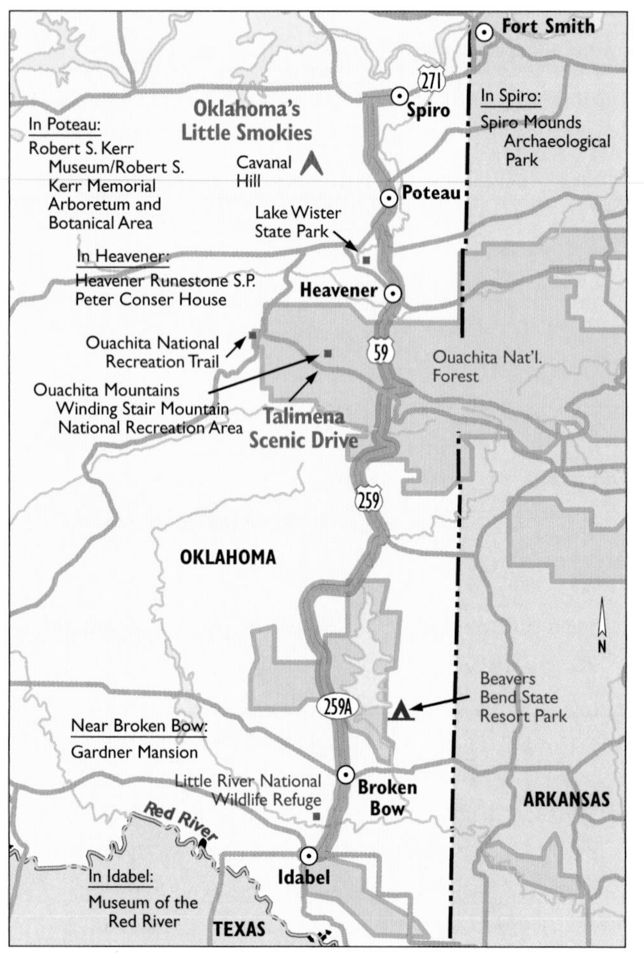


**Lake Wister State Park:** Wrapped by mountain slopes cloaked in dogwood, spruce, and ponderosa pine, the park takes full advantage of 7,300-acre Lake Wister. Park officials claim the fishing is among the best in the state. A beach invites swimming, and concessionaires provide bike rentals and waterskiing options.

**Heavener Runestone State Park:** A historical curiosity, the Heavener runestone is a 12-foot-tall slab of stone onto which eight letters have been carved. Research suggests the stone is a Norse land claim dating back to the 8th century. The theory is that Norse explorers entered the Gulf of Mexico, found the Mississippi River, and sailed up two tributaries, the Arkansas and Poteau Rivers, about 750. A visitor center at the 50-acre park on Poteau Mountain provides details.

**Peter Conser House:** Built in 1894, the two-story, white-frame house was the home of Peter Conser, a Choctaw statesman, wealthy landowner, and leading member of the Choctaw Lighthorsemen. A law-enforcement group, the Lighthorsemen are considered the Choctaw equivalent of the Texas Rangers; they patrolled the Choctaw region of the old American Indian Territory. The house, restored to pre-statehood condition, displays antiques and photographs of Oklahoma history.

**Talimena Scenic Drive:** This 54-mile drive (Oklahoma Route 1/Arkansas Route 88) winds along mountain ridge tops through the Ouachita National Forest. Cross this scenic drive as it dips between Winding Stair and Rich Mountains—about 18 miles south of Heavener. Make a detour west here to enjoy some of the panoramic vistas.

**Winding Stair Mountain National Recreation Area:** A part of Ouachita National Forest, the 26,445 acres of the Winding Stair Mountain National Recreation Area were set aside in 1988 for recreational purposes by President Ronald Reagan. A place of forest-clad mountains and majestic vistas, it is also noted for odd geologic formations, an abundance of lakes and streams, a rich natural and cultural history, and plentiful wildlife. The Ouachita is the South's oldest national forest.

**Beavers Bend State Resort Park:** Overlooking huge Broken Bow Lake, which boasts a 180-mile shoreline, the park is a popular vacation destination. A 40-room lodge and 47 cabins provide overnight lodging, and there's a wide choice of recreational activities, including paddleboating, horseback riding, hayrides, miniature golf, and trout fishing. The Forest Heritage Center Museum features dioramas describing the evolution of local forests.

**Gardner Mansion:** The antebellum-style mansion south of Broken Bow, completed in 1884, was the home of Jefferson Gardner, principal chief of the Choctaw Nation from 1894 to 1896. Choctaw artifacts and pioneer relics are displayed in the mansion.

**Little River National Wildlife Refuge:** A wet bottomland, this 15,000-acre refuge is habitat for waterfowl, principally mallard and wood duck. Ancient American Indian mounds exist on the refuge, but they have been disturbed by early forestry practices. A three-mile graded road leads though a forest to the hardwood bottomland and Little River.

**Museum of the Red River:** The museum houses a collection of more than 20,000 Native American objects. They focus both on the local mound-building groups and the Choctaw Indians. The Choctaws were moved into Oklahoma from their Mississippi homelands in the 1830s. The collection also includes contemporary native arts and crafts from throughout the Americas.

# Crowley's Ridge Parkway

*An odd geological formation duplicated only in Siberia, Crowley's Ridge rises and runs for miles. A forested region, it harbors five state parks and a national forest offering varied outdoor recreation.*

Part of a multistate byway; see also Missouri.

Imagine a geological wonder that took wind, water, and ice together 50 million years to create. Now imagine yourself enjoying the dramatic views and rolling topography you'll experience as you drive along on top of it! Named for the earliest settler in the area, Crowley's Ridge is one of only two such formations in the world, and the Crowley's Ridge Parkway allows you to experience it firsthand. This unique, crescent-shaped ridge rises 100 to 250 feet above the flat delta lands that surround it and boasts plants found nowhere else, along with many beautiful native wildflowers and cacti.

Along with its natural qualities, the ridge and surrounding areas are rich in Southern history and culture. Take the time to stop at one of the many fresh fruit and vegetable stands or browse the shelves at an old-fashioned country store. As you travel the byway, you will also find numerous museums, Civil War battlefields, African-American heritage sites, culture centers, and festivals. If you prefer the great outdoors, be sure to visit one of five nearby state parks or the St. Francis National Forest. Along the way, you'll discover opportunities for world-class waterfowl hunting, fishing, boating, picnicking, hunting, camping, golf, bird-watching, and more. With all of these recreational opportunities at your fingertips, you're sure to have a good time.

*The Hemingway barn studio in Piggott is on the National Historic Register. Part of Hemingway's* A Farewell to Arms *was written here.*

## Intrinsic Qualities

**Archaeological:** The earliest recorded cemetery in the new world is found in Greene County on Crowley's Ridge. Excavated in 1974, the Sloan Site was both home and burial ground for a small group of Native Americans who lived here approximately 10,500 years ago. Living in small bands and in semipermanent villages, they established the earliest documented cemetery in North America.

The Mississippian site of Parkin is now the Parkin Archaeological State Park in Cross Country, providing a museum, a visitor center, a walking tour, and a research station. This site features a rectangular planned village of 400 houses, with a plaza surrounding mounds and evidence of a large population that interacted with the DeSoto Expedition.

**Cultural:** Culturally, the most notable part of this byway is the historic development of the Delta Blues at Helena. The Delta Cultural Center and the annual King Biscuit Blues Festival keep the legacy alive.

**Historical:** The Civil War battlefield at Chalk Bluff plays a key role in understanding the historical importance of Crowley's Ridge. A site of significant battles, this area has remained largely undisturbed since Civil War times. The railroad also played a significant role in the history of Crowley's Ridge. The arrival of the railroads to remove harvested timber from the ridge and delta led to the beginning and end of many towns. After the railroads traversed the ridge, numerous towns were established along the tracks. Several county seats were abandoned and relocated near the railroads, as well.

Also significant is that one of the world's most-famous American authors had great connections with this area; the Hemingway-Pfeiffer Museum and Conference Center shares the story of Ernest Hemingway's time in Piggott.

**Natural:** The natural intrinsic qualities found along this byway

### Quick Facts

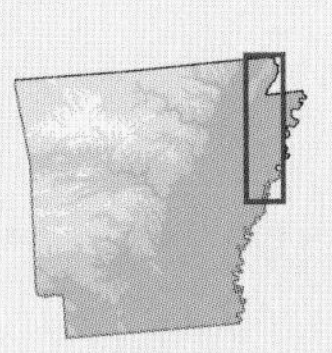

**Length:** 212 miles.

**Time to allow:** Six hours.

**Considerations:** The entire length of the route is paved, with the exception of an interesting $11\frac{1}{2}$-mile stretch of well-maintained gravel road through the St. Francis National Forest. An alternative to the gravel road is Route 1 south of Marianna. Watch your engine temperature so that you notice if it begins to increase.

are unique to the Crowley's Ridge geographic formation. Simply stated, this ridge is the only known erosional remnant in North America. This narrow ribbon of land, some 200 miles in length, was formed during the tremendous erosional action of the Pleistocene Period. The Mississippi and Ohio rivers formed huge glacial sluiceways that altered the face of the landscape. An amazing sliver of erosional remnant survived, with elevations up to 200 feet above the delta topography.

The combination of the loess soil deposited on the ridge and the ridge's topography did not support large-scale agriculture, thus preserving unique plant communities found here. Along Crowley's Ridge, a mixture of plant communities and a diversity of species respond to abrupt changes in soil type, exposure, soil moisture levels, and slope.

**Recreational:** In terms of recreation, the ridge is home to five state parks, world-class waterfowl hunting, and excellent fishing. Numerous trails and outdoor recreation areas abound.

**Scenic:** This byway's scenic intrinsic qualities are associated with the natural plant communities found on the ridge, as well as the rolling topography, which creates picturesque and dramatic viewsheds. Spring and fall find their most dramatic expressions in the foliage, providing beauty and aesthetics. In addition, the proliferation of wildflowers and unique plant communities in the spring, summer, and fall are enhanced by the wildflower trail.

## Highlights

Though Crowley's Ridge Parkway has a variety of stories to tell, ranging from geologic to human, ancient to modern, this itinerary gives a taste of how the Civil War affected the Confederate state of Arkansas, bordering the Union-aligned Missouri, as both sides used the road on Crowley's Ridge.

**Chalk Bluff Battlefield Park and Natural Area:** At the northernmost edge of the Arkansas section of Crowley's Ridge Parkway, begin the journey at Chalk Bluff Battlefield Park and Natural Area. A prosperous town before the railroad bypassed it in the 1880s, the village of Chalk Bluff saw many skirmishes during the Civil War. Interpretive signage along a walking trail explains the battles and history of Chalk Bluff.

**Crowley's Ridge State Park:** Crowley's Ridge State Park, though not having any particular Civil War sites, does give the visitor some spectacular bird's-eye views of the surrounding delta and an understanding of why this parkway was so important to travelers navigating the eastern edge of Arkansas. Campsites, picnic areas, and hiking trails along with year-round interpretive programs give visitors an opportunity to enjoy this park.

**Forrest City:** Farther south on the byway is the town of Forrest City, named for Confederate General Nathan Bedford Forrest. During the Civil War, soldiers stopped here near Stuart Springs, and those who were injured were treated in the spring's healing waters. Today Stuart Springs is a 16-acre park and is listed on the National Register of Historic Places.

**Helena:** The town of Helena, a picturesque town situated strategically along the Mississippi River, is at the southernmost part of the Crowley's Ridge Parkway and has several Civil War sites to visit.

**Civil War Batteries:** Helena was a Union stronghold coveted by the Confederates, and four Civil War batteries can be viewed by visitors.

**Helena Confederate Cemetery:** Helena Confederate Cemetery was created in 1869 in the southwest corner of Maple Hill Cemetery. More than half of those interred here were victims of the unsuccessful Confederate raid on the Union stronghold at Helena on July 4, 1863. Many veterans of the war, including Confederate General Patrick Cleburne, also chose to be buried here.

**Delta Cultural Center:** In the historic district of downtown Helena is the Delta Cultural Center located on Missouri Street. Housed in a historic railroad depot, the center features exhibits about frontier life, the unique culture of the people of the Mississippi River, railroading, and the Civil War story in Arkansas. The Delta Cultural Center also spreads out to encompass a visitor center on Cherry Street, the Moore-Hornor House, and the Cherry Street Pavilion.

# GREAT RIVER ROAD 

*The road navigates the state's delta, a region of rivers, lakes, and swamps. This is a cultural drive, glimpsing a southern culture in transition from agricultural to modern industrial.*

PART OF A MULTISTATE BYWAY; SEE ALSO ILLINOIS, IOWA, MINNESOTA, AND WISCONSIN.

## Quick Facts

**Length:** 159 miles.

**Time to Allow:** Three hours.

**Considerations:** During the winter, there may be some icy patches in rural parts of the roadway. There is one 11½-mile segment through the St. Francis National Forest that is gravel, but it is well maintained and accessible for all vehicles.

Look out over the river, and try to comprehend the complex layers of history that have been acted out along its banks. Imagine the large communities of the Hopewell Indian culture—the most complex society in North America (circa A.D. 700 to 1400)—and early French colonial settlements and fortifications. Or reflect on the frightened, cautious, and optimistic eyes of slaves seeking freedom on the Underground Railroad. Watch as nearly 15 percent of the nation's shipping passes through the river's complex system of locks and dams. And look upward and see that the river flows under the spreading wings of the newly thriving American bald eagle.

## Highlights

The Arkansas section of the Great River Road has some varied architectural highlights. You will want to be sure to see them as you travel from north to south on the southern part of the byway.

**Marianna:** Begin in Marianna at the Chamber of Commerce, and pick up a map of the walking tour of the historic downtown district. Around 45 of the buildings here are listed on the National Register of Historic Places. Also in Marianna is the Missouri–Pacific railroad depot, built in 1915.

**Helena:** Helena is a fascinating port town with a mixture of Mississippi River charm, blues music, Civil War history, and a generous blend of building styles. Helena's Delta Cultural Center tells the story of this area. Also downtown is the Cherry Street Pavilion, a former theater with grand Spanish Colonial Revival detailing, and more.

**First United Methodist Church:** In DeWitt is the First United Methodist Church. It is an excellent example of Charles Thompson architecture.

**Rohwer Relocation Center:** Though only a few scattered building foundations and the cemetery remain, the Rohwer Relocation Center had a very basic functional style of architecture. The camp was opened in 1942 to intern Japanese American evacuees from California during World War II. The Rohwer Memorial Cemetery is a National Historic Landmark.

**Arkansas City:** Arkansas City is one of the few remaining examples of an old Mississippi River town in eastern Arkansas. A walking tour of the historic downtown area yields a variety of building styles.

**Eudora:** Eudora has some interesting sites. The Dr. A. G. Anderson House is a restored 1901 home. The Rubye and Henry Connerly Museum offers a quaint bit of local history in a historic grocery store. And the American Legion Post is a 1934 rustic-style structure.

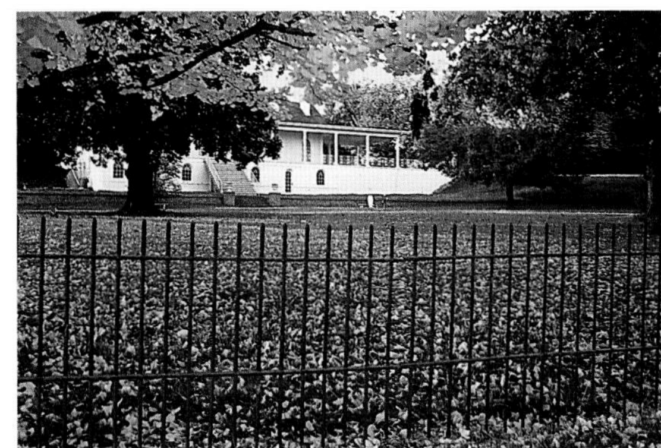

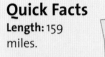

*This house in Helena was built in 1826 and is on the National Historic Register.*

# Cherohala Skyway

*Opened in 1996, the skyway yields mile-high mountain and woodland vistas as it winds into the heartland of the Cherokee Indian ancestral territories. Hiking, fishing, and wildlife spotting tempt you from behind the wheel.*

This is a multistate byway; it also runs through North Carolina.

Experience first-hand amazingly towering trees by traveling the Cherohala Skyway in North Carolina and Tennessee, and you will agree that nothing could be lovelier. Visit in the fall when vibrant vermilion, golden, and orange leaves drape the trees surrounding the skyway. Or plan a leisurely summer road trip, leaving plenty of time for picnics, hikes, fishing, or many of the other activities available on the Cherohala Skyway.

The Tellico River parallels part of the skyway, delighting canoeists and kayakers from all over. Follow the river with paddle in hand, and bask in the sunlight and beauty of the surrounding forests. With hundreds of miles of hiking trails traversing the national forests, you're bound to find a favorite. Botany lovers will want to whip out their sketchbooks to capture in ink some of the 2,000 native plant species that thrive around the Cherohala Skyway. Catch your breath by pausing to admire the wildflowers sprinkled throughout the landscape in the spring, or make camp at one of the many campgrounds and spend several days exploring the backwoods.



## Highlights

With spectacular views it is hard to leave the heights of the Cherohala Skyway, but some of the most interesting natural and Native American sites are just beyond the byway. A few of those venues are highlighted here.

**Fort Loudoun State Historic Park:** Nearby is Fort Loudoun State Historic Park. Operating from 1756 to 1760, Fort Loudoun was built by the British to protect the Cherokee during the French and Indian War. Though the original buildings are long gone, the current replica is historically accurate. Activities allow visitor participation, and a visitor center explains the fort's role in the French and Indian War.

**Sequoyah Birthplace Museum:** Learn about the lifestyle of the Overhill Cherokee at the Sequoyah Birthplace Museum. Born near where the museum stands and roaming the area as a boy, Sequoyah was born in 1776 and was the man who gave the Cherokee nation, formerly illiterate, its unique writing system. The museum is the only tribally owned and operated historical attraction in the state.

**Vonore Heritage Museum:** Before leaving the Tellico Lake area, be sure to stop at the Vonore Heritage Museum on Church Street. The museum features farm implements and tools, household items, and lovingly created miniature replicas of local historic venues. Also exhibited are many items donated by local citizens to help in the telling of the Vonore story.

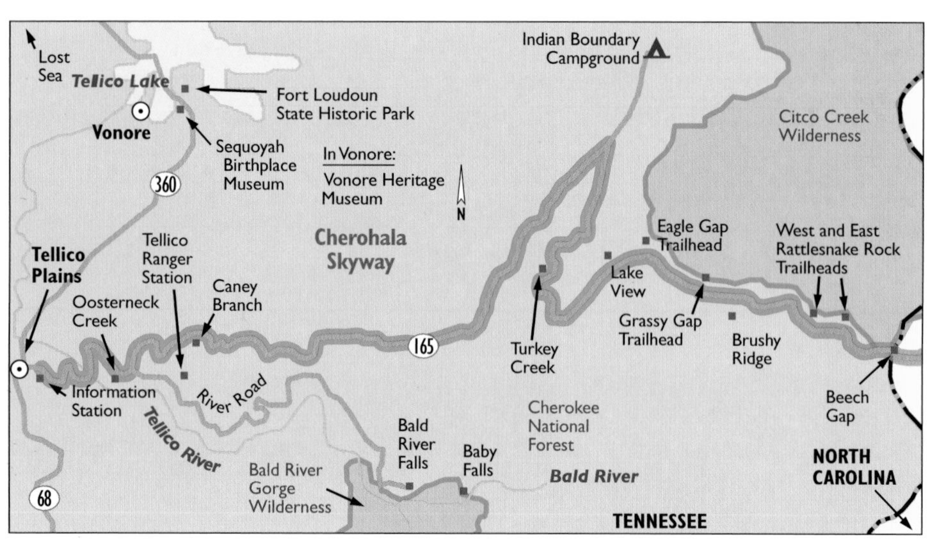


**Quick Facts**

**Length:** 43 miles.

**Time to Allow:** One hour and 45 minutes.

**Considerations:** There are no services available on the skyway. However, there are services available in Tellico Plains and Robbinsville in North Carolina. Byway visitors should be aware that there are some grades as steep as 9 percent. Use caution on the skyway, but take particular care during winter storms. Roads may close during heavy snows.

**Lost Sea:** Descending even farther from the heights of the Cherohala Skyway at the town of Sweetwater is the Lost Sea, America's largest underground lake. Part of the larger Craighead Cavern system known and used by the Cherokee, the lake is extensive, its depths never having been completely mapped. Glass-bottomed boats carry visitors into the Lost Sea, a Registered National Landmark, where rare and beautiful geologic formations in massive cavernous rooms can be seen.

**Bald River Falls and Baby Falls:** Viewable from the car or via hiking paths, Bald River Falls in the Cherokee National Forest is a stunning sight as the plunge over rock

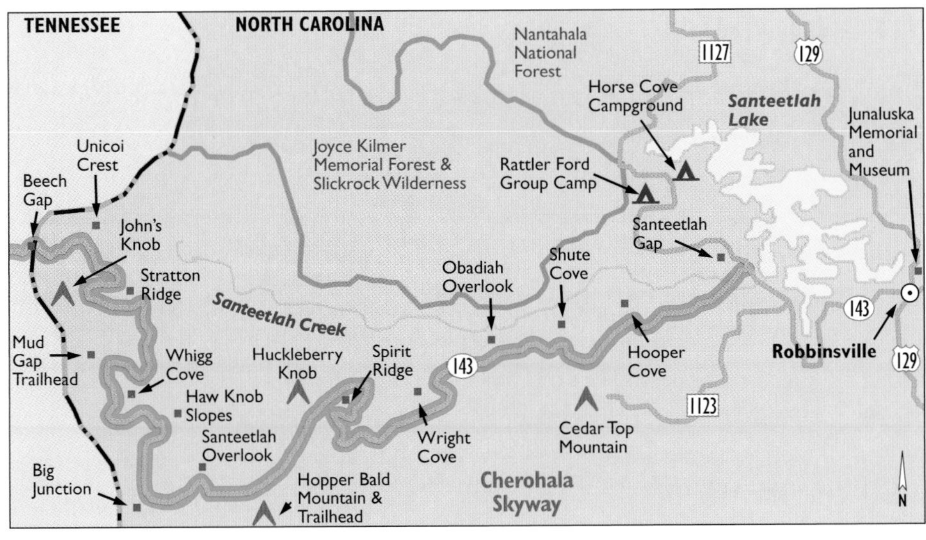


outcroppings makes for an 80-foot white-water falls. As an added bonus, just a quarter of a mile up the road is Baby Falls, a playpen for kayakers and swimmers.

**Stratton Ridge:** Be on the lookout on the left side of the road for the next noteworthy overlook. At 4,420 feet, Stratton Ridge looks over lower portions of the Cherohala Skyway and provides information about the byway and surrounding area on informational kiosks. Picnic tables and restroom facilities are also available here.

**Spirit Ridge Overlook:** From the roadway take a gentle walk less than a mile through the hardwood forest to the Spirit Ridge overlook. Here visitors get seemingly unending panoramas of splendid mountaintops. The trail leading to the overlook is wheelchair accessible and is appropriate for people of all ages.

**Hooper Cove:** Hooper Cove is an open area to get out and enjoy the view from this 3,100-foot high vantage point. Four picnic tables give visitors an opportunity to eat a bit while drinking in the beautiful vistas. This is a great location for fabulous photos of the Santeetlah Creek rushing below.

**Joyce Kilmer Memorial Forest:** Just north of the Cherohala Skyway is the Joyce Kilmer Memorial Forest. Once the uncharted hunting ground of the Cherokee, the best way to see the Memorial Forest is on foot using the Joyce Kilmer National Recreation Trail. It is an easy trail, possible for novices and families with small children to enjoy. A tribute to World War I soldier and author of the poem "Trees," the forest is a rare and outstanding gathering of virgin Appalachian hardwood trees, some as old as 400 years and as large as 20 feet in circumference at their base.

**Junaluska Memorial and Museum:** From Robbinsville just east of the Cherohala Skyway is the Junaluska Memorial and Museum. A warrior for both the Cherokee and Americans, Junaluska saved Andrew Jackson's life at the Battle of Horseshoe Bend. Ironically, it was Jackson who then turned around and ordered the forced relocation of the Cherokee to Oklahoma via what was to become known as the Trail of Tears. Not only does this memorial and museum honor Junaluska but it also portrays the history and culture of the Cherokee people.

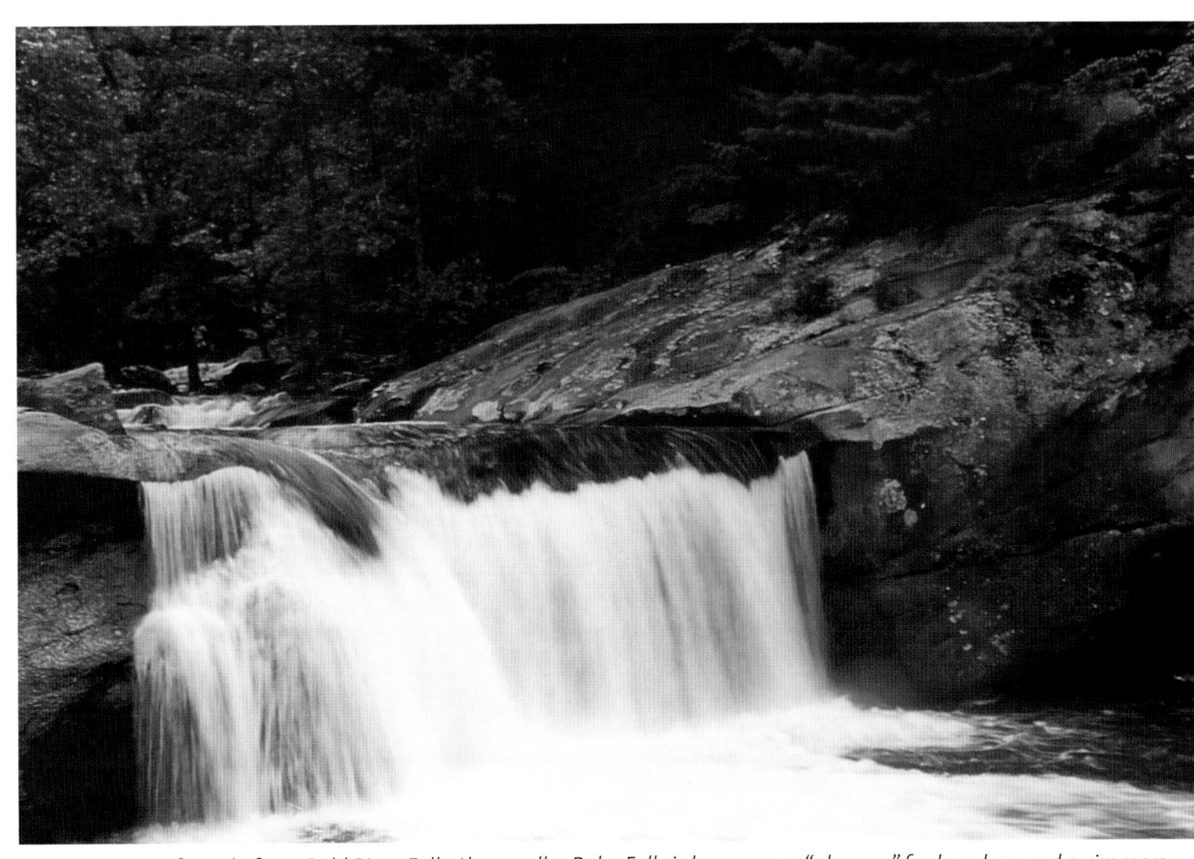
*Just a quarter of a mile from Bald River Falls, the smaller Baby Falls is known as a "playpen" for kayakers and swimmers.*

# Blue Ridge Parkway

*Unhampered by stop signs and stoplights, the parkway glides along mountain ridge tops, offering nonstop views right and left of quilted fields and toylike towns far below.*

The Blue Ridge Parkway is a scenic drive that crests the southern Appalachian Mountains and takes you through a myriad of natural, cultural, and recreational places. Many people drive the Blue Ridge Parkway for its natural botanical qualities. And where there is lush vegetation, there is also abundant wildlife.

The diverse history and culture of the southern Appalachians are described at many overlooks and facilities along the parkway.

*Many of the trees of Mount Mitchell are being destroyed by pests, including Balsam Woolly Adegid.*

## Intrinsic Qualities

**Archaeological:** You'll find many signs of Native American culture and influence along the Blue Ridge Parkway, including those of the Cherokee. Many of the fields still visible at the base of the mountains date back centuries to ancient Native American agricultural methods of burning and deadening the trees and underbrush to provide needed grazing and crop land. Mountain and river names along the parkway also reflect the Native American influence. In North Carolina, the parkway enters the Qualla Reservation. Remnants of early European settlements and homesteads are also found all along the parkway.

**Cultural:** Along the Blue Ridge Parkway, evidence of the local cultures is found in communities, museums, and shops.

Mountain handicrafts are one of the most popular attractions along the byway, and traditional and contemporary crafts and music thrive in the Blue Ridge Mountains. Along the parkway in North Carolina are several places to view and purchase locally made items. The Folk Art Center in Asheville offers an impressive collection of crafts.

**Historical:** The parkway was conceived as a link between the Shenandoah National Park in Virginia and the Great Smoky Mountains National Park in North Carolina and Tennessee. The vision came to fruition in 1935. The idea to build the parkway resulted from a combination of many factors, the primary one being the need to create jobs for those people suffering from the Great Depression and for poor mountain families.

World War II halted construction, but road-building resumed soon after the war ended. By 1968, the only task left was the completion of a seven-mile stretch around North Carolina's Grandfather Mountain. In order to preserve the fragile environment on the steep slopes of the mountain, the Linn Cove Viaduct, a 1,200-foot suspended section of the parkway, was designed and built. Considered an engineering marvel, it represents one of the most successful fusions of road and landscape on the parkway. The Blue Ridge Parkway was officially dedicated in 1987, 52 years after the groundbreaking.

**Natural:** The creation of the Blue Ridge Mountains, perhaps hundreds of millions of years in the geologic past, was both violent and dramatic. Today, you can witness the flip side to the mountain-building story—the mountain's gradual destruction. The slow, steady forces of wind, water, and chemical decomposition have reduced the Blue Ridge from Sierralike proportions to the low profile of the world's oldest mountain range.

Diversity is the key word when understanding the ecology of the Appalachian Mountains. Park

### Quick Facts

**Length:** 241 miles.

**Time to Allow:** Two to three days.

**Considerations:** Avoid traveling the parkway during periods of fog, snow, and ice. Bring a lightweight jacket for cool nights from spring through fall. Service stations are limited, but access points along the parkway allow for refueling in nearby communities. Also, watch for crossing deer. Swimming is not allowed in parkway lakes and ponds.

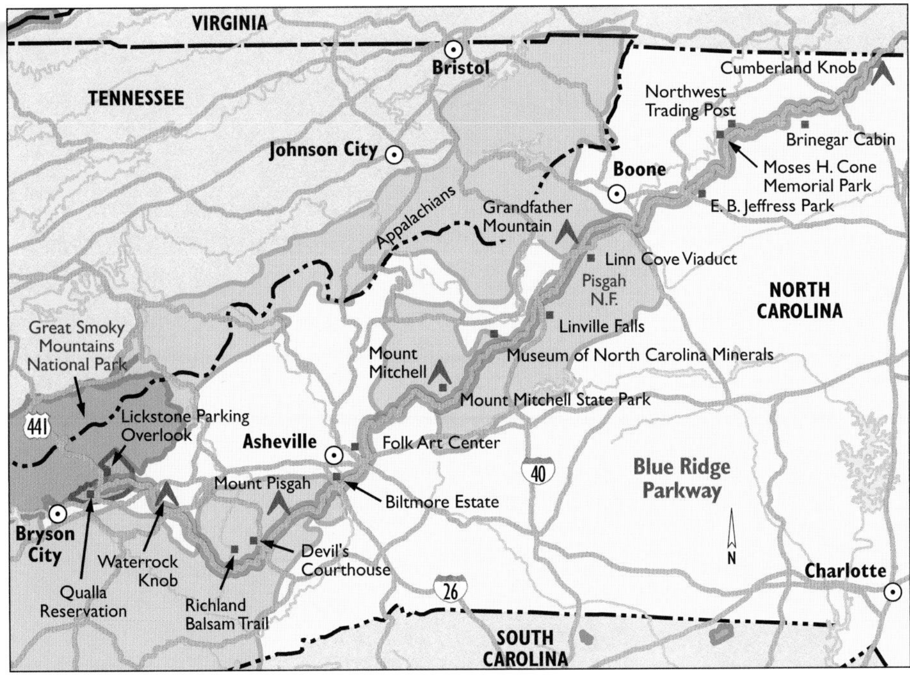


biologists have identified 1,250 kinds of vascular plants, 25 of which are rare or endangered. The reasons for this wide diversity are numerous. Elevation is a key factor, with parkway lands as low as 650 feet above sea level and as high as 6,047 feet above sea level. The parkway is also oriented on a north–south axis, with its two ends far apart.

Beginning at the parkway's lowest elevations and climbing up to its highest, you notice numerous transitions among a variety of forest types. Interspersed among these various forest types are small habitats, such as mountain bogs and heath balds. Many species of animals find their niche in these small pockets of habitat. Bog turtles and Gray's lily thrive in mountain bogs. Sheltered, wet coves are excellent for finding salamanders. A hemlock cove is a great place to find red squirrels.

Black-capped chickadees replace the Carolina chickadees as you climb up toward the spruce-fir forest. And of course, the Blue Ridge Mountains are also home to mountain lions, eagles, and even bears. For birding enthusiasts, the parkway offers a never-ending supply of beautiful birds.

**Recreational:** The very nature of the Blue Ridge Parkway allows for outstanding recreational opportunities, such as camping, hiking, cycling, swimming, and kayaking.

Festivals and events are often occurring in local towns and communities, from sports to outdoor adventure to drama to folk art.

**Scenic:** The parkway combines awesome natural beauty with the pioneer history of gristmills, weathered cabins, and split-rail fences to create the country's most popular national park. It encompasses a world of mountain forests, wildlife, and wildflowers thousands of feet above a patchwork of villages, fields, and farms.

## Highlights

The following points of interest are excellent sights along or just off of the byway.

**Cumberland Knob:** Cumberland Knob, at 2,885 feet, is a great spot to walk through fields and woodlands.

**Brinegar Cabin:** Brinegar Cabin was built by Martin Brinegar about 1880 and lived in until the 1930s; it is still standing.

**Northwest Trading Post:** Northwest Trading Post keeps alive the old crafts within North Carolina's 11 northwestern counties.

**Moses H. Cone Memorial Park:** This park has 25 miles of carriage roads that are ideal for hiking and horseback riding.

**E. B. Jeffress Park:** E. B. Jeffress Park has a self-guided trail to the Cascades and another trail to the old cabin and church.

**Linn Cove Viaduct:** Linn Cove Viaduct, a highlight of the parkway and a design and engineering marvel, skirts the side of Grandfather Mountain.

**Linville Falls:** Linville Falls roars through a dramatic, rugged gorge. Take trails to overlooks.

**Museum of North Carolina Minerals:** This museum has a display of the state's mineral wealth.

**Mount Mitchell State Park:** This park has a picnic area and a lookout tower. It is the highest point east of the Mississippi River.

**Folk Art Center:** This center offers sales and exhibits of traditional and contemporary crafts of the Appalachian Region.

**Biltmore Estate:** This is George Vanderbilt's impressive 250-room mansion and grounds landscaped by Frederick Law Olmstead, who was the designer of Central Park.

**Mount Pisgah:** Part of the Biltmore Estate became home of the first U.S. forestry school. That tract of land is the nucleus of the Pisgah National Forest.

**Devil's Courthouse:** Devil's Courthouse is a rugged exposed mountaintop rich in Cherokee legends. A walk to the bare rock summit yields a spectacular view.

**Richland Balsam Trail:** This trail takes you through a remnant spruce-fir forest. It's the highest point on the parkway at 6,047 feet.

**Waterrock Knob:** Waterrock Knob provides a panorama of the Great Smokies, as well as a trail, exhibits, and comfort station.

# San Antonio Missions Trail

*The Alamo is famous, but a chain of four other lovely Spanish frontier missions along the San Antonio River form the Missions Trail, a pleasant drive into an often-overlooked aspect of America's past.*

It must be noted up front that the San Antonio Missions Trail, a 25-mile loop south of San Antonio, is an urban drive that weaves its way at times through city traffic before reaching more open countryside dotted with farms. But the five missions—the Alamo, Concepcion, San Jose, San Juan, and Espada—and other historic structures, set in parklike grounds, provide scenic beauty enough. And each is a cool and relaxing oasis of quiet. Scattered along the San Antonio River, which the drive follows south from the city, the missions form San Antonio Missions National Historical Park.

The Alamo, established as a dusty outpost of the Spanish Empire in 1718, was the first of San Antonio's missions to be founded. It assumed legendary status in March 1836 when a small garrison of Texas independence fighters, including Davy Crockett and Jim Bowie, fought to the death rather than surrender to a Mexican army. Texans enter its cool adobe walls as if paying homage at a shrine.

The other four missions are less political but no less interesting. Each is different, but they all served the goal of introducing the local Tejas Indians (after whom Texas is named) to Spanish society and Christianity. Franciscan friars founded the four between 1718 and 1731, gathering scattered tribes into church-oriented communities near the river. These and Spain's many other New World missions went into decline during the Napoleonic wars in Europe, and their lands were redistributed in the 1820s when Mexico gained its independence from Spain. In Texas, preservation efforts began in the 1930s.

## Highlights

Begin your tour at The Alamo.

**The Alamo:** In the heart of San Antonio on Alamo Plaza, the sun-baked Alamo is the most historic spot in Texas, known as "The Cradle of Texas Liberty." Founded as the city's first mission in 1718, it served as a fortress in 1836 when Mexican General Santa Anna's army attacked. A total of 189 defenders died here. Today, only the chapel and the barracks remain, encircled by beautifully landscaped gardens. A hallowed site, The Alamo houses mementos of Texas history, including Davy Crockett's beaded buckskin vest with onyx buttons. A museum in the garden courtyard explains the origins of Texas, first as a republic and then as a state. It is maintained by the Daughters of the Republic of Texas.

**Paseo del Rio (River Walk):** The Paseo del Rio is an urban treasure, a masterful use of the city's river frontage. Cloistered 20 feet below street level in the midst of the busy commercial district, it winds

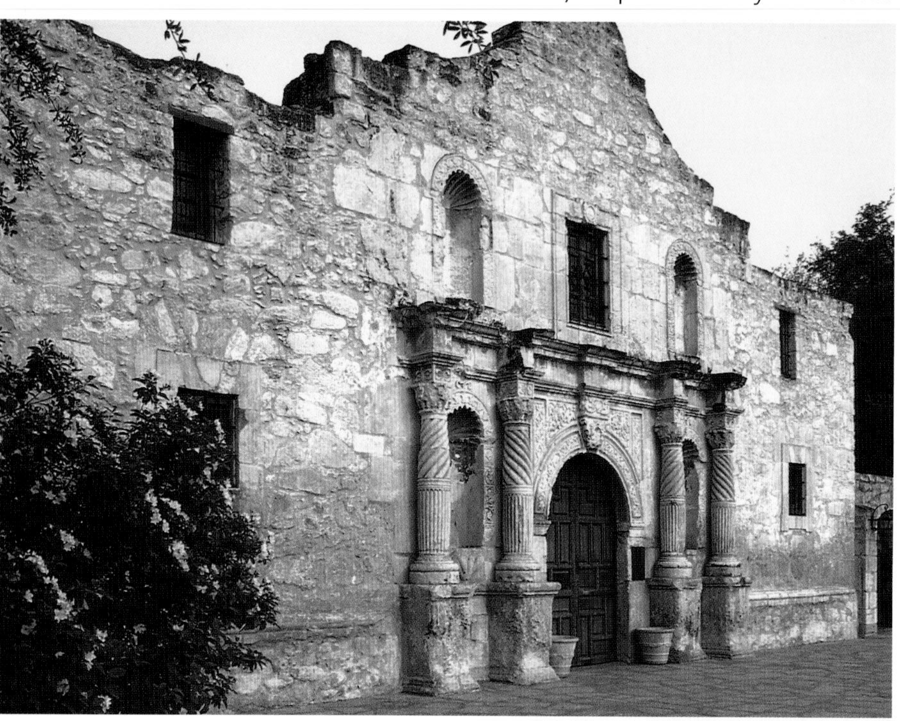

*Mission San Antonio de Valero, better known as The Alamo, represents nearly 300 years of human activity from early pre-colonial days to the modern landscape that surrounds it.*

### Quick Facts

**Length:** 25 miles roundtrip.

**Time to Allow:** Four hours if you take in the exhibits at each mission.

**Considerations:** Although signs point the way, the route that links the four missions can be confusing. This is especially true because there is now a new hiking and biking trail along the San Antonio River to connect the missions. Also, work is ongoing to realign the driving trail itself, eliminating much of the confusion and adding improved signage. Pick up a Missions Trail map before leaving Alamo Plaza. When rain causes the San Antonio River to rise, the route south to Mission San Jose can be closed to traffic. If so, ask at Mission Concepcion for an alternate route south.

for $2^1/_2$ flower-draped miles along both sides of the San Antonio River. Lovely arched bridges vault the slender river, and brightly painted motor barges pass beneath, carrying visitors. Milky green in color, the river is barely the width of a two-lane city street. Throngs stroll the cobblestone walks day and night.

**El Mercado:** A few blocks east of the river, El Mercado, San Antonio's historic Market Square, claims to be the largest Mexican market outside of Mexico. Inside a barnlike building, numerous individual stalls crammed along narrow aisles sell the typical tourist wares of Mexico—ceramics, serapes, sombreros, baskets of all sizes, pottery, leather goods, handworked silver, giant piñatas, and Mexican sugar cookies and other treats. Covering two city blocks, Market Square has been the site of a public market for more than a century.

**Institute of Texan Cultures:** A museum of Texas history, the Institute of Texan Cultures in HemisFair Park explores the culture of 27 ethnic groups who helped settle the state. The museum, which is sponsored by the University of Texas at San Antonio, features exhibits, photos, and multimedia presentations.

**San Antonio Museum of Art:** Of interest on the Missions Trail is the San Antonio Museum of Art's collection of Spanish colonial artworks and its Mexican and other Latin American folk art. The museum occupies a former Lone Star Beer brewery, which was remodeled into a dramatic showcase of art.

**Mission Concepcion:** This mission, the first one on the Missions Trail, preserves a lovely stone church built in 1755 with typical Spanish-colonial features: thick walls, Moorish windows, a pair of tall bell towers, and a solid stone staircase. It is the least restored of San Antonio's missions, looking much as it did more than two centuries ago. Its interior decoration is considered the finest of all the missions. The highlight is a ceiling painting of a starburst depicting God as a mestizo, a person of mixed European and American Indian ancestry. It is located in what is called the "God's Eye room," the mission's library, named for the decoration.

**Mission San Jose:** Down the trail, San Jose, founded in 1720, is the largest and best preserved of the missions. Known as the Queen of Missions, it houses a visitor's center for the Missions Trail. A 20-minute presentation depicts the early life at the mission. Inside its high walls is a huge open courtyard around which are numerous structures, including a large granary that could hold 5,000 bushels of corn, as well as the living quarters for the American Indians. In the mission's heyday, they may have numbered 300. Adobe hornos, or ovens, are scattered over the grounds, and in the far corner stands a magnificently ornate church that is still used for parish services. Each Sunday at noon, a Mariachi Mass is held, and visitors are invited. The church's wood doors were carved in 1937 to duplicate the ones removed in the 1880s. Its Rose Window is regarded as one of the finest representations of Spanish colonial ornamentation in the country. Elsewhere on the grounds, you can see a remnant of the acequia, or irrigation ditch, that brought water to the mission's farm fields.

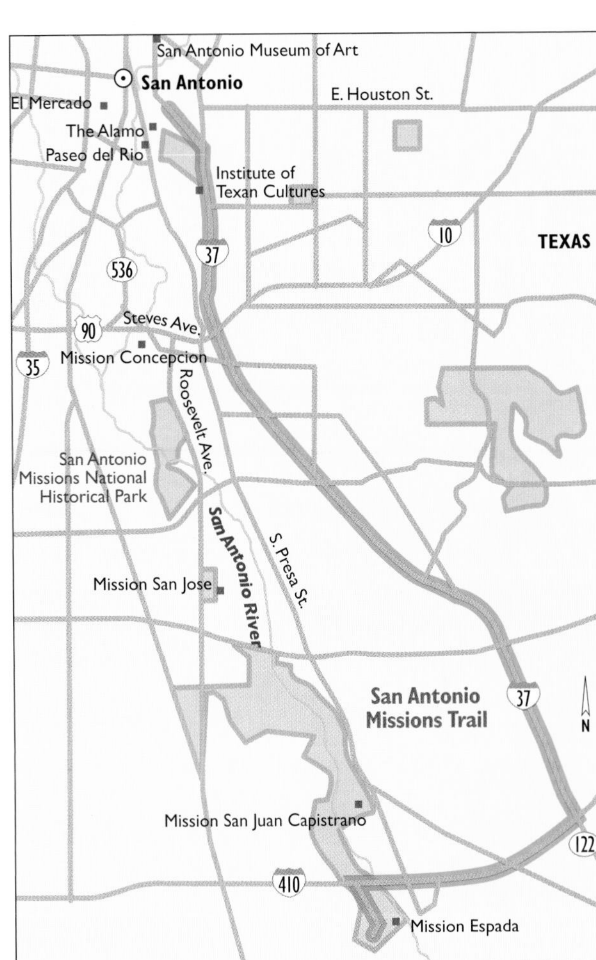


**Mission San Juan Capistrano:** Much simpler than the first two missions on the trail, San Juan Capistrano, established on its present site in 1731, offers its own rewards. A Romanesque arch marks the entrance to the courtyard, which is a quiet place to relax. Its little chapel supporting a bell tower is still in use. Built in an area of rich farm and pasturelands, the mission was a major supplier of produce for the region. Among the beneficiaries were the presidios, the military garrisons that helped protect the missions from raids by invading Apache and Comanche Indians. Look for the self-guided nature trail.

**Mission Espada:** Seemingly as remote as it was in 1731 when it was established, Mission Espada preserves segments of the historic acequias, the irrigation system built to provide water for crops. A marvel of Spanish colonial engineering, the Espada Aqueduct, completed in 1745, was built to carry water from the San Antonio River across a small creek. It is still used to bring water to fields near the mission.

# Creole Nature Trail

*In this unique world of water, encompassing thousands of acres of wetlands, explore three wildlife refuges and a bird sanctuary. Along the way, try your hand at crabbing, and keep an eye open for alligators.*

The Creole Nature Trail travels through thousands of acres of untouched wetlands that reflect an area blessed with some of the most beautiful scenery imaginable. If you like to photograph or hunt wildlife, the trail takes you to three different wildlife refuges and a bird sanctuary. If you aren't a duck hunter, you may like to try your hand at a little Louisiana fishing. The combination of fresh and saltwater areas provides a unique habitat for many of the plants and creatures that live along the byway.

Traveling the edge of the Gulf of Mexico, you will be enchanted by the entwining ecosystems of the coastland and the marshland. So drive the trail through Louisiana's very own outback and discover the culture, nature, and history awaiting you there.

## Intrinsic Qualities

**Archaeological:** Comparatively large concentrations of American Indian archaeological finds, such as pots, shards, and arrowheads, have been unearthed throughout Cameron Parish, and burial mounds were found on Little Chenier, indicating that the earlier American Indian populations must have been large and widespread.

*Sabine Pass Lighthouse was built in 1856 and served as a beacon for mariners for more than 90 years.*

**Cultural:** The culture along the Creole Nature Trail is one that has been mixing and evolving for hundreds of years. Spanish, French, and African influences have all collided here in this coastal outback where alligators roam and hurricanes are known to swallow entire villages. The people of southwest Louisiana understand the place they live in and they revel in it. Throughout the year more than 75 festivals celebrate living on the Creole Nature Trail. Visitors might learn how to skin an alligator or enjoy some real Cajun cooking. All along the byway, historic buildings, nature trails, and even wildlife refuges provide a few more details about the way people live and enjoy life on the byway.

Shrimp boats and ships in the Cameron Ship Channel reflect the importance of the Gulf in the area. Shrimp, crabs, oysters, and a host of fresh and saltwater fish are harvested daily. Visitors can sample these delicacies at area restaurants or purchase fresh seafood for their own recipes.

**Historical:** An infamous history prevails throughout much of the early 1800s on the byway. The pirate Jean Lafitte made a huge profit from capturing Spanish slave ships and selling the slaves to Louisiana cotton and sugar cane planters. His exploits involved everything from the African slave trade to liaisons with French spies. It is rumored that Lafitte buried riches and treasure chests all along the Calcasieu River.

When the Civil War came to Louisiana, battles were fought over Sabine Pass and Calcasieu Pass where the Confederates were successful. Standing today as a stalwart landmark, the Sabine Pass Lighthouse was built in 1856 and became a point of conflict during the Civil War.

### Quick Facts

**Length:** 180 miles.

**Time to Allow:** A self-guided tour could take a day or two.

**Considerations:** There is no parking on highway shoulders except where designated. It is a good idea to bring insect repellent. Also, some wildlife in the refuges may be dangerous. For example, do not try to feed, tease, or prod an American alligator; it is perfectly capable of defending itself. The best months for alligator watching are April through October. Wildlife refuges are closed on federal holidays. Some hunting and fishing grounds require permits. Also, it is advised not to take dogs along at Marsh Trail because alligators may consume them.

**Natural:** The marshlands of coastal Louisiana are teeming with wildlife. They are a bird-watcher's paradise and a photographer's dream. These marshes are filled with the songs of the cardinal and

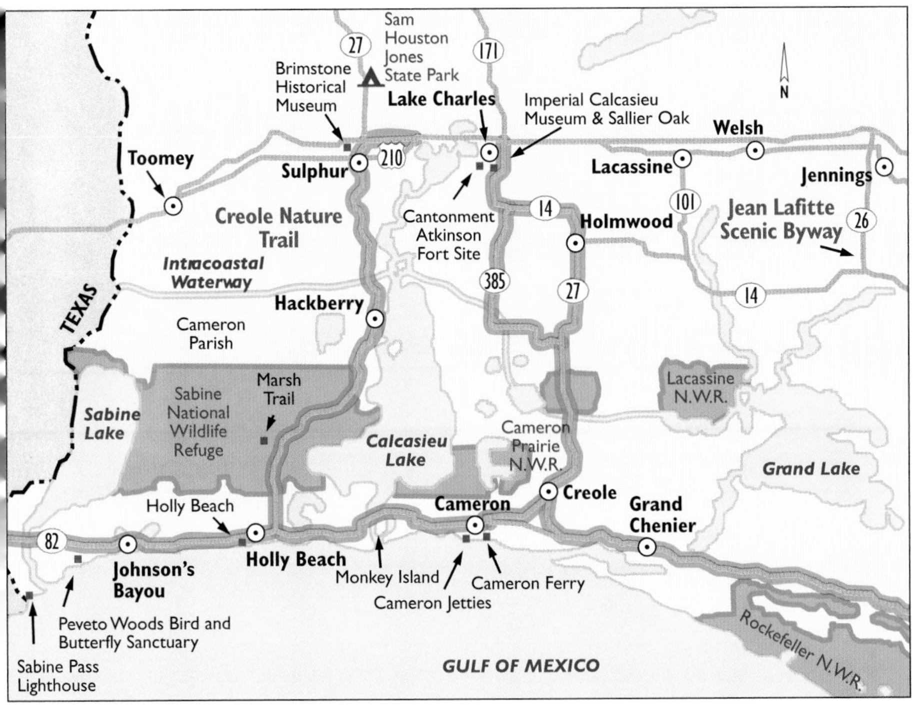


blackbird, the quacking and honking of ducks and geese, the chatter of squirrels, the croaking of frogs, and the bellowing of alligators.

In southwestern Louisiana, marshes and other wetlands can be viewed in the Sabine National Wildlife Refuge, the Rockefeller Wildlife Refuge, and the Cameron Prairie National Wildlife Refuge. At Peveto Woods Bird and Butterfly Sanctuary, visitors will find creatures living amid the cheniers. Beautiful butterflies find this habitat to be the perfect place to spend the winter.

As a coastal prairie, much of the land along the byway displays beautiful wildflowers throughout the warmer months. Many of the flowers have memorable names, like maypop passionflower and duck potato. Unique plants can be found growing everywhere along the byway. Cordgrass grows where nothing else will, and a plant called alligator weed is a food source for deer, herons, and egrets.

**Recreational:** One of the most popular activities for locals and visitors alike is the excellent fishing on Louisiana's coastline. Here, visitors will catch more than just fish. Crabs, shrimp, and oysters are also popular items to pull from the sea. Freshwater, saltwater, and brackish fishing are all available to travelers.

Even on the Creole Nature Trail, you may want a taste of civilization every now and then. Visitors love to stop in places such as Lake Charles or Cameron Parish just to take a look at the historic sites that make each town memorable.

**Scenic:** The Creole Nature Trail provides scenery just as it should be in an outback wilderness—untamed and intriguing. These characteristics are preserved in the way wetland birds roam freely across the countryside and in the way that the ocean waves curl into the salt marshes. Study the shapes of sculpted oak trees that reside on the chenier ridges along the byway. The Creole Nature Trail provides scenery of extraordinary natural quality formed from the interactions of the Gulf of Mexico and the lowlands of Louisiana.

Mineral soils and higher ground form beach ridges, or cheniers as they are called in Louisiana. The most significant of these ridges is Blue Buck Ridge. The chenier ridges are where the live oaks grow, offering a habitat for songbirds and a beautiful photography opportunity.

## Highlights

This tour of the Creole Nature Trail begins in Sulphur, Louisiana (or, if you prefer, start at the other end of the byway and read this list from the bottom up).

**Sulphur:** At Sulphur, the area is characterized by rolling pastureland that gradually turns to wetland. Small ponds and bayous begin to appear, as well.

**Cameron Parish:** Cameron Parish is the largest parish in the state. The vegetation in the area is mostly of the salt marsh variety. Additionally, the landscape is dotted with oil wells and oilfield pumping stations.

**Hackberry:** In Hackberry, you find an abundance of shrimp and crab houses along Kelso Bayou. Here, seafood is cheap and plentiful.

**Sabine National Wildlife Refuge:** At Sabine National Wildlife Refuge, you see views of birds and other marsh animals. The refuge includes the 1½-mile self-guided Marsh Trail with interpretation stations, an observation tower, and panoramic view of marsh terrain.

**Holly Beach:** Also known as the Cajun Riviera, Holly Beach provides 25 miles of year-round beaches, campsites, accommodations, and a variety of outdoor recreation.

**Rockefeller Wildlife Refuge:** The Rockefeller Wildlife Refuge is home to a variety of wintering waterfowl and resident mammals. The refuge is also an important area for research studies about a number of marsh-management strategies. Although you can enjoy recreational fishing in this area, hunting is strictly prohibited. Be cautious of the alligators that inhabit the area.

**Cameron Prairie National Wildlife Refuge:** From this area, you may choose to turn back west toward Cameron Prairie National Wildlife Refuge or continue east toward the western terminus of the byway.

# NATCHEZ TRACE PARKWAY 

*Part of a 445-mile, three-state route, the scenic parkway follows the historic late 18th- and early 19th-century footpath north from Natchez to the Ohio River Valley. Rock-studded hills line this segment.*

PART OF A MULTISTATE BYWAY; IT ALSO RUNS THROUGH ALABAMA AND TENNESSEE.

At first, the Natchez Trace Parkway was probably a series of hunters' paths that slowly came together to form a trail that led from the Mississippi River over the low hills into the Tennessee Valley. By 1785, Ohio River Valley farmers searching for markets had begun floating their crops and products down the rivers to Natchez or New Orleans. Since the late 1930s, the National Park Service has been constructing a modern parkway that closely follows the course of the original trail.

## Intrinsic Qualities

**Archaeological:** Archaeological sites in this area date from the Paleo-Indian period (12,000–8000 B.C.) through historic Natchez, Choctaw, and Chickasaw settlements (1540–1837). Campsites, village sites, stone quarry sites, rock shelters, shell heaps, and burial sites are among the archaeological treasures here.

**Cultural:** The people who live along this parkway embody its rich culture. Southern traditions and hospitality are apparent as you meander through the heart of Dixie. From Natchez to Memphis, you'll enjoy the people you meet along the Natchez Trace Parkway.

**Historical:** The Natchez Trace Parkway was established to commemorate the historical significance of the Old Natchez Trace as a primitive trail that stretched some 500 miles through the wilderness from Natchez, Mississippi, to Nashville, Tennessee. Although generally thought of as one trail, the Old Natchez Trace was actually a number of closely parallel routes. It probably evolved from the repeated use of meandering game trails by the earliest human inhabitants. Over time, these paths were gradually linked and used for transportation, communication, and trade.

**Natural:** The Natchez Trace Parkway encompasses a diversity of natural resources. The motor road cuts through six major forest types and four major watersheds.

Within the park, approximately 900 species of plants help to support 57 species of mammals, 216 species of birds, 57 species of reptiles, 36 species of amphibians, and a variety of other animals.

**Recreational:** Take in one of the many museums located throughout the byway or take a walk among the dogwoods. The byway has many historic battlefields, allowing you the chance to reminisce about the past. Pack a picnic and see the many Southern mansions along the route or hunt for souvenirs in one of the many quaint shops along the way.

*Monuments and artillery are reminders of the personal and tactical resources required by both Union and Confederate troops during the Battle of Vicksburg.*

### Quick Facts

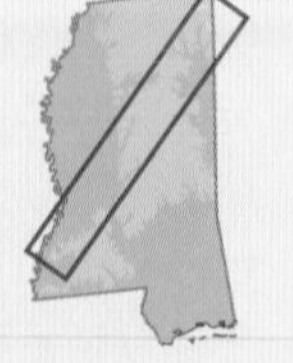

**Length:** 312 miles.

**Time to Allow:** Two days.

**Considerations:** Be alert for animals on the parkway. The parkway is a designated bike route, so please watch for bicyclists. Commercial trucking is not allowed, and tent and trailer camping is allowed at designated campgrounds only.

**Scenic:** From blossoming flowers and trees to historical Native American earthen mounds, the Natchez Trace Parkway offers scenic vistas at every turn and a variety of habitats and wildlife.

## Highlights

Start in Natchez, Mississippi, and end in Nashville, Tennessee.

**Natchez:** The historic Mississippi River port of Natchez boasts as many as 14 palatial homes open to the public. One of the finest is Melrose, a national park site.

**Emerald Mound:** Dating to 1250, 35-foot-high Emerald Mound is the second-largest American Indian temple. It covers eight acres.

**Mount Locust:** Take a quick tour of Mount Locust. It is a rustic inn, or "stand," one of the first that provided food and shelter along this trail.

**Sunken Trace:** Here are three sections of the original road that show how the route was relocated to avoid mudholes.

**Rocky Springs Site:** A church and cemetery mark the site of the once-prosperous town of Rocky Springs. In the 1790s, the rural community grew to more than 2,600 residents. But by 1920, the Civil War, yellow fever, the boll weevil, and erosion had devastated the town.

**Vicksburg National Military Park:** Vicksburg's major attraction is the national military park, where on July 4, 1863, Union General Ulysses S. Grant's army dealt a mortal blow to the local planter population.

**Jackson:** Mississippi's state capital is an attractive river city with fine museums and parks. Of particular note is the Old Capitol.

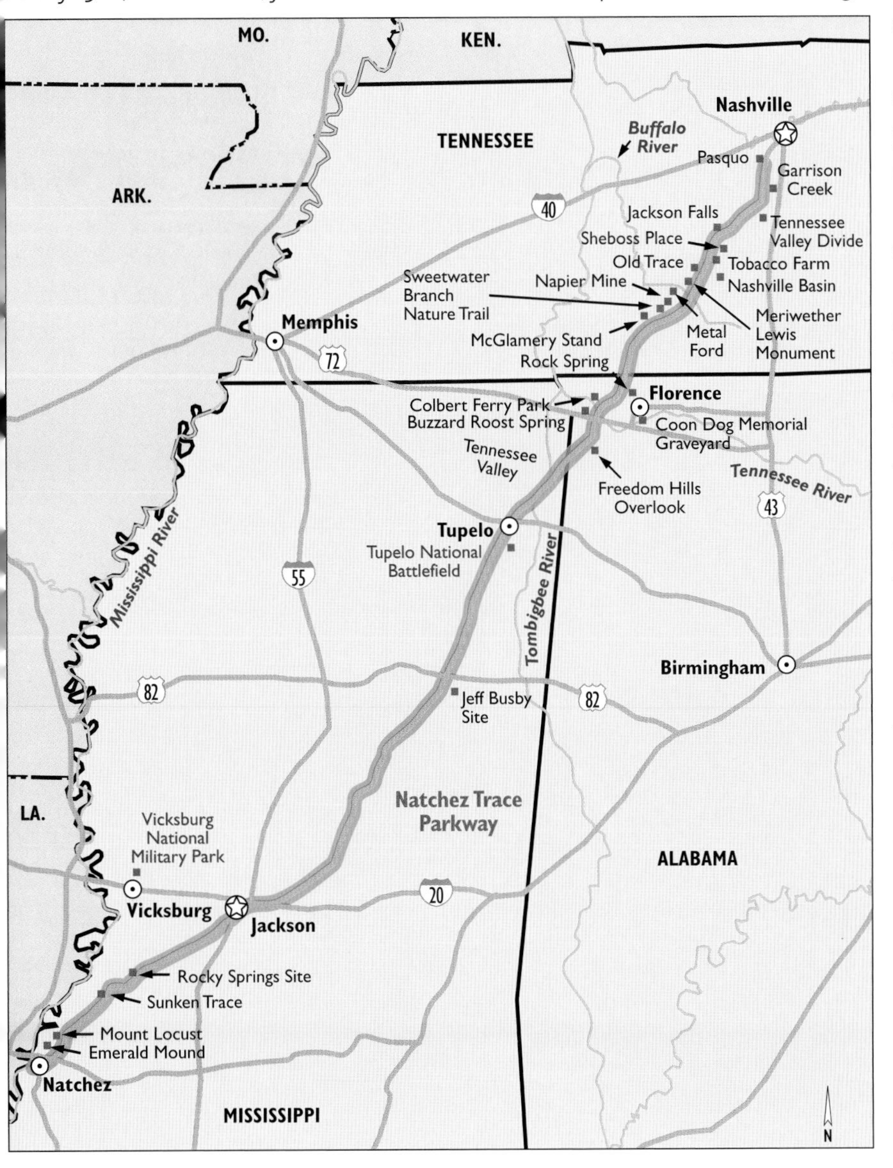


**Jeff Busby Site:** The campground at Jeff Busby Site is named for Thomas Jefferson Busby, who introduced a bill in Congress that led to the creation of the Natchez Trace Parkway.

**Tupelo National Battlefield:** Fought on July 13–15, 1864, the battle resulted in a Union victory.

**Freedom Hills Overlook:** A steep quarter-mile trail climbs to the highest point on the parkway—an altitude of 800 feet.

**Coon Dog Memorial Graveyard:** An Alabama curiosity, more than 100 coon dogs have been buried here since 1937.

**Buzzard Roost Spring:** Levi Colbert, a Chickasaw Indian chief, operated an inn, or "stand," nearby. His story is told in exhibits.

**Colbert Ferry Park:** In the trace's heyday, George Colbert operated an inn and a river ferry here. There are facilities for swimming, fishing, and boating.

**Rock Spring:** A short trail follows Colbert Creek. It is one of numerous easy trails along the trace that offer motorists a chance to climb out from behind the wheel.

**McGlamery Stand:** The nearby village still bears the name of this old stand.

**Sweetwater Branch Nature Trail:** A clear, fast-flowing stream parallels the route of this 20-minute walk.

**Napier Mine:** This open pit was worked during the 19th century.

**Metal Ford:** Travelers crossed the Buffalo River here; an ironworks and McLish's Stand were nearby.

**Meriwether Lewis Monument:** A campground, picnic area, ranger station, and Meriwether Lewis's grave are here.

**Old Trace:** Here the Trace marked the boundaries of the Chickasaw lands ceded to the United States in 1805 and 1816.

**Tobacco Farm:** Exhibits at the farm and barn explain tobacco growing.

**Sheboss Place:** This is the site of one of the stands that once served travelers on the trace.

**Jackson Falls:** Named for Andrew Jackson, the falls are on the intermittent Jackson Branch that empties into Duck River.

**Tennessee Valley Divide:** When Tennessee was admitted to the Union in 1796, this watershed was the boundary between the United States and the Chickasaw nation.

**Garrison Creek:** Named for a nearby 1801–1802 U.S. Army post, this area is a trailhead for horseback riders and hikers.

# SELMA TO MONTGOMERY MARCH BYWAY 

*This historical route, rich in poignant stories, honors the memory of civil rights marchers whose efforts helped Southern African-Americans gain access to the ballot box with passage of the 1965 Voting Rights Act.*

Designated as a National Historic Trail, this byway has known many facets of history in its years of existence. However, it wasn't until Dr. Martin Luther King, Jr., began leading voting rights demonstrations in Selma early in 1965, culminating with the historic Selma to Montgomery March, that the route became internationally known.

After a failed attempt just three weeks earlier, Dr. King marshaled a group of protesters who made their way 43 miles from the Edmund Pettus Bridge in Selma to Montgomery, giving birth to the most important piece of social legislation of the 20th century. This march helped bring access to the ballot box for many African-Americans in Southern states.



## Intrinsic Qualities

**Cultural:** Dr. Martin Luther King, Jr., stood on the platform in front of the stark-white state capitol in Montgomery, Alabama, and gazed out at the crowd of 30,000 people on March 25, 1965. The largest civil rights march ever to take place in the South had finally reached its destination after weeks of uncertainty and danger. Two blocks down the street, at the edge of the vast assemblage, was Dexter Avenue Baptist Church, from whose pulpit King had inspired black bus boycotters a decade earlier. Their year-long display of nonviolence and courage had not only earned blacks the right to sit where they wanted on the buses but it had also started a fire in the hearts of many Americans.

King did not refer directly to the brutal attack by state and local law officers just 18 days earlier. However, that attack, seen on national television, drew the attention of the world to this moment.

Less than five months later, the 1965 Voting Rights Act was signed, and African-Americans throughout the South streamed into courthouses to register as voters. They were at last exercising a fundamental promise of democracy, a promise that took our nation 178 years to fulfill.

### Quick Facts

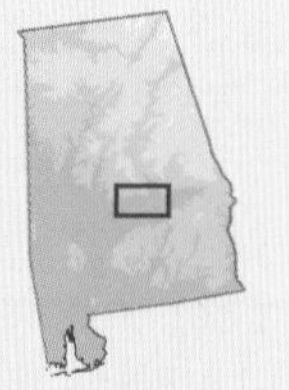

**Length:** 43 miles.

**Time to Allow:** One hour.

**Considerations:** Martin Luther King, Jr., Day, the third Monday in January, is an excellent time to visit the byway, with all of the associated activities.

**Historical:** African-Americans in Selma formed the Dallas County Voters League (DCVL) under the leadership of Samuel W. Boynton, a local agricultural extension agent and former president of the local chapter of the National Association for the Advancement of Colored People (NAACP).

Despite stiff resistance from white officials, local activists persisted. Their terrific courage attracted the attention of other African-American leaders. In early 1963, Bernard and Colia Lafayette of the Student Nonviolent Coordinating Committee (SNCC) went to Selma to help the DCVL register African-American voters.

The Selma activists quickly found themselves battling not only bureaucratic resistance, but also the intimidation tactics of Sheriff Jim Clark and his deputized posse. In 1961, the U.S. Justice Department filed a voter discrimination lawsuit against the County Board of Registrars and, two years later, sued Clark directly for the harassment of African-Americans attempting to register.

Fearful that more "outside agitators" would target Selma, State Circuit Judge James Hare on July 9, 1964, enjoined any group of more than three people from meeting in Dallas County.

As protests and meetings came to a virtual halt, local activists Amelia Platts Boynton and J. L. Chestnut asked Southern Christian Leadership Conference (SCLC)

*Overlooking the infamous Edmund Pettus Bridge, the Window of Fame in the National Voting Rights Museum and Institute memorializes those who participated in the Selma to Montgomery March.*

officials for help. SCLC leaders, following their hard-won victory in Birmingham, had already declared that their next push would be for a strong national voting rights law. Selma offered the perfect opportunity.

On January 2, 1965, Dr. King defied Judge Hare's injunction and led a rally at Brown Chapel African Methodist Episcopal (AME) Church, promising demonstrations and even another march on Washington if voting rights were not guaranteed for African-Americans in the South. Immediately, a series of mass meetings and protest marches began with renewed momentum in Selma and nearby Marion, the seat of Perry County.

Then, on February 18, a nighttime march in Marion ended in violence and death. Alabama State Troopers attacked African-Americans leaving a mass meeting at Zion Methodist Church. Several people, including Viola Jackson and her son Jimmie Lee, sought refuge in a small café, but troopers soon found them.

An officer moved to strike Viola Jackson, then turned on Jimmie Lee when he tried to protect her. Two troopers assaulted Jimmie Lee, shooting him at point blank range. On February 26, Jimmie Lee Jackson died in Selma from an infection caused by the shooting.

His death angered activists. Lucy Foster, a leader in Marion, bitterly proposed that residents take his body to the Alabama Capitol to gain the attention of Governor George Wallace—a proposal repeated later by SCLC's James Bevel. Bevel and others realized that some mass nonviolent action was necessary, not only to win the attention of political leaders but also to vent the anger and frustration of the activists.

Even as Jimmie Lee was buried, the idea for a Selma to Montgomery march was growing. By March 2, plans were confirmed that Dr. King would lead a march from Selma to Montgomery beginning on Sunday, March 7, 1965.

## Highlights

The following tour encompasses the first section of the byway beginning on the corner of Martin Luther King, Jr., Street and Jeff Davis Avenue and passes the George Washington Carver Home, historic landmark Brown AME Church, and the Martin Luther King, Jr., monument. Through the written word and vivid historic photographs, each of the 20 memorials along the route tells the story of the individuals who came together for a common cause.

**Cecil B. Jackson Public Safety Building:** On the byway, the first point of interest is the Cecil B. Jackson Public Safety Building, which was once the old Selma city hall. This building served as the city and county jail in which Dr. King and other protesters were imprisoned in 1965.

*Brown Chapel is commemorated as the starting point for the historic 1965 march for voting rights.*

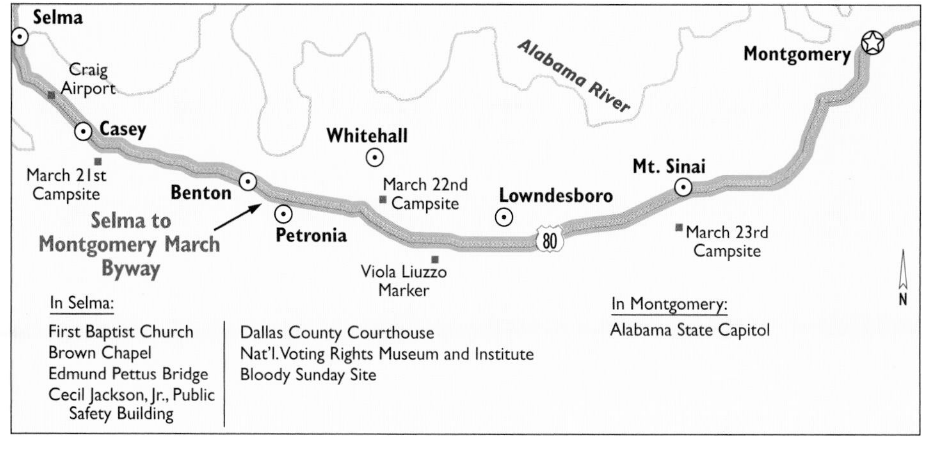


**Dallas County Courthouse:** The Dallas County Courthouse was the destination of most protest marches in an effort to register to vote.

**National Voting Rights Museum and Institute:** Just before the Alabama River is the National Voting Rights Museum and Institute, dedicated to honoring the attainment of voting rights.

**Edmund Pettus Bridge:** Crossing the Alabama River is the Edmund Pettus Bridge, the famous landmark where "Bloody Sunday" took place on March 7, 1965.

**Montgomery:** From here, the byway travels along Highway 80 to Montgomery, passing numerous campsites that were used by marchers during the historic event. Between the cities of Petronia and Lowndesboro stands the memorial to Viola Liuzzo, who was murdered while supporting the civil rights movement.

**Alabama State Capitol:** The final destination of the Selma to Montgomery March is the Alabama State Capitol in Montgomery. On the steps of this great building, Dr. Martin Luther King, Jr., told marchers that even though the journey was through, the struggle for civil rights was far from over. But it would be won, he said, and it wouldn't be long.

# Russell–Brasstown Scenic Byway 

*A mountainous loop, the byway passes numerous sparkling waterfalls, climbing to Brasstown Bald. It's the state's highest point, yielding a 360-degree view of rumpled green highlands.*

Cool in the summer, mild in the winter, this byway beckons you to lose yourself in its luscious timberland. Linger atop Brasstown Bald to absorb all 360 degrees of rolling highlands. Escape the crowds and retire to the cooling mists of the byway's numerous waterfalls. Got a hanker for a hike, but the Appalachian Trail isn't what you had in mind? Sparkling waterfalls and secluded valley views are just a short stroll from the main road. The average weekend hiker could spend years exploring these trails and never retrace a step. Share a meal at a cozy picnic site or break bread in a real Bavarian hamlet enveloped in the Georgian mountains. Whether you're looking to hike the hinterland or lounge in a lazy village, the Russell–Brasstown Scenic Byway is an ideal getaway.

*Meandering creeks and both large and small waterfalls are highlights of a visit to the Russell–Brasstown Scenic Byway.*

## Intrinsic Qualities

**Natural:** Two Forest Service Scenic Areas have been designated to protect their unique qualities and natural beauty. First, the High Shoals Creek Falls Scenic Area covers 170 heavily wooded acres that surround the numerous waterfalls along the creek. Second, the highlight of the Anna Ruby Falls Scenic Area is the dramatic 150-foot waterfall where Curtis and York creeks join to create Smith Creek. Protecting 1,600 acres, the Anna Ruby Falls Scenic Area is covered with poplars, white pines, rhododendrons, and many wildflower species.

Three Wildlife Management areas, including Chattahoochee, Swallow Creek, and Chestatee, are designed to provide an undisturbed habitat for many of the native plant and wildlife species of the region.

The Georgia Department of Natural Resources operates two state parks, as well as Smithgall Woods–Dukes Creek Conservation Area. These two parks and the conservation area collectively protect more than 6,800 acres of North Georgia wilderness. Unicoi and Vogel State Parks comprise 1,261 acres of protected lands and offer a variety of recreational and educational opportunities. The Smithgall Woods–Dukes Creek Conservation Area has been designated as a State Heritage Preserve; this designation will protect its 5,555 acres of trout streams, hiking trails, and wildlife habitats for future generations.

**Recreational:** Hiking trails that lead visitors to tumbling waterfalls or breathtaking mountain overlooks abound in the Chattahoochee National Forest of North Georgia. The most prominent of these is the Appalachian National Scenic Trail. Extending more than 2,000 miles from Georgia's Springer Mountain to Maine, traveling the entire Appalachian Trail is a goal for many hikers. The Russell–Brasstown Scenic Byway provides access to the trail, which covers nearly 80 miles in Georgia. Atop Brasstown Bald, hikers can explore the Jacks Knob, Arkaquah, and Wagon Train trails. These trails, ranging from 4½ to 6 miles in length, radiate from the visitor center parking area. Numerous smaller trails snake their way around the area and can be accessed from Andrews Cove, Chattahoochee Campground, Dukes Creek Falls, Raven Cliff Falls,

### Quick Facts

**Length:** 40½ miles.

**Time to Allow:** At least three hours.

**Considerations:** The only regular seasonal limitations are imposed on recreational facilities. Andrews Cove is closed from late November until early May, and the Chattahoochee River Campground is closed from early November until late March. The Chattahoochee Campground is open for Wildlife Management Area hunts in November and December. Also, the visitor center at Brasstown Bald is open daily from Memorial Day until early November, and on weekends during the spring and fall depending on weather conditions.

and the other state parks and scenic areas.

**Scenic:** Whether a deep summer green or an exploding autumn red and yellow, the Chattahoochee National Forest covers the area with slender pines, towering hardwoods, beautiful rhododendrons, and colorful wildflowers. Hidden beneath the forest's canopy, gentle streams wander down mountain sides and tumble down spectacular waterfalls on their journey to the sea. Dukes Creek Falls, High Shoals Creek Falls, and nearby Anna Ruby Falls offer dramatic examples of the power of nature.

## Highlights

The following itinerary offers a sampling of what the byway has to offer.

**Helen:** To begin your journey fully equipped with maps, brochures, and food and drink, stop at the charming town of Helen, just two miles before officially reaching the byway. Originally this area was a vibrant center of the indigenous Cherokee culture. When gold was discovered in the area in 1828, thousands of Europeans flooded the region. Gold mining and then the timber industry flourished until the mid-20th century. In the 1960s the village once again reinvented itself, this time as a quaint Bavarian hamlet.

**Smithgall Woods–Dukes Creek Conservation Area:** Formerly a private estate, this conservation area has been described as being home to one of North Georgia's best trout streams, as well as nature trails and wildlife viewing stands.

**Dukes Creek Falls:** Leaving the Smithgall Woods–Dukes Creek Conservation Area, turn north on State Route 348 for a half-mile to Dukes Hollow Road and follow the signs to Dukes Creek Falls. The falls are actually on Davis Creek before it joins Dukes Creek. Dropping 250 feet down a steep granite canyon, Dukes Creek Falls is a spectacular sight. A wheelchair-accessible trail from the parking lot to observation platforms gives an overview of the falls. Hikers can continue down Dukes Creek Gorge to the base of the falls for an up-close experience.

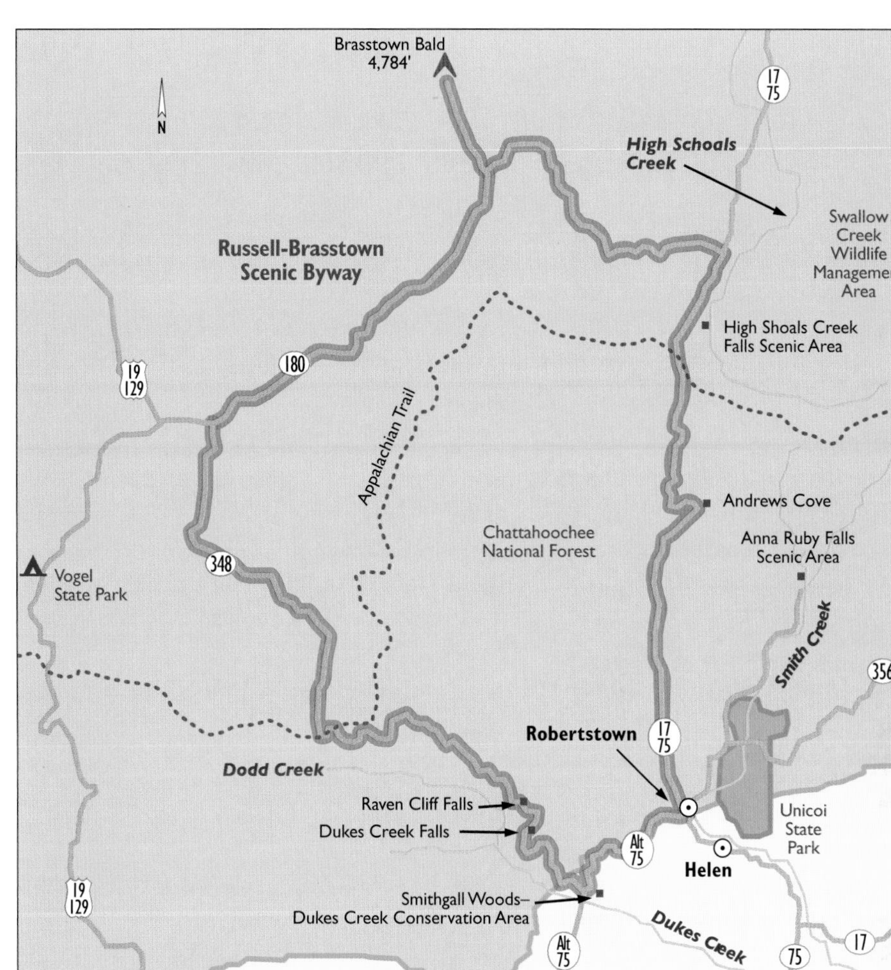


**Raven Cliff Falls:** Returning to State Route 348, continue another $2\frac{1}{2}$ miles north. Parking is available along the left side of the road. Follow the signs marking the trail to Raven Cliff Falls. Tumbling a total of 100 feet down Dodd Creek, Raven Cliff Falls is actually a series of three splendid waterfalls. The middle section flows through a split in a solid rock outcropping. Other waterfalls are found on the creek with the largest having a drop of 70 feet. The surrounding wilderness, measuring more than 9,100 acres, is federally protected.

**Brasstown Bald:** Brasstown Bald is Georgia's highest mountain. At 4,784 feet above sea level, this vantage point offers a commanding 360-degree view.

**High Shoals Creek Falls Scenic Area:** Near the intersection of State Routes 17/75 and 180, Forest Service Road 283 leads visitors through the Swallow Creek Wildlife Management Area to the High Shoals Creek Falls Scenic Area. A $1\frac{1}{4}$-mile trail takes visitors down to the High Shoals Creek Falls and Blue Hole Falls. It is highly recommended that the falls be viewed only from the established trails and observation platforms.

**Smith Creek:** From State Route 17/75, turn left on State Route 356 for $1\frac{1}{2}$ miles, and then left at the sign for Anna Ruby Falls. Follow this road for $3\frac{1}{2}$ miles to the parking area. Fed by underground springs, rain, and snow, Curtis Creek and York Creek thunder down Tray Mountain to form Smith Creek. Paths and trails traverse the area. Lion's Eye Trail gives people with visual impairments the opportunity to experience the Smith Creek environment with Braille signs.

# Ashley River Road 

*A short excursion from Charleston, the road tunnels beneath towering live oaks dripping in Spanish moss en route to a wealth of historic low-country gardens and mansions open to the public.*

## Quick Facts

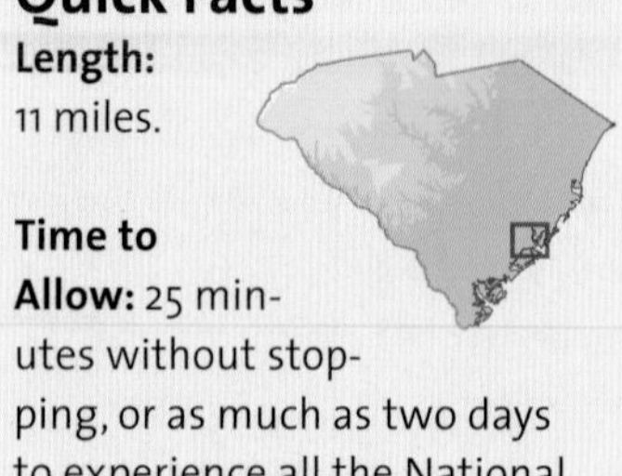

**Length:** 11 miles.

**Time to Allow:** 25 minutes without stopping, or as much as two days to experience all the National Historic Landmarks.

**Considerations:** There are no fees on this byway.

Covering a distance of only 11 miles, the Ashley River Road is a journey into the history, culture, and beauty of the South Carolina low country. Ancient live oaks, Spanish moss stirring in a warm summer breeze, and elegant brick gates hinting at the architecture within hearken back to days gone by. The Ashley River Road itself reflects the history and culture that has been at home along this great river.

## Intrinsic Qualities

**Cultural:** In addition to the grand architecture of the mansions and gardens of the area, the African-American churches that chronicle their religion from slavery to emancipation are no less remarkable. As the first non-native culture to live in the area, the early slave and subsequent emancipated African cultures contributed to the shaping of the Ashley River Road and the surrounding area.

The Springfield Baptist Church along the byway is a great example of community efforts of the African-American culture of the area. Coming together in the mid-1860s, African-American individuals established the first freely organized Baptist congregation. The Ashley River Road connected these congregations with rural African-American communities such as Red Top, Marysville, Sanders, Drayton, Bullfield, and Cherokee. This connection ensured the heritage of the people would remain intact by allowing open and free communication between people.

*Stately oaks form a scenic canopy over the road leading in to the grounds of the Magnolia Plantation.*

The plantation mansions and magnificent gardens are witnesses of the influence of English architecture for both mansion and garden. Drayton Hall is an example of the Georgian-Palladian architectural style, which meant that these homes were often rectangular in shape and that the rooms were arranged symmetrically around a spacious hall. The Middleton Place Gardens also illustrate order, geometry, and balance, with a variety of sweeping vistas and blooming flowers, shrubs, and trees.

**Historical:** An extraordinary blending of plantation, slave, religious, war, and mining history along the Ashley River Road secures this 11-mile stretch of road as an important snapshot of the history of South Carolina. The grand architecture of the plantation mansions, the road itself, and local historic churches speak of a time rich in tradition.

During the colonial period of U.S. history, the low country of South Carolina was ideal for rice plantations, and the nearby Ashley River was used to cultivate these rice fields. The fields were planted, flooded, and harvested at the hands of mainly African slaves.

In addition to work on the plantations, slave labor was an integral part of the construction and development of the Ashley River Road itself. Plantation owners were required to send their slaves to work on the road; consequently, while the funds generally came from the white landowners, the labor for the road is due to the work of the slave population.

The Ashley River Road saw dramatic changes when action at Fort Bull during the Civil War resulted in the abandonment of the fort to Union troops and the burning and looting of many of the great manor houses along the road. With the slave labor era waning, the search for new ways to make money resulted in the mining of nearby phosphate rock. Signs of this mining are seen today in low berms and high mounds of mining tailings from Drayton Hall to Middleton Place.

**Scenic:** The Ashley River Road provides a classic South Carolina low-country scenic experience. The live oak allée, with its ancient trees and Spanish moss, creates a kinesthetic experience of light and shadow as travelers pass beneath the spreading arms of each tree. Glimpses of tree-lined drives beyond the road or views of the Ashley River beyond a wide marsh further enhance the scenic experience for the visitor.

## Highlights

The following itinerary takes you from the beginning of the Ashley River right on in to the city of Charleston.

**Colonial Dorchester State Historic Site:** Not officially on the byway, but a significant site in the telling of the Ashley River history, and just six miles outside of Summerville on State Road 642 south is the 325-acre Colonial Dorchester State Historic Site. This historic park is the former location of a village founded in 1697 by a group of Congregationalists from Massachusetts who abandoned the community after the American Revolution. Attractions here include the site of the tabby fort, ruins of the once-thriving village, ongoing archaeological excavations, the tower of the St. George's Parish Church, and signage that explains the history of the town and the upper Ashley River area. The park is listed on the National Register of Historic Places.

**Middleton Place:** Originally constructed in the mid-1700s, this plantation survived the American Revolution, hurricanes, and an earthquake, but the manor house nearly didn't survive the Yankee troops intent on burning it to the ground in the Civil War. Today visitors can tour the surviving south wing of the manor with an elegant glimpse into the lives of the former residents, and the stableyards for demonstrations of slave life, skills, and crafts.

**Magnolia Plantation and Gardens:** Adjoining Drayton Hall and still in the possession of the original owners, the Drayton family, is Magnolia Plantation and Gardens. Dating back to 1676, the plantation offers tours of the manor house and the world-famous gardens, including the Barbados Tropical Garden and a horticultural maze. The entire 500 acres of Magnolia Plantation have been managed as a wildlife refuge since 1975. Nature trails offer a narrated tour of the wildlife refuge, and hiking trails and an observation tower afford other viewing opportunities. A petting zoo is available for children.

**Drayton Hall:** Drayton Hall, a National Historic Landmark, is the oldest preserved plantation house in America that is open to the public and has remained in nearly original condition. Jointly owned by the National Trust for Historic Preservation and the State of South Carolina, Drayton Hall is considered one of the finest examples of Georgian Palladian architecture in the nation. It was the only home along the Ashley River that was not vandalized by the invading Union troops during the Civil War.

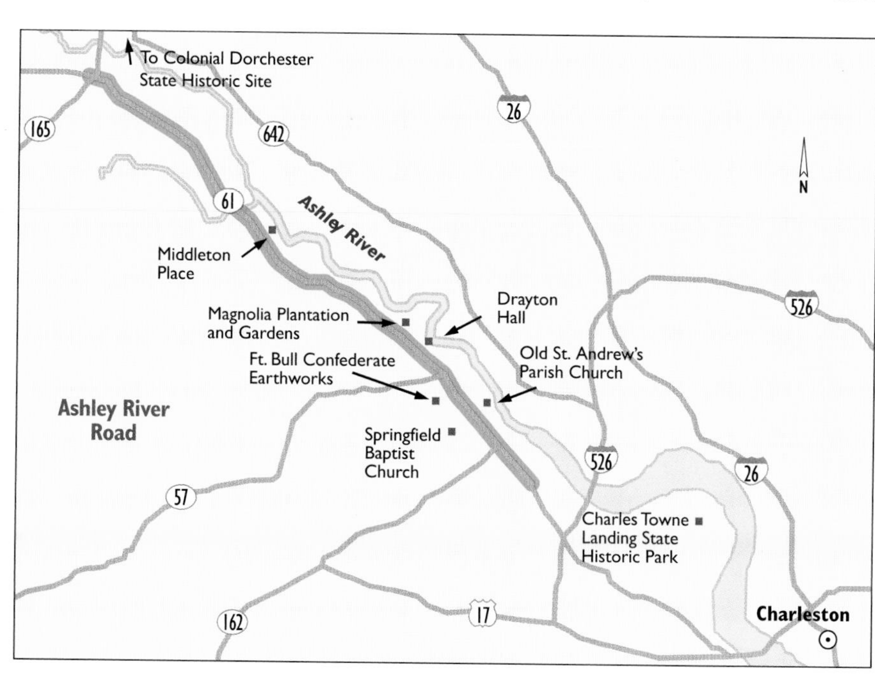


**Old Saint Andrew's Parish Church:** The oldest surviving church in South Carolina, Old Saint Andrew's Parish Church still retains many of its historic features, including original flooring and the original baptismal font. Nestled close to the Ashley River and containing ten acres of land, Old Saint Andrew's property is comprised of a cemetery, an education building, and the main building that dates back to 1706.

**Springfield Baptist Church:** Another historic church on the Ashley River Road is the Springfield Baptist Church. It was originally organized as St. Andrew's Baptist Church in 1863 on land donated by the owner of nearby Springfield plantation. Though enlarged and encased in a brick veneer in the mid-1900s, the present building actually dates back to 1865.

**Charles Towne Landing State Historic Site:** The Ashley River Road was developed by early settlers to travel down to Charles Towne Landing. Today travelers will find that a visit to Charles Towne Landing State Historic Site, though not officially part of the scenic byway, is an appropriate and enjoyable way to complete the Ashley River Road experience. This protected historic site includes a reproduction sailing vessel, a re-created settlement that portrays 1670s village life, Animal Forest, guided tram tours, foot and bicycle trails, and the original fortified town site from 1670 that established the first permanent English settlement in the Carolinas on these grounds.

# Savannah River Scenic Byway

*Skirting J. Strom Thurmond Lake, where you can swim, the byway continues north through a varied region of dense woods, rolling farmland, and historic villages, where antique shopping is popular.*

Outdoor excitement and historic adventures await you on the Savannah River Scenic Byway. Running along the western edge of South Carolina, the byway is a beautiful country drive through the dense wooded Hickory Knob State Resort Park and Sumter National Forest, quaint towns such as McCormick and Willington, and past rolling farmland dotted with historic churches. The J. Strom Thurmond Dam and Lake and the Savannah River are both only seconds off the byway, providing camping, fishing, and other recreational opportunities that you will be able to enjoy with the whole family.

For antique hounds and history buffs, a small side trip off the byway will be well worth your time. Head to the town of Abbeville, just a few miles off the byway, to experience some great shopping, dining, and historic architecture.

## Quick Facts

**Length:** 110 miles.

**Time to Allow:** One could easily spend three hours to all day exploring this byway.

**Considerations:** Lane widths and highway designs do not present problems for motor vehicles with standard clearances.

## Intrinsic Qualities

**Cultural:** The Savannah River Scenic Byway is the primary touring route within the upper regions of the South Carolina Heritage Corridor. As a key segment of the Heritage Corridor's "Nature Route," the scenic highway serves both as a touring route and as the major north/south pathway for visitors to the area.

Examples of this region's unique cultural traditions include basket making and shape-note singing. Numerous places along the route also offer cuisine that is unique to the region.

The visual character of the present-day landscape was shaped by many different cultural and economic influences. These influences include the early cotton-dependent economy, the introduction of the railroads, the creation of the lakes, and more recently, the completion of I-85 and the development of Savannah Lakes Village.

This corridor tells the vibrant story of South Carolina's (and the South's) evolution and culture. Visitors will learn about rice and indigo, pirates and patriots, slaves and freemen, cotton fields and mill villages, swamps and waterfalls, railroads and back roads, soul food and "pig-pickin's," and spirituals and bluegrass. Locations of natural beauty, recreational opportunities, military history, local arts and crafts, agricultural traditions, and the state's rich African-American heritage are identified and interpreted along the way.

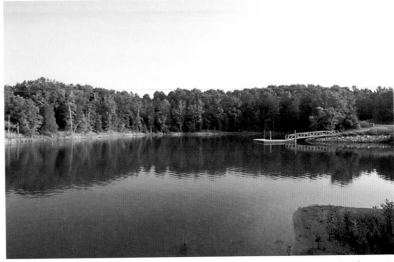

*Calhoun Falls State Park is located on Russell Lake, one of South Carolina's most popular fishing lakes.*

**Historical:** The Savannah River Scenic Highway winds more than 100 miles along the shores of three major lakes and through four counties. In the 18th century, this was the western frontier, and it was bustling with soldiers, American Indian traders, and adventurers when South Carolina's first battle of the Revolution erupted here.

Abbeville is a historically significant town along the byway. This town was so actively involved in events relating to the Civil War that it claims the title "Birthplace and Deathbed of the Confederacy." On November 22, 1860, Secession Hill was the site of the first public meeting organized to consider seceding from the Union. On May 2, 1865, at the Burt–Stark Mansion, Jefferson Davis met for the last time with his Council of War and agreed to disband his Confederate troops.

Edgefield is home to the Old Edgefield Pottery where a resident potter still makes alkaline-glazed stoneware in the Old Edgefield tradition. Antebellum homes, such as Oakley Park and Magnolia Dale, are open for tours. Nearby Johnston, with its Victorian architecture and antique shops, has designated itself "the Peach Capital of the World."

**Recreational:** The Savannah River Scenic Highway serves as a major recreational gateway to the freshwater coast. It includes more than 2,700 miles of shoreline along lakes Hartwell, Russell, and Thurmond. The scenic highway provides access to 59 recreation areas, including the developed recreational sites operated by the Corps of Engineers, SCPRT, and the U.S. Forest Service, as well as a few sites that are operated by local government.

In addition, the route connects to 104 recreational access sites that have boat ramps, campgrounds, welcome centers, or shoreline access points and other points of interest.

Some of the recreation areas accessible from the scenic highway include the five state parks associated with the freshwater coast. These parks are Sadlers Creek State Recreation Area, Calhoun Falls State Park, Hickory Knob State Resort Park, Baker Creek State Park, and Hamilton–Branch State Park.

## Highlights

With the Savannah River Scenic Byway offering a mix of natural wonders, historic treasures, and southern hospitality, this itinerary gives just a sampling of what there is to see and do on and near the byway.

**J. Strom Thurmond Dam and Lake:** West of the byway is the J. Strom Thurmond Dam and Lake, one of the ten most visited Corps of Engineers lakes in the nation. It is the largest Corps project east of the Mississippi River and offers camping, boating, fishing, hunting, and a variety of trails for up-close views of wildlife in their stunning natural habitats.

**McCormick's Historic District:** Directly on the byway, the former gold mining town of McCormick has several interesting and noteworthy buildings in its historic downtown district. Strom's Drug Store on Main Street still offers old-fashioned fountain sodas, ice cream, and shakes. And the McCormick Visitor's Center was the first service station in the county. Maps and information about the region can be picked up here.

**McCormick hotels:** Along with the historic depot, hotels from the turn of the 20th century have been preserved and restored and function now as an integral part of the business life of McCormick. The McCormick Hotel now serves hungry diners as a locally popular eatery. The old Keturah Hotel, a two-story structure with white Doric columns, draws new customers today as the MACK Art Gallery. The adjoining city park and amphitheater host plays and concerts during the summer months.

**Ninety Six National Historic Site:** Northeast of McCormick is the Ninety Six National Historic Site, a frontier settlement and battlefield from the Revolutionary War. The park site covers more than 989 acres and includes a visitor's center, self-guided tours, special events, interpretive trails, archaeological digs, and insightful restorations.

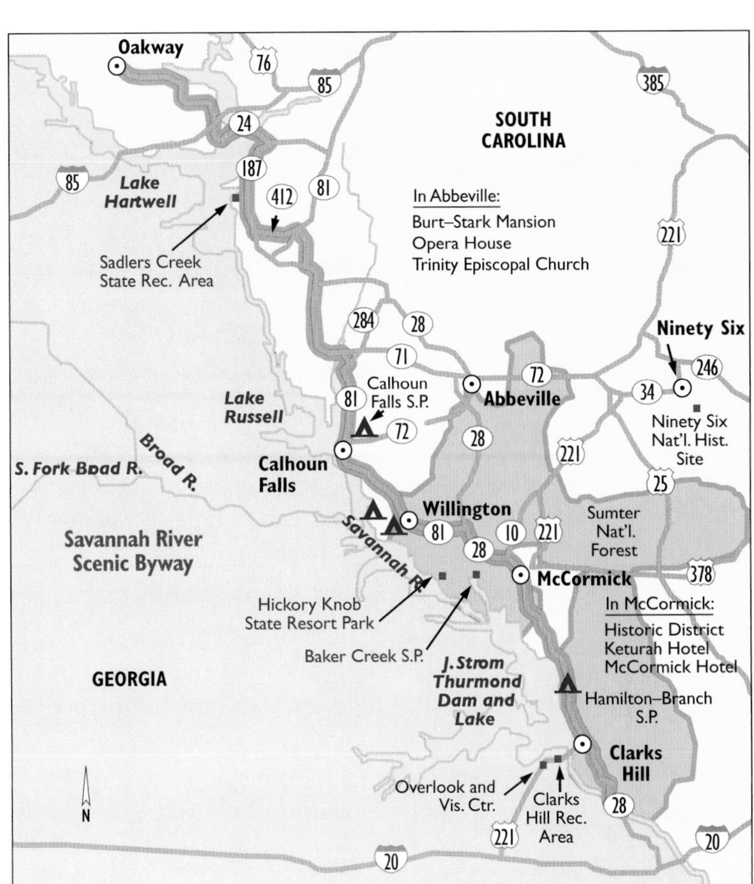


**Abbeville:** With more than 300 homes and buildings in the National Register Historic District, a stop at the Welcome Center is essential for maps and information about walking tours, attractions, and events. It is located opposite the courthouse and opera house in the extensively renovated Old Bank Building.

**Trinity Episcopal Church and Burt–Stark Mansion:** The Trinity Episcopal Church features a massive tracker organ, stunning stained-glass windows, original handmade pews, and a soaring 125-foot spire. The Burt–Stark Mansion, a National Historic Landmark, is where the secession papers for the state of South Carolina were read and where Jefferson Davis, former President of the Confederacy, held his final cabinet meeting and formally disbanded the Confederate armies.

**Calhoun Falls State Park:** The town of Calhoun Falls is the gateway to the Calhoun Falls State Park on the shores of popular Lake Russell. With 438 acres of woodlands, the park facilities include 100 campsites, a lighted marina, boat ramps, fishing pier, park store, seasonal swimming beach, bathhouses, restrooms, nature trails, picnic shelters, playgrounds, and tennis courts.

# A1A Scenic and Historic Coastal Highway

*Miles of white sand beaches invite splashing in the surf. Keep watch offshore for migrating whales and schools of dolphins. The highway also visits St. Augustine, a fascinating lesson in the Spanish exploration of the coast.*

Dip your toes in the ocean off the Florida coast during your journey along A1A Scenic and Historic Coastal Highway. With miles and miles of white sand beaches, you will have plenty of space to spread out with buckets and blankets. You can charter a fishing boat and dangle a line for flounder, snook, whiting, snapper, or blues, just to name a few varieties. Or swing your feet over the pier while fishing from land.

If you don't want to get your feet wet but still enjoy watching the ocean, try jogging, biking, roller blading, or strolling along the 19-mile path from Marineland to the Volusia County line. Or stash your binoculars in your beach bag for views of wildlife and birds.



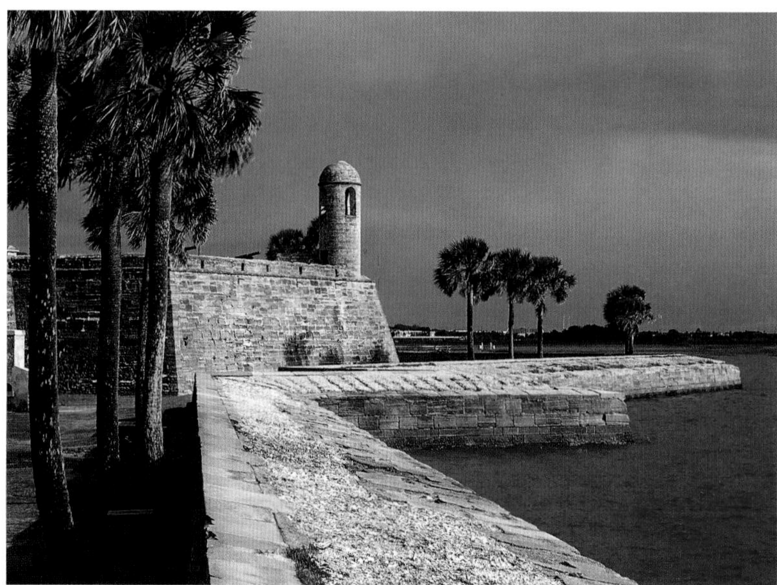

*The Castillo de San Marcos guarded the Spanish colonial interests in the settlement of St. Augustine against onslaughts of pirates and other nations.*

## Intrinsic Qualities

**Archaeological:** More than 75 archaeological sites have been formally recognized and recorded along this stretch of road, excluding the downtown St. Augustine area, which has hundreds more sites. Middens—mounds or deposits containing shells, animal bones, and other refuse, indicating sites of prehistoric human settlements—are located on publicly owned sites found in the River to Sea Preserve at Marineland, Washington Oaks Gardens State Park, Anastasia State Park, and Guana River State Park. Additionally, fossils have been found along the Intracoastal Waterway. These remains include mastodons, woolly mammoths, sloths, camels, birds, fish, beavers, snakes, tapirs, and deer.

**Cultural:** The A1A Scenic and Historic Coastal Highway stretches through an area whose culture is heavily influenced by its natural surroundings. The scenic ocean landscape certainly plays a part in this influence, as do the scents and sounds of the coast, giving shape to the art, architecture, and even livelihood of the inhabitants along the byway. This maritime culture is expressed in the byway's attractions, architecture, art, and festivals.

**Historical:** The byway traverses an area full of colorful history. Glorious hotels still stand as memorials to Henry Flagler's influence on tourism. Remnants of vast plantations allow views into the life of General Joseph Hernandez, Florida's first delegate to the U.S. Congress.

In 1565, Spanish Admiral Don Pedro Menendez de Aviles arrived with 600 soldiers and settlers, founding the city of St. Augustine at the site of the Timucuan Indian village of Seloy. He and the settlers successfully colonized Florida, 42 years before the English colony at Jamestown, Virginia, and 55 years before the arrival of the Pilgrims at Plymouth Rock, Massachusetts. St. Augustine today contains more than 2,500 historic structures.

### Quick Facts

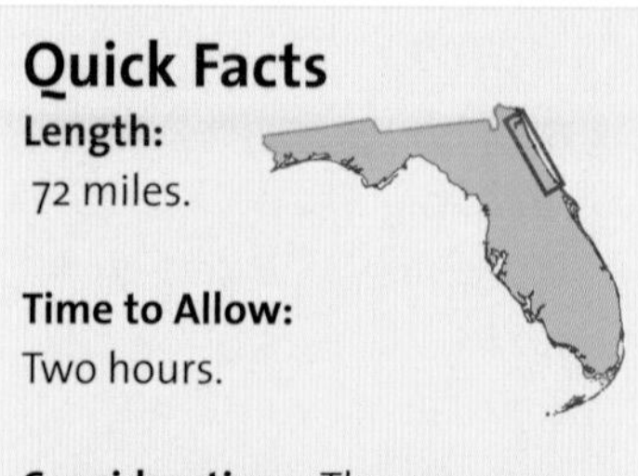

**Length:** 72 miles.

**Time to Allow:** Two hours.

**Considerations:** There are no seasonal limitations, except during the hurricane season (June–November) when the rare hurricane or tropical storm is within the vicinity.

**Natural:** The Atlantic Ocean, clean bays, rivers, marshes, and pristine beaches and dunes all play an important role in forming the natural qualities of the byway. These environmental characteristics have shaped and inspired the culture and livelihood of the area's inhabitants. Presently, numerous state parks and estuaries offer exceptional interaction with nature. Boardwalks and trails offer opportunities to explore the areas without damaging the habitat. Likewise, kayaking tours are available on the Intracoastal Waterway for an intimate look at the aquatic ecosystem.

The combination and variation of habitats in the area are home to an impressive variety of wildlife. More than 50 species of endangered or threatened animals live in the area, such as the gopher tortoise and tricolor heron. More than 300 species of fish and wildlife have been recorded in the area's reserves. Manatees, oystercatchers, green and leatherback turtles, dolphins, and even migrating northern right whales can be observed. The corridor has even been included on the Great Florida Birding Trail by the Florida Fish and Wildlife Conservation Commission. The marshes along the byway are home to their own unique animal life. Typical animals include marsh snails, fiddler crabs, otters, wading birds, ospreys, manatees, marsh wrens, alligators, turtles, great blue herons, and American egrets.

**Recreational:** There are miles and miles of beaches along the byway. Recreationalists can participate in beachcombing, sunning, beach strolling, and even beach driving; Crescent Beach allows motor vehicles on its expansive beaches.

With the ocean on one side and a river on the other along much of the byway, there is plenty of room for aquatic activities, including surfing, swimming, fishing, and boating, with free public boat launches such as the one found at Bing's Landing. Kayaking and canoeing are also popular activities, whether in the river or in shallow lakes and canals in the area. Other popular aquatic activities include sailing, taking a scenic cruise, and scuba diving. The traveler can even observe or interact with dolphins and sea turtles near the town of Marineland.

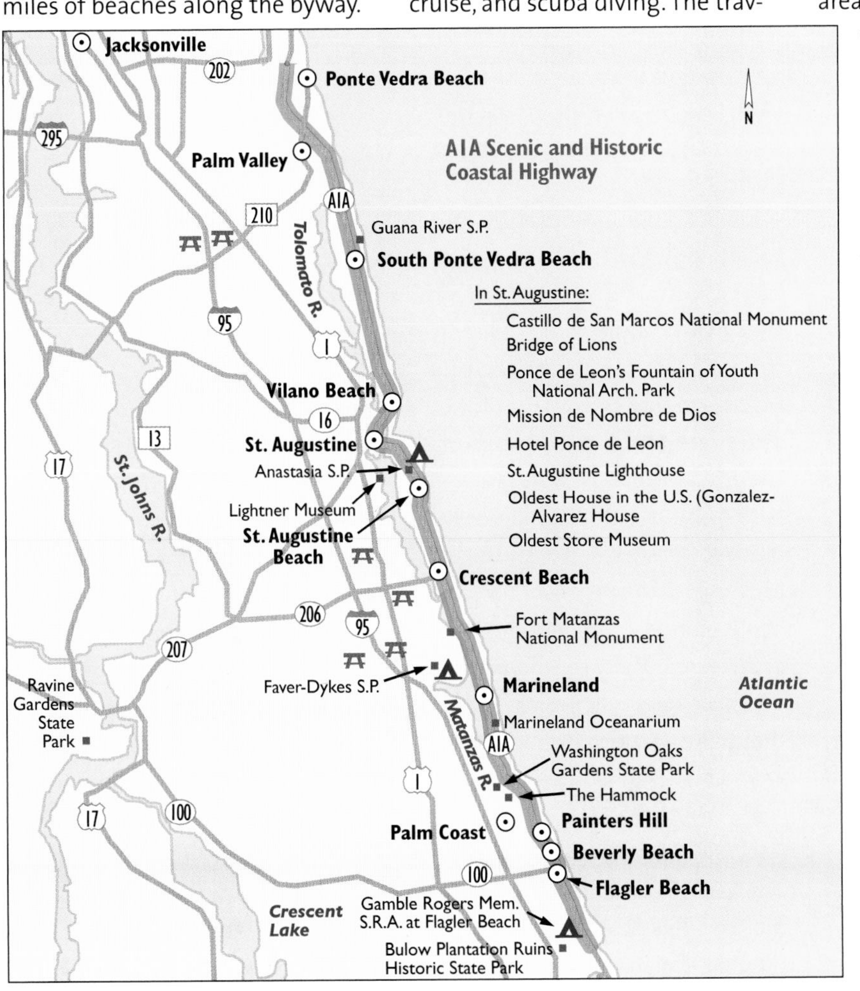


**Scenic:** The natural beauty in this byway varies from expansive ocean views, clean bays, and wide, white beaches. The most prominent of these features can be observed at the higher elevations offered at places such as the Guana River State Park dune crossover, where the Atlantic Ocean, Guana Lake, and native Florida vegetation (Coastal Strand) are visible. The sand dunes in the area reach heights of 35 to 40 feet. Dune crossovers provide perching areas to view migrating birds, right whales, and other wildlife.

## Highlights

Since being first explored by Ponce de Leon in 1513, this area has had a distinctly Spanish flair. With that in mind, here are a few of the highlights exploring that heritage.

**St. Augustine:** Start with a visit to the St. Augustine and St. Johns County Visitor Information Center. St. Augustine can be experienced by horse and buggy, tram/trolley, and on foot. Visitors may want to stop at the St. Augustine Historical Society, located in the "Oldest House in the United States" (the Gonzalez-Alvarez House).

**Ponce de Leon's Fountain of Youth National Archaeological Park:** Seeking the Fountain of Youth and believing he had found it, Ponce de Leon landed here in 1513 and planted a stone cross into the ground. Ponce de Leon's Fountain of Youth National Archaeological Park exhibits foundations and artifacts of the first St. Augustine mission and colony. Enjoy the Landmark Spring waters, a video presentation, and the Explorers Globe and Navigators' Planetarium.

**Mission de Nombre de Dios:** In 1565, Pedro Menendez de Aviles landed at what became the Mission de Nombre de Dios and claimed this site for Spain and the Church. It was on these grounds that Father Lopez would celebrate the first parish mass in the New World.

**Castillo de San Marcos National Monument:** The Castillo de San Marcos National Monument represents the oldest remaining European fortification in the continental United States. The masonry fort and its surrounding land comprise 25 acres in historic downtown St. Augustine. There is no visitor center in the park, but extensive museum exhibits are maintained within the casemates.

**Fort Matanzas National Monument:** Fort Matanzas National Monument, a former Spanish outpost fort, was built from 1740 to 1742 to guard Matanzas Inlet and to warn St. Augustine of enemies approaching from the south. Fort Matanzas now serves as a reminder of the early Spanish empire in the New World.

# Indian River Lagoon Scenic Highway

*This coastal loop explores Atlantic beaches and a diverse estuary, where you can take your pick of water sports. Then step into the Kennedy Space Center Visitors Complex for an update on America's space program.*

For a truly diverse adventure, travel the Indian River Lagoon Scenic Highway. Explore wildlife refuges, seashores, historic districts, and even the intricacies of the NASA Space Program. While traveling the highway, you will meander through three national wildlife refuges and several state and local parks and sanctuaries. And, speaking of diversity, while visiting the Indian River Lagoon, you will find yourself in the most biologically diverse estuary in North America. The lagoon is home to more than 4,000 species of plants and animals.

## Intrinsic Qualities

**Archaeological:** It is thought that Native Americans and their ancestors dwelt in the Indian River Lagoon area for as long as 15,000 years. The Ais Indians, encountered by the first Spanish explorers to Florida, are thought to be descendants of these earlier civilizations. The principal archaeological evidences of these aboriginal Indians are the middens, mounds or deposits containing shells, pottery, animal bones, and other refuse, which have been found and preserved in the area. The middens indicate that the site was once a human settlement.

Many of these shell and pottery middens were disturbed in the early years of Florida's development because they were an excellent source of shell for road building. However, the remaining middens are now carefully preserved. An abundance of middens can be found along the shores of the bluff at Ais Lookout Point.

*In the Rocket Garden at Kennedy Space Center visitors can experience the same rockets that first put NASA astronauts into space.*

**Cultural:** The Indian River Lagoon Scenic Highway is just as rich in cultural diversity as it is rich in natural diversity. From porch swings to surfboards, Florida's central coast is home to a wide variety of people. With a casual beach lifestyle, many have found Florida's space coast to be a refreshing getaway. Many communities along the byway have refurbished their historic districts into quaint shopping areas. The area is rich with theaters for the performing arts, and museums of art, history, natural science, and technology.

**Historical:** History comes alive on the Indian River Lagoon Scenic Highway. From the history of the space race to the preservation of the ecosystem, this byway is filled with museums that dynamically illustrate the lessons of the past. Each museum tells a vibrant story about Florida's rich heritage and biodiversity. Many communities also have restored historic districts that preserve the exceptional architectures of Florida.

**Natural:** The Indian River Lagoon Scenic Highway encompasses the most biodiverse estuary in North America, the Indian River Lagoon. The lagoon is host to more than 4,000 plant and animal species! The special waters of the estuary, consisting of freshwater from the river mixed with saltwater from the ocean, provide habitat for 700 species of fish and 310 species of birds, many migrating here in the winter through the Atlantic Fly Way. Many of the plants and animals are native only to the lagoon, and four species of fish breed only in the lagoon system. More than 75 rare, threatened, or endangered species survive at Indian River Lagoon, including

### Quick Facts

**Length:** 150 miles.

**Time to Allow:** Ten hours for a quick tour or two days for an exceptional adventure.

**Considerations:** Patrick Air Force Base (Cape Canaveral Air Station) does not allow through traffic. Visitors can take a bus onto the base and see the Space and Missile Museum. Florida has some of the greatest beaches in the world, with opportunities for contact with wildlife such as manatees, dolphins, and sea turtles. These are wild animals and may behave unpredictably. They may also be protected by law. For your safety and theirs, please do not approach them.

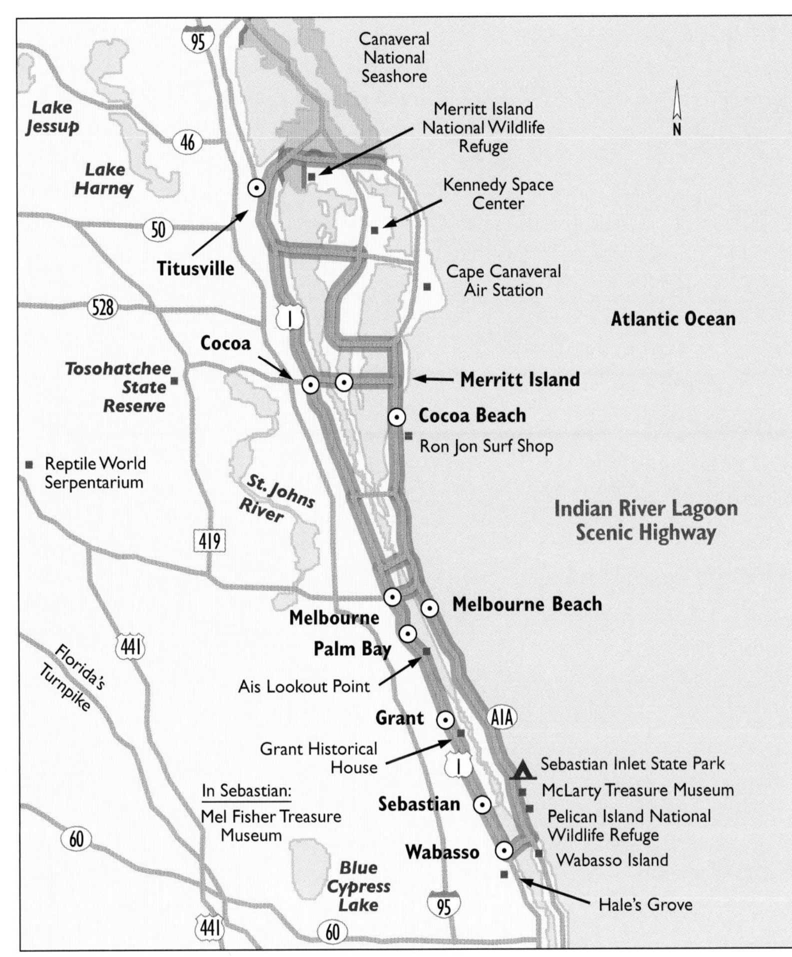


nearly one-third of the U.S. population of manatees. The area also sustains some of the most productive sea turtle nesting sites in the Western Hemisphere.

**Recreational:** In addition to showcasing shuttle launches, the byway is host to practically every recreational activity imaginable.

Surfing and scuba diving are enjoyed all along the coast, and those who like fishing will be amazed at the excellent fishing on Florida's central shore. The ocean also provides opportunities for sailing and other boating, and for swimming. Snorkeling is probably one of the most affordable yet one of the most rewarding activities.

The lagoon, on the other hand, offers its own activities. Travelers can rent an airboat or take a jungle cruise to see the wonders of Florida's unspoiled natural habitats. Travelers can also participate in waterskiing, boating, and fishing. One of the best ways to experience the peaceful appeal of Florida is to rent a canoe or kayak on the Indian River Lagoon and try your hand at paddling your way to pleasant adventures.

**Scenic:** The byway showcases a unique blend of pristine natural and recreational resources with the space-age technology of NASA, featuring alligators in front of a Space Shuttle backdrop. The traveler can stop at Ais Lookout Point and get a spectacular view. The drive out to the Kennedy Space Center provides unparalleled views of ancient orange groves and wooded hammocks.

The Canaveral National Seashore is one of the few pristine and undeveloped beaches remaining in Florida, and therefore offers an unusual look at Florida as it was in years gone by.

## Highlights

Working from south to north, travelers on the Indian River Lagoon Scenic Highway have a variety of opportunities for things to see and do. This itinerary features just a few.

**Wabasso Island:** Beginning at Wabasso Island, visit the Environmental Learning Center. Here there are hands-on learning opportunities, various nature trails with interpretive signage, wet and dry labs, and a butterfly garden.

**Sebastian:** Treasure hunters have two museums in Sebastian dedicated to adventure. At the Mel Fisher Treasure Museum visitors observe the preservation techniques used to save the recovered treasure that is currently being salvaged from the ocean floor. There are also artifacts from other discoveries.

**McLarty Treasure Museum:** This museum sits on the site of a salvaging camp created by the 1715 Spanish Plate Fleet. The museum exhibits include artifacts and displays re-creating the camps.

**Sebastian Inlet State Park:** Sebastian Inlet State Park is home to a fishing museum and beaches, as well as wildlife-viewing opportunities, nature trails, camping, and scuba diving. It also has the largest nesting assemblage of sea turtles in the United States and is part of the Great Florida Birding Trail.

**Kennedy Space Center:** Tours of the complex include IMAX Theater, the launch facilities, the Vehicle Assembly Building, and a full-size Space Shuttle mock-up. Also see an actual Gemini program capsule, view ten-story-high rockets from all eras of space exploration, and strap in and experience interactive space flight simulators.

**Merritt Island National Wildlife Refuge:** Stop first at the Visitor Information Center for details about hiking trails, the manatee observation deck, the seven-mile auto tour route, educational programs, boating, canoeing, fishing, and more.

**Canaveral National Seashore:** Canaveral National Seashore is on a barrier island that includes ocean, beach, dune, hammock, lagoon, salt marsh, and pine flatland habitats. Opportunities for recreational activities include lagoon and surf fishing, boating, canoeing, surfing, sunbathing, swimming, hiking, horseback riding, and backcountry camping.

# Tamiami Trail Scenic Highway

*A plunge into the subtropical climes of southern Florida, the highway edges Everglades National Park and bisects Big Cypress National Preserve. Huge cypress trees, 130 feet tall, line the horizon.*

Travel under a canopy of hardwood hammocks with bright splashes of tropical flowers and watch for kelly green tree frogs leaping across your trail. The Tamiami Trail Scenic Highway on the southern tip of Florida will lead the adventurous through a tropical landscape unlike any other in the United States. Venturing straight through the Big Cypress National Preserve, the Tamiami Trail offers visitors an opportunity to escape into the wilds of Florida, where you can search for endangered Florida panthers or cigar orchids. While in Big Cypress National Preserve, take advantage of opportunities to bike, hike, canoe, and picnic.

## Intrinsic Qualities

**Archaeological:** The Calusa people were the original inhabitants in the area long before the trail existed. Today, several small family-operated Native American craft shops are located along the trail. Most of the Native American villages along the edges of the trail are not open to the public. Most are visible from the trail and contain elements representative of their culture. The villages are usually communal family oriented that is also typical of their culture.

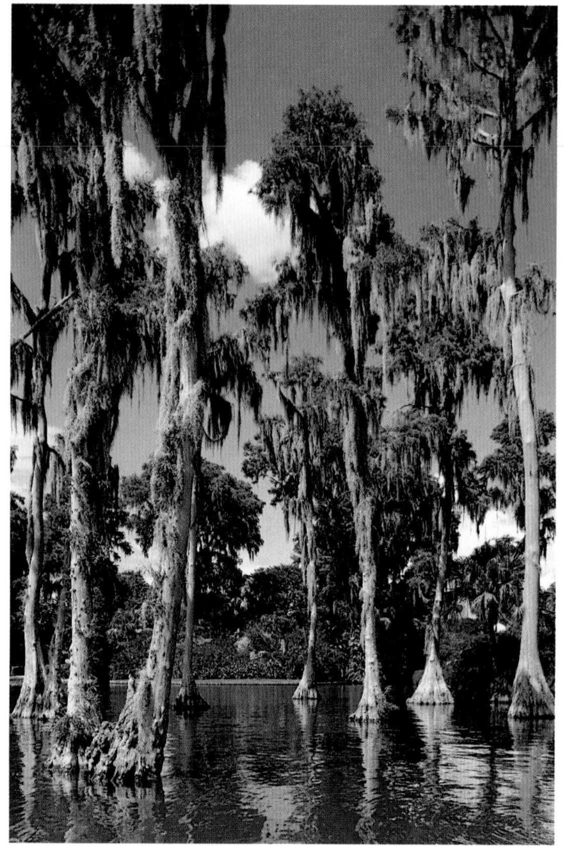

*The subtropical Everglades is a low-lying floodplain with cypress trees, mangrove thickets, and palms.*

The Seminole Monument is located one mile west of Monroe Station. This spot marks the location where Florida governor David Sholtz met with leaders of the Seminole and Miccosukee Nations. The Miccosukee Tribe's headquarters is located on the Tamiami Trail just east of the Dade County line.

**Historical:** The completion of the Tamiami Trail in 1928 led to the construction of the first buildings along the route, called way stations. These way stations, similar to gas or filling stations, were built along the trail specifically to assist stranded motorists. The stations were located at ten-mile intervals, and each one was operated by a husband and wife team. Five of the way station sites are found within the corridor limits, and include Royal Palm, Weavers, Monroe, Turner River, and Paolita stations. Royal Palm and Monroe stations have the original structures still in place, but they have been altered from the original design.

Settlements and businesses began to develop soon after the road was completed. Three sawmills were located along the trail to harvest cypress and pine trees. Lumbering activities became an important activity in Collier County in the 1930s. Other business opportunities developed around agriculture.

**Natural:** The Tamiami Trail Scenic Highway travels through the Everglades/Big Cypress region of Florida, which is the largest remaining subtropical wilderness in the United States. This particular section of land is home to unique palms and palm islands. About 80 percent of the land is owned by the public in the form of national parks, national preserves, and state parks. Visitors have a chance to see the natural habitat of south Florida, including mangroves, fresh- and saltwater marshes, sawgrass prairie, tropical hardwood hammocks, palm hammocks and islands, pinelands, and cypress strands. The combination of these unique features provides an unparalleled wildlife sanctuary.

The Everglades area boasts the largest mangrove forest in North America, and the cypress strands build a virtual canopy for the visitor to travel under. Abundant wildlife is also found throughout the byway area. For example, American alligators, soft-shell turtles, bald eagles, wood storks, great egrets,

### Quick Facts

**Length:** 49½ miles.

**Time to Allow:** Just three to four hours will allow you ample time to capture the charm of this byway.

**Considerations:** Portions of the trail are relatively isolated, so travelers should be sure they have plenty of gasoline.

great blue herons, Everglades mink, black bears, panthers, wild hogs, white-tailed deer, otters, roseate spoonbills, and manatees (along with various fish) are known inhabitants of the area.

**Recreational:** Recreational opportunities are abundant along the Tamiami Trail. The unique Everglades region, coupled with the 800,000 acres of public land located around the byway, give visitors and recreational enthusiasts a variety of chances to enjoy themselves. Picnic areas, wildlife viewing, photographic opportunities, and a visitor center area are all available for casual visitors. Canoe launch areas provide an avenue for the more adventurous traveler.

Fishers can try their hand at salt- or freshwater fishing via canoe or along the canal edges. The Florida National Scenic Trail crosses the byway and provides 31 miles of hiking for day hikers and overnight backpackers. There are primitive campgrounds that offer a few facilities, as well as many campgrounds with full facilities. Hunting and off-road vehicle exploration of the Big Cypress National Preserve is allowed. Permits and required licenses are necessary to hunt, fish, or operate an off-road vehicle.

**Scenic:** The trail traverses the middle of the Everglades region and offers an unrivaled view of the area's rich natural wonders. Common sightings of wildlife and scenic vistas along the trail have introduced countless travelers to the area and has drawn regional, state, and national attention to South Florida's unique ecosystems.

## Highlights

Here are some of the natural and historical highlights along Florida's Tamiami Trail Scenic Highway.

**Smallwood Trading Post:** Smallwood Trading Post was built in 1906, located on Chokoloskee Island on the western edge of the Everglades. One of the oldest standing buildings in southwest Florida and listed on the National Register of Historic Places, it is a time capsule of Florida pioneer history. When the business closed in 1982, 90 percent of the original goods remained in the store. Ted Smallwood's granddaughter reopened the store in recent years as a museum.

**Big Cypress National Preserve:** The Big Cypress National Preserve covers more than 729,000 acres of open prairie dotted with cypress trees, pinelands, and dark forested swamps. The most common tree species are bald cypress, which grow to heights of 130 feet with broad canopies. Visitors will want to start with the orientation video at the visitor center. Other opportunities include wildlife viewing and bird-watching; hiking, biking, and driving trails; and special ranger-guided programs.

**Big Cypress Swamp:** Experience this swamp on a swamp buggy or airboat. Swamp buggies provide a mechanical mode of transportation into the swamp, and airboats enable visitors to cruise atop grasses and marshes, covering great distances in little time. Also, canoeing and kayaking provide fun water exploration.

**Museum of the Everglades:** This museum showcases the history of the southwestern Everglades. Artifacts and displays in the recently restored laundry building tell the story of two millennia of human occupation. The building is the only remaining, unaltered structure original to the town. A company town built during the 1920s by Barron Gift Collier, the laundry served the workers who completed the Tamiami Trail to Miami. A tour of the museum is self-guided.

**Everglades National Park:** The Gulf Coast entrance to the Everglades National Park is located just a short distance from the Tamiami Trail. Everglades National Park has been designated a World Heritage Site, an International Biosphere Reserve, and a Wetland of International Importance. It is the only subtropical preserve in North America. Ranger-led boat trips, walks, and canoe programs allow you to learn more about this park's history.

**Ten Thousand Islands National Wildlife Refuge:** Though best accessed by boat, the Ten Thousand Islands National Wildlife Refuge is worth the trip. This 35,000-acre refuge protects important mangrove habitats and a rich diversity of native wildlife, including several endangered species.

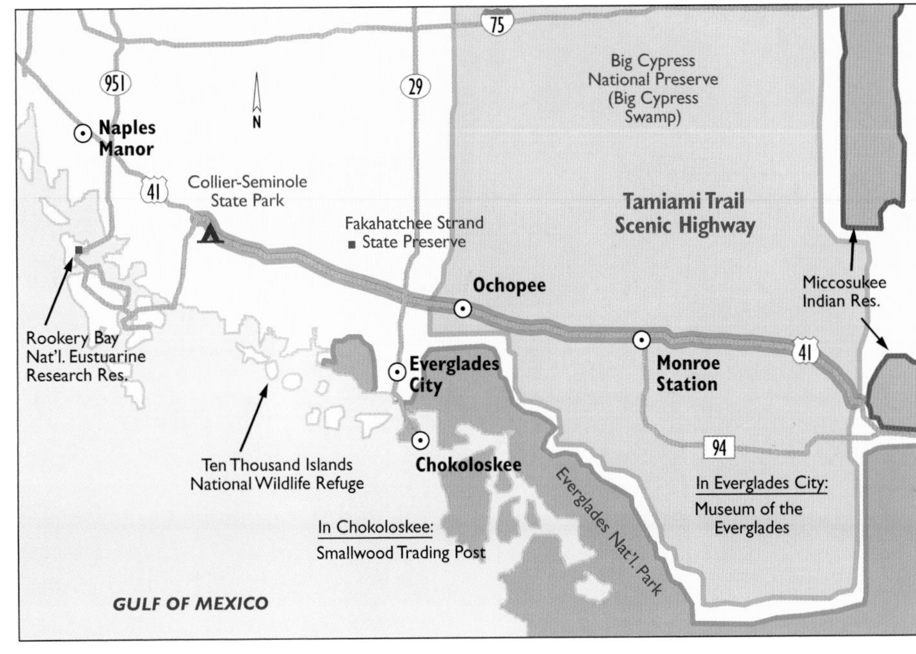

# Amazing Places to Take Your kids

NEW ENGLAND

## Acadia National Park

Acadia covers more than 47,000 scenic acres of islands and peninsulas at the northern tip of Maine. Its glacier-carved mountains, evergreen forests, inland lakes, and surf-tossed rocky shores lure nearly three million visitors annually. The Loop Road, which encircles the eastern side of the park, is the best way for newcomers to begin exploring. The road will take you past Sand Beach, which lifeguards patrol in the summer. It's a great place for the kids to swim in the chilly water or to take a stroll to stretch your legs.

## Bar Harbor

The Bar Harbor area, the gateway to Maine's Acadia National Park, has a terrific selection of family activities, including an oceanarium, kayak tours, nature programs, and a small museum that showcases an excellent collection of Native American artifacts. Visitors can also rent bicycles to explore the 55 miles of carriage trails that lace the area. Families can rent a canoe or kayak and explore on their own or take boat tours in search of whales, seals, and seabirds. Be sure to walk along Shore Path, a wide, winding trail that follows the shoreline for more than a half-mile.

## White Mountain National Forest

Located in central New Hampshire, White Mountain National Forest attracts more visitors than Yellowstone and Yosemite national parks combined. The forest's 770,000 acres includes the Presidential Range, so called because its peaks are each named for an early U.S. president.

The forest offers hiking, cycling, canoeing, climbing, and fishing in summer; and snowshoeing, snowmobiling, and cross-country and downhill skiing in winter. The towns and villages in the area contain plenty of other attractions for families, including the Conway Scenic Railroad, the New England Ski Museum, Story Land, Santa's Village, and a number of water parks.

*The spectacular scenery at Acadia National Park includes 26 mountains. Its rugged terrain and dramatic coastline make for some memorable sights.*

## Lake Winnipesaukee

Summers at Lake Winnipesaukee are all about cottages by the shore, leisurely boat rides to the store for groceries, moonlit swims on warm nights, and a rod and reel on the dock. Winnipesaukee is New Hampshire's largest lake and is dotted with 253 islands and edged with coves, deep inlets, and bays.

Each of the area's villages has something different to offer. For example, Weirs Beach is a perennial family favorite, where you'll find arcades, bumper cars, an old-fashioned drive-in movie theater, waterslides, and tour boats. On certain nights in the summer, fireworks explode high in the sky above hundreds of boats.

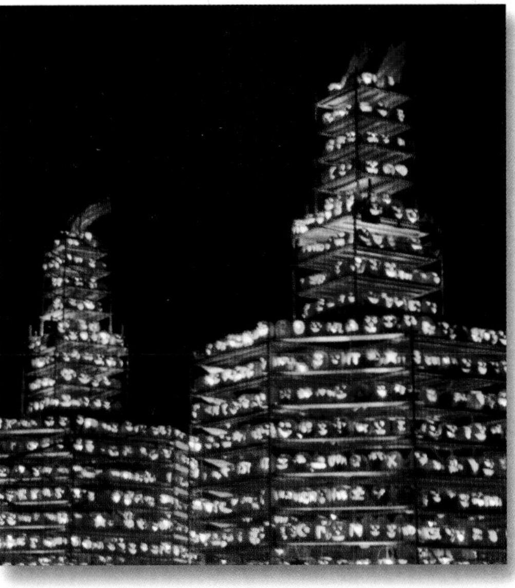

*Scary scowls and goofy grimaces adorn the collection of pumpkins at the Keene Pumpkin Festival. What began as a small-town festival now attracts thousands, with many attending the highlight of the event: the lighting of the pumpkin towers.*

## Keene Pumpkin Festival

After dark, when volunteers have lit the thousands of pumpkins in downtown Keene, New Hampshire, a switch is flipped and four immense towers of carved, light-filled pumpkins blaze in the night. During this annual late-October festival, there are pumpkins aplenty, and the carved gourds take all forms—classic peg-toothed grinners, leering witches, pop-culture celebrities, and even advertising slogans.

There is plenty of fun to occupy your time while you're waiting for the great pumpkin lights. The festival features trick-or-treating on Main Street, a pumpkin-pie-eating contest, a pumpkin-seed-spitting contest, a craft fair, food vendors, a climbing wall, and a kids' activity tent called Jack's House.

## Odiorne Point State Park

Visit Odiorne's Seacoast Science Center before going to the beach to give your family a leg up on identifying the many creatures you're likely to spot in the shoreline's intertidal zone. The center's

Gone, but not forgotten: The many ice cream flavors retired by Ben & Jerry's have been given a final resting place.

aquariums and animal exhibits showcase coastal habitats from tide pools to the seafloor. Other exhibits detail the natural and human history of Odiorne and the seacoast area.

The state park includes Odiorne Point, the largest undeveloped stretch of shore on New Hampshire's 18-mile coast. Its spectacular oceanfront is backed by marshes, sand dunes, and dense vegetation. An extensive network of trails, including a paved bike path, winds through the park.

## Sand Bar State Park

Sand Bar State Park in Vermont is named for a natural sandbar between South Hero Island in Grand Isle County and the town of Milton. Its smooth, sandy lake bottom remains shallow well out from shore, making this a perfect swimming spot for young children. The park's 2,000-foot stretch of sand is considered one of the best beaches on Lake Champlain, and one where the water tends to stay a bit warmer than other parts of the lake in midsummer. Families headquarter on the sand and can take a break to picnic in the tree-shaded spots near the beach.

## Ben & Jerry's Ice Cream Factory Tour

Vermont's top tourist attraction is the Ben & Jerry's Ice Cream Factory in Waterbury. The grounds of the brightly painted factory include a number of unusual items for children to climb on, a bubbles kiosk, spin art, and a small playground. The tour consists of a short video presentation followed by a walk through the factory to see the ice cream-making process. Everyone's favorite part of the tour comes at the end, when two rich and creamy samples are offered. Be sure to take the Stairway to Heaven to the Flavor Graveyard, where colorful tombstones honor dearly departed flavors, such as Fred and Ginger and Holy Cannoli.

## Shelburne Museum

Plan your day carefully at the Shelburne, nicknamed Vermont's Smithsonian, so you have plenty of time to enjoy its extensive collection of American folk art. You could get lost exploring its exhibition halls; restored barns; jail; and vehicle sheds with hundreds of horse-drawn stagecoaches, sleighs, and fire engines.

Most of the exhibits have touch-and-learn components designed for kids. In the Apothecary Shop, children can pretend to mix compounds. In the Hat and Fragrance Textile Gallery, they can make a quilt with magnetic patterns and feel the textures of different types of quilts. In the doll exhibit, there is a dollhouse they can play in.

## Freedom Trail

A walk along Boston's Freedom Trail is like a trip back in time to Colonial America. The 16 sites along the trail describe Boston's early patriots, their notion of liberty, and the journey to independence. Exploring the 2.5-mile-long Freedom Trail is a fascinating way to experience Boston's rich history, as well as the sights and sounds of the modern city.

A painted red line or red brick path connects the sites and buildings on the trail and serves as a guide on your journey. It begins in Boston Common, one of the nation's oldest public parks, and finishes at the Bunker Hill Monument.

## Plimoth Plantation

As you stroll the lanes of Plimoth Plantation in Plymouth, Massachusetts, it's easy to envision yourself living in this settlement just seven years after the *Mayflower* landed. Costumed interpreters go about their daily lives as they would have during the early years of Colonial America. Each person has a story to tell, and it's clear that they enjoy talking.

The living-history museum has two main components: the reconstructed English village the colonists occupied and a reconstructed Wampanoag Native American settlement, Hobbamock's Homesite. The homesite explores the life of one 17th-century Wampanoag person, Hobbamock, as well as traditional Wampanoag culture and history.

A member of the Wampanoag tribe at Plimoth Plantation shows visitors how to use fire to fortify a dugout canoe. This practice was an important part of the Wampanoag's culture, as they depended on the ocean for transportation and food.

## Boston Children's Museum

A 40-foot-high red and white wooden milk bottle marks the entry to the Boston Children's Museum, where hands-on discovery and uninhibited experimenta-

*The famous 40-foot-high Hood milk bottle greets visitors at the entrance of the Boston Children's Museum. The building actually houses a snack stand.*

tion are found on four floors of fun. The museum's centerpiece is the New Balance Climb, an elaborate three-story sculptural maze of brightly painted towers, colorful tubes, and wobbly walkways. Other educational attractions include the Science Playground, where principles of physics are creatively displayed; Construction Zone, where youngsters can dig, tunnel, build, and tear down; Kid Power, which inspires families to develop healthier habits; and Play-Space, an area created especially for preschoolers and toddlers.

## Boston's Public Garden

The biggest celebrities in Boston's Public Garden are characters from children's literature. In Robert McCloskey's beloved *Make Way for Ducklings,* a family of ducks travels from Boston's Charles River, with the help of local police officers, to the Public Garden, where they decide to live. The charming scene of Mrs. Mallard and her eight little ducklings all in a row waddling across the street is immortalized in a garden statue. The Public Garden pond is famous for its swan boats, which have been making leisurely pedal-powered cruises around the water in warmer months since 1877.

## Martha's Vineyard

Martha's Vineyard provides an old-fashioned beach vacation with miles of pristine beaches, clean salty air, lavish beachfront homes, and rolling farmland. New England's largest island is home to picturesque towns filled with ice-cream shops, stately sea captain's houses, art galleries, and winding lanes edged with plum trees and blackberry bushes.

Because of its gentle surf, one of the best public beaches for families with young children is State Beach. Older kids enjoy the high waves at the public Katama Beach, where surfboards, kayaks, sailboards, and sailboats can be rented. In Oak Bluffs, don't neglect to stop by the Flying Horses Carousel, the oldest operating carousel in the country.

## Old Sturbridge Village

Families who want to experience life in times past will be enthralled by Old Sturbridge Village, just an hour's drive outside of Boston. The largest outdoor living-history museum in the northeast, Old Sturbridge Village brings to life an 1830s New England rural community, down to the smallest details.

Its 200 acres contain 40 exhibits, including authentically restored homes, gardens, and meeting-houses; a working farm; a district school; blacksmith, pottery, and tin shops; a bank; and law and printing offices. Children can play historic games on the commons, or they can practice writing on slates in the old-time schoolhouse. Music programs, storytelling, and crafts are regularly featured.

## Salem

Salem, Massachusetts, calls itself "Witch City," because of that harrowing seven-month period in 1692 when the townspeople put 19 innocent people to death. Today, the town commemorates its history with a number of ghoulish attractions.

The Salem Witch Museum brings visitors back to early Salem through a dramatic presentation using stage sets with life-size figures, lighting, and narration. It also gives visitors an excellent overview of the Salem Witch Trials. Other witchy attractions include the Salem Wax Museum, the Witch Dungeon Museum, and the New England Pirate Museum. Some of these may be a bit scary for children younger than seven.

## Eric Carle Museum of Picture Book Art

Most children have seen the vibrant collage illustrations in Eric Carle's *The Very Hungry Caterpillar,* a book that has sold 25 million copies and has been translated into 35 languages. Carle and his wife founded this museum in Amherst, Massachusetts, to hold hundreds of his collages, sketches, and manuscripts. It's also home to original illustrations by other children's book artists, such as Dr. Seuss, Maurice Sendak, Chris Van Allsburg, and Leo Lionni.

One of the centerpieces of the museum is Art Studio, a bright space with worktables, nonslip floors, a cleanup station, and shelves containing various art supplies. A 130-seat auditorium hosts puppet shows, films, and lectures by visiting artists.

## Block Island

Off the coast of Rhode Island is Block Island, a family destination with 17 miles of beaches, windswept dunes, gently rolling hillsides, and hundreds of freshwater ponds. Even getting here is fun—the kids will love the ferry ride to the island.

Town Beach is filled with concession stands, lifeguards, and crowds; for a quieter alternative, check out Crescent Beach. Mansion Beach is wonderful for exploring tide pools, where you'll find crabs, starfish, and sand dollars. Sachem Pond is great for a freshwater swim, especially for toddlers. Many visitors enjoy biking, and rentals are plentiful. Kayaking, snorkeling, and horseback riding are popular, too.

## Newport

This historic Rhode Island seaport has beautiful beaches and a bustling wharf where lobster boats unload their catch. Be sure to amble along the town's famous Cliff Walk. You can pick up the trail along Newport's eastern shore, and you'll eventually end up at Easton's Beach, where you'll find a carousel, a skateboard park, and free weekly concerts in summer.

The extravagant summer homes of some of America's wealthiest families, such as the Vanderbilts, Astors, and Dukes, are great to explore. The family tour of The Breakers focuses on the more personal stories of the Vanderbilts, and older children will enjoy Belcourt Castle's intriguing Ghost Tour.

## Mystic Seaport

It's easy for children to fantasize about the life of an old-time sailor in this 19-acre Connecticut living-history museum. Kids can poke around in a ship's galley and climb into actual sailors' bunks. They can learn about sailors' knots and crafts, listen to old salts spin their yarns, and learn old-time sea chanteys.

The museum is set up as a re-created 19th-century seafaring village. It comprises historic buildings that have been transported from locations around New England. Families can stroll around the typical seacoast village and watch craftspeople at work, or they can explore its shipyard and port.

*The Yale Peabody Museum boasts an impresssive display of dinosaurs among its exhibits.*

*The Barker Character, Comic & Cartoon Museum features a number of collectibles to stir up a sense of nostalgia. Its exhibits include many current favorites, as well as plenty that grown-ups will remember from their own childhoods.*

## Barker Character, Comic & Cartoon Museum

This nostalgic museum located in Cheshire, Connecticut, tips its cap to beloved childhood icons, such as Mickey and Minnie, the Flintstones, Charlie McCarthy, Li'l Abner, and SpongeBob. The museum houses the more than 80,000 toys and other items that founders Herb and Gloria Barker have accumulated over the years.

A theater shows short animated films from the 1930s and 1940s featuring some of the beloved characters found in the museum. Large cartoon character cutouts are popular backdrops for photographs. An animation and sculpture gallery is located next door.

## Yale Peabody Museum of Natural History

Towering dinosaurs and a spine-tingling mummy are just a couple of the exhibits that have made this New Haven, Connecticut, museum a hit with families. The Great Hall of Dinosaurs has complete skeletons of a *Stegosaurus* and an *Archelon,* a minivan-size extinct turtle species. The tomb of a 2,000-year-old Egyptian mummy has also been re-created in the museum.

But the museum goes even further to lure children into the fascinating realm of natural science. Its special Discovery Room is designed just for families. Here, "please touch" is the rule—you can examine a 100-million-year-old fossil, walk in the tracks of a dinosaur, and connect the bones of a rabbit.

**THE MID-ATLANTIC**

## Statue of Liberty and Ellis Island

For more than 100 years, the Statue of Liberty has stood watch just off Manhattan as the country's most illustrious symbol of freedom. Although tours inside the statue have been discontinued since September 11, 2001, you can still visit the multilevel pedestal.

Another must-see is Ellis Island, the site through which 12 million immigrants passed between

1892 and 1954, beginning with 15-year-old Annie Moore and her two brothers from Ireland. Some 40 percent of today's Americans can trace at least one ancestor back to Ellis Island. An excellent short film describes why millions of people left their homes to come to America, and what the experience was like for them.

## American Museum of Natural History

A colossal collection of dinosaur skeletons is a huge attraction at this New York museum, where more than 30 million fossils and artifacts are spread throughout 40 exhibition halls. Children ages five through twelve should visit the hands-on Discovery Room, where they can reassemble a cast skeleton of a *Prestosuchus,* a 14-foot-long reptile from the late Triassic Period. Fledgling paleontologists will enjoy examining real fossils or unearthing an *Oviraptor* nest in a re-creation of a dig site. After all those earthbound adventures, it's time to head into the galaxies—through the museum's Rose Center for Earth and Space. Step into the Hayden Planetarium to explore the history of the universe.

## The Empire State Building

Completed in 1931 and soaring approximately a quarter of a mile into the sky, the Empire State Building, with its famous Art Deco spire, is one of the most recognized of all American landmarks. The building has two observation decks: an 86th floor observatory offering an open-air view and an enclosed deck on the 102nd floor. Both offer high-powered binoculars on their promenades. The New York Skyride, a virtual-tour ride, is located on the second floor. Be sure to look up at the Empire State Building at night, when its spire is bathed in colorful lights that change to honor various holidays and charities.

## Macy's Thanksgiving Day Parade

Nearly everyone in North America has heard of Macy's Thanksgiving Day Parade, with its fabulous and elaborate floats, dancing clowns, and brassy marching bands. But what it's really known for are the signature giant helium balloons featuring favorite characters such as Angelina Ballerina, the Statue of Liberty, Scooby-Doo, and Dora the Explorer. The New York City parade heralds the start of the holiday season—Santa Claus rides along in his sleigh as a special guest. More than 40 million people watch the parade on television, but nothing beats being there in person.

## Bronx Zoo

The Children's Zoo at this world-famous facility in New York lets children experience life from an animal's perspective. They can crawl through a prairie dog tunnel, listen for sounds through a fox's ear, climb a spiderweb, and shimmy up a tree to be eye to eye with the lemurs right next door.

Three times a day in the tiger area zookeepers bring behind-the-scenes activities front and center to show visitors how they keep animals stimulated and entertained. In winter, indoor exhibits such as the World of Reptiles, housed in an original 19th-century building, allow guests to stay toasty while they tour.

## Circle Line Tours

When New York's concrete jungle and nonstop hustle and bustle begin to wear down your children, plan a Circle Line Tour. You'll get a break from the action and relax in the fresh air while you view Manhattan's famous skyline from the water.

Children with short attention spans will prefer the 75-minute tour, which takes you around the lower half of Manhattan Island and offers excellent views of the Statue of Liberty. The three-hour sightseeing cruise takes you around the entire 35 miles of the island and passes many famous landmarks. Additional cruises cover other attractions in the city, and the sunset tour offers a nighttime perspective of the city.

## Adirondack Park

Upstate New York is the place to leave the fast pace of city life behind. That's where you'll find the six-million-acre Adirondack Park and its mountains, lakes, and rivers. Visitors flock here to enjoy canoeing, fishing, boating, horseback riding, hiking, mountain climbing, and swimming—and that's just in warm weather. When the snow falls, downhill and cross-country skiing, snowshoeing, ice-skating, iceboating, and snowmobiling take over as recreational favorites. Other attractions include ski resorts; century-old country estates; scenic railroad trips; and Fort Ticonderoga, which showcases numerous muskets, bayo-

*Mount Marcy, located in the Adirondacks, is the highest point in New York. It is situated near Lake Placid, twice the host of the Winter Olympics.*

nets, pistols, and swords from the 18th century.

## Lake Placid

Lake Placid, New York, hosted the 1932 and 1980 Winter Olympic Games, and visiting families can sample many of the same sports and venues enjoyed by world-class athletes. Whiteface Mountain lures skiers and snowboarders of all abilities, and ice-skaters can practice at the Olympic speed-skating oval. But for sheer thrills, nothing beats the luge and bobsled rides.

Climb into a fiberglass Luge Rocket, and after you've had a brief lesson, you can hurtle down a track at speeds approaching 80 miles per hour. The bobsled races down a half-mile track with a guide and a person at the brakes. Both rides are for children 48 inches and taller.

## Cooperstown

Cooperstown, New York, the site of baseball's holy shrine, is also a walkable, picturesque lakeside village at the southern tip of Lake Otsego, surrounded by miles of rolling farmland. The streets are lined with old-fashioned ice-cream parlors, baseball memorabilia shops, quaint bed-and-breakfasts, and historic buildings.

Three standout museums have earned Cooperstown the nickname, "The Village of Museums." The Fenimore Art Museum boasts an enviable collection of American folk art, photography, fine art, and Native American arts and crafts. Across the street, The Farmers' Museum celebrates the rural life of the area. And, of course, The National Baseball Hall of Fame and Museum pays tribute to the heroes of America's most beloved sport.

## Seaside Heights

Combine sandy white beaches and perfect ocean waves with a long boardwalk promenade and amusement park fun, and you have an enjoyable family beach town. Seaside Heights, just north of Long Beach Island, New Jersey, has all that and more.

Amusement parks are located at both ends of the mile-long boardwalk, which extends from the north end of Seaside Heights to the southern border of Island Beach State Park. Along the boardwalk are shops, arcades, seafood restaurants, and snack stands selling summertime classics such as cotton candy and saltwater taffy. The boardwalk bustles with families and fun-seekers all day and well into the evening.

## Six Flags Great Adventure

Six Flags Great Adventure in Jackson, New Jersey, is all about the biggest, the fastest, and the most. It is considered the largest regional amusement park in the country, covering 2,200 acres with more than 200 amusement rides, including some of the fastest thrill rides anywhere in the world. It encompasses two other parks: Wild Safari, the largest drive-through safari park outside of Africa, and Hurricane Harbor, one of the largest water parks in the world. The park caters to younger children, too, at Looney Tunes Seaport and Wiggles World. Plus, there are concerts and performances all season.

## Crayola Factory

The Crayola Factory in Easton, Pennsylvania, has made more than 110 billion crayons. But this place is much more than a factory tour—it's a hands-on discovery center complete with creative activities. Children can play with magic modeling clay, draw on the walls, illustrate on screens that project their work, and try out the latest Crayola products. The factory features a different theme each month, and projects are geared toward the themes.

Kids can take their projects home, and at the end of the tour they receive a marker and a four-pack of crayons. The Crayola Store outside carries the most complete line of Crayola products anywhere.

*What do you get when you combine the excitement of a carnival with the activity of a beach? Seaside Heights—a family favorite that appeals to children of all ages.*

## Gettysburg National Military Park

For three days in July 1863, 165,000 Union and Confederate soldiers fought in Gettysburg, Pennsylvania, to determine the future of the United States. More than 51,000 soldiers were killed, wounded, or captured. The battlefield has been preserved so visitors can tread the same varied terrain as the soldiers. The first stop on your visit should be the visitor's center, where you can begin one of the many battlefield tours, including a guided bus tour, private tours with guides who will accompany you in your car, an audio tape timed to the marked plaques, a guided bicycle trip, and a horseback riding tour.

## Hersheypark

Initially opened in 1907 by candy maker Milton Hershey as a picnic

Dozens of Mummers clubs work year-round to prepare the colorful costumes you'll see at the annual New Year's Day parade, a holiday favorite.

spot for his employees, Hersheypark in Hershey, Pennsylvania, is now a 110-acre theme park with more than 60 rides. Keep an eye out for seven-foot-tall costumed characters dressed as Hershey bars, Hershey's Kisses, and Reese's Peanut Butter Cups wandering around the park.

While the amusement park and adjacent zoo and gardens are closed during the winter months, you can still visit other attractions, such as the Hershey's Chocolate World Visitor's Center, which offers a factory tour. Visitors climb into mechanized cars to tour the chocolate-making process, from cocoa bean to molded bar.

## Kennywood Amusement Park

Founded in 1898, Kennywood Amusement Park is the quintessential American amusement park. Located in West Mifflin, Pennsylvania, Kennywood combines the best of an old-style park with the thrills of the new. Its classic wooden roller coasters are considered among the best in the world. The Racer is a particular favorite for kids—it is a single-track racing coaster, the only one of its kind in the United States. Kennywood is also famous for its homemade fudge, funnel cakes, dip cones, and "Potato Patch French fries" that are cut fresh and served in a basket with up to eight toppings.

## Mummers Parade

Take the extravagant costumes of a New Orleans Mardi Gras parade and add even more sequins, feathers, and fabric. After all, this parade takes place on New Year's Day, when the weather in Philadelphia can be frosty, if not downright freezing. Then add string-band music, dancing clowns, elaborate floats, brass bands, and an extra dose of humor, and you have the Mummers Parade, a Philadelphia institution that dates back to the late 1700s. Swedish immigrants began the tradition as part of their Christmas celebration. Many of Philadelphia's Mummers spend the entire year practicing dance and band routines and constructing their elaborate costumes.

## Independence Hall

The seeds of liberty were sown in Philadelphia's Independence Hall. It was here that the Declaration of Independence was signed in 1776, the Articles of Confederation uniting the 13 colonies was ratified in 1781, and the Constitution of the United States was adopted in 1787. The Declaration was first read in public in Independence Square a few days after its signing. The famous Liberty Bell, which is now on display in a pavilion across from the hall, was rung to announce the public reading.

## Please Touch Museum

The Please Touch Museum features thoughtfully designed exhibits geared toward kids ages seven and under. This engaging Philadelphia attraction is meant to inspire a lifelong appreciation for museums. Several enchanting exhibits are based on the classics of children's literature: A scene from *Alice's Adventures in Wonderland* lures visitors through the base of a tree and into the rabbit hole. In the hall of mirrors, your reflection becomes smaller or larger at the twist of a knob. The interactive Maurice Sendak exhibit includes oversize settings and characters from his books *Where the Wild Things Are* and *In the Night Kitchen*.

## Franklin Institute Science Museum

This Philadelphia museum's star attraction is a two-story human heart. Big enough to fit nicely inside the Statue of Liberty's chest, the heart has been the centerpiece of this museum for the past 50 years. Visitors walk through it, following the same route that blood would take, passing through chambers and veins to the ever-present sound of the beating organ. The eight-foot-long Crawl Through Arteries feature allows children to pretend they are blood cells navigating through clear and clogged arteries. All kinds of educational information about the heart lines the walls of the walkway and nearby exhibition space.

*Philadelphia's Franklin Institute of Science is the city's most visited museum. Its most famous exhibit is a giant replica of a human heart. Children enjoy walking through the display, which was built in 1953.*

*The first stop is fun! The Miniature Railroad & Village has been a popular attraction of the Carnegie Science Center for the past 50 years. Look closely at the amazing detail that goes into each display.*

## Sesame Place

Join Big Bird, Bert, Ernie, and other fuzzy favorites from the award-winning PBS show *Sesame Street* at Sesame Place, a theme park based on the popular television program. This Langhorne, Pennsylvania, amusement park features rides, 12 water attractions, exciting stage shows, parades, and plenty of opportunities to shake hands with Elmo, Snuffleupagus, and other life-size characters. You can also reserve dinner with the characters so your children are guaranteed to rub shoulders with their favorite cast members.

## Carnegie Science Center

There is so much for children to do at this imaginative science museum in Pittsburgh that they may never get to Exploration Station, the enormous fourth floor filled with interactive exhibits designed just for kids. Many children become sidetracked in SportsWorks, an entire building that emphasizes the physics of sports with virtual reality rides. Or they can design their own roller coaster on a special computer and then "ride" it in a simulator. At the Miniature Railroad & Village display, adults will marvel at the minute historical accuracy of familiar Pittsburgh neighborhoods, while kids will be spellbound by its special animated features.

## Pennsylvania Dutch Country

As you drive through this peaceful realm, you'll pass classic barns and silos, horse-drawn buggies, wooden covered bridges, and a pretty patchwork of farm fields and villages. You might even see girls in bonnets and boys in hats, but you won't see many kids riding bicycles to get to their one-room schoolhouses. Some children aren't allowed to have bicycles because their elders fear they might venture too far from home. That's just one of the many things that sets apart the Pennsylvania Dutch Country, which hearkens back in time to a simpler era.

## Winterthur Garden and Enchanted Woods

Many people visit Winterthur, the lavish former home of Henry Francis du Pont in northern Delaware, to see its collection of art and antiques and its elaborate formal gardens. Most popular with families is its Enchanted Woods, a three-acre fairy-tale garden. Children delight in the legend that fairies brought broken stones, old columns, crumbling millstones, and cast-off balustrades to this hilltop area to create a magical place of wonder for children. Kids will love the Tulip Tree House; the Faerie Cottage; and the magical mushroom ring, which according to fairy lore, will transport you to fairyland.

## Lewes

This Delaware seaport is situated where Delaware Bay meets the Atlantic Ocean. It is filled with both bay and ocean beaches where you can swim, surf, or comb the sand for old Spanish pieces-of-eight coins, which some say still wash up on shore from an old shipwreck. The village of Lewes is a charmer, lined with historic homes and quaint antique stores. At Fisherman's Wharf, families can drop a line to fish for flounder or sea bass, or board a boat to go whale- and dolphin-watching.

## Baltimore's Inner Harbor

The Inner Harbor has become Baltimore's top tourist destination, and you'll need at least a day to enjoy the museums, entertainment, and eateries at this lively, family-friendly seaport. Several attractions are related to Baltimore's 300-year history as a maritime

*A common sight in Pennsylvania Dutch Country, an Amish farmer plows his field with a team of horses. The area draws many visitors, curious to see a way of life that doesn't include modern conveniences.*

powerhouse. The USS *Constellation*, a restored 1854 wooden naval warship, is docked in the harbor and is open for tours.

The National Aquarium features marine life from Maryland's tidal marshes, as well as creatures of the deep from all over the planet. And a terrific children's museum, Port Discovery, is a hands-on delight located one block northeast of Inner Harbor.

## The B&O Railroad Museum

Anyone who has ever played Monopoly knows the B&O Railroad. But they may not know that "B&O" stands for "Baltimore & Ohio," a railroad company that at one time was one of the most important freight and passenger lines in the country. This heritage is honored at the B&O Railroad Museum in Baltimore, the largest railroad museum in the Western Hemisphere.

The museum features a large collection of railroad cars. Kids can climb in a caboose and a World War II troop sleeper car, and watch large toy trains make their way through an outdoor garden. Train rides are offered Tuesday–Sunday, April–December.

## Fourth of July Festivities

For America's finest Fourth of July birthday party, the place to be is Washington, D.C. The day begins with a rousing dramatic reading of the Declaration of Independence, followed by a parade complete with armed-forces bands, drill teams and marching groups from across the United States, VIPs, floats, and giant balloons.

At 8:00 P.M. the National Symphony Orchestra and other guest performers get the crowd in a patriotic mood with favorites such as John Philip Sousa's "Stars and Stripes Forever" and the "1812 Overture" in front of the U.S. Capitol. The grand finale is an amazing fireworks display against the picturesque backdrops of the U.S. Capitol and the Washington Monument.

## The National Mall

The National Mall is a tree-lined stretch of parkland that runs for 2.5 miles from the banks of the Potomac River to the U.S. Capitol. It is the center of every visitor's trip to Washington, D.C., because of its grand monuments, amazing memorials, and world-class museums. The most rousing night out on the town won't cost you a thing (nor will any other attraction on the mall). Pack a picnic dinner and arrive before the start of the 8:00 P.M. military band concert to claim your square of turf. The concerts are offered near the Capitol most summer weeknights, weather permitting.

## National Air and Space Museum

Showcasing the icons of space and aviation—Apollo modules, a Mercury space capsule, lunar landing probes, the Wright Brothers' 1903 Flyer, and full-size missiles—the most-visited museum in the world exhibits the real deal instead of models. At this Washington, D.C., museum children can touch a piece of real moon rock, activate a supersonic wind tunnel, and see John Glenn's flight suit.

One sure favorite is the At the Controls: Flight Simulator Zone, where visitors can flip over, twist, and turn as they pilot a full-motion flight simulator. Other simulation programs allow visitors to fly combat missions, experience a space walk, or pilot famous aircraft.

## Bureau of Engraving and Printing

The buck starts at this Washington, D.C. location. You can watch as bills evolve from large blank sheets of paper into complexly printed wallet-size notes. A fortune rolls off the presses every few minutes. Around $635 million is printed each day ($232 billion per year), mostly for the purpose of replacing worn bills already in circulation.

If you take the tour, you'll learn about the various steps involved in currency production; procedures the Bureau has put in place to thwart counterfeiting; and what type of durable paper is used that can withstand thousands of wallets, hands, and ATMs.

## International Spy Museum

Learn firsthand how a spy operates at the only museum in the United States dedicated to the world of espionage. Upon your arrival at Washington, D.C.'s International Spy Museum, you'll adopt a "cover" and receive a new identity. You'll need to remember this information to see how well you perform as a spy, particularly when border guards throughout the museum interrogate you.

Some of the family programs include workshops on disguise-

*Were you born to be a spy? Find out as you tour the International Spy Museum. You'll enjoy your journey into the world of disguises and mystery.*

making, as well as on making and breaking secret codes, and inventing concealment devices. On display are classic hidden spy craft tools, such as buttonhole cameras, lapel knives, lipstick pistols, and hollowed-out coins concealing microdots.

## The National Cherry Blossom Festival

This two-week celebration features a kite festival, a parade, daily traditional music and dance performances, martial arts demonstrations, bike tours of the pink and white blossoms, origami lessons, a Japanese street fair, and fireworks. The festival celebrates the arrival of spring and commemorates the gift of 3,000 cherry trees to the city of Washington, D.C., from the people of Tokyo in 1912.

The parade is the festival's biggest event and features spectacular floats, marching bands, taiko drum corps, costumed dance groups, and giant helium balloons. Sakura Matsuri, a Japanese street festival held after the parade, exhibits the traditions, arts, and food of Japan. Kids will enjoy playing Japanese games and learning all about Japanese paper- and doll-making.

## National Museum of the American Indian

This showplace of Native American cultures, from the Arctic Circle to Tierra del Fuego, is a must-see in Washington, D.C. Kids enjoy the journey through the museum's exhibits, which include steamy wetlands and lush green woodlands. They can participate in a Native American celebration of song and dance and listen to storytelling.

Exhibits at the museum include painted hides from the Plains Indians, woodcarvings from North America's northwest coast, basketry from the southwestern United States, carved jade from the Maya, and gold from the Andean cultures. Performances regularly feature storytellers, dancers, musicians, and informative talks by Native Americans.

## National Zoo

Washington, D.C.'s National Zoo opens at 6:00 A.M. so visitors can see the animals out and about when they are particularly lively. Get there early and it's easy to see the zoo's most popular guests: the adorable giant pandas from China, Mei Xiang, Tian Tian, and their offspring. Almost one-quarter of the zoo's animals are endangered species, including the pandas, Asian elephants, and western lowland gorillas.

Daily programs include animal training, feeding demonstrations, and animal-keeper talks. During the summer months, visitors can enjoy a popular free concert series, Sunset Serenades, performed on Lion and Tiger Hill.

*Scientists believe that fewer than 1,000 giant pandas remain in the wild. This panda is a popular resident of the National Zoo.*

# THE SOUTH

## Shenandoah National Park

Scenic Shenandoah National Park stretches along a particularly glorious section of the Blue Ridge Mountains in northeastern Virginia. It's an excellent park for families who like to hike—even young children can manage some of the easy, self-guided trails that wind past waterfalls, hemlocks, pines, and wildflowers.

More than 500 miles of hiking trails cut through the park, including 100 miles of the Appalachian Trail. The famous Skyline Drive runs 105 miles along the mountain crest of the entire park, and it offers stunning panoramas and opportunities to stretch your legs at each of the 75 viewpoints.

## Mount Vernon

George Washington's Virginia plantation on the banks of the Potomac River offers a fascinating glimpse of how America's first president lived toward the end of the 18th century. Visit the mansion to see Martha's tea service laid out in one of the parlors; the study, containing its original globe and desk; and the bedroom where George spent his final days. Be sure to explore the rest of the plantation grounds, including the stables, the overseer and slaves' quarters, and the Washingtons' graves. In spring and summer, you can journey from Washington, D.C., to Mount Vernon by boat along the scenic Potomac River.

## Colonial Williamsburg

This former capital of colonial Virginia is the world's largest living-history museum. The town appears much as it did during the Revolutionary War. You can explore many of its more than 500 restored and reconstructed buildings: Walk through dank jails, visit elegant government buildings, and tour simple homes and neighborhood taverns.

Many of the quaint shops offer fascinating hands-on demonstrations of trades such as boot-, barrel-, and wig-making. Interpreters of all ages wander the streets in period costumes, bringing to life the stories of the working people, families, slaves, and revolutionary firebrands who lived here 300 years ago.

## Historic Jamestowne and Jamestown Settlement

Historic Jamestowne, Virginia, is where the settlers formed the first permanent English colony. Archaeologists working at various locations have unearthed a wealth of artifacts, and visitors can tour its excavations and the few structures that remain. Jamestowne's glass-blowing industry is also depicted, with costumed workers applying their skills in the same manner as the early craftspeople.

Nearby is Jamestown Settlement. It features artifacts from the settlement, including a 17th-century child's hornbook; a wooden doll; clay marbles; and a small stoneware jug, dated 1590, which reportedly was given to Pocahontas. The settlement is best known for its re-created fort, the Powhatan Indian Village, and three ships that are open for exploration.

## Busch Gardens, Williamsburg

Many believe this Williamsburg, Virginia, attraction is the world's most beautiful theme park. Even though most young visitors care more about Busch Gardens' other features, their parents will appreciate the park's European-themed "lands," such as the Italian Renaissance hillside village. Each of the lands features its own music and dance shows, rides, exhibits, foods, and classic theme-park thrills.

Situated on 100 action-packed acres, Busch Gardens has more than 50 rides and attractions, with something special for all ages. It also has a small walk-through nature area that features gray wolves and other endangered animals.

*The Powhatan native people were the first residents of what was later called Jamestown. One of their huts has been re-created and is on display at Jamestown Settlement.*

## Assateague Island National Seashore

Assateague Island National Seashore lies on a long, narrow barrier island that straddles the coasts of Virginia and Maryland. The island is a peaceful, windswept sanctuary to a famous wild pony population. According to legend, these shaggy, sturdy animals survived the shipwreck of a Spanish galleon in the 1600s and then swam ashore to Assateague.

The ponies now share Assateague with an assortment of wildlife, including the unusual sika deer that make their home in the island's pine forests. The island is also known for its lovely beaches and hiking trails that allow for plenty of exploring.

*You're in for a splash landing on Escape from Pompeii, a popular ride at Busch Gardens. A visit to this beautiful amusement park will take you to many different lands and an assortment of exciting rides.*

## Virginia Beach

Virginia Beach, Virginia, is a timeless beach town, full of classic summer fun and miles of smooth, white sandy beaches. Its three-mile-long boardwalk is perfect for inline skating, bike riding, or ambling with a stroller. If you cover its entire length, you'll come across a variety of diversions that include an amusement park, the world's busiest Dairy Queen, a Beatles museum, taffy shops, and a 1903 Coast Guard Station with a rooftop "tower cam" that kids can use to get a closer look at the ships along the horizon.

## Steven F. Udvar-Hazy Center

The Steven F. Udvar–Hazy Center, an extension of the Smithsonian National Air and Space Museum, was built to display the thousands of aviation and space-travel artifacts that could not possibly fit into the popular Washington, D.C., museum. Opened in December 2003 in Chantilly, Virginia, it showcases famous aircraft, spacecraft, rockets, and satellites, and a

*Your kids will have a booming good time at the fireworks display that's part of the Kentucky Derby Festival. The event caps the first day of festival activities.*

wide assortment of other space-exploration memorabilia.

The centerpiece of the museum is a cavernous hangar that is more than three football fields in length and ten stories high. It houses the *Enola Gay*, the plane that dropped the atom bomb on Hiroshima; the world's fastest jet; and dozens of other aircraft displayed on three levels.

## Harpers Ferry National Historical Park

Harpers Ferry, West Virginia, was a key staging area for pioneers heading into the western frontier in colonial days—Lewis and Clark began their transcontinental trek here. But the town came to national attention in 1859, when abolitionist firebrand John Brown raided the federal armory in his effort to end slavery by arming slaves. Today the town is a National Historical Park, and it still looks as it did during the Civil War. Its mixture of historic events and recreational activities (including hiking, kayaking, and rock climbing) draws about one million visitors annually.

## Winter Festival of Lights

The Oglebay Park Winter Festival of Lights in West Virginia has grown into one of the nation's largest holiday light shows, attracting more than one million visitors per year during its November-to-January run. Featuring more than one million lights and 50 displays, the festival covers 300 acres.

Guests experience the display of lights via car. An animated Snowflake Tunnel glows with thousands of lights as visitors drive through the exhibit of twinkling snowflakes. Other displays lit up in holiday finery include a poinsettia wreath with candles that stands almost 60 feet high, making it the festival's tallest display.

## Kentucky Derby Festival

The Kentucky Derby Festival that precedes the famous horse race in Louisville is a two- to three-week extravaganza of family-friendly activity. It begins in mid-April and sets the pace for the excitement leading up to the race. The festival's trademark daylong Thunder Over Louisville Air Show dazzles viewers with more than 100 planes, as well as aerial acrobatic teams and daring skydiving teams performing breathtaking stunts. In addition, the 28-minute fireworks show is the largest annual pyrotechnic display in the country, and the colorful Pegasus Parade is full of floats, marching bands, and giant inflatables. All of these events and more lead up to the Kentucky Derby at Churchill Downs, which attracts more than 100,000 spectators each year.

## Louisville Slugger Museum and Factory

Ever since Bud Hillerich created the first Louisville Slugger baseball bat in his father's workshop in 1884, the sport's biggest stars have used these finely crafted pieces of smooth white ash. A collection of famous bats lines the walls of this factory and museum in Louisville, Kentucky; most notable is the 1927 Louisville Slugger bat Babe Ruth used to hit 21 home runs. You can still see the notches carved by Ruth himself on the top of the bat. The world's largest bat, a 120-foot-tall replica of Babe Ruth's, leans casually against the factory near its entrance.

## Mammoth Cave National Park

Mammoth Cave is the longest cave system in the world: It comprises 360 miles of caverns and passages in south-central Kentucky. Many of the rooms in the vast subterranean world are enormous. At 192 feet high, Mammoth Dome

*There is no mistaking the Louisville Slugger Museum and Factory. You'll also find the world's largest baseball glove nearby.*

is as big as a palace ballroom, while the Bottomless Pit plunges 105 feet into blackness.

The best way to visit the caves is to take a tour. A special tour just for children, the Trog Tour, explores the connections between the cave and the world above. Wearing hard hats and headlamps, children walk and crawl through various passageways as they learn how the cave was formed and what lives in it.

## The National Corvette Museum and Factory Tour

More than 75 Corvettes are on display at the National Corvette Museum in Bowling Green, Kentucky, from the first cars to roll off the assembly line to the super-sci-fi, finned Stingray. In addition to the cars, there are videos, scale models, Schwinn Corvette bicycles, and various rare memorabilia on display.

The Corvette assembly plant is across the street. Here you'll see robots welding the steel frame together and workers installing the seats, wheels, and roof. You'll also witness the "marriage," the point at which the chassis and the engine come together. Be sure to call ahead to verify tour times; tours are sometimes canceled during preproduction of future models.

## Tennessee Aquarium

The spectacular Tennessee Aquarium in Chattanooga is the biggest freshwater aquarium in the world. One section of the aquarium follows the course of the Tennessee River all the way from an Appalachian high-country stream down through the steamy Mississippi Delta and out into the Gulf of Mexico. Along the way, visitors see thousands of animals that live above and below the water's surface. The Rivers of the World gallery displays creatures from warm Eurasian waters, as well as from the Amazon, St. Lawrence, Volga, and Fly rivers. Here, visitors see colorful fish, anacondas, red-bellied piranhas, massive Beluga sturgeon, and pig-nosed and four-eyed turtles.

*At the National Civil Rights Museum your family will gain a new awareness of the people who have struggled for equality and fairness throughout the country's history. The museum opened in 1991.*

## Graceland

Many kids don't know much about Elvis Presley, but after touring his home and his two private jets, they definitely appreciate his over-the-top sense of grandeur. The Graceland Mansion is the biggest attraction in Memphis, Tennessee, and is one of the five most visited home museums in the United States. The house tour is great fun for kids, who love to see the flashy stage costumes and the gold records. The Automobile Museum includes a 1955 pink Cadillac and a 1956 purple Cadillac convertible, as well as motorcycles and other vehicles.

## National Civil Rights Museum

This Memphis, Tennessee, museum pays tribute to the many people involved in the struggle for civil rights in the United States. Built around the Lorraine Motel, where Dr. Martin Luther King, Jr., was assassinated in 1968, the museum chronicles the history of civil rights activities, from the beginnings of slavery through the end of the 20th century.

Exhibits focus on such events as the Civil War, the Supreme Court decision to desegregate schools, the lunch counter sit-ins, the Montgomery Bus Boycott, and the March on Washington. Multimedia presentations and full-scale exhibits bring the civil rights movement to life for children.

## Pigeon Forge and Dollywood

Pigeon Forge, Tennessee, is filled with the kind of flashy family fun (miniature golf, go-karts, laser games, and even an indoor skydiving simulator) that kids love. But the biggest draws are Dollywood and its neighboring water park, Dollywood's Splash Country, both of which are affiliated with Dolly Parton.

Dollywood is packed with more than 30 rides and attractions, and live shows feature the best bluegrass, Southern gospel, country, and mountain music you'll find in the area. Dollywood's Splash Country is a 30-acre water park open in the summer. The fun includes two play areas, a 25,000-square-foot wave pool, 23 waterslides, and other signature attractions.

## National Storytelling Festival

This event, which began in 1973, is traditionally held the first weekend of October in Jonesborough, Tennessee. Performance storytelling is as much an art as dancing, acting, or making music. The commitment and artistry can be seen and heard in this three-day festival devoted to the telling of traditional stories, multicultural folktales, and contemporary legends.

All ages, but especially kids, enjoy the Youthful Voices concert, where young storytellers between the ages of five and eighteen share their finest tales. Also popular are the Ghost Story Concerts that are held on Friday and Saturday nights. Audience members spread out on blankets and are captivated as professional storytellers relate creepy, astonishing tales.

## Great Smoky Mountains National Park

Great Smoky Mountains National Park runs northeast to southwest, stretching across the border of North Carolina and Tennessee. The park hosts more visitors than any other national park in the United States, thanks to its half-million acres that are filled with stately old-growth forests, wildflower-packed meadows, high mountain streams, and beautiful waterfalls. This national treasure is so rich in its variety of life that the United Nations has named the park an International Biosphere Reserve and World Heritage Site. Families traveling with younger children should try to hike to Laurel Falls. The 2.5-mile trail is partially paved and leads to a refreshing waterfall.

## Outer Banks

Beach-lovers visit the legendary islands of North Carolina's Outer Banks to enjoy the seemingly endless stretches of ocean and soft sand. Families who can tear themselves away from the beach should visit lively Roanoke Island Festival Park, which has a hands-on museum; free concerts and plays; and a replica of the ship that brought over the people of Roanoke Island, who settled and then mysteriously disappeared in the 1580s. In addition, the Wright Brothers National Memorial marks the site of the world's first successful airplane flight.

*Summer school just became a lot more fun! Wrightsville Beach, a popular surfing spot, has a number of camps that offer instruction on the finer points of catching a wave.*

*Forsyth Park is Savannah's oldest large park and home to The Fountain, which was featured in* Forrest Gump *and* Midnight in the Garden of Good and Evil.

## Wrightsville Beach

Wrightsville Beach is the premier family beach town on the popular Cape Fear coastline of North Carolina. Located about 15 minutes from historic and activity-filled Wilmington, this peaceful seaside community has a small-island feel and miles of pure white sand.

The Wrightsville area is considered one of the best surfing spots on the East Coast, and kids of all ages can take lessons at several surf camps. Boogie boarding and windsurfing are popular, too. Paddlers can take a marked five-mile kayak trail that winds throughout the island's marshes. Most of the public beaches have beach volleyball courts, and Wrightsville Beach Park has a children's playground.

## Charleston

Charleston, South Carolina, is one of the most beautifully preserved cities in America, full of antebellum mansions, quaint cobblestone alleys, and carefully preserved historic buildings. After the Civil War devastated the community, residents were so poor that they could not afford to rebuild, so the city simply adapted its old buildings, unknowingly protecting them as historical treasures for future generations to appreciate. Magnolia Plantation is particularly well suited for families to visit. It features a home tour, and its grounds and gardens are filled with extras that keep kids entertained for hours. There's a petting zoo, a garden maze, and a wildlife observation tower.

## Savannah

Savannah, Georgia's historic district is filled with elegant homes, one of which belonged to Juliette Gordon Low, the founder of the Girl Scouts. The home has been converted into a museum and is a popular destination for Girl Scout troops from across the United

States. Another highlight of the historic city is Old Fort Jackson, which was built in 1808 and helped protect the coast from British warships during the War of 1812.

You can tour Savannah by horse-drawn carriage, and guides will treat you to details about the city's famous characters. If your kids enjoy a good ghost story, they'll like the tours of the supposedly haunted areas of the city.

## The Golden Isles

Georgia's great barrier islands shelter the Atlantic Intracoastal Waterway and guard the coastal shoreline. The beauties known as the Golden Isles—Sea Island, Jekyll Island, St. Simons Island, Little St. Simons Island, and Cumberland Island—are about 20 minutes from each other by boat or car, and each has a slightly different personality. All have stunning beaches, as well as marshes and creeks that are great fun to explore by canoe and kayak—most outfitters can tailor their outings to fit a family's ages and interests. In addition, dolphin-watching tours depart from several of the islands, and along the way you might see manatees and other marine life.

## The Okefenokee National Wildlife Refuge

The Okefenokee's primitive wetlands in southeastern Georgia harbor hundreds of birds, mammals, reptiles, and amphibians. The refuge is crisscrossed with more than 100 miles of canoe trails, and visitors can best see its natural wonders by touring on the water.

Okefenokee's three main entrances all offer canoe rentals and boat tours, as well as wooden boardwalks and observation platforms. Day-trippers have plenty of paddling options because several canoe trails are short enough to traverse in an afternoon. Families who want to spend a night or two can reserve wooden platform tent sites along the canoe trails or book a room near the western entrance of the park.

## Fernbank Museum of Natural History

This Atlanta museum's main exhibit, A Walk Through Time in Georgia, reflects the story of Georgia's natural history and the development of our planet with a series of realistic dioramas covering roughly 1.5 billion years. The hands-on Sensing Nature exhibit playfully demonstrates the role of our senses in interpreting our environment. The exhibit is filled with lights, videos, lasers, mirrors, optical illusions, and more, and kids can create a giant soap bubble and witness a tornado forming as they learn about human perception.

## Georgia Aquarium

Whale sharks are the biggest stars of the Georgia Aquarium in Atlanta. It is the only aquarium outside of Asia to feature them. At nearly 20 feet long and growing, these creatures are members of the largest fish species on Earth. They roam the waters of a six-million-gallon tank they share with thousands of other fish, including sawfish, giant grouper, stingrays, and hammerhead sharks.

Elsewhere, the aquarium features 100,000 animals representing more than 500 species in 60 separate habitats and has several major viewing galleries, each arranged around a theme, such as cold water, Georgia's coast, and various rivers.

## Everglades National Park

This national treasure in south Florida encompasses 1.5 million acres of saw grass marshes, tangled mangrove forests, and fresh and brackish water wetlands. Tram tours and hiking trails are available in areas of the Everglades open to the public. However, this slow-moving "River of Grass" is best explored by boat. At Flamingo Marina you can rent a kayak, canoe, or skiff to see an incredible collection of animals up close: Turtles, marsh rabbits, manatees, crocodiles, otters, alligators, and hundreds of species of birds inhabit the area.

## St. Augustine

The beaches here are legendary stretches of soft sand bordered by calm, blue water. But St. Augustine, Florida's real claim to fame is that it is the oldest permanently inhabited city in the United States. Founded in 1565, it's filled with reminders of its early Spanish history. At the edge of the ocean is an authentic fort, Castillo de San Marcos. It boasts a moat, drawbridge, and huge cannons atop which kids can sit.

Other highlights include museums, the country's oldest wooden schoolhouse, and Ponce de Leon's Fountain of Youth. There are also several 17th- and 18th-century buildings that house ice-cream parlors and shops staffed by costumed interpreters who reenact 18th-century life.

*These two giants of the prehistoric world can be viewed at the Fernbank Museum of Natural History in Atlanta. It is one of the only museums in the world located in an old-growth forest.*

## Busch Gardens, Tampa Bay

What happens when you mix the adrenaline rush of an amusement park, the beauty of a tropical garden, and the excitement of wild animals? The result is Busch Gardens in Tampa Bay, Florida.

The animal exhibits have an African theme and are divided into eight different areas, with 2,000 exotic and endangered animals living in natural environments. Scattered throughout the park are world-class roller coasters, rides for very young children, Broadway-style live entertainment, and plenty of water rides to cool down visitors during the steamy summer months. The gardens have mature trees, beds thick with blooming flowers and shrubs, fountains, and plenty of benches in their many shady corners.

## Sanibel Island

Sanibel Island is a shell-collector's paradise. Areas of the soft sandy beaches are festooned with a variety of shells, including scallops, whelks, and kitten's paws. Shell-collectors easily assume the "Sanibel Stoop" as they comb for tiny treasures washed up by the tide. Don't become too engrossed in your collecting, or you'll miss the dolphins that frequently feed just offshore. Visit the island's Bailey–Matthews Shell Museum before you begin your beach-combing to learn the names of the shells you'll find.

## Kennedy Space Center

The Kennedy Space Center in Cape Canaveral, Florida, has been the launch site for all crewed U.S. space missions since 1962. It's still the busiest launch and landing facility in the country, as well as a government site where more than 10,000 people work to maintain the existing space program and push the boundaries of scientific knowledge.

In 1967, a small visitor's complex was built as a launch-viewing site for astronauts' families. Ever since, visitors have been coming to central Florida to get a glimpse of the American space program. The center has been expanded into a full-fledged spacecraft museum that is fascinating, fun, and educational.

*Venetian Pool has been a popular attraction for decades. During its heyday, movie stars and prominent politicians lounged poolside while gondolas glided across its waters.*

## Destin

Destin, Florida, is renowned for its deep-sea fishing, but kids also love its white-sand beaches that are great for collecting shells. In fact, Destin is considered one of the top five shell-collecting areas in the world. Many visitors believe it's the best beach in the South. Families come to Destin to enjoy its soft sand and clear emerald waters, which are suited to a range of recreational activities. The clarity of its warm waters makes it especially inviting for snorkeling and scuba diving enthusiasts.

## Venetian Pool

This unusual and enormous swimming pool in Coral Gables, Florida, is reminiscent of a Venetian grotto and looks like a movie set from an old-fashioned Hollywood musical. Honored with a listing on the National Register of Historic Places, the pool dates from the 1920s and was constructed out of an old limestone quarry.

The free-form coral rock lagoon is bordered by lavish displays of blooming bougainvilleas, birds of paradise, palms, and vine-covered loggias, as well as three-story Spanish porticos with viewing areas at their top. The Venetian Pool features lovely cascading waterfalls, a cobblestone bridge, and even a sandy beach.

## Walt Disney World

Four major theme parks (all of which have rides) make up Disney World in Orlando, Florida. The Magic Kingdom, with its Cinderella Castle centerpiece and costumed characters, is the best known and possibly best loved of all the Disney World parks. At Disney's MGM Studios, guests can tour the MGM back lot and see sets from favorite TV shows or visit the animation studios. Part zoo, part theme park, Disney's Animal Kingdom is a blend of nature and adventure packaged with imaginative touches. And finally, Epcot Center showcases world culture and technology in a unique mix of attractions and educational exhibits.

## Blizzard Beach and Typhoon Lagoon Water Parks

Legend has it that when an unexpected (and, of course, completely fictional) winter storm dumped a mountain of snow on Orlando, the folks at Disney decided to create Florida's first winter resort. When temperatures returned to normal, the snow began to melt, turning the slalom course, bobsled, and toboggan runs into waterslides. And so the winter resort was turned into Blizzard Beach.

*You won't need your boots, and leave your winter coats at home. Blizzard Beach may sound cold, but the Florida water park offers the best in refreshing fun.*

Nearby is another Disney water park, Typhoon Lagoon, which was supposedly "created" when a huge storm struck and a ship was stranded high on a mountain by a giant wave. Left in the typhoon's wake are twisting slides, roaring rapids, and a 2.5-acre wave pool, as well as tamer water fun.

## Universal Studios and Islands of Adventure

Universal Studios in Orlando, Florida, has two entertaining attractions that kids will love. Universal Studios Florida, which focuses on movie-based rides and behind-the-scenes displays, and Islands of Adventure, a theme park based on cartoon characters, which features thrill rides and play areas for young children.

Universal Studios has more than 40 rides, shows, and attractions, including Shrek 4-D and Revenge of the Mummy. Younger kids enjoy A Day in the Park with Barney and Fievel's Playland. At Islands of Adventure, two favorite rides are the Amazing Adventures of Spider-Man and The Incredible Hulk Coaster. Younger children like to linger in Seuss Landing, which is based on Dr. Seuss books.

## U.S. Space and Rocket Center

The U.S. Space and Rocket Center in Huntsville, Alabama, showcases a fascinating and comprehensive collection of rockets, missiles, boosters, and space memorabilia. On display are capsules and space suits used over the years in NASA missions and a mock-up of the Apollo II Saturn V, the 363-foot rocket that helped launch astronauts to the moon. There's also a full-size mock-up of a space shuttle and a lunar rover vehicle that features tires made of piano wire to ensure that they would be able to withstand extreme temperatures.

## Gulf Islands National Seashore

The 160-mile stretch of barrier islands and coastal shores that make up Gulf Islands National Seashore has been described as the Crown Jewel of Mississippi, and it's easy to see why. Visitors can enjoy miles of sparkling white-sand beaches, warm gulf waters, idyllic barrier islands, and fertile salt marshes. Bayous thick with alligators, turtles, and frogs are waiting to be explored. These areas are accessible by kayak and canoe. Trails wind through forests of magnolias, historic sites, and cozy campgrounds. Families can relax and spend their days swimming, sunning, fishing, boating, and paddling year-round.

## Hot Springs National Park

Hot Springs National Park in central Arkansas protects 47 different hot springs and their watershed on Hot Springs Mountain, as well as the eight historic bathhouses in the town of Hot Springs. For more than 200 years, vacationers have come to the waters in Bathhouse Row in hopes of curing all kinds of ills, and tourists can still enjoy a soak in several bathhouses that have remained open. The town of Hot Springs has a number of family attractions, including an alligator farm and petting zoo, an amusement park, a water park, a riverboat tour, a wax museum, go-karts, and horseback riding.

## Blanchard Springs Caverns

Blanchard Springs Caverns in north-central Arkansas is a living cave that continues to grow moment by moment as drops of water thick with minerals add to its columns and walls. The cave has two paved, lighted trails: The Dripstone Trail tour begins with an elevator trip down 200 feet. At the bottom, concrete pathways with handrails wind through water-carved passages. Forest Service guides lead the tour and provide interesting facts about Blanchard. Discovery Trail is more strenuous than Dripstone and explores the middle portion of the cave.

*Watch out—low ceiling. Older children will enjoy the guided tours of the more challenging parts of the Blanchard Springs Caverns.*

## Ozark Folk Center State Park

Take a step into the past with a visit to the Ozark Folk Center in Mountain View, Arkansas. You'll be treated to an old-fashioned way of life that was retained well into the 20th century. The center celebrates these traditions in a state park designated specifically to preserving the culture of the early pioneers in the Ozark Mountains.

You're likely to hear an assortment of foot-stomping folk tunes played on fiddles, banjos, autoharps, dulcimers, and other instruments throughout the day. And as you explore, you'll see craftspeople working in little cottages, where they make household goods such as soap, quilts, brooms, and barrels. Many of the items are for sale.

## New Orleans Jazz and Heritage Festival

Food and music are a winning combination, and the New Orleans Jazz and Heritage Festival serves up heaping portions of both at its spring celebration spanning two action-packed weekends in late April and early May. Twelve big stages and five performance tents offer an eclectic selection of jazz, blues, gospel, funk, Cajun, zydeco, bluegrass, and much more.

Food choices at the festival are even more mind-boggling: Muffulettas or po' boys? Crawfish Monica or the pheasant-quail-andouille gumbo? Pecan pralines, peach cobbler, or a New Orleans sno-ball? The tantalizing entrées, snacks, and desserts are influenced by local flavor and showcase New Orleans cuisine and Southern cooking at their best.

## Spooky Cemeteries and Haunted House Tours

Tours with mysterious, eerie, and downright scary themes are popular in New Orleans, and many tour companies take visitors through the city's bewitching old cemeteries and haunted buildings. Cemetery tours usually wind through St. Louis Cemetery #1, established in 1789 and the oldest existing cemetery in the city. Voodoo queen Marie Laveau is purportedly buried there.

Many tours also visit the crypts, tombs, and historic headstones of Lafayette Cemetery, depicted in many of Ann Rice's vampire novels. Ghost tours of the French Quarter share hair-raising tales about the ghosts, spirits, and phantoms of its various residences and businesses.

*Colorful feathers, fancy flowers, and beautiful beadwork—that's only a fraction of the items that go into your typical Mardi Gras parade float. At Mardi Gras World, you can see the preparation and work that is involved in these unique creations.*

## Mardi Gras World

Although the spectacular floats and the sequined-and-feathered costumes of Mardi Gras would appeal to just about any child, most parents find the parades and accompanying debauchery too racy for the kids. So, to get into the Mardi Gras spirit year-round, tour New Orleans's Mardi Gras World, an actual working studio where 80 percent of the floats that travel down the New Orleans streets during Carnival season are designed and built. You'll learn about the traditions surrounding Mardi Gras parades, balls, and music. King cake, a tasty Mardi Gras tradition, is served at the end of the tour.

## National World War II Museum

The National World War II Museum in New Orleans celebrates the courage and sacrifice of the American men and women of World War II. It tells the story of the war through multimedia: interactive exhibits that include letters from soldiers, films, and photographs; planes; battle gear; and a re-creation of a German lookout post on the Normandy coast.

Highlights include nine oral history stations that feature emotionally touching videotaped interviews with D-Day veterans and others who were involved in the war effort. Artifacts accompanied by the personal stories of those who owned them give audiences a rich insight to the veterans' experiences during the war.

**THE MIDWEST**

## Rock and Roll Hall of Fame and Museum

Known as "the house that rock built," the Rock and Roll Hall of Fame and Museum in Cleveland offers a range of activities that will appeal to your inner rock star. Memorabilia buffs can linger over Jimi Hendrix's handwritten lyrics; John Lennon's childhood report card; Tina Turner's memorable concert costumes; plus other artists' concert posters, ticket stubs, and more. Children enjoy the Hall of Fame wing; at the entrance visitors can see footage of past induction ceremonies. Once inside, kids hear the stories of the artists and view artifacts from the latest honorees. At the Hall of Fame exit, there are jukeboxes that play nearly every song by the inductees.

## The National Underground Railroad Freedom Center

Cincinnati was a major hub of Underground Railroad activity due to its location on the Ohio River. In the 1800s, the city offered refuge to thousands fleeing slavery in the South. The National Underground Railroad Freedom Center showcases the importance and relevance of human struggles for freedom in the United States and around the world, in the past and present.

Local educators helped design many of the exhibits to parallel the curriculum of area schools. As a result, the exhibits are child-friendly and use storytelling, role-playing, and hands-on activities to engage young visitors.

*Everyday Freedom Heroes is just one of the exhibits you'll find at The National Underground Railroad Freedom Center, which opened its doors in 2004. The center has three buildings that symbolize the cornerstones of freedom: courage, cooperation, and perseverance.*

## Cedar Point Amusement Park

Cedar Point is a 364-acre peninsula in Sandusky, Ohio, that first became popular in 1870 as a bathing beach. Today it is home to the planet's largest collection of rides and roller coasters. Many consider Cedar Point one of the best amusement parks in the world. Besides its menu of heart-pounding coasters and various other amusement park rides, Cedar Point boasts a water park, four resort hotels, a luxury RV campground that includes cottages and cabins, and two large marinas. In addition, the park has an entertainment complex, live shows, gift shops, restaurants, kids' areas, and much more.

*Roller-coaster enthusiasts believe it's not enough to build them—you have to build them BIG! That's what the folks at Cedar Point have been doing since 1892, when its first roller coaster was constructed.*

## Pro Football Hall of Fame Festival

Football fans who visit Canton, Ohio's Pro Football Hall of Fame in early August, just before induction time, can score extra fun points at the Pro Football Hall of Fame Festival. This ten-day celebration of everything football also includes plenty of activities, including seven football inflatables and a children's entertainment area that has a rock-climbing wall, kiddie rides, and more. The parade features spectacular floats, marching bands, clowns, costumed characters, returning Hall of Famers, and the current class of enshrinees. The highlights of the festival are the Hall of Fame Game and the induction of new Hall members.

## Kings Island

Kings Island is a 364-acre amusement and water park near Cincinnati with a number of rides based on movies. It also has seven themed areas, two of which are designed for visitors of all ages.

Rides for younger kids include a carousel and a swinging pirate ship. There's also Nickelodeon Universe and Hanna-Barbera lands with a variety of Dora the Explorer and SpongeBob SquarePants-themed attractions, as well as the Rugrats Runaway Reptar, the world's first suspended roller coaster designed for younger children. Older children will like The Beast, a legendary ride that's been called the best wooden roller coaster in the world by ride aficionados.

## Mackinac Island

Visitors take a step back in time when they arrive at this leisurely island escape in Michigan. Cars are prohibited on Mackinac

A friendly pioneer greeting awaits you at Conner Prairie, where kids can experience history firsthand.

Island—they were banned shortly after the first "horseless carriage" motored off the ferry in the early 20th century. Visitors tour the small island by bicycle, on foot, or in a horse-drawn taxi.

More than 75 percent of the island is Mackinac Island State Park, which includes 18th-century Fort Mackinac. Inside the fort you'll see enthusiastic reenactors and 14 original buildings with interesting displays that tell about life for American soldiers and their families circa 1880. In the Kids' Quarters, children can revisit the styles of the 1800s.

## Henry Ford Museum and Greenfield Village

The eclectic Henry Ford Museum in Dearborn, Michigan, was founded in 1929 by the Ford family as a place to house inventor Henry Ford's immense personal collection of Americana. It also serves to honor America's technological ingenuity and innovative thinking.

Both the museum and neighboring Greenfield Village reflect the quirks of their eccentric founder. The collection is diverse—from the bike shop where the Wright brothers designed and built their first airplane to Thomas Edison's last breath, captured in a test tube. It's wise to study the visitor's guide and pick out some of the museum's unique treasures for a closer look.

## Conner Prairie

Conner Prairie in Fishers, Indiana, lets families travel back in time to the 1800s, where they can experience firsthand how everyday life has changed over the past two centuries. This living-history museum has several different areas replete with costumed interpreters and hands-on experiences that bring the past to life.

Prairietown is a restored and re-created 1836 Indiana frontier village. Be sure to visit Pastport, where families can dip candles, churn butter, and wash clothes on a washboard. At the 1816 Lenape Indian Camp, you can enter a Native American wigwam, learn to throw a tomahawk, help make a dugout canoe, and even chat with a fur trader at the trading post.

## Indianapolis 500 and the 500 Festival

Mom and Dad can start their engines and take the family minivan—and the kids—for a lap around the famed Indianapolis Motor Speedway four days before the superstars of the raceway hit the track. Kids can pedal tiny racecars around a section of the official track, and the entire family can watch the actual crews practice their pit stops or get autographs from current Indy car drivers and past champions. It's all part of Community Day, one of the many 500 Festival events that precede the big race.

## Children's Museum of Indianapolis

This world-class collection of hands-on fun makes up the largest children's museum in the entire world. Its exhibits continue to amaze and entertain local children, as well as families who travel to Indianapolis just to visit this renowned attraction.

The astonishing "Fireworks of Glass," a blown-glass exhibit in the five-story atrium, is the largest permanent sculpture that artist Dale Chihuly has ever created. The 43-foot-tall glass tower rises above what appears to be a floating glass ceiling. Other popular exhibits here are Dinosphere, the Playscape Preschool Gallery, the Carousel Wishes and Dreams Gallery, and ScienceWorks.

## Holiday World

This holiday-themed fun spot geared toward preschoolers is appropriately located in Santa Claus, Indiana. It's a favorite of parents who enjoy its low-key pleasures. Built in 1946, the park was first known as Santa Claus Land and was billed as the nation's first amusement theme park. In 1984, the park was expanded to include three holiday motif sections: Christmas, Halloween, and

Everything seems to come alive at the Children's Museum of Indianapolis.

Fourth of July. A water park went in nine years later, and Thanksgiving was added in 2006.

Holiday World's child-friendly attention to detail makes parents happy: Soft drinks, lemonade, and water are free, and complimentary self-serve sunblock dispensers are found throughout the park.

## Shedd Aquarium

The exhibits at Chicago's amazing Shedd Aquarium, which feature 8,000 animals and an Oceanarium, get you as close to underwater environments as you can be without gills. The Waters of the World exhibit includes hundreds of different kinds of fish—from bighead and silver carp to clown anemonefish and sea stars. The 400,000-gallon Wild Reef habitat is a floor-to-ceiling aquarium that gives guests a diver's-eye view of a coral reef. Divers hand-feed the animals at scheduled times during the day at the Caribbean Coral Reef tank, and the expansive Oceanarium exhibit re-creates a Pacific Northwest marine environment, with dolphins, harbor seals, sea otters, penguins, and beluga whales visible through underwater viewing windows.

## Chicago International Children's Film Festival

North America's largest and longest-running festival of films for children, the Chicago International Children's Film Festival brings together some of the best

*Visitors to the Shedd Aquarium will be treated to a performance by the Oceanarium's dolphins that also demonstrates the care and training each one receives.*

animated and live action films from 40 different countries. The festival traditionally begins in October and spans an 11-day period. The films and videos compete for recognition and prizes, and children who attend the festival vote for their favorites. One of the categories is Child-Produced Work, which features the works of aspiring filmmakers younger than fourteen.

The films shown at the festival are carefully selected to present humanistic, nonexploitative, culturally diverse, and nonviolent work. The festival also sponsors a number of workshops for kids interested in making movies.

## ZooLights at Lincoln Park Zoo

During the holiday season, it's hard for a meerkat to get a good night's sleep when millions of tiny lights brighten the grounds of Chicago's Lincoln Park Zoo and add a festive glow. You can take in the sights on foot or jump aboard the Holiday Express train to view the more than 100 light displays and giant illuminated animal figures located throughout the zoo. Other highlights include ice-carving demonstrations and family crafts and activities. Children can visit Santa in his workshop, listen to stories and music, and ride the zoo's carousel. Carolers offer entertainment, and when little zoo-goers get hungry, there are plenty of hot treats.

## The Art Institute of Chicago

Some of the world's most famous paintings are housed in The Art Institute of Chicago. The collection includes the works of Impressionists and Post-Impressionists, as well as other notable works, such as Grant Wood's "American Gothic" and Edward Hopper's "Nighthawks." The collection of arms and armor, which contains shiny suits of armor, wicked swords and daggers, and ancient firearms, is a favorite among children.

Kids also love the 68 dollhouse-size rooms in the Thorne Miniature Rooms exhibit. The rooms are filled with exquisite tiny furniture, household objects, and works of art. Many of the rooms are duplicates of those found in European palaces and homes throughout the United States.

## Millennium Park

Along Chicago's lakefront is a stunning 24.5-acre urban jewel called Millennium Park. Among its major attractions are two extraordinary pieces of public art. One is a highly reflective 110-ton polished steel sculpture officially named "Cloud Gate" but affectionately called "The Bean." Visitors can wander under and around it to see the park and cityscape reflected in its curves. The other, the Crown Fountain, is a reflecting pool flanked by two 50-foot towers onto which close-up images of Chicagoans are projected. The lips on the faces purse, and water sprays from them, making the ever-changing faces look like giant gargoyles.

## Navy Pier

Chicago's lakefront playground is a fabulous 50-acre complex of parks, promenades, shops, and restaurants. Navy Pier is a wonderful place to bike or roller blade, and rental shops offer both.

The pier is home to a wide array of family-oriented events and entertainment. Its most visible attraction is a 150-foot-high Ferris wheel that was modeled after the one built for Chicago's 1893 World Columbian Exposition.

It is a great way to get a bird's-eye view of the area. Other attractions include a musical carousel, old-fashioned Viennese swings, miniature golf, a maze, an IMAX theater, and an excellent children's museum.

## Museum of Science and Industry

This innovative Chicago museum features a myriad of thoroughly engaging exhibits for family members of every age. You can climb through a cramped World War II German U-boat to get a feel for life undersea or descend into a coal mine like a real miner.

The astonishing Fairy Castle, designed by Colleen Moore, is a wonderland of miniature treasures from around the world. In the dining room, King Arthur's table is set with real gold plates, and the stitches in the Viennese tapestries lining the wall are so small that you can barely see them, even under a magnifying glass.

*Who's up for one more ride? Noah's Ark, the premier water park in the Wisconsin Dells, offers a huge selection of water rides and activities.*

## Wisconsin Dells

Nearly two dozen water parks lure families to the Dells in central Wisconsin year-round: It's considered to be the water park capital of the world. Many of them are indoors and themed—pirates, King Arthur, the lost world of Atlantis—and each one tries to outdo its neighbor.

Feeling a little waterlogged? Check out the Tommy Bartlett Show and watch the incredible feats of daredevil skiers and aerial performers. You can visit Ripley's Believe It or Not! Museum or the Circus World Museum in nearby Baraboo. Visitors can choose among plenty of other attractions, such as train rides, horseback riding, miniature golf, and go-karts.

## Boundary Waters Canoe Area Wilderness

If a perfect vacation for your family is paddling along a peaceful waterway, head to the Boundary Waters Canoe Area Wilderness in northern Minnesota and the Quetico Provincial Park in Ontario. Together they comprise one of the largest areas of protected wilderness in North America. Glaciers have carved out a breathtaking series of more than 1,000 interconnected waterways linked by portage trails.

There are more than 1,200 miles of canoe routes, and motorized boats are only allowed in certain areas. There are paddle-in campsites throughout the park. The rugged terrain is populated by moose, beavers, otters, mink, and loons, and the fishing is superb.

*It's the mall that has it all. The Mall of America attracts about 40 million visitors a year and boasts an indoor amusement park, an IMAX theater, and a major aquarium that is home to thousands of exotic animals. It's become one of the biggest tourist attractions in the country.*

## St. Paul Winter Carnival

This gala is a much-anticipated event in St. Paul, Minnesota, and it is the country's oldest and largest winter festival. The city is filled with parades, car races on ice, and ice-carving contests.

The carnival offers all kinds of sporting events, including ice hockey, softball played on ice, a children's ice fishing contest, ice skating, snow volleyball, ice golf, and more. A frozen winter playground and a giant snow slide are popular stops for younger children. The intricate and elaborate sculptures of the ice-carving competition are on display throughout the entire carnival.

## Mall of America

You can spend the whole day at Bloomington, Minnesota's Mall of America (MOA) and never even set foot in any of its more than 520 stores. The Park at MOA is a seven-acre playground with more than 30 rides and attractions for children. It is the nation's largest indoor theme park, complete with its own food court and restaurants. The MOA also houses a NASCAR simulator; a four-story Lego play area with more than 30 full-size Lego models; and a lively, interactive dinosaur museum. The mall also has the Underwater Adventures Aquarium, the world's largest underground aquarium. The 1.2-million-gallon tank teems with more than 4,500 sea creatures.

## Children's Theatre Company

North America's flagship theater for young people brings to the stage classic children's stories, such as *The Magic Mrs. Piggle-Wiggle, Pippi Longstocking,* and *How the Grinch Stole Christmas.* The productions are brilliantly staged with wildly imaginative, colorful sets and vivid costumes.

The Minneapolis theater company also commissions new works from significant artists, such as Pulitzer Prize-winning Nilo Cruz, who adapted for the stage the short story *A Very Old Man With Enormous Wings* by magical realist author Gabriel García Márquez. In 2003, the Children's Theatre Company was the first theater for young people to win a Regional Theatre Tony Award.

## Minneapolis Sculpture Garden

Dozens of extraordinary sculptures by 20th-century artists such as Henry Moore, Isamu Noguchi, and Frank Gehry are situated around the grassy landscape of the Minneapolis Sculpture Garden. Its most famous work is the playful "Spoonbridge and Cherry," a 50-foot-long teaspoon with a 15-foot-high, water-spouting, bright-red cherry perched on its rim. Created by Claes Oldenburg and Coosje van Bruggen, it sits in the middle of a lily pond.

The unique setting is the largest urban sculpture garden in the country. It's also a place where children can run around and blow off steam while enjoying some of the world's finest modern three-dimensional works of art.

## Iowa State Fair

When it comes to state fairs, Iowa brings home the blue ribbon. It has more competitive events—almost 900—than any other state fair in the nation. It seamlessly blends old favorites, such as pie baking, quilt making, and prettiest pig contests, with some unusual competitions that are great fun to see. The ugliest cake contest is a favorite for children. It's not judged on appearance only, however; the cake must be tasty, too. Other tests of skill include a yo-yo contest, a nail-driving competition, a rubber chicken-throwing contest, and a hog-calling competition. You'll also find rides and games on the fair's expansive midway, plus concerts featuring chart-topping performers.

## Branson

This country music hot spot in southwest Missouri calls itself "The Live Music Show Capital of the World," and it features dozens of performances daily, as well as a variety of attractions that can keep the fun going for days.

You'll find entertainment for all ages in Branson. The Dixie Stampede is a dinner theater that features costumed stunt riders on horseback, ostrich races, and live buffalo, while the Kirby Van Burch Show offers exotic animals and magic. There are also acrobatics shows, a lively 1950s music review, and family-friendly comedy shows. Amusement parks, go-kart tracks, train rides, and festivals add to the fun.

## The Magic House

This enchanting three-story Victorian house in St. Louis is jam-packed with hands-on learning disguised as fun. Ranked by *U.S. Family Travel Guide* and *FamilyFun* magazines as one of the top family destinations in the country, it has more than 100 exhibits, and most of them encourage children to touch, poke, push, pull, or play.

*Very impressive! First Impressions, now on exhibit at The Magic House, is one of the largest movable art sculptures in the United States. It stands eight feet tall and is made up of 75,000 plastic rods.*

The Magic House's interactive displays show kids how to lift themselves off the ground with pulley power and demonstrate the powerful force of air as they launch an air rocket. They also can change their shadows into a multitude of colors, tap out messages in Morse code, and crawl through tunnel mazes.

## The Gateway Arch

The soaring Gateway Arch in St. Louis is the tallest monument in the nation. This graceful 630-foot-high stainless-steel arch commemorates the city and the thousands of pioneers who stopped here to rest and replenish their provisions before continuing west. Visitors can take a tram up either side of the Arch to an observation room for views of the city, the Mississippi River, and the vast plains stretching out into the distance.

The Museum of Westward Expansion is located at the base of the monument and features exhibits about the exploration of the West and noteworthy people who formed its history, including Lewis and Clark, the Plains Indians, and the Buffalo Soldiers.

## St. Louis Zoo

Although the St. Louis Zoo takes its commitment to worldwide animal-conservation issues seriously, visiting the zoo is all about fun. In the children's zoo, kids can pretend they're animals. They'll enjoy navigating the strands of a giant spiderweb, digging in the sand like an aardvark, and measuring their height against that of a grizzly bear.

The zoo is filled with excellent exhibits that will take you right into the middle of the animals' habitats. For example, you're hit with a blast of cold air as you enter the indoor penguin habitat in the Penguin and Puffin Coast, and the ten-acre River's Edge exhibit features an underwater hippo tank.

*Don't bug the artist! Kaleidoscope invites children to create, create, and then create again. The Hallmark-sponsored activity center provides the materials, and the rest is up to the kids.*

## Kaleidoscope

Hallmark Cards, Inc., created an art studio for children right next door to its visitor's center in Kansas City, Missouri. Called Kaleidoscope, it's an 8,000-square-foot space divided into various colorful theme areas with all kinds of art supplies and creative materials. Children need only bring their imaginations and willingness to create. Ribbons, papers, melted crayons, cutout shapes, and all kinds of other craft materials are provided by the Hallmark studios so kids are all set up to get creative. Kaleidoscope features different projects every day.

## Dodge City

Back in the heyday of Dodge City, Kansas, gunslingers fought and died with their boots on. They took up permanent residence in Boot Hill Cemetery alongside paupers who couldn't afford a burial. The actual graves were moved, but the tombstones have been re-created. They now display colorful epitaphs, such as: "Here lies Lester Moore. Four slugs from a 44. No Les. No more."

The cemetery is part of Boot Hill Museum, a reconstruction of notorious Front Street in 1876, the business district of Old Dodge City. Carefully researched through photographs and diaries, the historic buildings include an 1879 cattle driver's home, the jail from Fort Dodge, and a one-room schoolhouse.

## The Oz Museum

You won't need a broomstick, a tornado, or even ruby slippers to visit this museum in Wamego, Kansas. Just step through the screen door of the old wooden farmhouse, where you'll be greeted by life-size figures of Dorothy and Toto. Other favorite Oz characters, such as the Scarecrow and Tin Man, are also in the museum, where thousands of Oz items from the classic children's book series by L. Frank Baum and the famous 1939 MGM production of *The Wizard of Oz* are on display.

## Henry Doorly Zoo

Workers at Omaha, Nebraska's award-winning zoo like to say the animals roam free and its visitors are captive. This claim is partially true. In Hubbard Gorilla Valley, a 520-foot-long window-lined tunnel allows visitors to travel into the middle of the three-acre gorilla habitat to observe these majestic creatures.

As you traverse an elevated treetop walkway through the award-winning Lied Jungle exhibit, you'll pass lush vegetation and fascinating animals native to the misty jungles of three continents. The authentically re-created habitat features waterfalls, cliffs, caves, medicinal plants, and giant trees. The zoo's Desert Dome has viewing areas at two levels. Kingdoms of the Night, the world's largest exhibit of nocturnal animals and their habitats, is located beneath the Desert Dome.

## Fort Robinson State Park

Fort Robinson in northwest Nebraska offers visitors modern-day dude ranch activities and a fascinating Old West background. Its 22,000 acres of wide-open plains, forested hills, and sandstone bluffs are home to herds of buffalo and longhorn sheep. Guests can explore on horseback, by stagecoach, by jeep, by mountain bike, or on foot.

Summers are packed with activities for families. The breakfast trail rides and fireside buffalo stew cookouts and sing-alongs are popular events. History buffs like to explore the Fort Robinson Museum and the Trailside Museum, which displays fossils that date back 200 million years. Other activities include swimming, trout fishing, and crafts. In winter, cross-country skiing is popular.

## Buffalo Bill Ranch State Historical Park

William "Buffalo Bill" Cody lived on a ranch just north of North Platte, Nebraska, and toured the United States and Europe with his famous Wild West Show. Today, his home

*You'll find Kingdoms of the Night housed in the Desert Dome at Henry Doorly Zoo. The exhibit covers 42,000 square feet and is home to 75 nocturnal animals.*

is part of the Buffalo Bill Ranch State Historical Park. When you tour the house and its outlying buildings, you'll find a wealth of memorabilia from the Wild West days, including original posters, costumes, and film clips from his show's tours. Families can camp in the park, and hiking trails and picnic areas are available.

## Wind Cave National Park

One of the world's longest and most complex caves, Wind Cave in southwest South Dakota was named for the eerie whistling noise that can be heard at its entrance. There are five tours of the caves. The Natural Entrance Tour is very popular among families with children. You enter through the hillside and exit by elevator. The tour provides an excellent opportunity to see boxwork, an unusual formation the cave is known for, which is composed of paper-thin calcite fins that resemble delicate honeycombs. Other tours go deeper into the caves, but they involve more stairs.

## Mount Rushmore

This presidential face-off of monumental proportions is a jaw-dropping feat of art and engineering. Blasted and chiseled out of granite, Mount Rushmore features four famous presidents: George Washington, Thomas Jefferson, Theodore Roosevelt, and Abraham Lincoln. The faces on the 5,725-foot-tall landmark tower over a majestic forest of pine, spruce, birch, and aspen trees in South Dakota's Black Hills.

The herculean effort began in 1927, with sculptor Gutzon Borglum and a team of dedicated South Dakota workers. They blasted and crafted this shrine to democracy over a 14-year period. The towering faces on Mount Rushmore are illuminated year-round. During the summer months, there is a nightly lighting ceremony in the park's spacious amphitheater.

## Mammoth Site

This treasure trove of fossils in Hot Springs, South Dakota, was discovered in 1974 when excavation for a housing development unearthed the remains of a woolly mammoth. Since then, budding paleontologists and their parents have visited the site to get hands-on experience in an actual dig.

To date, the fossilized skeletons of 55 mammoths have been identified, along with the remains of many other animals. Walkways throughout the excavation afford visitors close-up views of the skulls, ribs, tusks, femurs, and even nearly complete skeletons visible in the mass grave. A simulated excavation for junior paleontologists is held daily during the summer months.

## Theodore Roosevelt National Park

While visiting The Badlands in North Dakota on a hunting trip in 1883, Theodore Roosevelt became alarmed by the extent of damage to the land and its wildlife. Later, when he became president, Roosevelt established numerous national parks and protected areas. It's only fitting that this national park, where he had a home and ranch, was named to honor him.

*The fossils of animals that existed 26,000 years ago are revealed at the Mammoth Site. Your family will be fascinated by the in-depth tours.*

In the park's South Unit, families can visit one of Roosevelt's former ranch cabins next to the Medora Visitor Center. Children will find the town of Medora a fun stop, as it offers carriage and stagecoach tours of the area. Or they can saddle up a horse to explore the area.

**THE SOUTHWEST**

## Space Center Houston

Where on Earth—or any other planet, for that matter—can you dock a space shuttle, touch an authentic moon rock, and watch an astronaut train for a space mission all in the same day? Space Center Houston, that's where.

Located in the Johnson Space Center complex, Space Center Houston was designed by Walt Disney Imagineering with both entertainment and education in mind. It's a perfect place for space buffs to get a close-up look at the country's space program. Space Center Houston's interactive exhibits show what life in space is like, and younger children enjoy the center's expansive play areas.

## Houston Livestock Show and Rodeo

The biggest and best rodeo in Texas has star-quality bull riders, barrel racers, ropers, steer wrestlers, and bucking bronco riders competing for big cash prizes. The livestock show attracts the top stars of the animal world and features some of the finest examples of cattle, pigs, chickens, horses, donkeys, sheep, goats, rabbits, and llamas.

Several events are particularly popular with children. Fledgling bronco riders can try their skills on a mechanical bull, or go on pony rides. Kids can also watch pig races and see newborn animals as they attempt their first steps. At Rodeo University, children can meet rodeo athletes who give roping demonstrations and share their experiences.

## Houston Art Car Parade

Picture a car completely covered in singing fish—that's the Sashimi Tabernacle Choir car, and it's one of more than 250 outlandishly decorated automobiles, motorcycles, bicycles, and other contraptions that are featured in the Houston Art Car Parade. On the second weekend in May, approximately 200,000 people gather for this outlandish event, which features creative and outright crazy-looking vehicles parading through the city streets. You might see a car that looks like a giant dolphin, a car covered bumper-to-bumper in buttons, a racecar transformed into a sleek metallic lizard, and a car completely covered in grass from a recently mowed yard.

*"Orange you glad" you visited Houston? Where else could you see the eccentric Fruitmobile, one of the many imaginatively detailed and outrageously decorated automobiles that appear in the Houston Art Car Parade?*

## Schlitterbahn Waterpark Resort

Schlitterbahn is nestled on the banks of the spring-fed Comal River in New Braunfels, Texas, about 175 miles west of Houston, near San Antonio. Its natural setting amid towering trees gives it a unique character among water parks. Several of the rides make use of the river and its fresh springwater.

The Raging River Tube Chute transports riders through a tube and into twisting turns, then spills them out into another ride called the Congo River. Three of the park's water coasters actually shoot riders uphill, including the six-story Master Blaster. Many water park enthusiasts believe that this ride is the best of its kind. There are six shallow-water playgrounds for younger children.

## San Antonio

A visit to downtown San Antonio, Texas, will put you near the famous Paseo del Rio, or Riverwalk, where giant cypress trees shade 2.5 miles of meandering pathways, shops, and sidewalk cafés along the San Antonio River. Riverboats with narrated tours travel back and forth throughout the day and evening. Your kids may have heard of the most-famous San Antonio landmark, the Alamo, but they'll get the full story of its brave defenders by taking a tour.

*The Master Blaster, Schlitterbahn's high-tech water ride, uses a patented system of water jets to propel its riders through the looping and swooping course.*

There's plenty more to do in this scenic, multicultural city. The bustling Market Square is filled with mariachi bands, restaurants, and shops. Six Flags Fiesta Texas is a theme park with thrilling rides, country-western music shows, and a water park. To see everything San Antonio has to offer, take a ride to the top of the 750-foot-high Tower of the Americas at HemisFair Park.

## Fiesta San Antonio

This ten-day event that celebrates San Antonio's diverse culture and recognizes the heroes of the Alamo and the Battle of San Jacinto is held every April. Numerous ethnic groups have contributed to the rich culture and history of Texas, and just about every one of them is honored during the fiesta. More than 100 events are held throughout the city, including distinctly different parades (the Battle of Flowers Parade, the Texas Cavaliers River Parade, The Famous Fiesta Flambeau Night Parade, and the Fiesta Pooch Parade). Each one is worth seeing.

## SeaWorld

It's a four-in-one experience at the world's largest marine life adventure park. SeaWorld is 250 acres of fun in San Antonio, featuring an amusement park, a water park, animal attractions, and live entertainment. World-famous killer whale Shamu performs in a special stadium that has an overhead camera and plenty of splashing. Dolphin shows and beluga whale performances are also popular, as are the daring water-ski stunt shows. A water park keeps young visitors cool during the heat of the day, with daredevil slides and water play areas for little kids.

## Big Bend National Park

Big Bend is a land of dramatic contrasts. It covers 801,000 acres of west Texas and encompasses a vast section of the Chihuahuan Desert, approximately 69 serpentine miles of the Rio Grande Wild and Scenic River, and the Chisos Mountain range. The spectacular scenery includes deeply chiseled canyons, windblown dunes, and 60 species of cacti.

River rafting, kayaking, and canoeing through the canyons of the Rio Grande are activities you won't want to miss. There are several easy hikes that kids of all ages enjoy, including the Window View Trail and the Chihuahuan Desert Nature Trail. A 4.8-mile round-trip hike, Lost Mine Trail, provides a good challenge for older children, and it's an excellent day hike.

## Padre Island National Seashore

The pristine beaches, wind-sculpted dunes, and saltwater marshes of Padre Island National Seashore stretch for 80 miles along the Gulf of Mexico off of Texas. It's the longest span of undeveloped beach in the United States and the longest undeveloped barrier island in the world. A boardwalk stretches over a section of wetlands where kids can observe some of the many bird species that occupy the seashore.

Padre Island National Seashore is a fishing enthusiast's paradise. It offers speckled trout, black drum, redfish, and flounder. In addition, the saltwater lagoon between the island and the mainland is a perfect place to learn to windsurf—it's only three to five feet deep with a soft, sandy bottom.

## AIA Sandcastle Competition

The American Institute of Architects (AIA) sponsors a sand castle-building competition in Galveston, Texas, that puts all others to shame. On this one day in June, about 80 teams of architects, engineers, and students of these two professions each go to work on their own section of beach. They have just five hours to sculpt their creations.

*Take a group of design and building professionals, add a lot of imagination, and turn them loose on a beach, and you get a battle of the sands. The American Institute of Architects Sandcastle Competition is the largest event of its kind in the United States.*

The results of their painstaking efforts are elaborate, often humorous, eccentric creations that frequently reflect current attitudes. The results are judged on concept, artistic execution, technical difficulty, carving technique, and use of the site. Additional awards, such as Most Hilarious, Most Lifelike, and Public Favorite, are also given out.

## Red Earth Native American Cultural Festival

Every June, more than 100 Native American tribes from North America gather in Oklahoma City for a foot-stomping celebration of their culture, history, and artistic handiwork. A parade kicks off the festivities and features master drummers, dancers, and tribal princesses resplendent in feather headdresses, buckskins, and beads.

One of the highlights of this festival is the Red Earth Dance Competition, which features thousands of participants competing in war dances, victory dances, and more. Traditional storytelling, music, and crafts are a big part of the festival, too. The Red Earth Art Market features about 170 Native American artists selling both traditional and contemporary art and handcrafted pieces.

## Taos Pueblo

The Taos Pueblo in northern New Mexico is the oldest continuously occupied structure on the continent. Dating back to A.D. 1000, its adobe walls today house about 150 Taos Native Americans who maintain the ancient traditions of their ancestors. The Pueblo is not a historical artifact or a re-creation; it is an actual town that offers a fascinating introduction to Native American life.

The Pueblo consists of two long, multistory adobe structures, one on each side of a freshwater creek. Explore on your own or take an escorted tour that recounts the Pueblo's history, which includes occupation by Spanish conquistadors in 1540 and by Franciscan friars in the 1590s.

## Carlsbad Caverns

Nature's artistic streak takes a fanciful turn in this famous and enormous cave system in southeastern New Mexico that was created by water dripping through an ancient reef made of porous limestone. More than 30 miles of the main cavern have been explored, and the three miles of caves that are open to visitors are among the largest and most magnificent underground formations in the world. A variety of self-guided and ranger-led tours are available year-round, and high-speed elevators make the caves accessible to everyone.

## Santa Fe

Santa Fe, New Mexico, is the second-oldest city in the United States. It's a place where the merging of three cultures—Anglo, Hispanic, and Native American—can be seen in its vibrant art, architecture, and food. The town is filled with numerous galleries that exhibit exquisite southwestern art, shops that offer the best in fashion, and sophisticated restaurants.

The center of it all is the Plaza, which once marked the official end of the Old Santa Fe Trail. It is now lined with shade trees, famous landmarks, and museums, including the Palace of the Governors. Native American artisans sell silver-and-turquoise jewelry, pottery, leatherwork, and hand-woven blankets in front of the Palace.

## Albuquerque International Balloon Fiesta

Hot air balloons of all shapes, sizes, and colors fill the fall sky during Albuquerque's balloon festival, the largest of its kind in the world. You'll see a string of chili peppers, a reclining chair, Chinese pagodas, and Russian dolls as they ascend into the sky. For the best viewing, choose early morning when the majestic balloons are beginning their ascents. Certain mornings have mass ascensions—a simultaneous launch of all the festival balloons. Later in the day, book your own balloon flight and take your family up into the clear New Mexico sky.

*Your family will enjoy the dawn-to-dusk activities of the Albuquerque International Balloon Fiesta. The daytime sky is dotted with a rainbow of colors, and evening events include fireworks displays. On certain nights, there are dramatic presentations of illuminated balloons.*

## The Grand Canyon

Millions of years of erosion caused by wind and water have carved and sculpted Arizona's Grand Canyon, truly one of the world's most dramatic natural wonders. At 227 miles long and 18 miles across at its widest point, this breathtaking abyss plunges more than a mile from rim to river bottom at its deepest point.

*Reno's Whitewater Park offers a great kayaking experience. It's become a popular downtown attraction, as well.*

The Colorado River flows along the bottom of the canyon, but because of the canyon's depth, the river is visible only from certain viewpoints above. Families can book a rafting trip on the Colorado for one or more days, and it's an unforgettable way to explore the canyon.

## The Petrified Forest National Park and Painted Desert

This Arizona park encompasses portions of the Painted Desert and is one of the largest tracts of petrified wood in the world. The ancient log fragments are littered around the park, and visitors can see them as they hike or drive through the desolate dreamscape.

Visitors can travel through the park on a ten-mile paved road that runs through the Painted Desert. Signs that explain features of the park are located at various stops, and there's a visitor's center and the Rainbow Forest Museum. Kids particularly enjoy the museum's variety of ancient animal fossils and the huge, petrified logs found along the Giant Logs Trail.

## Whitewater Park and Kayak Slalom Racing Course

Cutting right through the middle of downtown Reno, Nevada, this white-water rafting course was created out of the Truckee River. It is open year-round for kayaking, rafting, canoeing, and tubing. The mile-long course features 11 drop pools and a slalom racing course, and there are 7,000 tons of smooth flat rocks along the riverbanks that are perfect for picnicking or watching the paddlers pass by. Concessionaires rent all types of watercraft, including tubes and riverboards, and kayaking lessons are available for all ages. A river festival in May brings out some of the world's best professional and Olympic kayakers for white-water competitions, clinics, and demonstrations.

THE ROCKY MOUNTAINS

## Mesa Verde National Park

Mesa Verde National Park in southwest Colorado offers visitors a spectacular opportunity to learn about the lives of the Pueblo people who lived in cliff dwellings they chiseled out of the solid mountainside before they mysteriously disappeared about 700 years ago. Visitors can hike to three of the dwellings with a ranger guide and crawl through tunnels and climb ladders to get a closer look at the ancient caves. These are physical tours that can be quite rigorous, so they're more appropriate for older children.

## Great Sand Dunes National Park

The ever-changing landscape of Great Sand Dunes National Park in south-central Colorado contains 39 square miles of dunes, some of which are more than 750 feet high. The park is set against a rugged backdrop of the Sangre de Cristo Mountains, the southernmost range of the Rockies.

Sledding is a popular pastime here; it's merely done without snow. Carrying their sleds, kids climb to the tops of the dunes and then slide down the steep sides. Many bring skis or snowboards to slalom down the sandy slopes. Forgot your sled? No problem, simply roll your way down, and ignore the sand in your pockets—it's part of the fun.

## Rocky Mountain National Park

The rugged grandeur of Colorado's Rocky Mountain National Park is only a 90-minute drive from Denver. Sixty mountains in the park rise above 12,000 feet, with Longs Peak reaching highest at 14,259 feet. Visitors have countless opportunities for hiking, mountain climbing, camping, horseback riding, and wildlife viewing in the summer; cross-country skiing and snowshoeing are popular in winter.

Estes Park, a town just east of the national park, features an abundance of family activities. A number of horseback-riding stables offer trail rides, and a small lake comes complete with boating and fishing. Other activities include bicycling and cultural events.

*Surrounded by the beautiful Rocky Mountains, mile-high Glenwood Hot Springs Pool is located along the banks of the Colorado River. President Theodore Roosevelt often spent summers here enjoying the soothing spring-fed waters.*

## The Manitou and Pikes Peak Cog Railway

Pikes Peak near Colorado Springs is second only to Mount Fuji in Japan for having the most travelers to its summit. And perhaps the best way to get there is to take the three-hour ride on the delightful old-fashioned cog railway. The railway began service in 1891, and it hasn't changed much since then. The view from the 14,110-foot summit is astonishing. You'll see Denver from 60 miles away; the Sangre de Cristo Mountains; the historic Cripple Creek Gold Camp; the majestic mountains that form the Continental Divide; as well as bighorn sheep, marmots, and deer.

## Glenwood Hot Springs Pool

Open all year, no matter what the weather, this king-size swimming pool in Glenwood Springs, Colorado, is more than three city blocks long. This is the world's largest hot mineral pool, and it's naturally heated to a comfortable 90 to 93 degrees Fahrenheit year-round.

Kids love cascading down the pool's two giant waterslides and playing in the warm, relaxing water. There are lanes for lap swimmers, diving boards, and a special shallow pool for younger kids. Tired from a day of hiking and sightseeing? You can relax in the therapy pool that's heated to 104 degrees Fahrenheit. Pop a quarter into the "bubble chairs" for a special massage.

## Buffalo Bill Historical Center

The five museums at the Buffalo Bill Historical Center in Cody, Wyoming, contain an internationally acclaimed collection of Western Americana. Featured within its walls are masterworks of Western art, a rich collection of Native American artifacts, exhibits about the natural history of the greater Yellowstone area, and an enormous Winchester gun collection.

The museum staff has developed materials, events, and exhibits just for the younger set. At the Whitney Gallery of Western Art, kids can pick up a family guidebook. After completing its questions, they can trade it in for a souvenir. In the Draper Museum of Natural History, kids receive a passport that gets stamped at various stations.

## Yellowstone National Park

The National Park Service doesn't hand out gold medals for special effects, but if it did, Yellowstone (most of which is in Wyoming, but parts are in Montana and Idaho,

*Ice and snow are helpful but not necessary. Kids love the high-speed twists and turns on the luge and skeleton tracks at Utah Olympic Park.*

too) would win, hands down. Its geothermal attractions, from one corner of the park to the other, dramatically spout, steam, and bubble. Old Faithful is the star, but a supporting cast includes 300 spouting geysers, plus boiling mud pots, hissing steam vents, steaming fumaroles, and billowing vapors. The park also contains the largest concentration of free-roaming wildlife in the lower 48 states. Bison, moose, elk, bighorn sheep, coyotes, wolves, antelope, and bears all call the park home.

## Grand Teton National Park

The spectacular, craggy, cloud-high peaks of the Tetons seem to rise out of nowhere into the endless Wyoming sky. These mountains offer a vacation experience of unspoiled nature, with ample opportunities to hike through untouched forests, fish for five kinds of trout, and splash in pure mountain streams and lakes. An abundance of wildlife thrives in the park's Jackson Hole Valley: Moose, elk, bison, and deer frequently graze in the area.

Ranger-led activities abound and are an excellent way to learn more about the park for free. There are wildlife walks and talks, daytime and twilight hikes, campfire programs, and special activities for children.

## Devils Tower National Monument

The sheer drama and spectacle of this vertical rock monolith in northeastern Wyoming has been a beacon to visitors for hundreds of years. Hiking through the adjacent meadows and exploring nearby forests and boulder fields are great, but climbing stands out as the most alluring activity.

A number of climbing schools are licensed to operate at Devils Tower. Each offers play days where visitors learn the basics of rock climbing. The play days are appropriate for children ages four and older, and kids as young as seven have climbed to the summit. Outfitters supply all the necessary equipment, including sticky-soled rubber climbing shoes.

## Arches National Park

Sculpted by wind and weather over millions of years, Arches National Park in Utah is a garden of geological formations. The park contains the largest concentration of natural sandstone arches in the world, including balanced rocks, towers, domes, fins, and pinnacles that preside over a dramatic desert landscape.

Children love the unusual names of some of the formations, such as Paul Bunyan's Potty, the Fiery Furnace, and the Parade of Elephants. The park's scenic drive, a paved road that runs 40 miles round-trip through the park, offers the easiest access to its major sights, with plenty of places to stop to get a closer look at the distinctive geological wonders.

## Utah Olympic Park

Kid visitors to this Park City attraction can test their mettle in some of the Olympic sports the venue hosted in 2002, including luge, bobsled, ski jumping, ice hockey, speed skating, freestyle skiing, biathlon, curling, and skeleton. They can also watch Olympic hopefuls train for the next winter games. The park is also a favorite with freestyle aerialist skiers, who train in the summer by landing from their flips, twists, and jumps in a 750,000-gallon splash pool.

## Best Friends Animal Sanctuary

The largest no-kill animal sanctuary in the United States, Best Friends is located in Kanab, Utah, at the heart of the famous Golden Circle of national parks: Zion, the Grand Canyon, Bryce Canyon, and Lake Powell. It houses about 1,500 dogs, cats, horses, donkeys, rabbits, birds, goats, and other animals. Each animal is named, fed, and housed in clean and comfortable surroundings, and a lucky 75 percent of them are adopted into happy homes. Guests who want to spend the night can reserve a cottage overlooking the horse pastures, and they are encouraged to take a dog for a sleepover in their cabins.

## Glacier National Park

This magnificent expanse of glacier-capped mountain peaks, forests, alpine meadows, and lakes in Montana is home to more than 70 species of mammals, including grizzly bears, mountain lions, and wolves. The park extends into Canada and connects with Waterton Lakes National Park to create one large protected area, which is officially called Waterton–Glacier International Peace Park.

Glacier has 13 campgrounds and many short, self-guided nature hikes that make it easy for families to enjoy the true beauty of the park. A variety of ranger programs operate year-round, and an expanded program is offered during the summer, when special guided hikes, evening slide presentations, campfire programs, and other family activities are available.

## Virginia City

At its peak, Virginia City, Montana, was a Gold Rush boomtown populated by vigilantes, villains, and desperadoes. Thanks to preser-

*High in the Rocky Mountains you'll find Virginia City. This remnant of the Gold Rush days once had a population of more than 10,000.*

vation efforts that started in the 1940s, the town is remarkably well preserved. More than 100 historic buildings replete with artifacts and furnishings are open to the public. Visitors can poke into 1860s barbershops and saloons or take a stagecoach ride around town. They can also see a gunfight reenactment or an old-fashioned melodrama. Children can even try their hand at panning gold, just as the prospectors once did.

## The Lewis and Clark National Historic Trail Interpretive Center

The center is the largest museum dedicated to the Meriwether Lewis and William Clark expedition and provides a wealth of information and exhibits about their famous journey.

Before beginning the tour of the museum, visitors can watch a reenactment of the meeting between President Thomas Jefferson and the two explorers. Then they follow the route the adventurers took all the way to the coast of Oregon. Along the way, children can crawl inside a miniature Native American lodge, where they listen to the sound of drums, inspect items made by Native Americans, and pull a rope as if they're portaging the falls.

## Craters of the Moon National Monument and Preserve

Called by an early visitor the strangest 75 square miles on the North American continent, Idaho's Craters of the Moon National Monument and Preserve is a remarkable volcanic landscape pockmarked with cinder cones, lava tubes, deep fissures, and lava fields. Rather than one large volcano cone, there are many small craters and fissures through which lava flowed at one time. In some places, the molten lava encased standing trees and then hardened. Eventually, the wood rotted, resulting in bizarre tree-shape lava molds. The landscape is so strange and lunar-like that American astronauts have actually trained at the site.

## River Rafting on the Salmon River

The Salmon River in Idaho is considered one of the continent's premier rafting destinations. Although early in the season it's too rough for families with small children, the Salmon warms up and calms down about mid-July, making it excellent for family rafting trips.

A number of outfitters offer special trips of the river that focus on family fun and amazing views of wildlife. On all trips, the river guides set up camp and prepare dinner, including child-friendly fare. Most family trips are four to six days long and include plenty of stops to get out and play, explore historical sites, take short hikes, fish, and swim.

## Sawtooth National Forest

Located in south-central Idaho, Sawtooth National Forest is named for its sharp, serrated peaks that can be seen silhouetted against the sky like the teeth of a saw. About 1,100 lakes and more than 3,000 miles of rivers famous for their salmon, steelhead, and native trout run through Sawtooth and make it a perfect spot for young fishing enthusiasts. In addition, numerous hiking trails wind through its rugged terrain. During the winter months, downhill skiing is a favorite pastime, particularly in Sun Valley. There are also plenty of trails for cross-country skiing, snowshoeing, and snowmobiling.

*Families will find the best of both worlds at Sawtooth National Forest—camping and hiking in the mountains and fishing in Redfish Lake.*

**THE PACIFIC**

## Disneyland

Walt Disney envisioned a place where parents could recapture childhood memories and enjoy a magical world of fantasy with their children. Disneyland in Anaheim, California, brought this vision to life. Many of its early rides and attractions are still in place and are as popular as ever, attesting to the power and longevity of Disney's imagination.

An adjacent park, Disney's California Adventure, features rides and attractions inspired by the Golden State, such as the California Screamin' roller coaster and Soarin' Over California, which takes you on a virtual hang-gliding ride over the state. Downtown Disney, located in the middle of the resort complex, is a shopping and dining hub of activity that will keep all ages entertained.

## Santa Catalina Island

Only 22 miles from Los Angeles, quiet Santa Catalina seems a world apart from the hustle and bustle of the city across the water. It's an ideal traffic-free, clean-air vacation spot for any active family that likes hiking, snorkeling, and exploring.

The Catalina Island Conservancy protects much of the interior of the island. It oversees the diverse island habitat that is home to plant and animal species found nowhere else in the world. The organization also sponsors a nature center at Avalon Canyon and conducts nature walks every evening. Kids will enjoy the center's hands-on exhibits that feature information about the island's native wildlife and hiking its many trails.

*Santa Catalina Island's beautiful Avalon Bay was named after the paradise described in the legend of King Arthur.*

## Sequoia and Kings Canyon National Parks

General Sherman is Sequoia's most famous resident and the largest living organism in the world. This huge tree is 275 feet tall and 36 feet in diameter. It's also approximately 2,500 years old. But the good general isn't alone—thousands of its relatives fill the pristine forests of these two spectacular national parks.

The best place to see these breathtaking giants is suitably named the Giant Forest. Visitors also enjoy the park's diverse landscape, which includes deep canyons, granite cliffs, wildflower-filled meadows, and a wild river. An easy 1.7-mile hike starts near the Giant Forest and leads to a 1,200-foot waterfall.

## Yosemite National Park

The awesome sights of Yosemite National Park's towering granite peaks, cascading waterfalls, glacial lakes, and giant trees attract families year after year. At the park's center in central California is the half-mile-deep Yosemite Valley, carved by glaciers during the last ice age. Sights like the soaring El Capitán, the majestic Half Dome, and the thundering waterfall of Bridal Veil are not to be missed. It's no wonder American nature photographer Ansel Adams found much of his inspiration here, popularizing many of Yosemite Valley's granite landmarks in his black-and-white photographs.

*The drive-through in Sequoia National Park is open 24 hours! Before this sequoia fell in 1937, it stood 275 feet high. Rather than attempt its removal, the park service carved a tunnel through it that measures 17 feet wide and 8 feet high.*

## Monterey Bay Aquarium

Monterey Bay Aquarium in Monterey, California, brings the mysterious marine world to its visitors with extraordinary exhibits that are sure to captivate families. Hands-on experiences are its hallmark. For example, a special petting pool lets children touch rubbery bat rays and nubby sea stars. The aquarium's Splash Zone is another special exhibit and play area where children can crawl through, climb on, and pop up in displays as they visit nearly 60 different sea creatures in their coral reef and rocky shore homes.

## SeaWorld

Beware the Soak Zone, or at least wear quick-drying clothing when you visit SeaWorld in San Diego. When everyone's favorite killer whale sends up its signature greeting, those closest to the tank will be deluged by a wall of water as Shamu leaps out of the air and belly smacks back into the pool.

Shamu is the main attraction, but SeaWorld also features other aquatic animals and a collection of rides that include water coasters, raft rides, and the Wild Arctic experience, where guests find themselves on a stomach-twirling simulated helicopter ride to a remote Arctic research station.

## San Diego Zoo

From the tiny shrew to the mighty elephant, the San Diego Zoo in picturesque Balboa Park offers visitors some of the world's most exceptional animals. It is considered one of the finest zoos on the continent and is home to more than 3,800 creatures representing 800 species from all over the globe.

Many of the animals at the Children's Zoo are trained as animal ambassadors and accept being observed and touched by children. And what mouse wouldn't feel at home at the San Diego Zoo? The Mouse House is made from a large loaf of bread, which is replaced each week as its residents chew their way through the walls.

## Tournament of Roses Parade

This annual New Year's tradition in Pasadena, California, draws about one million people, and millions more watch it on television. The lavishly decorated floats are a labor of love, and some builders spend all year on their elaborate creations. The parade, which consists of floats, a Rose Queen, spirited marching bands, equestrian units, and celebrity Grand Marshals, travels a 5.5-mile route through town. Before the parade, families can watch float-makers decorate their projects with thousands of blossoms, see award-winning marching bands, and get up close to the parade horses. The floats are on display for several days after the parade.

## California State Railroad Museum

The impact of the railroad and how it shaped the history, culture, and economy of California and the West is told through the various exhibits in this vast Sacramento museum. You'll find 21 meticulously restored railroad cars and locomotives on display here.

Several displays invite visitors to climb aboard for a closer look. Children can sit in the engineer's cab of a Santa Fe steam locomotive and experience the sounds and the rocking motion of a sleeping car on a pretend rail trip. Little ones can play with Thomas the Tank Engine trains and wooden Brio trains and tracks.

## Alcatraz Island

Atop Alcatraz Island sits the infamous prison that Al Capone once called home. Kids will love their visit to the country's most noted lockup that is now part of a national park. Audio tours discuss some of the various escape attempts that have become a part of the island's history. Even though Alcatraz is only about one mile off San Francisco's shore, most would-be escapees were swept out to sea by the treacherous currents of the San Francisco Bay or they died of exposure in the icy Pacific Ocean.

## Exploratorium

You'll never hear the words "hands off" or "don't touch" at this San Francisco family favorite. On the contrary, this wonderful museum teaches children about the world and the way it works through the hands-on, touch-and-tinker experiences of more than 650 permanent exhibits.

One crowd-pleaser is Shadow Box, a darkened room with phosphorescent vinyl wallpaper that freezes your shadow on the wall when a strobe light flashes. In another favorite exhibit, a ten-foot-tall tornado alters its shape when you place your hands in it. Make reservations to experience the Tactile Dome, an interactive excursion through total darkness where your sense of touch becomes your only guide.

## Hearst Castle

Hollywood celebrities, business tycoons, and political heavyweights of the 1920s and 1930s were all entertained by William Randolph Hearst at Hearst Castle, an opulent 165-room hilltop hideaway above the California coastline in San Simeon. Hearst was not one to live the simple life, and his home overflows with unbelievable treasures and priceless art from all over the world. He spent millions building his estate, and in its heyday, he entertained lavishly.

Hearst's heirs presented the home and its treasures to the state in 1958 for public exhibition. Some of the home's many rooms can be viewed on the five different tours offered to visitors.

## Santa Barbara

Blessed with a mild Mediterranean climate, this Spanish-style beach town is beautiful year-round. You can spend lazy days at the beach or visit the town's many parks and playgrounds. Other Santa Barbara favorites include a zoo and a stunning botanical garden. Rent bikes or skates or hire a surrey and cruise the three-mile paved beachfront path, kayak along the shore, or meander along the mile-long boardwalk, one of the state's oldest working piers.

## Legoland

The popular building blocks that have amused so many young builders are the inspiration behind this Carlsbad, California, amusement park. It's one of four Legoland parks around the world, and the only one located in North America.

*Isolation and solitude come to mind when you first see Alcatraz Island. This prison was designated for criminals who were the worst of the worst.*

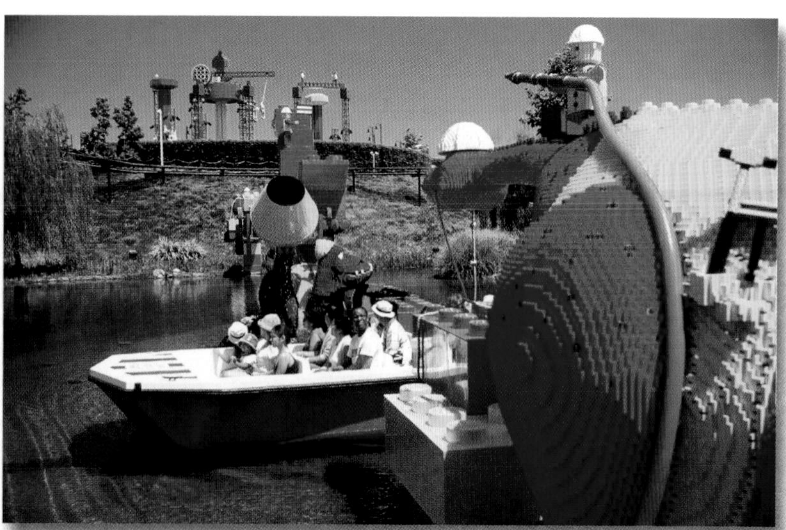

*Kids love the 120 acres of fun rides, entertaining shows, and imaginative buildings that make up Legoland. The Coast Cruise is one of the park's 50 rides.*

Many of the rides in the park use a supersize version of the signature design and colors of the bricks, while other attractions are actually made out of Lego pieces. Don't miss the amazing Miniland, USA, which displays seven regions of the United States, all animated and constructed completely out of 20 million Lego bricks.

## Big Sur Coastline

This scenic stretch of California coastline has a breathtaking beauty that invites many stops for family pictures. One minute you're standing atop a high cliff looking down at a crashing sapphire sea, and the next you're hiking through a misty redwood forest. The Big Sur coastline begins just south of Monterey, where Point Lobos Reserve encompasses a group of headlands, coves, and rolling meadows. Hiking trails follow the shoreline, where you'll probably catch a glimpse of sea otters floating on their backs and snacking on abalone. Migrating gray whales are a common sight between the months of December and May.

## Oregon Dunes National Recreation Area

This glorious national recreation area is filled with wind-sculpted dunes that tower nearly 500 feet above sea level and stretch for 40 miles along the Oregon coast. It's a popular spot for families who enjoy hiking, fishing, canoeing, horseback riding, and camping.

A major lure for many families is the chance to go roaring across the dunes in all-terrain vehicles (ATVs). Oregon Dunes National Recreation Area contains some of the best ATV and dune buggy areas in the United States. A number of rental locations can be found along the coast, from Florence to North Bend.

## Seaside

Seaside is a family favorite first discovered by vacationers in the mid-1800s. This coastal town in Oregon offers a wide, smooth beach dotted with playgrounds and volleyball nets. Its boardwalk has an aquarium and a classic amusement park with bumper cars and saltwater taffy. Seaside is a national landmark and marks the end of the Lewis and Clark National Historic Trail.

The ocean water here is a little too cold for swimming, so kite flying and bike riding are popular. A number of shops rent bikes, in-line skates, four-wheeled surreys, and three-wheeled FunCycles that are designed for pedaling on the packed sand during low tide.

## Crater Lake National Park

Your first glimpse of Crater Lake in southwest Oregon will be memorable. The caldera in which the sapphire blue lake sits was formed after a series of volcanic explosions; consequently, the landscape is quite rugged and varied. It's the deepest lake in the United States and the seventh-deepest in the world.

Rim Drive runs the 33-mile circumference of the lake and features more than 20 scenic overlooks with spectacular views. Camping and hiking through the park's old-growth forests are popular activities, and cross-country skiing is excellent during the eight-month-long winters.

## The Columbia River Gorge and Multnomah Falls

The Columbia River Gorge in northwest Oregon is an impressive river canyon carved by the Columbia as it flows into the Pacific Ocean. The gorge features dramatic cliffs and has the highest concentration of waterfalls in the Pacific Northwest. It's also a favorite location of windsurfers and kite surfers. A drive through the gorge is frequently enhanced by the sight of the colorful sails and kites.

*You'll find rustic campsites, as well as luxury hotels as you drive along Big Sur coastline. The scenery is fantastic—its dramatic, rocky beaches are quite a departure from those found in southern California.*

It's an easy hike to see Multnomah Falls, the second-highest continuous waterfall in the United States. The trail is paved and crosses a bridge before continuing to a viewpoint at the top.

## Portland Rose Festival and Rose Gardens

Portland, Oregon's climate is perfect for growing roses, and in 1889, local rose enthusiasts created the Portland Rose Society to encourage amateurs to cultivate the aromatic flower. A few years later, society members organized the festival and floral parade that has become an annual June tradition.

The present-day event includes the flower-festooned Grand Floral Parade. Other favorites are the evening Starlight Parade and the kids-only Junior Parade. The festival's program of events now has hundreds of family-friendly activities and performances, which include a children's stage complete with clowns, jugglers, magicians, and musicians.

## Olympic National Park

For most people, the term "rain forest" conjures up an image of a hot, steamy jungle located in the tropics. However, Olympic National Park in the northwest corner of Washington contains a temperate rain forest populated by ferns, lichens, salamanders, and stands of old-growth trees adorned with moss. The park actually embraces three distinctly different ecosystems: snowcapped mountains with alpine meadows that rise at its eastern flank, the rugged wilderness of the Pacific coast that sits at its western edge, and the emerald-colored rain forest between the two.

## Seattle Center

Seattle Center, home of the Space Needle, is the cultural heart of the city. Its 74 acres are filled with enough high-quality entertainment to keep a family happy for days.

For a view of Seattle Center and beyond, board the Space Needle's glass-enclosed elevator for the journey that stops 520 feet above ground. You can dine in a rotating restaurant and see a fabulous panorama of downtown Seattle, Puget Sound, Lake Union, and Mount Rainier.

Other popular stops in Seattle Center are the Pacific Science Center, the Seattle Children's Museum, the Seattle Children's Theatre, the Experience Music Project, and the International Fountain. The Fun Forest Amusement Park features a variety of children's rides and games.

## Northwest Folklife Festival

Under the Space Needle, the Northwest Folklife Festival sprawls across the 74 acres of Seattle Center every Memorial Day weekend. The event is a four-day extravaganza of ethnic music, dance, crafts, food, and folklore from more than 100 countries. Eighteen stages offer nonstop performances, demonstrations, and workshops for every imaginable cultural tradition. Street performers and artists are everywhere—you can find a musical saw player, a kilt-clad highland piper, and a punked-out preteen virtuoso on the violin.

Programs featuring circus acts, music, storytelling, and crafts are headquartered in the Discovery Zone. Here kids can participate in various activities, from creating Chinese dragon masks to building their own harmonica and learning how to play it.

## Pike Place Market

The fishmongers at Pike Place Market in Seattle put on one of the best shows in town. They toss the catch of the day through the air like a football as they engage the customers in all kinds of banter. They often pick up the largest fish they can shoulder and invite a visitor to pucker up for a kiss.

The market is one of Seattle's most famous landmarks and tourist attractions. More than 100 farmers and 200 artists and craftspeople occupy this spot, where you'll find an assortment of retail shops and the best of Washington's seasonal flowers and produce.

## San Juan Islands

North of Seattle in Puget Sound sits the San Juan Archipelago, a collection of 172 named islands and another several hundred rocky island outcroppings that appear at low tide. Although about 40 of these idyllic islands are inhabited, most people living here reside on the four that have ferry service: San Juan, Orcas, Lopez, and Shaw. Many families take bicycles aboard the ferry to explore the islands at a leisurely pace.

The islands' sheltered waters are home to harbor seals, sea lions, sea otters, dolphins, and orcas. Whale-watching is a popular

*Its eye-catching design makes it an instant landmark—explore the Experience Music Project and you'll find exciting exhibits that bring popular music to life.*

pastime, particularly around Friday Harbor on San Juan Island (the largest island of the group).

## Washington State International Kite Festival

The ornate and intricate kites featured in this weeklong festival are worlds away from the diamond-shape structures you used to make out of newspaper, string, and old rags. The festival takes place every August in Long Beach in the southwestern corner of Washington. The event attracts kite fanatics who come to show off their impressive flying skills and stunningly beautiful kites, as well as families looking for a novel way to enjoy a day at the beach. Children have their own section of the beach for flying kites, and there are kite-making workshops and all kinds of competitions.

## Denali National Park and Preserve

Denali's rugged, subarctic wilderness in south-central Alaska encompasses glaciers, tundra, and North America's tallest mountain: 20,320-foot-tall Mount McKinley. The park's six million acres are home to grizzly bears, wolves, caribou, and moose, all living in relatively undisturbed isolation. To maintain the stability of the environment, the park has been set up to minimize visitors' impact on the delicate, yet spectacular, ecosystem, and traffic is strictly controlled. Most tourists visit in summer, when they can hike, climb, and camp, but the park is also open in winter for dogsledding and ice climbing.

*First established as Mount McKinley National Park in 1917, Denali has been termed North America's last frontier. Adventure-seeking families will find plenty of opportunities to fish, hike, and camp during the summer months. Winter activities include cross-country skiing and dogsledding.*

## Glacier Bay National Park and Preserve

The bay and its tidewater glaciers and deep fjords are major attractions at Glacier Bay National Park and Preserve in southeast Alaska. Nearly one-fifth of this marine wilderness is made up of water, and it features the largest nonpolar ice field in the world. The park is best toured by boat, which allows you to see huge chunks of ice breaking off of glaciers and crashing into the sea. Touring by boat also affords the best chances to see the many animals that live in the water and along the shore.

*Beautiful, but only for a short time, the amazing sculptures created at the World Ice Art Championships will last until the first thaw.*

## World Ice Art Championships and Kid's Park

The world's best ice sculptors convene in Fairbanks, Alaska, in late February or early March to create dozens of frozen sculptures near the center of town. The ice in Fairbanks is considered some of the best in the business, and it is so crystal clear that you can read a newspaper through a block that is four feet thick.

For children, the best part of the festival is a captivating four-acre ice playground with an imaginatively carved entrance that may take the form of a fairyland castle or an icy fortress with ice-cream-cone turrets. Inside, kids will find an amazing world of slides, rides, mazes, and houses—all made of ice.

## Hawaii Volcanoes National Park

Hawaii Volcanoes National Park on the Big Island sets the standard for volcanoes, as it is home to the world's most massive volcano, Mauna Loa, as well as Kilauea, the world's most active volcano. Kilauea has been spewing lava constantly since 1983 and has added more than 500 acres of land to the Big Island. You can drive the Chain of Craters Road throughout the park, but exploring the area on foot is an exciting experience. Older children will enjoy the spectacle of a live lava flow, but families with young children should proceed with caution through the park, where a number of areas are closed to the public.

## The USS Arizona Memorial

The USS *Arizona* Memorial on the Hawaiian island of Oahu stretches across the water above the sunken midsection of the battleship on which 1,177 crewmembers died during the Pearl Harbor attack on December 7, 1941. It's a poignant and moving reminder of the tragic event that led to America's involvement in World War II. Children will learn about the attack in a 23-minute film that precedes a short boat ride on a Navy launch to the memorial.

While visiting, be sure to ask for the informative booklet specifically designed to help children understand what the monument represents. It guides young visitors through the events of the attack and explains the importance of remembering those who died.

## Waikiki Beach

This famous two-mile stretch of sand in Oahu, Hawaii, is home to scores of family-friendly beach hotels. Kids will enjoy strolling along the beachfront promenade, stopping for shaved ice or an ice-cream cone, taking a dip in the ocean, and checking out the parade of people. Waikiki is an excellent place to learn to surf, and lessons are available at just about every hotel or water sports center on the beach. If you can tear yourself away from the water, hike the landmark volcanic crater Diamond Head, visit the indigenous animals of Honolulu Zoo, or tour the Bishop Museum to view an interesting collection of Polynesian artifacts.

## Oahu's North Shore Big Surf Competitions

Some of the tallest ocean waves in the world are found at North Shore coastline of Oahu, Hawaii, during the winter months. These crashing walls of water are perfect for surfing and offer one of the best free shows on the islands. The North Shore is home to world-renowned surf contests, such as the Vans Triple Crown, which is held here from early November to late December and attracts the world's top surfers. Another contest, the impromptu Eddie Aikau Big Wave Invitational, is never scheduled in advance. This event is put together at the last minute anytime the waves reach heights of 20 feet or more.

*The verdant green beauty of Waimea Canyon can be appreciated by helicopter, from a car, or on foot along its 45 miles of hiking trails that crisscross the valley and outlying areas.*

## Polynesian Cultural Center

The colorful costumes, lively songs, and intricate dances of a number of Pacific region cultures are presented at the Polynesian Cultural Center in Oahu, Hawaii. You'll see Fiji, New Zealand, Marquesas, Samoa, Tahiti, Tonga, and Hawaii all represented in these authentically re-created island villages scattered around the 42-acre property.

Every stop has something for children to enjoy. They can fish, bowl, play shuffleboard, and take hula lessons. Natives in each village demonstrate crafts and skills, such as creating clothing from bark, sparking a fire by rubbing sticks together, and climbing a coconut tree. Each day ends with a lavish luau that features a show by more than 100 native performers.

## Waimea Canyon

Dubbed "The Grand Canyon of the Pacific" by Mark Twain, Waimea Canyon's sharply eroded cliffs reveal layers of vivid colors that seem to change in the sun. Unlike the Grand Canyon, plentiful rainfall keeps this canyon and its surrounding area thick with vegetation, and visitors are frequently treated to the sight of vivid rainbows. At ten miles long, one mile wide, and more than 3,500 feet deep, this Kauai landmark is the largest canyon in the Pacific.

## Kapalua Beach

Hawaii is home to hundreds of gorgeous sandy beaches, and the sunny island of Maui certainly has its fair share. But many consider the golden sand of Maui's Kapalua Beach to be the best of all the Hawaiian Islands.

Kapalua is especially well suited for families with small children. It is situated on a sheltered stretch of a crescent-shape bay that protects it from any rough surf. Coral reefs and rocky peninsulas further protect the shore. The calm water and an easily accessible reef make it an excellent place for children to learn to snorkel. They'll love the colorful tropical fish and vivid coral formations.

**CANADA & MEXICO**

## Old Quebec

Canada's walled city, Old Quebec, is the only fortified city in North America. A three-mile-long wall of ancient stone surrounds Old Quebec, and separates it from Quebec City. Historic Old Quebec features an abundance of 17th- and 18th-century buildings and is located on a steep hill, overlooking the St. Lawrence River.

Set aside some time to visit the Museum of Civilization and its Canadian Children's Museum. The International Village exhibit has numerous interactive displays, and during the summer children can play in Adventure World, an outdoor exhibit. Canada Hall has life-size displays from the daily life of Quebec's residents through the generations. Performers often interact with visitors in this area.

## Niagara Falls

This famous wall of water at the Canadian and U.S. border is the most powerful waterfall in North America. Once a popular honeymoon destination, Niagara Falls now attracts tourists and families from all over the world.

In Ontario, on the Canadian side, don a raincoat and visit the Journey Behind the Falls observation deck. As you peer out, the river explodes in front of you after it free-falls more than 13 stories. And don't miss seeing Niagara Falls after dark, when powerful spotlights bathe the water in ever-changing colors. The light catches the mist, giving the entire area an otherworldly glow. In summer, fireworks displays enhance the splendor of the setting.

## Hockey Hall of Fame

You'll need quick reflexes at the Hockey Hall of Fame in Toronto, Ontario—that way, you can block the shots from a virtual Wayne Gretzky and Mark Messier. Put on the pads and step into the action as the two legends launch lightning-fast foam pucks in your direction. Next, grab a stick, step onto the plastic "ice," and go up against a video version of goalie Ed Belfour. A machine records your reaction time, accuracy, and speed.

Kids are certain to enjoy the many interactive exhibits at the Hall of Fame, but don't overlook the other interesting hockey displays and memorabilia, such as the classic uniforms, equipment, and the original 1893 Stanley Cup.

## Calgary Stampede

The Calgary Stampede in Alberta is Canada's largest annual event. It's also the world's richest rodeo, awarding $1 million in prize money to the winners of such daring competitions as bareback and bull riding, barrel racing, steer wrestling, roping, and chuck wagon racing. The event draws rodeo champions from all over the world.

Most of the events take place in Stampede Park, a fairground that was specially built to accommodate the Stampede. Some of the attractions you'll find there are an amusement park, a petting zoo, a number of livestock barns, and musical entertainment on multiple stages. A Kid's Midway features rides and rodeo events for children ages four through twelve.

## Banff National Park

Banff National Park in southwestern Alberta is an extraordinary landscape of craggy, snowcapped peaks that make up the Alberta Rocky Mountains. During the summer, the most scenic areas can be reached on day hikes. Banff has more than 80 maintained trails that cover about 1,000 miles of park land, and they range from leisurely strolls to arduous long-distance treks. Banff is also a world-class ski resort and offers a wide variety of winter sports, including downhill skiing, cross-country skiing, snowshoe treks, toboggan rides, and dogsledding.

*Canoeing in the calm waters of Lake Louise is a great family outing. Don't forget the binoculars—you'll see a variety of wildlife along the lake's edge and in the surrounding mountains.*

## Lake Louise

Snowcapped mountain peaks and formidable glaciers cradle Lake Louise's emerald depths in a natural, icy amphitheater. Situated in Banff National Park in Alberta, it offers one of the most breathtaking views in the world and is a popular vacation site.

Teatime amid the splendor of Banff National Park awaits those who hike the 4.5-mile round-trip along Lake Agnes Trail, which begins at the shores of Lake Louise. The trail leads you through a magnificent old-growth forest past Mirror Lake and Bridal Veil Falls before reaching the Lake Agnes Teahouse. Farther up the trail, a longer and more arduous hike better suited for older children will take you to yet another teahouse, The Plain of Six Glaciers.

## West Edmonton Mall

Even though this mall in Edmonton, Alberta, contains 800 retail stores and businesses, shopping isn't what sets it apart. It features the world's largest indoor amusement park, a lagoon with a sea lion show, a professional-size ice rink, 21 movie theaters, and much more.

Even in winter, kids can spend the day in their swimsuits at World Waterpark, which boasts North America's biggest wave pool and all kinds of traditional water park fun. Galaxyland Amusement Park's 25 rides include Mindbender—a 14-story, triple-loop roller coaster—and Space Shot, a 120-foot, heart-pounding free fall. And the mall aquarium houses a shark exhibit as well as an assortment of other interesting creatures.

## Victoria and Vancouver Island

Most visitors travel to the friendly capital of British Columbia by ferry, and as they approach the town they see its beautiful Inner Harbour and the peaked roofline of the famous Empress Hotel. Victoria is also known for its Butchart Gardens, 55 acres of internationally acclaimed botanical gardens.

*Mayan statues remain in the archaeological sites at Xcaret, a destination that provides adventure and insight into the ancient people who once lived there.*

A favorite section for children is the Sunken Garden, where they descend a set of stairs into a valley of blooming flowers.

Bicycling around the island is a popular family pastime and an ideal way to take in its many sights. During your excursion, stop at Miniature World, where younger children will enjoy the tiny landscapes.

## Chichén Itzá

When you come upon the ancient city of Chichén Itzá, located on Mexico's Yucatán Peninsula, its role as the seat of power in the Mayan world is vividly clear. Massive pyramids, huge stone courts, dozens of temples, and wide plazas are spread out across a vast grassy plain.

Chichén Itzá is the most completely restored archaeological site in the Yucatán, and its scale is tremendous. The great stone pyramid known as El Castillo is the tallest structure on the site, at 75 feet. Climbing it is a highlight for most children, and from its peak they can survey the great city of Chichén Itzá and the jungles beyond.

## Xcaret and Xel-Ha

Xcaret and Xel-Ha in Cancún's Riviera Maya are theme parks that incorporate the assets of their tropical surroundings into exciting activities that introduce the heritage and history of Mexico to park visitors. Xcaret lets you bob through the same underground river passages that Mayan warriors used for stealth warfare. You can also snorkel in a lagoon, swim with the dolphins, see animal exhibits, and visit Mayan ruins. The smaller Xel-Ha park features a large lagoon for snorkeling, ruins to explore, hidden beaches with hammocks for relaxing, and a Mayan cave.

## Day of the Dead and Night of the Radishes Festivals

Located on Mexico's Pacific coast, the city of Oaxaca is known for its enthusiastic celebration of two very unusual festivals: Day of the Dead and Night of the Radishes. Day of the Dead is a joyful celebration that honors the spirits of deceased family members and friends. The town's marketplace comes alive on October 31 with handcrafted decorations and homemade treats that are used to decorate the graves of loved ones.

The Night of the Radishes festival began about 100 years ago during the Christmas season, as vegetable growers carved designs into their produce to attract customers. The practice became an annual tradition, and with it grew a friendly competition that has evolved into the annual Night of the Radishes Festival.

## Whale Watching in the Sea of Cortez

Every year, thousands of gray whales migrate to the warm coastal waters of Mexico's Baja Peninsula to mate and give birth. They migrate from their summer homes in the Bering and Chukchi seas between Alaska and Siberia, a journey of more than 6,000 miles.

Three locations on Baja's Pacific coast are great for watching grays. They include Scammon's Lagoon, about 430 miles south of the U.S.–Mexico border; San Ignacio Lagoon, about 525 miles south of the border; and Magdalena Bay, about 800 miles south of the border. These areas are protected marine parks, and whale-watching is restricted to boats operated by trained guides.

## Cozumel and Isla Mujeres

These two islands offer a quiet departure from nearby Cancún's fast-paced activities and busy beaches. Both islands offer plenty of amenities and are worth a visit in order to combine a relaxing, warm-weather beach vacation with a destination that has true Mexican character.

Cozumel is famous for idyllic soft white sand beaches and calm turquoise waters on its western shore. The island is surrounded by three massive reef systems, the Santa Rosa, Colombia, and Palancar, making it a mecca for snorkelers and divers. Isla Mujeres is just seven miles from Cancún, but it is a serene and peaceful retreat. Isla Mujeres is a popular spot for divers and snorkelers. It is bordered by two reef systems that create a natural aquarium.

*Many kids will believe it's just one more reason not to eat their vegetables—the celebration known as Night of the Radishes features some wonderful creations.*

**Acknowledgments**
Page 38: Verses from "The Bridge," from *Complete Poems of Hart Crane,* by Hart Crane, edited by Marc Simon. Copyright © 1933, 1958, 1966 by Liveright Publishing Corporation. Copyright © 1986 by Marc Simon. Reprinted by permission of Liveright Publishing Corporation.

Page 157: Quote by Carhenge creator Jim Reinders, from an interview with author Eric Peterson. Copyright © Eric Peterson. Reprinted by permission.

Page 163: Quote by Sturgis Motorcycle Rally attendee. Copyright © 2005 Sturgis Motorcycle Rally. Reprinted by permission.

Page 179: The Mission Statement for the National Cowboy & Western Heritage Museum. Copyright © the National Cowboy & Western Heritage Museum. Reprinted by permission.

Page 181: Memorial Mission Statement, the Oklahoma City National Memorial & Museum. Copyright © 1996 Oklahoma City National Memorial Foundation. Text and image reprinted by permission.

registered service mark of Virginia Beach Events Unlimited; Newport Folk Festival® is a registered trademark of Festival Productions, Inc.; Newport Jazz Festival® is a registered service mark of Wein,George d b a Festival Productions; NFL® is a registered trademark of the National Football League; Nieman Marcus® is a registered service mark of NM Nevada Trust; Olympic® is a registered trademark of the United States Olympic Committee; OMNIMAX® is a registered trademark of IMAX® Corporation; Peanuts® is a registered trademark of United Feature Syndicate, Inc.; Pike Place Market® is a registered service mark of Pike Place Market Preservation and Development Authority; PNC Park® is a registered service mark of PNC Financial Services Group, Inc.; Ponce de Leon's Fountain of Youth® is a registered trademark and service mark of Fountain of Youth Properties, Inc.; Porsche® is a registered trademark of Dr. Ing. h.c. F. Porsche AG; Port Discovery® is a registered service mark of The Baltimore Children's Museum; Preakness Stakes® is a registered service mark of Maryland Jockey Club of Baltimore City, The Corporation Maryland Pimlico Race Course; Professional Football Hall of Fame® is a registered service mark of the National Football Museum, Inc.; Punxsutawney Phil® is a registered service mark of Punxsutawney Groundhog Club, Inc.; Radio City Music Hall® is a registered trademark and service mark of Radio City Trademarks, LLC; Radio City® is a registered trademark of Radio City Trademark, LLC; Ralph Lauren® is a registered trademark of PRL USA Holdings, Inc.; Ringling Bros and Barnum & Bailey® is a registered trademark and service mark of Ringling Bros and Barnum & Bailey Combined Shows, Inc.; Rock and Roll Hall of Fame® is a registered trademark and service mark of Rock and Roll Hall of Fame Foundation, Inc.; Rock and Roll Hall of Fame Museum® is a registered trademark and service mark of Rock and Roll Hall of Fame Foundation, Inc.; Rockefeller Center® is a registered service mark of Rockefeller Center, Inc.; Rockettes® is a registered trademark and service mark of Radio City Trademark, LLC; Rose Bowl Parade® is a registered trademark and service mark of Pasadena Tournament of Roses Association; Rose Bowl® is a registered service mark of the City of Pasadena; Ryman Auditorium® is a registered service mark of Gaylord Entertainment Company; San Diego Zoo® is a registered service mark of the Zoological Society of San Diego, Inc.; Smithsonian Institution® is a registered service mark of Smithsonian Institution Trust; Smithsonian® is a registered trademark and service mark of Smithsonian Institution; Snoopy® is a registered trademark of United Feature Syndicate, Inc.; Space Needle® is a registered trademark of Space Needle Corporation; Sturgis® is a registered trademark and service mark of the Sturgis Area Chamber of Commerce; Sun Studio® is a registered service mark of Sun Studio, Inc.; Super Bowl® is a registered trademark of the National Football League; Superman® is a registered trademark and service mark of DC Comics Inc.; Taliesin® is a registered trademark of the Frank Lloyd Wright Foundation; Tall Ships® is a registered service mark of The American Sail Training Association; TelePrompTer® is a registered trademark of Teleprompter Corporation; Telluride® is a registered trademark of TSG SKI & GOLF, LLC LTD; The American Museum of Natural History® is a registered service mark of the American Museum of Natural History; The Art Institute of Chicago® is a registered service mark of The Art Institute of Chicago; The Beatles® is a registered trademark of Apple Corps Limited; The Chrysler Building® is a registered trademark of TST/TMW 405 Lexington; The Farmer's Museum® is a registered service mark of The Farmers' Museum; The Great Stupa of Dharmakaya® is a registered trademark of Shambhala/Nalanda Foundation; The Metropolitan Museum of Art® is a registered service mark of The Metropolitan Museum of Art; The Metropolitan Opera® is a registered trademark of The Metropolitan Opera; The Museum of Modern Art® is a registered service mark of the Museum of Modern Art; The Solomon R Guggenheim Museum® is a registered trademark and service mark of the Solomon R Guggenheim Foundation; The World of Coca-Cola® is a registered service mark of the Coca-Cola Company; The World Series® is a registered trademark of the Office of the Commissioner of Baseball; Tiffany and Company® is a registered trademark of Tiffany (NJ) Inc.; Tournament of Roses® is a registered service mark of Pasadena Tournament of Roses Association; Triple Crown Challenge® is a registered service mark of Triple Crown Productions, LLC; Trump Taj Mahal Casino-Resort® is a registered service mark of Donald J Trump; Willys® is a registered trademark of Daimler/Chrysler; Woody Guthrie® is a registered trademark of Woody Guthrie Publications, Inc.; World Trade Center® is a registered service mark of World Trade Centers Association; Wynn Las Vegas® is a registered trademark of Wynn Resorts Holdings, LLC; Yosemite National Park® is a registered trademark of Yosemite Concession Services Corporation.

**Trademark acknowledgments for pages 588–627:**
500 Festival® is a registered service mark of Brickyard Trademarks, Inc.; AIA® is a registered trademark, service mark and collective membership mark of The American Institute of Architects; Al Capone® is a registered service mark of Dillinger, LLC; American Institute of Architects® is a registered collective membership mark of The American Institute of Architects; American Museum of Natural History® is a registered service mark of the American Museum of Natural History; Angelina Ballerina® is a registered trademark and service mark of Helen Craig, Katharine Holabird, and HIT Entertainment, PLC; Baltimore & Ohio Railroad Museum® is a registered service mark of the Baltimore & Ohio Railroad Museum; Ben & Jerry's® is a registered trademark and service mark of Ben & Jerry's Homemade Holdings, Inc.; Bert® is a registered trademark of Muppets, Inc.; Best Friends® is a registered trademark and service mark of Best Friends Animal Sanctuary; Big Bird® is a registered trademark of Muppets, Inc.; Blizzard Beach® is a registered service mark of The Walt Disney Company; Bronx Zoo® is a registered trademark of the Wildlife Conservation Society; Busch Gardens® is a registered service mark of Anheuser-Busch, Inc.; Cadillac® is a registered trademark of the General Motors Corporation; Calgary Stampede® is a pending registered trademark of Calgary Exhibition and Stampede; California Screamin'® is a registered service mark of Disney Enterprises, Inc.; Canadian Museum of Civilization® is a pending registered trademark of Musee Canadien des Civilisations/Canadian Museum of Civilization; Cedar Point® is a registered service mark of Cedar Fair LP; Colonial Williamsburg® is a registered service mark of Colonial Williamsburg Foundation; Conner Prairie® is a registered service mark of Earlham College; Corvette® is a registered trademark of General Motors Corporation; Crayola® is a registered service mark of Binney & Smith Properties, Inc.; Dairy Queen® is a registered trademark and service mark of American Dairy Queen Corporation; Derby Festival® is a registered service mark of Kentucky Derby Festival, Inc.; Dinosphere® is a registered service mark of The Children's Museum of Indianapolis, Inc.; Disney® is a registered trademark of Disney Enterprises, Inc.; Disney World® is a registered service mark of Disney Enterprises, Inc.; Disneyland® is a registered trademark and service mark of Disney Enterprises, Inc.; Disney's Animal Kingdom® is a registered service mark of Disney Enterprises, Inc.; Disney's California Adventure® is a registered service mark of Disney Enterprises, Inc.; Dixie Stampede® is a registered service mark of Dixie Stampede, Inc.; Dolly Parton® is a registered service mark of Dolly Parton; Dollywood® is a registered trademark and service mark of Dolly Parton Productions, Inc.; Donald Duck® is a registered service mark of Disney Enterprises, Inc.; Dora the Explorer® is a registered trademark and service mark of Viacom International Inc.; Dorothy® is a registered trademark of Turner Entertainment Co.; Downtown Disney® is a registered service mark of Disney Enterprises, Inc.; Dr. Seuss® is a registered trademark of Dr. Seuss Enterprises, LP; Dr. Seuss' How the Grinch Stole Christmas!® is a registered trademark of Dr. Seuss Enterprises, LP Geisel-Seuss Enterprises, Inc.; Eddie Aikau® is a registered trademark of Clyde Aikau; Ellis Island: The National Museum of Immigration® is a registered service mark of The Statute of Liberty-Ellis Island Foundation; Elvis Presley Automobile Museum® is a registered service mark of Elvis Presley Enterprises, Inc.; Elvis Presley® is a registered trademark and service mark of Elvis Presley Enterprises, Inc.; Elvis® is a registered trademark and service mark of Elvis Presley Enterprises, Inc.; Empire State Building® is a registered service mark of the Empire State Building Company; Enchanted Woods® is a registered service mark of Henry Francis du Pont Winterthur Museum, Inc.; Epcot® is a registered service mark of Disney Enterprises, Inc.; Epcot® is a registered trademark of Walt Disney Productions; Eric Carle® is a registered trademark of Eric Carle; Ernie® is a registered trademark of Muppets, Inc.; Escape from Pompeii® is a registered service mark of Busch Entertainment Corporation; Experience Music Project® is a registered trademark and service mark of Experience Learning Community; Exploration Station® is a registered service mark of the Bourbonnais Township Park District; Exploratorium® is a registered service mark of The Palace of Arts and Science; Exploratorium® is a registered trademark of The Exploratorium; FamilyFun® is a registered trademark of Disney Enterprises, Inc.; Fernbank Museum of Natural History® is a registered trademark and service mark of Fernbank, Inc.; Flintstones® is a registered trademark and service mark of Hanna-Barbera Productions, Inc.; Ford® is a registered trademark and service mark of Ford Motor Company; Galaxyland® is a registered trademark and service mark of West Edmonton Mall Property, Inc.; Girl Scouts® is a registered trademark of Girl Scouts of the United States of America, Inc.; Graceland® is a registered trademark and service mark of Elvis Presley Enterprises, Inc.; Grand Floral Parade® is a registered service mark of the Portland Rose Festival Association; Greenfield Village® is a registered service mark of The Edison Institute; Hallmark® is a registered service mark of Hallmark Cards, Inc.; Hanna-Barbera® is a registered trademark of Hanna-Barbera Productions, Inc.; Hearst Castle® is a registered trademark of the State of California Department of Parks and Recreation; HemisFair Park® is a registered service mark of City of San Antonio; Henry Doorly Zoo® is a registered service mark of

Omaha Zoological Society; Henry Ford Museum® is a registered service mark of The Edison Institute; HERSHEYPARK® is a registered service mark of Hershey Foods Corporation; HERSHEY'S KISSES® is a registered trademark of the Hershey Chocolate & Confectionery Corporation; HERSHEY'S is a registered trademark of the Hershey Chocolate & Confectionery Corporation; Historic Jamestowne® is a registered trademark and service mark of The Association for the Preservation of Virginia Antiquities; Hockey Hall of Fame® is a pending registered trademark of the Hockey Hall of Fame and Museum; Holiday World® is a registered service mark of Santa Claus Land, Inc.; Hurricane Harbor® is a registered service mark of Six Flags Theme Parks, Inc.; IMAX® is a registered trademark and service mark of Imax Corporation; Indianapolis 500® is a registered trademark and service mark of the Indianapolis Motor Speedway Corporation; Indy® is a registered trademark and service mark of the Indianapolis Motor Speedway Corporation; International Spy Museum® is a registered trademark and service mark of The House On F Street, LLC; Jamestown Settlement® is a registered trademark of Jamestown-Yorktown Foundation; Jimi Hendrix® is a registered trademark and service mark of Experience Hendrix, LLC; John Philip Sousa® is a registered trademark of The Instrumentalist Co.; Journey Behind the Falls is a pending registered trademark of The Niagara Parks Commission; Kaleidoscope® is a registered service mark of Hallmark Cards, Inc.; Kentucky Derby® is a registered trademark of Churchill Downs, Inc.; Kingdoms of the Night® is a registered service mark of Omaha Zoological Society; Kings Island® is a registered service mark of Paramount Parks, Inc.; LEGO® is a registered trademark of Kirkbi AG; LEGO® is a registered trademark and service mark of Interlego A.G.; LEGOLAND® is a registered service mark of Kirkbi AG; LEGOLAND® is a registered trademark of Interlego A.G.; Li'l Abner® is a registered trademark of Capp Enterprises, Inc.; Looney Tunes® is a registered trademark of Time Warner Entertainment Company, LP; Louisville Slugger Museum & Factory® is a registered service mark of Hillerich & Bradsby Co.; Louisville Slugger® is a registered trademark of Hillerich & Bradsby Co.; Macy's Thanksgiving Day Parade® is a registered service mark of Federated Department Stores, Inc.; Magic Kingdom® is a registered service mark of Walt Disney Productions; Mall of America® is a registered trademark and service mark of the Mall of America Company; MasterBlaster® is a registered service mark of Henry, Jeffery W.; Mei Xiang® is a registered trademark of Smithsonian Institution; MGM® is a registered trademark and service mark of Metro-Goldwyn-Mayer Lion Corp.; Mickey Mouse® is a registered trademark of Disney Enterprises, Inc.; Miniature Railroad & Village® is a registered service mark of Carnegie Institute; Miniature World® is a registered trademark and service mark of Lin Rite Enterprises, Ltd; Minnie Mouse® is a registered trademark of Disney Enterprises, Inc.; Monopoly® is a registered trademark of Hasbro, Inc.; Monterey Bay Aquarium® is a registered trademark and service mark of Monterey Bay Aquarium Foundation; Mount Vernon® is a registered trademark of the Mount Vernon Ladies' Association of the Union; Muppets® is a registered trademark and service mark of The Muppets Holding Company, LLC; Mystic Seaport® is a registered service mark of Mystic Seaport Museum, Inc.; NASCAR® is a registered trademark and service mark of the National Association for Stock Car Auto Racing, Inc.; National Air and Space Museum® is a registered trademark of Smithsonian Institution; National Aquarium in Baltimore® is a registered service mark of National Aquarium in Baltimore, Inc.; National Baseball Hall of Fame and Museum® is a registered service mark of National Baseball Hall of Fame and Museum, Inc.; National Cherry Blossom Festival® is a registered service mark of National Cherry Blossom Festival, Inc.; National Storytelling Festival® is a registered service mark of the National Association for the Preservation and Perpetuation of Storytelling; National Symphony Orchestra® is a registered trademark and service mark of The Trustees of the John F. Kennedy Center for the Performing Arts; National Underground Railroad Freedom Center® is a registered service mark of National Underground Railroad Freedom Center, Inc.; Navy Pier® is a registered trademark and service mark of Metropolitan Pier and Exposition Authority; New Orleans Jazz & Heritage Festival® is a registered service mark of New Orleans Jazz & Heritage Foundation, Inc.; Nickelodeon Universe® is a registered service mark of Viacom International, Inc.; Old Sturbridge Village® is a registered trademark and service mark of Old Sturbridge, Inc.; Olympic® is a registered trademark of the United States Olympic Committee; Pike Place Market® is a registered service mark of Pike Place Market Preservation and Development Authority; Pikes Peak Cog Railway® is a registered service mark of Manitou & Pikes Peak Railway Company; Pippi Longstocking® is a registered trademark and service mark of Tre Lindgren AB; Please Touch Museum® is a registered service mark of Please Touch Museum; Plimoth Plantation® is a registered service mark of Plimoth Plantation, Inc.; Polynesian Cultural Center® is a registered service mark of Polynesian Cultural Center; Ponce de Leon's Fountain of Youth® is a registered trademark and service mark of Fountain of Youth Properties, Inc.; Port Discovery® is a registered service mark of The Baltimore Children's Museum, Inc.; Portland Rose Festival® is a registered service mark of Portland Rose Festival Association; Pro Football Hall of Fame® is a registered service mark of the National Football Museum, Inc.; Red Earth® is a registered service mark of Red Earth, Inc.; REESE'S® is a registered trademark of the Hershey Chocolate & Confectionery Corporation; Revenge of the Mummy® is a registered service mark of Universal City Studios, LLLP; Ripley's Believe It or Not® is a registered trademark and service mark of Ripley International Limited; Rock and Roll Hall of Fame and Museum® is a registered trademark and service mark of Rock and Roll Hall of Fame Foundation, Inc.; Rugrats® is a registered trademark and service mark of Viacom International, Inc.; Salem Witch Museum® is a registered service mark of BPM Productions, Inc.; San Diego Zoo® is a registered trademark and service mark of Zoological Society of San Diego, Inc.; Scarecrow® is a registered trademark of Turner Entertainment Co.; Schlitterbahn® is a registered trademark and service mark of Bad Schloss, Inc.; Schwinn® is a registered trademark of Schwinn Cycling & Fitness Inc.; Scooby-Doo® is a registered trademark and service mark of Hanna-Barbera Productions, Inc.; SeaWorld® is a registered trademark of Sea World, Inc.; Sesame Place® is a registered service mark of Children's Television Workshop; Sesame Street® is a registered trademark and service mark of Children's Television Workshop; Seuss Landing® is a registered service mark of Dr. Seuss Enterprises, L.P. Geisel-Seuss Enterprises, Inc.; Shamu® is a registered trademark and service mark of Sea World, Inc.; Shedd Aquarium® is a registered trademark and service mark of the Shedd Aquarium Society; Shrek 4-D Presented in Ogre-Vision® is a registered service mark of DreamWorks LLC; Six Flags Great Adventure® is a registered service mark of Six Flags Theme Parks, Inc.; Six Flags® is a registered service mark of Six Flags Theme Parks, Inc.; Smithsonian Institution® is a registered service mark of Smithsonian Institution; Smithsonian® is a registered trademark and service mark of Smithsonian Institution; Soarin' Over California® is a registered service mark of Disney Enterprises, Inc.; Space Needle® is a registered trademark and service mark of Space Needle Corporation; SpongeBob SquarePants® is a registered trademark and service mark of Viacom International, Inc.; SportsWorks® is a registered service mark of Carnegie Institute; Stanley Cup® is a registered trademark and service mark of the National Hockey League; Tennessee Aquarium® is a registered trademark and service mark of Tennessee Aquarium; The Amazing Adventures of Spider-Man® is a registered service mark of Marvel Characters, Inc.; The Art Institute of Chicago® is a registered service mark of The Art Institute of Chicago; The Beast® is a registered service mark of Paramount Parks Inc.; The Butchart Gardens® is a registered trademark and service mark of The Butchart Gardens Ltd; The Crayola Factory® is a registered service mark of Binney & Smith Properties, Inc.; The Empress® is a registered service mark of Legacy EF Inc.; The Farmers' Museum® is a registered service mark of The Farmers' Museum; The Fenimore Art Museum® is a registered service mark of the New York State Historical Association; The Freedom Trail® is a registered service mark of Freedom Trail Foundation, Inc.; The Incredible Hulk Coaster® is a registered service mark of Marvel Characters, Inc.; The Magic House® is a registered service mark of The Magic House; The Mammoth Site® is a registered trademark of Mammoth Site of Hot Springs, SD Inc.; The Tournament of Roses® is a registered service mark of Pasadena Tournament of Roses Association, Inc.; The Wright Brothers® is a registered trademark and service mark of The Wright Family Fund; Tian Tian® is a registered trademark of Smithsonian Institution; Tin Man® is a registered trademark of Turner Entertainment Co.; Tina Turner® is a registered trademark and service mark of Tina Turner; Tony Awards® is a registered service mark of American Theatre Wing, Inc.; Tower of the Americas® is a registered service mark of City of San Antonio; U.S. Olympic Winter Challenge® is a registered service mark of the United States Olympic Committee; U.S. Space & Rocket Center® is a registered service mark of the Alabama Space Science Exhibit Commission; Universal Studios Islands of Adventure® is a registered trademark and service mark of Universal City Studios Inc.; Universal Studios® is a registered service mark of Universal City Studios Inc.; Walt Disney World® is a registered service mark of Disney Enterprises, Inc.; West Edmonton Mall® is a registered trademark and service mark of West Edmonton Mall Property, Inc.; Where the Wild Things Are® is a registered service mark of Maurice Sendak; Wild Arctic® is a registered trademark and service mark of Sea World, Inc.; Wizard of Oz® is a registered trademark and service mark of Turner Entertainment Co.; Yosemite National Park® is a registered trademark of Yosemite Concession Services Corporation; ZooLights® is a registered service mark of The Lincoln Park Zoological Society.

# Index

## D



## E



## F

## N

# Amazing Places to Take Your Kids Index

*This index covers only the Amazing Places to Take Your Kids section. The general book index begins on page 631.*